The Illustrated

ROCK
HANDBOOK

KU-591-142

The Illustrated ROCK HANDBOOK

Consultant: Mike Clifford

Authors: Pete Frame, John Tobler, Ed Hanel, Roger St. Pierre, Chris Trengove, John Beecher, Clive Richardson, Gary Cooper, Marsha Hanlon, Linda Sandahl.

a Salamander book

Published by Salamander Books Limited
LONDON

A Salamander Book

Published by
Salamander Books Ltd.,
Salamander House,
27 Old Gloucester Street,
London WC1N 3AF,
United Kingdom.

©1983 by Salamander Books Ltd.

All rights reserved. No part of this book may be produced, stored in a retrieval system or transmitted in any form or by any means, electronic, mechanical, photocopying, recording or otherwise, without prior permission of Salamander Books Ltd.

ISBN 0-86101-186-4 (cloth)
ISBN 0-86101-191-0 (paper)

Distributed by Hodder & Stoughton Services, PO Box 6, Mill Road, Dunton Green, Sevenoaks, Kent TN13 2XX.

All correspondence concerning the content of this volume should be addressed to Salamander Books Ltd.

Credits

Managing Editor: Ray Bonds
Editor: Roxane Streeter
Designer: Philip Gorton
Family Trees: Pete Frame
Picture Research: Joe McCarthy
Filmset by Modern Text Typesetting Ltd.
Colour Reproduction by Rodney Howe Ltd.
Printed in Belgium by Henri Proost et Cie.

Acknowledgments

The publishers wish to thank all the record companies and publicity/management agencies who supplied and gave their permission to use promotional photos and record sleeves. All other photos by Pictorial Press, Terry Lott, Phil Gorton, Keith Bernstein, Tom Sheehan, Trinifold, Chris Morphet, Adrian Boot, Michael Putland, Robert Ellis, John Timbers, Victor Skrebneski, MTV, Jill Furmanovsky, Barry Plummer, Paul Slattery, Fin Costello, Martin Godard, Duane Michaels, Peter Anderson, Scope Features, Brian Aris, Simon Fowler, Eric Watson, Rex Features, and DeMonde Advertising.

US chart positions © 1955 through 1983 by Billboard Publications, Inc. Compiled by the Billboard Research Department and reprinted with permission. UK chart positions from 1956 through 1983 by kind permission of Music And Video Week/BBC/Gallup.

We would also like to recognise the contributions and assistance of the Schwann Music Catalog, the Music Master Catalogue, and Joel Whitburn.

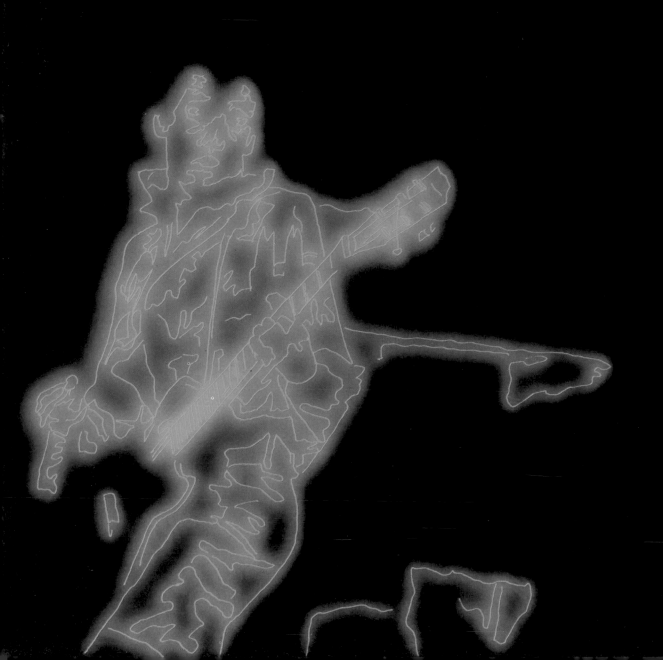

Contents

The Consultant

MIKE CLIFFORD played bass with '60s soul outfit the Errol Dixon Band. He has worked with Bad Company and Led Zeppelin and handled public relations for Aretha Franklin, James Brown, the Drifters, Richie Havens, and many other performers. Mike has written extensively on rock 'n' roll and was chief author and consultant of Salamander's 'Black Music' and consultant co-author of their 'Illustrated Encyclopedia of Rock' (third edition).

The Authors

PETE FRAME is probably best known for his intricate Rock Family Trees, but he has also been a freelance rock journalist since 1969 when he founded Zig Zag magazine, which he edited for several years. Following work for Charisma and Stiff Records in the '70s, he specialized in group genealogies. Three volumes of his Rock Family Trees have been published to date.

JOHN TOBLER has written for all the major music weeklies in the UK at one time or another, but concentrates on rock books, such as '25 Years Of Rock' (co-written with Pete Frame), 'The Record Producers', and 'Guitar Greats', all of which have also been successful BBC Radio One series. He has also written books on the Beach Boys, Buddy Holly, Cliff Richard, and Elvis Presley, plus rock trivia books such as 'The Rock Lists Album'.

ED HANEL plunged into rock journalism when he founded the Who fanzine 'Who's News'. Still a fan himself and an avid record collector, Ed specializes in discographies. He has contributed to various US and UK rock publications, including 'Trouser Press', 'Zig Zag', and the 'History of Rock' series. He is the author of 'The Omnibus Rock Bibiography' and 'The Who: The Illustrated Discography'.

ROGER ST. PIERRE has worked for nearly 20 years in the music industry, mostly as a publicist for such acts as the Drifters, Johnnie Ray, Frankie Laine, Marvin Gaye, the Temptations, Diana Ross, and the Jacksons. He is also the author of several books, has contributed to 'Record Mirror', 'Blues And Soul', and 'New Musical Express', written several hundred sleeve notes, and was a co-author of Salamander's 'Black Music'.

CHRIS TRENGOVE played tenor sax with soul band Lester Square and the GTs and the John Dummer Blues in the '60s. In the '70s he worked as a publicist for Status Quo, Thin Lizzy, and Bill Withers, among others. He has co-authored two novels and a biography of Keith Moon, and has contributed to 'Beat Instrumental' 'Album Tracking', 'Black Echoes', and Salamander's 'Black Music' and 'Illustrated Encyclopedia of Rock'.

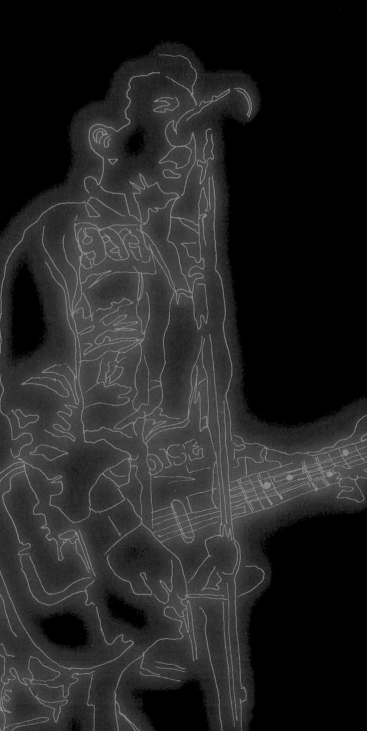

JOHN BEECHER is a rock historian, rock music publisher, and owner of an oldies record shop. He compiled the comprehensive boxed set of Buddy Holly LPs.

CLIVE RICHARDSON was editor of 'Shout' soul magazine from 1967 until its demise in 1976. He then became a regular contributor to 'Black Echoes' and 'Blues Unlimited' and has written sleeve notes for numerous soul and R&B albums. He was a contributor to Salamander's 'Black Music' and 'Illustrated Encyclopedia of Rock' publications.

GARY COOPER became editor of 'Beat Instrumental' in the '70s and since then has been writing for musical instrument/musicians magazines throughout the world, including 'Spotlight' (West Germany), 'Music Maker' (Holland), and 'Sonix' (Australia), and UK publications 'Sounds', 'Music World', and 'Sound International'. In 1981 co-founded and became editor of 'Music UK'.

MARSHA HANLON has been a rock 'n' roll fan since she danced in the aisles of New York's Paramount in the '50s. In the '60s she co-founded a weekly entertainment newspaper in Boston. She has worked as a freelance publicist/journalist since.

LINDA SANDAHL gained her early writing experience as assistant to James Robert Parish. Since then she has worked on Steven H. Scheuer's 'Movies On TV', of which she is now an associate editor. Linda recently began researching and writing for the collector's magazine 'Goldmine'.

Introduction

uring the week that this book went to press, David Crosby (C,S, & N) was sentenced to a five-year prison term, Culture Club added a member, Bauhaus split up, K.C. and the Sunshine Band came back out of nowhere and scored a UK No. 1, ELO drummer Bev Bevan joined Black Sabbath, the reformed Animals signed to Miles Copeland's IRS label, and James Brown, the Tom Tom Club, War, Herbie Hancock, Depeche Mode, AC/DC, the Stray Cats, and Neil Young all released new albums—not to mention the new singles released. These examples illustrate the complexity involved in trying to produce an up-to-date rock encyclopedia. However, apart from trying to keep current, the real challenge is getting the past right. Legends, backstage stories, and publicity stunts are rampant in rock, an fabricators of such so-called facts have an audience of fans eager to believe and retell the outrageous. We have endeavoured to confirm and cross-check our information with our team of well-seasoned rock writers.

When it comes to rock 'n' roll, every fan is a critic and every critic a fan. Therefore we're bound to upset someone in trying to choose 600 performers from thousands. The selection was somewhat subjective; our team had to fight it out amongst themselves to narrow down the list. There are a few 'borderline cases', which have been chosen either because of their originality, influence on other artists, or contribution to rock rather than popularity or chart success. To give recognition to some of the lesser-known performers, 'One Hit Wonders', and faded glories, we have put together an appendix including notes on no fewer tha 00 additional personalities.

Another 80 entries on the managers, producers, promoters, DJs, executives, and others in the business recognize the people behind the scenes who are responsible in part for the success of a performer.

A directory of Record Companies follows, giving their addresses, a brief history, and listing major artists (past and present).

To complete this reference work, we've included a section which reviews the musical instruments (guitars, drums, keyboards) of rock, both those used in the past and those currently available to the musician.

How To Read this Book:

1. Within the main text, individual artists are listed under their surnames, groups under group name. The name of an individual performer is followed by his/her country of origin and a description of talents (US vocalist, producer, composer) in order of renown. His/her date and place of birth and real name (if known by a pseudonym) comes next. Group headings are followed by place of origin, year founded, and the original line-up listing members and instruments ed. In cases where a musician is particularly well known, his preference of instrument is listed, i.e. Guitar: Fender Stratocaster. (Where an artist has his/her own entry separate to group, this instrument would be listed in their own entry.)

2. The biography beneath the heading outlines the career of the artist(s). Within the entry, the symbol(▶) is likely to appear; this indicates that the reader may refer to a related entry in the main text of the book.

The industry terms AOR, MOR, Gold Record, and Platinum Record also appear frequently.

AOR stands for 'Adult Oriented Rock', meaning that which is easily digested by the record buying public (the Eagles, Billy Joel, rather than Motorhead, Kiss, or the Ramones). MOR stands for 'Middle of the Road', meaning easy-listening music which isn't heavy metal, rock, blues, or any other distinct sound.

Gold and Platinum albums are awarded by the RIAA (Recording Industry Association of America) in the US and the BPI (British Phonographic Industries Association) in the UK, and the criteria required by each country differs slightly. In the US, a million singles sold earns a Gold record; two million singles earns Platinum. An LP which goes gold in the US has sold half a million copies. If it goes on to sell a million copies, it becomes Platinum (12″ singles are awarded in the same way).

In the UK, the singles system is based on sales figures, or 'pounds sterling', thus: £250,000 = Silver, £500,000 = Gold, and one million pounds = Platinum. For LPs however, awards are based on units (as in the US) rather than sales, 60,000 copies sold = Silver, 100,000 = Gold, and 300,000 = Platinum. But then, things have changed over the years as values change.

3. A discography follows the biography, beginning with Hit Singles. To be listed in this category, a single must have made the Top 20 in either the US or UK charts. If so, the position it reached in the

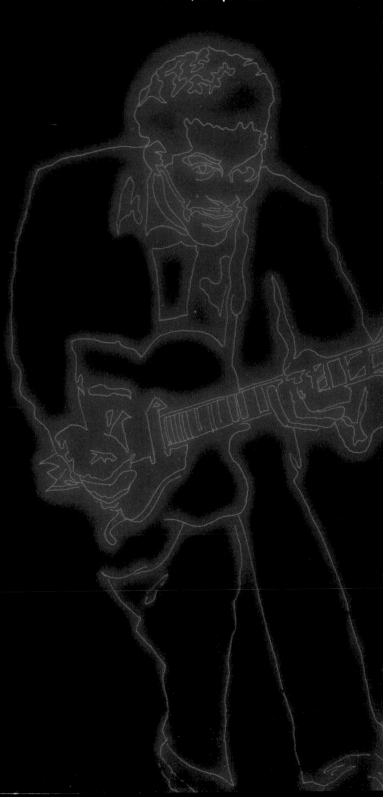

Foreword

corresponding chart, up to and including No. 60 (but not 61-100) would also be listed. Single positions were taken from the most respected chart compilers/publications in the trade, Billboard (US) and Music And Video Week/BBC/Gallup (UK). Billboard began a regular Hot 100 chart in November 1955, while Music And Video Week commenced their charts in January 1956 (figures were compiled by Record Mirror, now owned by Music And Video Week, at that time).

In the case where a record came out in time to make the Billboard chart but not the UK chart, this symbol ✳ will appear in place of a figure. We are aware that some artists included in this book had million-sellers prior to the publication of charts; in such cases we have mentioned their biggest hits within their biography. Our official cut-off date for charts was June 1, 1983, though we have followed through the positions of any singles in the charts at that time.

4. Albums listed are those currently available according to the trade catalogues, Schwann (US) and Music Master (UK) through June 1, 1983. We have added on new LP releases through to press date whenever possible. In certain cases, (selected) appears after the 'Albums' heading; such instances usually involve a 'fringe' artist from country, R&B, soul, etc, and therefore we have listed only the pertinent albums. Albums not available but which are essential to the understanding and appreciation of a performer and therefore merit looking in second hand record shops for, appear under the heading 'Worth Searching Out'. Following the title of an album is the label it is currently available on. (Atlantic) would mean the album is available on Atlantic in both the US and the UK; (MCA, Polydor) means the album is available on MCA in the US and on Polydor in the UK.

5. Group geneology expert Pete Frame was specially commissioned to draw 12 Family Trees exclusively for this book. These trees serve as a visual aid in attempting to keep track of the complex evolutions and intricate relationships of several groups, and allow us to introduce some of the more obscure performers in rock.

Enough of the technicalities, read on . . .

Mike Clifford
Roxane Streeter

August 1983

The seeds of rock were sown in the southern states of America at the turn of the century when slaves, transported from Africa against their will, used field hollers, chants, and work songs to communicate with each other, in a way that only they, and not their white masters, could understand. These were accompanied by African drum rhythms which eventually became the back-beat. The slaves were able to sing the latest news, latest gossip, and latest goings on from field to field.

After the American Civil War, the freed blacks taught themselves to play whatever European instruments they could find. They played them the only way they knew how—making a discordant, synchopated rhythm. This eventually evolved into jazz.

At the same time, the same basic chants and hollers from the fields were revitalized and became rhythm 'n' blues.

Most rhythm 'n' blues singers were devils in disguise. They could sing at your woman from the stage, go past you with a secret message, and go right in her ear and say 'I wanna rock you baby all night long'. The R&B singer put the secrets learned by the slaves to use. He knew he'd got his message across when your woman started dancing and left you standing at the bar.

Sometimes the R&B singer would get himself into trouble, so he'd move on down the line to another town, which led to another major part of the rock 'n' roll life—travel. If it's rock, it's gotta go on the road. If it don't travel, it ain't rock.

As a kid in my hometown Newcastle in Northern England, I went to many jazz concerts. A time came in every jazz concert when a blues singer got up in front of the jazz band. They all united behind him and riffed away. A back beat was laid down. The blues singer moved more permanently to the fore. Rock 'n' roll was born.

One night I heard jazz entrepreneur Norman Grantz explain from the stage of the Newcastle City Hall that if jazz was a bright shining diamond, then rock 'n' roll was a lump of coal which did nothing more than generate heat and a lot of smoke. From that moment on I was an avid rocker.

Rock 'n' roll hit me in the abdominal region, not the brain. Rock 'n' roll is sexuality. It communicates all the basic drives. The back-beat equals the heartbeat. The blues can represent the ups and downs of a romantic love affair. Heavy metal can be related to S&M. Punk is like losing your virginity. Reggae is political and spiritual.

Rock 'n' roll can be a gathering of the tribes like Woodstock. It can be a chance to just rock-out every Saturday night at your local gig.

Rock 'n' roll is the poetry of Bob Dylan and Chuck Berry. It's the genius of Ray Charles. It can be a fad like the Beatles—or something magnificent like the writing of Lennon and McCartney.

Rock can be fun. It can also be hell. Rock 'n' roll is a game with no rules, because the rules keep changing all the time.

The soul of rock 'n' roll gets drowned from time to time and people think it's dead, but then like a disease, it crops up again, totally unexpected, in another powerful form.

ABC

UK group formed 1980.

Original line-up: Martin Fry, vocals; Mark Lickley, bass; David Robinson, drums; Stephen Singleton, saxophone; Mark White, guitar.

Career: Martin Fry formed ABC out of demise of synth band Vice Versa. From experience gained as editor of fanzine ('Modern Drugs') began creating an image of glamour and style for group. A year after signing with Phonogram, Fry had led ABC into UK pop charts with three hit singles and a gold album.

**The Lexicon Of Love, ABC.
Courtesy Mercury Records.**

Band won widespread acceptance with American audience via MTV through strong, well-made videos. ABC's sound combines clever lyrics and good melody but relies heavily on Fry's excellent vocals as well as good production. With the collapse of Squeeze(▶), ABC seem heir apparent in the pop sweepstakes. Only problem is that sound is a little too smooth, just a bit glib, and live performances probably will not hold same paying audience attraction as videos.

Current line-up: Fry; Singleton; White.

Hit Singles:	US	UK
Tears Are Not Enough, 1981	—	19
Poison Arrow, 1982	—	6
The Look Of Love, 1982	19	4
All Of My Heart, 1982	—	5

Albums:
The Lexicon Of Love (Mercury/
   Neutron), 1982

AC/DC

Australian group formed 1974.

Original line-up: Malcolm Young, guitar; Angus Young, Gibson SG guitar; Phil Rudd, drums; Mark Evans, bass; Bon Scott, vocals.

Career: Malcolm and Angus Young formed band in Sydney, Australia, but moved to Melbourne where original line-up evolved. Malcolm and Angus are younger brothers of George Young of '60s pop outfit Easybeats. This connection has proved invaluable to AC/DC in terms of experience and production. However, there is no trace of the Easybeats' pop melodies in the sonic, frontal assaults of AC/DC.

Now superstars on heavy-metal circuit, AC/DC were instrumental in breaking down prejudices against Australian rock. Strong home following was gained via release of two 1975 albums: **High Voltage** and **TNT**. Then came low-budget, hard-working tour of UK which earned enough favourable response for UK album release. (Entitled **High Voltage**, UK LP is actually **TNT** minus two tracks, with two added from the Australian release **High Voltage**.)

Making every performance an athletic endurance contest for both band and audience, AD/DC gained notoriety in US. Clearly everyone else was back-up to Scott's rivet-driving vocals and Angus' head-bobbing gyrotechnics. (Change in bass players in 1977 from Mark Evans to Cliff Williams almost went unnoticed.) Bon Scott's death from alcohol abuse in April 1980 occurred when AC/DC was on fringe of super-group status. In a fortunate twist of fate, AC/DC hired Scott-soundalike Brian Johnson (from band Geordie).

Back In Black set proved band could overcome loss of one of its main attractions, and led to less hectic touring and recording schedule. AC/DC are real heavy-metal heavies, with deserved success and should be a force for many years to come.

Current line-up: Malcolm Young; Angus Young; Rudd; Cliff Williams, bass; Brian Johnson, vocals.

Hit Singles:	US	UK
Rock'n'Roll Ain't Noise Pollution, 1981	—	15
Let's Get It Up, 1982	44	13
For Those About To Rock, 1982	—	15

Albums:
High Voltage (ATCO/Atlantic), 1976
Dirty Deeds Done Dirt Cheap (Atlantic), 1976
Let There Be Rock (ATCO/Atlantic), 1977
Powerage (Atlantic), 1978
If You Want Blood (Atlantic), 1978
Highway To Hell (Atlantic), 1979
Back In Black (Atlantic), 1980
For Those About To Rock (Atlantic), 1981

Abba

Swedish group formed 1971.

Original/Current line-up: Agnetha Ulvaeus, vocals; Anni-Frid Lyngstad-Fredriksson, vocals; Bjorn Ulvaeus, guitar, vocals; Benny Andersson, keyboards, synthesiser, vocals.

Career: Reputed to earn more for the Swedish economy each year than the vast Volvo car and truck company, Abba leapt to international prominence when they won the 1974 Eurovision Song Contest. Before that, they had already put in long service as leading figures of Swedish pop scene.

Anni-Frid (born Norway, November 15, 1945; raised in Toshala, Sweden) moved to Stockholm in 1967 to start singing career. Agnetha (born Jonkopping, April 5, 1950) started recording at 17 and had several local hits. Bjorn (born Gothenburg, April 25, 1945) was the star of successful Hootenanny Singers in late '60s. Benny (born Stockholm, December 16, 1946) was leader of popular rock band the Hep Cats.

Pop industry entrepreneur Stikkan Andersson persuaded Bjorn, whom he already had under contract to his Polar Music company, and Benny to leave their groups and pool resources. Benny and Anni-Frid had been living together in Stockholm since 1970; Bjorn and Agnetha married in July 1971, a major event on Sweden's pop scene as both were already national figures. After Benny and Bjorn cut **Lycka** album as duo, Abba gradually came into being. The girls had been doing vocal back-ups on Benny and Bjorn recordings and as foursome had made some stage appearances.

Anni-Frid was unsuccessful solo entrant in 1971 Eurovision song contest; for next two years foursome worked hard on their act with view to using that event as springboard to stardom. Name Abba was chosen in 1973 and the group represented Sweden in that year's Eurovision with **Ring Ring** but failed to win. Next year, despite strongest ever competition, they came out on top with **Waterloo.** The event was televised from Brighton, England, to an audience of some 500 million. Eurovision triumph does not automatically spell big record sales but in Abba's case it did. **Waterloo** not only went to No. 1 in most European countries, but made No. 6 in the US where Eurovision is unknown.

However, Eurovision's market is not normally the same as the pop market, its appeal being largely to mums and dads rather than young rock fans. It was 18 months before Abba could crack the true pop market. They did it with **S.O.S.**, which made charts all over Europe, precipitating them to superstardom. **Mama Mia, Fernando, Dancing Queen** and **Knowing Me, Knowing You** were all UK No. l's, while **Money, Money, Money** went to No. 2. In 1977 **Dancing Queen** gave them their first American chart-topper. Every record was a perfectly crafted piece of pop commercialism, employing perfect harmonies, irresistible hooks, and impeccable pro-

Left: Angus Young of AC/DC adds to the group's visual image with his schoolboy shorts and head banging.

duction. Their accompanying promotional videos utilised equally flawless formula.

When they finally embarked on a world tour in 1977 it was done in the grandest manner with 14 musicians, elaborate sets and full-blown productions. Hits continued to flow, both albums and singles racking amazing sales. Personal problems, however, began to overshadow their artistic and commercial success (besides musical activities they invested heavily in property and other business spheres).

Bjorn and Agnetha divorced in 1979. Agnetha reverted to maiden name Fältskog. Anni-Frid and Benny divorced in 1981. For some time they did not allow this to interfere with their career as a group, but the foursome eventually drifted apart as artists, embarking on solo ventures, though they have not officially called end to group.

Hit Singles:	US	UK
Waterloo, 1974	6	1
S.O.S., 1975	15	6
Mamma Mia, 1975	32	1
Fernando, 1976	13	1
I Do I Do I Do I Do, 1976	15	38
Dancing Queen, 1976	1	1
Money Money Money, 1976	56	3
Knowing Me Knowing You, 1977	14	1
The Name Of The Game, 1977	12	1
Take A Chance On Me, 1978	3	1
Summer Night City, 1978	—	15
Chiquitita, 1979	29	2
Does Your Mother Know, 1979	19	4
Angeleyes/Voulez-Vous, 1979	—	3
Gimme Gimme Gimme (A Man After Midnight), 1979	—	3
I Have A Dream, 1979	-	2
The Winner Takes It All, 1980	8	1
Super Trouper, 1980	45	1
Lay All Your Love On Me, 1981	—	7
One Of Us, 1981	—	3

Albums:
Waterloo (Atlantic/Epic), 1974
Abba (Atlantic/Epic), 1975
Arrival (Atlantic/Epic), 1976
Greatest Hits (Atlantic/Epic), 1976
The Album (Atlantic/Epic), 1978
Greatest Hits Volume II (Atlantic/Epic), 1979
Voulez-Vous (Atlantic/Epic), 1979
Super Trouper (Atlantic/Epic), 1980
The Visitors (Atlantic/Epic), 1981
Gracias Pour La Musica (—/Epic), 1981
The Singles (Atlantic/Epic), 1982

Frida Solo:
Something's Going On (Atlantic/Epic), 1982

Agnetha Fältskog Solo:
Wrap Your Arms Around Me (Atlantic/Epic), 1983

Adam Ant

UK vocalist, composer.

Born Stuart Leslie Goddard, London, November 3, 1954.

Career: Idol of the pre-teens, Adam Ant ended up filling same kind of role as Donny Osmond(▶) had done decade earlier, though, ironically, he had emerged from London's rebellious punk movement of late '70s.

While at art college in North London, Goddard joined Bazooka Joe but left group to form new band, the B-Sides. Though commercial failure, outfit proved catalyst for Adam and the Ants.

Andy Warren and Lester Square from B-Sides were original Ants. Group's early material was largely about punk fetishes; members adopted black leather bondage image through links with clothing store 'Sex' in London's Kings Road (owned by Malcolm

McLaren of Sex Pistols(▶) renown). 'Sex' shop assistant Jordan managed emergent band. She helped create stage identity and appeared with them on gigs to sing **Red Scab** and **Lou,** latter dedicated to Lou Reed(▶). Group's first gig was at 'Man In The Moon' pub in Kings Road. Entire audience walked out save Jordan and Siouxsie and Steve Severin of the Banshees(▶); the show was that bad.

In 1977 cut single **Young Parisians** and unreleased sides for Decca; in 1978 cut **Xerox** on independent Do It label.

Support roles with Siouxsie and the Banshees and gradually softening look—pirate theme replacing bondage,—saw band building commercial base. Cut debut LP **Dirk Wears White Sox** (Do It, 1979). McLaren was temporary manager before he split group and turned part of it (Matthew Ashman, guitar, and Dave Barbarossa, drums) into nucleus of Bow Wow Wow(▶).

New band comprising Adam, Marco Perrone, guitar, Gary Tibbs (from Roxy Music(▶)), bass, and two drummers, Lee Merrick and Terry Lee Miall, did widely acclaimed small-club Ants Invasion tour early '80. Followed with minor hit **Kings Of The Wild Frontier.** **Dog Eat Dog** provided first Top 20 record, bringing wide TV exposure.

Ant Music (1980), **Stand And Deliver** (1981), chart-topping **Prince Charming** (1981) and **Ant Rap** (1981) were helped by inventive lavishly produced promotional videos. Sense of theatrics and wide variety of thematic costumes—highwayman, pirate, beau—gave enormous visual impact to almost primeval thudding rhythms of records.

In summer 1982, Adam dissolved Ants and went solo, scoring with **Goody Two Shoes, Friend Or Foe,** and minor hit **Desperate But Not Serious.** He retained songwriting partnership with Marco Perrone.

As fame grew, Adam and the Ants' audiences had grown younger and younger, original fans not wanting to know group after **Kings Of The Wild Frontier.** Whether as solo Adam can regain more mature rock following remains to be seen, though he has broken into the US market of late via MTV; his videos are among most requested by viewers.

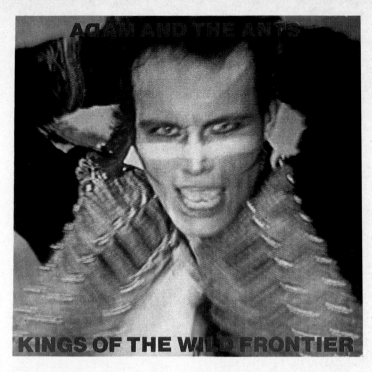

KINGS OF THE WILD FRONTIER

Hit Singles:	US	UK
As Adam And The Ants:		
Dog Eat Dog, 1980	—	4
Ant Music, 1981	—	2
Young Parisians, 1981	—	9
Kings Of The Wild Frontier, 1981	—	2
Stand And Deliver, 1981	—	1
Prince Charming, 1981	—	1
Ant Rap, 1981	—	3
Deutscher Girls, 1982	—	13
As Adam Ant:		
Goody Two Shoes, 1982	12	1
Friend Or Foe, 1982	—	9

Albums:
As Adam And The Ants:
Dirk Wears White Sox (—/Do It), 1979

Kings Of The Wild Frontier (—/CBS), 1980
Solo:
Friend Or Foe (Epic/CBS), 1982

Kings Of The Wild Frontier, Adam and the Ants. Courtesy CBS Records. Adam has since gone solo.

FLOWERS OF ROMANCE
BUZZCOCKS · BANSHEES ANTS & ULTRAVOX

SLIK LATE 74 to SEPT 77
- JIM McGINLAY (rep by RUSSELL WEBB) bass/voc
- RUSSELL WEBB bass/voc
- KENNY HYSLOP drums/voc
- BILLY McISAAC keybd/voc
- MIDGE URE gtr/voc

cabaret — formed The Zones

SEX PISTOLS AUG 75 to FEB 77
- GLEN MATLOCK bass
- JOHNNY ROTTEN vocals
- PAUL COOK drums
- STEVE JONES guitar

continued with Sid Vicious

BUZZCOCKS #1 JUL 76 to JAN 77
- HOWARD DEVOTO vocals
- PETE SHELLEY gtr/voc
- STEVE DIGGLE bass
- JOHN MAHER drums

SIOUXSIE AND THE BANSHEES SEPT 76 ONLY
- SID VICIOUS drums
- SIOUXSIE vocals
- STEVEN SEVERIN bass
- MARCO PIRRONI guitar

to Sex Pistols

ADAM & THE ANTS #1 APR 77 to OCT 79
- JOHNNY BINOUAC guitar
- MARK GAUMONT guitar
- PAUL FLANAGAN drums
- ADAM ANT vocals
- ANDY WARREN bass
- LESTER SQUARE guitar

various Ants came and went — Monochrome Set

ULTRAVOX #1 (formerly TIGER LILY) APR 74 to FEB 78
- STEVE SHEARS guitar
- JOHN FOXX vocals
- CHRIS CROSS bass/voc
- WARREN CANN drums/voc
- BILLY CURRIE violin/keybd

Cowboys Int

RICH KIDS SEPT 77 to NOV 78
- GLEN MATLOCK bass/voc
- MIDGE URE gtr/voc
- RUSTY EGAN drums
- STEVE NEW guitar

The Spectres

BUZZCOCKS #2 FEB 77 to MAR 81
- PETE SHELLEY gtr/voc
- STEVE DIGGLE gtr/voc
- JOHN MAHER drums
- STEVE GARVEY (rep by GARTH SMITH) bass
- GARTH SMITH bass

solo — Flag of Convenience

MODELS OCT 76 to APR 78
- CLIFF HARRIS gtr/voc
- MICK ALLEN bass
- MARCO PIRRONI guitar
- TERRY LEE MIALL drums

Music Club — Rema Rema

ULTRAVOX #2 MAR 78 to MAR 79
- ROBIN SIMON guitar
- JOHN FOXX vocals
- CHRIS CROSS bass/synth
- WARREN CANN drums/voc
- BILLY CURRIE keybd/violin

Magazine — solo

MAGAZINE #1 APR 77 to OCT 78
- BOB DICKINSON (rep by DAVE FORMULA) keybds
- DAVE FORMULA keybds
- BARRY ADAMSON bass
- JOHN McGEOCH guitar
- HOWARD DEVOTO vocals
- MARTIN JACKSON drums
- PAUL SPENCER (rep by) guitar

SIOUXSIE AND THE BANSHEES NOV 76 to JUL 77
- SIOUXSIE vocals
- STEVEN SEVERIN bass
- KENNY MORRIS drums
- P.T. FENTON guitar

The Heroes

ADAM & THE ANTS #2 OCT 79 to JAN 80
- ADAM ANT vocals
- LEIGH GORMAN bass
- DAVE BARBE drums
- MATTHEW ASHMAN guitar

TUBEWAY ARMY MAR 77 to JULY 78
- GARY NUMAN vocals
- PAUL GARDINER bass
- OTHER GUYS various

VISAGE LATE 78 to JAN 82 (STUDIO GROUP ONLY)
- BILLY CURRIE keybds
- MIDGE URE gtr/synth
- STEVE STRANGE vocals
- RUSTY EGAN drums
- DAVE FORMULA keybds
- BARRY ADAMSON bass
- JOHN McGEOCH gtr/sax

gay blades about town

SIOUXSIE AND THE BANSHEES #3 JUL 77 to SEP 79
- JOHN McKAY guitar
- SIOUXSIE vocals
- STEVEN SEVERIN bass
- KENNY MORRIS drums

BOW-WOW-WOW FEB 80-NOW
- ANNABELLA LU-WIN vocals
- LEIGH GORMAN bass/voc
- DAVE BARBE drums
- MATTHEW ASHMAN gtr/voc

GARY NUMAN JUN 79 to OCT 79
- GARY NUMAN vocals
- FOUR OTHERS various
- BILLY CURRIE synth

continued solo career

THIN LIZZY #7 JUL 79 to AUG 79
- GARY MOORE (rep by MIDGE URE) guitar
- MIDGE URE guitar
- PHIL LYNOTT bass/voc
- SCOTT GORHAM gtr/voc
- BRIAN DOWNEY drums

continued with Snowy White

MAGAZINE #2 OCT 78 to JUL 80
- BARRY ADAMSON bass
- DAVE FORMULA keybds
- HOWARD DEVOTO vocals
- JOHN DOYLE drums

SIOUXSIE AND THE BANSHEES SEPT 79 to JULY 80
- JOHN McGEOCH guitar
- SIOUXSIE vocals
- STEVEN SEVERIN bass
- BUDGIE drums
- ROBERT SMITH guitar

on loan from The Cure

ADAM & THE ANTS #3 FEB 80 to FEB 81
- MARCO PIRRONI guitar
- TERRY LEE MIALL drums
- MERRICK drums
- ADAM ANT vocals
- KEVIN MOONEY bass

ULTRAVOX #3 OCT 79 to NOW
- BILLY CURRIE keyb'd/viol
- WARREN CANN drums/voc
- CHRIS CROSS bass/synth
- MIDGE URE gtr/voc

MAGAZINE #3 JULY 80 to MAY 81
- BEN MANDELSON gtr/violin
- ROBIN SIMON (rep by) guitar
- BARRY ADAMSON bass
- DAVE FORMULA keyb'd
- HOWARD DEVOTO vocals
- JOHN DOYLE drums

SIOUXSIE AND THE BANSHEES JULY 80 to DEC 82
- JOHN McGEOCH guitar
- SIOUXSIE vocals
- STEVEN SEVERIN bass
- BUDGIE drums

ADAM & THE ANTS #4 FEB 81 to JAN 82
- ADAM ANT vocals
- MARCO PIRRONI gtr/voc
- TERRY LEE MIALL drums
- MERRICK drums
- GARY TIBBS bass

Pete Frame

Aerosmith

US group formed 1970.

Original line-up: Steve Tyler, vocals; Joe Perry, guitar; Tom Hamilton, bass; Joey Kramer, drums; Brad Whitford, guitar.

Career: Legend has band forming in Sunapee, New Hampshire, during summer 1970. Lots of local gigging in Boston led to dates at Max's Kansas City where they were seen and signed by Clive Davis for CBS in late 1972. Despite emphasis on group participation, focal point was Jagger look-alike Tyler and guitarist Perry. Duo were main writers of original material and also took brunt of universal criticism as Rolling Stones(▶)/Yardbirds(▶) rip-offs.

Long-term liaison with producer Jack Douglas began with widely criticised second album **Get Your Wings**. By 1975 extensive touring

**Aerosmith's Draw The Line.
Courtesy CBS Records.**

finally paid off with success in American singles and album charts. **Toys In The Attic** went platinum within months of release and stayed in charts for two years. This sparked interest in first two albums which went platinum by the release of **Rocks**. 1976 saw re-issue of **Dream On**, which earned gold record three years after first appearance. Aerosmith seemed destined for long run as high-class Grand Funk Railroad(▶), a people's band, working diligently for fans. But success brought problems.

A well-deserved rest from touring may have caused **Draw The Line** to miss the fire of earlier albums. Original LP sleeve, which featured only a cartoon of band, also seemed ego trip which did not mesh with spirit of '77 punk revolution. Instead of being allowed to enjoy hard-won success, Aerosmith found themselves part of establishment about to be assaulted by new wave.

Dissension broke out publicly in 1979 when Perry began spending more time on solo project than on band's newest recording. Packaging of **Night In The Ruts** with inner sleeve advert for Aerosmith merchandise indicated widening gulf between band and its populist roots. Perry left soon afterwards and has released two US albums as Joe Perry Project.

With the loss of Perry's guitar sound and songwriting, it might have seemed a good time to stop. Whitford did, partway through recording new album. Tyler pressed on. Significantly, he re-joined Jack Douglas (who was absent on Ruts) and 1982 set **Rock In A Hard Place** marked return to power of earlier albums.

Current line-up: Tyler; Hamilton; Kramer.

Hit Singles:	US	UK
Dream On, 1976	6	—
Walk This Way, 1977	10	—

Albums:
Aerosmith (Columbia/CBS), 1973
Get Your Wings (Columbia/CBS), 1974
Toys In The Attic (Columbia/CBS), 1975
Rocks (Columbia/CBS), 1976
Draw The Line (Columbia/CBS), 1977
Live! Bootleg (Columbia/CBS), 1978
Greatest Hits (Columbia/CBS), 1980
Rock In A Hard Place (Columbia/CBS), 1982

Air Supply

Australian group formed 1976.

Career: Graham Russell (born Nottingham, England) and Russell Hitchcock met when in Australian production of 'Jesus Christ Superstar'; cut demos with aid of show's musical director, Frank Esler-Smith. Adopted group name as contrast to preponderance of heavy metal in Australia, and released debut single **Love And Other Bruises** there in 1976. Single made No. 2 in chart while Russell and Hitchcock were still in 'Superstar'. LP was recorded after leaving show, and went gold in Australia. By end of 1976, group were major local attraction; but when they appeared as support act on Rod Stewart(▶) tour of US, early fans saw this as 'selling out', and fame evaporated.

Russell retreated to write songs, including **Lost In Love** and **All Out Of Love** which became group's first two monster US hits in 1980, while Graham returned to UK to write rock opera about Robin Hood. At Midem Festival in early 1980 Graham attempted to generate European interest in group, who seemed close to folding when he left Australia; he noticed that a trade magazine was featuring Air Supply on front cover—Arista Records (US) had released **Lost In Love** as single. Graham quickly returned to Australia via US, where Arista boss Clive Davis sanctioned making of LP.

Subsequently, Air Supply, despite somewhat easy listening sound, scored seven consecutive Top 10 singles in US—although bubble showed signs of bursting towards end of 1982—and three highly successful albums (all gold or better). US success failed to impress UK market, though original Australian fans have now returned in force. Air Supply, as major spearhead of Australian invasion of US charts, are probably most tuneful of Antipodean acts.

Current line-up: Russell Hitchcock, vocals; Graham Russell, vocals, guitar; Frank Esler-Smith, keyboards; David Moyse, lead guitar; David Green, bass; Ralph Cooper, drums.

Hit Singles:	US	UK
Lost In Love, 1980	3	—
All Out Of Love, 1980	1	11
Every Woman In The World, 1980	3	—
The One That You Love, 1981	1	—
Here I Am (Just When I Thought I Was Over You), 1981	4	—
Sweet Dreams, 1981	6	—
Even The Nights Are Better, 1982	5	44

Albums:
Lost In Love (Arista), 1980
The One That You Love (Arista), 1981
Now And Forever (Arista), 1982

Jan Akkerman

Dutch guitarist, composer.
Born Holland, December 24, 1946.

Career: Former member of Focus(▶) whose frantic but precise playing considerably enhanced this adventurous Dutch outfit. He left band in 1976 to better pursue solo career, which reached artistic peak in 1980 with release of **Jan Akkerman 3**.

A reticent, introverted character who epitomises the phrase 'let's his playing do the talking', Akkerman seems to have settled into jazz/rock groove, with considerable classical leanings. In addition to guitar, plays bass, piano, and lute.

Various recorded projects include LPs with Dutch vocalist Kaz Lux (**Eli**) and German arranger Claus Ogerman (**Aranjuez**), and live set **Jan Akkerman Live** featuring Cees Van Der Laarse (bass), Bruno Castelucci (drums), Neppia Nova (percussion), William Kennes (keyboards), Jasper Van't Hof (keyboards) and Tom Barlage (tenor sax).

Akkerman's one concession to commercialism was first Atlantic LP (second solo effort) **Tabernakel** in 1974, which included bassist Tim Bogert and drummer Carmine Appice in line-up, produced with former Columbia University professor of music George Flynn, who co-wrote much of the material.

This flying Dutchman's ability will mean longevity if not pop star status.

Guitar: Gibson Les Paul.

Albums (selected):
Profile (Sire/Harvest), 1972
Guitar For Sale (—/Bovema), 1973
Eli (Atlantic), 1977
Aranjuez (—/CBS), 1978
Live (Atlantic), 1979
Jan Akkerman 3 (Atlantic), 1980

Alabama

US group formed 1970.

Original/Current line-up: Randy Owen, guitar, vocals; Jeff Cook, guitar, fiddle, keyboards, vocals; Teddy Gentry, bass, vocals; Mark Herndon, drums, vocals.

Career: Alabama are a perplexing success story; after years of determined work, they have topped US country charts consistently since breaking in 1980, although their music can be described as bland at best. They've prospered apparently through sheer persistence.

Formed in early '70s, band spent nearly ten years playing a gruelling treadmill of small gigs. Demo tapes were repeatedly rejected in Nashville. Still they held out, convinced that a larger audience waited for their brand of slightly rock-tinged, 'easy listening' country. Their patience was rewarded when RCA signed them in 1980, and first album, **My Home's In Alabama**, was enormous suc-

Below: Original line-up of the Allman Brothers Band (1970) makers of fine R&B/rock music.

cess. It was quickly followed up by two more platinum albums; they eventually became the most popular country/rock group in US, touring constantly, and reaping huge concert sales.

Hit Singles:	US	UK
Feels So Right, 1981	20	—
Love In The First Degree, 1981	15	—
Take Me Down, 1982	18	—

Albums:
My Home's In Alabama (RCA), 1980
Feels So Right (RCA), 1981
Mountain Music (RCA), 1982

Allman Brothers Band

US group formed 1969.

Original line-up: Duane Allman, Gibson Les Paul, Fender Stratocaster guitar; Gregg Allman, guitar, vocals, keyboards; Dickie Betts, Gibson Les Paul guitar; Berry Oakley, bass; Jai Johnny Johanson, drums; Butch Trucks, drums.

Career: Duane Allman (born Nashville, November 20, 1946) was raised in Daytona Beach, Florida; moved to Los Angeles in '60s. Formed Hour Glass with brother Gregg (born December 8, 1947) on keyboards, guitar, vocals; Paul Hornsby, keyboards, guitar, vocals; Jesse Willard Carr, bass, vocals; John Sandlin, drums, guitar. Debut Liberty album was cut at label's own LA studio. Band recorded follow-up at Rick Hall's Muscle Shoals Studio. Duane Allman had previously worked there as session guitarist (on Clarence Carter's 1967 **Road Of Love** sessions). Tapes for second album were rejected by Liberty and band broke up.

Allman stayed at Fame to work on sessions with Percy Sledge, Aretha Franklin(▶), Boz Scaggs(▶), Wilson Pickett and others. Also cut material for projected but unreleased Atlantic solo album before signing to Phil Walden's Capricorn label (based in nearby Macon, Georgia, and distributed by Atlantic).

Walden had previously managed the late Otis Redding(▶) and helped Allman put together what became Allman Brothers Band. The Brothers had been working informally with Butch Truck's band 31st February; when outfit jammed with Betts and Oakley's band Second Coming, in Jacksonville, foundations of Allman Brothers band were laid.

New band gigged around Southern States building big following. Debut album **The Allman Brothers Band**, 1969 (cut in New York), was potent mixture of progressive rock and R&B/blues roots. Interplay between Duane Allman's potent slide work and forceful

technique of Dickie Betts was focal point of band's attractive new sound. From **Idlewild South** album (1970) single **Midnight Rider** was smash, pushing LP to gold status.

While band's reputation grew ever bigger, Duane Allman continued session work, both at Muscle Shoals and elsewhere. Among artists who benefited from his creative playing were Johnny Jenkins, Delaney and Bonnie and Friends(▶), King Curtis(▶), Lulu(▶), Herbie Mann(▶), Ronnie Hawkins(▶), Sam Samudio, the Duck and the Bear (a pseudonym for Canned Heat's Al Wilson), blues legend Otis Rush and, most especially, Eric Clapton(▶). Allman's trading-off of licks with Clapton on the Derek and the Dominoes' **Layla** album was among his finest work.

Tragedy hit band when Duane Allman died in motorcycle crash on October 29, 1971; he was just 24 years old. Last testament was superlative **The Allman Brothers Band At Fillmore East** album, recorded shortly before. Contained superb versions of blues standards **Statesboro' Blues** and **Stormy Monday** plus a 22-minute 40-second workout on **Whipping Post** which filled whole of one side of double LP set.

Three tracks for **Eat A Peach** had been laid down before Duane's death; it was decided to finish album without recruiting replacement guitarist. LP proved another massive seller.

Unbelievably, lightning struck twice: on November 11, 1972, Berry Oakley died in another motorcycle accident, also in Macon.

Band subsequently added Chuck Leavill, keyboards, and Lamar Williams, bass. Sound softened out into more medlodic country-rock idiom for **Brothers And Sisters** album. From this, **Jessica** instrumental hit proved to be Betts' tour-de-force; revealed depth of talent which had previously been, to some degree, overshadowed by Duane Allman.

Following **Win, Lose Or Draw,** Betts and Gregg Allman embarked on solo projects. Gregg toured States under own name with new band. Allman Brothers' Band LP **The Road Goes On Forever** was compilation rather than new material.

End seemed to have arrived when Allman testified against his personal road manager Scooter Herring who received a 75-year sentence on narcotics' charges. 'There is no way we can ever work with Gregg again', aggrieved Betts told 'Rolling Stone' magazine. Betts promptly departed to form own band, Great Southern, with debut album on Arista (1977). Jazz-rock group Sea Level was formed by Johnson, Williams and Leavill, plus guitarist Jimmy Nalls.

Above: Duane Allman, who died in a motorcycle crash at 24.

By now married to Cher Bono, Gregg Allman issued **Playin' Up A Storm** under own name in 1977. Rift was healed, however, when at a Great Southern concert in Central Park, Betts was joined on stage for finale by Gregg and Butch Trucks. Soon after, at Capricorn Records' annual barbecue, core of Allman Brothers Band, plus David Goldflies, bass, and Dan Toler, drums, played 90-minute set; band was back in business with a vengeance.

Regular Atlantic producer Tom Dowd was on hand for **Enlightened Rogues** (1979), their sixth gold album. In 1980 the Allman Brothers signed to Arista for **Reach For The Sky** album and have continued with further first-class product.

Current line-up: Gregg Allman; Betts; Trucks; Dan Toler, guitar; David Goldflies, bass; Jim Essery, harmonica. David 'Frankie' Toler, drums

Hit Singles:

	US	UK
Ramblin' Man, 1973	2	—

Albums:
The Allman Brothers Band (Capricorn), 1969
Idlewild South (Capricorn), 1970
At Fillmore East (Capricorn), 1971
Eat A Peach (Capricorn), 1972
Beginnings (Capricorn), 1973
Brothers And Sisters (Capricorn), 1973
Win, Loose Or Draw (Capricorn), 1975
The Road Goes On Forever (Capricorn), 1975
Wipe The Windows, Check The Oil, Dollar Gas (Capricorn), 1976
Enlightened Rogues (Capricorn) 1979
Best Of (Capricorn), 1980
Reach For The Sky (Arista), 1980
Brothers Of The Road (Arista), 1981

Duane Allman Solo:
Anthology (Polydor/Capricorn), 1972
Anthology Volume 2 (Polydor/Capricorn), 1974
Best Of (Polydor/Capricorn), 1979

Gregg Allman:
Laid Back (Polydor/Capricorn), 1973
Playing Up A Storm (Polydor/Capricorn), 1977
Dickie Betts And The Great Southern (Arista), 1977

Worth Searching Out:
The Hour Glass (Liberty), 1968
Duane And Gregg Allman (Bold/Polydor), 1972

Herb Alpert

US trumpeter, bandleader, composer, vocalist, executive.
Born Los Angeles, California, March 31, 1937.

Career: A trumpeter from age eight, Alpert entered music business as songwriter in partnership with Lou Adler. Close friends of Sam Cooke(▶), they co-wrote his hit **Wonderful World** and produced early Jan and Dean(▶) hits on Dore before setting up Shardee label with soul singer Lou Rawls.

As Dore Alpert, he cut two vocal flop singles for RCA in early '60s before splitting with Adler and setting up new partnership with promotion man/producer Jerry Moss on new label Carnival (later A&M).

Alpert's vocal effort **Tell It To The Birds** (1962) was among first A&M releases. While watching bull-fight in Tijuana, Mexico, he had idea of recording audience 'ole' roars and over-dubbing them on earlier instrumental **Twinkle Star**. Re-titled **The Lonely Bull**, record went gold and established his unique 'Ameriachi' sound, a blend of rock'n'roll, jazz and Mexican music achieved by over-dubbing one trumpet solo on top of another and using maracas, tambourines and mandolin sounds.

Herb Alpert & The Tijuana Brass, Greatest Hits. Courtesy A&M Records.

First four albums, **The Lonely Bull** (a gold LP), **Going Places**, **South Of The Border** (also gold and 167 weeks on US chart) and **Whipped Cream And Other Delights** were massive sellers as was **What Now My Love**, US No. 1 for 12 weeks and first gold cartridge tape. Alpert's success was reflected in turnover of A&M, jumping from $600,000 gross in third year (1964) to $7,600,000 in 1965, $25 million in 1966 and $50 million in 1967.

Alpert starred in April 1968 CBS TV Special, and accompanying album **The Beat Of The Brass** went gold, while single **This Guy's In Love With You** was released following public response and gave Alpert first vocal smash (four weeks at No. 1) and writers Burt Bacharach and Hal David their first US chart-topper.

Alpert's musicians Lou Pagani (piano), John Pisano (guitar), Tonni Kalash (trumpet), Pat Senatore (guitar), Bob Edmondson (trombone) and Nick Ceroli (drums) were reputedly highest-paid sidemen of their era, each earning between $50,000 and $100,000 a year.

Alpert disbanded group in 1969 to concentrate on A&M, quickly turning the Carpenters(▶) into major act and scoring with music spanning MOR, pop, rock, soul and jazz.

America's undisputed King of MOR instrumentals during '60s, when his LPs outsold even those of Beatles(▶), Alpert found rebirth returning to studio in the '80s; he scored in discos with **Rise** (second US chart-topper) and then **Fandango**, co-produced by Jose Quitana (who had 17 of top 25 sellers in Latin America in '81), and his jazz-funk albums were critically acclaimed.

Hit Singles:

	US	UK
The Lonely Bull, 1962	6	22
Spanish Flea, 1965	27	3
Taste Of Honey, 1965	7	—
Zorba The Greek, 1966	11	—
The Work Song, 1966	18	—
Mame, 1966	19	—
This Guy's In Love With You, 1968	1	3
Rise, 1979	1	13

Albums (selected):
Greatest Hits (A&M), 1969
Greatest Hits Volume II (A&M/—), 1970
40 Greatest (—/K-Tel), 1977
Rise (A&M), 1979
Magic Man (A&M), 1981

America

US group formed 1971.

Original line-up: Dewey Bunnell, guitar; vocals; Gerry Beckley, guitar, vocals; Dan Peek, guitar vocals.

Career: Members first met each other in 1967 while stationed with parents at US Air Force base in UK. Mutual interest in rock'n'roll kept up the acquaintance as trio passed through various local bands.

In early 1971 trio formed acoustic group and named it after homeland they hardly knew.

They secured contract with Warner Bros, and first single was harmless Crosby, Still and Nash(▶) soundalike **Horse With No Name**, which made No.3 in UK. This encouraged Warner to release cut in US, and song with no meaning went to No. 1.

America (A Horse With No Name) Courtesy Warner Bros Records.

Despite two follow-up singles which made US Top 10, everything else was somewhat anti-climactic, becoming rather MOR. Peek left in late 1977, leaving America a duo. Then to everyone's surprise, regrouped America returned to US charts in 1982 with Top 10 hit, **You Can Do Magic**.

Current line-up: Bunnel; Beckley; Peek.

Hit Singles:

	US	UK
Horse With No Name, 1972	1	3
I Need You, 1972	9	—
Ventura Highway, 1972	8	43
You Can Do Magic, 1982	8	59

Albums:
America (Horse With No Name) (Warner Bros), 1971
Homecoming (Warner Bros), 1972
Hat Trick (Warner Bros), 1973
Holiday (Warner Bros), 1974
Hearts (Warner Bros), 1975
History: Greatest Hits (Warner Bros), 1975
Live (Warner Bros), 1977
View From The Bottom (Warner Bros), 1982

Dan Peek Solo:
All Things Are Possible (World/Lamb And Lion), 1979

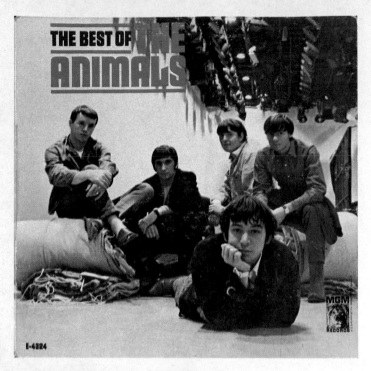

THE BEST OF THE ANIMALS

I-4324

**The Best Of The Animals, Courtesy MGM Records.
The 1983 reformation was enormously successful.**

The Animals

UK group formed 1960.

Original line-up: Eric Burdon, vocals; Alan Price, keyboards; Hilton Valentine, guitar; Chas Chandler, bass; John Steel, drums.

Career: One of several important groups to emerge from vibrant British R&B scene of early '60s, the band started out with Saturday residency at Newcastle's Downbeat Club around 1960 before moving to city centre Club A Go-Go, changing name from Alan Price(▶) Combo to the Animals when Eric Burdon joined in 1962.

Cutting a demo disc they sold 500 copies to local fans while their manager took a copy to London where it impressed producer Mickie Most enough to persuade him to travel North to see group. Most brought them to London to record cover of **Baby Let Me Take You Home** (from the first Bob Dylan(▶) album), and it charted in April 1964, winning the group a slot on that month's Chuck Berry(▶) tour. (As the Alan Price Combo they had backed Jerry Lee Lewis(▶) on tour.)

A semi-residency at London's Scene Club cemented their following and for their second release they lifted another song from same Dylan LP, the traditional New Orleans number **House Of The Rising Sun**. This plaintive blues ballad shot straight to No. 1 both sides of Atlantic, leading to debut US tour that summer. (Both re-issues have charted.)

1965 produced succession of hits kicking off with brilliant reading of Nina Simone(▶) masterpiece **Don't Let Me Be Misunderstood**, but despite the success he had brought them, band—and Burdon in particular—were unhappy with Most's choice of material and when their Columbia contract expired they refused to renew it, switching to Decca.

Never keen on air travel, Alan Price quit group to form the Alan Price Set, touring solely in UK, going on to work prodigiously with Georgie Fame(▶), while Dave Rowberry was drafted in from the Mike Cotton Sound to replace him. In February 1966 John Steel was replaced by Barry Jenkins.

After two more hits, **Inside—Looking Out** and **Don't Bring Me Down**, the Animals split in July, largely due to rows over Burdon's hard drinking and heavy flirtation with LSD.

Burdon moved to Los Angeles, then to San Francisco where he formed the New Animals with Jenkins and newcomers Mick Briggs (ex-

Below: The Animals in 1966, minus Alan Price, with Burdon in centre.

Steampacket), guitar, and Danny McCullough, bass.

The New Animals made UK charts with **Help Me Girl** (1966), **Good Times** (1967) and **San Francisco Nights** (1967) before Burdon disbanded them to gig around LA rock scene with Jimi Hendrix(▶) (Andy Summers of Police(▶) was a member briefly in 1968). He met up with producers Jerry Goldstein and Steve Gold who teamed him with the rhythm section of black LA band Nite Shift to form new unit known as War(▶) featuring the brilliant Danish harmonica player Lee Oskar and Burdon's hoarse vocals. (Hilton Valentine worked as unit's roadie.)

War went on to become one of the most successful of new wave of black funk bands. The wild-natured Burdon once more went into limbo, drifting round the rock scene, recording with blues veteran Jimmy Witherspoon, touring UK in 1973 and 1976, retiring to France for a time, then returning to California.

Back in Britain, Alan Price had become TV regular while Chas Chandler had sold his bass guitars to launch Jimi Hendrix's solo career, then masterminded road to stardom for Slade.

During his 1976 UK visit, Burdon and the other original Animals got together to cut **Before We Were So Rudely Interrupted** album, released in 1977 on Jet in US.

Original Animals line-up reformed in 1983 and undertook six-week tour of America in summer '83.

Current line-up: Original line-up plus sessioneers.

Hit Singles:	US	UK
House Of The Rising Sun, 1964	1	1
I'm Crying, 1964	19	8
Don't Let Me Be Misunderstood, 1965	15	5
Bring It On Home To Me, 1965	32	7
We Gotta Get Out Of This Place, 1965	13	2
It's My Life, 1965	23	7
Inside—Looking Out, 1966	34	12
Don't Bring Me Down, 1966	12	6
See See Rider, 1966	10	—
When I Was Young, 1967	15	—
San Francisco Nights, 1967	9	—
Monterey, 1968	15	—
Sky Pilot, 1968	14	—

Albums (selected):
The Animals (—/Starline), 1969
Most Of The Animals (—/MFP), 1971
Best Of (Abcko/—), 1975
Newcastle December 1963 (with Sonny Boy Williamson) (—/Charly), 1977

Below: The original Animals line-up two decades later.

April Wine

Canadian group formed 1970.

1974 line-up: Myles Goodwyn, vocals, guitar; Gary Moffett, guitar, vocals; Jim Clench, bass, vocals; Jerry Mercer, drums, vocals.

Career: Goodwyn, then teenager, formed band in Nova Scotia with two brothers and cousin from Henman family. Highly successful in native land, had gained seven gold, three platinum and one double platinum LPs by 1978. Early albums, although probably not released outside Canada, were produced by ex-members of (Young) Rascals. Mid-'70s LPs (produced by Goodwyn) include **Stand Back** and **The Whole World's Going Crazy.** During this period, personnel gradually altered to above line-up, most recent addition being Greenway in 1977.

Group first attracted non-North American attention when supporting Rolling Stones(▶) at El Mocambo Club, Toronto. Result was first listed LP and signing with Capitol Records. Albums began appearing worldwide, with some success.

April Wine are a typical North American hard rock/heavy metal band, with little to obviously differentiate them from numerous competitors, although their wider exposure has resulted in some LP chart action during early '80s.

Current line-up: Goodwyn; Moffet; Mercer; Brian Greenaway, guitar; Steve Lang, bass.

Hit Singles:	US	UK
Just Between You And Me, 1981	16	52

Albums:
Goin' Crazy (London), 1976
First Glance (Capitol), 1978
Harder...Faster (Capitol), 1979
The Nature Of The Beast (Capitol), 1981
Power Play (Capitol), 1982

Worth Searching Out:
Live At The El Mocambo (London), 1977

Argent

UK group formed 1969.

Original line-up: Rod Argent, vocals, keyboards; Russ Ballard, guitar, piano; Jim Rodford, bass; Robert Henrit, drums.

Career: Rod Argent sprang to national fame in 1964 as member of the ill-fated Zombies(▶). Following a beat group competition sponsored by London's 'Evening News', they were

Above: Canadian group April Wine like the sound of three guitars. Though popular in the US, have yet to make an impression in the UK.

signed to Decca. Group folded after short-lived success.

While Zombies singer Colin Blunstone plotted solo career, Rod Argent formed new unit under own name. First album **Argent** (1970) was heavily reliant on old Zombies sound, but succeeded in producing US hit via Three Dog Night's(▶) cover of **Liar**. An American tour followed, quickly taking in New York's Fillmore East, the Boston Tea Party, Chicago's Kinetic Playground and LA's Whisky-A-Go-Go. It was not until 1971's **Ring Of Hands** that Argent discovered own identity. Album fared extremely well critically and the distinctive heavy keyboard sound suggested they might exploit highly lucrative Yes/ELP/Genesis market. Unfortunately, third album **All Together**

Below: West Indian vocalist, guitarist, composer, Joan Armatrading.

Now (1972) was spoilt by over-indulgent extended solos and tedious arrangements.

A sudden change of fortune brought two hit singles, **Hold Your Head Up** and **God Gave Rock 'n' Roll To You.** Unfortunately, ill-focused **In Deep** prevented band from taking full advantage of chart status.

Following release of **Nexus,** talented chief songwriter Russ Ballard quit in favour of solo career. Guitarists John Verity and John Grimaldi were enlisted to stop musical gap, but without Ballard's writing ability, future looked bleak. **Circus** (1975) and **Counterpoint** (1976) failed to recommend themselves to critics and when Grimaldi left in early 1976, Argent folded. Rod embarked on solo career encompassing session/film/television/theatrical work. Also runs keyboard shop in London's West End.

Final line-up: Argent; Henrit; Rodford; John Verity, vocals; John Grimaldi, guitar.

Hit Singles: US UK
Hold Your Head Up, 1972 — 5 — 5
God Gave Rock 'n' Roll To You, 1973 — — — 18

Albums:
All Together Now (Epic), 1972
The Best Of Argent—An Anthology (Epic), 1976
Hold Your Head Up (—/Embassy), 1977

Joan Armatrading

West Indian vocalist, guitarist, composer. Born St Kitts, December 9, 1950.

Career: One of five children, Joan emigrated to Birmingham, UK, with her family in 1958. She starred in local production of rock musical 'Hair' and formed songwriting partnership with fellow West Indian immigrant Pam Nester.

Moving to London in 1971, duo signed production and management deal with Cube Records but, when Gus Dudgeon-produced **Whatever's For Us** album appeared, Nester

Joan Armatrading's 1976 album. Courtesy A&M Records.

received no label credit and resultant friction led to break-up of both partnership and Cube deal.

After two years in limbo, Joan was signed by A&M and, adding own lyrics to previous melody-writing, came up with praised **Back To The Night** album (1975). Lack of sales success led A&M to team her with legendary producer Glyn Johns (Rolling Stones(▶), the Who(▶), Eagles(▶), Steve Miller(▶), etc) whose work proved totally sympathetic to her mood-laden introverted style. **Joan Armatrading** (1976) yielded **Love And Affection** hit single; and her third album **Show Some Emotion** spent four months on US charts, breaking her into American market.

A third Glyn Johns-produced LP, **To The Limit** (1978), introduced harder cutting edge while in 1980 **Me, Myself I** was successful single and album (produced by Richard Gottehrer of Blondie(▶), Link Wray, and Robert Johnson fame).

Since 1978 Joan has played to increasingly larger audiences in cities all over Europe.

Hit Singles: US UK
Love And Affection, 1976 — — — 10

Albums:
Whatever's For Us (Hifly/Cube), 1974
Back To The Night (A&M), 1975
Joan Armatrading (A&M), 1976
Show Some Emotion (A&M), 1977
To The Limit (A&M), 1978
Stepping Out (A&M), 1979
Me Myself I (A&M), 1980
Walk Under Ladders (A&M), 1981
The Key (A&M), 1983

Ashford And Simpson

US vocal duo, composers.

Career: Moving from Detroit to New York, Nick Ashford met Valerie Simpson, then a member of Followers gospel group, at White Rock Church, Harlem. They began songwriting together and landed staff job at Florence Greenberg's Scepter/Wand Records, composing R&B hits for, notably, Maxine Brown and Chuck Jackson.

Writing **Let's Go Get Stoned** on a day when everything was going wrong, they managed to place song with Ray Charles(▶), who made it international smash. Gained staff positions at Tamla Motown in Detroit where they wrote classic songs **Ain't No Mountain High Enough, You're All I Need To Get By, Ain't Nothing Like The Real Thing, Reach Out And Touch Somebody's Hand** and **The Boss,** giving hits to other black performers Marvin Gaye(▶), Tammi Terrell, Diana Ross(▶) and others.

Embarked on own career as recording duo via deal with Warner Bros, which has given them Top 100 transatlantic hits **(Don't Cost Nothing, It Seems To Hang On, Flashback)** and succession of highly listenable soft soul albums.

Albums:
Gimme Something Real (Warner Bros), 1973
I Wanna Be Selfish (Warner Bros), 1974
Come As You Are (Warner Bros), 1976
Send It (Warner Bros), 1977
So So Satisfied (Warner Bros), 1977
Keep It Coming (Tamla) 1978/79
Stay Free (Warner Bros), 1979
Is It Still Good To Ya (Warner Bros), 1979
A Musical Affair (Warner Bros), 1980
Street Opera (Capitol), 1982

Asia

UK group formed 1981.

Original line-up: John Wetton, bass, vocals; Steve Howe, guitar; Geoffrey Downes, keyboards; Carl Palmer, drums.

Career: Wetton was England's premier utility man, playing in Family(▶), King Crimson(▶), Roxy Music(▶), Uriah Heep(▶) and UK. In late 1980 he teamed up with Steve Howe who was free following the break-up of Yes(▶). Last line-up of Yes had merged with UK band, Buggles (who had No.1 UK single **Video Killed The Radio Star**). Geoff Downes was re-forming Buggles when Howe asked him to join Wetton's group.

Carl Palmer's past included original King Crimson and megastardom with Emerson, Lake and Palmer(▶). After 1979 demise of ELP, Palmer tried solo career. Grand style of playing seemed anachronistic and 1981 UK tour/album flopped. Asia beckoned.

Self-named album appeared in early 1982 to universal condemnation *before* release. Critics judged public would not support 'supergroup' of dinosaur rockers from '70s. Through word of mouth, US sales rocketed, LP zooming to platinum despite recession and critics. After nine weeks at No.1, criticism shifted to complaints of selling out to undiscriminating youth of America.

Asia began selling well in UK and critics griped about ease of success. Even worse, band was instant sell-out attraction at large venues in US and UK.

In 1983 Asia began recording second album, quite happy to continue defying critics and pleasing public.

Hit Singles:

	US	UK
Heat Of The Moment, 1982	4	46
Only Time Will Tell, 1982	17	54

Albums:
Asia (Geffen), 1982

Chet Atkins

US guitarist, composer, producer, executive. Born Luttrell, Tennessee, June 20, 1924.

Career: RCA's dominance of American country music scene is in large part attributed to work of Chet Atkins, both as musician and—more importantly—as catalyst. Atkins has been involved, as composer, arranger, producer, musician and general factotum, with countless RCA recordings by such diverse talents as Elvis Presley(▶), Jim Reeves(▶), Floyd Kramer, Hank Snow, Waylon Jennings(▶) and Dolly Parton(▶).

Music was in his family; father James Arley Atkins was a musician while guitarist half-brother Jim played with Les Paul(▶). (Atkins himself recorded LP **Chester And Les** with Les Paul in 1976.) At 18, Atkins worked on Knoxville, Tennessee's Radio WNOX as fiddle player before touring with Archie Campbell and Bill Carlisle and moving to guitar.

He failed audition for Roy Acuff's band but in 1946 joined Red Foley and was signed to RCA by Steve Sholes. He moved base to Nashville in 1950 by which time he was company's leading session guitarist, becoming Shole's A&R assistant in 1952. First solo album **Gallopin' Shoes**, released 1953, was followed by profusion of best-selling LPs over the years. After involvement in Presley's 1955 **Heartbreak Hotel** sessions Atkins took charge of RCA's new studio and became company's Nashville A&R head in 1960, and company vice-president in 1968.

Winner of Cashbox magazine's 'Best Instrumentalist' poll for 14 consecutive years, Atkins has explored the far parameters of country music—he even played at Newport Jazz Festival—but greatest claim to fame is for evolving familiar 'Nashville Sound' with massed strings and wide use of pedal steel guitar.

Guitar: Gretsch Country Gentleman.

Albums (Selected):
Best Of (RCA), 1964
Best Of Volume 2 (RCA), 1965
The Best Of Chet And Friends (RCA), 1976
First Nashville Guitar Quartet (RCA), 1979

Frankie Avalon

US vocalist, actor.

Born Frank Avallone, Philadelphia, Pennsylvania, September 18, 1940.

Career: 'American Bandstand', an enormously popular US television programme in mid-'50s, provided opportunity for new pop and rock singers to perform. In addition, programme featured ordinary schoolkids from largely working class/ethnic Philadelphia neighbourhood around broadcasting studio. Kids danced, chatted, commented on new records and became popular with teenage audiences around country. Viewers (who numbered 40 million) were ready for idol from this milieu, and Chancellor Records' Bob Marcucci and Peter de Angelis provided them with Avalon, whom they discovered in 1956.

An experienced performer before 'discovery', Avalon began career winning talent show at six. After learning trumpet, he played local dance halls and Atlantic City with band at 12, then sung on TV and at family night club. Unlike friend Fabian(▶), Avalon needed little grooming before 'Bandstand' appearance shot him to stardom. Between 1958 and 1962 he had 24 US hit singles like **Dede Dinah** (on which he pinched his nose to get nasal sound), **Venus** and **Why**.

Although Avalon rapidly faded as teen dream, slick performance style and pleasant singing voice led to night club success during '60s, combined with acting in summer stock theatre and films, including 'The Alamo', 'The Carpetbaggers', 'Voyage To The Bottom Of The Sea' and various beach and bikini movies.

During '70s, Avalon appeared in US television dramas and musical specials, and was featured in 1978 film 'Grease'.

Hit Singles	US	UK
Dede Dinah, 1958	7	—
Ginger Bread, 1958	9	30
I'll Wait For You, 1958	15	—
Venus, 1959	1	16
Bobby Sox To Stockings/A Boy Without A Girl, 1959	8	
A Boy Without A Girl/Bobby Sox To Stockings, 1959	10	—
Just Ask Your Heart, 1959	7	—
Why, 1960	1	20

Albums:
Stars Of The Sixties (—/Bovema/EMI), 1974

The Average White Band

US group formed 1972.

Original line-up: Hamish Stuart, lead vocals, guitar; Alan Gorrie, lead vocals, bass; Onnie McIntyre, lead guitar; Robbie McIntosh, drums; Roger Ball, alto and baritone saxophone; Malcolm 'Molly' Duncan, tenor and soprano saxophone.

Career: Formed by six experienced Scottish musicians who had gigged with various bands in Scottish lowlands since mid-'60s. Supported Eric Clapton(▶) on comeback performance at Rainbow Theatre in January 1973. Ecstatic reviews for their brand of blue-eyed soul, plus workmanlike debut album **Show Your Hand** for MCA, got career rolling. LP included classy vocal version of Crusaders'(▶) **Put It Where You Want It**, which won airplay (re-titled after single when re-issued in 1975).

Switch to Atlantic in 1974 saw AWB benefit

Below: 'American Bandstand' discovery Frankie Avalon wows 'teen' crowd with '59 smash 'Venus'.

First Average White Band. Courtesy Atlantic Records.

from major Stateside push. Debut album **Average White Band** was produced by Arif Mardin. **Pick Up The Pieces** single went gold and captured enthusiasm of both black and white audiences. By February 1975, album and single were atop respective American charts. However, in time between release and success, Robbie McIntosh had died of heroin overdose at Los Angeles party in September 1974.

Black, Brighton-born British drummer Steve Verrone (ex-Brian Auger's Oblivion Express and American band Bloodstone) came in as temporary replacement; fit so well that gig became permanent.

Enormous American success plus tax advantages caused band to re-locate permanently in Los Angeles. **Cut The Cake** album (1975) cemented position as leading white band in soul/funk idiom; most of material penned in-house by Gorrie and Stuart. Unfortunately, initial innovation of image and sound became somewhat clichéd.

Joint album with black soul veteran Ben E. King, **Benny And Us,** was pleasant but undistinguished; group also toured Europe with King. Band switched to RCA for final album with Mardin at helm, **Warmer Communication,** which included brilliant cut **Big City Lights.**

Cupid's In Fashion, Average White Band. Courtesy RCA Records.

Subsequently self-produced, AWB have continued to cut classy but not overly exciting albums and occasional single hits (like **Let's Go Round Again** from **Shine** LP). Sheer sparkle of **Pick Up The Pieces** still seems to elude them.

Current line-up: Stuart; Gorrie; McIntyre; Ball; Duncan; Steve Verrone, drums.

Hit Singles:

	US	UK
Pick Up The Pieces, 1975	1	6
Cut The Cake, 1975	10	31
Let's Go Round Again, 1980	53	12

Albums:
Average White Band (Atlantic), 1974
Cut The Cake (Atlantic), 1975

Soul Searchin' (Atlantic), 1976
Person To Person (Atlantic), 1976
Warmer Communications (Atlantic), 1978
Feel No Fret (RCA), 1979
Shine (RCA), 1980
Best Of (—/RCA), 1981
Cupid's In Fashion (Arista/RCA), 1982

With Ben E. King
Benny And Us (Atlantic), 1977

Worth Searching Out:
Put It Where You Want It (MCA), 1975*
*Originally **Show Your Hand** (MCA), 1973
with some changes

Bachman-Turner Overdrive

Canadian group formed 1972.
Original line-up: Randy Bachman, guitars, vocals; Fred Turner, bass, vocals; Robbie Bachman, drums; Tim Bachman, guitar.

Career: Randy Bachman (pronounced *Back*man) founded Guess Who(▶) in mid-'60s and seemed destined for superstar status when Guess Who cracked American Top 10 market in 1969. Never one to do the expected, Bachman left in 1970, cutting solo effort **Axe**.

Keith Emerson asked him to join a new band for which Emerson needed special guitarist. Bachman's Chet Atkins(▶)-jazz-infuenced sound seemed perfect for project, but Bachman became seriously ill and regretfully declined invitation. Emerson found Greg Lake and went on to form Emerson, Lake and Palmer(▶).

Bachman next produced an album for old friend Chad Allen. Allen had been original vocalist in Guess Who and welcomed chance to work with Bachman again. Bachman's involvement grew to point of playing guitars on album and Allen asked him to join group called Brave Belt Band released two albums but did not generate any response, so Allen quit. Bachman and bass player Fred Turner decided to reorganise, and founded Bachman-Turner Overdrive with Randy's brothers Robbie and Tim in late 1972.

Bachman's flair for melody which kept hard

edge and loud volume in control helped win large following within heavy metal hierarchy In six months Tim Bachman was replaced by Blair Thornton (guitar) who played on second album. BTO became a sell-out concert attraction whose every album guaranteed large sales. But formulas never suited Bachman and he left band in late 1977. Despite one subsequent and pointless LP, as well as ironically titled anthology **The Best Of BTO (So Far)**, BTO now seems a thing of the past.

Above: Astute management earned Bad Company near decade of album chart action.

Hit Singles:	US	UK
Takin' Care Of Business, 1974	12	—
You Ain't Seen Nothing Yet, 1974	1	2
Roll On Down The Highway, 1975	14	22

Albums:
Bachman-Turner Overdrive (Mercury), 1973
Bachman-Turner Overdrive II (Mercury), 1973
Not Fragile (Mercury), 1974
Four Wheel Drive (Mercury), 1975
Head On (Mercury), 1975
The Best Of BTO (So Far) (Mercury), 1976
Freeways (Mercury), 1977

Bad Company

UK group formed 1973.
Original/Final line-up: Paul Rodgers, guitar, vocals; Mick Ralphs, guitar; Boz Burrell, bass; Simon Kirke, drums.

Career: Formed from the remnants of Free(▶) (Kirke and Rodgers), Bad Company—named after the Robert Benton western—carved no new ground in their lifetime but made one hell of a dent on the British and American markets during '70s.

The sparse, tight rhythm section of Burrell (ex King Crimson(▶)), Kirke and Ralphs (ex-Mott the Hoople(▶)) was the perfect foil for Rodgers' explosive vocal talents, and on the right night they were among the best of live bands.

After brief breaking-in period, Bad Company hit the road in March 1974, debuting at Rodgers' home gig, Newcastle Town Hall (which remained group's favourite venue until their demise).

First album **Bad Company** went platinum in States, with debut single **Can't Get Enough** making US Top 10 and UK Top 20. All material released on manager Peter Grant(▶)'s and Led Zeppelin(▶)'s Swan Song label, breaking Company in States, and furthering Grant's managerial reputation.

Desolation Angels, Bad Company. Courtesy Swan Song Records.

Grant's policy of a world tour every two years kept audiences hungry, and explained group's life-span of nearly ten years. Their later material was certainly not worthy of the adulation it received.

Apart from sax player Mel Collins' contribution to first album, Bad Company was a completely self-contained unit, working both studio and live with minimum of frills.

Although Rodgers was an aggressive powerhouse front man (not unlike his personality) and centre of attention, Ralphs, Burrell and Kirke always turned in some memorable riffs and melodies.

1979 release **Desolation Angels** was surrounded by rumour of split, although this was not confirmed until summer 1982 (after successful **Rough Diamond** set), when Kirke and Burrell began putting together new bands.

Below: Every mother's favourite son, 'Buster' Bloodvessel (in chair) leads Bad Manners with aggression, wit and not inconsiderable style.

Hit Singles:	US	UK
Can't Get Enough, 1974	5	15
Movin' On, 1975	19	—
Feel Like Making Love, 1975	10	20
Young Blood, 1976	20	—
Rock'n'Roll Fantasy, 1979	13	—

Albums:
Bad Company (Swan Song/Island), 1974
Straight Shooter (Swan Song/Island), 1975
Run With The Pack (Swan Song/Island), 1976
Burning Sky (Swan Song/Island), 1977
Desolation Angels (Swan Song), 1979
Rough Diamonds (Swan Song), 1981

Bad Manners

UK group formed 1980.
Line-up: Fatty 'Buster' Bloodvessel (Doug Trendle), vocals; Gus 'Hot Lips' Herman, trumpet; Andrew 'Marcus Absent' Marson, saxophone; Chris Kane, saxophone; Louis Alphonso (L. Cook), guitar; David Farren, bass; Martin Stewart, keyboards; Brian Chew-It (Brian Tuitt), drums; Winston Bazoomies (Alan Sayag), harmonica.

Career: Formed in North London, Bad Manners quickly gained success as part of ska revival movement along with Madness(▶) and the Specials(▶). Despite controversy at one time surrounding 'skinhead' following, band relies on showmanship, raucous enthusiasm and easily assimilable music to make impact. Stage act is based around antics of bald, 17-stone Buster Bloodvessel, one of Britain's most unlikely pop stars. Extrovert to outrageous degree, Bloodvessel is given to wearing dresses and other outlandish costumes along with Doctor Marten 'bovver' boots.

'Good time' image sometimes obscures fact that band are solid musicians capable of exciting music. Knack for picking hit singles seem likely to ensure reasonable longevity, although very 'British' nature of act might preclude major international success.

Hit Singles:	US	UK
Lip Up Fatty, 1980	—	15
Special Brew, 1980	—	3

15

Gosh It's, Bad Manners. Courtesy Magnet Records.

Just A Feeling, 1981	—	13
Can Can, 1981	—	3
Walkin' In The Sunshine, 1981	—	10
My Girl Lollipop (My Boy Lollipop), 1982	—	9

Albums:
Ska'n'B (—/Magnet), 1980
Loonee Tunes (—/Magnet), 1981
Gosh It's . . . (—/Magnet), 1981
Forging Ahead (—/Magnet), 1982

Joan Baez

US vocalist, guitarist, composer.
Born Staten Island, New York, January 9, 1941.

Career: When 19-year-old Baez was invited by Bob Gibson, champion of many young singers, to join him in duets during evening concert at 1959 Newport Folk Festival, her pure soprano voice and performance of traditional ballads staggered the audience. Vanguard's Festival album, her first recording, contains two of these numbers: **Virgin Mary Had One Son** and **We Are Crossing The Jordan River.** Until then Baez was unknown except to growing following in Boston-area folk clubs, but even most loyal fan was unlikely to predict that three years later she would be featured on cover of 'Time' magazine.

First albums were filled with British and Spanish ballads, reflecting English-Scottish and Mexican (though middle-class) heritage. Urged on by Bob Dylan(▶) (whom she helped bring to notice, toured with and with whom she had intense personal relationship), she began to express political sentiments previously confined to non-singing life. Dylan's **With God On Our Side** was included in her concerts. Later albums were peppered with contemporary and protest songs. In 1965 had hit single with Phil Ochs'(▶) **There But For Fortune.**

Moving musically in new directions with 1967 **Joan,** having orchestrated arrangements of songs by Paul Simon(▶), Lennon/McCartney(▶) and Jacques Brel, Baez then went through Nashville phase. However, she remained deeply involved in political arena, founding The Institute For The Study Of Non-Violence in 1965, participating in civil rights and peace demonstrations, and refusing to pay taxes because the money would be used towards Vietnam War. In 1968 she married draft resister David Harris, who was jailed for three years. During same year published autobiography 'Daybreak' and book of poems. At Woodstock Festival in 1969, her pure, unfailing voice, unaccompanied, went out to half a million people listening silently in the dark. Film about her life and politics was made in 1970. After having son Gabriel, marriage ended in 1971.

Although Baez' own compositions had been

included on albums since **Blessed Are,** it was with move from Vanguard to A&M that she was really encouraged to write, with songs becoming more personal while still showing deep social concern. **Come From The Shadows** (1971) was critical of Dylan's move from political commitment. After several years of heavy involvement in politics, both personally and musically, she became interested in string and horn arrangements and use of synthesiser. In 1975, entertaining and commercial LP **Diamonds And Rust** was released. Using jazz-rock group the Crusaders (▶) and including songs by Janis Ian(▶), Jackson Browne(▶) and Stevie Wonder(▶), in addition to own compositions, album achieved gold status.

Baez went on tour later that year and released double-album of concert tracks. Next album **Gulf Winds** was entirely self-penned. Changing labels again, Baez signed with Columbia's Portrait Records, for whom she has released several albums. Although renowned as leader of protest movement and, more recently, for achieving success as songwriter, perhaps Baez' most distinguishing characteristic is her extraordinarily clear and beautiful voice, enabling her to record everything from country blues to classical works like Villa-Lobos' **Bachianas Brasileiras No. 5 Aria**.

Hit Singles:	US	UK
There But For Fortune, 1967	50	8
The Night They Drove Old Dixie Down, 1971	3	6

Albums (selected):
In Concert Volume I (Vanguard), 1962
In Concert Volume II (Vanguard), 1963
Any Day Now (Vanguard), 1969
Come From The Shadows (A&M), 1971
Best Of (A&M), 1977
Very Early Joan (61-63) (Vanguard), 1981
European Tour (Portrait), 1981

Worth Searching Out:
Diamond And Rust (A&M), 1975
Gulf Winds (A&M), 1976
Honest Lullaby (Portrait), 1979

Below: The man of a thousand bands, Ginger Baker, has had mixed fortunes since heady days of Cream.

'Ginger' Baker

UK drummer.
Born Peter Baker, London, August 19, 1939.

Career: One sight of his orange hair and it's obvious where Baker's nickname came from. Began musical career as trumpeter for local air cadets. By 16, Baker was playing drums, first with local Storyville Jazzmen, which later earned invitations to play with England's premier trad-jazz bands, including Acker Bilk's Paramount Jazz Band. Also played as resident drummer at Ronnie Scott's 100 Club.

In Bert Courtley Band Baker came across Jack Bruce(▶). Bruce began sitting in with Alexis Korner's Blues Incorporated and brought Baker along. In 1963 pair tried forming more permanent arrangement with organist/vocalist Graham Bond. The Graham Bond Organization picked up small, but loyal, cult following and strong reputation as musician's group.

Bruce left in August 1965 but Baker stayed on. During this period he played on B-side of Who's(▶) **Substitute**. (For short while both Who and original B-side were under court injunction. Rather than halting sales completely, Who's record company paid Graham Bond Organization to record alternative B-side.) Eric Clapton(▶) and Bruce asked Baker to join them in Cream(▶) soon after.

Following Cream's break-up in 1968, Baker joined Eric Clapton's short-lived Blind Faith(▶) in February 1969. Baker took direction of remnants and formed Airforce. To press and public, it was 'Ginger Baker's Airforce' and Cream connection ensured ready-made audience. Airforce proved unwieldy, suggesting that no rock band could support 10 members. The volatile mixture of Baker, Steve Winwood(▶), Chris Wood, Denny Lane and others failed to come up with explosive musical ideas. Two lacklustre albums, released in 1970, destroyed Baker's street credibility as well as raising the question of whether he could ever surpass Cream.

Baker responded by removing himself to Nigeria, Africa. For next three years he tried variety of activities: recording African music, managing Nigerian band, running trucking company, and opening recording studio.

When he returned to England in 1974, he found rock littered with Cream-influenced heavy-metal bands. To consternation of fans, he joined one of them (Three Man Army) to form the Baker-Gurvitz Army. After three typical heavy-metal albums, the band broke up in 1976. 1977 solo LP **Eleven Sides Of Baker** was highly self-indulgent in view of changes going on in punk music. Baker then quit the music business.

However, 1981 saw his return with short-lived Ginger Baker's Nutters. Moving on to Italy in 1982, he formed Bakerland which quickly fell apart amid rumours and denials that he was joining Hawkwind(▶). A man with Baker's unique talents can never be counted out, but it does seem that Cream is an unbeatable past.

Albums:
The Baker/Gurvitz Army (Mountain), 1977

Worth Searching Out:
At His Best (Polydor), 1973

The Band

Canadian group formed late '50s.
Original/final line-up: Jamie 'Robbie' Robertson, guitar; Garth Hudson, organ, saxophone; Richard Manuel, piano, vocals; Rick Danko, bass, vocals; Levon Helm, drums, vocals, mandolin.

Career: Leader Helm came from Arkansas, rest are Canadians. Group started as backing band for Toronto-based rock 'n' roller Ronnie Hawkins(▶), with whom they recorded covers of urban blues hits featuring Helm's vocals and Robertson's incisive guitar (classic example, Hawkins' **Who Do You Love**). Billed first as Canadian Squires then as Levon and the Hawks, they left Hawkins and toured Canada and US. Recorded classic single **The Stones I Throw** while in New York, where they met white blues singer John Hammond Jr, whose father was A&R boss of Columbia.

Through the Hammond connection, the Band met Bob Dylan(▶), who was then moving more heavily into electric music and saw their musical versatility (all play several instruments) as ideal backing. First collaboration was single **Can You Please Crawl Out**

The Band. Courtesy Capitol Records.

Your Window some members played on **Blonde On Blonde** album. With Mickey Jones playing drums instead of Helm, the Band accompanied Dylan on 1965-66 US/European tour. A motorcycle accident in July 1966 put Dylan out of action and the Band settled in Woodstock, New York. Rehearsed and recorded with him while he recovered, the results being heard on **The Basement Tapes,** a bootleg so successful that much of its material was officially released on LP of same name by Columbia in 1975.

The crossflow influence between Dylan and the Band can be heard on Dylan's **John Wesley Harding** album and the Band's own **Music From Big Pink** (Capitol, 1968), from which **The Weight** remains true classic.

Robertson's songs for second LP, **The Band,** included **Up On Cripple Creek** and **The Night They Drove Old Dixie Down,** both subtle yet powerfully evocative traditional-style, truly American songs. Became first North American band to make the cover of 'Time' magazine.

Undertaking lengthy tours on their own led to **Stage Fright** LP; titletrack told of perils of being on road. **Cahoots** (1971) reflected their weariness at then current American values, but seemed a trifle pretentious; it included track cut in collaboration with Van Morrison(▶).

There followed four-year hiatus before Robertson came up with new material; after December 1971 concert at New York Academy Of Music (recorded live as **Rock Of Ages),** Band made no appearances until Watkins Glen Festival of July 1973. Their studio efforts, a planned thematic work by Robertson, was shelved and next record release was **Moondog Matinee,** a tribute to their rock 'n' roll roots.

Before The Flood encapsulated live work with Dylan on 1974 tour; they provided all back-up work on his **Planet Waves** album. In late 1975, own long-awaited album of new material hit stores, but **Northern Lights Southern Cross** did not quite have stunning effect expected, though musicianship remained superb.

In late 1976 came shock announcement—their current tour was to be the Band's last and stage career was to climax with a special Thanksgiving Day concert at San Francisco's Winterland, to be dubbed 'The Last Waltz'. It was a triumphant occasion with such friends and collaborators as Bob Dylan, Ronnie Hawkins, Neil Young, Bobby Charles, Van Morrison, Joni Mitchell, Eric Clapton, Dr John, Neil Diamond and Muddy Waters turning out. (Robertson had produced two Neil Diamond(▶) albums, **Beautiful Noise** (1976) and **Love At The Greek** (1977), while Helm had produced **Muddy Waters in Woodstock,** 1976.)

Islands (1977), a very laid-back effort, completed group's contractual obligations to Capitol and they embarked on solo projects leaving the album and movie of 'The Last Waltz' as their testament. Robbie Robertson co-wrote, produced and starred in 'Carny' with Gary Busey and Jodi Foster in 1980. Levon Helm received critical approval for role in 'Coal Miner's Daughter' in 1980; recently starred in Tom Woolf's 'The Right Stuff' and is currently filming 'The Dollmaker' with Jane Fonda. Helm (mandolin) and Danko (guitar) are now appearing as country-based duo.

Hit Singles:

	US	UK
Rag Mama Rag, 1970	57	16

Albums:
Music From Big Pink (Capitol), 1968
The Band (Capitol), 1969

Below: Northant's outfit Bauhaus looked to Ziggy for chart status. Main man Peter Murphy on left.

Stage Fright (Capitol), 1970
Cahoots (Capitol), 1971
Rock Of Ages (Capitol), 1972
Rock Of Ages Volume II (-/Capitol), 1972
Moondog Matinee (Capitol), 1973
Northern Lights, Southern Cross (Capitol), 1975
Best Of (Capitol/Fame), 1976
Islands (Capitol), 1977
The Last Waltz (Warner Bros), 1978
Anthology Volume I (Capitol), 1978
Anthology Volume II (Capitol), 1980

Levon Helm Solo:
American Son (MCA), 1978
The Legend of Jesse James (A&M), 1980*
*With various artists

Rick Danko Solo:
Rick Danko (Arista), 1978

Bauhaus

UK group formed 1978.

Original/Current line-up: Peter Murphy, vocals; Kevin Haskins, drums; Daniel Ash, guitar, vocals; David Jay, bass, vocals.

Career: Formed in Northampton, following stints in various punk outfits during 1977. Haskins and Jay were part of the Submerged Tenth, before forming the Craze with Daniel Ash as additional vocalist. With Murphy they became Bauhaus 1919, then Bauhaus.

Debut at Cromwell Pub, Wellingborough, on New Year's Eve 1978, led to series of gigs at Billy's Club in Soho's Dean Street. Tour of Germany, Holland and Belgium in April '80 was followed by US sojourn in September. Well-received session on John Peel Show bolstered success of first two singles, **Bela Lugosi's Dead** and **Dark Entries,** in independent chart. First album, **In The Flat Field,** proved equally durable.

A move to parent company, Beggar's Banquet, resulted in more percussive **Mask.** Third album, **The Sky's Gone Out,** showed a substantial improvement. Initial copies included free live album, **Press The Eject And Give Me The Tape,** later released in own right.

Television debut, on BBC's 'Riverside' (January 1982), was quickly followed by Murphy's appearance in Maxell Tape TV ads. Cameo appearance in David Bowie/Catherine Deneuve film, 'The Hunger', further underlined growing cult acceptance. Still regarded as primarily a live act, their Gothic horror routine led to sell-out performances at London's Hammersmith Palais and the Lyceum, Old Vic and Adelphi Theatres.

Heavily influenced by early '70s work of Bowie(▶) and Iggy Pop(▶) Bauhaus have built up noticeable young cult following since 1978. Their bleak, nihilistic, neo-Germanic style repertoire has led many critics to dismiss them as outdated punks. Others have derided them as Thin White Duke clones, totally lacking in originality. Success of single **Ziggy Stardust,** a veritable carbon copy of the original, will only reinforce such prejudices, but should enable Bauhaus to break free of their cult status and reach wider audience.

Hit Singles:

	US	UK
Ziggy Stardust, 1982	—	15

Albums:
In The Flat Field (4.A.D.), 1980
Mask (—/Beggar's Banquet), 1981
The Sky's Gone Out (A&M/Beggar's Banquet), 1982
Press The Eject And Give Me The Tape (—/Beggar's Banquet), 1982
Burning From The Inside (—/Beggars Banquet), 1983

The Bay City Rollers

UK group formed 1970.

Original line-up: Leslie McKeown, vocals; Stuart 'Woody' Wood, guitar; Eric Faulkner, guitar; Alan Longmuir, bass; Derek Longmuir, drums.

Career: The epitomy of a mediocre pop group turned into superstars by astute management, the Rollers were good-looking youngsters carefully manipulated by hard-headed svengali Tam Paton. His ruthlessness paired with immaturity of group members was to lead to personality problems when group made it big.

Formed in 1970 in Edinburgh where they held residencies as cover-version band the Saxons. Changing name to Bay City Rollers, had first UK hit with **Keep On Dancing,** 1971, (produced by Jonathan King). Then after hiatus, benefited from songwriting talents of Bill Martin and Phil Coulter who had earlier composed Eurovision Song Contest winning titles **Puppet On A String** (for Sandie Shaw), **Congratulations** (Cliff Richard), **All Kings Of Everything** (Dana), aided by session musicians; it was rumoured that Rollers did not play on their hits.

From then on their teen appeal and image took style of football fan 'bovver boys' (with tartan scarves, hats, etc) and was carefully nurtured until they reached zenith of career in early 1975 with Phil Wainman—produced revival of Four Seasons' **Bye Bye Baby.** Aided by massive media exposure and, especially, support of teen-girl magazines, Rollermania burst forth in 1975 with as much fervour as the Beatles' explosion more than a decade earlier. Setting out to conquer US, group topped chart there with **Saturday Night.**

Having reached 26, Longmuir was deemed too old for the band; 18-year-old bass player Ian Mitchell came in, being in turn replaced by Pat McGlynn in April 1977. Attempts by record company to widen appeal to more adult rock audience failed, and by 1980 Leslie McKeown had left for solo career (had some success in Japan). Rest of band continued working mainly abroad, but by now reduced to cashing in on nostalgia for earlier heady times.

Final line-up: Wood; Faulkner; Derek Longmuir; Pat McGlynn, bass.

Hit Singles:

	US	UK
Keep On Dancing, 1971	—	9
Remember (Sha-La-La), 1974	—	6
Shang-A-Lang, 1974	—	2
Summer Love Sensation, 1974	—	3
All Of Me Loves All Of You, 1974		4
Bye Bye Baby, 1975	—	1
Give A Little Love, 1975	—	1
Money Honey, 1975	9	3
Saturday Night, 1975	1	—
Love Me Like I Love You, 1976		4
I Only Wanna Be With You, 1976	12	4
It's A Game, 1977	—	16
You Made Me Believe In Magic, 1977	10	34

Albums:
Once Upon A Star (—/Bell), 1975
Wouldn't You Like It (—/Bell), 1975
Dedication (—/Bell), 1976
It's A Game (Arista), 1977
Greatest Hits (Arista/—), 1977
Strangers In The Wind (Arista), 1978

The Beach Boys

US group formed 1950s.

Original line-up: Brian Wilson, vocals; Dennis Wilson, vocals, drums; Carl Wilson, vocals, guitar; Mike Love, vocals; Al Jardine, vocals, guitar.

Career: Sons of California's 1960s surfing boom, the Beach Boys were based around the Wilson brothers. Songwriting genius Brian Wilson (born June 20, 1942), Dennis Wilson (born December 4, 1944), Carl Wilson (born December 21, 1946), cousin Mike Love (born March 15, 1941) and friend Al Jardine (born September 3, 1942) grew up in middle-class Los Angeles district of Hawthorne. Started out singing barber-shop/Four Freshmen-styled harmonies at homes of friends and relatives. Then launched themselves as Carl and the Passions; name soon changed to Kenny and the Cadets (Brian being Kenny).

Dennis, already a surfing addict, suggested to Brian and Mike that they write a song about the cult sport. Result was **Surfin'**. The Wilson brothers' father Murray, himself an established songwriter, took them along to his music publisher. A cheapo production found Carl on guitar, Al on acoustic bass and Brian providing percussion courtesy of a garbage can. Record was issued on tiny local X label then switched to slightly bigger Candix label. It hung around low limits of US Hot 100 for six weeks.

Group worked for while as the Pendletones, a name taken from a make of heavy plaid shirt which was standard surfer wear and which they adopted as stage garb. Candix promotion man suggested the Beach Boys as better tag. First appearance under new name was at Ritchie Valens'(▶) Memorial Concert, Long Beach Municipal Auditorium, December 31, 1961 (Mexicano rock singer Valens had perished in recent air-crash along with Buddy Holly(▶) and the Big Bopper).

Al Jardine left group to take up dental studies at college and he was temporarily replaced by neigbour David L. Marks (featured on sleeve pics of debut album).

Candix folded early 1962. Murray per-

Above: These are Boys? (Left to right) Carl Wilson, Bruce Johnston, Al Jardine, Dennis Wilson, Mike Love—the Beach Boys during the late 1970s.

suaded Capitol Records' producer Nik Venet to pick up group. With smooth harmonies, his own falsetto and a twangy guitar, Brian Wilson had created a whole new sound. What's more, his songs went beyond Tin Pan Alley-style romance and dealt with real teenage concerns—and fantasies—like surfing, hot rod cars and motorcycles.

First Capitol release, **Surfin' Safari**, went US Top 20. **Ten Little Indians** bombed, then **Surfin' USA** (a clever parody of Chuck Berry's(▶) **Sweet Little Sixteen**) went all the way to No. 3. **Surfin' USA** album (1963) brought the group first gold record. In same year Brian Wilson had further success when his composition **Surf City** gave his friends Jan and Dean(▶) a million-seller.

Al Jardine rejoined the fold, Marks passing

into rock history. Meanwhile, ballad **Surfer Girl, Fun Fun Fun, Little Honda** and chart-topping **I Get Around** continued run of hits. The Beach Boys' flawless harmonies impressed and influenced many artists, and group's success opened flood-gates for profusion of imitators. When Wilson switched from songs about the wild surf to songs about drag strips, imitators followed suit.

When I Grow Up To Be A Man, Dance Dance Dance, Help Me Rhonda (another chart-topper) kept things going but Brian, always something of an introvert, was feeling the strain. Suffering from working pressures, he had nervous breakdown in early 1965; also suffered loss of hearing in one ear. He decided to stop touring with band, though he continued to mastermind their records. Glen

Campbell(▶) joined group as temporary replacement but left following argument over uneven split of income. He was replaced by Bruce Johnston who, as Bruce and Terry (with Terry Melcher), had been among Beach Boys imitators.

Increasingly influenced by Phil Spector's 'Wall Of Sound' technique (Beach Boys eventually cut version of Spector song **Then I Kissed Her**), Brian Wilson's productions became ever more inventive (with occasional relapses, like the beach party sing-along **Barbara Ann**). This sophistication helped band compete successfully with British invasion of US charts.

However, when Brian came up with his tour-de-force **Pet Sounds,** (a monumental concept album on which he worked with lyricist Tony Asher) it was totally upstaged by the Beatles'(▶) **Sergeant Pepper**, which came right on its heels. Brian was by now hanging out with Van Dyke Parks, who later wrote Beach Boys lyrics. Brian got into the drug scene, dropping acid, and drifted away from his brothers. (They had been on tour overseas at time of **Pet Sounds** release, of which they did not totally approve.)

Good Vibrations proved to be *the* classic Beach Boys' single but it took nine months to piece together. Complex though record was, this time-lag was due more to Brian's untogetherness than anything else.

Follow-up album project **Smile,** which eventually appeared as **Smiley Smile,** found Van Dyke Parks heavily involved with Brian, to disapproval of rest of group. Rather than being Brian's dreamed-of masterwork LP was eclipsed by emergent West Coast psychedelia movement; it seemed old hat.

With Brian more and more out of things the Beach Boys continued to churn out pleasant if time-warped singles—including **Wild Honey, Do It Again** and **I Can Hear Music.** Their albums also maintained totally distinctive sound. In 1967 formed own Brother Records label but ran into immediate legal problems. Their dispute with Capitol did not end until 1970 when label's distribution was switched to Warner Bros/Reprise. Brother was one of first artist-owned labels (preceding Beatles' Apple set-up but meeting similar problems).

Below: This is how it all began—the three Wilson brothers, Dennis (drums), Brian (bass) and Carl (lead guitar, partially obscured) in the early 1960s.

Below: Bruce Johnston (left) and Carl Wilson during recent years, perhaps wondering if they would ever make a completely new LP.

Courtesy Capitol Records—this was the LP which appeared in place of the legendary 'Smile', possibly the lost musical masterpiece of the '60s.

New management by Jack Rieley, who also wrote lyrics for them, helped put group back on course. Rieley dug up some old, incomplete tapes for a song called **Surf's Up**, which had been intended as part of **Smile.** He got group to finish it off and make it titletrack of new album. Rieley also encouraged group to drop stage uniforms and come up with less structured stage show. Sets now ran for as much as two hours and included newer, more obscure material alongside hits.

Bruce Johnston quit group after **Surf's Up.** In 1972 Rieley took band off to the Netherlands to cut critically applauded but commercially unspectacular **Holland** album. This led to his split from group. (Band had moved Brother studios to Holland—then Brian decided to return to California.)

At this time, a new rhythm section was formed, including black South Africans Blondie Champlin, guitar, and Ricky Fataar, drums (both of SA Group Fire), making group more potent in concert, but the hits stopped.

Chaplin and Fataar quit in 1974. James Guercio, who had been associated with both Blood Sweat and Tears(▶) and Chicago(▶), came in as manager also played bass on-stage in line-up which reverted to original format.

Dennis and Carl Wilson were proving to be songwriters of some talent but magic spark of Brian Wilson was missing. Numerous attempts were made to tempt him out of his hermit-like existence at Bel-Air mansion. After nearly a decade of virtual inactivity, and following course of therapeutic songwriting prescribed by an analyst, 1976 album **15 Big Ones** (title referring both to number of tracks and the group's age) found Brian back with Beach Boys as singer, songwriter and 'director'. LP won plenty of publicity but did not really stand up. 1977's **The Beach Boys Love You** was more promising. Brian was now firmly back in command of his faculties, composing and producing all material; performed on US tour in summer 1977.

1978's **M.I.U.** album sold poorly and members of band seemed to be going off in own directions. Bruce Johnston came back to help with first Caribou/CBS album **The Beach Boys L.A. Light Album**; and also helped on **Keepin' The Summer Alive** project. Explained Carl: 'He was exactly what

Beach Boy Carl Wilson, who cut two solo albums in the early 1980s.

we needed. He helped us sort the good from the bad and get back to the basics—the vocals and harmonies—which have been our strength from the beginning.'

It was truly a joint effort: Carl Wilson and Randy Bachman of Guess Who and Bachman Turnover Overdrive fame wrote title cut; Brian Wilson/Al Jardine co-wrote five songs and did a new arrangement of Chuck Berry's **School Day;** and Bruce Johnston contributed **Endless Harmony**—an apt Beach Boys' theme.

Keepin' The Summer Alive (1979) and **Ten Years Of Harmony** (1981) kept show rolling, but Beach Boys became shadows of former selves and failed to live up to past glories. Most probably the time for surf music has passed—or maybe the tide's just gone out for a while.

Current line-up: Brian Wilson; Dennis Wilson; Carl Wilson; Love; Jardine; plus sessioneers.

Hit Singles:

	US	UK
Surfin' Safari, 1962	14	—
Surfin' USA, 1963	3	34
Surfer Girl, 1963	7	—
Little Deuce Coupe, 1963	15	—
Be True To Your School, 1963	6	—
Fun Fun Fun, 1964	5	—
I Get Around, 1964	1	7
When I Grow Up (To Be A Man), 1964	9	27
Dance Dance Dance, 1964	8	24
Do You Wanna Dance, 1965	12	—
Help Me Rhonda, 1965	1	27
California Girls, 1965	3	26
The Little Girl I Once Knew, 1965	20	—
Barbara Ann, 1966	2	3
Sloop John B., 1966	3	2
Wouldn't It Be Nice, 1966	8	—
God Only Knows, 1966	39	2
Good Vibrations, 1966	1	1
Then I Kissed Her, 1967	—	4
Heroes And Villains, 1967	12	8
Darlin', 1968	19	11
Do It Again, 1968	20	1
I Can Hear Music, 1969	24	10
Break Away, 1969	—	6
Cottonfields, 1970	—	5
Good Vibrations, 1976	—	8
Rock And Roll Music, 1976	5	36
Lady Lynda, 1979	—	6
Beach Boys Medley, 1981	12	47
Come Go With Me, 1981	18	—

Albums:
Surfin' Safari (Capitol/Greenlight), 1962
Surfin' USA (Capitol), 1963
Surfer Girl (Capitol/Pickwick), 1963
Little Deuce Coupe (Capitol/Greenlight), 1963
All Summer Long (Capitol/MFP), 1964
Concert (Capitol/—), 1964*
Party (Capitol), 1965
Pet Sounds (Capitol/Greenlight), 1966
Best Of (Capitol), 1966
Smiley Smile (Capitol), 1967
Best Of Volume 2 (Capitol), 1967
Wild Honey (Capitol), 1967
Friends (Capitol), 1968
20/20 (Capitol), 1969
Sunflower (Reprise/Caribou), 1970
Surf's Up (Reprise/Caribou), 1971
Live In London (Capitol/MFP), 1972
Endless Summer (Capitol/MFP), 1974
Spirit Of America (Capitol), 1975
The Beach Boys Love You (Reprise), 1977
Fun Fun Fun (Capitol), 1978
California Girls (Capitol/—), 1978
Keepin' The Summer Alive (Caribou), 1979
L.A. (Light Album) (Caribou), 1979
Ten Years Of Harmony (Caribou), 1981
Sunshine Dream (Capitol/—), 1982
*Live

Worth Searching Out:
Surf's Up (Reprise/Stateside), 1971
Holland (Reprise), 1972

Dennis Wilson Solo:
Pacific Ocean Blue (Caribou), 1977
One Of Those People (Elektra), 1979

Carl Wilson Solo:
Carl Wilson (Caribou), 1981

The Beat

UK group formed 1978.

Original line-up: Dave Wakeling, vocals, guitar; Andy Cox, guitar; David Steele, bass; Everett Morton, drums.

Career: Along with fellow-Midlanders the Specials(▶) and the Selecter, the Beat ('The English Beat' in US') were part of multi-racial ska-influenced two-tone movement in late '70s. After first gig in March 1979, they began to take on more members; first 'toaster' Ranking Roger, then 50-year-old saxophone player 'Saxa'.

First single released on Two-Tone in autumn 1979 was individualistic treatment of Smokey Robinson(▶) classic, **Tears Of A Clown**. Record made Top 10 and inaugurated run of successful singles. After **Clown**, singles were self-composed and combined dance beat with better-than-average socially aware lyrics (qv **Stand Down Margaret**). At same time they notched up considerable album success.

Band toured regularly, and gained reputation as premier live act; they gig for causes like Rock For Jobs, and are articulate spokesmen on youth and social issues.

1982 saw further alterations to personnel, Wesley Magoogan replacing ailing Saxa on saxophone, former tour manager Blockhead joining on keyboards. Band have recently kept relatively low profile in UK, while introducing US audiences to 'Two-Tone'.

Commercially and critically successful, the Beat have gained wide and loyal audience through combination of originality, danceability and intelligence. However, Wakeling left band in summer 1983.

Current line-up: Ranking Roger, vocals; Cox; Steele; Morton; Blockhead, keyboards; Wesley Magoogan, saxophone.

Hit Singles:

	US	UK
Tears Of A Clown/Ranking Full Stop, 1979	—	6
Hands Off—She's Mine, 1980	—	9
Mirror In The Bathroom, 1980	—	4
Too Nice To Talk To, 1981	—	7
Can't Get Used To Losing You, 1983	—	7

Albums:
I Just Can't Stop (—/Go Feet), 1980
The Beat (Columbia/—), 1980
Wha'ppen (—/Go Feet), 1981
Special Beat Service (Go Feet), 1982
What Is Beat (Arista/Go Feet), 1983

The Beat—(from left) Andy Cox, Everett Morton, Wakeling, David Steele and Ranking Roger, Saxa.

The Beatles

UK group formed 1959.

Original line-up: John Lennon, vocals, guitar; Paul McCartney, guitar, vocals; George Harrison, guitar, vocals; Stuart Sutcliffe, bass; Pete Best, drums.

Career: Formed in Liverpool area: influenced strongly by American rock 'n' roll and R&B records brought to port by sailors. After becoming local success, began to work in Hamburg, West Germany, where bookings involved playing 8-10 hours per night for little money. However, this experience perfected crowd-pleasing ability (recordings from era are high on energy, short on polish). First studio records were in Germany 1961 as backing group for Tony Sheridan, legendary UK rocker. Sessions also provided first genuine Beatles tracks, notably **Ain't She Sweet,** although tracks not released until much later.

Discovered by Liverpool record shop manager Brian Epstein in late 1961, by which time Sutcliffe had left group, preferring to remain in Germany. McCartney(▶) then moved to bass, and group became quartet (Sutcliffe died of brain haemorrhage, 1962). Epstein tried to acquire recording contract for Beatles, but without success. Group cut demo tracks for Decca Records, but were rejected in favour of Brian Poole & Tremeloes. Finally, Epstein convinced then minor Parlophone label to provide audition. George Martin, head of label, signed group in late 1962, but suggested replacement of Pete Best—rest of band not unhappy, and recruited Ringo Starr(▶) from Rory Storme and the Hurricanes, fellow Merseyside group.

Prior to this, group had gone through several name changes—initially known as the Quarrymen (after school which Lennon(▶) attended), they became Silver Beatles, then simply the Beatles (name inspired by the Crickets, Buddy Holly's(▶) group). Sessions for Parlophone proved promising—first single, **Love Me Do,** released October 1962, reached No. 17 in UK while follow-up, **Please Please Me**, released early 1962, became huge hit. Similarly titled debut LP topped UK charts. Three further chart-toppers, **From Me To You**, **She Loves You**, and **I Want To Hold Your Hand**, followed in 1963.

US success delayed until 1964 when **I Want To Hold Your Hand** (fifth UK hit) topped US singles chart, beginning deluge of releases in US, almost all becoming major hits. At one point in first half of 1964, the Beatles held positions 1, 2, 3, 4 and 5 in US chart, with seven *other* singles in Top 100, and LPs at No. 1 and No. 2. While this success was never equalled, group enjoyed enormous worldwide success through mid-'60s, with strings of chart-toppers in both US and UK. Almost all Beatles B-sides charted on their own in US.

Beatles' success opened floodgates for the 'British Invasion', when numerous British acts broke through in US charts, including Rolling Stones(▶), Gerry & the Pacemakers, Dave Clark Five(▶) and many more. Beatles also starred in pair of ground-breaking rock films, 'A Hard Day's Night' and 'Help!', which were enormously successful both artistically and commercially. Lennon and McCartney were recognised as most potent songwriting partnership of rock'n'roll era; besides providing all Beatle hits, they also wrote chart-toppers for Billy J. Kramer and Peter & Gordon.

Early beat group style, influenced by Chuck Berry(▶), Everly Brothers(▶), Carl Perkins(▶) and Tamla-Motown, evolved by 1966 LP **Rubber Soul** into much more original sound and approach, without affecting commercial success; by late 1966, as psychedelic album **Revolver** released, group gave up touring, mostly because hysterical fans made it too risky. This led to lengthy studio experimentation (and often, in retrospect, self-indulgence) culminating in arguably finest LP ever made.

Sergeant Pepper's Lonely Hearts Club Band, released in June 1967. Group also got involved with Indian guru Maharishi Mahesh Yogi; during their attendance at transcendental meditation course in August, Brian Epstein, who had directed group's career throughout hugely successful period, died (of alcohol/drug overdose).

Beatles plunged back into work, creating **Magical Mystery Tour** LP and TV film, an extension of **Sergeant Pepper,** and equally influenced by hallucinogenic drugs. It received critical roasting but latterly has been regarded as legendary. Although group by this time beginning to argue internally, they created remarkable double LP in 1968, known as **The White Album** because of completely white sleeve; it was preceded by **Lady Madonna** single, which heralded return to more basic rock 'n' roll, and by anthemic **Hey Jude,** single lasting seven minutes plus. Year also saw formation of Beatles' company, Apple Corps, with record label, shop, film company etc. 'Yellow Submarine' cartoon movie was created around fictional characters suggested by Beatle songs.

1969 was final year of Beatles activities, including fated film project 'Let It Be' which produced two chart-topping singles in title song and **Get Back.** Apple Records achieved great success with Mary Hopkin (recommended to Paul McCartney by Twiggy), but 'Let It Be' film was virtually abandoned, as each Beatle wanted to work without the others. Having left producer and svengali George Martin for **Let It Be,** group returned to him for final classic LP, **Abbey Road,** but opposing business interests, particularly of Lennon and McCartney, were becoming impossible.

Lennon and new wife, Japanese avant-garde artist Yoko Ono, formed splinter group, Plastic Ono Band, who scored with first single, **Give Peace A Chance.** Eventually, in 1970, new manager Allen Klein and famed record producer Phil Spector pulled together **Let It Be** project, but this further annoyed McCartney, who announced that he was leaving group. Subsequently, each Beatle enjoyed solo success to a greater or lesser extent. Compilations, re-issues and a few new recordings have kept group in charts ever since, although solo careers (see under individual entries) have in some cases tarnished reputation of undoubtedly most popular group of rock 'n' roll era, whose success and influence are unlikely ever to be equalled.

Rumours of unreleased material being made available arose during refitting of Abbey Road Studios (July 1983) and subsequent opening to public.

Final line-up: Lennon; McCartney; bass, Harrison; Ringo Starr, drums.

Right: US release Meet The Beatles. Courtesy Capitol Records.

Below: Vastly underrated as a 'live' band, the Beatles paid dues with gruelling schedule of German clubs in early days.

The American issue, Beatles' 65.
Courtesy Capitol Records.

Hit Singles:

	US	UK
Love Me Do, 1962	1	17
Please Please Me, 1963	3	2
From Me To You, 1963	41	1
She Loves You, 1963	1	1
I Want To Hold Your Hand, 1963	1	1
Can't Buy Me Love, 1964	1	1
I Saw Her Standing There, 1964	14	—
Twist & Shout, 1964	2	—
Do You Want To Know A Secret, 1964,	2	—
P.S. I Love You, 1964	10	—
A Hard Day's Night, 1964	1	1
Ain't She Sweet, 1964	19	29
And I Love Her, 1964	12	—
Matchbox, 1964	17	—
I Feel Fine, 1964	1	1
She's A Woman, 1964	4	—
Eight Days A Week, 1965	1	—
Ticket To Ride, 1965	1	1
Help, 1965	1	1
Yesterday, 1965	1	—
Day Tripper/We Can Work It Out, 1965	—	1
Day Tripper, 1966	5	—
We Can Work It Out, 1966	1	—
Nowhere Man, 1966	3	—
Paperback Writer, 1966	1	1
Yellow Submarine/Eleanor Rigby, 1966	—	1
Yellow Submarine, 1966	2	—
Eleanor Rigby, 1966	11	—
Penny Lane/Strawberry Fields Forever, 1967	—	2
Penny Lane, 1967	1	—
Strawberry Fields Forever, 1967	8	—
All You Need Is Love, 1967	1	1
Hello Goodbye, 1967	1	1
Magical Mystery Tour (EP), 1967	—	2
Lady Madonna, 1968	1	1
Hey Jude, 1968	1	1
Revolution, 1968	12	—
Get Back, 1969	1	1
Ballad Of John And Yoko, 1969	8	1
Something/Come Together, 1969	—	4
Come Together/Something, 1969	1	—
Let It Be, 1970	1	2
Long And Winding Road, 1970	1	—
Yesterday, 1976	—	8
Got To Get You Into My Life, 1976	7	—
Back In The U.S.S.R., 1976	—	19
Beatles Movie Medley, 1982	12	9

Albums:

UK:
Please Please Me (Parlophone), 1963
With The Beatles (Parlophone), 1963
A Hard Day's Night (Parlophone), 1964
Beatles For Sale (Parlophone), 1964
Help (Parlophone), 1965
Rubber Soul (Parlophone), 1965
Revolver (Parlophone), 1966
A Collection of Beatles' Oldies (But Goldies) (Parlophone), 1966
Sergeant Pepper's Lonely Hearts Club Band (Parlophone), 1967
The Beatles (White Album) (Parlophone), 1968
Yellow Submarine (Parlophone), 1969
Abbey Road (Parlophone), 1969
Let It Be (Parlophone), 1970
The Beatles 1962-1966 (Parlophone), 1973
The Beatles 1967-1970 (Parlophone), 1973
Rock 'n' Roll Music (Parlophone, 1976
Magical Mystery Tour, (Parlophone), 1976
The Beatles At The Hollywood Bowl, (Parlophone), 1977
Love Songs (Parlophone), 1977
Hey Jude (Parlophone), 1979
Rarities, 1979
The Beatles Ballads (Parlophone), 1980
Reel Music (Parlophone), 1982
20 Greatest Hits (Parlophone), 1982

Below: Near the end. One of the last publicity shots issued by Parlophone.

US:
(excluding Boxed Sets and superfluous compilations)
Introducing The Beatles (Capitol), 1963
Meet The Beatles (Capitol), 1964
The Beatles' Second Album (Capitol), 1964
A Hard Day's Night (Capitol), 1964
Something New (Capitol), 1964
The Beatles Story (Capitol), 1964
Beatles '65 (Capitol), 1965
The Early Beatles (Capitol), 1965
Beatles VI (Capitol), 1965
Help (Capitol), 1965

Below: The changing face of pop and the Beatles—one and the same thing. Top: Inside of Sergeant Pepper album. Bottom: Two early Parlophone press shots, circa 1962. Most early shots were by Dezo Hoffman.

Rubber Soul (Capitol), 1965
Yesterday And Today (Capitol), 1966
Revolver (Capitol), 1966
Sergeant Pepper's Lonely Hearts Club Band (Capitol), 1967
Magical Mystery Tour (Capitol), 1967
The Beatles (White Album) (Capitol), 1968
Yellow Submarine (Capitol), 1969
Abbey Road (Capitol), 1969
Hey Jude (Capitol), 1970
Let It Be (Capitol), 1970
The Beatles 1962-1966 (Capitol), 1973
The Beatles 1967-1970 (Capitol), 1973
Rock 'n' Roll Music (Capitol), 1976
The Beatles At The Hollywood Bowl, (Capitol), 1977
Love Songs (Capitol), 1977
The Beatles Rarities (Capitol), 1980
Reel Music (Capitol), 1982
20 Greatest Hits (Capitol), 1982

The classic '60s album, Sergeant Pepper's Lonely Hearts Club Band. Courtesy Parlophone Records.

Help!, the soundtrack album from the enormously successful fab four film. Courtesy Capitol Records.

Jeff Beck

UK guitarist, composer, vocalist.
Born Surrey, June 24, 1944.

Career: Studied at Wimbledon Art College. Played lead guitar for Tridents before being recommended to Yardbirds(▶) by Jimmy Page as replacement for Eric Clapton(▶). Spent two years with group, contributing to new, more experimental, sound on singles like **Shapes Of Things To Come** and **Over Under Sideways Down**.

Left Yardbirds in December 1966 to sign solo deal on EMI's Columbia label. Scored with out-of-character sing along **Hi Ho Silver Lining** (again hit on re-release via Rak in 1972 and still a UK disco/pub/juke-box/party standard). Also cut version of **Love Is Blue** and played guitar solo on Donovan's(▶) hit **Goo Goo Barabajagel** before forming Jeff Beck Group featuring Rod Stewart(▶), vocals; Ron Wood, bass; Ray Cook, drums. (Cook was replaced by Mickey Waller after group was thrown off Roy Orbison/Small Faces(▶) package tour in March 1967.)

Nicky Hopkins (keyboards) joined later, and group won big reputation in US with **Truth** and **Beck-Ola** LPs. Playing biting, R&B-edged heavy rock, group had exciting but tempestuous career, developing reputation for potent music and bawdy life-style. Wood and Stewart split to join Faces(▶) in 1969.

Beck planned new group with ex-Vanilla Fudge(▶) players Tim Bogert (bass) and Carmine Appice (drums) — friends met on early Yardbirds visit to New York — but when car accident kept Beck out of action for 18 months the other two formed Cactus.

Beck-Ola, Jeff Beck. Courtesy Columbia Records.

Beck re-appeared in late 1971 to form new Jeff Beck Group with Robert Tench, vocals; Max Middleton, piano; Clive Chaman, bass, and Cozy Powell, drums. After two albums he declared band wasn't what he wanted and, on break-up of Cactus, formed trio with Bogert and Appice. This broke up after one album, **Beck Bogert Appice** (1973), and tour.

Beck retired again until, in 1975, George Martin produced **Blow By Blow** set, which found Beck experimenting heavily with jazz/rock fusion. Joining Jan Hammer Group for co-billing tour (which produced joint album **Live** in 1977), Beck featured Hammer's synthesiser work on 1976 album **Wired**.

Yet another inactive period ended in 1980 with appearance of **There And Back** album, again featuring Hammer, plus Tony Hymas, keyboards; Mo Foster, bass, and Simon Phillips, drums (Beck's first all-British band since Yardbirds).

Beck stands among greats of rock guitar like Eric Clapton(▶) and Jimi Hendrix(▶) for his creativity, style and sheer fluidity of playing, even if his career has been fragmented. Guitars: Gibson Les Paul, Schecter, Fender Stratocaster.

Above: Jeff Beck laces into his favourite Strat.

Hit Singles:	US	UK
Hi Ho Silver Lining, 1967	—	14
Hi Ho Silver Lining, 1972	—	17

Albums:
Truth (Epic/Columbia), 1968*
Beck-Ola (Epic/Columbia), 1969*
Rough And Ready (Epic), 1971
Jeff Beck Group (Epic), 1972
Beck, Bogert, Appice (Epic), 1973
Wired (Epic), 1976
Live (with the Jan Hammer Group), (Epic), 1977
There And Back (Epic), 1980
Early Anthology (Accord/—), 1981
*Released as double LP (Epic/—), 1975

The Bee Gees

UK group formed 1950s.

Original line-up: Barry Gibb, vocals, guitar; Robin Gibb, vocals; Maurice Gibb, vocals, guitar; Vince Melouney, guitar; Colin Petersen, drums.

Career: Formed in Manchester, England (Barry born September, 1946; non-identical twins Robin and Maurice born December 1949), Bee Gees performed on-stage in home city as pre-teens (father, Hugh, was bandleader). Emigrated to Australia with parents in 1958.

After winning radio talent contest, trio graduated to hosting own TV show. First single **Three Kisses Of Love** (1963) was mildly successful. Group's name was taken from Barry Gibbs' initials. By 1966 they were top Antipodean group but market had limitations. Australian pomoter/manager/entrepreneur Robert Stigwood decided to take band to UK in 1967 as challenge to Beatles. Former child actor Colin Petersen was recruited to go with them as drummer. On arrival in London, another Australian, Vince Melouney, was added on guitar. Their **Spicks and Specks** reached top of Australian charts after they arrived in UK.

This group scored almost immediately with **New York Mining Disaster 1941** in both Britain and America. Follow-ups **To Love Somebody** and **Holiday** were hits, while **Massachusetts** topped UK charts. **I've Got To Get A Message To You** confirmed brothers' songwriting talent. On one early Royal Albert Hall concert they had support from 60-piece orchestra, huge choir and Royal Air Force Brass Band.

Melouney left to form own short-lived band in 1969. Robin Gibb fell out with others and went solo; scored with **Robin's Reign** album and hit single **Saved By The Bell** but career soon floundered. His brothers remained relatively inactive (Maurice married Scottish singer Lulu; they subsequently divorced); Colin Petersen had departed amid much acrimony. Brothers reunited as trio in late 1970.

Bee Gees had two million-selling American singles in 1971, with **Lonely Days** and **How Can You Mend A Broken Heart** but then languished. It was mid-'70s disco explosion which not only revived their career but made them superstars.

Switching from somewhat self-pitying storyline-songs to an emasculated brand of soul/disco did trick. Robin's high-pitched lead matched to nasal falsetto harmonies gave unique sound. 1975 Arif Mardin-produced album **Main Course** went platinum. **Jive Talkin'** was the disco smash of 1975.

Follow-up set **Children Of The Night** was self-produced; contained **You Should Be Dancing** and **Love So Right** monster singles.

Their music for RSO movies 'Saturday Night awards in 1979; **Saturday Night Fever**

soundtrack included three No. 1s for group. Two further chart-toppers from studio album **Spirits Having Flown** made it a remarkable six No. 1s in a row. Bee Gees-penned title song from 'Grease' gave Frankie Valli No. 1 in 1978.

Their 1979 'Music For Unicef' charity project found them headlining worldwide televised New York spectacular. Also on bill were Abba(▶), John Denver(▶), Rod Stewart (▶), Earth, Wind And Fire(▶), Elton John(▶) and other major artists. Youngest Gibb brother Andy had four hit singles and became teenybopper hearthrob in late '70s. In 1980 Barry Gibb co-wrote, co-produced and contributed vocals to Barbra Streisand's(▶) smash album **Guilty**; he went on to revive Dionne Warwick's (▶) career as her new producer. Robin Gibb produced an LP on soul star Jimmy Ruffin and wrote, performed and produced **Help Me** for movie 'Times Square'. Group appeared in Stigwood's 'Sgt. Pepper' film with Peter Frampton(▶).

Bee Gees now live and work in Miami where they have own recording studio. Shared lead vocals on 1981 album **Living Eyes**.

In a 20-year career, the brothers have written more than 1,000 published songs. Authorised biography 'The Illustrated Bee Gees' was published in 1979.

Current line-up: Barry Gibb; Maurice Gibb; Robin Gibb.

Hit Singles:	US	UK
New York Mining Disaster 1941, 1967	12	12
To Love Somebody, 1967	15	41
(The Lights Went Out In) Massachusetts, 1967	11	1
World, 1967	—	9
Holiday, 1967	16	—
Words, 1968	15	8
I've Gotta Get A Message To You, 1968	8	1
I Started A Joke, 1969	6	—
First Of May, 1969	37	6
Don't Forget To Remember, 1969	—	2
Lonely Days, 1971	3	33
How Can You Mend A Broken Heart, 1971	1	—
My World, 1972	16	16
Run To Me, 1972	16	9
Jive Talkin', 1975	1	5

Spirits Having Flown, the Bee Gees. Courtesy RSO Records.

Fanny (Be Tender With My Love), 1976	12	—
You Should Be Dancing, 1976	1	5
Love So Right, 1976	3	41
Boogie Child, 1977	12	—
How Deep Is Your Love, 1977	1	3
Stayin' Alive, 1978	1	4
Night Fever, 1978	1	1
Too Much Heaven, 1978	1	3
Tragedy, 1979	1	1
Love You Inside Out, 1979	1	13
Spirits Having Flown, 1980	—	16

Robin Gibb Solo:
Saved By The Bell, 1969   —   2
Oh! Darling, 1978*   15   —
*From Sgt. Pepper soundtrack featuring all Bee Gees.

Albums:
Odessa (RSO/Polydor), 1969
Best Of (—/RSO), 1969
Best Of Volume 2 (RSO), 1973
Main Course (RSO), 1975
Children Of The World (RSO), 1976
Gold (RSO/—), 1976
Massachusetts (—/Contour), 1976
Here At Last—Live (RSO), 1977
I've Gotta Get A Message To You (—/Contour), 1977
Bonanza—Early Days (—/Pickwick), 1978
Greatest Hits (RSO), 1979
Spirits Having Flown (RSO), 1979
The Bee Gees (—/Impact), 1979
Early Days Volume 1 (—/Pickwick), 1979
Early Days Volume 2 (—/Pickwick), 1979
Early Days Volume 3 (—/Pickwick), 1979
Living Eyes (RSO), 1981

Worth Searching Out:
Bee Gees First (Polydor), 1967

Pat Benatar

US vocalist.
Born Pat Andrejewski, Brooklyn, New York, 1953.

Career: Possessed of undeniably unusual vocal ability, Pat Benatar trained in opera, but never actually attempted professional classical career. After short early marriage, she supported herself by singing in nightclubs, and quickly found her voice as the ultimate female hard-rocker.

Her musical and performing stance is original only in that she *is* female, however. Whether the power-chord clichés and humorless posturing of heavy metal are rendered any more interesting when performed by a tiny, spandex-clad redhead (even with natural talent) rather than by the usual macho howlers is questionable.

Still, Benatar's appearance on the rock scene in 1979 certainly filled a niche. **In The Heat Of The Night** was surprisingly successful, and was followed by two hit singles in 1980 and 1981, **Heartbreaker** and **Hit Me With Your Best Shot.** Her second album, **Crimes of Passion,** went straight to the top in 1981; quick follow-up LP **Precious Time** did just as well. She made acting debut in 'Union City Blues' same year.

Handicapped by not being a proficient songwriter, Benatar's own attempts have been naive, and guitarist-producer (and new husband) Neil Geraldo's writing seldom rises above clichés of the genre. Nevertheless, she has shown taste and daring in her selection of covers, which include John Cougar's(▶) **I Need A Lover Who Won't Drive Me Crazy,** Lennon and McCartney's **Helter Skelter** and Kate Bush's(▶) **Wuthering Heights.**

Hit Singles:	US	UK
Hit Me With Your Best Shot, 1981	5	—
Treat Me Right, 1981	13	—
Fire And Ice, 1981	5	—
Shadows In The Night, 1982	13	—

Albums:
In The Heat Of The Night (Mobile/Chrysalis), 1979
Crimes Of Passion (Chrysalis), 1980
Precious Time (Chrysalis), 1981
Get Nervous (Chrysalis), 1982

Right: Pat Benatar quickly dispensed with operatic background.

George Benson

US guitarist, vocalist.
Born Pittsburgh, Pennsylvania, March 22, 1943.

Career: Began learning guitar at eight, and played and sang with several Pittsburgh R&B outfits during teens. However, models for guitar style were jazz men like Charlie Christian and Wes Montgomery rather than R&B practitioners.

Benson moved to New York in 1963 and joined band of organist Brother Jack McDuff; two years on road with McDuff's funky tenor- and organ-led outfit honed Benson's guitar style. In mid-60s recorded for Columbia with own group, before forming working relationship with Creed Taylor's CTI label in 1970, becoming 'house guitarist' and releasing albums under own name.

CTI period resulted in recognition of Benson's skills, and moderate success, including Grammy nomination for album **White Rabbit**. His vocal talents, however, were largely ignored.

Real success came when Benson joined Warner Bros in mid-'70s, and was teamed with producer Tommy LiPuma. Result was **Breezin'**, a lightweight jazz-funk effort that struck lucrative chord with record-buying public. Eventually going double platinum, it yielded two hit singles in title track (an instrumental) and **This Masqerade**, on which Benson exhibited his attractive Stevie Wonder(▶)-influenced voice. Next album, **In Flight**, followed similar formula and also achieved double platinum sales.

Further hit singles and albums ensued, and

Benson established himself as major concert draw throughout world. Always accompanied by the very best musicians, Benson vocalises to good effect, plays inventive guitar in effortless style, and occasionally combines both in unison scat-singing/guitar improvisations.

In 1980, partnership with renowned musician and producer Quincy Jones brought about renewed success with **Give Me The Night** LP and further hit singles through early '80s.

One of handful of jazz-orientated musicians to have achieved wide crossover success, Benson continues to sell out concerts world wide. He has opened up large market for well-crafted, easy-listening funk, bringing a touch of jazz sophistication to popular music.

Above: Master guitarist George Benson now vocal superstar.

Guitars: Ibanez G310, Gibson Super 400 CES.

Hit Singles:	US	UK
This Masquerade, 1976	10	—
On Broadway, 1978	7	—
Love Ballad, 1979	18	29
Give Me The Night, 1980	4	7
Love X Love, 1980	—	10
Turn Your Love Around, 1981	5	29
Never Give Up, 1982	52	17

Albums:
George Benson & Jack McDuff (Prestige/—), 1960s
It's Uptown (Columbia/—), 1965
Cookbook (Columbia/—), 1966
Shape Of Things To Come (A&M), 1968
White Rabbit (CTI), 1973
Breezin' (Warner Bros), 1977
Summertime: In Concert (CTI), 1977
In Flight (Warner Bros), 1977
Best Of (A&M/—), 1978
Stormy Weather (—/Embassy), 1978
Weekend In L.A. (Warner Bros), 1978
Livin' Inside Your Love (Warner Bros), 1979
Cast Your Fate To The Wind (CTI/—), 1979
Blue Benson (Polydor/—), 1980
New Boss Guitar (Prestige/—), 1980
Give Me The Night (Warner Bros), 1980
The George Benson Collection (Warner Bros), 1981

Chuck Berry

US vocalist, guitarist, composer.
Born Charles Edward Berry, San Jose, California, October 18, 1926.

Career: Arguably the most influential guitarist and songwriter of the entire rock genre; a musically adequate vocalist, his highly articulate diction ensured maximum impact from inventive lyrics. Many of his songs became anthems of teenage life.

Family moved to St Louis, Missouri, in 1930s; young Berry gained musical experience in school glee-clubs and church choirs. Trained as hairdresser, then worked in car factory; performed with small group evenings and weekends.

In 1955 recorded some songs for audition tape and travelled North to Chicago to look for successful bluesman Muddy Waters(▶). Muddy suggested Berry take tape to Chess Records. Leonard Chess was interested in embryonic version of **Maybellene** and had the young hopeful record polished version for Chess debut; disc topped R&B chart and

began prolific succession of hits like **Brown Eyed Handsome Man, Roll Over Beethoven, Sweet Little Sixteen, School Day, Johnny B. Goode, Rock 'n' Roll Music, Reelin' & Rockin'** and **Memphis Tennessee.**

Berry's records are notable for their lyrical content and distinctive guitar style; most discs had guitar introductions and incisive solos midway. On stage, Berry played solo while hopping around in squatting posture; this came to be described as a 'duckwalk'.

Consistency of hit singles resulted in several movie parts; Chuck was committed to celluloid in 'Go Johnny Go' and 'Rock Rock Rock'; also featured in film of 1958 Newport Jazz Festival 'Jazz On A Summers Day' singing **Sweet Little Sixteen.** His performance considered quite revolutionary in such context! Convicted for immorality offence (for taking underage girl across state lines) in 1959; Chess still issued Berry singles but with minimal sales.

Recorded fresh material upon release in 1964; scored hits with **Nadine, No Particular Place To Go** and **You Never Can Tell.** Made first overseas tour and played in England with Carl Perkins(▶). Left Chess after financial temptation from Mercury but only decent Mercury disc was **Club Nitty Gritty** — others were mainly re-hashes of old hits; returned to Chess in 1969. During 1972 toured England and recorded 'live' and studio material; from live set, **My Ding A Ling** was issued as single. This version of old blues song with suggestive lyric topped US and UK charts (sadly Berry's only No. 1).

As Chess label faded, Chuck cut final **Bio** LP. Began to concentrate more on tours than recording; gained reputation for being hard to deal with financially. Has become regular attraction at cosmopolitan music festivals. Brief contract with Atlantic yielded solitary 1979 LP **Rock It,** patchy in quality, a commercial failure.

Although now becoming something of a self-parody, Chuck Berry will always be remembered as one of the giants of rock'n'roll.
Guitar: Gibson 335.

Above: Chuck Berry glides into the 'duckwalk'.

Hit Singles:

	US	UK
Maybellene, 1955	5	—
School Day, 1957	3	24
Rock 'n' Roll Music, 1957	8	—
Sweet Little Sixteen, 1958	2	16
Johnny B. Goode, 1958	8	—
Carol	18	—
Let It Rock/Memphis Tennessee, 1963	—	16
No Particular Place To Go, 1964	10	3
You Never Can Tell, 1964	14	23
My Ding-A-Ling, 1972	1	1
Reelin' And Rockin', 1972	27	18

Albums:
Golden Hits (Mercury/—), 1967
Greatest Hits (Archive Of Folk And Jazz Music/—), 1967
Chuck Berry Volume 1 (—/Impact), 1979
Chuck Berry Volume 2 (—/Impact), 1979

Worth Searching Out:
After School Sessions (Chess/—), 1958
One Dozen Berry's (Chess/—), 1958
Golden Decade Volumes 1-3 (—/Chess), 1973

Bill Black

US bassist, bandleader, composer.
Born Memphis, Tennessee, September 17, 1926; died October 1965.

Career: Session bass player at Sun Records in Memphis, Black played an important role in early success of Elvis Presley(▶), along with guitarist Scotty Moore and drummer D.J. Fontana. He played on all early Elvis hits, at that time using a stand-up bass, his insistently pulsating sound laying perfect background for Presley's potent vocals. Besides supporting the star on recording dates and concert tours, Black appeared in the film 'Loving You'.

Switching to electric bass, he formed his own Bill Black Combo in 1959, signing to local Hi label and innovating emergent Memphis

Sound of R&B (though in his case there was also strong country music flavour).

Smokie (1959), **White Silver Sound** (1960) and **Tuff** (1962), the latter strongly featuring Ace Cannon's raunchy saxophone playing, were all an influence on such other Memphis instrumental groups as the Mar-Keys Booker T and the MGs(▶) and the Willie Mitchell Combo.

Besides having their own hits, the Bill Black Combo backed Gene Simmons on his 1964 hit **Haunted House**.

Following Black's death, group was disbanded but Bill Black Combo name was retained by Hi Records who released flow of recordings actually cut by labelmate Willie Mitchell under the Bill Black banner.

Hit Singles:

	US	UK
Smokie Pt 2, 1960	17	—
White Silver Sands, 1960	9	50
Josephine, 1960	18	—
Don't Be Cruel, 1960	11	32
Blue Tango, 1960	16	—
Hearts Of Stone, 1961	20	—

Albums:
Memphis Tennessee (Hi/—), '60s
Award Winners (Hi/—), '60s

Black Sabbath
UK group formed 1969.

Original line-up: Ozzy Osbourne, vocals; Tony Iommi, Jay-dee guitar; Terry 'Geezer' Butler, bass; Bill Ward, drums.

Career: Started in Birmingham as blues band Earth; in late 1969 they changed name to Black Sabbath and recorded first album of same name, developing quasi occult, 'evil' image. Although album was largely ignored by radio and media, word of mouth eventually hoisted it into UK charts where it remained for 13 weeks.

International success followed quickly with release of 1970 album **Paranoid**; LP and single of same name hit on both sides of Atlantic. Band played first successful American tour in autumn 1970.

From that time until 1973, band toured regularly and recorded prolifically, establishing themselves as one of world's foremost heavy metal bands, though critical acclaim continued to elude them.

In 1973 managerial problems forced cessation of activities until 1975 release of album **Sabotage** re-established band as major force in heavy metal, a position they have maintained ever since.

Since 1978 band has undergone several

Below: They sold their souls for rock'n'roll—Black Sabbath.

personnel changes. Ozzy Osbourne(▶) left, to return a few months later, but in 1979 he departed for good to form own band, Ozzy Osbourne's Blizzard of Oz, which has achieved considerable success. He was replaced by Ronnie James Dio, formerly singer with Ritchie Blackmore's Rainbow(▶). At end of 1980 Bill Ward left for personal reasons, and Vinnie Appice, brother of the more famous Carmine, was recruited.

Technical Ecstacy, Black Sabbath. Courtesy Warner Bros Records.

At the time of writing, both Dio and Appice had split. Ward returned and Butler and Iommi announced that ex-Deep Purple(▶) and Gillan(▶) vocalist Ian Gillan would replace Dio.

Black Sabbath can certainly lay claim to be among originators of heavy metal music, and there is no doubt that their particular brand of sledgehammer rock still commands wide and loyal following. To non-aficionados, however, much of their output seems both monotonous and simple-minded.

Current line-up: Iommi; Butler; Ward; Ian Gillan, vocals.

Hit Singles:

	US	UK
Paranoid, 1970	—	4
Paranoid, 1980	—	14

Albums:
Black Sabbath (Nems/Warner Bros), 1970
Paranoid (Nems/Warner Bros), 1970
Master Of Reality (Nems/Warner Bros), 1971
Black Sabbath 4 (Nems/Warner Bros), 1972
Sabbath Bloody Sabbath (Nems/Warner Bros), 1973
Sabotage (Nems/Warner Bros), 1975
We Sold Our Souls For Rock 'N' Roll (Nems/Warner Bros), 1975
Technical Ecstacy (Nems/Warner Bros), 1976
Greatest Hits (Nems/Warner Bros), 1977
Never Say Die (Vertigo/Warner Bros), 1978
Heaven & Hell (Vertigo/Warner Bros), 1980
Mob Rules (Vertigo/Warner Bros), 1981
Live Evil (Vertigo/Warner Bros), 1983

Bobby Bland

US vocalist.
Born Rosemark, Tennessee, January 27, 1930.

Career: Settling in Memphis with his family in 1944, Bland had spell with a gospel group. From 1949-50 he was valet to B.B. King(▶), then to Rosco Gordon for three years.

Bland worked with Earl Forrest, Johnny Ace, Rosco Gordon, and Billy Duncan in loose-knit aggregation known as the Beale Streeters, which lasted six years but never recorded. Under aegis of Ike Turner(▶), he cut first records for LA-based Modern label, but company bosses, the Biharri Brothers, had no real faith in his talents and records were not pushed.

While serving with the army, Bland appeared on show in Houston, Texas, and was spotted and signed by Duke Records' boss Don Robey in 1954. It was 1957 before Bland started making impact on charts, the breakthrough coming with powerful **Farther Up The Road**.

The following years brought run of more than 30 chart successes. During first eight years with Duke, Bland worked closely with labelmate Little Junior Parker, sharing same stage band (featuring Pat Hare on guitar), but from 1962 onwards he fronted own 10- or 12-piece outfit, with Wayne Bennett and sax player Mel Jackson prominently featured. Jackson has stayed with Bland to this day while Bennett returned to band in 1982 after 15-year absence.

In 1972, following Don Robey's death, Duke was bought out by ABC which, in turn, was taken over by MCA. Bland's contract was retained and, with B.B. King also on roster, MCA paired the old friends for two albums.

Showcased by superb arrangements from trumpeter Joe Scott which fully exploited brass-laden Bill Harvey Band and featuring stunningly innovative guitar solos of Wayne Bennett, Bobby 'Blue' Bland's prolific recordings for Duke label through '60s were absolute masterworks of R&B genre, making him permanent fixture in American R&B/soul charts.

Bland's latter-day albums have ranged from ordinary to excellent and have included a handful of numbers which match the majesty of his earlier work. Ironically, despite having

Above: R&B legend Bobby Bland still stirs crowds in the '80s. Pictured in London, 1982.

fervent and faithful following in UK, as evidenced by his reception on first British visit in 1982, Bland has yet to achieve a British chart entry.

Hit Singles:	US	UK
Ain't Nothing You Can Do, 1964	20	—

Albums:
Two Steps From The Blues (Duke/—), '60s
Here's The Man (MCA/—), '60s
Ain't Nothing You Can Do (MCA/—), '60s
Soul Of The Man (Duke/—), '60s
Touch Of The Blues (Duke/—), 1968
Spotlighting The Man (Duke/—), 1969
Best Of Volume 1 (Duke/—), 1973
Best Of Volume 2 (Duke/—), 1977
Introspective Of The Early Years (MCA/—), '70s
Reflections In Blue (MCA), 1977
Come Fly With Me (MCA), 1978
I Feel Good, I Feel Fine (MCA/—), 1979
Sweet Vibrations (MCA/—), 1980
Woke Up Screaming (—/Ace), 1981
Here We Go Again (MCA/—), 1982
Try Me, I'm Real (MCA/—), 1982

With B.B. King:
Together For The First Time (MCA), 1974
Together Again (MCA), 1976

Worth Searching Out:
The California Album (ABC Dunhill/ABC), 1973

The Blasters

US group formed 1978.
Original/Current line-up: Phil Alvin, guitar, vocals; Dave Alvin, guitar; Gene Taylor, piano; Steve Berlin, bass; Lee Allen, saxophone.

Career: Brothers Dave and Phil Alvin grew up in LA suburb Downey. Became passionately interested in R&B and traditional country music. When other teenagers were into the Beatles, they were searching out obscure songs by T-Bone Walker and Lowell Fulsom. Both took up guitar; Dave started writing.

By late '70s, Blasters were popular act on LA punk scene. Among other new bands like X, Black Flag and Gun Club, Blasters were unusual: they were a new band with a traditional sound. Not a rockabilly group, being too wedded to rougher forms of R&B and disdainful of costumes and posturing that rockabilly often relies upon, Blasters are probably most pure rock 'n' roll band to come out of new wave.

In 1979, recorded **American Music** for Ronnie Weiser's Rollin' Rock Company, a small independent outfit devoted to archival rock (some of Gene Vincent's(▶) last recordings were on this label). The album was cheaply made and poorly produced, but contained two of Dave Alvin's best songs, **Marie Marie** and **American Music.** Signed to Slash records, an independent but quite important label generally associated with LA punk. Released **The Blasters** (1981), a far better album, with new versions of Alvin's two songs, and **I'm Shakin'**, which featured sax player Lee Allen.

An integral part of New Orleans R&B scene in '50s (played on hits by Fats Domino(▶), Little Richard(▶), and countless others, as well as having a big instrumental hit with his own band, **Walkin' With Mr. Lee**), Allen had retired to LA, doing occasional session work when Blasters convinced him to join band permanently.

In 1982, Slash made deal with Warner Bros, and album was picked up and given national distribution; received critical raves and quite respectable sales airplay. Band went on major tour to support album; in 1982 recorded live EP at the Venue in London (which made album charts in US as 'mini-album'). Live show is not to be missed.

A third album of all new material was released in May 1983.

Though deeply rooted in classic rock forms, the Blasters' sound is unique—particularly because they avoid archivist's trap of imitation, and rely on their own individuality and original material.

Albums:
American Music (Rollin' Rock/—), 1980
The Blasters (Slash/Warner Bros), 1981
Live In London (EP) (Warner Bros), 1983
Non-Fiction (Warner Bros), 1983

Blind Faith

UK group formed 1969.
Original/Final line-up: Steve Winwood, keyboards, guitar, vocals; Eric Clapton, guitar, vocals; Ginger Baker, drums; Rick Grech, bass, violin, vocals.

Career: The emergent heavy rock movement of late '60s spawned crop of so-called 'supergroups' formed from the remains of previous major (or well-respected) acts. Cream was one of the first, bringing together erstwhile R&B players Eric Clapton (who had

US release Blind Faith. Courtesy Atco. The band's only release.

been working in John Mayall's band after leaving Yardbirds), Ginger Baker and Jack Bruce (from Graham Bond Organization).

Supergroups were usually short-lived due to personality clashes and Cream was no exception. But Clapton and Baker immediately set up another megaband, this time with Stevie Winwood (ex-leader of Traffic and, before that, with Spencer Davis) and Rick Grech (lifted from Family in mid-tour) under the working title Blind Faith.

In true supergroup style, band got off to mega-hype start, with their debut (and only) album selling a million and their June '69 gig in London's Hyde Park drawing 100,000 devotees; but their American tour resulted in major rows which led to break up only months after formation. Though not the major landmark it was first hailed, the album remains highly listenable and reveals promise of what could have developed into major creative force given more cohesive personalities.

Albums:
Blind Faith (RSO/Polydor), 1969

Blondie

US group formed 1975.
Original line-up: Debbie Harry, vocals; Chris Stein, guitar; Jimmy Destri, keyboards; Gary Valentine, bass; Clem Burke, drums.

Career: Band born out of mid-'70s New York new wave, a splinter group of punk/sleaze outfit the Stilettoes. Lead singer was Debbie Harry, one-time front person of folk-rock band the Wind In The Willows, and well-known figure around New York music/art/night-life scene. Briefly calling themselves Angel and the Snake, band consisted of Harry, Chris Stein (guitar), Billy O'Connor (drums), Fred Smith (bass), and two back-up singers, Tish and Snooky. By 1975 had reached line-up (above) known as Blondie.

Plastic Letters, Blondie. Courtesy Chrysalis Records.

In 1976 band signed with producer Richard Gottehrer and released first single, **X Offender/In The Sun**. In October same year they contracted to Private Stock, and released first album, **Blondie**. Promotion concentrated on Monroesque good looks of Debbie Harry, as much of the publicity throughout life of band.

Lack of success with Private Stock prompted move to Chrysalis, who re-released first album and followed it with **Plastic Letters** in 1978. Gary Valentine had left, and was replaced by guitarist Frank Infante, who played bass on **Letters**. Album spawned international hits **Denis** and **(I'm Always Touched By Your) Presence Dear** and set band on road to success. Next album, **Parallel Lines**, with addition of bassist Nigel Harrison, established band as top international attraction and went on to eventually sell 20 million copies.

From 1978 to 1981 band was among most

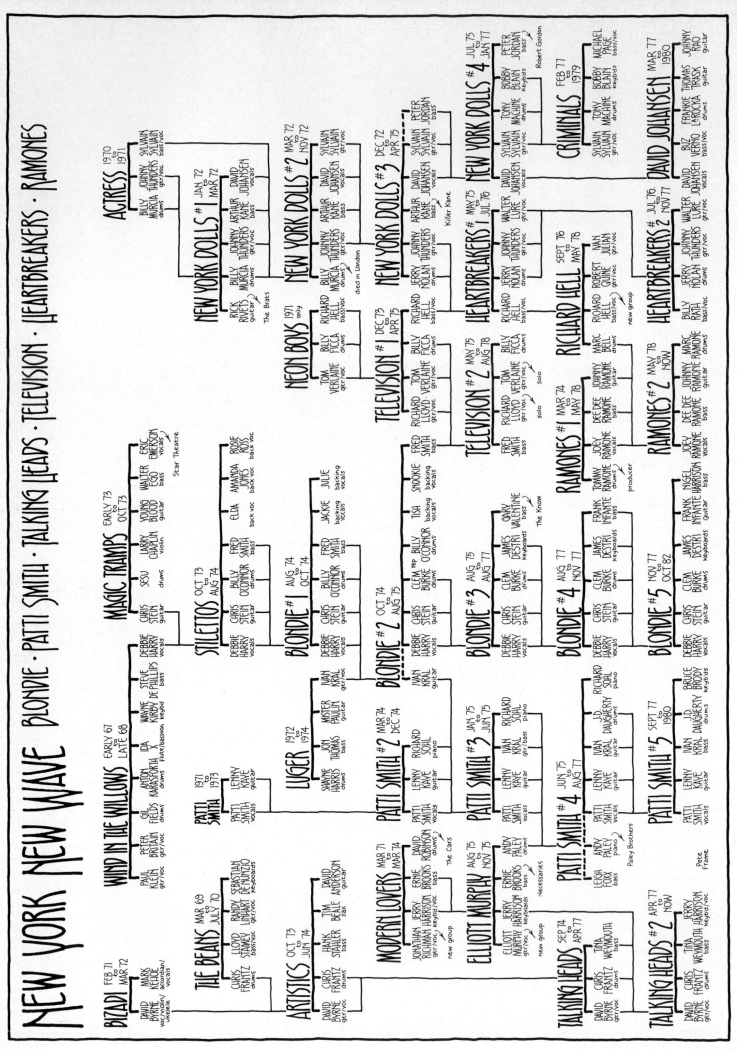

successful in world. Winning formula combined commercial material, clear, pop-style vocals, and rock backing with hint of punk aggression. Audiences were drawn from both pop and rock aficionados. Harry became much-photographed sex symbol of rock.

In 1982, however, it became apparent that runaway pace of success was slowing down. Album **The Hunter** was relatively unsuccessful (although it still made UK Top 10 and US Top 40), and British tour was cancelled because it failed to attract interest anticipated. Critics cited lack of regular live work.

In meantime, Debbie Harry had some success with solo album **Koo Koo** (produced by Chic(▶) supremos Nile Rodgers and Bernard Edwards) and acting debut in 'Union City Blues' and 'Roadie' (1980). (Her career on Broadway lasted precisely one evening in 1983 New York play.) Other members of Blondie also branched out into production and projects with other musicians. In February 1983 band announced break-up. Burke went on to play with Eurythmics(▶).

Final line-up: Harry; Stein; Destri; Frank Infante, guitar; Nigel Harrison, bass; Burke.

Hit Singles:

	US	UK
Denis, 1978	—	2
(I'm Always Touched By Your) Presence Dear, 1978	—	10
Picture This, 1978	—	12
Hanging On The Telephone, 1978	—	5
Heart Of Glass, 1979	1	1
Sunday Girl, 1979	—	1
Dreaming, 1979	27	2
Union City Blues, 1979	—	13
Atomic, 1980	39	1
Call Me, 1980	1	1
The Tide Is High, 1980	1	1
Rapture, 1981	1	5
Island Of Lost Souls, 1982	37	11

Albums:
Blondie (Chrysalis), 1978
Plastic Letters (Chrysalis), 1978
Parallel Lines (Chrysalis), 1978
Eat To The Beat (Chrysalis), 1979
Autoamerican (Chrysalis), 1980
The Best Of (Chrysalis), 1981
The Hunter (Chrysalis), 1982

Blood Sweat and Tears

US group formed 1967.
Original line-up: Steve Katz, guitar, lute, vocals; Al Kooper, organ, piano, vocals; Fred Lipsius, alto sax, piano; Randy Brecker, trumpet, flugelhorn; Dick Halligan, trombone; Jerry Weiss, trumpet, fluegelhorn; Jim Fielder, bass; Bobby Colomby, drums, percussion, vocals.

Career: Conceived as jazz-rock big-band fusion, Blood Sweat and Tears were brainchild of Al Kooper(▶) and Steve Katz, after they quit Blues Project.

First album **Child Is Father To The Man** was hard-hitting, raw power, with Kooper handling most of vocals. As group headed in more commercial direction he quit to make 'supersession' albums with Mike Bloomfield(▶). Husky-voiced Canadian blue-eyed soul singer David Clayton-Thomas was brought in to front group and second album **Blood Sweat And Tears** found massive commercial success. Music was now highly arranged, brassy and almost orchestral in form. **You Made Me So Very Happy, Spinning Wheel** and **When I Die** were all culled from album to become million-selling singles.

Steadily evolving line-up saw band's early fire gradually extinguished. After Clayton-Thomas quit for solo career in 1972, only Colomby remained from early line-up.

Bobby Doyle, Jerry Fisher and Jerry Le Croix all had stints at lead singer role before Clayton-Thomas rejoined in 1974 for **New City** album.

By 1980 **Nuclear Blues** album and none-too-successful double-header UK tour with War(▶), band had changed enormously though still rooting itself in brass-heavy style.

Final line-up: David Clayton-Thomas, vocals; Bruce Cassidy, trumpet, fluegelhorn; Robert Piltch, guitar; Richard Martinez, keyboards; Earl Seymour, baritone and tenor saxophone; Vernon Dorge, alto and soprano saxophone, flute; David Piltch, bass; Bobby Economou, drums.

Hit Singles:

	US	UK
You've Made Me So Very Happy, 1969	2	35
Spinning Wheel, 1969	2	—
And When I Die, 1969	2	—
Hi Di Ho, 1970	14	—

Albums:
"3" (Columbia/CBS), 1970
Greatest Hits (Columbia/CBS), 1972
The First Album (Columbia/Embassy), 1973*
Blood Sweat And Tears (Columbia/Hallmark), 1978
Nuclear Blues (Lax/MCA), 1980

*originally titled **Child Is Father To The Man,** 1968

Mike Bloomfield

US guitarist, vocalist, composer.
Born Chicago, 1943; died February 14, 1981.

Career: As guitarist for the legendary Paul Butterfield Blues Band(▶) and leader of the brilliant but short-lived Electric Flag, Bloomfield had carved formidable reputation by the time he embarked on solo career in 1968.

His first venture was on album with Stephen Stills(▶) and Al Kooper(▶) called **Super Session,** a glorified jam which featured Stills (on guitar) on one side and Bloomfield on the other. Despite Kooper's less than inspired vocals and often over-elaborate production, set was enormous success, and contained some of Bloomfield's best-ever work. This 1968 offering was followed in 1969 by live double album, **The Live Adventures Of Mike Bloomfield And Al Kooper,** which suffered from similar defects but was equally successful.

Bloomfield's career then went into slow but steady decline. He veered off into film music, collaborating with former Electric Flag colleague Nick Gravenites on score of Fonda-Sutherland movie 'Steelyard Blues'. He cut another three-handed album, this time with blues singer John Paul Hammond and keyboards ace Dr John(▶), but it failed to repeat success of **Super Session.** By end of '70s he could no longer be regarded as major contender on American music scene.

In 1977 he recorded an album intended as primer for aspiring blues guitarists, **If You Love These Blues, Play 'Em As You Please.** It was probably the most worthwhile work he did during '70s, effectively demonstrating the styles of the blues masters. It was also testimony to a never-fully-realised talent, for Bloomfield died in February 1981, another rock'n'roll casualty rather than an enduring influence.

Guitars: Gibson 335, Les Paul.

Above: Blondie, in better days. Debbie Harry's solo career has not yet matched former success with group.

Albums:
If You Love These Blues . . .(Guitar Player/ Sonet), 1977
Analine (Takoma/Sonet), 1977
Bloomfield And Harris (with Woody Harris) (Kicking Mule), 1980
Between The Hard Place (Takoma/—), 1981
Michael Bloomfield (Takoma/—), 1981
Living In The Fast Lane (Waterhouse), 1982

Worth Searching Out:
Super Session (with Al Kooper and Stephen Stills) (Columbia/CBS), 1968
Live At Bill Graham's Fillmore West (Columbia/CBS), 1969

Blue Mink

UK group formed 1969.
Original line-up: Madeline Bell, vocals; Roger Cook, vocals; Herbie Flowers, bass; Roger Coulman, keyboards; Alan Parker, guitar; Barry Morgan, drums.

Career: In 1969 a group of leading London session musicians came together to record an album of instrumentals they had penned. One number, **Melting Pot**, written by Roger Cook and his composing partner Roger Greenaway (they had earlier scored as a recording duo under name David And Johnathan with singles **Michelle** and **Lovers Of The World Unite**), called for vocals on which Cook and black American singer Madeline Bell were featured.

Melting Pot, with its plea for racial harmony, was immediate success, reaching No.3, and led to run of hits including **Good Morning Freedom, Our World, Banner Man, Stay With Me, By The Devil** and **Randy**, which encouraged the studio group to go out on the road, playing leading UK cabaret spots. Preferring to concentrate on session work, Roger Coulman left in April 1973 (replaced by Ann Odell) while percussionist Ray Cooper joined soon after for a reasonably well-received debut US tour.

Outside interests caused band to break up in 1975, Cook returning to songwriting and establishing base in Nashville; Parker and Morgan concentrated on session work and their highly successful Morgan Studios in North London; Flowers guested on a wide variety of recordings, issuing his own solo efforts and eventually becoming founder member of classical-rock band Sky; and Madeline Bell became established solo act as

well as contributing voice-overs on numerous TV commercials and working for a time on BBC Radio One as DJ.

Ann Odell now spends time doing sessions and working with Madeline Bell's vocal back-up group, while Ray Cooper has worked regularly with Elton John(▶).

Final line-up: Bell; Cook; Flowers; Parker; Morgan; Ann Odel, keyboards; Ray Cooper, percussion.

Hit Singles:

	US	UK
Melting Pot, 1969	—	3
Good Morning Freedom, 1970	—	10
Our World, 1970	—	17
Banner Man, 1971	—	3
Stay With Me, 1972	—	11
Randy, 1973	—	9

Albums:
Hit Making Sounds (—/Gull), 1977

Blue Oyster Cult

US group formed 1970.

Original/Current line-up: Eric Bloom, vocals, guitar; Allen Lanier, keyboards, synthesiser; Donald 'Buck Dharma' Roeser, guitar, vocals; Joe Bouchard, bass, vocals; Albert Bouchard, drums, vocals.

Career: America's prime exponents of heavy-metal idiom started in New York as Stalk Forrest Group and Soft White Underbelly. Recorded two unreleased albums for Elektra before name change and Columbia contract, earned via mentor Sandy Pearlman, 'Crawdaddy' magazine critic, in 1971. Released eponymous debut album.

Breakthrough came with third album **Secret Treaties** in 1974, which included Patti Smith(▶)-penned **Career Of Evil**; 1975 live

Secret Treaties, Blue Oyster Cult. Courtesy CBS Records.

double set **On Your Feet Or On Your Knees** captured their explosive stage presence—screaming vocals and savage guitar riffs overlaying a pounding rhythm section.

Patti Smith wrote two songs and guested on 1976 album **Agents Of Fortune** from which **(Don't Fear) The Reaper** was US hit. Since then, somewhat sinister mysticism of lyrics, album cover designs and image, and increasingly heavy playing has marked work. They have won an increasing reputation as heavy-metal cult band among head bangers on both sides of the Atlantic.

Hit Singles:

	US	UK
(Don't Fear) The Reaper, 1976	12	—
(Don't Fear) The Reaper, 1978	—	16

Albums:
Blue Oyster Cult (Columbia/CBS), 1972
Tyranny And Mutation (Columbia/CBS), 1974
Secret Treaties (Columbia/CBS), 1974
On Your Feet Or On Your Knees (Columbia/CBS), 1975
Agents Of Fortune (Columbia/CBS), 1976
Spectres (Columbia/CBS), 1977
Some Enchanted Evening (Columbia/CBS), 1978
Mirrors (Columbia/CBS), 1979
Cultasaurus Erectus (Columbia/CBS), 1980
Buck Dharma Solo:
Fire Of Unknown Origin (Columbia/CBS), 1981
Flat Out (Columbia), 1982
Extraterrestrial/Live (Columbia/CBS), 1982

Blues Brothers

US group formed 1978.

Original/Final line-up: Joliet 'Jake' Blues (John Belushi), lead vocals; Elwood Blues (Dan Aykroyd, harmonica, vocals; Paul Shaffer, piano, organ; Steve Cropper, guitar; Matt 'Guitar' Murphy, guitar; Donald 'Duck' Dunn, bass, Steve Jordan, drums; Lou Marini, tenor sax; Lan Rubin, trumpet; Tom Scott, tenor sax; Tom Malone, tenor and baritone sax, trumpet, trombone.

Career: Turned on to blues and soul music in 1977 while making 'Animal House', Belushi decided it was time to hit out against 'preprogrammed electronic disco'; with fellow actor Dan Aykroyd created the Blues Brothers (Jake and Elwood). Belushi and Aykroyd were known for connection with *National Lampoon* team and cult show 'Saturday Night Live' in US, on which they had performed early versions of Blues Brothers.

First live gig was at Universal Amphitheatre, LA, in 1978 with headliner comedian Steve Martin. Behind Jake and Elwood was a great R&B band (some musicians had played on original versions of soul classics). Belushi was right, there were a lot of people who wanted to break from disco—band went down a storm and from this cut first live album, **Briefcase Full Of Blues,** which topped American charts; Aykroyd was signed by Universal to co-write film about band ('The Blues Brothers').

The demure duo provided strong vocal front to great band treating Stax and Chicago blues with respect it deserved, while adding many, often amusing, improvisations. Music not perfect, but emotional.

In 1980 'The Blues Brothers' appeared to generally bad reviews from film critics, but did well with music fans and now has large cult following. A musical comedy, the film is largely tribute to soul music of '60s with guest appearances from James Brown,(▶) Cab Calloway, Ray Charles(▶), Aretha Franklin(▶) and John Lee Hooker(▶). Belushi died from drug overdose in 1982—a sad waste of talent. Ackroyd continues to act in films.

Hit Singles:

	US	UK
Soul Man, 1978	14	—

Albums:
Briefcase Full Of Blues (Atlantic), 1978
The Blues Brothers (soundtrack) (Atlantic), 1980
Made In America (Atlantic), 1980
Best Of The Blues Brothers (Atlantic), 1982

Marc Bolan

UK vocalist, guitarist, composer.
Born Mark Feld, London, July 30, 1947; died September 16, 1977.

Career: Always adept at self-promotion, in early '60s then 15-year-old Feld managed to win wide exposure in media as archetypal mod, which led to brief career as male model. Later dropped sharp besuited image for loose-fitting flowery clothes, beads and espousal of 'flower power'. Changed name to Bolan for debut single **The Wizard** on Decca (1966). Briefly joined pioneer glam-rock band John's Children, scoring with **Desdemona**. Their **Go Go Girl** backing track was used for Bolan's later **Mustang Ford**. On leaving group, Bolan cut sides for Track which did not surface until 1974, as **Beginning Of Doves** LP.

Joined by Steve Peregrine Took, Bolan attempted to form five-piece electronic band but hire-purchase company snatched back equipment. Bolan and Took consequently started working in 1968 as acoustic folksy-rock duo Tyrannosaurus Rex. Full of elves, fairies and flower-power mythology, Tyrannosaurus Rex albums **My People Were Fair And Had Sky In Their Hair But Now They're Content To Wear Stars On Their Brows** (1968), **Prophets, Seers And Sages** (1969), **The Angels Of The Ages** (1969) and **Unicorn** (1969) may have been somewhat pretentious, but captured essence of the love-and-peace philosophy. Duo also benefited from support of influential BBC radio DJ John Peel (as did Bolan's book of poetry).

Overshadowed in duo by Bolan, Took quit in 1970, replaced by Mickey Finn (who met Bolan in a health food restaurant). On their

Below: Marc Bolan—a master of the changing pop genre, in at the start of punk. Photo from inside of T. Rex album.

Beard Of Stars album Bolan switched to electric guitar. Later that year, with name shortened to T.Rex, they notched surprise UK No. 2 with soft-rock but uptempo **Ride A White Swan.** Added drummer Bill Legend and bass player Steve Currie in time for next single **Hot Love.** Aimed direct at teenybop pop audience, it topped chart for six weeks in early 1971. **Get It On** was second No. 1 later same year; re-titled **Bang A Gong,** became group's biggest US success.

You Scare Me To Death, Marc Bolan. Courtesy Decca Records.

T. Rex had now fully undergone transition from esoteric folk-rock outfit to rocking pop band. Bolan had become pre-teen idol to rival earlier Beatles(▶) and Monkees(▶).

Though **Jeepster** made UK No. 2, Fly Records had pulled it from **Electric Warrior** album without consulting Bolan. Angered, he split to start own T.Rex label, via EMI. String of UK hits made 1972 big year. In 1973 ex-Beatle Ringo Starr(▶) directed movie, 'Born To Boogie', about T.Rex phenomenon but it flopped. By end of year Bolan's fickle young audiences were deserting him in droves for younger artists like the Osmonds(▶) and David Cassidy, and more exciting bands like Slade(▶).

The glamour and glitter became tarnished. Bolan left wife June Child to live with black American soul singer Gloria Jones (who bore him a child). He put on weight alarmingly, churned out ever less satisfying material, split with Finn (in March 1975) and broke up T.Rex before slinking off to tax exile in Los Angeles.

Bolan undertook comeback tour with Jones early in 1976 and formed new T.Rex with veteran studio musicians Herbie Flowers, Miller Anderson and Tony Newman, and keyboard player Dino Dines.

Seeking rising star to hitch on to, Marc tried to become self-proclaimed guru of British new-wave movement and used the Damned(▶) as support on his spring 1977 tour. Hosted a rather unsatisfactory weekly TV music show and fought hard to rebuild career. Early one September morning in 1977, the mini car driven by Gloria Jones careered off road on dangerous bend and passenger Bolan was killed, aged 30. Totally shattered, Jones—who blamed tragedy on herself—had hard time until, with help of songwriter brother, she rebuilt career, wrote hit records for several artists, notably British soul act Gonzales (worldwide disco smash **Haven't Stopped Dancing Yet**). Her composition **Tainted Love,** written back in '60s, became big 1981 hit for Soft Cell.

Hit Singles:

	US	UK
As Tyrannosaurus Rex:		
Deborah/One Inch Rock, 1972	—	7
As T.Rex:		
Ride A White Swan, 1970	—	2
Hot Love, 1971	—	1
Get It On, 1971	10	1
Jeepster, 1971	—	2
Telegram Sam, 1972	—	1

	US	UK
Metal Guru, 1972	—	1
Children Of The Revolution, 1972	—	2
Solid Gold Easy Action, 1972	—	2
20th Century Boy, 1973	—	3
The Groover, 1973	—	4
Truck On (Tyke), 1973	—	12
Teenage Dream, 1974	—	13
New York City, 1975	—	15
I Love To Boogie, 1976	—	13

Albums:
As Tyrannosaurus Rex:
Prophet/My People (—/Cube), 1972*
Beard Of Stars/Unicorn (—/Cube), 1972*
As T.Rex:
T.Rex (—/Cube), 1970
Electric Warrior (Reprise/Cube), 1971
Bolan Boogie (—/Cube), 1972
The Slider (Reprise/EMI), 1972
Greatest Hits Volume I (—/Hallmark), 1978
Collection (—/Hallmark), 1978
Solid Gold (—/Fame), 1979
Unobtainable (—/Nut), 1980
In Concert (—/Marc), 1981
Patinum Collection (—/Cube), 1981
*Released as double albums two years after original release as singles.

Gary 'US' Bonds

US vocalist.
Born Gary Anderson, Jacksonville, Florida, June 6, 1939.

Career: Former street-corner singer who found success after ingenious 'con' by producer Frank Guida. Guida sent promotional copies of Anderson's first single **New Orleans** to record stations in a sleeve marked 'Buy US Bonds'. Gary had no idea his new name was being taken in vain, although quickly accepted this promotional device as record charted.

Bonds followed **New Orleans** with similar series of raucous R&B belters, amateurishly but effectively produced by enthusiastic Guida.

When hits dried up, Bonds moved to lounge circuit, where he was 're-discovered' by Bruce Springsteen(▶) in 1980. With producer Miami Steve Van Zandt and Springsteen at the helm, Bonds went back into the studio to cut **Dedication** LP, which understandably paid homage to Bonds' earlier recordings, provided minor chart action, and led to further Springsteen/Van Zandt assistance on 1982 album, **On The Line.**

Greatest Hits, Gary 'US' Bonds. Courtesy Ensign Records.

Hit Singles:

	US	UK
New Orleans, 1960	6	16
Quarter To Three, 1961	1	7
School Is Out, 1961	5	—
Dear Lady Twist, 1962	9	—
Twist Twist Senora, 1962	9	—

Albums:
Certified Soul (Rhino/—), 1980s
Dedication (EMI), 1981
Greatest Hits (—/Ensign), 1981
On The Line (Capitol), 1982

Booker T and the MGs

US band formed 1960.

Original line-up: Booker T. Jones, keyboards; Steve Cropper, Fender Telecaster guitar; Donald 'Duck' Dunn, Fender Precision bass; Al Jackson, drums.

Career: Originally brought together as house rhythm section for Stax Records, Booker T and the MGs went on to cut some '60s classic soul sides, both with Stax artists and on their own. Purveyors of lean, spare funk that became one of the most instantly recognisable sounds of the era, band first emerged from studio to find themselves in spotlight with release of **Green Onions** in 1962.

A great instrumental based on simplest of riffs, **Green Onions** set pattern for string of hits which were to follow: Booker T's bluesy organ alternated with Cropper's raw guitar, while bass and drums provided rock-solid back-up. Although band undertook some live appearances, they still spent most of their time cloistered in Stax studios, backing artists like Otis Redding(▶), William Bell and Rufus Thomas.

1968 provided interesting challenge when band were asked to compose and perform soundtrack for film 'Uptight', a re-working of 'The Informer' set in ghetto Cleveland. The music played a considerable part in film's success, and single taken from soundtrack, **Time Is Tight**, became international hit.

It seemed that film music might be another direction which Booker T and the MGs could profitably follow, but in fact **Uptight** was to be their only movie score. Although band hit with **Soul Clap '69** and produced several more albums, their most creative days were over by turn of decade, and members went separate ways in 1972. Dunn and Jackson stayed on in Memphis and continued playing sessions, while Booker T moved to California and made several mediocre albums with wife Priscilla Coolidge. Cropper concentrated on producing other artists.

Latterly, Booker T. Jones has recorded under his own name with varying success, while Dunn and Cropper were recently featured in movie 'The Blues Brothers' as part of Blues Brothers Band(▶). Unhappily, Al Jackson was killed by an intruder at his home in 1975. 1976 reunion album, **Universal Language**, with Willie Hall replacing Jackson, was not successful.

Anyone who appreciates instrumental work with both taste and soul should have a couple of Booker T albums in their collection. Never reliant on technique for its own sake, band was a model of cohesion, tight yet relaxed, and set a standard for soul rhythm sections that is still relevant today.

Final line-up: Booker T. Jones; Cropper; Dunn; Willie Hall, drums.

Hit Singles:	US	UK
Green Onions, 1962	3	—
Soul Limbo, 168	17	30
Hang 'Em High, 1969	9	—
Time Is Tight, 1969	6	4
Green Onions, 1979	—	7

Albums:
Best Of (Atlantic/—), 1968
1968
Soul Bimbo (Stax), 1968
Free Ride (Stax/—), 1970
Greatest Hits (Stax/—), 1982

Worth Searching Out:
Green Onions (Stax/Atlantic), 1966

Boomtown Rats

UK group formed 1975.

Original line-up: Bob Geldof, vocals; Garry Roberts, guitar; Gerry Cott, guitar; Johnny Fingers, keyboards; Pete Briquette, bass; Simon Crowe, drums, Albe Donnelly, saxophone.

Career: Formed in Dun Laoghaire, port town near Dublin in Southern Ireland. In early stages Geldof was manager, Roberts lead singer. Once Geldof had taken over vocal duties, band started to attract attention from record companies, eventually signing with Ensign and making move to London.

Although offering more variety and more coherence than run-of-mill punk outfits, Rats rose to fame on crest of New Wave. After establishing reputation as exciting and often wild live act, band had major hit with first single release, **Looking After No. 1,** in summer 1977.

Several more Top 20 singles preceded first No. 1, **Rat Trap,** in October 1978. This year also saw chart action with album **Tonic For The Troops,** and band became major attraction. Geldof, intelligent and articulate, became spokesman and sought-after interviewee. Donnelly and Cott left and were not replaced.

Finest hour came with next single, **I Don't Like Mondays,** a song based on true story of homicidal San Diego schoolgirl. **Mondays** broke band in many foreign territories, and was voted Single of Year in British Rock And Pop Awards. Extended foreign touring ensued.

Several more successful singles and further albums followed, but band has been relatively quiet since 1982 album release **Five Deep.** Geldof received mixed reviews for his venture into acting in Alan Parker's film version of Pink Floyd's(▶) 'The Wall', and lately has seemed content to take back seat to partner, media starlet Paula Yates.

Current line-up: Geldof; Roberts; Fingers; Briquette; Crowe.

Hit Singles:	US	UK
Looking After No. 1, 1977	—	11
Mary Of The Fourth Form, 1977	—	15
She's So Modern, 1978	—	12
Like Clockwork, 1978	—	6
Rat Trap, 1978	—	1
I Don't Like Mondays, 1979	—	1
Diamond Smiles, 1979	—	13
Someone's Looking At You, 1980	—	4
Banana Republic, 1980	—	3

Above: Gucci-punk as purveyed by Geldof and the Boomtown Rats.

Albums:
The Boomtown Rats (Mercury/Ensign), 1977
Tonic For The Troops (Columbia/Ensign), 1978
The Fine Art Of Surfacing (Columbia/Ensign), 1979
Mondo Bongo (Columbia/Mercury), 1981
Five Deep (Columbia/Mercury), 1982

Boston

US group formed 1975.

Original/Final line-up: Tom Scholz, guitar, keyboards; Brad Delp, guitar, vocals; Barry Goudreau, guitar; Fran Sheehan, bass; Sib Hashian, drums.

Career: Band formed around Tom Scholz who utilised own 12-track studio to prepare meticulous demo tapes. After series of record company rejections Scholz signed to Epic, and duly formed Boston. A recording phenomenon (though members only played in part on first LP), band earned double platinum album within first year for debut set **Boston** which included worldwide hit **More Than A Feeling**.

Boston. Courtesy Epic Records.

Despite Massachusetts origins Boston had a typical West Coast sound—tight harmonies, echo-laden guitars and reverberating percussion, and, not least, enterprising material.

Not surprisingly, Boston could not sustain career surge, and split after best-forgotten second offering **Don't Look Back**.

Guitarist Goudreau re-surfaced with own album **Barry Goudreau** in 1980, featuring other original band members. Scholz, Delp, Goudreau and Hashian worked with Sammy Hagar(▶) in 1980.

Hit Singles:	US	UK
More Than A Feeling, 1976	5	22
Don't Look Back, 1978	4	43

Albums:
Boston (Epic), 1976
Don't Look Back (Epic), 1978

Bow Wow Wow

UK group formed 1979

Original/Current line-up: Annabella Lwin, vocals; Matthew Ashman, guitar; Leroy Gorman, bass; Dave Barbarossa, drums.

Career: Put together by entrepreneur extraordinaire and former Sex Pistols(▶) supremo Malcolm McLaren, Bow Wow Wow were intended to duplicate for '80s Pistols '70s impact. Focal point of band is teenage Burmese vocalist Annabella Lwin (born October 31, 1965), discovered by McLaren, so legend goes, in London launderette.

McLaren's genius for promotion ensured large advance from EMI, and controversy surrounded band from start. First 'single' **C30, C60, C90 Go** was available only on cassette and advocated illegal home taping. Having moved from EMI via another large advance to RCA, band caused uproar with cover art for first RCA album **See Jungle;** a modern version of Manet's classic painting *Déjeuner Sur L'Herbe*, it featured naked Annabella (then only 16) and provoked first of many outbursts of complaint from singer's redoubtable mother.

Nevertheless, by 1981 band had built up considerable following, offering fairly simple musical formula based on 'burundi beat' and image based on Annabella's youthful but bizarre (hair cut in unique mohawk) sex appeal. Toured with acts like Police(▶) and Pretenders(▶), and 1982 brought reward of two major UK hits, **Go Wild In The Country** and **I Want Candy.**

Nevertheless, at time of writing band needed major commercial boost to ensure longevity. Step in that direction was taken with enlistment of Blondie(▶) producer Mike Chapman for early 1983 album **When The Going Gets Tough The Tough Get Going.** Though not very successful on US tour with Pretenders(▶), recent MTV exposure has brought Bow Wow Wow more US popularity.

Hit Singles:	US	UK
Go Wild In The Country, 1982	—	7
I Want Candy, 1982	—	9

Albums:
12 Original Recordings (Harvest/—), 1981
See Jungle! Join Your Gang Yeah, City All Over! Go Ape Crazy! (RCA), 1981*
Last Of The Mohicans (RCA/—), 1982
I Want Candy (RCA/EMI), 1982
When The Going Gets Tough The Tough Get Going (RCA), 1983
*Wild In The Country in US

When The Going Get's Tough . . . Bow Wow Wow. Courtesy RCA Records.

29

David Bowie

UK vocalist, composer, producer, actor.
Born David Robert Jones, London, January 8, 1947.

Career: Began musical career playing tenor sax in school group. Suffered eye injury following a fight; subsequent surgery left him with paralysed pupil. Leaving Bromley High School, secured job as commercial artist before forming succession of progressive R&B groups: Davie Jones and the King Bees, the Manish Boys, and the Lower Third. All recorded without success. Upsurge of Monkees(▶) forced name change from Jones to Bowie.

Subsequent contract with Pye and Decca as soloist produced series of pop/love songs, strongly influenced by Anthony Newley. Originally issued as **The World Of David Bowie,** these were re-released in 1973 as **Images 1966/67.** Included in set was embarrassing **The Laughing Gnome,** which actually reached Top 10 on re-release in 1973.

For brief period Bowie dropped out of music and flirted with Buddhism. Also joined Lindsay Kemp's mime company, a move that would greatly influence his later theatrical work. Re-emerged in 1969 and started an arts lab in Beckenham, recording **Space Oddity** for Mercury during same period. Song became surprise hit, followed by average album of same title. Toured as support act, but returned, disillusioned, to one-man show in Beckenham. Failure to follow up novelty **Space Oddity** strongly indicated that he was little more than a one-hit-wonder.

By 1970, Bowie had consolidated resources, combining interest in mime, Buddhism, novelty and whatever else to produce epic **The Man Who Sold The World.**

Album was complete contrast to predecessor; acoustic strumming was replaced by heavy guitar work of Mick Ronson. Thematically, work was chilling: an Orwellian vision of a future riddled with sexual perversion, dominance by machines, loneliness and helplessness. Many of these themes would be extended to produce later albums, not least the Nietzschean vision of **The Supermen.**

Although initially a relatively poor seller, **The Man Who Sold The World** gave Bowie cult following and was hailed as excellent work by more perceptive buyers/critics of the period. An important and much-publicised US tour followed, with Bowie decked out as 1970s Garbo, complete with flowing dress. Switch to RCA proved timely, and with further publicity critics were well-primed for release of **Hunky Dory.** Work was more mellow than its predecessor but still haunting, original and commercially appealing in range of themes.

1972 was year of the breakthrough with most commerical work to date, **The Rise And Fall Of Ziggy Stardust And The Spiders From Mars.** Where he had used a number of different ideas/personae on previous LPs, Bowie now created a single figure, Ziggy, the ultimate rock superstar destroyed by the fanaticism he creates. Negotiating ground between the heaviness of **The Man Who Sold The World** and the diverse quirkiness of **Hunky Dory,** an image of Ziggy was created that almost subsumed Bowie in later years. Artist and art, actor and part were inextricably linked. From this point on Bowie became the most important rock figure of '70s.

Activities broadened following hit single **Starman** and Bowie took on role as producer, literally saving the faltering career of Lou Reed(▶) (**Transformer**) and resurrecting the already dead Mott the Hoople(▶) (**All The Young Dudes**). 1972 US tour provided ideas for next conceptual work, **Aladdin Sane.** Album was not classic, though Ronson's work was exceptional and two hit singles were forthcoming via **Jean Genie** and Drive In Saturday. **Pin Ups** was a surprise *volte face* that brought suspicion from some critical quarters; a re-working of selected oldies from 1964-67 pop scene, it seemed rather too lightweight as concept. Period of uncertainty was punctuated by 'retirement' following Hammersmith Odeon concert in July 1973.

Later in year, recorded an NBC Midnight Special at London's Marquee Club titled 'The 1980 Floor Show'. Production inspired next album **Diamond Dogs** (1974), a return to Orwellian gloom of **Man Who Sold The World,** but minus fine guitar work of Ronson. Show was taken on road in US and performance at Philadelphia's Tower Theatre was used for double **David Live.** During tour, a new course was charted as Bowie picked up on soul/R&B style. Results were evident enough on Philly-influenced **Young Americans,** which included another couple of hit singles in titletrack and **Fame.** Latter, co-written by John Lennon(▶), provided first US No. 1 single. Incredibly, 1975 UK re-release of first hit **Space Oddity** went to top in same year, the slowest No. 1 of all time (6 years 63 days!).

For remainder of 1975 Bowie involved himself in filming 'The Man Who Fell To Earth' (directed by Nicholas Roeg), released the following year. Long-awaited return to England in spring '76 provided memorable gigs at Wembley Empire Pool. Having re-established himself commercially, Bowie felt free to record more adventurous material. **Station To Station,** consisting of six lengthy cuts, was return to top form, paving way for three albums recorded under supervision of Brian Eno(▶). **Low,** originally titled **New Music: Night And Day,** was essentially a mood piece, consisting largely of instrumental music. (Nick Lowe(▶) 'retaliated' by calling his 1977 EP **Bowi.**) The experiment was continued on **Heroes,** but with enough conventional rock to attract larger listening audience. Trilogy was interrupted by **Stage,** an uninspired double LP documenting 1978 tour. Final Bowie/Eno collaboration **Lodger** proved only partially successful in spite of strong tracks (**Boys Keep Swingin', Repetition**).

Right: Contemporary Bowie — the return of the Thin White Duke in 1976.

Below: The unlikely hit-making duo of David Bowie and Bing Crosby.

Right: Scary Monsters, David Bowie. Courtesy RCA Records.

Young Americans, David Bowie. Courtesy RCA Records.

Above: Bowie circa 1965. 'Ground control to Major...Fred? Joe?'

Above: Bowie models a dress — androgynous?

With **Scary Monsters (And Super Creeps),** commitment and commerciality were neatly fused in old tradition. Album spawned several hit singles, including excellent **Ashes To Ashes,** which hit No. 1 in UK in August '80. Since then there have been a series of re-issues, re-packages and film soundtracks, though for his next album, Bowie promised some positive dance-orientated music as reaction against apocalyptic themes of yore.

This was forthcoming in 1983 Nile Rodgers produced album **Let's Dance,** a worldwide chart topper with its titletrack single. Soon after release, Bowie toured Europe and UK for first time in seven years.

Rightly acknowledged as '70s rock's most important figure, Bowie continues to wield enormous influence on '80s rock scene. Acting commitments and extra-curricular work may prove distracting enough to lose musical direction, though this seems unlikely. Acting credits include films 'The Man Who Fell To Earth' (1975), 'Just A Gigolo' (1979), and, most recently, 'The Hunger' (1983) and 'Merry Christmas Mr. Lawrence (1983). Played main role of disfigured John Merrick in Broadway play 'The Elephant Man' (1980) and the lead in BBC TV's production of Berthold Brecht's 'Baal' (1981).

Hit Singles:	US	UK
Space Oddity, 1969	—	5
Starman, 1972	—	10
John I'm Only Dancing, 1972	—	12
The Jean Genie, 1972	—	2
Space Oddity, 1973	15	—
Drive In Saturday, 1973	—	3
Life On Mars, 1973	—	3
The Laughing Gnome, 1973	—	6
Sorrow, 1973	—	3
Rebel Rebel, 1974	—	5
Knock On Wood, 1974	—	10
Space Oddity, 1975	—	1
Young Americans, 1975	—	18
Fame, 1975	1	17
Golden Years, 1975	10	8
Sound And Vision, 1977	—	3
Boys Keep Swinging, 1979	—	7
John I'm Only Dancing (Again), 1979	—	12
Ashes To Ashes, 1980	—	1
Fashion, 1980	—	5
Scary Monsters, 1981	—	20
Let's Dance, 1983	2	1
China Girl, 1983	—	2

**Let's Dance , Bowie's 1983 LP.
Courtesy EMI—America Records.**

With Queen:

	US	UK
Under Pressure, 1981	29	1

With Bing Crosby:

	US	UK
Peace On Earth, 1982	—	3

Albums:
The World Of David Bowie (Decca), 1970
The Man Who Sold The World (Mercury/RSA), 1971
Hunky Dory (RCA), 1971
The Rise And Fall Of Ziggy Stardust And The Spiders From Mars (RCA), 1972
Space Oddity (RCA), 1972
Aladin Sane (RCA), 1973
Pin Ups (RCA), 1973
Diamond Dogs (RCA), 1974
David Live (RCA), 1974
Young Americans (RCA), 1975
Images (Decca), 1975
Station To Station (RCA), 1976
Changesonebowie (RCA), 1976
Low (RCA), 1977
Starting Point (London/—), 1977
Heroes (RCA), 1977
Stage (RCA), 1978
Lodger (RCA), 1979
Scary Monsters (And Super Creeps) (RCA), 1980
The Best Of (—/K-Tel), 1980
Another Face (Decca), 1981
Don't Be Fooled By The Name (PRT), 1981*
Changes (RCA), 1981†
Christianne F (Soundtrack) (RCA), 1981
Changestwobowie (RCA), 1981
The Manish Boys, Davy Jones And The Lower Third (Charly), 1981
Rare Bowie (RCA), 1982
Let's Dance (EMI), 1983

*Tracks From 1966
†Hunky Dory & Ziggy Stardust

Below: Ziggy with Stratocaster on stage in 1974.

**David Live , David Bowie.
Courtesy RCA Records.**

Bread

US group formed 1969.

Original line-up: David Gates, vocals, guitar, keyboards, synthesiser; Robb Royer, vocals, guitar; James Griffin, vocals, guitar.

Career: The sensitive songwriting of David Gates was backbone of Bread's success. Born in Tulsa, Oklahoma, on December 11, 1940, Gates organised high-school band which included Leon Russell(▶), and worked in group backing Chuck Berry(▶), Carl Perkins(▶), Johnny Burnette(▶) and others on local visits.

Moving to Los Angeles to work as session musician and arranger, Gates scored an Elvis Presley(▶) film, produced Pat Boone and played on records by Duane Eddy(▶), Glen Campbell(▶) and Merle Haggard(▶).

Griffin had used pseudonym Arthur James when writing the Oscar-winning 'Best Film Song 1969' **For All We Know** for movie 'Lovers And Other Strangers', and his production credits included work with Johnny Burnette and the Crickets.

Starting out as a pure studio band in soft-rock idiom, Gates/Griffin/Royer trio changed name from Pleasure Faire to Bread in 1969 and signed to Elektra, recording debut album with addition of sessioneer Jim Gordon on drums.

Bread. Courtesy Elektra Records.

With emphasis on strong yet gentle songs, harmonics and melodic style, album won immediate following and when **Make It With You** from second LP, **On The Water**, went gold in US, and silver in UK, Bread's popularity pushed them into becoming a performing band, with Mike Botts added to complete stage line-up.

Respected session-man Larry Knechtel—who had played piano on Simon and Garfunkel(▶)'s monumental classic **Bridge Over Troubled Water**—replaced Royer immediately following million-selling **Manna** set, which included Bread's most covered song, **If**.

Baby I'm A Want You, titletrack from Knechtel's first LP with group, went gold as did album and Bread seemed destined for long run when music world was shocked by their disbandment in 1973.

Griffin made unsuccessful solo album in 1974, while Gates enjoyed solo success before band got together again in 1976 for reasonably successful **Lost Without Your Love** album, but they soon went own ways once more.

Final line-up: Gates; Griffin; Larry Knechtel, keyboards; Mike Botts, drums.

Hit Singles:

	US	UK
Make It With You, 1970	1	5
It Don't Matter To Me, 1970	10	—
If, 1971	4	—
Baby, I'm A Want You, 1971	3	14
Everything I Own, 1972	5	32
Diary, 1972	15	—
The Guitar Man, 1972	11	16
Sweet Surrender, 1972	15	—
Aubrey, 1973	15	—
Lost Without Your Love, 1976	9	27

David Gates Solo:

Goodbye Girl, 1978	15	—

Albums:
On The Water (Elektra), 1970
Manna (Elektra), 1971
Baby I'm A-Want You (Elektra), 1972
Guitar Man (Elektra), 1972
Best Of (Elektra), 1974
Best Of Volume 2 (Elektra), 1974
Lost Without Your Love (Elektra), 1976
The Sound Of Bread (Elektra), 1977

David Gates Solo:
First (Elektra), 1976
Never Let Her Go (Elektra), 1976
Goodbye Girl (Elektra), 1978
Falling In Love Again (Elektra), 1980
Take Me Now (Arista/—), 1981

Above: David Gates, lead singer of Bread, solo artist and prolific songwriter.

James Brown

US vocalist, composer, also arranger, multi-instrumentalist.
Born Macon, Georgia, May 3, 1933.

Career: Born into rural poverty, Brown first came to music via gospel. He formed first version of Famous Flames, which included long-time colleague Bobby Byrd, in 1954. Group quickly gained local reputation, Brown already showing impassioned style that was to become trademark. Gospel material gradually shelved in favour of secular songs; **Please Please Please** came to attention of King Records, who signed Brown and Flames and released it as single. Record became major R&B chart success.

Successful follow-up was elusive, and group spent next few years touring small-time club circuit. In September 1958 they went to New York to record; result was gospel-flavoured **Try Me**, group's second hit. Brown consolidated success with string of hit records between 1959 and 1961.

By 1962 Famous Flames had metamorphosised into entire revue, consisting of back-up singers, sizeable band and even own

support acts. Brown had developed dynamic stage act and offered most exciting live performance of era. Exhilaration of Brown live in front of black audience is captured on seminal double album, **Live At The Apollo**. One of the first live recordings, it was also one of the most successful records by a black artist up to that point and marked beginning of acceptance by white American and international markets.

Hits continued throughout '60s, Brown achieving position as number one black superstar and figurehead for American black consciousness movement. He also acquired reputation as no-nonsense businessman and disciplinarian employer. He toured to capacity audiences all over world, and was especially successful in UK.

After disappearance of King Records in 1970, Brown signed to Polydor; hits continued unabated. During '70s his influence was discernible in work of many newer soul/rock/funk bands. Sly and the Family Stone(▶) adapted Brown rhythmic patterns and combined them with rock sensibility; others such as Kool and the Gang(▶), Ohio Players, Blackbyrds and Earth, Wind and Fire(▶) evolved directly out of Brown's musical approach, creating new funk/dance movement. Brown himself enjoyed massive success with **Body Heat** LP in 1976.

Late '70s saw some diminution of Brown's appeal, although he hit back in 1981 with **Rap Payback**, his answer to success of New York 'rapper' cult. Most recently he has been label-hopping in search of right context for his talents in the '80s.

Whether or not Brown ever again achieves heights of late '60s/early '70s, his place in the history of popular music is assured. One of black music's most charismatic stars, an innovator whose influence spreads over three decades, he is to a large extent responsible for current popularity of black music and, latterly, the revival of dance music. Definitely an all-time great.

Hit Singles:

	US	UK
Prisoner Of Love, 1963	18	—
Papa's Got A Brand New Bag, —Pt 1, 1965	8	25
I Got You (I Feel Good), 1965	3	29
It's A Man's Man's World, 1966	8	13
Cold Sweat—Pt 1, 1967	7	—
I Got The Feelin', 1968	6	—
Licking Stick—Pt 1, 1968	14	—
Say It Loud—I'm Black And I'm Proud, 1968	10	—
Give It Up Or Turnit A Loose, 1969	15	—
I Don't Want Nobody To Give Me Nothing (Open Up The Door, I'll Get It Myself), 1969	20	—
Mother Popcorn—Pt 1, 1969	11	—
Get Up I Feel Like Being A Sex Machine, 1970	15	32
Super Bad (Pts I & II), 1970	13	—
Hot Pants (She Got To Use What She Got To Get What She Wants)—Pt 1, 1971	15	—

Below: Jackson Browne—one of America's favourite pop poets.

Above: Guv'nor bassist Jack Bruce still looking for a second Cream.

Get On The Good Foot—Pt 1,
1972   18   —

Albums (selected):
Live At The Apollo (Polydor), 1962
Best Of (Polydor), 1975
Body Heat (Polydor), 1977
Solid Gold (Polydor), 1977
Special (Polydor), 1981
Soul Syndrome (RCA), 1980

Worth Searching Out:
It's A Man's Man's World (Polydor), 1966
Say It Loud I'm Black And I'm Proud (King/
   Polydor), 1968
Get On The Good Foot (Polydor), 1973
Sex Machine Today (Polydor), 1975

Jackson Browne

US composer, vocalist, guitarist.
Born Heidelberg, Germany, October 9, 1948.

Career: Raised in Los Angeles, Browne moved to New York in 1967 and began playing guitar for Nico. She liked his original songs and used three on **Chelsea Girl** album. Soon Browne was placing songs with folk-rock artists such as Johnny Rivers, Nitty Gritty Dirt Band(▶) and Tom Rush(▶). Although now largely forgotten or overlooked, Tom Rush was then important musician whose opinion carried great weight in folk community; if Rush was recording songs by somebody named Browne, then Browne must be good.

Browne's multi-talents could never be channelled into one area, so it's not surprising that he signed with Asylum in his own right. **Jackson Browne** LP (1971) contained mostly material already recorded by others. Sales not impressive, but critical reviews were strongly favourable. Browne worked closely with newly formed Eagles(▶), co-writing first major hit, **Take It Easy**. His version is on his second LP, 1973's **For Everyman**. Again reviews bordered on ecstatic; again sales bordered on non-existent. Browne seemed doomed to cult status as excellent composer. His low-key stage performance also seemed antithetical to usual excess prevalent in rock.

But Browne's reputation for heartfelt emotion began spreading and with 1974 release **Late For The Sky** his back catalogue

began selling well. Browne's careful approach is not conducive to dashing off albums. His next effort was delayed even further by March 1976 suicide of his wife. **The Pretender** seemed to strip Browne to essentials and suddenly he was a big star.

Refusing to cash in on success, he made extended tour of US and Europe, releasing **Running On Empty** in 1978. This album seemed radical departure from past work in that it had rough edges not normally associated

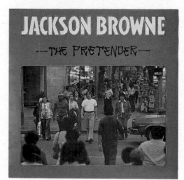

The Pretender, Jackson Browne. Courtesy Asylum Records.

with Browne. Critics did not know quite what to make of it, so emphasised risk Browne took in recording under adverse conditions while on tour. The public loved it and sales boomed.

Hold Out seemed to mark return of some peace in Jackson's personal life. Only time will tell if **The Pretender** and **Running On Empty** marked high point of Browne's career. But he has firmly established himself as intellectual lyricist with compassionate eye on concerns and problems of the person in the street.

Hit Singles: US   UK
Doctor My Eyes, 1972   8   —
Running On Empty, 1978   11   —
Stay, 1978   20   12
Somebody's Baby, 1982   7   —

Albums:
Jackson Browne, Saturate Before Using
   (Asylum), 1971
For Everyman (Asylum), 1973
Late For The Sky (Asylum), 1974
The Pretender (Asylum), 1976
Running On Empty (Asylum), 1978
Hold Out (Asylum), 1980

Jack Bruce

UK bass player, vocalist, composer.
Born John Bruce, Lanarkshire, Scotland,
May 14, 1943.

Career: Early experience came in Glasgow dance halls, playing acoustic bass with Jim McHarg's Scotsville Jazzband, and studies from age 17 at Royal Scottish Academy Of Music.

Moving to London in 1962, Bruce joined Alexis Korner's Blues Incorporated R&B group, quitting in February 1963 with alto-sax player/organist Graham Bond and drummer Ginger Baker(▶) to form Graham Bond Organization. He worked with GBO until 1965 when he left for short stint with John Mayall(▶)'s Bluesbreakers, followed by six months with Manfred Mann(▶) before rejoining Baker to form supergroup trio Cream(▶), with guitarist Eric Clapton(▶).

After Cream's creative but short-lived existence (Clapton and Baker forming Blind Faith(▶) with Stevie Winwood), Bruce, under guidance of entrepreneur and RSO Records' founder Robert Stigwood, embarked on solo career with patchy but in parts brilliant **Songs For A Tailor** set (1969). Later he brought in such redoubtable luminaries as John McLaughlin(▶), Jon Hiseman, Larry Coryell(▶), Mike Mandel, Graham Bond, Dick Heckstall-Smith and Chris Spedding to guest on projects.

Spending a stint with Tony Williams' Lifetime, he recruited services of Coryell, Mandel and Jimi Hendrix's(▶) former drummer Mitch Mitchell for concerts to promote

Songs For A Tailor, Jack Bruce. Courtesy Polydor Records.

second LP **Harmony Row**.

Jazzers Carla Bley and Paul Haines were brought in for **Escalator Over The Rock** LP. In 1972 Bruce became part of West Bruce Laing triumvirate with guitarist Leslie West and drummer 'Corky' Laing from US rock band Mountain(▶). Adopting same heavy-rock approach as Cream, trio cut two none-too-hot studio albums (on Windfall/CBS and Columbia/RSO) and live set before Bruce split in 1973. West and Laing returned to States and re-formed Mountain.

For third solo LP, **Out Of The Storm** (1974), Bruce brought in ex-Rolling Stone(▶) Mick Taylor on guitar, Carla Bley and Ronnie Leahy on keyboards and Bruce Gary on drums, but Taylor and Bley walked out after handful of traumatic gigs and Bruce dropped into virtual retirement for two years, re-emerging in 1977 for the **How's Tricks** set. His most recent recording efforts have been in collaboration with Robin Trower(▶).

An idiosyncratic yet highly creative bass-player, Jack Bruce has floated round music scene for two decades as sideman, session guest, supergroup member and solo artist, venturing beyond rock and into jazz. His somewhat fiery and unpredictable personality has contributed to the ups and downs of his career, but he deserves credit as one of rock's great innovators.

Albums:
Things We Like (Atco/Polydor), 1970
I've Always Wanted To Do This (Epic), 1980

With Robin Trower:
BLT (Chrysalis), 1981
Truce (Chrysalis), 1982

Worth Searching Out:
Songs For A Tailor (Polydor), 1969

Tim Buckley

US vocalist, guitarist, composer.
Born Washington D.C. April 12, 1947; died
June 29, 1975.

Career: One of rock's great might-have-beens, Buckley started his career gigging in clubs around Los Angeles. Elektra Records, impressed both by his voice and his material, signed him in 1966; result was first album, **Tim Buckley**.

Album increased interest in the talented 19-year old, but commercial success was not to come until release of second album **Goodbye And Hello** in 1967. Its affirmation of 'life and love' values touched nerve in new generation of liberated youth, both in US and then UK, and Buckley was hailed as major new singing and songwriting force.

However, instead of developing creative direction of **Goodbye And Hello**, Buckley veered off into uncharted realms of jazz-folk fusion. With next few albums, he largely lost audience he had built up, and reverted to relative obscurity.

It was not until release of 1972 album, **Greetings From LA**, that Buckley made major impact again. A powerful and commercial rock album, it re-established Buckley's career and is probably his best album. **Sefronia** and **Look At The Fool** followed, but the latter proved to be Buckley's last record. He died in 1975 from an overdose of heroin and morphine, another tragic rock statistic.

Albums:
Goodbye And Hello (Elektra), 1971
Happy Sad (Elektra), 1969
Greetings From LA (Warner Bros), 1972
Sefronia (Warner Bros/Discreet), 1974

Worth Searching Out:
Blue Afternoon (Warner Bros/Straight), 1970

Buffalo Springfield

US group formed 1966.

Original line-up: Neil Young, guitar, vocals; Stephen Stills, guitar, vocals; Richie Furay; guitar, vocals; Dewey Martin, drums, vocals; Bruce Palmer, bass.

Career: Notable as first major outfit for three future first-division performers: Young(▶), Stills(▶), and Furay. Formed around Stills and Furay, who had moved to West Coast after period in New York with the Au Go Go Singers. Young and Palmer were working together, and quartet joined forces in Los Angeles. Ex-Dillard Martin completed line-up.

Debut album **Buffalo Springfield** included band's only major chart success **For What It's Worth** (written by Stills). Palmer departed before completion (visa ran out, returned to Canada) of second LP, to be replaced by Jim Messina. Temporary additions included bassist Jim Fielder (later Blood Sweat & Tears(▶)) and guitarist Doug Hastings (founder member of Rhinoceros).

Internal aggravation hastened band's demise. Young failed to show for 1968 Monterey Festival gig, and band soon split. Aptly

Buffalo Springfield. Courtesy Atco Records.

titled set **Last Time Around** was released afterwards in 1969.

Stills, Young, Furay and Messina maintained group's melodic, disciplined vocal work in their various band/solo projects. Martin formed short-lived Medicine Ball before moving to session work, while Palmer cut ordinary solo album.

Final line-up: Stills; Young; Furay; Martin; Jim Messina, bass, vocals.

Hit Singles:

	US	UK
For What It's Worth (Stop, Hey What's That Sound), 1967	7	—

Albums:
Buffalo Springfield (Atco/Atlantic), 1967
Buffalo Springfield Again (Atco/Atlantic), 1968
Last Time Around (Atco/Atlantic), 1969
Retrospective (Atco/Atlantic), 1972

Eric Burdon

UK vocalist.
Born Newcastle, May 11, 1941.

Career: Raised in Newcastle, Burdon discovered black music via a merchant seaman living in flat below who brought records home from US. Finding friends had developed same interest in R&B Burdon joined with them to set up band, originally as Alan Price Combo, which became the Animals(▶). Burdon soon built reputation as hard-drinking, hard-talking

Last Time Around, Buffalo Springfield. Courtesy Atco Records.

Geordie with brash, husky blues-laced vocal delivery. His frenetic stage demeanour led to his being described as 'a black man in a white skin'.

On break-up of original Animals in 1966 following tempestuous US tour, Burdon moved from hard-edged R&B to then emergent acid-rock format with new band known as Eric Burdon and the Animals (Denny McCulloch, guitar; Vic Briggs, keyboards; John Weider, bass; Barry Jenkins, drums). Burdon espoused flower-power and, like John Lennon(▶) switched reputation as brawling boozer for that of gentle prophet of love image. Concentrated activities in America, and US hits **San Franciscan Nights** and **Sky Pilot** summed up his new philosophy.

After **Love Is** album (double set in US, single in Britain), Burdon dropped out from music scene and went into obscurity on West Coast amid rumours of drug problems. He suddenly re-emerged in 1970 as front-man for War(▶), an aggressive black progressive band with whom he enjoyed US chart-topper **Spill The Wine** from **Eric Burdon Declares War** album. After follow-up set, **Black Man's Burdon,** War went own way as heavy

R&B group. Burdon, still closely associated with War's management/production team of Steve Gold and Jerry Goldstein, fulfilled personal ambition by working with their artist, blues veteran Jimmy Witherspoon, on joint album **Guilty.**

In 1973, Burdon returned to stage scene, playing three gigs in Britain and some dates in US with Aaron Butler (guitar), Randy Rice (bass) and Alvin Taylor (drums) in heavy-rock idiom.

Various abortive comebacks in '70s, together with contractual entanglements and personal problems, kept Burdon's name in press but out of charts. In 1983 the original Animals re-formed and Burdon settled in London again, but whether past glories can be repeated remains to be seen.

Hit Singles:

	US	UK
San Franciscan Nights, 1967	—	7

Albums:
Survivor (Polydor), 1978
Black And White Blues (MCA), 1979

Below: Eric Burdon making 1983 comeback with reformed Animals.

Johnny Burnette

US vocalist, composer, guitarist.
Born Memphis, Tennessee, March 25, 1943; died 1964.

Career: Johnny Burnette, his older brother Dorsey (stand-up bass), and Paul Burlison (guitar) formed original rock 'n' roll trio, the Texans in Memphis, 1956. Had regional success, playing constantly in small clubs and rough bars; broadcasted live on local radio.

Johnny felt they needed national exposure so they drove to New York City in search of work. Landed appearance on Ted Mack's 'Amateur Hour' (TV show); and won first prize three times in row. This quickly led to contract with Coral Records, and group's first sessions in New York.

Records failed commercially, partly due to lack of support and promotion by Coral. However, the more raucous side of rockabilly was cooling down anyway; the show business establishment preferred something a bit more manageable. Despite stature today, and despite a few local hits, the Rock 'n' Roll Trio were a complete failure on a national level.

The brothers began to disagree between themselves. Dorsey was a good singer in own right, and felt confined just backing up Johnny occasionally and playing bass. He left group for solo career in country music; replacement was Johnny Black.

Johnny fronted various line-ups until 1960, when his approach changed radically; mushy rock ballad **Dreamin'** was a worldwide hit. The following year, **You're Sixteen** was biggest hit yet, making Top 10 in US and UK. Johnny had found a formula for pop-rock, and no doubt he would surely have had further success but for his death in a boating accident in 1964 while on vacation.

Hit Singles:

	US	UK
Dreamin', 1960	11	5
You're Sixteen, 1961	8	3
Little Boy Sad, 1961	17	12
God, Country And My Baby, 1961	18	—

Albums:
Tear It Up (Solid Smoke/Coral), 1975
The Johnny Burnette Rock 'n' Roll Trio (Solid Smoke), 1979

James Burton

US guitarist.
Born Shreveport, Louisiana, August 21, 1939.

Career: One of the longest-serving West Coast session guitar giants, James Burton has appeared on numerous major recordings and was mainstay of Elvis Presley's(▶) backing band during the rock'n'roll star's later years, but has had only two LPs released in his own right.

Burton's grounding came, like that of fellow sessioneers Al Casey and Roy Buchanan, in the rockabilly music of the Deep South, working out of Shreveport, Louisiana. At 16 he featured on Dale Hawkin's classic 1957 rocker **Suzie Q** (Checker). Moving to California he joined Rick Nelson's(▶) regular backing band, playing on many of the young singer's hits, yielding solos with strong 'Sun Sound' (the sound of Sam Philip's Studios where Presley, Jerry Lee Lewis and others recorded in the '50s) influence gleaned from listening to work of Scotty Moore, Carl Perkins(▶) and other Memphis rockabillies.

Burton has recorded with Delaney and Bonnie(▶), Gram Parsons, the Everly Brothers (▶) and many others working the country rock idiom and, with another Presley sideman,

The Guitar Sounds Of James Burton. Courtesy A&M Records.

Glen D. Hardin, was backbone of Emmylou Harris's(▶) Hot Band back-up group.

Guitar: Fender Telecaster.

Albums:
Worth Searching Out:
Corn Pickin' And Slick Slidin' (Capitol/—), 1960s
The Guitar Sounds Of James Burton (A&M), 1971

Kate Bush
UK vocalist, composer.
Born London, July 30, 1958.

Career: Born into a musical family, Kate studied violin and piano. Leaving school at 16, she signed to EMI having recorded demo tape under aegis of Pink Floyd's(▶) Dave Gilmour. She then spent several years writing, making demos, and studying dance and mime.

Recorded first album, **The Kick Inside**, in 1977. Single from album, **Wuthering Heights**, shot to top of UK charts on release in early 1978. Instant impact of record was due partly to originality of subject matter and musical treatment, partly to unearthly quality of Bush's voice. Critics were divided as to worth of artist, some decrying record as mere gimmickry.

However, **Heights** was first of string of hit singles for Bush, which established her as highly creative and innovative artist. Bush's writing style and vocal delivery are instantly recognisable, and her individuality is stamped on clutch of big-selling albums. She has also become renowned for her showmanship and idiosyncratic stage act, which involves elements of dance and mime.

Kate Bush is now regarded as all-round professional, and looks set to sustain career into '80s. Her most recent LP, **The Dreaming**, made No.3 in UK but had little impact in US, a territory which has so far largely resisted her undoubted talents.

Hit Singles:	US	UK
Wuthering Heights, 1978	—	1
Man With The Child In His Eyes, 1978	—	6
Wow, 1979	—	14
Kate Bush On Stage (EP), 1979	—	10
Breathing, 1980	—	16
Babooshka, 1980	—	5
Army Dreamers, 1980	—	16
Sat In Your Lap, 1981	—	11

Albums:
The Kick Inside (EMI), 1978
Lionheart (EMI), 1978
Never For Ever (—/EMI), 1980
The Dreaming (EMI), 1982

Prince Buster
Jamaican vocalist, composer.
Born Buster Campbell, Kingston, Jamaica, May 24, 1938.

Career: First great hero of ethnic Jamaican pop music, Buster's early love was boxing and he earned title 'Prince' after particularly bloody street brawl between rival gangs of 'rude boys' in Kingston's Orange Street (where years later he opened his renowned record store).

After weight training each evening, young Buster (named after great Jamaican statesman Bustamente) worked out with small 'spasm' combo, beating out rhythm on old saucepans. Entering talent contest at Tilly Blackman's Glass Bucket Club he won three weeks running and earned spot with resident band which featured fellow vocalists Derrick Morgan and Eric 'Humpty Dumpty' Morris.

Band's drummer Drumbago (Arkland Park) eased Buster into recording in early '60s, formative years of emergent ska (blue beat) style. Backed by Drumbago All Stars, Les Dawson Blues Unit or Rico Rodriguez Blues Band on various cuts, 1963 debut album **I Feel The Spirit** remains a Jamaican classic, including **Run Man Run, Madness** (something of anthem at mod discos of era) and **Lucky Old Sun**.

Buster toured UK, France, and Spain to ecstatic response despite ethnic nature of his

Below: Kate Bush—the girl with the 'wow' in her eyes.

work, much of it politically motivated (as on **Black Head Chinaman**). Other Buster themes ranged from the lewd **Big Five** through his paean of male chauvinism **Ten Commandments** to **Al Capone** (concerned with Jamaican gang violence). 1967 hit **Rough Rider** sold more than 130,000 copies (massive sales for a Jamaican record) and cover version by UK pop/ska outfit the Beat(▶) appeared in '80s.

Since '60s hey-day, the enigmatic Buster has concentrated on production (Alton Ellis, Heptones, Ethiopians, Dennis Brown, John Holt), his 10 record stores ,and virtual monopoly of supplying records to Jamaica's jukebox operators. He made fresh recordings in early '80s in vain attempt to cash in on British 2-Tone ska/rock-steady revival movement.

Hit Singles:	US	UK
Al Capone, 1967	—	18

Albums:
Fabulous Greatest Hits (—/Melodisc), 1976
Wreck A Pum Pum (—/Blue Beat), 1976
She Was A Rough Rider (—/Melodisc), 1978

Paul Butterfield
US vocalist, harmonica player, composer.
Born Chicago, December 17, 1942.

Career: Though white, Paul Butterfield served musical apprenticeship in black blues clubs of Southside Chicago. Learned harmonica craft from such greats as Little Walter,

Golden Butter, Paul Butterfield Blues Band. Courtesy Elektra Records.

Walter 'Shakey' Horton, Junior Wells and James Cotton. Formed first band with black musicians Jerome Arnold (bass) and Sam Lay (drums), who had been playing with Howlin' Wolf(▶), and guitarist Smokey Smothers. Smothers was replaced by white guitarist Elvin Bishop and when another white guitarist, Mike Bloomfield(▶), joined in 1965, the classic Paul Butterfield(▶) Blues Band was born.

Basically a sampler of folk music, the Elektra compilation album **What's Shakin'** included boisterous electric blues cuts from Butterfield's band. Instant acclaim as best of emergent revivalist R&B bands led to swift release of band's debut album by the label (keyboard player Mark Naftalin having joined and Billy Davenport replacing Lay on drums).

First electric band to appear at Newport Folk Festival, outfit caused storm both for own performance and as backing band for Bob Dylan(▶). Folk purists hated it, but a whole new audience was created.

In 1965 band backed Chuck Berry's(▶) return-to-form **It Wasn't Me.** Following year their best album **East-West** appeared. Highlight was 13-minute titletrack instrumental which mixed an Indian raga scale with bluesy feel. In Britain band met little response from audiences then into blue-eyed soul stylings, though Butterfield did cut an EP with John Mayall's(▶) Bluesbreakers, with Peter Green(▶)

on guitar.

With addition of brass section (David Sanborn, tenor sax; Keith Johnson, trumpet; Charles Dinwiddie, tenor sax), Bloomfield moved towards soul music with **Resurrection Of Pigboy Cranshaw** album.

When Bloomfield quit to form Electric Flag, Elvin Bishop took over lead guitar for **In My Own Dream** LP. Then he too left for solo career.

Produced by Jerry Ragovoy, **Keep On Moving** ventured deeper into soul territory before Butterfield's return to blues roots for a role in Chess's **Father And Sons** double album project. This showcased Muddy Waters, backed by the younger generation, and reunited Butterfield with Mike Bloomfield.

Butterfield cut live double album, produced by Todd Rundgren(▶), at Los Angeles' Troubadour in 1971. Soon after cut final Elektra album, **Sometimes I Just Feel Like Smilin'.** Disbanded outfit in 1972.

Moved to Woodstock, New York; recruited Bobby Charles, Ronnie Barron, Amos Garrett and Geoff Muldaur to form short-lived Better Days. They recorded two not altogether satisfactory albums for Bearsville.

Butterfield has since contented himself with occasional guest appearances, notably at the Band's farewell concert and on albums by Bonnie Raitt(▶) and Maria Muldaur(▶).

Albums:
Paul Butterfield Blues Band (Elektra), 1965
East West (Elektra), 1966
Resurrection Of Pigboy Cranshaw (Elektra), 1967
Live (Elektra), 1970
Golden Butter (Best Of) (Elektra), 1972
North South (Warner Bros/—), 1981

With Walter Horton:
An Offer You Can't Refuse (—/Red Lightnin'), 1982

The Byrds
US group formed 1964.

Original line-up: Roger McGuinn, lead guitar, vocals; David Crosby, rhythm guitar, vocals; Gene Clark, vocals, tambourine; Chris Hillman, bass; Michael Clarke, drums.

Career: Originally called the Jet Set before arrival of Hillman and Clarke; recorded series of demos for World Pacific, later released as **Preflyte.** As trio, cut one unsuccessful single for Elektra, **Please Let Me Love You,** then signed to Columbia as the Byrds. Acclaimed as America's answer to the Beatles(▶) they successfully combined the lyrical genius of Dylan(▶) with the Beatles' melodic expertise to produce a distinctive style exemplified by million-selling **Mr Tambourine Man,** which topped US and UK charts during summer 1965.

Generally acknowledged as pioneers of 'folk rock', Byrds produced a string of consistently excellent singles during 1965-67, including **Turn! Turn! Turn!, Eight Miles High, So You Want To Be A Rock 'n' Roll Star** and **My Back Pages.** First two albums consisted mainly of Dylan covers and love songs from the prolific Gene Clark.

By early 1966, folk-rock repertoire was extended to include a number of jazz and hard-rock items. The seminal **Eight Miles High** rivalled the output of such contemporaries as the Beatles and the Stones(▶) but Byrds suffered from radio bans; some numbers were unjustly labelled 'drug songs'.

In March, career development was further complicated by shock departure of Gene

35

Clark. Continuing as quartet, they released **Fifth Dimension**—a neat amalgam of folk-rock orchestration, jazz and raga-tinged rock that fully demonstrated their ability to survive and thrive.

In late 1966, Byrds retired temporarily from live appearances amid speculation that they were breaking up.

1967 was most crucial year in their history, beginning with brilliant **Younger Than Yesterday** LP, which fully demonstrated David Crosby's growing importance as singer/songwriter. More surprisingly, album featured several country-flavoured songs from Chris Hillman, the fourth singer/songwriter to emerge from original line-up. Creative tensions in group led to several flare ups and a struggle for leadership between McGuinn and Crosby. Loss of management team, Jim Dickson and Eddie Tickner, only made matters worse.

The Byrds Greatest Hits. Courtesy Columbia Records.

Arguments over musical direction precipitated Crosby's sacking in October 1967. He was replaced by former Byrd Gene Clark, who lasted only three weeks before quitting due to ever-present fear of flying. Drummer Michael Clarke quit in disillusionment shortly afterwards, leaving McGuinn and Hillman to complete the excellent **Notoriuos Byrd Brothers,** generally hailed as a creative peak in their illustrious career.

Early in 1968, McGuinn and Hillman recruited Kevin Kelley (drums) and Gram Parsons (guitar/vocals) and plunged headlong into new musical direction. Although McGuinn was intent on recording an electronic-jazz album, it was Parsons and Hillman who proved strongest in determining group's subsequent musical policy. Country and western styled **Sweetheart Of The Rodeo** was a perfectly timed reaction against the excesses of psychedelia, predating Dylan's **Nashville Skyline** by a year. The Byrds' interest in country music continued, even after Parsons decided to quit on eve of an abortive South African tour.

Late 1968 was another period of flux, culminating in departure of Hillman following a dispute with McGuinn. By end of year, group was almost totally restructured with introduction of bluegrass virtuoso Clarence White (guitar), John York (bass) and Gene Parsons (drums).

From 1969 onwards, McGuinn assumed sole control of Byrds while ex-members went on to fame and fortune in offshoot groups, including Flying Burrito Brothers(▶), Dillard and Clark, Crosby Stills Nash & Young(▶), Manassas, the Souther-Hillman Furay Band and Firefall.

Recruitment of bassist Skip Battin (replacing York) produced settled line-up during early '70s, but quality of group's work declined significantly. There were, however, occasional highpoints, particularly the double album **(Untitled)** which included group's last hit single, **Chestnut Mare.**

By 1972, several members had drifted into various unproductive solo ventures and group shortly disbanded. Original quintet re-formed for one album, but results were not encouraging enough to inspire follow-up. During same disastrous year, former members Clarence White and Gram Parsons died in tragic circumstances: White in hit and run accident, Parsons of drug overdose.

Following an erratic series of solo outings, McGuinn, Clark and Hillman reunited during late '70s but failed to establish themselves as supergroup. All five original Byrds have found difficulty in securing record contracts in recent years and save Crosby—safe with CSN—their futures seem uncertain. Although Byrds were plagued by ego clashes and disputes, there is little doubt that at their peak in mid-'60s, they were the most important group in American rock music.

Having pioneered folk rock, raga rock and space rock, Byrds must also be credited for spearheading country rock boom of late '60s/early '70s. Influence on such units as Poco(▶) and the Eagles(▶) is probably incalculable.

Final line-up: McGuinn; Clarence White, guitar, vocals; Skip Battin, bass, vocals; John Guerin, drums.

Hit Singles:

	US	UK
Mr Tambourine Man, 1965	1	1
All I Really Want To Do, 1965	40	4
Turn! Turn! Turn!, 1965	1	—
Eight Miles High, 1966	14	—
Chestnut Mare, 1971	—	19

Albums:
Preflyte (Together) (Columbia/CBS), 1969
Mr Tambourine Man (Columbia/CBS), 1965*
Turn! Turn! Turn! (Columbia/CBS), 1965*
Fifth Dimension (Columbia/CBS), 1966
Younger Than Yesterday (Columbia/CBS), 1967
Greatest Hits (Columbia/CBS), 1967
The Notorious Byrd Brothers (Columbia/CBS), 1968†
Sweetheart Of The Rodeo (Columbia/CBS), 1968†
Dr Bryds And Mr Hyde (Columbia/CBS), 1969
Ballad Of Easy Rider (Columbia/CBS), 1969

Mr. Tambourine Man, the Byrds. Courtesy Columbia Records.

Greatest Hits Volume II (Columbia/CBS), 1971
(Columbia/CBS), 1971
History Of The Byrds (CBS), 1973
The Byrds Play Dylan (Columbia/CBS), 1979
The Original Singles Volume I (Columbia/CBS), 1980
The Original Singles Volume II (Columbia/CBS), 1982
*Available as double LP set (Columbia) US only.
†Available as double album, UK only, 1976.

Worth Searching Out:
(Untitled) (Columbia/CBS), 1970

John Cale

UK vocalist, composer, multi-instrumentalist. Born Garnant, South Wales, 1942.

Career: Studied viola and keyboards at Goldsmith's College, London. Moved to US on scholarship and worked alongside avant-garde composer La Monte Young. Founder member of Velvet Underground(▶) with whom he stayed for two albums. Influence can be observed most fully on **Sister Ray** and **European Son To Delmore Schwartz.** Leaving Velvets, worked as producer for Iggy(▶) and the Stooges and Nico before taking up employment as staff producer/A&R man at Columbia and Warner Bros. Signed recording contract with Columbia; resulting **Vintage Violence** was unusual mixture of melodic pop and oddly sinister music. Collaboration with Terry Riley, **Church Of Anthrax** (1971), was an intriguing gothic experimental work, though no classic.

Following work on albums by Nick Drake, Mike Heron and Nico, Cale moved to Warners. **The Academy In Peril** (1972), an incomplete symphony, with Cale conducting the Royal Philharmonic, proved anticlimactic, but **Paris 1919,** released following year, was critical triumph, combining musical invention with surreal lyrics.

Returned to London in 1974; signed with Island and recorded **Fear,** employing services of Eno and Phil Manzanera. Work was more aggressive, featuring metallic sound, ably complementing bleak images. Appearance with Nico, Kevin Ayers and Eno at London's Rainbow can be heard on **June 1 1974.** Cale also contributed to films 'La Cicatrice Interieure' and 'Heat'.

Since mid-70s his output has been erratic in quality. **Slow Dazzle** utilised backing group of Chris Spedding (guitar), Timi Donald (drums), Pat Donaldson (bass) and Chris Thomas (keyboards/violin), whom Cale took on road for 1975 European tour. Follow-up **Helen Of Troy** fared less well because it was rushed venture, completed only days before tour. Split with Island Records resulted from Cale's insistence on producing Patti Smith(▶) rather than concentrating on own work.

While many of his contemporaries fell from grace, Cale found himself in favourable position during mid-'70s punk-rock era. Velvets work had been applauded and his production credits on albums by Iggy Pop, Jonathan Richman, Patti Smith and later Squeeze(▶), enhanced his reputation. He had even plumbed depths of punk excess by chopping up a chicken on-stage in London, an incident which provided inspiration for 1977 EP, **Animal Justice.**

Moving away from majors, Cale formed his own label, Spy Records, for 1979's **Sabotage/Live,** a heavier work than its predecessors. Continued to impress critics during US tour and promoted new album in punk stores throughout country. Move to A&M led to 'drum' record **Honi Soit,** another pile-driving album with production by Mike Thorne.

Cale's most recent album, **Music For A New Society,** released on ZE, is a more sombre work, boasting impressive list of backing musicians/engineers, including Marc Acron (lead guitar); Joe Bidewell (keyboards/vocals); Deerfrance (percussion/vocals); George Scott (bass/vocals) and Doug Bowne (drums/vocals). LP also included collaboration with playwright/actor Sam Shephard, for whom Cale had previously written music for operetta 'The Sad Lament Of Pecos Bill On The Eve Of Killing His Wife'.

Cale has been important influence on rock since mid-'60s, though his work has often been peripheral. Since 1977 there has been a discernible move away from the occasional romanticism of his early '70s songwriting towards riff-style rock. Recent work suggests further radical changes.

Albums:
With Velvet Underground:
The Velvet Underground And Nico (Verve), 1967
White Light/White Heat (Verve), 1967

Solo:
Vintage Violence (Columbia/CBS), 1971
Church Of Anthrax (Columbia/CBS), 1971
The Academy In Peril (Warner Bros), 1972
Paris 1919 (Warner Bros), 1973
Fear (Island), 1974
Slow Dazzle (Island), 1975
Helen Of Troy (Island), 1975
Sabotage/Live (Spy), 1979
Honi Soit (A&M), 1981
Music For A New Society (ZE/Island), 1982

With Nico, Eno and Kevin Ayers:
June 1, 1974 (Island), 1974

J.J. Cale

US singer, guitarist, composer. Born Tulsa, Oklahoma, 1939.

Career: Started playing guitar at 10. Professional career began with Gene Crose and the Rockets and own band, J.J. Cale and the Valentines. In late '50s he moved to Nashville and made unsuccessful stab as country singer.

Next move was to Los Angeles to join Tulsa colleagues Leon Russell(▶), Carl Radle and Chuck Blackwell. He played small-time clubs

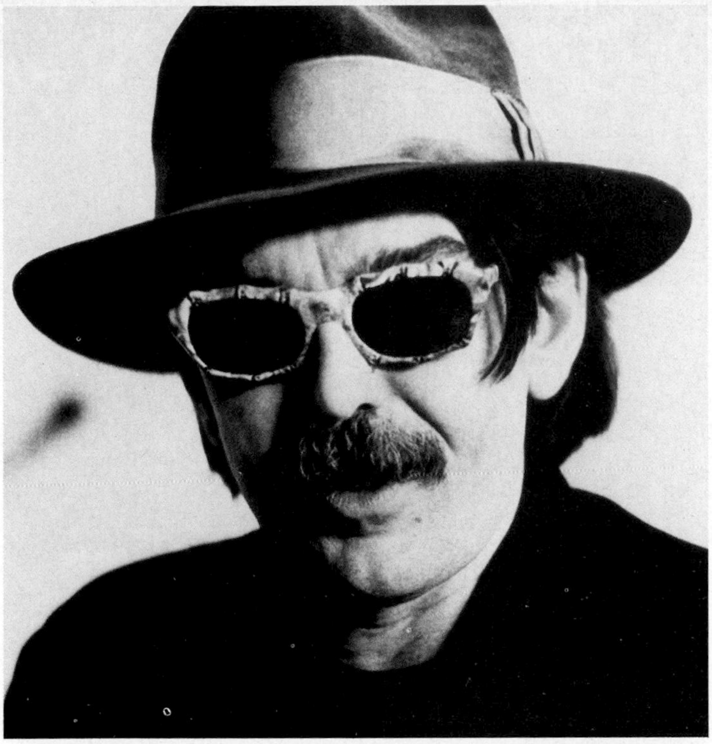

Above: Don Van Vliet, alias the notorious Captain Beefheart.

and bars and developed writing, arranging and producing skills. In 1963 he wrote and recorded **After Midnight**, but song remained obscure until 1970 Eric Clapton(▶) version made Top 10.

In 1967 Cale moved back to Tulsa, continuing to write and occasionally playing local clubs. He built home studio for demos, eventually giving tapes of songs to Carl Radle who took them to Nashville. Result was recording and management deal and first album, **Naturally**, which was critically acclaimed and yielded Top 30 single **Crazy Mama**. The laid-back, down-home blend of blues, country, rock'n'roll and cajun behind Cale's smokey voice and fluid guitar-playing set pattern for further releases.

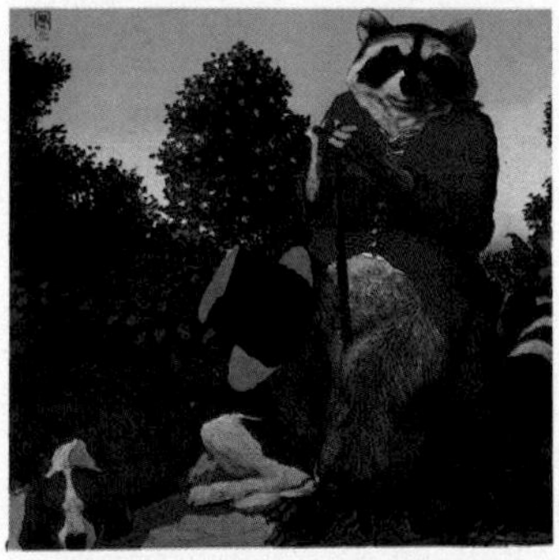

Naturally, J.J. Cale. Courtesy Shelter Records.

Despite continued moderate success, Cale remains reluctant to tour and shuns publicity. Now something of cult figure, he seems likely to continue to produce appealingly relaxed music which is as well thought of by fellow musicians as by loyal audience.

Albums:
Naturally (MCA/Shelter), 1971
Really (MCA/Shelter), 1972
Okie (MCA/Shelter), 1974
Troubadour (MCA/Shelter), 1976
Five (MCA/Shelter), 1979
Shades (MCA/Shelter), 1981
Grasshopper (Mercury/Shelter), 1982

Glen Campbell

US vocalist, guitarist, composer, mutli-intrumentalist.
Born Billstown, Arkansas, April 22, 1936.

Career: Seventh of 11 children, learned 12-string and six-string guitar, banjo, mandolin and bass before teens. Joined his uncle Dick Bill's band working radio and TV at 15; set up own Glen Campbell And His Western Ranglers at 19. Played clubs around Albuquerque before moving to LA and joining short-lived rock 'n' roll band formed by Jerry Naylor.

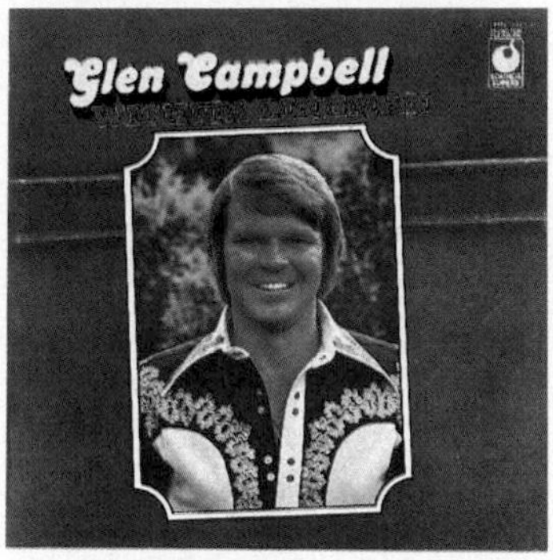

Wichita Lineman, Glen Campbell. Courtesy Capitol Records.

Graduated to lead guitar and vocal role with legendary band the Champs but with arrival of first child decided to quit road work and make it as studio musician, working on records by Frank Sinatra(▶), Bobby Darin(▶) and others. Joined Beach Boys(▶) for short stint in 1965 as replacement for Brian Wilson and before arrival of Bruce Johnston.

First solo success was **Turn Around, Look At Me** which led to deal with major label Capitol but first 20 records were unsuccessful until he was allowed to select own material. In 1967, broke through with **Gentle On My Mind** and **By The Time I Get To Phoenix** (also establishing writer Jim Webb as major composer).

In UK, Capitol's outlet EMI did not believe Campbell's country-flavoured style would find market, so they allowed Jeff Kruger to lease product for his Ember label. Kruger broke Campbell as major act in Britain. Association with Campbell's career continued after artist returned to EMI fold, and on into '80s via succession of major tours.

In 1969 Campbell made movie debut in John Wayne's box-office smash 'True Grit' and hosted first of long run of US TV shows. 'Norwood' and 'Strange Homecoming' have given Campbell further success as movie actor.

Campbell has had 13 million-selling singles and run of chart albums. Successful duets have been cut with Bobbie Gentry, Anne Murray, Rita Coolidge(▶), his one-time lady Tanya Tucker and Diane Solomon. He signed to Atlantic Records in 1983.

Though his records are in straightforward MOR genre, Campbell's stage shows are a revelation, encompassing country, rock and even heavy blues.

Hit Singles:	US	UK
Wichita Lineman, 1968	3	7
All I Have To Do Is Dream, (With Bobby Gentry),1969	27	3
Galveston, 1969	4	14
Honey Come Back, 1970	19	4
It's Only Make Believe, 1970	10	4
Rhinestone Cowboy, 1975	1	4
Country Boy (You Got Your Feet in LA) 1976	11	—
Southern Nights, 1977	1	28

Albums:
(not including repetitive budget albums)
Best Of (Capitol), 1965
Wichita Lineman (Capitol/Ember), 1969
Try A Little Kindness (Capitol), 1970
Greatest Hits (Capitol), 1971
Glen Travis Campbell (Capitol), 1972
Rhinestone Cowboy (Capitol), 1975
Southern Nights (Capitol), 1977
Astounding 12-string Guitar (Capitol), 1978
Collection (—/Ember), 1978
Live (—/MFP), 1978
It's The World Gone Crazy (Capitol), 1981
20 Classic Tracks (—/MFP), 1981
Old Home Town (Atlantic), 1982
By The Time I Get To Pheonix (Capitol/ Ember), 1982
Hey, Little Girl (Capitol), 1982

Canned Heat

US group formed 1966.

Original line-up: Bob 'The Bear' Hite, vocals, harmonica; Henry Vestine, guitar; Larry Taylor, bass; Al 'Blind Owl' Wilson, guitar, harmonica, vocals; Frank Cook, drums.

Career: Eventually recognised as two of world's leading authorities on blues music, record-store manager Hite and music student Wilson met through passionate interest in collecting old records (Hite eventually boasted what was claimed as world's largest private collection). With Cook formed jug band in Los Angeles in 1965; with addition of Vestine (from Mothers Of Invention) became Canned Heat. Adding bassist Larry Taylor, group veered towards blues/R&B and cut first album **Canned Heat** for Liberty in 1967 before making major impact at Monterey Festival.

For second album, Cook was replaced by Mexican drummer Fito De La Parra and, showcasing Wilson's high-pitched vocals, **On The Road Again** (penned by Wilson) cracked singles charts. Followed with **Going Up The Country.** Vestine left mid-1969 to form new band, replaced by Detroit's Harvey Mandel. Larry Taylor split to join John Mayall(▶) band in May 1970.

Exploiting country-blues-styled material in electric blues setting, group cut numerous albums, including one with veteran bluesman John Lee Hooker(▶). Had international smash in 1970 with version of Wilbert Harrison's **Let's Work Together** but Wilson's death on September 3, 1970, hit them hard and welter of personnel changes ensued: Vestine returned, Joel Scott Hill replaced Wilson; Mexican bass-player Antonio De La Barreda came in briefly; Larry Taylor returned then quit again; Joel Scott Hill left; Hite's brother Richard (guitar, bass, vocals) joined. In late 1975 Vestine departed once more. Other brief members included Ed Beyer, keyboards, James Shane, guitar, and Chris Morgan. After spell with John Mayall then stint as solo, Harvey Mandell rejoined in summer 1976. By that time band had lost its earlier vitality; eventually broke up.

Bob Hite became second founder member to die when he succumbed to heart attack (drug-related) at 38 in April 1981.

Final line-up: Bob Hite; Richard Hite, bass; Adolfo 'Fito' de la Palma, drums; Chris Morgan, rhythm guitar; Mark Skyer, lead guitar; Ronnie Baron, piano.

Hit Singles:	US	UK
On The Road Again, 1968	16	8
Going Up The Country, 1969	11	19
Let's Work Together, 1970	26	2

Albums:
Boogie With Canned Heat (Liberty, 1968
Cookbook (The Best of Canned Heat) (Liberty), 1970

Worth Searching Out:
Very Best Of (United Artists/—), 1973

Captain Beefheart

US composer, vocalist, multi-instrumentalist.
Born Don Van Vliet, Glendale, California, January 15, 1941.

Career: As young man in California Van Vliet tried playing straight with group called Blackouts. Assuming name Captain Beefheart (a name not so unusual now, but rather outrageous in 1964) he formed loose confederation of forever-changing musicians called the Magic Band. In what some called his last touch with reality, he released 'commercial' single **Diddy Wah Diddy** on A&M. Then he began changing record labels almost as fast as he changed band members.

Safe As Milk in spring 1967 was very avant-garde, very original, and very much an inside joke. Critics like to consider themselves insiders and Beefheart quickly became known as someone to like, not because you listened to his records, but to be 'cool'.

Beefheart recorded **Mirror Man** next but no one would release it until Buddah took a chance in 1973. With third line-up in 12 months, Beefheart recorded **Strictly Personal** which he got Blue Thumb to release in

Safe As Milk, Captain Beefheart. Courtesy Kama Sutra Records.

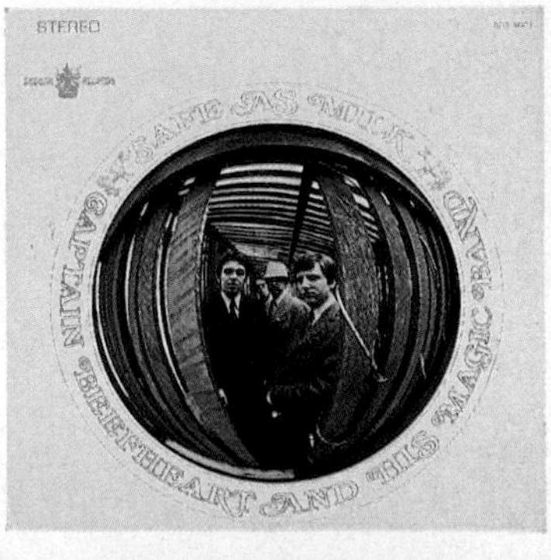

December 1968. Beefheart's excuse for this one was that it was mixed without his supervision. Next record was definitely going to be it. He signed with old friend Frank Zappa(▶)'s label, Straight.

Trout Mask Replica was made with no restraints, and no effort to be commerical. This was art. Critics fell over themselves praising it as one of rock's truly innovative moments; rock public fell over itself avoiding it. Zappa and Beefheart fell out over who was responsible. Straight released a second Beefheart album with one of rock's better titles, Lick My Decals Off, Baby.

Moving to Reprise, Captain released somewhat blues-based The Spotlight Kid, then Clear Spot. Both were departures in containing some identifiable tunes. Another record deal in 1974 (Mercury/Virgin) launched Captain yet again. Unconditionally Guaranteed was commercial sell-out of his career. To avoid falling into rut, he quickly followed up with demented Blue Jeans And Moonbeams.

In 1975 he dissolved Magic Band (who resented dismissal and went on to fail on own as Mallard). Beefheart collaborated with Zappa on Bongo Fury album and in 1976 recorded 'solo' effort. (Warner Bros eventually released Shiney Beast Bat Chain Puller in 1978.) With new Magic Band, Beefheart released 1980 Doc At The Radar Station and has continued to record since.

Some call this music with a personal vision; others call it eccentric nonsense. Beefheart would probably agree with both. In any case Captain has always been original, and remained somewhat immune to criticism. Rave on Captain.

Albums:
Safe As Milk (Kama Sutra/Pye), 1967
Strictly Personal (Blue Thumb/Liberty), 1968
Trout Mask Replica (Straight), 1970
Lick My Decals Off, Baby (Straight), 1970*
The Spotlight Kid (Reprise), 1972*
Clear Spot (Reprise), 1972
Mirror Man (Buddah/Pye), 1973
Unconditionally Guaranteed (Mercury/Fame), 1974
The Captain Beefheart File (—/Pye), 1977
Shiney Beast Bat Chain Puller (Warner Bros/Virgin, 1978)
Two Originals Of . . .(—/Reprise), 1979
Doc At The Radar Station (Virgin), 1980
Ice Cream For Crow (Virgin), 1982

*Released as double album set (—/Reprise), 1976

Larry Carlton

US guitarist, composer, vocalist.
Born Lawrence Eugene Carlton, Torrance, California, March 2, 1948.

Career: Definitive session guitar player, who has successfully recorded as solo performer.

Former Disneyland band member in California, Carlton toured with Fifth Dimension before recording first album for Uni Records in 1969. He became musical director of American NBC-TV children's show in December '69 and also appeared on camera as 'Johnny Guitar'.

He moved into lucrative session field in 1970, and has recorded countless jingles and TV film scores, and worked with leading rock performers, including Art Garfunkel(▶), Ray Manzarek (ex-Doors(▶)), Steely Dan(▶) (Katy Lied, The Royal Scam, Aja, Gaucho), Seals & Crofts(▶), Joni Mitchell(▶), Glen Campbell(▶), David Blue, Hoyt Axton(▶), Terence Boylen, Grammy award winner Christopher Cross'(▶) debut album and Donald Fagen (The Nightfly).

As member of the Crusaders(▶) (1973-76),

he appeared on Crusaders, Second Crusade, Unsung Heroes, Scratch, Southern Comfort, Chain Reaction, Those Southern Nights, Free As The Wind.

Most notable commercial success as guitarist was on Mike Post's 'Hill Street Blues' TV theme. He has huge following in Japan, where

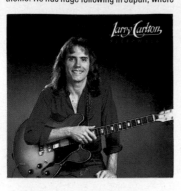

Sleepwalk, Larry Carlton. Courtesy Warner Bros Records.

he cut Mr 335 Live In Japan in 1978.

A fluid, stylish player, Carlton seems to have dispensed with his ordinary vocals and will no doubt continue as influence in '80s.

Guitars: Gibson ES 335 stereo, Valley Arts Stratocaster.

Albums:
Larry Carlton (Warner Bros), 1978
Strikes Twice (Warner Bros/—), 1979
Mr 335 Live In Japan (Warner Bros), 1979
Sleepwalk (Warner Bros), 1982

Eric Carmen

US vocalist, guitarist, composer, producer.
Born Cleveland, Ohio, August 11, 1949.

Career: First achieved success as lead singer and prime mover of the Raspberries, a Cleveland band formed in 1970. Band specialised in home-grown version of 'English sound', formula which brought them string of hits (Go All The Way, I Wanna Be With You, Let's Pretend, Overnight Sensation) in early '70s. Other members were Wallace Bryson (guitar), David Smalley (guitar) and Jim Bonfanti (drums).

Carmen quit band in 1975 to pursue solo career, and was almost immediately rewarded by major success. Ballad All By Myself became worldwide hit, and was followed by further chart entries in US.

Since that time career has been more erratic. Change Of Heart became Top 20 hit in 1978, but by end of decade Carmen was having only minor chart success and had turned hand to producing other artists (e.g. Euclid Beach Band).

A versatile artist and possessor of strong voice, Carmen could surface again at any time. Raspberries' material worth checking out for period charm and excellent example of power pop.

Hit Singles:		US	UK
Raspberries:		
Go All The Way, 1972		5	—
I Wanna Be With You, 1973		16	—
Overnight Sensation (Hit Record), 1974		18	—
Solo:		
All By Myself, 1976		2	12
Never Gonna Fall In Love Again, 1976		11	—
Change Of Heart, 1978		19	—

Albums:
Eric Carmen (Arista), 1976
Boats Against The Current (Arista), 1977
Change Of Heart (Arista), 1978
Tonight You're Mine (Arista), 1980

Worth Searching Out:
Raspberries (Capitol), 1972
Fresh (Capitol), 1973
Best Of (Capitol), 1975

Kim Carnes

US vocalist, pianist, composer.
Born Los Angeles, July 20, 1945.

Career: Former member of New Christy Minstrel, Carnes' career was taking a distinctly MOR direction when Bette Davis Eyes cut loose in 1981.

One-time commercials writer/performer, Carnes first attracted attention with A&M albums Kim Carnes and Sailin', produced by Mentor Williams and Jerry Wexler respectively. A prolific writer (with husband David Ellingson), her material has been recorded by Anne Murray, Frank Sinatra(▶) and Barbra Streisand(▶).

Cut Don't Fall In Love With A Dreamer with Kenny Rogers(▶), another ex-New Christy Minstrel, in '79. Rogers subsequently recorded album of Carnes/Ellingson material, Gideon (1980).

Below: The late Karen Carpenter with brother Richard.

Bette Davis Eyes (written by Jackie De Shannon, whose husky vocals Carnes successfully emulated) pushed the LA native into the rock mainstream where she has continued to flourish.

Hit Singles:	US	UK
More Love, 1980	10	—
Bette Davis Eyes, 1981	1	10

With Kenny Rogers:
Don't Fall In Love With A Dreamer, 1980 | | 4 |

Albums:
Kim Carnes (A&M), 1976
Sailin' (A&M), 1977
St Vincents Court (EMI), 1979
Romance Dance (EMI), 1980
Best Of (A&M), 1981
Mistaken Identity (EMI), 1981
Voyeur (EMI), 1982

The Carpenters

US duo formed 1969.
Richard Carpenter, vocals, keyboards; born New Haven, Connecticut, October 15, 1945.
Karen Carpenter, vocals, drums; born New Haven, Connecticut, March 2, 1950; died December, 1982.

Career: Richard began playing piano at 12, while younger sister Karen developed interest in drums. When Carpenter family moved to Downey, California, in early '60s brother and sister recruited bass player to form jazz outfit.

A Song For You, the Carpenters. Courtesy A&M Records.

Trio won Hollywood Battle Of The Bands contest, but was soon disbanded as Richard and Karen developed interest in vocal harmonies. Next band, Spectrum, comprised Richard and Karen plus four others, and was equally short-lived.

Duo decided to experiment on their own with vocal harmony effects, using overdubbing techniques. Demo tapes were eventually heard by Herb Alpert(▶) of A&M Records, who signed pair as the Carpenters. Success was almost immediate; 1970 Bacharach-David million-seller Close To You set pattern for string of hit singles lasting into mid-'70s. At same time duo notched up massive album sales worldwide (1973 album The Singles 1969-73 became one of the all-time biggest-selling albums). Concert appearances were equally successful.

Appeal of act was based on Karen Carpenter's limpid voice, excellent material from writers such as Bacharach-David and Paul Williams, and unique vocal harmony blend. Richard Carpenter was mainly responsible for arranging and musical direction. Although often critically berated for blandness and wholesome, clean-cut image, the Carpenters were praised by musicians and industry insiders for musicianship, excellent choice of sidemen (e.g. virtuoso guitarist Tony Peluso) and professionalism.

In late '70s duo kept relatively low profile, although 1981 album **Made In America** brought them back into limelight (especially in UK where it made No.12). Unfortunately, career ended in December 1982 with death of Karen Carpenter (caused by heart trouble/anorexia).

Hit Singles:	US	UK
(They Long To Be) Close To You, 1970	1	6
We've Only Just Begun, 1970	2	28
For All We Know, 1971	3	—
Rainy Days And Mondays, 1971	2	—
Superstar/For All We Know, 1971	—	18
Superstar, 1971	2	—
Hurting Each Other, 1972	2	—
It's Going To Take Some Time, 1972	12	—
I Won't Last A Day Without You/ Goodbye To Love, 1972	—	9
Goodbye To Love, 1972	7	—
Sing, 1973	3	—
Yesterday Once More, 1973	2	2
Top Of The World, 1973	1	5
Jambalaya/Mr Guder, 1974	—	12
I Won't Last A Day Without You, 1974	11	32
Please Mr Postman, 1975	1	2
Only Yesterday, 1975	4	7
Solitaire, 1975	17	32
There's A Kind Of Hush, 1976	12	22
Calling Occupants Of Interplanetary Craft, 1977	32	9
Touch Me When We're Dancing, 1981	16	—

Albums:
Close To You (A&M), 1971
The Carpenters (A&M), 1971
Ticket To Ride (A&M), 1972
A Song For You (A&M), 1972
Now And Then (A&M), 1973
The Singles 1969-73 (A&M), 1974
Greatest Hits (—/Hallmark), 1974
Horizon (A&M), 1975
Live In Japan (A&M), 1975
A Kind Of Hush (A&M), 1976
The Carpenters Collection (—/A&M), 1976
Live At The Palladium (A&M), 1977
Passage (A&M), 1977
The Singles 1974-78 (A&M), 1978
Made In America (A&M), 1981

The Cars
US group formed 1976.
Original/Current line-up: Ric Ocasek, guitar, vocals; Ben Orr, bass, vocals; Greg Hawkes, keyboards, sax, percussion; Elliot Easton, guitar; David Robinson, drums.

Career: Richard Otcasek was born and raised near Cleveland, Ohio. He went East to Boston and became Ric Ocasek. In early '70s he met and began working with Ben Orr in various small local bands. Mid-'70s brought in Greg Hawkes. Ocasek was clearly focal point of this melting pot but he was also very much open to others' ideas and opinions. Trio did various demo tapes and kept in touch with each other while Ocasek came across Elliot Easton in another local band.

Meanwhile Bostonian David Robinson, who had been playing in Jonathan Richman's Modern Lovers, moved to Los Angeles. After short time with highly underrated the Pop, he returned to Boston. There he joined Ocasek's group, was impressed by team spirit and offered up name he had been saving: the Cars.

In February 1977 Cars began playing at Boston's 'The Rat' where ability to mix enthusiasm with professional musicianship marked them as special. In 1978 they signed

to Elektra who teamed them with Roy Thomas Baker as producer, and first album followed. As strong as album became after several plays, several tracks were masterpieces in own right as singles. Even new-wave orientated UK proved susceptible to Cars' music and made **My Best Friend's Girl** No.3.

Candy-O (1979) could only prove anti-climactic, especially as recorded quickly between tours. But Cars proved their commitment to rock by refusing to do US TV's 'Midnight Special' unless they got complete control of guests and presentation. They turned fall '79 show into masterpiece of what rock *could* be on television.

The Cars. Courtesy Elektra Records.

Panorama (1980) seemed a reaction to the critics who complained Cars were too slick and too mechanical. 1981 saw release of **Shake It Up** which almost recaptured first album's balance. Despite public effort to present Cars in group image, Ocasek's personality is too strong not to emerge as head Car. 1982 proved this as no new Cars album appeared. US got **Beatitude**, Ocasek solo album sounding a lot like . . .a new Cars album.

Like cross-town compatriots, Boston, Cars are loaded with talent. Both won their deserved success relatively quickly, but as so often happens, band has had difficulty matching thrill and power of first album.

Hit Singles:	US	UK
My Best Friend's Girl, 1978	35	3
Just What I Needed, 1979	27	17
Let's Go, 1979	14	—
Shake It Up, 1982	4	—

Albums:
The Cars (Elektra), 1978
Candy-O (Elektra), 1979
Panorama (Elektra), 1980
Shake It Up (Elektra), 1981

Ric Ocasek Solo:
Beatitude, 1982

Johnny Cash
US vocalist, guitarist, composer.
Born Kingsland, Arkansas, February 26, 1932.

Career: Having suffered through Depression as son of cotton farmer, Cash joined Air Force during Korean War, where he learned guitar and began songwriting. Discharged in 1954, he married and sold electrical goods while studying to be DJ. Switching to performing, he was signed by Sam Phillips of Sun Records about same time as Presley(▶). Phillips re-arranged mournful **I Walk The Line** into uptempo single and Cash had million-seller that turned him from country singer into crossover success.

After several more hits, Cash acted in unmemorable film 'Five Minutes To Live',

Above: Front-line American unit the Cars, bumper to bumper.

playing a killer. Toured Canada and Australia and, in 1960, added drummer to increase back-up group to Tennessee Three. Doing 300 gigs a year, he began pill-popping, an addiction that nearly destroyed career and life until cured in late 1960s with help of second wife, country star June Carter. (Cash and Carter recorded hit single **Jackson** before marriage, and successful duet **If I Was A Carpenter**, 1970.)

Despite sympathy for prisoners, including albums recorded at Folsom and San Quentin prisons, Cash only spent few days in jail for his peculiar behaviour caused by taking pills that would have been legal with prescription. **Folsom Prison Blues** was written after seeing movie 'Inside The Walls Of Folsom Prison'. Other sympathies include plight of American Indian; Cash claims to have Cherokee blood.

Singing with Bob Dylan(▶) at Newport in 1964 and on **Nashville Skyline** album

Below: Young Johnny Cash with young Elvis.

widened his audience, as did ABC-TV series. Cash helped popularise Kris Kristofferson(▶) by introducing him at 1969 Newport Folk Festival and recorded **Sunday Morning Coming Down** with great success.

During Vietnam War, when US political polarisation was echoed in the protest songs of folk-based singers and super-patriotism of country music in vein of Merle Haggard's(▶) **(Okie From Muskogee)**, Cash found middle ground with satirical number about musical trio, **The One On The Right Is On The Left.** Recording success resumed with **A Boy Named Sue,** which went gold in US and was selected by Country Music Association as single of the year (1969). When singing at White House in 1970, Cash reportedly turned down Richard Nixon's request for **Okie** with polite excuse.

Since re-marriage and end of drugs and drink excess, Cash has returned to simplistic religious faith of childhood, but his obvious sincerity gives dignity to hymn-singing and to 1971 movie 'Gospel Road', filmed in Israel and distributed by evangelist Billy Graham. He also returned to acting in films, including 'The Gunfight' with Kirk Douglas (1970), and on television where he has played opposite Peter Falk in 'Columbo' and starred with wife June in TV film 'Thadeus Rose and Eddie'.

Gone Girl, 1979 album, includes Jagger/ Richards'(▶) **No Expectations,** blues number done in Cash's uptempo rockabilly style. Cash continued to record in early '80s, particularly with other artists.

Craggy, tortured, insolent face and deep, doom-laden voice combined with stylish costumes and splendid Martin guitar, initialled in mother-of-pearl, have made Cash intriguing as well as talented performer. He was subject of 1969 biopic 'Johnny Cash! The Man, His World, His Music', which included duet with Dylan, 1974 biography 'Winners Got Scars Too' and 1975 autobiography 'Man In Black'.

Hit Singles:	US	UK
I Walk The Line, 1956	17	—
Ballad Of A Teenage Queen, 1958	14	—
Guess Things Happen That Way, 1958	11	—
Ring Of Fire, 1963	17	—
A Boy Named Sue, 1969	2	4
What Is Truth, 1970	19	21
A Thing Called Love, 1972	—	4

Albums (selected):
Ring Of Fire (Columbia/CBS), 1963
I Walk The Line (Accord/CBS), 1964
Greatest Hits (Columbia/CBS), 1967
At Folsom Prison (Columbia/CBS), 1968
At San Quentin (Columbia/CBS), 1969
Greatest Hits (Sun/—), 1970
The Original (—/Charly), 1970
The Baron (Columbia/CBS), 1981

With Jerry Lee Lewis and Carl Perkins:
The Survivors (Columbia/CBS), 1982

With Marty Robbins:
The Cowboys (—/Ronco), 1982

Harry Chapin
US vocalist, composer.
Born Greenwich Village, New York, December 7, 1942; died July 16, 1981.

Career: Born into musical family, Chapin's first public exposure was with Brooklyn Heights Boys Choir. After graduating from Cornell University he went into film industry and made critically successful 'Legendary Champions'. Eventually returned to first love, music. In 1964 he formed group with two brothers and father to play Greenwich Village clubs. Outfit

disbanded when brothers split to avoid draft. Subsequently formed new band which attracted strong local following. He then signed to Elektra Records and first album **Heads And Tales** yielded hit single, **Taxi.**

Further albums increased audience for Chapin's music, building up strong if somewhat cultish following. Songs generally stuck to narrative format, varying between genuinely perceptive vignettes of American life and over-whimsical melodrama. Unlike many composer/performers, Chapin projected well in live performance, and his record success was matched by successful concert appearances both in US and abroad. Versatility was demonstrated further by appearance in 'The Night That Made America Famous', an experimental musical revue for which he wrote several songs.

By mid-70's Chapin had several big-selling albums and hit singles under his belt, and had established loyal audience in US—although he never sold many records in rest of world. He commanded a substantial faithful following when his life was cut tragically short by car crash in 1981.

Rather an acquired taste, Chapin's work can be both overly sentimental and hectoring in tone. Nevertheless, he followed individualistic path through jungle of singer/songwriter clichés, and often succeeded in creating original and arresting music. His lyrics revealed him to be socially concerned, and he did extensive benefit tours for the W.H.O.

Hit Singles:	US	UK
Cat's In The Cradle, 1974	1	—

Albums:
Heads And Tales (Elektra), 1971
Sniper And Other Love Songs (Elektra), 1972
Short Stories (Elektra), 1973
Verities And Balderdash (Elektra), 1974
Portrait Gallery (Elektra), 1975
On The Road To Kingdom Come (Elektra), 1976
Greatest Stories—Live (Elektra), 1976
Dance Band On The Titanic (Elektra), 1977
Living Room Suite (Elektra), 1978
Legends Of The Lost And Found (Elektra), 1979
Sequel (Boardwalk/Epic), 1980

Ray Charles
US vocalist, pianist, composer, arranger.
Born Ray Charles Robinson, Albany, Georgia, September 23, 1930.

Career: Brought up in Greenville, Florida, Charles was blinded by glaucoma at age six. He showed early signs of musical talent, and was sent to State School for Blind at seven. He remained until 15, concentrating on musical studies, and by early teens was already playing piano semi-professionally. On death of his mother in 1945 he became full-time musician.

Early experience on road included stint as part of blues singer Lowell Fulsom's band. First band Charles led was called McSon Trio. Recorded number of Nat Cole(▶)-influenced sides for small local labels.

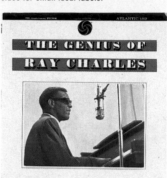

The Genuis Of Ray Charles. Courtesy Atlantic Records.

Big career break was signing with nascent black music label Atlantic; **It Should Have Been Me**, a semi-humorous blues number, was R&B hit in 1954.

During this period Charles began to move away from Cole influence and developed idiosyncratic style based on mixture of secularised gospel and blues. At same time he put together

Below: The legendary 'Brother' Ray Charles, R&B giant of four decades, a great influence on rock singers.

band of top-echelon jazz musicians; result was commercial success and respect from critics.

Charles broke pop market in 1959 with **What'd I Say**, a wildly exciting single that synthesised blues, gospel, and rock'n'roll in one dynamic package. Made Top 10 of pop charts and started Charles' career as performer of wide appeal.

Following big money offer, Charles left Atlantic for ABC-Paramount at end of 1959. He continued to make excellent recordings, particularly of blues-based material, and notch up major hits. **Georgia On My Mind**, a reading of Hoagy Carmichael standard which set Charles' emotion-filled voice against strings backing, was Top-30 hit in UK and established Charles internationally.

Further landmark was created in 1962 when Charles recorded album of country songs, **Modern Sounds In Country And Western**. Idea of black R&B star covering country songs seemed outlandish at time, but concept was successful both artistically and commercially, and resulted in huge album sales and hit singles like **I Can't Stop Loving You**. That year Charles sold then phenomenal amount of eight million dollars worth of records (he has had nearly 70 US chart singles), and became major international star, in demand for TV and concert dates all over world.

During '60s Charles' career assumed fairly consistent pattern; albums contained mixture of R&B and more pop-orientated material, and live appearances became well-oiled and disciplined runthroughs of hits. Nevertheless, Charles' power as vocalist continued unabated.

The '70s saw changes in record company arrangements. In 1973, he severed connections with ABC to form own label, Crossover, and in 1977 Crossover became distributed and marketed by his old company, Atlantic.

In '80s Charles seems content to follow formula which has kept him at top for 20 years. A living legend, he is still capable of powerful music and remains an important influence on many contemporary rock singers —particularly Joe Cocker(▶). His Atlantic and early ABC material is a testimony to one of the most exhilarating talents in popular music.

Hit Singles:	US	UK
What'd I Say, 1959	6	—
Georgia On My Mind, 1960	1	24
One Mint Julep, 1961	8	—
Hit The Road Jack, 1961	1	6
Unchain My Heart, 1961	9	—
Hide Nor Hair, 1962	20	—
I Can't Stop Loving You, 1962	1	1
You Don't Know Me, 1962	2	9
You Are My Sunshine, 1962	7	—
Your Cheating Heart, 1962	29	13
Don't Set Me Free, 1963	20	37
Take These Chains From My Heart, 1963	8	5
Busted, 1963	4	21
That Lucky Old Sun, 1964	20	—
Crying Time, 1966	6	50
Together Again, 1966	19	48
Here We Go Again, 1967	15	38

Albums:
Ray Charles At Newport (Atlantic), 1958
The Great Ray Charles (Atlantic/London), 1958
Genius Of Ray Charles (Atlantic/Boulevard), 1958
Ray Charles Live (Atlantic/—), 1965
25th Anniversary In Showbusiness (ABC/Atlantic), 1971
Come Live With Me (Crossover/London), 1974
World Of (—/Decca), 1974
World Of Volume 2 (—/Decca), 1975
Focus On Ray Charles (London), 1975
My Kind Of Jazz Volume 3 (Crossover/—), 1975

Renaissance (Crossover/London), 1975
Porgy And Bess (with Cleo Laine)
   (RCA/London), 1976
What Have I Done To Their Songs (London),
   1977
True To Life (Atlantic/London), 1977
Love And Peace (Atco/London), 1978
Ray Charles Blues (—/Ember), 1978
20 Golden Pieces Of (—/Bulldog), 1979
Ain't It So (—/London), 1979
A Ray Of Hope (—/Manhattan), 1980
Brother Ray (London), 1980
Everything (—/Manhattan), 1980
I Can't Stop Loving You (—/Pickwick), 1980
Simply Ray (—/Manhattan), 1980
Great Hits (—/Phoenix), 1982

With Milt Jackson:
Soul Brothers (Atlantic/London), 1959
Soul Meeting (Atlantic), 1962

Worth Searching Out:
Yes Indeed (Atlantic/London), 1958
What'd I Say (Atlantic/London), 1959
Ray Charles And Betty Carter (HMV/ABC),
   1960
Genius + Soul = Jazz (Atlantic/HMV), 1961
Modern Sounds In Country & Western
   (ABC/HMV), 1962

Cheap Trick

US group formed 1972.
Original line-up: Rick Nielsen, guitar, vocals;
Robin Zander, vocals, guitar; Bun E. Carlos,
drums; Tom Peterson, bass, vocals.

Career: Nielsen and Peterson started out in
1967 Mid-Western band Grim Reaper; Epic
signed group in 1968, changed name to Fuse
and released little-noted LP in January 1969.
Nielsen and Peterson then joined forces with
several musicians from Nazz for a couple of
years, spending some time in Europe.

By 1972, Nielsen was back home in
Rockford, Illinois, where he started Cheap
Trick. Rest of band consisted of local friends:
Bun E. Carlos on drums, Zeno on vocals and
someone now forgotten on bass. Nielsen
called Peterson in Europe and told him band
was on brink of stardom. Peterson was not
amused on learning truth after his arrival, but
agreed to take over on bass. In 1974, Xeno
was fired as vocalist; he recommended Robin
Zander as replacement.

This line-up began endless tours of Midwest
and earned reputation as exciting live act.
Jack Douglas (Aerosmith▶) producer) saw
performance and convinced Columbia to sign
band. With an eye for image and humorous
flair for invention, band created a fake history
for itself: Peterson added an 's' to surname;
bio claimed Carlos was son of a Venezuelan
industrialist, etc. Punk music was just about to
introduce a whole new range of assumed
names and aliases — Cheap Trick's 'revised'
past helped identify them as part of new music
rather than re-hash of older bands.

Douglas rushed first album through production in five weeks in deliberate attempt to

Cheap Trick. Courtesy Epic Records.

capture raw energy of 'live' Cheap Trick.
Overlooked by general press, sales depended
on word of mouth but **Cheap Trick** LP was
too rough to get US air play needed for
massive sales.

In frenzy of work band opened national
tours for Queen(▶), Kinks(▶), Santana(▶),
Journey(▶) and Kiss(▶), setting aside six weeks
in Los Angeles to record second LP. Tom
Werman took over production and went for
smoother (more commercial) sound. Released within months of first LP, **In Color**
received favourable press and more air play.

Cheap Trick returned to touring for rest of
1977, then spent a month recording **Heaven
Tonight** LP, finished the day before band left
for successful tour of small European/UK
venues. Later, in Japan, Cheap Trick found
themselves in midst of 10-day 'Beatlemania'
tour. Overwhelming response convinced band
to call over Jack Douglas to record a concert
for Japanese release. Band returned to US for

**Above: Cheap Trick in the line-up for the
'Dream Police'.**

headlining tour.

The end of 1978 continued at same pace,
with band recording **Dream Police** LP.
Meanwhile the live LP recorded in Japan sold
so well as US import that bootleg copies
began selling at prices close to the original.
Epic Records decided to hold up release of
Dream Police while issuing domestic version
of the live LP. **At Budokan** quickly became Cheap Trick's biggest seller and went
platinum.

When **Dream Police** was eventually released, it sounded anti-climactic. With its
carefully crafted, smoothly produced rock, the
simple, zany excitement of live album was
totally lost. Cheap Trick thus alienated some
of old audience, without managing to attract a
new one. The rest of 1979 continued with
rather routine touring.

When next LP, **All Shook Up** (produced by
George Martin), was released, it lacked
unique wit and feel of Cheap Trick, and
signalled Tom Petersson's growing disenchantment. He subsequently quit band and
Pete Comita, who had subbed for him on fall
1980 Japan tour, soon took his place. But by
time band began recording **One On One**, Jon
Brant was bassist. To promote this LP, band
resorted to 'cheap trick' of issuing it in 'limited'
red vinyl edition; album barely made US Top
40.

Cheap Trick is one of America's most
interesting bands to emerge in last 10 years,
and one of the most difficult to describe. New
wave only in name, too melodic for heavy
metal, and too raw for pop, it stands in a
category all its own.
Current line-up: Nielsen (one of largest
private guitar collectors in US); Zander;
Carlos; Jon Brant, bass.

Hit Singles:	US	UK
I Want You To Want Me, 1979	7	—

Albums:
Cheap Trick (Epic), 1977
In Color (Epic), 1977
Heaven Tonight (Epic), 1978
At Budokan (Epic), 1979
Dream Police (Epic), 1979
All Shook Up (Epic), 1980
One On One (Epic), 1982

Chic

US group formed 1977.
Original/Current line-up: Nile Rodgers,
guitar, producer; Bernard Edwards, producer,
bass.

Career: New York-born Nile Rodgers was
brought up in Greenwich Village and Hollywood. Played with New York rock band New
World Rising in mid-'60s, and later became
regular member of Apollo Theatre house
band.

Born in Greenville, North Carolina, Bernard
Edwards moved to New York at 10; studied
tenor sax in junior high, then took up electric
bass. Played small-time gigs around New
York.

Two met through mutual acquaintance and
started working together in various clubs.
Eventually both joined Big Apple Band in
1972, backing then successful group New
York City (**I'm Doing Fine Now**). Toured US
and Europe from 1972 to 1975.

On demise of New York City, Rodgers and
Edwards kept band together, recording demos
and backing singer Carol Douglas. Demo
tapes attracted attention of Atlantic Records,
and company signed group in 1977. Re-
named Chic, group now also featured drummer
Tony Thompson and vocalist Alfa Anderson
and Luci Martin.

Debut single **Dance Dance Dance** was
huge international hit, and heralded run of
major successes. **Le Freak**, for example,
became biggest-selling single in history of
WEA Records, sales eventually totalling over

Chic. Courtesy Atlantic Records.

four million copies. Album success was for a while equally spectacular, and Rodgers and Edwards became in demand as producers. Artists to receive the Chic treatment included Sister Sledge, Sheila B. Devotion, Diana Ross(▶) and Debby Harry(▶).

Chic's highly recognisable sound — pared-down rhythm section, repetitive, syncopated melody lines — may be the cause of band's relative eclipse in the '80s. At its best, the Chic concept added wit, sophistication and musicality to disco, but its begetters seemed reluctant to adapt sufficiently to changing audience demands.

Latterly, however, Nile Rodgers has co-produced the massively successful David Bowie(▶) album **Let's Dance**, with Bernard Edwards contributing on bass. It seems likely that wide-ranging talent and astute business acumen will keep duo in limelight in foreseeable future.

Hit Singles:

	US	UK
Dance Dance Dance, 1977	6	6
Everybody Dance, 1978	38	9
Le Freak, 1978	1	7
I Want Your Love, 1979	7	4
Good Times, 1979	1	5
My Forbidden Lover, 1979	43	15

Albums:
Chic (Atlantic), 1978
C'est Chic (Atlantic), 1978
Risque (Atlantic), 1979
Les Plus Grandes Succes De Chic — Greatest Hits (Atlantic), 1979
Real People (Atlantic), 1980
Take It Off (Atlantic), 1981
Tongue In Chic (Atlantic), 1982

Chicago

US group formed 1968.

Original line-up: Robert Lamm, keyboards, lead vocals; Terry Kath, guitar, lead vocals; Peter Cetera, bass, lead vocals; Lee Loughnana, trumpet, background vocals; James Pankow, trombone; Walter Parazaider, woodwinds, background vocals; Daniel Seraphine, drums.

Career: Formed as the Big Thin in 1968, name changed to Chicago Transit Authority. Made big reputation in Chicago (shortening name to simply 'Chicago' when sued by Mayor Daley) before moving to Los Angeles and

If You Leave Me Now, Chicago. Courtesy CBS Records.

linking with producer/manager James William Guercio. Debut album **Chicago Transit Authority** (1969) won immediate acclaim for its blend of black-influenced rhythm section and jazzy brass section—in similar mode to also emergent Blood Sweat And Tears(▶). Album was massive seller, staying in chart for amazing six years.

Subsequent albums, called Chicago I-VIII etc., appeared at regular annual intervals and run of singles like **I'm A Man** (a punchy 1970

version of Spencer Davis Group(▶) oldie), **Make Me Smile, 25 Or 6 To 4** and romantic chart-topping ballad **If You Leave Me Now** have made them one of the highest-earning groups in rock. They are reputed to have generated more than $160 million in sales, their 14 albums selling 20 million copies.

Following death of guitarist Terry Kath (playing Russian roulette), band went into limbo for short time. He was eventually replaced by Donnie Dacus. Comeback 1980 world tour included concert before 150,000 audience at Chicago Festival.

Group's music has often been criticised as being somewhat antiseptic, especially compared to inventiveness of other jazz-rock orientated groups in late '70- early '80s. Nevertheless, it has found long-standing audience.

Chicago moved to Full Moon label in 1982.

Current line-up: Lamm; Cetera; Loughnana; Pankow; Parazaider; Seraphine; Donnie Dacus, guitar, lead vocals.

Hit Singles:

	US	UK
I'm A Man, 1970	—	8
Make Me Smile, 1970	9	—
25 Or 6 To 4, 1970	4	7
Does Anybody Really Know What Time It Is? 1970	7	—
Free, 1971	20	—
Beginnings/Colour My World, 1971	7	—
Saturday In The Park, 1972	3	—
Feelin' Stronger Every Day, 1973	10	—
Just You 'n' Me, 1973	4	—
(I've Been) Searchin' So Long, 1974	9	—
Call On Me, 1974	6	—
Wishing You Were Here, 1974	11	—
Harry Truman, 1975	13	—
Old Days, 1975	5	—
If You Leave Me Now, 1976	1	1
Baby What A Big Surprise, 1977	4	41
Live Again, 1978	14	—
No Tell Lover, 1979	14	—
Hard For Me To Say I'm Sorry, 1982	1	4

Albums:
Chicago Transit Authority (Columbia/CBS), 1968
Chicago (Columbia/CBS), 1970
III (Columbia/CBS), 1971
IV Live At Carnegie Hall* (Columbia/CBS), 1971

V (Columbia/CBS), 1972
VI (Columbia/CBS), 1973
VII (Columbia/CBS), 1974
VIII (Columbia/CBS), 1975
IX Greatest Hits (Columbia/CBS), 1975
X (Columbia/CBS), 1976
XI (Columbia/CBS), 1977
Hot Streets (Columbia/CBS), 1978
XIII (Columbia/CBS), 1979
XIV (Columbia/CBS), 1980
Greatest Hits Volume 2 (Columbia/CBS), 1982
If You Leave Me Now (—/CBS), 1982
Love Songs (—/TV), 1982
XVI (Full Moon), 1982
Toronto Rock 'n' Roll Revival 1969, Volume 1 (Accord/—), 1982
*4 album live set

Eric Clapton

UK guitarist, vocalist, composer.
Born Ripley, Surrey, March 30, 1945.

Career: Brought up by foster-parents. At 15 he started to listen to blues recordings by Muddy Waters(▶), Chuck Berry(▶), Big Bill Broonzy et al, and bought first guitar at 17. Taught himself to play while studying at Kingston Art College.

Formed first band in 1963, an R&B outfit called Roosters which also included at various times Paul Jones and Tom McGuinness later of Manfred Mann(▶) and Brian Jones later of Rolling Stones(▶). Band was short-lived; and in late 1963 Clapton spent two weeks with Casey Jones and the Engineers before replacing Anthony 'Top'

Backless, Eric Clapton. Courtesy RSO Records.

Above: Chicago earned the wrath of Mayor Daly before moving to L.A.

Topham as lead guitarist in recently formed Yardbirds(▶).

While with Yardbirds Clapton established reputation as blues stylist, and recorded **Five Live Yardbirds** and **Sonny Boy Williamson & The Yardbirds** albums. But when band took more commercial direction with 1965 single **For Your Love,** Clapton took off for more purist environment of John Mayall's(▶) Bluesbreakers.

Money And Cigarettes, Eric Clapton. Courtesy Warner Bros Records.

Straight-down-the-line blues approach of Mayall's band provided perfect backdrop for Clapton, and the guitarist attracted even more fervent following. Shown to good effect on **Bluesbreakers** album, Clapton's playing began to influence other British players; he became widely regarded as *the* guitar hero.

Sitters-in with Bluesbreakers included Jack Bruce(▶) and Ginger Baker(▶) , bass player and drummer respectively, with Graham Bond Organization. Empathy with both musicians led to break from Mayall (Clapton replaced by Peter Green(▶)) and formation of Cream(▶) in 1967.

With Cream Clapton enjoyed first major commercial success and fully blown rock star status. Although band was important link in development of heavy rock—the first power trio—it was relatively short-lived, and folded in November 1968.

Period which followed saw Clapton involved with variety of projects, including ill-fated Blind Faith(▶) supergroup, touring and recording with Delaney & Bonnie(▶), guesting on other artists' albums, and his first solo album in 1970. From this time onwards Clapton seemed to be trying to live down his axe hero past. He immersed himself in group as Derek of Derek and the Dominoes(▶) December 1970 Dominoes album featured Duane Allman(▶) and is regarded by many as Clapton's best recorded effort. Single **Layla**—dedicated to then wife of George Harrison(▶), Patti, whom Clapton was later to marry—has achieved classic status.

Nevertheless, Derek and the Dominoes were not huge commercial success, and this relative failure plus increasing drug problem took Clapton off music scene for several years. Eventually, with help of friends like Pete Townshend(▶) and course of electro-acupuncture, Clapton regained health.

Since 1974 Clapton has pursued fairly low-profile career, making relaxed, down-home albums, occasionally coming up with hit singles, and working live sporadically. He has continued to play down guitar hero persona, and has developed pleasing J.J. Cale(▶)-like voice to go with his simple but appealing compositions. Nowadays as often influenced by country and other forms of blues (he is for example fan of super-relaxed country artist Don Williams(▶)), Clapton appeals both to AOR audiences and diehard rock fans. One of the most important British musicians to have come out of rock, he has been as influential to many young players as the blues masters he originally emulated.

Guitars: Fender Stratocaster, Gibson Les Paul.

Hit Singles:

	US	UK
After Midnight, 1970	18	—
I Shot The Sherriff, 1974	1	9
Swing Low Sweet Chariot, 1975	—	19
Lay Down Sally, 1978	3	39
Wonderful Tonight, 1978	16	—
Promises, 1979	9	37
I Can't Stand it, 1981	10	—

Below: Eric Clapton, with Ron Wood and Freddie King at the Crystal Palace Garden Party.

Albums:
Eric Clapton (Polydor), 1970
History of Eric Clapton (Polydor), 1972
Eric Clapton At His Best (Polydor), 1973
Eric Clapton's Rainbow Concert (RSO), 1973
461 Ocean Boulevard* (RSO), 1974
There's One In Every Crowd (RSO), 1975
E.C. Was Here (RSO), 1975
The Blues World Of (—/Decca), 1975
No Reason To Cry (RSO), 1976
Slowhand* (RSO), 1977
Backless* (RSO), 1978
Just One Night (RSO), 1980
Another Ticket (RSO), 1981
Steppin' Out (—/Decca), 1981
Time Pieces (Best Of) (RSO), 1982
Money And Cigarettes (Warner Bros), 1983
Time Pieces, Volume II (RSO), 1983

*Available as triple album set.

The Dave Clark Five

UK group formed 1963.
Original/Final line-up: Dave Clark, drums, vocals; Lenny Davidson, guitar; Rick Huxley, guitar, banjo; Dennis Payton, saxophone, guitar, clarinet, harmonica; Mike Smith, keyboards, vibraphone, vocals.

Career: This 'British invasion' group followed the Beatles(▶) to US and found great, if temporary, fame and fortune there. Nowadays often considered pale imitation of Beatles, but in fact the Five had distinctive sound (called 'Tottenham Sound') of their own, based on Clark's steadily thudding drums and chanting vocals. Smash hit single **Glad All Over** was amazingly considered rather risqué at the time. Group became involved in a ridiculous publicity war with the Beatles, the Five being touted as a neat, well-groomed London alternative. Then the Rolling Stones(▶) arrived. It was all a contrived tempest in a teapot, anyway, indicative of the innocent controversies that filled the pages of

teen magazines at the time.

Band also starred in what turned out to be one of the best rock movies, 'Having A Wild Weekend', directed by then unknown John Boorman in 1965. Despite title, it is a bitter-sweet story that looks at the price of sudden fame and at the hysteria that briefly surrounds popular young musicians. There's no great acting here, of course, but it is one of the few rock exploitation films that holds up.

Group had several hit singles in the States, including **Do You Love Me**, a cover of the 1962 dance hit by the Contours, and raucous stomper **Bits And Pieces**. After that, popularity faded; although the Five had an original and identifiable sound, it never varied. They weren't capable of the changes that more lasting bands were beginning to explore. They

The Best of the Dave Clark Five. Courtesy EMI Records.

stayed together, a constant live attraction (going temporarily hippie in '68 like everyone else, and replacing their signature turtleneck pullovers with flowered shirts and medallions), eventually splitting for good in 1973.

Hit Singles:

	US	UK
Glad All Over, 1963	6	1
Bits And Pieces, 1964	4	2
Can't You See That She's Mine, 1964,	4	10
Do You Love Me, 1964	11	30
Because, 1964	3	—
Everybody Knows (I Still Love, You), 1964	15	37
Any Way You Want It, 1964	14	25
Come Home, 1965	14	16
I Like It Like That, 1965	7	—
Catch Us If You Can, 1965	4	5

Above: London's answer to the 'Mersey' sound, the Dave Clark Five with Ed Sullivan, who introduced many UK acts.

Over And Over, 1965	1	45
At The Scene, 1966	18	—
Try Too Hard, 1966	12	—
You Got What It Takes, 1967	7	28
Everybody Knows (I Still Love You) 1967	43	2
Red Balloon, 1968	—	7
Good Old Rock 'n' Roll, 1969	—	7
Everybody Get Together, 1970	—	8

Albums:
Best Of (—/Starline), 1970
Plays Good Old Rock 'n' Roll (—/MFP), 1975
25 Thumping Great Hits (—/Polydor), 1978

Worth Searching Out:
Greatest Hits (Epic/Columbia), 1966

Stanley Clarke

US bass guitarist, producer, vocalist.
Born Philadelphia, June 30, 1951.

Career: Major figure of jazz-funk movement as artist/producer/sideman, Stanley Clarke has been involved with such diverse projects as a Roy Buchanan rock album and soul singer Dee Dee Bridgewater and Lenny White's **Echoes Of An Era** album, which featured current jazz stars re-vamping classic jazz standards.

Classically trained, Clarke mastered violin, cello and double-bass by 13 and went on to study at Philadelphia Musical Academy. Moving to New York in 1970 he joined Horace Silver's group, then Joe Henderson's band where he met Chick Corea. The two formed highly-touted Return To Forever, which included Lenny White, drums, and Al Di Meola(▶), guitar, and cut seven classy albums.

During stint with band, Clarke found time to play gigs and record dates with Aretha Franklin(▶), Carlos Santana(▶), Stan Getz, Dexter Gordon, Art Blakey and others, exposing himself to wide spectrum of music. Often using Return To Forever cohorts as sidemen, he started his solo career, debuting in 1974 with **Stanley Clarke**, notching R&B hit with **Silly Putty** from his second album, a cut which showcased his ability to carry a central melody

on bass. Along with Louis Johnson of Brothers Johnson, he has pioneered inventive way of playing electric bass, 'popping' the strings and playing lead fills.

Particularly through his work since 1981, with keyboard player George Duke in Clarke/Duke Project, Clarke has become major concert attraction as well as enjoying chart success and albums.

Guitar: Alembic bass.

Albums:
Stanley Clarke (Columbia/Epic), 1974
Journey To Love (Columbia/Epic), 1975
School Days (Columbia/Atlantic), 1976
Modern Man (Nemporer/Epic), 1978
I Wanna Play For You (Nemporer/Epic), 1979
Rocks, Pebbles And Sand (Epic), 1980
With Chick Corea:
Children Of Forever (Polydor), 1972
With George Duke:
The Clarke/Duke Project (Epic), 1981
Let Me Know You (Epic), 1982

The Clash

UK group formed 1976.

Original line-up: Joe Strummer, vocals, guitar; Paul Simonon, bass; Mick Jones, guitar; Keith Levine, guitar; Terry Chimes, drums.

Career: Group formed in squat in London's Shepherd's Bush area in May 1976. Simonon and Jones were previously part of prototype punk unit, London SS, and approached Strummer, then a member of pub-rock band, the 101ers. Keith Levine became group's second guitarist but soon left. He re-emerged in Flowers Of Romance and, later, Public Image Ltd. After several auditions, Terry Chimes (drums) completed line-up.

Moving headquarters to disused warehouse in Camden Town, group rehearsed under direction and guidance of manager Bernie Rhodes. An unpublicised appearance with the Sex Pistols(▶) was followed by their official unveiling in August 1976. The publicity afforded the Pistols and punk led to lucrative contract with CBS. Move regarded as treason by some hard-core punk fans. Nevertheless, the Clash quickly established themselves as one of the most forceful and committed spokesmen of the new wave; their impact was immediately felt.

First single '**White Riot**' reached No. 38 and was hailed as mini-classic of punk genre. Debut album **The Clash** entered LP chart at No. 12. During same period, drummer Terry Chimes left, disillusioned with trappings of punk; antipathy felt by other members reflected on LP sleeve where Chimes is renamed Tory Crimes. An endless series of auditions followed before Nicky 'Topper' Headon was brought in as replacement.

Third single **Complete Control**, a riposte to CBS, was produced by Lee Perry and reached Top 30. Tour with Richard Hell and the Voidoids was followed by publicity in the form of group arrests on charges of petty vandalism and shooting racing pigeons. Another tour, appropriately titled 'The Clash Out On Parole', and new single, **White Man In Hammersmith Palais/The Prisoner,** maintained momentum.

Second LP **Give 'Em Enough Rope** hit No. 2 on album charts and provided first Top 20 hit single, **Tommy Gun.** Production by Sandy Pearlman caused further controversy amongst punk elite, who feared that Clash were being transformed into heavy-metal unit. Following split with manager Rhodes, group embarked on first US visit, dubbed the 'Pearl Harbour Tour'. Positive response from US critics helped subsequent career prospects.

Returning to UK, began work on film 'Rude Boy' (1980). On the day of Britain's General Election (May 11, 1979) **The Cost Of Living** (EP) was issued. Included a version of Bobby Fuller's **I Fought The Law.** Group's political credibility was promoted further by appearances at Rock Against Racism gigs. Another US tour saw group augmented by Blockheads' keyboardist Micky Gallagher.

Third LP, produced by Guy Stevens, was scheduled as **The New Testament,** a pretentious title finally dropped in favour of **London Calling.** Released in Christmas 1979 as a two for the price of one, the work was a strong seller. Follow up **Sandinista,** a triple album, followed same pattern, though less successfully.

Headon's increasingly idiosyncratic (drug related) behaviour resulted in his removal from group on eve of crucial US tour in May 1982. At short notice, Terry Chimes agreed to return to drummer's seat—a position he filled ably until December, when close-knit trio were once again diverted to search for a compatible cohort. Former Cold Fish Peter Howard was named in 1983.

Clash have continued to reach wider audience without greatly diverging from original punk stance. Purists, however, would contend this. Their appearance on the cover of **Rolling Stone** caused strong ripples of indignation among punk hard core, but most mainstream critics accepted their political integrity and credited them for commitment and lack of obvious compromise. Their most recent album **Combat Rock** saw US Top 10 breakthrough, while in Britain they remain the most popular of the 1976 new wave/punk pioneers. Most recently supported several dates on Who's(▶) 1982 'Farewell' Tour of US; accused by some of selling out, shows nevertheless exposed Clash to more diverse US audience.

Current line-up: Strummer; Simonon; Jones; Peter Howard, drums.

Hit Singles:	US	UK
Tommy Gun, 1978	—	19
London Calling, 1979	—	11
Bank Robber, 1980	—	12
Should I Stay Or Should I Go Straight To Hell, 1982	—	17
Rock The Casbah, 1982	15	30

Below: Survivors of the London punk movement, the Clash.

Albums:
The Clash (Columbia/CBS), 1977
Give 'Em Enough Rope (Columbia/CBS), 1978
London Calling (Columbia/CBS), 1979
Sandinista (Columbia/CBS), 1980
Combat Rock (Columbia/CBS), 1982

Jimmy Cliff

Jamaican vocalist, composer.
Born James Chambers, St Catherine, Jamaica, 1948.

Career: Dropped out of college and moved to Kingston in search of music stardom in 1962. Career began to move forward after meeting ace producer Leslie Kong; **Hurricane Hattie** became local hit.

While touring US in 1964 Cliff met Island Records boss Chris Blackwell who persuaded him to try his luck in UK. In 1969 Cliff had hit with **Wonderful World, Beautiful People,** which also made Top 30 in US. Next year consolidated success with version of Cat Stevens' **Wild World**.

Sandanista, the Clash. Courtesy Columbia/CBS Records.

With two hits under his belt and other artists like the Pioneers and Desmond Dekker recording his material, '70s opened hopefully for Cliff. Nevertheless, artist never seemed to find direction. First LP of decade was **Another Cycle**, a non-reggae album which was not strong enough for soul audiences. Next step was starring role in Perry Henzell's movie, 'The Harder They Come'. Film was a major success in Jamaica and critical success everywhere, but failed to make commerical impact worldwide. Soundtrack album was probably best ever reggae compilation, with Cliff well to the fore, but again did not register major sales.

In 1973 Cliff left Island and embarked on series of albums that never quite lived up to early promise. Attempting too many styles and falling between too many stools, Cliff never managed to broaden his loyal following. To date, his finest moment was probably **The Harder They Come,** but his undoubted talent may well still bring him to the forefront of today's music scene.

Hit Singles:	US	UK
Wonderful World, Beautiful People, 1969	25	6
Wild World, 1970	—	8

Albums:
Another Cycle (—/Island), 1971
The Harder They Come (Mango/Island), 1972
Unlimited (—/EMI), 1973
Strugglin' Man (Mango/Island), 1974
House Of Exile (—/EMI), 1974
Brave Warrior (—/EMI), 1975
Best Of (—/Island), 1976
Follow My Mind (—/Reprise), 1976
Oh Jamaica (—/EMI), 1976
In Concert—Best Of Jimmy Cliff (Reprise), 1976
Jimmy Cliff (—/Island), 1977
Give Thanx (Warner Bros), 1978
I Am The Living (Warner Bros/MCA), 1980
Give The People What They Want (Warner Bros/MCA), 1981
Special (Columbia/CBS), 1982

George Clinton

US composer, producer, vocalist.
Born Blainfield, Ohio, July 22, 1940.

Career: The mastermind behind the P.Funk(▶) organisation, George Clinton brought fantasy into realms of funk via his various acts: Parliament, Funkadelic, Parlet, the Brides Of Funkenstein, et al.

Parliament were founded in Detroit in mid-'50s as doo-wop group. Had releases on ABC and New, and cut un-released sides for Motown. Had no sucess until catchy soul efforts **(I Wanna) Testify** and **All Your Goodies Are Gone** for local Revilot label in 1967.

By 1969, Clinton and cohorts had evolved Funkadelic as alter-ego for Parliament, carrying music into more progressively orientated vein. Contracts with Westbound (as Funkadelic) and Invictus (1971-72), then Casablanca (as Parliament), made room for prolific output.

Despite bizarre nature of much material, commercial success was attained, notably with Parliament's **Up For The Down Stroke** (1975) and Funkadelic's **One Nation Under A Groove** (1975).

Clad in futuristic space-age clothes and sporting all manner of strange accessories (emphasis on glitter and sparkle), Clinton plus motley crew of nearly 40 singers and musicians entered '80s as the P.Funk All-Stars.

Hit Singles:	US	UK
Parliament:		
(I Wanna) Testify, 1967	20	—
Tear The Roof Off The Sucker (Give Up The Funk), 1976	15	—
Flashlight, 1978	16	6
Funkadelic:		
One Nation Under A Groove—Part One, 1978	28	9

Albums:
Parliament:
Motor Booty Affair (Casablanca), 1978
Funkadelic:
One Nation Under A Groove (Warner Bros), 1978
Uncle Jam Wants You (Warner Bros), 1979
Electric Spanking Of War Babies, (Warner Bros), 1981
Connections And Disconnections (Lax/CBS), 1982
Worth Searching Out:
Free Your Mind And Your Ass Will Follow (Westbound/Pye), 1970
Maggot Brain (Westbound), 1971

Above: James Chambers, better known as Jimmy Cliff.

The Coasters

US vocal group formed 1955.
Original line-up: Carl Gardner; Bobby Nunn; Billy Guy; Leon Hughes.

Career: Legendary vocal quartet who added large dose of fun to classic age of rock 'n' roll. Group have such an involved history that it took whole book ('The Coasters' by Bill Millar) to explain. The legend began in 1949 with Los Angeles group the Robins; they had local R&B hits on Savoy and RCA. Moving to Spark Records, incepted in 1954, scored big with R&B **Smokey Joe's Cafe**. Jerry Leiber and Mike Stoller's material became major factor in Coasters' success.

When Atlantic negotiated for acquisition

The Coasters' Greatest Hits. Courtesy Atco Records.

of Spark, Robins' management didn't approve; Leiber and Stoller persudaded lead voice Carl Gardner and bassman Bobby Nunn to leave group. Joined Billy Guy and Leon Hughes to form Coasters; name derived from their west-coast origins. Debut **Down In Mexico** hit R&B Top 10. String of smash hits followed over next five years, with varying personnel; Nunn and Hughes left, replaced by Cornel Gunter and Will 'Dub' Jones, first session yielding **Yakety Yak,** Coasters' first pop chart topper in summer 1958.

Magical ingredients were Gardner's earthy, good-humoured tenor lead contrasted by Jones' rumbling bass; inventive Leiber/Stoller lyrics were punctuated by King Curtis'(▶) raunchy tenor sax solos and embellished by Mickey Baker's catchy guitar phrases. Songs like **Searching, Charlie Brown, Poison Ivy** and **Little Egypt** are rock 'n' roll classics.

Hits dwindled by late 1961; Cornel Gunter

left, replaced by Earl Carroll from Cadillacs. Standards declined until 1964 when **'Tain't Nothin' To Me,** cut 'live' at the Apollo Theatre, was hit.

Connections with Leiber and Stoller were severed. Final Atco release revived Louis Jordan's jumping **Saturday Night Fish Fry.** In 1967 group signed with Columbia soul subsidiary Date; produced again by Leiber and Stoller in contemporary idiom. **Soul Pad** and **She Can** resulted, artistically excellent but commercial failures. Solitary single appeared on Lloyd's Price's Turntable label in 1969.

In 1971 King Records bought all Date material, did doctoring in studio with overdubs, and hit with group's revival of Clovers' **Love Potion No. 9.** Coasters continue to tour with varying personnel; managed another disc outing in 1976 on Wilson Pickett's Wicked label.

1974 line-up: Gardner; Earl Carroll; Ronnie Bright; Jimmy Norman.

Hit Singles:	US	UK
Searchin'/Young Blood, 1957	3	30
Young Blood/Searchin', 1957	8	—
Yakkety Yak, 1958	1	12
Charlie Brown, 1959	2	6
Along Came Jones, 1959	9	—
Poison Ivy, 1959	7	15

Albums (selected):
Greatest Hits (Atco/London), 1962
Greatest Hits (Power/—), 1979
Greatest Recordings/The Early Years (Atco/Atlantic), 1978
20 Great Originals (—/Atlantic), 1978

Billy Cobham

US drummer, composer, arranger.
Born Panama, May 16, 1944.

Career: New York-raised Cobham gigged with Billy Taylor and New York Jazz Sextet in 1967-68 as well as playing with assorted R&B bands. Joining Miles Davis in 1968, he appeared on three albums before leaving for Dreams, a jazz-rock combo. Became much in demand as a session drummer, working with James Brown(▶), Larry Coryell, Sam and Dave(▶), Herbie Mann(▶) and others. He was then invited by John McLaughlin(▶)—another

former Davis sideman—to join Mahavishnu Orchestra.

First solo album, **Spectrum,** appeared in 1974 and featured rock guitarist Tommy Bolin, winning Cobham crossover appeal. A band based around the Brecker Brothers—a white horn section—gave him three exciting and commercially successful albums **(Crosswinds, Total Eclipse** and **Shabazz).** He then formed new aggregation which included keyboard player George Duke(▶), but with music now showing lack of direction, straddling fields of jazz-funk, rock and disco and failing to please any specific audience, band was short-lived. Return to success came with aptly named **Magic** album (1977).

Above: Premier session-drummer Billy Cobham.

A highly competent and innovative drummer/percussionist with dazzling technique, he has made his name as much through Billy Cobham Drum Clinics held around world, as for recordings. He is also a respected composer/arranger.

Albums:
Spectrum (Atlantic), 1973
Crosswinds (Atlantic), 1974
Live On Tour In Europe (Atlantic), 1976*
Best of (CBS), 1980
*With George Duke

Eddie Cochran

US vocalist, guitarist, composer.
Born Oklahoma City, October 3, 1938;
died April 17, 1960.

Career: Teamed with Hank Cochran (unrelated) as Cochran Brothers in 1954; recorded first single for Ekko label in hillbilly style. Met songwriter (later manager) Jerry Capehart in 1956 and signed to Crest Records in Los Angeles as solo. When first Crest single failed, Capehart negotiated contract with Liberty Records on strength of Cochran's successful audition for appearance in movie 'The Girl Can't Help It'. First Liberty single **Sittin' In The Balcony** became hit, and album that followed revealed soft pop style. Returned, however, to rock 'n' roll with subsequent singles and biggest US hit **Summertime Blues.**

Two further cameo appearances in typical exploitive rock 'n' roll movies failed to capture dynamic stage performance, but nationwide tours soon established Cochran as teen idol. Made first British appearances early in 1960 with Gene Vincent(▶) and popularity in UK much increased by spots on 'Boy Meets Girl' television show and tour of major UK theatres. During tour many British guitarists were influenced by Cochran's individual style and tuning of Gretsch semi-acoustic guitar with humbucker pickup.

Above; Rock'n'Roll legend Eddie Cochran. Died at early age of 22.

Interrupted British tour in April 1960 intending to make brief visit to Los Angeles; died as result of injuries received in car crash when returning to London for flight. Biggest UK hit in May marked beginning of cult following and subsequent releases included material culled from demo sessions and studio jams. Cochran had recorded extensively as solo and as sideman and tapes of hitherto unheard of performances are still being discovered and released.

Cochran's involvement in studio production and arranging (he was first artist to make own demos, and innovated multi-tracking techniques) revealed talents which could hardly have failed to influence popular music had he lived. However, his death did not stop his influence through songs and style which found reflection in New Wave records of '70s, notably the Sex Pistols(▶) covers of **Somethin' Else** and **C'mon Everybody.**

Guitar: Semi-acoustic Gretsch.

Hit Singles:

	US	UK
Sittin' In The Balcony, 1957	18	—
Summertime Blues, 1958	8	18
C'mon Everybody, 1959	35	6
Three Steps To Heaven, 1960	—	1
Weekend, 1961	—	15

Albums:
Memorial Album (Liberty), 1960
C'mon Everybody (—/Sunset), 1970
Legendary Masters (United Artists), 1971
Very Best Of (15th Anniversary), 1975
  Anniversary), 1975
Many Sides Of (—/Rollercoaster), 1979
A Legend In Our Time (Union Pacific), 1979

The Eddie Cochran Singles Album (United Artists), 1979
20th Anniversary Album (—/United Artists), 1980
Gene Vincent & Eddie Cochran—Together Again (Capitol), 1980
Gene Vincent & Eddie Cochran—Rock 'n' Roll Heroes (Rockstar), 1981
Words and Music (Rockstar), (United Artists 1982

Joe Cocker

UK vocalist, composer.
Born Sheffield, May 20, 1944.

Career: 'Blue-eyed soul' exponent Cocker joined brother Victor's Cavaliers skiffle group at 12 as drummer/harmonica player. Became hooked on rock 'n' roll, blues and, especially, music of Ray Charles(▶), on whom he based subsequent vocal style. First pro band was Big Blues, which evolved into Vance Arnold and the Avengers. Cocker was given six months' leave of absence by employers (the gas board), while he worked with band as support act for Rolling Stones(▶), Manfred Mann(▶) and Hollies(▶). Group's debut single, Beatles'(▶) song **I'll Cry Instead,** on Decca (1964), flopped. Cocker went back to work as gas fitter then as packer for magazine distributor before co-writing **Marjorine** with fellow Sheffield musician Chris Stainton; they sent demo to Denny Cordell (producer of Move and Procol Harum), who secured release via Deram.

Cocker and bass player Stainton headed semi-pro Grease Band with Henry McCullough, guitar, Tommy Eyre, keyboards, and Kenny Slade, drums, playing Northern clubs and residency at Sheffield's King Mojo Club.

Recorded limited issue live single for Sheffield University Rag Week. With **Marjorine,** issued under his name, hitting UK Top-50, Cocker moved to London. Follow-up single, a Ray Charles-styled cover of Lennon/McCartney's **With A Little Help From My Friends,** was massive European hit and title cut from debut album. It featured Grease Band plus guest musicians, including Jimmy Page, Stevie Winwood(▶), Albert Lee and Procol Harum's(▶) drummer B.J. Wilson (who

Joe Cocker! Courtesy A&M Records.

later became member of Cocker's touring band).

Success of record, plus appearance at Windsor Jazz and Blues Festival, made international reputation. During 1969 US tour Cocker appeared at Woodstock Festival and met Leon Russell(▶) who co-produced (with Cordell) his second album and hit single **Delta Lady**.

When Grease Band (except Stainton), went own way a year later, Bruce Rowland and Alan Spenner having replaced Eyre and Slade, Russell put together ambitious 40-strong musical entourage under title **Mad Dogs And Englishmen.** Tour yielded double album and movie of same title for Cocker. Excellent single **High Time We Went** made it to No. 22 in US.

Unfortunately, Cocker failed to follow-up on success; though it seemed he was used to handling cigarettes and booze, he couldn't cope with drugs. His hyper-energetic stage performances and emotion-laden recordings contributed to near mental and physical collapse. Became temporary recluse on West Coast at end of Mad Dogs tour, later slipping home to UK to live with parents. Made one fleeting live appearance when called up on-stage by Rita Coolidge(▶) and the Dixie Flyers during their 1971 tour as support to the Byrds(▶).

With help of Stainton, Cocker formed new 12-piece band for 1972 comeback tour of US, Britain and Australia, where he was busted on drugs charge. When band split, Stainton helped his friend put together combination of concert tapes and studio material for **Something To Say** album.

Had 1974 US hit with Billy Preston's(▶) **You Are So Beautiful.** Regular album releases were counterbalanced by repeated on and off-stage traumas and a succession of abortive comeback attempts as major live act. Made guest vocal appearance on Crusaders' Top 100 single **I'm So Glad** (1981).

Cocker's 1982 Island album, **Sheffield Steel,** mixed soul, rock and ballads and following its success Cocker contributed to soundtrack of hit movie 'An Officer And A Gentleman', recording ballad **Up Where We Belong** with Jennifer Warnes for his first US chart-topper. Hopefully, this means a rejuvenated career for a man who has often seemed one of the saddest casualties of rock's pressures.

Hit Singles:

	US	UK
With A Little Help From My Friends, 1968	—	1
Delta Lady, 1969	—	10
The Letter, 1970	7	39
Cry Me A River, 1970	11	—
You Are So Beautiful, 1974	5	—

With Jennifer Warnes:
| Up Where We Belong, 1983 | 1 | 4 |

Below: "Who's nicked me guitar?" Joe Cocker belts it out.

Albums:
With A Little Help From My Friends
(A&M), 1969
Joe Cocker! (A&M), 1970
Mad Dogs And Englishmen (A&M), 1971
I Can Stand A Little Rain (A&M), 1974
Stingray (A&M), 1976
Luxury You Can Afford (Asylum), 1978
Platinum Collection (—/Cube), 1981
Sheffield Steel (Island), 1982
Space Captain (—/Cube), 1982

Leonard Cohen

Canadian composer, vocalist, guitarist.
Born Montreal, September 21, 1934.

Career: After studying English literature at McGill and Columbia Universities, Cohen took up literary career and established reputation in Canada as poet and novelist. Musical experience was limited to playing in square dance group in teens, but he started to set poems to music in mid-twenties. Had little success initially, but eventually Judy Collins(▶) recorded **Suzanne** in 1966 and fostered his musical career.

Signed to Columbia in 1968, he released first album **Songs Of Leonard Cohen.** Very personal, somewhat doom-laden songs, sung in Cohen's flat, droning voice, struck instant chord with bed-sit depressives everywhere. After **Songs From A Room** became equally successful, Cohen began to undertake live appearances in Canada, US and Europe.

Never a prolific recording artist, Cohen released only two albums between 1968 and 1973, one a 'live' collection. 1974 saw move closer to rock direction with **New Skin For The Old Ceremony.** In 1977 Cohen collaborated with legendary producer Phil Spector (▶) on **Death Of A Ladies' Man,** but result did not live up to expectations, including Cohen's.

Recent Songs saw return to atmosphere of his early records; since its release Cohen has kept low profile on musical front.

Hailed in some quarters as major musician-poet, yet often castigated as tedious, pretentious and unmusical, Leonard Cohen has certainly come up with several semi-classics: **Suzanne, So Long Marianne, Hey That's No Way To Say Goodbye.** His sporadic recordings and live appearances will no doubt continue to attract a loyal and devoted audience.

Albums:
The Songs Of Leonard Cohen (Columbia/CBS) 1968
Songs From A Room (Columbia/CBS), 1968
Songs Of Love And Hate (Columbia/CBS), 1970
Live Songs (Columbia/CBS), 1973
New Skin For The Old Ceremony (Columbia/CBS), 1974
Greatest Hits (Columbia/CBS), 1975
Death Of A Ladies' Man (Columbia/CBS), 1977
Recent Songs (Columbia/CBS), 1979

Nat King Cole

US vocalist, pianist, composer.
Born Nathaniel Adams Cole, Montgomery, Alabama, March 17, 1919; died February 15, 1965.

Career: Arguably the first black pop star, Cole made his public debut at the tender age of four, playing piano talent show at Chicago's Regal Theatre. Made recording debut in 1936 as pianist with brother Eddie Cole's band, The Rogues of Rhythm.

Above: "Wake Me When It's Over" — Cohen in concert.

Featuring Oscar Moore, guitar, Wesley Price, bass, and Cole's classy piano stylings, the Nat Cole Swingsters Three (formed 1937) became major force on West Coast jazz scene in '40s, earning Cole name 'King' and securing Capitol Records contract in 1943 (after unsuccessful stint with Decca from 1940). Early instrumental outings gave way to Cole's suave vocal stylings (he didn't start singing until around 1943) and trio disbanded in 1948 when lushly orchestrated **Nature Boy** made Cole solo million-seller. (The trio's own gold record of same year, **Little Girl,** had relied on Cole's vocals for appeal.) **Nature Boy** topped US charts for seven weeks and set pattern for an amazing career which saw total sales of more than 75 million records before Cole died of cancer in 1965.

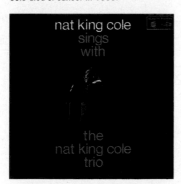

Nat 'King' Cole Sings With The Nat 'King' Cole Trio. Courtesy Capitol Records.

Most of Cole's records, including million-selling **Mona Lisa** (1950), **Too Young** (1951), **Answer Me, My Love,** (1954) and British-written **A Blossom Fell** (1955), were in smooth ballad style. Still, it could be argued that his best record was the soul-flavoured **Let There Be Love,** with a superb piano solo, not, ironically, from his own fingers, but by blind British jazzman George Shearing.

In 1964, Cole appeared in and sang theme for spoof Western 'Cat Ballou.' His first movie appearance was in starring role of legendary blues composer W.C. Handy in 'St Louis Blues'.

Since Cole's death, daughter Natalie has become major soul artist in her own right.

Hit Singles:	US	UK
Forgive My Heart/Someone You Love, 1955	16	*
Dreams Can Tell A Lie, 1956	—	10
Ask Me, 1956	18	—
Too Young To Go Steady, 1956	21	8
That's All There Is To That, 1956	16	—
Love Me As If There Were No Tomorrow, 1956	—	11
Night Lights, 1956	11	—
Ballerina, 1957	18	—
When I Fall In Love, 1957	—	2
Send For Me, 1957	6	—
Looking Back, 1958	5	—
That's You, 1960	—	10
Just As Much As Ever, 1960	—	18
Let There Be Love (with George Shearing), 1962	—	11
Ramblin' Rose, 1962	2	5
Dear Lonely Hearts, 1962	13	37
Those Lazy Hazy Crazy Days Of Summer, 1963	12	—
That Sunday, That Summer, 1963	12	—

Albums (selected):
Trio Days (Capitol/—), N/A
Best Of Volume 1 (Capitol), 1968
Best Of Volume 2 (Capitol), 1970

Judy Collins

US vocalist, composer, guitarist.
Born Denver, Colorado, May 1, 1939.

Career: Born into musical family; first studied classical piano and took up guitar as teenager. Developed interest in folk music and began singing in folk clubs around Colorado in late '50s.

Following move to Chicago, came to attention of Elektra Records and started recording career with **Maid Of Constant Sorrow,** a collection of folk standards. It was followed by similar effort, **Golden Apples Of The Sun,** in 1963.

However, with third album, Collins began to move into different area, drawing on more contemporary repertoire. During whole of '60s she continued to record distinctively personal versions of songs by writers like Leonard Cohen(▶), Joni Mitchell(▶) and

Jacques Brel, and was often first to interpret work of new writers. Landmark came with **Wildflowers,** which included two of her own songs, **Since You've Asked** and **Albatross.** It was also Collins' first gold album.

Always something of a polymath, Collins made acting debut in 1969, in New York production of 'Peer Gynt,' and in early '70s was involved in award-winning documentary film about her former piano teacher Antonia Bricas. Following international hit **Amazing Grace,** Collins began to develop into more commercially orientated artist, drawing on material from writers as diverse as Rogers and Hart, Stephen Sondheim (she enjoyed a mid-'70s hit with his **Send In The Clowns),** the Eagles(▶) and Randy Newman(▶).

Collins continues to record with considerable success, and tours regularly, usually accompanied by small group. During her career she has always been concerned with various political causes, and despite recent softening of musical direction, humanitarian concerns are still represented. A sensitive, many-sided artist she has pursued dignified course through musical changes of two decades.

Hit Singles:	US	UK
Both Sides Now, 1968	8	—
Both Sides Now, 1970	—	14
Amazing Grace, 1970	15	5
Amazing Grace, 1972	—	20
Send In The Clowns, 1975	—	6
Send In The Clowns, 1977	19	—

Albums:
A Maid Of Constant Sorrow (Elektra), 1962
Golden Apples Of The Sun (Elektra), 1963
Judy Collins No. 3 (Elektra), 1963
The Judy Collins Concert (Elektra), 1964
Fifth Album (Elektra), 1965
Wild Flowers (Elektra), 1967
In My Life (Elektra), 1968
Who Knows Where The Time Goes (Elektra), 1968
Recollections (Best Of) (Elektra), 1969
Whales And Nightingales (Elektra), 1971
Living (Elektra), 1972
Colors Of The Day (The Best Of Judy Collins) (Elektra/—), 1972
True Stories And Other Dreams (Elektra), 1973
Judith (Elektra), 1975
Bread And Roses (Elektra), 1976
So Early In Spring (Elektra), 1977
Hard Time For Lovers (Elektra), 1979
Running For My Life (Elektra), 1980
Time Of Our Lives (Elektra), 1982

Phil Collins

UK drummer, vocalist, composer.
Born London, January 31, 1951.

Career: Former child actor—he played the Artful Dodger in stage version of 'Oliver Twist'—Collins joined Genesis(▶) as drummer after stint with Flaming Youth. He was brought forward as vocalist for group's 1976 album **A Trick Of The Tail** which promptly revived their flagging career.

In tandem with work as member of Genesis, Collins has played drums on all but one of six albums released by jazz-rock outfit Brand X.

In February 1981, issued first solo album **Face Value;** shot to top of UK album charts. In totally different musical vein to Genesis, Collins' solo sound got him UK No. 2 hit with **In The Air Tonight.** Then worked reggae backbeat and heavy percussion for compulsive **I Missed Again** hit single; also scored with **If Leaving Me Is Easy.** Magic of Earth Wind And Fire's(▶) brass section, great

Face Value, Phil Collins. Courtesy Virgin Records.

melodic songs and Collins' soul-tinged vocals added up to potent package. Not so inventive, however, was second solo set. Single **You Can't Hurry Love** was straight re-make of Supremes(▶) soul oldie, but it was what public wanted, rocketing to No. 1. Its success was aided by clever promotional video in which Collins appeared as cross between the Supremes and the Blues Brothers(▶).

Hit Singles:

	US	UK
In The Air Tonight, 1981	19	2
I Missed Again, 1981	19	14
If Leaving Me Is Easy, 1981	—	17
You Can't Hurry Love, 1982	10	1

Albums:
Face Value (Atlantic/Virgin), 1981
Hello I Must Be Going (Atlantic/Virgin), 1982

Commander Cody And His Lost Planet Airmen

US group formed 1967.

1971 line-up: George Frayne, piano, vocals; John Tichy, guitar; Andy Stein, fiddle, sax; Billy C. Farlow, harmonica, vocals; 'Buffalo' Bruce Barlow, bass, vocals; Lance Dickerson, drums; The West Virginia Creeper, steel guitar; Bill Kirchen, guitar, vocals.

Career: George Frayne and John Tichy began by entertaining fellow students at University of Michigan in '60s. Their sense of humour was reflected in band names (the Fantastic Surfing Beavers and Lorenzo Lightfoot among others). They were somewhat surprised to find easy stage banter and C&W flavoured songs could keep barrooms entertained. First Stein, then Farlow joined ever changing line-up. Whole conglomeration settled down to nucleus listed above after Bill Kirchen visited West Coast in 1969 and felt band could do well in San Francisco.

Best bar band in town signed contract two years later and released **Lost In The Ozone**. Whether this was really rock'n'roll did not matter: easy-going gait foreshadowed mellow sound of mid-'70s Southern California. Band also hit with cover of old novelty song **Hot Rod Lincoln** in 1972. Bobby Black replaced The West Virginia Creeper on second album and this line-up produced four more albums' worth of lazy jaunts through spaced-out, country-western, truck-drivin' blues.

John Tichy left before 1976 European tour. Gigs from tour made up **We've Got A Live One Here** LP with John Higgenbotham on guitar and Norton Buffalo on horns. Band broke up after tour and Commander signed solo contract deal with Arista.

Lack of response to **Midnight Man** led Frayne to reorganise band (with only Barlow

and Black from old outfit). Using various guest and session artists two more albums appeared on Arista.

Final line-up: Frayne; Barlow; Bobby Black, pedal steel guitar.

Hit Singles:

	US	UK
Hot Rod Lincoln, 1972	9	—

Albums:
Lost In The Ozone (ABC/Paramount), 1971
Hot Licks, Cold Steel And Truckers Favourites (ABC/Paramount), 1972
Country Casanova (ABC/Paramount), 1973
Live From Deep In The Heart Of Texas (ABC/Paramount), 1974
Tales From The Ozone (Warner Bros), 1975
We've Got A Live One Here (Warner Bros), 1976
Rock'n'Roll Again (Arista), 1977
Flying Dreams (Arista), 1978
Lose It Tonight (Peter Pan/—), 1981

George Frayne Solo:
Midnight Man (Arista), 1977

Commodores

US group formed 1960s.

Original line-up: Lionel Richie, vocals, tenor saxophone; William King, trumpet; Thomas McClary, guitar; Milan Williams, keyboards.

Career: Original four were school-friends in Tuskegee, Alabama; formed Commodores after merger of two other school groups, Mystics and Jays. With two additional musicians played local gigs and gained strong reputation.

Eventually signed management deal with Benjamin Ashburn who secured band New York gigs. At one of these, Commodores were spotted by Suzanne DePasse, Motown vice-president; result was support spot on Jackson Five(▶) worldwide tour. In 1972, band signed contract with Motown; two latest recruits had by this time moved on and been replaced by drummer and vocalist Walter 'Clyde' Orange and bass player Ronald LaPread.

Zoom, the Commodores. Courtesy Motown Records.

After three singles had made impact on soul market, simple but effective instrumental **Machine Gun** became hit on both sides of Atlantic. This and another single, **Do The Bump**, helped **Machine Gun** LP to eventual gold status. Following initial success band toured with Rolling Stones(▶) and Stevie Wonder(▶).

From that time Commodores diversified material; **Sweet Love,** from 1975 album **Movin' On,** was melodic ballad, and showed direction in which writer Lionel Richie(▶) would lead group.

By late '70s group were a headlining international act, shipping platinum with every album. Band had also made impact with

Above: The electric combination of Ry Cooder and his Fender Stratocaster.

appearance in disco film 'Thank God It's Friday' with Donna Summer(▶); but high spot was 1978 single **Three Times A Lady.** Beautiful Richie-composed song went double platinum in US and became biggest-ever Motown single in UK; also gained numerous songwriting awards.

In '80s, band maintained impact—the only black acts to equal them in popular appeal being Earth, Wind and Fire(▶) and Hot Chocolate(▶). Lionel Richie, following massive international hit with Diana Ross(▶) with movie theme **Endless Love,** split to pursue successful solo career. It remains to be seen whether Commodores can sustain impetus without their talented writer and frontman.

Current line-up: King; McClary; Williams; Walter 'Clyde' Orange, drums, vocals; Ronald La Pread, bass.

Hit Singles:

	US	UK
Machine Gun, 1974	22	20
Slippery When Wet, 1975	19	—
Sweet Love, 1976	5	—
Easy, 1977	4	9
Brickhouse/Sweet Love, 1977	5	32
Three Times A Lady, 1978	1	1
Just To Be Close To You, 1978	7	—
Sail On, 1979	4	8
Still, 1979	1	4
Old Fashioned Love, 1980	20	—
Lady (You Bring Me Up), 1981	8	56
Oh No, 1981	4	44

Albums:
Machine Gun (Motown), 1974
Caught In The Act (Motown), 1975
Movin' On (Motown), 1975
Hot On The Tracks (Motown), 1976
Commodores* (Motown), 1977
Live (Motown), 1978
Natural High (Motown), 1978
Greatest Hits (Motown), 1978
Midnight Magic (Motown), 1979
Heroes (Motown), 1980
In The Pocket (Motown), 1981
All The Greatest Hits (Motown), 1982
*Titled **Zoom** in UK.

Ry Cooder

US guitarist, vocalist, producer, arranger. Born Los Angeles, March 15, 1947.

Career: Former session player (predominantly slide guitar, also mandolin); one-time member of Taj Mahal(▶) and Captain Beefheart(▶) bands. Now fronts formidable R&B group consisting of keyboard players Jim Dickenson and William D. Smith, bass guitarist Tim Drummond, drummer Jim Keltner, percussionist Baboo and vocalists Bobby King, Willie Greene and Herman Johnson.

Worked on film scores 'Candy' and 'Performances' (which starred Mick Jagger) and made notable contribution to Rolling Stones'(▶) **Let It Bleed** album. Other sessions include Marc Benno, Crazy Horse(▶), Randy Newman(▶), John Sebastian(▶) and Maria Muldaur(▶).

First solo LP **Ry Cooder** released by Reprise in 1970. Established Cooder's mean bottle-neck guitar style and strangled, authentic R&B vocalising. Has run entire musical heritage of America with more than a smattering of cajun and country, '20s and '30s swing (**Jazz**), eclectic (**Chicken Skin Music**), down-home R&B (**Borderline**) and further soundtrack albums (**The Long Riders, Southern Comfort** and **The Border**).

Borderline, Ry Cooder. Courtesy Warner Bros Records. The versatile Ry Cooder has experimented with Cajun, country, R&B, swing, and even rock.

Cooder's work has never fallen into rock mainstream, and this has prevented permanent niche in upper reaches of album charts. Concerts, however, are a different matter, with Cooder now established as major stage performer, particularly in Britain; on bi-annual pilgrimage plays to capacity audiences.

True spirit of R&B is deeply implanted in this multi-talented veteran, and never better expounded than on Jimmy Reed's(▶) **How Can A Poor Man Stand Such Times And Live** from live **Show Time** album.

Guitars: Various Fenders, primarily 1968 Stratocaster, Washburn solid-body electric, Martin and Ovation acoustics; also Gibson F-style mandolin.

The Long Riders Soundtrack, Ry Cooder. Courtesy Warner Bros Records.

Albums:
Ry Cooder (Reprise) 1970
Into The Purple Valley (Reprise), 1971
Boomer's Story (Reprise), 1972
Paradise And Lunch (Reprise), 1974
Chicken Skin Music (Warner Bros), 1976
Show Time (Warner Bros), 1977*
Jazz (Warner Bros), 1978
Bop Till You Drop (Warner Bros), 1979
Borderline (Warner Bros), 1980
The Long Riders (Warner Bros), 1980**
Southern Comfort (Warner Bros), 1981**
The Border (Warner Bros), 1982**
The Slide Area (Warner Bros), 1982
* Live
** Soundtracks

Sam Cooke
US vocalist, composer.
Born Chicago, Illinois, January 22, 1931; died December 11, 1964.

Career: Influential black performer/writer whose songs and vocal style have remained in vogue over three decades. Originally member of Soul Stirrers gospel group, Cooke turned to secular music in late '50s.

First hit **You Send Me** (1957) was followed by classics **Only Sixteen, Wonderful World, Cupid, Bring It On Home To Me** and **A Change Is Gonna Come**. He started own label Sar in 1960, recording Sims Twins,

Twistin' The Night Away, Sam Cooke. Courtesy Everest Records.

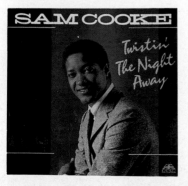

Johnnie Taylor, and the Valentinos.

Under aegis of Hugo & Luigi (who later groomed the Stylistics(▶)), Cooke remained chart-bound until his untimely demise: he was shot by a woman in December 1964, after entering wrong motel room. The courts ruled the shooting 'justifiable homicide'.

Cooke is still considered the definitive soul vocalist some 20 years after his death. His phrasing and articulation may never be surpassed. His material has since been recorded by Aretha Franklin(▶), Otis Redding(▶), Dawn, Rod Stewart(▶) and countless others.

Hit Singles: US UK
You Send Me/Summertime, 1957 1 29
(I Love You) For Sentimental Reasons, 1958 17 —
I'll Come Running Back To You, 1958 18 —
Only Sixteen, 1959 28 13
Wonderful World, 1960 12 27
Chain Gang, 1960 2 9
Cupid, 1961 17 7
Twistin' The Night Away, 1962 9 6
Having A Party, 1962 17 —
Bring It On Home To Me, 1963 10 23
Nothing Can Change This Love, 1962 12 —
Another Saturday Night, 1963 10 23
Frankie And Johnny, 1963 14 30
Send Me Some Lovin', 1963 13 —
Little Red Rooster, 1963 11 —
Good News, 1964 11 —
Good Times, 1964 11 —
Shake, 1965 7 —

Albums:
Twistin' The Night Away (RCA), 1961
Best Of (RCA/—), 1961
Golden Age Of (RCA/—), 1969
Two Sides Of (Specialty/Sonet), 1971
This Is Sam Cooke (RCA), 1971
When I Fall In Love (—/EMI), 1979
Mr Soul (—/RCA), 1980

Rita Coolidge
US vocalist.
Born Nashville, Tennessee, May 1, 1944.

Career: Daughter of Baptist minister, sang in church choirs from early age. While studying at Florida State University formed band called RC and the Moonpies; eventually dropped out of college to pursue musical career.

Following family move to Memphis, Rita and sister Priscilla started doing radio jingles. Priscilla met and married Booker T. of Booker T and the MG's(▶), while Rita moved to Los Angeles where she met Delaney and Bonnie(▶).

Rita toured and recorded with Delaney and Bonnie as one of Friends' entourage. After operation folded, Rita and most of other Friends joined infamous Joe Cocker(▶)/Leon Russell(▶) package Mad Dogs And Englishmen.

Having become in-demand session singer, Coolidge released first solo album on A&M in 1971, following it with series of albums that combined elements of rock, country and easy listening.

In meantime, Coolidge had met Kris Kristofferson(▶). She married him in 1973, and for several years pair ran their careers in tandem, making several albums as duo and appearing together in concert.

Although steady seller, Coolidge did not have major record success until 1977 and release of **Anytime, Anywhere.** Album spawned hits, notably Boz Scaggs(▶)-penned **We're All Alone,** and established artist as major international attraction. Unfortunately professional success was not reflected in

personal life, as marriage to Kristofferson broke up at this time.

Since then Coolidge has maintained position as classy MOR/rock singer, her dark good looks being no hindrance to her career. Although not major talent, Coolidge uses her mellifluous voice to good effect and generally chooses worthwhile material. Most recently she sang theme to James Bond movie 'Octopussy'.

Hit Singles: US UK
We're All Alone, 1977 7 6
(Your Love Has Lifted Me)
Higher And Higher, 1977 2 48
The Way You Do The Things You Do, 1978 20 —

Albums:
Rita Coolidge (A&M), 1971
Nice Feeling' (A&M), 1971
The Lady's Not For Sale (A&M), 1972
Fall Into Spring (A&M), 1974
It's Only Love (A&M), 1975
Anytime, Anywhere (A&M), 1977
Love Me Again (A&M), 1978
Satisfied (A&M), 1979
Heartbreak Radio (A&M), 1981
The Very Best Of (—/A&M), 1981

With Kris Kristofferson:
(See separate entry.)

Alice Cooper
US vocalist, composer.
Born Vincent Furnier, Detroit, Michigan, February 4, 1948.

Career: Raised in Phoenix, Arizona. Formed first band at high school, which performed variously as Spiders, Earwigs, Nazz. Members included Glen Buxton (guitar), Michael Bruce (guitar, keyboards), Dennis Dunaway (bass), and Neal Smith (drums). Recorded locally with minor success.

After move to Los Angeles, group changed name to Alice Cooper. Signed to Frank Zappa's Straight label in 1969 by manager Shep Gordon. Debut LP **Pretties For You** released 1969.

After running up massive debts, outfit shifted to Detroit, working under aegis of Bob Ezrin. First album produced by Ezrin **Love It To Death** earned group instant credibility, and first chart single **I'm 18.**

As a live act, Alice Cooper's (his name alone attracted enough attention) bizarre antics disguised mediocrity of performance. Nevertheless, band was now on frontline of rock scene; scored further chart successes including million-selling **School's Out.**

Above: Vincent Furnier, aka Alice Cooper.

1974 saw wholesale change of group personnel; Cooper recruited former Lou Reed(▶) sidemen Dick Wagner (guitar), Prakash John (bass), Steve Hunter (guitar), Whitney (Panti) Glan (drums), and Josef Chirowski (keyboards) (later replaced by Fred Mandel).

Last major tour undertaken in 1975 after release of **Welcome To My Nightmare.** Cooper's long-term drink problem caused period of inactivity. Had re-think in face of developing punk scene (which made band's formerly outrageous tactics seem about as revolutionary as a Pat Boone concert).

Cooper re-surfaced in 1982 with new band and album, **Special Forces,** turning the rock clock back 10 years.

Hit Singles: US UK
School's Out, 1972 7 —
Only Women Bleed, 1975 12 —
I Never Cry, 1976 12 —
You And Me, 1977 9 —
How You Gonna See Me Now, 1978 12 —

Albums:
Love It To Death (Warner Bros), 1971
Killer (Warner Bros), 1971
School's Out (Warner Bros), 1972
Billion Dollar Babies (Warner Bros), 1973
Greatest Hits (Warner Bros), 1974
Welcome To My Nightmare (ATCO/Anchor), 1974
Goes To Hell (Warner Bros), 1976
Lace And Whiskey (Warner Bros), 1977
Alice Cooper Show (Warner Bros), 1977
From The Inside (Warner Bros), 1978
Flush The Fashion (Warner Bros), 1980
Special Forces (Warner Bros), 1981
Zipper Catches Skin (Warner Bros), 1982

Below: A very satisfied lady, Rita Coolidge.

Larry Coryell

US guitarist, composer.
Born Galveston, Texas, April 2, 1943.

Career: Spirited self-taught jazz guitarist who has flirted with jazz rock, fusion and hard rock. Staccato solos burst from his exemplary technique, which has received acclaim from contemporaries.

He worked in several groups, notably with Chico Hamilton, Gary Burton and Herbie Mann, and has recorded with John McLaughlin(▶), Chick Corea, Steve Kahn, Jack Bruce(▶), Steve Gadd and Tony Williams. Own units have been Free Spirits (mid-'60s), Foreplay (early '70s), and 11th House (formed 1973).

Coryell's insistence on moving in and out of conventional jazz framework has made him less commerically acceptable than other less talented guitarists.

Guitars: Hagstrom, Gibson.

Albums:
Larry Coryell (Vanguard), 1969
Coryell (Vanguard), 1970
Barefoot Boy (Vanguard/Philips), 1972
Spaces (with John McLaughlin) (Vanguard), 1974
Introducing 11th House (Vanguard), 1974
At Village Gate (Vanguard), 1975
Restful Mind (Vanguard), 1975
Essential (Vanguard), 1975
Planet End (Vanguard), 1976
Level One (Arista), 1976
Aspects (Arista), 1976
Back Together Again (with Alphonse Mouzon) (Atlantic), 1977
11th House At Montreux (Vanguard), 1978
Return (Vanguard), 1980
Standing Ovation (Arista), 1981

With Philip Catherine:
Twin House (Atlantic), 1977
Splendid (Atlantic), 1978

Elvis Costello

UK composer, vocalist, guitarist.
Born Declan McManus, London, August 25, 1954.

Career: After unsuccessful early career in pub/country-rock band Hip City, Costello (son of erstwhile Joe Loss Band singer Ross McManus) took demo tapes in 1976 to then fledgling Stiff label. Jake Riviera was impressed enough not only to sign Declan, but also to manage him. With name change to Elvis Costello, first three singles built strong cult following, and debut LP reached UK Top 20, backing provided by San Francisco band Clover, performing under name of the Shamrocks.

June 1977 saw formation of permanent backing group, the Attractions. Pete Thomas (drums, ex-Chilli Willi), Bruce Thomas (bass, ex-Quiver) and Steve Nieve (keyboards, ex-Royal Academy of Music). Elvis and band toured with first Stiff Records package along with Ian Dury(▶) Nick Lowe(▶) (who had produced all Costello records up to this point), Dave Edmunds(▶) and Wreckless Eric—concurrently scored first Top 20 hit with **Watching The Detectives.**

By early 1978 had made major US impact; moved with Riviera and Lowe to newly formed Radar label; three Top 30 hits followed in 1978, plus second acclaimed album; third LP released during first days of 1979. Biggest UK hit so far was **Oliver's Army;** 1979 also saw production of first LP by the Specials(▶) and collapse of Radar Records. Riviera subsequently set up new F-Beat label, launched

with Top 5 Costello single, **I Can't Stand Up For Falling Down** (cover of ancient Sam & Dave song). Made further hit singles (although smaller successes) during 1980, plus classic LP **Get Happy.**

1981 chiefly notable for release of Billy Sherrill-produced country LP **Almost Blue,** which polarised fans. Played concert at Royal Albert Hall with Royal Philharmonic Orchestra at start of 1982. Rest of year saw return to original abrasive style—thoughtful, meaningful, but often bitter songs—with **Imperial Bedroom** LP. Prospects of Beatlesque success have probably disappeared, but Elvis (an inspired choice of pseudonym) looks likely to enjoy similar status to that of Bob Dylan(▶)

Imperial Bedroom, Elvis Costello.
Courtesy F-Beat Records.

(prior to his religious conversion). In mid-1983, released single under name of The Imposter, while F-Beat negotiated to change distribution deal. Single charted despite being available for only very limited period.

Guitar: Fender Jaguar.

Hit Singles:	US	UK
Watching The Detectives, 1977	—	15
(I Don't Want To Go To) Chelsea, 1977	—	16
Oliver's Army, 1979	—	2
I Can't Stand Up For Falling Down, 1980	—	4
Good Year For The Roses, 1981	—	6

Albums:
My Aim Is True (Columbia/Stiff), 1977
This Year's Model (Columbia/F-Beat), 1978
Armed Forces (Columbia/Radar), 1979
Get Happy (Columbia/F-Beat), 1980

Trust (Columbia/F-Beat), 1981
Almost Blue (Columbia/F-Beat), 1981
Imperial Bedroom (Columbia/F-Beat), 1982

John Cougar

US vocalist, composer.
Born John Mellencamp, Seymour, Indiana.

Career: Married at 17, a father at 19, Mellencamp worked at various jobs before launching himself into music scene in 1975. On strength of demo tapes, was signed by Tony De Fries—then David Bowie's(▶) manager—who renamed him Johnny Cougar and signed him to MCA. First album **Chestnut Street Incident** combined new tracks with raw demos; split from De Fries swiftly followed.

Cougar then met up with Billy Gaff (then Rod Stewart's(▶) manager), head of Riva Records. Signed to Riva, Cougar achieved some impact with album **A Biography,** which yielded international chart single in **I Need A Lover,** and follow-up **Nothin' Matters And What If It Did,** which made US Top 50. Latter also provided two Top 40 singles, **This Time** and **Ain't Even Done With The Night.**

Steve Cropper produced **Nothin' Matters,** but Cougar decided that time had come to take full musical control. With Don Gehman

Above: John Cougar, a scruffy superstar for the '80s, came to fame in 1982, largely due to MTV airplay.

co-producing, put together **American Fool;** album became one of the sensations of 1982, reaching No. 1 and achieving platinum status. Three singles which all received heavy MTV airplay were also hugely successful.

In meantime, Cougar had been touring regularly with band the Zones, and established himself as good live attraction. His music has wide appeal for rock and pop audiences, combining melodic sense, macho/boyish image, modicum of intelligence and evocative, quintessentially American lyrics. Rock star who is tailor-made for '80s, at time of writing Cougar has yet to make major impact in UK.

Hit Singles:	US	UK
Ain't Even Done With The Night, 1981	17	—
Hurt So Good, 1982	2	—
Jack And Diane, 1982	1	25
Hand To Hold On To, 1983	3	—

Albums:
A Biography (Riva), 1978
John Cougar (Riva), 1979
Nothin' Matters And What If It Did (Riva), 1980
American Fool (Riva), 1982

Below: The Imposter, alias Elvis Costello and his band the Attractions.

Crazy Horse

US group formed 1968.

Original line-up: Billy Talbot, bass; Ralph Molina, drums; Danny Whitten, vocals, guitar.

Career: Formed on the West Coast, group first attracted interest when they backed Neil Young(▶) on his solo album **Everybody Knows This Is Nowhere.** Also acclaimed as live act supporting Young.

Released first album **Crazy Horse** (1971) as group (on Young's label, Reprise), joined by Jack Nitzsche, keyboards, vocals, and Nils Lofgren(▶), guitar, vocals. Cut three more albums which excited critics, but not record buyers; broke up in discouragement when guitarist Whitten died of drug overdose.

Re-formed in 1975, with Frank Sampedro on guitar, to support Neil Young on excellent **Tonight's The Night;** the album was dedicated to Whitten.

Band continued to tour and record backing Young; their work on his **Zuma** album is particularly effective. In 1977, with Karl Himmell, drums, Tim Drummond, bass, Ben Keith, guitar, dobro, and Sampedro, they signed with RCA and released **Crazy Moon,** another highly praised non-seller.

Current line-up: Talbot; Molina; Tim Drummond, bass; Ben Keith, guitar, dobro; Frank Sampedro, guitar; Joe Lala, percussion; Bruce Palmer, bass.

Worth Searching Out:
Crazy Horse (Reprise), 1971
Crazy Moon (RCA), 1977

Randy Crawford

US vocalist, composer.
Born Macon, Georgia, 1952.

Career: Prime claimant to title 'Queen of '80s Soul', Randy Crawford manages to mix deep-soul stylings of South with urban disco-slant.

Raised in Cincinnati, Ohio, grounded in gospel, she became regular night club performer from 15. During school holidays she had two-week gig in St Tropez, France, which was extended to three months and brought record deal offers, but she returned to US to complete education and take six-night-a-week stint at Cincinnati's Buccaneer Club.

On graduation, moved to New York where she sang with George Benson(▶) before signing with Cannonball Adderley's manager John Levy and guesting on Adderley's final album **Big Man.**

Shifting base to Los Angeles, Randy appeared before capacity 5,500 audience at Shrine Auditorium as part of World Jazz Association all-star package in tribute concert to Adderley who had just died. Show was taped and some of her set was used on her 1980s' Warner Bros album, **Everything Must Change,** acceptance of which led to formation of own five-piece band.

First writer credit came with **I Got Myself A Happy Song** on second album **Raw Silk** (1979).

Though uncredited on label, Randy was chosen to sing vocal on titletrack of Crusaders' (▶) **Street Life** album, a transatlantic hit which established her reputation. Subsequently she undertook two successful European tours with Crusaders, who became involved with producing **Now We May Begin** set, star cut of which was haunting Joe Sample ballad **One Day I'll Fly Away**, Crawford's first major hit single (winning her

Most Outstanding Performance award at 1980 Tokyo Music Festival).

Veteran West Coast producer Tommy LiPuma came in for **Secret Combination** LP from which **You Might Need Somebody** was perfect sample of her wistful and soul-searching style.

Though lacking raw power of Etta James or Aretha Franklin(▶), or pure commericalism of Diana Ross(▶), Randy Crawford has displayed rare penchant for understated performances which nevertheless wring last drop of emotion from a song.

Hit Singles:

	US	UK
Street Life (featured vocalist with Crusaders), 1979	36	5
One Day I'll Fly Away, 1980	—	2
You Might Need Somebody, 1981	—	11
Rainy Night In Georgia, 1981	—	18

Albums:

Miss Randy Crawford (Warner Bros), 1977
Raw Silk (Warner Bros), 1979
Now We May Begin (Warner Bros), 1980
Everything Must Change (Warner Bros), 1980
Secret Combination (Warner Bros), 1981
Windsong (Warner Bros), 1982

Cream

UK group formed 1966.

Original/final line-up: Eric Clapton, guitar; Jack Bruce, vocals, bass; Ginger Baker, drums.

Career: Clapton(▶), previously with John Mayall's Bluesbreakers(▶), joined forces with former Graham Bond Organization sidemen Bruce(▶) and Baker(▶) with object of forming blues supergroup. Immediate acclaim followed first gig at 1966 Windsor Festival.

First album, **Fresh Cream,** revealed winning format of blues-influenced songs plus extended improvised solos. Group also had ability to come up with hit singles, and during just over two years of existence scored with handful of unusual but effective cuts.

From 1967, however, band spent most of time in US where they had quickly gained huge reputation. Every Cream album exceeded sales of one million dollars, and gigs

Below: Southern soulstress Randy Crawford is quickly assuming 'Queen of R&B' mantle.

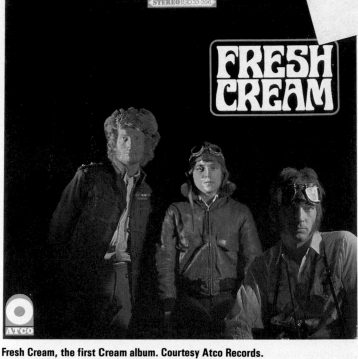

STEREO SD33-206

Fresh Cream, the first Cream album. Courtesy Atco Records.

throughout country were standing room only.

In 1968, however, members decided that outfit had run its course, and in autumn played farewell concert at London's Royal Albert Hall. Shortly afterwards recorded last album, **Goodbye.**

Although somewhat given to overstatement, especially in live context—thunderous volume and seemingly endless solos being order of day—Cream were highly influential band; they set pattern for 'power trio' format, later endlessly copied by generally lesser talents. Group also acted as springboard to superstardom for Clapton, and to lesser extent for other members. Immediately following demise of band Clapton and Baker became involved in short-lived Blind Faith(▶), while Bruce took up solo career.

Hit Singles:

	US	UK
I Feel Free, 1966	—	11
Strange Brew, 1967	—	17
Sunshine Of Your Love, 1968	5	25
White Room, 1968	6	28
Badge, 1969	60	18

Albums:

Fresh Cream (RSO/Polydor), 1966
Disraeli Gears (RSO/Polydor), 1967
Wheels Of Fire (RSO/Polydor), 1968
Goodbye (RSO/Polydor), 1969
Cream Live (RSO/Polydor), 1970
Cream Live 2 (RSO/Polydor), 1972
Off The Top (RSO/—), 1972
Heavy Cream (RSO/Polydor), 1973
Cream (—/Polydor), 1975
Cream Volume 2 (—/RSO), 1978
Original version of Fresh Cream on Atco has more tracks.

Creedence Clearwater Revival

US group, formed 1967.

Original line-up: John Fogerty, vocals, guitar; Tom Fogerty, rhythm guitar; Stu Cook, bass; Doug 'Cosmo' Clifford, drums.

Career: While attending junior high school in San Francisco Bay area of El Cerritto, foursome got together as Tommy Fogerty and the Blue Velvets. Locally based Fantasy Records offered recording deal on proviso that band changed name to the Golliwogs (in attempt to cash-in on then current British beat boom). Band reluctantly agreed and debut single was released in 1965. Further singles followed but none made impact except local hit **Brown Eyed Girl.** Group evolved new 'swamp rock' style based on mixture of R&B and cajun rhythms. They persuaded label's new boss Saul Zaentz to agree to change of name to Creedence Clearwater Revival.

New sound and image coincided with San Francisco rock music explosion. Band's eponymous debut album, a mix of rock 'n' roll/R&B standards and John Fogerty originals, made immediate impression. Two singles were lifted simultaneously. A version of Dale Hawkins' oldie **Suzie Q** registered first in charts then classy reading of Screamin' Jay Hawkins' **I Put A Spell On You** also scored.

Group's albums were essentially collections of potential hits and CCR went against then current trend by remaining singles-orientated. John Fogerty-penned **Proud Mary** became instant rock/soul standard, eliciting superb cover versions by Solomon Burke, Arif Mardin,

Ike and Tina Turner(▶) and others. Checkmates Limited's version of song (masterminded by Phil Spector) was reputed to be most expensively produced single ever, several hundred musicians having been used on sessions.

Despite CCR's San Francisco origins, their spiritual home was deep in bayou country of the Southern states. Their songs like **Bad Moon Rising, Lodi, Born On The Bayou** and **Green River** were epics of swamp rock genre.

Fifth CCR album **Cosmo's Factory** included three gold singles (**Travellin' Band, Up Around The Bend** and **Lookin' Out My Back Door**) plus incisive 11-minute version of Marvin Gaye(▶)/Gladys Knight and the Pips'(▶) Motown classic **I Heard It Through The Grapevine.**

Produced, arranged and largely written by John Fogerty, CCR's music was amazingly tight. It relied almost entirely on band's own integral musicianship rather than depending on studio over-dubs (aside from occasional addition of saxophone). Musical togetherness was not matched on personal front, however. Tom Fogerty quit following differences with others. They continued as trio for world tour which yielded **Creedence—Live In Europe** album.

John Fogerty's increasing dominance caused further dissension. In what has come to be known as 'Fogerty's Revenge', he allowed Cook and Clifford equal creative participation in **Mardi Gras** album. Result was total disaster, lambasted by critics and leading to band's dissolution in October 1972.

Tom Fogerty went on to record moderately successful albums and his **Joyful Resurrection** single, cut with Cook and Clifford, was, he said, the story of CCR.

Cosmo's Factory, Creedence Clearwater Revival. Courtesy Fantasy Records.

Clifford's solo outing was far less satisfactory. He continued working with Cook, however, as respected session rhythm team. They went on to join the Don Harrison Band.

Meanwhile, John Fogerty made low-key solo debut with **Blue Ride Rangers** album; he claimed it was made by group of that name but LP proved to be all his own work: he arranged, produced, played all instruments and sang. His re-make of Hank Williams'(▶) country oldie **Jambalaya** was US hit, as was version of **Hearts Of Stone.**

Protracted dispute with Fantasy Records caused three-year gap before he emerged with new Asylum deal, Top 30 hit single **Rockin' All Over The World** (covered in UK by Dave Edmunds)(▶) and applauded **John Fogerty** album. It was again strictly a solo effort but very much in CCR vein.

Final line-up: John Fogerty; Cook; Clifford.

Hit Singles:	US	UK
Suzie Q (Part 1), 1968	11	—
Proud Mary, 1969	2	8
Bad Moon Rising, 1969	2	1
Green River, 1969	2	19

Above: Creedence Clearwater Revival, the boys with the bayou sound.

Down On The Corner/Fortunate Son, 1969	3	31
Fortunate Son/Down On The Corner, 1969	14	—
Travellin' Band/Who'll Stop The Rain, 1970	2	8
Who'll Stop The Rain/Travellin' Band, 1970	13	—
Up Around The Bend, 1970	4	3
Lookin' Out My Back Door, 1970	2	—
Have You Ever Seen The Rain, 1971	8	36
Sweet Hitchhiker, 1971	6	36

Albums:
Creedence Clearwater Revival (Fantasy), 1968
Bayou Country (Fantasy), 1969
Green River (Fantasy), 1969
Willie And The Poor Boys (Fantasy), 1969
Cosmo's Factory (Fantasy), 1970
Pendulum (Fantasy), 1971
Mardi Gras (Fantasy), 1972
Gold (Fantasy), 1972
More Gold (Fantasy), 1973
Live In Europe (Fantasy), 1973
Golliwogs (Fantasy), 1975.

John Fogerty Solo:
John Fogerty (Asylum), 1975

Worth Searching Out:
Tom Fogerty:
Tom Fogerty (Fantasy), 1972
John Fogerty:
Blue Ridge Rangers (Fantasy), 1973
Doug Clifford:
Doug 'Cosmo' Clifford (Fantasy), 1972

Marshall Crenshaw

US composer, vocalist, guitarist.
Born Detroit, Michigan, 1954.

Career: First heard live rock 'n' roll when parents took him to shows and concerts. Detroit was source of great rock and soul throughout '60s and young Crenshaw absorbed it all.

During teens played guitar in typical high-school 'copy' band. In 1976 won role of John Lennon(▶) in road show of 'Beatlemania'. Soon began to write prolifically; three songs were recorded by Robert Gordon, whose single of Crenshaw's **Someday Someway** was minor hit and brought Crenshaw favourable attention.

Small independent record company Shake signed him, and recorded what is now collector's item **Something's Gonna Happen/She Can't Dance.** On strength of this cut was signed to Warner Bros; first album, produced by Richard Gottehrer, was extraordinarily successful.

LP consisted of ten original songs, one

collaboration and one cover (**Soldier Of Love,** first recorded by Arthur Alexander, later performed by Beatles but never recorded by them); music critics had to brush up their adjectives; most of them described album's sound as bright, fresh and sparkling. Crenshaw's three-piece band (brother Robert, drums; Chris Donato, bass) handled everything with style (with no assistance from session players).

Guitar: Fender Stratocaster, Vox 12-string.

Albums:
Marshall Crenshaw (Warner Bros), 1982

Jim Croce

US vocalist, composer, guitarist.
Born Philadelphia, January 10, 1932; died September 20, 1973.

Career: Played in bands and ran radio show while attending University of Villanova. After graduating supported himself with manual jobs while trying to get break in music.

Gigs in coffee-houses led to contract with Capitol and unsuccessful first album, released in 1967. More years of dues-paying followed, during which time Croce made living by driving trucks. In 1971 he submitted collection of songs to New York production team Cashman and West (one of whom, Tommy West, was old friend from college days). End result was **You Don't Mess Around With Jim,** a successful album which yielded two hit singles in title track and **Operator**.

The combination of Croce's craftsmanlike, appealing songwriting and Cashman and West's production expertise bore even more fruit on 1973 outing **Life And Times.** A hit album, it also yielded No. 1 single in **Bad Bad Leroy Brown**—a song which has since gone on to become a standard, being recorded by among others Frank Sinatra(▶).

With their carefully crafted lyrics, memorable melodies and irresistible hooks, Croce's songs appealed to rock/pop audiences, and it seemed that he was on brink of superstardom.

I Got A Name. Courtesy Lifesong.

Sadly, he and long-time partner Maury Muehleisen were killed when their light plane crashed on take-off at Natchitoches in Louisiana in September 1973.

Last album, **I Got A Name**, was released late in 1973 and became instant best-seller, as did compilation albums **Photographs And Memories** and **Time In A Bottle.** An artist of genuine talent, refreshingly without pretention, Jim Croce was one of rock's and pop's most regretted casualties.

Hit Singles:	US	UK
You Don't Mess Around With Jim, 1972	8	—
Operator (That's Not The Way It Feels), 1972	17	—
Bad Bad Leroy Brown, 1973	1	—
I Got A Name, 1972	10	—
Time In A Bottle, 1973	1	—
I'll Have To Say I Love You In A Song, 1974	9	—

Albums (selected):
The Faces I've Been (Lifesong), 1977
His Greatest Hits (—/Lifesong), 1977
His Greatest Songs (—/K-Tel), 1980

Worth Searching Out:
You Don't Mess Around With Jim (Lifesong/Vertigo), 1971

Crosby, Stills, Nash & Young

US group formed 1968.

Original/Current line-up: David Crosby, guitar; Stephen Stills, vocals, guitar; Graham Nash, vocals, guitar.

Career: Band formed without Young(▶) as Crosby, Stills and Nash; Crosby came from Byrds(▶), Stills(▶) from Buffalo Springfield(▶) and Nash from UK 'beat group' The Hollies(▶). Debut album **Crosby Stills And Nash** released in 1969 to critical and commercial success. Semi-acoustic soft-rock with accent on vocal harmonies, music combined commercial appeal with 'sensitivity'; occasional banality camouflaged by slickness. Album went gold and single from it, **Marrakesh Express**, charted in US and UK.

Looking to fill out sound, band recruited another ex-Buffalo Springfield alumnus, Neil Young(▶), then pursuing solo career. Young's chunky guitar and sombre vocals became major asset, and his songwriting ability gave authority to repertoire. **Deja Vu,** with added talents of bass-player Greg Reeves and drummer Dallas Taylor, also went gold. Critical plaudits tipped in favour of Young's contributions. Lyrical content was timely and in keeping with appearance at Woodstock festival.

Disappointing live set, **Four Way Street,** followed in 1971, but band members were already beginning to take individual directions and CSN & Y folded that year. Crosby and Nash continued to work as duo until late '70s; Stills took up threads of erratically successful solo career; and Young went on to become enigmatic rock superstar.

In retrospect, what was good about Crosby, Stills, Nash & Young was very often what was good about Neil Young or Stephen Stills. Otherwise, band was too often guilty of peculiar combination of naivety and pretentiousness to be serious contenders for hall of fame. Nevertheless, they left behind collection of melodic, easy-on-the-ear music that is at least usually harmless if no longer relevant.

So Far is best-of collection. Crosby, Stills and Nash came together for reunion album, **CSN,** in 1977; regrouped again in 1982.

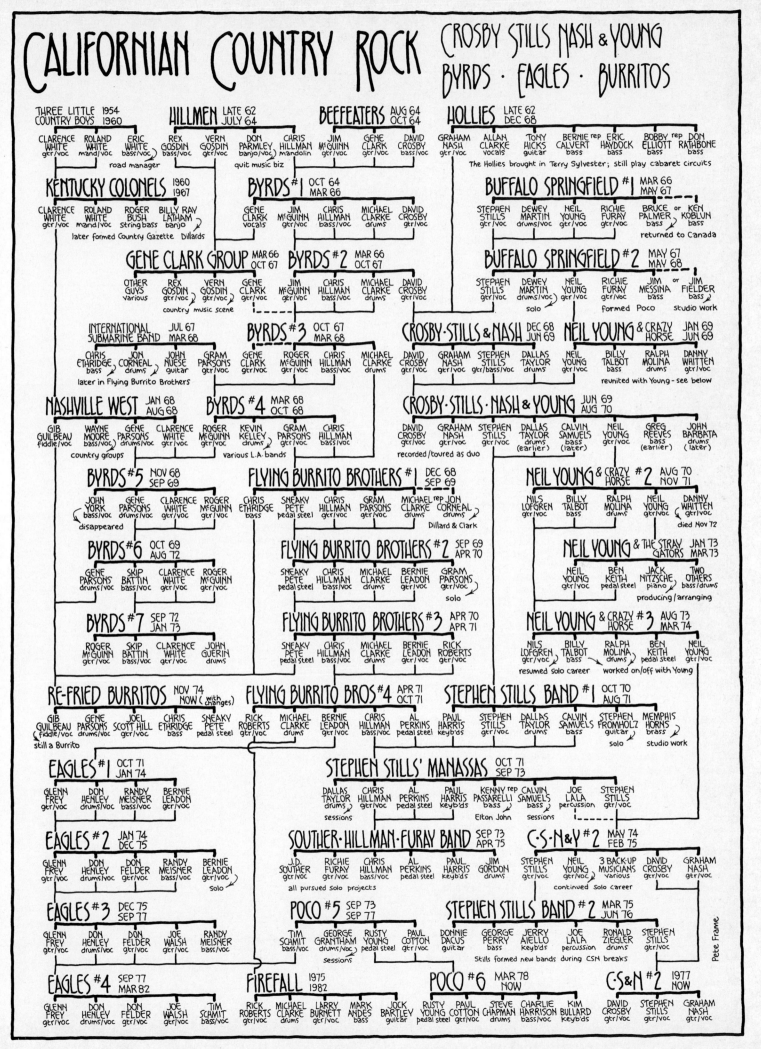

CALIFORNIAN COUNTRY ROCK

CROSBY STILLS NASH & YOUNG
BYRDS · EAGLES · BURRITOS

Pete Frame.

Current line-up; Crosby; Stills; Nash.

Hit Singles:	US	UK
Marrakesh Express (without Young), 1969	—	17
Woodstock, 1970	11	—
Teach Your Children, 1970	16	—
Ohio, 1970	14	—
Just A Song Before I Go (without Young), 1977	7	—

Albums:
Crosby, Stills & Nash (Atlantic), 1969
Deja Vu (Atlantic), 1970
Four Way Street (Atlantic), 1972
So Far (Atlantic), 1974
CSN (Atlantic), 1977
Replay (Atlantic), 1980
Daylight Again (Atlantic), 1982
Allies (Atlantic), 1983

Crosby/Nash:
Graham Nash & David Crosby (Atlantic), 1972
Wind On The Water (Polydor), 1975

David Crosby Solo:
If I Could Only Remember My Name (Atlantic), 1971

Graham Nash Solo:
Tales For Beginners (Atlantic), 1971
Wild Tales (Atlantic), 1973
Earth And Sky (Capitol), 1980

Stephen Stills Solo:
(See separate entry).

Neil Young: Solo:
(See separate entry).

Christopher Cross

US vocalist, guitarist, composer.
Born Austin, Texas.

Career: First US phenomenon of '80s, Cross dominated 1981 Grammy Awards when he won in five categories on strength of debut solo LP **Christopher Cross** and its two Top 3 US singles, plus chart-topping theme from Dudley Moore movie vehicle 'Arthur', **Best That You Can Do.**

Prior to overnight success, Cross had been singer/guitarist with Flash, from San Antonio, Texas, known locally as suitable opening act for superstars. Finding his material not really suitable for Flash, Cross left band in 1973 to feature own songs more, picking up with group of friends: Rob Meurer (keyboards), Andy Salmon (bass), and Tommy Taylor (drums). Attracted attention of musical entrepreneur Michael Brovsky, who took band into studios for long period to refine material/performance.

Cross signed with Warner Bros in late 1978; first LP attracted help from country/rock mafia, including J.D. Souther and Eagle(▶) Don Henley. **Sailing** (second single) was giant US hit. Cross was rated fifth biggest artist of 1980 by 'Billboard' in first year on chart.

Subsequently, pace has slowed somewhat, although second LP almost as successful as first. However, British success limited.

Hit Singles:	US	UK
Ride Like The Wind, 1980	—	2
Sailing, 1980	1	48
Never Be The Same, 1980	10	—
Arthur's Theme (Best That You Can Do), 1981	1	7
All Right, 1983	12	—

Albums:
Christopher Cross (Warner Bros), 1980
Arthur—The Album (Soundtrack) (Warner Bros), 1981
Another Page (Warner Bros), 1983

Rodney Crowell

US composer, vocalist, producer, guitarist. Born Houston, Texas.

Career: Track record as songwriter and producer of hits, despite lack of publicity, grows more impressive yearly. Started out playing drums, but switched to guitar. Moved to Nashville in early '70 (just missing the Texas-based 'outlaw' movement), where he honed his songwriting skills and made contacts; his material was cut by country artists such as Guy Clark and Jerry Reed. Met Emmylou Harris(▶) via producer Brian Ahern and became resident songwriter and rhythm guitar player for Hot Band.

Crowell provided Harris with such songs as **Leaving Louisiana In The Broad Daylight** (hit version later recorded by Oak Ridge Boys(▶)), **Ain't Livin' Long Like This** (Waylon Jennings(▶) country hit) and **Till I Gain Control Again** (memorably performed by Willie Nelson(▶)). Quit Harris' band to record first solo albmu for Warner Bros, **Ain't Livin' Long Like This** included single **Elvira,** which became a pop and country hit when covered by Oak Ridge Boys(▶). Second album **But What Will The Neighbors Think** was also critically approved and drew music industry's attention to range of Crowell's talent.

Married Roseanne Cash, daughter of Johnny Cash(▶), a rising country star in her own right; produced her million-selling album **Seven Year Ache,** and hit single of same title.

In 1981, Crowell released self-titled, self-produced third album; band included guest appearances on guitars by Hank DeVito, Vince Gill and Albert Lee. Album, which consists of nearly all original material, sold better than earlier work and again provided smash hits for other artists. Bob Seger's(▶) cover of **Shame On The Moon** made No.2 in US singles chart in 1983.

Albums:
Ain't Livin' Long Like This (Warner Bros), 1978
But What Will The Neighbors Think (Warner Bros), 1980
Rodney Crowell (Warner Bros), 1981

The Crusaders

US group formed 1961.
Original line-up: Wilton Felder, reeds; Wayne Henderson, trombone; Joe Sample, keyboards; Nesbert 'Stix' Hooper, drums.

Career: Band originally formed in Houston, Texas, in early '50s and was known as the Swingsters. Performed jazz, blues and R&B on small-time circuit.

By 1961 quartet was called Jazz Crusaders. They moved to California and signed contract with Pacific. Over next decade they recorded number of albums in funky jazz genre, using top musicians to fill bass chair, and also worked on many West Coast sessions.

In 1970 band dropped 'Jazz' from name and started developing characteristic sound of machine-tooled, precision rhythms and sinuous horn improvisations. During early '70s they began to garner commerical success, helped by endorsement of top rock and soul artists such as Average White Band. Continued to be in demand for sessions, recording with wide variety of artists.

In 1975 Wayne Henderson left to pursue solo career, since which time band has carried on with nucleus of three, hiring other musicians as necessary. Among other top

Crusaders 1. Courtesy MCA Records.

names, Robert 'Pops' Popwell filled bass chair for number of years, and top guitarist Larry Carlton(▶) was featured during late '70s.

By late '70s band had become major live attraction, playing to SRO audiences worldwide. 1978 album **Images** was first to gain gold status. This period also saw solo efforts by each band member.

1979 started trend of using name vocalists on Crusaders' singles. Randy Crawford(▶) gained stardom on strength of inspired performance on **Street Life**, Bill Withers(▶) sang evocative **Soul Shadows** in 1980, and Joe Cocker(▶) came back into limelight with **I'm So Glad I'm Standing Here Today**, released in 1981.

Highly respected by musicians, critics and public alike, Crusaders are among rare examples of virtuoso musicians who have gained commerical acceptance. Original progenitors of jazz-funk form, Crusaders possess sufficient talent, creativity and acumen to remain at or near top indefinitely, though Hooper quit in summer 1983.

Current line-up: Felder; Sample.

Hit Singles:	US	UK
Street Life, 1979	36	5

Albums:
Crusaders 1 (MCA), 1971
Second Crusade (MCA), 1972
Scratch (MCA), 1975
Southern Comfort (MCA), 1975
Chain Reaction (MCA), 1975
Those Southern Knights (MCA), 1976
Young Rabbits (Blue Note), 1976
Best Of (MCA), 1976
Free As The Wind (MCA), 1977
Images (MCA), 1978
Street Life (MCA), 1979
Rhapsody & Blues (MCA), 1980
Standing Tall (MCA), 1981
Live Sides (Blue Note/—), 1981
Ongaku-Kai: Live In Japan (Crusader/—), 1982

Culture Club

UK group formed 1981.

Original/Current line-up: Boy George, (George O'Dowd) vocals; Jon Moss, drums, percussion; Roy Hay, guitar, keyboards; Michael Craig, bass.

Career: Modern-day Myra Breckinridge Boy George (ex-Bow Wow Wow(▶)) formed Culture Club with drummer Jon Moss (ex-Clash(▶), Damned(▶), Adam & Ants(▶)) from remnants of Praise of Lemmings. Recruiting Roy Hay and Mickey Craig, band recorded debut

Below: Crusader's reed man (and occasional bass player) Wilton Felder.

Kissing To Be Clever, Culture Club. Courtesy Virgin Records.

Kissing To Be Clever set in 1982 and scored in US/UK single charts with **Do You Really Want To Hurt Me**, a slick piece of pop reggae.

Striving for missing link between soul and modern white electronic music, the Club came close with second single, **Time (Clock Of The Heart)**. They seem assured of solid future while in guiding manicured hands of flamboyant ex-window dresser Boy George.

Hit Singles:

	US	UK
Do You Really Want To Hurt Me, 1982	3	1
Time (Clock Of The Heart), 1982	2	1

Albums:
Kissing To Be Clever (Epic/Virgin), 1982
Colour By Numbers (Epic/Virgin), 1983

King Curtis

US saxophonist, bandleader, composer. Born Curtis Ousley, Fort Worth, Texas, 1934; died August 31, 1971.

Career: Master reedman Curtis started career playing sessions in New York in the '50s. Following tradition of 'honkers and screamers' like Sil Austin, Red Prysock and Hal 'Cornbread' Singer, but adding healthy dash of taste and invention, Curtis was featured on records by artists as diverse as Buddy Holly(▶) and the Coasters(▶). His superior musicianship also kept him in demand as bandleader for tours and one-nighters.

Curtis also cut number of jazz sides under own name but soon turned to his forte, instrumental R&B. Standout tracks from this period include Curtis' versions of Jimmy Forrest's **Night Train**, Bill Doggett's(▶) **Honky Tonk**, and the self-composed **Soul Serenade** and **Soul Twist** (the latter a hit during twist craze of 1962).

By mid-'60s Curtis had found niche at Atlantic Records, where he provided back-up for label's stars Donny Hathaway(▶) and Aretha Franklin(▶), and brought out series of albums under own name. These generally consisted of instrumental versions of pop and soul hits with sprinkling of originals, and featured cream of session musicians, including guitarist Cornell Dupree, bassists Jerry Jemmott and Chuck Rainey, keyboardsman Richard Tee and legendary drummer Bernard 'Pretty' Purdie(▶). Most of these albums were extremely listenable as examples of cohesive but relaxed instrumental R&B, the sidemen providing impeccable backing to Curtis' tough tenor.

Curtis' most important legacy, however, was 1971 release **Live At The Fillmore West**, one of the most exhilarating instrumental albums ever. Recorded at the same gig as Aretha Franklin's equally memorable **Live At Fillmore West**, it features Curtis at his storming best, backed by ace band that included Billy Preston(▶) on organ, Cornell Dupree,

Above: Boy George (at left) and his Culture Club.

Jerry Jemmott, Bernard Purdie and the Memphis Horns.

Sadly, King Curtis was struck down at height of his powers. In summer 1971 he was stabbed to death at a New York apartment building he owned. An R&B player who could turn his hand to virtually any form of popular music, King Curtis has had some influence on practically every saxophone player in popular music today. In a sense, he invented a new voice for the instrument.

Hit Singles:

	US	UK
Soul Twist, 1962	17	—

Albums:
Best Of (Prestige/—), 1968
One More Time (The Best Of King Curtis) (Prestige/—), 1969
Jazz Groove (Prestige), 1974
Twenty Golden Pieces Of (—/Bulldog), 1979

Worth Searching Out:
Soul Serenade (Capitol/—), 1964
Get Ready (Atco/Atlantic), 1970
King Curtis Live At The Fillmore West (Atco/Atlantic), 1971
Everybody's Talkin' (Atco/Atlantic), 1971

Roger Daltrey

UK vocalist, actor.
Born London, March 1, 1944.

Career: Daltrey grew up in non-musical family in working-class neighbourhood of London's Shepherd's Bush. Around 12 he

Best Bits, Roger Daltrey. Courtesy Polydor Records.

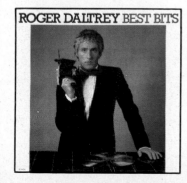

began playing self-made guitars. Thrown out of school at 15, he formed his own band, the Detours, later to become the Who(▶). After playing guitar in Detours for nearly two years, he became a singer and has remained so ever since, generally as lead vocalist with the Who.

Daltrey's first solo project was singing part of Tommy with Lou Reizner's London Symphony Orchestra production of the Who opera. His single **I'm Free** from this version went to No. 13 in UK. First completely solo venture came in 1973 when he sang compositions of then unknown writers such as Leo Sayer(▶) on **Daltrey,** his best solo effort to date. Produced by Adam Faith(▶) the album yielded a No.5 hit in UK, **Giving It All Away,** a great boost to Sayer. Away from the Who, Daltrey was able to expand his vocal range, abandoning screaming style he was best known for within band, and proving his ability to sing softer ballads. Daltrey was also interested in singing material written by other artists, as he'd been the vehicle for Pete Townshend's(▶) compositions/lyrics for 10 years.

1975 was a big year for Daltrey: he starred in his first film, the highly successful 'Tommy', and millions again identified the golden-maned Daltrey as the central character. To erase this impression, Daltrey starred in second Ken Russell film, 'Lisztomania,' portraying Franz Liszt as decadent 19th century pop star. Besides being heavily featured on the 'Lisztomania' and 'Tommy' soundtrack

LPs, Daltrey also had another solo LP out that year, **Ride A Rock Horse.** Apart from award-winning cover, the LP broke no new ground, but was well-received. Daltrey again utilised unknown composers, giving them opportunities to expand. **One Of The Boys** (1977) was more of the same—a collection of songs sung quite well, but not surpassing his work with the Who.

Daltrey's other film roles included a ghastly performance in the low-budget horror flick 'The Legacy' in 1978 and the lead part in 'McVicar' in 1980 opposite Adam Faith, for which he received generally good reviews.

In 1983 Daltrey continues to record and act, starring in the Jonathan Miller production of 'The Beggar's Opera' for British TV, and working on another solo album, **Pop Songs.**

Hit Singles:

	US	UK
Giving It All Away, 1973	—	5
I'm Free (London Symphony Tommy), 1973	—	13

Albums:
Daltrey (MCA/Track), 1973
Ride A Rock Horse (MCA/Polydor), 1975
Lisztomania (A&M Ode/A&M), 1975
One Of The Boys (MCA/Polydor), 1977
McVicar (Soundtrack) (Polydor), 1980
Best Bits (Greatest Hits) (MCA/Polydor), 1983

The Damned

UK group formed 1976.
Original line-up: Rat Scabies, drums; Captain Sensible, bass; Dave Vanian, vocals; Brian James, guitar.

Career: Close on heels of Sex Pistols(▶), Damned were in forefront of mid-'70s' assault on established rock. Line-up had settled down by May 1976 and signed to Stiff in September. **New Rose/Help** was released in October and revolution was on. First 'punk' album was **Damned, Damned, Damned** released in February 1977.

In August 1977, Lu Edmunds joined as second guitarist. Pink Floyd's(▶) Nick Mason produced second album, **Music For Pleasure.** Then band seemed to sink into superstar trauma but without reaching super success. Rat Scabies left in October 1977. Dave Berk sat in on loan from Johnny Moped for tour in November. John Moss joined as permanent drummer in late 1977. Loss of street credibility and lack of sales resulted in Stiff dropping

Below: The Damned. Captain Sensible (far left) went on to solo success.

band in January 1978. Within month Captain Sensible and Brian James had usual musical differences and band folded. James eventually re-emerged with Deadboys Stiv Bators as Lords Of The New Church.

Within six months of Rainbow farewell concert on April 8, 1978, Sensible and Vanian were back together. Sensible had talked Rat Scabies and Vanian into playing with him and Lemmy (from Motorhead(▶)) for one gig at Electric Ballroom. Damned alumni continued on with other musicians and appeared as the Damned while acquiring rights to old name.

In November 1978 re-vamped band appeared, with Sensible now on guitar, sharing vocals with Vanian. Rat Scabies on drums and Algy Ward from the Saints on bass completed line-up. Chiswick signed them and got a UK No.20 with **Love Song** in April 1979. **Machine Gun Etiquette** LP did not appear until November. Ward left in early 1980 to enter heavy-metal sweepstakes with Tank. His place was taken by Eddie and the Hot Rods' bass player Paul Gray. This line-up released critically acclaimed **The Black Album** in November 1980. Arguably album is stronger as single LP in US version. Band seemed continually on road and new popularity prompted November 1981 release of **Best Of The Damned** which featured early work.

In early October 1982 Damned released excellent, but patchy, **Strawberries** album. Captain Sensible's vaudeville tendencies still sought other outlet. In July 1982 his cover of old Rodgers/Hammerstein tune **Happy Talk** was UK No.1 and second single as well as album followed. This schizoid approach plagued Damned from earliest days. Captain's success and band's relative commerical failure caused new label, Bronze, to drop Damned in April 1983. Paul Gray left and once again the Damned's future is doubtful.

Current line-up: Sensible, guitar; Scabies; Vanian.

Hit Singles: | | US | UK |
Love Song, 1979 | | — | 20 |

Captain Sensible Solo:
Happy Talk, 1982 | — | 1 |

Albums:
Damned, Damned, Damned (—/Stiff), 1977
Music For Pleasure (—/Stiff), 1977
Machine Gun Etiquette (—/Chiswick), 1979
The Black Album (—/Chiswick), 1980
The Best Of The Damned (—/Stiff), 1981
Strawberries (—/Bronze), 1982

Captain Sensible Solo:
Women And Captains First (A&M), 1982

Charlie Daniels Band

US group formed 1973.
Original line-up: Charlie Daniels, vocals, guitar, violin; Barry Barnes, guitar; Mark Fitzgerald, bass; Joel DiGregorio, keyboards; Fred Edwards, drums; Gary Allen, drums.

Career: Band is brainchild of Charlie Daniels, born Wilmington, North Carolina, 1937. Daniels grew up listening to bluegrass and rock 'n' roll; learned guitar at early age. By 20, was on road playing honky-tonks throughout Washington, South and Mid-West.

In 1967 in Texas, Daniels met producer Bob Johnston, who suggested he try session work in Nashville. Work on Johnston's Dylan(▶) albums ensued; Daniels played on albums for artists as varied as Ringo Starr(▶), Leonard Cohen(▶) and Youngbloods.

In 1970 started writing songs and initiated solo career, signing with Kama Sutra. **Uneasy Rider,** from album **Honey In The Rock,** established him in US Top 10 in 1973; formed band as above shortly afterwards.

Charlie Daniels Band steadily built up reputation as hard-working Southern country/rock outfit, and album sales gradually increased. 1975 hit single **The South's Gonna Do It** further boosted commercial

Volunteer Jam VII, Charlie Daniels. Courtesy Capricorn Records.

credibility. That year Daniels inaugurated annual jam of Southern bands in Murfreesboro, Tennessee, the 'Volunteer Jam'; event has been commemorated on live albums.

By late '70s, despite several personnel changes, Daniels Band was regular sell-out as live act, and in 1979 achieved its biggest hit to date with **The Devil Went Down To Georgia,** a semi-novelty fiddle feature. Outfit continues to straddle country, rock 'n' roll, Western swing, boogie and blues, and is excellent example of way in which versatility, craftsmanship and good-time feeling can still prove highly commercial commodities. Daniels himself, a rotund, jovial figure, remains one of music scene's more endearing personalities.

Current line-up: Daniels; DiGregorio; Edwards; Charlie Hayward, bass; James Marshall, drums; Tom Crain, guitar, vocals.

Hit Singles: | | US | UK |
Uneasy Rider, 1973 | | 9 | — |
The Devil Went Down To Georgia, 1979 | | 3 | 14 |
In America, 1980 | | 11 | — |

Albums:
TeJohn, Grease And Wolfman (Kama Sutra/—), 1970
Charlie Daniels (Capitol/—), 1970
Fire On The Mountain (Kama Sutra), 1974
Nightrider (Kama Sutra), 1975
Saddle Tramp (Epic), 1976
Uneasy River (Epic/—), 1976
Volunteer Jam (Capricorn), 1976
High & Lonesome (Epic), 1976
Whiskey (Epic/—), 1977
Midnight Wind (Epic), 1977
Volunteer Jam 3 & 4 (Epic), 1978
Million Mile Reflections (Epic), 1979
Full Moon (Epic), 1980
Windows (Epic), 1982
Volunteer Jam VII (Capricorn), 1982

Bobby Darin

US vocalist, composer, actor.
Born Robert Walden Cassotto, New York, May 14, 1936; died December 20, 1973.

Career: Darin's career was balanced precariously between jazz and pop music, and acting, although success in the American and British singles charts from 1958-66 placed him firmly in pop mould.

Unsure of what path to travel, Darin flirted with rock'n'roll (recording **Early In The Morning** as the Rinky Dinks), before scoring with teen anthems **Splish Splash** (Atlantic's first white hit record, produced by Ahmet Ertegun) and **Queen Of The Hop**. He then

moved to jazz standards like **Mack The Knife** (a two million-selling single). **Bill Bailey** and **Lazy River**.

In 1960 he married Sandra Dee (marriage lasted until 1967).

He tried country (**Things**, 1962) and folk-rock (**If I Were A Carpenter**, 1966) before shedding his toupee and baring his soul for the album **Robert Walden Cassotto**, 1971. (Picked name 'Bobby Darin' from a phone book.)

Record success presented Darin with opportunity to move into films, like so many of his contemporaries, although he was singularly more effective than most rock singers-turned-movie stars. Between 1960 and 1973 he appeared in 13 movies and was nominated for an Oscar for his performance in the 1964 film 'Captain Newman MD'.

He died in December 1973, following a long period of heart trouble.

Hit Singles: | | US | UK |
Splish Splash, 1958 | | 3 | 17 |
Queen Of The Hop, 1958 | | 9 | 24 |
Dream Lover, 1959 | | 2 | 1 |
Mack The Knife, 1959 | | 1 | 1 |
Beyond The Sea, 1960 | | 6 | 8 |
Clementine, 1960 | | 21 | 8 |
Bill Bailey, 1960 | | 19 | 34 |
Artificial Flowers, 1960 | | 20 | — |
Lazy River, 1961 | | 14 | 2 |
You Must Have Been A Beautiful Baby, 1961 | | 5 | 10 |
Multiplication, 1961 | | 30 | 5 |
Irresistible You, 1962 | | 15 | — |
Things, 1962 | | 3 | 2 |
You're The Reason I'm Leaving, 1963 | | 3 | — |
Eighteen Yellow Roses, 1963 | | 10 | 37 |
If I Were A Carpenter, 1966 | | 8 | 9 |

Albums:
Bobby Darin Story (Atco/—), 1961
Greatest Moments (Atlantic), 1974
At The Copa (Bainbridge/—), 1981

Below: The mid-period cabaret persona of the great Bobby Darin.

Spencer Davis Group

UK group formed 1963.

Original line-up: Spencer Davis, guitar; Stevie Winwood, guitar, keyboards, vocals; Muff Winwood, bass; Pete York, drums.

Career: Birmingham-raised members had jazz and folk-blues background before developing interest in emergent R&B scene. They landed residency in city's Golden Eagle pub playing versions of material by Sonny Boy Williamson, Muddy Waters(▶), Bo Diddley(▶) and other black Americans.

Chris Blackwell, then trying to set up his own Island label to cater for the West Indian market in UK, discovered the group during visit to Birmingham and, realising the ethnic basis of his own label, signed them instead to Fontana.

Their first three singles were minor hits then Blackwell teamed them with songwriting talents of Jamaican ska star Wilfred 'Jackie' Edwards and first collaboration, **Keep On**

Their First LP, Spencer Davis Group. Courtesy Fontana Records.

Running, took them to British No.1 slot in December 1965. The compulsive **Gimme Some Loving** helped them attain Stateside success while they became an established act on UK club circuit.

Their final hit came in February 1967 with the Stevie Winwood(▶) composition **I'm A Man** (later covered successfully by Santana (▶)). By then, pyschedelia and flower-power had burst onto the scene and, like so many of his contemporaries, Stevie Winwood decided to move from a style of music totally derivative of American sources into something more original, if, in retrospect, far less exciting.

The result was formation of Traffic(▶) with which Winwood achieved considerable success. His brother Muff moved into record production, inititally with Island and later as head of A&R at Epic Records' London office. Attempting to keep group going, Spencer Davis brought in Eddie Hardin, keyboards, Phil Sawyer, guitar, and Charlie McCracken, bass.

A late LP by the Spencer Davis Group. Courtesy United Artists Records.

Hardin and York soon left to form Hardin-York duo and, after several further line-up changes and lack of success, Davis disbanded group in 1969. He emigrated first to Germany, then to California where he formed trio with Peter Jameson and Alun Davies (even working with rural blues veteran Mississippi Fred McDowell at one stage).

In 1973, Davis met up again with Eddie Hardin in Los Angeles and re-formed Spencer Davis Group but, despite reasonably well-received UK and US tours, this new incarnation was short-lived and Spencer Davis gave up his rock star aspirations to work as West Coast recording executive.

Final line-up: Davis; Eddie Hardin, keyboards; Phil Sawyer, guitar; Charlie McCracken, bass.

Hit Singles:	US	UK
Keep On Running, 1965	—	1
Somebody Help Me, 1966	47	1
When I Come Home, 1966	—	12
Gimme Some Lovin', 1966	7	2
I'm A Man, 1967	10	9

Albums:
Best Of (—/Island), 1972

Dead Kennedys

US group formed 1979.

Original line-up: Jello Biafra, vocals; Ray Valium aka East Bay Ray, guitar; Klaus Floride, bass, vocals; Ted, drums.

Career: Jello Biafra formed band in late '70s around nucleus of Ray and Klaus. Immediately formed own record company, Alternative Tentacles, avoiding pressure to change name or soften lyrics. With first single **California Uber Alles**, DKs' established objective was to provoke and remain outside mainstream rock.

Fresh Fruit For Rotting Vegetables LP moved DKs to forefront of US punks and earned critical success in UK. Sound was minimal and fast. Intelligent lyrics tended to

The folded-out cover of Deep Purple. Courtesy Harvest Records.

be over the top, attacking every possible political, social and fashionable attitude in sight.

Subsequent singles also provided something to offend everyone: **Holiday In Cambodia** lambasted left, **Nazi Punks** ridiculed right; **Kill The Poor** and **Moral Majority** took on rich and middle classes. **Too Drunk To Fuck** earned UK exposure and Top 40 hit thanks to BBC banning. Maintaining stance against traditional methods meant DKs appeared on obscure compilation LPs (Walking Dead Records' 1980 **Can You Hear Me? Music From The Deaf Club** and No Nukes/Pax Records' 1981 **Wargasm**). Second LP did not appear until early 1983 but retained high-intensity level of previous work.

So far Biafra has stuck to commitment to go own way which has earned him label as spokesman for hardcore movement. Dead Kennedys are set as America's rebel youth of the '80s. Their sound, titles and lyrics should keep that image safe for some time to come.

Current line-up: Biafra; Ray; Floride; D.H. Peligro, drums.

Albums:
Fresh Fruit For Rotting Vegetables (IRS/Cherry Red), 1980
Plastic Surgery Disasters (Alternative Tentacles/Cherry Red), 1982

Deep Purple

UK group formed 1968.
Original line-up: Rod Evans, vocals; Ritchie Blackmore, guitar; Jon Lord, keyboards; Nick Simper, bass; Ian Paice, drums.

Career: Formed in Germany from remnants of UK band Roundabout (Blackmore; Lord; Dave Curtis, bass; Chris Curtis, vocals; Bobby Clark, drums) as pop-rock outfit. First single (with line-up above), **Hush**, made Top 5 in US as did next two singles. First albums also achieved American success. However, band did not gain credibility in homeland until 1970 when Ian Gillan(▶) and Roger Glover replaced Evans and Simper for ambitious **Concerto For Group And Orchestra** album, recorded at Albert Hall with Royal Philharmonic Orchestra. New line-up also gained single success with **Black Night** in August of that year.

Pursuing a heavier rock direction, Purple quickly became one of the most successful and influential bands of early '70s; joined Black Sabbath(▶) and Led Zeppelin(▶) in spreading gospel of multi-decibel, piledriver British rock around the world. Main asset was Blackmore, who, although somewhat derivative, established reputation as guitar hero.

However, by 1972 band was beset by various ego problems; a year later Gillan left (later to achieve considerable success with his own band), followed shortly by Glover (who went into production). Glenn Hughes, bassist with moderately successful band Trapeze, replaced Glover, while Gillan was replaced by complete unknown David Coverdale. In 1975 Ritchie Blackmore also quit to form Rainbow(▶) (where he was later joined by Glover), and American Tommy Bolin, formerly of James Gang(▶), was recruited in his place.

By 1976, audience for Purple's music was beginning to diminish, and band died natural death that year. Coverdale, Lord and Paice eventually became three-fifths of Whitesnake(▶). Glenn Hughes recorded a solo album and undertook session work. Tommy Bolin died suddenly in Miami in 1976.

At press time there was speculation that band might re-form with several of original members (though Gillan joined Black Sabbath(▶)). Although prone to 'everything-but-

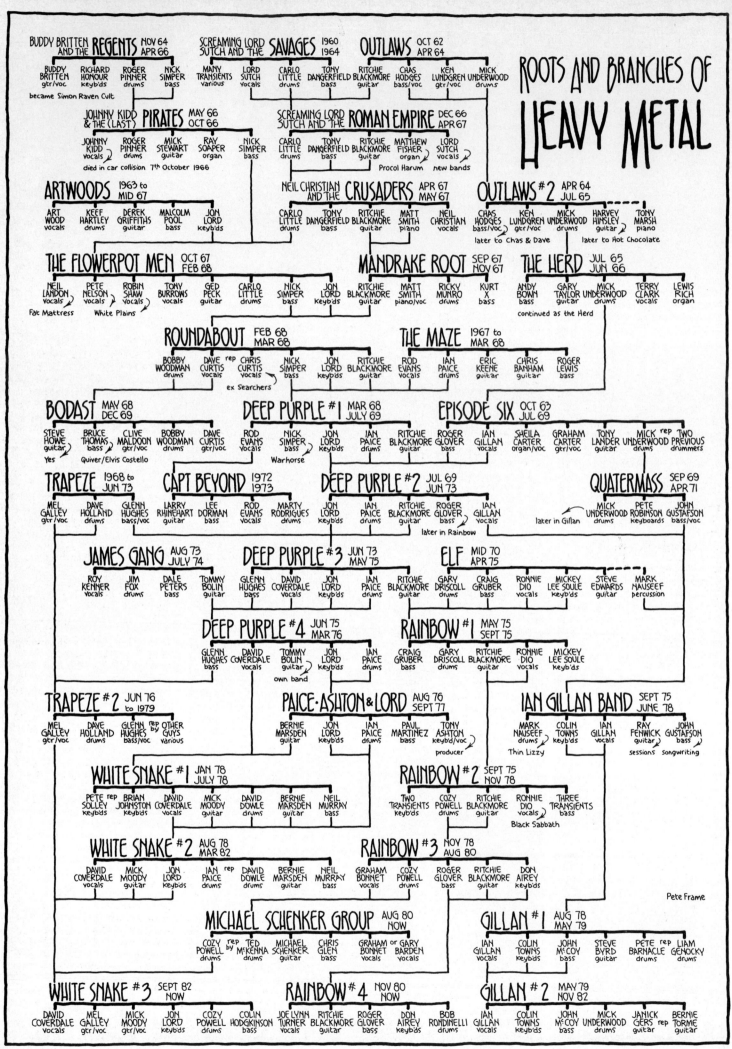

Roots and Branches of Heavy Metal

Pete Frame

the-kitchen-sink' approach, incorporating wide range of influences from psychedelic to classical, Deep Purple were basically band of hard-rockers who on good day could create fair amount of excitement. Among the more interesting musically of heavy brigade, they were considerable influence on '70s rock.

Final line-up: Lord; Paice; David Coverdale, vocals; Glenn Hughes, bass, vocals; Tommy Bolin, guitar.

Hit Singles:	US	UK
Hush, 1968	4	
Black Night, 1970	—	2
Strange Kind Of Woman, 1971		8
Fireball, 1971	—	15
Smoke On The Water, 1973	4	21

Albums:
Shades Of Deep Purple (Tetragrammaton/ Harvest), 1968
Book Of Taliesyn (Tetragrammaton/Harvest), 1969
Deep Purple (Tetragrammaton/Harvest), 1969
In Concert (Portrait/Harvest), 1970
Concerto For Group & Orchestra (Warner Bros/ Harvest), 1970
In Rock (Warner Bros/Harvest), 1970
Fireball (Deep Purple/Harvest), 1971
Machine Head (Warner Bros/Purple), 1972
Made In Japan (Deep Purple/Purple), 1972
Who Do We Think We Are (Deep Purple/ Purple), 1973
Burn (Deep Purple/Purple), 1974
Stormbringer (Deep Purple/Purple), 1974
Come Taste The Band (Deep Purple/Purple), 1975
24 Carat Purple (—/Purple), 1975
Purple Passages (Warner Bros), 1975
Made In Europe (Deep Purple/Purple), 1976
Powerhouse (—/Purple), 1977
Singles (—/Harvest), 1978
When We Rock We Rock (Warner Bros/—), 1978
Live In London (—/Harvest), 1982

Def Leppard

UK group formed 1978.

Original line-up: Steve Clark, guitar; Rick Savage, bass; Pete Willis, guitar; Rick Allen, drums; Joe Elliot, vocals.

Career: Sheffield lads, Def Leppard cut an impressive debut album **On Through The Night** with twin guitar leads which owed as

much to Wishbone Ash(▶) as new wave of British heavy metal.

Immediate attention brought by 'overnight success' caused problems. 1981 set **High 'n' Dry** sounded rather sedated, just another heavy metal album, and Pete Willis developed personal problems which resulted in his being fired during recording of crucial third album. Band continued recording as foursome when Elliot heard that guitarist Phil Collen (ex-Girl) was available.

Despite delays and problems, **Pyromania** matched scope of first album and climbed into America's Top 10. Def Leppard are back in top form.

Current line-up: Clark; Savage; Allen; Elliot; Phil Collen, guitar.

Albums:
On Through The Night (Mercury/Vertigo), 1980
High 'n' Dry (Mercury/Vertigo), 1981
Pyromania (Mercury/Vertigo), 1983

Desmond Dekker

Jamaican vocalist, composer.
Born Kingston, Jamaica, 1943.

Career: Desmond Dekker was reggae's first superstar, responsible for carrying Jamaica's ethnic pop music to a massive white audience in both UK and US. Credit for his impact, however, must be shared with his guardian/ mentor Leslie Kong who produced all Dekker's classic recordings from 1967 until 1971 when Kong died, aged 38, of heart attack.

Orphaned as small child, Dekker worked as welder before, in mid-'60s, joining the Aces, a studio group used by producers Duke Reid and Lloyd 'The Matador' Daley.

Portraying the Jamaican 'rude boy' cult, **007 (Shanty Town)** was one of the first rock-steady hits, bringing Desmond Dekker and the Aces to prominence not only in Jamaica but in UK, where record charted in 1967.

007 was the first of more than 20 consecutive chart-toppers for Dekker in his home country. In 1969, he became first reggae artist to top UK charts, with **The Israelites** which also made No.9 spot in US, despite strange

patois of its lyrics. **The Israelites** charted twice more on re-release in UK while **It Mek**, first released in Britain before **The Israelites**, also became a smash hit when given second chance.

Pickney Gal, **You Can Get It If You Really Want It** (featured in critically acclaimed Jimmy Cliff(▶) movie 'The Harder They Come') and, in 1975, **Sing A Little Song** were all UK hits but despite moving to London after Kong's death, Dekker's fortunes waned as Bob Marley assumed the title of reggae's numero uno.

In 1980 there were signs of new interest via the second generation of skinheads (he had been the original skinheads' cult hero) and an album with Stiff ensued, but neither that nor subsequent set produced by Robert Palmer(▶) made real impact.

Hit Singles:	US	UK
007 (Shanty Town), 1967	—	14
The Israelites, 1969	9	1
It Mek, 1969	—	7
You Can Get It If You Really Want It, 1970	—	2
The Israelites (re-issue), 1975	—	10
Sing A Little Song, 1975	—	16

Albums:
Dekker's Sweet 16 Hits (—/Trojan), 1979
Black And Dekker (—/Stiff), 1980
Israelites (—/Cactus), 1980
Compass Point (—/Stiff), 1981

Delaney And Bonnie

US vocal duo.
Delaney Bramlett, born Pontotoc County, Mississippi, July 1, 1939.
Bonnie Bramlett, born Acton, Illinois, November 8, 1944.

Career: Masters of blue-eyed soul idiom, husband-and-wife team Delaney and Bonnie met in Los Angeles via Jack Good's ABC TV show 'Shindig'. Delaney was partner of Joey Cooper in show's resident Shindogs duo. Bonnie (Lynn) had been session singer at Stax-Volt studios in Memphis, gigged with Albert King and Fontella Bass, then joined Ike and Tina Turner's(▶) Revue as only white member ever of Ikettes vocal group.

Married within seven days of meeting, Delaney and Bonnie became one of first white acts signed to Stax (they were preceded by MarKeys, one of whose members, Don Nix, co-produced with Duck Dunn their debut album **Down Home** on which Dunn and rest of Booker T and the MGs(▶) provided backings). It was vast improvement on duo's earlier album effort for Independence label in 1968 but was not released till after they came to fame.

Through their contacts on Los Angeles session scene, duo put together the casual, ever-changing group Friends, which included at various times Leon Russell(▶), ex-Ventures(▶)' guitarist Jerry McGhee, Rita Coolidge(▶), Englishman Dave Mason(▶) (ex-Traffic), Jim Price, Bobby Keyes, Jim Keltner, Duane Allman, Carl Radle and Bobby Whitlock.

Signed to Elektra, the duo's **Accept No Substitute—The Original Delaney And Bonnie** LP was widely acclaimed, pulling together soul, gospel, country and rock elements into a totally pleasing sound.

Friendship with Eric Clapton(▶) led to the **On Tour (With Eric Clapton)** set and switch to Atlantic Records. Clapton (and, on some gigs, George Harrison(▶)) joined them for UK tour during which they played London's Lyceum as guest members of John and

Yoko's Plastic Ono Band. Duo also featured on Clapton's solo album **Eric Clapton**.

Friends (without Delaney and Bonnie) became nucleus of legendary Mad Dogs and Englishmen tour (1970), after which Whitlock, Radle and Jim Gordon became Eric Clapton's Dominoes, while Price and Keyes toured with the Rolling Stones(▶).

Delaney & Bonnie's classic LP. Courtesy Elektra Records.

Delaney and Bonnie continued to record together until their professional and working divorce in 1972. Bonnie cut solo albums for Phil Walden's Capricorn label while Delaney made one solo set for Columbia then went into semi-retirement on his Californian ranch.

Delaney re-emerged in 1977 on Motown's Prodigal label for **Delaney And Friends— Class Reunion** LP set which featured Eric Clapton, George Harrison, Leon Russell, Billy Preston(▶) and Ringo Starr(▶).

Hit Singles:	US	UK
Comin' Home, 1969	—	16
Never Ending Song Of Love, 1971	13	—
Only You And I Know, 1971	20	—

Albums:
On Tour (Atco/Atlantic), 1970
Genesis (GNP/—), 1971
Best Of (Atco/Atlantic), 1972

Delaney Bramlett solo:
Delaney And Friends—Class Reunion (Prodigal), 1977

John Denver

Singer, composer, guitarist.
Born John Henry Deutschendorf Jr., Rockwell, New Mexico, December 31, 1943.

Career: Son of USAF pilot who held three world aviation records, Denver spent youth moving from one base to another throughout America. First performed as folk singer in Lubbock, Texas, where he majored in architecture at college.

Moving to Los Angeles in 1964, he auditioned successfully as replacement for Chad Mitchell in Chad Mitchell Trio and toured with them for five years before going solo. First album in 1969 featured original composition **Leaving On A Jet Plane,** which became international hit for Peter, Paul and Mary(▶), the same year.

By 1971 Denver was major star thanks to million-selling self-penned **Take Me Home Country Roads** and gold album **Poems, Prayers And Promises.** Million-selling **Annie's Song** (1974) gave him UK chart debut and in 1975 he starred in series of major TV specials and in Lake Tahoe cabaret alongside Frank Sinatra.

Windsong album went gold on pre-release orders alone, while 'Rocky Mountain Christmas' TV special captured audience of 30 million. Film debut came in 1977 with 'Oh God', starring George Burns.

Below: Britain's most successful latter-day heavy metal export to America, Def Leppard.

Country music's version of the All-American Boy, John Denver's ecology-minded material and easy-listening style have made him a show-business phenomenon and a major figure in field of country rock.

Hit Singles:	US	UK
Take Me Home, Country Roads, 1971	2	—
Rocky Mountain High, 1973	9	—
Sunshine On My Shoulders, 1974	1	—
Annie's Song, 1974	1	1
Back Home Again, 1974	5	—
Sweet Surrender, 1975	13	—
Thank God I'm A Country Boy, 1975	1	—
I'm Sorry, 1975	1	—
Fly Away, 1976	13	—

Albums:
Poems, Prayers And Promises (RCA), 1971
Aerie (RCA), 1971
Rocky Mountain High (RCA), 1972
Farewell Andromeda (RCA), 1973
Greatest Hits (RCA/—), 1973
Back Home Again (RCA), 1974
Best Of (—/RCA), 1974
An Evening With (RCA), 1975
Windsong (RCA), 1975
Rocky Mountain Xmas (RCA), 1975
Spirit (RCA), 1976
Greatest Hits Volume II (RCA), 1977
I Want To Live (RCA), 1977
Best Of Volume II (—/RCA), 1977
Autograph (RCA), 1980
Some Days Are Diamonds (RCA), 1981
Perhaps Love (with Placido Domingo) (Columbia/CBS), 1981

Deodato

Brazilian keyboard player, composer, arranger, producer.
Born Eumir Deodato, Rio De Janeiro, June 22, 1942.

Career: Entered recording as arranger/conductor at 17; mixed classical and jazz influences, composing tone poems, string quartets, film scores and ballets before emigrating to US in 1967. Worked on TV jingles until introduced by Brazilian star Astrud Gilberto to jazz producer Creed Taylor.

Taylor hired Deodato to work on three cuts of classic Wes Montgomery album **Down Here On The Ground**. This led to mass of studio work, notably with arrangements for Aretha Franklin(▶), Frank Sinatra(▶), Bette Midler(▶) and others.

First solo album appeared in 1973, followed by string of US singles (minor hits) and LPs, as well as film scores for 'Gentle Rain', 'The Adventurers', 'Target Risk', 'The Black Pearl' and 'The Onion Field', and work with acts like Roberta Flack(▶) and Kool and the Gang(▶).

Deodato is premier background musician, where he seems content to remain.

Hit Singles:	US	UK
Also Sprach Zarathustra (2001), 1973	2	7

Albums:
Prelude (CTI), 1973
Deodato II (CTI), 1973
Whirlwinds (MCA), 1974
Artistry (MCA), 1975
First Cuckoo (MCA), 1975
Very Together (MCA), 1976
Love Island (Warner Bros), 1978
Night Cruiser (Warner Bros), 1980
Knights Of Fantasy (Warner Bros/—), 1981
Happy Hour (Warner Bros), 1982

Depeche Mode

UK group formed 1980.

Original line-up: Andy Fletcher, guitar, vocals; Martin Gore, guitar, vocals; Vince Clarke, synthesisers, vocals; Dave Gahan, vocals.

Career: Formed by Fletcher, Gore and Clarke in Basildon, Essex, under forgotten name. Acquired Depeche Mode tag from French fashion magazine. In 1981, dispensed with guitars to become all-electronic band. Early demo tapes met with zero response, until group began to play 'futurist' nights at Bridge House pub in East London. Seen by group entrepreneur Stevo who included a track, **Photographic,** on semi-legendary **Some Bizzare** compilation LP; others on album included Soft Cell(▶), Blancmange, the The and Naked Lunch. Also approached by Daniel Miller of Mute Records, who became group's svengali/record producer.

First Mute single, **Dreaming Of Me,** was minor hit in early 1981, since when six singles and two albums have reached UK Top 10, despite departure, after release of first LP, of Vince Clarke, who had been main songwriter to this point. Martin Gore assumed this role and success continued unabated, while Vince Clarke formed Yazoo (or 'Yaz' in US) with Alison 'Alf' Moyet.

In early 1982, Alan Wilder (ex-Hitmen)

Below: The totally synthesised Depeche Mode, who have yet to miss the UK chart with a single release.

recruited for US tour, and later became full member of band. Departure of Vince Clarke (and especially his songwriting talent) led many to write off Depeche Mode, but they have contrived to remain very popular, both in Britain and in several overseas territories, although their heavily electronic sound shows signs of becoming over familiar.

Current line-up: Gahan; Fletcher; Gore; Alan Wilder, electronics.

Hit Singles:	US	UK
New Life, 1981	—	11
Just Can't Get Enough, 1981	—	8
See You, 1982	—	6
The Meaning Of Love, 1982	—	12
Leave In Silence, 1982	—	18
Get The Balance Right, 1983	—	13

Albums:
Speak And Spell (Sire/Mute), 1981
A Broken Frame (Sire/Mute), 1982

Derek And The Dominoes

US/UK group formed 1970.

Original/Final line-up: Eric Clapton, guitars, vocals; Bobby Whitlock, keyboards, vocals, acoustic guitar; Jim Gordon, drums, percussion, piano; Carl Radle, Fender Precision bass, percussion.

Career: Reacting to stardom of Cream(▶) and media over-exposure of Blind Faith(▶), Eric Clapton tried finding happiness as guitar

Above: Eric Clapton (aka Derek) puts the short lived Derek & the Dominoes through their paces.

player with Delaney and Bonnie(▶) in 1970. This introduced him to excellent session men Whitlock, Radle and Gordon. In May 1970 Clapton gathered them and fellow Brit, Dave Mason(▶) to form Derek And The Dominoes (Mason quitting immediately after first show).

While recording debut **Layla** album, quartet recruited Duane Allman and his presence tied effort together into cohesive whole. Released December 1970, double album got good reviews but no public notice. **Layla**, written for and about Patti Harrison, was chosen as obvious single in February 1971. It missed the Top 50.

Layla, Derek & the Dominoes. Courtesy Atco Records.

Work on a second album ground to a halt when Clapton lost interest in project. Ironically, **Layla** was re-issued a year later and climbed to Top 10 in US/UK.

Live album recorded at Fillmore East in 1972 reflected belated interest in saga of Derek and Layla, but lacked any subtle texture or classic musicianship.

Hit Singles:	US	UK
Layla, 1972	10	7

Albums:
Layla And Other Assorted Love Songs (ATCO/Polydor), 1970
In Concert (ATCO/Polydor), 1973

Rick Derringer

US guitarist, producer.
Born Richard Zehringer, Celina, Ohio, August 5, 1947.

Career: Zehringer, his brother and friends formed McCoys (name inspired by Ventures'

The McCoy) in Indiana, 1962. This was before arrival of Beatles and band played American rock'n'roll throughout midwest while British invasion changed rock'n'roll into rock.

In 1965 group signed with Bang Records and released ditty by 18-year-old Zehringer, **Hang On Sloopy.** Name of group and sound of song certainly did not reflect British influence expected in 1965. Still, within months it was worldwide monster hit.

Four years later in 1969 McCoys were reduced to house band status at New York's Scene Club. Scene's owner, Steve Paul, re-organised band and arranged for them to back blues-rock guitarist Johnny Winter(▶). Rick changed his name to Derringer, became involved with producing Winter's recordings and subsequently began working for Edgar Winter(▶).

As guitarist for Edgar Winter's White Trash and the Edgar Winter Group, Derringer got reasonable amount of press as an exception-ally able guitarist. This led to his releasing several solo albums and formation of own group. Technically very good, Derringer lacks that extra something to set him apart and above other competent guitarists.

Albums:
All American Boy (Blue Sky), 1973
Derringer (Blue Sky), 1976
Live (Blue Sky), 1977
If I Weren't So Romantic, (Blue Sky), 1978
Guitars And Women (Blue Sky), 1979

Below: Are We Not Men? We are Devo!

Devo
US group formed 1976.
Original/Current line-up: Jerry Casale, bass; Mark Mothersbough, vocals, guitar, keyboards; Bob Casale, guitar; Bob Mothersbough, guitar; Alan Meyers, drums.

Career: Jerry and Mark met at Kent State in early '70s and began experimental non-musical approach to music. Mid-'70s upheaval provided chance for hearing. Bob Casale (brother of Jerry) and Bob Mothersbough (brother of Mark), and fellow Akron friend Myers completed line-up.

In 1977 Iggy Pop(▶), then David Bowie(▶), befriended band which won cult status. Self-released early singles (**Jocko Homo, Mongoloid,** and jerky, electronic cover of Stones' **Satisfaction)** with clinical, icy edge spread underground reputation. As befitting former Fine Art majors, Jerry and Mark marketed Devo with multi-media campaign incorporating masks, films, in-jokes about potatoes, philosophies of devolution, science and flower pots, as well as a self-developed language.

High Tech gloss was enhanced by Eno-produced first album. With Ken Scott-produced **Duty Now For The Future,** band took things more seriously, to its detriment, and **Freedom Of Choice** signified a shift to dance music with disco hit **Whip It.** Devo's electronic bop continued through quirky live mini LP and into precision beat of **New**

Traditionalists.

Latest LP **Oh No! It's Devo** sums up band: staccato synthesisers with at least one outstanding cut, but marketing and jokes wearing thin. First taste of Devo is disconcert-ing but interesting. Second bite is like undercooked spuds: hard and in need of warmth.

Hit Singles:	US	UK
Whip It, 1980	14	51

Albums:
Q: Are We Not Men? A: We Are Devo (Warner Bros/Virgin), 1978
Duty Now For The Future (Warner Bros/Virgin), 1979
Freedom Of Choice (Warner Bros/Virgin), 1980
Live (mini-album) (Warner Bros/Virgin), 1981
New Traditionalists (Warner Bros/Virgin), 1981
Oh No! It's Devo (Warner Bros/Virgin), 1982

Dexy's Midnight Runners
UK group formed 1978.
Original line-up: Kevin Rowland, vocals, guitar; Al Archer, guitar; Jimmy Paterson, trombone; Pete Saunders, organ; J.B., tenor saxophone; Steve 'Babyface' Spooner, alto saxophone; Pete Williams, bass; Andy Grow-cott, drums.

Career: Group's main-man Kevin Rowland (born Wolverhampton, August 17, 1953) started in Lucy and Lovers then joined the Killjoys. Made one record, **Johnny Won't Get To Heaven.** In July 1978 Birmingham-based Rowlands decided to form new band in '60s soul mould. Result was Dexy's Midnight Runners. Image was based on New York '60s street gangs—inspired by movie 'Mean Streets'.

Former Clash(▶) manager Bernie Rhodes was called in to help; got group onto Specials' tour as support. Via his own Oddball label, Rhodes secured an EMI/Parlophone re-cording contract leading to release of **Dance Stance** in October 1979. Brass-laden record, with lyrics about bigotry towards Irish, made UK Top 40. This capitalised on small but dedicated following built via controversial 44-date 'Straight From The Heart' tour where Rowland's uncompromising attitude to audiences angered some, delighted others.

Having parted company with Rhodes, band issued second single. A-side **Geno** was tribute to '60s British soul club hero Geno Washington; flip-side was re-make of Johnny

Above: Kevin Rowland, chief Midnight Runner.

Johnson and the Bandwagon's soul oldie **Breaking Down The Walls Of Heartache.** On last day of recording debut LP, band snatched master-tapes from producer Pete Wingfield and refused to give them to EMI unless company came up with better contract; their nerve won out. Finally released in July 1980, **Searching For The Young Soul Rebels** stayed on charts for three months and was strong showcase for Rowland's stance—so strong that Rowland thought he would never be able to surpass it and made tentative plans to move into films. Third single **There There My Dear** was another hit.

Rowland continued to create controversy. Group took out full page adverts in which they slated music papers and rock writers as being 'dishonest and hippy'. They stated that in future they would communicate with fans by submitting their own essays to the press and by including written handouts with their records.

Band set off on aptly titled 'Midnight Runners Intense Emotion Revue Tour'. Tired from exhaustive recording sessions and under-rehearsed for the road, group met hostile reaction from audience. Rowland repaid compliment by abusing the crowd each night.

Massive row broke out in group during European tour. Rowland had decided to release **Keep It Part 2** as next single. Rest of band disagreed and when Rowland insisted on having own way they quit, with exception of Paterson.

Rowland returned to Birmingham to put together new line-up. (Rowland; Paterson; Micky Billingham, keyboards; Paul Speare, tenor sax; Brian Maurice, alto sax; Billy Adams, guitar; Seb Shelton, drums). He asked that group's recent recordings should not be exploited but EMI decided to release **Plan,** a song which they rightly thought would prove Dexy's ability to come up with the goods. In protest, Rowland decided to walk out on contract. New manager Paul Burton spent two days studying small print before he found loophole that enabled Rowland to get away with it.

When group returned to stage there was whole new look. Hooded anoraks, tracksuit trousers and boxing boots replaced previous gang image. In keeping with this 'keep fit' style, group banned consumption of alcohol at their gigs. 'Midnight Runners Projected Passion Revue' climaxed with three nights at London's hallowed Old Vic theatre, the first rock band to play there.

New deal with Phonogram saw somewhat below par **Show Me** single make charts. Like

image, the music was also changing direction. Rowland had been experimenting for some time with use of violins (playing riffs rather than as an orchestra). First result was **Liars A To E,** which was none too successful. Next time out, though, was the superb **The Celtic Soul Singers/Love Part Two.** On this, the fiddles of the Emerald Express—Helen O'Hara, Steve Brennan and Roger Macduff—replaced familiar Dexy's brass sound. Record only reached lower limits of chart but die was cast.

Too-Rye-Ay, Dexy's Midnight Runners. Courtesy Mercury Records.

Yet another new image emerged: dungarees, neckerchiefs and leather jerkins to fit almost folksy bent of much of the new music. **Come On Eileen** (first US hit) shot group back to top in early summer 1982. **Too-Rye-Ay** album featured neat blend of acoustic guitar and violins with soft brass and included brilliant brassy version of Van Morrison's(▶) **Jackie Wilson Said (I'm In Heaven When You Smile).**

Current line-up: Rowland; Helen O'Hara, violin; Steve Brennan, violin; Billy Adams, guitar; Seb Shelton, drums.

Hit Singles:	US	UK
Geno, 1980	—	1
There There My Dear, 1980	—	7
Show Me, 1981	—	16
Come On Eileen, 1982	1	1

As Kevin Rowland and Dexy's Midnight Runners:

Jackie Wilson Said,1982	—	5
Let's Get This Straight (From The Start), 1982	—	17

Albums:
Searching For Young Soul Rebels (EMI/ Fame), 1980
Too-Rye-Ay (Mercury), 1982
Geno (—/EMI), 1983

Al Di Meola
US guitarist, arranger, composer.
Born Jersey City, New Jersey, July 22, 1954.

Career: Premier fusion guitarist, now part of McLaughlin(▶) de Lucia, Di Meola triumvirate. Initially studied percussion, before moving to guitar at age seven. Early influence was super country picker Doc Watson. Jazz interest spurred by Larry Coryell(▶), whom he replaced, ironically, in current trio.

Joined Chick Corea's Return To Forever after studying at Boston's Berkley School Of Music, and had period with Barry Miles' band. Debut solo album **Land Of The Midnight Sun** (1976), released on RTF's demise, included two acoustic guitar cuts with Corea. (First played acoustic guitar on RTF's **No Mystery,** 1975.)

Duet with de Lucia on 1977 LP **Elegant Gypsy** paved way for guitar trio. Threesome

joined forces in 1980, playing sell-out concerts in Europe and America, and earning 750,000 sales of first album **Friday Night In San Francisco**'.

Di Meola's various awards include three

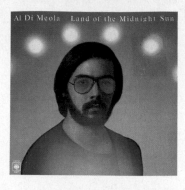

Land Of The Midnight Sun, Al Di Meola. Courtesy Columbia Records.

Best Album trophies from 'Guitar Player' magazine and Best New Jazz Group (with trio) from trade papers 'Cashbox' and 'Record World'.

With De Lucia and McLaughlin, has pushed acoustic guitar to new plane. Inventive, with flawless technique (his book 'Al Di Meola's Picking Techniques' was published by Noonzio Productions), Di Meola (not yet 30 himself) is the new inspiration for thousands of budding rock/jazz stars.

Guitars: Ovation Balladeer, Legend and Cutaway models.

Albums:
Land Of The Midnight Sun (Columbia/CBS), 1976
Elegant Gypsy (Columbia/CBS), 1977
Casino (Columbia/CBS), 1978
Splendido Hotel (Columbia/CBS), 1979
Electric Rendezvous (Columbia/CBS), 1982
Tour De Force—Live (Columbia/CBS), 1982

WIth Paco De Lucia and John McLaughlin:
Friday Night In San Francisco (Columbia/CBS), 1981

With Chick Corea:
Touchstone (Warner Bros), 1970s

Neil Diamond
US vocalist, composer, guitarist.
Born Brooklyn, New York, January 24, 1941.

Career: Became staff songwriter with Sunbeam Music in New York City's legendary Brill Building 'hit factory' in early '60s. Earned biggest successes with **I'm A Believer** and **A Little Bit Me, A Little Bit You** for Monkees(▶).

Fellow writers Ellie Greenwich and Jeff Barry recognised Diamond's potential as artist and took him to Bert Berns' new Bang label in late 1965. Debut single **Solitary Man** (1966) set off train of hits, including **Cherry Cherry, Sweet Caroline** and **Cracklin' Rosie,** all cut after switch to Uni label. Meanwhile, **Kentucky Woman** (Elvis Presley(▶) and Deep Purple(▶)) and **The Boat That I Row** (Lulu(▶)) gave Diamond further rewards as writer.

With **Tap Root Manuscript** album (1970), Diamond ventured beyond realms of pure pop for imaginative (if trifle pretentious) **African Trilogy** song cycle.

Earlier projected as a clean-cut 'all-American boy', Diamond grew hair longer and cultivated new image as introspective folk-poet; built ever wider audience. In 1973, earned record multi-million dollar advance on

signing to Columbia for conceptual **Jonathan Livingston Seagull** soundtrack album. This was followed by **Serenade** (1974), then two years of silence before superb **Beautiful Noise** set, produced by Bond's(▶) Robbie Robertson, as was **Love At The Greek** live double album.

Teaming up with Barbra Streisand(▶) in late 1978, Diamond had huge hit with duet titletrack from **You Don't Bring Me Flowers** LP. (Diamond and Streisand had both recorded **Flowers** single; Colombia decided to record duet when they heard a DJ splice two versions together). Worked with Four Seasons' producer Bob Gaudio for follow-up set **September Morn** (1979).

The 1980 re-make of the classic Al Jolson movie 'The Jazz Singer', co-starring Sir Laurence Olivier, took Diamond to new heights and revealed his acting talents. Spine-tingling hit single **Love On The Rocks** from film showed his mastery of mood and innate soulfulness.

In earlier times often dismissed as a purveyor of somewhat trite efforts at artiness, Diamond has emerged as a totally distinctive and creative songwriter, and a performer of major stature.

Hit Singles:	US	UK
Cherry Cherry, 1966	6	—
I Got The Feelin' (Oh No No), 1966	16	—
You Got To Me, 1967	18	—
Girl, You'll Be A Woman Soon, 1967	10	—
I Thank The Lord For The Night Time, 1967	13	—
Sweet Caroline, 1969	4	—
Holly Holy, 1969	6	—
Cracklin' Rosie, 1970	1	3
He Ain't Heavy—He's My Brother, 1970	20	—
Sweet Caroline, 1971	—	8
I Am. . . I Said, 1971	4	4
Stones/Crunchy Granada Suite, 1971	14	—
Song Sung Blue, 1972	1	14
Play Me, 1972	11	—
Walk On Water, 1972	17	—
Longfellow Serenade, 1974	5	—
If You Know What I Mean, 1976	11	35
Beautiful Noise, 1976	—	13
Desiree, 1978	16	39
Forever In Blue Jeans, 1979	20	16
September Morn, 1979	17	—
Love On The Rocks, 1980	2	17
Hello Again, 1981	6	51
America, 1981	8	—
Yesterday's Song, 1981	11	—
Heartlight, 1982	5	47

With Barbra Streisand:

You Don't Bring Me Flowers, 1978	1	5

Albums:
(Excluding budget reissues)
The Feel Of Neil Diamond (Bang/—), 1966
Just For You (Bang/-), 1967
Greatest Hits (Bang/Joy), 1968
Velvet Gloves And Spit (MCA), 1968
Brother Love's Travelling Salvation Show (MCA), 1969
Touching You Touching Me (MCA), 1969
Gold (MCA), 1970
Shiloh/Solitary Man (Bang/—), 1970
Tap Root Manuscript (MCA), 1970
Do It (Bang/—), 1971
Moods (MCA), 1972
Hot August Night (MCA), 1972
Double Gold (Bang/—), 1973
Rainbow (MCA), 1973
Jonathan Livingston Seagull (Soundtrack), 1973
Stones (MCA), 1974

Below: Bo Diddley (right) holding one of his home made guitars.

His 12 Greatest Hits (Direct/MCA), 1974
Serenade (Columbia/CBS), 1974
Beautiful Noise (Columbia/CBS), 1976
And The Singer Sings His Song (MCA), 1976
Love At the Greek (Columbia/CBS), 1977
20 Golden Greats (MCA), 1978
September Morn (Columbia/CBS), 1980
The Jazz Singer (songs from the soundtrack) (Capitol), 1980
Love Songs (Columbia/CBS), 1981
On The Way To The Sky (Columbia/CBS), 1981
12 Greatest Hits, Volume II (Columbia/CBS), 1982
Heartlight (Columbia/CBS), 1982
Live Diamond (—/MCA), 1982

With Barbra Streisand:
You Don't Bring Me Flowers (Columbia/CBS), 1978

Bo Diddley

US vocalist, guitarist, composer.
Born Ellas McDaniel, McComb, Mississippi, December 30, 1928.

Career: Raised by mother's cousin, Mrs Gussie McDaniel; taken to Chicago aged five. Studied classical violin for 12 years but also absorbed music of Baptist church services. Rhythm and blues influences were in complete contrast—balladry of Nat Cole(▶), humour of Louis Jordan, guitar of John Lee Hooker(▶). Streets of Chicago brought contact with Mississippi Delta blues style of Muddy Waters(▶) and Little Walter, who gigged in local clubs.

Given guitar by sister as teenager; taught himself to play and formed small group in early 1950s. Played on street corners: Diddley, vocals, guitar; Frank Kirkland, drums (Jerome Green, maraccas; Billy Boy Arnold sometimes on harp).

Earned money as boxer, then construction worker, before realising that music could also pay bills. Auditioned for Chess in 1954, cutting **I'm A Man** and **Bo Diddley,** a landmark with its throbbing jungle rhythm. Disc was released on Checker in spring 1955. A Top 10 R&B hit, it provided foundation for years of inimitable material. Regular band included half-sister 'The Duchess' on rhythm guitar. Diddley maintained phenomenal output of original, lyrically unorthodox material with strong humour content; **Cracking Up** provided Bo's first crossover pop hit in summer 1959; then **Say Man** became Top 20 smash. In early 1960s Diddley's repertoire was used by many British beat groups, songs like **Road Runner, Pretty Thing, Mona, Who Do You Love, I Can Tell** and **You Can't Judge A Book By The Cover** clocking up good mileage. Diddley released prodigious quantity of LPs, mainly during '60s. Material was still mainly original, often predictable, but artist's humour and enthusiasm ooze from the grooves.

Distinctive pair of albums cut in 1967; **Super Blues,** with Bo, Muddy Waters and Little Walter, and **The Super Super Blues Band** with Bo, Muddy and Howlin' Wolf. Around 1970 Bo tried heavier musical context for LP **Another Dimension,** with uncomfortable results; similarly uninspiring was **Big Bad Bo** in 1974. In 1972 and 1973, his stage performance was filmed for **Let The Good Times Roll** and **Keep On Rockin'.**

Continued heavy schedule of live shows in US and Europe; disc career less active. With demise of Chess, signed with RCA; cut disappointing LP **20th Anniversary Of Rock 'n' Roll,** and **Not Fade Away,** a flop 45. Now tours as support to British 'new wave' bands who mirror his energy if not his talent.

Guitars: Various custom-bodied Gibsons.

Hit Singles:	US	UK
Say Man, 1959	20	—

Albums:
Golden Decade (—/Chess),1973
Toronto Rock 'N' Roll Revival 1969 Volume 5 (Accord/—), 1981

Worth Searching Out:
Have Guitar Will Travel (Checker/—), 1962
Bo Diddley Is A Gunslinger (Checker/Pye), 1963
Black Gladiator (Checker/—), 1971

Dion

US vocalist, songwriter.
Born Dion Di Mucci, Bronx, New York, July 18, 1939.

Career: First professional appearance was at 15 on Paul Whiteman's 'Teen Club' TV show in Philadelphia. First group the Timberlanes formed 1957; recorded one single for Mohawk label without success. During 1958 formed new group the Belmonts, named after Belmont Avenue in NY; recorded further single for Mohawk, which also failed. Moved to Laurie label where **I Wonder Why** (released as Dion and the Belmonts) quickly became hit, followed by two Top 50 entries. Then, in 1959, had first Top 10 hit, **A Teenager In Love.** All were in pure, if 'white', doo-wop style.

Dion and the Belmonts became most

Dion & the Belmonts' reunion LP. Courtesy B & C Records.

Above: Dire Straits, led by Knopfler (bottom left) started the 1980s as one of the top groups in the world.

popular white vocal group of rock 'n' roll era, although chart successes were somewhat erratic. Biggest hit **Where Or When** preceded Dion's departure from Belmonts in 1960, and first solo hit in similar style, **Lonely Teenager.** Despite failure of immediate follow-ups, achieved even greater success when **Runaround Sue** reached No. 1 in 1961, consolidating popularity both in US and UK.

Moved to CBS Records in 1962. Continued to hit charts with singles still sounding like extension of Belmonts' style, until venture into MOR and, later, R&B, style failed to maintain popularity. Drugs problem forced semi-retirement during 1964 but returned in 1967 to re-unite with Belmonts, recording minor hit **My Girl The Month of May** for ABC; failed to equal past glories.

By 1969 had re-signed with Laurie Records and regained magic touch, with **Abraham, Martin & John** reaching No. 4 and heralding turn to 'folk-protest' style for remainder of Laurie output. Signed to Warner Bros in 1970. Apart from further reunion with Belmonts, which resulted in fine live LP (1972), recorded in contemporary singer-songwriter style without commercial success.

Despite highly regarded recordings with Phil Spector in late '70s and several attempts at comeback singles and albums, Dion has failed to break out of 'oldies' market; looks set to remain in demand only for revival concerts and periodic reunions with Belmonts.

Hit Singles:	US	UK
No One Knows,* 1958	19	—
A Teenager In Love,* 1959	5	—
Where Or When*, Dion, 1960	3	—
Lonely Teenager, 1960	12	—
Runaround Sue, 1961	1	11
The Wanderer, 1961	2	10
Lovers Who Wander, 1962	3	—
Little Diane, 1962	8	—
Love Came To Me, 1962	10	—
Ruby Baby, 1963	2	—
Donna The Prima Donna, 1963	6	—
Drip Drop, 1963	6	—
Abraham, Martin & John, 1968	4	—
The Wanderer, 1976	—	16
*With the Belmonts	

Albums:
Dion's Greatest Hits (Laurie), 1964
Dion And The Belmonts Greatest Hits (Laurie), 1982.
Greatest Hits (Columbia/—), 1978.

Dire Straits

UK group formed 1977.

Original line-up: Mark Knopfler, Schecter, Fernandez guitars, vocals, producer; Dave Knopfler, guitar; John Illsley, bass; Pick Withers, drums.

Career: Originally formed by Mark Knopfler with brother Dave on guitars, Illsley on bass, and Pick Withers on drums. Dire Straits burst on music scene with unlikely hit single, an affectionate rock song about a jazz band, **Sultans Of Swing.** In year dominated by punk in UK and arena-rock in US, record was surprising and refreshing, with simple arrangement and cool, silky Stratocaster solos by Mark Knopfler. Self-titled first album, released in 1978, was immediately successful, eventually going platinum in several countries, as did **Communique**, released later that year. Dave Knopfler then left band; replaced by Hal Lindes.

Mark Knopfler composes all Straits material and his husky, semi-spoken (Dylan-influenced) vocals, and instantly recognisable lead guitar are the Dire Straits sound, though he doesn't take limelight on stage. (Knopfler has played on sessions with, among others, Bob Dylan(▶) and Steely Dan(▶).

Communique, Dire Straits. Courtesy Vertigo Records.

With third album **Making Movies,** band's sound expanded with effective addition of keyboards, played on record by E Street Band's Roy Bittan. Knopfler's songwriting also continued to grow, ranging from **Tunnel Of Love,** a lyrical carnival romance (introduced by a haunting few bars of Richard Rodgers' 'Carousel Waltz') to **Skateaway,** a chuckling appreciation of a city girl on rollerskates.

The next album, **Love Over Gold** (1982), went to top of US LP charts, remaining in Top 100 for months. With addition to permanent line-up of keyboardist Alan Clark, Dire Straits found neat, tight organisation with the flexibility of an orchestra. Knopfler's ever more powerful songs needed that flexibility. **Love Over Gold** took on more difficult subjects than personal passions. In it Knopfler explored, with some pain, not only states of the heart but state of the world, and the force of history. Album met with great critical approval, especially in UK. After **Gold,** respected drummer Terry Williams (ex-Man, Rockpile) joined as tour started.

Mark Knopfler is one of the new guitar heroes, a breed which almost perished in the first wash of the New Wave. In Dire Straits first appearance, he was a devoted user of the Fender Stratocaster; but recently he has been using several custom-made Schecter guitars with different pick-ups and tonal qualities, and a Japanese Strat copy, a Fernandez. His score for film 'Local Hero' earned him further plaudits for his ever-evolving technique in 1983.

Current line-up: Mark Knopfler; Hal Lindes, guitar; Alan Clark, keyboards; Terry Williams, drums.

Hit Singles:	US	UK
Sultans Of Swing, 1979	4	8
Romeo And Juliet, 1981	—	11
Private Investigations, 1982	—	2

Albums:
Dire Straits (Warner Bros/Vertigo), 1978
Communique (Warner Bros/Vertigo), 1979
Making Movies (Warner Bros/Vertigo), 1980
Love Over Gold (Warner Bros/Vertigo),1982

Mark Knopfler Solo:
Local Hero (soundtrack) (Vertigo), 1983

Bill Doggett

US organist, bandleader, composer.
Born Philadelphia, February 16, 1916; died late '70s.

Career: The man who popularised use of Hammond electric organ in R&B started as pianist with Jimmy Gorman's Band in 1935. Took over leadership in 1938 but soon relinquished position to Lucky Millinder. Remained with band until 1942; worked from then until 1944 as pianist with the Ink Spots. Then replaced Bill Davis in Tympani 5 led by Louis Jordan. Davis went off to study Hammond organ and was brought back on that instrument at huge salary by Jordan; in protest, Doggett quit band and bought himself a Hammond!

Forming own combo in 1952, signed with Cincinnati-based King label and recorded prolifically. Hit peak with perky **Honky Tonk** (1956). Record hinged round Clifford Scott's rooting saxophone and Billy Butler's guitar work as well as Doggett's own organ vamping. It sold three-million-plus copies and was later revived by James Brown(▶). After nine years with King, Doggett switched to Warner Bros in 1961, then recorded for succession of labels, including Columbia, Sue, ABC ad Roulette. Toured Europe in 1964 package with Miles Davis and Sarah Vaughan. Has worked as backing musician and arranger with Ella Fitzgerald. He died in late '70s.

Hit Singles:	US	UK
Honky Tonk (Parts 1 and 2) 1956	2	—

Albums:
Worth Searching Out:
Honky Tonk (King/—), early '60s
Fingertips (ABC Paramount/HMV), 1963
Honky Tonk à la Mode (Roulette/—), 1964
Wow! (ABC Paramount/HMV), 1965

Fats Domino

US vocalist, pianist, composer.
Born Antoine Domino, New Orleans, February 26, 1928.

Career: One of nine children in family with little musical background. Became interested in piano at early age; taught to play by his brother-in-law Harrison Verrett. Quickly gained proficiency; played and sang in local clubs. At 17, was in Billy Diamond's band; leader tagged him 'Fats' and it stuck. Played nights in juke-joints and worked days in factory when spotted by trumpeter/bandleader Dave Bartholomew.

Success began in 1949 with Imperial

Records. December session yielded **The Fat Man,** a hit early in 1950. Fats had R&B hits for five years; style influenced by Albert Ammons,Meade Lux Lewis, Pleasant Joseph, Leon T.Gross (Archibald), Little Willie Little-field.

Hit national charts in late 1955 with **Ain't That A Shame;** for next eight years was regular in US Top 50. Hits included **I'm In Love Again, Blueberry Hill, Blue Monday, Whole Lotta Loving, I'm Ready, Walking To New Orleans** and **Be My Guest.** Also had parts in rock movies 'Shake Rattle & Roll,' 'Disc Jockey Jamboree', 'The Big Beat,' 'The Girl Can't Help It'.

1960s saw dilution of music with occasional strings; material less convincing in aesthetic content. At end of 1962 declining sales brought parting with Imperial. Signed to ABC Paramount, output tailored to contemporary needs; **Red Sails In The Sunset** was Top 50 hit, combining piano triplets with swirling strings. A dozen releases yielded one more hit, **Heartbreak Hill;** by late 1964 Fats and Paramount had parted. Joined Mercury in 1965; brief association yielded a couple of abysmal singles.

Company taped Domino in Las Vegas, producing excellent 'live' LP. Made British debut at the Saville Theatre, March 1967. Following two years of recording inactivity formed own label, Broadmoor. Cut two singles before being signed by Reprise in 1968. Reprise album **Fats Is Back** was produced by Richard Perry; half-a-dozen singles had small sales; **Lady Madonna** made Top 100 in US charts.

Fats now seems content to live quietly at home with wife Rosemary and their eight children. Takes his pick of cabaret dates and occasional overseas tours; in 1978 went to Sea-Saint Studios to cut LP **Sleeping On The Job** for Sonet. Rumours of more new material in vintage New Orleans style have yet to be realised.

Hit Singles:	US	UK
Ain't That A Shame, 1955	10	23*
I'm In Love Again/My Blue Heaven, 1956	3	12
My Blue Heaven/I'm In Love Again, 1956	19	—
When My Dreamboat Comes Home, 1956	14	—
Blueberry Hill, 1956	2	6

	US	UK
Blue Monday, 1957	5	23
I'm Walkin', 1957	4	19
Valley Of Tears/It's You I Love, 1957	8	25
It's You I Love/Valley Of Tears, 1957	8	25
The Big Beat, 1958	26	20
Whole Lotta Loving, 1959	6	—
Margie/I'm Ready, 1959	51	18
I'm Ready/Margie, 1959	16	—
I Want To Walk You Home/I'm Gonna Be A Wheel Someday, 1959	8	14
I'm Gonna Be A Wheel Someday/ I'm Gonna Walk You Home, 1959	17	—
Be My Guest, 1959	8	11
Country Boy, 1960	25	19
Walking To New Orleans, 1960	6	19
Three Nights A Week, 1960	15	45
My Girl Josephine, 1960	14	32
Let The Four Winds Blow, 1961	15	—
*1957 in UK		

Albums (selected):
Million Sellers (Liberty), 1962
Fats Domino (Archive Of Folk And Jazz Music/—), 1966
Fats Domino Volume 2 (Archive Of Folk And Jazz Music/—), 1967
Legendary Masters (United Artists), 1972
The Fats Domino Story Volumes 1-6 (—/United Artists), 1977
Sleeping On The Job (Polydor/Sonet), 1979

Above: The veteran rocker from New Orleans, Fats Domino.

Lonnie Donegan

UK vocalist, guitarist, composer, banjoist.
Born Glasgow, April 29, 1931.

Career: Following family move to London, took up guitar at age 15. Turned to drums and banjo during Army service. First professional appearances in 1952 with Ken Colyer's Jazzmen, playing banjo and later singing in own skiffle music segment of Colyer's engagements. Band became Chris Barber Jazz Band after Colyer's departure in 1954, and recorded first album for Decca—**Rock Island Line** was credited to 'Lonnie Donegan Skiffle Group'. Track later released as single and became first hit (1956) after contract with Decca had expired. With **Rock Island Line** making inroads on US charts, Donegan was swiftly signed by Pye Records as solo act. First release **Lost John** soon became hit.

Tours of UK and US followed, with Donegan at head of skiffle music boom inspired by folksy simplicity of music and cheapness of instruments required for accompaniment. Throughout late '50s appeared regularly in charts with skiffle material. Songs were based mostly on traditional melodies but with arrangements bordering on rock 'n' roll. Got British kids to start thinking of groups, rather than just individuals (Presley, Berry, etc.).

Biggest hit **My Old Man's A Dustman** at end of skiffle era (1960) was followed by huge US success with another novelty, **Does Your Chewing Gum Lose Its Flavour.** By 1962 career had waned somewhat despite effectively turning to more adult material. Remained popular live performer throughout '60s with regular television appearances and new recordings. Awareness of value in song copyrights had prompted formation of own publishing company in '50s. Income from own songs, together with other writers signed to company, was considerable, with **Nights In White Satin** becoming modern 'standard'— this copyright was reputedly purchased for $500.

In recent years Donegan has recorded erratically, few later recordings have equalled previous material, despite assistance of several 'superstars'. Notable exception was 1981 single with rockabilly band Shakin' Pyramids, which proved Donegan was still capable of energetic performance.

Although hardly an innovator in strict

Left: Lonnie Donegan, the only superstar of skiffle.

sense, Donegan was one of the most success-full UK solo artists, second only to Cliff Richard(▶) in late '50's/early '60's and can take credit for several 'firsts'. Most notable was his ability to sell skiffle back to America in days when US charts were dominated by home-grown artists.

Hit Singles:

	US	UK
Rock Island Line, 1956	8	8
Lost John, 1956	—	2
Skiffle Session (EP), 1956	—	20
Bring A Little Water Sylvie, 1957	—	7
Don't You Rock Me Daddy-O, 1957	—	4
Cumberland Gap, 1957	—	1
Puttin' On The Style, 1957	—	1
My Dixie Darling, 1957	—	10
Jack O'Diamonds, 1957	—	14
Grand Coolie Dam, 1958	—	6
Sally Don't You Grieve, 1958	—	11
Tom Dooley, 1958	—	3
Does Your Chewing Gum Lose Its Flavour, 1959	5*	3
Fort Worth Jail, 1959	—	14
Battle of New Orleans, 1959	—	2
Sal's Got A Sugar Lip, 1959	—	13
San Miguel, 1959	—	19
My Old Man's A Dustman, 1960	—	1
I Wanna Go Home, 1960	—	5
Lorelei, 1960	—	10
Lively, 1960	—	13
Have A Drink On Me, 1961	—	8
Michael Row The Boat, 1961	—	6
The Comancheros, 1962	—	14
The Party's Over, 1962	—	9
Pick A Bale Of Cotton, 1962	—	11

*1961 in US

Albums:
Golden Hour of Golden Hits (—/Golden Hour), 1971
Golden Hour of Golden Hits Volume 2 (—/Golden Hour), 1973
Lonnie Donegan File (—/PRT), 1977
Jubilee Concert, (—/Dakota), 1981

Donovan

UK vocalist, guitarist.
Born Donovan Leitch, Glasgow, Scotland, May 10, 1946.

Career: Launched via ITV's 'Ready Steady Go' pop show (1965) as Britain's answer to Bob Dylan(▶), Donovan projected diluted version of then fashionable 'protest singer' image. His imitation extended to denim dungarees, flat denim hat, harmonica harness and acoustic guitar bearing legend 'This machine kills' (which Dylan himself had borrowed from Woody

Donovan's Greatest Hits. Courtesy Epic Records.

Guthrie(▶) who included the important extra word 'fascists'). Switching to flower-power in 1966 he became very much own man, with delightful results.

Signed to Pye Records, his first big hit, **Catch The Wind**, was still in Dylan mould, but by **Sunshine Superman** (1966) and

Mellow Yellow (a US chart-topper in 1967) Donovan had evolved extremely catchy folk-pop sound, and consequent **Sunshine Superman** LP, produced by Mickie Most, was a gem, as was **A Gift From A Flower To A Garden** set. By this time Donovan had injected into his work a large measure of mysticism and colourful imagery.

After 1969 Jeff Beck(▶) collaboration on **Barabajagal** hit single, Donovan renounced drug culture, took up Eastern mysticism (following Beatles' lead) and retired to Ireland, emerging a year later to score movie 'If It's Tuesday This Must Be Belgium'.

In 1972 he scored 'The Pied Piper' (which he appeared in) and in '73 'Brother Sun, Sister Moon'. Also released in '73 was acclaimed **Cosmic Wheels** LP. However, most of Donovan's '70s LPs were poorly received in US, where the flower power image was 'out'.

Moving to US, he wrote stage show'7-Tease' in 1974 and cut concept album in Nashville before virtual retirement. Re-emerging at Edinburgh Festival, he toured Germany and France, and appeared on London Palladium charity Christmas show with Ralph McTell and Billy Connolly which led to 1981 UK concert tour and new album.

Hit Singles:

	US	UK
Catch The Wind, 1965	23	4
Colours, 1965	—	4
Sunshine Superman, 1966	1	3
Mellow Yellow, 1966	2	8
Epistle To Dippy, 1967	19	—
There Is A Mountain, 1967	11	8
Jennifer Juniper, 1968	26	5
Hurdy Gurdy Man, 1968	5	4
Atlantis, 1969	7	23
Barabajagal, 1969	—	12

Albums:
Catch The Wind (Hickory/Hallmark), 1965
Sunshine Superman (Epic/Pye), 1966
In Concert (Epic/Pye), 1968
Hurdy Gurdy Man (Epic/—), 1968

From A Flower To A Garden (Epic/Pye), 1968
Barabajagal (with Jeff Beck) (Epic/—), 1968
Greatest Hits (Epic/Pye), 1969
Colours (—/Hallmark), 1972
Cosmic Wheels (—/Epic), 1973
Donovan (—/Rak), 1977
The Donovan File (—/Pye), 1977
Greatest Hits (—/Embassy), 1979

Doobie Brothers

US group formed 1970.
Original line-up: Tom Johnston, guitar, vocals; John Hartman, drums; Pat Simmons, guitar vocals; Dave Shogren, bass.

Career: Founded in San Jose, California, from remnants of band Pud; first line-up included Johnston, Hartman and bassist Gregory Murphy. Shogren quickly replaced Murphy, and with acquisition of Simmons group cut debut album for Warner Bros in 1971.

Additional drummer Mike Hossack joined soon after release of **The Doobie Bros;** Tiran Porter recruited for departing Dave Shogren (who joined Dave Gardner group). Quintet soon earned reputation on West Coast, basing themselves in San Francisco, latterly San Anselmo.

Twin guitars of Simmons and Johnston courted comparison with Allman Bros(▶). Doobies, however, were altogether lighter and less blues-influenced. Second album **Toulouse Street** introduced band to charts, both album and single (**Listen To The Music**) confirming hard-driving, but commercial, approach.

Now prominent concert attraction, band debuted in UK using new drummer Keith Knudsen (ex-Lee Michaels); Hossack moved to short-lived Bonaroo in 1975. Reviews were mixed but audiences enthusiastic. This line-up cut **The Captain & Me** LP, which followed **Toulouse Street** as second gold

Above: The Doobie Brothers 'Takin' It To The Streets' in the late 1970s.

record. Band's long-time favourite **Long Train Running** was major single success from album.

What Were Once Vices Are Now Habits included session work from Jeff 'Skunk' Baxter, former Steely Dan(▶) guitarist. Baxter joined Doobies permanently shortly

Stampede, The Doobie Brothers. Courtesy Warner Bros Records.

after album's release. Two-million seller **Black Water** (another band anthem) was US No. 1 culled from **Vices** set.

Another former Steely Dan member, keyboard player/vocalist Michael McDonald, joined group in 1976; he had temporarily stood in for Johnston during '75 US tour. McDonald's inclusion took band into new era, with emphasis on R&B-styled rythms behind his high, impassioned voice—McDonald stands apart as one of the finest rock vocalists in the business, with phenomenal control and range.

Never the rock critic's favourite outfit, Doobies reversed opinion with stunning **Minute By Minute** album. With group now trimmed to six-piece (Johnston having left permanently in 1978), and McDonald and Simmons splitting lead vocal role, **Minute** earned four Grammy awards. Titletrack and **What A Fool Believes** are now rock classics, having been covered by various prominent performers (Aretha Franklin(▶) had minor US hit with **Fool**).

Doobies' ever-evolving line-up saw further changes in 1979, when Baxter and Hartman quit. Baxter is now producing (Nazareth(▶), Terry Boylan) and doing session work after stint with Four On The Floor (with Al Kooper(▶), Rich Schlosser, Neil Stubenhaus). Replacements were Cornelius Bumpus (ex-Moby Grape(▶)), keyboards and sax; John McFee (ex-Clover, sessions for Steve Miller(▶) and Bill Wyman) guitar; and drummer Chet

Minute By Minute, The Doobie Bros. Courtesy Warner Bros Records.

McCracken (ex-Don Randi Band, Nick Gilder). Seven-piece Doobies recorded **One Step Closer** in 1980, with long-time producer Ted Templeman still at helm. Album included Top 10 US hit **Real Love**.

Lack of studio recording since **Closer** (**Best of Volume 2** released in interim) has enabled McDonald to release debut solo album **If That's What It Takes** (1982) which features leading session players Steve Gadd, drums; Willie Weeks, bass; Dean Parks, guitar; Louis Johnson, bass; and Edgar Winter and Jeff and Mike Porcaro (Toto(▶)). McDonald has also recorded with Gary Wright, Elton John(▶), Jackie DeShannon, Christopher Cross(▶) and Kenny Loggins(▶) (with whom he wrote **What A**

Fool Believes). Added keyboards to Tom Johnston's solo album **Everything You Feel Is True** (1979).

Although derivative in early days, latter work (particularly after introduction of McDonald) has been exemplary, and Doobies remain a major live attraction. Certain inductees into the Rock Hall Of Fame. No doubt they will release a 'Best Of' Volume 3 in a few years.

Current line-up: Simmons; Michael McDonald, keyboards, vocals; John McFee, guitar; Keith Knudsen, drums; Chet McCracken, drums, percussion; Tiran Porter bass; Cornelius Bumpus, saxophones, keyboards.

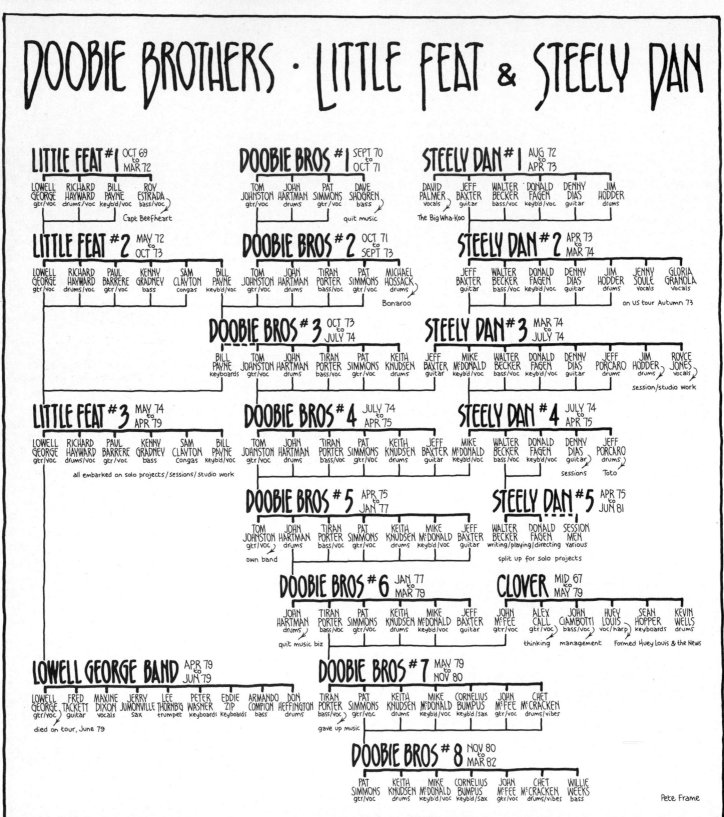

Hit Singles:	US	UK
Listen To The Music, 1972	11	29
Long Train Runnin', 1973	8	—
China Grove 1973,	15	—
Black Water, 1975	1	—
Take Me In Your Arms (Rock Me), 1975	11	29
Takin' It To The Streets, 1976	13	—
What A Fool Believes, 1979	1	31
Minute By Minute, 1979	14	47
Real Love, 1980	5	—

Albums:
Doobie Brothers (Warner Bros), 1971
Toulouse Street (Warner Bros), 1972
The Captain And Me (Warner Bros) 1973
What Were Once Vices (Warner Bros), 1974
Stampeded (Warner Bros), 1975
Takin' It To The Streets (Warner Bros), 1976
Best Of (Warner Bros), 1976
Livin' On The Fault Line (Warner Bros), 1977
Minute By Minute (Warner Bros), 1979
One Step Closer (Warner Bros),1980
Best Of Volume 2 (Warner Bros), 1981

Michael McDonald Solo:
If That's What It Takes (Warner Bros), 1982

Doors

US group formed 1965.

Original line-up: Jim Morrison, vocals; Ray Manzarek, keyboards; Robby Krieger, bass; John Densmore, drums.

Career: Leader and focus of band, Jim Morrison was born James Douglas Morrisson in Melbourne, Florida, on December 8, 1943. Graduated from George Washington High School in 1961, spent year at St Petersburg Junior College, then moved to Los Angeles to major in film techniques at UCLA. Met Chicago-born keyboard player Ray Manzarek who was running blues-flavoured band, Rick and the Ravens. They met LA native John Densmore, then playing with Psychedelic Rangers, and Robby Kreiger, at local meditation centre, and Doors opened career with gig at London Fog Club on Sunset Boulevard.

Early warning of subsequent tempestuous career came when they were banned from Los Angeles' prestigious rock club, Whiskey A Go-Go, for performance of **The End,** a

Below: Inside Morrison Hotel, The Doors. Courtesy Elektra Records.

half-spoken, half-improvised free-form epic song of apocalyptic imagery in which a young man murders his parents. A born rebel, Morisson claimed his own parents were dead and dropped one 's' from surname. His father was, in fact, a successful Rear Admiral from establishment family of long military standing.

The Doors' name was well chosen from William Blake: 'If the doors of perception were cleansed/All things would appear infinite'. Morrison's sense of theatrics aided him in acting out the fantasies, visions and fears of late '60s young America, from the innocuousness of flower power to the often frightening aspects of psychedelia and the self-destructiveness of drug culture. A charismatic figure on-stage, Morrison exuded animal sexuality with a mere glance.

Jack Holzman, who had been busy transforming his Elektra label from an esoteric folk outlet to major rock company, signed Doors; sensational debut album **Doors** included unedited version of **The End** as well as **Light My Fire**, which gave group US chart-topping single.

From sleeve art-work featuring various freaks, to bizarre lyrical content, second album, **Strange Days**, was archetypal Doors. Third set, **Waiting For The Sun**, yielded further No. 1 single **Hello I Love You** (only Doors recording which used a bass player — Doug Lubahn; Manzarek usually supplied bass lines through bass pedal of electric organ). Ray Davies of Kinks(▶)sued Doors, claiming **Hello** was rip-off of **All Day And All Of The Night**; UK royalties of **Hello I Love You** went to Davies instead of Doors. Featured on inner sleeve was full libretto of **The Celebration Of The Lizard King** but only small sampling, in form of **Not To Touch The Earth,** appeared on album, and plans for theatrical presentation were unfulfilled. Morrison did venture into movie world via 'A Feast Of Friends' (in collaboration with two acquaintances from UCLA days) and two promotional films, 'Break On Through' and 'The Unknown Soldier'. He had also completed another screenplay (with novelist Michael McClure) shortly before his death.

Hippy generation felt Morrison's political and philosophical statements were diluted by an innate commercialism. Those in authority rated them anarchical heresies and when, on stage, he not only urged violent resistance to police repression but advocated blatant sexualism, he soon ran into trouble. He was arrested for using obscene language in New

Haven, Connecticut, in December 1967, and for indecent exposure on stage in Miami in March 1969.

While court proceedings continued apace, rock critics alleged that Doors were merely pop outfit masquerading as leaders of youth revolution; this was confirmed in part when 1969 album **The Soft Parade** emerged with lightweight chart-style material and lack of direction. However, following album **Morrison Hotel** threw pretension to the wind, revealing hard edge of raw R&B. **Absolutely Live** set finally gave life to Morrison's reptilian fantasy (and alter-ego) via **The Celebration Of The Lizard**.

With LA Woman (1971), Doors reached creative zenith, blending brash rock 'n' roll with imagery of Morrison's lyrics in set which found them at most powerful and disturbing. From it came classic track **Riders On The Storm**.

Four years of over-indulgence in sex, drugs, drink, philosophising, soul-searching and rock 'n' roll were taking their toll. An angry, depressed and world-weary Morrison quit group to live in Paris and write poetry (published as two books 'The Lords' and 'The New Creatures' in 1971).

Fittingly, Morrison's death is shrouded in mystery and there are even rumours that he still lives. According to official records he died of a heart attack in his bath on July 3, 1971. He is buried in Perè Lachaise cemetery in Paris, which also houses remains of many of France's most famous artists, musicians, statesmen and legendary eccentrics. Morrison's tomb has become a point of pilgrimage for latter-day hippies.

Though lacking Morrison's touch of demented genius, **Other Voices** album was commendable effort from the three surviving Doors. **Full Circle** was sub-standard and trio broke up (though Manzarek made aborted effort to re-form group later with Iggy Stooge(▶) as vocalist).

Manzarek continued career with solo albums for Mercury in 1975 — **The Golden Scarab** and **The Whole Thing Started With Rock 'N' Roll And Now It's Out Of Control**, a title that could well stand as most fitting epitaph for Jim Morrison.

Krieger and Densmore produced album for the Comfortable Chairs then formed short-lived Butts Band, Krieger re-emerging in 1977 with jazz/rock outfit for **Bobby Krieger And Friends** album on Blue Note. Manzarek continues to work in California as producer/

manager for bands, notably LA group 'X'.

Greatest Hits (1980) went platinum in US, attesting to Doors dedicated following and new audience despite lack of new material or any chance of reunion.

Final line-up: Manzarek; Krieger; Densmore.

Hit Singles:	US	UK
Light My Fire, 1967	1	49
People Are Strange, 1967	12	—
Hello, I Love You, 1968	1	15
Touch Me, 1969	3	—
Love Her Madly, 1971	11	—
Riders On The Storm,	14	22

Albums:
Doors (Elektra), 1967*
Strange Days (Elektra), 1967
Waiting For The Sun (Elektra), 1968
The Soft Parade (Elektra), 1969
Morrison Hotel/Hard Rock Café (Elektra), 1970
Absolutely Live (Elektra), 1970
'13' (Elektra), 1971
LA Woman (Elektra), 1971
Weird Scenes Inside The Goldmine (Elektra), 1971
Best Of (Elektra), 1973
An American Prayer (Elektra), 1978
Greatest Hits (Elektra), 1980**
*Re-mastered version available under same title (Mobile/—), 1982
**Includes remixed versions of singles.

Worth Searching Out:
Other Voices (Elektra), 1971

Ray Manzarek Solo:
The Golden Scarab (Mercury), 1975

Dr Feelgood

UK group formed 1971.

Original line-up: Lee Brilleaux, vocals, guitar;
Wilko Johnson (John Wilkinson), guitar;
John B. Sparks, bass; The Big Figure (Johnny Martin), drums.

Career: Formed by local musicians in Southend/Canvey Island area; took name from blues by Piano Red. Attracted local following as result of wild performances, particularly by Wilko, who held guitar like a machine gun and moved like a robot. Fame

spread to nearby London, where pub rock phenomenon was in full bloom. Feelgood became popular live attraction; signed with Liberty/United Artists in 1974.

Early records were somewhat pale compared with strong live sound, emphasised by ecstatic reaction to band on 1975 pub rock package tour. Decision made to release live LP **Stupidity**, which topped UK charts at end of 1976. Soon afterwards, Wilko (by this time best-known member of group) left, after disagreements over material, to form own band with limited success. With replacement John 'Gypie' Mayo (spring 1977) chart success continued through 1979. In mid-1981, Mayo quit, replaced by Johnny Guitar (ex-Count Bishops). Since then, while remaining major live draw, Feelgood have rarely featured in charts. In 1982, Sparks and Figure also departed, replaced by Buzz Barwell (drums, ex-Lew Lewis Band) and Pat McCullan (bass, ex-Count Bishops), leaving Brilleaux as sole original.

New line-up was short lived—by mid-1983,

Malpractice, Dr. Feelgood. Courtesy United Artists Records.

Phil Mitchell (bass) had replaced McMullan, and Gordon Russell had superseded Johnny Guitar. Sadly, Dr Feelgood appear in 1983 as dated anachronism compared with early '70s reputation as authentic R&B band, hailed by punks and hippies alike as ultimate street-credible act of era. It is difficult to see this status returning without major policy changes, which seem unlikely to occur.

Current line-up: Brilleaux; Gordon Russell, guitar; Phil Mitchell, bass; Buzz Barwell, drums.

Hit Singles:

	US	UK
Milk And Alcohol, 1979	—	9

Albums:
Down By The Jetty (—UA), 1975
Malpractice (Columbia/UA), 1975
Stupidity (—/UA), 1976
Private Practice (—/UA), 1978
As It Happens (—/UA), 1979
Let It Roll (—/UA), 1979
A Case Of The Shakes (—/UA), 1980
On The Job (—/Liberty), 1981
Dr Feelgood's Casebook (—/Liberty), 1981
Fast Women And Slow Horses (—/Chiswick), 1982

Dr Hook

US group formed 1969.

Original line-up: Dennis Locorriere, vocals, guitar; Ray Sawyer, vocals, guitar; George Cummings, guitar, pedal steel guitar; Billy Francis, keyboards; Jay David, drums.

Career: Group was formed by former R&B singer Sawyer and ex-folkie Locorriere to play New Jersey club circuit. Shifting nucleus of musicians included other three as above.

First break was 'discovery' by Playboy

cartoonist and songwriter Shel Silverstein, who got band to perform soundtrack he had scored for Dustin Hoffman movie ('Who Is Harry Kellerman'). Columbia recording contract followed.

First two albums were entirely Silverstein-written, and vindicated Hook/Silverstein collaboration both artistically and commercially. Silverstein's compositions were wry, often humorous songs with strong country flavour, well suited to Locorriere's impassioned delivery. Debut album (credited to Dr Hook and Medicine Show, an appellation later dropped) yielded international hit in **Sylvia's Mother.** Follow-up **Sloppy Seconds** yielded major US hit with **The Cover Of Rolling Stone,** another unusual and humorous Silverstein song. They subsequently did get on the cover of Rolling Stone.

Next album, **Belly Up,** saw introduction of band's own songs; subsequent albums had compositions from variety of sources (still including Silverstein). By 1975 band's personnel comprised Locorriere; Francis; Cumming; Sawyer; Rik Elswit (1972), guitar; Billy Francis, keyboards; Jance Garfat (1972), bass; and John Wolters (1975), drums. Cummings left in 1976; Rob 'Willard' Henke played guitar from 1978-1980. Band switched labels to Capitol in 1976, move which resulted in renewed run of international hits.

In latter half of '70s Dr Hook's music evolved somewhat, becoming more dance orientated and more acceptable to pop audiences. Result was number of massive international hits that established band as major-league attraction, particularly in UK. Switched labels to Casablanca in 1980. Although progress has slowed slightly in last couple of years, Dr Hook have talent and, just as important, experience, to weather most fluctuations. Refreshingly unpretentious, they have provided many bright moments in course of lengthy career.

Current line-up: Locorriere; Sawyer; Francis; John Wolters, drums; Rik Elswit, guitar; Jance Garfat, bass; Rod Smarr, guitar.

Hit Singles:

	US	UK
Sylvia's Mother, 1972	5	2
The Cover Of Rolling Stone, 1972	6	—
Only Sixteen, 1976	6	—
A Little Bit More, 1976	11	2
If Not You, 1976	55	5
More Like The Movies, 1978	—	14
Sharing The Night Together, 1978	6	—
When You're In Love With A Beautiful Woman, 1979	6	1
Better Love Next Time, 1980	12	8
Sexy Eyes, 1980	5	4

Above: The voices of Dr. Hook—Sawyer (left) and Locorriere.

Albums:
Dr Hook And The Medicine Show (Columbia/CBS), 1971
Sloppy Seconds (Columbia/CBS), 1972
Belly Up (Columbia/CBS), 1973
Bankrupt (Capitol), 1976
A Little Bit More (Capitol), 1976
Makin' Love And Music (Capitol), 1977
Revisited (Columbia/CBS), 1977
Pleasure And Pain (Capitol), 1978
Sometimes You Win (Capitol), 1979
Rising (Casablanca), 1980
Greatest Hits (Capitol), 1980
Live In The UK (Capitol), 1981
Players In The Dark (Casablanca), 1982

Dr John

US vocalist, multi-instrumentalist, composer. Born Malcolm John 'Mac' Rebennack, New Orleans, 1941.

Career: Son of model and record store owner; appeared in soap ads as baby. Learnt guitar from Sister Eustace at Temple Of The Innocent Blood in home city. Entered music business while teenager as session guitarist and producer with Johnny Vincent's Ace Records, working under Red Tyler. Local sax player Lee Allen, famed for work with Fats Domino and Little Richard, introduced him to regular session crew working on R&B product at Cosimo Matassa's New Orleans studio. Played guitar on sides for Ebb, Specialty, Ric and Ronn labels, and wrote and arranged, notably Jerry Byrne's rock 'n' roll hit **Lights Out.** Worked on road in bands of Byrne and Frankie Ford and cut instrumental single **Storm Warning** (Rex) leading to albums for Ace and Rex. Shot in finger in 1961, he switched to electric bass, working in Dixieland band, before learning organ; backed strippers in French Quarter. Returned to session work for Harold Battiste's AFO ('All For One') black co-operative (though white); cut organ album for AFO label.

With Battiste, split for Los Angeles in 1962, taking other musicians with them, including drummer John Boudreaux (later a mainstay of Dr John band) and Mel Lasty (who later played cornet with King Curtis(▶)). Detoured via Texas and became hung up on drugs. Companions became back-up team for Sam Cooke(▶) but by time Rebennack arrived on West Coast Cooke had been shot dead. Cooke's manager J.W. Alexander helped Rebennack break into LA session

scene; he was soon playing guitar on record and on stage for Sonny and Cher(▶) as well as working with other New Orleans exiles Jesse Hill, Alvin Robinson, Shirley Goodman). Also worked with such producer/arrangers as H.B. Barnum, Gene Page and Rene Hall.

Formed own bands, Drits And Dravy (with Ronnie Barron), the Zu Zu Band (with Jessie Hill) and Morgus and the Three Ghouls. With Battiste's help, developed new mystic identity as Dr John Creux, The Night Tripper. This involved witch-doctor clothes, weird head dresses and self-proclamation as 'The Grand Zombie'. Image heightened by his vast bushy beard and considerable bulk.

Sonny Bono (of Sonny and Cher) financed first Dr John album, which was leased to Atlantic (1968) in one-off deal; included weird rhythms and hypnotic chants and eerie classic **Walk On Guilded Splinters.**

After further obscure album, Dr John joined Atlantic's regular roster thanks to producer Jerry Wexler, but he had become victim of drug abuse. A doctor from psychiatric ward of UCLA Medical Centre called Wexler who took him in hand; he was put on Atlantic staff as session musician, he cut organ for Aretha Franklin's (▶) **Spanish Harlem.**

Further Dr John recordings were cut and such musicians as Mick Jagger and Eric Clapton(▶) (who appeared on his 1971 album **Sun, Moon And Herbs)** helped spread the word.

Mixing voodoo, Creole, African and R&B influences, Dr John was one of pioneers of 'swamp rock' style (Doug Kershaw, Tony Joe White and Creedence Clearwater Revival(▶)) were other exponents, though none sounded quite like him). In 1973 **Right Time, Wrong Place** single made big impact leading to major tours, including one of Europe backed by New Orleans' R&B giants the Meters. In 1978 recorded **City Lights** album for A&M.

Since that zenith, Dr John has maintained low profile, while guesting on albums; remains a revered session pianist.

Hit Singles:

	US	UK
Right Place, Wrong Time, 1973	9	—

Albums:
City Lights (A&M), 1978
Love Potion (Accord/—), 1981
Plays (Clean Cuts/—), 1981

Worth Searching Out:
Gris Gris (Atco/Atlantic), 1968
Babylon (Atco/Atlantic), 1972
Cut Me While I'm Hot (—/DJM), 1976

The Drifters

US vocal group formed 1953.

Original line-up: Clyde McPhatter; Gerhardt Thrasher; Andrew Thrasher; Bill Pinkney.

Career: More like a football side than a group, the Drifters have featured constantly changing line-up. More than 40 individuals have worked with the official group over past three decades. Several breakaway groups have exploited name, notably Bill Pinkney's Original Drifters.

Masterminded by manager George Treadwell, then husband of Sarah Vaughan, group was launched to showcase lead singer Clyde McPhatter. First six releases, via Atlantic, were R&B hits.

In 1955, McPhatter left for military service, being replaced as lead singer briefly by David Baughn, then by Johnny Moore, who was in turn drafted. Bill Pinkney, Gerhardt Thrasher and Bobby Hendricks also sang lead at various times but most records flopped. The best was **Flip Flop,** led by Moore, and **Drip Drop,** led by Hendricks. Significantly, both songs were penned by Jerry Leiber and Mike Stoller. When Treadwell sacked his group in 1968 and set about finding a new set of Drifters, he turned to Leiber and Stoller for material.

Group chosen—Ben E. King, Doc Green, Charlie Thomas, Elsbeary Hobbs—had been working with no real success as the Crowns. Moving King to lead singer and using Leiber/Stoller songs proved masterstroke and 1959 smash hit **There Goes My Baby** set in train whole gamut of big records.

King left for solo career, also with Atlantic, in 1960 and Rudy Lewis was brought in from Clara Ward Singers as new lead voice. Lewis held job for next three years. Rest of group was blended with female back-up quartet of Dionne and Dee Dee Warwick, Doris Troy and Cissy Houston. Arrangements by Phil Spector, Burt Bacharach, Bert Berns and Gary Sherman and songs from Gerry Goffin and Carole King(▶), Burt Bacharach and Hal David, and Barry Mann and Cynthia Weil added to potent format, producing classic hits like **Up On The Roof, Sweets For My Sweet** and **Let The Music Play.**

Lewis died on eve of session for **Under The Boardwalk** and Johnnie Moore, who had returned to group, stepped into breach as new lead singer. Though no longer with Drifters, Moore can claim to have sung lead on more than 80% of all their records to date.

Group had capitalised on coming together of black and white teenage tastes in early '60s, but subsequent polarisation of audiences saw their run of success subside. Then, in 1972, UK Atlantic started to score on charts with re-issues of their earlier classics.

Consequent recording deal with Bell, and link with British songwriters Roger Cook, Roger Greenaway and Tony Macauley, brought new run of hits, reviving the teen-ballad story-line themes of their Atlantic classics. **Saturday Night At The Movies** inspired **Kissin' In The Back Row Of The Movies, and Under The Boardwalk** and **Sand In My Shoes** provided theme for **Down On The Beach Tonight**.

With group now under management of Treadwell's second wife (and widow) Faye, a steady living was made playing cabaret venues around the world—helping people revive fond memories of their teens. Moore remained only constant factor in perpetually evolving line-up.

In 1980 Moore left for short-lived solo career. He rejoined for short spell then left again to form Slightly Adrift, with fellow Drifter Joe Blunt and former member Clyde Brown, when Faye Treadwell decided to sever 11-year business relationship with group's UK promoter Henry Sellers.

Treadwell brought Ben E. King back into the Drifters as lead singer, also re-recruiting Bill Fredericks, who had sung lead on some of the group's Bell recordings.

Current line-up:
Ben E. King; Bill Fredericks.

Hit Singles:	US	UK
There Goes My Baby, 1959	2	—
Dance With Me, 1959	15	17
This Magic Moment, 1960	16	—
Save The Last Dance For Me, 1960	1	2
I Count The Years, 1961	17	28
Please Stay, 1961	14	—
Sweets For My Sweet, 1961	16	—
Up On The Roof, 1963	5	—
On Broadway, 1963	9	—
Under The Boardwalk, 1964	4	45
Saturday Night At The Movies, 1964	18	—
At The Club/Saturday Night At The Movies, 1972	—	3
Come On Over To My Place, 1972	—	9
Like Sister And Brother, 1973	—	7
Kissin' In The Back Row Of The Movies, 1974	—	2
Down On The Beach Tonight, 1974	—	7
There Goes My First Love, 1975	—	3
Can I Take You Home Little Girl, 1975	—	10
Hello Happiness, 1976	—	12
You're More Than A Number In My Little Red Book, 1976	—	5

Albums:
Golden Hits (Atlantic), 1966
Greatest Recordings—The Early Years (Atco/—), 1960
Love Games (—/Bell), 1975
24 Original Hits (Atlantic), 1975
Juke Box Giants (—/Audio Fidelity), 1982

Sly Dunbar and Robbie Shakespeare

Jamaican session duo formed 1975.
Sly (Noel Charles) Dunbar, drums; born Jamaica, May 10, 1952.
Robbie Shakespeare, bass; born Jamaica.

Career: Dunbar earned 'Sly' nickname for penchant for Sly and the Family Stone(▶) records. At 15, joined first band, the Yardbrooms. Stints followed with RHT Invincibles, the Volcanoes, and four-year residency at Kingston's Tit for Tat Club with Skin, Flesh And Bones (later re-named the Revolutionaries).

Dunbar's first recording session was on Dave and Ansell Collins' international reggae hit **Double Barrel.** Also played on Joy White's **The First Cut Is The Deepest,** the Upsetters' **Night Doctor** and Jimmy London's **I'm Your Puppet,** a reggae version of James and Bobby Purify's soul classic.

The Revolutionaries, with Dunbar's inventive double-rimshot drum style to the fore, became established session band for producer Jo Jo Hookim at Channel One Studio. A term with the Aggrovators introduced Dunbar to Robbie Shakespeare whose bass playing proved ideal foil, making them most in-demand session team in Jamaica.

After producing, arranging and playing on Mighty Diamonds' **The Right Time** (1976) album, duo went on to work with numerous other artists. These included Bunny Wailer, Gregory Isaacs, Dennis Brown, Johnny Clarke, Wailin' Souls, Black Uhuru, Gwen Guthrie and

Below: The faces that cover teenage bedroom walls in '80s—Duran Duran.

the reggae/funk hybrid music of Grace Jones(▶).

Albums:
Sly Dunbar solo.*
Simple Sly Man (—/Frontline), 1978
Sly Wicked And Slick (—/Frontline), 1979
Sly-Go-Ville (—/Island), 1982
*Shakespeare is featured on all Sly Dunbar's solo albums.

Duran Duran

UK group formed 1980.
Original/current line-up: Simon Le Bon, vocals; Andy Taylor, guitar; Nick Rhodes, synthesiser; John Taylor, bass; Roger Taylor, drums.

Career: Nick (born 1962) and John (born 1960) formed early version of band (name taken from villain in Jane Fonda film 'Bar-

Rio, Duran Duran. Courtesy EMI Records.

barella') with Steve Duffy (vocals) and Simon Colley (bass)—John played guitar at this point. Duffy and Colley left, replaced by Andy Wickett (vocals, ex-TV Eye) and Roger Taylor (born 1960, ex-Scent Organs). At this stage, band all from Birmingham area. Wickett left, John Taylor moved to bass, and Andy Taylor (born 1961) from Newcastle joined as a result of 'Melody Maker' advert. Simon (born 1958, Hertfordshire), then studying drama at Birmingham University, became final piece of jigsaw, assuming lyricist's role as well as singing.

In autumn 1980 toured as support act to Hazel O'Connor(▶). Group subsequently signed with EMI, and have been hugely successful ever since with eight consecutive original hit singles and two chart albums, reinforced by series of notable (if sometimes unnecessarily risqué) videos. Today Duran

Duran are arguably the biggest homegrown act in Britain, while their influence is spreading around the world. Most recently, MTV has brought them huge US following. Where such styles as 'futurism' and 'new romanticism' are catching on, group's photogenic qualities have placed them in a position of popularity similar to that enjoyed by the Bay City Rollers(▶) and the Osmonds(▶) in early '70s. However, Duran Duran seem better equipped musically and boast broader audience than their teenybop forbears.

Hit Singles:	US	UK
Planet Earth, 1981	—	12
Girls On Film, 1981	—	5
My Own Way, 1981	—	14
Hungry Like The Wolf, 1982	3	5
Save A Prayer, 1982	—	2
Rio, 1982	14	9
Is There Something I Should Know, 1983	—	1

Albums:
Duran Duran (Harvest/EMI), 1981
Rio (Harvest/EMI), 1982
Carnival Harvest, 1982

Ian Dury

UK vocalist, composer.
Born Billericay, Essex, 1942.

Career: Crippled by polio at age seven, Dury spent early youth at institution for disabled until going to grammar school. At 17 he went to Walthamstow Art College; then on to Royal College of Art for postgraduate course.

While teaching he formed band Kilburn and the High Roads, which cut a couple of albums and achieved considerable cult following. After Kilburn folded, Dury signed with Stiff Records and released **New Boots And Panties** with new band. Blockheads (Chas Jankel, guitar; Mickey Gallagher, keyboards; Davey Payne, sax; Norman Watt-Roy, bass; Charley Charles, drums). Dury and co-writer/musical director Chas Jankel combined intriguing new blend of soul/disco musical feel with English music-hall lyrical approach.

Boots eventually sold almost half a million copies, mainly in UK, and spawned classic rock 'n' roll anthem **Sex And Drugs And Rock And Roll.**

By now Blockheads had established reputation as hot live act, and were touring in US and Europe. First major single hit came in 1978 with **What A Waste,** which was followed by No. 1 **Hit Me With Your Rhythm Stick.**

Reasons To Be Cheerful Pt.3 in 1979 was band's last big hit, and subsequent releases have been less successful. Dury switched label to Polydor in 1980, a move which has as yet to pay big dividends. An idiosyncratic artist whose music is difficult to pigeonhole, Dury could regain impetus of career at any time.

Hit Singles:	US	UK
What A Waste, 1978	—	9
Hit Me With Your Rhythm Stick, 1978	—	1
Reasons To Be Cheerful, Pt. 3, 1979	—	3

Albums:
New Boots And Panties (Stiff), 1977
Do It Yourself (—/Stiff), 1979
Laughter (—/Stiff), 1980
Lord Upminster (Polydor), 1981

Worth Searching Out;
Kilburn and the High Roads:
Handsome (—/Pye), 1975
Wot A Bunch (—/Warner Bros), 1978

Bob Dylan

US composer, vocalist, guitarist, harmonica player.
Born Robert Allen Zimmerman, Duluth, Minnesota, May 24, 1941.

Career: Quiet, serious Bobby Zimmerman got good grades, participated in school activities and graduated from Hibbing High in 1959. However, listened to blues and country music, and was more interested in becoming rock 'n' roll star. At University of Minnesota discovered remnants of beat era in nearby Dinkytown with its folk music coffee-houses. Seeing this as route to success, began playing at local folk clubs. Read Woody Guthrie's(▶) 'Bound For Glory', began calling himself Bob Dylan, and invented past as runaway with Okie roots.

With rambling boy image down pat, got blessing—and fare—from parents for December 1960 visit to Guthrie in hospital. Remained in New York, singing traditional songs in Greenwich Village clubs. 'Village Voice' and 'New York Times' predicted success, while others thought him Guthrie clone—but uncool, uncaring and mannered.

Played back-up harmonica on titletrack of Harry Belafonte's **Midnight Special** album, and for Carolyn Hester. Signed by Columbia Records' John Hammond in October 1961. First album **Bob Dylan,** including own compositions **Song To Woody** and **Talkin' New York,** plus traditional numbers, sold only 5,000 copies in first year.

Dylan predicted direction music was heading and took civil rights/anti-war stance, often using 'borrowed' tunes for self-righteous, moralising topical songs filled with brilliant imagery and caustic irony. By March 1963 reputation was growing, and **The Freewheelin' Bob Dylan** was released (after power struggle between Hammond and Dylan's manager Albert Grossman led to Hammond's departure in mid-recording, replaced by Tom Wilson).

Album includes **Blowin' In The Wind,** highlight of Newport Folk Festival that summer when Dylan sang it with Peter, Paul and Mary(▶). Trio's cover version became Top 10 hit, selling 320,000 copies in first eight days of release. Personal relationship developed with Joan Baez(▶) and Dylan appeared at her concerts. Becoming hot property, he headlined Carnegie Hall concert; **The Times They Are A-Changin'** album made him hero of protest movement. Because of public pressure, by February 1964 Dylan became recluse, using bodyguards and drugs as protection from outside world.

With success as folk singer achieved, Dylan began changing image. During British visits, he heard English rock (and had small role in BBC-TV play). As usual, he had eye on barometer: though acoustic, 1964 LP **Another Side of Bob Dylan** was first step toward rock. Self-pitying and cruel, but vividly powerful, lyrics emphasised personal rather than political sentiments on songs like **All I Really Want To Do** and **It Ain't Me, Babe.** Folk fans and political protesters felt betrayed and album did not do as well as first two.

Spending much time in Woodstock, NY, Dylan wrote 18 new songs for 1965 **Bringing It All Back Home,** which completed switch from folk to rock, and from travelling to tripping. One side had four solo tracks, including **Mr Tambourine Man** and **It's All Over Now, Baby Blue;** other side with electric guitar and backup band featured **Subterranean Homesick Blues.** Released as single, this surreal, apocalyptic vision ultimately became Dylan's first gold record. The Byrds'(▶) two-minute version of **Mr Tambourine Man** went to No. 1 in US and UK, leading new folk-rock trend.

Although losing fans among protesters, Dylan gained wider audience of alienated young people who responded to funky music and sneering rejection of American Dream. May 1965 film 'Don't Look Back' showed on-stage and backstage dramas, including split with Baez, during Dylan's English tour. Returning to US, recorded **Like A Rolling Stone,** which gave him international stardom, with Mike Bloomfield(▶) on guitar and Al Kooper(▶) on organ. Single was released before rest of **Highway 61 Revisited,** produced by Bob Johnston.

Unveiling electric sound and Carnaby Street clothes at Newport and Forest Hills that summer, Dylan was booed by audience who saw prancing rock 'n' roller as sell-out. Next single **Positively 4th Street** was described as 'most vicious song ever to reach the Hit Parade'. Double album **Blonde on Blonde** was characterised by intense, poetic songs of drugs, dreams and nightmares about identity. Toured with the Hawks, later called the Band(▶); and married Sara Lowndes. Dylan admitted to being a millionaire with over 10 million records sold worldwide.

In July 1966, shortly after his 25th birthday, motorcycle crash led to 18-month disappearance; while recuperating in Woodstock from broken neck, rumours of death, disfigurement and drug addiction abounded. During this period Dylan recorded **Basement Tapes** with the Band (not officially released until eight years later). Early 1968 saw his appearance at benefit concert for Woody Guthrie, the birth of his first child, and release of **John Wesley Harding,** recorded in Nashville with country instrumentation. Voice had mellowed, lyrics were more accessible and gave hint of compassion, and tunes were melodic. **Nashville Skyline** continued songs in praise of living and gave last Top 10 single with **Lay Lady Lay.** During summer 1969 he split with Grossman; performed for huge crowds at Isle of Wight and Woodstock Festivals.

Moving back to Greenwich Village, released two disappointing records in 1970, although **Self Portrait** became seventh gold album. Over next two years kept low profile, while books, fanzines and Dylanology clubs interpreted his words and scavengers searched his garbage for significance. Meanwhile, bootleg records proliferated, Dylan's book Tarantula was published, and he visited Israel. Performed at Madison Square Garden benefit for Bangla Desh; recorded both electric and acoustic versions of **George Jackson** single, and did sessions for friends. **Greatest Hits II** was released.

Went to West Coast for small role in film 'Pat Garrett and Billy the Kid', and wrote score, including **Knocking On Heaven's Door.** When Columbia contract expired, recorded **Planet Waves** for Asylum; tour with the Band resulted in exciting live album **Before The Flood.**

Below: Bob Dylan during the early '70s—the classic electric era.

The Times They Are A-Changin'. Bob Dylan. Courtesy CBS Records.

Right: John Wesley Harding. Bob Dylan. Courtesy CBS Records.

Above right: Bob Dylan on stage during the late 1970s.

Re-signing with Columbia, recorded **Blood On The Tracks.** Filled with pain and bitterness (his marriage was breaking up), album was seen as return to form after recent simplistic good-time music. After recording new album **Desire,** toured with old friends and stars of 1960s in 1975-76 Rolling Thunder Revue. Dylan praised as charismatic entertainer; television special and live album **Hard Rain** released. During tour Dylan also created four-hour poetically rambling film 'Renaldo and Clara', screened in 1968.

At end of 1970s Dylan became born-again Christian. Somewhat self-righteously aimed moralising at non-believers (including fellow rock 'n' rollers). First post-conversion album **Slow Train Coming** (1979) featured talented instrumentalists. Later albums added gospel flavour, but didn't create much excitement. 'A creature of collective need', according to the 'New York Times', Bob Dylan has been a major influence on music and philosophy of young people for over 20 years. Whether his was a liberating influence that opened the mind to exploring new channels, or a polarising one that urged retreat and alienation is argued in sizeable collection of articles and books.

Hit Singles:	US	UK
Times They Are A-Changin', 1965	—	9
Subterranean Homesick Blues, 1965	39	9
Maggie's Farm, 1965	—	22
Like A Rolling Stone, 1965	2	4
Positively 4th Street, 1965	7	8
Can You Please Crawl Out Your Window!, 1966	58	17
Rainy Day Women, Nos 12 & 35, 1966	2	7
I Want You, 1966	20	16
Lay Lady Lay, 1969	7	5
Knockin' On Heaven's Door, 1973	12	14
Baby Stop Crying, 1978	—	13

Albums:

Bob Dylan (Columbia/CBS), 1962
Freewheelin' Bob Dylan (Columbia/CBS), 1963
Times They Are A-Changin' (Columbia/CBS), 1964
Another Side Of Bob Dylan (Columbia/CBS), 1964
Bringing It All Back Home (Columbia/CBS), 1965
Highway 61 Revisited (Columbia/CBS), 1965
Blonde On Blonde (Columbia/CBS), 1966
Greatest Hits (Columbia/CBS), 1967
John Wesley Harding (Columbia/CBS), 1968
Nashville Skyline (Columbia/CBS), 1969
Self Portrait (Columbia/CBS), 1970
New Morning (Columbia/CBS), 1970
Greatest Hits Volume II (Columbia/CBS), 1971
Pat Garrett & Billy The Kid (soundtrack) (Columbia/CBS), 1973
Dylan (Columbia/CBS), 1973
Planet Waves (Columbia/CBS), 1974
Before The Flood (Asylum/Island), 1974
Blood On The Tracks (Columbia/CBS), 1974
Desire (Columbia/CBS), 1975
Hard Rain (Columbia/CBS), 1976
Street Legal (Columbia/CBS), 1978
At Budokan (Columbia/CBS), 1978
Slow Train Coming (Columbia/CBS), 1979
Saved (Columbia/CBS) 1980
Shot Of Love (Columbia/CBS), 1981

Above: Dylan as he appeared in the 'Rolling Thunder' Revue of 1976.

Left: Street Legal, Bob Dylan. Courtesy CBS Records.

Inset above: Self Portrait, Bob Dylan. Courtesy CBS Records.

Above: Robert Allen Zimmerman Circa 1963, a 'freewheelin' folkie.

BIRMINGHAM BEATSTERS ELO · THE MOVE & MOODY BLUES

GERRY LEVENE AND THE AVENGERS 1963 to MAY 64

ROY WOOD guitar	GERRY LEVENE vocals	JIM ONSLOW bass	MIKE HOPKINS guitar	GRAEME EDGE drums

quit music business — to Idle Race

DENNY LAINE AND THE DIPLOMATS SEP 62 to MAY 64

PHIL ACKRILL gtr/voc	BEV BEVAN drums	STEVE HORTON bass	DENNY LAINE gtr/voc

UGLYS #1 1958 to 1965

STEVE GIBBONS vocals	JIMMY HOLDEN drums	JOHN GORDON keyboards	BOB BURNETT guitar	JOHN HUSTWAYTE bass

EL RIOT & THE REBELS 1957 to 1963

MIKE PINDER keyboards	RAY THOMAS voc/harp	MICKEY HERD guitar	BRIAN BETTERIDGE guitar	BOBBY SHURE drums	JOHN LODGE bass

MIKE SHERIDAN'S NIGHTRIDERS MAY 64 to JAN 66

GREG MASTERS bass/voc	DAVE PRITCHARD gtr/voc	ROGER SPENCER drums	MIKE SHERIDAN vocals	ROY WOOD gtr/voc

quit music biz

CARL WAYNE'S VIKINGS MAY 64 to JAN 66

CARL WAYNE vocals	ACE KEFFORD bass	BEV BEVAN drums	JOHNNY MANN guitar

DANNY KING AND THE MAYFAIR SET 1964 to JAN 66

TREVOR BURTON guitar	DANNY KING vocals	DENIS BALL bass	ROGER HARRIS keyb'ds	KEITH SMART drums

various groups — to the Sorcerers

MOODYBLUES #1 MAY 64 to NOV 66

DENNY LAINE gtr/voc	RAY THOMAS voc/harp	MIKE PINDER keyb'ds	GRAEME EDGE drums	CLINT WARWICK bass

SORCERERS 1965 to APR 68

COZY POWELL drums	DENIS BALL bass	THREE OTHERS various

MOVE #1 FEB 66 to APR 68

ACE KEFFORD bass/voc	CARL WAYNE vocals	ROY WOOD gtr/voc	BEV BEVAN drums	TREVOR BURTON gtr/voc

UGLYS #2 1966 to MAR 68

ROGER HILL guitar	JIMMY O'NEIL keyb'ds	DAVE PEGG bass	JIMMY HOLDEN drums	STEVE GIBBONS vocals

Mongrel · Mindbenders · Fairport Convention

MOODYBLUES #2 NOV 66 to JULY 78

RAY THOMAS voc/flute	JOHN LODGE bass/voc	GRAEME EDGE drums	RICK HAYWARD gtr/voc	MIKE PINDER keyb'ds

pulled out

THE ACE KEFFORD STAND APR 68 to JUN 69

COZY POWELL drums	DENIS BALL bass	DAVE BALL guitar	ACE KEFFORD gtr/voc

Jeff Beck/Rainbow · Procol Harum

MOVE #2 APR 68 to FEB 69

CARL WAYNE vocals	ROY WOOD gtr/voc	BEV BEVAN drums	TREVOR BURTON bass/voc

SIGHT 'N' SOUND 1964 to NOW

RICK PRICE gtr/voc	KELLY GROUCUTT bass/voc	GEOFF TURTON vocals	JOE DIGNAM drums	MANY OTHERS various

to E.L.O.

MOODYBLUES #3 JULY 78 to NOW

RAY THOMAS voc/flute	JOHN LODGE bass/voc	GRAEME EDGE drums	RICK HAYWARD gtr/voc	PATRICK MORAZ keyb'ds

IDLE RACE #1 MAY 66 to JAN 70

GREG MASTERS bass/voc	DAVE PRITCHARD gtr/voc	ROGER SPENCER drums	JEFF LYNNE gtr/voc

MOVE #3 FEB 69 to JAN 70

CARL WAYNE vocals	RICK PRICE bass/voc	ROY WOOD gtr/voc	BEV BEVAN drums

UGLYS #3 MAR 68 to FEB 69

WILLIE HAMMOND guitar	RICHARD TANDY keyb'ds	DAVE MORGAN bass	STEVE GIBBONS vocals	KEITH SMART drums

IDLE RACE #2 JAN 70 to FEB 72

GREG MASTERS bass/voc	DAVE PRITCHARD gtr/voc	ROGER SPENCER drums	MIKE HOPKINS guitar	DAVE WALKER vocals

MOVE #4 JAN 70 to OCT 71

RICK PRICE bass/voc	ROY WOOD gtr/voc	JEFF LYNNE gtr/voc	BEV BEVAN drums

BALLS #1 FEB 69 to DEC 69

RICHARD TANDY keyboards	DAVE MORGAN bass	KEITH SMART drums	TREVOR BURTON gtr/voc	DENNY LAINE gtr/voc	STEVE GIBBONS vocals

E.L.O. road band · Mongrel

MONGREL NOV 71 to JUL 72

BOB BRADY keyboards	ROGER HILL guitar	RICK PRICE bass/voc	CHARLIE GRIMA percussion	KEITH SMART drums	STUART SCOTT guitar

Fairports

E.L.O. #1 OCT 71 to JUL 72

ROY WOOD voc/various	BILL HUNT keyb'd	HUGH McDOWELL cello	JEFF LYNNE voc/gtr	BEV BEVAN drums/voc	RICHARD TANDY bass/voc	WILF GIBSON violin	ANDY CRAIG cello

BALLS #2 DEC 69 to FEB 71

JACKIE LOMAX vocals	DENNY LAINE gtr/voc	STEVE GIBBONS vocals	TREVOR BURTON bass/voc	ALAN WHITE drums

solo · to Wings · later in Yes

WIZZARD #1 AUG 72 to NOV 73

ROY WOOD gtr/voc	RICK PRICE bass/voc	CHARLIE GRIMA drums	KEITH SMART drums	NICK PENTELOW sax	MIKE BURNEY sax	BILL HUNT keyboards	HUGH McDOWELL cello

teacher

E.L.O. #2 AUG 72 to SEP 73

JEFF LYNNE gtr/voc	BEV BEVAN drums/voc	RICHARD TANDY keyb'ds	M. DE ALBUQUE bass	MIKE EDWARDS cello	WILF GIBSON violin

sessions · teacher

STEVE GIBBONS JUN 71 to 1980

COLIN WALKER cello	STEVE GIBBONS vocals	TREVOR BURTON bass/voc	DAVE CARROLL gtr/voc	BOB LAMB drums	BOB WILSON gtr/voc

formed new band; still popular locally

WIZZARD #2 NOV 73 to FEB 75

BOB BRADY keyboards	ROY WOOD gtr/voc	RICK PRICE bass/voc	CHARLIE GRIMA drums	KEITH SMART drums	NICK PENTELOW sax	MIKE BURNEY sax

Fairports · acting · Rockin' Berries · sessions

E.L.O. #3 SEP 73 to OCT 74

HUGH McDOWELL cello	JEFF LYNNE gtr/voc	BEV BEVAN drums/voc	RICHARD TANDY keyb'ds	MIK KAMINSKI violin	MIKE EDWARDS cello	M. DE ALBUQUE bass/voc

pursued own projects

WIZZO BAND APR 77 to MAR 78

ROY WOOD gtr/voc	RICK PRICE pedal steel	DAVE DONOVAN drums	BILLY PAUL alto	GRAHAM GALLERY bass	PAUL ROBBINS keyb'ds	BOBBY WILSON trombone

E.L.O. #4 OCT 74 to DEC 79

HUGH McDOWELL cello	JEFF LYNNE gtr/voc	BEV BEVAN drums/voc	RICHARD TANDY keyb'ds	KELLY GROUCUTT bass/voc	MIK KAMINSKI violin	MELVYN GALE cello

formed own group

ROY WOOD'S HELICOPTERS SEPT 81 to NOW

ROY WOOD gtr/voc	JOHN CAMP bass	MIKE DEACON or TERRY ROWLEY keyb'ds	KEK GORIN or TOM FARNELL drums	ROBIN GEORGE guitar

E.L.O. #5 DEC 79 to NOW

JEFF LYNNE gtr/voc	BEV BEVAN drums/voc	RICHARD TANDY keyb'ds	KELLY GROUCUTT bass/voc

Pete Frame

ELO (Electric Light Orchestra)

UK group formed 1971.

Original line-up: Jeff Lynne, vocals, guitar; Roy Wood, vocals, guitar; Bev Bevan, drums, vocals.

Career: Band was formed out of remnants of Move(▶); idea was to expand boundaries of orchestral rock. First album, **Electric Light Orchestra**, was recorded over considerable period of time with various string players; yielded hit single in **10538 Overture.**

Although Roy Wood(▶) split to form Wizzard, Lynne decided to rebuild group from scratch, hiring motley collection of musicians, some with rock and some with classical backgrounds. **ELO II** was released in 1973 to critical indifference, but it yielded another hit single, an updated and highly orchestrated version of Chuck Berry's warhorse **Roll Over Beethoven.**

By this time recognisable style was being set, and it was proving to be commercially acceptable. Pop-orientated but with thick, dense texture overlaid by characteristic strings, ELO sound became mid-'70s winner. 1974 album **Eldorado** went gold in US, feat that most of following albums repeated or surpassed. At same time, band released almost unbroken string of Top 20 hit singles.

By end of decade it appeared that ELO could virtually do no wrong. Although involved in catastrophic movie 'Xanadu', band managed to walk away with massive hit single (with Olivia Newton-John(▶)), and retained most of their credibility. One time member violinist Mick Kaminski (1976) scored solo success in 1979 with **Violinski.**

Very much brainchild of Jeff Lynne, ELO have become giants of market that lies between pop and rock, to some extent filling gap left by Beatles. In fact, much of Lynne's work shows considerable Beatles influence. Although it seems likely that band would be success even without string section—because of Lynne's commercial songs and well-honed pop sensibility—basic concept generally works well. Success will doubtless continue through '80s.

Current line-up: Lynne; Bevan; Richard Tannoy, keyboards; Melvyn Gale, cello; Kelly Groucutt, bass.

Hit Singles:	US	UK
10538 Overture, 1972	—	9
Roll Over Beethoven, 1973	42	6
Showdown, 1973	53	12
Can't Get It Out Of My Head, 1975	9	—
Evil Woman, 1976	10	10
Strange Magic, 1976	14	38
Livin' Thing, 1976	13	4
Rockaria, 1977	—	9
Telephone Line, 1977	7	8
Turn To Stone, 1977	13	18
Mister Blue Sky, 1978	35	6
Sweet Talkin' Woman, 1978	17	6
Wild West Hero, 1978	—	6
Shine A Little Love, 1979	8	6
The Diary Of Horace Wimp, 1979	—	8
Don't Bring Me Down, 1979	4	3
Confusion/Last Train To London, 1979	—	8
Confusion, 1979	37	—
Last Train To London, 1979	38	—
I'm Alive, 1980	16	20
All Over The World, 1980	13	11
Hold On Tight, 1981	10	4

With Olivia Newton-John:

Xanadu, 1980	8	1

Desperado, The Eagles. Courtesy Asylum Records.

Albums:
Electric Light Orchestra (Jet/Harvest), 1971*
ELO (Jet/Fame), 1973
On The Third Day (Jet), 1973
Face The Music (Jet), 1975
Eldorado (Jet), 1975
Olé ELO (Jet), 1976
New World Record (Jet), 1976
Out Of The Blue (Jet), 1977
The Light Shines On (—/Harvest), 1977
The Light Shines On Volume 2 (—/Harvest), 1979
Discovery (Jet), 1979
Greatest Hits (Jet), 1979
A Box Of Their Best (Jet/—), 1980**
Time (Jet), 1981
Secret Messages (Jet), 1983

*Titled **No Answer** in US.
**Four LP set.

The Eagles

US band formed 1971.

Original line-up: Glenn Frey, vocals, guitar; Randy Meisner, vocals, bass; Bernie Leadon, guitar, vocals; Don Henley, drums, vocals.

Career: Frey and Henley met as members of Linda Ronstadt's(▶) backing band. Following recruitment of former Poco(▶) member Meisner and former Flying Burrito Brother(▶) Leadon, four flew to London to record first album as Eagles for Asylum.

Album **The Eagles** made major impact, as did single **Take It Easy**, co-written by Frey and stablemate Jackson Browne(▶). **Desperado** consolidated success, and crystallised Eagles' image as laid-back California outlaws. By now band had become major live attraction, adding large orchestra for some concerts.

Having contributed to sessions for third album **On The Border**, guitarist Don Felder added as fifth member. Band went from strength to strength, breaking British market for first time in 1975 with single **One Of These Nights**. Same year saw first No.1 single in US, **Best Of My Love**.

During mid-'70s band could do no wrong, achieving status of mega-group with across-board appeal. Heaped with gold and platinum records, garlanded with awards, only problem was meeting demand for product and live appearances. Strain proved too much for Bernie Leadon, who quit at end of 1975 to pursue unspectacular solo career. Slightly surprising choice of replacement was former James Gang(▶) guitarist Joe Walsh(▶), who had more recently been pursuing solo career; Walsh's songwriting/guitar work gave their 'laid-back' California sound a shot in the arm. In 1977 Randy Meisner also quit to go solo, and in came Timothy B. Schmidt, another former Poco stalwart.

By end of decade, by which time line-up had been further augmented by long-time friend Joe Vitale on keyboards, Eagles had become one of the most successful American recording acts of the '70s. Band has sold 40 million albums worldwide since inception; **Hotel California** sold nine million in year of release, **Greatest Hits** seven million. All concerts were immediate sell-outs.

1982 saw band in abeyance as both Glenn Frey and Don Henley had success with solo releases (Henley's **Dirty Laundry** (1982) in particular becoming major hit) but fans had consolation of **Greatest Hits Volume 2** album. While current split in ranks has lasted over a year now, band are always likely to return as permanent unit.

Although often criticised as epitome of unchallenging AOR, Eagles have over the years delivered impressively consistent body of work and shown that genré doesn't have to be moronic. Songwriting ability, musicianship and vocal harmonies combine in package that is irresistible to millions.

Current line-up: Frey; Henley; Don Felder, guitar, vocals; Joe Walsh, guitar, vocals; Timothy B. Schmidt, bass, vocals; Joe Vitale, keyboards.

Hit Singles:	US	UK
Take It Easy, 1972	12	—
Witchy Woman, 1972	9	—
Best Of My Love, 1975	1	—
One Of These Nights, 1975	1	23
Lyin' Eyes, 1975	2	23
Take It To The Limit, 1976	4	12
New Kid In Town, 1977	1	20
Hotel California, 1977	1	8
Life In The Fast Lane, 1977	11	—
Please Come Home For Christmas, 1978	18	30
Heartache Tonight, 1979	1	40
The Long Run, 1979	8	—
I Can't Tell You Why, 1980	8	—

Don Henley Solo:

Leather And Lace, 1981*	6	—
Dirty Laundry, 1982	3	—

*with Stevie Nicks

Albums:
The Eagles (Asylum), 1972
Desperado (Asylum), 1973
On The Border (Asylum), 1974
One Of These Nights (Asylum), 1975
Their Greatest Hits (Asylum), 1975
Hotel California (Asylum), 1976
The Long Run (Asylum), 1979
Eagles Live (Asylum), 1980
Greatest Hits Volume 2 (Asylum), 1982

Don Henley Solo:
I Can't Stand Still (Asylum/—), 1982

Joe Walsh Solo:
(see separate entry)

Earth, Wind And Fire

US group formed 1970.

Original line-up: Maurice White, drums, vocals, sax, Verdine White, bass; Ronnie Laws, guitar; Roland Bautista, guitar; Jessica Cleaves, vocals; Wade Flemons, keyboards; Donald Whitehead, keyboards.

Career: The guiding light and musical talent of one man has been behind the phenomenal success of Earth, Wind And Fire's soul/rock/jazz fusion—Maurice White. Born in Memphis,

Below: Maurice White fronting the group he leads, Earth, Wind & Fire.

Tennessee, on December 19, 1941, White started singing gospel at age four. He played drums in band led by Booker T. Jones (of Booker T. & The MGs(▶) from age 10 and at 15 moved with family to Chicago. Doctor father wanted him to study medicine but White quit Roosevelt University to enrol at Chicago Conservatory Of Music. In 1963 began working as session drummer for city's Chess Records, recording with Chuck Berry(▶), Etta James, Howlin' Wolf(▶), the Dells, Muddy Waters(▶) and outside artists, including John

**I Am, Earth Wind And Fire.
Courtesy CBS Records.**

Coltrane, Sonny Stitt, Jackie Wilson(▶), and Curtis Mayfield(▶) and the Impressions.

When Eldee Young and Red Holt quit Ramsey Lewis to form Young Holt Unlimited, Lewis invited White to take over drummer's chair in his trio. During four-year tenure, White played on 10 Ramsey Lewis albums and classic single **Wade In The Water**. Trips with group to Africa and Middle East gave White abiding interest in Egyptology and mysticism, which was to have major influence on Earth, Wind And Fire's music—and their album sleeves. He also discovered the kalimba, an African finger piano which he subsequently used extensively, and which gave its name to his publishing company.

Studying under mystic masters, White decided to form own group and, as the Salty Peppers, they had local Chicago hits with **La La Time** and **Love Is Life** (on Warner Bros) before name change to Earth, Wind And Fire. Flemons and Whitehead left and were replaced by Philip Bailey (percussion, vocals) and Larry Dunn (keyboards). Major Columbia contract yielded **Last Days And Time** debut album (1972). Following year Bautista and Laws (who went on to solo success) were replaced by Johnny Graham and Al McKay on guitars, Andrew Woolfolk (horns) and Ralph Johnson (percussion) were added. Cleaves left in late '73. Continuing association with Ramsey Lewis, White produced his **Sun Goddess** hit album in 1974. Maurice and Verdine's brother Fred White joined as extra drummer in time for Grammy-winning **That's The Way Of The World** set (1975), which topped US pop charts and went double

**Open Our Eyes, Earth, Wind And Fire.
Courtesy CBS Records.**

platinum, leading to debut European tour with Santana(▶). 1976 album **Spirit** was dedicated to producer Charles Stepney, who died before completion—the album was another two-million seller.

In 1979, White launched American Recording Company as extension of Kalimba Productions and signed the Emotions, Deniece Williams, Weather Report and D.J. Williams to label, as well as building major recording complex. **Boogie Wonderland**, recorded with the Emotions, continued run of Earth, Wind And Fire hit singles.

Original guitarist Roland Bautista rejoined in 1981 replacing Al McKay. **Let's Groove**, from **Raise** album, hit charts worldwide, making Top 3 in several countries. Measure of group's stature was shown by sell-out of six nights at London's huge Wembley Arena within days of box office opening.

A combination of stunning stage effects (White being a master of theatrics), with shows costing hundreds of thousands of dollars, and superbly rhythmic music have made Earth, Wind And Fire the most consistently successful black music group of past decade. Their Phenix Horns brass section has featured on recordings by numerous other artists.

Current line-up: Maurice White; Verdine White; Bautista; Philip Bailey, vocals, percussion; Larry Dunn, keyboards; Johnny Graham, guitar; Ralph Johnson, drums, percussion; Fred White, drums, percussion; Andrew Woolfolk, horns.

Hit Singles:	US	UK
Shining Star, 1975	1	—
That's The Way Of The World, 1975	12	—
Sing A Song, 1976	5	—
Getaway, 1976	12	—
Saturday Nite, 1977	21	17
Fantasy, 1978	32	14
Got To Get You Into My life, 1978	9	33
September, 1978	8	3
Boogie Wonderland (with the Emotions), 1979	6	4
After The Love Has Gone, 1979	2	4
Star, 1979	—	16
Let's Groove, 1981	3	—

Albums:
Last Days And Time (Columbia/CBS), 1972
Head To The Sky (Columbia/CBS), 1973
Open Our Eyes (Columbia/CBS), 1974
That's The Way Of The World (Coumbia/CBS), 1975
Gratitude (Columbia/CBS), 1975
Spirit (Columbia/CBS), 1976
All And All (Columbia/CBS), 1977
Best Of, Volume I (Columbia/CBS), 1978
I Am (Columbia/CBS), 1979
Faces (Columbia/CBS), 1980
Raise (Columbia/CBS), 1981
Powerlight (Columbia/CBS), 1983

Above: Front-runners of the Liverpool sound of the '80s, Echo & the Bunnymen.

Sheena Easton

UK vocalist.
Born Bellshill, Glasgow, April 27, 1959.

Career: Chosen as subject for BBC television's 'The Big Time'—a documentary tracing aspiring singer's struggle for stardom—Sheena Easton lived out the part to establish herself as major international artist.

While studying at Royal Scottish Academy Of Music And Drama, she spent evenings working local pub/club circuit before auditioning for 'The Big Time'.

Signed to EMI, second single **9 To 5** became THE summer hit of 1980 and screening of 'The Big Time' in July focused attention on debut single **Modern Girl**, earlier a minor hit, which joined **9 To 5**, making her first British female singer to have two Top 10 hits at same time. In America she went one better: her first three singles all featured simultaneously in Top 50.

Easton's first year was topped off by Royal Variety Show appearance, while debut album quickly went gold in US and UK, and platinum in Japan and Canada, leading to awards as Best Female Singer of 1981 and Female Personality of Year in UK and Best Female Newcomer in US.

She not only sang theme to James Bond movie 'For Your Eyes Only' but appeared in opening sequence, and later performed song at 1982 Oscar ceremony.

Extensive world tours and numerous TV appearances are being crowned in 1983 with her own US coast-to-coast TV special.

Below: The phenomenally successful Sheena Easton 'Modern Girl' of the '80s.

Hit Singles:	US	UK
9 To 5*, 1980	1	3
Modern Girl, 1980	18	8
One Man Woman, 1980	—	14
When He Shines, 1981	—	12
For Your Eyes Only, 1981	4	8
You Could Have Been With Me, 1981	15	54

*Known as 'Morning Train' in US

Albums:
Take My Time (EMI), 1981
You Could Have Been With Me (EMI), 1981
Madness, Money And Music (EMI), 1982

Echo & the Bunnymen

UK group formed 1978.

Original/Current line-up: Ian McCulloch, vocals, guitar; Will Sergeant, guitar; Les Pattinson, bass; Pete de Freitas, drums.

Career: Remnants of several local Liverpool bands provided nucleus of Echo & the Bunnymen. First show was at Eric's Club in Liverpool in November 1978. Despite lack of experience, debut single, **Pictures On My Wall,** attracted much critical acclaim. Extensive work in Liverpool area toned down haunting, emotive music and got long-term record contract with Sire at end of 1979. Mid-1980 saw first LP, **Crocodiles;** press drew comparisons between Bunnymen, Doors(▶) and Lou Reed(▶). Massive coverage followed.

Band amazingly avoided 'superstar' pressure; instead they continued touring and building up following. In January 1981 outfit filmed 30-minute movie from poorly planned secret gig. Result disappointed group and seemed to indicate some loss of direction. However, excellent EP was salvaged from show.

In May 1981 **Heaven Up Here** LP was heralded as *the* album of the year. Excellent cut **A Promise** followed as single. Again showing acumen for avoiding usual rock pitfalls, Bunnymen exercised restraint in producing crucial third LP. **Porcupine** wasn't released until 1983 and proved worth wait. Excellent video matched single **The Cutting** and added to band's stature.

Despite comparisons with various '60 bands, Echo & The Bunnymen are unique, original talent. Every Liverpool band since 1962 has lived in shadow of Beatles(▶); Echo beat this by ignoring Beatles tradition entirely. Strong sense of independence and self-preservation seems to provide knack for retaining approval of fickle UK press and ensures stability needed for long-term success.

Hit Singles: US UK
The Back Of Love, 1982 — 19

Albums:
Crocodiles (Korova/Sire), 1980
Heaven Up Here (Korova/Sire), 1981
Porcupine (Korova/Sire), 1983

Duane Eddy

US guitarist, composer.
Born Corning, New York, April 28, 1938.

Career: Raised in Phoenix, Arizona, Eddy began playing guitar at five and at 16 was working in local dance bands before coming under influence of ace session guitarist Al Casey.

After tuition from jazz guitarist Jim Wybele, Eddy was signed by local DJ Lee Hazlewood—later a recording star/producer himself—and Lester Sill in 1957. He cut debut **Movin 'N' Groovin'** for Jamie with his backing band the Rebels (Larry Knechtel, Steve Douglas and Al Casey).

Eddy developed unique 'twangy' guitar sound by tuning normal six-string guitar down an octave and playing melody on bass rather than top strings. As much a part of his records' appeal were the raunchy sax solos of Steve Douglas and Jim Horn and the rebel yells of Ben De Moto. The overall effect was potent blend of rock'n'roll, R&B and Southern States' influences.

Second release **Rebel Rouser** (1958)

went gold and led to string of big sellers (12 million records sold by 1963, total sales having now topped 30 million from some 25 singles, 21 of which made UK charts). More than half his hits were self-penned.

Eddy acted in TV western series 'Have Gun Will Travel', and movies 'Because They're Young' (his theme for which was 1960 million-seller), 'A Thunder Of Drums' and 'The Wild Westerner'. He also composed the theme for 1961 movie 'Ring Of Fire'.

Though his record career waned towards

Twangin' The Golden Hits, Duane Eddy compilation. Courtesy RCA Records.

end of '60s, Eddy continued to tour extensively, undertook session work and moved into production. He is a frequent visitor to Europe. Guitar: Gretsch.

Hit Singles:	US	UK
Rebel Rouser, 1958	6	19
Cannon Ball, 1958	15	22
Peter Gunn Theme, 1959	—	6
Yep!, 1959	30	17
40 Miles Of Bad Road, 1959	9	11
Some Kinda Earthquake, 1959	37	12
Bonnie Come Back, 1960	26	12
Shazam!, 1960	45	4
Because They're Young, 1960	4	2
Kommotion, 1960	—	13
Peter Gunn Theme, 1960	27	—
Pepe, 1961	18	2
Theme From Dixie, 1961	39	7
Ring Of Fire, 1961	—	17
Drivin' Home, 1961	—	18
Deep In The Heart Of Texas, 1962	—	19
Ballad Of Paladin, 1962	33	10
(Dance With The) Guitar Man, 1962	12	4
Play Me Like You Play Your Guitar, 1975	—	9

Albums:
Have Twangy Guitar, Will Travel (Jamie/London), 1958
Especially For You (Jamie/London), 1958
Twang's The Thang (Jamie/London), 1959
Songs For Our Heritage (Jamie/London), 1960
$1,000,000 Worth Of Twang (Jamie/London), 1961
Girls, Girls, Girls (Jamie/London), 1961
$1,000,000 Worth Of Twang Volume 2 (Jamie/London), 1962
Twistin' (Jamie/—), 1962
In Person (Jamie/—), 1962
16 Greatest Hits (Jamie/—), 1962
Pure Gold (RCA), 1965
Best Of (RCA/Camden), 1965
Movin' 'N' Groovin' (—/London), 1970
Twangy Guitar (RCA), 1970
Duane Eddy Guitar Man (—/GTO), 1975
Legend Of Rock (—/Deram), 1975
Duane Eddy Collection (—/Pickwick), 1978
Greatest Hits Of (—/Ronco), 1979
20 Terrific Twangies (—/RCA), 1980

Below: The great Dave Edmunds, whose career stretches over three decades, despite his comparative youth.

Dave Edmunds

UK vocalist, guitarist, composer, producer.
Born Cardiff, Wales, April 15, 1944.

Career: Served eight-year musical apprenticeship in various local bands. Formed Love Sculpture with John Williams, bass, and Bob Jones, drums; their frenetic rock instrumental adaptation of Khatchaturian's **Sabre Dance** on Parlophone skated to six on UK chart in 1968 and was band's only hit. Love Sculpture broke up following American tour.

Edmunds signed as solo to Gordon Mills' MAM agency before moving back to South Wales with Kingsley Ward to build own Rockfield Studio in Monmouthshire. After months of experimentation, Rockfield developed unique sound, making it one of Britain's most active studios. Edmunds learned to exactly reproduce sounds of his favourite oldies. Re-make of Smiley Lewis's R&B classic **I Hear You Knocking** gave him three-million selling UK No.1 in 1970. Debut album **Rockpile** (1972) featured John Williams and former Amen Corner leader Andy Fairweather-Low.

Besides own work, Edmunds produced Brinsley Schwarz, Ducks Deluxe, Flamin' Groovies, Shakin' Stevens(▶) and the Sunsets, and American legend Del Shannon(▶). Re-creating classic Phil Spector 'Wall Of Sound', had further hits of own with versions of Spector oldies **Baby I Love You** and **Born To Be With You**.

Appeared in 1975 David Essex(▶) movie 'Stardust'. He wrote much of the film score. Second album **Subtle As A Flying Mallet** appeared in 1975.

Former Brinsley Schwarz member Nick Lowe(▶) contributed to Edmunds' debut album

with Led Zeppelin's Swan Song label, **Get It** (1975). Lowe also became member of Rockpile road band formed by Edmunds, and featured heavily on 1980 Rockpile LP **Seconds Of Pleasure**, a big US success. Rockpile included Edmunds (vocals, guitar), Lowe (vocals, bass), Terry Williams (drums), and Billy Bremner (vocals, guitar).

1979 **Repeat When Necessary** album included chart singles **Girls Talk, Queen Of**

Subtle As A Flying Mallet, Dave Edmunds. Courtesy RCA Records.

Hearts and **Crawling From The Wreckage.** Edmunds enjoyed further UK Top 30 hit with version of Guy Mitchell's **Singing The Blues** in following year.

He signed to Arista's F. Beat label in 1980. Although not a major solo artist, Edmunds stays busy among peers and has own stalwart following.

Guitars: Gibson 335, also Gibson J200 acoustics, Fender Telecaster, Martin D45.

Hit Singles:

	US	UK
I Hear You Knocking, 1970	4	1
Baby I Love You, 1973	—	8
Born To Be With You, 1973	—	5
Queen Of Hearts, 1979	—	11

Albums:
With Love Sculpture:
Classic Tracks 68-72 (—/One-Up),1974
Singles, A's and B's (—/Harvest), 1980

Solo:
Subtle As A Flying Mallet (RCA), 1975
Get It (Swan Song), 1977
Tracks On Wax (Swan Song), 1978
Repeat When Necessary (Swan Song), 1979
Twangin' (Swan Song), 1981
Best Of (Swan Song), 1981
D.E. 7 (Columbia/Arista), 1982
Information (Swan Song), 1983

Rockpile:
Seconds Of Pleasure (Columbia/F-Beat), 1980

Worth Searching Out:
Rockpile (NAM/Regal Zonophone), 1972

Emerson, Lake And Palmer

UK group formed 1969.
Original line-up: Keith Emerson, keyboards; Greg Lake, bass, guitar, vocals; Carl Palmer, drums.

Career: Keith Emerson revealed classical background while with Nice and used that group to introduce knife-throwing, organ thrashing, musical mayhem act. Nice broke up in late '60s and Emerson began search for special talent to make up next venture.

He met Lake, then with the original King Crimson(▶), and convinced him to join. They then tried to enlist Randy Bachman, late of Guess Who(▶), and discussed union with Jimi

Above: Keith Emerson (left) and Greg Lake during their time together as two thirds of Emerson, Lake & Palmer.

Hendrix/Mitch Mitchell. Eventually Carl Palmer, whose background (ex-Chris Farlowe, Atomic Rooster and Arthur Brown) prepared him for Emerson's dynamic stage show, was recruited.

Band's live debut was 1970 Isle Of Wight festival followed shortly by first album. Both recordings and stage shows became grandiose and flamboyant displays of technical skill. But after third album, **Pictures**, sameness crept in. ELP could still sell albums, but could they come up with anything new? They released live set (**Welcome Back, My Friends, To The Show That Never Ends**) for fans and then disappeared: no tours and no recordings.

In 1977, **Works Volume 1** appeared. Large sales, despite album's overly pretentious base, seemed to indicate ELP's fans were still there, but ELP was apparently stranded in 1969/1970 time zone and grand orchestral style clashed with musical revolution of late '70s. Wise enough to know when to quit, ELP planned extravaganza farewell tour. Naturally, live set was recorded and **In Concert** appeared for the memories.

Hit Singles:

	US	UK
Fanfare For The Common Man, 1977	—	2

Albums:
Emerson, Lake And Palmer (Cotillion/Island), 1970
Tarkus (Cotillion/Island), 1971
Pictures At An Exhibition (Cotillion/Island), 1971
Trilogy (Cotillion/Island), 1972
Brain Salad Surgery (Manticore), 1973
Welcome Back, My Friends, To The Show That Never Ends (Manticore), 1974
Works Volume I (Atlantic/Manticore), 1977
Works Volume II (Atlantic), 1978
Love Beach (Atlantic), 1978
In Concert (Atlantic), 1979

Brian Eno

UK producer, composer, vocalist, electronic multi-instrumentalist.
Born Woodbridge, Suffolk, 1948.

Career: Quit Roxy Music(▶) in July 1973 and embarked on productive solo career, occasionally working with other artists on diverse projects. Loose partnership with Robert Fripp throughout '70s resulted in some bizarre and interesting albums. **No Pussyfooting**, released March 1973, was both avant garde and commercially successful, even reaching Top 30. Tour to promote album featured duo in total darkness with background film loops! A more commerical work followed with **Here Come The Warm Jets**, which included entire Roxy line-up, bar Ferry. Following recording of prototype punk single, **Seven Deadly Finns**, Eno teamed up with pub rockers, the Winkies; collaboration ended when his right lung collapsed and he was confined to hospital.

Moving to States, Eno worked with John Cale(▶), late of Velvet Underground(▶), contributing to both **Slow Dazzle** and **Helen Of**

Troy. Fraternisation with old Velvets reached fruition at the Rainbow on June 1, 1974, when Eno played alongside Kevin Ayers, John Cale and Nico, aided by Robert Wyatt and Mike Oldfield(▶). In spite of flattering press reports, individual egos outweighed collective musical accomplishments.

Eno's interest in stream-of-consciousness writing partly inspired **Talking Tiger Mountain (By Strategy)**, an interesting and occasionally humorous work. It was not until 1975, however, that his career began to develop fully. In January he was knocked down by a car and while in hospital hit upon idea of transforming muzak into serious musical form. Following the founding of Obscure Records, Eno experimented with Environmental Music. **Discreet Music** was an elongated synthesiser piece, deliberately recorded at an almost inaudible volume. Coining the term 'ambient music', Eno went on to record several mood pieces, including **Music For Films** and **Music For Airports**. At same time, he has revealed less esoteric

Below: Brian Eno, who left Roxy Music, but subsequently went on to work with David Bowie.

Above: Possibly the best bass player in rock, John Entwistle of the Who.

side on such works as **Another Green World** and **Before And After Science**.

In recent years, Eno has become more famous by virtue of the number of artists with whom he has collaborated. His friendship with Phil Manzanera resulted in appearances on **Diamond Head, Mainstream** and, of course, the formation of 801. As collaborator/producer he has worked with David Bowie(▶) (**Low** and **Heroes**), Robert Wyatt, Bob Calvert, Ultravox(▶), Devo(▶), Moebius and Roedelius, Quiet Sun, Jon Hassell, Harold Budd and the Neu/Cluster group of musicians among other artists. As producer, achieved considerable commerical success with Talking Heads(▶) on **More Songs About Buildings And Food, Fear of Music** and **Remain In Light**. An obsessive interest in African music resulted in extraordinary Eno/David Byrne collaboration, **My Life In The Bush Of Ghosts**, with experimental use of 'found voices'.

Although a great experimentalist, Eno has frequently suffered from having work placed in a 'rock' context. While many of his albums have proved deliberately obscure, accusations of 'over clinical' sometimes levelled at his work seem unfair. Nevertheless, his long-standing belief in systems and over-rigid theories of art may well have prevented production of singularly majestic piece of work.

Albums:
Here Come The Warm Jets (Island), 1974
Taking Tiger Mountain (By Strategy) (Island), 1974
Another Green World (Island), 1975
Before And After Science (EG/Polydor), 1977
Discreet Music (Island/Obscure), 1975
Music For Films (EG/Polydor), 1977
Music For Airports (PVC/Ambient), 1979
On Land (PVC/Ambient), 1982

Collaborative Works:
No Pussyfooting (with Robert Fripp) (Island), 1973
June 1st 1974 (with Kevin Ayers, Nico, etc) (Island), 1974
Evening Star (with Robert Fripp) (Antilles/Island), 1975
801 Live (with 801) (Island), 1976
Cluster And Eno (Sky), 1978
Eno, Moebius And Roedelius—After The Heat (Sky), 1979

Fourth World (Possible Musics) Volume 1 (with Jon Hassell) (Editions), 1980
The Plateaux Of Mirrors (with Harold Budd) (Editions), 1980
My Life In The Bush Of Ghosts (with David Byrne) (Sire), 1981

John Entwistle

UK bass player, vocalist, composer.
Born London, October 9, 1944.

Career: Entwistle pioneered new roles for bass players with lead runs on early Who(▶) singles. Developed now standard rotosound strings and was one of the first in rock to experiment with six and eight-string bass. Entwistle was only member of Who to undergo formal musical training (french horn), which led to brilliant terse horn work in Who from **Circles** through **Tommy** to solo efforts.

Nicknamed 'The Ox' and 'The Quiet One', Entwistle was known for fast-moving fingers accompanied by incongruous shock-still pose and general 'bored-with-it-all' look on stage. In fact, he lives to perform. As anchor man for Who, he also began writing B-sides of Who singles **In The City, I've Been Away, Doctor, Doctor, Someone's Coming.** He favoured humorous/macabre subjects on second Who LP, (**Boris The Spider, Whiskey Man**) but was pushed by Townshend to write **Cousin Kevin** and **Uncle Ernie** for **Tommy** project.

With '70s success of Who and slowdown in work schedule, Entwistle took chance to branch out in solo direction. **Smash Your Head Against The Wall** was first Who solo LP and met fair amount of support in States. **Whistle Rymes** (punning misspelt credits on Who recordings) showed promising musical developments. Next LP, **Rigor Mortis Sets In**, lamented state of rock in mid-'70s three years before punks, but did so by falling back on '50s style. **Made In Japan** is notable track.

His band Rigor Mortis went on road with overlarge production and failed to complete US tour. Entwistle compiled Who's **Odds'n' Sods** LP while rest of Who worked on 'Tommy' film. He next put together band Ox and released poorly received **Mad Dog** LP.

Death of Keith Moon spurred Who activity and Entwistle worked sporadically for next few years on **Too Late The Hero** with Joe Walsh. When released in 1981, it seemed too polished, too finished. Title cut was released

in pic-disc, individually autographed by Entwistle. Issue disappeared in weeks from London shops but never charted.

Entwistle has also acted as music director on Who soundtracks (**Quadrophenia, Kids Are Alright**, both 1979).

Entwistle's solo career has been sideline to Who. With imminent retirement of Who, interest will be there for more of his work.

Bass: Fender Precision, Custom Alembic with spider web inlay (since 1975). (Entwistle has finest collection of antique guitars and basses in the UK.)

Albums:
Smash Your Head Against The Wall (Decca/Track), 1971

Worth Searching Out:
Whistle Rymes (Decca/Track), 1972
Rigor Mortis Sets In (MCA/Track), 1973
Mad Dog (MCA/Track), 1975
Too Late The Hero (ATCO/WEA), 1981

David Essex

UK vocalist, composer.
Born London, July 23, 1947.

Career: During teens Essex played drums and sang in various semi-professional groups in East London. Lack of success in music led to change of direction in favour of acting, and stints in small-time theatre followed.

He landed leading role in American musical 'Godspell', and played in London's West End from 1971 to 1973. Attracting favourable attention from critics, he won central role in movie 'That'll Be The Day'. Movie's success prompted re-launch of singing career with self-composed **Rock On**. The record, a carefully crafted evocation of '50s atmosphere, became major hit in UK and US, establishing Essex as star.

Further hits and album successes followed, and in 1974 Essex starred in 'Stardust', sequel to 'That'll Be The Day'. By end of year Essex was attracting teenybopper attention comparable to Beatlemania, in UK and abroad.

Teenage fervour died down, and Essex's career has since alternated between well-crafted, listenable albums, hit singles of varying quality and film and theatre stints ('Evita', 'Silver Dream Racer', 'Childe Byron'). Despite continuing success in each area, Essex seems to spread his not inconsiderable talent too thinly to achieve international superstar status. Nevertheless, there seems no reason why he should not pursue career in middleweight section of rock and pop for years to come.

Hit Singles:

	US	UK
Rock On, 1973	5	3
Lamplight, 1973	—	7
Gonna Make You A Star, 1974	—	1
Stardust, 1974	—	7
Rollin' Stone, 1975	—	5
Hold Me Close, 1975	—	1
If I Could, 1975	—	13
Oh What A Circus, 1978	—	3
Silver Dream Machine (Part 1), 1980	—	4
Me And My Girl, 1982	—	13
A Winters Tale, 1982	—	2

Albums:
Hold Me Close (Columbia/CBS), 1979
The David Essex Album (Columbia/CBS), 1979
Silver Dream Racer (Mercury), 1980
The David Essex Collection (—/Pickwick), 1980
Be-Bop The Future (Mercury), 1981
Stage Struck (Mercury), 1982
The Very Best Of David Essex (—/TV), 1982

Eurythmics

UK duo formed 1981.

David A. Stewart, guitar, keyboards, synthesiser, bass, composer; born Sunderland 1952.
Annie Lennox, vocals, composer, keyboards, flute, synthesiser; born Aberdeen, December 25, 1954.

Above: Annie Lennox, once a Tourist — more successful as a Eurythmic.

Career: Duo were both members of the Tourists, promising pop-styled band 1977-80 scoring five hit singles, including Top 10 items **I Only Want To Be With You** (Dusty Springfield(▶) cover) and **So Good To Be Back Home Again,** plus three interesting LPs. Prior to forming Tourists, Stewart had worked in folk music, then had spell in Longdancer (early signing to Elton John's(▶) Rocket label). Lennox had studied at Royal Academy of Music (piano, flute) before working as part-time cabaret singer/waitress; met Stewart while working in restaurant.

When Tourists folded, duo started writing (which neither had previously done seriously) and recorded first Eurythmics LP, **In The Garden**, in Cologne, produced by Tourists' mentor Conny Plank. Instrumental help provided by Clem Burke (drums) of Blondie(▶) plus members of Can and D.A.F. Although LP not huge success, it effectively laid ghost of Tourists. 1981-82 saw minor chart action but in 1983 duo came of age with two major hit singles, **Sweet Dreams Are Made Of This** (titletrack of second LP) and **Love Is A Stranger** (reissued after success of **Sweet Dreams**).

With their highly distinctive appearance (Lennox like a white Grace Jones), hybrid soul/electronics, plus multi-instrumental

The David Essex Album. Courtesy Columbia Records.

capacity, Eurythmics seem destined for healthy future. However, same prediction was made about Tourists. . .

Hit Singles:

	US	UK
Love Is A Stranger, 1982	—	6
Sweet Dreams Are Made Of This, 1983	2	2
Who's That Girl, 1983	—	3

Albums:
In The Garden (—/RCA), 1981
Sweet Dreams (—/RCA), 1983

The Everly Brothers

US vocal duo, guitarists, composers.
Don Everly born Brownie, Kentucky, February 1, 1937.
Phil Everly born Chicago, Illinois, January 19, 1939.

Career: Both Don and Phil had early experience appearing on parents Ike & Margaret's radio show in Knoxville, 1955, singing hillbilly gospel material. First recordings for US Columbia label in 1956 came as result of encouragement from family friend Chet Atkins(▶). First single **The Sun Keeps Shining** not successful but featured same harmonising later to bring them to charts. In 1956, auditioned for publisher Wesley Rose and soon signed to Cadence Records. First release in 1957, Felice and Boudleaux Bryant's **Bye Bye Love**, became major hit, followed by others in similar high-register harmony style. Rarely adventurous, material explored teen romance to limit with appropriately simple backing. Use of Gibson guitars prompted Gibson company to produce Jumbo style Everly model in limited quantities.

Everlys signed to newly formed Warner Bros Records at peak of career in 1960, quickly expanding musical horizons with material and accompaniment. Continued to reach charts throughout early and mid-'60s with imaginative and well-produced singles and albums, surviving where other '50s artists retired. Toured US and UK regularly even when singles failed to chart in late '60s.

Strain of touring may have contributed to friction between brothers, resulting in on-stage row and final split in 1973. Although both have pursued separate careers and produced

Roots, The Everly Brothers. Courtesy Warner Bros Records.

some fine recordings, neither have equalled success they enjoyed together. Phil recently recorded in England with Cliff Richard(▶), and resulting duet single **She Means Nothing To Me** returned Everly name to charts. With current plans for reunion concerts likely to bear fruit, return of Everly Brothers to fame cannot be discounted.

Influence of Everlys can be heard in many later groups who use harmony style, including Beatles(▶), Beach Boys(▶), Hollies(▶), Simon and Garfunkel(▶) and the Eagles(▶).

Ironically, duo themselves had popularised 'brother' harmonies of '50s bluegrass teams like Louvin Brothers and Lilly Brothers.

Hit Singles:

	US	UK
Bye Bye Love, 1957	2	6
Wake Up Little Susie, 1957	1	2
All I Have To Do Is Dream, 1957	1	1
Bird Dog/Devoted To You, 1958	—	10
Devoted To You/Bird Dog, 1958	10	—
Problems, 1958	2	6
Take A Message To Mary, 1959	16	29
('Til) I Kissed You, 1959	4	2
Let It Be Me, 1960	7	13
Cathy's Clown, 1960	1	1
When Will I Be Loved, 1960	8	4
So Sad/Lucille, 1960	7	4
Lucille/So Sad, 1960	21	4
Like Strangers, 1960	—	11
Walk Right Back/Ebony Eyes, 1961	7	1
Ebony Eyes/Walk Right Back, 1961	8	—
Temptation, 1961	27	1
Don't Blame Me/Muskrat, 1961	20	20
Cryin' In The Rain, 1962	6	6
That's Old Fashioned/How Can I Meet Her, 1962	9	12
No-One Can Make My Sunshine Smile, 1962	—	11
The Price Of Love, 1965	—	2
Love Is Strange, 1965	—	11

Albums:
Very Best Of The Everly Brothers (Warner Bros), 1965
Golden Hits (Warner Bros), 1971
Walk Right Back With The Everlys (Warner Bros), 1975
Rock'n'Roll Forever (Warner Bros), 1981
The Everly Brothers (Warner Bros), 1981
Rip It Up (Ace), 1983

Fabian

Born Fabiano Forte, Philadelphia, Pennsylvania, February 6, 1943.

Career: In 1957 Frankie Avalon(▶) mentioned 15-year-old friend who looked like cross between Elvis(▶) and Ricky Nelson(▶) to Chancellor Records' Bob Marcucci and Peter de Angelis; they agreed to see him. Despite having a voice which couldn't match pretty face and boyish charm, Fabian was coached, packaged and promoted to stardom, helped by appearances on 'American Bandstand' which turned him into teenyboppers' delight.

Singles like **I'm A Man** and **Turn Me Loose,** followed by million-selling **Tiger,** led to film career beginning with 'Houng Dog Man'. Since then Fabian has acted regularly in movies and on TV, including '60s series 'Bus Stop'. Resuming surname after 1970, Fabian Forte continues to work successfully, mostly in made-for-TV films.

Hit Singles:

	US	UK
Turn Me Loose, 1959	9	—
Tiger, 1959	3	—
Hound Dog Man/This Friendly World	9	46
This Friendly World/Hound Dog Man	12	—

Albums:
Worth Searching Out:
Stars Of The Sixties (—/Bovema-EMI), 1974

Below: The Everly Brothers with their trademark Jumbo Gibsons.

Fabulous Thunderbirds

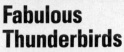

US group formed 1977.

Original line-up: Jimmy Vaughn, guitar; Ken Wilson, vocals, harmonica; Keith Ferguson, bass; Mike Buck, drums.

Career: Vaughn, Wilson and Ferguson formed nucleus of Texan band which played straight-ahead R&B with no pretentions and no adornment. Upheavals in establishment rock provided T-Birds with opportunity to record as part of new wave. First LP provided excellent example of band's stripped-down approach to basic rock music. Comparisons with George Thorogood(▶) come to mind as both expound simple, honest love of blues influence on rock music.

What's The Word, Fabulous Thunderbirds. Courtesy Chrysalis Records.

What's The Word saw departure of drummer Buck; half of LP has Fran Christina filling in as session drummer. Excellent **Butt Rockin'** included Christina as full-time member and line-up has remained constant since. Nick Lowe(▶) indicated critical breakthrough of band by agreeing to produce strongest effort yet, **T-Bird Rhythm.**

Band works best in small, intimate context; just as well perhaps, since audience for T-Birds' music may remain limited, though recent airplay on MTV has greatly expanded US audience. Buy the records but see them live.

Current line-up: Vaughn; Wilson; Ferguson.

Albums:
Girls Go Wild (—/Chrysalis), 1979
The Fabulous Thunderbirds (Takoma/—), 1979
What's The Word (Chrysalis), 1980
Butt Rockin' (Chrysalis), 1981
T-Bird Rhythm (Chrysalis), 1982

The Faces

UK group formed 1968.

Original line-up: Rod Stewart, vocals; Ron Wood, guitar; Ronnie Lane, bass; Kenney Jones, drums; Ian MacLagan, keyboards.

Career: When lead singer Steve Marriott left Small Faces to form Humble Pie(▶) with Peter Frampton(▶) in 1968, his erstwhile partners, Jones, MacLagan and Lane, brought in Rod Stewart(▶) and Ron Wood from the Jeff Beck Group(▶) and became simply the Faces (though first LP was released as Small Faces to keep old audience). Wood switch back to lead guitar, having played bass with Beck.

Signed by Warner Bros in early 1969, band spent two years establishing themselves via UK university and club circuits. They turned out high-energy, if inconsistent albums. Repu-

tation as a mischievous, free-boozing party band, plus growing success of Stewart's parallel solo career, made them one of the most popular on-stage outfits in UK/US during 1972-75.

Disappointing 1973 **Ooh La La** set was last album of fresh material Faces made together. Stewart's widely reported remarks that he didn't like it helped neither its commercial acceptability nor band's future as working unit.

Fed up with Stewart's dominance of band, Lane left (pursuing solo career) and was replaced by Japanese bass-player Tetsu Yamauchi (ex-Free); Stewart concentrated more on solo career. Wood released own solo effort **I've Got My Own Album To Do** (title meant as slap at Stewart's solo efforts) in 1974, guested on London dates with friends Keith Richard, Andy Newmark and Willie Weeks, and became increasingly involved with the Rolling Stones(▶). All this pointed to imminent demise of Faces. In 1975, Wood toured States as guest replacement for departed Mick Taylor in Rolling Stones and then joined Faces for their tour there. He also recorded second solo album **Now Look**, on which Bobby Womack and other names guested. In 1976 Wood and Lane recorded **Mahoney's Last Stand** (originally to be a soundtrack) with Jones and MacLagan sessioning on LP.

Having degenerated into a drinking club rather than a working band, Faces finally broke up December 1975 when Stewart announced his official departure.

Successful re-release of Small Faces' 1967 single **Itchycoo Park** led to temporary re-union of that outfit in 1977, while Wood became permanent member of Rolling Stones. Ronnie Lane made several solo LPs with his Slim Chance band. Kenney Jones joined the Who(▶) in 1979. Ian McLagan is now married to Keith Moon's ex-wife, Kim.

Final line-up: Stewart; Wood; Jones; MacLagan; Testu Yamauchi, bass.

Hit Singles:	US	UK
Stay With Me, 1971	17	6
Cindy Incidentally, 1973	48	2
Pool Hall Richard/I Wish It Would Rain, 1973	—	8

Ooh La La, The Faces. Courtesy Warner Bros Records.

First Step, (no longer Small) Faces. Courtesy Warner Bros Records.

You Can Make Me Dance Or Sing
Or Anything, 1974   —   12
Albums:
Faces:
First Step/Long Player (Warner Bros), 1975*
A Nod Is As Good As A Wink. . .To A Blind
  Horse (Warner Bros), 1971
Best Of (—/Riva), 1977
Faces (featuring Rod Stewart) (—/Pickwick),
  1980

Rod Stewart Solo:
See separate entry.

Ronnie Lane Solo:
Rough Mix (with Pete Townshend) (MCA/
  Polydor), 1977

Worth Searching Out:
Anymore For Anymore (GM), 1974
Slim Chance (A&M/Island), 1975
One For The Road (—/Island), 1976
See Me (—/GEM), 1979

Ron Wood Solo:
Gimme Some Neck (Columbia/CBS), 1979

Worth Searching out:
Mahoney's Last Stand (Atco/Atlantic), 1976

Ian McLagan Solo:
Troublemaker (Mercury/—), 1979
Bump In The Night (Mercury/—), 1981
*Available as double album, UK only.
Originally 1970/1971.

Fairport Convention

UK group formed 1967.

Original line-up: Simon Nichol, guitar, vocals; Richard Thompson, guitar, vocals; Ashley Hutchings, bass; Shaun Frater, drums; Judy Dyble, autoharp, vocals.

Career: 12-year career of Fairport involved 14 different line-ups and 20 members. Undoubtedly one of the most talented UK musical ensembles, their repertoire extends far beyond term 'folk-rock' to embrace rock 'n' roll, blues, country, cajun and bluegrass.

Original line-up (above) played debut gig in spring 1967. By November, Martin Lamble (drums) and lead singer Ian Matthews(▶)

were recruited for first album, **Fairport Convention,** produced by manager Joe Boyd. Early repertoire consisted of contemporary American folk-rock and original material. Dyble was replaced by the Strawbs'(▶) Sandy Denny in 1968, and group began eventual conversion to traditional British folk music. **What We Did On Our Holidays** revealed Thompson(▶) as major songwriting talent, while demonstrating healthy balance of original interpretations of traditional songs and excellent Joni Mitchell(▶)/Bob Dylan(▶) covers.

Disillusioned by musical policy, Matthews quit in January 1969, and was replaced by established folkie Dave Swarbrick (violin/vocals), who became Fairport's longest serving member. Traditionally based **Unhalfbricking** was succeeded by **Liege And Lief,** the definitive British folk-rock album, generally acknowledged as Fairport's finest work.

In June 1969, following a Birmingham gig, the group's van skidded from motorway and Lamble was killed. By the end of the year, Sandy Denny had quit to form Fotheringay, while Ashley Hutchings left to start Steeleye Span. New members Dave Mattacks (drums) and Dave Pegg (bass) kept unit stable for a year during which **Full House** and **Live At The L.A. Troubadour** were recorded. The former, their first album without a female singer, revealed Swarbrick/Thompson partnership at its best. By January '71, Richard Thompson had gone on to pursue highly acclaimed solo career, later duetting with wife Linda. Following two more British folk/rock albums, **Angel Delight** and **Babbacombe Lee,** the last of the original Fairports, Simon Nichol left to form Albion Country Band with Ashley Hutchings.

From March-July 1972 group went through unprecedented period of flux with line-up changes involving Roger Hill (guitar), Tom Farnell (drums), and David Rea (guitar), before Trevor Lucas (guitar/vocals) and Jerry Donahue (guitar) settled long enough to complete two albums, **Rosie** and **Nine.** Latter proved their best post-Thompson effort. Group's somewhat fading credibility was improved by dramatic return of Sandy Denny in March 1974. The disappointing **Live Convention** was followed by **Rising For The Moon,** a showcase for Denny insufficiently integrated into group context.

Mattacks left to join Etchingham Steam Band, and in January 1976 Denny returned

to solo career. Lucas and Donahue also quit, precipitating Fairport's demise. New members were recruited, including Bruce Rowland (drums), Bob Brady (piano), Dan Ar Bras (guitar) and Roger Burridge (mandolin/fiddle). Final Island album, **Gottle O'Geer**, originally intended as Swarbrick solo, was recorded as contractual filler. A brief period with Vertigo in 1977 resulted in two averge works, **The Bonny Bunch Of Roses** and **Tipplers Tales**, before anti-climactic **Farewell Farewell.** Former Fairports all succeeded at various levels with spin off/solo ventures. Sandy Denny died tragically of a brain haemorrhage on April 21, 1978, after falling downstairs at a friend's house.

Although Fairport's later work was decidedly patchy in comparison with earlier pioneering achievements, their influence on development of British electric folk music is inestimable. Various members still reunite for one-off gigs.

Final line-up: Nichol; Bruce Rowland, drums, vocals; Dave Swarbrick, violin, vocals; Dave Pegg, bass, vocals;

Albums:
Fairport Convention (A&M/Polydor), 1968
What We Did On Our Holidays (—/Island),
  1969
Unhalfbricking (A&M/Island), 1969
Liege And Lief (A&M/Island), 1969
Full House (A&M/Island), 1970
Angel Delight (A&M/Island), 1971
Babbacombe Lee (A&M/Island), 1971
A History Of Fairport Convention (—/Island),
  1972
Rosie (A&M/Island), 1973
Nine (A&M/Island), 1973
Fairport Live—A Moveable Beast (Island),
  1974
Rising For The Moon (Island), 1974
Gottle O'Geer (Antilles/Island), 1976
Fairport Chronicles (A&M/—), 1976
Live At The LA Troubadour (—/Island),
  1976
The Bonny Bunch Of Roses (—/Vertigo),
  1977
Tipplers Tales (—/Vertigo), 1978
Farewell Farewell (—/Simons), 1979

Adam Faith

UK vocalist, actor, manager, producer.
Born Terry Nelhams, London, June 23, 1940.

Career: A messenger in film business, at Rank Screen Services, he joined workmates in Worried Men skiffle group before TV pop producer Jack Good suggested he go solo as Adam Faith.

After two '6.5 Special' TV appearances, spell on road and flop HMV singles, he lost heart and returned to Rank as assistant film cutter before bandleader John Barry recommended him for TV series 'Drumbeat'. Faith

I Survive, Adam Faith. Courtesy Warner Bros Records.

Above: Adam Faith, born Terry Nelhams, succeeded as singer, actor and manager.

stayed for entire 22 week run and cut futher flop single, for Top Rank, as well as appearing in 'Beat Girl' teen movie.

Raindrops' member and songwriter John Worth offered Faith catchy song **What Do You Want?** Exaggerating hiccupy style of Buddy Holly(▶) over unusual John Barry-arranged pizzicato string backing, Faith cut song in late '59 and made it biggest selling British record of 1960. However, although one of biggest stars of '50s in UK, never had US success. Exploiting same vocal treatment and little-boy-lost lyrics, he had further chart-topper with **Poor Me**, then charted **Someone Else's Baby, Lonely Pup** and **Who Am I?**

Becoming increasingly interested in acting, he appeared in appalling 'What A Whopper' before critically applauded dramatic role as condemned man in 'Mix Me A Person'. In 1965, with recording career flagging, he turned full-time to the stage, touring for two years in relative obscurity of repertory, before regaining national limelight as loser/tarnished hero of 'Budgie' TV series.

In 1973 produced Roger Daltrey's(▶) solo LP **Daltrey** featuring Leo Sayer (whom Faith manages) compositions. He made recording comeback in 1974 with **I Survive** album (artistically far superior to earlier work). Returned to film in 1975 starring with David Essex in 'Stardust'. 1977 saw Faith produce comeback album of erstwhile skiffle idol Lonnie Donegan(▶) and in 1979 he starred with Roger Daltrey in 'McVicar'.

Hit Singles:

	US	UK
What Do You Want?, 1959	—	1
Poor Me, 1960	—	1
Someone Else's Baby, 1960	—	2
When Johnny Comes Marching Home/Made You, 1960	—	5
How About That, 1960	—	4
Lonely Pup, 1960	—	4
This Is It/Who Am I, 1961	—	5
Easy Going Me, 1961	—	12
Don't You Know It?, 1961	—	12
The Time Has Come, 1961	—	4
Lonesome, 1962	—	12
As You Like It, 1962	—	5
Don't That Beat All, 1962	—	8
The First Time, 1963	—	5
We Are In Love, 1963	—	11
Message To Martha, 1964	—	12

Albums:
24 Golden Greats (—/Warwick), 1981

Worth Searching Out:
I Survive (Warner Bros/WEA), 1974

Georgie Fame

UK vocalist, keyboards, composer.
Born Clive Powell, Leigh, Lancashire, June 26, 1943.

Career: British pop impresario Larry Parnes had penchant for giving evocative names to his emergent artists: Billy Fury(▶), Duffy Power, Marty Wilde, Johnny Gentle et al. When he decided to use Billy Fury's then pianist as front man, Parnes came up with name Georgie Fame, with Blue Flames as backing band.

Not an immediate sensation, the group was treading water until they landed residency at London's Flamingo Club. There they developed a cult following for their then innovative mix of various (mainly American) influences ranging from R&B, jazz and soul to West Indian

20 Beat Classics, Georgie Fame. Courtesy RSO Records.

reggae, with white R&B star Mose Allison and jazz vocal team Lambert, Hendricks and Bavan as particular influences. Fame in many ways copied Allison's vocal phrasing while his organ style showed heavy Jimmy Smith/John Patton influence.

Blue Flames included some of finest musicians on London scene, notably Colin Green (guitar), Mick Eve (sax), Red Reece (drums), John McLaughlin(▶)(guitar), Big Jim Sullivan (guitar) and Mitch Mitchell (later of Jimi Hendrix(▶) Experience) (drums) during stint at Flamingo which brought group under management of John and Rick Gunnell with Andrew Loog Oldham (subsequently Rolling Stones' manager) as publicist.

First two albums, one cut live at Flamingo, were released before first hit single **Yeh Yeh** (cover of a Lambert/Hendricks/Bavan classic), which toppled Beatles from No.1 slot on UK chart.

Mid-1966 brought second UK No.1 with **Get Away** and Top-10 cover of Bobby Hebb's **Sunny**, with Fame moving away from small-combo R&B format to work with big bands of both Harry South and Count Basie.

The Ballad Of Bonnie And Clyde (1967) completed his trio of British chart-toppers but his ever-broadening musical base led to decline in sales appeal, though it made him a TV regular and brought him into partnership with former Animals' organist Alan Price(▶) as duo working cabaret circuit. Fame also cut UK TV jingles, notably for Maxwell House coffee.

Following split with Price in 1973, Fame returned to R&B roots with re-formed Blue Flames and Island contract but no new chart success though he continues to work club circuit.

Hit Singles:

	US	UK
Yeh Yeh, 1964	21	1
Get Away, 1966	—	1
Sunny, 1966	—	13
Sittin' In The Park, 1966	—	12
Because I Love You, 1967	—	15
Ballad Of Bonnie And Clyde, 1967	7	1
Peaceful, 1969	—	16
Rosetta (with Alan Price), 1971	—	11

Albums:
Right Now (—/Pye), 1979
That's What Friends Are For (—/Pye), 1979
Closing The Gap (—/Piccadilly), 1980
In Hoagland '81 (with Annie Ross) (—/Bald Eagle), 1981
20 Beat Classics (—/RSO), 1982

Family

UK group formed 1966.

Original line-up: Roger Chapman, vocals, harmonica; Charlie Whitney, guitar; Rob Townsend, drums; Jim King, reed instruments; Rick Grech, bass, vocals, violin.

Career: Two local groups in Leicester merged in 1966 as Jim King and the Farinas. Soon changed name to Family and cut two critically successful albums. Band seemed in vanguard of experimental rock with use of eastern and traditional English instruments; they backed Dave Mason's(▶)(ex-Traffic) solo single without using any electrical instruments. As progressive band, Family seemed destined for success internationally.

Group began series of personnel changes even before second LP appeared. Rick Grech left for Blind Faith(▶) and King returned to Leicester. John Weider (ex-New Animals) on bass and violin took Grech's place and John 'Poli' Palmer, keyboards and winds, replaced King. This line-up lasted three years and two albums.

Band was precluded from US exposure

after row with promoter Bill Graham in April 1969 on American tour. Despite minor UK singles success, this spelt disaster for any '70s band. Weider left in June 1971 and was replaced by journeyman John Wetton (King Crimson(▶), Roxy Music(▶), Uriah Heep(▶), Asia(▶).

Fearless and **Bandstand** LPs restored part of band's lost ground but in 1972 Wetton and Palmer left. Jim Cregan (bass) and Tony Ashton (ex-Ashton, Gardner & Dyke, Remo Four) joined. Family then undertook more relaxed approach, toured US/UK and cut excellent album, **It's Only A Movie**.

Band called quits in October 1973, following successful UK tour. Cregan and Ashton's session commitments, problems lining up US tours, and Chapman's independence of action put future career out of question. Family are fondly remembered by loyal following; they are mostly of interest because of various members' subsequent successes.

Final line-up: Chapman; Whitney; Townsend; Jim Cregan, bass; Tony Ashton, keyboards, vocals.

Hit Singles:

	US	UK
Stange Band, 1970	—	11
In My Own Time, 1971	—	4
Burlesque, 1972	-	13

Albums:
Music In A Doll's House (Reprise), 1968
Family Entertainment (Reprise), 1969
Anyway (Reprise), 1970
Old Songs New Songs (Reprise), 1971
Fearless (Reprise), 1971
Bandstand (Reprise), 1972
Best Of (Reprise), 1974

Jose Feliciano

Latin/US vocalist, guitarist, composer.
Born Puerto Rico, September 10, 1945.

Career: Blind since birth, Feliciano was brought up in Harlem, New York. Interested in music from early age, he experimented with accordion before taking up guitar. In late teens he started working New York folk clubs and coffee houses. Residency at Greenwich Village's Café Id led to RCA contract in 1964.

First albums were generally in Spanish and he soon garnered major following in Latin American countries. Pop success came with 1968 version of Doors(▶) classic **Light My Fire**. An enormous international hit,this—regarded by many as definitive version of song—showcased Feliciano's expressive, melismatic voice and virtuoso acoustic guitar technique.

Since that time Feliciano has based career on album sales and concert and TV appearances rather than hit singles. Over course of years he has earned two Grammy awards and many gold and platinum albums worldwide. In 1981 Feliciano signed to Motown Latino, and 1982 saw the release of Spanish language album **Escenas De Amor**. Although highly talented—his guitar playing alone has won him handful of awards—and a mesmeric concert performer, Feliciano has always suffered from lack of direction.

Like that of Nina Simone(▶), Ray Charles(▶) and other electric performers, his audience is now firmly middle-of-the-road.

Hit Singles:

	US	UK
Light My Fire, 1968	3	6

Albums:
Feliciano (RCA), 1969
Encore! (RCA), 1971
Fireworks (RCA), 1974
Escenas De Amor (Motown), 1982

Above: The immaculately stylish Bryan Ferry.

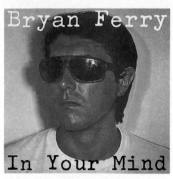

In Your Mind, Bryan Ferry. Courtesy Polydor Records.

Bryan Ferry

UK vocalist.
Born Washington, County Durham, September 26, 1945.

Career: Ferry had life-long interest in music which found outlet in singing for small local groups. Upon graduation from Newcastle University, worked as teacher. By 1970 he had committed self to professional music with formation of Roxy Music(▶).

Band held his full-time attention until solo release in 1973 of **These Foolish Things**, featuring Ferry singing covers of his favourite rock songs. His second solo album featured original material which appeared to be Roxy cast-offs.

Inability to balance both careers resulted in dissolution of Roxy Music in 1976. Instead of waiting to produce proper release, Ferry offered strange collection from his earlier solo singles as well as reworked Roxy Music material. (The LP was really a compilation for US market.) Yet holding pattern of **Let's Stick Together** sounded interesting in comparison to next planned album, **In Your Mind**. Tours of UK/US failed to win any support for this material and made demise of Roxy Music all the more regrettable.

Just as public interest in Ferry reached low point, he produced superb **The Bride Stripped Bare** which reflected emotional trauma of break-up with girlfriend Jerry Hall. In August 1978 Ferry re-formed Roxy Music and began impressive return to public and critical favour.

Although many consider Roxy Music and Bryan Ferry to be one and the same, Ferry's fling at solo stardom shows they're not. Content to channel his creativity into group dynamics instead of controlling *everything*, Ferry is now in position to be lasting influence throughout '80s.

Hit Singles:

	US	UK
A Hard Rain's Gonna Fall, 1973	—	10
The In Crowd, 1974	—	13
Smoke Gets In Your Eyes, 1974	—	17
Let's Stick Together, 1976	—	4
Extended Play (EP), 1976	—	7
This Is Tomorrow, 1977	—	9
Tokyo Joe, 1977	—	15

Albums:
These Foolish Things (Atlantic/Island), 1973
Another Time Another Place (Atlantic/Island), 1974
Let's Stick Together (Atlantic/Island), 1976
In Your Mind (Atlantic/Polydor), 1977
The Bride Stripped Bare (Polydor), 1978

Roberta Flack

US vocalist, pianist, composer.
Born Asheville, North Carolina, February 2, 1937.

Career: Born into musical family (her mother was a church organist), Roberta started piano lessons at nine and by 13 was a competent player. She won music scholarship to Howard University at 15 and subsequently graduated with degrees in music and education. From early to mid-'60s Flack taught in schools in North Carolina and Washington, eventually moving onto club circuit playing blues and R&B.

By summer of 1968 Flack was successful club performer and attracted attention of Atlantic Records. First album, **First Take**, was released in 1969, and included delicate version of Scottish folksinger Ewan McColl's ballad **The First Time Ever I Saw Your Face**. Album aroused interest, but major success came in 1972 when **Face** was featured in Clint Eastwood movie 'Play Misty For Me'; single topped US charts and made Flack's reputation.

In the meantime Flack released second LP and started collaboration with fellow Atlantic artist Donny Hathaway(▶). By 1975 Flack was fully established as major international artist, by now also producing own albums.

Association with Hathaway came to end with his untimely death in 1979. Duet album with Peabo Bryson was success in 1981, and in 1982 Flack was back in Top 20 singles chart with titletrack of movie **Making Love**. Difficult to categorise, Flack's music combines blues, jazz and soul elements with classical influence. Her somewhat detached voice can be ethereally effective on ballad material but is less convincing on uptempo songs. Talent and versatility ensure longevity of career.

Below: Roberta Flack dueted with both Donny Hathaway and Peabo Bryson.

Hit Singles:

	US	UK
The First Time Ever I Saw Your Face, 1972	1	14
Killing Me Softly With His Song, 1973	1	6
Feel Like Makin' Love, 1974	3	34
Making Love, 1982	13	—

With Donny Hathaway:

	US	UK
Where Is The Love, 1972	5	29
The Closer I Get To You, 1978	2	42
Back Together Again, 1980	56	3

Albums:
First Take (Atlantic), 1969*
Chapter Two (Atlantic), 1970*
Quiet Fire (Atlantic), 1971
Killing Me Softly (Atlantic), 1973
Blue Lights In The Basement (Atlantic), 1977
Roberta Flack (Atlantic), 1978
The Best Of Roberta Flack (Atlantic), 1981
I'm The One (Atlantic), 1982

*Available as double set (—/Atlantic), 1972

With Donny Hathaway:
Flack And Hathaway (Atlantic), 1972
Featuring Donny Hathaway (Atlantic), 1980

With Peabo Bryson:
Live And More (Atlantic), 1981

Flatt & Scruggs

US vocal/instrumental duo formed 1948.
Lester Raymond Flatt, guitar, vocals, born Overton County, Tennessee June 19, 1914; Earl Eugene Scruggs, banjo, born Cleveland County, North Carolina, January 6, 1924.

Career: Influential, pioneering bluegrass duo who joined forces after a period with Bill Monroe's(▶) band. Both enjoyed strong musical family heritage, and were brought up in country music strongholds.

Flatt's powerful high tenor delivery compensated for an average 'picking' technique, although he was a solid rhythm guitarist. Scruggs, however, was an instrumental virtuoso and he perfected a three-finger banjo 'roll' which has influenced four subsequent generations of banjo players.

They first recorded for Mercury Records (1948), calling themselves the Foggy Mountain Boys, cutting legendary **Foggy Mountain Breakdown** a year later; this music was revived after 20 years as soundtrack for film, 'Bonnie & Clyde', and made both UK and US Top 60.

Major chart hit was theme from the 'Beverly Hillbillies' TV series, **The Ballad Of Jed Clampett**, which enjoyed three-month stay at top of C&W charts in 1962.

Flatt & Scruggs split in 1969, Scruggs to lead the rock-orientated Earl Scruggs review (which included his sons), Flatt remaining within established bluegrass boundaries. Scruggs subsequently formed group with guitarist/vocalist Doug Dillard. Flatt died in Nashville in May 1979.

Instruments: Lester Flatt, Martin acoustic guitars; Earl Scruggs, Gibson Mastertone banjo, OME banjo.

Albums (selected):
The Golden Era (1950/55) (Rounder), 1977
Foggy Mountain Banjo (Bluegrass), 1978
Blue Ridge Cabin Home (County), 1979
Flatt & Scruggs (Columbia/CBS), 1982
Lester Flatt:
Heavens Bluegrass Band (Checkmate), 1977
Lester Flatt (—/Sonet), 1977
Earl Scruggs:
Earl Scruggs Review—Anniversary Special, Volume 1 (Columbia/CBS), 1975
The Story Teller And The Banjo Man (with Tom T. Hall) (Columbia/CBS), 1982

Fleetwood Mac, Fleetwood Mac (1968). Courtesy Blue Horizon Records.

Fleetwood Mac

UK group formed 1967.
Original line-up: Peter Green, Gibson Les Paul guitar, vocals; John McVie, bass; Mick Fleetwood, drums; Jeremy Spencer, guitar, vocals.

Career: Peter Green(▶) formed band when he, McVie and Fleetwood quit (or were fired from) Mayall's(▶) Bluesbreakers. For short period McVie considered re-joining Mayall and Fleetwood Mac's debut performance at Windsor Festival (August 1967) featured temporary bassist Bob Brunning (who also recorded B-side on band's first single).

First LP featured straight-ahead blues and became instant steady seller for over a year. Green then added third guitarist, Danny Kirwan, for third album. Many consider this classic line-up to be band's best.

In UK, band released **Then Play On, Pious Bird Of Good Omen** and **Blues Jam At Chess** before Green left in May 1970 to join religious sect. From this period came No. 1 UK single **Albatross, Man Of The World,** and concert favourite **Oh Well.**

Spencer and Kirwan assumed leadership roles and produced excellent set **Kiln House**.

Below: Christine McVie joined husband John in Fleetwood Mac in 1970.

For all practical purposes, McVie's wife, Christine Perfect (ex-Chicken Shack), joined as full-time member.

Band was beginning to recover self-confidence by February 1971 when Jeremy Spencer jolted Mac with conversion to religious cult, Children of God. Like Green, he renounced his past and swore to leave rock business. Green stepped in to help band complete US tour. Permanent guitar duties were assumed in April 1971 by Bob Welch and with him Mac released spotty **Future Games** and highly underrated **Bare Trees.**

Next casualty was Kirwan who was fired in summer 1972 because of growing disenchantment with road life. Welch's influence took Mac from blues-based rock towards softer California sound. This trend was accelerated by Kirwan's replacements, Americans Bob Weston (guitar, vocals) and Dave Walker (vocals). Walker had been lead singer with Savoy Brown and his addition was experiment to re-organise traditional frontman vocalist lines. Mac released **Penguin,** indicating McVie's fascination for the Antarctic bird which became band's symbol.

By June 1973 Walker had left to work with Kirwan, and band floundered. **Mystery To Me** was critically disappointing and is of interest only because original pressing included **Good Things (Come To Those Who Wait)** which was immediately replaced by cover of Yardbirds(▶) hit, **For Your Love.** Weston left after recording this LP and resulting internal upheavals caused band to cancel US autumn 1973 tour. Their manager formed bogus group to tour in their place at start of 1974. Band seemed to disappear for good as litigation ensued over various claims to name Fleetwood Mac. They reappeared with **Heroes Are Hard To Find** but seemed doomed to perennial flux as Bob Welch left shortly after.

Legend has it that Mick Fleetwood was checking out LA studio to record Mac's next album when he was introduced to Lindsey Buckingham, who was working next door with Stevie Nicks on their second album **Buckingham Nicks.** Fleetwood asked them to join his group. Somewhat reluctantly, duo accepted. Result was smash hit LP, **Fleetwood Mac.** Album maintained sales as nearly every track proved to be strong single in own right. Any

doubts about Mac's ability to sustain this success was dispelled by even better and bigger hit, **Rumours.**

Mac's capacity to survive is evidenced by **Rumours** since it followed break-up of John and Christine McVie's marriage, as well as Fleetwood's. Buckingham and Nicks also broke off long-term relationship. **Rumours'** strength is its ability to convey hurt and loss without resorting to sentimentalism.

New success of Mac pushed band into realm of superstars. Certain air of self-indulgence appeared in long-awaited follow up, **Tusk. Fleetwood Mac Live** broke no new ground and Mac seemed to lose direction again as Nicks, Fleetwood and Buckingham all released solo offerings.

Mirage returned band to top form and continued Buckingham's gradual take-over of group's musical direction.

Rumours, Fleetwood Mac. Courtesy Warner Bros Records.

Current line-up: John McVie; Fleetwood; Christine McVie, keyboards, vocals; Lindsey Buckingham, guitar, vocals; Stevie Nicks, vocals.

Hit Singles:	US	UK
Albatross, 1968	—	1
Man Of The World, 1969	—	2
Oh Well, 1969	55	2
The Green Manalishi, 1970	—	10
Albatross, 1973	—	2
Rhiannon, 1976	11	46
Say You Love Me, 1976	11	40
Go Your Own Way, 1976	10	38
Don't Stop, 1977	3	32
Tusk, 1979	8	2
Sara, 1979	7	37
Think About Me, 1980	20	—
Hold Me, 1982	4	—
Gypsy, 1982	12	46
Oh Diane, 1982	—	9

Stevie Nicks with Don Henley:

Leather And Lace, 1981	6	—

Stevie Nicks with Tom Petty:

Stop Draggin' My Heart Around, 1981	3	—

Fleetwood Mac's Greatest Hits. Courtesy CBS.

Albums:
English Rose (Epic/—), 1969
Then Play On (Reprise), 1969
Fleetwood Mac In Chicago* (Sire/Blue Horizon),1969
Kiln House (Reprise), 1970
The Original Fleetwood Mac (Sire/CBS), 1971
Black Magic Woman† (Columbia/CBS), 1971
Future Games (Reprise), 1971
Greatest Hits (Epic/CBS), 1971
Bare Trees (Reprise), 1972
Penguin (Reprise), 1973
Mystery To Me (Reprise), 1974
Heroes Are Hard To Find (Reprise), 1974
Fleetwood Mac (Reprise), 1975
Vintage Years (Columbia/CBS), 1975
Albatross (—/Embassy), 1977
Rumours (Warner Bros), 1977
Tusk (Warner Bros), 1979
Fleetwood Mac Live (Warner Bros), 1980
Mirage (Warner Bros), 1982

*UK title: Blues Jam At Chess
†Compilation of first two US LPs

Selected Solo Albums:
Christine McVie:
Christine Perfect (Sire/Blue Horizon), 1970
Jeremy Spencer:
Jeremy Spencer (Reprise), 1970
Jeremy Spencer & The Children Of God (Columbia/CBS), 1972
Flee (—/Alantic), 1979
Lindsey Buckingham/Stevie Nicks:
Buckingham Nicks (Polydor), 1973
Stevie Nicks:
Bella Donna (Modern/WEA), 1981
Lindsey Buckingham:
Law & Order (Asylum/Mercury), 1982
Danny Kirwin:
Second Chapter (DJM), 1975
Midnight In San Juan (DJM), 1976
Hello There Big Boy (DJM), 1979
Mick Fleetwood:
The Visitor (RCA), 1981
Peter Green:
(See separate entry)

Below: An early line-up of Fleetwood Mac, with Peter Green in red robe.

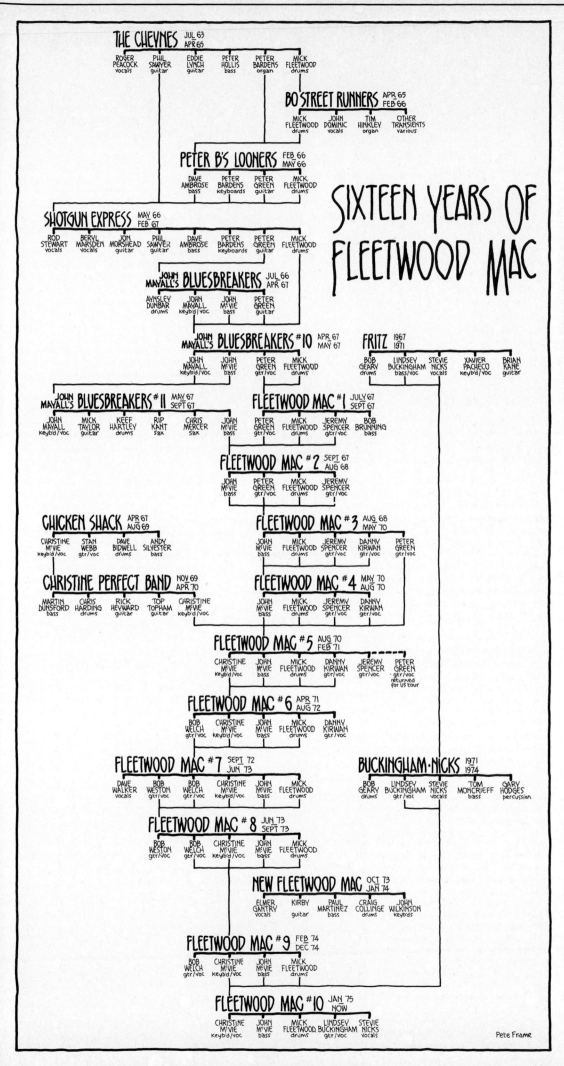

A Flock Of Seagulls

UK group formed 1980.

Original/Current line-up: Mike Score, vocals, keyboards; Frank Maudsley, bass, vocals; Paul Reynolds, guitar, vocals; Ali Score, drums.

Career: Mike Score (of striking stage hair-do), owned Liverpool hairdressing shop. He told employee Maudsley of plans for group named after Richard Bach's book 'Jonathan Livingston Seagull'. Score recruited brother Ali and Maudsley met Reynolds in night-club.

Listen, A Flock Of Seagulls. Courtesy Jive Records.

Seagulls found Liverpool had little room for their aggressive pop and moved to London. This led to more work, a record contract, and support slot on Squeeze's(▶) American tour. What was to be short US stay turned into seven months of solid work and massive concerts with big breakthrough coming from excellent videos played on US 24-hour music/video subscription TV channel, MTV.

Album was released in May 1982; ignored in UK, it made Top 10 in US, signalling belated American acceptance of post-1976 UK bands. Seagulls soon had US hit singles, but UK press criticised their 'sell-out'.

Seagulls have proved they can go own way, and demonstrate variety of talents Liverpool has to offer when Merseybeat is only historical memory. Continued perseverance should eventually win more success in homeland.

Hit Singles:	US	UK
I Ran (So Far Away), 1982	9	43
Wishing (If I Had A Photograph), 1982	26	10

Albums:
A Flock Of Seagulls (Jive), 1982
Listen (Jive), 1983

Flying Burrito Brothers

US group formed 1968.

Original line-up: Gram Parsons, guitar, vocals; Chris Hillman, guitar, bass, mandolin, vocals; Sneeky Pete Kleinow, pedal steel guitar; Chris Etheridge, bass.

Career: Basically the brainchild of ex-Byrd(▶) Gram Parsons, Flying Burrito Brothers were one of first bands to synthesise rock and country music and find audience for it. In relatively short working life band underwent numerous personnel changes, encompassing many of the best-known names of country rock.

The original line-up with various session drummers cut **The Gilded Palace Of Sin** in

1969, and immediately established band as something special. The combination of Parsons' idiosyncratic, almost fragile vocals, Sneeky Pete's southern fried pedal steel and Parsons/Hillman (Hillman also ex-Byrds) compositions created unique sound that was nevertheless too close to pure country for many rock-orientated listeners.

There were many changes before the next album; another ex-Byrd, Michael Clarke, joined as permanent drummer, while Etheridge left to return to session work. Hillman moved over to bass and Bernie Leadon (ex Dillard and Clarke) joined on guitar. This aggregation produced **Burrito De Luxe**, released in May 1970, a tighter, rockier collection that garnered band many more fans.

At this time founder-member and main inspiration Gram Parsons left, but band con-

Airborne. The Flying Burrito Bros. Courtesy Columbia Records.

tinued with Rick Roberts as replacement. This line-up lasted a year, before Sneeky Pete left to be replaced by Al Perkins. A few months later Bernie Leadon quit to become founder member of the Eagles(▶). In the meantime third album, **The Flying Burrito Brothers**, was released, featuring Roberts' more pop-orientated singing and compositions.

It was obvious, however, that Burritos were soon to be grounded. Ego clashes and legendary wild lifestyle meant stability was not band's forte. Remaining members drafted champion fiddler Byron Berline, bassist Roger Bush, and guitarist Kenny Wertz from Country Gazette, and recorded exciting live album, **Last Of The Red Hot Burritos**, before throwing in towel in October 1971. Hillman and Perkins went on to join Stephen Stills'(▶) Manassas, Hillman later pursuing solo career.

Red Hot Burritos was the last 'true' Burrito album, although most of Country Gazette plus Rick Roberts undertook European tour as the Flying Burrito Brothers, and several live albums ensued. Two 'reunion' albums, **Flying Again**, which featured Kleinow and Etheridge, and **Airborne**, were both critical and commercial failures.

More than any other band, the Flying Burrito Brothers drew country music into mainstream of American rock, paving way for bands like Poco(▶), the Ozark Mountain Daredevils(▶) and indeed the Eagles.

Final line-up: Al Perkins, pedal steel guitar; Kenny Wertz, guitar, banjo; Chris Hillman; Rick Roberts, guitar; Michael Clarke, drums.

Albums:
Gilded Palace Of Sin (A&M), 1969
Burrito De Luxe (A&M), 1970
Flying Burrito Brothers (A&M), 1971
Last Of The Red Hot Burritos (A&M), 1971
Close Up The Honky Tonks (A&M), 1974
Flying Again (Columbia/CBS), 1975
Airborne (Columbia/CBS), 1976
Sleepless Nights (with Gram Parsons) (A&M), 1976
Live From Tokyo (Regency/—), 1978

Dan Fogelberg

US vocalist, composer.
Born Peoria, Illinois, 1954.

Career: Abandoned art studies at University of Illinois in order to pursue singer/songwriter career in late '60s. Achieving minimal success on folk circuit, moved to Los Angeles to secure lucrative work as sessioneer. Impressed Van Morrison(▶) enough to be invited to join touring troupe.

Moving from LA to Nashville, Fogelberg was eventually offered contract by Columbia. Under aegis of Nashville producer Norbert Putnam, work was completed on debut **Home Free**. Poor promotion blighted record's chances and Fogelberg was dropped from label shortly afterwards.

Returning to Nashville session work, Fogelberg's luck changed when he was signed to management by Irv Azoff, whose other clients included Joe Walsh(▶) and the Eagles(▶). Using business contacts, Azoff finalised deal with Epic. Next album **Souvenirs** boasted impressive back-up team, including Graham Nash and various Eagles, plus Joe Walsh as producer.

Critical and commercial success followed as Fogelberg was accepted into US singer/songwriter mafia. Guested on several albums, including Jackson Browne's(▶) **Late For The Sky**. **Captured Angel**, released following year, trod same ground as **Souvenirs**, with pleasant melodies, soft vocal, standard lovelorn lyrics and accomplished musicianship. Since then, Fogelberg has released several albums. Support tours with Eagles have boosted following.

Over the years, there has been little sign of any development from original formula. Essentially, Fobelberg is a second-division singer/songwriter, somewhat outclassed by artists with whom he has had tenuous connections. Nevertheless, his records still sporadically make US Top 20, and he receives much airplay on MOR radio.

Above: Champion fiddler Byron Berline onstage with the Flying Burritos.

Hit Singles:	US	UK
Same Olde Lang Syne, 1981	9	—
Hard To Say, 1981	10	—
Leader Of The Band, 1982	9	—
Run For The Roses, 1982	18	—

Albums:
Home Free (Columbia), 1972
Souvenirs (Epic), 1974
Captured Angel (Epic), 1975
Netherlands (Epic), 1977
Phoenix (Epic), 1980
The Innocent Age (Epic/—), 1981
Greatest Hits (Epic/—), 1981

With Tim Weisberg:
Twin Sons Of Different Mothers (Epic), 1978

Tennessee Ernie Ford

US vocalist.
Born Bristol, Tennessee, February 13, 1919.

Career: A radio announcer DJ in Pasadena, California, before joining US Air Force in 1941, Ford worked in quartet on 'Hometown Jamboree Show' in Pasadena on return to civilian life. A Capitol Records' talent scout heard Ford on his car radio and signed him to solo contract.

His first recording, **Mule Train**, in 1949 was a hit, and follow-ups **I'll Never Be Free** (with Kay Starr) and own composition **Shotgun Boogie** (a 1950 million-seller which topped US country charts) established his reputation.

In 1955 Ford picked up a song by fellow country artist Merl Travis, a Kentucky coalminer's son. The sardonic tale of **Sixteen Tons** proved to be one of the fastest selling records of all time, leaping to top of US charts (where it stayed for seven weeks) and spending four weeks at No.1 in Britain. In first 11 days 400,000 records were sold and total world sales exceeded four million.

In many ways the record paved way for emergent rockabilly sound of Elvis Presley(▶) but for the main part Ford stayed firmly in country and western mould. An amazing number of his recordings were also religiously inspired; of his 26 albums released by Capitol up to 1966, 16 were of inspirational nature, the most successful being **Hymns**, which went gold in 1956, stayed on American charts for a sensational 276 weeks and was still selling steadily more than a decade later.

Hit Singles:	US	UK
Give Me Your Word, 1955	—	11
Ballad Of Davy Crockett, 1955	5	3
Sixteen Tons, 1955	1	1
That's All, 1956	17	—

Albums (selected):
The Very Best Of (Capitol), 1974
Yesterday-Today 25th Anniversary (Capitol), 1974
He Touched Me (Word), 1978

Worth Searching Out:
Hymns (Capitol/—), 1956

Below: One time protege of Joe Walsh, Dan Fogelberg's fame has only accrued in his native land.

Foreigner

US/UK group formed 1976.

Original line-up: Mick Jones, guitar; Ian McDonald, guitar, keyboards; Dennis Elliot, drums; Lou Gamm, vocals; Al Greenwood, keyboards; Ed Gagliardi, bass.

Career: Formed in New York by two Englishmen — Jones (ex-Spooky Tooth, Leslie West Band) and McDonald (ex-King Crimson(▶), McDonald & Giles). Adding English drummer Elliot (also ex-King Crimson) and three Americans — Gamm, Greenwood and Gagliardi — band recorded debut album in 1977.

Foreigner LP spawned hits **Feels Like The First Time** and **Cold As Ice**; established Gamm as premier rock vocalist and Jones as melodic composer in mêlée of heavy-metal outfits. After steady stream of chart singles and two further albums, Jones withdrew band from recording and touring in 1980.

With departure of McDonald, Greenwood and Gagliardi, Foreigner re-formed as four piece; Rick Wills (ex-Peter Frampton(▶)) took Gagliardi's bass spot. New line-up topped US album charts with **4** during winter 1981. Maintained single success, 1981 being most productive year since band's inception. Both **Urgent** (with stirring tenor solo by Junior Walker(▶)) and **Waiting For A Girl Like You** made US Top 5, the latter giving group first UK Top 20 chart entry.

Best Of (1982) set in absence of new studio album suggested serious planning of band's future. With Gamm's asbestos-throated vocals injecting undiminished passion into Jones' songs, Foreigner can afford all the time they want.

Current line-up: Jones; Elliot; Gamm; Rick Wills, bass.

Hit Singles:

	US	UK
Feels Like The First Time, 1977	4	39
Cold As Ice, 1977	6	24
Long, Long Way From Home, 1978	20	—
Hot Blooded, 1978	3	42
Double Vision, 1978	2	—
Blue Morning, Blue Day, 1979	15	45
Dirty White Boy, 1979	12	—
Head Games, 1979	14	—
Urgent, 1981	3	—
Waiting For A Girl Like You, 1981	2	8

Albums:

Foreigner (Atlantic), 1977
Double Vision (Atlantic), 1978
Head Games (Atlantic), 1979
4 (Atlantic), 1981
Best Of (Atlantic), 1982

Four Seasons

US group formed 1962.

Original line-up: Frankie Valli, lead vocals; Bob Gaudio, vocals, keyboard; Nick Massi, vocals; Tommy De Vito, vocals.

Career: America's closest challengers to the Beatles(▶) (for short time both groups' records appeared on same US label, Vee-Jay). The Four Seasons' appeal hinged on unique falsetto-style lead vocals of Valli and songwriting talents of group member Bob Gaudio and producer Bob Crewe.

Record sales of more than 80 million copies, plus a career which outlasted that of their British rivals, make the Four Seasons arguably the greatest pop (as opposed to rock) group of all time.

Frankie Valli (born Francis Castelluccio, Newark, New Jersey, May 3, 1937) began career in 1953 joining local Variatone Trio (Nick and Tommy De Vito, Hank Magenski). Changing name to Four Lovers, group enjoyed minor hit in 1956 with **Apple Of My Eye** by black songwriter Otis Blackwell (who wrote several Presley hits).

Dropped by RCA in 1959 after three lean years, they met New York/Philadelphia based Bob Crewe. Four Lovers were intially used as back-up singers on sessions for Bob Crewe/Frank Slay-owned Swan label in Philly. Label had success with Freddy Cannon and launched careers of Mitch Ryder and the Toys (as well as being Bealtes' first US label).

Nick Massi replaced Magenski and Nick De Vito was replaced by Charles Callelo, who in turn gave way to Bob Gaudio. A protégé of Crewe's, Gaudio (born Bronx, New York, November 17, 1942) had been member of the Royal Teens.

With new line-up and new name—the Four Seasons—group began to record, debut appearing on Gone. Signed to fast-rising Chicago-based independent Vee-Jay Records for second single **Sherry** (1962) for which Gaudio persuaded Valli to use his subsequent trademark falsetto sound.

Record shot to No. 1 in US, No. 8 in UK. **Big Girls Don't Cry** gave them second 1962 million seller followed in early 1963 by **Walk Like A Man**, making it three American chart-toppers in a row.

Four Seasons' emergence coincided with the 'Merseymania' explosion and they plus the equally nascent Beach Boys(▶) were the only groups able to challenge British domination of transatlantic charts.

Contractual arguments with Vee-Jay led to switch to Philips label in 1964. Vee-Jay, who also had US rights to Beatles material, issued lavish double album set featuring both acts and billed as 'The International Battle Of The Century'.

Dawn (Go Away) made No. 3, and **Rag Doll** (1964) saw the Four Seasons back at top of charts. 1965's **Let's Hang On** was fifth chart-topping million-seller and marked move into a blue-eyed soul flavoured style which made subsequent **Workin' My Way Back To You** such a classic. Song was successfully covered years later by black superstars the Detroit Spinners.

Parallel to group's continuing stardom, Valli issued solo record, scoring big with **The Proud One** and MOR slanted **Can't Take My Eyes Off You**. Group also recorded anonymously as the Wonder Who with quirky version of Bob Dylan's(▶) **Don't Think Twice It's Alright** with view to proving that it was their music and not their image which gave them hits; record went to Top 20 in US.

With both the Beatles and the Beach Boys veering towards progressive pop/rock and issuing concept albums, the Four Seasons came up with ambitious **Genuine Imitation Life Gazette** (1969) project in answer to **Sergeant Pepper** and **Pet Sounds**. Lavishly produced—reputedly one of most expensive recordings ever—it lacked conviction. Album failed dismally in commerical as well as artistic terms, leading to split with both Bob Crewe and Philips.

The Four Seasons spent some years in recording retirement, contenting themselves with playing cabaret venues and cashing in on nostalgia market. They were then signed by Berry Gordy for Motown's new West Coast label Mowest. **Chameleon** album and several singles passed relatively unnoticed at time though they have since become collectors' items.

Motown refused to release Valli's solo effort **My Eyes Adored You**, so he took it to Private Stock and was rewarded with massive transatlantic hit in late 1974. While Private Stock picked up Valli as solo artist and bought rights to all old Philips' material (re-packaged as hit album **The Four Seasons Story**), group itself signed new deal with Warner Bros. 1976 was good year for big comeback; cover versions of Four Seasons' oldies (**Bye Bye Baby** by the Bay City Rollers(▶), **Sherry** by Adrian Baker and Valli's **The Proud One** by the Osmonds(▶)) were peppering UK charts when their Motown oldie **The Night** was re-issued, reaching No. 3. Copies of the original pressing had been changing hands for £10 in British Northern Soul collectors' circles.

Classy Warner Bros album **Who Loves You** capitalised on both nostalgia of older audiences and emergent disco boom. The Four Seasons, albeit with much revised line-up, were right back on top. Follow-up single to **Who Loves You** was **December '63** on which new drummer Gerry Polci handled bulk of vocal; it became Four Seasons' first UK chart-topper. **Silver Star** also went Top 5 and resultant British tour was pure magic.

Though Bob Gaudio wrote all songs for **Who Loves You** album (with Judy Parker) he was no longer working member of group (except on record). Valli was still part-and-parcel of their greatness and the balance between his totally distinctive falsetto and the more gutsy voice of Polci added whole new dimension. Album's line-up comprised; Frankie Valli, vocals; Gerry Polci, drums, vocals; John Paiva, guitar; Lee Shapiro, keyboards; Don Ciccone, bass.

Spring 1976 saw same team, with more Gaudio songs, involved in **Hellicon** album. However, it lacked sparkle of its predecessor. In September 1977 Valli announced he was ending his long stint as leader of the Four Seasons to concentrate on solo projects. Had US No. 1, UK No. 3 in 1978 with theme from movie 'Grease'.

Like their erstwhile rivals the Beatles, the Four Seasons' appeal has remained strong through the years. They have consistently attracted new audiences. The group's shows have always been crowd-pullers even at times when they have had no chart success; in early '70s they filled Madison Square Gardens for eight shows in a row.

Final line-up: Valli; Gerry Polci, drums, vocals; John Paiva, guitar; Lee Shapiro, keyboards; Don Ciccone, bass.

Hit Singles:

	US	UK
Sherry, 1962	1	8
Big Girls Don't Cry, 1962	1	13
Walk Like A Man, 1963	1	12
Candy Girl, 1963	3	—
Dawn (Go Away), 1964	3	—
Stay, 1964	16	—
Ronnie, 1964	6	—
Rag Doll, 1964	1	2
Save It For Me, 1964	10	—
Big Man In Town, 1964	20	—
Bye Bye Baby, 1965	12	—
Let's Hang On, 1965	3	4
Working My Way Back To You, 1966	9	50
Opus 17 (Don't Worry 'Bout Me), 1966	13	20
I've Got You Under My Skin, 1966	9	12
Tell It To The Rain, 1967	10	37
Beggin', 1967	16	—
Come On Marianne, 1967	9	—
Night, 1967	—	7
Who Loves You, 1975	3	6
December '63 (Oh What A Night), 1976	1	1
Silver Star, 1976	38	3

As The Wonder Who:

	US	UK
Don't Think Twice It's Alright, 1965	12	—

Frankie Valli Solo:

	US	UK
Can't Take My Eyes Off You, 1967	2	—
I Make A Fool Of Myself, 1967	18	—
You're Ready Now, 1970	—	11
My Eyes Adored You, 1975	1	5

Below: The Four Seasons, with the great Frankie Valli (centre).

Swearin' To God, 1975	6	31
Our Day Will Come, 1975	11	—
Fallen Angel, 1976	36	11
Grease, 1978	1	3

Albums:
Chameleon (Mowest), 1972
Who Loves You (Warner Bros), 1975
Greatest Hits (—/K-Tel), 1976
Story (Private Stock), 1976
Helicon (Warner Bros), 1977
Reunited Live (Warner Bros), 1981
Frankie Valli And The Four Seasons (K-Tel), 1982

Frankie Valli Solo:
Heaven Above Me (MCA), 1980
The Very Best Of (MCA), 1980

Worth Searching Out:
Sherry (Vee-Jay/Atlantic), 1963
Gold Vault (Philips), 1965
Working My Way Back To You (Philips), 1965

The Four Tops

US vocal group formed 1954.
Original/Current line-up: Levi Stubbs, lead vocals; Renaldo Benson, vocals; Abdul 'Duke' Fakir, vocals; Lawrence Payton, vocals.

Career: Formed as the Four Aims in Detroit, during period 1954-64, group signed to Chess, Singular, Riverside and Columbia without significant success. Eventually joined Motown in 1964, and changed name to Four Tops. Famed Motown team Holland/Dozier/Holland(▶) were assigned to writing and production duties; first release, **Baby I Need Your Loving**, was hit.

Success was consolidated in 1965 with **I Can't Help Myself**, US No.1, international hit and million-seller. Next few releases established Tops as major headlining act, much of spotlight falling on Levi Stubbs as particularly powerful and distinctive lead singer.

Group was forging style as fairly conventional Motown act, and thus surprised public and critics in 1966 with landmark record **Reach Out I'll Be There**. Superb production, with innovative rhythmic pattern and searing vocal by Stubbs, blasted record to No.1 spot on both sides of Atlantic. It established Motown as force in contemporary music as well as highly successful commercial company.

Further hits followed, continuing even after Tops lost Holland/Dozier/Holland when team split to form Invictus Records. By 1969 Tops began to feel overlooked among large number of acts now signed to Motown, particularly as musical supremo Norman Whitfield was concentrating on following rock-influenced directions with Temptations(▶). Tops split from Motown, apparently relatively amicably.

Group eventually signed with ABC/Dunhill in 1972, and achieved minor hits in early '70s. Their recorded output was not up to quality of Motown releases, but they continued to record throughout '70s with varying degrees of success. Meanwhile, they continued to tour steadily, being particularly popular in UK.

By end of '70s it seemed group were headed towards gold-plated semi-retirement on lucrative cabaret circuit, but events turned out differently. Having signed to Casablanca in 1981, they released **Tonight**, a classy collection of relaxed pop-soul songs that recaptured great deal of magic of Tops' great days. Album yielded hit singles which re-established act as credible force.

Now seems likely that Tops will go on forever as perennial mainstays of good black pop music. Although not overly innovative or sociologically significant, the Four Tops have in their time produced some superb and memorable music, much of which has achieved classic status.

Hit Singles:

	US	UK
Baby I Need Your Loving, 1964	11	—
I Can't Help Myself, 1965	1	23
It's The Same Old Song, 1965	5	—
Something About You, 1965	19	—
Shake Me Wake Me (When It's Over), 1966	18	—
Reach Out I'll Be There, 1966	1	1
Standing In The Shadows Of Love, 1966	6	6
Bernadette, 1967	4	8
Seven Rooms Of Gloom, 1967	14	12
You Keep Running Away, 1967	19	26
Walk Away Renee, 1967	14	3
If I Were A Carpenter, 1968	20	7
Yesterday's Dreams, 1968	49	20
What Is A Man, 1969	53	16
Do What You Gotta Do, 1969	—	20
I Can't Help Myself (re-issue), 1970	—	10
It's All In The Game, 1970	24	5
Still Water (Love), 1970	11	10
Simple Game, 1971	—	3
Keeper Of The Castle, 1972	10	18
Ain't No Woman (Like The One I've Got), 1973	4	—
Are You Man Enough, 1973	15	—
When She Was My Girl, 1981	12	3
Don't Walk Away, 1982	—	16

With Supremes:

River Deep Mountain High, 1970	14	11

Albums:
Four Tops Second Album (Tamla Motown), 1966
Reach Out (Tamla Motown), 1967
Greatest Hits (Tamla Motown), 1968
Still Waters Run Deep (Tamla Motown), 1970
Greatest Hits Volume 2 (Tamla Motown), 1971
The Magnificent Seven (with Supremes) (Tamla Motown), 1971
Keep Of The Castle (Dunhill/MFP), 1972
Four Tops Story (—/Tamla Motown), 1973
Main Street People (Dunhill/Probe), 1973
Shaft In Africa (Probe/Anchor), 1974
Live In Concert (Dunhill/Anchor), 1974
Night Lights Harmony (ABC/Anchor), 1974
Super Hits (—/Tamla Motown), 1976
Anthology (Tamla Motown), 1976
Catfish (ABC), 1976
The Show Must Go On (ABC/Anchor), 1977
Motown Special (—/Tamla Motown), 1977
At The Top (ABC), 1978
It's All In The Game (—/MFP), 1979
20 Golden Greats (—/Tamla Motown), 1980

Below: The Four Tops, one of Motown's most consistent acts of the '60s.

Tonight (Casablanca), 1981		
Greatest Hits (ABC), 1982		
Hits Of Gold (—/Pickwick), 1982		
One More Mountain (Casablanca), 1982		
Best Of The Four Tops (K-Tel), 1982		
The Fabulous Four Tops (—/Pickwick), 1982		

Peter Frampton

UK vocalist, guitarist, composer.
Born Beckenham, England, April 22, 1950.

Career: British pop music press traditionally seized cute faces to pump up, and cherubic-faced Peter Frampton was their choice for 'Face of '68' teen idol. He was then leader of the Herd who hit with **From The Underworld** (1967), **Paradise Lost** (1968) and **I Don't Want Our Loving To Die** (1968). But Frampton had other ideas, seeking recognition as talented musician rather than mere pin-up. He quit Herd to form highly rated Humble Pie(▶) with former Small Faces(▶) leader Steve Marriott, Greg Ridley (bass) and Jerry Shirley (drums), with hard-driving R&B-influenced style.

In 1971 Frampton left to pursue more melodic and romantic direction with increasing emphasis on tasteful guitar work and songs with potent hooklines. He also guested on George Harrison's(▶) **All Things Must Pass**, Harry Nilsson's(▶) **Son Of Schmilsson** and other projects.

First solo album, **Frampton**, featured Ringo Starr(▶), Billy Preston(▶), Klaus Voorman, former Herd cohort Andy Brown, ex-Spooky Tooth member Mike Kellie and Rick Wills from Cochise. Kellie and Wills were drafted into Frampton's new band Camel with Mick Gallagher, ex-Bell'n'Arc. Kellie soon moved back to re-formed Spooky Tooth, being replaced by American drummer John Siomos (ex-Voices of East Harlem and Mitch Ryder).

Camel toured US and concentrated on American market till break-up in 1974, Frampton continuing to record solo albums and tour with various back-up bands, scoring best-selling live album of all time (10 million) with 1976 **Frampton Comes Alive!** LP which included hit singles **Show Me The Way**, **Baby I Love Your Way** and **Do You Feel**. Mick Jagger, Stevie Wonder(▶) and other names helped on 1977 success **I'm In You**. Frampton's role in Stigwood's poorly received film 'Sgt. Pepper's Lonely Hearts Club Band', put him back to pre-**Comes Alive!** status.

Near-fatal 1978 car smash took him off road. He re-emerged in 1981 with new direction of **Breaking All The Rules** set, exploring wider dimensions in guitar work and vocal stylings.

Hit Singles:

	US	UK
Show Me The Way, 1976	6	10
Baby I Love Your Way, 1976	12	43
Do You Feel Like We Do, 1976	10	39
I'm In You, 1977	2	41
Signed, Sealed, Delivered (I'm Yours), 1977	18	—

Albums:
Wind Of Change (A&M), 1972
Frampton's Camel (A&M), 1973
Frampton (A&M), 1975
Comes Alive! (A&M), 1975
I'm In You (A&M), 1977
Where I Should Be (A&M), 1979
Super Disc Of Peter Frampton (—/A&M), 1979
Breaking All The Rules (A&M), 1981
The Art Of Control (A&M), 1982

Connie Francis

US vocalist.
Born Constance Franconero, Belleville, New Jersey, December 12, 1938.

Career: Of Italian descent, Connie Francis, made stage debut at five, wrote and produced musical while at school, and won TV talent contest at 11 (playing accordion and singing on 'Startime'). Further success on Arthur Godfrey Talent Show led to four-year stint as featured vocalist on NBC-TV Startime series and, at 17, a MGM recording contract. First hit (1957) was **Majesty Of Love** duet with Marvin Rainwater, scoring first of seven solo gold hits year later with **Who's Sorry Now**.

In 1960 she had distinction of three double-sided million-sellers: **Mama/Teddy, Everybody's Somebody's Fool/Jealous Of You** and **My Heart Has A Mind Of Its Own/Many Tears Ago**. Steady string of hits reached total of 35 million sales by 1967, at which time her recording career stagnated, though she remained major cabaret draw.

Made native language hits aimed at France, Germany, Spain, Italy and Japan and starred in 1961 movie 'Where The Boys Are'. Had short-lived but much-publicised romance with Bobby Darin(▶).

By 1974 she was on third marriage. After a miscarriage, husband Joe Garzilli suggested comeback as therapy but, tragically, on night

of first gig, she was raped at knife-point (subsequently being awarded $3,055,000 in damages for hotel owners' negligence). She became recluse and spent two and a half years under psychiatric treatment before bravely making another comeback in 1978, only to lose $50,000 worth of jewelry in London hotel burglary. (She had suffered similar $85,000 loss in New York 11 years earlier.)

Gifted with pleasant, if unspectacular voice, Connie Francis had across-the-board appeal which made her the major female star of the '60s.

Hit Singles:	US	UK
Who's Sorry Now? 1958	4	1
I'm Sorry I Made You Cry, 1958	36	11
Stupid Cupid/Carolina Moon, 1958	17	1
I'll Get By, 1958	—	19
Fallin', 1958	30	20
You Always Hurt The One You Love, 1958	—	13
My Happiness, 1958	2	4
Lipstick On Your Collar, 1959	5	3
Frankie/Lipstick On Your Collar, 1959	9	—
Plenty Good Lovin', 1959	—	18
Among My Souvenirs, 1959	7	11
Mama/Teddy, 1960	8	—
Mama/Robot Man, 1960	—	2
Teddy/Mama, 1960	17	—
Everybody's Somebody Fool/Jealous Of You, 1960	1	6
Jealous Of You/Everybody's Somebody's Fool, 1960	19	—
My Heart Has A Mind Of Its Own, 1960	1	3
Many Tears Ago, 1960	7	12
Where The Boys Are/Baby Roo, 1961	4	5
Breaking' In A Brand New Broken Heart, 1961	7	12
Together, 1961	6	10
He's My (Dreamboat), 1961	14	—
When The Boy In Your Arms/Baby's First Christmas, 1961	10	—
Baby's First Christmas/When The Boy In Your Arms, 1961	—	17
Don't Break The Heart That Loves You, 1962	1	39
Secondhand Love, 1962	7	—
Vacation, 1962	9	10
I'm Gonna Be Warm This Winter, 1962	18	48
Follow The Boys, 1963	17	—

Albums (selected):
The Very Best Of (MGM/—), 1972 1972
Sings Great Country Hits Volume 2 (MGM), 1973
Sings Great Country Hits (with Hank Williams Jnr) (MGM), 1976
20 All Time Greats (MGM), 1977
I'm Me Again—Silver Anniversary Album (—/Polydor), 1981
Greatest Hits Volumes 1 & 2 (—/Polydor MGM), 1982

Aretha Franklin

US vocalist, pianist, composer.
Born Memphis, Tennessee, March 25, 1942.

Career: 'Lady Soul' is daughter of Rev. C.L. Franklin, who has had more than 80 albums of sermons released in US. Along with sisters Erma and Carolyn—both subsequently successful soul artists—Aretha sang in choir at father's New Bethel Church in Detroit.

Her aunt was renowned gospel singer Clara Ward; legendary black singer Sam Cooke(▶) was family friend. With their encouragement she began recording career with local JVP label and Checker; then cut

demos with Major Holly, bass player with jazz pianist Teddy Wilson. These brought her to attention of Columbia Records' A&R man John Hammond, who pronounced her 'Best natural singer since Billie Holiday'.

Debut Columbia album was mix of jazz, R&B and show-business standards. Entire six-year period of her stay with Columbia showed lack of direction, though every album contained its share of gems.

Love All The Hurt Away, Aretha Franklin. Courtesy Arista Records.

When then husband/manager Ted White signed her to Atlantic in early 1967, Aretha's career took off. Atlantic vice president Jerry Wexler took personal charge of project. Debut album **I Never Loved A Man (The Way I Love You)**, hinged around single of same title, was masterpiece. Wexler had taken Aretha to Muscle Shoals, Alabama, for recordings, and classy studio team there were at best. By end of '67, further gold had been mined with **Respect**, **Baby I Love You** and **Chain Of Fools**. Second album also sold over a million copies as did third LP **Lady Soul**, which used Atlantic's own New York session crew and featured masterful Eric Clapton(▶) guitar solo on **Good To Me As I Am To You**. LP helped earn Aretha accolade as 'R&B Singer Of The Year' in Grammy Awards.

1968 European tour—which yielded **Aretha In Paris** live album—helped **Think**, co-penned with her husband, to international hit status, but marriage was heading for rocks. After **Soul '69** album, Aretha was out of studios for more than a year before recording patchy **This Girl's In Love With You** LP in Miami and New York. Her stage shows too were less than satisfying as she reverted to mixing show-biz standards with solid soul.

Re-marriage and scrapping of large orchestra in favour of small, all-star combo led by King Curtis(▶), seemed to put fire back into the lady. By late 1970 Aretha was back on top, thanks to some great records and exciting stage performances (one of which was captured on **Live At Fillmore West** album).

In 1972, Aretha returned to gospel roots for **Amazing Grace** album. This was recorded live at Temple Missionary Baptist Church in Los Angeles with gospel superstar James Cleveland and Southern California Community Choir.

Subsequent work saw gradual diminution in her magic. At her best when fronting a small Southern-soul flavoured combo, Franklin was recorded in increasingly sophisticated settings. While following general trend in soul music of the era, these were not the best frame for talent. Despite working with such redoubtable producers as Quincy Jones(▶), Van McCoy, Lamont Dozier and Curtis Mayfield (▶), vast majority of her mid-to-late '70s output was below par.

Switch of labels to Arista in 1980 began steady revival of fortunes. From first Arista album **Aretha** came frenetic version of Otis

Redding's oldie **I Can't Turn You Loose**. This recalled feel of her '60s triumphs. Re-work of Sam and Dave's(▶) **Hold On, I'm Coming** from next album was even more potent. Also scored in duet with guitarist/vocalist George Benson on **Love All The Hurt Away**, the album's title cut. Appeared in 'Blues Brothers' film in 1980 (and on LP).

Although once unchallenged position as foremost female singer in black music has been lost, Aretha Franklin still seems capable of delivering goods. Perhaps greatest tribute to her unique abilities comes from dozens of cover versions she has made of other people's big hits; these have breathed new life into familiar material. Don Covay's **See Saw**, Ben E. King's **Spanish Harlem** and **Don't Play That Song**, the Band's **The Weight** (featuring a brilliant guitar solo by Duane Allman) and Stevie Wonder's(▶) **Until You Come Back To Me** are prime examples. On rousing uptempo dance numbers or smouldering deep-soul ballads, Aretha Franklin has more than earned her title 'Lady Soul'.

Hit Singles:	US	UK
I Never Loved A Man (The Way I Love You), 1967	9	—
Respect, 1967	1	10
Baby I Love You, 1967	4	39
A Natural Woman, 1967	8	—
Chain Of Fools, 1968	2	43
(Sweet Sweet Baby) Since You've Been Gone/Ain't No Way, 1968	5	47
Ain't No Way/(Sweet Sweet Baby) Since You've Been Gone, 1968	16	—
Think, 1968	7	26
I Say A Little Prayer/The House That Jack Built, 1968	10	4
The House That Jack Built/I Say A Little Prayer, 1968	6	—
See Saw, 1968	14	—
The Weight, 1969	19	—
Share Your Love With Me, 1969	13	—
Eleanor Rigby, 1969	17	—
Call Me, 1970	13	—
Don't Play That Song, 1970	11	13
You're All I Need To Get By, 1971	19	—
Bridge Over Troubled Water, 1971	6	—
Spanish Harlem, 1971	2	14
Rock Steady, 1971	9	—
Day Dreaming, 1972	5	—
Until You Come Back To Me (That's What I'm Gonna Do), 1974	3	26
I'm In Love, 1974	19	—

Above: Lady Soul circa 1960. Aretha Franklin has earned her title.

Albums:
I Never Loved A Man (Atlantic), 1967
Aretha's Gold (Atlantic), 1969
Greatest Hits (Atlantic), 1971
Amazing Grace (Atlantic), 1972
Ten Years Of Gold (Atlantic), 1976
Aretha (Arista), 1980
Sweet Bitter Love (Columbia/—), 1981
Love All The Hurt Away (Arista), 1981
Jump To It (Arista), 1982
The Legendary Queen Of Soul (Columbia/CBS), 1983

Worth Searching Out:
Aretha Arrives (Atlantic), 1967
Lady Soul (Atlantic), 1968
Soul '69 (Atlantic), 1969
Spirit In The Dark (Atlantic), 1970*
Live At Fillmore West (Atlantic), 1971

*Issued as **Don't Play That Song** in UK

Free

UK group formed 1968.

Original line-up: Paul Kossoff, Gibson Les Paul guitar; Simon Kirke, drums; Andy Fraser, bass; Paul Rodgers, vocals.

Career: Kossoff and Kirke were in second division band Black Cat Bones. They saw Rodgers perform with Brown Sugar and asked him to join. Young Andy Fraser (then only 15) was in Mayall's(▶) Bluesbreakers

Fire And Water, Free. Courtesy Island Records.

but dissatisfied with jazz direction. Mutual friend contacted him and the four got together for jamming session; first evening produced four songs and group decided to make unit permanent.

Alexis Korner supported group and provided name from band he called Free At Last while with Ginger Baker(▶) and Graham Bond UK gigs impressed Island Records who signed band. First LP made substantial UK impact but second, **Free**, won massive US support; **All Right Now** single went Top 10 everywhere. Sudden success seemed to bring out friction as members strove for limelight. After **Highway** album, band split. Rogers' solo effort flopped as did Fraser's. Kossoff and Texan keyboards man Rabbit Bundrick for

Free Live!, Free. Courtesy Island Records.

Kossoff, Kirke, Tetsu And Rabbit LP.
In 1972 original band re-formed for **Free At Last** album. During tour Kossoff's drug habit and Rodgers/Fraser fights split group again. Kossoff and Fraser left, Tetsu and Rabbit replacing them. This line-up recorded **Heartbreaker** (Kossoff helped with guitar work). Single from LP, **Wishing Well**, prompted tour. Kossoff started but again collapsed and Wendell Richardson (ex-Osibisa) stepped in. At end of US tour, Free folded for good.

Fraser failed to follow up success with either Andy Fraser Band or Sharks. Kossoff died in 1976 of drug-induced heart failure shortly after setting up Back Street Crawler. Tetsu joined Rod Stewart's Faces(▶) and Rabbit did session work and two solo LPs before joining Who(▶) as tour 'member', 1978-'82. Rodgers and Kirke set up Bad Company(▶).

Certainly one of UK's finer bands, with understated, sparse arrangements and high energy spirit, Free has had far-ranging influence. Unfortunately, it is yet another story of talent which failed to reach its potential; drugs and egos doomed Free from the start.

Final line-up: Rodgers: Kirke; Wendell Richardson, guitar; Tetsu Kamauchi, bass; Rabbit Bundrick, keyboards.

Hit Singles:	US	UK
All Right Now, 1970	4	2
My Brother Jake, 1971	—	4
Little Bit Of Love, 1972	—	13
Wishing Well, 1973	—	7
All Right Now, 1973	—	15
Free (EP), 1978	—	11

Albums:
Tons Of Sobs (A&M/Island), 1969
Free (A&M/Island), 1969
Fire And Water (A&M/Island), 1970
Highway (A&M/Island), 1970
Live (A&M/Island), 1971
Free At Last (A&M/Island), 1972

Heartbreaker (A&M/Island), 1973
Best Of (A&M/—), 1975
Completely Free (A&M/Island), 1983*
*Compilation

Fun Boy Three
UK group formed 1981.

Original/Current line-up: Terry Hall, vocals; Neville Staples, percussion, vocals; Lynval Golding, guitar.

Career: Trio were founder members of the Specials(▶), original Coventry-based 2-Tone band. After apparent policy problems, Hall, Staples and Golding split off to form Fun Boy Three; since their departure Specials have been far less active.

After immediate success with debut single **The Lunatics Have Taken Over The Asylum** (seen as condemnation of UK's decline), have charted with all eight singles (all but one reaching Top 20), plus two Top 20 LPs. Despite inability to be self-contained group instrumentally, trio have contrived to use electronics and mostly female (in true non-sexist style) back-up singers/musicians to complete sound. Second single featured girl trio Bananarama as co-vocalists, and FB3 returned favour for next Bananarama single.

Second LP (recorded during latter half of 1982) included Nicky Holland (keyboards, ex-Ravishing Beauties) and June Kingston (drums, ex Modettes), with production by David Byrne of Talking Heads(▶).

While first year of band saw no live appearances, early 1983 found group performing on stage (rather than video/TV); predictably, response was ecstatic.

The music of Fun Boy Three always verged on cynical/political lyrically and trio captured the imagination of British youth. However, as their approach was peculiarly British (despite Golding and Staples being of Jamaican extraction) never made impact in US before Terry Hall announced he was quitting band in summer 1983.

Below: Early rockers Billy Fury (left), Eddie Cochran and Joe Brown, the only one of the trio still alive.

Hit Singles:	US	UK
The Lunatics Have Taken Over The Asylum, 1981	—	20
The Telephone Always Rings, 1982	—	17
Summertime, 1982	—	18
Tunnel Of Love, 1983	—	10
Our Lips Are Sealed, 1983	—	7
Really Saying Something, 1982	—	5

With Bananarama:

	US	UK
It Ain't What You Do It's The Way That You Do It, 1982	—	4

Albums:
The Fun Boy Three (—/Chrysalis), 1982
Waiting (—/Chrysalis), 1983

Billy Fury
UK singer.
Born Ronald Wycherly, Liverpool, April 17, 1941; died January 28, 1983.

Career: Talking his way into Marty Wilde's dressing room at Liverpool package show concert, Wycherly met promoter/manager Larry Parnes and impressed him with his material and his voice. Parnes added the youngster to rest of tour and gave him name Billy Fury (he had also named Wilde, Georgie Fame, and others).

Originally a tugboat worker, Fury leapt into rock'n'roll limelight, his debut **Maybe Tomorrow** charting in April 1959 when he was just 18.

After a couple of flops he charted in UK again in 1960 with self-penned **Colette** and **That's Love.** Then came his majestic rockabilly album **The Sound Of Fury** which, despite authentic American sound, consisted entirely of Fury's own songs and featured subsequent solo star Joe Brown on guitar.

Fury found greatest success, however, when he turned from raucous rock'n'roll to big-ballad cover versions of American Tin Pan Alley standards, (though he remains nearly unknown US), notably **Halfway To Paradise** and **Jealousy,** entering UK Top 20 on 19 occasions.

When chart success ended, Fury made successful switch to steady living on cabaret scene, and appeared as rock'n'roll singer in David Essex movie 'That'll Be The Day' (1973).

Long dogged by ill-health, he died of a heart attack in 1983 amid attempts at comeback.

Hit Singles:	US	UK
Maybe Tomorrow, 1959	—	18
Colette, 1960	—	9
That's Love, 1960	—	19
A Thousand Stars, 1961	—	14
Halfway To Paradise, 1961	—	3
Jealousy, 1961	—	2
I'd Never Find Another You, 1961	—	5
Last Night Was Made For Love, 1962	—	4
Once Upon A Dream, 1962	—	7
Because Of Love, 1962	—	18
Like I've Never Been Gone, 1963	—	3
When Will You Say I Love You, 1963	—	3
In Summer, 1963	—	5
Somebody Else's Girl, 1963	—	18
Do You Really Love Me Too, 1964	—	13
I Will, 1964	—	14
It's Only Make Believe, 1964	—	10
I'm Lost Without You, 1965	—	16
In Thoughts Of You, 1965	—	9

Albums:
The Sound Of Fury (—/Decca), 1960
We Want Billy (with the Tornados) (—/Decca), 1963
World Of (—/Decca), 1972
The Billy Fury Story (—/Decca), 1977
The Golden Years (Dash/K-Tel), 1979
World Of, Volume 2 (—/Decca), 1980
The Billy Fury Hit Parade (—/Decca), 1982
The One And Only (—/Polydor), 1983

Peter Gabriel
UK vocalist, composer, producer.
Born London, May 13, 1950.

Career: Musical career began at Charterhouse Public School in the Garden Wall, a short-lived unit featuring Tony Banks (piano)

The first Peter Gabriel. Courtesy Charisma Records.

and Chris Stewart (drums). Group was formed primarily as vehicle for Gabriel's songwriting; dressed in kaftan, beads and flowers he already revealed theatrical bent. Love of soul music, particularly Otis Redding(▶), James Brown(▶) and Nina Simone(▶), was major musical influence.

Garden Wall gradually evolved into Genesis(▶) and Gabriel systematically steered group's musical direction in early '70s; contributed much to their visual/theatrical appeal, as well as penning their best work. From 1970's **Trespass** through to 1974's **The Lamb Lies Down On Broadway,** Genesis emerged as one of UK's most popular groups. An elaborate tour to promote **Lamb Lies Down On Broadway,** featuring Gabriel playing album's leading character, proved enormously successful in both UK and US.

In May 1975, Gabriel shocked rock world by announcing his departure from band to pursue solo career. Debut **Peter Gabriel,** an intelligent and adventurous work, was well received and spawned hit single **Solsbury Hill.** For second album, replaced producer Bob Ezrin with Robert Fripp. A less accessible work, album showed collaboration to best effect on **Exposure,** a clever amalgam of Frippertronics and Gabriel experimentation.

Third and fourth albums, also titled **Peter Gabriel,** showed growing confidence, with artist taking control of production. Two evocative hits from third album established reputation in singles charts. **Games Without Frontiers,** a scathing anti-jingoistic comment inspired by BBC television programme 'It's A Knockout', was followed by 33 rpm single **Biko,** a protest song about the controversial death of South African political activist Stephen Biko.

Peter Gabriel's Security. Courtesy Geffen Records.

Sometimes criticised for lack of spontaneity, Gabriel's work still shows greater adventure and experimentation than Genesis days. Freed from commercial restraints, he has frequently worked on rock/avant-garde fringe; allied himself closely with such contemporaries as Robert Fripp and Brian Eno(▶) . In recent years has successfully broadened his musical and lyrical frames of reference

encompassing a variety of contrasting ethnic sounds deriving from the Californian Indians, Central Africa and industrial Europe. Ever inventive, he has simultaneously incorporated unusual rhythms and sounds from factories, scrapyards, and even smashing television screens to complement his studio experimentation. Recently acclaimed for his role in organising WOMAD (World of Music, Arts and Dance) Festival which proved significant gathering of artists from all over the world. 1982 LP **Security** yielded successful US single **Shock The Monkey**; accompanying video, played frequently by MTV, is one of most imaginative and evocative ever made. One of the least compromising figures working in rock music, always seeking to widen frontiers of sound and visuals, Gabriel's finest moment may well lie in the future.

Hit Singles:		US	UK
Solsbury Hill, 1977		—	13
Games Without Frontiers, 1980		—	4

Albums:
Peter Gabriel (Atco/Charisma), 1977
Peter Gabriel (Mercury/Charisma), 1978
Peter Gabriel (Charisma), 1980
Peter Gabriel (Charisma), 1982
Security (Geffen/—), 1982
Peter Gabriel Plays Live (Charisma), 1983

Eric Gale

US guitarist.
Born Brooklyn, New York, September 20, 1938.

Career: Started playing guitar in early teens, and while still at school worked club circuit with artists like Maxine Brown, Jackie Wilson(▶) and Flamingoes.

Gale became full-time musician after leaving university, and served apprenticeship on road before breaking into circle of New York session musicians. Early work included sessions with King Curtis(▶) and Jimmy Smith(▶) and in late '60s and early '70s he worked with wide range of major artists, including Marvin Gaye(▶), Diana Ross(▶), Steely Dan(▶), Paul Simon(▶) and Aretha Franklin(▶).

In 1973 he joined Creed Taylor's CTI Records as house producer, and released **Forecast** LP under own name. He moved to CBS in 1976, and continued policy of making albums matching excellent musicianship with commerical appeal. More recently Gale has combined sessions and solo projects with membership of top session man's band Stuff. He also appeared in Paul Simon(▶) movie 'One Trick Pony'.

A guitarist's guitarist who combines taste, technique and fluid blues feeling, Gale is asset to any record he is featured on. His own recordings, while sometimes bland, showcase excellent playing in easy-listening context.

Guitar: Gibson Super 400 CES.

Albums:
Ginseng Woman (Columbia/CBS), 1977
Multiplication (Columbia/CBS), 1978
Part Of You (Columbia/CBS), 1979
Touch Of Silk (Columbia/CBS), 1980
Best Of (Columbia/CBS), 1980
Blue Horizon (Elektra Musician), 1982

Gallagher And Lyle

UK duo formed 1972.
Benny Gallagher, vocalist, guitarist, composer, multi-instrumentalist;
Graham Lyle, vocalist, guitarist, composer, multi-instrumentalist.

Career: Both born in Largs, Scotland, originally worked together in various local bands. After decamping to London, they were signed by Beatles'(▶) Apple Corps as writers, providing material for Mary Hopkins among others.

Following expiry of Apple contract, pair joined former Manfred Mann(▶) bass player Tom McGuinness in McGuinness Flint. Wrote band's two hits, **When I'm Dead And Gone** and **Malt And Barley Blues**; split after 18 months to pursue career as duo.

Signed with A&M, they steadily built up

Below: Rory Gallagher, the blues star who refuses to compromise.

reputation as live act and purveyors of well-crafted, charming songs on record. After four albums, enjoyed success with 1976 offering **Breakaway**. Titletrack was recorded by Art Garfunkel(▶), and duo enjoyed major hits with two other tracks from album.

However, act was unable to sustain success, and after moving to Mercury in 1979 for **Lonesome No More**, faded from public sight. Those with taste for melodic soft rock with folk influence will find albums worth searching out.

Hit Singles:	US	UK
I Wanna Stay With You, 1976	49	6
Heart On My Sleeve, 1976	—	6

Albums:
Gallagher And Lyle (A&M), 1972
Willie And The Lap Dog (A&M), 1973
Seeds (A&M), 1973
The Last Cowboy (A&M), 1974
Breakaway (A&M), 1976
Love On The Airwaves (MFP), 1976
Showdown (A&M), 1978
Gone Crazy (A&M), 1979
Lonesome No More (—/Mercury), 1979
Best Of (—/Warwick), 1980

Rory Gallagher

UK guitarist, vocalist, composer.
Born Ballyshannon, County Donegal, Ireland, March 2, 1948.

Career: One of rock's true grafters. Raised in Cork; played in local bands until 15. Joined the Fontana Showband, an amalgam of brass and guitars which played pop hits to enthusiastic dance-hall crowds.

With Charlie McCracken (bass) and John Wilson (drums) formed Taste, high-energy blues/rock trio. Band learned trade in Hamburg and home country before moving to UK in 1969.

Polydor recording contract produced several spirited albums. As live act, band headlined throughout Britain and Europe. Earned ecstatic reviews for Gallagher's dominant acrobatic stage presence and dazzling guitar technique; McCracken and Wilson provided energetic rhythm section.

With Gallagher taking central role, dissension in group grew to extreme proportions, a situation aggravated by unsympathetic management. Wilson often refused to take stage for group encores, leaving Gallagher and McCracken to appease audience. Trio split in 1971, Wilson and McCracken forming short-lived Stud with Jim Cregan (future Family(▶), Rod Stewart(▶) Band).

Gallagher took to road with Wilgar Campbell (drums) and Gerry McAvoy (bass), using own name as band title. Line-up completed three successful albums before Campbell was replaced by Rod De'Ath. Lou Martin was added on keyboards.

Pursuing a hectic touring schedule, Rory Gallagher Band secured reputation in Europe and America. Steady album sales meant considerable output, with several memorable highlights. Live album **Irish Tour 74** captured gregarious Gallagher at his best. Director Tony Palmer filmed gigs for his movie 'Rory Gallagher—Irish Tour '74' which premiered at prestigious Cork Film Festival that year.

After '76 set **Calling Card**, De'Ath and Martin quit. Drummer Ted Mckenna (ex-Alex Harvey Band(▶)) joined for **Photo Finish** (1978). 1980 world tour provided live cuts for **Stage Struck** (1980). Album showed Gallagher still loved the road.

Complete absence from both UK/US singles charts during recording career belies Gallagher's popular appeal. Steadfastly refusing to 'commercialise' his work and rejecting

'pop' format TV shows, which he feels could not do his work justice, Gallagher is secure in knowledge that he is playing authentic rock-based blues to undiminished ecstatic audiences.
Guitar: Fender Stratocaster

Albums:
With Taste:
Taste (Atco/Polydor), 1969
On The Boards (Atco/Polydor), 1970
Live Taste (–/Polydor), 1971
Live At The Isle Of Wight (–/Polydor), 1972
Taste (–/Polydor), 1977

Solo:
Rory Gallagher (–/Polydor), 1971
Deuce (–/Chrysalis), 1971
Live In Europe (Chrysalis), 1973*
Blueprint (Chrysalis), 1973
Tattoo (Chrysalis), 1973
Irish Tour '74 (Chrysalis), 1974*
In The Beginning (–/Emerald Gem), 1974
Against The Grain (Chrysalis), 1975
Calling Card (Chrysalis), 1976
Photo Finish (Chrysalis), 1978
Top Priority (Chrysalis), 1979
Stage Struck (Chrysalis), 1980*
Jinx (Chrysalis), 1982
*Live

Gang Of Four

UK group formed 1978.
Original line-up: Jon King, vocals, melodica; Dave Allen, bass, vocals; Andy Gill, guitar, vocals; Hugo Burnham, drums, vocals.

Career: Formed in Leeds after meeting in 1977, when all but Allen were at university. Band became darlings of critics in late '70s due to recorded debut on super-hip Fast Product label (early labelmates include Human League(▶), Scars and Mekons). In 1979, signed with EMI, and scored minor hit with **At Home He's A Tourist**, although lyrical reference in song to contraceptives (which group would not amend) prevented exposure on 'Top Of The Pops'.

Various injuries sustained by members in accidents and fights halted group's progress during 1980, although LPs became minor hits. Allen left band in July 1981, replaced by Sara Lee (who had played with both Robert Fripp and Jane Aire and the Belvederes). Third LP, **Songs Of The Free**, produced by Mike Howlett, provided minor hit single, **I Love A Man In Uniform**.

Gang Of Four are difficult to categorise — contain essence of R&B, disco and various other elements — and perhaps this inability for potential fans to pigeonhole band has prevented greater success, although tie-up with Bennett Glotzer (Frank Zappa's manager) may assist future market penetration.

Current line-up: King; Gill; Burnham; Sara Lee, bass, vocals.

Albums:
Entertainment (Warner Bros/EMI), 1979
Solid Gold (Warner Bros/EMI), 1981
Songs Of The Free (Warner Bros/EMI), 1982

Art Garfunkel

US vocalist, actor.
Born Forest Hills, New York, November 5, 1941.

Career: Although responsible for arranging highly-praised two-part vocal harmonies as well as being half of singing duo, Garfunkel felt like junior partner of Simon and Garfunkel(▶) as Simon(▶) wrote both words

and music and played guitar. Having acted in one film, 'Catch-22', Art began moving in independent direction. In light of Simon's desire to attempt solo career split in 1970 seemed logical decision for duo.

After some time on Scottish farm, Garfunkel returned to US West Coast to pursue both acting and recording career. His performance in films 'Carnal Knowledge' (1971) and 'Bad Timing' (1979) (the latter more successful in Europe than US) were critically well received.

Solo recording career began with 1973 **Angel Clare**, produced by Simon and Garfunkel's Roy Halee, which went gold. **Breakaway** in 1975, under influence of new producer Richard Perry, surpassed it and resulted in UK No.1 with **I Only Have Eyes For You**. Album included one-off reunion with Paul Simon on **My Little Town** (also released on Simon's LP **Still Crazy After All These Years**).

Angel Clare, Art Garfunkel. Courtesy Columbia Records.

Self-produced **Watermark** in 1978 featured James Taylor(▶) (for whom Garfunkel had done session in 1976) and Paul Simon on **(What A) Wonderful World**, one of few tracks not by Jimmy Webb. **Fate For Breakfast**, partly recorded in London, featured Cliff Richard(▶) hit **Miss You Nights**. Single **Bright Eyes** from movie 'Watership Down' gave him second UK No.1 in 1979, and **Since I Don't Have You** made charts same year. **Scissors Cut** album was ignored.

As solo artist Garfunkel gained respect for interpreting wide range of material, but career hit doldrums until revitalised by 1981 Simon and Garfunkel reunion concert in Central Park.

Hit Singles:	US	UK
All I Know, 1973	9	–
I Only Have Eyes For You, 1975	18	1
(What A) Wonderful World (with James Taylor and Paul Simon), 1978	17	–
Bright Eyes, 1979	–	1

Above: Art Garfunkel, owner of one of the purest voices in rock music.

Albums:
Angel Clare (Columbia/CBS), 1973
Breakaway (Columbia/CBS), 1975
Watermark (Columbia/CBS), 1977
Fate For Breakfast (Columbia/CBS), 1979
Scissors Cut (Columbia/CBS), 1981

Marvin Gaye

US vocalist, composer, keyboard player, drummer.
Born Marvin Pentz Gaye Jr, Washington DC, April 2, 1939.

Career: Son of a minister, began singing in church choir and learned organ. After spell in US Air Force sang in various doo-wop bands before joining seminal black vocal group Rainbows. (Membership has also included soul legends Don Covay and Billy 'Fat Boy' Stewart.) Formed Marquis in 1957 with two other former Rainbows. With help from Bo Diddley, cut album for Okeh. In 1959, Harvey Fuqua — later major figure at Motown Records — invited Marquis to become his backing group, the Moonglows. This new line-up made two singles for Chess (some years earlier, Gaye had won a Fuqua-judged talent contest singing Moonglows' classic **Ten Commandments Of Love**).

When Fuqua moved from Chicago to Detroit in 1960, to set up his Tri-Phi and Harvey labels, Gaye joined him. The labels were soon to come into fledgling Motown Records' fold. Fuqua married Gwen Gordy, sister of Motown founder Berry Gordy Jr; soon after Gaye married another Gordy sister, Anna.

In 1961, Gaye's contract with Gwen Gordy's label, Anna, was taken over by brother Berry. While waiting for recording career to flower, Gaye filled in time as drummer for Motown sessions and for stage appearances of Smokey Robinson and the Miracles (for two years). He also sang back-up, notably on Marvelettes' recordings, and displayed talent as multi-instrumentalist.

Gaye's fourth single in own right, the mid-tempo **Stubborn Kind Of Fellow** (1962), was breakthrough — first of nearly 30 Top 50 hits over next decade. First hit's producer Mickey Stevenson, was also involved in **Hitch Hike** and **Pride And Joy** successes before Berry Gordy, then the Holland/Dozier/Holland team, took over reins.

Can I Get A Witness (covered by Rolling Stones) and **You're A Wonderful One** were classics of Motown's Detroit Sound idiom. In 1964, Gaye was teamed with Mary Wells for

duet album from which both sides of single scored. This was first of several successful Gaye partnerships with Motown ladies — Kim Weston, Tammi Terrell, Diana Ross.

Gaye/Terrell partnership was longest lasting (from 1967-70) and most fruitful. Terminated tragically when Tammi died following several operations for brain tumour. The then 24-year-old Gaye was deeply affected and became something of a hermit, dropping out of touring scene and rarely appearing in studio. In 1971, he returned with introspective **What's Going On** album, a landmark in development of black music and, particularly, of the Motown Sound, being a conceptual LP rather than a collection of singles.Morever, Gaye produced/wrote album himself. Songs were covered by such major black artists as Diana Ross(▶) (**Save The Children**), Quincy Jones(▶) (**What's Going On**), Aretha Franklin(▶) (**Wholly Holy**) and Gil Scott-Heron (**Inner City Blues**).

1972 movie soundtrack **Trouble Man** continued vein as did sensual concept album **Let's Get It On**, before release of duo album with Diana Ross, **Diana And Marvin**.

What's Going On, Marvin Gaye. Courtesy Motown Records.

By 1974, Gaye was established as leading solo vocalist in black music. Fronted 34-piece orchestra at Oakland Coliseum, California, for first stage appearance in four years.

Personal problems over break-up of his second marriage led to further stage/recording hiatus, and eventually to the self-pitying concept album **Here My Dear**.

Wife's affair with Teddy Prendergrass (one of Gaye's closest friends), troubles over alimony, tax arrears (which led to seizure of his recording studio) and disagreements with Motown resulted in inner turmoil and an increasingly unpredictable personality. Gaye even disappeared to Hawaii for time to live in a converted bread van.

Visit to UK for 1980 tour saw contrast between sensationally exciting performances and series of blown TV dates and late appearances (he kept HRH Princess Margaret waiting hours for scheduled dinner date and cabaret appearance).

Virtually unmanageable, Gaye was released by Motown; moved base to Belgium and lapsed into obscurity for a while.

New deal with CBS was fruit of two years of careful re-assessment; resultant 1982 album **Midnight Love** showed all his old mastery. Single **(Sexual) Healing** brought him back into charts with vengeance.

Hit Singles:	US	UK
Pride And Joy, 1963	10	–
You're A Wonderful One, 1964	15	–
Try It Baby, 1964	15	–
How Sweet It Is (To Be Loved By You), 1964	6	49
I'll Be Doggone, 1965	8	–
Ain't That Peculiar, 1965	8	–
I Heard It Through The Grapevine, 1968	1	1

	US	UK
Too Busy Thinking About My Baby, 1969	4	5
That's The Way Love Is, 1969	7	—
Abraham Martin And John, 1970	—	9
What's Going On, 1971	2	—
Mercy Mercy Me (The Ecology), (1971)	4	—
Inner City Blues (Make Me Wanna Holler), 1971	9	—
Trouble Man, 1972	7	—
Let's Get It On, 1973	1	31
You're A Special Part Of Me, 1973	12	—
My Mistake (Was To Love You), 1974	19	—
Got To Give It Up, Pt. 1, 1977	1	7
(Sexual) Healing, 1982	3	4

With Mary Wells:

	US	UK
What's The Matter With You Baby, 1964	17	—
Once Upon A Time, 1964	19	50

With Kim Weston:

	US	UK
It Takes Two, 1967	14	16

With Tammi Terrell:

	US	UK
Ain't No Mountain High Enough, 1967	19	—
Your Precious Love, 1967	5	—
If I Could Build My Whole World Around You, 1968	10	41
Ain't Nothing Like The Real Thing, 1968	8	34
You're All I Need To Get By, 1968	7	19

With Diana Ross:

	US	UK
You're A Special Part Of Me, 1973	12	—
You Are Everything, 1974	—	5
My Mistake (Was To Love You), 1974	19	—

Albums:
M.P.G., Greatest Hits (Tamla Motown), 1970
What's Going On (Tamla Motown), 1971
Let's Get It On (Tamla Motown), 1973
Anthology (Tamla Motown), 1974
Best Of (Tamla Motown), 1976
I Want You (Tamla Motown), 1976
Here My Dear (Tamla Motown), 1979
Early Years (Tamla Motown), 1980
Motown Superstar Series Volume 15 (Motown/), 1981
In Our Lifetime (Tamla Motown), 1981
Magic Of (—/Pickwick), 1982

Midnight Love (Columbia/CBS), 1982

With Tammi Terrell:
United (Tamla Motown), 1966
Greatest Hits (Tamla Motown), 1969
Motown Superstar Series, Volume 2 (Motown/—), 1970

With Diana Ross:
Marvin & Diana (Tamla Motown), 1973

Worth Searching Out:
How Sweet It Is (Tamla/MFP), 1964
Moods Of (Tamla Motown), 1966

Genesis
UK group formed 1967.

Original line-up: Anthony Phillips, guitar, vocals; Michael Rutherford, bass, guitar, vocals; Tony Banks, keyboards, vocals; Peter Gabriel, vocals; Chris Stewart, drums.

Career: Original members were attending Charterhouse public school when they met in mid-'60s. Passing demo tapes to Charterhouse alumnus Jonathan King led to first contract, with Decca. King suggested name Genesis. Two early singles did little and Stewart was replaced with John Silver. King produced first album and when told to change group's name (because of American group of same name) he refused and worked up LP title **From Genesis To Revelations**. King's production muddled Genesis sound and as LP was poorly received, King and Decca lost interest.

Band almost broke up. Instead 'Melody Maker' ad found John Mayhew to take over drums and ex-school mate Richard MacPhail took over as road manager. Besides providing transportation, he rented cottage in October 1969 where band lived, wrote and rehearsed **Trespass** LP. Charisma boss Tony Stratton-Smith became interested in their live work and signed them in spring 1970; **Trespass** appeared in October.

Both Phillips and Mayhew quit soon after and another MM ad came up with Phil Collins (▶), who was added as drummer. It was

Below: Marvin Gaye, still testifying in the 1980s, and still a hit artist.

not until December 1970 that band settled on Steve Hackett as guitarist. Band was still very 'art-rock' orientated, but 1971 **Nursery Cryme** showed sense of adventure and began to define mature Genesis sound. Gabriel(▶) had started wearing stage costumes, which were becoming more and more outrageous, but won favour with audiences. 1972 **Foxtrot** finally pushed them into major league and band started drawing larger crowds. 1973 **Genesis Live** is excellent account of band development at this point. Same year saw release of **Selling England**

Abacab, Genesis. Courtesy Charisma Records.

By The Pound and UK hit single **I Know What I Like**.

Band was clearly at forefront of progressive rock upon release of double LP, **Lamb Lies Down On Broadway**, with American interest sparked by elaborate stage show in which Gabriel acted out story-line. Rumours of Gabriel's loss of interest were confusing considering band's success, but were confirmed by shock announcement in June 1975 that he had quit.

Press assumption that band could not survive without Gabriel failed to deter members who began long series of auditions to locate replacement. Eventual announcement puzzled fans and critics alike: Gabriel's replacement would be Phil Collins. Many backing vocals since 1971 had been by Collins, but at time it seemed unlikely Collins could replace Gabriel with any self-assurance. Even release of excellent **Trick Of The Tail** LP and two-month US tour (assisted by Bill Bruford (ex-Yes(▶) on drums) could not put down rumour band would completely fold. But within 11 months **Wind And Wuthering** was released and Genesis seemed permanently on road, this time with Chester Thompson (ex-Zappa(▶), Weather Report) assisting on drums. Paris dates were recorded and produced double live set **Seconds Out**.

Mid-1977 brought more adjustments when Hackett left after 45-city US tour and three 'sold out' Earls Court, London, gigs, again raising speculation that band's days were over. But **And Then There Were Three . . .**

Nursery Cryme, Genesis. Courtesy Charisma Records.

became band's biggest seller and produced UK Top 10 hit, **Follow Me Follow You.** Supergroups seemed out of touch with musical upheavals of late '70s, and band wisely took recording break. Bank's 1979 solo LP **A Curious Feeling** and Rutherford's **Small Creeps Day** (1980) filled void. **Duke**, when released in 1980, proved Genesis could maintain energy levels, and if anything, become more accessible with rhythmic melodies. '70s pretensions disappeared as band successfully moved back into smaller venues on UK '80 and '82 tours (including surprise London Marquee gig).

Phil Collins' personal problems and ultimate divorce made up the content of highly successful solo LP, **Face Value**. 1981 also saw group release **Abacab** which continued healthy trend toward group compositions. Collins, resident workaholic, managed to record another solo LP, **Hello I Must Be Going**, which yielded No.1 hit with old standard **You Can't Hurry Love**. (A clever video with three Phil Collins' singing à la Supremes(▶) helped greatly.) Rutherford's **Acting Very Strange** was also solid but failed to attract as much attention.

Three Sides Live actually improved already high quality of **Duke** and **Abacab** tracks, demonstrating enthusiasm and energy of live Genesis even after 14 years on stage. As treat for (or exploitation of) fans, fourth side contains different material on US/UK versions. Genesis is more than a rock institution. Like an old family friend, they are always dependable, always faithful and, hopefully, always there. With room for solo projects, that should be the case for some time to come.

Current line-up: Collins, drums, vocals; Rutherford; Banks; Chester Thompson, drums (on tour).

Hit Singles:

	US	UK
Spot The Pigeon (EP), 1977	—	14
Follow You Follow Me, 1978	23	7
Misunderstanding, 1980	14	42
Turn It On Again, 1980	58	8
Abacab, 1981	—	19
Paperlate (EP), 1982	32	10

Albums:
Trespass (ABC/Charisma), 1970
Nursery Cryme (Charisma), 1971
Foxtrot (Charisma), 1972
Genesis Live (Charisma), 1973
Selling England By The Pound (Charisma), 1973
In The Beginning (1st LP retitled) (London/Decca), 1974
The Lamb Lies Down On Broadway (ATCO/Charisma), 1974
A Trick Of The Tail (ATCO/Charisma), 1976
Wind And Wuthering (ATCO/Charisma), 1976
Seconds Out (ATCO/Charisma), 1977
'. . . And Then There Were Three . . .' (ATCO/Charisma), 1978
Duke (ATCO/Charisma), 1980
Abacab (ATCO/Charisma), 1981
Three Sides Live (ATCO/Charisma), 1982

Gerry And The Pacemakers
UK group formed 1961.

Original/Final line-up: Gerry Marsden, vocals, guitar; Freddie Marsden, drums; Leslie Maguire, piano; Les Chadwick, bass.

Career: After stints, often with brother Freddie, in various skiffle and rock'n'roll bands, Gerry Marsden formed Mars-Bars in hometown of Liverpool, playing local clubs for six months before break-up. Following split the

Marsdens were joined by Les Chadwick to form Pacemakers trio.

After two months at Top Ten Club in Hamburg they returned to Merseyside, added Leslie Maguire and were signed by Beatles'(▶) manager Brian Epstein in June 1962.

Beatles' producer and Parlophone A&R chief George Martin saw performance at Birkenhead and chose to record Mitch Murray song **How Do You Do It?** which he had earlier tried to record with the Beatles (but they preferred to cut own material). Song climbed quickly to No.1, as did another Mitch Murray song, **I Like It**, and their reading of Rodgers and Hammerstein ballad standard, **You'll Never Walk Alone**, making them only group ever to top charts with each of their first three records.

A Gerry & the Pacemakers compilation. Courtesy EMI Records.

The belated Merseymania movie 'Ferry Cross The Mersey' (1965) gave them a showcase and the theme (penned by Gerry Marsden) was their sixth and final Top-10 single.

Band was equally popular in US (after first US single success **Don't Let The Sun Catch You Crying**, their earlier singles were released there), but quickly faded from limelight and broke up in 1968. Marsden embarked on solo career which yielded no hits but five-year starring role opposite Anna Neagle in West End musical production 'Charlie Girl' before leaving to host children's TV series.

In 1975 Gerry and the Pacemakers reformed for triumphant 'Mersey Beat' revival tour of US and again for similar 'Sounds Of The Sixties' tour of UK in 1979.

Marsden's solo career has continued with appearances in variety, pantomime and cabaret.

Hit Singles:

	US	UK
How Do You Do It? 1963	9	1
I Like It, 1963	17	1
You'll Never Walk Alone, 1963	48	1
I'm The One, 1964	—	2
Don't Let The Sun Catch You Crying, 1964	4	6
Ferry Cross The Mersey, 1964	6	8
I'll Be There, 1965	14	12

Albums:
Best Of (Capitol/Nut), 1977

Don Gibson
US vocalist, guitarist, composer.
Born Shelby, North Carolina, April 3, 1928.

Career: Prolific country writer/performer, Gibson is best known for his compositions **I Can't Stop Loving You** (Kitty Wells, Ray Charles(▶)), **Oh Lonesome Me**, **Sweet Dreams** (Faron Young, Elvis Costello(▶)) and **Legend In My Time** (Ronnie Mislap (▶)).

Crossover country/pop hits like **Sea Of Heartbreak** and **Lonesome Number One** established Gibson's baritone style in early '60s. Although not maintaining Top-20 chart

success, he is nevertheless a regular in country listings.

Consistent live performer (and fair guitarist), Gibson has been long-time attraction at Grand Old Opry (although once dismissed for failing to make set number of contracted appearances). He is also a regular at London's Wembley Festival.

Hit Singles:

	US	UK
Oh Lonesome Me, 1958	7	—
Blue Blue Day, 1958	20	—
Sea Of Heartbreak, 1961	21	14

Albums (selected):
Four Sides Of Don Gibson (—/DJM), 1976
Don't Stop Loving Me (—/DJM), 1976
Famous Country Music Makers (RCA), 1977
I'm All Wrapped Up In You (DJM), 1977
Country Number One (—/Warwick), 1980
Country My Way (—/Warwick), 1981

Gillan
UK group formed 1975.

Original line-up: Ian Gillan, vocals; Ray Fenwick, guitar; John Gustafson, bass; Mark Nauseef, drums.

Career: Ian Gillan was originally lead singer with Deep Purple; he left in 1973 and two years later formed Ian Gillan Band with above line-up and released **Child In Time** album. Band released two more albums under same name. Major personnel shake-up and shortening of name to Gillan heralded 1979 Top 20 album **Mr Universe**. Line-up on this album: Gillan; Steve Bird, guitar; John McCoy, bass; Pete Barnacle, drums; Colin Towns, keyboards.

Success was consolidated by 1980 signing to Virgin Records, although by this time personnel had changed again; Bernie Torme had replaced Steve Bird on guitar, and Mick Underwood had taken over drums. 1981 was successful year with two Top 20 LPs and Top 20 single, a version of Gary US Bonds' classic **New Orleans**. In the summer Torme quit and was replaced by Janick Gers.

Below: Girlschool, the acceptable face of female heavy metal music.

By this time Gillan had established reputation as hard-working live act, undertaking gruelling tours in UK and abroad. 1982 saw consolidation of UK success with album **Magic**, but in 1983 Gillan disbanded; Ian Gillan joined Black Sabbath(▶).

Although not in heavy rock's major league Gillan (band failed to crack American market) still has large and loyal audience among aficionados.

Final line-up: Gillan; Janick Gers, guitar; John McCoy, Fender Precision bass; Colin Towns, keyboards; Mick Underwood, drums.

Hit Singles:

	US	UK
Trouble, 1980	—	14
New Orleans, 1981	—	17

Albums:
Clear Air Turbulence (Virgin), 1977
Scarabus (Virgin), 1977.
Live (—/Island), 1978
Mr Universe (—/Acrobat), 1979
Gillan (—/Flyover), 1979
Glory Road (—/Virgin), 1980
Future Shock (Virgin), 1981
Double Trouble (Virgin), 1981
Magic (Virgin), 1982

Girlschool
UK group formed 1978.

Original line-up: Kim McAuliffe, vocals, guitar; Enid Williams, bass, vocals, Kelly Johnson, guitar, vocals; Denise Dufort, drums

Career: McAuliffe and Williams were in 1977 group Painted Lady. After several personnel shifts band had settled down by March 1978 with change of name to Girlschool, emphasising heavy-metal music (rather than Runaways image of girls playing at rock'n'roll game).

First single, **Take It All Away**, caught attention of Motorhead(▶) manager Doug Smith who put them on that band's 1980 tour and acquired Bronze recording deal. **Demolition** appeared in UK in June 1980 while band was on tour; within two weeks LP hit Top 30. Motorhead connection peaked with excellent

Saint Valentine's Massacre EP, which includes superb cover **Please Don't Touch**. **Hit And Run** expanded audience and proved Girlschool's staying power.

Williams left in 1982 and was replaced by Gil Weston, following her recommendation by Motorhead bassist Lemmy. This line-up recorded band's best effort so far, **Screaming Blue Murder**. LP continued in thunder-and-swagger tradition of hard rock, but several cuts had touch of irony, humour and understanding.

With success of Girlschool, distinctions between men and women playing rock are hopefully fading. There are many all-male bands who'd be glad to sound as strong or as interesting as this one.

Current line-up: McAuliffe; Johnson; Dufort; Gil Weston, bass, vocals.

Albums:
Demolition (Bronze), 1980
Hit And Run (Bronze), 1981
Screaming Blue Murder (Bronze), 1982

Gary Glitter
UK vocalist.
Born Paul Gadd, Banbury, Oxfordshire, May 8, 1940.

Career: As Paul Raven, he pursued undistinguished early career with string of unsuccessful solo singles for Decca and then Parlophone. In 1965 he joined TV pop show 'Ready Steady Go' as programme assistant and met writer/producer Mike Leander, later to become his mentor.

In 1967, again as Paul Raven, he signed with MCA and released yet more flop singles. Total lack of success continued until 1971 when he signed with teenybop specialists Bell Records and met up with Leander again.

Leander and Gadd set out to capitalise on then-current glitter-rock fad. Gadd created character 'Gary Glitter' and came up with sound to go with persona. First single, **Rock & Roll (Parts 1 & 2)**, was a spare, atmospheric opus, heavily reliant on bass and drums; public response was slow but eventually record made British charts, reaching No. 2 in June 1972. (It also became a No. 1 in US but remained his only major transatlantic success.)

Between June 1972 and June 1975 Glitter turned in 11 UK Top-10 hits, including three No.1s. All followed basic style set by **Rock & Roll**, and seemed to touch lucrative chord among pubescent Britons. Stranger perhaps than Glitter's long-awaited record success was his elevation to sex symbol. Apart from the fact that his birthdate was rumoured to be considerably earlier than that given on his biography, he had something of a weight problem; stuffed into his shimmering jumpsuits and platform heels he often seemed more comic than sexy. (His backing group the Glitter Band also scored in UK during this period.)

In 1976 Glitter announced retirement 'for personal reasons', but returned to performing in December that year, and switched labels to Arista in 1977 for a couple more minor hits. During years of stardom he was a big spender, and profligacy took its toll when he was declared bankrupt. A circus tent tour with Gerry Cottle brought him back to the public but was a financial failure. Latterly he has been making strenuous efforts to re-establish himself as major attraction, and has become something of father figure to post-punk musicians. (Joan Jett and the Blackhearts(▶) had a US hit with **Do You Wanna Touch Me** in 1982.) Never one to take himself too seriously, Glitter seems destined to be the rock equivalent of the 'old trouper', working on as long as audiences will turn out to see him.

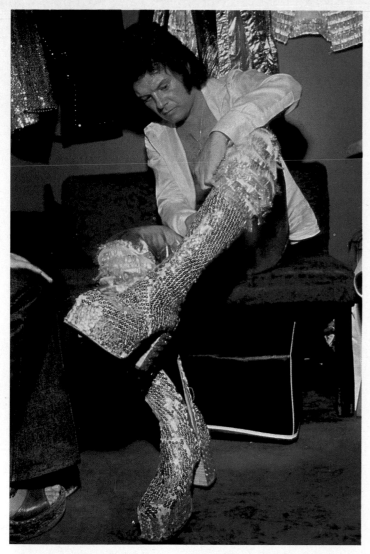

Above: Gary Glitter was a superstar during the phase which bore his name, but vanished when it ended.

Hit Singles:	US	UK
Rock & Roll (Parts 1 & 2), 1972	1	2
I Didn't Know I Loved You (Till I Saw You Rock'n'Roll), 1972	35	4
Do You Wanna Touch Me (Oh Yeah), 1973	—	2
Hello Hello I'm Back Again, 1973	—	2
I'm The Leader Of The Gang (I Am), 1973	—	1
I Love You Love Me Love, 1973	—	1
Remember Me This Way, 1974	—	3
Always Yours, 1974	—	1
Oh Yes! You're Beautiful, 1974	—	2
Love Like You And Me, 1975	—	10
Doing Alright With The Boys, 1975	—	6

Albums:
Remember Me This Way (Bell), 1974
G.G. (Bell), 1975
Greatest Hits (Bell), 1976
Gary Glitter's Golden Greats (—/GTO), 1977
I Love You Love Me Love (—/Hallmark), 1977
The Leader (—/GTO), 1980

Go Gos

US group formed 1978.
Original line-up: Belinda Carlisle, vocals; Charlotte Caffey, lead guitar; Jane Wiedlin, rhythm guitar; Elissa, drums; Margot Olavera, bass.

Career: Formed to open for the Dickies, May 1978, in Los Angeles. Struggled around LA club scene under original name of the Misfits, before changing to Go Gos. Prior to this, Belinda invited to join the Germs (prevented from doing so by illness!); performed with Black Randy and the Metro Squad. Charlotte played with both the Eyes and Manual and the Gardeners, but rest of band were novices.

During 1980, signed one-off singles deal with Stiff for **We Got The Beat**, but expected major record deal failed to transpire. Shortly before single, Elissa was replaced by Gina Shock; and shortly afterwards, Margot replaced by Kathy Valentine (ex-Textones).

By 1981, group signed with I.R.S. label and recorded **Beauty And The Beat** LP, from which came first hit single **Our Lips Are Sealed**, co-written by Jane and Terry Hall (then of Specials(▶)—with whom Go Gos toured UK—now of Fun Boy Three(▶)).

1982 was amazing year for band, with two Top 10 US singles, and **Beauty And The Beat** topping chart. Follow-up LP **Vacation** made Top 10 of LP chart, although UK success remains extremely limited. Go Gos are first big time self-contained all-girl group in rock'n'roll history, having topped US album chart with their '60s-styled pop sound, like unusual cross between the Beatles and the Shangri-Las.

Current line-up: Carlisle; Caffey; Wiedlin; Kathy Valentine, bass; Gina Shock, drums.

Hit Singles:	US	UK
Our Lips Are Sealed, 1981	20	47
We Got The Beat, 1982	2	—
Vacation, 1982	8	—

Albums:
Beauty And The Beat (IRS), 1981
Vacation (IRS), 1982

Andrew Gold

US vocalist, composer, guitarist, keyboard player, producer.
Born Burbank, California, August 2, 1951.

Career: LA session musician; worked with Karla Bonoff and Art Garfunkel(▶), among others. Joined Linda Ronstadt's(▶) slick, professional back-up band in early '70s; contributed keyboards, backing vocals, and arrangements.

Went solo in 1975, recording first album **Andrew Gold** for Asylum in 1976. Second LP **What's Wrong With This Picture** came out later that year; contained hit single, **Lonely Boy**.

Albums were similar to bland Eagles(▶) style and to LA studio sound of a dozen other artists despite excellent production/execution. As songwriter Gold has little that's original to say; his strongest talents probably lie in arrangement and production.

Released two more fairly unsuccessful albums for Asylum, but has since been dropped by label. Still tours with Ronstadt as guitarist and keyboard player.

Hit Singles:	US	UK
Lonely Boy, 1976	7	11
Never Let Her Slip Away, 1978	—	5
How Can This Be Love, 1978	—	19

Albums:
Andrew Gold (Asylum), 1976
What's Wrong With This Picture (Asylum), 1976
All This And Heaven Too (Asylum), 1978
Whirlwind (Asylum), 1980

Grand Funk

US group formed 1968.

Original line-up: Mark Farner, vocals, guitar; Mel Schacher, bass; Don Brewer, drums.

Career: Probably the most critically savaged successful band in rock history, Grand Funk began as Grand Funk Railroad. Members played with various local bands around Michigan until formation of Grand Funk in late 1968. Crucial move was appointment of Terry Knight as business manager (Knight was lead singer of Brewer's former band the Pack).

Knight secured band a spot at Atlanta Pop Festival in 1969, where their brand of sledge-hammer rock went down a storm. Contract with Capitol followed, and first album **On Time** was released same year. Although ignored by radio stations and reviled by press, album reached top of American charts and achieved gold status. Two singles, **Time Machine** and **Mr Limousine Driver**, were also smash hits.

Two years of astounding success followed. Albums notched up mega-sales, and singles were equally successful. As live act, Funk became huge attraction nationwide, selling

Good Singin', Good Playin', Grand Funk Railroad. Courtesy EMI Records.

out massive venues such as New York's Shea Stadium.

In late 1971, however, band decided they could manage without Terry Knight and fired him. He counteracted with legal proceedings, but eventually lost. Once removed from Knight's Midas-like commercial influence, band sought 'artistic' respectability. Craig Frost (keyboards) joined at time of self-produced **Phoenix** album.

Of remainder of output, **We're An American Band** (1973) is notable in that it was produced by Todd Rundgren and yielded half-way decent hard-rock single in title track. **Good Singin' Good Playin'** featured production talents of Frank Zappa, but even he was unable to make much out of the unpromising material.

Grand Funk eventually folded in 1976 after the Zappa album. The theory 'right place, right time' goes some way towards explaining phenomenal success of this mediocre head-banging outfit. As a home-grown American band at time of invasion by British heavy rock outfits like Zeppelin(▶) and Black Sabbath(▶) they filled a lucrative if temporary gap. Re-formed in 1981 for **Grand Funk Lives** LP.

Current line-up: Farner; Brewer; Frost, keyboards; Dennis Bellinger, bass.

Hit Singles:	US	UK
We're An American Band, 1973	1	—
Walk Like A Man, 1974	19	—
Locomotion, 1974	1	—
Shinin' On, 1974	11	—
Some Kind Of Wonderful, 1975	3	—
Bad Time, 1975	4	—

Albums:
On Time (Capitol/—), 1970
Grand Funk (Capitol), 1970
Closer To Home (Capitol), 1970
Live Album (Capitol), 1970
Survival (Capitol), 1971
E Pluribus Funk (Capitol), 1972
Mark, Don And Mel 1969-71 (Capitol), 1972
Phoenix (Capitol), 1973
We're An American Band (Capitol), 1973
Shinin' On (Capitol), 1974
Masters Of Rock (—/EMI), 1975
Caught In The Act (Capitol), 1975
Good Singin' Good Playin' (MCA/EMI), 1976
Hits (Capitol), 1977
Lives (Full Moon), 1981
What's Funk (WEA), 1983

Eddy Grant

Guyanese vocalist, composer, guitarist, keyboard player.
Born Edmond Montague Grant, Plaisance, Guyana, March 5, 1948.

Career: Moved to London with parents in 1960. Made first guitar; played trumpet and piano in jazz group at school. Helped form Equals with whom he knocked up eight UK hits between 1968-70. These included chart-topping **Baby Come Back, Viva Bobby Joe** and **Black Skin Blue Eyed Boys**.

Grant was dominant personalty in group of Lincoln Gordon (guitar), Derv Gordon (vocals), Pat Lloyd (bass and rhythm guitar) and John Hall (drums). He quit in 1972 to form production company and produce artists, including Pioneers, 96 Degrees, Inclusive, as well as Equals, with view to setting up own independent label, recording complex and distribution network.

A clever businessman, he had invested royalties in property which funded Ice Records, based initially in Guyana, and his Coach House Studios, located in London.

In 1977, issued debut solo album, **Message Man**, on which, by using multi-tracking and over-dubs, Grant played virtually all the music himself (as he has done for subsequent efforts).

Walking On Sunshine album (1979) spawned breakthrough hit, **Living On The Front Line,** a compulsive effort containing a strong reggae flavour; titletrack has since been covered successfully by Rockers Revenge.

In early '80s Grant decided to move himself, his family, and his recording studio to Barbados. Though he's left cold Britain, the nation hasn't forgotten him, and subsequent releases, including **I Don't Wanna Dance** and **(I'm Gonna Rock On To) Electric Avenue**, have made Grant the most successful black solo artist to have been nurtured by UK music scene.

Hit Singles:

	US	UK
With Equals:		
Baby Come Back, 1968	32	1
Viva Bobby Joe, 1969	—	6
Black Skin Blue Eyed Boys, 1970	—	9
Solo:		
Living On The Front Line, 1979	—	11
Do You Feel My Love, 1980	—	11
Can't Get Enough Of You, 1981	—	13
I Don't Wanna Dance, 1982	—	1
(I'm Gonna Rock On To) Electric Avenue, 1983	2	—

Albums:
Eddy Grant (—/Torpedo), 1975
Message Man (—/Ice), 1977
Walking On Sunshine (Epc/Ice), 1979
Live In Exile (—/Ice), 1980
Can't Get Enough (—/Ice), 1981
Killer On The Rampage (Portrait/Ice), 1982

Grateful Dead

US group formed 1966

Original line-up: Jerry Garcia, guitar; Phil Lesh, bass; Ron 'Pigpen' McKernan, keyboards Bob Weir, guitar; Bill Kreutzmann (aka Bill Sommers), drums; Robert Hunter, lyrics.

Career: Grateful Dead burst forth from San Francisco's hippy scene as amalgamation of several community bands. Garcia joined up with Hunter at San Mateo Junior College in early '60s. While playing blues in local spots, they came across Weir and Pigpen. Garcia met Kreutzmann when working in record store.

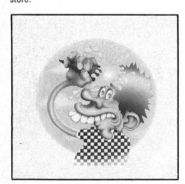

Back of Europe '72, The Grateful Dead. Courtesy Warner Bros Records.

Kreutzmann and Pigpen formed rock band Zodiacs, while Garcia and Hunter joined David Nelson (later New Riders of the Purple Sage(▶)) and Pete Albin (later Big Brother & The Holding Co.). This collection played bluegrass as Wildwood Boys and later as Hart Valley Drifters.

Garcia then formed Mother McCree's Uptown Jug Champions with Pigpen, Weir and John Dawson. Pigpen convinced band to

change from ethnic music to electric blues and came up with name Warlocks. Dawson was replaced by Kreutzmann and after several gigs Phil Lesh joined on bass.

Warlocks were befriended by Tom Wolfe who documented the social milieu and cultural influences on band in his book 'The Electric Kool-Aid Acid Test'. In 1966 band chose name Grateful Dead and began the long, loose concert format so closely associated with group.

Garcia refused to commit himself to standard recording contract and band remained unsigned while other Bay area bands 'sold out' to commercial world. Finally signing with Warner Bros in 1967 and recording first LP in three days, Dead became known as band who did things their own way.

Unsatisfied with sound on first album, Garcia took six months to record follow-up, **Anthem Of The Sun.** Mickey Hart joined as second drummer for recording and soon after Tom Constanten added keyboards to band's sound. Third LP **Aoxomoxoa** put band even deeper into debt as Warner Bros had yet to recover studio costs for second release. Problem was inability to capture atmosphere of band on stage. Next effort attempted to correct that by presenting double live set, **Live Dead.**

Band now entered what many consider to be classic period. Constanten dropped out. Remaining line-up switched studio work from drawn-out jams to short, structured songs. **Working Man's Dead** and **American Beauty** reflect this care and attention and remain among Dead's best efforts.

Unfortunate incident involving embezzlement charges against manager (Hart's father), caused Hart to leave band. Drug charges after bust in New Orleans raised question of band's future. But Dead played in Europe and continued to perform from three to five hours per set. Fans of the band became known as 'Dead Heads' and were famous for their incredible loyalty—they would travel anywhere band was playing.

Growing reputation ensured success of **The Grateful Dead,** band's second live album; it marked peak which in many ways Dead has not regained. **Europe '72** was

Above: A Caribbean superstar to rival Bob Marley, Eddy Grant, who first found fame in England.

triple live set featuring some of Pigpen's last days with Dead and introduced Keith Godchaux (keyboards) and wife Donna Godchaux (vocals) who began filling in for Pigpen. Pigpen had liver disease which became serious and was shortly to force his retirement. He died in May 1973. Although outsiders might not appreciate his influence, this loss marked start of rough period for Dead.

Warners released **History Of The Grateful Dead, Volume I (Bear's Choice)** from February 1970 Fillmore East shows. It hardly seemed up to quality demanded when band had been with label. Yet band's own effort, **Wake Of The Flood,** did nothing to dispel concern about Dead's falling standards.

Continuing outside activities took attention away from group. However, excellent **Blues For Allah** LP proved Dead could still try for new sounds. It also marked Mickey Hart's return to fold.

In March 1976 Dead and Who(▶) were paired by Bill Graham for massive 100,000 strong two-day outdoor concert in Oakland, California. Although critically in same class, difference in styles seemed to make this a strange coupling, but it worked (and was repeated for March 1981 gig in Essen, Germany).

Band continued to record and was willing to take new approaches; **Terrapin Station** was first Dead LP to use outside producer (Keith Olsen) and **Shakedown Street** was recorded at band's private studio, using producer Lowell George, in effort to get 'live' feel. This period also saw Warners release nostalgic restrospective, **What A Long Strange Trip It's Been.**

In 1978 Dead set up special night concert in front of Great Pyramid, Cairo, Egypt. **Go To Heaven** was last appearance of the late Keith Godchaux and wife Donna. Most artists who've been associated with Dead cannot be ruled out from future work. **Heaven** also featured keyboards by Brent Myland who has toured and recorded with band since.

Reckoning is interesting side aspect of Dead which presents all-acoustic live work.

With loyal fans, Dead are guaranteed certain level of success forever. Yet degree of disappointment hangs over band—they have strongest claim to title of people's band but are still not widely appreciated. The multi-influences and '60s cultural ties seem to preclude any future breakthrough. But Grateful Dead, with pedigree that reads like directory for San Francisco's counterculture, are special band who will always evoke memories of long, lazy days and community spirit of the summer of love.

Current line-up: Garcia; Weir; Lesh; Kreutzmann; Mikey Hart, percussion; Brent Myland, keyboards.

Albums:
Grateful Dead (Warner Bros/—), 1967
Anthem For The Sun (Warner Bros), 1968
Aoxomoxoa (Warner Bros), 1969
Live Dead (Warner Bros), 1970
Workingman's Dead (Warner Bros), 1970
American Beauty (Warner Bros), 1970
The Grateful Dead (Warner Bros), 1971
Europe '72 (Warner Bros), 1972
History Of The Grateful Dead, Volume 1— Bear's Choice (Warner Bros), 1973
Wake Of The Flood (Grateful Dead), 1973*
Grateful Dead From The Mars Hotel (Grateful Dead), 1974*
Blues For Allah (Grateful Dead), 1975
Steal Your Face (Grateful Dead), 1976
Terrapin Station (Arista), 1977
What A Long Strange Trip It's Been (Warner Bros), 1977
Shakedown Street (Arista), 1978
Go To Heaven (Arista), 1980
Reckoning (Arista), 1981
Dead Set (Arista), 1981

*Available as double album in UK only

Dobie Gray

US vocalist.
Born Brookshire, Texas, 1943.

Career: One of eight children of black share-cropping parents, Gray travelled to California in 1964 to pursue singing career. He answered ad placed by Sonny Bono(▶), then at Specialty Records, and single **Look At Me** followed, then **The In Crowd**, a major hit in both US and UK. Nevertheless, follow-ups were elusive, and Gray took up career as actor. Jobs included two years in cast of 'Hair'.

Gray kept links with music business by singing with group called Pollution; he also cut demos for Paul Williams. His eventual return to the recording scene was via Paul's writer/ producer brother, Mentor Williams, who produced Gray's first album for MCA in 1973.

Drift Away was recorded in Nashville and teamed Gray's husky, soul-inflected voice with country musicians and rock/country arrangements. This unusual combination led to success for album and US Top 5 for title track. The album and follow-up LP **Loving Arms** were both beautifully crafted collections of songs, now regarded as minor classics. After one more album for MCA, Gray moved on to Capricorn in 1975, and finally to Infinity for **Midnight Diamond** in 1979. This album spawned disco hit **You Can Do It.**

Since then Gray has kept low profile and seems to be suffering from the problem which has dogged his career—lack of direction. Possessor of a fine, distinctive voice, he seems uncertain which musical context suits it best. Nevertheless, **Drift Away** and **Loving Arms** are albums which should be in the collection of anyone with taste for well-crafted soft-rock with country flavour.

Hit Singles:	US	UK
The 'In' Crowd, 1965	13	25
Drift Away, 1973	5	—

Albums:
Dobie Gray (Infinity), 1979
Midnight (Infinity), 1979

Worth Searching Out:
Drift Away (MCA), 1973
Loving Arms (MCA), 1974

Al Green

US vocalist.
Born Forrest City, Arkansas, April 13, 1946.

Career: Musical grounding came singing in family gospel group the Greene Brothers from age nine; family moved north to Grand Rapids, Michigan, in 1959. There Al made initial foray into secular musical styles, joining local group Creations (aged 17), recording some sides for Zodiac.

Progress was slow, until early 1967 when two group members, Palmer Jones and Curtis Rodgers, persuaded Al to sing a song of theirs so they could produce disc for Hot Line Music Journal label; thus emerged **Back Up Train**, a gently haunting love song, credited to Al Greene (with third 'e') and the Soul Mates, which climbed into R&B Top 10 early in 1968, crossing over to Top 50 in pop charts. Two subsequent singles in similar style, **Don' Hurt Me No More** and **Lover's Hideaway**, sold well enough locally, but failed to break nationally.

Let's Stay Together, Al Green. Courtesy London Records.

Group became unsettled at failure to maintain initial impact; Soul Mates split, leaving Al high and dry. Continued as solo performer; soon noticed at Texas gig by Willie Mitchell(▶), renowned R&B musician/writer/producer scouting for Hi Records in Memphis.

Initial product dabbled in variety of styles from impassioned deep soul balladry **One Woman** and crisp funky **You Say It** to thumping power of **Right Now Right Now**. Also evident was blues influence (he cut version of Roosevelt Syke's vintage **Driving Wheel**); it was an interesting combination of blues and funk which yielded first major hit on Hi—Al Green's (now minus third 'e') powerful, ponderous treatment of **I Can't Get Next To You**, reviving Temptation's(▶) 1969 chart-topper.

In summer 1971, Al was back in upper reaches of charts with yet another change of musical direction; **Tired Of Being Alone** returned to Green's gospel roots—his tenor delivery, partly restrained, almost tearful, drawing on soaring emotional falsetto and crooning soulful melismatic sound lifted from Baptist choir heritage. Top 10 R&B, Top 20 pop was the result. Formula generated

lengthy succession of smash hits over the next half-dozen years. **Let's Stay Together** topped R&B and pop charts in February 1972. Sound began to stagnate, slipping into predictable groove; main relief came with occasional burst of down-home gospel like **Have A Good Time**.

Al's vocals began to suffer from overkill of wistful introversion; became almost parody of himself. On stage he purveyed image of eternal romeo, playing heavily to female element in audience. Love-man image was to be his Waterloo however; a jealous female fan broke into Al's apartment while he was taking bath and tipped basin of boiling grits down his back; Al suffered severe skin burns, was unable to record or perform for some time. During lay-off, he 'found' religion again, and took to preaching around Memphis.

In 1977 cut highly-rated **Belle Album**; titletrack single, an intense soulful ballad, charted. 1978 brought fresh approach with LP **Truth'n'Time**. Ballad **To Sir With Love** had some chart action, while funky flip **Wait Here** had crisp, punchy beat; Al produced himself with more vigour than ever Willie Mitchell had generated.

By 1980 Al Green had forsaken R&B, leaving Hi to sign with religious organisation, Word's Myrrh label. His 'born-again' gospel LPs have enjoyed good sales, gaining chart placings and Grammy nominations.

Hit Singles:	US	UK
Tired Of Being Alone, 1971	11	4
Let's Stay Together, 1972	1	7
Look What You Done For Me, 1972	4	44
I'm Still In Love With You, 1972	3	35
You Ought To Be With Me, 1972	3	—
Call Me (Come Back Home), 1973	10	—
Here I Am (Come And Take Me), 1973	10	—
Livin' For You, 1974	19	—
Sha La La (Make Me Happy), 1974	7	20
L.O.V.E., 1975	13	24

Albums:
Greatest Hits Volume 1 (Hi/—), 1976
Greatest Hits Volume 2 (Hi/—), 1978
Cream Of (Hi-Cream), 1980
Tokyo/Live (Hi-Cream), 1981
The Lord Will Make A Way (Myrrh/—), 1982
Precious Lord (Hi-Cream), 1982
Higher Plane (Hi-Cream), 1982

Peter Green

UK guitarist, vocalist, composer.
Born Peter Greenbaum, London, October 29, 1946.

Career: In February 1966 Peter Bardens (later of Camel) finished short stint with Them(▶) and returned to London to form new band. he contacted Mick Fleetwood who had drummed for him in previous local group and got young Peter Green to fill in on bass. The Peter Bees folded within months, but Green and Fleetwood stayed on to join Bardens and unknown Rod Stewart(▶) in Shotgun Express.

By now Green was playing guitar and playing well enough to gain the attention of John Mayall(▶). Green was given unenviable task of assuming Eric Clapton's(▶) place in Mayall's Bluesbreakers. He appeared on **A Hard Road** and put a halt to the cries 'bring back Eric'.

Fleetwood sat in with Mayall's band and shortly after, in rather unclear circumstances, Green, McVie and Fleetwood began forming what was to become Fleetwood Mac(▶). After brilliant run in that group, Green's history becomes difficult to pin down. He left Mac to join US fundamentalist religious group. His

sincerity was beyond doubt as he began donating royalties to charity. **The End Of The Game** LP appeared in late 1970, but showed none of the ability expected of Green. He filled in awhile for Mac in 1971 after Jeremy Spencer left and did some one-off gigs around London.

Amid various rumoured activities, Green appeared in court in February 1977 following incident in which he belligerently renounced continued royalties from Fleetwood Mac. Following commitment to mental institution, he began recording again for first time in nearly 10 years. Unfortunately nothing has matched grace and style of his early years.

Guitar: Gibson Les Paul

Albums:
The End Of The Game (Reprise), 1970
In The skies (Sail/PVK), 1979
Little Dreamer (Sail/PVK), 1980
Whatcha Gonna Do? (Sail/PVK), 1981
Blue Skies (Sail/PVK), 1981

The Guess Who

Canadian group formed 1965.

Original line-up: Randy Bachman, guitar; Chad Allen, vocals; Gary Peterson, drums; James Kale, bass.

Career: In 1959 Randy Bachman and Chad Allen formed Al and the Silvertones in Winnipeg, Manitoba. Bachman finished high school and entered Manitoba Institute of Technology while he and Allen gathered together Peterson and Kale, two of Manitoba's best musicians. Bachman visited London and saw the Who(▶) at Marquee Club. His band began calling themselves the Guess Who.

Pop direction did not please Allen and he was replaced by Burton Cummings. Bachman-Cummings discovered mutual talent for writing strong, punchy songs. Songs began selling throughout Canada and Guess Who took over weekly TV show in 1967.

Strong pro-Canadian stance kept them in Canada (and out of ears of everyone else) until RCA released **These Eyes** in 1969. Guess Who became hot radio product in US. They achieved classic US No. 1 with **American Woman**, which chastised US neglect of its Northern neighbour.

Just as Guess Who seemed destined for great things, Bachman left for personal reasons in 1970. He eventually overshadowed former mates with Bachman-Turner Overdrive(▶). Cummings took control and replaced Bachman with two guitarists: Kurt Winter and Greg Leskiw. Leskiw provided hit **Hand Me Down World** and for a while it seemed Guess Who would improve, but Bachman split was never made good. In 1972 Leskiw left, and Kale decided to quit music completely. Re-

Below: Arlo Guthrie, famous son of an even more famous father.

placements Don McDougal (guitars) and Bill Wallace (bass) did not offer anything exciting, although this line-up recorded underrated live album at tiny Seattle Paramount.

In 1973 McDougal left and was replaced by Dom Trolano from the James Gang(▶). 1975 saw Winter quit and band fell apart as Cummings launched solo career. There have been several Guess Who efforts since

A Guess Who compilation album. Courtesy RCA Records.

then, with various line-ups, though without Bachman or Cummings such efforts seem pointless. The Bachman-Cummings Guess Who, highly underrated, are now acknowledged as forerunners of many new bands who are proud to be Canadian.

Final line-up: Peterson; Bill Wallace, bass; Don Trolano, guitar; Kurt Winter, guitar; Burton Cummings, vocals.

Hit Singles:	US	UK
These Eyes, 1969	6	—
Laughing, 1969	10	—
No Time, 1969	5	—
American Woman, 1970	1	19
Hand Me Down World, 1970	17	—
Share The Land, 1970	10	—
Rain Dance, 1971	19	—
Clap For The Wolfman, 1974	6	—

Albums:
American Woman (RCA), 1970
Best Of The Guess Who (RCA), 1971
Greatest of (RCA/—), 1975

Arlo Guthrie

US vocalist, guitarist, pianist, harmonica player, composer.
Born Coney Island, New York, July 10, 1947.

Career: Alice's Restaurant, performed at 1967 Newport Folk Festival, established Guthrie as major talent within one weekend. Sung first at topical song workshop, story of 'massacree' went on to such success at afternoon concert that Guthrie was added to evening concert where headliners joined in

chorus to rapturous reception from audience. Filling up entire side of album recorded later that year, delightfully ironic song tells auto-biographical tale of being convicted for littering, which US Army considered sufficient cause for refusing to induct him to fight him in Vietnam: he wasn't moral enough to kill women and children. Story was later expanded into popular film (and cookbook) which allowed him to further celebrate alternative life style while satirising police and army.

Success led to expensive penthouse apartment and Arlo's mother bemoaned that such indulgence didn't reflect the way he was brought up to live. Indeed, as son of influential folk singer Woody Guthrie(▶), Arlo's childhood was filled with his father's dedication to cause of migrant workers and other displaced people, and the music of America's finest folk musicians, resulting in probably the only hootenanny Bar Mitzvah in history.

While avoiding identificaiton with father's style by looking at world from contemporary perspective, Arlo involved himself in environmental and peace causes, often performing with Woody's colleague Pete Seeger(▶). Songs, though, are characterised by refreshing humour and friendliness which made him a highlight of 'Woodstock' festival/film.

Third album **Running Down The Road** (1969) incorporated Nashville accompaniment and rock track. Latest album **Power Of Love**, in addition to own composition, features songs by T-Bone Burnett, Jimmy Webb and Richard Thompson(▶), and adds Rickie Lee Jones(▶), Phil Everly(▶) and Leah Kunkel on vocals. An accomplished guitarist, Guthrie has played sessions for Doobie Brothers(▶) and for Sonny Terry and Brownie McGhee. He now lives with wife and children on Massachusetts farm, not far from Alice's Restaurant setting, and continues to tour, write and record.

Hit Singles: US UK
The City of New Orleans, 1972 18 —

Albums:
Alice's Restaurant (Reprise), 1967
Hobo's Lullaby (Reprise), 1972
Last Of The Brooklyn Cowboys (Reprise), 1973
Amigo (Reprise), 1975
Best Of (Warner Bros), 1977
One Night (Warner Bros/—), 1978
Outlasting The Blues (Warner Bros), 1979
Power Of Love (Warner Bros), 1981

With Peter Seeger:
In Concert (Reprise), 1975
Precious Friend (Warner Bros/—), 1981

Woody Guthrie

US vocalist, guitarist, composer.
Born Woodrow Wilson Guthrie, Okemah, Oklahoma, July 12, 1912; died October 3, 1967.

Career: Arguably America's greatest and certainly most influential folk poet, Woody Guthrie provided inspiration for many later musicians, in particular Bob Dylan(▶) who sang his material and copied his affectations. More than a thousand songs, several books, hundreds of poems and articles remain testament to a man who lived and died in relative poverty and whose work enshrined the spirit of America's mobility and its working class. Although sung in a flat nasal twang, his songs were incredibly moving.

Guthrie took to the road at an early age, alongside dustbowl refugees and hopeful emigrants to California (on seeing film of John Steinbeck's 'Grapes Of Wrath' starring Henry Fonda, Guthrie left cinema and composed his

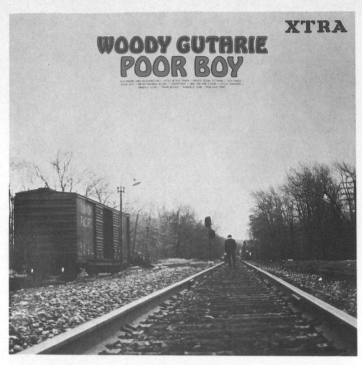

Poor Boy, Woody Guthrie. Courtesy Xtra Records.

classic **Dustbowl Ballads**).

After a spell of dollar-a-day radio shows for WKVD Los Angeles, Guthrie moved East and became major figure of left-wing folk music movement, recording for Alan Lomax and Library of Congress, singing with Burl Ives and the Almanac Singers. He teamed up with Pete Seeger(▶) for numerous treks across USA, recording for RCA Victor, Stinson and Folkways, working in trade union movement and writing for The People's World. His 1943 autobiography 'Bound For Glory' remains giant work of American literature (made into a film starring David Carradine in 1976). But he was already falling prey to a degenerative disease, Huntingdon's chorea (which had killed his mother), and his work tailed off. Bedridden for two decades, he died in October 1967.

His son Arlo(▶) continued family's involvement in music, though in more contemporary folk-rock vein.

Albums (selected):
Bound For Glory (Folkways/—), 1960
Dustbowl Ballads (Folkways/RCA Victor), 1964
Woody Guthrie (Folkways/Pye), 1966
Poor Boy—13 Of His Folk Songs (Folkways/Xtra), '60s

Worth Searching Out:
Library Of Congress (Elektra/), '60s

Sammy Hagar

US guitarist, vocalist, composer.
Born October 13, 1947.

Career: Son of a prizefighter, Hagar first came to prominence as guitarist in Montrose(▶). Left in 1975 to pursue solo career as heavy metal guitarist. Debut **Nine On A Ten Scale** showed promise with some interesting echobox phrasing, particularly on **Urban Gorilla**. 1977's eponymous album, recorded at Abbey Road, was less impressive and led to predictable mundane material on subsequent **Musical Chairs**. Within seven months **All Night Long** appeared, a rushed work seemingly bereft of new ideas.

His popularity having declined considerably, Hagar waited a year before releasing next work; **Street Machine** was distinct improvement, with Hagar taking control of production.

Set included his paeon to fast cars, **Trans-Am**, which became great audience favourite. Fortunes continued to improve in 1979 and he enjoyed hugely successful appearances on Boston's(▶) US tour. a brief UK visit gained him some commendation and with resurgence

there of interest in heavy metal he was pushed into limelight. Christmas single, **This Planet's On Fire/Space Station No. 5**, provided minor hit, and two months later **I've Done Everything For You** climbed into UK Top 50, paving way for sell-out tour in April.

Release of live **Loud And Clear** (March '80) was an inspired move, indicating that faulty earlier work could still sound impressive in live setting. Set included nine Hagar numbers, seven of which had originally appeared on swiftly deleted **All Night Long**; a version of Montrose's driving **Bad Motor Scooter** was another clever addition.

Completed Capitol contract with **Danger Zone**, regarded by some as his finest album. Although limited by scope of heavy metal, Hagar's career has progressed surprisingly since 1978. He recently signed to Geffen Records alongside wealth of rock talent. **Standing Hampton**, a US Top 30 album, suggests that he may not get lost in the shuffle.

Guitar: Various custom models

Albums:
Nine On A Ten Scale (Capitol), 1976
Sammy Hagar (Capitol), 1977
Musical Chairs (Capitol), 1978
All Night Long (Live) (Capitol), 1978
Street Machine (Capitol), 1979
Danger Zone (Capitol), 1979
Loud And Clear (Capitol), 1980
Standing Hampton (Geffen), 1982
Three Lock Box (Geffen), 1982

Merle Haggard

US vocalist, composer, guitarist.
Born Bakersfield, California, April 6, 1937.

Career: Former petty criminal who saw the light in San Quentin (while serving six months to 15 years) after Johnny Cash's(▶) famed performance at the prison.

Best known for staunch pro-US anthem **Okie From Muskogee**, which antagonised anti-Vietnam War rock generation in 1970, Haggard first recorded for Fuzzy Owen's (now Haggard's manager) Tally label, scoring initial Top 10 country hit in 1965 with **All My Friends Are Gonna Be Strangers.**

Haggard's songs have been recorded by countless C&W performers, including Willie Nelson(▶), Emmylou Harris(▶), Jerry Lee Lewis(▶) and Dolly Parton(▶). He also wrote theme music to John Wayne movie 'Chisum'.

Haggard is fast approaching reputation of 1976 and did tours supporting Marvin

Above: Sammy Hagar, on red street from 'Blow Up' film. Courtesy Capitol Records.
Below: Haircut 100 prior to their split with frontman Nick Heyward (seated in chair).

his two idols, Hank Williams(▶) and, particularly, Jimmie Rodgers(▶), for whom he recorded tribute album **Same Train, A Different Time** (1969).

A consistent hit-maker, his mellow, relaxed baritone is still cutting traditional country fare, although occasional excursions into rock have proved unsatisfactory.

Albums (selected):
Mama Tried (Capitol), 1968
Same Train, A Different Time (Capitol), 1969
Okie From Muskogee (Capitol/C&W), 1970
Capitol Country Classics—Merle Haggard (Capitol), 1979
The Way I Am (Capitol), 1980

Haircut 100

UK group formed 1980.

Original line-up: Nick Heyward, lead vocals, guitar; Graham Jones, guitar; Les Nemes, bass; Blair Cunningham, drums; Phil Smith, saxophone; Mark 'Ilford' Fox, percussion.

Career: Friends since schooldays, Heyward, Jones and Nemes had girlfriends who knew each other. When the three girls elbowed the three lads in the same week, the trio decided to console themselves by forming a group.

The first gig came in early 1981, a private concert at the Ski Club, a gentleman's club in London's Eaton Square. Around same time, recording engineer Karl Adams, who later became their manager, offered them some studio time and hawked resultant tape round the record companies. Phil Smith, who had been doing session work with various artists, was at studio when Haircut 100 came in, was drafted into session, then into group. Soon after, he invited old friend Mark Fox, a schoolteacher, to a rehearsal which led to Fox joining (initially part-time).

Line-up was completed with addition of American drummer Blair Cunningham. Born and raised in Memphis, Tennessee, Cunningham had joined Stax act the Soul Children in 1976 and did tours supporting Marvin Gaye(▶), the O'Jays(▶) and other major acts. He left group to work as session drummer, recording with Rufus Thomas, Eddie Floyd, Anita Ward and others. Cunnginham then joined band of Columbia artis Greg Sutton. While on rehearsals in LA, played with Michael Jackson(▶) and the Doobie Brothers(▶) at that group's anniversary party. On leaving Sutton's band, he went to Phil Rambow's group; did two UK tours with Rambow, plus another with Pearl Harbour. Cunningham was playing with a band called Shake Shake when invited to join Haircut.

Arista Records won race to sign group; issued their first single **Favourite Shirts (Boy Meets Girl)**, produced by Beat's producer Bob Sargeant, in September 1981. Single went silver in November and by end of year was international hit. Follow-up **Love Plus One**, released January 1982, was succeeded by debut album.

In early 1983 Nick Heyward (born Beckenham, Kent, May 20, 1961) split from band to work solo. Arista offered him a deal which led to major row with group; band negotiated new deal for themselves with Polydor which led to law-suit; fortunately resolved to everyone's satsifaction within a couple of months.

Heyward's father was jazz buff and encouraged youngster to break free from earlier ambitions (in commercial art) and go into full-time music. Heyward's original songs and image of vulnerable adolescence were focal point of Haircut 100's appeal. Material had an air of '60s nostalgia to it, yet was very much contemporary dance music. First solo release was immediate hit **Whistle Down The Wind.**

Heyward's solo material has proved to be in same vein as Haircut. He played all guitar parts himself and co-produced with Geoff Emerick. His first stage gig as solo was at Albany Empire, Deptford, South London, on March 22, 1983. Billed as Morris and the Jazz Reasons he was joined by Pino Palladino, bass, Morris Pert, percussion, Mark Pinder, drums, and a brass section led by sax man Chris White. Club host and ex-Squeeze(▶) member Glen Tilbrook joined in for the encore. Among material specially written for occasion was **Take That Situation** which was recorded soon after and gave Heyward his second hit. Heyward often makes appearances with the The at London's Marquee.

In summer 1983 Haircut 100 released first single without Heyward.

Current line-up: Jones; Nemes; Cunningham; Smith; Fox.

Hit Singles:	US	UK
Favourite Shirts (Boy Meets Girl), 1981	—	4
Love Plus One, 1982	37	3
Fantastic Day, 1982	—	9
Nobody's Fool, 1982	—	9
Nick Heyward Solo:		
Whistle Down The Wind, 1983	—	3
Take That Situation, 1983	—	11

Album:
Pelican West (Arista/Haricut 100), 1982

Bill Haley

US vocalist, guitarist, composer.
Born William John Clifton Haley Jr., Detroit, July 6, 1927; died February 9, 1981.

Career: Bill Haley's career lived up to name of his backing group, the Comets. It was his classic single **Rock Around The Clock** (arguably the all-time anthem of rock music— and its biggest and most consistent selling single with total sales of more than 20 million copies) which really triggered off rock 'n' roll revolution when featured in 1955 movie 'The Blackboard Jungle'.

Moving to Booth-Winn Pennsylvania, at four and raised on parents' farm, Haley played hillbilly music at local country fairs as teenager and spent two years in early '40s as guitarist in cousin Lee's band. Cut first solo record, **Candy Kisses**, in 1945 when 18.

After four years with various country and western bands, in 1949 Haley became DJ at Radio WPWA in Chester, Pennsylvania. Formed own group, the Four Aces Of Western Swing, to broadcast for station. Recorded for various labels (including one single on Atlantic) before signing to Dave Miller's Essex label in Philadelphia.

Jackie Brenston's 1951 R&B single **Rocket 88** has often been cited as first rock 'n' roll hit and Haley covered it for white audiences in rockabilly style, selling 10,000 copies, then notched 75,000 sales for follow-up, **Rock The Joint**, another R&B cover.

Sensing innate commercial potential of R&B/C&W hybrid, Haley stopped recording hillbilly material, changed band's name to Comets and made national charts in 1953 with **Crazy Man Crazy**, a pulsating record which formulated his successful and instantly recognisable style.

Already long past teens, his moon-shaped face crowned by a soon-to-be-famous kiss curl, Haley fronted band of seasoned musicians: John Grande, Al Reed, Francis Beecher, Billy Williamson, Don Raymond and Rudy Pompelli. Although belonging to dif-

ferent age group they touched chord of rising youth cult and suddenly became hottest property in music business.

Rock Around The Clock, recorded in April 1954 after move from Essex Records to Decca, was cut as favour to Haley's manager Dave Myers, who had written song 18 months earlier for Sunny Dae. Released late 1954, record reached No. 17 in UK in January 1955, then quickly dropped from chart. After follow-up **Shake Rattle And Roll** (re-make of Joe Turner R&B hit) scored on both sides of Atlantic, it was re-issued to top charts in June (US) and October (UK). It has subsequently been re-released several times, most recent chart revival being 1974 when it reached No. 12 in UK.

1955 saw no fewer than six Haley records scorch up charts. 1956 produced a further five hits with two final hit recordings in 1957.

Haley's American success was surpassed in UK where in February 1957 he was mobbed by many thousands of fans on arrival in a train specially chartered by the Daily Mirror newspaper at London's Waterloo Station. Cinema audience had rioted at showings of the two exploitation movies 'Rock Around The Clock' and 'Don't Knock The Rock' in which Haley starred. Concert tour produced similar scenes with theatre seats being ripped out and fans going into hysterics.

However, despite sometimes wild live act which saw Pompelli cavorting all over stage, playing saxophone flat on his back and the like, group couldn't hide fact that they were essentially mddle-aged musicians pandering to kids. With arrival of Presley(▶), Haley's comet burned out, since these kids now had a hero of their generation. Haley's fate was sealed. A chubby-faced, rather sedate, happily married man, he could offer the excitement of his music but not the sex appeal of his younger rival. His music also soon lost its edge, later recordings lapsing into lightweight MOR genre.

Moving to Rio Grande Valley, Haley contented himself with occasional nostalgia-appeal tours with Comets. He was set for one such in Autumn 1980 but it was called off due to illness and in November he was admitted to an LA hospital with suspected brain tumour. Three months later the first hero of rock 'n' roll — a man who sold nearly 70 million records — was dead at early age of 54.

Hit Singles:	US	UK
Crazy Man Crazy, 1953	12	—
Shake Rattle And Roll, 1954	7	4
Rock Around The Clock, 1955	1	1
Dim, Dim The Lights, 1955	11	—
Birth Of The Boogie, Mambo Rock 1955	17	—
Mambo Rock, 1955	18	14
Razzle-Dazzle, 1955	15	—
Rock-A-Beatin' Boogie, 1955	23	4
Burn The Candle, 1955	9	—

Above: The first rock'n'roll superstar, Bill Haley, third from left with kiss curl, on stage with the Comets.

	US	UK
See You Later Alligator, 1956	6	7
R-O-C-K/The Saints Rock'n'Roll, 1956	16	—
The Saints Rock'n'Roll, 1956	18	5
Rockin' Thru The Rye, 1956	—	3
Razzle-Dazzle, 1956	—	13
Rock Around The Clock, 1956	—	5
Rip It Up, 1956	25	4
Rockin' Thru The Rye, 1957	—	19
Rock The Joint, 1957	—	20
Don't Knock The Rock, 1957	—	7
Rock Around The Clock, 1968	—	20
Rock Around The Clock, 1974	39	12

Albums:
Rock Around The Clock (Decca/MCA Coral), 1955
Twistin' Knights At The Round Table (Roulette/PRT), 1961
Rock The Joint (London/Roller Coaster), 1963
Greatest Hits (MCA), 1968
Rock 'n' Roll (GNP/—), 1970
On Stage (—/Hallmark), 1970
Rock Around The Country (GNP/Sonet), 1971
Golden King of Rock (—/Hallmark), 1972
Just Rock & Roll Music (—/Sonet), 1973
Mister Rock 'n' Roll (—/Ember), 1974
Golden Hits (MCA), 1974
Bill Haley Collection (—/Pickwick), 1976
R.O.C.K. (—/Sonet), 1976
Armchair Rock 'n' Roll (MCA), 1978
Everyone Can Rock 'n' Roll (—/Sonet), 1979
Golden Country Origins (—/Roller Coaster), 1979
20 Golden Pieces (—/Bulldog), 1979
Rockin' And Rollin' (Accord/Bear Family), 1981
Greatest Hits (Piccadilly/—), 1981
Tribute (—/MCA), 1981

Hall & Oates

US vocal/instrumental duo.
Daryl Hall, vocals, keyboards; born Phildephia, October 11, 1948; John Oates, vocals, guitar; born New York, April 7, 1949

Career: Hall doubled working with Philadelphia Orchestra and singing back-up for soul artists recording in the city. Mage first record with the Romeos, a group led by Kenny Gamble. When Gamble and the Romeos' keyboard player Leon Huff started producing records, firstly for Jimmy Bishop's Arctic label then for their own Neptune and Philadelphia International labels, they used Hall as a

Bigger Than Both Of Us, Hall & Oates. Courtesy RCA Records.

regular back-up musician. As habitué of Sigma Sound Studios, Hall also worked on records by the Stylistics(▶), the Temptations(▶) and others.

Hall and Oates first met at teenage dance, later they sang together in various doo-wop outfits. While Oates went to college to get a degree in journalism, Hall teamed with singer/songwriter Tim Moore and producer Tim Sellers to record an album for Elektra as Gulliver. Oates occasionally played with band; he started to play regularly with Hall when it broke up. Duo landed contract with Atlantic in 1972, cutting folksy debut album in New York with Arif Mardin producing. 1973 saw them on US charts with soulful **She's Gone** from more R&B flavoured **Abandoned Luncheonette** album. Third Atlantic LP, the Todd Rundgren(▶)-produced **War Babies'** was in heavy-rock mould.

A more precise sense of direction came with move to RCA in 1975 for **Hall And Oates** set which yielded **Sara Smile** hit. Charted on both sides of Atlantic with **Bigger Than Both Of Us** LP (1976) from which came 1977 US chart-topper **Rich Girl**. 1980 found duo producing themselves, and next two albums, **Voices** and **Private Eyes**, contained eight hit singles of which **I Can't Go For That (No Can Do)** was an amazing crossover phenomenon, topping US pop, adult contemprary, R&B and dance charts.

In 1980 Hall had success with Robert Fripp-produced solo album **Sacred Songs**, while Oates wrote soundtrack for film 'Outlaw Blues'.

Private Eyes, Hall & Oates. Courtesy RCA Records.

Hit Singles:

	US	UK
Sarah Smile, 1976	4	—
She's Gone, 1976	7	42
Rich Girl, 1977	1	—
It's A Laugh, 1978	20	—
Wait For Me, 1979	18	—
You've Lost That Lovin' Feeling, 1980	12	55
Kiss On My List, 1981	1	33
You Make My Dreams, 1981	5	—
Private Eyes, 1981	1	32
I Can't Go For That (No Can Do), 1981	1	8
Did It In A Minute, 1982	9	—
Maneater, 1982	1	6
One On One, 1983	9	—

Albums:
Whole Oates (Atlantic), 1972
Abandoned Luncheonette (Atlantic), 1973
War Babies (Atlantic), 1974
Hall & Oates (Atlantic), 1975
Bigger Than Both Of Us (RCA), 1976
Beauty On A Backstreet (RCA), 1977
Past Times Behind (Chelsea), 1977*
Live Time (RCA), 1978
Along The Red Ledge (RCA), 1978
X-Static (RCA), 1979
Voices (RCA), 1980
Private Eyes (RCA), 1981
H₂0 (RCA), 1982

Daryl Hall Solo:
Sacred Songs (RCA), 1980

*Material from 1971-72

Herbie Hancock

US keyboard player, composer, vocalist.
Born Chicago, April 12, 1940.

Career: Classically trained as child; formed first band while studying engineering at Grinnel College, Iowa, in late '50s. Resigned from engineering course to take up music composition.

Returned to Chicago after college and began gigging locally. Eventually joined trumpeter Donald Byrd's band as pianist. While still playing with Byrd, signed long-term solo contract with Blue Note and released first album, **Takin' Off**. Hancock composition from album, **Watermelon Man**, was covered by Mongo Santamaria and became major hit.

From 1963-68 Hancock was member of vintage Miles Davis band with Wayne Shorter, Ron Carter and Tony Williams. As well as contributing to classic Davis albums **The Sorcerer, Nefertiti, Miles In The Sky, Filles De Kilimanjaro** and **In A Silent Way**, Hancock continued to record highly rated albums for Blue Note. From this period, **Empyrean Isles** and **Maiden Voyage** were particularly well received.

In 1968 Hancock left Davis and formed own band, Herbie Hancock Sextet. Album **Mwandishi** (1971) continued development of electronic keyboard sounds that he had first started experimenting with while with Davis. Jazz purists were offended, but album was voted among year's best by 'Time' magazine.

Commercial breakthrough came with release of 1973 LP **Headhunters**; in jazz-funk mode, it outsold all previous Hancock albums put together and was certified gold. Several further albums successfully repeated formula.

Perhaps surprisingly, Hancock followed this commercial success by going back to jazz roots. He reunited Miles Davis Quintet (with Freddie Hubbard on trumpet instead of Davis), played Newport Jazz Festival in 1976 and undertook US tour in 1977. Critics were ecstatic about live appearances and spin-off albums **The Quintet** and **V.S.O.P.**

Continuing with electronic experiments, Hancock registered UK singles hits with **I Thought It Was You** and **You Bet Your Love** using vocoder (type of voice synthesiser). As Hancock moved into '80s, he concentrated music and gained many new fans. Worked with Rod Temperton for **Lite Me Up** LP.

Lite Me Up, Herbie Hancock. Courtesy Columbia Records.

Immensely talented, Hancock will undoubtedly create interesting music for years to come. Like Quincy Jones(▶), he is classic example of new breed of jazzmen able to turn hand to any genre.

Hit Singles:

	US	UK
I Thought It Was You, 1978	—	15
You Bet Your Love, 1979	—	18

Albums (selected):
Best Of (Blue Note), 1974
Headhunters (Columbia/CBS), 1974
Thrust (Columbia/CBS), 1974
The Quintet (Columbia/CBS), 1977
V.S.O.P. (Columbia/CBS), 1977
Sunlight (Columbia/CBS), 1978
Feets Don't Fail Me Now (Columbia/CBS), 1979
Monster (Columbia/CBS), 1980
Greatest Hits (Columbia/CBS), 1980
Lite Me Up (Columbia/CBS), 1982

Tim Hardin

US composer, vocalist, guitarist.
Born Eugene, Oregon, 1940; died December 29, 1980.

Career: One of rock's lost souls, Hardin was a sad, often pathetic figure whose writing/vocal talent has been undervalued.

Raised in musical environment, this former US marine (and relative of notorious outlaw John Wesley Hardin) joined folk boom on New York's East Coast in early '60s after brief attempt at acting career.

An appearance at 1966 Newport Folk Festival prompted Verve to sign him, and he quickly established cult following, if only for interpretations of his songs by other performers. His best-known composition, **If I Were A Carpenter**, was hit for Bobby Darin(▶) in 1966 and for the Four Tops(▶) in 1968.

Hardin dismissed own recordings, particularly the Verve output, claiming overproduction and lack of sympathetic arrangements. He is said to have burst into tears upon hearing final master of **Tim Hardin 1** with additional strings.

Albums for Columbia and Antilles became increasingly maudlin, and it seemed that the talent which had produced songs like **Hang On To A Dream**, **The Lady Came From Baltimore**, **Don't Make Promises** and **Misty Roses** had evaporated.

'Tim Hardin 1'. Courtesy Verve Records.

Brief flirtation with success in the mid-'70s, prompted by the Rod Stewart(▶) recording of **Reason To Believe**, was spoiled by Hardin's increasing abuse of drugs. He died in 1980, leaving a fine legacy of material, but an underlying regret for 'what might have been'.

Albums:
Best Of . . . (Polydor), 1974
Nine (Antilles/GM), 1974
The Shock Of Grace (Columbia/—), 1981
Memorial Album (Polydor), 1982

Roy Harper

UK composer, guitarist.
Born Manchester, June 12, 1941.

Career: Briefly played in skiffle group with brother David during adolescence. Left home to join Air Force at 15; secured discharge by feigning madness, underwent electric shock treatment, followed by group therapy in Surrey. Entered Lancaster Moor Mental Institution, then drifted around Blackpool. Suffered year-long jail sentence in process.

After release, took up busking, wandered around Europe, sang blues in Scandinavia, began writing poetry. Returning to London, secured residency at Les Cousins folk club where he sang repertoire of powerful songs, bemoaning his physical and mental injuries. Recorded **The Sophisticated Beggar** and **Come Out Fighting Genghis Smith**, both revealing distinctive guitar technique and self-mythologising lyrics. Frequent appearances at free festivals brought cult following and hippie poet status. Two further works, **Folkjokeopus** (1969) and **Flat, Baroque And Berserk** (1970), consolidated this position.

Finest work, **Stormcock** (1971), included guest appearance by Jimmy Page on guitar. Both Page and Jethro Tull's(▶) Ian Anderson have frequently championed Harper's work; the former even included appreciative **Hats Off To Harper** on third Led Zeppelin(▶) album. Subsequently, Harper's critical and commercial reputation grew, but he remained self-obsessed and often self-indulgent in much-touted 'honesty'. Occasionally, stream-of-consciousness revelation has been used to great effect (**Stormcock**), but equally frequently, results were embarrassing. His monologues often alienated audiences and concerts have been reduced to slanging matches. Even prestigious debut at Festival Hall saw mass walk-out by disgruntled punters.

In 1972, Harper dabbled with acting in UK film 'Made', completed gruelling tour and was subsequently hospitalised with circulation complaint which led to rumours of imminent death. Recovered to play comeback at

Left: Herbie Hancock, a jazz superstar who moved into rock in the 1970s, and has now progressed into the commercial field of jazz/funk.

London's Royal Albert Hall. Next album **Valentine**, appropriately released on February 14, 1974, was another strong work. Album was promoted with much publicised appearance at London's Rainbow, where Harper was backed by orchestra conducted by David Bedford and joined on-stage by Jimmy Page, John Paul Jones, Dave Gilmour, Ronnie Lane and Keith Moon(▶). Concert was far from classic, in spite of all-star line-up, but live double **Flashes From The Archives Of Oblivion** sold reasonably on strength of publicity.

For 1975's **HQ** Harper briefly put together backing group, Trigger, comprising Chris Spedding, Bill Bruford and Dave Cochran. 1976 US tour saw recruitment of Andy Roberts (in place of Spedding). Harper gained further publicity when he was invited to sing lead vocal on **Have A Cigar** on Pink Floyd's(▶) million-selling **Wish You Were Here** LP. Since late '70s, Harper has consolidated position, but penchant for self-destruction means that mass popularity is probably beyond him. A social misfit and eccentric, Harper is prone to strange happenings; he once contracted rare disease from a sheep and was subsequently hospitalised.

The Unknown Soldier in 1980 was another bleak work, and failed commercially. Harper's commercial decline since mid-'70s has continued, yet, ironically, his work seems peculiarly suited to the austere '80s.

Albums:
The Sophisticated Beggar (Strike/ Youngblood), 1967
Come Out Fighting Genghis Smith (—/Embassy), 1967
Lifemask (—/Harvest), 1973
Valentine (—/Harvest), 1974
Flashes From The Archives Of Oblivion (—/Harvest), 1974
HQ (retitled When An Old Cricketer Leaves The Crease) (Chrysalis/Harvest), 1975
Bullinamingvase (—/Harvest), 1977
The Early Years (—/CBS), 1979
The Unknown Soldier (—/Harvest), 1980
Work Of Heart (Public Recordings), 1981

Worth Searching Out:
Folkjokeopus (World Pacific/Liberty), 1969
Flat, Baroque And Berserk (—/Harvest), 1970
Stormcock (—/Harvest), 1971

Emmylou Harris

US vocalist, composer guitarist.
Born Birmingham, Alabama, April 2, 1947.

Career: Developed early interest in country music; when family moved to Washington DC, played folk and country material in East Coast clubs and coffee-houses. 1969 album on Jubilee made little impression.

Break came at end of 1970 when Flying

Evangeline, Emmylou Harris. Courtesy Reprise Records.

Burrito Brothers(▶) saw Harris performing at Cellar Door Club in Washington; Cellar Door was tiny club which has featured such local talent as Link Wray, Roy Buchanan, Nils Lofgren(▶) and Grin, and George Thorogood(▶). Met and went into partnership with Gram Parsons. Harris sang on his first solo album **G.P.,** shared vocal duties with him on next album **Grievous Angel**, and became member of his touring band.

On death of Parsons in September 1973, Harris returned to Washington and formed own outfit, Angelband. However, in 1974 she was offered contract by Reprise and recorded **Pieces Of The Sky**, a well-balanced and craftsmanlike album that immediately established her as important new voice in contemporary country music. On strength of LP success Harris formed appositely named backing group Hot Band. Members comprised legendary guitarist James Burton(▶), Glen D. Hardin on piano, Hank De Vito on pedal steel, Rodney Crowell(▶) on guitar and harmony vocals, Emory Gordy on bass and John Ware on drums.

During '70s Harris gained international success with series of albums that combined her plaintive voice with excellent choice of material and superlative instrumental back-up. (In 1976 James Burton left Hot Band to be replaced by another outstanding guitarist, Albert Lee.) Albums from **Luxury Liner** (1977) onwards show rock leanings, but in general Harris is true to her country roots. She appeals to rock audiences because she avoids sentimentality and redneck stance of straight country artists, keeping music appealingly honest and straightforward.

In 1980 Harris won Country Music Association award for best female vocalist, and during '80s has continued to crossover between country and rock with great success.

Albums:
Pieces Of The Sky (Reprise), 1975
Elite Hotel (Reprise), 1976
Luxury Liner (Reprise), 1977
Quarter Moon In A Ten Cent Town (Reprise), 1978
Profile — Best Of Emmylou (Reprise), 1978
Blue Kentucky Girl (Reprise), 1979
Gliding Bird (Jubilee/Pye), 1979
Roses In The Snow (Reprise), 1980
Light Of The Stable (Reprise), 1980
Her Best Songs (—/K-Tel), 1980
Evangeline (Reprise), 1981
Cimarron (Reprise), 1981
Last Date (Reprise), 1982

Above: George Harrison either teaching or being taught how to use the studio.

George Harrison

UK vocalist, guitarist, composer.
Born Liverpool, February 25, 1943.

Career: As youngest member of Beatles(▶) spent several years in shadow of Lennon(▶) and McCartney(▶) and in early days was rarely allowed to demonstrate not inconsiderable songwriting talent on Beatle records. In fact, achieved first single A-side for Beatles (**Something**) on last Beatle LP, **Abbey Road**. Even before that, Harrison had released solo Beatle record in shape of rather tedious soundtrack for film 'Wonderwall' first LP to be released on Apple label, in 1968. Also released experimental and similarly unlistenable LP, **Electronic Sounds**, before Beatles split up.

In late 1969, became involved with US white soulsters Delaney & Bonnie(▶), touring and recording with them. Perhaps curiously, Harrison was last of four Beatles to release genuinely musical album, triple set **All Things Must Pass**, in 1970. Set was immediate success, particularly **My Sweet Lord**, which was released as single, and topped charts around world. However, this song was to become notorious in view of court case over its similarity to **He's So Fine**, '60s hit for the Chiffons. Harrison lost case and in late '70s had to pay damages of more than half a million dollars to publishers of **He's So Fine**.

During later Beatle years, Harrison became besotted by India, leading to interest in transcendental meditation and the sitar. This aspect of his work was thankfully mostly absent from **All Things Must Pass**, but when leading Indian sitar player Ravi Shankar asked for help for starving people of Bangla Desh in form of charity concert, Harrison was delighted to oblige. With star-studded line-up, including Bob Dylan(▶), Eric Clapton(▶), Billy Preston, Leon Russell(▶) and Ringo Starr(▶), Harrison organised two concerts at Madison Square Garden, New York, which were recorded and filmed, with all proceeds theoretically going to assist Bangla Desh victims. In reality, prevarication on part of record companies to which other stars contracted meant long delays, although eventually substantial sum was donated.

By next LP, Harrison's interest in Eastern religion had largely changed musical direction, resulting in very poor LP. His marriage to '60s model Patti Boyd also fell apart; Patti moved in with Eric Clapton. 1974 LP, **Dark Horse**, was still overly religious and thus not popular; next LP was no improvement.

In 1976, launched own Dark Horse label with A&M Records. By end of year, disagreements with A&M meant that Dark Horse (and George) moved to Warner Bros amid heavy lawsuits, although first Dark Horse LP by Harrison, **33⅓** was best thing since Bangla Desh days. After long hiatus, next LP, **George Harrison** (1979), appeared to little success. Harrison is rarely seen in public, and only emerged following John Lennon's murder with tribute single **All Those Years Ago**, on which Paul McCartney and Ringo also guested. Follow-up LP, **Somewhere In England**, failed to improve much on previous few years' output, and most recent releases, **Gone Troppo** LP and **Wake Up My Love** single, were released almost secretly in late 1982. At time of writing, Harrison seems to be a spent force, although spare-time activites, which include great interest in Grand Prix motor racing and film-making with Monty Python team (especially 'Time Bandits' movie), as well as presumed domestic bliss with second wife Olivia Arias, no doubt consume his time adequately.

Hit Singles:

	US	UK
My Sweet Lord, 1970	1	1
What Is Life, 1971	10	—
Bangla Desh, 1971	23	10
Give Me Love (Give Me Peace On Earth), 1973	1	8
Dark Horse, 1974	15	—
You, 1975	20	38
Crackerbox Palace, 1977	19	—
Blow Away, 1979	16	51
All Those Years Ago, 1981	3	13

Albums:
Wonderwall (Apple), 1968
Electronic Sounds (Apple), 1969
All Things Must Pass (Apple), 1970
Concert For Bangla Desh (Apple), 1972
Living In The Material World (Apple), 1973
Dark Horse (Pathe), 1974
Extra Texture (Apple), 1975
33⅓ (Dark Horse), 1976
The Best Of (Capitol/Parlophone), 1977
    Parlophone), 1977
George Harrison (Dark Horse), 1979
Somewhere In England (Dark Horse), 1981
Gone Troppo (Dark Horse), 1982

Alex Harvey

UK vocalist, guitarist, composer, banjoist.
Born Glasgow, February 5, 1935; died February 4, 1981.
SAHB: Alex Harvey, guitar, vocals; Zal Cleminson, guitar, vocals; Chris Glen, bass; Ted McKenna, drums; Hugh McKenna, keyboards.

Career: Spent childhood in Gorbals district of Glasgow. Left school at 15 to take up innumerable jobs, including brief stint as lion tamer. Turned to music in 1954, playing in various Dixieland/jazz groups. Two years later, won newspaper competition to find Scotland's answer to Tommy Steele. This was followed by long period in skiffle groups playing Big Bill Broonzy and Jimmie Rodgers(▶) covers.

In 1959 formed Alex Harvey Soul Band (aka Alex Harvey Big Soul Band) and played regularly in Glasgow and Edinburgh. Also backed American visitors such as Eddie Cochran(▶), Gene Vincent(▶) and John Lee Hooker(▶). Residency at Hamburg's legendary Top Ten Club led to Polydor contract in 1963. Live album **Alex Harvey And His Soul Band,** featuring Liverpudlians Bobby Thompson (bass) and Gibson Kemp (drums), released same year. A number of obscure singles were recorded under various names

for German club owners, before group returned to UK in 1963.

By early 1964, Harvey had achieved modicum of success playing rock and blues on club circuit; failed to break big with other R&B based acts. When group finally split, Harvey became solo artist, briefly teaming up with brother Leslie to cut **The Blues**. Returned to Glasgow with Leslie in 1966 and formed short-lived unit with Bobby Patrick, Blues Council, but lost direction. Couple of solo singles and flirtation with psychedelia in Giant Moth led to steady job in pit band of London musical 'Hair'.

After third LP **Roman Wall Blues** (1969) Harvey teamed up with bassist Ian Ellis (ex-Clouds) and drummer Dave Dufort (ex-Velvet Opera) for another ill-fated venture. Career looked to be in decline until discovery of Tear Gas — a financially distressed progressive group from his Scottish hometown — provided necessary inspiration for formation of the Sensational Alex Harvey Band in 1972. During same year, brother Leslie (then member of Stone The Crows) was electrocuted on stage in Swansea. His death served as catalyst in encouraging Harvey to develop new group, amid gruelling work schedule on club/college circuit. Group gradually attracted cult following and effectively combined theatre and rock. Although seldom able to capture drama and humour of live work on vinyl, group achieved Top 10 hit in July 1975 with melodramatic reworking of Tom Jones' 1968 hit **Delilah**. Couple of minor hits followed, including impressive **Boston Tea Party** (1976).

A hugely successful international billtopper, Harvey was forced into periods of convalescence by recurrent back trouble (he was injured on stage during characteristically frenetic performance). In October 1977 announced retirement from full time rock 'n' roll.

On February 4, 1981, a day before his 47th birthday, he suffered heart attack in Zeebruggen, Belgium, following rare European tour, and rock lost one of its most ebullient characters.

Below: The remarkable Alex Harvey, whose few hit singles in no way reflected his avid live following.

Hit Singles:

	US	UK
Delilah, 1975	—	7
The Boston Tea Party, 1976	—	13

Albums:
As Sensational Alex Harvey Band:
Framed (—/Mountain), 1972
Next (Vertigo/Mountain), 1973
The Impossible Dream (Vertigo/Mountain), 1974
Tomorrow Belongs To Me (Vertigo/Mountain), 1975
Live (Atlantic/Mountain), 1975
The Penthouse Tapes (Vertigo/Mountain), 1976
Big Hits And Close Shaves (—/Vertigo), 1977
Rock Drill (—/Mountain), 1978
Collectors Item (—/Mountain), 1980

SAHB without Alex Harvey:
Fourplay (Vertigo), 1977

Alex Harvey Solo:
The Mafia Stole My Guitar (—/RCA), 1979

Worth Searching Out:
As Alex Harvey Soul Band:
Alex Harvey And His Soul Band (—/Polydor), 1964
The Blues (—/Polydor), 1964
Roman Wall Blues (—/Fontana), 1969

Donny Hathaway

US vocalist, keyboard player, composer, arranger, producer.
Born Chicago, October 1, 1945; died 1979.

Career: It is a near certainty that but for his tragic suicide jump from a high building at relatively early age, Donny Hathaway would have emerged as one of greatest figures in history of black music; such was the level of his creativity as session musician, composer, arranger, producer and artist.

Raised in St Louis, Hathaway majored in musical theory at Howard University in Washington DC. While there he played with the Ric Powell Trio jazz outfit and met Roberta Flack(▶) with whom he later worked as producer and arranger; as a duo the pair scored several major hits in '70s including **Where**

Is The Love, The Closer I Get To You and Back Together Again.

Hathaway also met Curtis Mayfield(▶) while in Washington. Mayfield invited the youngster to Chicago to join staff of his new Curtom label as producer, during which collaboration Hathaway recorded duets with June Conquest.

Live, Donny Hathaway. Courtesy Atlantic Records.

After a staff stint at neighbouring Chess label, Hathaway worked as freelance for Uni, Kapp, Stax and other labels and with artists such as Jerry Butler, Woody Herman, Carla Thomas and Staple Singers, before meeting up with King Curtis at music-industry convention.

Curtis took the new talent to Atlantic who promptly signed Hathaway as songwriter, producer and artist. Big breakthrough came with black consciousness song **The Ghetto** in 1970 and partnership with Roberta Flack started same year.

Hit Singles:
With Roberta Flack:
(see separate entry)

Albums:
Everything Is Everything (Atco/Atlantic), 1970
Live (Atco/Atlantic), 1972
Best Of (Atco/Atlantic), 1979
With Robert Flack:
(see separate entry)

Richie Havens

US guitarist, vocalist, composer.
Born Bedford-Stuyvesant, New York, January 21, 1941.

Career: Possessing intense, diverse talent, Havens followed a path which he considered pre-destined, which may explain patchy career short of high spots.

Poor environment deprived Havens of formal musical training, despite pianist father. He began singing as one of McCrae gospel singers when 14. He moved to Greenwich Village in early '60s, initially as an artist, but was soon

Richard P. Havens 1983, Richie Havens. Courtesy MGM Records.

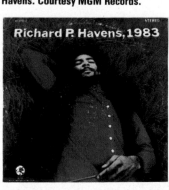

caught up in folk boom, turning to guitar as way of earning a living.

Early albums (**Richie Havens Record** and **Electric Havens**) sunk without trace, although they prompted a contract with Verve who launched Havens into series of notable LPs, particularly **Something Else Again**.

Havens was also gaining considerable reputation as live performer, being particularly successful at Newport Folk Festivals, the stage version of the Who's(▶) opera **Tommy,** and Woodstock, where his after midnight set was a major highlight of the festival. His energetic live act featuring percussive guitar-playing (with open E tuning) is still highly recommended.

Many consider Havens' interpretations of others' material his forté (at least it rewarded him with chart hit, **Here Comes The Sun** in 1971), but he always sounded happier, and more competent, with own biting material.

Formed own production company 'Stormy Forest' in early '70s, which signalled the end of any noteworthy recordings. Has most recently popped up as an actor after a promising debut with Richard Pryor in 'The Bingo Long Travelling All Stars and Motor Kings'.

Hit Singles:

	US	UK
Here Comes The Sun, 1971	16	—

Albums:
Richie Havens (Polydor), 1976
The End Of The Beginning (A&M), 1976

Worth Searching Out:
Something Else Again (Verve), 1968
Richard P. Havens 1983 (Verve), 1969

Ronnie Hawkins

US vocalist, harmonica player.
Born Huntsville, Arkansas, January 10, 1935.

Career: Chunky rock'n'roller, best known for frenzied **Forty Days**, who once boasted 'my parties would embarrass Nero'. He formed the first Hawks while at University in 1952, then moved to Canada where he is still based. Later line-up became the Band(▶)—Levon Helm joined Hawks in 1956, Robbie Robertson in 1963. (Hawkins appeared at the Band's farewell concert in 1976.)

Despite the occasional comeback, most notably a set for Cotillion in 1970, Hawkins is now content to have a good time on the proceeds of land investments and his own club, the Hawk's Nest.

Albums:
Rockin' (—/Pye), 1978
Rrrrackett Time (—/Charly), 1980

Worth Searching Out:
Ronnie Hawkins (Cotillion/Atlantic), 1970
The Hawk (Cotillion/—), 1971

Screamin' Jay Hawkins

US vocalist, pianist, saxophonist.
Born Jalacy Hawkins, Cleveland, Ohio, 1929.

Career: Brought up in orphanage; took up boxing; powerful fists enabled him to win 1947 Golden Gloves title; learned to play piano at early age and later took up saxophone. Gained first musical experience as singer/pianist with Tiny Grimes band in late 1940s. Moved on to Lynn Hope's band in early '50s before launching solo career.

Made first solo discs on Timely in 1953; wrote most of material. Created powerful stage image with throaty baritone vocals and rocking band arrangements; typical titles were **Baptize Me In Wine** (Timely/Apollo) and **She Put The Wammee On Me** (Mercury). Signed with Okeh in 1956, debuting with demonic **I Put A Spell On You**, adding demented snorts and screams to baritone delivery for gimmick effect.

Adopted outrageous live act, leaping from coffin to open shows and wielding skull containing smoke and lighting effects; gimmick image haunted disc career as he label-hopped from Grand, Chancellor and Enrica, attempting to emulate **Spell** with songs like **Ashes** and **I Hear Voices**; then quit New York to live in Hawaii.

Returned to spotlight in 1965 singing to Roulette; cut fresh version of **The Whammy** which attracted attention and brought UK tour. In London, cut LP for Planet using straight vocal ability and less gimmickry. Back in US signed with Philips to make **What That Is** LP in 1969, including **Constipation Blues**, the ultimate in lavatory humor. Music recreated spirit of '50s, as did second Philips LP produced by Huey P. Meaux in Texas.

During early '70s recorded for Hot Line in Nashville, then for London before making new versions of **Spell**, first on Decca, then RCA. Featured briefly in 'American Hot Wax' movie-biog of DJ Alan Freed. Returned to NY and became resident. Further resurgence in 1980 brought tour of Europe, and yet another revival of **Spell** for Polydor. Jay continues to play rock 'n' roll revival shows in US made return visit to England in mid-1983.

Over the years, Hawkins' influence and gimmickry have provided basis of careers for several plagiarists, primarily Screaming Lord Sutch and Arthur Brown.

Albums:
Screamin' The Blues (—/Red Lightnin'), 1979
Frenzy (—/Edsel), 1982

Worth Searching Out:
The Night And Day Of (Planet/—), 1950s
Screamin' Jay Hawkins (Philips/—), 1960

Hawkwind

UK group formed 1969.

Original line-up: Dave Brock, guitar, vocals; Huw Lloyd Langton, guitar; Terry Ollis, drums; Nik Turner, saxophone; John Harrison, bass; Dik Mik, electronics.

Career: Founded by Brock and Turner, unit emerged from Ladbroke Grove area of London as Group X, then Hawkwind Zoo and, finally, Hawkwind. Quickly established themselves as darlings of Notting Hill long-hair set. Manager Doug Smith negotiated recording contract with United Artists.

First album **Hawkwind** (1970) proved inauspicious, but strong live following boosted sales. Group's improvisational style was widely known after appearances at numerous festivals, including 1970 Isle Of Wight where they played free for fans outside the site's fence. Even national press latched onto Nik Turner's silver-painted face, and publicity helped to increased devoted following.

Group soon emerged as heroes of underground, playing community gigs and benefit concerts at every opportunity. Reputation and/or notoriety was further increased after newspaper reports about their apparent drug habits, prompting numerous police investigations.

In June 1971, played at Glastonbury Fayre Festival, aided by poet/painter/vocalist Bob Calvert, whose presence attracted interest from Sci-fi writer Michael Moorcock. This performance also introduced dancer Stacia, later to become regular feature at live gigs. Group's cosmic/space rock phase was evinced on 1971's **In Search Of Space**, with complex sleeve design by Barney Bubbles.

By early 1972, 'resident poet' Calvert joined as full-time member. In February, played London's Roundhouse alternative music spectacle, otherwise known as the 'Greasy Trucker's Party', later double album featured one side of Hawkwind performing **Masters Of The Universe** and **Born To Go**. Also played on triple album set **Glastonbury Fayre** with a host of celebrated rock heroes. Their highest single placing occurred during same period with No. 3 hit **Silver Machine**. Flushed with success, they financed their own Space Ritual Road Show which spawned **Space Ritual Live,** released following year.

Sonic Attack, Hawkwind. Courtesy RCA Records.

As youthful following increased, group suffered series of personnel upheavals. Langton, Harrison and Ollis drifted away, replaced by Simon King (drums), Del Detmar (electronics) and a series of bassists: Thomas Crimble, Dave Anderson and, finally, Ian 'Lemmy' Kilminster. Keyboard player Dik Mik left as did Calvert for an on/off solo career. Detmar was himself replaced by Simon House (ex-Third Ear Band), who joined for spring 1974 US tour.

During Stateside jaunt, larger-than-life Lemmy was caught in possession of amphetamine sulphate, mistaken for cocaine by Canadian officials. Resulting fracas led to his dismissal and he flew back to England to form heavy-metal band Motorhead(▶). Pink Fairies' Paul Rudolph was selected as replacement, having previously played with group on ad-hoc basis. When King suffered an accident following soccer match, Alan Powell (ex-Chicken Shack/Vinegar Joe) was granted permanent membership.

In 1976, signed deal with Charisma Records, and **Astounding Sounds Amazing Music** was released shortly afterwards. Further changes followed: Nik Turner left to form Sphinx and soon after Rudolph and Powell were fired because their playing was deemed 'too funky'.

While departing duo went on to Kicks, Adrian Shaw (bass/vocals) was recruited in time for **Quark, Strangeness And Charm.** Next album, **PXR5**, was not released until May 1979, by which time Hawkwind had effectively split. While Simon House went on to join Bowie's(▶) backing band, remaining members (with successive keyboards players Paul Hayles and Steve Swindells) met legal problems using group name. For brief period they became Hawklords, recording album under that title.

By September 1979, Hawklords had been replaced by revamped Hawkwind, comprising Dave Brock, Harvey Bainbridge, Simon King, Huw Lloyd Langton and Tim Blake. Played first gig at Futurama Festival in Leeds, introducing lasers to Hawkwind set for first time.

In 1980 signed to Bronze, releasing **Live '79**, which restored them to album charts.

Ginger Baker(▶) replaced King on drums. Next album, **Levitation**, hit Top 20. Further line-up changes followed with departure of Blake (replaced by Keith Hale) and Baker (replaced by Martin Griffin).

In July 1981 signed long-term deal with RCA and have produced three albums since. Sell-out tours followed; recently Griffin was replaced by Andy Anderson. '80s albums have revealed Hawkwind trapped in early '70s timewarp, endlessly re-running **Silver Machine** to ever-appreciative audiences.

Current line-up: Brock; Langton; Andy Anderson, drums; Harvey Bainbridge, Keith Hale.

Hit Single:

	US	UK
Silver Machine, 1972	—	3

Albums:
Hawkwind (Liberty/UA), 1970
In Search Of Space (Liberty/UA), 1971
Greasy Trucker's Party (Liberty/UA), 1972
Doremi Fasol Latido (Liberty/UA), 1972
Space Ritual Live (Liberty/UA), 1973
Hall Of The Mountain Grill (Liberty/UA), 1974
Warrior On The Edge Of Time (Liberty/UA), 1975
Roadhawks (Liberty/UA), 1976
Astounding Sounds Amazing Music (—/Charisma), 1976
Masters Of The Universe (—/UA), 1977
Quark, Strangeness And Charm (Sire/Charisma), 1977
Hawklords (—/Charisma), 1978
PXR 5 (—/Charisma), 1979
Repeat Performance (—/Charisma), 1980
Hawkwind Live 1979 (—/Bronze), 1980
Levitation (—/Bronze), 1980
Sonic Attack (—/RCA), 1981
Church Of Hawkwind (—/RCA), 1982
Choose Your Masques (—/RCA), 1982

With Various Artists:
Glastonbury Fayre (—/Revelation), 1972

Isaac Hayes

US vocalist, composer, instrumentalist.
Born Covington, Tennessee, August 20, 1943.

Career: Born into rural poverty, family moved to Memphis when Hayes was in teens. Hayes played saxophone in high school band; also played piano. He formed group Sir Isaac and the Doodads which undertook local gigs.

Eventually Hayes infiltrated elite session musicians of Stax studio, playing on many classic Stax soul cuts of early '60s, most notably with Otis Redding(▶) and Sam and Dave(▶). With David Porter, he wrote many of Sam and Dave's classic songs, including **Hold On I'm Comin'** and **Soul Man**. Porter and Hayes also produced duo, and wrote for other Stax artists.

Hayes' own first LP **Presenting Isaac Hayes** (later re-titled **Blue Hayes**), a straight-forward blues offering, made little impact. 1969 album **Hot Buttered Soul** was entirely different. One of the seminal albums in the development of modern black music, it was both innovative and exceptionally commercial. By stretching numbers to great length (**By The Time I Get To Phoenix** lasted 18 minutes), adding a soulful 'rap' prologue and wrapping song in atmospheric, string-laden arrangement, Hayes produced sexy, high-class mood music that showed off his deep brown voice to best advantage. Album went platinum by end of 1970.

Concept was repeated on next two LPs, and was extended for Hayes' soundtrack to black 'tec movie 'Shaft'. Titletrack became international hit and established 'sound' for thriller soundtracks throughout '70s.

By 1971 Hayes was touring with massive road-show, and had assumed mantle of 'Black Moses' (also title of 1971 double album). His macho, stripped-to-the-waist stage persona and no-expense-spared lifestyle combined to create somewhat overblown image. Period from '71 to '73 was peak of career.

By 1974 Hayes' appeal was beginning to wane (while that of his imitator Barry White(▶) was beginning to take off). After a couple of only moderately successful soundtracks that year, he moved to ABC in 1975. Since that time he has released series of largely disco-orientated albums with varying degrees of success. Duet albums with Dionne Warwick(▶) and Millie Jackson have helped keep his name in public eye.

Stax went bankrupt, and Hayes soon did same. Recently he seems to have been concentrating on acting ('Escape From New York') rather than music. Accused by many of being more concerned with style than content, Hayes nevertheless earned significant niche in the history of black music, and helped make it the dominant influence it is today.

Hit Singles:

	US	UK
Theme From 'Shaft', 1971	1	4
Disco Connection, 1976	—	10

Albums:
Hot Buttered Soul (Stax), 1969
. . . To Be Continued (Stax), 1970
Isaac Hayes Movement (Stax), 1971
Shaft (Stax), 1971

With Dionne Warwick:
A Man And A Woman (MCA), 1977

Heart
US group formed 1973.

Original line-up: Ann Wilson, guitar, keyboards, vocals; Nancy Wilson, vocals, guitar; Michael Derosier, drums; Howard Leese, guitar, keyboards; Steve Fossen, bass; Roger Fisher, guitar.

Career: Wilson sisters grew up on British-influenced rock of '60s. Began playing Seattle bars when women's role in rock was strictly limited to vocals. They knocked this concept on the head by playing Led Zeppelin(▶) covers with flair and gusto. Despite growing popularity, band pulled up roots and moved to British Columbia, primarily to avoid draft problems of Roger Fisher. While in Canada, Heart signed with small new Mushroom label. **Dreamboat Annie** became word of mouth hit and Heart found it was picking up national radio play. Debut LP was unusual in that it ranged from easy, quiet ballads to heavy metal without sounding unfocused or without direction.

With new, larger audience, band returned to US and found that Mushroom's distribution system couldn't handle demand for first LP, so signed to Portrait Records. Mushroom promptly sued for breach of contract. Heart countersued over rights to recording for second LP, alleging Mushroom was about to release rough, unfinished demo work. While case was being settled in Seattle's Federal District Court, Portrait released excellent **Little Queen** LP.

Bootleg copies of second Mushroom LP began fetching ridiculous amounts and Mushroom released **Magazine** with its original mix outside US. With wisdom of Solomon, Seattle federal judge settled suit out of court by suggesting Heart had overstepped bounds in signing to Portrait but that Heart had the right to mix second Mushroom LP as they deemed artistically suitable; Mushroom finally released this new version of **Magazine** in US during 1978. Whether or not aesthetic differences

between two versions make any sense outside of legal flail is questionable, but principle sets important precedent for other artists.

Next official LP, **Dog And Butterfly,** began with classic live cut, then seemed to fall apart. This time switch between hard rock and ballads didn't work as well and resulting confusion stalled band's career. **Bebe Le Strange** acknowledged break-up of Wilson/Fisher romance with Fisher's departure from band. His guitar work was missed and Heart's studio work seemed to continue downward. **Greatest And Live** compounded confusion by including a few new tracks, re-issuing some old selections, and adding nearly an entire LP's worth of live stage work; LP was cut down to single album a year later and released in UK as **Heart.** Taking time to re-organize their thoughts and ideas, Wilson sisters took two-year break before releasing **Private Edition.** This marked a return to spirit of early band as well as making Top 30 in US LP charts.

Heart has always centred on Anne and Nancy Wilson. Past failure to live up to early potential can be partly attributed to legal problems. But with Wilsons clearly in charge at last, long-time followers are expecting more than just another rock band. **Private Edition** is hopefully start of creative period which will ensure Heart is remembered for its often excellent music rather than simply as one of early bands to introduce women as rock instrumentalists.

Current line-up: Ann Wilson; Nancy Wilson; Derosier; Leese; Fossen.

Hit Singles:

	US	UK
Magic Man, 1976	9	—
Barracuda, 1977	11	—
Straight On, 1978	15	—
Tell It Like It Is, 1980	8	—

Albums:
Dreamboat Annie (Mushroom/Arista), 1975
Little Queen (Portrait), 1977
Dog And Butterfly (Portrait), 1979
Bebe Le Strange (Epic), 1980
Greatest And Live (Epic/—), 1980
Heart (—/Epic), 1981
Private Edition (Epic), 1982

Worth Searching Out:
Magazine (remixed) (Mushroom/Arista), 1978

Heatwave
Multi-national group formed 1975.

Original line-up: Johnnie Wilder, vocals, conga; Keith Wilder, vocals; Rod Temperton, keyboards; Eric Johns, guitar; Mario Mantese, bass; Jessie Whitten, guitar; Ernest 'Bilbo' Berger, drums.

Career: Dayton, Ohio, born Wilder brothers served with US Army in Germany and decided

Too Hot To Handle, Heatwave. Courtesy GTO Records.

Above: The unique Jimi Hendrix (foreground) with Noel Redding (left) and Mitch Mitchell—the Jimi Hendrix Experience.

to form band and stay in Europe when discharged. Placed an advert in British music paper and Hull-born Rod Temperton, who had been playing in a German band, answered. So did Los Angeles-born Eric Johns. Johnnie Wilder recruited Spanish-born Mario Mantese and refugee Czechoslovakian Ernest Berger in Switzerland; line-up was completed by Jessie Whitten from Chicago.

Playing mix of soul and pop cover versions and Temperton originals, Heatwave found success on UK club curcuit and at USAF bases. Signed in 1976 to GTO for debut album, produced by erstwhile pop star Barry Blue, which yielded three hit singles, **Too Hot To Handle, Always And Forever** and **Boogie Nights,** the latter earning platinum disc and establishing band in US.

Whitten was stabbed to death while on visit home to Chicago; British-born former Foundations member Roy Carter replaced him.

Central Heating LP was released in 1977. Subsequently, reggae artist Tyrone of its tracks, **Mind Blowing Decisions.** Johnnie Wilder was sufficiently impressed with cover to rush-release a 12-inch version of original with extended reggae version dubbed on end. This enterprise proceeded to dominate discotheques around the world.

Developing partial paralysis following car accident, Mantase was forced to leave and Keith Bramble came in. Johns also left, to be replaced by the Wilders' cousin Billy Jones for a highly successful US tour and third album, produced by Phil Ramone.

Preferring to concentrate on his burgeoning carer as songwriter (he was to achieve major success under tutelage of Quincy Jones(▶), notably with Michael Jackson, George

Benson, Aretha Franklin and Herbie Hancock, as well as continuing to write for Heatwave), Rod Temperton left band in 1977, as did Roy Carter. Former Fatback Band member Calvin Duke and Keith Harrison were brought in.

A car accident once again tragically marred Heatwave's progress when, in 1979, Johnnie Wilder was involved in crash which left him paralysed from neck down. Fighting back with incredible bravery, and with help of specially designed wheelchair with wide variety of functions controlled by facial movements, he has continued in band. He still produces their records, singing on studio dates and directing their stage shows from the wings, though British-born J. D. Nicholas assumes Wilder's stage role.

Vocals on fourth Heatwave album, **Candles,** were shared by the Wilder brothers and Nicholas; five of the songs were written by Rod Temperton.

Current line-up: Johnnie Wilder; Keith Wilder; Berger; Keith Bramble, bass; Billy Jones, guitar; Calvin Duke, keyboards; Keith Harrison, guitar; J. D. Nicholas, vocals.

Hit Singles:

	US	UK
Boogie Nights, 1977	2	2
Too Hot To Handle/Slip Your Disc To This, 1977	—	15
The Groove Line, 1978	7	12
Always And Forever, 1978	18	—
Mind Blowing Decisions, 1978	—	12
Always And Forever/Mind Blowing Decisions, 1978	—	9
Gangsters Of The Groove, 1981	—	19

Albums:
Too Hot To Handle (Epic/GTO), 1976
Central Heating (Epic/GTO), 1977
Hot Property (Epic/GTO), 1978
Candles (Epic/GTOO), 1981
Current (Epic), 1982

Jimi Hendrix

US guitarist/vocalist.
Born Johnny Allen Hendrix (name changed to James Marshall Hendrix in 1946), Seattle, Washington, November 27, 1942; died September 18, 1970.

Career: The most legendary guitarist in rock music, Jimi Hendrix spent early years, following military service, as back-up musician for R&B luminaries B.B. King(▶), Ike and Tina Turner(▶), Solomon Burke, Jackie Wilson, Tommy Tucker, Sam Cooke(▶), Little Richard(▶), Wilson Pickett(▶), the Isley Brothers(▶) and King Curtis(▶).

Settling in New York, Hendrix was heard playing in club by then girlfriend of Rolling Stone(▶) Keith Richard who persuaded former Animals'(▶) bass player turned manager, Chas Chandler, to check him out. Chandler decided to forgo own playing career and sold his bass guitars to buy equipment for Hendrix. He took the young black musician to London and embarked on major publicity campaign, bringing the Beatles(▶), Pete Townshend(▶) and Eric Clapton(▶) to 'in' clubs to see Hendrix's outrageously flashy performances.

A master showman, Hendrix exploited tricks learned from watching T. Bone Walker, Johnny Guitar Watson and other relatively unknown black American musicians, playing the guitar behind his neck or with his teeth, and experimenting with a whole new range of sound effects on his Fender Stratocaster. Polydor Records rushed to sign him and debut single **Hey Joe** stormed UK charts. In 1967 Hendrix debuted in his own country at the Monterey Pop Festival. His guitar-burning act (preserved in film 'Monterey Pop') left the audience stunned.

Switching to associated Track label, Hendrix had further single success before becoming major album artist, reaching zenith of commercial success and artistic creativity in 1968 with classic **Axis Bold As Love** and **Electric Ladyland** LPs. (In the studio, session man Alan Douglas added to Hendrix's basic tracks and was later responsible for **Crash Landing**, **Midnight Lightning** and **I Go To The Universe**, released, like the vast majority of Hendrix LPs, after his death.)

Experience, Jimi Hendrix soundtrack album. Courtesy Ember Records. Hendrix's act was almost as visual as aural.

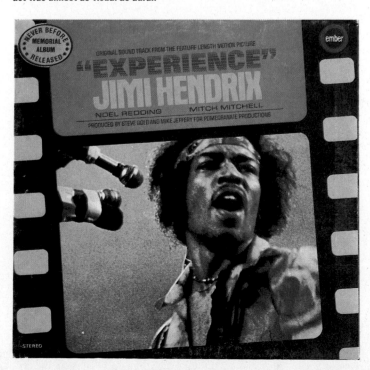

After masterful appearance at Woodstock in August 1969, the Jimi Hendrix Experience (British musicians Noel Redding (bass); Mitch Mitchell (drums)) broke up amid welter of personal and business problems, as well as drug-linked difficulties with the authorities. Mostly, however, Hendrix felt cornered by the style of music.

Under some pressure from Black Power movement in US, Hendrix decided to form Band Of Gypsys (Billy Cox, bass; Buddy Miles, drums) but despite phenomenal powers as concert draw band was short-lived, Hendrix walking out on 19,000 fans in middle of second number at Madison Square Garden gig in January 1970. That summer Hendrix played to nearly a quarter of a million people at the Isle Of Wight Festival, his last major concert and one which met with poor response from critics.

Three years of incredibly hard touring, recording and drink and drug abuse took their toll and on September 18, 1970, Hendrix was found dead in his London flat, suffocated by his own vomit.

Rainbow Bridge (soundtrack LP) Jimi Hendrix. Courtesy Reprise Records.

At times verging on the totally self-indulgent, Hendrix's guitar work nevertheless showed touch of sheer genius, opening up new musical horizons for a generation of rock musicians, while his vocals, despite their limited scope, oozed raw power.

Without a doubt Hendrix remains one of the most influential and popular artists in rock, as evidenced by the vast catalogue of his work still available.

Guitar: Fender Stratocaster.

Hit Singles:

	US	UK
Hey Joe, 1967	—	6
Purple Haze, 1967	—	3
The Wind Cries Mary, 1967	—	6
Burning Of The Midnight Lamp, 1967	—	18
All Along The Watchtower, 1968	20	5
Voodoo Chile, 1970	—	1

Albums:

Are You Experienced (Reprise/Polydor), 1967
Axis—Bold As Love (Reprise/Polydor), 1967
Smash Hits (Reprise/Polydor), 1968
Electric Ladyland (Reprise/Polydor), 1968
Electric Ladyland 2 (—/Polydor), 1968
Band Of Gypsys (Capitol/Polydor), 1970
Monterey (one side only; other side featured Otis Redding) (Reprise), 1970
Cry Of Love (Reprise/Polydor), 1971
Rainbow Bridge (soundtrack) (Reprise), 1971
Isle Of Wight (—/Polydor), 1971
Eternal Fire Of (—/Hallmark), 1971
Experience (soundtrack) (Mode/Bulldog), 1971
Friends From The Beginning (with Little Richard) (—/Bulldog), 1971
In The West (Reprise/Polydor), 1972
Jimi Hendrix (—/Polydor), 1973
Loose Ends (—/Polydor), 1973
Jimi Hendrix Volume 1 (—/Pan), 1973
Jimi Hendrix Volume 2 (—/Pan), 1973
Jimi Hendrix Volume 3 (—/Pan), 1973
War Heroes (Reprise/Polydor), 1973
The Wild One (with Curtis Knight) (—/Hallmark), 1973
Crash Landing (Reprise/Polydor), 1975
Rare Hendrix (Explosive/Enterprise), 1975
Jimi Hendrix 2 (—/Polydor), 1975
Midnight Lightning (Reprise/Polydor), 1976
For Real (—/DJM), 1976
The Essential (Reprise/Polydor), 1978
The Essential Volume 2 (Reprise/Polydor), 1978
More Experience (—/Bulldog), 1979
Recordings From Jimi (—/Reprise), 1979
20 Pieces Of Jimi Hendrix (—/Bulldog), 1979
10th Anniversary Box (—/Polydor), 1980
9 To The Universe (Warner Bros/Polydor), 1980
Woke Up This Morning And Found Myself Dead (Red Lightnin'), 1980*
Hendrix '66 (—/President), 1980
Free Spirit (Accord/Phoenix), 1981
Cosmic Turnaround (—/AFE), 1981
Cosmic Feeling (Accord/—), 1982
The Jimi Hendrix Concerts (Reprise/CBS), 1982
Moods (—/Phoenix), 1982
Roots Of (—/Phoenix), 1982
Voodoo Chile (—/Polydor), 1982
20 Golden Pieces Of, Volume 2 (—/Bulldog), 1982
The Singles Album (—/Polydor), 1983

*Jam with Jim Morrison

Herman's Hermits

UK group formed 1963.

Original/Final line-up: Peter Noone, vocals; Keith Hopwood, guitar; Derek Leckenby, guitar; Karl Green, bass; Barry Whitwarm, drums.

Career: with his little-boy looks, wide grin and big shiny teeth, Peter Noone (born November 5, 1947) was prototype for Donny Osmond(▶), David Cassidy and other teeny-bopper pin-ups to come. Producer Mickie Most saw Noone's appearance as actor in massively popular 'Coronation Street' TV soap opera series and decided Noone's was to be the face of 1964.

Group had been formed a year earlier as

Above: Peter Noone, who came to fame as Herman, leader of the Hermits, but later reverted to his real name.

the Heartbeats; Most changed Noone's name to Herman and effectively projected him as front-man. Indeed, the Hermits didn't even play on most of their records (**Mrs Brown You've Got A Lovely Daughter, I'm Into Something Good** and **I'm Henry The VIII I Am** being exceptions). Instead he used such luminaries as Big Jim Sullivan and, later, Led Zeppelin(▶) founders Jimmy Page and John Paul Jones (Jones also did all the arranging).

Debut single **I'm Into Something Good** (1964) went to UK No. 1 and made low-key breakthrough in US where they eventually became far more popular than in home market.

Despite 10 entries in UK Top 20 in just three years, Herman's Hermits had unobtrusive image there, and records made more impact than group. In America, however, Herman's return to clean-cut polite boy-next-door image of early Beatles days (while most British acts of era were into brash, rebellious R&B mould of Stones(▶), the Who(▶), et al) was a relief to parents, and just what American media were looking for. **Mrs Brown** and **I'm Henry The VIII** both sailed to No. 1 while Herman became TV and magazine personality of first order.

By 1967 American bubble had burst and title of US Top 20 entry **There's A Kind Of Hush** proved prophetic. However, UK hits continued before Noone went solo in 1970 (using real name).

He rejoined group briefly in 1973 for Richard Nader's English Invasion Revival tour while Hermits remained in America purveying their lightweight, happy style of innocuous pop. In 1979 Noone formed band the Tremblers (Noone, vocals, guitar, piano, bass; Gregg Inhofer, keyboards, guitar, vocals; Robert Williams, drums; George Williams, drums; George Connor, guitar, vocals; Mark Browne, bass) and in 1980 they recorded **Twice Nightly** LP. In 1983, Noone starred in new hit musical version of 'The Pirates Of Penzance'.

Hit Singles:

	US	UK
I'm Into Something Good, 1964	13	1
Show Me Girl, 1964	—	19
Can't You Hear My Heart Beat, 1965	—	2
Silhouettes, 1965	5	3
Mrs Brown You've Got A Lovely Daughter, 1965	1	—
Wonderful World, 1965	4	7
I'm Henry The VIII I Am, 1965	1	—
Just A Little Bit Better, 1965	7	15
A Must To Avoid, 1965	8	6
Listen People, 1966	3	—
You Won't Be Leaving, 1966	—	20
Leaning On The Lamp Post, 1966	9	—
This Door Swings Both Ways, 1966	12	18
No Milk Today, 1966	35	7
Dandy, 1966	5	—
There's A Kind Of Hush, 1967	4	7
Don't Go Out Into The Rain (You're Going To Melt), 1967	18	
I Can Take Or Leave Your Loving, 1968	22	11
Sleepy Joe, 1968	—	12
Sunshine Girl, 1968	—	8
Something's Happening, 1968	—	6
My Sentimental Friend, 1969	—	2
Years May Come, Years May Go, 1970		7
Lady Barbara, 1970	—	13

Peter Noone solo:

	US	UK
Oh You Pretty Thing, 1971	—	12

Albums:

Greatest Hits (Abcko/—), 1973
20 Greatest Hits (—/K-Tel), 1977

Steve Hillage

UK guitarist, composer, producer.
Born August 2, 1951.

Career: While at University of Kent in 1970, Hillage fell in with crowd that later became Gong, Caravan, Henry Cow, and Hatfield and the North. They encouraged him to return to musical career, having already recorded 1969 album **Arzachal** on Uriel label. He formed Khan and played lead guitar on 1971 **Space Shanties**. He then did session work, notably as guest guitarist on Kevin Ayers' **Bananamour**.

While touring with Ayers in France, Hillage jammed with Gong and switched bands. His role in Gong grew over their first three albums and by end of third he was preparing first solo album. **Fish Rising** came out in 1975 and represents rather eclectic approach, some songs going back to never recorded Khan album. Not generally known is fact that Hillage also appeared on Gong's fourth LP **Shamal**.

Hillage's interest in production came to the fore when he asked Todd Rundgren(▶) to produce next album. **L** was excellent progressive rock LP but 1976 was not year for such efforts. **Motivation Radio** and **Green** introduced spacy funk rhythm to Hillage's music. Between tours, Hillage recorded **Live Herald, Rainbow Dome Musick** and **Open**.

In 1980 Hillage took break from recording career. He picked up production experience with newer musicians such as Ken Lockie, Positive Noise and Simple Minds. He also began spending extensive time on personal computers. His return to recording in 1983 reflected this new pursuit with computer jargon title, **For To Next/And Not Or**.

Hillage is extremely gifted musician who fits in esoteric category labelled: 'Not For Use By The General Public'. His free-form music often goes far beyond the bounds of traditional rock or changing styles. He will be a musical force for long time to come.

Guitar: Fender Stratocaster.

Albums:

Fish Rising (Virgin), 1975
L (Atlantic/Virgin), 1976
Motivation Radio (Virgin), 1977
Green (Virgin), 1978
Live Herald (Virgin), 1979
Rainbow Dome Musick (Virgin), 1979
Open (Virgin), 1979
For To Next/And Not Or (Virgin), 1983

With Gong

Flying Teapot (—/Virgin), 1973
Angel's Egg (Virgin), 1973
You (Virgin), 1974

Worth Searching Out:

Arzachal (Uriel), 1969
Space Shanties (with Khan) (—/Dream), 1971
Bananamour (with Kevin Ayers) (Sire/Harvest), 1972

Holland/Dozier/Holland

US songwriters, producers, vocalists.
Eddie Holland born Detroit, October 30, 1939.
Lamont Dozier born Detroit, June 16, 1941.
Brian Holland born Detroit, February 15, 1941.

Career: One of Motown Records' most prodigious songwriting/production teams during golden era of 'the Detroit Sound' in mid-to-late-'60s, Trio went on to launch own short-lived but highly successful Invictus/Hot Wax operation which brought stardom to Freda Payne, Honey Cone, Chairmen Of The Board, Laura Lee and other Detroit-based soul acts. They also enjoyed some success with own solo efforts, starting off with Eddie Holland's 1962 Motown hit **Jamie**.

Eddie had dropped out of college to sing demos of Berry Gordy compositions and write. Gordy signed him as artist and leased early efforts to United Artists before forming Tamla Motown and switching Eddie to new company. After eight singles and three minor hits, Eddie teamed with brother Brian and Lamont Dozier to form highly potent team which from 1962 on enjoyed run of hits with the Supremes(▶), the Temptations(▶), the Four Tops(▶), Marvin Gaye(▶), the Isley Brothers(▶), Martha and the Vandellas and others to establish Motown as *the* major black record company.

Dozier had made first records as member of Romeos (on Fox) in 1956 at 15, marrying and moving to New York when group split. Back in Detroit in 1958, he met Berry Gordy and was signed to Anna Records, recording as Lamont Anthony on Anna and Melody with no real success. Brian Holland had been co-producing for Gordy with Robert Bateman (they scored with Marvelettes' **Please Mr Postman** in 1961). When Bateman left company, Dozier and Brian Holland were teamed to write and produce, being joined within months by Eddie Holland.

In 1968, Holland/Dozier/Holland were part of what became a somewhat general exodus from Motown which denuded label of several of its major artists and production teams. A lawsuit alleging breach of contract was settled out of court and Invictus/Hot Wax, backed by Columbia money, took full flight gaining first chart-topper with Honey Cone's **Want Ads** (1971).

Brian and Lamont recorded duets with success in 1972-3 but Lamont then left the brothers to pursue a solo recording career with ABC with help from Four Tops who had earlier joined that company from Motown.

Lamont Dozier's subsequent albums have met much critical acclaim if only minor success.

Hit Singles:

	US	UK
Lamont Dozier:		
Trying to Hold On To My Woman, 1974	15	—

Albums:

Lamont Dozier:

Out Here On My Own (ABC), 1974
Peddlin' Music On The Side (Warner Bros/—), 1975
Right There (Warner Bros), 1976
Bitter Sweet (Warner Bros), 1979

The Hollies

UK group formed 1962.
Original line-up: Allan Clarke, vocals; Tony Hicks, vocals, guitar; Graham Nash, vocals, guitar; Eric Haydock, bass; Don Rathbone, drums.

Career: Formed from members of two other Manchester groups, the Deltas and the Dolphins (Rathbone was almost immediately replaced by Bobby Elliot), like many British beat groups they took early material from US R&B catalogue. First two singles were covers of Coasters(▶) hits, second of which, **Searchin'**, started long run of UK Top 20 hits.

Lacking positive image, band's appeal was based on Clarke's strong lead vocals, distinctive harmonies and excellent choice of single material. Most early material came from outside band, from top writers like Graham Gouldman, but by 1966 they were writing own songs with considerable success. **But Stop** reached American Top 5, and established group as regular US hitmakers.

In 1966 Haydock left to be replaced by former Dolphins bass player Bernie Calvert. As 'psychedelic' era dawned, problems over musical direction arose. While band were still massive singles sellers, they were unable to break LP market despite making several interesting albums at this time (**Evolution** and **Butterfly** are both worth a listen).

Disillusioned by band's failure to compete with newer, critically rated album bands, Graham Nash left in 1968 to join forces with David Crosby and Stephen Stills to form Crosby, Still and Nash(▶). Former Swinging Blue Jeans Terry Sylvester replaced Nash; hits continued, although American success tailed off.

By 1971, band had reached something of a plateau; single releases were only moderately successful. Clarke left to pursue solo career. Replacement was Swedish singer Michael Rickfors. In 1972, however, single recorded with Clarke as lead singer, **Long Cool Woman In A Black Dress**, make No.1 spot in America (although strangely only 32 in UK). Rickfors was ousted and Clarke rejoined band, which signed new contract with Polydor. Band's last major hit was **The Air That I Breathe**.

Band continued to record throughout '70s, however, and found lucrative niche on cabaret circuit. In late 1981 **Holliedaze**, a single combining old hits in segued disco style, was minor hit in UK.

One of the longest-lasting pop-orientated British band, the Hollies can still turn in creditable performance, and given the right material, could still be chart force. As purveyors of finely crafted, memorable singles they probably have a more secure place in pop history than many of the more pretentious 'artists' they strove to emulate in late '60s.

Current line-up: Clarke; Hicks; Terry Sylvester, guitar, vocals; Bernie Calvert, bass; Bobby Elliot, drums.

Hit Singles:

	US	UK
Searchin', 1963	—	12
Stay, 1963	—	8
Just One Look, 1964	—	2
Here I Go Again, 1964	—	4
We're Through, 1964	—	7
Yes I Will, 1965	—	9
I'm Alive, 1965	—	1
Look Through Any Window, 1965	32	4
If I Needed Someone, 1965	—	20
I Can't Let Go, 1966	42	2
Bus Stop, 1966	5	5
Stop Stop Stop, 1966	7	2
On A Carousel, 1967	11	4
Carrie-Anne, 1967	9	3
King Midas In Reverse, 1967	51	18
Jennifer Eccles, 1968	40	7
Listen To Me, 1968	—	11
Sorry Suzanne, 1969	56	3
He Ain't Heavy He's My Brother, 1969	7	3
I Can't Tell The Bottom From The Top, 1970	—	7
Gasoline Alley Bred, 1970	—	14
The Air That I Breathe, 1974	6	2

Hollies' Greatest, The Hollies. Courtesy Parlophone Records.

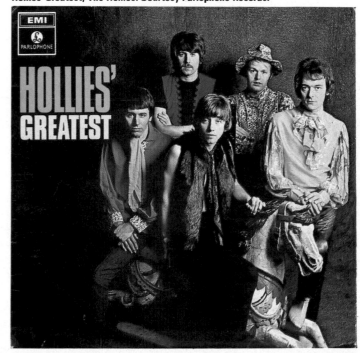

The Complete Buddy Holly (6 LP boxed set), one of the most comprehensive collections ever released on record. Courtesy MCA Records.

Albums:
Hollies' Greatest (Capitol/Parlophone), 1968
Sing Dylan (Epic/Parlophone), 1969
Stop Stop Stop (Imperial/Starline), 1971
Greatest Hits (Epic/Polydor), 1974
I Can't Let Go (—/MFP), 1974
Another Night (Epic/Polydor), 1975
The Best Of The Hollies EPs (—/Nut), 1975
Russian Roulette (—/Polydor), 1976
Live Hits (—/Polydor), 1977
A Crazy Steal (—/Polydor), 1978
20 Golden Greats (—/EMI), 1978
Long Cool Woman In A Black Dress (—/MFP), 1979
Five Three One-Double Seven O Four (—/Polydor), 1979
Sing Buddy Holly (—/Polydor), 1980

Buddy Holly

US vocalist, guitarist, composer.
Born Charles Hardin Holley, Lubbock, Texas, September 7, 1936. Died Feb. 3, 1959.

Career: During 1954-55 appeared on home-town radio station KDA, with partner Bob Montgomery. Played on package shows visiting towns who used local talent as warm-up acts to major artists. Spotted by Nashville talent scout on show headlined by Bill Haley(▶) and signed as solo to Decca Records. Early recordings for label showed promise but failed commercially.

Dissatisfaction with company and producers encouraged Holly to record independently at Norman Petty's Clovis, New Mexico, studio. Master of **That'll Be The Day** made there subsequently sold to New York subsidiaries of Decca where group recordings as the Crickets (Joe B. Mauldin, bass; Niki Sullivan, guitar (replaced by Tommy Allsop in 1959); Jerry Allison, drums) were released on Brunswick; Holly's solo efforts appeared on Coral. Resulting hits gave Holly dual career strengthened by own writing talents and those of Crickets, notably Allison.

Several US package tours and short visit to Australia preceded tour of UK in March 1958. Many UK musicians were impressed with his guitar style and then unknown Fender Strato-caster which, together with horn-rimmed glasses, became Holly's trademark.

Management problems and move to New York following marriage to Maria Elena Santiago in 1958 forced split with Crickets (who went on to record many more LPs without Holly). Recorded trendsetting session with Dick Jacobs Orchestra in New York and planned to record with Ray Charles(▶) Band. Produced Waylon Jennings' first single in 1958 and co-produced Lou Giordano with Phil Everly(▶).

Royalty disputes and lack of funds forced Holly into uncomfortable ballroom tour through frozen Mid-West states during early 1959. Halfway through tour chartered small plane with Ritchie Valens(▶) and Big Bopper to escape discomfort of tour buses. All three killed when plane crashed into snow-covered field.

Single coupling **It Doesn't Matter Anymore** and **Raining In My Heart** from orchestral session soon became biggest solo hit. Holly disappeared from US charts but had many further hits in UK helped by fanatical followers. Many posthumous releases were primitive demos enhanced by overdubbing under direction of Norman Petty.

Holly's influence is acknowledged by many artists, and his compositions are still extensively recorded.

Guitar: Fender Stratocaster.

Hit Singles:

	US	UK
That'll Be The Day*, 1957	1	1
Peggy Sue, 1957	3	6
Listen To Me, 1958	—	16
Oh Boy*, 1958	10	3
Maybe Baby*, 1958	17	4
Rave On, 1958	37	5
Think It Over*, 1958	27	11
Early In The Morning, 1958	32	17
It Doesn't Matter Anymore, 1959	13	1
Peggy Sue Got Married, 1959	—	13
Baby I Don't Care, 1961	—	12
Reminiscing, 1962	—	17
Brown Eyed Handsome Man, 1963	—	3
Bo Diddley, 1963	—	4
Wishing, 1963	—	10
*With Crickets		

Crickets:

Don't Ever Change, 1962	—	5
My Little Girl, 1963	—	17

Albums:
Buddy Holly (MCA), 1958
The Chirping Crickets (MCA), 1958
Legend (MCA), 1974
Greatest Hits (MCA), 1974
The Nashville Sessions (MCA), 1975
20 Golden Greats (MCA), 1978
The Complete Buddy Holly* (MCA), 1979
Love Songs (MCA), 1981
For The First Time Anywhere (MCA). 1983
*6 LP box set

John Lee Hooker

US vocalist, guitarist.
Born Clarksdale, Mississippi, August 22, 1917.

Career: John Lee Hooker worked with Robert Nighthawk and other Memphis blues luminaries before moving to Detroit in 1943 to work in car factories.

His first recording session for Modern (originally on local Sensation label) in 1948 produced the compulsively rocking **Boogie Chillun** and the million-selling **I'm In The Mood** (the echo effect being achieved by placing a microphone inside a toilet bowl!).

In 1952, while working as radio DJ, Hooker was signed by Vee-Jay, under which label released much of his finest work including **Dimples**, a minor UK hit in 1964, **Boom Boom** and **San Francisco** (featuring fellow Detroit act Martha and the Vandellas on back-up vocals).

Chess, King, De Luxe, Chance, Liberty, Stax, Probe, ABC, Tomato and MCA have all recorded Hooker and he cut for others under assumed names; because of Hooker's prolific recording output, record companies thought he would saturate market, so he used the names John Lee Hooker (on Chance), Birmingham Sam (on Regent), Texas Slim (on King) and Johnny Williams (on Staff). While best known for hard-rocking urban R&B items, he has been most creative with often spine-chilling blues ballads straight from the Deep South rural tradition. Hooker influenced many R&B based bands of the early '60s including the Animals(▶), the Who(▶), the Small Faces(▶), the Yardbirds(▶) and Canned

Below: Legendary bluesman John Lee Hooker onstage in Britain (1982), where he remains revered.

Heat, whom Hooker recorded **Hooker 'n' Heat** with.

In 1982 Hooker visited UK on same bill as Bobby Bland and B. B. King and proved a sensation, his playing and singing remaining as incisive as ever.

Albums (selected):
Folklore Of John Lee Hooker (Vee-Jay/Joy), 1962
Big Soul Of John Lee Hooker (Vee-Jay/Joy), 1964
No Friend Around (—/Red Lightning), 1970
Best Of (Vee-Jay/Joy), 1974
This Is Hip (Charly), 1980
Tantalising With The Blues (MCA), 1982

Hot Chocolate

UK group formed 1970
Original line-up: Errol Brown, vocals; Patrick Olive, bass; Larry Ferguson, keyboards; Harvey Hinsley, guitar.

Career: Essentially a singles' band, Hot Chocolate have been consistent hitmakers for the past decade, testimony both to their own abilities and the astute masterminding of their career by producer Mickie Most, owner of Rak Records.

Formed by Errol Brown in 1970, Hot Chocolate broke into recording with short-lived deal with the Beatles'(▶) Apple label for which they recorded version of John Lennon's(▶) **Give Peace A Chance.** Immediately afterwards they switched to Rak. First release, **Love Is Life,** made No.6 in UK.

Connor, who had previously been with Audience for three years, joined group in 1973. Tony Wilson, who played bass, sang and wrote most of the early material with Brown; left in 1975 to become the first British signing for Albert Grossman's Bearsville label.

US band Stories covered Hot Chocolate's(▶) **Brother Louie,** a clever story song about mixed marriage, and took it to top of American charts, paving way for Hot Chocolate's own Stateside success with **Emma** (1974).

With their heavy concentration on singles' market, group's first album, **Cicero Park**, did not appear until 1974.

Groups' continuing success has yielded such hits as **You Sexy Thing**, **So You Win Again**, **Every 1's A Winner** and the ballad **I'll Put You Together Again**, each song marked by an attractive melody, perceptive lyrics and Brown's highly distinctive vocal stylings which cut across usual barriers of black music and pure pop.

Current line-up: Brown; Ferguson; Hinsley; Olive; Tony Connor, drums.

Hit Singles:

	US	UK
Love Is Life, 1970	—	6
I Believe (In Love), 1971	—	8
Brother Louie, 1973	—	7
Emma, 1974	8	3
Disco Queen, 1975	28	11
A Child's Prayer, 1975	—	7
You Sexy Thing, 1975	3	2
Don't Stop It Now, 1976	42	11
Man To Man, 1976	—	14
So You Win Again, 1977	31	1
Put Your Love In Me, 1977	—	10
Every 1's A Winner, 1978	6	12
I'll Put You Back Together Again, 1978	—	13
No Doubt About It, 1980	—	2
Are You Getting Enough Of What Makes You Happy, 1980	—	17
Girl Crazy, 1982	—	7
It Started With A Kiss, 1982	—	5

Albums:
Cicero Park (—/Rak), 1974
Hot Chocolate (—/Rak), 1975
Man To Man (—/Rak), 1976
Greatest Hits (—/Rak), 1976
Everyone's A Winner (Infinity/Rak, 1978
Going Through The Motions (Infinity/Rak), 1979
Twenty Hottest Hits (—/Rak-EMI), 1979
Mystery (—/Rak), 1982

Howlin' Wolf

US vocalist, composer, guitarist, harmonica player.
Born Chester Arthur Burnett, Aberdeen, Mississippi, June 10, 1910; died January 10, 1976.

Career: Grew up around Mississippi and Arkansas making living initially as farmer. Learned to play guitar from legendary Charley Patton in 1928; began touring area as musician, building reputation for dynamic performance. Met Sonny Boy Williamson II (Rice Miller) from whom he learned harmonica.

By 1948 Wolf had moved to West Memphis, Arkansas; established own band playing electric guitar, with guys like Pat Hare, Matt Murphy, Junior Parker, Willie Johnson and Willie Steele as sidemen. Gained regular radio spot on KWEM in Memphis; interest resulted in recordings supervised by Ike Turner at Sun Records Studios in Memphis. Some released on Sun label, some leased to Modern Records in California, and some to Chess in Chicago, where **How Many More Years** hit R&B Top 10 in 1952. Earned

'**Live And Cookin''**, Howlin' Wolf.
Courtesy Chess Records.

nickname Howlin' Wolf for gutteral falsetto vocal effects.

Around 1953 Wolf moved north to Chicago; signed with Chess and gathered talented band, including Hubert Sumlin (guitar) and various rhythm players like Fred Below, Earl Phillips (drums), Otis Spann and Hosea Lee Kennard (piano). By 1956 was major force in Chicago blues, charting another R&B Top 10 with now classic **Smokestack Lightning** (later a UK Top 50 pop entry in 1964). **Smokestack** was an intense, rumbling blues showcase for 'howling' vocal pushed by hypnotic rhythm riff and punctuated by sombre harp.

Howlin' Wolf. Courtesy Chess Records.

Howlin' Wolf was a massive man, 6 feet 3 inches tall and weighing over 270 pounds, but surprisingly agile and animated on stage.

1954-1964 brought profusion of discs, many songs becoming blues standards. Wrote much of his own material, but also made good use of Willie Dixon's composing talents; songs like **Spoonful**, **Back Door Man**, **Red Rooster**, **Wang Dang Doodle**, **Evil**, **Killing Floor** and **Tail Dragger** have become staple diet on disc and in live shows for numerous blues and rock bands in recent years.

Somehow Wolf managed to transcend passage of time; his later Chess sides were not dissimilar to those of 20 years ago. Chess wanted to move with the times, however, and attempted to record some blues acts in contemporary electric fashion in late '60s Wolf was so dismayed at result of his session

that he described LP as 'dogshit'; released on Cadet Concept label, it actually yielded small R&B hit single **Evil**. Trip to London in 1972 resulted in album with English sessioneers and sidemen like Eric Clapton(▶), Ringo Starr(▶) and Steve Winwood(▶). Health was failing, however, and Wolf suffered heart-attacks. Then in 1973 car-smash he was badly injured and sustained kidney damage. Continued performing after release from hospital but was obliged to ration activities. Howlin' Wolf died in January 1976 from kidney failure. His memory and influence are indelibly inscribed on many modern musicians, particularly R&B-influenced bands of the early '60s.

Albums (selected):
London Sessions (Chess/Rolling Stones), 1971
Going Back Home (Syndicate), 1979
Legendary Sun Performers (—/Sun), 1978

With Little Milton:
Sam's Blues (—/Charly), 1976

Worth Searching Out:
A.K.A. Chester Burnett (Chess), 1971

Human League

UK group formed 1977.

Original line-up: Philip Oakey, vocals; Ian Craig Marsh, synthesisers; Martyn Ware, synthesisers; Adrian Wright, visual director, synthesisers.

Career: Computer operators Marsh and Ware and hospital porter Oakey made up original nucleus of band, formed in Sheffield to explore possibilities of electronic music. Wright joined slightly later.

Almost immediately band began to gain reputation for innovation; first single **Electronically Yours** was released in June 1978 on independent Fast label. Following exposure on Siouxsie and Banshees(▶) tour, band was signed to Virgin in April 1979. First album **Reproduction** released in late 1979.

Below: The Human League, with leader Phil Oakey (second left), who sprang to fame in 1981.

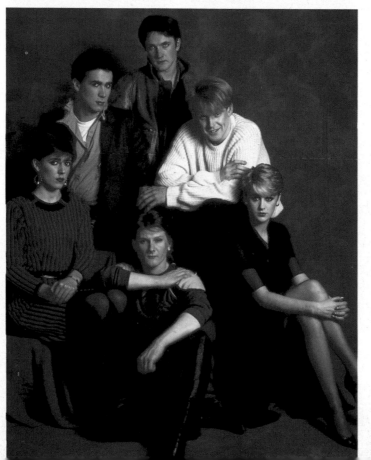

Dare, The Human League. Courtesy Virgin Records.

Boys And Girls at beginning of 1981. That year saw band go from strength to strength, with addition of guitarist Jo Callis (ex-Rezillos). Huge breakthrough came with single **Don't You Want Me** and album **Dare**. Both topped UK charts, and at beginning of 1982 repeated feat in territories all around world, most notably in US.

Since that time, there has been no stopping band; Human League have established themselves as stylish electronic pop outfit that can combine irresistibly catchy tunes with lyrics of above average intelligence. Oakey and the two girls provide striking and increasingly sophisticated visual image.

Current line-up: Oakey; Wright; Ian Burden, synthesisers; Jo Callis, guitar; Joanne Catherall, vocals; Susanne Sulley, vocals.

Hit Singles:

	US	UK
The Sound Of The Crowd, 1981	—	12
Love Action (I Believe In Love), 1981	—	3
Open Your Heart, 1981	—	6
Don't You Want Me, 1981	1	1
Being Boiled, 1982	—	6
Mirror Man, 1982	—	2
Fascination, 1983	8	2

Albums:
Reproduction (—/Virgin), 1979
Travelogue (—/Virgin), 1980
Dare (A&M/Virgin), 1981

Humble Pie

UK group formed 1969.

Original line-up: Peter Frampton, guitar, vocals; Steve Marriot, guitar, vocals; Greg Ridley, bass, vocals; Jerry Shirley, drums.

Career: Began in blaze of publicity as late '60s supergroup with Frampton(▶), 'the face of '68', from the Herd, and Marriot from the fashionable Small Faces(▶). Ridley (ex-Spooky Tooth) provided underground musical credibility to offset hype.

Arduous rehearsals at Marriot's house preceded release of first album, **As Safe As Yesterday,** on Small Faces' former label, Immediate. In spite of early Top 5 hit, **Natural Born Bugie,** Humble Pie were

1980 saw beginnings of chart success with low placings for **Holiday '80** and **Empire State Human**, but in autumn of that year band broke up; Ware and Marsh left to establish Heaven 17 and British Electric Foundation. Oakey and Wright took new direction, recruiting old friend (actually bass-player) Ian Burden to play synthesisers, and adding two girl dancers, Joanne Catherall and Susanne Sulley (spotted by Oakey in Sheffield disco).

The girls quickly became vocalists; new sound was featured on first Top 50 single plagued by 'supergroup' publicity and LPs failed to fulfill critics' expectations. Much hoped-for early US success did not materialise and following liquidation of Immediate, group almost folded, but eventually resurfaced on A&M, simultaneously acquiring services of manager Dee Anthony.

Through extensive gigging, group gradually enlarged following in States, and record sales increased with each successive release. Marriot slowly achieved greater control of unit, moving away from Frampton's somewhat lightweight material towards heavymetal sound. Policy proved commercially and aesthetically sound, with **Performance— Rockin' At The Fillmore** selling in vast quantities. Inevitably, Frampton quit to pursue lucrative solo career, replaced by more musically/socially compatible Dave 'Clem' Clempson from Colosseum.

Early '70s album **Smokin'** and live double **Eat It** revealed increasing move towards heavy rock. Group briefly experimented with soul during 1973, employing vocal trio the Blackbirds (Venetta Fields, Clydie King and Billie Barnum) for live revue.

With no new musical direction forthcoming, group gradually stagnated, in spite of some flattering gig reviews in States. Clempson quit to form Strange Brew, tolling death knell for Humble Pie, who finally broke up in July 1975. Marriot went on to form Steve Marriot All Stars, before involving himself in Small Faces reunion in 1978. Marriot then got involved in Humble Pie reunion with Bob Tench (guitar, vocals), Anthony Jones (bass, vocals) and Jerry Shirley (drums). This line-up released **On To Victory** LP in 1980.

Final line-up: Marriott; Ridley; Shirley; Dave Clempson, guitar.

Hit Singles:

	US	UK
Natural Born Bugie, 1969	—	4

Albums:
Humble Pie (A&M), 1970
Rock On (A&M), 1971
Performance—Rockin' At The Fillmore (A&M), 1971
Smokin' (A&M), 1972
Eat It (A&M), 1973
Thunderbox (A&M), 1974
Lost And Found (A&M/—), 1976
Back Home Again (—/Immediate), 1976

Ian Hunter

UK vocalist, composer, pianist, guitarist. Born Shewsbury, Shropshire, June 3, 1946.

Career: Established reputation as front man in Mott the Hoople, which he left dramatically in 1974, taking former Bowie(▶) guitarist Mick Ronson to form new group. Instead, solo careers ensued, with Ronson contributing to **Ian Hunter** —which included UK Top 20 single **Once Bitten Twice Shy**—in May 1975.

An impressive backing group comprising Hunter, Ronson, Jeff Appleby (bass), Dennis Elliot (drums) and Peter Arnesen (keyboards) was assembled for UK/US tour, but folded shortly afterwards (following Hunter's decision to reside permanently in upstate New York). Second album **All American Alien Boy** received critical acclaim but sales proved disappointing. In same year, literary credibility of sorts was gained in US with re-publication of Hunter's 1973 **Diary Of A Rock'n'Roll Star** retitled **Reflections Of A Rock'n'Roll Star.**

Hunter returned for long-awaited UK tour in May 1977 with backing group the Overnight Angels, comprising Earl Slick (guitar), Peter Oxendale (keyboards), Curly Smith (drums)

and Bob Rawlinson (bass, vocals). Album **Overnight Angels**, released to coincide with tour, ably displayed influence of US producer Roy Thomas Baker. Bad UK sales prompted Columbia to forego US release, and Hunter was soon dropped from label.

Returned to US for 18 months venturing out to produce Generation X's second album. Fraternisation with various members of British New Wave (on whom he was major influence) inspired his return to recording studio. Following move to Chrysalis, Hunter has attempted more contemporary sound with some success. **You're Never Alone With A Schizophrenic** included John Cale and Ellen Foley among credits, while **Short Back 'n' Sides** revealed number of different styles, with contributions from Todd Rundgren(▶) and the Clash's(▶) Topper Headon and Mick Jones. Hardly a classic solo career, but albums show continued determination to avoid extinction.

Hit Single:

	US	UK
Once Bitten Twice Shy, 1975	—	14

Albums:
Ian Hunter (Columbia/CBS), 1975
All American Alien Boy (Columbia/CBS), 1976
Overnight Angels (Columbia/CBS), 1977
Shades Of Ian Hunter (Columbia/CBS), 1980*
You're Never Alone With A Schizophrenic (Chrysalis), 1979
Welcome To The Club (Live) (Chrysalis), 1980
Short Back'n'Sides (Chrysalis), 1981
*Compilation of tracks from **Overnight Angels.**

Janis Ian

US vocalist, composer, guitarist, pianist. Born New York, April 7, 1951.

Career: At age 14 wrote **Society's Child,** dealing with racial discrimination, narrowness of educational system, parental pressure and hypocrisy. Released first as single, then included in first album **Janis Ian** which made charts in 1967. Sung in delicate, detached, almost alienated voice, it is often incorrectly assumed to be autobiographical. Based on observation, not experience, **Society's Child** was work of experienced songwriter; **Hair Of Spun Gold** (written at age 12½) was published in influential folk magazine 'Broadside'. Successful appearances at New York's Village Gate and Gaslight preceded first record.

Although beginning in Baez(▶)/Seeger(▶) folk tradition, even early albums used guitar, bass, organ, harpsichord and drums, including Richie Havens(▶) as drummer on **The Secret Life Of J. Eddy Fink** (1668). Critical enthusiasm waned until **Stars** in 1974, which once again added brilliance to skill and indicated new maturity. Title song has been recorded by Cher, Glen Campbell(▶) and Mel Torme, and **Jesse** was included on Joan Baez'(▶) **Diamonds And Rust.** Development confirmed by **Between The Lines** (1975) from which double-Grammy winner **At Seventeen** was US No. 1 single, going platinum in US and Japan. Renewed success, including Roberta Flack's(▶) version of **Jesse** which reached Top 10, led to 1976 re-issue of long-deleted early work.

Subsequent albums continued to show evidence of growing sophistication, incorporating jazz and blues into Ian's distinctive blend of vocals and instrumentation. **Night Rains** features theme songs used by films 'The Foxes' and 'The Bell Jar', and highlights include solos by E Street Band saxophonist Clarence Clemmons and piano duet shared by Ian and Chick Corea.

Unhappy with increasing dependence on complex instrumentation, Ian's recent songs

Above: Punk Godfather Iggy Pop, whose reputation and outrageous stage performances have so far outweighed his commercial appeal.

have been written to be performed by full band or simply with guitar or piano accompaniment. However, as recorded on 1981 **Restless Eyes,** backing musicians have been used to good effect.

Hit Singles:

	US	UK
Society's Child, 1967	14	—
At Seventeen, 1975	3	—

Albums:
Janis Ian (Polydor/Verve), 1967
Present Company (Capitol), 1971
Stars (Columbia/CBS), 1974
Between The Lines (Columbia/CBS), 1975
Aftertones (Columbia/CBS), 1975
Miracle Row (Columbia/CBS), 1977
Night Rains (Columbia/CBS), 1979
The Best Of (Columbia/CBS), 1980
Restless Eyes (Columbia/CBS), 1981

Icehouse

Australian group formed 1978.

Original line-up: Ira Davies, vocals, guitar; Keith Welsh, bass, vocals, keyboards; Anthony Smith, keyboards, vocals; John Lloyd, drums, vocals.

Career: Originally formed by Davies as the Flowers, who played cover versions of Roxy Music(▶), Bowie(▶), Kings, etc. Became major live attraction in Australia, touring with Elvis Costello(▶). Scored hits locally from 1980. That year saw release of first album **Icehouse** (band still known as the Flowers).

In mid-1981 signed worldwide deal with Chrysalis, but name change necessary as another act named Flowers had registered name in US, thus they became Icehouse. Group toured US (with slight chart success) and UK (to fierce anti-Australian backlash). After tour, Davies disbanded group, and embarked on solo career.

Primitive Man, Davies' solo LP, recorded in 1982 and mixed by Keith Forsey (associate of Giorgio Moroder). Meanwhile, video of **Icehouse** track from first LP provoked fresh UK interest, and Davies formed new group: John Lloyd (retained from previous line-up); Michael Hoste, keyboards (brought back from much earlier band incarnation; notable Australian musician Bob Kretshmer, guitar; Guy Pratt (ex-Killing Joke); Andy Qunta (ex-Hazel O'Connor(▶)). Pratt and Qunta both UK musicians.

Solo LP released to zero interest in UK, minor chart position in US. In early 1983, however, **Hey Little Girl** became Top 20 UK hit, partially due to impressive video directed by fellow Australian Russell Mulcahy, at which point **Primitive Man** LP, retitled **Love In Motion,** finally charted. Follow-up single **Street Cafe** became minor hit. At time when Australian acts are fashionable and successful, Icehouse are not yet among front runners, although Ira Davies' music has been likened to numerous more famous acts, including Roxy Music, Television and Japan(▶) major success may yet arrive.

Current line up: Davis; Bob Kretshmer, guitar; Michael Hoste, keyboards; Guy Pratt, bass; Andy Qunta, keyboards.

Hit Singles:

	US	UK
Hey Little Girl, 1983	—	17

Albums:
Icehouse (—/Chrysalis), 1981
Primitive Man (—/Chrysalis), 1982*
*Retitled **Love In Motion**

Iggy Pop

US vocalist, composer.
Born James Jewel Osterberg, Ann Arbor, Michigan, April 21, 1947.

Career: Iggy Pop is a rock icon of sorts; can justifiably be called 'grandfather' of punk. Fans and critics alike are polarised by Pop; one either loves him or hates him. His personality can only be truly appreciated on stage, where he routinely rants, screams, falls down, knocks into the musicians and invites— or commands—the audience to perform unnatural acts. Has been known to flail about so desperately that he ends show dripping with blood. Audiences often respond by hurling not just abuse, but beer bottles and anything else that's handy.

Osterberg named himself Iggy in early days in Detroit, when he performed with band called the Prime Movers. When he joined the infamous pre-punk band the Stooges (Ron Asheton, guitar; Dave Alexander, bass; Scott

Asheton, drums; Steve McKay, sax) became Iggy Stooge. Iggy and the Stooges were a band (and a philosophy) whose time had not yet come. Had moderate cult success, but lost inspiration and eventually fizzled out, leaving the albums **The Stooges** (1968), **Funhouse** (1969), and **Raw Power** (1973).

Iggy was rediscovered as an 'artist' by David Bowie(▶) in 1977. He changed his name symbolically to Iggy Pop, and toured with new mentor. This led to contract with RCA, for whom he recorded three albums in 1978. **The Idiot** and **Lust for Life** met with critical approval, but limited sales; switched to Arista in 1979, cutting two albums. Has most recently signed to Animal Records (Chris Stein's Blondie(▶) label).

Now a frequent and popular attraction on New York club scene, Iggy draws faithful and encouraging audiences wherever he goes.

Albums:
With Stooges:
The Stooges (Elektra), 1968
Funhouse (Elektra), 1969
Raw Power (Columbia/CBS), 1973
Metallic KO (Sky Dog/—), 1976

Iggy Solo:
The Idiot (RCA), 1976
TV Eye (RCA), 1978
Lust For Life (RCA), 1978
New Values (Arista), 1979
Soldier (Arista), 1979
No Fun (Elektra), 1980

Worth Searching Out:
With James Williamson:
Killer City (Radar), 1977

The Impressions

US vocal group formed 1958.
Original line-up: Jerry Butler, Curtis Mayfield, Sam Gooden, Fred Cash.

Career: The Impressions first won fame through lead voice of Jerry Butler but are best remembered as vehicle for softly understated falsetto soul vocals and highly perceptive songwriting of Curtis Mayfield(▶). Their roots lay in a Chatanooga, Tennessee group, the Roosters, which featured Gooden and Cash with brothers Richard and Arthur Brooks.

Big Sixteen, The Impressions. Courtesy EMI Records.

Gooden moved to Chicago in 1956 and Cash followed in 1958. Teaming with Butler and 14-year-old Mayfield to form the Impressions, they landed Vee-Jay contract. **For Your Precious Love** was massive debut hit but label credit to 'Jerry Butler and the Impressions' led to Butler launching highly successful solo career.

The Brooks brothers travelled North to join the Impressions, Richard Brooks sharing lead with Gooden on numerous unsuccessful recordings for Abner, Bandera and Swirl, while Mayfield concentrated on songwriting and playing guitar on Butler's solo records.

Down to a trio with departure of the Brooks, the Impressions signed to ABC Paramount in 1961, scoring immediately with New York-recorded, Mayfield-penned **Gypsy Woman** (a pop hit later for Brian Hyland).

Thanks to Johnny Pate's totally sympathetic orchestral arrangements, Mayfield's class as writer/lead singer, and group's overall sound, a string of successes followed to make them black music's premier vocal group till emergence of Temptations(▶).

For Your Precious Love, Impressions. Courtesy Charly Records.

It's All Right, **Keep On Pushing** and **People Get Ready** had underlying themes of social consciousness, while **You Must Believe Me** was a pure love song and **Amen** a gospel-inspired soul anthem. On switching to Mayfield's own newly-formed Curtom label in 1968, group concentrated increasingly on black awareness, in tune with mood of times, and **This Is My Country**, **Choice Of Colours** and **Mighty Mighty Spade And Whitey** were all classics of the idiom.

Mayfield left group in 1970 for solo recordings and commitment to running Curtom, but continued to mastermind the Impressions' work, calling in Leroy Hutson as his replacement.

Two years later, Hutson also went and Reggie Torrian and Ralph Johnson were recruited to join Gooden and Cash for **Three The Hard Way** film soundtrack.

In 1974, new line-up scored with **Finally Got Myself Together** and had big 1975 British hit with **First Impressions** but without Mayfield's involvement soon faded.

Current line-up: Gooden; Cash; Reggie Torrian; Ralph Johnson.

Hit Singles:

	US	UK
For Your Precious Love, 1958	11	—
Gypsy Woman, 1961	20	—
It's Alright, 1963	4	—
Talking About My Baby, 1964	12	—
I'm So Proud, 1964	14	—
Keep On Pushing, 1964	10	—
You Must Believe Me, 1964	15	—
Amen, 1964	7	—
People Get Ready, 1965	14	—
We're A Winner, 1968	14	—
Finally Got Myself Together (I'm A Changed Man), 1974	17	—
First Impressions, 1975	—	16

Albums:
Greatest Hits (MCA/—), 1965
Fan The Fire (20th Century), 1981
For Your Precious Love (—/Charly), 1981
In The Heat Of The Night (MCA/—), 1982

Worth Searching Out:
Big Sixteen (—/HMV), 1965

Iron Butterfly

US group formed 1968.
Original line-up: Doug Ingle, keyboards; Ron Bushy, drums; Jerry Penrod, bass; Danny Weis, guitar; Darryl DeLoach, guitar.

Career: Competent, but pretentious heavy metal aggregation whose career was built around million-selling album **In A-Gadda-Da-Vida** (In The Garden Of Life) (1968).

The original line-up cut debut set, aptly named **Heavy**, in early '68. Personnel changes saw Penrod, Weis (both ex-Rhinoceros) and DeLoach replaced by 17-year-old guitarist Erik Braunn and bassist Lee Dorman. This unit cut **Gadda**, a meandering cacophony whose title track (written by Ingle) stretched for a 17-minute life-time. Butterfly's most productive period musically

Below: Iron Maiden may look like peaceful hippies—but definitely aren't when they're onstage . . .

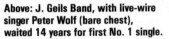

Above: J. Geils Band, with live-wire singer Peter Wolf (bare chest), waited 14 years for first No. 1 single.

came with recruitment of guitarists Mike Pinera (ex-Blues Image) and Larry Reinhardt, for departing Braunn.

The re-structured five-piece made some attempt at melody with 1970 **Metamorphosis** album. Headlining a European tour with Yes(▶) in early '71, they found some critical favour despite competition from the high-flying English band.

Unable to repeat platinum success of **Gadda**, Butterfly split at the end of farewell US tour in summer '71. An ill-advised comeback in 1974 with Braunn, Bushy, Phil Kramer (bass) and Howard Reitzes (keyboards) led to ordinary **Scorching Beauty** LP. Final line-up adjustment saw Bill De Martinez replace Reitzes for 1975 album **Sun And Steel**.

Iron Butterfly satisfactorily mirrored late '60s US musical direction, but were hardly competition for flourishing UK market led by Cream(▶) and Led Zeppelin(▶).

Final line-up: Erik Braunn, guitar; Phil Kramer, bass; Bill De Martinez, keyboards.

Albums:
In-A-Gadda-Da-Vida (Atco/Atlantic), 1968
Iron Butterfly — Live (Atlantic), 1970

Worth Searching Out:
Metamorphosis (Atlantic), 1970

Iron Maiden

UK group formed 1977.
Original line-up: Steve Harris, bass, vocals; Paul Di'anno, vocals; Dave Murray, guitar; Doug Sampson, drums.

Career: Steve Harris formed Iron Maiden amid new wave/punk breeding ground of London's East End. Harris went for deliberate high-energy, power-driven sound. Taking name from medieval torture cage. Iron Maiden went through numerous personnel changes; settled down to line-up above by mid-1979.

Harris refused lucrative offer for gigs and record contract that required him to remould Maiden into fashionable new wave band. Instead, band released **Soundhouse Tapes** EP on own label which sold quite well via mail order. Sampson left to be replaced by Clive Burr (drums), and Dennis Stratton (guitar) joined, adding even stronger drive to band.

EMI signed group in December 1979 amid growing signs that new wave wasn't as all-pervasive as it had first seemed. **Running Free** made UK Top 30 which led to Maiden's

historic live appearance on BBC TV's 'Top Of The Pops' — the first live gig since the Who in 1973. March 1980 found Maiden on road supporting Judas Priest(▶). Their impact was soon seen: debut album entered UK charts at No. 4. Album success led to headlining UK tour and European tour opening for Kiss(▶). Stratton left at this point and Dave Murray brought in old friend Adrian Smith, to keep twin guitar sound.

Killers LP, released in January 1981, broke band internationally; extensive world tour took most of year. Band now seemed deservedly ready for superstardom when departure of vocalist Di'anno was announced. What could have been devastating blow turned into even stronger line-up as Bruce Dickinson (ex-Samson) took over vocals. March 1982 saw release of excellent **Number Of The Beast** and another massive world tour.

Iron Maiden offer sonic assault, but heavy metal is tag which is too limiting for a band with interesting lyrics and a melody or two between the riffs. Critics who dismiss this band's hard rock miss much excitement and good music.

Current line-up: Harris; Murray; Bruce Dickinson, vocals; Adrian Smith, guitar; Clive Burr, drums.

Hit Singles:

	US	UK
Run To The Hills, 1982	—	7
The Number Of The Beast, 1982	—	18

Albums:
Iron Maiden (Harvest/EMI), 1980
Killers (Harvest/EMI), 1981
The Number Of The Beast (Capitol/EMI), 1982
Piece Of Mind (Capitol/EMI), 1983

Isley Brothers

US group formed 1957.

Original line-up: Ronald Isley, vocals; Rudolph Isley, vocals; Kelly Isley, vocals.

Career: Began performing gospel around hometown of Cincinnati. Moved to New York in 1957, changed to more secular style and recorded for several small labels. Eventually signed with RCA in 1959, and released **Shout,** wild gospel-flavoured stomper that made Top 50 and spawned several later cover versions.

Although group continued to build up reputation as hot live act, no more hits were forthcoming until 1962 release of **Twist And Shout** on Wand. Record made US Top 20 and was later covered by Beatles(▶) (who were great Isley fans).

Slump again followed, during which time Isleys formed own label, T-Neck. This period also saw group employing Jimi Hendrix(▶) as session guitarist. Continued success only came after signing to Motown in 1965. First release, **This Old Heart Of Mine,** became US hit (and major hit in Britain two years later). Over course of four-year period, band notched up variety of single successes on both sides of Atlantic, with greater consistency in UK charts.

Nevertheless, group eventually felt constricted by Motown formula and split from company in 1969. Simultaneously they revived dormant T-Neck operation and signed, distribution deal with Buddah. New business arrangements were matched by new approach to music, influenced by West Coast psychedelic bands, Hendrix and Sly and Family Stone(▶).

Ronald, Rudolph and Kelly recruited younger brothers Ernie on guitar and drums and Marvin on bass, plus cousin Chris Jasper on keyboards. Revitalised outfit exploded into new era of creativity and impact. Final barrier to international pop success was crossed with signing to Columbia in 1973. Superb album

3 Plus 3, The Isley Brothers. Courtesy Epic Records.

3+3 heralded string of gold and platinum records that has lasted into '80s. Recent albums have provided little more than variations on sound established in 1973, but Isley Brothers are now established in top echelon of soul and pop. Sales have slowed in last year or two, but talent and experience ensure likelihood of further worthwhile work.

Current line-up: Ronald Isley; Rudolph Isley; Kelly Isley; Ernie Isley, guitar, drums. Marvin Isley, bass; Chris Jasper, keyboards.

Hit Singles:

	US	UK
Twist And Shout, 1962	17	—
This Old Heart Of Mine, (Is Weak For You), 1966	12	47
This Old Heart Of Mine, (Is Weak For You), 1968	—	3
I Guess I'll Always Love You, 1969	—	11
Behind A Painted Smile, 1969	—	5
It's Your Thing, 1969	2	30
Put Yourself In My Place, 1969	—	13
Love The One You're With, 1971	18	—
That Lady, 1973	6	14
Summer Breeze, 1974	60	16
Fight The Power, 1975	4	—
Harvest For The World, 1976	—	10
It's A Disco Night (Rock Don't Stop), 1979	—	14

Albums:
Twist And Shout (Wand/DJM), 1962
This Old Heart Of Mine (Tamla Motown), 1966
3+3 (Featuring That Lady) (T-Neck/Epic), 1973
Live It Up (T-Neck/Epic), 1974
The Heat Is On (T-Neck/Epic), 1975
Harvest For The World (T-Neck/Epic), 1976
Super Hits (—/Tamla Motown), 1976
Go For Your Guns (T-Neck/Epic), 1977
Forever Gold (T-Neck/Epic), 1977
Showroom (T-Neck/Epic), 1978
Winner Takes All (T-Neck/Epic), 1979
Go All The Way (T-Neck/Epic), 1980
Grand Slam (T-Neck/Epic), 1981
Inside You (T-Neck/Epic), 1981
Motown Superstar Series Volume 6 (Motown/—) 1982
The Real Deal (T-Neck/Epic), 1982

J. Geils Band

US group formed 1967.

Original line-up: Peter Wolf, vocals; J. Geils, guitar; Magic Dick, harmonica; Danny Klein, bass; Stephen Bladd, drums.

Career: Formed in Boston, Massachusetts; originally known as J. Geils Blues Band. Dropped 'blues' tag in 1969, and added keyboards player Seth Justman. Gained strong local following playing no-nonsense synthesis of blues, R&B and rock.

Spotted by Atlantic Records on Dr John(▶) bill, band was signed, and released first album, **The J. Geils Band**, in 1971. Outfit showed direct approach reminiscent of Rolling Stones' (▶) attitude, which has persisted throughout recording career. **Bloodshot**, released in 1973, was band's first gold album, and also yielded first hit single, **Give It To Me**.

Further albums consolidated band's reputation, and **Monkey Island** (1977) took them qualitative step forward. Album showcased writing abilities of Justman and Wolf, and veered more towards hard rock ethos. It also heralded split from Atlantic and move to EMI America. (Changed name to simply Geils for **Monkey**, then went back to J. Geils.)

Shift seemed to revitalize band for they immediately produced 1978 gold album, **Sanctuary**. **Love Stinks** was equally successful, but it was only prelude to massive acceptance of album released at end of 1981, **Freeze Frame**. After 14 years of dues-paying, band reaped benefit of LP that topped charts all over the world, and yielded three hit singles, **Centrefold, Freeze Frame** and **Angel in Blue**. Nationwide US tour broke box-office records, and European tour with Rolling Stones(▶) brought wide acclaim.

Band had finally found formula to wed hard-rocking approach to commercial appeal. They look set to continue successful career into foreseeable future. Possessing charismatic frontman in Peter Wolf (once gossip-column fodder during lengthy courtship of and short marriage to Faye Dunaway), and excellent musicians in Magic Dick and J. Geils, J. Geils Band are classic example of band who have made it through talent and sheer hard work.

Current line-up: Wolf; Geils; Magic Dick; Klein; Bladd; Seth Justman, keyboards.

Hit Singles:

	US	UK
Must Of Got Lost, 1974	12	—
Centrefold, 1981	1	1
Freeze Frame, 1982	27	4
Do I Do, 1982	13	—

Albums:
J. Geils Band (Atlantic), 1971
The Morning After (Atlantic), 1971
Full House (Atlantic), 1972
Bloodshot (Atlantic), 1973
Ladies Invited (Atlantic), 1973
Nightmares And Other Tales From The Vinyl Jungle (Atlantic), 1974
Blow Your Face Out (Atlantic), 1976*
Monkey Island (Atlantic), 1977
Sanctuary (EMI), 1978
Love Stinks (EMI), 1980
Freeze Frame (EMI), 1981
Showtime (EMI), 1982
*Live

Joe Jackson

UK vocalist, pianist, composer. Born Portsmouth, 1956.

Career: Taught himself piano as child; undertook formal musical training at Royal Academy of Music. Early musical career included stints with various pub-rock outfits and Top 40 cover bands. While musical director of Portsmouth Playboy Club masterminded success of 'Opportunity Knocks' talent contest winners Coffee and Cream.

In meantime, Jackson was writing songs, and was signed to A&M in 1978. 1979 hit single **Is She Really Going Out With Him** showed emergence of distinctive new talent, combining deadpan vocal styling with wry lyric and strong melodic sense. Album **Look Sharp** confirmed success, gaining Top 20 chart placing in US.

Second LP **I'm The Man** won further acclaim, and early 1980 saw international success of single **It's Different For Girls.**

I'm The Man, Joe Jackson, Courtesy A&M Records.

Although superstardom was in sight, following year Jackson made bold decision to fold band and form new outfit, Jumpin' Jive. Band featured horns and was devoted to Louis Jordan-style swing and jump numbers from late '40s. Perhaps surprisingly, idea was successful. Jumpin' Jive played to full and ecstatic houses, and album of same name made UK Top 20 and US Top 60. However, Jackson had made it clear at outset that concept was one-off, and in due course folded band.

Ever ready to absorb new influences and environments, in 1982 Jackson left UK for New York. Album that resulted, **Night And**

Joe Jackson's Jumpin' Jive. Courtesy A&M Records.

Day, became one of 1982's sensations, achieving No. 4 position in US charts. Single **Steppin' Out** was equally successful. Unusual in that it does not feature guitar, **Night And Day** shows jazz, funk and salsa influence and eclecticism typical of Jackson. At same time, album has wide AOR appeal.

With his original talent and determination to follow own musical path, Jackson could become one of biggest names of '80s. Latterly he has been writing songs for a movie soundtrack, showing yet another likely direction for his abilities.

Hit Singles:

	US	UK
Is She Really Going Out With Him?, 1979	21	13
It's Different For Girls, 1980	—	5
Steppin' Out, 1982	6	—

Albums:
Look Sharp (A&M), 1979
I'm The Man (A&M), 1979
Beat Crazy (A&M), 1980
Jumpin' Jive (A&M), 1981
Night And Day (A&M), 1982

The Jacksons

US group formed 1966.

Original line-up: Michael Jackson, lead vocals; Jackie Jackson, vocals, guitar; Tito Jackson, vocals, guitar; Marlon Jackson, vocals; Jermaine Jackson, vocals, bass.

Career: Black America's answer to the Osmonds, the Jackson Five proved to have international, multi-racial appeal. Sons of Joe Jackson, once guitarist with Falcons soul group, and clarinettist Kathy, family grew up in Gary, Indiana, where they were all born (Jackie, May 4, 1951; Tito, October 15, 1953; Jermaine December 11, 1954; Marlon, March 12, 1957; Michael, August 29, 1958; Randy, October 29, 1962), Boys have three sisters of whom two youngest, La Toya and Janet, have now made careers in show business.

Tito had intense interest in music and persuaded others to form family group. Gigged in nearby Chicago and won several talent competitions, culminating in campaign benefit show for Gary's Mayor, Richard Hatcher. Diana Ross(▶) was in attendance and brought group to attention of Motown boss Berry Gordy. They had already recorded

Greatest Hits, Jackson Five. Courtesy Motown Records.

unsuccessfully for small local label, but Gordy saw them as major potential talent, especially with then nine-year-old Michael brought out front.

Debut single, **I Want You Back**, was immediate smash, Michael(▶) earning comparison with former child prodigy Stevie Wonner. **Diana Ross Presents The Jackson 5** album and group's inclusion in her 90-minute TV spectacular 'Diana' in 1971 helped build immediate fame. Following singles poured out at rapid rate giving them hits nearly every three months. Early material was all written and produced by 'The Corporation', i.e. Motown's multi-talented songwriting, arranging and production team.

Rivalry with Osmonds and resultant fan mania helped both groups; so did electric stage presence featuring colourful outfits and dazzling dance routines. The Jacksons were even made into a cartoon series.

Parallel—and ever more important—solo career for Michael began at 13 with 1972 hit **I'll Be There**. Tito and Jermaine also had solo releases but made less impact.

Steady flow of albums and singles led to multi-million dollar contract offer from Epic in 1976, which took group from Motown fold. Having married Hazel, daughter of Motown boss Berry Gordy Jr, Jermaine opted to stay and left group. Name was changed to simply the Jacksons, addition of youngest brother Randy kept number at five.

First Epic album **The Jacksons** went gold; hit singles continued. In 1978 hit highest spot yet with superb **Destiny** album; smash singles **Blame It On The Boogie** and

Shake Your Body (Down To The Ground) set world's discos alight. Album was self-produced, using cream of West Coast session musicians. During sell-out UK tour band played in front of the Queen at Silver Jubilee celebrations in Glasgow.

Meanwhile, sister LaToya, who in earlier years had often appeared on stage with brothers (whose stage band, incidentally, featured their cousins), made her recording debut. **If You Feel The Funk**, on Polydor, gave LaToya big hit. Youngest sister Janet, who has become popular TV child actress, has also since entered recording world.

Prior to release of group's aptly titled **Triumph** album, Michael Jackson released own **Off The Wall** LP. Produced by Quincy Jones(▶) it is reputed to be biggest seller ever in field of black music. LP spawned string of hit singles. 1983 solo album **Thriller** is continuing in same vein. Michael's ever-growing success in own right leads to speculation that he will soon stop working as part of Jacksons.

The magic of the Jacksons' stage performances was captured on 1981 double album **Live**.

Current line-up: Michael; Jackie; Tito; Marlon; Randy Jackson, vocals.

Hit Singles:	US	UK
As Jackson Five:		
I Want You Back, 1970	1	2
ABC, 1970	1	8
The Love You Save, 1970	1	7
I'll Be There, 1970	1	4
Mama's Pearl, 1971	2	25
Never Can Say Goodbye, 1971	2	33
Maybe Tomorrow, 1971	20	—
Sugar Daddy, 1972	10	—
Little Bitty Pretty One, 1972	13	—
Lookin' Through The Windows, 1972	16	9
Corner Of The Sky, 1972	18	—
Doctor My Eyes, 1973	—	9
Hallelujah Day, 1973	28	20
Dancing Machine, 1974	2	—
I Am Love (Parts 1 & 2), 1975	15	—
As the Jacksons:		
Enjoy Yourself, 1977	6	42
Show You The Way To Go, 1977	28	1
Blame It On The Boogie, 1978	54	8
Shake Your Body (Down To The Ground), 1979	7	4
Lovely One, 1980	12	29
Can You Feel It, 1981	—	6
Walk Right Now, 1981	—	7

Below: The Jacksons, hitmakers (as the Jackson 5) on Motown, now on Epic.

Jermaine Jackson solo:		
Daddy's Home, 1973	9	—
Let's Get Serious, 1980	9	8

Michael Jackson solo:
(See separate entry)

Albums:

As Jackson Five:
ABC (Tamla/Motown), 1970
Lookin' Through The Windows (Tamla/Motown), 1972
Greatest Hits (Tamla/Motown), 1972
Anthology (Tamla/Motown), 1977
20 Golden Greats (—/Motown), 1979
Motown Superstar Series Volume 12 (Tamla/—), 1981

As The Jacksons:
The Jacksons (Epic), 1976
Goin' Places (Epic), 1977
Destiny (Epic), 1978
Triumph (Epic), 1981
Live (Epic), 1982

Jermaine Jackson solo:
Jermaine (Tamla/Motown), 1980
Let's Get Serious (Tamla/Motown), 1980
I Like Your Style (Tamla/Motown), 1981
Let Me Tickle Your Fancy (Tamla/Motown), 1982

Michael Jackson solo:
(See separate entry)

Michael Jackson

US vocalist, composer.
Born Gary, Indiana, August 29, 1958.

Career: Dominant brother of the Jacksons(▶), Michael was youngest in original line-up (before Randy joined) and was heralded as infant genius by his Motown mentors. Just as Little Stevie Wonder's(▶) early promise reached potential so Michael Jackson's talent has stood test of time.

Besides singing lead on the Jacksons' amazing run of hits, Michael has achieved enormous success in own right. He has earned reputed $40 million to date.

First solo hit was **Got To Be There** (1971). Other successes included theme from movie **Ben**, a ballad which contrasted with usual uptempo style of Jackson Five. Between 1971-1976 enjoyed six best-selling albums with Motown. His last collaboration with the company was starring as the scarecrow, opposite Diana Ross in 'The Wiz' black re-make of the classic movie 'The Wizard Of Oz'. The film was heavily criticised but Jackson won applause for his role. His duet with Diana Ross, **Ease On Down The Road**, was hit single.

Moving with his family to Epic label, Michael continued to front the Jacksons. He was also teamed up with producer Quincy Jones(▶) (whom he had met while both worked on 'The Wiz') for the appropriately epic **Off The Wall** solo album. This included superb material by Paul McCartney(▶), British writer Rod Temperton (ex-Heatwave(▶)) and Jackson himself. Claimed as biggest selling album by a black artist of all time, the Los Angeles-recorded album had no weak spots. In US a number of tracks were lifted as singles. In one week three singles from the LP were in US Top 10, a unique achievement. Cashing in on this phenomenal success, Motown reissued old track **One Day In Your Life** for 1981 UK chart-topper. In 1982 Michael scored US/UK duet hit with Paul McCartney on McCartney's composition **The Girl Is Mine**.

Follow-up album **Thriller** (also produced by Quincy Jones in Los Angeles) appeared in 1983 and proceeded to emulate success of **Off The Wall**. Jackson co-produced three of the songs and contributed to vocals, synthesiser and rhythm arrangements. 1983 singles **Billie Jean** and **Beat It** (featuring Eddie Van Halen(▶) on guitar) both became US No. 1s proving Jackson will continue to be a major artist of the '80s.

Jackson, meantime, has become something of a hermit. A long-time vegetarian he has little contact with brothers or outside world and has surrounded his luxurious Hollywood mansion with exotic pets.

Hit Singles:	US	UK
Got To Be There, 1971	4	5
Rockin' Robin, 1972	2	3
I Wanna Be Where You Are, 1972	16	—
Ain't No Sunshine, 1972	—	8
Ben, 1972	1	7
Don't Stop Till You Get Enough, 1979	1	3
Off The Wall, 1979	10	7
Rock With You, 1979	1	7
She's Out Of My Life, 1980	10	3
One Day In Your Life, 1981	55	1
Billie Jean, 1983	1	1
Beat It, 1983	1	3
With Paul McCartney:		
The Girl Is Mine, 1982	2	8

Albums:
Ben (Tamla Motown), 1972
Got To Be There (Tamla Motown), 1972
Best Of (—/Motown), 1975
One Day In Your Life (—/Motown), 1981
Off The Wall (Epic), 1979
Thriller (Epic), 1982
Ain't No Sunshine (—/Pickwick), 1982

The Jam

UK group formed 1976.

Original line-up: Paul Weller vocals, bass; Steve Brookes, guitar; Bruce Foxton, guitar; Rick Buckler, drums.

Career: Above quartet got together while at school in Woking, Surrey, to play rock 'n' roll and R&B. Youth and social club gigs followed; after Steve Brookes left, Weller switched to guitar, Foxton to bass.

Line-up in this form made London debut in summer 1976, displaying image based on early '60s 'mod' look and playing sharp, well-crafted rock songs that showed songwriter Weller's debt to Pete Townshend(▶). Although band had little in common with most of 'New Wave' outfits, Jam won contract as part of mass record company signings that followed 'summer of punk'. Contracted to Polydor in February 1977.

First single **In The City** hovered around bottom of chart, but follow-up **All Around**

In The City, the first Jam album, with a very 'mod' sleeve. Courtesy Polydor Records.

The World made No. 13. In meantime, debut album, also called **In The City**, made No. 20 in album chart. During next three years band became chart regulars with both singles and albums, establishing themselves as one of most interesting new outfits of late '70s. Weller (born May 25, 1958) set direction of band, and showed himself to be perceptive and socially aware writer and spokesman.

1980 saw further triumphs for band, with first No. 1 single **Going Underground/The Dreams Of Children** and title of 'Best Group' in the New Musical Express Readers' Poll. Next single, **Start**, also made No. 1 and group were not out of Top 10 until their demise.

Despite massive success during 1982 — they swept board in all British polls and toured Britain and abroad to universal acclaim — Jam announced that band would fold at end of year. Apparently Weller found format too constricting and wished to move on to other things. During December band undertook farewell tour to usual ecstatic crowds, and retired from scene. 1982 LP **The Gift** entered UK charts at No. 1. Jam singles/sleeves are such collector's items that Polydor recently re-issued entire catalogue for third time.

Weller has already found further success with new band, the Style Council, and other acts such as Tracie on his own Respond label. Other members are involved with solo projects.

Although they never achieved more than cult status in US, Jam, always an intense live act, became one of most important bands in UK in '80s. Success was largely due to Paul Weller; his current projects and any future ones he may be involved in should be worth watching.

Above: The Jam, pictured before they split at the end of 1982 and Weller formed The Style Council.

Final line-up: Weller, vocals, guitar; Foxton, bass; Buckler.

Hit Singles:	US	UK
All Around The World, 1977	—	13
Down In The Tube Station At Midnight, 1978	—	15
Strange Town, 1979	—	15
When You're Young, 1979	—	17
The Eton Rifles, 1979	—	3
Going Underground/The Dreams Of Children, 1980	—	1
Start, 1980	—	1
Funeral Pyre, 1981	—	4
Absolute Beginners, 1981	—	4
Town Called Malice/Precious, 1982	—	1
Just Who Is The 5 O'Clock Hero, 1982*	—	8
The Bitterest Pill (I Ever Had To Swallow), 1982	—	2
Beat Surrender, 1982	—	1
*German import

Albums:
In The City (Polydor), 1977
This Is The Modern World (Polydor), 1977*
All Mod Cons (Polydor), 1978*
Setting Sons (Polydor), 1979
Sound Affects (Polydor), 1980
The Gift (Polydor), 1982
Dig The New Breed (Polydor), 1982†
*One track different on US/UK versions.
†Live

Bob James

US keyboard player, composer, arranger, producer.
Born Marshall, Montana, December 25, 1939.

Career: Forerunner of jazz/funk movement, James' contribution has been technical excellence rather than passion.

Former accompanist for Sarah Vaughan and staff composer for Association of Producing Artists Repertoire in New York, he entered session field in late '60s, and has since recorded with Quincy Jones(▶), Dionne Warwick(▶), Roberta Flack(▶), Ron Carter, Mark Colby, Neil Diamond(▶), and Paul Simon(▶) among others.

James joined CTI(▶) in 1973 as house arranger/producer, supervising albums for Eric Gale(▶), Grover Washington(▶), Hank Crawford, Johnny Hammond, Idris

Muhammad, Gabor Szabo and Stanley Turrentine. First of four solo albums for CTI, **One**, was released in 1976. (Debut recording, the experimental **Explosions** set issued a decade earlier, was unsuccessful.)

His own work has been littered with star performers, notably drummers Harvey Mason and Steve Gadd(▶), flautist Hubert Laws, saxophonists David Sanborn and Mike Brecker, trumpeter Thad Jones, and com-

Sign Of The Times, Bob James. Courtesy Columbia Records.

poser/keyboard star Rod Temperton, ex-Heatwave(▶).

Formed own label Tappan Zee in 1977, recruiting notable jazz and fusion acts like Wilbert Longmire, Richard Tee and Mongo Santamaria.

Prolific composer who has scored for Broadway ('The Selling Of The President'), and movies ('Serpico'), James is currently working with guitarist Earl Klugh(▶) a collaboration which has produced two successful albums.

Albums:
One (CTI), 1975
Two (CTI), 1975
Three (CTI), 1976
Four (CTI), 1977
Heads (Columbia/CBS), 1977
Touchdown (Columbia/CBS), 1978
Lucky Seven (Tappan Zee), 1979
Best of Bob James (CTI), 1978
'H' (Tappan Zee), 1980
All Around The Town — Live (Columbia/CBS), 1981
Sign Of The Times (Columbia/CBS), 1981
Hands Down (Columbia/CBS), 1982

With Earl Klugh:
One On One (Columbia/CBS), 1979
Two Of A Kind (Columbia/CBS), 1982

The James Gang

US group formed 1967.
Original line-up: Jim Fox, drums, vocals; Tom Kriss, bass; Glen Schwartz, guitar.

Career: Cleveland, Ohio, band formed by Jim

Yer Album, The James Gang, Courtesy Stateside Records.

Fox out of several local bands. Group settled as trio and established strong reputation throughout Ohio area.

In April 1969 Schwartz grew frustrated with band's slow development and left, later joining Pacific, Gas, and Electric Co. Kent State part-time student and local guitar wizard Joe Walsh(▶) joined group. His unique sound attracted Bill Szymczyk, then a fledgling producer, who convinced his record company, ABC, to sign band. He produced their first LP **Yer Album**, a strong debut which made Billboard's album chart in 1969 (remaining for five months).

Kriss decided to quit music in 1970 and Fox replaced him with old friend Dale Peters. This 'classic' James Gang line-up recorded next three albums and came closest to making superstar status which had been widely predicted. **The James Gang Rides Again** album was a showcase for Walsh's flourishing writing/playing talent and set made US Top 10. From this peak, Gang began to slip. Tour of Europe was disappointing.

Thirds album seemed diluted with a variety of sounds, as if to show band's progression. Its relative failure after **Rides Again** found band retreating to heavy-handed, thrashing guitars live LP, **James Gang Live At Carnegie Hall**. In response, Walsh left band in November 1971.

Fox hired two Canadians, Dom Trolano (guitar) and Roy Kenner (vocals), and this line-up recorded two weak albums: **Straight Shooter** (February 1972) and **Passin' Thru'** (August 1972). In 1973 Trolano quit—soon to join Guess Who(▶)—and was replaced by Tommy Bolin. New outfit recorded two much stronger albums **Bang** (1973) and **Miami** (1974).

Bolin's erratic behaviour caused Gang to fold as he left to join Deep Purple(▶). Fox and Peters tried yet again in 1975 with new vocalist Bubba Keith and guitarist Richard Shack. Two nondescript albums later, James Gang finally surrendered.

Final line-up: Fox; Dale Peters; Bubba Keith, vocals; Richard Shack, guitar.

Albums:
The James Gang Rides Again (ABC/Probe), 1970
Best Of (MCA/ABC), 1973
Bang (ATCO/Atlantic), 1973
16 Greatest Hits (MCA), 1974

Rick James

US vocalist, guitarist, composer.
Born James Johnson, Buffalo, New York, February 1, 1955.

Career: King of new-wave punk-funk, James joined US Navy at 15 but went AWOL and fled to Canada. There he shared apartment with then unknown Neil Young(▶). Together they formed rock band the Mynah Birds but found no success.

Slipping back into US, James found employment at Motown in Detroit as producer/songwriter, working with Bobby Taylor and the Vancouvers, the Originals, the (Detroit) Spinners, the Marvelettes and others. On expiry of contract, flitted between Canada, South America and London where he formed blues band called Main Line; played guitar and harmonica as well as singing. Returning to hometown of Buffalo, James decided to come up with an even funkier version of what then popular George Clinton(▶) and Funkadelic/Parliament were doing.

He cut some sides at Cross Eyed Bear Studios in neighbouring town of Clarence. Took tapes to old employers Motown who decided they were strong enough to release in album form under title **Come Get It!** Lifted from LP, **You And I** gave James big hit single.

James' bizarre image — a mix of eroticism, outrage and sheer eccentricity — struck responsive chord. He put together Stone City Band backing group (has since produced them in their own right) and the Punk Funk Chorus in time for second album **Bustin' Out Of L. Seven**.

A bout of severe hepatitis kept him out of action until he bounced back in December 1979 with **Fire It Up**, which outsold previous efforts. James also masterminded career of Teena Marie, producing her **Wild And Peaceful** LP featuring **I'm Just A Sucker For Your Love** hit single.

Jazz funk from Bob James, the Street Songs album. Courtesy Motown Records.

James put together songs for his fourth album **Garden Of Love** while holidaying in Barbados. In a more laid-back vein, it wasn't what his audiences wanted. Fifth album **Street Songs** (1981) was back in the urban gutter — gritty, ballsy music that went double platinum in US. Successful singles **Give It To Me Baby** and **Super Freak** led to sensational standing-room-only US tour with Cameo, Teena Marie and the Sugarhill Gang. British tour was well received but cynics saw act as being full of 'get down, do it y'all, put your hands together' clichés. In May 1982 he was guest singer on Temptations'(▶) Top 100 **Standing On The Top** single.

Hit Singles:

	US	UK
You And I, 1978	13	46
Super Freak Part 1, 1981	16	—

Albums:
Come Get It (Gordy/Motown), 1979
Fire It Up (Gordy/Motown), 1979
Garden Of Love (Gordy/Motown), 1981
Street Songs (Gordy/Motown), 1981
Throwin' Down (Gordy/Motown), 1982

Jan And Dean

US vocal duo formed 1958.
Jan Berry, born Los Angeles, April 3, 1941.
Dean Torrence, born Los Angeles, March 10, 1940.

Career: Major figures of California surf-music scene, Jan and Dean's career was abruptly terminated when a horrific car smash in 1966 left Jan with serious brain damage and considerable loss of mobility.

By no means originators, Jan and Dean were as much reliant on talents of their songwriters and producers as on own vocal abilities, but records like **Surf City, Little Old Lady From Pasadena** and **Dead Man's Curve** remain classics of their idiom — the totally unpretentious, fun-music West—Coast sound of the early '60s.

They started singing together in shower room after football practice at Emerson Junior High School in Los Angeles, and recorded on a twin-track machine in garage with help from friend Bruce Johnston, later to become a Beach Boy(▶).

In 1958, Berry managed to place **Jenny Lee** (which featured Berry, Torrence and Arnie Ginsburg as trio but appeared as Jan and Arnie on label because Torrence was in Army and unavailable to sign contract), a song about a burlesque stripper, with Arwin, and it became US Top 10 hit. A year later Berry was back with Dean Torrence as Jan and Dean, with **Baby Talk**, produced by Lou Adler and Herb Alpert(▶). Concurrently, they attended college, Berry studying medicine, Torrence design.

Music soon took over, however, and after Top-30 hit on Challenge with **Heart And Soul** in 1961 they signed to Liberty the following year and started singing about their big passion — surfing.

After a show with the Beach Boys, Brian Wilson played them demo of his composition **Surf City**. Their rendition went to No. 1 and was quickly followed by string of surf and hot-rod flavoured high-school epics, many of them written or produced by Brian Wilson. They repaid the favour, Jan Berry singing lead on the Beach Boys' live recording of **Barbara Ann**.

Golden Hits, Jan & Dean. Courtesy Liberty Records.

While filming 'Easy Come Easy Go' in spring 1966 Berry crashed his car into a parked truck. Since then it has been a long, slow path to partial recovery. Despite some sides recorded for A&M and recent stage appearances with erstwhile partner (where they were somewhat cruelly accused of going for sympathy market), Jan Berry's contribution to rock music remains rooted in his brief spell of '60s stardom. Dean Torrence was involved with the Legendary Masked Surfers and now runs a design studio which specialises in pop posters.

Hit Singles:

	US	UK
Jenny Lee (As Jan and Arnie), 1958	8	—
Baby Talk, 1959	10	—
Surf City, 1963	1	26
Honolulu Lulu, 1963	11	—
Drag City, 1964	10	—
Dead Man's Curve, 1964	8	—
Little Old Lady From Pasadena, 1964	3	—
Ride The Wild Surf, 1964	16	—

Albums:
Dead Man's Curve (Liberty/—), 1964
Ride The Wild Surf (Liberty/Greenlight-Liberty), 1964
Little Old Lady From Pasadena (Liberty/—), 1964
Legendary Masters (Liberty/—), 1971
The Very Best Of (—/Sunset), 1974
The Jan And Dean Story (—/Past), 1980
The Best Of (Liberty/—), 1982

Japan

UK group formed 1974.
Original line-up: David Sylvian, vocals, guitar, keyboards; Richard Barbieri, keyboards, synthesisers; Rob Dean, guitar; Mick Karn, bass, saxophone; Steve Jansen, drums.

Career: Formed by brothers Sylvian and Jansen (real surname Batt) from London, Cyprus-born Karn (real name Anthony Michaelides) and Barbieri. Dean joined via music press advertisement in 1977. During same year, group entered talent contest sponsored by Hansa record label, and were duly signed. Early recorded work completely unsuccessful commercially, since image (latter-day glamrock look and Sylvian's arty vocals) inappropriate to era dominated by punks. However, met some success in various European countries as well as in namesake Japan. After three LPs and five singles, group decided that answer to problems was change of record label; signed with Virgin.

Move coincided with group becoming fashionable (as New Romantics came to fore), to point where old and new labels interweaved releases with band's partial approval, as both old and new material dented charts. Although Dean left during year, 1981 was UK breakthrough period; three hit singles and two chart LPs. 1982 saw six hit singles and two more hit LPs; no US chart success.

1982 was also year band decided, if not to split, then to have trial separation. Barbieri produced Swedish band Lustans Lakejer; Jansen worked with various Japanese musicians; Karn released solo LP; Sylvian released single **Forbidden Colours** recorded with Riuichi Sakamoto of Yellow Magic Orchestra, and featured in film 'Merry Christmas Mr. Lawrence' with solo LP projected for late 1983. Karn became highly fashionable guest star for other acts in 1982-83, working with Gary Numan(▶) and Midge Ure among others. Also presented exhibition of own sculpture.

Japan's decision to splinter when they did was regarded by some as ultimate folly, especially after struggling for first four years of career and only enjoying brief period of success. However, if solo careers remain less than triumphant, band could easily re-form and regain position as ultra-fashionable modern electronic-based act in UK; US success still seems unlikely.

Current/Final line-up: Sylvian; Barbieri; Karn; Jansen.

Below: Japan, with David Sylvian (fourth from left) and Mick Karn (in shades) its two biggest stars.

Hit Singles:

	US	UK
Quiet Life, 1981	—	19
Ghosts, 1982	—	5
I Second That Emotion, 1982	—	9

Albums:
Adolescent Sex (—/Ariola), 1978
Obscure Alternatives (—/Ariola), 1978
Quiet Life (—/Ariola), 1980
Gentlemen Take Polaroids (—/Virgin), 1980
Tin Drum (—/Virgin), 1981
Assemblage (—/Ariola), 1981*
Japan (Virgin/Epic/—), 1981
Oil On The Canvas (Virgin), 1983
*Compilation of early tracks

Mick Karn Solo:
Titles (—/Virgin), 1982

Jean-Michel Jarre

French composer, multi-instrumentalist.
Born Lyon, France, August 24, 1948.

Career: Child prodigy from musical family, Jarre started to learn piano and guitar at five. Attended Conservatoire de Paris taking lessons in music structure and harmony. Heavily influenced by '60s English pop music during his latter school years. Played lead guitar in number of groups in western suburbs of Paris before moving on to more experimental music.

In 1968, Jarre enrolled at Group of Musical Research (GMR) and began thesis on non-European music (African, Amazonian and Oceanian). His increasing interest in synthesisers and free-form music conflicted with pursuits of GMR. Unsuited for classical career and disillusioned by clinical research, Jarre abandoned studies. Working in own recording studio with a number of technicians and sound engineers, Jarre built various instruments to own specification and worked out new ideas on the synthesiser.

For his debut in 1971, Jarre sensationally introduced electronic music to the opera; became youngest composer ever to have played at Palais Garnier. Impressed by public's reaction, Jarre sought wider acclaim. Extended activities to other areas: radio jingles, Pepsi commercials, and background music for department stores and airports. Gradually, he succeeded in writing film and ballet music ('Dorian Gray' by Norbert Schmucki; 'Le Labyrinthe' by Joseph Lazzini).

More success followed with music and lyrical contribution for such artists as Gerard Lenorman, Christophe, Patrick Juvet and Françoise Hardy.

With such a long apprenticeship, Jarre was in perfect position to produce appealing, if undemanding, music for mass consumption.

Oxygene, released in 1976, sold six million copies worldwide, as did successor **Equinoxe.** On July 14, 1979, Jarre erected an original spectacular show from **Oxygene** and **Equinoxe** at Place de la Concorde. The event attracted one million spectators (from the Etoile to the Tuileries) and 100 million telespectators (from Europe to Japan). In 1981, **Magnetic Fields** confirmed his position as one of the most commercially successful composers in his field. Played series of concerts in China in October 1981 which were broadcast to 500 million radio listeners and 30 million television viewers.

Jarre's phenomenal success has been all but ignored by the rock world, where he is still regarded as a purveyor of muzak.

Hit Singles:	US	UK
Oxygene Part IV, 1977	—	4

Albums:
Oxygene (Polydor), 1977
Equinoxe (Polydor), 1978
Magnetic Fields (Polydor), 1981
The Concerts In China (Polydor), 1982

Jefferson Airplane/Starship

US group formed 1965.

Original line-up: Marty Balin, vocals; Paul Kantner, guitar; Signe Anderson, vocals; Jorma Kaukonen, guitar; Jack Casady, bass; Skip Spence, drums.

Career: Balin and Kantner met on San Francisco's folk coffee-house circuit in early 1965. Balin felt it was time to return to his roots and explore rock 'n' roll of Elvis(▶), Jerry Lee Lewis(▶) and Little Richard(▶). Anderson joined, then Kaukonen. Balin called Washington, D.C., and asked long-time friend Casady to join on bass. Spence was recruited in mid-'65 and Airplane began building local reputation as band who played folk lyrics to rock beat. Bill Graham helped foster exciting, vibrant image by providing priority booking at new Fillmore Hall. This lead to RCA contract, the first for Bay area band.

Spencer Dryden replaced Spence (later to form Moby Grape(▶)) while band recorded **Jefferson Airplane Takes Off.** National promotion helped 'folk-rock' sound achieve gold LP status and aroused industry interest in West Coast bands. Anderson left due to pregnancy and Kantner recruited Grace Slick (ex-Great Society) from band who used to open for Airplane.

This classic line-up scored big US hit with **Somebody To Love.** This song and **White Rabbit** were old Great Society songs. Slick's vocals made them, and whole of **Surrealistic Pillow** LP, haunting, emotive experience. To band's delight, critics and fans fell in love with album and it is marked as essential listening for understanding '60s.

Sudden success meant band could live in communal bliss, but community living also brought problems. **After Bathing At Baxter's** reflected this by reducing Balin's songwriting contributions and by trying new sounds and formats. Unlike previous LP, **Baxter's** experiments no longer hold interest upon re-hearing today.

Slick and Kantner had become lovers; when they began assuming full leadership roles, Balin backed off. **Crown of Creation** reduced Balin's role even further by including weak Slick song, **Lather,** and non-rock David Crosby song, **Triad.** Daring at time of release, and containing some good harmony, this LP is high point of early Airplane.

Bless Its Pointed Little Head is average

live set. Next album, **Volunteers,** pushed band into forefront of counterculture's political stance. Considering shallow, preachy tone, LP has remained surprisingly interesting. Balin felt band was becoming too big and too smooth and left. Several US tours followed (including playing at Stones'(▶) Altamont concert), then band seemed to lose all sense of direction. Balin's loss, Slick's pregnancy with Kantner's child and Dryden's departure left Airplane grounded. Kaukonen and Casady began electric blues country band, Hot Tuna. At first a part-time affair, project eventually removed duo from Airplane altogether. In telling omen for the future, Slick and Kantner used several famous 'session' players (Jerry Garcia, David Crosby, Graham Nash) to record LP **Blows Against The Empire,** which they credited to 'Paul Kantner and the Jefferson Starship'.

Airplane returned with Joey Covington (drums) on **Bark** LP. State of Airplane is reflected by superior Slick-Kantner solo, **Sunfighter,** released at same time. With one more sub-par set, **Long John Silver,** Airplane finally crashed. David Frieberg, ex-Quicksilver Messenger Service(▶), added vocals on live but uninspired **Thirty Seconds Over Winterland.** Then with no formal announcement, Airplane disappeared. Casady and Kaukonen worked full time turning Hot Tuna into early heavy-metal band. Slick, Kantner and Frieberg produced weak solo effort, and Slick released unsatisfactory **Manhole** LP.

Winds Of Change, Jefferson Starship Courtesy RCA 'Grunt Records. Still in the biz after nearly twenty years.

Two years later in 1974, Slick and Kantner decided to re-form band. Using Frieberg, 'Papa' John Creach (fiddler Hot Tuna had introduced to Airplane on **Bark**) ex-Turtles(▶) John Barbata (drums), Peter Sears (bass) and Craig Chaquico (guitar), new formation took name Jefferson Starship.

US tour, using early Airplane and solo material, convinced Slick and Kantner that band was viable proposition. **Dragon Fly** wasn't overly brilliant but sold well. More importantly, it had one Balin credit and indicated reunion with his creative influence; Balin began appearing with Starship and contributing efforts to recording sessions. However, he refused to sign with group or formally commit self to Starship. His **Miracles** became mammoth US hit in summer 1975 and pushed LP **Red Octopus** to US No. 1 (Airplane/Starship's first after 10 years of work).

The success of **Octopus** obviously influenced sales of next LP **Spitfire,** but album was inferior and seemed a sell-out/cash-in. **Earth** reflected growing personal problems and confusion over what to do next. Slick, Balin and Barbata all left and there seemed no reason to continue.

Kantner recruited Aynsley Dunbar (drums) and Mickey Thomas (vocals). **Freedom At**

Point Zero was first Airplane/Starship line-up not to feature female lead vocals. Critically dismissed, Kantner pushed on to **Modern Times;** Slick provided some backing vocals. Having resolved bout with alcohol and various personal problems, she rejoined full time on **Winds Of Change** (after release of two solo LPs).

Jefferson Airplane/Starship have been up to top and back down several times. Any attempt to write off Kantner misses his proven ability to find new combinations and interesting situations to explore. If old '60s political and '70s love ballad audiences won't follow along, Kantner will probably find way to win over new fans in '80s, as heavy video play on MTV indicates already.

Current line-up: Kantner; Slick, vocals; Craig Chaquico, Carvin guitar; Pete Sears, bass; Aynsley Dunbar, drums; David Frieberg, vocals; Mickey Thomas, vocals.

Hit Singles:	US	UK
As Airplane:		
Somebody to Love, 1967	5	—
White Rabbit, 1967	8	—
As Starship:		
Miracles, 1975	3	—
With Your Love, 1976	12	—
Runaway, 1978	12	—
Count On Me, 1978	8	—
Jane, 1979	14	—

Albums:
As Airplane:
Jefferson Airplane Takes Off (RCA), 1966
Surrealistic Pillow (RCA), 1967
After Bathing At Baxter's (RCA), 1968
Crown Of Creation (RCA), 1968
Bless Its Pointed Little Head (RCA), 1969
Volunteers (RCA), 1969
The Worst Of The Jefferson Airplane (RCA), 1970
Bark (Grunt), 1971
Thirty Seconds Over Winterland — Live (Grunt), 1973

As Starship:
Dragon Fly (Grunt), 1974
Red Octopus (Grunt), 1975
Spitfire (Grunt), 1976
Earth (Grunt), 1978
Gold (Grunt), 1979
Freedom At Ground Zero (Grunt), 1980
Modern Times (Grunt), 1981
Winds Of Change (Grunt), 1982

Kantner-Slick:
Blows Against The Empire (RCA), 1970
Sunfighter (Grunt), 1971

Grace Slick:
Dreams (RCA), 1980
Welcome To The Wrecking Ball (RCA), 1981

Waylon Jennings

US vocalist, guitarist, composer.
Born Littlefield, Texas, June 15, 1937.

Career: Showed early promise in country music; by teens was DJ on local radio, and singing at local gigs. At 21, moved to Lubbock, Texas, where he met up with Buddy Holly(▶) and joined his band as bass player. Following Holly's death, Jennings moved to Phoenix, Arizona, where he worked local bars and recorded for Ramco label.

After short stint with A&M, who tried to push him towards pop market, Jennings signed with RCA in 1965. Started by cutting folk-tinged country albums; began to move away from production-line Nashville music in early '70s. With fellow artist Willie Nelson(▶) and a handful of others, Jennings pioneered a grittier, more individualistic approach to

country that became known as 'outlaw music'. By time of release of 1973 album **Honky Tonk Heroes,** new direction had been fully realised, prompting misgivings among Nashville establishment but attracting attention of many outside normal country audience.

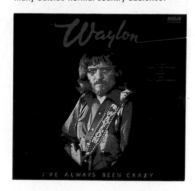

I've Always Been Crazy, Waylon Jennings. Courtesy RCA Records.

Major pay-off came with release of 1976 album **Outlaws,** featuring Jennings, Willie Nelson, Jennings' wife Jessi Colter, and Tompall Glaser, which reached No. 10 in US pop charts.

Since then Jennings has been accepted by country music establishment again, having helped to create a looser, less reactionary ambience around the music. At same time, he has continued to notch up pop success, and is comfortable performing in front of rock audiences. With his rich, powerful voice and charismatic personality, Jennings is now one of country's biggest crossover stars, and looks likely to maintain that status.

Albums (Selected):
Best Of (RCA), 1970
Ladies Love Outlaws (RCA), 1972
Honky Tonk Heroes (RCA), 1973
Waylon Live (RCA), 1976
Ole Waylon (RCA), 1977
Waylon Music (RCA), 1980
Music Man (RCA), 1980

Outlaws:
The Outlaws (RCA), 1976

With Willie Nelson:
Waylon And Willie (RCA), 1978

With Jessi Colter:
Leather And Lace (RCA), 1981

Jethro Tull

UK group formed 1968.

Original line-up: Ian Anderson, vocals, flute; Glenn Cornick, bass; Mick Abrahams, guitar; Clive Bunker, drums.

Career: Ian Anderson joined John Evan Band in native Blackpool in early 1966. Rapidly changing personnel brought him in contact with various musicians who would later work for him in Tull.

John Evan Band moved to London in winter 1967 and tried to break into club scene. Lack of success caused band's break-up, leaving Anderson and Cornick on their own. Abrahams and Bunker joined them in early 1968 and Anderson named band after 18th Century author/agriculturist Jethro Tull. Anderson's eccentric vocals and image caught attention of MGM records. Single **Aeroplane/ Sunshine Day** was fortunate flop in that band's name was misprinted as Jethro Toe. Island Records released next single, **Song For Jeffery,** which gathered bigger following and put band on road to success. Tull's albums began selling well as 'art-rock' in US and provided large, loyal following.

Abrahams left in late 1968 (forming Blodwyn Pig). Tony Iommi (later Black Sabbath(▶)) filled in for few weeks until Martin Barre was picked from auditions as permanent guitarist. This line-up recorded excellent **Stand Up** LP which was first indication of Anderson's true talent as songwriter. Adding old mate John Evan as session keyboard player, band recorded equally strong **Benefit** LP.

With flamboyant dress (usually like that of a mad jester) and leg-hopping antics, Anderson was now critical and popular success. Extended himself with rock opera **Aqualung** which took on typical early '70s targets (organised religion, society in general), but offered no substitute. Despite overblown, almost pretentious tone, LP **Aqualung** became huge US success and continues to sell well today. For this album John Evan became full member but co-founder Cornick was replaced by yet another Blackpool mate, Jeffery Hammond-Hammond. Cornick formed Wild Turkey; later he co-founded Paris with ex-Fleetwood Mac(▶) Bob Welch. By late 1971 Bunker had left and his place was taken by last ex-John Evan Band recruit, Barriemore Barlow.

Concept album ideas were extended in live show through use of stage props and pre-recorded films. After **Thick As A Brick,** Anderson threw caution to wind and presented **A Passion Play.** Rather than playing old hits or catering to any audience desire, Jethro Tull played new opera to astonished crowds.

Move proved to be rock'n'roll suicide as both fans and critics turned off. In retaliation Anderson announced break-up of group. When there was no public call to reconsider, Anderson realised mistake and explained he really only meant group would take break from touring. Using same basic line-up from **A Passion Play,** Anderson recorded 'comeback' LP **War Child,** as part of film project. Finally realising rock opera and concept albums were passé, film was abandoned and LP was released by itself.

Despite this background, **War Child** recaptured early Tull flavour and seemed excellent indication for band's future. More surprising was LP's single, **Bungle In The Jungle,** which became big US Hit, an event rare for Tull even when band played huge stadium concerts.

Unfortunately, it turned out to be Tull's last serious fling at critical or popular success. Using old line-up one more time, Anderson released disappointing **Minstrel In The Gallery.** Successive albums with various personnel changes periodically appear, usually just when it seems Tull are gone forever.

Anderson's talent is original enough (in use

of flute sound and almost manic vocals, in particular) to ensure modicum of interest whenever he wants to put out Jethro Tull releases or go on road (a break from his duty as a farmer/landowner). His past works are sometimes pretentious, but **Stand Up, Benefit, Aqualung** and **War Child** form basis of important contribution to rock's past.

Current line-up: Anderson; Martin Barre, guitar; David Pegg, bass, mandolin; Gerry Conway, drums; Peter-John Vettese, keyboards.

Hit Singles:	US	UK
Living In The Past, 1969	11	3
Sweet Dream, 1969	—	9
The Witch's Promise/Teacher, 1970	—	4
Life Is A Long Song/Up The Pool, 1971	—	11
Bungle In The Jungle, 1974	12	—

Albums:
This Was (Reprise/Island), 1968
Stand Up (Reprise/Island), 1969
Benefit (Reprise/Island), 1970
Aqualung (Chrysalis), 1971
Thick As A Brick (Chrysalis), 1972
Living In The Past (Chrysalis), 1972
A Passion Play (Chrysalis), 1973
War Child (Chrysalis), 1974
M.U. The Best Of Jethro Tull (Chrysalis), 1975
Minstrel In The Gallery (Chrysalis), 1975
Too Old To Rock'n'Roll: Too Young To Die (Chrysalis), 1976
Songs From The Wood (Chrysalis), 1977
Repeat: The Best Of Jethro Tull: Volume II (Chrysalis), 1977
Heavy Horses (Chrysalis), 1978
Live: Bursting Out (Chrysalis), 1978
Stormwatch (Chrysalis), 1979
A (Chrysalis), 1980
Broadsword And The Beast (Chrysalis), 1982

Joan Jett And The Blackhearts

US group formed 1979.

Original line-up: Joan Jett, guitar, vocals; Eric Amble, guitar; Lee Crystal, drums; Gary Ryan, bass.

Career: As young teenager, Joan Jett fell in love with heavy side of rock. T. Rex(▶), Black

Below: Contrary to popular belief, this man is not named Jethro Tull, but Ian Anderson.

Sabbath(▶) albums were early influence. After seeing Suzi Quatro(▶) in 1975, she decided to play rock instead of listening to it. Mutual friend linked up Kim Fowley and together they created the Runaways. Despite some promise, Runaways cashed in on being young girls in rock business rather than talented musicians. By 1979 Runaways had collapsed.

Jett became involved with Henry Laguna and Ritchie Cordell who were producing soundtrack for unreleased movie. Their music experience had been session/production work for Tommy James & the Shondells. This led to decision to do a Joan Jett album. Laguna/Cordell lined up various musicians, booked Who's Ramport Studios for December 1979/January 1980, and arranged European record deal. Back in March 1979, Jett had recorded three tracks with Paul Cook and Steve Jones, both free following Sex Pistols(▶) demise, resulting EP died and Jett used two tracks for new album.

Joan Jett LP first appeared in Europe. Jett auditioned line-up above and went on road. LP was pressed in limited quantity on private Blackheart label for US market. Over 20 companies saw no promise in Jett's music and refused to sign band. Neil Bogart, then president of Boardwalk Records, finally took chance. LP was re-issued under new title, **Bad Reputation.** Jett then built up following by sheer hard work, playing anywhere whenever gigs were available. For second album, Blackhearts re-recorded the final song Jett had played with Cook and Jones, **I Love Rock 'n' Roll.** It slowly picked up radio play and eventually reached No. 1. This broke second LP and in turn generated sufficient interest to chart **Bad Reputation. I Love Rock 'n' Roll** single subsequently made UK Top 5 but tour fared poorly.

Band continues to hold interest in US where any contrast to corporate rock must seem interesting. Whether Jett has peaked is hard to say, but she has outpaced the Runaways..

Current line-up: Jett; Crystal; Ricky Byrd, guitar.

Hit Singles:	US	UK
I Love Rock 'n' Roll, 1982	1	4
Crimson And Clover, 1982	7	60
Do You Wanna Touch Me (Oh Yeah), 1982	20	—

Albums:
Joan Jett (Blackheart/Ariola), 1980
Bad Reputation (Boardwalk/Epic), 1982
I Love Rock 'n' Roll (Boardwalk/Epic), 1982
Album (Boardwalk/Epic), 1983

Billy Joel

US vocalist, pianist, composer.
Born Long Island, New York, May 9, 1949.

Career: Encouraged by German-born father, Joel learnt piano from age four. In 1964, joined first group, the Echoes, which later became Lost Souls. Further early aggregations included the Hassles, who recorded two albums for United Artists, and Attila, a duo which made one album for Epic.

In 1971, demo tape of own songs gained Joel contract with Family Productions, and year later first solo album, **Cold Spring Harbor,** was released. Record created some interest despite appalling production, but business problems led to Joel's exodus to California. During this time he performed in bars and hotels under name Bill Martin.

However, song called **Captain Jack** had come to attention of Columbia records, and company traced Joel to California and signed him. Album **Piano Man** was released in

1973, providing Top 30 single in titletrack. Album eventually went platinum.

Strangely, next album, **Street Life Serenade,** did not do as well, and Joel decided to return to familiar environment of New York. 1976 album **Turnstiles** reflected home town lifestyle and furthered Joel's reputation as writer of memorable melodies and often perceptive story-telling lyrics.

Streetlife Serenade , Billy Joel. Courtesy Columbia Records. More melodies telling stories.

Massive breakthrough came with release of next album, **The Stranger.** It eventually became Columbia's biggest-selling album in US, surpassing even **Bridge Over Troubled Water.** LP also yielded instant standard in **Just The Way You Are,** covered by every artist from Englebert Humperdinck to Barry White(▶).

Since that time Joel has perched at or near top of pop and rock tree, alternating between effective ballads and more uptempo material. Somewhat lacking in identifiable image, Joel

The Stranger , Billy Joel. Courtesy Columbia Records.

nevertheless appeals to enormous number of people, cutting across rock and MOR markets. In 1982, success was as great as ever with three Top 40 singles and two hit albums in US.

Hit Singles:	US	UK
Just The Way You Are, 1978	3	19
Movin' Out (Anthony's Song), 1978	17	35
She's Always A Woman, 1978	17	—
My Life, 1978	3	12
Big Shot, 1979	14	—
You May Be Right, 1980	7	—
It's Still Rock And Roll To Me, 1980	1	14
Say Goodbye To Hollywood, 1981	17	—
Pressure, 1982	20	—
Allentown, 1983	17	—

Albums:
Piano Man (Columbia/CBS), 1973
Street Life Serenade (Columbia/CBS), 1975
Turnstiles (Columbia/CBS) 1976
The Stranger (Columbia/CBS), 1977
52nd Street (Columbia/CBS), 1978
Glass Houses (Columbia/CBS), 1980
Songs In The Attic (Columbia/CBS), 1981
The Nylon Curtain (Columbia/CBS), 1982

Elton John

UK vocalist, composer, pianist.
Born Reginald Kenneth Dwight, Pinner, Middlesex, March 25, 1947.

Career: Took piano lessons at early age. After leaving school in 1964, combined day job as messenger for music publisher with evening gig playing piano in pub. Following year joined local band Bluesology, which specialised in providing backing for visiting US soul stars like Billy Stewart, Patti Labelle and Major Lance. Band eventually became permanent backing outfit for Long John Baldry; this situation lasted until Baldry achieved pop stardom (albiet fleetingly) with **Let The Heartaches Begin** in late 1967.

By now John was collaborating as songwriter with lyricist Bernie Taupin, both having answered advertisement for talent placed by Liberty Records. Although Liberty lost interest, pair were signed by music publisher Dick James. After two years of attempting to write MOR material for other artists, John and Taupin concentrated on songs suitable for John's own voice. First single, **Lady Samantha**, was released in 1969 by Phillips.

Although it failed to chart, single created enough interest to boost first album, **Empty Sky**. Produced by DJM staffer Steve Brown on four-track machine, this in turn furthered John's growing reputation. But real breakthrough came with **Elton John**, more elaborately produced by Gus Dudgeon and featuring sensitive **Your Song**. Released as single, this became smash in UK and US.

A few months later, **Tumbleweed Connection** was released to almost universal acclaim. Atmospheric, evocative, filled with images of old American West, album made UK Top 20 and was soon joined in chart by earlier **Elton John**.

In meantime, John had formed Elton John Band with bass player Dee Murray and drummer Nigel Olsson. Outfit played Troubadour Club in Los Angeles to ecstatic audiences in August 1970; around same time **Elton John** and **Tumbleweed Connection** made US charts, and Elton John had made first steps towards huge American success.

Live album **17-10-70,** and **Friends,** soundtrack for obscure movie ,were next two issues, but **Madman Across The Water,** released in October 1971, was regarded as next 'official' release. Top 10 album on both sides of Atlantic, it initiated period lasting until 1976 during which artist could virtually do no wrong. John became one of world's most famous and highest-paid solo rock performers, breaking records for sales and live performance audiences. Singles and albums met with equal success. He established reputation for elaborate stage shows and over-the-top costumes, becoming in many ways the 'Liberace' of rock.

During 1973 John set up own record company Rocket Records (although artist himself did not start releasing product on label until 1976 when contract with DJM ran out) When Elton asked Lennon(▶) for permission to record 1974 cover hit **Lucy In The Sky With Diamonds.** Lennon agreed to appear on stage with Elton if it reached No. 1; when it did Lennon joined Elton in NYC concert—Lennon's last public performance.

In 1975 Elton participated in Ken Russell's movie 'Tommy' as Pinball Wizard and in 1976 topped UK singles chart for first time, via duet with Rocket artist Kiki Dee, **Don't Go Breaking My Heart.**

Commercially, John peaked around 1976; in late '70s began to keep a lower profile. In 1977 after years of punishing schedules and massive stage shows, played series of concerts accompanied only by percussionist Ray Cooper, an exercise he repeated in 1979 for tour of USSR.

Below: In the '70s, Elton became the 'Liberace of Rock'.

Above: Elton autographing Don't Shoot Me, I'm Only The Piano Player, 1973.

Above right: Captain Fantastic, still on top in the '80s.

Below: Elton with lyricist Bernie Taupin in the late '60s.

Inset Below:
Goodbye Yellow
Brick Road.
Courtesy MCA Records.

In 1978 partnership with Bernie Taupin terminated, and John began new collaboration with lyricist Gary Osborne. Although many critics predicted that departure of Taupin would have significant effect on John's career, in fact he continued to turn out hits, albeit less spectacularly. Work became more commercial and pop.

At present time Elton John is still highly successful act; 1982 saw Top 20 album in UK and US with **Jump Up**, as well as handful of hit singles, and reunion with Taupin. One of rock and pop's more endearing personalities, he is never far from news pages, and is now almost as well known for energetic chairmanship of Watford Football Club and difficulties with receding hairline as for music. Historically, he will probably be seen as most typical representative of '70s, a purveyor of glamour, spectacle and pretty tunes during beginnings of recession. Nevertheless, much of his work is of classic quality.

Hit Singles:	US	UK
Your Song, 1970	8	7
Rocket Man, 1972	6	2
Honky Cat, 1972	8	31
Crocodile Rock, 1972	1	5
Daniel, 1973	2	4
Saturday Night's Alright For Fighting, 1973	12	7
Goodbye Yellow Brick Road, 1973	2	6
Bennie And The Jets, 1974	1	37
Don't Let The Sun Go Down On Me, 1974	2	16
The Bitch Is Back, 1974	4	15
Lucy In The Sky With Diamonds, 1974	1	10
Philadelphia Freedom, 1975	1	12
Someone Saved My Life Tonight, 1975	4	22
Island Girl, 1975	1	14
Grow Some Funk Of Your Own/ I Feel Like A Bullet (In The Gun of Robert Ford), 1976	14	—
I Feel Like A Bullet (In The Gun Of Robert Ford)/Grow Some Funk Of Your Own, 1976	18	—
Pinball Wizard, 1976	—	7
Sorry Seems To Be The Hardest Word, 1976	6	11
Part Time Love, 1978	22	15
Song For Guy, 1978	—	4
Mama Can't Buy You Love, 1979	9	—
Little Jeannie, 1980	3	33
Empty Garden, 1982	13	51
Blue Eyes, 1982	12	8
I Guess That's Why They Call It The Blues, 1983	—	5
I'm Still Standing, 1983	12	42

With Kiki Dee:	US	UK
Don't Go Breaking My Heart, 1976	1	1

Albums:
Empty Sky (MCA/DJM), 1969
Elton John (MCA/DJM), 1970
Tumbleweed Connection (MCA/DJM), 1970
17-11-70 (MCA/DJM), 1971
Madman Across The Water (MCA/DJM), 1971
Honky Chateau (MCA/DJM), 1972
Don't Shoot Me, I'm Only The Piano Player (MCA/DJM), 1973
Goodbye Yellow Brick Road (MCA/DJM), 1973
Caribou (MCA/DJM), 1974
Captain Fantastic And The Brown Dirt Cowboy (MCA/DJM), 1974
Rock Of The Westies (MCA/DJM), 1975
Here And There (MCA/DJM), 1976
Blue Moves (MCXA/Rocket), 1976
Greatest Hits (MCA/DJM), 1977
Single Man (MCA/Rocket), 1978
Greatest Hits Volume 2 (MCA/DJM), 1979
Victim Of Love (Rocket), 1979
Live Collection (—/Pickwick), 1979
21 at 33 (Rocket), 1980
The Very Best Of Elton John (—/K-Tel), 1980
The Fox (Geffen/Rocket), 1981
Jump Up (Geffen/Rocket), 1982
Love Songs (—/TV), 1982
Too Low For Zero (MCA/Rocket), 1983

Below: The Piano Man, always excellent live in the early '70s.

Inset Below: Jump Up, Elton John. Courtesy MCA Records.

117

Johnny And The Hurricanes

US group formed 1958

Original line-up: Johnny Paris, tenor sax; Paul Tesluk, organ; Dave Yorko, guitar; Lionel 'Butch' Mattice, bass; Don Straczek, drums.

Career: Formed at high school in Toledo, Ohio, group played school hops and as back-up for a singer at city's Pearson Park. They were taken on in early 1959 by astute Detroit-based management team of Irving Micahnik and Harry Balk, who wrote or arranged most of group's material—often up-dates of old standards — under pseudonyms Tom King and Ira Mack.

Signed to Morty Craft's Warwick label, Hurricanes hit 23 in US charts in July 1959 with **Crossfire** before introducing organ sound in October with **Red River Rock** (a re-arrangement of C&W/folk number **Red River Valley**), a million-seller which reached No.3 in UK.

Staczek was replaced by Bill 'Little Joe' Savitch from the Royaltones and hits with **Revielle Rock** and **Beatnik Fly** followed before label switch to New York-based Big Top and big UK hit with **Rocking Goose**(which only made it to No. 60 in US). Group enjoyed continued success with **Ja-Ja** and **Old Smokey** before original line-up broke up in 1961.

Only Johnny Paris remained of originals in frequently changing touring band which exploited the hits during 1962 and '63 (visiting UK in latter year), while further records were made by session men, as had been the hit **Beatnik Fly** in 1960.

First rock 'n' roll instrumental band to steal a lead from contemporary R&B and heavily feature electric organ, counterpointing already fashionable raunchy sax sound, Johnny and the Hurricanes discs are now highly collectable among oldies freaks.

Final line-up: Paris; Tesluk; Yorko; Mattice; Kill 'Little Joe' Savitch, drums.

Hit Singles:

	US	UK
Red River Rock, 1959	5	3
Revielle Rock, 1959	25	14
Beatnik Fly, 1960	15	8
Down Yonder, 1960	48	8
Rocking Goose, 1960	60	3
Ja-Da, 1961	—	14

Albums:
Johnny And The Hurricanes (—/London), 1981
Johnny And The Hurricanes (—/Phoenix), 1982

Worth Searching Out:
Johnny And The Hurricanes (Warwick/—), 1960

Robert Johnson

US vocalist, guitarist, composer.
Born Robinsville, Mississippi between 1908-1917; died 1938.

Career: Robert Johnson completed five recording sessions, three in November 1936, two in June 1937. From these came 29 sides which are regarded as classics of the Delta blues idiom. Not only blues artists but many major rock stars have recorded his material: the Rolling Stones(▶) (**Love In Vain**), John Mayall(▶) (**Rambling On My Mid** and **Dust My Blues**), Cream(▶) (**Crossroads** and **From Four Till Late**). Johnny Winter(▶) is said to have learned slide guitar from listening

to Robert Johnson records.

Johnson's life is shrouded in mystery. Planning hits 'Spirituals To Swing' concert for Carnegie Hall in 1938, John Hammond decided to include the man who has been described as 'The King Of The Delta Blues Singers'. Hammond asked American Recording Corporation's field A&R man Don Law, who had recorded Johnson for Vocalion, to track Johnson down . Law discovered that this bluesman had died weeks before the concert was scheduled to take place — poisoned by a jealous lover. It is believed Johnson was not yet 21 at time of his death though estimates go as high as age 30.

Albums:
King Of The Delta Blues Singers (Columbia/CBS), 1966
King Of The Delta Blues Singers Volume 2 (Columbìa/CBS), 1970

George Jones

US vocalist, guitarist, composer.
Born Saratoga, Texas, September 12, 1931.

Career: Generally held to be greatest country singer of all time. Born into musical family; by early teens he was singing and playing guitar at local functions.

Served in Marines in Korea; following discharge did odd jobs while continuing to perform. Eventually signed with Starday Records, and gained first country hit in 1955 with **Why Baby Why**.

Although Jones flirted with rockabilly in '50s, recording under pseudonyms Thumper Jones and Hank Smith, he has generally stuck to pure country music. After Starday, Jones signed with Mercury, turning out more country hits; switched to United Artists in 1961. Early '60s saw Jones at height of career; he was voted top country singer by several trade papers, and continued to release classic country sides like **Window Up Above** and

She Thinks I Still Care.

In 1965 Jones teamed up with 'Pappy' Daly (formerly of Starday) to form Musicor Records; two-year collaboration resulted in music many regard as Jones' finest. Nevertheless, in 1967 artist switched yet again, to Epic.

In that year he married top female country singer Tammy Wynette(▶), forming an instant Royal Family of country. Pair recorded number of duet sides, and continued to record together even after divorce in 1973 (an event marked by Wynette classic single **D.I.V.O.R.C.E.**).

During '70s Jones consolidated success; unlike many others he remained unmoved by rock and pop influences and stayed strictly within country form. Nevertheless, his stylish vocalising has made him favourite among rockers who appreciate country (e.g. Elvis Costello). Somewhat belatedly, Country Music Association voted him Male Vocalist Of The Year for first time in 1980.

Albums (selected)
Best Of (Epic), 1975
All-Time Greatest Hits (—/Embassy), 1977
I Am What I Am (Epic), 1981
Still The Same Ole Me (Epic), 1982

With Tammy Wynette:
Greatest Hits (Epic), 1977

With Merle Haggard:
A Taste Of Yesterday's Wine (Epic), 1982

Grace Jones

West Indian vocalist, composer.
Born Jamaica, May 17, 19??

Career: Epitomising new genre of assertive sexually dominant women, Grace Jones embodies the bi-sexual, unisex concept. She has been dubbed 'The Dietrich of the new decade'.

Raised in Syracuse, New York, from age 12. Studied acting before becoming model for

prestigious Manhattan agency and appearing in movie 'Gordon's War'. Followed twin brother to Paris and became top model, appearing on covers of 'Vogue', 'Elle' and 'Der Stern'. Earned worldwide assignments before turning to singing with a French label.

Switching to Island Records Grace capitalised on disco boom. Became darling of New York's jet set and first artist to perform live at Studio 54.

Bizarre conceptual stage act, with undertones of sado-masochistic fantasy, masterminded by French artist Jean-Paul Goude, outrageous outfits (though best known for sleek men's trousers and suit jacket look) and decadent sensuality made her cult figure. Records became increasingly more commercially successful. Her recordings, which incorporate semi-reggae rhythms, feature vocals often half-spoken or whispered, are provocative. In UK her infamous appearance on Russell Harty's TV chat show, when she attacked her interviewer, brought her nationwide notoriety.

Grace's masterly theatrics more than compensate for any limitations in her singing voice.

Hit Singles:

	US	UK
Private Life, 1980	—	17

Albums:
Portfolio (Island), 1977
Fame (Island), 1978
Warm Leatherette (Island), 1980
Night Clubbing (Island), 1981
Living My Life (Island), 1982

Quincy Jones

US conductor, composer, arranger, producer.
Born Chicago, 1934.

Career: When Ray Charles(▶) moved to Seattle in 1948 at age 16 he was befriended by local resident Quincy Jones. Jones was destined to play major role in the emergent soul star's future career but their paths diverged for a while as Jones chose to enrol in Berkley School of Music in Boston rather than go out with Charles on black club touring circuit.

Regular visits to New York furthered Jones' enthusiasm for jazz. Before graduation he landed job as trumpeter with the Lionel Hampton Big Band, which took him around world. Following visit to France he decided to settle in Paris to further his studies in writing and arranging, working under teacher Nadia Boulanger, who also counted classical genius Stravinsky among her pupils.

Jones worked for Discques Barclay and won numerous European awards for work as composer, arranger and conductor during six-year sojourn in Paris. Attempts to run 18-piece big band, however, brought him close to bankruptcy in 1961. On his return to US, Mercury Records employed him as musical director, and he became first black to hold job as Mercury's vice president in charge of A&R.

Lesley Gore's **It's My Party** in May 1963 gave Jones his first pop chart-topper as producer; his own album **Big Band Bossa Nova** charted at same time. Further success at Mercury came with productions for Brook Benton, Billy Eckstine, Sarah Vaughan and others, as well as run of own albums. Jones also undertook freelance work for Frank Sinatra(▶), Johnny Mathis(▶), Tony Bennett and Ray Charles (including his **Genius + Soul = Jazz** album, an R&B masterpiece).

The mid-'60s found Jones branching successfully into sphere of movie score writing, which was to take up most of his time for some seven years. Starting with music for 'The

Below: Few rock stars of the 1980s have matched Grace Jones visually.

Pawnbroker' work included 'Bob And Carol And Ted And Alice', 'The Anderson Tapes', 'Cactus Flower', 'In The Heat Of The Night' (a particularly inventive effort which featured elements of country, pop, soul, jazz and electronic free-form, again working with Ray Charles), 'They Call Me Mr Tibbs', 'Mirage', 'Walk, Don't Run', 'Dollars' and 'The New Centurions'. Also scored TV series 'Ironside', 'I Spy' and, most recently 'Roots' (1977).

Moving back into popular music mainstream in 1969, Jones signed recording deal with A&M and began series of jazz-funk albums. Charted for first time since 1962 with

You've Got It Bad Girl, Quincy Jones. Courtesy A&M Records.

Walking In Space LP, which won Grammy Award.

Using finest West Coast jazz session-men, Jones was largely responsible for creating the jazz-funk explosion. In 1973 he once more turned to producing other artists, notably fellow A&M act the Brothers Johnson, whose career he masterminded, Rufus(▶), and Michael Jackson(▶) **(Off The Wall** was soul's most successful album of all time). He also nurtured careers of British songwriter Rod Temperton (from Heatwave) and singers Patti Austin, James Ingram, Jim Gilstrap, Al Jarreau and Leon Ware.

Jones' own Qwest label was launched in 1980, and he produced run of monster hits by jazz guitarist/vocalist George Benson(▶).

Jones scooped nearly all the 1982 Grammy Awards with his hit album **The Dude,** adding to a collection of more than 30 Grammys and Oscars.

Hit Singles:

	US	UK
Ai No Corrida, 1981	—	14
Razzamatazz, 1981	—	11
Just Once (featuring James Ingram), 1981	17	—
One Hundred Ways (featuring James Ingram), 1981	14	—

Albums (selected):
Smackwater Jack (A&M), 1974
Mellow Madness (A&M), 1975
I Heard That! (A&M), 1976
Quintessential Charts (Impulse/—), 1976
Sounds. . . And Stuff Like That (A&M), 1978
Body Heat (A&M), 1979
Great Wide World Of (Mercury), 1981
The Dude (A&M), 1981
Best Of (A&M), 1982

Rickie Lee Jones

US vocalist, composer, guitarist, keyboard player.
Born Los Angeles, 1958.

Career: Burst on scene with flair and originality in 1979 with self-titled album for Warner Bros. As youthful 'hanger-out' in seemier areas of LA, Jones began writing beat-influenced poetry; set it to music in jazzy,

boppy style that was catchy and listenable. Heavily influenced by fellow LA denizen Tom Waits(▶), showed tendency to write about wry street scenes populated with colourful, jive-talking characters. Her first album made Top 50, and from it came single **Chuck E's In Love,** still a standard on US FM radio.

Despite support of excellent band, suffered from stage-fright and shyness, refusing interviews and publicity, much to her record company's chagrin. After success of first album, retreated to Hills of LA to write poetry. Finally coaxed into studio when she had worked and re-worked enough material.

Second album showed different approach; in place of somewhat juvenile and simplistic cheery street scenarios were more mature, more perceptive compositions.

Hit Singles:

	US	UK
Chuck E's In Love, 1979	4	—

Albums:
Rickie Lee Jones (Warner Bros), 1979
Pirates (Warner Bros), 1981

Janis Joplin

US vocalist.
Born Port Arthur, Texas, January 19, 1943; died Los Angeles, October 4, 1970.

Career: An early fan of old Bessie Smith and Leadbelly blues records, Joplin started out in early '60s singing country and blues with bluegrass band in Texas. In 1966 she settled in hippy mecca of San Francisco and became lead vocalist of Big Brother and the Holding Company which featured James Gurley, guitar; Sam Andrew, guitar; Pete Albin, bass; and

Above: Always a loner, Janis Joplin was on the verge of huge stardom when she tragically overdosed in 1970.

David Getz, drums.

Raucous, ill-disciplined, and, in some areas, musically inept, band nonetheless had rare brand of raw energy which showcased Janis to good effect, especially on her classic reading of Erma Franklin's soul opus **Piece Of My Heart.** This set, from the 1968 Columbia album **Cheap Thrills,** confirmed the promise shown on the band's earlier LP for Mainstream (which Columbia re-released in 1970). **Cheap Thrills** sold more than a million copies and the management talents of Albert Grossman (man behind Dylan(▶) and others) made them Stateside superstars, though neither band nor Janis ever made it big in UK.

Janis Joplin's stature rapidly outgrew that of Big Brother (but band carried on for several years, Nick 'The Greek' Gravenites joining as vocalist in 1972) and in 1969 she went solo, earning immediate plaudits for **I Got Dem Ol' Kozmic Blues Again** set.

Her career was meteoric in its rapid rise, heights of adulation, and tragic fall. Seemingly trying to live up to her image, she became increasingly outrageous, drinking heavily, indulging in drug abuse and, in March 1970, being fined for using profane language on-stage. Seven months later she was found dead in a Hollywood hotel room of a heroine overdose. The album she had been working on with new backing outfit, the Full Tilt Boogie Band (comprising Richard Bell, piano; Ken Pearson, organ; John Till, guitar; Brad Campbell, bass; and Clark Pierson, drums), was issued under title **Pearl** (Janis' nickname) and included her memorable inter-

pretation of Kris Kristofferson's(▶) **Me And Bobby McGhee** which featured her vocals at their most spine-tinglingly soulful, and became posthumous US No. 1.

The 11-track album included two tracks for which she had not yet recorded vocals. Nick Gravenites was invited to sing them but declined so they appeared as instrumentals.

On her death, an immediate legend was created. A documentary titled 'Janis' was released in 1974, along with double-album soundtrack and biographies 'Buried Alive' by Myra Friedman and 'Going Down With Janis' by Peggy Caserta were widely read. Her tumultuous career and lonely private life were the inspiration for the film, 'The Rose', starring soundtrack, and biographies 'Buried Alive' by Bette Midler(▶) as Joplin. Both a product and a victim of the drug culture, Janis remains female personification of psychedelic/acid rock/hippie era.

Hit Singles:

	US	UK
With Big Brother And The Holding Company:		
Piece Of My Heart, 1968	12	—
Solo		
Me And Bobby McGhee, 1971	1	—

Albums:
Cheap Thrills (originally released as by Big Brother And The Holding Company) (Columbia/CBS), 1968
I Got Dem Ol' Kozmic Blues Again (Columbia/CBS), 1969
Pearl (Columbia/CBS), 1971
In Concert (Columbia/CBS), 1972
Janis (Columbia/CBS), 1974
Anthology (Columbia/CBS), 1982
Farewell Song (Columbia/CBS), 1982

Journey

US group formed 1973.

Original line-up: Gregg Rolie, vocals, keyboards, guitar; Neal Schon, guitar; George Tickner, guitar; Ross Valory, bass; Aynsley Dunbar, drums.

Career: Rolie and Schon were together in Santana(▶) when jazz influence created musical conflict of interest. They ran across Walter 'Herbie' Herbert who was attempting to assemble supergroup to play San Francisco area. Valory had played with Steve Miller(▶), and Dunbar with nearly every rock band with a drum kit — John Mayall(▶), Jeff Beck(▶), Zappa(▶) among others. Tickner was excellent session man.

For first gig, Journey played San Francisco's Winterland on last day of 1973. Interest from Columbia Records followed extensive touring, and first LP **Journey** appeared in spring 1975. Lack of response was discouraging and Tickner and Valory left band. Valory soon returned, however, and band continued year-round touring.

Next two albums (**Look Into The Future** and **Next**) were released in '75 and '76 with little notice. Manager Herbert suggested addition of lead vocalist Steve Perry, leaving Rolie free to fill out band's sound. **Infinity** can be considered Journey's first real album with powerful vocals and synthesised riffs. Perry's contribution also earned band US Top 20 hit, **Lovin' Touchin' Squeezin'**.

Live shows shifted from interminable solos to tight format. Such restraint never fitted Dunbar's style and he quit. Steve Smith (who had played with Ronnie Montrose(▶) who opened **Infinity** tour) took Dunbar's place. Subsequent albums increased band's popularity, although not with critics, who still dismiss Journey as 'commercial product'.

Renewed interest in band's history resulted in compilation LP, **In The Beginning. Captured** is strong live set and **Escape** introduced keyboard player Johnathan Cain. He is also songwriter, and co-wrote hit single **Who's Crying Now**. Journey's transition from guitar hard-rock sound to melodic hit-maker has turned group into US superstars. With smooth business machinery behind band, the 'trip' may be far from over.

Current line-up: Schon; Valory; Steve Perry, vocals; Steve Smith, drums; Johnathan Cain, keyboards.

Below: Lead singer Perry (second from right) also writes for Journey.

Hit Singles:	US	UK
Lovin' Touchin' Squeezin', 1979	16	—
Who's Crying Now, 1981	4	—
Don't Stop Believin', 1981	9	—
Open Arms, 1982	2	—
Still They ride, 1982	14	—

Steve Perry with Kenny Loggins:
Don't Fight It, 1982	17	—

Albums:
Journey (Columbia/CBS), 1975
Look Into The Future (Columbia/CBS), 1975
Next (Columbia/CBS), 1976
Infinity (Columbia/CBS), 1978
Evolution (Columbia/CBS), 1979
In The Beginning (Columbia/CBS), 1979
Departure (Columbia/CBS), 1980
Captured (Columbia/CBS), 1980
Escape (Columbia/CBS), 1981
Frontiers (Columbia/CBS), 1983

Joy Division

US group formed 1977.

Original line-up: Ian Curtis, vocals; Bernard Albrecht (né Dicken), guitar; Stephen Morris, drums; Peter Hook, bass.

Career: In 1977 Curtis, Albrecht, Morris came together and called themselves Warsaw. Early career consisted of nondescript playing throughout Manchester. They changed name to Joy Division, though there was never anything joyful about their sound, Curtis' flat voice being backed by depressing dirge-like instrumentals. Indications of things to come appear on live 10-inch compilation album **Short Circuit**. (**At A Later Date** is track by band while still Warsaw.)

Joy Division released four-track EP **An Ideal For Living** on own label Enigma. (Also released as 12-inch with vast improvement in sound quality on Anonymous Records.) Bands real potential for stark, sheer realism appeared first on new Factory label. **A Factory Sample** was EP to show off label's new talent. Two Joy Division tracks **Glass** and **Digital** were EP's high point.

National interest stirred by Martin Hannett-produced **Unknown Pleasures**, a bleak, troublesome, yet powerful debut album. Two out-takes given to Fast Records (Edinburgh) were released on **Earcom Two** compilation. Another two, **Atmosphere** and **DeadSouls**, appeared in 1,000 copy edition on small French Sordid Sentimentale label.

Joy Division's 1979 UK tour with Buzzcocks earned ecstatic response from critics and audience alike but the suicide of Curtis (in May 1980) curtailed planned US tour. Single **Love Will Tear Us Apart** and second album appeared after his death. Another out-take, **Komankino/Incubation**, appeared for awhile as free flexi-disc from Factory. Excellent **Still** release (1981) included live/studio material, covering the band's entire career.

Joy Division had agreed to 'kill' the name should any member leave the group, and remaining line-up thus became New Order.

Current line-up (New Order): Albrecht; Morris; Hook.

Hit Singles:	US	UK
Love Will Tear Us Apart, 1980	—	13

Albums:
Unknown Pleasures (—/Factory), 1979
Close (—/Factory), 1980
Still (—/Factory), 1981

Worth Searching Out:
An Ideal For Living (12-inch EP) (Anonymous), 1977
The Ideal Beginning (EP, released 1981, as Warsaw (Enigma)

Sin After Sin, Judas Priest. Courtesy Columbia Records.

Judas Priest

UK group formed 1973.

Original line-up: Rob Halford, vocals; Ken 'KK' Downing, Gibson Flying 'V' guitar; Ian Hill, bass; John Hinch, drums.

Career: One of Birmingham's local bands, Judas Priest always had extra spark setting them apart from usual heavy-rock treadmill. First album wears quickly but gained enough attention at the time to put group on first rung of ladder.

Initial change in drummers came as Alan Moore replaced Hinch; this line-up released second LP which got UK support but left band unknown in US. Simon Phillips played drums on band's debut CBS album **Sin After Sin**. Band spent 1978 in frenzied counter-attack on growing influence of new wave. **Stained Glass**, then **Killing Machine**, sounded the bombardment (Les Binks was now on drums).

Critics tended to dismiss band as outdated, but younger audience began picking up on TNWOBHM (The New Wave Of British Heavy Metal). This became apparent with single success of **Take On The World** in January 1979. Live recording from Japanese tour, **Unleashed In The East**, was 1979 LP and indicated band was rethinking direction. **British Steel** proved this to be true by providing balance of melody and vocal ballistics (with yet another new drummer, Dave Holland). Critics realised band was for real and sales finally improved in US. Appropriately titled album **Screaming For Vengeance** dispelled any doubt regarding band's commitment to heavy metal. It also became band's first platinum success in US which led to release of **Rocka Rolla**, nine years after UK release.

Aware of the need to experiment and to challenge audience, Judas Priest have proven long-lasting talent and have so far avoided becoming caricatures of themselves. Like Motorhead(▶) and Iron Maiden(▶), Judas Priest make narrow-minded heavy-metal category pointless.

Current line-up: Halford; Downing; Hill; Glen Tipton, Gibson SG guitar; Dave Holland, drums.

Hit Singles:

	US	UK
Take On The World, 1979	—	14
Living After Midnight, 1980	—	12
Breaking The Law, 1980	—	12

Albums:
Rocka Rolla (—/Gull), 1974
Sad Wings Of Destiny (Janus/Gull), 1976
Sin After Sin (Columbia/CBS), 1977
The Best Of Judas Priest (—/Gull), 1978
Stained Glass (Columbia/CBS), 1978
Killing Machine (Columbia/CBS), 1978
Unleashed In The East (Columbia/CBS), 1978
Hell Bent For Leather* (Columbia/—), 1979
British Steel (Columbia/CBS), 1980
Point Of Entry (Columbia/CBS), 1981
Screaming For Vengeance (Columbia/CBS), 1982
*US version of **Killing Machine** with extra track

Kansas

US group formed 1972.

Original line-up: Phil Ehart, drums; Dave Hope, bass; Kerry Livgren, guitar, keyboards; Steve Walsh, keyboards, vocals; Rich Williams, guitar.

Career: A prime example of US corporate/conglomerate rock. It comes as no surprise that Kansas' success was masterminded by Don Kirshner, the man behind success of the Monkees(▶) and the Archies. Unlike their predecessors, Kansas were no mere manufactured group, but a fairly strong musical unit, capable of challenging such contemporaries, as Foreigner(▶), Journey(▶) and REO Speedwagon(▶). Nameless faces, their albums

Below: Steve Walsh, the joker in the Kansas pack. The group have yet to emulate their great American success in the rest of the world.

have been uniformly acceptable but invariably bland, appealing to teenyboppers, over 20s and American AOR/FM audiences. Regularly appeared in single/LP charts.

Totally ignored by English rock press and public, the group almost reaped UK chart success with **Carry On Wayward Son**, which scraped Top 50 in July '78. Lyrics tend towards portentous, but occasionally Kansas have produced memorable cut, most notably the existential/nihilistic **Dust In The Wind** from fifth album **Point Of Know Return**.

Current line-up: Ehart; Hope; Livgren; Walsh; Williams; Robby Steinhardt, vocals, violins.

Hit Singles:

	US	UK
Carry On Our Wayward Son, 1976	11	51
Dust In The Wind, 1978	6	—
Play The Game Tonight, 1982	17	—

Albums:
Kansas (Epic), 1974
Masque (Epic), 1975
Song For America (Epic), 1975
Leftoverture (Epic), 1976
Point Of Know Return (Kirshner), 1977
Two For The Show (Kirshner), 1978
Monolith (Kirshner), 1979
Audio Visions (Kirshner), 1981
Visual Confessions (Kirshner), 1982

Chaka Khan

US vocalist.
Born Chicago, March 23, 1953.

Career: Consistently successful in field of black music, notably with 1978 mega-hits **I'm Every Woman** and **We Got The Love** (the latter a duet with guitarist/singer George Benson), Chaka Khan started out fronting multi-racial band which played mixture of soul, rock and pop.

Under name Rufus, band won major recording deal and made heavy impact as much for electric stage presence as for atmospherically classy, funk-slanted records like **Tell Me Something Good, You Got The Love** and **Once You Get Started**, which kept them in US charts from 1972-77.

With her often bizarre stage outfits, belting vocals and stage charisma, the petite and curvaceous Chaka became focal point of Rufus and in 1978 group's then label, Warner Bros, offered her solo deal under production aegis of talented Turkish emigré Arif Mardin.

A succession of acclaimed albums and singles, and her participation in Lenny White's ambitious 1982 project **Echoes Of An Era** which recreated '50s jazz classics using contemporary artists, has kept Khan in musical forefront.

Above: Chaka Khan, a 1980s black superstar in America, despite poor record sales.

Ht Singles:

	US	UK
With Rufus:		
Tell Me Something Good, 1974	3	—
You Got The Love, 1974	11	—
Once You Get Started, 1975	10	—
Sweet Thing, 1976	5	—
Solo:		
I'm Every Woman, 1978	21	11

Albums (selected):
With Rufus:
Rags To Rufus (MCA), 1974
Rufus Featuring Chaka Khan (MCA), 1975
Solo:
Chaka (Warner Bros), 1979
Naughty (Warner Bros), 1980
Whatcha' Gonna Do For Me (Warner Bros), 1981
Chaka Khan (Warner Bros/—), 1982

Kid Creole And The Coconuts

US group formed 1979.

Original line-up: August Darnell, vocals; 'Sugar-coated' Andy Hernandez, aka Coati Mundi, percussion, vibraphone; Adriana Kaegi, Brooksie Wells, Lourdes Cotto, Fonda Rae, backing vocals.

Career: Band is brainchild of vocalist/guitarist/composer August Darnell, aka Kid Creole. Haitian-born, New York raised, Darnell first came to prominence with seminal mid-'70s disco outfit Dr Buzzard's Original Savannah Band, which cut pair of albums for RCA and one for Elektra.

Following collapse of Savannah Band amid litigation, Darnell and ex-Savannah Andy Hernandez recruited three female vocalists (including wife Adriana) to form Coconuts. Concept of outfit was fashionable version of pre-war tropical night-life — Darnell has said that his vision is based on night-club scenes in 'King Kong'.

Signed to hip East Coast label Ze, outfit

released **Off The Coast Of Me** in 1980 to considerable critical enthusiasm but little public reaction. Album yielded minor hit in **Maladie D'Amour**. But it was not until release of 1982 album **Tropical Gangsters** that Creole and Coconuts started to gain commercial success, and then largely in UK.

Tropical Gangsters, Kid Creole & the Coconuts. Courtesy Island Records.

Very much a personal creation of Darnell, he fronts stage full of props in '40s suits as playboy to three ladies, Creole and Coconuts offer originality, imagination and whimsical fantasy, all qualities which are not over-abundant on pop and rock scene. Nevertheless, Latin-based music has never enjoyed extended commercial success, and it remains to be seen whether outfit can sustain commercial appeal.

Current line-up: Darnell; Hernandez; Kaegi; Cheryl Poirier and Taryn Haegy, backing vocals.

Hit Singles:	US	UK
I'm A Wonderful Thing Baby, 1982	—	4
Stool Pigeon, 1982	—	7
Annie, I'm Not Your Daddy, 1982	—	2

Albums:
Off The Coast Of Me (Ze), 1980
Fresh Fruit In Foreign Places (Ze), 1981
Tropical Gangsters (Ze), 1982

Kids From Fame
US TV series/group formed 1981.

Career: In 1980, English director Alan Parker's movie 'Fame' was big success. Story was of goings-on at an arts school (based on New York's Academy of the Performing Arts). Film's reception led to TV series written by Linda Elstad and directed by Mel Swope.

Series did not do well in US television ratings but was very well-received in Britain. Capitalising on this, **Fame** theme was released and became instant hit. It was, however, the version used in the movie, sung by Irene Cara, not that from TV series.

Cara had declined proffered role in TV series and there were several other differences in casting. Main characters in the TV series are: Coco (the singer/dancer; Carol Mayo), Lydia (the dance instructress; Debbie Allen), Doris (the diminutive but dynamic actress; Varelie Landsberg), Julie (the Chellist; Lori Singer), Leroy (the black dancer; Gene Anthony Ray), Danny (the funny guy; Carlo Imperato) and Sharofsky (the professor; Albert Hague).

When the spin-off album appeared, and charted, it did not include the original theme as the TV producers did not have rights to recording.

The Fame team have toured UK twice, their appeal proving to be mainly to teenybopper (the show being of the somewhat twee 'family entertainment' genre).

In meantime, Irene Cara, who for while seemed to have made a blunder by not joining the TV cast, bounced back to prominence by singing theme from smash hit movie 'Flashdance'. **Flashdance — What A Feeling** took this dynamic young singer to top of US and UK charts. Unfortunately, nobody in the TV series possesses the same level of vocal talent, though several Kids from Fame songs have charted in UK.

Hit Singles:	US	UK
Hi-Fidelity, 1981	—	5
Starmaker, 1981	—	3

Irene Cara:

Fame, 1980	4	1
Flashdance, 1983	1	2

Albums:
Fame (Film Soundtrack) (RSO), 1980
Fame (TV Series) (RCA/BBC), 1982
From Fame Again (—/BBC), 1982
Live (—/BBC), 1983

B. B. King
US vocalist, guitarist, composer.
Born Itta Bena, Indianola, Mississippi, September 16, 1925.

Career: Truly living up to his name, Riley B. 'Blues Boy' King has majestically dominated the blues scene for more than 30 years, gigging an average of 300 days a year and spending most of the other 65 in the recording studio.

King has matched talents with finest of musicians, from black American greats the Crusaders(▶) to rock stars like Leon Russell(▶), Carole King(▶), Ringo Starr(▶) and Nicky Hopkins. He has recorded hits in a hotel room, in a garage, and in the world's foremost studios. His material has ranged from pure blues (both urban and rural), to country songs (his cousin is country blues legend Bukka White) rock numbers, pop songs and even Broadway material, though in every case transferred to the blues idiom.

His emergent style was heavily influenced by both T. Bone Walker and the jazz of Charlie Christian. Joining Radio WGRM in Greenwood, Mississippi, in late '50s, he was spotted by Sonny Boy Williamson (Rice Miller) who took him to the far more important Memphis station WDIA. King became resident DJ and was dubbed 'The Beale Street Blues Boy', later shortened to 'B.B.', by station manager Don Kearn.

King's recording debut came with **Miss Martha King** (1949). Then talent scout Ike Turner(▶) signed him to Modern Records' RPM subsidiary where he enjoyed 11-year stint, soaring to No. 1 on R&B charts in 1950 with **Three O'Clock Blues** which featured Turner on piano, Hank Crawford on saxophone and Willie Mitchell on trumpet.

Quickly becoming most in-demand artist on blues circuit, King quit WDIA. (His show was taken over by Rufus Thomas who went on to fame as a soul singer.)

King's flashy guitar lines with their torrent of notes were matched to the response of his highly emotive vocals, a mix of falsetto wailing and rich gospel-flavoured tenor. Despite a couple of quirks (he can neither play particularly good rhythm nor sing while playing) King has clearly been maestro of his chosen music, influencing countless other players, notably Buddy Guy, Otis Rush and Eric Clapton(▶).

In 1961 he switched to major ABC Paramount label who sought to broaden his appeal (as they were for Ray Charles(▶)) by adding a more sophisticated flavour to his music through lush arrangements by Johnny

Below: The great B.B. King, pictured onstage in London during 1982 on the same bill as Bobby Bland.

Pate (the Impressions(▶) producer) and Quincy Jones(▶) (who was concurrently working with Charles), and even adding string sections on several recordings.

In 1969, strings were used in stunning fashion for epic smash **The Thrill Is Gone**, and the **Completely Well** album, which

Live At The Regal, considered to be the classic B.B. King album. Courtesy ABC Records.

included single, was arguably his best ever.

Commanding an increasingly broad-based audience through '70s, his concerts drawing both white and black, young and old, King's recorded output became somewhat inconsistent. Often ill-matched with material and musicians as he tried to please wider following by diversity of music, at times he seemed in danger of sinking into MOR mire. Duets with Bobby Bland(▶) — an old friend from Memphis days — did little justice to either, but recent live appearances have shown that he retains old potential and remains King among the blues kings. (Neither Albert King nor the late Freddie King managed to reach his heights despite their undoubted class.)

Guitar: Gibson 335.

Hit Singles:

	US	UK
The Thrill Is Gone, 1970	15	—

Albums (selected):
Live At The Regale (MCA/HMV), 1965
His Best: The Electric B. B. King (MCA/ABC), 1969
Live And Well (MCA/ABC), 1970
Completely Well (MCA/ABC), 1970
Live At Cook County Jail (MCA/Probe), 1971
Back In The Alley (MCA/ABC), 1973
The Best Of B. B. King (—/Ace Cadet), 1981
Love Me Tender (MCA), 1982
Alive In London (with the Crusaders) (MCA), 1982

With Bobby Bland:
Together For The First Time (MCA), 1974
Together Again (MCA), 1976

Worth Searching Out:
Indianola Mississippi (MCA/ABC), 1970

Carole King

US composer, vocalist, pianist.
Born Carole Klein, Brooklyn, New York, February 9, 1942.

Career: Played piano from age four; smitten by rock 'n' roll in early teens, started hanging out at rock 'n' roll shows. Formed own group in high school. After school, attended Queen's College, where she met aspirant songwriter (later her husband) Gerry Goffin. Personal and musical collaboration followed, resulting in first hit **Will You Still Love Me Tomorrow**; recorded by Shirelles, song made No. 1 in US and No. 3 in UK.

Goffin and King then became part of 'Brill Building' stable of writers under aegis of entrepreneur/publisher Don Kirshner. During this period pair wrote seemingly endless series of classic hits, including **Up On The Roof** and **When My Little Girl Is Smiling** for Drifters(▶), **Take Good Care Of My Baby** for Bobby Vee(▶), **One Fine Day** for Chiffons (▶), **Halfway To Paradise** for Tony Orlando and Billy Fury(▶), **Every Breath I Take** for Gene Pitney(▶) and **The Locomotion** for little Eva (actually pair's babysitter, Eva Boyd).

Don Kirshner launched King as solo recording artist in 1962 with **It Might As Well Rain Until September**. Despite this international hit, follow-ups were not successful and King was not to make serious attempt to become artist as well as writer until end of decade. Having moved to West Coast, in 1970 King recorded first solo album, **Writer**.

Although not huge success, it paved way for next offering, **Tapestry**, which was to become one of most successful albums ever. Released in 1971, **Tapestry** stuck chord with post-psychedelic generation with its emphasis on simple life and values. Spawning clutch of hit singles, it went on to sell somewhere

Above: Carole King exchanged a career as a top notch songwriter for equal fame in the 1970s as a recording artist in her own right.

around 13 million units over course of next decade.

After **Tapestry**, King never quite achieved same heights. Despite recording and working live with varying success, she only had two further major hits as artist (**Jazzman** in 1974, **Nightingale** in 1975). However, **Tapestry** and equally valid body of work from early '60s ensure continued veneration among fans of good pop songs. Not one of the great singers, King is nevertheless convincing interpreter of self-penned material.

Hit Singles:

	US	UK
It Might As Well Rain Until September, 1962	22	3
It's Too Late, 1971	1	6
So Far Away, 1971	14	—
Sweet Seasons, 1972	9	—
Jazzman, 1974	2	—
Nightingale, 1975	9	—

Albums:
Writer (Ode), 1970
Tapestry (Ode), 1972
Music (Ode), 1972
Rhymes And Reasons (Ode), 1972
Fantasy (Ode), 1973
Wrap Around Joy (Ode), 1974
Thoroughbred (Ode), 1976
Simple Things (Capitol), 1977
Welcome Home (Capitol), 1978
Greatest Hits (Ode), 1978
Touch The Sky (Capitol), 1979
Pearls — Songs Of Goffin & King (Capitol), 1980
One To One (Atlantic), 1982

King Crimson

UK group formed 1969.

Original line-up: Robert Fripp, guitar, mellotron; Ian McDonald, reeds, keyboards; Greg Lake, bass, vocals; Peter Sinfield, lyricist; Mike Giles, drums.

Career: Evolved from Giles, Giles And Fripp, a pop-influenced trio from Dorset that recorded two singles and one barely noticed album, **The Cheerful Insanity Of Giles Giles And Fripp**. Group split in November 1968, Peter Giles temporarily quitting business; brother Mike and Fripp founded King Crimson. With new members McDonald and Lake (aided by lyricist Sinfield) rehearsals were completed below cafe in London's Fulham Road. Debut gig at Speakeasy (April 1969) established small cult following, dramatically increased following appearance at Rolling Stones'(▶) celebrated Hyde Park concert in July. First album **In The Court Of The Crimson King** received ecstatic response and established

unit as one of most progressive of era. From this point on, group were dogged by series of personnel changes/upheavals.

An 11-day US tour in November/December 1969 took its toll; on return to London both Giles and McDonald quit. While seeking permanent line-up, Fripp employed a number of session men/friends to complete second LP **In The Wake Of Poseidon**. Giles returned as bassist, jazzer Keith Tippett played piano, Mel Collins added saxophone and Gordon Haskell contributed vocals. Sinfield was by this time credited as lyricist, light show operator and synthesiser player. Prior to album's release Fripp had declined invitations to join Yes(▶) and Aynsley Dunbar's Blue Whale. Lukewarm response afforded **Poseidon** meant that only Collins and Haskell were retained for third album, aided by drummer Andy McCullough. **Lizard** was noticeable improvement on predecessor, but following recording sessions Haskell and McCullough quit.

Fripp and Sinfield again restructured group, with Mel Collins, Ian Wallace (drums) and Boz Burrell, a singer whom Fripp taught to play bass. Following release of **Islands**, Sinfield left to reappear as Roxy Music's(▶) producer. Less than successful US tour killed off remaining members, leaving live **Earthbound** as final comment.

The ever-eccentric Fripp returned to England and, following period of hibernation, introduced another unit, comprising Bill Bruford (former Yes drummer), bassist John Wetton (ex-Family(▶)), percussionist James Muir and David Cross (violin/mellotron). The power and promise of line-up was fully revealed on excellent **Lark's Tongue In Aspic** and vindicated in concert performances. Unfortunately, Muir quit, leaving four-piece Crimson to record acceptable **Starless And Bible Black**.

In July 1974, Crimson closed tour with concert in NY's Central Park, captured for posterity on second live album, **USA**. In September, Fripp officially announced that Crimson no longer existed. A posthumous album, **Red**, was released in 1974 and saw return of original member Ian McDonald.

Few would disagree that Crimson split at the right time; they would have been in danger of losing credibility had they continued. Unlike their contemporaries, group managed to avoid worst excesses of self-indulgent '70s art rock. Their reputation as one of truly

innovative progressive rock groups was aided by Fripp's forays into avant garde and ambient music. Between 1974-80, Fripp worked with number of artists, most notably Eno(▶) (collaborated on **No Pussyfooting** and **Evening Star**). Work with Peter Gabriel(▶) and David Bowie(▶) also attracted great interest, leading to new-found respect from previous detractors.

In 1981, Fripp took unusual step of reforming King Crimson with Adrian Belew (guitar/lead vocal), Robert Fripp (guitar/devices!), Tony Levin (bass/vocals) and Bill Bruford (drums). Album **Discipline** was released in September 1981 amid critical arguments about whether Crimson were an anachronism, a seminal progressive rock band, or both. **Beat**, released following year, was first Crimson studio album to have same personnel on two consecutive releases. Since then, group have laid any misconceptions about a possible 'cash in' on the King Crimson name.

Their work continues to command respect, attracting younger audiences as well as the old die-hards. Though unlikely to make any impact on the development of rock at this stage, Crimson have demonstrated that re-formation need not necessarily imply retrogression.

Current line-up: Fripp, guitar, keyboards; Bill Bruford, drums; Adrian Belew, guitar; Tony Levin, bass.

Albums:
In The Court Of The Crimson King (Island), 1969
In The Wake Of Poseidon (Island), 1970
Lizard (Island), 1970
Islands (Island), 1971
Earthbound (Island), 1972
Lark's Tongue In Aspic (Island), 1973
Starless And Bible Black (Island), 1974
Red (Island), 1974
USA (Island), 1975
A Young Person's Guide To King Crimson (Island), 1976
Discipline (EG/Polydor), 1981
Beat (EG/Polydor), 1982

Robert Fripp with Andy Summers:
I Advance Masked (A&M), 1982

Below: One of the many line-ups of King Crimson, formed in the '60s by guitarist Robert Fripp, left.

The Kinks

UK group formed 1964.

Original line-up: Ray Davies, vocals, guitar; Dave Davies, guitar, vocals; Peter Quaife, bass; Mick Avory, drums.

Career: Dressed in red huntsman's jackets and sporting mod haircuts, the Kinks were launched on British public as an image-heavy beat band. Debut Pye single **Long Tall Sally** was straight copy of Beatles' cover of Little Richard's(▶) classic; it bombed, as did follow-up **You Do Something To Me**, which only sold 127 copies. The rough, propulsive **You Really Got Me** was something quite different. Close in form to the Kingsmen's **Louie, Louie**, it had an R&B edge which British audiences were looking for at time and shot to No.1.

Producer Shel Talmy had found a golden vein and exploited it well over next 18 months with string of charters, mostly written by Ray Davies. From straightforward pop songs, Davies started composing ever more pictorial lyrics, strongly British in inspiration yet with a wide appeal. The humorous **Dedicated Follower Of Fashion** (taking off '60s fashion fanatics) the atmospheric **Waterloo Sunset** (which proved songs didn't have to have American locations to be effective), **Autumn Almanac** and others showed depth of his writing talent, which some rated on par with Lennon/McCartney.

As band began touring less, Ray Davies involved himself in solo projects, including score for 'The Virgin Soldiers'. Brother Dave had solo UK hit (backed by Kinks and issued as Kinks single in US) in 1967 with **Death Of A Clown**. This was included along with **Waterloo Sunset** and the funny yet perceptive **David Watts** on brilliant **Something Else By The Kinks** album, marking end of group's partnership with Shel Talmy.

With Ray Davies now producing, the Kinks followed Beatles and others into realms of concept albums, notably with **The Kinks Are The Village Green Preservation Society** and **Arthur (Or The Decline And Fall Of The British Empire)**; latter was originally commissioned as TV soundtrack. By then Peter Quaife had been replaced by John Dalton. In 1970 group returned to singles' charts with controversial but excellent **Lola**, a song about transvestism and a hit on both sides of Atlantic. **Kinks Part 1: Lola Versus Powerman And The Moneygoround** had biting lyrics about rampant manipulation in pop music scene. Meanwhile, Ray Davies completed soundtrack of 'Percy' and had main role in television play 'The Long Distance Piano Player'.

Getting out of current management deal and Pye record contract, group pacted with RCA. Opening RCA album, **Muswell Hillbillies**, introduced John Gosling on keyboards plus brass section from the Mike Cotton Sound. Laurie Brown, Alan Holmes and John Beecham subsequently became regular members of the Kinks. Despite including **Alcohol** and **Skin And Bone**, two of most atypical Kink's classics, album sold poorly. Ironically, their following in America was burgeoning. Increasingly theatrical in concept, with strong roots in music-hall traditions, the Kinks' subsequent albums were often somewhat grandiose projects. **Sleepwalker** (1977) found group switching to Arista Records and album was another in string of Stateside successes.

In 1974 the Kinks had formed own Konk label, signing Claire Hamill. Ray Davies produced her **Stage Door Johnnies** album, and debut set by Cafe Society, also on Konk. 1977 label move to Arista saw departure of John Dalton; Davies then dropped horn section. Andy Pyle (ex-Savoy Brown(▶)) took up bass for a while but left by May 1978. Jim Rodford has filled spot since. John Gosling also left and was replaced on keyboards by Gordon Edwards, then Ian Gibbons. In 1979 group recorded **Low Budget**, their first venture in an American studio, and the following year issued **One For The Road**, a live double LP of their best-known material, recorded while on tour in US; a live version of **Lola** made US Hot 100 in 1980.

With recent **Give The People What They Want** album, the writing powers of Ray Davies showed sad decline, being full of clichés and cheap laughs. However, his previous output fully justifies his rating as one of most important figures in history of British pop music, and US success remains unabated.

Current line-up: Ray Davies; Dave Davies; Avory; Jim Rodford, bass; Ian Gibbons, keyboards.

Above: Raymond Douglas Davies, leader of The Kinks, and composer of some of the finest, though possibly least appreciated, songs of the rock'n'roll era.

Above: The first LP released by The Kinks, back in 1964. Courtesy Pye Records.

Below: The Kinks perform for British TV show 'Ready Steady Go' during the mid-'60s. (Left to right) Ray Davies, Mick Avory, Dave Davies, Pete Quaife.

Hit Singles:

	US	UK
You Really Got Me, 1964	7	1
All Day And All Of The Night, 1964	7	2
Tired Of Waiting For You, 1965	6	1
Everybody's Gonna Be Happy, 1965	—	17
Set Me Free, 1965	23	9
See My Friend, 1965	—	10
A Well Respected Man 1965	13	—
Till The End Of The Day, 1965	50	8
Dedicated Follower Of Fashion, 1966	36	4
Sunny Afternoon, 1966	14	1
Dead End Street, 1966	—	5
Waterloo Sunset, 1967	—	2
Autumn Almanac, 1967	—	3
Days, 1968	—	12
Lola, 1970	9	2
Apeman, 1970	45	5
Supersonic Rocket Ship, 1972	—	16
Come Dancing, 1983	—	6

Dave Davies Solo:

	US	UK
Death Of A Clown, 1967	—	3
Susannah's Still Alive, 1967	—	20

Albums:

The Kinks (—/Hallmark), 1964
You Really Got Me (Reprise/Pye), 1965
Live At The Kelvin Hall (Reprise/Pye), 1967
Something Else (Reprise/Pye), 1967
Village Green Preservation Society (Reprise/Pye), 1968
Arthur (Or The Decline And Fall Of The British Empire) (Reprise/Pye), 1969
Kinks Part 1: Lola Versus Powerman And The Moneygoround (Reprise/Pye), 1970
Lola (—/Hallmark), 1971
Everybody's In Showbiz (RCA), 1972
Kink Kronikles (Reprise/—), 1972
Soap Opera (RCA), 1975
Schoolboys In Disgrace (RCA), 1975
Celluloid Heroes—The Kinks' Greatest (RCA), 1976
The Kinks File (—/Pye), 1977
Sleepwalker (Arista/Fame), 1977
Misfits (Arista), 1978
20 Golden Greats (—/Ronco), 1978
Low Budget (Arista), 1979
Second Time Around (RCA/—), 1979
One For The Road (Arista), 1980*
Collection (—/Pickwick), 1980
Give The People What They Want (Arista), 1982
State Of Confusion (Arista), 1983
*Live double.

Worth Searching Out:

Kinks-size (Reprise/—), 1965
Kinda Kinks (Reprise/Pye), 1965
Muswell Hillbillies (RCA), 1971
The Great Lost Kinks Album (Reprise/—), 1973
Preservation Act I (RCA), 1973

Kiss

US group formed 1973.
Original line-up: Ace Frehley, guitar; Paul Stanley, guitar; Gene Simmons, bass; Peter Criss, drums.

Career: Kiss began by taking Lou Reed(▶)/David Bowie(▶) glitter rock and pushing it to extreme. Band obliterated members' past by hiding behind comic-book costumes and greasepaint. With first concerts, Kiss managed to alienate rock press, offend parents and win undying loyalty of New York's younger rock fans.

Albums emphasised gothic, bigger-than-life aspects of rock music. Live shows had massive drum kits rising 40 feet into air and explosives flashing everywhere, while Simmons spit fire (real) and blood (fake) or just rolled out his foot-long tongue. Critics wondered what this had to do with the music while kids made Kiss hottest selling band of decade.

Japan in particular took to Kiss early on and band showed appreciation by putting Japanese credits on second album in late 1974. **Alive** LP had giant **Rock And Roll All Nite** single and showed band was not all flash. Next LP, **Destroyer**, proved even more of surprise by including excellent ballad, **Beth**. Super hero/hidden identify ploy, enhanced by band's

Kiss Alive II, Kiss. Courtesy Casablanca Records.

refusal to be photographed or interviewed without make-up, finally went over top by actually including comic-book history of band in **The Originals** (special re-issue of first three LPs). Next two album covers, **Rock And Roll Over** (1976) and **Love Gun** (1977), also had comic style covers instead of usual pictures.

By 1977, Kiss management had organised fans into Kiss Army and provided them with range of Kiss memorabilia and products. Disdain of other bands and managers had suspicion of jealousy. First sign that Kiss fans were possibly outgrowing their heroes came in 1978. Amid much publicity, four solo LPs, one from each member of Kiss, went platinum before day of release. All four began appearing in cut-out racks shortly after. **Dynasty** (1979) and **Unmasked** (1980) lacked outrageousness of early Kiss. Perhaps rock world found Kiss passé after Sid Vicious & Co. Peter Criss quit, claiming face could no longer cope with make-up; band had first photos taken without it.

Surprisingly, Criss's replacement Eric Carr not only filled position well, but band produced excellent **The Elder**. It seemed to be rock-opera soundtrack for non-existent movie. Such a concept would drag down any album in 1981 and **The Elder** flopped. **Creatures Of The Night** returned to old Kiss style; problem was finding audience for it. One puzzling aspect is why this most visual of bands hasn't translated well into video age, though **Creatures Of The Night** video is superb.

Early Kiss were loud and crude but in hindsight innovative, even original. Professional management set standards for all to

Rock And Roll Over, Kiss. Courtesy Casablanca Records.

follow; to some this represents complete sell-out of rock's once powerful potential, to others it's the only way to run an entertainment business.

In early 1983 Ace Frehley left and was replaced by Vinny Vincent.

Current line-up: Simmons; Stanley; Eric Carr, drums; Vinny Vincent, guitar.

Hit Singles:

	US	UK
Rock And Roll All Nite (Live), 1976	12	—
Beth, 1976	7	—
Hard Luck Woman, 1977	15	—
Calling Dr Love, 1977	16	—
I Was Made For Lovin' You, 1979	11	50

Albums:

Kiss (Casablanca), 1974
Hotter Than Hell (Casablanca), 1974
Dressed To Kill (Casablanca), 1975
Alive (Casablanca), 1975
Destroyer (Casablanca), 1976
Rock And Roll Over (Casablanca), 1976
Love Gun (Casablanca), 1977
Kiss Alive II (Casablanca), 1977
Dynasty (Casablanca), 1979
The Best Of The Solo Albums (Casablanca), 1981
The Elder (Casablanca), 1981
Killers (Casablanca), 1982*
Creatures Of The Night (Casablanca), 1982
*compilation

Worth Searching Out:
The Originals (Casablanca), 1976

Earl Klugh

US guitarist, composer.
Born Detroit, Michigan, 1953.

Career: Klugh took up guitar at age of 10, inspired by then-current folk boom. Influenced originally by Chet Atkins, he developed individualistic jazz/funk/easy-listening style for acoustic guitar.

First professional experience came at 16, playing on record date with jazz reedman Yusef Lateef. Later he joined George Benson(▶) band, and toured with master guitarist for 18 months.

He signed with Blue Note in 1977, and has since released succession of LPs which have earned him wide international audience. Featuring ace sidemen like Steve Gadd, Ralph MacDonald and Phil Upchurch, Klugh's albums have strong crossover/MOR appeal. Interesting compositions and above-average inventiveness ensure that his output is worth more than cursory attention.

One On One, with Bob James(▶), earned Klugh first gold album. Artist looks set to continue to increase popularity of acoustic guitar as jazz/funk instrument.
Guitars: Velasquez classical, Takamine classical, Gibson Chet Atkins, solid body classical, Ibanez classical, Alvaraz classical.

Albums:
Earl Klugh (Blue Note/—), 1977
Living Inside Your Love (Blue Note), 1977
Finger Painting (Blue Note), 1977
Magic In Your Eyes (Liberty/United Artists), 1978
Heartstring (Liberty/United Artists), 1979
Dream Come True (Lberty/United Artists), 1980
Late Night Guitar (Liberty/United Artists), 1980
Crazy For You (Liberty/United Artists), 1981
Low Ride (Capitol), 1983

With Bob James:
One On One (Columbia/CBS), 1980
Two Of A Kind (Capitol), 1982

Gladys Knight And The Pips

US vocal group formed 1952.
Original line-up: Gladys Knight; Merald (Bubba) Knight; Brenda Knight; William Guest; Elenor Guest.

Career: Gladys Knight (born Atlanta, Georgia, May 28, 1944) was child singing prodigy, winning talent contests and peforming with gospel groups; sang with Atlanta gospel group the Morris Brown Choir at four, won 'Ted Mack Amateur Hour' TV talent competition at seven. Gladys Knight and the Pips was formed following family celebration when Gladys was only eight; Bubba and Brenda were Gladys' brother and sister, William and Elenor Guest her cousins. Group were soon playing local gigs, and made first national tour (with Sam Cooke(▶) and Jackie Wilson) in 1956.

After unsuccessful releases on Brunswick, Brenda and Elenor left group, to be replaced by Edward Patten, another cousin, and Langston George. This line-up had major hit with **Every Beat Of My Heart** in 1961.

Further hits on Fury followed, and group became sought-after live attraction. George left group and current line-up stabilised. Signing to Maxx Records consolidated R&B success. Following label's demise group signed to Motown in 1966.

Motown started group off on route to international success; version of classic **I Heard It Through The Grapevine** went to No. 2 in US charts in 1967, and was followed by string of major hits. Nevertheless, when Motown deal expired in 1973 group moved to Buddah; period of unprecedented success followed.

First album, **Imagination**, produced three hit singles and made group America's most successful vocal outfit of 1973. Since then, acclaim and chart honours have been virtually automatic. Versatility and talent of group have received wide exposure in top venues and on TV. Vocal prowess of Gladys Knight ensures continued respect of black music fans. Unusually, Gladys and her family group manage to successfully straddle both cabaret/MOR and gutsier, more soul-orientated fields.

At end of '70s Gladys and Pips drifted apart temporarily, Pips making album on their own, but they soon reunited and signed new deal with Columbia/CBS in 1980. Success continues, although hit singles have been less in evidence of late. Gladys and the Pips are one of the longest surviving acts, with over 30 years of showbiz behind them.

Current line-up: Gladys Knight; Bubba Knight; William Guest; Edward Patten.

Hit Singles:

	US	UK
Every Beat Of My Heart, 1961	6	—
Letter Full Of Tears, 1962	19	—
Take Me In Your Arms And Love Me, 1967	—	13
I Heard It Through The Grapevine, 1967	2	47
The End Of Our Road, 1968	15	—
The Nitty Gritty, 1969	19	—
Friendship Train, 1969	17	—
If I Were Your Woman, 1971	9	—
I Don't Want To Do Wrong, 1971	17	—
Help Me Make It Through The Night, 1972	33	11
Neither One Of Us (Can Be The First To Say Goodbye), 1973	2	31
Daddy Could Swear, I Declare, 1973	19	—
Midnight Train To Georgia, 1973	1	—
I've Got To Use My Imagination, 1974	4	—

The Best Thing That Ever Happened To Me, 1974	3	7
On And On, 1974	5	—
Try To Remember/The Way We Were, 1975	11	4
Midnight Train To Georgia, 1976	—	10
So Sad The Song, 1976	47	20
Baby Don't Change Your Mind, 1977	52	4
Come Back And Finish What You Started, 1978	—	15

Albums (selected):
Imagination (Buddah), 1973
Anthology (Tamla Motown), 1974
Best Of (Buddah), 1976
Thirty Greatest (—/K-Tel), 1977
Collection (Buddah), 1978
Memories Of The Way We Were (Buddah), 1979
Touch (Columbia/CBS), 1981
Looking Back — The Fury Years (—/Bulldog), 1982

Kool And The Gang

US group formed 1969.

Original line-up: Robert 'Kool' Bell, bass; Robert Mickens, trumpet; Michael Ray, trumpet; Dennis Thomas, alto saxophone; Ronald Bell, tenor saxophone; Clifford Adams, trombone; Amir Bayyan, keyboards; Charles 'Claydes' Smith, guitar; George Brown, drums.

Career: In 1964 Robert 'Kool' Bell formed band called Jazziacs in Jersey City. Band included brother Ronald Bell, Dennis Thomas and Robert Mickens, and played jazz-influenced dance music for local gigs.

During next five years they gained experience, tried out various names and expanded line-up. Eventually line-up as above signed as Kool And The Gang with De-Lite in 1969.

They continued policy of funky instrumental R&B with jazz influence, gaining popularity without achieving spectacular success. But fifth album, **Wild And Peaceful**, spawned trio of big-selling singles — **Jungle Boogie, Funky Stuff** and **Hollywood Swinging**.

Although among progenitors of whole style, Kool And The Gang were not among main beneficiaries of mid-'70s disco boom. They did, however, feature on best-selling **Saturday**

Below: A typically robotic pose from German funsters Kraftwerk.

Night Fever soundtrack album. Career finally took off in big way when band took on lead singer James 'J.T.' Taylor and combined forces with producer Eumir Deodato. Result was **Ladies Night**, major hit album which spawned several smash singles.

Since that time band has gone from strength to strength, conquering markets worldwide and becoming one of biggest attractions in black music. Slick but relaxed stage show is major strength, and band have found formula which cleverly combines dance potential with real musicality.

Current line-up: 'Kool' Bell; Mickens; Ray; Thomas; Ronald Bell; Adams; Bayyan; Smith; Brown; James 'J.T.' Taylor, vocals.

Hit Singles:	US	UK
Jungle Boogie, 1974	4	—
Hollywood Swinging, 1974	6	—
Ladies Night, 1979	8	9
Too Hot, 1980	5	23
Celebration, 1980	1	7
Jones Vs. Jones, 1981	39	17
Take My Heart (You Can Have It If You Want), 1981	17	—
Take It To The Top, 1981	—	15
Steppin' Out, 1981	—	12
Get Down On It, 1982	10	3
Big Fun, 1982	21	14
Let's Go Dancin' (Ooh La La La), 1982	9	6

Albums:
Spin Their Top Hits (De-Lite/—), 1978
Ladies Night (De-Lite), 1979
Everybody's Dancing (De-Lite/—), 1979
Celebrate (De-Lite), 1980
Something Special (De-Lite), 1981
As One (De-Lite), 1982
Kool Kuts (De-Lite), 1982
Twice As Kool—The Hits Of (De-Lite/Phonogram), 1983

Al Kooper

US vocalist, keyboard player, guitarist, composer.
Born Brooklyn, New York, February 5, 1944.

Career: At 13 Kooper had Top 10 hit with **Short Shorts** (1958) as member of Royal Teens on ABC. In late teens worked as session guitarist. Left college at 19 to work as studio engineer and songwriter. Co-penned **This Diamond Ring** chart-topper for Gary Lewis and the Playboys in 1965, and began working folk club circuit.

Producer Tom Wilson invited Kooper to attend Bob Dylan(▶) session. He turned up with his guitar, but Mike Bloomfield(▶) had been booked to play guitar. Determined to take part in session Kooper offered to lay down organ tracks though he hadn't played that instrument seriously before. Dylan was impressed with amateurish but fresh sound and used it on classic **Like A Rolling Stone** single; Kooper contributed to rest of **Highway 61 Revisited** album sessions.

Kooper joined Dylan's back-up band (basically Paul Butterfield(▶) Blues Band for controversial 1965 Newport Folk Festival set when when Dylan went electric to disapproval of folk purists, but approbation of rock fans. Kooper later worked on Dylan's **Blonde On Blonde** (1966) and **New Morning** (1970) sessions.

Through Tom Wilson, Kooper became involved in Blues Project. Featured on two live albums and studio set **Projections** before friction with guitarist Danny Kalb caused Kooper and Steve Katz to leave. They moved to Los Angeles to work on material for proposed new band; unveiled songs at 1967 Big Sur Folk Festival. Legend has it that band was formed solely to play one week at New York club to fund proposed trip to Britain. Band however, became more permanent unit as Blood, Sweat And Tears(▶). Kooper helped put line-up together and produced classic debut album **Child Is Father To The Man** (1969). Commercial success led to group moving in direction which did not suit Kooper; he quit to work as Columbia staff producer.

Kooper started trend for superstar jam sessions by recording **Super Session** album with Mike Bloomfield and Stephen Stills(▶) who had just left Buffalo Springfield, which led to series of concerts with Bloomfield and **Live Adventures Of Al Kooper And Mike Bloomfield** set (1969).

As session guitarist and keyboard player, Kooper appeared on Jimi Hendrix'(▶) **Electric Ladyland** and the Rolling Stones'(▶) **Let It Bleed**. Also recorded with Taj Mahal(▶) and B. B. King(▶), and did further Dylan sessions. Produced Don Ellis Band in jazz idiom and recorded series of solo albums of much-varied quality; **New York City You're A Woman**, largely recorded in London with members of Elton John's(▶) band, was among best. On 1969 **Kooper Session** he unveiled the emergent guitar talents of R&B veteran Johnny Otis's then 15-year-old son Shuggie Otis.

The '70s found Kooper concentrating increasingly on producing others, notably the Tubes(▶), Nils Lofgren(▶) and Lynyrd Skynyrd(▶). He moved base to Atlanta, Georgia, to set up his own Sounds Of The South label. Published a highly enjoyable autobiography under title 'Backstage Passes'.

Albums:
Super Session (with Mike Bloomfield and Stephen Stills) (Columbia/CBS), 1969
Live Adventures (with Mike Bloomfield) (Columbia/CBS), 1969
Championship Wrestling (Columbia/—), 1981
(See also Blood, Sweat and Tears)

Leo Kottke

US guitarist, composer.
Born Athens, Georgia,

Career: Kottke learned guitar during teens; heavily influenced by Delta Blues singers, particularly Mississippi-born John Hurt. While in high school, played in various groups, most notably Sun House. Enlisted in US Navy (Submarine Service), but suffered accident during training manoeuvre in Atlantic, resulting in permanent hearing damage.

Following discharge, played Minneapolis clubs and began recording for local labels. **Circle Round The Sun**, originally released in 1970 on Oblivion, was subsequently picked up by Symposium. Gained support from guitarist John Fahey, who proved willing to release Kottke's work on his ethnic-orientated Takoma Records. **Six And Twelve String Guitar** (1971) was stepping stone needed to attract interest of major companies. While still working as part-time packer for Takoma, Kottke was picked up by Capitol.

Small following increased with each album

Mudlark, Leo Kottke. Courtesy Capitol Records.

and Kottke is now respected as one of America's finest acoustic guitarists. His annual transatlantic trips have also earned him European audience. After several successful years with Capitol, his most recent albums have been for Chrysalis.

Guitar: Various acoustics.

Albums:
Circle Round The Sun (Symposium), 1970*
Six And Twelve String Guitar (Takoma/Sonet), 1971
Mudlark (Capitol), 1971
Green House (Capitol), 1973
My Feet Are Smiling (Capitol), 1973*
Ice Water (Capitol), 1974
Dreams And All That Stuff (Capitol), 1974
Chewing Pine (Capitol), 1975
Leo Kottke (Chrysalis), 1976
1971-76 (Capitol/—), 1976
Burnt Lips (Chrysalis), 1978
Balance (Chrysalis), 1979
Best Of (Capitol), 1979
Guitar Music (Chrysalis), 1981
Time Step (Chrysalis), 1983
*Live

Worth Searching Out:
(Recent Capitol re-issues tend to delete certain tracks from originals, making first issues worth searching out)

Kraftwerk

German duo formed 1970.

Ralf Hutter and Florian Schneider, vocals, keyboards, string-wind instruments, drums, electronics.

Career: Began recording in Connie Plank's studio in Dusseldorf oil refinery. Experimented with tape recorders and radios, gradually assimilating knowledge of German electronics. Formed five-piece Organisation, strongly influenced by early Tangerine Dream(▶) and Pink Floyd(▶). Organisation's **Tone Float** (1970) gave some indication of future work. Kraftwerk (literally 'Powerplant') first came to prominence when Vertigo released original two albums as double eponymous debut in Britain. LPs showed myriad of influences from Pink Floyd to avant-garde composers such as

John Cage and Karl-Heinz Stockhausen. Speeded-up tapes, producing unusual sounds representing grim mechanised alienation of modern industrial life, dominated set. Duo identified strongly with Bauhaus movement of 1920s and committed themselves to synthesising music and machinery.

Since 1973 have gradually extended activities to achieve greater commercial appeal. **Ralf And Florian** paved way for excellent **Autobahn**, which broke duo in US and UK. An edited single of titletrack was an international hit in 1975. Two new members, Klaus Roeder (violin/guitar) and Wolfgang Flur (percussion), were added, the former being replaced by Karl Bartos for concept album **Radio Activity**. **Activity** proved unusual combination of easy listening/experimental music, indicating dilemma that faced group in producing later work.

Successful move to Capitol resulted in series of best-selling works, less experimental than previous albums. **Trans Europe Express** and **The Man Machine** were sober and musically dour, underlining need for new direction. Group went into hibernation for three years before re-emerging with **Computer World**, a serio-comic look at the technological age. Their fortunes improved following inspired double A-side **The Model/Computer Love**, which provided surprise chart-topping UK hit in 1982. Celebrated series of gigs followed as Kraftwerk succeeded in transforming their studio into an elaborate mobile unit, complete with space-age gadgetry.

The Man Machine, Kraftwerk. Courtesy Capitol Records.

Work has proved extremely influential in recent years, seriously affecting the development of British electro-pop as well as numerous acts, including David Bowie, Eno, Gary Numan and Donna Summer. Recently, further attention was focused on Kraftwerk's innovation following the release of Neil Young's(▶) **Trans** which borrowed heavily from **Computer World**.

Current line-up: Hutter; Schneider; Klaus Roeder, violin, guitar; Wolfgang Flur, percussion.

Hit Singles:	UK	US
Autobahn, 1975	—	11
The Model/Computer Love, 1983	—	1

Albums:
Ralf And Florian (—/Vertigo), 1973
Autobahn (Mercury/Vertigo), 1974
Radio Activity (Capitol), 1975
Exceller 8 (—/Vertigo), 1975
Trans Europe Express (Capitol), 1977
The Man Machine (Capitol), 1978
Computer World (EMI), 1981

Worth Searching Out:
Var (Vertigo), 1971
Kraftwerk (Vertigo), 1972

Kris Kristofferson

US vocalist, guitarist, composer, actor.
Born Brownsville, Texas, June 22, 1936.

Career: Moved to California while in high school. After attending Pomona College went to England to take up Rhodes Scholarship at Oxford University. Started writing while at college; first fiction and later songs were under name of Kris Carson.

On return to US joined army and was eventually posted to Germany to fly helicopters. During German sojourn resumed songwriting and started to play in local clubs.

Back in US, joined West Point military academy for short period as English teacher, but made permanent move to Nashville in 1965.

For several years Kristofferson took menial jobs while songs (sent to Nashville publisher) made usual rounds. Eventually Roger Miller(▶) recorded some of his compositions, including **Me And Bobby McGee,** and Kristofferson was on his way. Janis Joplin's(▶) cover of **Bobby McGee** brought him to the youth/rock market.

In 1970 he was offered contract by Monument, and by time of marriage to Rita Coolidge(▶) in 1973 was major record seller. For next few years he and Coolidge ran careers together, using same band for touring, and cutting duet albums, **Full Moon** (1973) and **Breakaway** (1974). Dual appearance in Peckinpah movie 'Pat Garratt And Billy The Kid' started off Kristofferson's film career, which rapidly assumed major importance. Starring roles in movies like 'Alice Doesn't Live Here Anymore', 'A Star Is Born' (with Barbra Streisand) and 'Rollover' (with Jane Fonda) ensued.

Late '70s was bad period for Kristofferson personally, heavy drinking problems and break-up of marriage being widely publicised. However, latterly he has been as busy as ever, with both recording and film projects.

Although a passable singer and competent actor, Kristofferson's real claim to fame lies in clutch of classic and much-covered songs. **Me And Bobby McGee, Help Me Make It Through The Night, Sunday Morning Coming Down, For The Good Times** and others ensure continuing reputation as songwriter.

Hit Singles:	US	UK
Why Me, 1973	16	—

Albums:
Me And Bobby McGee (Monument), 1970
The Silver Tongued Devil And I (Monument), 1971
Border Lord (Monument), 1972
Jesus Was A Capricorn (Monument), 1973
Spooky Lady's Sideshow (Monument), 1974
Songs Of Kristofferson (Monument), 1977
Easter Island (Monument), 1978
Shake Hands With The Devil (Monument), 1979
To The Bone (Monument), 1981

With Rita Coolidge:
Full Moon (A&M), 1973
Natural Act (A&M), 1978

With Barbra Streisand:
A Star Is Born (Soundtrack) (Columbia/CBS), 1977

Krokus

Swiss group formed 1978.

Original line-up: Marc Storace, vocals; Tommy Kiefer, guitar, vocals; Fernando Von Arb, Fender Stratocaster guitar, vocals; Chris Von Rohr, Fender Precision bass, vocals; Freddy Steady, drums; Juerg Naegelli, keyboards.

Career: According to many critics, anybody who knows three chords can play heavy metal. Krokus shows the problems with such a theory. Debut **Metal Rendez-vouz** had all the ingredients: crashing guitars, songs about

Metal Rendez-Vous, Krokus. Courtesy Arista Records.

Below: Country superstar Kris Kristofferson, who has also made a major impact on the silver screen.

rock 'n' roll, macho posing, a stab at humour; but combination wasn't right. **Hardware** was better but not enough to warrant notice. So by the time Krokus released decent album, **One Vice At A Time**, they couldn't generate sales even with some strongly supportive reviews.

Despite weak lyrics on cover of Guess Who's **American Woman**, **Vice** is outing which proves even a Swiss band can rock. Mark Kohler replaced Kiefer on third LP and Steve Pace took over drums on the most recent release, **Headhunter.**

Current line-up: Storace; Von Arb; Von Rohr; Mark Kohler, guitar; Steve Pace, drums.

Albums:
Metal Rendez-vous (Arista/Ariola), 1980
Hardware (Arista/Ariola), 1981
One Vice At A Time (Arista/Ariola), 1982
Headhunter (Arista/Ariola), 1983

Frankie Laine

US vocalist.
Born Frank Lo Vecchio, Chicago, March 30, 1913.

Career: Though it's some time since he enjoyed major hit, Frankie Laine remains major concert draw and can look back on career spanning more than 40 years and record sales totalling over 100 million.

He won early fame by setting all-time marathon dancing record of 145 days in 1932. His professional singing career started five years later when he replaced Perry Como as resident singer with Freddie Carlone's band.

Going solo, he moved to New York and became staff singer in a city radio station. He headed for Hollywood immediately after World War II, developing an act with aid of pianist Carl Fischer, and was discovered singing in night club by Hoagy Carmichael.

Signed to Mercury in 1947, Laine immediately scored million-seller with **My Desire**, more gold following with **Shine** (1948), the pounding novelty song **Mule Train** (1948), the poignant **That Lucky Old Sun** (1949) and **Cry Of The Wild Goose** (1950).

In 1951, Mitch Miller signed Laine to Columbia and exploited mix of big balladry with hint of country and western. Laine's first year with new label yielded three million-sellers: **Jezebel, Jalousie** (a Danish composition) and **Rose, Rose I Love You** (adapted by British DJ Wilfred Thomas from traditional Chinese melody **Mei Kuei**).

The golden hits continued: the epic movie theme **High Noon** and **Sugarbush**, a duet with Doris Day (1952), the religious **I Believe, Tell Me A Story** (a duet with Jimmy Boyd) in 1953, and **Moonlight Gambler** (1956).

In more recent times Laine has concentrated on religious material.

Hit Singles:	US	UK
(Most of Laine's hits were prior to official charts)	
Humming Bird, 1955	17	16*
Hawkeye, 1955	30	7*
Sixteen Tons, 1956	—	10
A Woman In Love, 1956	19	1
Moonlight Gambler, 1956	3	13
Love Is A Golden Ring, 1957	10	19
Rawhide, 1959	—	6

Albums (selected):
Greatest Hits (Columbia/CBS), 1958
Golden Hits (Mercury/—), N/A
The Best Of Frankie Laine (—/Hallmark), 1967

Led Zeppelin

UK group formed 1968.

Original/final line-up: Robert Plant, vocals; Jimmy Page, Gibson Les Paul guitar; John Paul Jones, keyboards, Fender Precision bass; John Bonham, drums.

Career: Formed by Jimmy Page upon demise of Yardbirds(▶) to complete scheduled dates in Northern Europe. Quartet completed by session bass-player John Paul Jones, Birmingham drummer John Bonham, and ex-Band Of Joy vocalist Robert Plant.

Page and Jones were both prominent studio players. Page's credits include Kinks(▶), Stones(▶), Georgie Fame(▶) and the Who(▶) (featured on **I Can't Explain**). Joined Yardbirds as replacement bass player for departing Paul Samwell-Smith; switched to guitar when Jeff Beck quit. Jones supplied bass/keyboards for Stones, Lulu, Dusty Springfield(▶) and many others; formerly bass player for Jet Harris/Tony Meehan, ex-Shadows(▶) duo.

As New Yardbirds, band fulfilled Swedish/ Finnish dates. With manager Peter Grant, group selected new name Led Zeppelin suggested by Keith Moon(▶) (John Entwistle(▶) has also been credited). Grant quickly secured recording contract with Ahmet Ertegun of Atlantic (originally turned down by Atlantic's distribution company in UK Polydor); Grant and Ertegun have since arrived at arm's length respect for each other.

First album **Led Zeppelin** was released in 1968; went gold early following year. Mixture of blues and orchestrated rock riffs filled in void left by Cream; superb musicianship and beginning of Plant's 'macho' bare-to-the-waist image saw them streets ahead of US contemporaries. Album's crisp production set it apart from myriad of ponderous, muddy-sounding heavy metal merchants. Single **Good Times Bad Times** culled from LP earned group first US Top 100 entry.

Reputation secured by **Led Zeppelin II** which included band's anthem **Whole Lotta Love**, a US Top 10. Band has never had singles success in UK, though **Love** was theme for BBC's 'Top Of The Pops' TV show for several years; band never officially endorsed singles culled by record company.

Zeppelin completed major tour of US in '73, compounding success of further albums **III** and **IV**. Tracks **Immigrant Song** (from **III**) and now all-time classic **Stairway To Heaven** (from **IV**) extracted phenomenal reaction from audiences. Band now at peak, with Grant turning down telephone number-size deals which conflicted with his long-term strategy.

Assuming Presley/Beatles-type publicity and sales, group spent over a year away from studio after release of **Houses Of The Holy** (1973). Returned in '75 with **Physical Graffiti**. Album was packaged in 'moveable' sleeve, revealing various objects/individuals in windows of tenement block, and was as impressive musically as visually, attracting more favourable critical reaction; band have always been at loggerheads with 'knowledgeable' music press.

Own label Swan Song launched with release of **Graffiti**; Bad Company(▶), Maggie Bell and Pretty Things also signed to label. Acts distributed by Atlantic and Island. Swan Song office in Kings Road, London, saw much frantic wheeling and dealing by Grant. Reportedly turned down one million pounds for worldwide satellite TV concert of band.

1975 saw Plant injured in car crash during Greek holiday. Second personal tragedy for group's singer occurred in 1977 when his son Karac died of virus infection. Plant's incapacity kept band off road for two years, although album **Presence** (1976) maintained momentum. LP had biggest advance orders ever in US, going platinum upon issue.

In 1976 movie/soundtrack album **The Song Remains The Same** released. Film captured explosive stage act to the full, despite some 'live' footage being shot at Pinewood Studios, England.

Massive US tour saw Zeppelin gross over one million dollars for New York dates (at Madison Square Garden) alone. 10 dates were cancelled, however, when Plant had to fly home on son's death. First rumours of break-up denied by Page. Band had meticulously worked schedule, with periods of inactivity which fuelled 'split' stories.

The turning cover of Led Zeppelin III.
Courtesy Atlantic Records.

Ninth album **In Through The Out Door** cut in Sweden at end of '78 for spring '79 release. Unlikely hosts in frozen North were Abba(▶), who had invited band to record in their studio.

Major outdoor concert at stately home Knebworth House in August 1979 saw band re-conquer homeland. **In Through The Out Door** LP was released shortly after. Album's unique packaging (wrapped in brown paper and featuring six different covers) won major marketing award in US.

Led Zeppelin II featured Whole Lotta Love. Courtesy Atlantic Records.

Coda the last Led Zeppelin album. Courtesy Atlantic Records.

Band's future put in doubt after death of drummer John Bonham (attributed to heart attack brought on by drink) in September 1980; group had just completed major European tour to capacity crowds and were planning new album. A cursory press release in December 1980 announced end of Zeppelin.

Rumours have continued to circulate that band will re-form, with Who's Kenney Jones named as likely drummer. Cozy Powell, ex-Jeff Beck(▶), Rainbow(▶), put himself forward as man for drum seat after working on Plant's 1982 solo LP **Pictures At Eleven.** Album features Phil Collins, Robbie Blunt (ex-Bronco, Broken Glass, Steve Gibbons Band) guitar, Paul Martinez (ex-Paice Ashton Lord) bass, and Jezz Woodruffe. Plant released second solo LP **The Principle Of Moments** in 1983.

Most recently, Jimmy Page penned Michael Winner's 'Deathwish II' soundtrack. Impeccable music deserved better vehicle.

With Swan Song's premier act now dissolved, label has been run down to little more than administration in both US/UK. Individual ability of Zeppelin and shrewd judgements of Grant will ensure maximum attention. The bonus is a legacy of the finest mainstream rock ever recorded.

Below: Led Zeppelin as they were at the height of their fame in the '70s. (Left to right) John Paul Jones, Robert Plant, Jimmy Page, John Bonham.

Above: Houses Of The Holy, Led Zeppelin. Courtesy of Atlantic Records.

Below: Jimmy Page of Led Zeppelin onstage with his Les Paul.

Hit Singles:

	UK	US
Whole Lotta Love, 1970	4	—
Immigrant Song, 1971	16	—
Black Dog, 1972	15	—
D'Yer Mak'er, 1973	20	—

Robert Plant Solo:

Big Log, 1983	—	15

Albums:

Led Zeppelin (Atlantic), 1968
Led Zeppelin II (Atlantic), 1969
Led Zeppelin III (Atlantic), 1970
Led Zeppelin IV (Atlantic), 1971
House Of The Holy (Atlantic), 1973
Physical Graffiti (Swan Song), 1975
Presence (Swan Song), 1976
The Song Remains The Same (Swan Song), 1976
In Through The Out Door (Swan Song), 1979
Coda (Swan Song), 1982

Robert Plant Solo:

Pictures At Eleven (Swan Song), 1982
The Principle Of Moments, (Swan Song), 1983

Jimmy Page Solo:

Deathwish II Soundtrack (Swan Song), 1982

Brenda Lee

US vocalist.
Born Brenda Mae Tarpley, Atlanta, Georgia, December 11, 1944.

Career: Lee's musical talent was already in evidence at age six when she won local talent contest in home town Nashville. Heard by country star Red Foley at 12, spot on his TV programme 'Ozark Jubilee Show' followed. Success was instantaneous, and further TV dates and Decca (later MCA) recording contract followed.

First releases were country-orientated and moderately successful, but when Lee turned to rock 'n' roll her career took off. **Dynamite** was first of several international hits that carried her into mid-'60s. Probably the best female white rock singer of her generation, she also showed winning style on pop ballads like **I'm Sorry** and **As Usual**.

When chart success began to die down, Lee, like many white '50s rock 'n' rollers (Bob Luman, Conway Twitty(▶)), turned back to roots and started recording country material again. In recent years career has been low profile, but she continues to undertake TV and live work.

Always a strong, distinctive singer, Brenda Lee combined genuine talent with appealing, chirpy personality. Her early '80s singles remain among some of most evocative discs of period.

Hit Singles:

	US	UK
Sweet Nuthins, 1960	4	4
I'm Sorry/That's All You Gotta Do, 1960	1	12
That's All You Gotta Do/I'm Sorry, 1960	6	—
I Want To Be Wanted, 1960	1	31
Rockin' Around The Christmas Tree, 1960	14	—
Let's Jump The Broomstick, 1961	—	12
Emotions, 1961	7	45
You Can Depend On Me, 1961	6	—
Dum Dum, 1961	4	22
Fool No. 1, 1961	3	38
Break It To Me Gently, 1962	4	46
Speak To Me Pretty, 1962	—	3
Everybody Loves You But You, 1962	6	—
Here Comes That Feeling, 1962	—	5
Heart In Hand, 1962	15	—
It Started All Over Again, 1962	29	15
All Alone Am I, 1962	3	7
Rockin' Around The Christmas Tree, 1962	—	6
Losing You, 1963	6	10
I Wonder, 1963	25	14
The Grass Is Greener, 1963	17	—
As Usual, 1964	12	5
Is It True, 1964	17	17
Too Many Rivers, 1965	13	22
Coming On Strong, 1966	11	—

Albums:

Here's Brenda Lee (Vocalion/—), 1967
Let It Be Me (Coral/—), 1968
Brenda (MCA), 1973
Brenda Lee Story (MCA/Decca), 1974
Little Miss Dynamite (MCA/Warwick), 1976
Take Me Back (MCA), 1979
Even Better (MCA), 1980
16 Classic Tracks (-/MFP), 1982
25th Anniversary (MCA), 1982
Greatest Country Hits (—/MCA), 1982
Only When I Laugh (—/MCA), 1982

John Lennon

UK composer, vocalist, guitarist.
Born John Winston Lennon, Liverpool, October 9, 1940; died December 8, 1980.

Career: After achieving worldwide success with the Beatles during the '60s, Lennon, under influence of second wife, Yoko Ono(▶), began recording without rest of group in 1968. First LP, recorded with Yoko, featured full frontal nude picture of duo, resulting in LP being sold in brown paper bag, while contents—avant-garde inspired non-music— alienated Beatle fans around the world. Follow-up LP was no better, but in between, hit single by Plastic Ono Band (John, Yoko and friends), **Give Peace A Chance**, was substantial hit. Several follow-up singles were successful over years until 1976. LPs often unlistenable before **John Lennon/ Plastic Ono Band**, released in 1970, in which John, under influence of primal therapy, tried to release all supposedly suppressed feelings about early life.

Next LP, **Imagine**, generally agreed to be Lennon's best solo album. Thereafter output was patchy—Lennon felt to be too easily influenced by those around him, leading to involvement with peace movement, exotic religions, and many other things which prevented him making classic rock'n'roll records of which everyone knew he was capable.

On November 28, 1974, Lennon joined Elton John(▶) on stage at NY's Madison Square Gardens for three numbers (**Lucy In The Sky With Diamonds, I Saw Her Standing There,** and **Whatever Gets You**

Below: Mr. and Mrs. John Lennon at the time of the former's comeback.

Through The Night); this turned out to be his last live performance.

On birth of second child (first by Yoko), Lennon vowed to cease recording for five years. On return to active service in 1980, produced half LP (other half by Yoko) spawning rather disappointing single hit

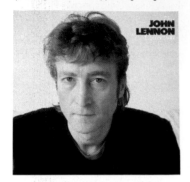

The John Lennon Collection. Courtesy EMI Records/Geffen Records.

(Just Like) Starting Over. As single began to descend chart, John was murdered by so-called fan outside New York apartment building. The entire world was shocked. Chart was soon deluged with Lennon/Beatles material for several months. While his post-Beatles work was very inconsistent, Lennon is regarded as most notable Beatle by majority of fans, making his quite senseless murder probably *the* ultimate tragedy of rock'n'roll.
Guitar: Rickenbacker

Hit Singles:	UK	US
Give Peace A Chance, 1969	2	14
Cold Turkey, 1969	14	30
Instant Karma, 1970	5	3
Power To The People, 1970	7	11
Imagine, 1971	—	3
Happy Xmas (War Is Over), 1972	4	—
Mind Games, 1973	26	18
Whatever Gets You Thru The Night, 1974	36	1
Number 9 Dream, 1975	23	9
Stand By Me, 1975	30	20
Imagine, 1975	6	—
Happy Xmas (War Is Over) (3rd entry), 1980	2	—
Imagine, 1980	1	—
(Just Like) Starting Over, 1981	3	1
Woman, 1981	1	2
Watching The Wheels, 1981	30	18

Rock'n'Roll, John Lennon. Courtesy Capitol Records.

Albums:
Unfinished Music No.1—Two Virgins (Apple), 1968
Unfinished Music No.2—Life With The Lions, (Capitol/Parlophone), 1969
The Wedding Album (Capitol/Parlophone), 1969
Plastic Ono Band/Live Peace In Toronto, (Capitol/Parlophone), 1969

John Lennon/Plastic Ono Band (Capitol/Parlophone), 1970
Imagine(Capitol/Parlophone), 1971
Some Time In New York City (Capitol/Parlophone), 1972
Mind Games (Capitol/MFP), 1973
Walls And Bridges (Capitol/Parlophone), 1974
Rock'n'Roll (Capitol/Parlophone), 1975
Shaved Fish (Collectable Lennon) (Capitol/Parlophone), 1975*
Double Fantasy (Capitol/Parlophone), 1980
The John Lennon Collection (Capitol/Parlophone), 1980*

*Compilations

Jerry Lee Lewis

US vocalist, pianist, composer.
Born Ferriday, Louisiana, September 29, 1935.

Career: Although Lewis made early start playing country style piano in bars and clubs, recording career did not commence until 1956 with signing to Sun Records in Memphis and first single Crazy Arms. Somewhat wilder style surfaced in 1957, with second single Whole Lotta Shakin' Goin' On becoming first hit and setting pattern for 'pumpin' piano' style, which rapidly became trademark.

Several hits and tours later, arrived in Britain in May 1958 for nationwide tour just as news broke of marriage to 13-year-old cousin, Myra. Resulting publicity effectively stalled career for over two years; made comeback with What'd I Say in 1961.

Began recording for Mercury in 1963 and style mellowed considerably over next five years as Lewis turned to country music with increasing success. New career followed with major hits in country charts and occasional excursions into rock 'n' roll.

Continued to tour US and UK regularly, and to appear in headlines as a result of lifestyle in keeping with reputation as wild man of rock. His various drug, booze and gun offences reached climax in 1976 when Lewis was arrested for brandishing a pistol outside Elvis

Above: "Rock'n'roll's the thing, Jerry Lee's the King"—Jerry Lee Lewis.

Presley's(▶) home in Memphis.

Following signing to Elektra label in 1977, appeared to have adopted quieter lifestyle; relationship with label was strained, however, ultimately leading to lawsuits from both sides. During 1981 was rushed to hospital for extensive stomach surgery, reportedly close to death, but recovered sufficiently to resume stage appearances and record first album for MCA.

Recent concerts reveal only slightly re-served stage performance and the same self-confidence—Lewis has always asserted that 'The Killer' is the 'King of Rock 'n' Roll'. This title may have been hotly contested in the '50s, now it would appear to belong to Lewis alone, for he remains one of the few active rock 'n' roll exponents.

Hit Singles:	US	UK
Whole Lotta Shakin' Goin' On, 1957	2	8
Great Balls Of Fire, 1957	3	1
Breathless, 1958	7	8
High School Confidential, 1959	21	12
What'd I Say, 1961	30	10

Albums:
Whole Lotta Shakin' Goin' On (Sun), 1963
Live At The Star Club, Hamburg (Philips), 1964
Best Of The Country Music Hall Of Fame Hits (Mercury), 1969
Jerry Lee Lewis And His Pumping Piano (—/Charly), 1975
Rare Jerry Lee Lewis Volume 1 (—/Charly), 1975
Rare Jerry Lee Lewis Volume 2 (—/Charly), 1975
Good Rockin' Tonite (Sun), 1975
The Original Jerry Lee Lewis (—/Charly), 1976
Nuggets (—/Charly), 1977
Nuggets Volume 2 (—/Charly), 1977
The Essential Jerry Lee Lewis (—/Charly), 1978
Jerry Lee Lewis And Friends—Duets (Sun/Charly), 1978
Jerry Lee's Greatest (—/Charly), 1980

The Sun Years (12 LP Box Set) Sun), 1980
Killer Country (Elektra), 1980
Pumpin' Piano Cat (Sun), 1983
The Great Ball Of Fire (Sun), 1983
The Wild One (Sun), 1983
My Fingers Do The Talking (MCA), 1983
Jerry Lee Lewis (—/Ditto), 1983

Gordon Lightfoot

Canadian vocalist, composer, guitarist, pianist.
Born Orillia, Ontario, November 17, 1938.

Career: One of the few artists to survive the folk-rock boom and establish lasting popularity in pop music during successive decades. Even more remarkably, Lightfoot has neither had to drastically change his musical style nor leave his native Canada to maintain success.

Learned piano at early age. Studied orchestration at Westlake College, Los Angeles. Spent much time at Hollywood recording studio arranging vocal material for singers and composing jingles for television. Cut demos of own songs and gradually abandoned college work.

Learned guitar in 1960, inspired by Pete Seeger(▶) and Bob Gibson. Interest in folk led to tentative appearances in Toronto coffee-houses. Championed by currently popular Ian and Sylvia, Lightfoot released series of

Best Of Gordon Lightfoot. Courtesy Warner Bros Records.

singles on various labels, before signing with their manager, Albert Grossman. His songs were soon picked up by other Grossman acts, most notably Peter, Paul and Mary(▶) who cut **For Lovin' Me** and **Early Morning Rain**.

While retaining country and western orientation, Lightfoot diversified in late '60s with material ranging from blues to ballads. Increasingly in demand as songwriter, songs were covered by number of acts including Johnny Cash(▶), Judy Collins(▶), Harry Belafonte, George Hamilton IV, Ronnie Hawkins(▶), Waylon Jennings(▶) and Richie Havens(▶).

Released five albums for United Artists from 1965-1969 before moving to Warners in 1970. Working with producer Lenny Waronker, success was immediate and **Sit Down Young Stranger**, which included first recording of Kristofferson's(▶) **Me And Bobby McGhee**, was good seller.

Lightfoot increased his popularity during '70s thanks to selected concert/television appearances, and in 1971 **If You Could Read My Mind, Summer Side Of Life** and **Classic Lightfoot** all charted in quick succession. Title track of 1974's **Sundown** provided US No. 1. Highly regarded by contemporaries, Lightfoot was invited by Bob Dylan(▶) to appear as part of the celebrated Rolling Thunder Revue. In spite of credentials and several exceptional songs, Lightfoot's music has veered rather too close to easy listening to attract much interest from rock audiences.

Hit Singles:

	US	UK
If You Could Read My Mind, 1970	5	30
Sundown, 1974	1	33
Carefree Highway, 1974	10	—
The Wreck Of The Edmund Fitzgerald, 1976	2	40

Albums:
Lightfoot (Liberty/—), 1966
The Way I Feel (Liberty/Sunset), 1967
Did She Mention My Name (Liberty/UA), 1968
Back Here On Earth (Liberty/UA), 1969
Sunday Concert (Liberty/UA), 1969
Best Of Volume I (Liberty/UA), 1975
If You Could Read My Mind (Reprise), 1971
Summer Side Of Life (Reprise), 1971
Don Quixote (Reprise), 1972
Sundown (Reprise/Warner Bros), 1974
Cold On Your Shoulder (Reprise), 1975
Gord's Gold (Reprise), 1975
Two Originals Of (—/Reprise), 1976
Summertime Dream (Reprise), 1976
Endless Wire (Warner Bros), 1978
Dream Street Rose (Warner Bros), 1980

Lightnin' Hopkins

US vocalist, guitarist, composer.
Born Sam Hopkins, Centerville, Texas, March 15, 1912; died 1979.

Career: Most prolifically recorded of all country-blues singers. Learned guitar from cousin Texas Alexander and legendary Blind Lemon Jefferson. Moved from rural East Texas to urban Houston to work clubs and record with Alexander and pianist Thunder Smith. Smith and Hopkins then went to Los Angeles to work and record as duo Thunder And Ligntning. Hopkins' early records were heavily amplified but with late '50s folk boom and discovery of country blues by white student and intellectual audiences he exploited acoustic style (he had suffered lean time between advent of rock 'n' roll and rediscovery by folklorist Mack McCormick in 1958).

Often recorded solo, his guitar style and

vocals accompanied by 'tap-dance' sound of beer bottle tops fixed to soles of shoes, Also played piano on some recordings. Aladdin, Gold Star, Jax, Mercury, Shad, RPM, Decca, Harlem, Chart, TNT, Ace, Prestige, Folkways, Bluesville were among many labels for which he recorded. Visited Europe for first time in 1964 with Folk Blues Festival. Died in 1979.

Albums (selected):
Country Blues (Tradition/—), 1960
Greatest Hits (Prestige/—), 1964
Lightning Strikes (Tradition/Mayfair), 1964
Best Of (Tradition/—), 1967
Live At The Bird Lounge (—/Bulldog), 1976
At His Natural Best (—/Rhapsody), 1980

Lindisfarne

UK group formed 1967.
Original/Current line-up: Alan Hull, vocals; Ray Jackson, guitar, mandolin, vocals; Simon Cowe, guitar, mandolin, vocals; Rod Clements, bass, violin, vocals; Ray Laidlaw, drums.

Career: Folk-rock band formed in Newcastle, had various names before signing as Lindisfarne to Charisma in 1969. First album, **Nicely Out Of Tune**, met with good reception, and steady gigging on college and festival circuit during 1969 and '70 paved way for commercial success.

Dingly Dell, Lindisfarne. Courtesy Elektra Records.

Next album, **Fog On The Tyne**, was produced by Bob Johnston and became biggest-selling British album of 1970. Also spawned hit single **Meet Me On The Corner**. Earlier unsuccessful single **Lady Eleanor** was re-released and this time became major hit.

However, band faltered after this success and original line-up split in 1973. Clements, Laidlaw and Cowe went on to form relatively unsuccessful Jack The Lad, while Hull and Jackson pulled in other musicians for a couple of albums. Success was not forthcomng.

In late '70s original line-up re-formed, but widespread support had dropped. Latterly band again played folk festivals which had provided original impetus to career. Rise and fall of talented if unspectacular outfit remains something of an enigma.

Hit Singles:

	US	UK
Meet Me On The Corner, 1972	—	5
Lady Eleanor, 1972	—	3
Run For Home, 1978	33	10

Albums:
Fog On The Tyne (—/Charisma), 1971
Dingly Dell (—/Charisma), 1972
Lady Eleanor (—/Hallmark), 1976
Back And Forth (Atco/Mercury), 1978
The News (—/Mercury), 1979
The Singles Album (—/Charisma), 1981
Lindisfarne Live (—/Charisma), 1982
Sleepless Nights (—/LMP), 1982

Little Feat

US group formed 1969.
Original line-up: Lowell George, guitar, harmonica, vocals; Bill Payne, keyboards, vocals; Richard Hayward, drums; Roy Estrada, bass.

Career: Lowell George (born 1945) played in mid-'60s folk rock group Factory (with Hayward and bassist Martin Kibbee) and, two years later, the Standells (**Dirty Water**), then Seeds (**Pushin' Too Hard**) briefly. George left to take over from singer Ray Collins in Mothers of Invention, playing on both **Weasels Ripped My Flesh** and **Hot Rats** (uncredited).

While in Mothers, wrote/recorded several demos, including **Willing** and **Truck Stop Girl**, the latter being picked up by Clarence White of the Byrds(▶) for inclusion on **(Untitled)**. Other covers followed by numerous US acts, including Seatrain, Linda Ronstadt(▶) and Commander Cody(▶).

During same period, George teamed up with Bill Payne, and both contributed to Fraternity Of Man's second LP, **Get It On**. Interest in George's demos eventually led to recording deal with Warners. Above line-up was assembled. (Group name apparently came from Mother's drummer Jimmy Carl Black and sarcastically refers to size of George's feet.)

First album **Little Feat**, released December 1969, was surprisingly mature work for debut and attracted some critical acclaim, though sales were poor. Same fate befell follow-up **Sailin' Shoes**, in spite of increased media coverage. Disillusioned, Estrada left to join Captain Beefheart's Magic Band. The others re-grouped in new six-piece line-up, including Ken Gradney (bass), Sam Clayton (congas) and Paul Barrere (guitar). Third album **Dixie Chicken** also saw minimal success and members lost interest and drifted into other projects.

George was in constant demand as sessioneer/songwriter, but declined invitation to join projected group with John Sebastian and Phil Everly as well as similar request from Jackson Browne. Contributed to albums by the Meters(▶), Jimmy Webb, Carly Simon(▶), John Sebastian(▶), Kathy Dalton, Chico Hamilton, Nilsson(▶), Robert Palmer(▶) (**Sneaking Sally Through The Alley**), John Cale(▶) (**Paris 1919**) and Van Dyke Parks (**Discover America**). Payne, meanwhile, went on road and appeared on albums with Doobie Brothers(▶) (**Toulouse Street** and **The Captain And Me**) and Bonnie Raitt(▶)

(**Taking My Time** and **Streetlights**).

Little Feat re-formed in 1974 to cut excellent **Feats Don't Fail Me Now**. Followed with critically acclaimed tour of England as part of Warner Bros Music Show in early 1975. Returned to England in May 1976 to support the Who at Charlton Football Ground. Subsequently toured Europe with the Outlaws. During group's final years, Lowell George's role appeared to diminish. Contributed only three songs to **The Last Record Album**, including the memorable **Long Distance Love**.

Feats Don't Fail Me Now, Little Feat. Courtesy Warner Bros Records.

Hepatitis precluded extensive involvement in next album, **Time Loves A Hero**, generally regarded as least impressive. Live double, **Waiting For Columbus** (1978), was also poor in relation to earlier work, which was hardly surprising since George was travelling separately during tours. Produced Grateful Dead's **Shakedown Street** LP the same year.

Group finally split in April 1979 while recording final album. George, meanwhile, had begun solo career with average **Thanks I'll Eat It Here,** better work being anticipated in the future. On June 29, 1979, Lowell George died, age 34, from drug-induced heart failure in Arlington, Virginia; last gig had taken place at George Washington University in Washington DC the previous evening.

Ironically, posthumously released **Down On The Farm** revealed group's finest moments since early days. Since then, a further double album of new material has surfaced, **Hoy Hoy!**. Remnants of group were rumoured to be re-forming to promote work but, thankfully, idea was abandoned.

Below: The mercurial Lowell George, leading light of Little Feat, died on June 29, 1979.

Final line-up: George; Hayward; Paul Barrere, guitar, vocals; Sam Clayton, vocals, percussion; Ken Gradney, bass; Bill Payne, keyboards, vocals, percussion.

Albums:
Little Feat (Warner Bros), 1971
Sailin' Shoes (Warner Bros), 1972
Dixie Chicken (Warner Bros), 1973
Feats Don't Fail Me Now (Warner Bros), 1974
The Last Record Album (Warner Bros), 1975
Time Loves A Hero (Warner Bros), 1977
Waiting For Columbus (Warner Bros), 1978
Down On The Farm (Warner Bros), 1979
Hoy Hoy! (Warner Bros), 1981

Lowell George Solo:
Thanks, I'll Eat It Here (Warner Bros), 1979

Little Richard

US vocalist, composer, pianist.
Born Richard Wayne Penniman, Macon, Georgia, December 5, 1935.

Career: Family had heavily religious background; Richard grew up a Seventh Day Adventist then ran away from home to perform in a 'medicine show'. Adopted by a white Macon couple, Ann and Enotris Johnson. Both were to feature in his subsequent musical career, 'Miss Ann' in an intense, bluesy song, and Enotris as co-writer of smash hit **Long Tall Sally**.

Musical career began in 1951. Won talent contest in Atlanta as 'Little Richard'; the prize was a contract with RCA. Two sessions yielded eight songs, mostly ballads and frantic jump-blues. Richard's intense tenor voice was influenced by rich, throaty Roy Brown and gospelly blues-wailer Billy Wright.

Success was very limited, and by late 1953 he signed with Peacock Records. During three years recording with the Tempo Toppers vocal group, singles made only local sales. Richard sent demo tape to Art Rupe at Specialty Records. Rupe negotiated release from Peacock, and sent producer Robert 'Bumps' Blackwell to New Orleans to cut some sides with Richard. Results wrote new chapter in annals of rock'n'roll; debut **Tutti Frutti** charted in late 1955, followed by gems like

The Second Coming, Little Richard. Courtesy Reprise Records.

Long Tall Sally, Rip It Up, Ready Teddy, **Lucille**, **Good Golly Miss Molly** and **The Girl Can't Help It**; latter also became a movie title with Richard in cameo performance. ('Don't Knock The Rock' and 'Mr Rock And Roll' also featured him briefly.)

In 1957 Richard suddenly relinquished rock'n'roll and turned to religion. Career became patchy; Specialty lifted LP tracks for pop hits; he cut gospel songs for various labels, including Coral, End, Goldisc and Mercury (Mercury under the direction of Quincy Jones).

The Georgia Peach, Little Richard. Courtesy Charly Records.

By 1962 Richard's vocals were heard on Little Star singles credited to his band the Upsetters. Then came Mercury single **He Got What He Wanted** with just gospel undertones. 1963 deal with Atlantic yielded gospel sides. 1964 took Richard back to Specialty with storming rocker **Bama Lama Bama Loo**. Moved to Vee Jay to record mixture of soul-tinged new material and crass re-hashes of Specialty classics. Among worthwhile singles were **Without Love** and **I Don't Know What You've Got But It's Got Me**, his only chart hit on Vee Jay.

Richard then made some interesting raunchy soul sides for Modern and Kent; moved on to Okeh in 1966. Debut **Poor Dog** charted briefly. Toured UK and recorded **Get Down With It**, his most torrid rocker in years.

Lean times ensued—brash soul dancers on Brunswick, contemporary production on Reprise; subsequent discs appeared on Green

Mountain, Manticore and Mainstream. Richard's live performances have ranged from stand-up pianist in baggy suit to embarrassing poseur in tight pink jumpsuit and headband emblazoned 'The King'. He has returned to religion as touring evangelist.

Hit Singles:	US	UK
Tutti Frutti, 1956	17	29
Long Tall Sally, 1956	6	3
Rip It Up, 1956	17	30
She's Got It, 1957	—	15
The Girl Can't Help It, 1957	49	9
Lucille, 1957	21	10
Jenny Jenny, 1957	10	11
Keep A Knockin', 1957	8	21
Good Golly Miss Molly, 1958	10	8
Baby Face, 1959	41	2
By The Light Of The Silvery Moon, 1959	—	17
Bama Lama Bama Loo, 1964	—	20

Albums:
His Biggest Hits (Specialty/London), 1957
The Fabulous Little Richard (Specialty/London), 1959
Well Alright (Specialty/—), 1959
Grooviest 17 hits (Speciality/—), 1960
The Original (—/Sonet), 1972
All Time Hits (—/Sonet), 1972
22 Original Hits (—/Warwick), 1977
Greatest Hits (—/Embassy), 1977
Tutti Frutti (Accord/—), 1981

Little River Band

Australian group formed 1974.

Original line-up: Glenn Shorrock, vocals; Rick Formosa, guitar; Beeb Birtles, guitar, vocals; Graham Goble, guitar vocals; Roger McLachlan, bass; Derek Pellicci, drum.

Career: Originally formed by Shorrock (ex-Twilights, Axiom, Esperanto), Birtles (ex-Zoom, which also featured Rick Springfield) and Goble (ex-Mississippi with Birtles). Pellicci, also ex-Mississipi, was next to join; band completed by New Zealander McLachlan

Time Exposure, Little River Band. Courtesy Capitol Records.

who came to Australia with touring version of 'Godspell', and Formosa, classically trained Italian guitarist who arrived in Australia via Canada.

Debut domestic single **Curiosity** was Australian Top 10 hit in late 1975. First eponymous LP, featuring Californian country/rock harmonies, made reasonable chart impact in US, but less in UK, where punk rock was about to boil over. By second LP in 1977, Formosa was replaced by David Briggs, McLachlan by George McArdle; album reached US Top 50 and achieved gold status. Subsequent LPs (one per year from 1978 to **Greatest Hits**, 1983) have all charted in US Top 50 without achieving any chart action in UK. Various personnel changes have occurred during this time without really altering basic

soft rock sound of band.

Birtles, Goble and Pellicci remain from original line-up, while most important newcomer John Farnham replaced Shorrock in 1982. Apparently a veteran of Australian music scene since '60s, Farnham joined Little River Band after Goble produced his solo LP, **Uncovered**, in 1981.

Current line-up: Birtles; Goble; Pellicci; Steve Housden, lead guitar; Wayne Nelson, bass; John Farnham, vocals.

Hit Singles:	US	UK
Help Is On Its Way, 1977	14	—
Happy Anniversary, 1978	16	—
Reminiscing, 1978	3	—
Lady, 1979	10	—
Lonesome Lover, 1979	6	—
Cool Change, 1979	10	—
The Night Owls, 1981	6	—
Take It Easy On Me, 1981	10	—
Man On Your Mind, 1982	14	—
The Other Guy, 1982	11	—

Albums:
Little River Band (Harvest/—), 1976
Diamantina Cocktail (Harvest/—), 1977
Sleeper Catcher (Capitol), 1978
First Under The Wire (Capitol), 1979
Backstage Pass (Capitol), 1980
After Hours (Capitol), 1980
Time Exposure (Capitol), 1981
Greatest Hits (Capitol), 1982
The Net (Capitol), 1983

Nils Lofgren

US vocalist, composer, guitarist, pianist.
Born Chicago, 1953.

Career: Lofgren's parents moved to Maryland when he was a teenager. He and his brother began playng in local DC bands, Nils' talents came to attention of Crazy Horse(▶) who featured him on their first album. (**Crazy Horse** remains strong upon hearing even today, thanks in part to Lofgren's lead runs.) This association led to work with Neil Young(▶) who used Lofgren on **After The Goldrush.**

18-year-old Lofgren returned to DC to set up own band, Grin. (From this era, LP **1 + 1** and compilation **The Best Of Grin** are worth a listen.) Grin had split by 1973 and Lofgren was happy to join Neil Young's(▶) **Tonight's The Night** tour.

I Came To Dance, Nils Lofgren. Courtesy A&M Records.

Lofgren spent good part of 1974 re-forming Grin and watching it fall apart again. This background ensured modicum of interest when **Nils Lofgren** was released in 1975. Follow-up tour developed cult following and Lofgren seemed ready for stardom. Curious LP, **Back It Up**, appeared, which was 'authorised bootleg' pressed as promo only item. It became overnight collectors' item.

Left: Nils Lofgren, the boy wonder who made his name playing with Neil Young as a teenager. Despite critical acclaim, Lofgren seems never to have achieved the position which has so often been claimed for him.

Despite this, even excellent 1976 **Cry Tough** and tour as opening act for Boston failed to gain expected results. Subsequent LPs are all of interest, **Night After Night** being live. 1979 LP **Nils** managed a lot of US airplay, but didn't chart well. Lofgren again played for Neil Young on 1982 **Trans** LP and joined Young's touring schedule. As expected, Lofgren played with great economy and style, which makes his only slightly successful solo career all the more perplexing.

Guitar: Fender Stratocaster

Albums:
1+1 (SpinDizzy/Epic), 1971
Nils Lofgren (A&M), 1975
Cry Tough (A&M), 1976
The Best Of Grin Featuring Nils Lofgren (Epic/CBS), 1976
I Came To Dance (A&M), 1977
Night After Night (A&M), 1977*
Nils (A&M), 1979
The Best Of (A&M), 1981
Night Fades Away (Backstreet), 1983
*Live

Loggins & Messina

US duo formed 1972.
Jim Messina, guitar, vocals, composer; born Maywood, California, December 5, 1947.
Kenny Loggins, guitar, vocals, composer; born Everett, Washington, January 7, 1948.

Career: Joined forces when (Messina (ex-Buffalo Springfield(▶), co-founder of Poco(▶)) was recruited to produce Loggins' debut solo LP. Album **Sittin' In**, with Jim Messina, was credited 'Kenny Loggins, with Jim Messina'. Duo formed band (Merle Bergante, drums; Al Garth, reeds, violin; Larry Sims, bass; Jon Clarke, reeds; Michael Omartian, keyboards) and established reputation, initially on West Coast. **Sittin' In** subsequently went gold; included original of Ann Murray's hit **Danny's Song**.

Purveyors of typical California soft rock, pair nevertheless reached inspired heights. **Your Mamma Don't Dance** from **Loggins And Messina** LP made US Top 5. Further Top 40 hits and gold albums ensued before partnership announced break in 1976.

Both have subsequently enjoyed varied solo success. Loggins charted in 1978 with single **Whenever I Call You Friend** (with Stevie Nicks as back-up vocal) and co-wrote **What A Fool Believes** with Michael

McDonald of Dobbie Brothers(▶); provided backing vocals/writing credits for McDonald's solo album (1982).

McDonald had supplied harmonies for Loggins' magnificent soul-styled **This Is It** from **Keep The Fire** album. Single made US Top 20 (1979). Theme from movie 'Caddyshack', **I'm Alright**, was further US Top 10 (1980).

Messina recorded **Oasis** (1979) for Columbia. Sessions include actor Stuart Margolin and Hoyt Axton.

Loggins' powerful R&B-infuenced vocals have found favour with more discriminating AOR audience. Messina has never left his country rock roots; consequently has found solo career a tougher proposition.

Hit Singles:	US	UK
Your Mama Don't Dance, 1973	4	—
Thinking Of You, 1973	16	—
My Music, 1973	16	—

Kenny Loggins Solo:

Whenever I Call You Friend, 1978	5	—
This Is It, 1979	11	—
I'm Alright, 1980	7	—
Don't Fight It, 1982	17	—

Albums:
Sittin' In (Columbia/CBS), 1972
Loggins & Messina (Columbia/CBS), 1972
Full Sail (Columbia/CBS), 1973
On Stage (Columbia/CBS), 1974
Mother Lode (Columbia/CBS), 1974
So Fine (Columbia/CBS), 1975
Best Of Friends (Columbia/CBS), 1976
Finale (Columbia/CBS), 1977

Kenny Loggins Solo:
Celebrate Me Home (Columbia/CBS), 1977
Keep The Fire (Columbia/CBS), 1979
Nightwatch (Columbia/CBS), 1978
Alive (Columbia/CBS), 1980

Jim Messina Solo:
Oasis (Columbia/CBS), 1979
Messina (Warner Bros), 1981

Love

US group formed 1965.

Original line-up: Arthur Lee, vocals, guitar, keyboards; Bryan Maclean, guitar, vocals; Ken Forssi, bass; Alban 'Snoopy' Pfisterer, drums; John Echols, guitar.

Career: Arthur Lee grew up in Memphis but moved to West Coast after British invasion

(before it became de rigueur for aspiring American musicians). Was part of nascent music scene in California with several small groups like the LAGs (Los Angeles Group, a name inspired by his hometown success Booker T and the MGs(▶) — Memphis Group) and American Four. He saw Byrds(▶) perform and decided to explore their style. With Byrds' roadie Bryan Maclean he lined up Forssi, Echols and a drummer named Don Conka.

At first they called themselves the Grass Roots, but changed to Love when another band appeared with same name (later to become strong US singles band). At some point Conka was thrown out and 'Snoopy' brought in.

Live Love was always hit or miss and this edge of uncertainty made them a joy to watch. Loyal LA following (group had residency at Bido Lito's in Hollywood) provided strong local reputation. This led Jac Holzman to sign them when he decided Elektra labels should expand into growing rock field. First album was recorded late 1965 and released March 1966. Generally original material, Beatles-Byrds sound and cohesive impact provided very strong debut as well as sounding out growing American response to British rock. **My Little Red Book** became minor hit and **Signed D.C.** (a nod to Don Conka) got some FM play.

Lee already planned to push sound even further on next album. **Da Capo** had two additional players: Tjay Cantrelli (horns) and Michael Stuart (drums), with Snoopy on keyboards. They provided the fuller sound Lee sought. Heavy metal had not yet been invented but Lee laid some groundwork with **7 And 7 Is**. He can also take some blame for all magna opera of progressive rock for

Da Capo, Love. Courtesy Elektra Records.

recording 19-minute **Revelation** over entire second side.

Big-time success failed to come. Uneven live performances and lack of proper tours kept Love an 'underground' (i.e. unknown) band. Love came to be appreciated more in UK than at home (best evidenced by availability of Love albums in UK after US deletion). Size of band also became cumbersome and thrown together make-up took on 'hired hands' atmosphere as Snoopy was fired and Cantrelli disappeared. With remaining members, Lee recorded one of rock's finest albums, **Forever Changes**. It had everything: highs, lows, loud, soft, fast, slow — all mixed into symphonic excitement as fresh today as in 1967. Equally important then, it had lyrics and themes deep enough in year of Beatles(▶) **Sgt. Pepper** LP. Continued availability confirms its timelessness. However, it failed to win massive

audience Lee felt his masterpiece deserved. Within months Love was gone.

In 1968 Lee produced new Love with Jay Donnellan (guitar), Frank Fayad (bass) and George Suranovich (drums). Lee again tried single-handedly to invent heavy metal. This Love lost British-influenced harmonies, replacing them with erratic volume on **Four Sail**. With this album's failure, Lee moved to Blue Thumb Records which later (1969) released double set, **Out Here**. Using recordings from same session as **Four Sail**, it hardly seemed auspicious start on new label.

1970 saw replacement of Donnellan (a.k.a. Jay Lewis) with Gary Rowles, and Love made rare visit to England. This line-up recorded **False Start**, unnotable but for one track, **The Everlasting First**, from Lee's collaboration with Jimi Hendrix(▶) during UK visit. (Supposedly an album's worth of material was recorded with Hendrix but results have never been released.) Weakness of **False Start** doomed Love; Lee broke up band before end of 1971. Using old mate Frank Fayad, he released solo album, **Vindicator** (1972), which showed some return to humour and enthusiasm of early Love, but still missed earlier standards and was generally ignored.

In 1973 Elektra released UK compilation **Love Masters,** worth finding for John Tobler's liner notes. Lee recorded another solo album in late '73 but financial problems prevented its appearance.

Love re-appeared in 1974; Lee, Melvan Whittington (guitars), John Sterling (guitars), Joe Blocker (drums), Sherwood Akuna (bass), Robert Rozelle (bass) and some guests/session musicians recorded the poor **Reel-To-Real**. Love deservedly disappeared again. Lee continued to play various one-off dates, trying to live down past.

One musician with whom he worked was John Sterling. In 1977 he got Lee and Maclean to re-form Love with himself, Kim Kesterton (bass) and George Suranovich (drums) from Love 2. Band tried recapturing the feel of early Love but perhaps should have been more inventive. (Bruce Gary (The Knack) drummed at some point for this version of Love.)

Interest in Love never died out as **Forever Changes** remained in Elektra catalogue, and Rhino Records sold a reasonable amount of 1980 compilation, **Best Of Love**. This led Rhino to release **Arthur Lee** in 1981 — interesting but totally out of sync with times. MCA released curious LP in 1982 with one side featuring eight tracks from **Out Here** and live side from Fillmore East with no recording dates or personnel listed. The undying loyalty and unfailing interest in Love is justifiable since they were a brilliant band with several excellent albums, and classic **Forever Changes** LP is a must for any record collection.

Final line-up: Lee; Maclean; John Sterling, guitar; Kim Kesterton, bass; George Suranovich, drums.

Albums:
Love (Elektra), 1966
Da Capo (Elektra), 1967
Forever Changes (Elektra), 1967
Four Sail (Elektra), 1969
Out Here (Blue Thumb/Harvest), 1969
False Start (Blue Thumb/Harvest), 1970
Love Revisited (Elektra), 1970
Love Masters (—/Elektra), 1973
Reel-To-Real (RSO), 1974
Best Of Love (Rhino/—), 1980
Love Live (Rhino/—), 1982
Love (MCA/—), 1982

Lee Solo:
Vindicator (A&M), 1972
Arthur Lee (Rhino/Beggars Banquet), 1982

Loverboy

Canadian group formed 1979.

Original/Current line-up: Mike Reno, vocals; Paul Dean, guitar, vocals; Doug Johnson, keyboards; Scott Smith, bass; Matt Frenette, drums.

Career: After slow start — debut LP not released until 1980 — Loverboy have become typical of North American heavy-metal scene. Based in Vancouver, Dean and Reno started songwriting together in 1979; soon afterwards were joined by session drummer Frenette. Seemingly none of group had achieved much prior to Loverboy. It wasn't until early 1981 that eponymous debut LP began to storm US charts (although already triple platinum in native Canada).

Eventually, **Loverboy** featured in US LP charts for over a year, peaking at 13. Second LP **Get Lucky**, released end of 1981, reached Top 10 in US. While Loverboy are certainly adept and professional at what they do (material written exclusively within group with contributions from a few friends), it seems unlikely that influence will spread beyond North American continent. Band have little that is unique or sufficiently different to distinguish them from vast bulk of insufficiently inspired heavy metal outfits, despite platinum status of both LPs in US and Canada.

Albums:
Loverboy (Columbia/CBS), 1980
Get Lucky (Columbia/CBS), 1981

Lovin' Spoonful

US group formed 1964.

Original line-up: John Sebastian, guitar, vocals, harmonica, autoharp; Zal Yanovsky, guitar; Joe Butler, drums; Steve Boone, bass.

Career: Sebastian and Yanovsky were together in folk group Mugwumps. Rest of band went on to form Mamas And Papas(▶); Sebastian travelled south. Upon return to New York in 1965, producer Eric Jacobson suggested Sebastian record his own songs. Lovin' Spoonful became New York club circuit favourites and record deal with Kama Sutra followed.

Greetest Hits, The Lovin' Spoonful. Courtesy Kama Sutra Records.

Band refused to dress or sound like popular English groups of time, although British invasion influence is obvious in band's rock fusion of folk and blues. Sebastian's **Do You Believe In Magic?** reflected excitement and energy of growing rock scene. **Daydream** broke group in UK and **Summer In The City** became classic out-of-school, good time paean, as well as US No. 1. Establishment wanted to tap rock's enthusiasm and Sebastian found himself in demand for scoring 'with it' movies (Francis Ford Coppola's 'You're A Big

Above: The much missed Lovin' Spoonful as they appeared on British TV show 'Ready Steady Go' in the 1960s.

Boy Now' and Woody Allen's 'What's Up Tiger Lily?').

Drug culture was still hidden side of rock music and Yanovsky's bust in 1967 proved devastating blow to popularity. Worse, Yanovsky went free by naming others involved and band's reputation within rock business was finished. Jerry Yester (brother of Association's Jim Yester) replaced Yanovsky for **Everything Playing** LP. By 1968, group had collapsed. Subsequent careers have been checkered. Sebastian appeared at Woodstock in 1969, and even got US hit with TV theme **Welcome Back, Kotter** in 1976, but generally failed to match expectations. Butler tried using Lovin' Spoonful name for flop 1969 LP. Yester has produced Tom Waits(▶).

With hindsight it can be said that there was little progression in band's career. Sebastian's songs seem lightweight now and it's hard to see what all the excitement was about. Still, their infectious sound influenced nearly everyone from the Beatles to Dylan. It is that widespread impact which makes up Lovin' Spoonful's legacy.

Final line-up: Sebastian; Butler; Boone; Jerry Yester, guitar.

Hit Singles:	US	UK
Do You Believe In Magic?, 1965	9	—
You Didn't Have To Be So Nice, 1965	10	—
Daydream, 1966	2	2
Did You Ever Have To Make Up Your Mind, 1966	2	—
Summer In The City, 1966	1	8
Rain On The Roof, 1966	10	—
Nashville Cats, 1966	8	26
Darling Be Home Soon, 1967	15	44
Six O'Clock, 1967	18	—

John Sebastian Solo:

Welcome Back, 1976	1	—

Albums:
The Best . . . Lovin' Spoonful (Kama Sutra/—), 1967
File (—/Pye), 1977

Worth Searching Out:
Hums (Kama Sutra), 1967
You're A Big Boy Now (Kama Sutra), 1967
Greatest Hits (Golden Hour), 1975
Golden Hour Of The Lovin' Spoonful's Greatest Hits (—/Golden Hour), 1977

Nick Lowe

UK vocalist, bassist, producer.
Born Woolridge, Suffolk, March 24, 1949.

Career: First significant group was Kippington Lodge, from Tunbridge Wells area; also included Brinsley Schwarz, guitar, Bob Andrews, keyboards. Recorded series of singles during second half of '60s without success, so decided at end of decade to change group name to Brinsley Schwarz. Management company Famepushers Ltd tried to launch 'new' group with debut gig at Fillmore East,

Jesus Of Cool, Nick Lowe. Courtesy Radar Records.

New York, to coincide with release of first LP. This resulted in few taking group seriously, and career blighted thereafter, despite five more LPs, several of which were of above average quality, with many Lowe songs. Group folded in March 1975.

Lowe worked as songwriter and record producer (for Graham Parker(▶) & The Rumour, which included Schwarz and Andrews) and released pseudonymous singles, then joined new manager Jake Riviera (real name Andrew Jakeman) in launch of Stiff Records with ex-Brinsley manager Dave Robinson.

First Stiff release was Lowe's classic single **So It Goes**, and much of label's early output involved Lowe either as artist or producer (for The Damned(▶), Wreckless Eric, etc) until Riviera signed Elvis Costello(▶), whose records Lowe produced for several years with great success. Also worked as producer for Dr Feelgood(▶), plus further Graham Parker album. Formed alliance with Dave Edmunds(▶) in group Rockpile, featured with Costello,

Edmunds and Ian Dury in Stiff package tour at end of 1977.

Left Stiff with Riviera and Costello in late 1977, signed with Radar label; made UK Top 10 with first Radar release; had further hits by end of 1979. Continued to produce Costello, and recorded own albums and Edmunds albums using Rockpile musicians. Also produced first single by Pretenders(▶). Married Carlene Carter (step-daughter of Johnny Cash).

During 1980, contractual hassles which had prevented Rockpile recording under group name resolved, but this only resulted in group splitting up after single LP. Lowe made third solo album; produced LPs for Costello and Dr Feelgood, as well as for wife during 1981, and in 1982 formed band Noise To Go, with Paul Carrack (ex-Ace, Squeeze(▶)), who was achieving solo success on his own account. Also produced Carrack and Fabulous Thunderbirds(▶). Cut fourth LP. After much touring, spent time during first half of 1983 producing John Hiatt.

Nick Lowe is regarded as a man of many talents—producer, songwriter, singer, musician—but has only achieved major success consistently as record producer. He is well known around the world, but conceivably has yet to reach full artistic potential due to diversification. At his best, his 'pure pop for now people' has few equals in history of rock music.

Hit Singles:	US	UK
I Love The Sound Of Breaking Glass, 1978	—	7
Cruel To Be Kind, 1979	12	12

Albums:
With Brinsley Schwarz:
Nervous On The Road (Liberty), 1972
New Favourites Of Brinsley Schwarz (Liberty), 1974

Solo:
Jesus Of Cool (Columbia/Radar) (US title — Pure Pop For Now People), 1978
Labour Of Lust (Columbia/Radar), 1979
Nick The Knife (Columbia/F-Beat), 1982
The Abominable Showman (Columbia/F-Beat), 1983

With Rockpile:
Seconds Of Pleasure (Columbia/F-Beat), 1980

Worth Searching Out:
With Brinsley Schwarz:
Fifteen Thoughts Of Brinsley Schwarz (compilation) (UA), 1978

Lulu

UK vocalist.
Born Marie McDonald McLaughlin Lawrie, Glasgow, Scotland, November 3, 1948.

Career: With Luvvers, scored first hit, cover of Isley Brothers(▶) **Shout**, in 1964 (band members included Jim Dewar, ex-Stone the Crows, Robin Trower(▶)). Had prolific period in charts under Mickie Most production in mid-'60s. Starred in movie 'To Sir With Love' with Sydney Poitier, and scored US No. 1 (five weeks) with titletrack; song was written by prominent lyricist Don Black and her current producer Mark London.

Trite **Boom Bang-A-Bang**, Eurovision Song Contest entry for 1968, preceded impressive work for Atlantic under Jerry Wexler; **Oh Me Oh Mi** made US Top 30.

Collaboration with David Bowie(▶) returned artist to pop listings in 1974 with **The Man Who Sold The World**. After chart hiatus, hit with **I Could Never Miss You** in 1981. Earned Grammy nomination year later for

Who's Fooling Who from **Lulu** album on Japanese label Alfa.

A permanent fixture on British TV — once had own show which featured 'live' rock music, including Hendrix(▶) and other premier performers — MOR reputation belies powerful soul-styled vocals and dynamic presentation. Career has been moulded to encompass wide audience, hence UK longevity.

Now married to leading London hairdresser John Frieda; first husband was Bee Gee Maurice Gibb.

Hit Singles:

	US	UK
Shout, 1964	—	7
Leave A Little Love, 1965	—	8
The Boat That I Row, 1967	—	6
Let's Pretend, 1967	—	11
To Sir With Love, 1967	1	—
Me The Peaceful Heart, 1968	53	9
Boy, 1968	—	15
I'm A Tiger, 1968	—	9
Boom-Bang-A-Bang, 1969	—	2
The Man Who Sold The World, 1974	—	3
I Could Never Miss You (More Than I Do Know), 1981	19	—

Albums:
Don't Take Love For Granted (Rocket), 1979
Very Best (—/Warwick), 1980
Lulu (Alfa), 1981

Loretta Lynn

US vocalist, composer, guitarist.
Born Loretta Webb, Butcher Hollow, Kentucky, April 14, 1935.

Career: Second of eight children of coal miner Melvin Webb and wife Clara. Although extremely poor, family was musical, and by the time she was 13, Loretta was singing at local functions. She met Oliver 'Mooney' Lynn at one such function and married him just before her 14th birthday. By 18 she had four children.

Musical ambitions were not forgotten, however. Encouraged by Mooney, Loretta learned guitar and started to write. By 24 she was singing professionally in clubs around Custer, Washington, where family now lived.

Lynn's appearance on Buck Owen's TV show was seen by Norm Burley of Zero Records; session for Zero followed, resulting in first single **I'm A Honky Tonk Girl**, which reached Top 20 of US country charts in July 1960. October 1960 saw first appearance on 'Grand Ole Opry'. By 1961 Lynn had landed contract with US Decca (later MCA). Under supervision of veteran producer Owen Bradley, she recorded **Success**, which became Top 10 country hit.

Unbroken run of charting records and accolades followed, making Lynn one of country music's most successful performers. In addition to solo efforts, she recorded many duets with Ernest Tubb and later, extremely successfully, with Conway Twitty(▶). She has regularly toured in US and throughout world and was first woman to receive Country Music Association's sought-after Entertainer Of The Year award (1972).

Now regarded as virtual godmother of modern country music, Lynn received worldwide acclaim in 1980 when 'Coal Miner's Daughter', a movie based on her autobiography, was released. Starring Sissy Spacek and Tommy Lee Jones, it was among year's top-grossing films.

Although in many ways the archetypal country artist, Lynn broke the boundaries of this naturally conservative form with prefeminist songs of aggrieved wifehood, like **Don't Come Home A Drinkin' (With Lovin'**

On Your Mind) and **The Pill**. Unlike Dolly Parton(▶) and others, she has stuck strictly to country form and is one of its most accomplished writers and performers.

Albums (selected):
You Ain't Woman Enough (MCA), 1960
Greatest Hits (MCA), 1968
Who Says God Is Dead (MCA), 1968
Coal Miner's Daughter (MCA), 1974
The Loretta Lynn Story (—/MFP), 1981
Alone With You (MCA/—), 1982

With Conway Twitty:
(See separate entry)

Lynyrd Skynyrd

US group formed 1965.
Original line-up: Ronnie Van Zant, vocals; Gary Rossington, guitar; Allen Collins, guitar.

Career: Originally formed in Jacksonville, Florida, as high-school trio, named after their authoritarian PE teacher, Leonard Skinner. By 1972, full line-up completed with Leon Wilkeson (bass), Billy Powell (keyboards) and Robert Burns (drums). Discovered playing Southern bars and clubs by Al Kooper(▶), who immediately signed them to his Sounds of the South label. Session bassist Ed King (ex-Strawberry Alarm Clock) brought in by Kooper as full-time member. First album, **Pronounced Loh-nerd Skin-nerd**, received favourable response. Closing cut **Free Bird** later became group anthem, achieving minor chart placings following several re-releases.

Career boosted by playing support on Who's(▶) 1973 US tour. Quickly established themselves as one of America's most celebrated boogie bands, boasting three guitarists. Next album, **Second Helping**, went gold. Set included US hit single, **Sweet Home Alabama**, their famous riposte to Neil Young's(▶) scathing **Southern Man** and **Alabama** put downs. Third album, **Nuthin' Fancy**, also went gold and included another US hit with Lee Clayton's **Saturday Night Special**.

Extensive touring schedules consistently drained group's energies, prompting Burns' departure, replaced by Artimus Pyle. Not surprisingly, seasoned sessioneer Ed King left shortly afterwards. Undeterred, Skynyrd kept on boogieing and their increasingly raucous behaviour inspired strong, devoted following.

On October 20, 1977, a week after the release of the notable **Street Survivors** LP, Skynyrd embarked on lengthy US tour. Their private plane took off from Greenville, South Carolina, en route for Baton Rouge, Louisiana; approaching Gillsburg, Mississippi, the plane crashed in a wood, 200 yards from an open field. Casualties included Ronnie Van Zant, Steve Gaines, roadie Dean Kirkpatrick, and backing single Cassie Gaines. The tragedy shook the rock world, for the group had always been much loved for their aggressive, uncom-

Recalled cover of Street Survivors, Lynyrd Skynyrd. Courtesy MCA Records.

promising approach: MCA quickly stopped release of **Survivors** LP with its sadly prophetic cover. Even Neil Young sang **Sweet Home Alabama** at one of his concerts in their memory.

The Rossington Collins Band emerged with some remaining members of Skynyrd, retaining the spirit of the original group.

Final line-up: Van Zant; Rossington; Collins; Artimus Pyle, drums; Leo Wilkeson, bass; Billy Powell, keyboards; Steve Gaines, guitar.

Hit Singles:

	US	UK
Sweet Home Alabama, 1974	8	—
Free Bird, 1974	19	—

Albums:
Pronounced Leh-nerd Skin-nerd (MCA), 1974
Second Helping (MCA), 1974
Nuthin' Fancy (MCA), 1975
Gimme Back My Bullets (MCA), 1976
One More From The Road (MCA), 1976*
Street Survivors (MCA), 1977
First And Last (MCA), 1978

*Double Live LP

MC5

US group formed 1967.
Original/Final line-up: Wayne Kramer, guitar; Fred 'Sonic' Smith, guitar; Rob Tyner, vocals, harmonica; Michael Davis, bass; Denis Thompson, drums.

Career: MC5 (Motor City Five) were part of Detroit's 1967 vibrant local scene when John Sinclair took them under wing and proclaimed

them stars of his White Panther Party. This mixing of politics and music continued with release of first album. Recorded live, it immediately caused headaches for Elektra with opening lines, 'Kick Out The Jams, Motherfuckers!' The band's decision to record new opening seemed compromise incompatible with their political stance. In any event Elektra dropped them soon after.

After breaking with Sinclair, band tried to settle down by signing with Atlantic. Jon Landau then produced **Back In The USA**. Its failure to sell well is ironic in light of later far-reaching influence among bands of 1976 London. Next LP **High Time** also failed and Atlantic terminated contract. Fred Smith eventually married Patti Smith(▶). Kramer and Davis went to prison on drug charges.

In hindsight, unschooled, crudely aggressive music of MC5 was most important part of their 'revolutionary' stance. Despite changing fashions, MC5 remain powerful influence and inspiration to anyone interested in high-energy rock.

Albums:
Worth Searching Out:
Kick Out The Jams (Elektra), 1969
Back In The USA (Atlantic), 1970
High Time (Atlantic), 1971

Madness

UK group formed 1978.
Original/Current line-up: Suggs (Graham McPherson), vocals; Chas Smash, vocals, compere, dancer; Chris Foreman, guitar; Lee 'Kix' Thompson, saxophone; Mark Bedford, bass; Dan Woodgate, drums.

Career: Formed in North London as the Invaders, changed name to Madness (after song by ska hero Prince Buster). In 1979, Specials(▶) launched 2 Tone records; Madness invited to cut single **The Prince/Madness**, which scored first hit. Group then signed by Stiff and became biggest act on label by far with 13 further consecutive UK hits and five Top 10 LPs by end of 1982, mostly composed within band.

With appealing mixture of ska (now largely abandoned), music hall, pop, R&B, visual

Below: Madness, Stiff Records biggest hitmakers, live in London.

Madness, a US compilation. Courtesy Geffen Records.

comedy and biting yet amusing social comment, Madness have become most consistent UK hitmakers of '80s, guaranteed sell-out shows wherever they appear in UK, and to some extent in Europe. American success eluded them until 1983, perhaps because of curiously British lyrical content/humour and appearance. In 1981 made feature film financed by Stiff, 'Take It Or Leave It', which predictably achieved mammoth sales for video medium. **Complete Madness**, TV-advertised hits compilation, topped UK album charts for three weeks during 1982. Group's only problem may be sustaining remarkable success. Should eventually conquer US, provided rumours of internal discord are proved incorrect.

Hit Singles:	US	UK
The Prince, 1979	—	16
One Step Beyond, 1979	—	7
My Girl, 1980	—	3
Work Rest And Play, 1980	—	6
Baggy Trousers, 1980	—	3
Embarrassment, 1980	—	4
Return Of The Los Palmas 7, 1981	—	7
Grey Day, 1981	—	4
Shut Up, 1981	—	7
It Must Be Love, 1981	—	4
Cardiac Arrest, 1982	—	14
House Of Fun, 1982	—	1
Driving In My Car, 1982	—	4
Our House, 1982	—	5

Albums:
One Step Beyond (Sire/Stiff), 1980
Absolutely (Sire/Stiff), 1980
Seven (—/Stiff), 1981
Complete Madness (—/Stiff), 1982
The Rise And Fall (—/Stiff), 1982

Taj Mahal

US multi-instrumentalist, vocalist, composer. Born New York, May 17, 1942.

Career: Taj Mahal immersed himself in traditional blues forms, but when that music regained social respectability, he promptly went off in another direction, exploring such roots as African and Caribbean music.

Unlike most blues singers (often semi-

literates from rural Doop South, though they may later base themselves in Northern industrial ghettos), Mahal came from educated black middle class, being raised in Springfield, Massachusetts, and has a university background. He majored in animal husbandry and studied folk music history, becoming an acknowledged expert on subject.

In Los Angeles he formed first band, the Rising Sons, with Ry Cooder(▶), which soon broke up. Then he landed Columbia contract and for debut album **Taj Mahal** put together superlative multi-racial backing band featuring Cooder (guitar, mandolin) and Jessie Ed Davis (guitar).

The Natch'l Blues, Taj Mahal. Courtesy Columbia Records.

Subsequent albums further explored country blues, notably double sets **Giant Step/De Ole Folks At Home** and **The Real Thing**, while African elements were introduced with **Recycling The Blues**, and **Music Keeps Me Together** had West Indian flavour.

Mahal, who also plays guitar, harmonica, piano, bass, banjo and fife, developed a penchant for exploiting potential of often obscure traditional instruments.

In 1977, left Columbia for Warner Bros and did **Music Fuh Ya** set. He scored movies 'Sounder' (in which he appeared) and 'Brothers'.

A towering 6ft 4in, Mahal featured prominently in many outdoor rock festivals of the '70s and can be given much credit for re-awakening public interest in traditional black music forms.

Albums:
Taj Mahal (Columbia/Direction), 1967
Natch'l Blues (Columbia/Direction), 1968
Giant Step/De Ole Folks At Home (Columbia/CBS), 1971
Recycling The Blues (Columbia/CBS), 1973
Ooh So Good 'n' Blues (Columbia/CBS), 1973
Mo' Roots (Columbia/CBS), 1974
Live And Direct (Crystal Clear), 1979
Best Of (Columbia/—), 1980
Going Home (Columbia/CBS), 1980

The Mamas And The Papas

US vocal group formed 1965

Original/Final line-up: John Philips, Michelle Phillips, Cass Elliott, Denny Doherty.

Career: One of first aggregations to make freewheeling, California hippie image commercially acceptable, with series of records that combined strong, memorable melodies with soaring vocal harmonies and distinctive folk-rock sound.

Ex-folkie John Phillips and wife Michelle came together with Cass Elliott and Denny Doherty, former members of New York band the Mugwumps, in Virgin Islands. Almost immediately guiding light Phillips moved outfit to LA and arranged record deal with Lou Adler's newly formed Dunhill label.

Hits Of Gold, The Mamas And The Papas. Courtesy ABC Records.

First single was Phillips' **California Dreamin'**, a key flower-power cut almost as evocative as **San Francisco (Wear Some Flowers In Your Hair)** which Phillips also composed. Top 10 hit in US and substantial hit elsewhere, it set group on road to success, including three more major hits in 1966.

Despite single success and several gold albums, group was not destined for longevity. John and Michelle Phillips' marriage started teetering in 1966, and problems caused by this and other internal dissensions led to break-up in 1968. Subsequently John Phillips went into film production and took up lifestyle of California pop aristocrat. Michelle Phillips has sporadically surfaced as an actress ('Dillinger', 'Valentino'), while providing staple fare for gossip columns; Denny Doherty more or less disappeared from sight, while Cass Elliott died in 1974 of a heart attack, after patchy solo ventures.

Despite their brief career, the Mamas and the Papas had considerable influence on '60s music scene, paving way for more heavyweight protagonists of Aquarian age. Furthermore, they left behind cuts which have become much-played classics, notably **California Dreamin'**, **Monday Monday**, **Dedicated To The One I Love** and **Creeque Alley**.

Although there were reports in 1982 that reunion was being planned, nothing seemed to come of idea.

Hit Singles:	US	UK
California Dreamin', 1966	4	23
Monday Monday, 1966	1	3
I Saw Her Again, 1966	5	11
Words Of Love, 1966	5	47
Dedicated To The One I Love, 1967	2	2
Creeque Alley, 1967	5	9
Twelve Thirty, 1967	20	—

Albums:
Farewell To The First Golden Era (Dunhill/—), 1968
The Papas And The Mamas (Dunhill/RCA), 1968
Hits Of Gold (ABC), 1969
A Gathering Of Flowers (Dunhill/Probe), 1970
Sixteen Of Their Greatest Hits (Dunhill/—), 1970
Twenty Golden Hits (Dunhill/Probe), 1972
The Best Of The Mamas And The Papas (—/Arcade), 1977

Worth Searching Out:
If You Can Believe Your Eyes And Ears (Dunhill/RCA), 1966

Manfred Mann

UK band formed 1962.

Original line-up: Manfred Mann, keyboards; Paul Jones, vocals, harmonica; Mike Vickers, reeds, guitar; Dave Richmond, bass; Mike Hugg, drums.

Career: South African-born Mann and Mike Hugg put together Mann-Hugg Blues Brothers in late 1962 and started gigging on burgeoning London blues circuit. Changing name to Manfred Mann, band signed with HMV and recorded first single, **Why Should We Not**, in 1963.

Tom McGuinness replaced Dave Richmond on bass on release of third single, **5-4-3-2-1**. Track, which featured Paul Jones' harmonica, was adopted as theme tune for TV show 'Ready Steady Go' and became major hit. From that time until end of '60s, band were rarely out of singles charts, with succession of songs from wide variety of sources, particularly US soul material (**Doo Wah Diddy Diddy, Oh No Not My Baby**) and Bob Dylan (**If You Gotta Go, Go Now, Just Like A Woman, Mighty Quinn**).

Changes took place during this period, however; Mike Vickers left at end of 1965, McGuinness switched to lead guitar and Jack Bruce joined on bass; six months later Jones left to pursue solo career as singer (and later actor), and Bruce quit to join supergroup Cream(▶). Their respective replacements were Mike D'Abo from Band Of Angels and Klaus Voorman (a Beatles(▶) cohort).

However, by end of decade, after 18 hit singles, members were tired of restrictions of pop formula. Mann folded band, and he and Hugg put together more ambitious Manfred Mann Chapter Three. More orientated towards albums, outfit lasted for couple of years. Mann then put together yet another outfit, Manfred's Mann's Earth Band. Original line-up comprised Mann, Colin Pattenden (bass), Mick Rogers (guitar), and Chris Slade (drums).

From beginning, band followed ambitious rock direction, backing album releases with heavy touring schedules in UK and US. In 1973 they had first hit single with **Joybringer**, based on theme from Holst's 'Planets', and in mid-'70s scored with cover of Bruce Springsteen's(▶) **Blinded By The Light.**

Davy's On The Road Again was also major hit, and since that time Earth Band has gone on recording and touring with continued moderate success. There have been several personnel changes, but the slightly enigmatic figure of Mann has given continuity.

Rarely less than interesting, Mann-led aggregations have provided much worthwhile music over last two decades.

Current line-up: (Manfred Mann's Earth Band): Mann; John Lingwood, drums; Chris Thompson, vocals; Steve Waller, guitar; Matt Irving, bass.

Hit Singles:

	US	UK
Manfred Mann:		
5-4-3-2-1, 1964	—	5
Hubble Bubble Toil And Trouble, 1964	—	11
Doo Wah Diddy Diddy, 1964	1	1
Sha La La, 1964	12	3
Come Tomorrow, 1965	50	4
Oh No Not My Baby, 1965	—	11
If You Gotta Go, Go Now, 1965	—	2
Pretty Flamingo, 1966	29	1
Just Like A Woman, 1966	—	10
Semi-Detached Suburban Mr James, 1966	—	2
Ha! Ha! Said The Clown, 1967	—	4
Mighty Quinn, 1968	10	1
My Name Is Jack, 1968	—	8
Fox On The Run, 1968	—	5
Ragamuffin Man, 1969	—	8
Manfred Mann's Earth Band:		
Joybringer, 1973	—	9
Blinded By The Light, 1976	1	6
Davy's On The Road Again, 1978	—	6

Albums:
Manfred Mann:
The Best Of Manfred Mann (Mercury/Nut), 1977

Manfred Mann Chapter Three:
Worth Searching Out:
Chapter Three (Polydor), 1970

Manfred Mann's Earth Band:
Earth Band (Bronze), 1972
Glorified, Magnified (Bronze), 1972
Messin' (Bronze), 1973
Solar Fire (Polydor/Bronze), 1973
The Good Earth (Warner Bros/Bronze), 1974
Nightingales And Bombers (Warner Bros/Bronze), 1975
Mannerisms (—/Sonic), 1976
The Roaring Silence (Warner Bros/Bronze), 1976
Watch (Warner Bros/Bronze), 1978
Angel Station (Warner Bros/Bronze), 1979
The R&B Years (—/See For Miles), 1982
Semi-Detached Suburban (—/EMI), 1979
Chance (Warner Bros/Bronze), 1980
Somewhere In Afrika (—/Bronze), 1983

Manhattan Transfer

US vocal group formed 1969.
Original line-up: Tim Hauser; Janis Siegel; Alan Paul; Laurel Masse.

Career: Originally signed to Capitol Records in 1969; 1971 set **Junkin'** initially failed miserably; Re-vamped, re-styled and with only Hauser remaining, group earned reputation in early '70s in New York.

Hauser had been with R&B vocal group the

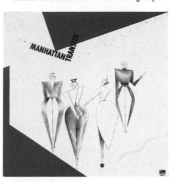

Extensions, Manhattan Transfer. Courtesy Atlantic Records.

Criterions in '50s; later worked as producer and actor. Paul (with BA in Music and Drama) was film and stage actor; appearing on Broadway in 'Camelot', 'The King & I' and 'Oliver'. Masse and Siegel had singing backgrounds — primarily jingles and session vocals. Siegel had recorded for Leiber & Stoller with the Young Generation on Red Bird R&B label.

After period in gay bars and bath houses, quartet developed kitsch swing era image, but vocal ability partially swamped by grandiose stage act. Transfer, however, took good advice on album material; have charted sporadically since **Operator** (1975). Main success was in Europe, particularly France, and UK. Scored eight British Top 50 entries between 1976 and 1980. Lyrical ballad **Chanson D'Amour** made No. 1 in UK.

With Cheryl Bentyne replacing Masse,

Below: Manfred Mann (left) with late '60s line-up (Paul Jones singing) of group which bore his name.

Transfer entered new era with '79 set **Extensions**. Produced by guitarist Jay Graydon, album had futuristic air while retaining strong jazz roots. Included stage favourite **Birdland** (used as jingle for Akai stereo), rock-flavoured **Nothin' You Can do About It** and electronic **Twilight Zone**, which returned outfit to US charts.

Reputation confirmed by Grammy awards and 'Downbeat' magazine honour of Best Vocal Group in 1980 poll. Chart status maintained with 1981 LP **Mecca for Moderns**, which made US Top 40. **Best Of** collection charted following year.

Unit's powerful live act has been refined in recent years; camp nostalgia 'feel' has in part been replaced by contemporary styling and design. Vocally, group use perfect mix of jazz, R&B and rock material. Paul's soulful reading of classic doo-wop numbers from '50s has earned him comparisons with leading black performers.

Current line-up: Hauser; Paul; Siegel; Cheryl Bentyne.

Hit Singles:

	US	UK
Chanson D'Amour, 1977	—	1
Walk In Love, 1978	—	12
On A Little Street In Singapore, 1978	—	20

Albums:
Junkin' (with Gene Pistilli) (Capitol/MFP), 1971
Manhattan Transfer (Atlantic), 1975
Coming Out (Atlantic), 1976
Pastiche (Atlantic), 1978
Live (Atlantic), 1978
Extensions (Atlantic), 1979
Mecca For Moderns (Atlantic), 1981
Best Of (Atlantic), 1982

Barry Manilow

US vocalist, pianist, composer.
Born Brooklyn, New York, June 17, 1946.

Career: While studying at New York College of Music and Juilliard Academy, Manilow had part-time job in mail room at Columbia Records. After working on 'Callback' series of talent shows for WCBS-TV, in 1967 became conductor/arranger for Ed Sullivan TV specials. Met Bette Midler(▶) when working as pianist at New York's Continental Baths in 1972. Manilow arranged and co-produced her first two albums as well as joining her 1973 US tour as musical director and pianist. Tour gave him chance to showcase own talents as opening act, leading to own tour in 1974 and recording deal with Arista Records.

Mandy topped US charts in January 1975 within nine months of release, and was first of string of hits which showed crossover appeal between pop and MOR with audiences ranging from young girls to mums and dads.

Manilow's slick and rather schmaltzy stage shows—in the Liberace mould though not quite so over the top — have won him major international audience while at same time nauseating many critics. His records have been consistently well crafted and there is real talent behind the manufactured show-biz image.

Besides his records, Manilow has been prolific writer of TV and radio advertising jingles, including the famous 'You Deserve A Break Today' for McDonald's hamburgers.

He holds Broadway box-office records with $782,000 for one show.

Hit Singles:

	US	UK
Mandy, 1975	1	11
It's A Miracle, 1975	12	—
Could It Be Magic, 1975	6	25*
I Write The Songs, 1976	1	—
Tryin' To Get The Feeling Again, 1976	10	—
Weekend In New England, 1977	10	—
Looks Like We Made It, 1977	1	—
Can't Smile Without You, 1978	3	43
Even Now, 1978	19	—
Copacabana, 1978†	8	42
Ready To Take A Chance Again, 1978	11	—
Somewhere In The Night, 1979	1	42
Ships, 1979	9	—
When I Wanted You, 1979	20	—
I Made It Through The Rain, 1980	10	6
Bermuda Triangle, 1981	—	15
Let's Hang On, 1981	32	12
The Old Songs, 1981	15	48
I Wanna Do It With You, 1982	—	8

*1978 UK.
†Double A-side in UK.

Albums:
Barry Manilow I (Arista), 1973
Barry Manilow II (Arista/—), 1974
Mandy (—/Arista), 1975
This One's For You (Arista), 1976
Trying To Get The Feeling (Arista/Fame), 1975
Manilow Magic—The Best Of (—/Arista), 1976
Greatest Hits (Arista), 1978
Even Now (Arista), 1978
One Voice (Arista), 1979
All The Best—Barry (Arista), 1980
If I Should Love Again (Arista), 1981
Here Comes The Night (Arista/—), 1981
Barry Live In Britain (Arista), 1982
Oh, Julie! (Arista), 1982
I Wanna Do It with You (Arista), 1982

Herbie Mann

US flautist, tenor saxophonist, bandleader, composer.
Born Brooklyn, New York, April 16, 1930.

Career: Like John Mayall(▶) in British R&B movement, Herbie Mann's importance to jazz scene lies more in the musicians he has brought together than in own playing talents.

Roy Ayers, Larry Coryell(▶), Duane Allman(▶), Dave 'Fathead' Newman, reggae sax ace Tommy McCook, famed Muscle Shoals Rhythm Section (Eddie Hinton, Barry Beckett, David Hood, Roger Hawkins) have appeared on his prodigious output of albums. Covered gamut of styles with elements of Latin American, Afro, Middle Eastern, R&B, soul, salsa and disco thrown into jazz melting pot.

Mann always brought commercial edge to jazz. Using his regulars (Roy Ayers, vibes; Larry Coryell, guitar; Sonny Sharrock, guitar) plus Memphis R&B sessioneers (including Reggie Young, Bobby Emmons, Bobby Wood, Tommy Cogbill, Mike Leech), 1969 LP **Memphis Underground** was big seller as well as his best artistically.

His Family Of Mann group emerged in '73, featuring Pat Rebillot (keyboards) and Dave Newman (tenor sax). In '74 he recorded with UK rock musicians, notching disco hit following year with **Hi-Jack**.

He has recorded Ron Carter, Miroslav Vitous and Attila Zoller (all appearing on his LPs) for his Atlantic-distributed Embryo label.

Hit Singles:

	US	UK
Hi-Jack, 1975	14	—

Albums:
Memphis Underground (Atlantic), 1969
Best Of (Atlantic), 1973

Bob Marley

Jamaican vocalist, composer.
Born Robert Nesta Marley, St Anns, Jamaica, 1945 (passport gave exact date as February 6, but Marley said this was inaccurate); died May 11, 1980.

Career: Son of an English army captain and Jamaican mother, Bob Marley was undoubtedly *the* giant figure in the evolution of reggae music.

While at Jamaica's Stepney School, became friendly with Winston Hubert McIntosh and Neville O'Reiley Livingstone; as Peter Tosh(▶) and Bunny Wailer they were later to join Marley in forming the Wailers.

At 16 cut debut record **Judge Not,** co-written with mentor Joe Higgs, at Ken Khouri's Federal Studio in Kingston. Then with Leslie Kong producing covered Brook Benton's **One Cup Of Coffee** after seeing the American star in concert with Dinah Washington.

Teaming with Tosh and Wailer, plus Junior Braithwaite and Beverly Kelso, Marley formed the Wailin' Wailers; signed to Clement Coxsone Dodds' Studio One label and sold more than 80,000 copies of first single **Simmer Down.**

Backed by studio band the Skatalites, quintet worked through ska and rock-steady eras towards dawn of reggae style. However, they broke up in 1966 following wrangles over payment for their recordings.

Marley joined his mother in Delaware, US, and worked in Chrysler car factory before returning to Jamaica to avoid service in Vietnam. Re-uniting with Tosh and Wailer, Marley recorded again with Leslie Kong who, via work with Desmond Dekker(▶), had become island's top producer. Following Kong's death from cancer, trio began work with Lee Perry who helped form Marley's distinctive style. Earned first international hit with **Small Axe**.

Espousing teachings of Jamaican politico/ folk legend Marcus Garvey, Marley and friends became devout Rastafarians. In 1968 Marley was busted for possession of marijuana, the first of many subsequent clashes with Jamaican establishment.

Quitting Perry's label, trio took his ace musicians, brothers Carlton and Aston 'Family Man' Barrett, with them and formed own short-lived Wailing Soul label.

When Wailer was sent to prison for year following another drugs bust, Marley signed as songwriter to American soul star Johnny Nash's(▶) Jad label. He helped Nash develop unique blend of soul and reggae which gave the American a UK No. 1 with **Stir It Up**.

Marley used resultant income to set up Tuff Gong label with Tosh and Wailer. Subsequent records won them an international deal with Island Records thanks to that company's Jamaican-born boss Chris Blackwell.

Blackwell's carefully orchestrated promotion put Bob Marley and Wailers in vogue with rock critics, musicians and audiences alike. **Catch A Fire** album (1973) led to well-received UK visit and Stateside tour with Sly and the Family Stone(▶). Though not quite so strong, follow-up set **Burnin'** did include **I Shot The Sheriff**, covered very successfully by Eric Clapton(▶).

Wailer and Tosh then quit group though they remained firm friends with Marley they were unhappy with Island deal.

Inset Below: Uprising, Marley and the Wailers. Courtesy Island Records.
Bottom Inset: Marley swings his dreadlocks.

Below: Robert Nesta Marley, the number one figure in reggae.

Inset Below: Exodus, the 1977 album. Courtesy Island Records.

Marley brought in his wife Rita plus Judy Mowatt and Marcia Griffiths (the I-Threes) as back-up vocalists and in 1975 recorded classic **Natty Dread** album. This set seal on his growing reputation as Jamaica's most important artist. Superb live LP, **Jah Live**, recorded at London's Lyceum, included version of **No Woman No Cry**, which became major UK pop hit, as well as brilliant **Lively Up Yourself**.

Marley's stature as spokesman for Jamaican masses — his songs were often full of social and political comment — made him target of political gangs. In December 1976 he was shot four times in the arm by a group who burst into his home on eve of concert he was to give for then ruling left-wing PNP party led by Michael Manley. Marley appeared in concert but immediately after went into exile in Miami for 18 months. Recorded 1976 album **Exodus** partly in that city, partly in London.

Marley's return to homeland was triumphant. Before 20,000 people at Kingston's National Stadium he joined Manley and political rival (now premier) Edward Seaga in symbolic handshake at concert which commemorated visit to Jamaica 12 years earlier by Emperor Haile Selassie of Ethiopia, figurehead of the Rastafarian movement. Marley also appeared in a special concert to celebrate birth of new African nation of Zimbabwe.

Towards end of his 1980 world tour he collapsed following performance at NY's Madison Square Gardens and was rushed to hospital. Three years earlier he had had cancerous toe removed, but now it seemed the cancer had spread. Despite treatment at famed Josef Issels Clinic in Bavaria, Marley's condition was incurable. He died during May 1980 at Cedars Lebanon Hospital in Miami where he had flown to visit his mother en-route for Jamaica.

During long stint with Island, Marley had recorded 10 albums; his music spanned whole gamut of Jamaican experience, both on national and international level. Material ranged from pure love songs to strident political statements. Marvellously evocative lyrics — even when full of patois they struck chord with both multi-national and multi-racial audiences — were matched by catchiest of melodies. His popularity and influence have not waned—if anything his impact is possibly stronger today.

Above: Natty Dread, Marley and the Wailers. Courtesy Island Records.

Left: Marley's music was both religious and political.

Hit Singles:	US	UK
Exodus, 1977	—	14
Jamming/Punky Reggae Party, 1977	—	9
Is This Love, 1978	—	9
Could You Be Loved, 1980	—	5
No Woman No Cry, 1981	—	8
Buffalo Soldier, 1983	—	4

Rasta Revolution, Marley and the Wailers. Courtesy Island Records.

Albums:
Catch A Fire (Island), 1972
African Herbsman (—/Trojan), 1973
Burnin' (Island), 1973
Rasta Revolution (—/Trojan), 1974
Natty Dread (Island), 1975
Jah Live (Island), 1975
Rasta Man Vibration (Island), 1976
Exodus (Island), 1977
Birth Of A Legend (Epic), 1977
Early Music (—/Embassy), 1977
Babylon By Bus (Island), 1978
Kaya (Island), 1978
Bob Marley And The Wailers (—/Hammer), 1979
Survival (Island), 1979
Uprising (Island), 1980
Soul Rebel (—/New Cross), 1981
Chances Are (Warner Bros), 1981
Confrontation (Island), 1983

John Martyn

UK vocalist, composer, guitarist.
Born Glasgow, Scotland, June 28, 1946.

Career: Began playing acoustic guitar and singing in folk clubs in early 1967. Signed to Island Records, immediately began work on folk-based **London Conversation**, released in 1968. **The Tumbler** was in similar vein, with addition of Harold McNair on flute and saxophone. Next two albums, **Stormbringer** (released at same time as Deep Purple's LP of same name, the only time such a coincidence has occured in rock) and **The Road To Ruin** (both 1970), were recorded with wife Beverly. Former was cut in New York with number of well-known session musicians, including the Band's(▶) Garth Hudson and Levon Helm, helping Martyn reach wider audience.

Beverly reverted to solo career, while John plunged into jazz-influenced **Bless The Weather**, a logical development from its predecessors. **Solid Air** (1972) proved strongest to date, continuing experiments with amplified guitar and scat singing. Extensive tour followed with former Pentangle bassist, Danny Thompson.

Inside Out (1973) and **Sunday's Child** (1974) completed Martyn's gradual assimilation of folk/jazz styles, establishing him as important and imaginative writer/arranger. Ever on fringes of music business, his 1975 LP **Live At Leeds** (amusingly repeating title of the Who's(▶) best-selling live album) was available on mail order only from Martyn's Hastings home. Island later released limited pressing.

Well Kept Secret, John Martyn. Courtesy WEA Records. Most Martin is jazz/folk flavoured.

Three years elapsed before release of next studio work, **So Far So Good**. **One World** LP quickly followed and was critically acclaimed in many quarters as his finest, most mature work. Cult following has substantially increased Stateside, but major breakthrough there still seems unlikely.

Final album with Island, **Grace And Danger**, was a disturbing but exceptional work, documenting break-up of his marriage with Beverly. (Apparently, LP was shelved for a year by Island, due to bleak subject-matter.)

Switch to Warner Bros brought **Glorious Fool**, a further musical development, produced by Phil Collins (who also supplied drums/additional vocals). Titletrack, a satirical attack on Ronald Reagan, saw Martyn aggressively entering political arena. In 1981 he took his first permanent group on road, refusing to be confined by myopic classification 'folk artist'. Latest work, **Well Kept Secret**, boasts impressive line-up of musicians and indicates Martyn's desire to retain musical quality while experimenting with new ideas.

A sporadic recording artist, his post-**One World** output has alienated many old-style Martyn purists; others maintain that his recent exploits are a natural and aesthetically acceptable development.

Albums:
Solo:
London Conversation (—/Island), 1968
The Tumbler (—/Island), 1968
Bless The Weather (—/Island), 1971
Solid Air (—/Island), 1973
Inside Out (—/Island), 1973
Sunday's Child (—/Island), 1974
Live At Leeds (—/Island), 1975
So Far So Good (—/Island), 1977
One World (—/Island), 1977
Grace And Danger (Atlantic/Island), 1980
Glorious Fool (—/Warner Bros), 1981
Well Kept Secret (Duke/Warner Bros), 1982
The Electric John Martyn (Island), 1982

With Beverly Martyn:
Stormbringer (—/Island), 1970
The Road To Ruin (—/Island), 1970

Dave Mason

UK vocalist, guitarist, composer.
Born Worcester, England, May 10, 1945.

Career: Played with Shadows-inspired Jaguars before founding Hellions with Jim Capaldi, Luther Grosvenor and Poli Palmer. Recorded one single, **Daydreaming Of You**, under auspices of Kim Fowley, before evolving into Birmingham-based Deep Feeling.

Friendship with fellow Midlander Stevie Winwood(▶) of Spencer Davis Group(▶) led to uncredited vocal appearance on No. 1 hit **Someone Help Me**, and tambourine accompaniment on **I'm A Man**. While Winwood plotted his departure from Spencer Davis, Mason briefly roadied for them.

Formation of Traffic(▶) in 1967 gave Mason opportunity to reveal talents as songwriter/guitarist/singer. Contributed three songs to **Mr Fantasy** (**Utterly Simple, Hope I Never Find Me There** and **House For Everyone**) and penned second hit single **Hole In My Shoe**, which reached No. 2 in UK chart. Disenchantment with Traffic's direction precipitated his departure in December 1967. He then produced Family's(▶) seminal **Music In A Doll's House**. Returned to Traffic in May 1968, contributing **You Can All Join In, Don't Be Sad, Cryin' To Be Heard** and **Feelin' Alright'** to their second album. Ousted by others in October 1968.

Cut one solo single, **Little Woman**; played sessions on Hendrix' **Electric Ladybird**, Stones' **Beggar's Banquet** and (later) Harrison's **All Things Must Pass**. When Winwood dissolved Traffic, Mason allied himself with Capaldi, Wood and (Wynder K.) Frog for short-lived project.

Became involved with Delaney and Bonnie(▶), guesting on their highly acclaimed US/UK tour of 1969. His playing alongside Clapton can be heard on their **On Tour** album; collaboration would later encourage very brief period in celebrated Derek and the Dominoes(▶).

Along with Delaney and Bonnie's Friends, Mason recorded the classic **Alone Together** (known to collectors for its limited edition multi-coloured 'vomit' vinyl, preceding flood of coloured discs), released on Blue Thumb. In early 1971, recorded album with Mama Cass Elliot — an intriguing coupling, but results proved less than memorable. Drifted back to England for six gigs with Traffic, resulting in sometimes excellent **Welcome To The Canteen** live LP.

Formed own group back in States and recorded projected studio/live double **Headkeeper**. Problems at Blue Thumb resulted in work being released in two parts — **Head-**

keeper (1972) and **Dave Mason Is Alive** (1973). Leaving record company in dis-illusionment Mason signed long-term deal with Columbia. '70s albums proved solid, but generally unspectacular. Erratic solo activities were partly result of various problems with record companies. First album still regarded as definitive statement, though subsequent releases well received, particularly in US.

Albums:
With Traffic:
Mr Fantasy (Island), 1967
Traffic (Island), 1968
Welcome To The Canteen (Island), 1971

With Cass Elliot:
Dave Mason And Cass Elliot, (Blue Thumb) 1971

Solo:
Alone Together (MCA), 1970
Headkeeper (MCA), 1972
Scrapbook (Island), 1972
Dave Mason Is Alive (MCA), 1973
It's Like You Never Left (Columbia/CBS), 1973
Best Of (Blue Thumb/—), 1974
Dave Mason (Columbia/CBS), 1974
At His Best (MCA), 1975
Split Coconut (Columbia/CBS), 1975
Certified Live (Columbia/CBS), 1976
Let It Flow (Columbia/CBS), 1977
Marisopa De Oro (Columbia/CBS), 1978
Very Best (MCA/—), 1978
Old Crest On A New Wave (CBS), 1980
Best Of (Columbia/CBS), 1981

Johnny Mathis
US vocalist.
Born San Francisco, September 30, 1935.

Career: Believed to be first black entertainer to achieve millionaire status, Mathis was taught singing by his vaudeville artist father and started his recording career in jazz vein, before Mitch Miller decided the young star should switch his attention to ballad singing —which brought immediate success. Had previously been outstanding athlete at college; was potential Olympian at high jump.

His 1956 gold single **Wonderful, Wonderful** (backed by Ray Coniff's orchestra). **The Shadow Of Your Smile** and **The Twelfth Of Never** were among big hits which made Mathis natural successor to Nat King Cole(▶). However, one of his most memorable outings was a decidedly uptempo version of the show song **I'm Getting Married In The Morning** from 'My Fair Lady'.

His 1958 **Greatest Hits** album was still on American charts a decade later, topping two million mark during 490-week record chart run (making it the longest charting LP until Pink Floyd's(▶) **Dark Side Of The Moon.**

Originally cast in mould of Frank Sinatra(▶), Tony Bennett, Vic Damone and Sammy Davis Jr, Mathis entered '80s as authentic soul singer working with producer Thom Bell out of Sigma Sound Studios in Philadelphia. He cut string of fine records, including moving Christmas song **When A Child Is Born** (re-make of Stylistics'(▶) superb **I'm Stone In Love With You,** disco hit **Gone, Gone, Gone** and some laudable duets with Deniece Williams, making his 25th anniversary of his recording with Columbia in 1980 a real landmark.

Hit Singles:	US	UK
Wonderful, Wonderful, 1957	14	—
It's Not For Me To Say, 1957	5	—
Chances Are/The Twelfth Of Never, 1957	1	—

The Twelfth Of Never/Chances		
Are, 1957	9	—
A Certain Smile, 1958	14	4
Winter Wonderland, 1958	—	17
Someone, 1959	35	6
Small World, 1959	20	—
Misty, 1959	12	12
My Love For You, 1960	47	9
Gina, 1962	6	—
What Will Mary Say, 1963	9	49
I'm Stone In Love With You, 1975	—	10
When A Child Is Born, 1976	—	1
Too Much Too Little Too Late (with Deniece Williams), 1978	1	3
Gone Gone Gone, 1979	—	15

Albums (selected):
Heavenly (Columbia/Embassy), 1959
All Time Greatest Hits (Columbia/CBS), 1972
You've Got A Friend — Today's Great Hits (Columbia/CBS), 1974
You Light Up My Life (with Deniece Williams) (Columbia/CBS), 1978
That's What Friends Are For (with Deniece Williams) (Columbia/CBS), 1978
Friends In Love (Columbia/CBS), 1982

Ian Matthews
US comoser, vocalist, guitarist.
Born Ian Matthews MacDonald, Lincolnshire, England, June 16, 1945.

Career: First worked professionally with mid-'60s vocal group, Pyramid. Joined Fairport Convention(▶) with whom he stayed for over two years, appearing on **Fairport Convention, What We Did On Our Holidays** and **Unhalfbricking**. Moved on to solo career, recording **Matthew's Southern Comfort** for MCA's Uni label, partly written and produced by Howard and Blakeley Sessions were so successful that new group emerged bearing album's title and comprising Gordon Huntley (pedel steel guitar), Carl Barnwell (guitar/vocals), Mark Griffiths (guitar/vocals), Andy Leigh (bass/vocals) and Ray Duffy (drums). Group recorded two further albums, **Second Spring** and **Later That Same Year,** as well as scoring surprise UK No. 1 hit with cover of Joni Mitchell's **Woodstock.**

Disappointed by group's increasingly commercial direction, Matthews resumed solo career and cut two albums for Vertigo, **If You Saw Thro' My Eyes** and **Tigers Will Survive.** Relations with Vertigo worsened

Above: Dave Mason, who left Traffic for solo success which soon faded.

and third album, **Journeys From Gospel Oak,** did not appear until 1974 (on Mooncrest label).

Having made relatively small impact as soloist, Matthews involved himself in another group venture with Plainsong, line-up completed by Andy Roberts (guitar), Dave Richards (bass) and Bob Ronga (guitar). Released excellent and much-neglected **In Search Of Amelia Earheart,** inspired by Fred Goerner's book of same title. After break-up of Plainsong, Matthews signed with Elektra and concentrated activities on US market. A much-touted collaboration with former Monkee Mike Nesmith as producer resulted in critically acclaimed **Valley Hi.** Elektra contract expired after acceptable **Some Days You Eat The Bear . . . And Some Days The Bear Eats You,** following which Matthews almost moved to Arista but left due to irreconcilable differences with label chief Clive Davis.

Before recording new group touring unit, Ian Matthews and Another Fine Mess, with Joel Tepp (guitar), John Ware (drums), Don Whaley (bass) and Tommy Nunes (guitar). New deal with Columbia produced **Go For**

Broke, but again failed to acheve commercial success. Subsequent works, including **Hit And Run, Stealin' Home, Siamese Friends** and **Spot Of Interference,** suffered same fate.

For years Matthews has been a cult figure, always tipped for success, but never able to break through. Frequent changes of backing musicians, management and record companies have not aided his cause. Although a talented writer with excellent taste in cover material, his work has never quite reached standard of US contemporaries.

Hit Single:	US	UK
Woodstock, 1977	—	1

Albums:
With Fairport Convention:
Fairport Convention (Island), 1968
What We Did On Our Holidays (Island), 1969
Unhalfbricking (Island), 1969

With Matthews Southern Comfort:
Matthews Southern Comfort (UNI), 1970
Second Spring (UNI), 1970
Later That Same Year (UNI), 1970

With Plainsong:
In Search Of Amelia Earhart (Elektra), 1972

Solo:
Valley Hi (Elektra), 1973
Some Days You Eat The Bear. . . And Some Days The Bear Eats You (Elektra), 1974
Journeys From Gospel Oak (—/Mooncrest), 1974
Hit And Run (CBS), 1977
Stealin' Home (—/Rockburgh), 1978
Siamese Friends (—/Rockburgh), 1979
Discreet Repeat (—/Rockburgh), 1980*
Spot Of Interference (RSO/Rockburgh), 1980
*compilation

John Mayall
UK vocalist, guitarist, keyboard player, band-leader, composer.
Born Manchester, November 23, 1933.

Career: Mayall formed his first band, Powerhouse Four, at college after national service, building reputation backing US bluesmen John Lee Hooker(▶) and Sonny Boy Williamson(▶) on UK tours.

Below: A 1960s line-up of John Mayall's ever changing Bluesbreakers, which included John McVie and Mick Taylor.

His career has two distinct segments: the years on British R&B club scene, during which Eric Clapton(▶), Mick Taylor, Jack Bruce(▶), Peter Green(▶), Jon Hiseman and other luminaries were featured in his Bluesbreakers working band; and his time as exile in California working with Rick Vito, Larry Taylor, Harvey Mandel, Don 'Sugarcane' Harris and Blue Mitchell in bands that were also chameleon-like in personnel and musical direction, but more studio orientated.

Encouraged by Alexis Korner to move to London in 1962, he formed Bluesbreakers with John McVie (bass) and Bernie Watson (guitar), cutting first album **Live At Klooks Kleek** 18 months later, Roger Dean replacing Watson and Hughie Flint joining on drums.

Succession of critically applauded singles and exhaustive club tours led to major breakthrough in 1966 when Eric Clapton of Yardbirds(▶) joined. **Bluesbreakers—John Mayall With Eric Clapton** won quick cult-status hitting No. 6 on UK album charts.

Mayall/Clapton/McVie/Flint line-up was arguably best British R&B band of all time. McVie was temporarily replaced by Jack Bruce and Clapton left to join emergent psychedelic movement, forming Cream(▶) with Bruce and Ginger Baker(▶). McVie rejoined. Peter Green coming in on guitar. Aynsley Dunbar on drums. Dunbar was soon replaced by Mick Fleetwood, the new line-up lasting till May 1967 when Fleetwood and Green left to form Fleetwood Mac(▶), soon to be joined by McVie.

The then unknown Mick Taylor joined Mayall from the Gods, staying till 1969 when he replaced late Brian Jones in the Rolling Stones(▶).

Changing musical direction, Mayall brought in Keef Hartley's powerhouse drumming and strong brass section for jazz-slanted sound. He also cut back-to-the-roots solo album, **The Blues Alone**.

USA Union, John Mayall. Courtesy Polydor Records.

Chris Mercer, who left for Juicy Luicy, Jon Hiseman and Dick Heckstall-Smith, who formed Colosseum, Andy Fraser, who became member of Free(▶), Jon Mark and Johnny Almond, who set-up Mark-Almond, all spent time with Mayall before July 1968 when he decided to go back to tighter backing group with new line-up of Mick Taylor, Stephen Thompson (bass) and Colin Allen (drums) from Zoot Money's band. This line-up cut **Blues From Laurel Canyon** set, inspired by brief holiday in Los Angeles. With Taylor leaving, Mayall moved to California, signed new deal with Polydor (after five years with Decca) and put together first of many American line-ups.

In 1975, Mayall switched to ABC and later cut album with legendary New Orleans producer Allen Toussaint.

A charismatic catalyst of some of the finest white/multi-racial R&B line-ups ever, Mayall is remembered for knack of nurturing emergent major talents as much as for his own work.

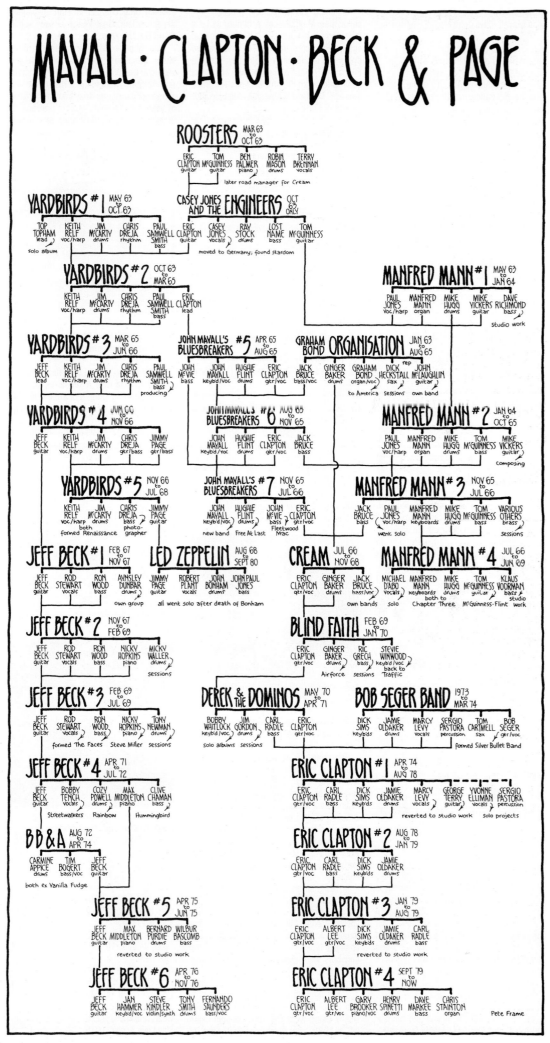

Albums:
John Mayall Plays John Mayall (—/Decca), 1965
Bluesbreakers (London/Decca), 1965
A Hard Road (London/Decca), 1967
Crusade (London/Decca), 1967
Blues Alone (London/Ace Of Hearts), 1967
Raw Blues (London/Ace Of Hearts), 1967
Bare Wires (London/Decca), 1968
Blues From Laurel Canyon (London/Decca), 1969
Diary Of A Band Volume 1 (—/Decca), 1968
Looking Back (London/Decca), 1969
Empty Rooms (Polydor), 1970
Turning Point (Polydor), 1970
World Of Volume 1 (—/World Of), 1970
World Of Volume 2 (—/World Of), 1971
Beyond The Turning Point (Polydor/—), 1971
Diary Of A Band Volume 2 (—/Decca), 1972
Jazz Blues Fusion (Polydor), 1972
Through The Years (London/Decca), 1972
Best Of (Polydor), 1973
Notice To Appear (ABC), 1975
John Mayall (Polydor), 1976
A Hard Core Package (MCA/—), 1977
Primal Solos (London/—), 1977
Last Of The British Blues (MCA/—), 1978
No More Interviews (—/DJM), 1979
Bottom Line (—/DJM), 1979

Curtis Mayfield

US composer, vocalist, guitarist.
Born Chicago, June 3, 1942.

Career: Led own group, the Alphatones, as teenager. Met Jerry Butler in his grandmother's church choir. On moving to North Side of Chicago in 1956 renewed acquaintances with Butler, leaving Alphatones to link up with him and group known as the Roosters.

This team evolved into the Impressions(▶) with Butler as lead singer. Following **For Your Precious Love** smash, Butler went solo. Mayfield had stints as Butler's backing guitarist and wrote material for him while trying to hold the Impressions together. With Mayfield elevated to lead singer, the Impressions became one of most successful vocal groups in black music history.

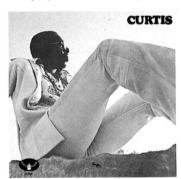

Curtis, Curtis Mayfield. Courtesy Buddah Records.

In 1968 Mayfield formed own Curtom label and two years later left the Impressions, though he continued to produce them. Debut solo album went gold and single **Move On Up** took him into UK charts. His soundtrack for **Superfly** movie stood up in own right and spawned two gold singles, **Freddie's Dead** and **Superfly**. He also wrote and produced scores for 'Claudine' movie (performed by Gladys Knight(▶) and the Pips) and Staple Singer's(▶) (**Let's Do It Again**). He appeared as actor in 'Short Eyes', writing the score, as he did for 'A Piece Of The Action' and 'Sparkle', which featured singing of Aretha Franklin(▶).

As record company boss, producer and songwriter, Mayfield has continued to be a major force in black music. His own somewhat lightweight recordings have, however, lacked dynamism of the Impressions' days, despite their often potent lyrical content which has dealt widely with the problems of black urban America. Mayfield is now signed to Epic after demise of Curtom.

Hit Singles:	US	UK
Move On Up, 1971	—	12
Freddie's Dead (Theme From Superfly), 1972	4	—
Superfly, 1972	8	—

Albums:
Superfly (Buddah/RSO), 1974
Never Say You Can't Survive (Curtom), 1977
Heartbeat (Curtom), 1979
Something To Believe In (RSO), 1980
Honesty (Epic), 1983
Worth Searching Out:
Roots (Curtom), 1974
Curtis (Curtom), 1974

Paul McCartney

UK composer, vocalist, bass player.
Born James Paul McCartney, Liverpool, June 8, 1942.

Career: As half of the world-dominating Lennon/McCartney songwriting partnership (there were reportedly nearly 2,000 cover versions of their songs by 1965) seemed particularly alienated when Yoko Ono(▶) began exerting strong influence over Lennon(▶) in late '60s. Although not first member of Beatles(▶) to release solo record, McCartney sued rest of group for freedom from group contracts.

Tug Of War, Paul McCartney. Courtesy Parlophone Records.

First solo LP released 1970, opening floodgates for virtual barrage of hit singles and inconsistent albums — indicating that break-up of group and particularly of songwriting team was major loss to rock 'n' roll — although singles especially not without controversy. **Give Ireland Back To The Irish** was banned by BBC on political grounds, for example, while **Hi Hi Hi** (1972) was banned for potential lyrical endorsement of drug usage.

In 1971, formed Wings (Paul, vocals, bass; wife Linda McCartney, keyboards, vocals; Denny Laine (ex Moody Blues(▶)), guitar, vocals; Denny Seiwell, drums), which first appeared on **Wild Life** LP. Various personnel changes took place during '70s — among members were guitarists Henry McCullough, Jimmy McCulloch (who died in January 1979 of drug related heart failure) and Laurence Juber, drummers Geoff Britton, Joe English and Steve Holley. However Paul, Linda and Denny Laine were ever present until Laine left in 1980, after much publicised arrest of

Paul on drug charges at start of planned Japanese tour. Best Wings LP was superb **Band On The Run**.

Subsequently, McCartney has recorded either completely solo, or with help from superstar friends, including Stevie Wonder(▶) and Michael Jackson(▶). His music has shown definite moves away from the hard rock of years with Beatles, but his praiseworthy organisation of annual events to commemorate Buddy Holly(▶) (whose music publishing

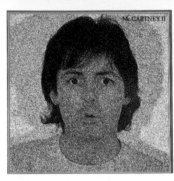

McCartney II, Paul McCartney. Courtesy Parlophone Records.

is owned by McCartney) indicates continuing love for spirit of rock 'n' roll, if not for actual musical involvement. McCartney in '80s regarded as past best by rockers, but he is probably biggest AOR/pop star in world, as well as reputedly a multi-millionaire. Operates own company MPL from prestigious office in Soho Square in London's West End.
Bass: Höfner violin.

Hit Singles:	US	UK
Solo:		
Another Day, 1971	5	2
Uncle Albert/Admiral Halsey, 1971	1	—
Wonderful Christmastime, 1979	—	6
Coming Up, 1980	1	2
Waterfalls, 1980	—	9
Ebony And Ivory, 1982*	1	1
The Girl Is Mine, 1982†	2	8

*With Stevie Wonder
†With Michael Jackson

Back To The Egg, Paul McCartney & Wings. Courtesy Parlophone Records.

McCartney and Wings:		
Give Ireland Back To The Irish, 1972	21	16
Mary Had A Little Lamb, 1972	28	9
Hi Hi Hi/C Moon, 1972	10	5
My Love, 1973	1	9
Live And Let Die, 1973	2	9
Helen Wheels, 1973	10	12
Jet, 1974	7	7
Band On The Run, 1974	1	3
Junior's Farm, 1974	3	16
Listen To What The Man Said, 1975	1	6
Venus And Mars/Rock Show, 1975	12	—
Silly Love Songs, 1976	1	2

Let 'Em In, 1976	3	2
Maybe I'm Amazed, 1977	10	28
Mull Of Kintyre/Girls School, 1977	33	1
With A Little Luck, 1978	1	5
Goodnight Tonight, 1979	5	5
Getting Closer, 1979	20	60

Albums:
Solo:
McCartney (Columbia/Parlophone), 1970
Ram (Columbia/Parlophone), 1971
McCartney II (Columbia/Parlophone), 1980
Tug Of War (Columbia/Parlophone), 1982

McCartney and Wings:
Wild Life (Columbia/Parliaphone), 1971
Red Rose Speedway (Columbia/Parlophone), 1973
Band On The Run (Columbia/Parlophone), 1974
Venus And Mars (Columbia/Parlophone), 1975
Wings Over America (Capitol/Parlophone), 1976*
London Town (Capitol/Parlophone), 1978
Wings' Greatest (Capitol/Parlophone), 1978 (Compilation)
Back To The Egg (Columbia/Parlophone), 1979
*Triple live set

Country Joe McDonald

US vocalist, composer, guitarist.
Born Joseph McDonald, El Monte, California, January 1, 1942.

Career: Named by leftist parents for Joseph Stalin. Grew up listing to country and folk. Served tour in US Navy and then began working as folk singer in Berkeley, California area. Recorded obscure, unknown solo in 1964, then met guitarist Barry Melton while working in folk band. Like many folk performers duo turned to rock, forming Country Joe & the Fish with Barry Melton, guitar; David Cohen, keyboards; Bruce Barthol, bass; Chicken Hirsh, drums.

Band's first recordings were EPs made to accompany McDonald's self-produced magazine. Gigs at Fillmore attracted folk label Vanguard, who signed band in late 1966. Fish eventually recorded four LPs which at time were highly regarded for political stance,

Here We Are Again, Country Joe & The Fish. Courtesy Vanguard Records.

social satire and commitment to counterculture. First LP, **Electric Music For The Mind And Body,** stand up best. Second (**Fixin' To Die**) is fondly remembered by nostalgists for Fish cheer ('Give us an 'F'. Give us a 'U', etc.')

Close identification with protest and Berkeley area ultimately backfired and band broke up for good in 1970. McDonald began variety of activities; he wrote music for several movies, briefly worked with Jane Fonda and returned to early style of folk music. Moving to Paris, he played variety of venues and clubs, seeking support for ecological and environmental causes.

Late 1974 included brief reunion with Melton for UK gigs. After period in London, McDonald returned to San Francisco.

As time passes, McDonald's contribution makes smaller and smaller impact. It is difficult to recall political and social milieu which made him seem so vital in 1966-67. His excellent solo efforts are always overshadowed by his days with the Fish.

Albums:
With Fish:
Electric Music For The Mind And Body (Vanguard), 1967
I-Feel-Like-I'm-Fixin'-To-Die (Vanguard), 1967

Country Joe Solo:
Paradise With An Ocean View (Fantasy), 1975
Love Is A Fire (Fantasy), 1976
Goodbye Blues (Fantasy), 1977
Best Of Country (—/Golden Hour), 1977
Rock 'n' Roll Music From Planet Earth (Fantasy), 1978
Leisure Suite (Fantasy), 1979
The Early Years (Piccadilly/—), 1980

Kate And Anna McGarrigle

Canadian duo formed 1976.
Kate McGarrigle, vocals, guitar, keyboards, banjo, composer.
Anna McGarrigle, vocals, keyboards, banjo, composer.

Career: Grew up in French quarter of Quebec; joined group in Montreal called Mountain City Four, and started to write songs.

In early '70s, compositions started to attract attention. Anna's **Heart Like A**

Wheel was recorded in 1972 by McKendree Spring, and later became Linda Ronstadt(▶) favourite. Maria Muldaur(▶) also used several McGarrigle songs.

Eventually attracted notice of Warner Bros, who flew sisters to West Coast to record first album, **Kate And Anna McGarrigle**. Despite presence of West Coast session mafia, album was delightful montage of folk, cajun and French Canadian influences, and was critically acclaimed. Sisters were hailed as highly promising new act.

McGarrigles found it difficult to reproduce delicate charm of recordings live, however, and tours were not universally praised. Next two albums did not live up to promise of first, and although reputation was largely restored by **French Record**, McGarrigles remain minority taste.

Albums:
Kate And Anna McGarrigle (Warner Bros), 1975
Dancer With Bruised Knees (Warner Bros), 1977
Pronto Monto (Warner Bros), 1978
The French Record (Hannibal), 1981
Love Over And Over (—/Polydor), 1982

John McLaughlin

UK guitarist, composer.
Born Yorkshire, January 4, 1942.

Career: McLaughlin came from musical family. Self-taught, played first in trad jazz band of Big Pete Deuchar. Joined British R&B movement of mid-'60s working with Graham Bond, Herbie Goins and Brian Auger.

Shortly after emigrating to States in 1968 joined Tony Williams' Lifetime (Williams, drums; Larry Young (aka Khalid Yasin), keyboards. Also featured on Miles Davis(▶) classic **Bitches Brew** and **In A Silent Way** sets.

Below: Don McLean — 'American Pie' and 'Vincent' are unforgettable.

Followed first solo album **Extrapolation** (1969), with **Devotion** (1971). Recorded in France, it included Buddy Miles(▶) on drums and Lifetime sideman Young.

Formed Mahavishnu Orchestra in 1971. Name suggested by guru Sri Chimnoy of whom McLaughlin was devotee. Band comprised Jerry Goodman (ex-Flock), violin; Billy Cobman(▶), drums; Jan Hammer, keyboards, and Rick Laird, bass. Goodman and Cobham had previously cut **My Goals Beyond** (1971) with McLaughlin, an acoustic album which explored Indian rhythms and scales.

Group's best work **Birds Of Fire** pushed jazz-rock genre to new heights; McLaughlin's flawless technique set yardstick for contemporaries. However, line-up split after three LPs, McLaughlin seemingly losing his spiritual inclination.

Recorded self-indulgent **Love Devotion Surrender** with fellow Chimnoy disciple Carlos Santana(▶) in 1973. Final Orchestra LP, **Between Nothingness And Eternity**, was cut live at NY's Central Park same year.

Anxious to work with larger unit, created multi-talented aggregation for 1974 LP **Apocalypse**. The 'new' Mahavishnu group featured Michael Walden (now 'Narada') drums; Ralph Armstrong, bass; Gayle Moran, keyboards, and French violin virtuoso Jean Luc-Ponty (ex-Mothers Of Invention). Recruitment of London Symphony Orchestra made **Apocalypse** a spectacular if cumbersome work.

Emerged from unwieldy unit after **Visions Of Emerald Beyond** (1975) for **Inner Words** (1976). Recorded at Château d'Heronville in France. Album retained Walden, Armstrong, Moran and added Stu Goldberg, keyboards.

McLaughlin had left Chimnoy in 1975 and future of MO was in doubt from that time. **Inner Worlds** proved last work from group. Free of responsibility of being band-leader/ focal point, McLaughlin settled quietly into Indian acoustic trio Shakti. Remained until 1978, cutting three LPs, **Shakti, Handful Of Beauty** and **Natural Elements**.

Now firmly entrenched in acoustic guitar, McLaughlin joined forces with Paco De Lucia and Larry Coryell — and later Al Di Meola(▶) — for 'supergroup' guitar trio, formed 1980. His phenomenal speed has been matched note for note by his partners in this definitive musical co-operative. That it remains melodic beyond the 100 mph phrases is a testimony to these guitar legends.
Guitars: Ovation acoustic/electric.

Above: John McLaughlin, one of the fastest most accurate guitarists around.

Albums:
Mahavishnu Orchestra:
Inner Mountain Flame (Columbia/CBS), 1971
Birds Of Fire (Columbia/CBS), 1973
Best Of (Columbia/—), 1980

With Carlos Santana:
Love Devotion Surrender (Columbia/CBS), 1973

Solo:
Extrapolation (Polydor), 1969
My Goals Beyond (Douglas/Elektra Musician), 1971
Inner Worlds (Columbia/CBS), 1976
Electric Guitarist (Columbia/CBS), 1978
Electric Dreams (Columbia/CBS), 1979
Music Spoken Here (Warner Bros/—), 1981
Belo Horizonte (Warner Bros), 1982
Best Of (Columbia/CBS), 1980

Shakti:
Shakti (Columbia/CBS), 1976
Handful Of Beauty (Columbia/CBS), 1977
Natural Elements (Columbia/CBS), 1978
(See also Al Di Meola)

Don McLean

US vocalist, guitarist, composer.
Born New Rochelle, New York, October, 2, 1945.

Career: Developed early interest in all forms of American music, particularly folk. On leaving school in 1963 started singing and playing in clubs.

By end of '60s MacLean had built up excellent reputation within his field and become a prolific songwriter. After spending two years knocking on record company doors, he made album **Tapestry** for small company which soon folded (although record was later re-released by United Artists, who signed him in 1971).

Breakthrough came with late '71 release of extraordinary single, **American Pie.** Despite McLean's folky background, record was symbolic 'history' of rock'n'roll, using evocative images tied to highly commercial hookline. Record was worldwide smash, catapulting McLean to instant stardom. Follow-up, **Vincent,** a highly personal song celebrating genius of painter Vincent Van Gogh, was almost as successful. Both songs were excellent showcases for McLean's attractively plaintive voice.

Career received further boost in 1973 when MOR singer Perry Como had huge hit with **And I Love You So,** another McLean song. In meantime, McLean had become in-demand live performer, years of small-time gigs paying off in controlled, well-paced performances.

During remainder of '70s McLean consolidated career, although he was never elevated to 'bed-sit philosophy' status of singer-songwriters such as Cat Stevens(▶) and Leonard Cohen(▶). Perhaps strangely, he became more popular in UK than in homeland, and regular tours were always sellouts.

In 1980 McLean's career entered new phase with massive pop success of his cover of Roy Orbison's(▶) **Crying.** (True to form record became hit in UK well before it did in US.) However, he will no doubt always be best known for now classic **American Pie.**

Hit Singles:	US	UK
American Pie, 1972	1	2
Vincent, 1972	12	1
Crying, 1980	5	1

Albums:
Tapestry (United Artists), 1972
American Pie (United Artists), 1972
Playin' Favourites (United Artists), 1973
Homeless Brother (United Artists), 1974
Solo (United Artists), 1976
Chain Lightning (Arista), 1979
Very Best Of (United Artists), 1980
Believers (Arista), 1982

Meat Loaf
US vocalist, actor.
Born Marvin Lee Aday, Dallas, Texas, September 27, 1948.

Career: Bat Out Of Hell was released in 1977 and very slowly began working way up through US/UK charts. Operatic, bombastic, with comic-book hero on cover, album seemed to combine pomp of early '70s with enthusiasm of punk. As album settled in for what seemed permanent place in charts, interest grew in larger-than-life figure behind it.

Meat Loaf, it happened, had been around for sometime. He had released rather weak R&B album for Tamla in 1970; **Featuring Stoney And Meat Loaf** quickly disappeared. So did Meat Loaf as he ventured into theatre. In 1976 he appeared in cult film 'Rocky Horror Picture Show'. It was through acting that he met Jim Steinman. Meat Loaf liked Steinman's songs and together they began assaulting record companies with demo tapes. CBS eventually signed them.

After success of first CBS LP (produced by

Todd Rundgren(▶)) **Bat Out Of Hell,** Meat Loaf toured (with back-up singers and band) until he ruined his voice. Wait for follow-up LP grew to point Steinman released separate opus **Bad For Good** in May 1981. Meanwhile Meat Loaf appeared in movie 'Roadie' after their first album.

Dead Ringer finally arrived in 1982 as continuation of gothic texture which made up **Bat**. Some claimed **Dead Ringer** was formalistic repeat while others called it brilliant return. Fans wondered if Meat Loaf really underwent rumoured exotic treatments (including drinking his own urine) to save his voice. Whatever the cure, it seems to have worked.

Hit Singles:	US	UK
Two Out Of Three Ain't Bad, 1978	11	32
Bat Out Of Hell, 1979	—	15
Dead Ringer For Love, 1982	—	5

Albums:
Featuring Stoney And Meatloaf (Prodigal), 1970
Bat Out Of Hell (Epic), 1978
Dead Ringer (Epic), 1982
Midnight At The Lost And Found (Epic), 1983

Melanie
US vocalist, composer, guitarist.
Born Melanie Safka, New York, February 3, 1947.

Career: A true flower-child, Melanie's sensitive little-girl image made her darling of the peace-and-love movement of early '70s.

Daughter of former jazz singer, Melanie's first ambition was to be an actress, but when going to audition for a play she mistakenly entered a music publisher's office. As she had guitar with her she was asked to sing. This led to Buddah Records' contract and introduction to Peter Schekeryck who became her producer, then her husband.

Candles In The Rain album, with its pensive and sincere songs, went gold, while hit singles were in Edith Piaf vocal mould, particularly **What Have They Done To My Song Ma.** Further hits with Jagger/Richard song **Ruby Tuesday** and US chart-topping **Brand New Key** won her an audience beyond confines of hippy movement.

With husband, formed Neighbourhood Records in 1972 as outlet for own material plus other acts. Only Mike Heron's Reputation and Melanie's own records got anywhere and label folded in 1975. She then signed to Atlantic. **Photograph** LP was produced by Ahmet Ertegun. Since then she has slipped from prominence.

Below: The gang from down under—Men At Work. Lead singer Colin Hay—centre.

Hit Singles:	US	UK
Lay Down (Candles In The Rain) (with Edwin Hawkins singers), 1970	6	—
Ruby Tuesday, 1970	52	9
Brand New Key, 1971	1	4

Albums:
Very Best Of (Buddah), 1974
Beautiful People (Accord/—), 1982
Want Have They Done To My Song Ma? (Accord/—), 1982

Men At Work
Australian group formed 1982.

Original/Current line-up: Colin Hay, vocals, guitar; Ron Strykert, guitar, vocals; Jerry Speiser, drums, vocals; Greg Ham, saxophone, keyboards; vocals, wind instruments; John Rees, bass, vocals.

Career: Men At Work's witty **Business As Usual** was released in US in mid-1982. Single **Who Can It Be Now?** was picked up by MTV and slowly began creating interest. Three months later it was No. 1, and album followed to take over what seemed permanent spot at top of US charts.

Business As Usual , Men At Work. Courtesy Epic Records.

UK press wondered what was going on; Men At Work wasn't usual Australian heavy metal popularised by AC/DC. **Down Under,** next single from album, had excellent video which gained UK exposure on 'Top Of The Pops'. MAW achieved what was becoming rare event in rock: a simultaneous No. 1 in US/UK charts.

Spring 1983 saw release of **Cargo** LP. Immediate reaction was that it lacked strong video material, though **Overkill** single was UK hit. Question now is whether or not Men At Work can eventually surpass debut album. For rock in general, problem is whether an accompanying video is essential to success of music.

Hit Singles:	US	UK
Who Can It Be Now?, 1982	1	45
Down Under, 1982	1	1
Overkill, 1983	3	22
It's A Mistake, 1983	15	33

Albums:
Business As Usual (Epic), 1982
Cargo (Epic), 1983

The Meters
US group formed 1969.

Original/Current line-up: Art Neville, keyboards; Leo Nocentelli, guitar; Joseph Modeliste, drums; George Porter, bass.

Career: The Meters have been regular studio band for ace producer Allen Toussaint and

partner Marshall Sehorn since mid-'60s (prior to which they started as Hawkettes, backing Fats Domino(▶), and worked as Art Neville Sound). Their brand of syncopated funk backed Lee Dorsey's string of '60s hits (**Ride Your Pony, Get Out Of My Life Woman, Everythin' I Do Gonna Be Funky**), and supported leader Art Neville's hit-making brother Aaron, Betty Harris, Irma Thomas and Toussaint's own recorded efforts.

Signed to Jubilee subsidiary Josie, Meters had first hit in 1968 with **Sophisticated Sissy.** Other R&B hits included **Sissy Strut, Look-Ka Py-Py, Chicken Strut** and (for Reprise) **Cabbage Alley,** which later veered them towards rock influence.

They supported Dr John(▶) and Rolling Stones(▶) on tour and also recorded with Robert Palmer(▶) and Paul McCartney(▶), which brought them to wider audience.

Whether doing backing work for other artists or own recordings and live appearances, the Meters personify unique soul sound of New Orleans through their quirky clipped rhythms, bare-boned funk and emphasis on the off-beat (emphasising strong link between the Crescent City and reggae).

Albums:
Good Old Funky Music (—/Pye), 1979

Worth Searching Out:
Look-Ka-Py-Py (Josie/Charly), 1972
Best Of (Reprise), 1975

Bette Midler
US vocalist, actress.
Born Honolulu, Hawaii, December 1, 1945.

Career: Trash with flash, sleaze with ease, the Divine Miss M's over-the-top high camp style led to Grammy for newcomer of the year eight years after Bette Midler came to New York from Hawaii where she grew up. Unhappy childhood as 'plain little fat Jewish kid in working-class Samoan neighbourhood' led to daydreams of stardom.

After one year at University of Hawaii and summer job in pineapple cannery, Midler landed small part in film 'Hawaii', saving every penny for fare to New York, where she arrived end of 1965. While typing, filing and working as go-go girl, she also studied acting, singing, dancing and appeared in Off-Off-Broadway plays. Got job in chorus of 'Fiddler On The Roof' on Broadway, then moved up to role of Tzeitel. At same time, Midler sang at two late-night supper clubs, researching old songs at Lincoln Center Library and learning style of torch singers to incorporate in act.

Began appearing on TV chat shows, played clubs in Boston and Chicago, then got 16-weekend booking that led to stardom: singing for gay men in towels at Upper West Side's Continental Baths. During these four months in 1970, Midler learned how to relate to audience, developed comic patter and turned her act from bluesy to up-beat.

The Divine Miss M took shape as Midler's alter-ego, and Barry Manilow(▶) joined as pianist and arranger. In following year night-club bookings increased. Sold-out Carnegie Hall concert introduced three-women vocal back-up group by time of Philharmonic concert at end of 1972, Harlettes had become integral to style of Midler's tightly rehearsed shows. High-powered Aaron Russo had taken over as manager, resulting in tempestuous personal and professional relationship that nonetheless led to wider audience.

Co-produced by Manilow, first album **The Divine Miss M** was released in November 1972, followed by **Bette Midler.** Although albums were criticised as offering something

for everyone and not conveying exuberance of stage personality, Midler won best newcomer Grammy.

City-by-city tour was next, culminating in award-winning show at Palace Theatre. Among her fans was reputed to be Laurence Olivier. Who better could appreciate the drama and theatricality Midler brought to pop music, her touching vulnerability under the comic vulgarity, the respect and daring with which she enacted a repertoire from the Andrews sisters to Bob Dylan(▶), the energetic and lavish, yet fun production numbers?

After Palace, when Manilow left to pursue solo career, subsequent shows were somewhat repetitious. Although albums, tours and TV special kept her in front of adoring international public, it was with sense of needing new direction that Midler decided to star in 'The Rose'. This 1979 film about Janis Joplin(▶) like character confirmed acting ability hinted at since cabaret days.

The following year 'Divine Madness' concert film brought Midler's extraordinary showmanship full distance from camp coterie to high-street movie house. **Fire Down Below** was released as single from soundtrack album.

Hit Singles:	US	UK
Do You Want To Dance?, 1973	17	—
Boogie Woogie Bugle Boy, 1973	8	—

Albums:
The Divine Miss M (Atlantic), 1974
Songs For The New Depression (Warner Bros), 1976
Live At Last (Atlantic), 1977
The Best Of Bette (Atlantic), 1978
Thighs And Whispers (Atlantic), 1979
The Rose (Atlantic), 1979
Divine Madness (Atlantic), 1980

Buddy Miles

US drummer, vocalist.
Born Omaha, Nebraska, September 5, 1946.

Career: A huge man with a powerful drum sound and husky voice, Miles worked professionally from age 13 backing the Ink Spots,

Above: The Divine Ms. Bette Midler with her prominent features to the fore.

Bryan Hyland, Conway Twitty(▶), the Dick Clark Revue and others, and appeared on classic Jaynetts' R&B single **Sally Go Round The Roses**.

In 1965 he joined soulman Wilson Pickett's(▶) band. A year later he was linked by legendary manager Albert Grossman (the man behind Dylan(▶) and others) with white blues/rock musicians Mike Bloomfield(▶), Nick 'The Greek' Gravenites, Barry Goldberg and Roger 'Jellyroll' Troy, to form short-lived but potent Electric Flag on Atlantic.

Miles moved on to join Jimi Hendrix(▶) and Billy Cox in ill-starred Band Of Gypsys, featuring on album of that title as well as on Hendrix's **Electric Ladyland, The Jimi Hendrix Experience** (a soundtrack called **Soundtrack From The Film 'Jimi Hendrix'** in the US) and **Cry Of Love** albums.

Following Hendrix's tragic death, Miles returned to R&B roots, though with rock undertones, to form brass-laden Buddy Miles Band (with Cox on bass). In 1970, he came up with storming album, **Them Changes**, which resided in US charts for nearly 18 months.

Re-named Buddy Miles Express, his band put out a series of fine albums on Mercury and Columbia, including 1972 venture with Carlos Santana(▶), recorded live in a Hawaiian volcano crater.

Miles joined re-formed Electric Flag in 1974 but group was short-lived and following year he was again leading own band, recording **More Miles Per Gallon** set for Casablanca.

Prolifically recorded in own right, Miles has also been a highly active session drummer, appearing on Wilson Pickett's(▶) **In The Midnight Hour**, Eddie Floyd's **Knock On Wood**, Aretha Franklin's **Respect**, as well as playing on record or on stage with Ben E. King, Gladys Knight and the Pips(▶), Joe Tex, Percy Sledge, James Brown(▶), Billy Stewart, and other major soul artists.

Albums:
Them Changes (Mercury), 1970
Live (with Carlos Santana) (Columbia/CBS), 1972
Sneak Attack (Atlantic), 1981

Frankie Miller

UK vocalist, composer, guitarist, actor.
Born Glasgow, Scotland,

Career: Began singing/writing at 10, and by 14 was gigging in Scotland. Heavily influenced by Little Richard and such Stax/Volt artists as Wilson Pickett(▶) and Otis Redding(▶) After brief period as electrician's apprentice, toured Scotland and Europe in various short-lived bands including the Deljacks, the Sabres and the Stoics. Moved to London to cut demos for Chrysalis and teamed up with Robin Trower(▶), ex-Procol Harum(▶), who was in process of forming Jude, a new group with Clive Bunker, ex-Jethro Tull(▶) , and Stone the Crows' bassist Jim Dewar. Jude's career ended almost before it had begun, but Miller's potential secured solo deal with Chrysalis in 1972.

Debut **Once In A Blue Moon** featured Brinsley Schwarz as backing group, which led to guest appearances with such pub rockers as Bees Make Honey and Ducks Deluxe. Full talent emerged on **High Life,** produced by Allen Toussaint in New Orleans; LP highlighted Miller's soulful vocals. Strong material produced several tracks which later became hit singles for Betty Wright and Three Dog Night(▶). Seeking permanent group, Miller assembled the Frankie Miller Band: Henry McCullough (guitar), Mick Weaver (keyboards), Chrissie Stewart (bass) and Stu Perry (drums) for **The Rock**, credited to band and produced by Elliot Mazer.

Poor sales prompted dissolution and on returning to England, new unit Full House was formed, comprising Ray Minhinnitt (guitar), Charles Harrison (bass), James Hall (keyboards) and Graham Deacon (drums). 1977's **Full House** LP presented same problems as ever — mediocre reviews; bad **Double Trouble** merely underlined Miller's inability to combine his fiery vocals with series of impressive songs. Yet his material has frequently been covered by artists such as Kim Carnes(▶), Ry Cooder(▶), Delbert Mc Clinton and Bob Seger(▶) who recorded excellent version of **Ain't Got No Money** on **Stranger In Town**). Although achieving three Top 50 entries during late '70s, only **Darlin'** made any strong impact. Meanwhile, Miller toured relentlessly, fronting series of pick-up bands.

He eventually moved to Capitol, cutting **Standing On The Edge** with highly respected Muscle Shoals rhythm section, featuring Barry Beckett (producer/keyboardist), David Hood (bass) and Roger Hawkins (drums). Against, commercial success proved elusive, indicating that Miller may remain second-division rock singer, or devote more energy to his concurrent career as actor.

Hit Single:	US	UK
Darlin', 1978	—	6

Albums:
Once In A Blue Moon (Chrysalis), 1973
High Life (Chrysalis), 1974
The Rock (Chrysalis), 1975
Full House (Chrysalis), 1977
Double Trouble (Chrysalis), 1978
Falling In Love (Chrysalis), 1979
Easy Money (Chrysalis), 1980
Standing On The Edge (Capitol), 1982

Steve Miller

US guitarist, vocalist, composer.
Born Milwaukee, Wisconsin, October 5, 1943.

Career: Began playing guitar at four under auspices of legendary Les Paul(▶) and T-Bone Walker, both friends of Miller's father. Formed first band before teens. This blues outfit, which included Boz Scaggs(▶), was known as the Marksmen Combo.

Returning from adopted home state of Texas, Miller enrolled at University of Wisconsin to study literature, playing guitar part-time in the Ardells and then the Fabulous Knight Train (re-uniting Miller with Scaggs).

After studying in Denmark for a year, Miller moved to Chicago's burgeoning blues scene. He got involved with fleeting projects — the Goldberg/Miller Blues Band (with Barry Goldberg) and the World War Three Blues Band — but spent most of his time jamming with blues greats Muddy Waters(▶), Buddy Guy, Junior Wells and Otis Rush.

A brief respite back in Texas introduced Miller to recording; working as janitor for a local studio, he cut demos in spare time, before heading for San Francisco in 1966.

Below: The king of comebacks, Steve 'Guitar' Miller, who survived a four year rest to return to the top.

Recruiting Lonnie Turner (bass), Tim Davis (drums) and James 'Curly' Cooke (guitar) he formed Steve Miller Band, debuting at the Matrix after frantic period rehearsing in basement on Berkeley University campus.

Band attained strong local following at Avalon Ballroom and Bill Graham's(▶) Fillmore Auditorium (where they backed Chuck Berry(▶) for a live album). In summer 1967 they appeared at Monterey Pop Festival.

With other San Franciscan outfits Mother Earth and Quicksilver Messenger Service(▶), they made recording debut with **Revolution** soundtrack album.

Signed with Capitol Records in 1967, band released first album **Children Of The Future** in May 1968, with Scaggs re-joining Miller (replacing Cooke) and Jim Peterman providing keyboards.

Children Of The Future, Steve Miller. Courtesy Capitol Records.

Stunning **Sailor** set (1968), produced by Glyn Johns, included classic material **Living In The USA, Gangster Of Love** and haunting **Song For Our Ancestors**, pushing Miller's band to top of West Coast pile.

Various personnel changes (a continuing feature of Miller's outfits) saw Scaggs go solo and Peterman turn to production. Subsequent Miller aggregations have included Nicky Hopkins, Ben Sidran (one-time member of Marksmen) and dextrous bassist Gerald Johnson.

Overcoming serious bout of hepatitis (one of several extended breaks due to health problems), Miller progressed steadily, if not prolifically, through '70s with gold albums **The Joker** and **Fly Like An Eagle**. A four-year hiatus from '77 to '81 ended with **Circle Of Love** Miller returning from extended period spent farming his estate in Oregon.

Maintaining that the best was yet to come, he set out to make '82 his own, with **Abracadabra** single storming US/UK charts.

Often dismissed as 'lightweight', Miller could be criticised for repetition, but his manipulation of memorable licks and sharp simple lyrics remain undisputedly close to heavyweight.

Guitars: Fender Stratocaster, Gibson Les Paul.

Hit Singles:	US	UK
The Joker, 1974	1	—
Take The Money And Run, 1976	11	—
Rock'n Me, 1976	1	11
Fly Like An Eagle, 1977	2	—
Jet Airliner, 1977	8	—
Swingtown, 1977	17	—
Abracadabra, 1982	1	2

Albums:
Children Of The Future (Capitol), 1968
Sailor (Capitol), 1969
Brave New World (Capitol), 1969
Your Saving Grace (Capitol), 1970
Number Five (Capitol), 1970
Rock Love (Capitol), 1971
Recall The Beginning (Capitol), 1973
Living In The USA (Capitol), 1973

The Joker (Capitol), 1973
Anthology (Capitol), 1973
Fly Like An Eagle (Capitol/Mercury), 1976
Book Of Dreams (Capitol/Mercury), 1977
Best Of 1968-73 (Capitol), 1977
Greatest Hits '74-'78 (Capitol/Mercury), 1978
Circle Of Love (Capitol/Mercury), 1981
Abracadabra (Capitol/Mercury), 1982
Steve Miller Band Live (Mercury), 1983

Ronnie Milsap

US vocalist, pianist, composer, multi-instrumentalist.
Born Robbinsville, North Carolina.

Career: Outstanding crossover country performer, blind since birth, now making regular appearance on American pop charts.

Initially learned violin; proficient on piano and guitar before teens. Formed first band the Apparitions at Raleigh State School for the Blind. Curtailed studies to join J.J. Cale(▶) before forming own group and signing deal with Scepter Records.

Initial cuts were R&B influenced, and Milsap and his band were booked for soul shows featuring the Miracles(▶) and Bobby Bland(▶). Moved to Memphis in 1969, earning residency at TJ's night-club. First minor hit, **Loving You Is A Natural Thing,** recorded for the Chips label in 1970.

Turned to country music full-time after moving to Nashville; played weekly at Roger Miller's King Of The Road Motel. Career went on upward spiral after signing with Charly Pride's(▶) manager Jack D. Johnson. Pacted with RCA in 1973. Debut single for label **I Hate You** made C&W Top 10. Has subsequently remained a permanent fixture in country charts.

Milsap is frequent recipient of Country Music Awards (vocalist, album, entertainer) and won Grammys in '74, '76 and '81 for Best Country Vocal Performance. Received Gold Records for **It Was Almost Like A Song** and **Only One Love In My Life** in 1978. Earned Gold Album in 1979 for **Ronnie Milsap Live.**

Combining effortless R&B-styled vocals with the best in country songs has made Milsap heir apparent to the legendary George Jones(▶).

Hit Singles:	US	UK
It Was Almost Like A Love Song, 1977	16	—
(There's) No Gettin' Over Me, 1981	5	—
I Wouldn't Have Missed It For The World, 1981	20	—
Any Day Now, 1982	14	—

Albums (selected):
20-20 Vision (RCA), 1976
Live (RCA), 1977
Greatest Hits (RCA), 1980
There's No Getting Over Me (RCA/—), 1981
Inside (RCA), 1982

Missing Persons

US group formed 1980.

Original/Current line-up: Dale Bozzio, vocals; Terry Bozzio, drums, keyboards; Warren Cuccurullo, guitar; Patrick O'Hearn, bass; Chuck Wild, keyboards.

Career: Terry Bozzio's pedigree includes spells with George Duke(▶), Eddie Henderson, Frank Zappa(▶) and UK. Cuccurullo is a Zappa grad who joined Bozzio and his wife Dale in 1980 to form band. Dale sang lead on Zappa's **I Don't Want To Get Drafted** but her primary former experience was as Playboy bunny.

Trio worked on material for 18 months in LA, adding fellow ex-Zappa mate O'Hearn and long-time session man Wild. Ken Scott (Kansas(▶), Supertramp(▶), Bowie(▶), Devo(▶) and more) produced and released EP, following rejection by record companies. Capitol reconsidered and released EP with **Words** in place of Doors(▶) cover, **Hello, I Love You**.

EP did well in US album charts and provided two Top 50 singles. Follow-up album made US Top 30. So far band has had no UK impact. Stage show relies as much on Dale's (lack of) costume as on music, though husband Terry's drumming (in manic style of Keith Moon), often steals spotlight.

Apart from Dale's squeaky, high-pitched vocals, Missing Persons are rather derivative, but popularity would seem to confirm that US market finds their electro-pop sound quite comfortably familiar.

Albums:
Spring Session M (Capitol), 1982

Worth Searching Out:
Missing Persons (EP) (KoMos/—), 1981

Joni Mitchell

US vocalist, composer, guitarist, pianist.
Born Roberta Joan Anderson, Fort McLeod, Alberta, Canada, November 7, 1943.

Career: Attended Alberta College of Art with intention of becoming commercial artist. Learned to play ukelele for personal enjoy-

ment, then developed serious interest in folk music/songwriting. Securing gig at the Depression coffee-house, Joni gradually gained confidence. Following performance at Mariposa Folk Festival in Ontario, she wrote her first song, **Day After Day.** Professional career began in Toronto, where she quickly became a leading figure of the Yorktown set.

Married Chuck Mitchell in June 1965; couple moved to Detroit, achieving some acclaim as duo on local folk circuit. After break-up of marriage, Joni continued as soloist, securing engagements in New York; signed to Reprise in 1967. Under aegis of Elliot Roberts, she gained reputation as star songwriter with a series of covers by such artists as Judy Collins(▶), Gordon Lightfoot(▶), Johnny Cash(▶), Tom Rush(▶) and Fairport Convention(▶).

Wild Things Run Fast, Joni Mitchell. Courtesy Geffen Records.

Employing services of ex-Byrd(▶) David Crosby as producer, Mitchell recorded **Songs To A Seagull,** a brilliant debut displaying talent as singer/songwriter. Early albums were essentially acoustic, melodic works, sharpened by poetic lyrics. Although a product of the singer/songwriter boom of the late '60s, Mitchell revealed a maturity and incisiveness that separated her from most of her contemporaries. While others wallowed in their own narcissism, Mitchell was careful to bring a cutting edge to many of her lines. She continually struggled to find meaning in her much-publicised broken relationships, without falling into self-indulgence.

Third album, **Ladies Of The Canyon,** provided the breakthrough that Mitchell needed for continued success in the '70s. Sales were boosted by surprise hit single, **Big Yellow Taxi,** and cover versions of **Woodstock** by Crosby, Stills, Nash & Young(▶) and Matthew's Southern Comfort (who took song to No. 1 in UK). More importantly, **Ladies Of The Canyon** included piano accompaniment to match her acoustic guitar work.

Successive albums, **Blue, For The Roses** and **Court And Spark,** showed greater confidence in her own writing and a willingness to explore new musical ideas. Introduction of Tom Scott on wind instruments on **For The Roses** LP revealed first recorded signs of an interest in jazz as possible avenue for later work. Significantly, the only non-Mitchell song of the set was a re-make of Annie Ross' **Twisted.**

By 1975, Mitchell was moving too fast for many of her older fans. **The Hissing Of Summer Lawns,** in many respects her best work to date, featured an array of new musical effects, including synthesiser and the African drums of Burundi. The lyrics contained many of the old themes presented in different points of view. By this time, her songwriting talent was probably unmatched

Left: Joni Mitchell casting a spell with her guitar—her unique talent is too little heard in the '80s.

by any artist in rock, bar Dylan(▶). In spite of such achievements, her more myopic critics were crying for a return to the folky songs of the late '60s. Instead, Mitchell pushed forward; **Hejira** was another dense work, less tuneful than its predecessor, but still commercially successful.

Her attraction to jazz was fully expressed in late '70s LPs **Don Juan's Reckless Daughter** and, more noticeably, **Mingus.** Realising, perhaps, that her interests were becoming increasingly incompatible with the mainstream rock audience, Mitchell threatened to retire at the end of decade to devote more energy to her first love, painting. (Virtually all her albums feature her original paintings.)

Just as it seemed that her career was nearing a close, Mitchell returned in 1982 with **Wild Things Run Fast** on David Geffen's label. Surprisingly, it was a return to the more melodic work of the early '70s and fared well chart wise. Mitchell is reputed to be under five-year contract to Geffen, but the prospect of an increased recording output seems extremely unlikely.

Hit Singles:	US	UK
Big Yellow Taxi, 1970	—	11
Help Me, 1974	7	—

Albums:
Joni Mitchell, aka Songs To A Seagull, (Reprise), 1968
Clouds (Reprise), 1969
Ladies Of The Canyon (Reprise), 1970
Blue (Reprise), 1971
For The Roses (Asylum), 1972
Court And Spark (Electra/Asylum), 1974
Miles Of Aisles (Asylum), 1974
The Hissing Of Summer Lawns (Asylum), 1975
Hejira (Asylum), 1976
Don Juan's Reckless Daughter (Asylum), 1977
Mingus (Asylum), 1979
Shadows And Light (Asylum), 1980
Wild Things Run Fast (Geffen), 1982

Willie Mitchell

US trumpeter, keyboard player, composer, arranger, producer.
Born Ashland, Mississipi, 1928.

Career: A major cornerstone of the Memphis Sound in R&B/soul music for 30 years, Willie Mitchell has made his mark as record company boss, record producer, arranger and songwriter, as well as recording steady stream of own albums showcasing his trumpet playing (and, to a lesser extent, his keyboard work).

Though internationally best-known as the man behind black superstars Al Green(▶) and Ann Peebles, Mitchell has had considerable success in his own right, both through his own Willie Mitchell combo and, incognito, as the Bill Black Combo(▶); took group as alter ego following Black's death.

Mitchell played in bands of Tuff Green and Al Jackson (father of later Al Jackson Jr, drummer with Booker T and the MGs(▶)) before forming own outfit in 1954, which became resident backing band at House of the Blues Records. Invited to join Hi records by Joe Cuoghi in 1961.

Mitchell's driving R&B dance music style made him a regular feature in black music charts with originals like **20-45, Everything Is Gonna Be Alright** and **Soul Serenade**, and with cover versions of contemporary soul hits.

Al Jackson Jr was Mitchell's original drummer; role was later taken by Howard 'Tiny' Grimes who became fixture with outfit

along with the Hodges Brothers — Mabon 'Teenie' Hodges, guitar; Charles 'Dufunny' Hodges, organ; and Leroy 'Flick' Hodges, bass — and his own saxophonist brother James. This band played on virtually all Hi Records' output through label's most successful period from late '60s to mid-'70s.

On Cuoghi's death, Mitchell became president of Hi and in recent years his own recording has become rather sporadic. However, his reputation as a creative force remains untarnished.

Album:
Best Of . . . (Hi/—), 1980

Moby Grape

US group formed 1966.

Original line-up: Alexander 'Skip' Spence, guitar, vocals; Peter Lewis, guitar, vocals; Jerry Miller, guitar, vocals; Bob Mosely, bass, vocals; Don Stevenson, drums.

Career: Group formed by Peter Lewis (ex-Peter and the Wolves) and Bob Mosely (ex-Frantics) in conjunction with Jefferson Airplane(▶) manager Matthew Katz. Miller and Stevenson also former Frantics were brought in and quintet was completed with induction of Spence, who had recently quit Airplane. Debut at the Ark, Marin County, in 1966, led to prestigious and well-received gigs at San Francisco's Fillmore West and Winterland, during city's commercial heyday.

Moby Grape immediately gained small cult following, and won reputation for their vocal dexterity (particularly Moby's R&B styling) and imaginative guitar work. Attracted interest from Elektra, Kama Sutra and Columbia Records, who were all invited by Katz to see group play at the Fillmore, Columbia finally secured Grape, mainly through enthusiasm of producer David Rubinson.

Unfortunately, Rubinson was also responsible for masterminding mind-boggling publicity campaign to coincide with release of their debut, **Moby Grape**. A purple elephants, paraded Sunset Strip, helium balloons bearing group's logo were hoisted in Golden Gate Park; a horse and cart delivered bunches of grapes to prominent Hollywood journalists. Most bizarre of all was the simultaneous release of five singles (none of them hits), consisting of every track from the album. Press were unimpressed and excellent debut was buried amid cries of record company hype. Grape never truly recovered from this bitter blow.

Grape played extensively for next 12 months, determined to bury memory of promotional overkill. In 1968 released **Wow** which included a free album, **Grape Jam**, and featured services of supersessioneers Al Kooper(▶) and Mike Bloomfield(▶). It was inventive work, highlighting the distinctive guitar sound that had made debut a classic. Poor sales blighted group's chances and Skip Spence left shortly afterwards to record solo album **Oar**, a cult classic and collectors' item. Now in artistic decline, group recorded **Moby Grape '69**, a distinctly lacklustre effort, and after a series of erratic gigs Mosely quit and joined the Marines, re-emerging later with an eponymous solo album. Remaining trio moved to Nashville to cut uninspired **Truly Fine Citizen** with Bob Moore on bass. Reputation had not been helped by appearance at Altamont of a bogus Moby Grape, apparently engineered by former manager Katz who still owned name.

After dissolution in spring 1969, group re-formed in 1971 to complete disappointing **20 Granite Creek**. Miller, Mosely and Lewis re-formed Grape again in 1974, but that and

Above: Heads down Southern boogie as Molly Hatchet purvey it.

subsequent attempts to relive halcyon '60s days were confined to local bar gigs around Santa Cruz, California. One late version of band, calling itself the Grape, released LP **Live Grape** on own label in 1978.

For all their early promise, Moby Grape failed to achieve the mass popularity for which they once seemed destined. Their rapid decline following brilliant start remains one of the saddest tales in the history of '60s American rock.

Final line-up: Mosely; Miller; Lewis; Stevenson; Spence; Gordon Stevens, viola, dobro, mandolin.

Albums:
Worth Searching Out:
Moby Grape (Columbia/CBS), 1967
Wow (Columbia/CBS), 1968
Wow/Grape Jam (Columbia/—), 1968

Molly Hatchet

US group formed 1971.

Original line-up: Dave Hlubek, lead guitar; Steve Holland, lead guitar; Banner Thomas, bass.

Career: Hlubek, from Jacksonville, Florida, met Holland (at that time rhythm guitarist of Ice), from Virginia. By 1973, bass Banner Thomas, also from Jacksonville, had joined. Third lead guitarist Duane Roland guested with band for one early '70s gig, but group had constant changes of personnel and name through early years. By end of 1975, Hlubek and Thomas had introduced drummer Bruce Crump and contacted Holland, who had earlier left band. Up to this point, band had been one of many using huge Jacksonville talent pool along with Lynyrd Skynyrd(▶) and .38 Special(▶).

In 1976, four piece group played first gig of second phase of band's career — name Molly Hatchet taken from 17th century resident of Salem, Missouri, with penchant for chopping off lovers' heads. In late 1975, recruited singer

Danny Joe Brown (ex-Rum Creek), and in 1976, Duane Roland formally completed line-up at end of year. In 1977, signed with Epic Records, and in early 1978 recorded debut LP produced by Tom Werman, producer of Cheap Trick(▶) and Ted Nugent(▶). Album released with eye-catching sleeve painting by Frank Frazetta; later sleeves equally lurid. First LP minor chart item in US, but second album, also produced by Werman, reached US Top 20. For 1980 LP, **Beatin' The Odds**, Brown replaced by Jimmy Farrar, but both his and 1981 album, **Take No Prisoners**, were still major US hits. Latest LP, **No Guts . . .**

Take No Prisoners, Molly Hatchet. Courtesy Epic Records.

No Glory, featured more personnel changes, with return of Danny Joe Brown as singer, plus new rhythm section of Riff West, bass, and B. B. Bordan, drums.

While Molly Hatchet are major heavy metal/hard rock stars in the US, they have made minimal impact in Europe, and probably have only minor interest in altering that situation.

Current line-up: Danny Joe Brown, vocals; Dave Hlubek, lead guitar; Steve Holland, lead guitar; Duane Roland, lead guitar; Riff West, bass; B. B. Bordan, drums.

Albums:
Molly Hatchet (Epic/—), 1978
Flirtin' With Disaster (Epic/—), 1979
Beatin' The Odds (Epic), 1980
Take No Prisoners (Epic/—), 1981
No Guts . . . No Glory (Epic), 1983

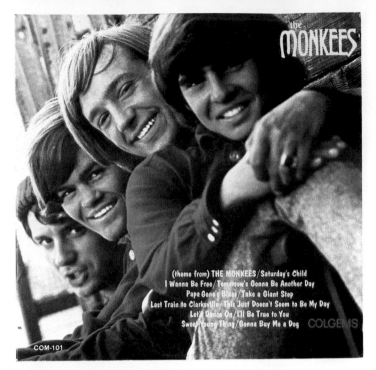

The Monkees (debut album). Courtesy Colgems/RCA Records.

The Monkees

US group formed 1966.
Original/final line-up: Davy Jones, vocals; Mike Nesmith, guitar, vocals; Peter Tork, bass, vocals; Mickey Dolenz, drums, vocals.

Career: Following its conquest by the Beatles, Stones, Kinks and slew of lesser British talents like Herman's Hermits, by 1966 America was ready for home-grown pop phenomenon. What was needed was group along lines of the Limey invaders — mop-topped, cute and lovable — but *American*. British invasion had spawned imitators like Beau Brummells, but there was still a yawning gap. With typical transatlantic ingenuity, Americans decided to create their own Beatles from scratch—and the Monkees were born.

The Monkees phenomenon, although lasting a scant two years, was a brilliant exercise in marketing. The giant NBC-TV network was prime mover — what it wanted was a TV series that would tap same youth market as the Beatles' phenomenally successful 'A Hard Day's Night' and 'Help' featuring zany, vaguely anti-establishment 'beat group'. Music featured in the show could be marketed in its own right — the show could promote the records, and vice-versa. It was decided that existing groups could cause too many problems, so after auditioning hundreds of hopeful unknowns, NBC picked Dolenz and English-born Jones, former child actors, and small-time musicians Tork and Nesmith.

Considering how dire it could have been, the TV series was surprisingly entertaining as well as extremely successful. Music from the show was translated into a series of singles that were worldwide hits.

In fact, the Monkees' music, particularly the singles, stands up as an excellent example of superbly crafted mid-'60s pop — not so surprising perhaps considering that writing duties were in hands of people like Neil Diamond(▶), Tommy Boyce and Bobby Hart, and back-up production was taken care of by top talents of the day. (Needless to say, band resented not being allowed to play on their first few singles.) Nesmith penned several songs on their later LPs.

Ultimately, it was over as quickly as it had begun. Tork left after badly received movie

'Head', and the others split after hits dried up in 1969. Mike Nesmith went on to forge successful career with own brand of country rock and is now a video/film producer. Dolenz eventually moved to England to become an in-demand commercials TV director. Attempt by Jones and Dolenz to re-create band with Tommy Boyce and Bobby Hart in 1975 was needless to say a failure.

The Monkees may not have been important, but they were fun. They left behind body of music which may well continue to be played when more pretentious outpourings of the '60s are long forgotten. The original TV series has been rerun on US and UK television several times in the past 15 years, and the group continues to have a small cult following.

Hit Singles:

	US	UK
I'm A Believer (I'm Not Your) Steppin' Stone, 1967	1	1
(I'm Not Your) Steppin' Stone/I'm A Believer, 1967	20	—
Last Train To Clarksville, 1967	1	23
A Little Bit Me, A Little Bit You, 1967	2	3
Alternate Title, 1967	—	2
Pleasant Valley Sunday/Words, 1967	3	11
Words/Pleasant Valley Sunday, 1967	11	—
Daydream Believer, 1967	1	5
Valleri, 1968	3	12
D. W. Washburn, 1968	19	17

Albums:
Monkees (—/Sounds Superb), 1974
The Best Of The Monkees (—/MFP), 1981
The Monkees (Arista), 1981
20 Golden Greats (—/Ronco), 1982

Bill Monroe

US mandolinist, vocalist, composer.
Born William Smith Monroe, Rosine, Kentucky, September 13, 1911.

Career: Generally regarded as the father of bluegrass, Monroe started Monroe Brothers (with brother Charlie on guitar) in 1934, working on local radio stations in Chicago and Carolina. Brothers split in 1938, Bill forming the Kentuckians, and then first of the legend-

ary Blue Grass Boys, which later included Flatt & Scruggs(▶).

As a writer, Monroe's best-known work is **Blue Moon Of Kentucky**, made popular by Elvis Presley(▶). His bluegrass standards include **Kentucky Waltz, Will You Be Loving Another Man, Uncle Pen, Gotta Travel On** and **Cheyenne.**

A member of the Country Music Hall Of Fame, and 'Grand Ole Opry' regular (since 1939), Monroe's high tenor vocal delivery and dazzling mandolin technique are still much in demand at country festivals and on record.
Mandolin: Gibson 'Lloyd Loar' F5.

Albums (selected):
Bean Blossom (MCA/—), 1950s
Mr Bluegrass (MCA), 1961
Greatest Hits (MCA/—), 1968
Sings Country Songs (MCA), 1973

Montrose

US group formed 1974.
Original line-up: Ronnie Montrose, guitar; Sam Hagar, vocals; Denny Carmassi, drums; Bill Church, bass.

Career: Brainchild of Ronnie Montrose, a session musician from Bay Area of San Francisco. Having played on Beaver and Krause's **Gandharva**, Montrose joined Van Morrison's(▶) backing group, playing on both **Tupelo Honey** and **St Dominic's Preview**. Stints with Boz Scaggs(▶) and Edgar Winter(▶) culminated in offer to join Mott the Hoople(▶); but Montrose preferred to form heavier group.

Debut LP **Montrose** revealed that unit could hold their own on US hard-rock circuit. Basically a derivative boogie band, impetus was lost following departure of Hagar(▶) (replaced by Bob James) after 1974's **Paper Money**. Group made celebrated appearance in England as part of Warner Bros' Music Show with labelmates Doobie Brothers(▶), Little Feat(▶) and Graham Central Station. Jim Alcivar (keyboards) was recruited in 1975 to add musical depth, and following Church's departure, both Alan Fitzgerald and Randy Jo Hobbs did spells on bass. However, by this point, Montrose had already outlived their usefulness.

Montrose. Courtesy Warner Bros Records.

In 1976, they split, allowing Montrose to ruminate before forming Gamma in 1979. A hard rock/blues outfit tempered with synthesiser and intricate vocal arrangements, it has so far failed to break through, despite three interesting albums released on the Elektra label.

Final line-up (Montrose): Montrose; Carmassi; Bob James, vocals; Jim Alcivar, keyboards; Randy Jo Hobbs, bass.
Gamma line-up: Montrose; Alcivar; Alan Fitzgerald, bass; Davey Pattison, vocals; Skip Gillette, drums.

Albums:
Montrose (Warner Bros), 1974
Paper Money (Warner Bros), 1974
Warner Bros Presents Montrose (Warner Bros), 1975
Jump On It (Warner Bros), 1976

Gamma:
Gamma I (Elektra), 1980
Gamma II (Elektra), 1980
Gamma III (Elektra), 1982

Moody Blues

UK group formed 1964.
Original line-up: Mike Pinder, vocals, keyboards; Denny Laine, vocals, guitar; Ray Thomas, flute, vocals; Clint Warwick, bass, vocals; Graeme Edge, drums.

Career: Line-up above formed R&B group in Birmingham; second single release, cover of classic Bessie Banks song **Go Now**, leapt to No. 1 in British charts, No. 10 in US.

Although band scored couple more minor hits, after two albums Laine and Warwick both quite (Laine later becoming mainstay of Paul McCartney's Wings(▶)). They were replaced by Justin Hayward and John Lodge. Following period of reappraisal, band came up with **Days Of Future Passed**, album which united group with London Symphony Orchestra. Total departure from pattern of previous work, album was heavy on portentous philosophising, light on rock 'n' roll. However, it caught mood of time (1967) and proved to be total success, re-establishing group in big way and spawning classic single in **Nights In White Satin** (a hit several times over, and since covered by many artists).

From that time on Moodies cornered market in pomp-rock; albums generally repeated formula of pop philosophy dressed up in high-flown, often orchestral, arrangements. Occasional hit singles boosted sales, whch ran into multi-millions all over world. From 1969 Moodies' product was released on own Threshold lable, which didn't alter winning formula.

After 1972 album **Seventh Sojourn**, group did not record any fresh material for six years, spending intervening period on various solo projects. Most viable of these was Lodge/Hayward album, **Blue Jays**, which spawned major hit single **Blue Guitar** in 1975.

Compilation album **This Is The Moody Blues** and collection of bits and pieces called **Caught Live And Five** kept Moodies' public simmering until their return in force in 1978 with **Octave**. Predictably successful album heralded further live work, with ex-Yes(▶) keyboard man Patrick Moraz taking place of Mike Pinder. **Long Distance Voyager** LP, featuring Moraz, took Moodies into '80s. It made No. 1 in US, No. 7 in UK, showing that market for group's particular brand of music was far from moribund.

Not always most critically praised band, Moody Blues nevertheless consistently give public what it wants. Skill and craft have never been in question, although it does seem that band could occasionally afford to introduce new ideas.

Current line-up: Thomas; Edge; Justin Hayward, vocals, guitar; John Lodge, bass, vocals; Patrick Moraz, keyboards.

Hit Singles:

	US	UK
Go Now, 1964	10	1
Nights In White Satin, 1967	—	19
Question, 1970	21	2
Isn't Life Strange, 1972	29	13
Nights In White Satin, 1972	2	9

I'm Just A Singer (In A Rock And Roll Band), 1973	12	36
Nights In White Satin, 1979	—	14
Gemini Dream, 1981	14	—
The Voice, 1981	16	—

Albums:
The Magnificent Moodies (London/Decca), 1966
Days Of Future Passed (Deram), 1967
In Search Of The Lost Chord (Deram), 1968
On The Threshold Of A Dream (Decca), 1969
To Our Children's Children (Threshold), 1969
A Question Of Balance (Threshold), 1970
Seventh Sojourn (Threshold), 1972
This Is The Moody Blues (Threshold), 1974
Caught Live & Five (London/Decca), 1977
Octave (London/Threshold), 1978
Out Of This World (K-Tel), 1979
Long Distance Voyager (Threshold), 1981

Worth Searching Out:
Moody Blues:
Go Now (London/—), 1965

Justin Hayward & John Lodge:
Blue Jays (Threshold), 1975

Graeme Edge Band with Adrian Gurvits:
Kick Off Your Muddy Boots (Threshold), 1975

Ray Thomas Solo:
Hopes, Wishes And Dreams (Threshold), 1976

Michael Pinder Solo:
The Promise (Threshold), 1976

Keith Moon

UK drummer, actor.
Born London, August 23, 1946; died London, September 7, 1978.

Career: Moon began musical career in Harrow, playing with local friends in band not serious enough to merit name. Recorded obscure 1963 single, **Mad Goose/ You Can't Sit Down**, with the Beachcombers. Later joined Roger Daltrey(▶), John Entwistle(▶) and Pete Townshend(▶) in the Who(▶).

Two Sides Of The Moon, Keith Moon. Courtesy Polydor Records.

Moon quickly earned well-deserved reputation for being one of rock's most exciting, innovative drummers. Entirely self-taught, he had natural gift for using each arm and leg independently. Consequently, he was one of rock's first drummers to employ double bass drums and a myriad of cymbals. Unlike many later imitators with big flashy kits, Moon used all his equipment.

Equally deserved was Moon's growing reputation for crazy, over-the-top antics. His practical jokes, real-life adventures and deathy-defying feats are legendary .This aspect of Moon's life is detailed in personal manager/minder Peter 'Dougal' Butler's book (co-authored by Chris Trengove), 'Moon the

Loon' ('Full Moon' in US). However, the larger-than-life image surrounding Moon not only covered up some insecurity and personal unhappiness but also downplayed wide variety of unfortunate incidents which affected those who had to live or work with him. In 1967, the Who had to cancel studio sessions because of injuries suffered by Moon. He was directly involved in the death of his driver during a pub brawl. Such incidents were not nearly so isolated as suggested by the nothing-can-hurt me facade Moon was so found of projecting.

Moon's growing party reputation soon jeopardised his private life. He had married in 1966, but kept the marriage secret for two years. By early '70s, he had moved his wife and daughter into country estate where they too were caught up with never-ending party atmosphere. Keith's mother, however, recalls his visits home to Harrow when he would arrive alone, and ask only for tea and biscuits. After a few hours of quiet chatter Keith would leave and resume behaviour pattern expected by public.

By mid-1974, Moon's wife Kim could handle no more and left. In many ways, Moon never recovered from the loss. At this particular time, Who reached a two-year hiatus. While Townshend, Daltrey and Entwistle got involved in film or solo LPs, Moon, apart for brief role in 'Tommy' film, had nothing to do. In September 1974, Moon moved to Los Angeles to be near drinking partners Ringo Starr(▶) and Harry Nilsson(▶).

Moon convinced MCA he could be solo star, and managed to collect sizeable advance. Using money to party in studio, he began collecting every available LA musician he could and proceeded to record superstar session that defies description. MCA became concerned when single released in October 1974 proved a disaster. **Don't Worry Baby** was a cover of Moon's heroes the Beach Boys (▶) even expected hard core Who/Beach Boys fans weren't buying. Producer and former Beatles associate Mal Evans was replaced by Skip Taylor and John Stronack, who re-mixed entire album. Released in April 1975, LP's rapid appearance in cut-out bins announced end of Moon's party.

Moon returned to UK in 1978. His pudgy face and generally sloppy appearance were price of his relentless lifestyle. The death of possibly the greatest drummer in rock came as a kind of anticipated shock, but no surprise to those who knew him well. The Who con-

tinued with ex-Face(▶) Kenney Jones, but magic was lost.

Notable 'session' work includes: **Truth** (Jeff Beck(▶)), **Flash Fearless, Pussy Cats** (Nilsson(▶)), **All This & World War Two** soundtrack, **Sometime In New York** (John Lennon(▶)) and **The 20th Anniversary of Rock and Roll** (Bo Diddley(▶)).
Drums: Premier.

Albums:
Worth Searching Out:
Two Sides Of The Moon (MCA/Polydor), 1975

Van Morrison

UK vocalist, composer, guitarist.
Born George Ivan, Belfast, N. Ireland, August 31, 1945.

Career: Irish music played little part in Morrison's upbringing. Raised to the sounds of America's Deep South (his mother a blues

Them Featuring Van Morrison. Courtesy Decca Records.

and jazz singer, his father a fanatical record collector with love for rural blues), Morrison mastered guitar, saxophone and harmonica while at school, playing in skiffle bands from age 11 at local dance halls.

Leaving school in 1960 for career as professional musician, he joined Monarchs for tour of US air bases in Germany and in 1963 returned to Belfast to form Them with two Monarchs members and two other friends. Installed as house band at R&B club in Belfast's Maritime Hotel, Billy Harrison (guitar), Ronnie Millings (drums), and Eric Wisksen (piano), fronted by Morrison's vocals, built cult following for frenetic brand of blues-flavoured beat music.

Astral Weeks, Van Morrison. Courtesy Warner Bros Records.

A version of Slim Harpo's **Don't Start Crying Now** was Irish hit and, signed to Decca, band moved base to London and followed through with up-beat version of Big Joe Williams' classic **Baby Please Don't Go** which climbed high into UK national charts.

Ace American producer Bert Berns (co-writer of **Twist And Shout, Tell Him, Cry Baby** and other '60s soul classics) was brought in for Morrison's own composition **Here Comes The Night**, group's first transatlantic hit. Though never a UK hit, Them's **Gloria**, another Morrison original, helped establish band's reputation and is regarded as true classic. On debut album, session men, including guitarist Jimmy Page (later of Led Zeppelin(▶)), were brought in while Jackie McAuley replaced Wicksen.

Below: Keith Moon, rock's 'premier' drummer, and madman of the Who.

By second album, band was on verge of collapsing and session men laid down most of tracks behind Morrison's vocals. Following unsatisfactory US tour Morrison disbanded Them and returned to Ulster.

Having formed own Bang label, Berns sent Morrison air ticket and took him into New York studios to cut solo sides from which sessions **Brown-Eyed Girl** was US hit in mid-'67. Them later re-formed for short period, but without Morrison, whose solo career took full flight.

Berns died of heart attack on December 1, 1967, and Morrison signed to Warner Bros, who gave him complete creative control. Resulting **Astral Weeks** album, cut in New York in just 48 hours, is one of all-time great rock albums, though with no obvious hit singles, it only sold modestly.

Moondance (containing hit single **Into The Mystic**) and **Van Morrison — His Band And Street Choir** (producing **Domino** hit) forged solid reputation and built Morrison into major US concert attraction, touring with large 11-piece band including strings. Close to the mike, eyes half-closed, lips barely parted, chubby face crowned by mass of rust-red hair, his vocals have always oozed soulfulness and personal conviction.

Veedon Fleece, Van Morrison. Courtesy Warner Bros Records.

Tupelo Honey (1971), which included suite of love songs to wife Janet Planet, and further albums — especially the exceptionally strong **It's Too Late To Stop Now** live double LP (following hugely successful 1974 US and European tour) which was truly live with no over-dubs — brought Morrison to his zenith.

Personal and professional hassles continued, however. He divorced in 1973 and in 1974 suddenly broke up applauded Caledonia Soul Orchestra, carrying out next European tour with five-piece band, playing sax and harmonica himself.

Morrison had returned to Ireland in 1973 for first time in seven years and songs written there emerged as 1974 album **Veedon Fleece**, arguably his best work since **Astral Weeks**. Followed by several aborted album ventures (including one featuring the Crusaders(▶)), it was not till spring 1977 that **A Period Of Transition** surfaced (with Dr John(▶) guesting).

Since then, Morrison has continued to release artistically creative albums and carry out widely acclaimed live gigs.

Hit Singles:	US	UK
With Them:		
Baby Please Don't Go, 1965	—	10
Here Comes The Night, 1965	24	2
Solo:		
Brown-Eyed Girl, 1967	10	—
Domino, 1970	9	—

Albums:
Astral Weeks (Warner Bros), 1968
Best Of (Bang/President), 1970
Moondance (Warner Bros), 1970
His Band And Street Choir (Warner Bros), 1970
Tupelo Honey (Warner Bros), 1971
St Dominic's Preview (Warner Bros), 1972
Hard Nose The Highway (Warner Bros), 1973
It's Too Late To Stop Now (Warner Bros), 1974
Veedon Fleece (Warner Bros), 1974
Period Of Transition (Warner Bros), 1977
Wavelength (Warner Bros), 1978
Into The Music (Warner Bros), 1978
Common One (Warner Bros/Mercury), 1980
Beautiful Vision (Warner Bros/Mercury), 1982
Inarticulate Speech Of The Heart (Mercury), 1983

The Motels
US group formed 1977.

Original line-up: Martha Davis, vocals; Marty Jourard, sax, keyboards; Tim ,McGovern, guitar; Brian Glascock, drums; Michael Goodroe, bass; Jeff Jourard, guitar.

Career: Power-pop quintet who project essentially smooth, 'dark side of LA' atmosphere. Motels' sound is based on deep voice of singer/songwriter Davis. A native of Berkeley, Davis moved to LA and joined band called Warfield Foxes, who changed name to Motels and promptly broke up (none are in present group).

In 1977, Davis teamed up with guitarist Jeff Jourard; they co-wrote most of material on first Motels album and assembled band consisting of Jourard's brother Marty on sax, drummer Glascock, and bassist Goodroe. Signed with Capitol Records; LP **The Motels** was produced by staff producer John Carter.

Davis and Jeff Jourard soon ran into serious creative arguments, resulting in the guitarist leaving group. He was replaced by Tim McGovern who produced next album **Careful**, which, like their first, was an interesting failure. Capitol was interested in a third album, but suggested bringing in different producer. This turned out to be Val Garay, still unknown at the time, who had just recorded **Bette Davis Eyes** for Kim Carnes(▶). The result was **All Four One**, from which came smash hit single, **Only The Lonely**.

Embarking on successful tour, the Motels added guitarist Guy Perry to line-up. The Motels' showmanship is fairly well demonstrated by their fine video of **Only The Lonely**, popular on America's MTV. Overall sound is cool, passionate and serious. Perhaps a hopeful sign for the future is Martha Davis' independent collaboration with the Tubes(▶), a hilarious single re-make of **Monkey Time**, revealing Davis' sense of humour as well as her talent as singer.

Current line-up: Davis; Marty Jourard; Jeff Jourard; Glascock; Goodroe; Guy Perry, guitar.

Hit Singles:	US	UK
Only The Lonely, 1982	9	—

Albums:
The Motels (Capitol), 1979
Careful (Capitol), 1980
All Four One (Capitol), 1982

Motorhead
UK group formed 1975.

Original line-up: Ian 'Lemmy' Kilmister; Larry Wallis, guitar; Lucas Fox, drums.

Career: Lemmy worked as roadie for Hawkwind(▶) and without prior experience took over group's bass spot. In 1974 he involved band with drug bust at US/Canadian border and got fired. Upon returning to UK, he formed Bastard. Journalist Mick Farren introduced him to ex-Pink Fairies Wallis, and then Fox.

Manager Doug Smith convinced trio to pick more viable name. Lemmy came up with Americanism for speed freak, Motorhead. Band debuted at Camden Town's Roundhouse on July 20, 1975 and promptly went on tour. Opening for Blue Oyster Cult's(▶) London October 1975 show they earned critical assessment as 'worst band in the world'. Motorhead never looked back.

Overkill, Motorhead. Courtesy Bronze Records.

Trio began recording LP for United Artists in December '75. Lemmy asked friend Phil Taylor for ride to Rockfield Studios and explained his dissatisfaction with Fox. Taylor volunteered to sit in and found himself re-recording entire album (except for one track). United Artists accepted tapes but refused to release LP. Phil introduced 'Fast' Eddie Clarke to band as second guitarist. Wallis left shortly afterwards and band was back to trio.

Giving up on United Artists, band recorded **White Line Fever/Leavin' Here** for Stiff Records in mid-1976. United Artists, although still refusing to support band, raised contractual objections and killed release. (Both cuts were eventually issued in 1977 on compilation LPs, **Bunch Of Stiffs** and **Hits Greatest Stiffs**.)

Band almost broke up but Ted Carroll of Chiswick Records asked them to record single and provided two days' studio time. Band worked around clock and presented Carroll with 13 backing tracks. He liked them and agreed for band to finish them off.

Single **Motorhead/City Kids** appeared in June 1977, and album **Motorhead** in August.

Instead of finding success, Lemmy became involved in management problems with inter-loper Tony Secunda (ex-Move(▶)) and band found itself without label in spring 1978. Doug Smith stepped back in and arranged recording contract with Bronze Records. Single **Louie, Louie** was released and paved way for sonic assault of **Overkill** LP.

By now band was developing fanatical following whose loyalty rivals that of any group. Continuing tours opened up new audiences and **Bomber** album made No. 12 in UK charts. Tour supporting this release featured bomber lighting rig with replica of German airplane acrobats, which became exciting part of band's performance.

Not too surprisingly, United Artists noted Motorhead's growing stature and released band's first recordings as **On Parole**. Although hardly representative of band's current abilities, it provided insight into early days of Motorhead's history.

April 1980 saw release of live material on EP **The Golden Years**. Motorhead's live shows have always been strong point and EP became band's first Top 10 hit. **Ace of Spades** set became band's biggest seller so far and Motorhead was hot property. Chiswick released **Beer Drinkers** EP with four tracks recorded at time of **Motorhead** album.

Injury to Taylor caused cancellation of late 1980 tour, while Lemmy and Clarke joined Girlschool(▶) to record **Valentines Day Massacre** EP. Year ended with band being voted No. 1 (as were **Ace of Spaces** LP and single) in Sounds Readers Poll.

Band returned to touring in March 1981, and while at Leeds Queen Hall/Newcastle City Hall recorded material for live LP, **No Sleep 'Till Hammersmith**. Described as guaranteed to melt speakers, fuse amps and short circuit turntables, album can claim to be best example of recorded high energy since Who's(▶) **Live at Leeds**. Hammersmith went to UK No. 1 within one week of issue. Just prior to its release, Motorhead opened Ozzie Osbourne's(▶) US Blizzard of Oz tour. Band returned again in 1982 and seemed poised to crack US market. Instead, late May 1982 brought announcement that Clarke was leaving group in middle of tour (because of disagreement with Lemmy's ongoing plans for Motorhead's involvement in outside activities).

Lemmy's 'try anything once' attitude produced successful **Valentines Day Massacre** release as well as more bizarre single **Don't Do That** featuring himself, Nolan Sisters, Cozy Powell and others. But his disregard of doing the expected reached new height. He joined Wendy O. Williams of the Plasmatics to do send-up version of several-times-divorced

Below: The very lovely Motorhead—(left to right) Phil Taylor, Lemmy, Brian Robertson.

Tammy Wynette's **Stand By Your Man.** This was too much for Clarke and he left (later to form Fastway). This crisis disrupted band's progression, although Brian Robertson (ex-Thin Lizzy(▶)) filled in so band could complete US tour.

Motorhead disappeared for last part of 1982 to work Robertson in as permanent replacement. New LP is due at press time and Motorhead will continue to build on past success. This band is one of the most exciting current rock acts.

Current line-up: Lemmy; Phil Taylor, drums; Brian Robertson, guitar, vocals.

Hit Singles:

	US	UK
The Golden Years (EP), 1980	—	8
Ace Of Spaces, 1980	—	15
Motorhead (Live), 1981	—	6

Albums (selected):
Motorhead (—/Chiswick), 1977
Overkill (—/Bronze), 1979
On Parole (—/United Artists), 1979
Bomber (—/Bronze), 1979
Ace Of Spades (Mercury/Bronze), 1980
No Sleep 'Til Hammersmith (Mercury/Bronze), 1981
Iron Fist (Mercury/Bronze), 1982
What's Words Worth (—/Big Beat), 1983*
Another Perfect Day (—/Bronze), 1983
*Live At The Roundhouse, 1973

Mott the Hoople

UK group formed 1969.

Original line-up: Mick Ralphs, guitar; Dale 'Buffin' Griffin, drums; Pete 'Overend' Watts, bass; Verden 'Phally' Allen, organ; Ian Hunter, vocals, guitar, keyboards.

Career: Evolved from Herefordshire group Silence, featuring Ralphs, Griffin, Watts, Allen and vocalist Stan Tippens. Signed to Island by A&R head Guy Stevens, who changed name to Mott the Hoople (from novel by Willard Manus). Following Stevens' suggestion, Tippens reverted to road manager, replaced by Ian Hunter(▶) (recruited from auditions).

Mott, Mott The Hoople. Courtesy Columbia Records.

Debut **Mott The Hoople** relied heavily on Hunter's rasping Dylanesque vocals, recalling sound of **Blonde On Blonde.** Next two albums, **Mad Shadows** (1970) and **Wildlife** (1971), revealed contrasting hard/soft rock styles of Hunter and Ralphs respectively. In spite of loyal following on London club circuit, album sales remained poor. **Brain Capers** (1971) was followed by barren period; group finally split in March 1972. Later that year, recent Hoople fan, David Bowie(▶), encouraged and nurtured re-formation. Following an introduction to Bowie's manager Tony De Fries, a new contract was signed with CBS. Bowie wrote/produced hit single **All The Young Dudes,** which climbed to No. 3.

Success of fifth album gave group new lease of life and following Bowie's retreat as svengali, they continued to chart until 1974. During interim, charismatic Hunter took over as leader, resulting in departure of Allen. Original leader Mick Ralphs left shortly afterwards to form Bad Company(▶).

New members were recruited: guitarist Ariel Bender (actually Luther Grosvenor of Spooky Tooth) and keyboards player Morgan Fisher, formerly of Love Affair. 1973 US summer tour proved particularly memorable with an array of costumes and theatrical effects; group subsequently played a week in a Broadway theatre. New line-up cut one studio album, **The Hoople,** and a Top 50 single, **Saturday Gig,** before Grosvenor left, to be replaced by Bowie sideman Mick Ronson. Shortly afterwards, Hunter was hospitalised in New York suffering from exhaustion, and important British tour was cancelled. Amid rumour and confusion, Hunter and Ronson left to form new group just as **Live** LP was released and became band's biggest seller.

Six months later, renamed Mott regrouped with singer Nigel Benjamin and guitarist Ray Major. Two patchy albums appeared before Benjamin quit; CBS then dropped Mott from roster. Remaining members, minus Nigel Benjamin, teamed up with John Fiddler (ex-Medicine Head) for brief career as British Lions.

Final line-up: Watts; Griffin; Morgan Fisher, keyboards; Ray Major, vocals, guitar; Nigel Benjamin, vocals.

Hit Singles:

	US	UK
All The Young Dudes, 1972	—	3
Honaloochie Boogie, 1973	—	12
All The Way From Memphis, 1973	—	10
Roll Away The Stone, 1973	—	8
Golden Age Of Rock And Roll, 1974	—	16

Albums:
Mott The Hoople (Atlantic Island), 1969
Mad Shadows (Island), 1970
Wild Life (Island), 1971
Brain Capers (Island), 1971
All The Young Dudes (Columbia/CBS), 1972
Rock 'n' Roll Queen (Columbia/CBS), 1972
Mott (Columbia/CBS), 1973
Live (Columbia/CBS), 1974
Greatest Hits (Columbia/CBS), 1976

As Mott:
Worth Searching Out:
Drive On (CBS), 1975
Shouting And Pointing (CBS), 1976

Above: Head Hoopler Ian Hunter—after he left Mott The Hoople, group's commercial success soon departed.

Mountain

US group formed 1969.

Original line-up: Leslie Wright, Gibson Les Paul guitar; Felix Pappalardi, bass; Steve Knight, keyboards; Norman Smart, drums.

Career: One of the more respected American heavy-metal groups, Mountain had short but auspicious career between 1969 and 1974. Pappalardi had established a reputation as producer and bass guitarist with such acts as Joan Baez(▶), Tim Hardin(▶), the Lovin' Spoonful(▶) and the Youngbloods, but it was production work with Cream(▶) that brought him to international attention.

In early 1967, Atlantic had enlisted Pappalardi to produce single by newly signed New York group, the Vagrants, featuring distinctive guitarist Leslie West. Two years later, West went solo and Pappalardi returned to produce first LP **Leslie West—Mountain.** Pappalardi then left for England to produce Jack Bruce's(▶) **Songs For A Tailor** but returned to States with idea of forming own group. West was recruited, along with keyboards player Steve Knight (from '60s unit Devil's Anvil) and Boston drummer Norman Smart.

Nantucket Sleighride, Mountain. Courtesy Windfall Records.

Taking their name from West's solo, Mountain quickly rehearsed set of hard-rock guitar pieces which impressed several critics attending their Fillmore West debut in July 1969. A prestigious appearance at Woodstock Festival in August thrust Mountain into limelight, and further tours increased following. First album, **Mountain Climbing,** went

gold; shortly after its release drummer Norman Smart was replaced by Canadian Corky Laing.

Building on reputation as heavy but talented unit, Mountain achieved considerable commercial success in US and had several minor hit singles, including **Mississippi Queen** and **The Animal Trainer And The Toad. Nantucket Sleighride,** the band's best work, also went gold. In 1972 after two impressive albums, the group split. Pappalardi, now suffering from partial deafness, returned to studio work while West and Laing joined forces with Cream bassist Jack Bruce.

The short-lived West, Bruce and Laing trio released three LPs before break-up in summer of '73. West and Laing worked briefly as Leslie West's Wild West Show before evolving into re-formed Mountain with the return of Pappalardi, aided by rhythm guitarist David Perry. **Avalanche** failed to prevent second dissolution. West returned to solo work, but his subsequent albums were disappointing compared to Mountain. Pappalardi was shot dead in New York in April 1983.

Final line-up: West; Pappalardi; Corky Laing, drums; David Perry, rhythm guitar.

Albums:
Best Of (Windfall/Island), 1973
Avalanche (Columbia/Epic), 1974
Twin Peaks (Columbia/CBS), 1977

Worth Searching Out:
Nantucket Sleighride (Windfall/Island), 1971

The Move

UK group formed 1965.

Original line-up: Carl Wayne, vocals; Roy Wood, guitar, vocals; Trevor Burton, guitar, vocals; Ace Kefford, bass; Bev Bevan, drums.

Career: Formed in Birmingham out of some of city's top musicians, the Move nevertheless first made their mark at London's Marquee Club in 1966. Their exciting stage show/ pop-art image created much interest, and band was quickly signed to Deram Records.

Something Else From The Move. Courtesy Harvest Records.

First single, Roy Wood's **Night Of Fear,** reached No. 2 in UK charts in January 1967.

A troupe of seasoned gigsters, the somewhat fey mantle of psychedelia sat uneasily upon them. However, helped by remarkable song-writing facility of Roy Wood, the Move took up flower-power banner and produced series of hits which to many sum up spirit of '60s.

From **Fire Brigade** onwards, Wood began handling lead vocals and it became obvious that band was coming more and more under his influence. 1968 saw first of series of personnel changes — Ace Kefford left, followed in early 1969 by Trevor Burton (who later went on to Steve Gibbons Band). Rick

Price, another Birmingham musician, joined on bass.

Hits continued through the late '60s and early '70s with **Curly, Brontosaurus, Tonight, Chinatown** and **California Man** all charting heavily in UK. Strangely, the Move never made much impact in US, being regarded as cult underground group rather than pop band.

By 1970, however, band was practically falling apart. Jeff Lynne came in to replace Carl Wayne, and by 1971 band was reduced to Wood, Bevan and Lynne. The stage was set for end of the Move and beginning of Electric Light Orchestra(▶), a concept which Wood had been kicking around for some time (Wood/Lynne originally planned to run Move and ELO simultaneously). Wood eventually left ELO to form Wizzard, and achieved considerable success with Spector-influenced sound up to mid-'70s.

Always plagued by problem of falling between several stools, not to mention personality clashes and wrangling over musical direction, the Move were never likely candidates in longevity stakes. However, they were important influence at a time when rock was beginning to emerge and become a separate form, and they leave behind collection of singles which stand up to repeated listening.

Final line-up: Roy Wood; Bevan; Jeff Lynne, guitar, vocals.

Hit Singles:

	US	UK
Night Of Fear, 1967	—	2
I Can Hear The Grass Grow, 1967	—	5
Flowers In The Rain, 1967	—	2
Fire Brigade, 1968	—	3
Blackberry Way, 1968	—	1
Curly, 1969	—	12
Brontosaurus, 1970	—	7
Tonight, 1971	—	11
California Man, 1972	—	7

Albums:
The Best Of (A&M), 1974
The Greatest Hits (—/Hallmark), 1978
The Move (Shines On) (—/Harvest), 1979
Platinum Collection (—/Cube), 1981

Worth Searching Out:
Something Else (Live EP) (Regal/Zonophone), 1968

Maria Muldaur

US vocalist, fiddler, percussionist.
Born Maria Grazia Rosa Domenica d'Amato, New York City, September 12, 1943.

Career: Surprisingly, the woman behind the mellow and sensual voice on **Midnight At The Oasis** actually began her professional career doing jug band music — a good-time sound played on fiddle, guitar, banjo, washboard, gut-bucket (tin tub, broom handle and string) and, of course, a stoneware jug (otherwise used for 'corn likker'). In addition to providing vocals, Maria d'Amato played kazoo and tambourine. While with Even Dozen Jug Band, she recorded **Jug Band Music And Rags Of The South** with pianist Joshua Rifkin, who later made name with Scott Joplin's piano rags.

Married Geoff Muldaur, guitarist and fellow-vocalist in Jim Kweskin's Jug Band, a popular New England group in early '60s which recorded several albums. When Kweskin got involved with Boston-based quasi-religious cult, the Muldaurs left to record duo albums. Geoff joined Paul Butterfield's(▶) Better Days and Maria played session on group's first LP before marriage ended. First solo album **Maria Muldaur** went platinum, and provided

Above: Birmingham beatsters The Move, with the great Roy Wood pictured second from left.

Oasis single, featuring solo by Better Days' guitarist Amos Garrett. Ry Cooder(▶) plays guitar on another track. Muldaur's uptempo bluesy voice covers wide range of contemporary songs while giving scope for talents of excellent session players.

Next album, **Waitress In The Donut Shop**, again featured top artists: Benny Carter arranging and conducting jazz numbers, Doc and Merle Watson on guitar, Paul Butterfield playing harmonica, and Linda Ronstadt(▶) doing background vocals. Third LP, **Sweet Harmony** (produced, like the first two, by Lenny Waronker and Joe Boyd), although containing equally loving arrangements of songs by such diverse writers as Hoagy Carmichael, Neil Sedaka(▶) and Smokey Robinson(▶), was less successful.

Subsequent albums, although admired, haven't returned her to early popularity. In addition to own records, Maria Muldaur did sessions during late '70s for the Doobie Brothers(▶), Elvin Bishop, Leon Russell(▶) and Willie Nelson(▶).

Hit Singles:

	US	UK
Midnight At The Oasis, 1974	6	21
I'm A Woman, 1975	12	—

Albums:
Maria Muldaur (Reprise), 1973
Waitress In The Donut Shop (Reprise), 1974
Sweet Harmony (Reprise), 1976
Southern Winds (Warner Bros), 1978
Open Your Eyes (Warner Bros), 1979
Gospel Nights (Takoma/—), 1980
There Is A Love (Myrrh), 1982

Musical Youth

US group formed 1980.

Original/Current line-up: Dennis Seaton, vocals; Kelvin Grant, guitar; Michael Grant, keyboards; Patrick Waite, bass; Junior Waite, drums.

Career: Composed of two pairs of brothers and a friend, all from black families in Birmingham. Became phenomenon of autumn 1982 when debut single, cover version of reggae singer Jackie Mittoo's **Full Up** and/or Mighty Diamonds' **Pass The Kutchie**, retitled **Pass The Dutchie**, topped UK singles chart for three weeks in October. Follow-up single also made Top 20; debut LP charted substantially.

However, group not without certain controversy — despite extreme youth of members

(oldest, Dennis and Junior, born 1967; yongest, Kelvin, born 1971) — lyrics of chart-topping hit interpreted as 'pass the joint', causing popular press furore, as band of West Indian extraction. Additionally, young age of Kelvin and Michael (born 1969) prevent them from working (including recording) for more than very limited number of days per year, in order to protect their education.

Group visited Japan and then US, where single reached Top 10 in early 1983. Third UK single returned group to Top 10, but obviously new material is needed (within the work limits referred to above) before group can reach full potential. While early Jackson Five(▶) image has launched their career with great success, some expansion of horizons may be necessary to prevent fame being all too brief. Have recently recorded with Donna Summer(▶), which will help confirm international reputation.

Hit Singles:

	US	UK
Pass The Dutchie, 1982	10	1
Youth Of Today, 1982	—	13
Never Gonna Give You Up, 1983	—	6

Albums:
The Youth Of Today (MCA), 1982

Johnny Nash

US vocalist, composer.
Born Houston, Texas, August 19, 1940.

Career: The major mark of Nash's long and varied career came in early '70s when his involvement with Jamaican music, backed by reputation as black American soul singer, not only carried reggae into US charts but also

propelled Bob Marley(▶) and the Wailers, then working as his back-up unit, to eventual stardom.

Nash had started out as a teen idol, breaking racial barriers on Texan TV when he starred in KPRC's Matinée Show which won him ABC Paramount recording contract, and seven year stint on Arthur Godfrey TV talent show which took him through the '50s. His records of that era were very much in teenage pop idiom (he even recorded with Paul Anka and George Hamilton IV).

Strongly influenced by Sam Cooke(▶), Nash followed his lead in mixing shows tunes and MOR material with soul flavoured material during early '60s when his efforts appeared on such labels as Warner Bros, Argo and MGM.

In 1965 he set up own Jad label in New York with business partner Danny Sims, producing Sam and Bill's US soul hit **For Your Love** that year.

While on location in Caribbean during filming of Burt Lancaster movie 'Take A Giant Step', when he was 17, Nash had fallen in love with Jamaica and in 1968 he visited Byron Lee's studio in Kingston to record own composition **Hold Me Tight**, utilising gently rhythmic reggae beat and scoring Stateside smash, which also took him into UK charts for the first time.

He repeated the musical format with **You Got Soul** and a reggae re-make of Sam Cooke's **Cupid** while sticking closer to conventional soul on album of duets with ex-Motown star Kim Weston, produced by her husband Mickey Stevenson.

Refining soul/reggae mix even further, Nash reached peak of creativity in 1971 (by which time he was signed to CBS in London, released on Columbia in US) with attractive Bob Marley(▶) composition **Stir It Up** and self-written American chart-topper **I Can See Clearly Now**. Followed with succesion of fine records using the same hauntingly wistful style, including UK No. 1, **Tears On My Pillow** in 1975.

Hit Singles:

	US	UK
Hold Me Tight, 1968	5	5
You Got Soul, 1969	58	6
Cupid, 1969	39	6
Stir It Up, 1971	12	13
I Can See Clearly Now, 1972	1	5
There Are More Questions Than Answers, 1972	—	9
Tears On My Pillow, 1975	—	1

Albums:
My Merry Go Round (Epic/—), 1973
I Can See Clearly Now (Epic), 1974
Greatest Hits (Epic), 1974
The Johnny Nash Album (Epic), 1980
Stir It Up (Hallmark), 1981

Nazareth

UK group formed 1969.

Original/Current line-up: Dan McCafferty, vocals; Manny Charlton, guitar; Pete Agnew, bass; Darryl Sweet, drums.

Career: McCafferty, Agnew and Sweet played in Dunfermline, Scotland, semi-pro band the Shadettes, changing name to Nazareth when Charlton joined in 1969.

They became known on club circuit as no-nonsense hard rock outfit, with strong following in Scotland. Recorded two albums before making breakthrough with 1973 LP **Razamanaz** which yielded two British hit

Left: Johnny Nash, who sang like Sam Cooke, but was unable to capitalise on his early breakthrough.

singles in **Broken Down Angel** and **Bad Bad Boy**. Follow-up album **Loud 'n' Proud** gained international success (especially in Europe).

By mid-'70s group had established presence in US market, helped by hit version of old Everly Brothers(▶) number **Love Hurts**. Continued to sell records and work steadily at home and abroad without establishing super-star status.

Fool Circle, Nazareth. Courtesy NEMS Records.

Dismissed by many critics as essentially a second-division band, Nazareth nevertheless obviously provided straight-down-the-line musical fare that many people wanted. When Mountain label folded in 1981, they switched to NEMS but failed to match earlier single success, despite increased following in US, where they now reside.

Hit Singles:

	US	UK
Broken Down Angel, 1973	—	9
Bad Bad Boy, 1973	—	10
This Flight Tonight, 1973	—	11
My White Bicycle, 1975	—	14
Love Hurts, 1975	8	—
Hot Tracks (EP), 1977	1	15

Albums:
Nazareth (A&M/Mountain), 1971
Exercises (A&M/Mountain), 1972
Razamanaz (A&M/Mountain), 1973
Loud 'n' Proud (A&M/Mountain), 1974
Rampant (A&M/Mountain), 1974
Hair Of The Dog (A&M/Mountain), 1975
Greatest Hits (—/Mountain), 1975
Close Enough For Rock 'n' Roll (A&M/Mountain), 1976
Play 'n' The Game (A&M/Mountain), 1977
Expect No Mercy (A&M/Mountain), 1977
No Mean City (A&M/Mountain), 1978
Malice In Wonderland (A&M/Mountain), 1980
Whatever You Want, Babe (—/Mountain), 1980
Fool Circle (A&M), 1981
It's Naz (A&M/NEMS), 1981
2X5 (A&M/—), 1982

Rick Nelson

US vocalist, guitarist, composer, actor.
Born Eric Hilliard Nelson, Teaneck, New Jersey, May 8, 1940.

Career: Joined parents' radio show at four; made transition to television's 'Adventures of Ozzie and Harriet' in early '50s. Signed first record contract as Ricky Nelson with Verve in 1956, scoring first hit **I'm Walkin'**. Signed to Imperial Records 1957; consistently appeared in US and UK charts until early '60s.

Initial appeal was to young teens. He had some good looks as Presley(▶) but his clean-cut image was less threatening to middle-American morals. Records were somewhat subdued but well-crafted due to fine

musicians, notably guitarist James Burton(▶), who contributed classic solos to sides that would have been classified as rockabilly had they been recorded in Memphis.

Change of image followed shortening of name to Rick in 1961 and recording deal with US Decca in 1963. Later material appealed more to young adults, including effective recording of Dylan's(▶) **She Belongs To Me** (1969). Formed own group, the Stone Canyon Band (1971), with leanings towards country rock. Had major hit in 1972 with autobiographical **Garden Party** summing up his feelings about audiences who regarded him as a rock'n'roller and nothing else. Since then Nelson has failed to make chart contribution, but has recorded several fine albums, including a recent debut on Capitol, **Playing To Win**.

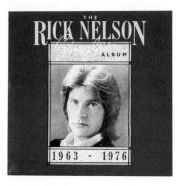

The Rick Nelson Singles Album. Courtesy MCA Records.

Although Nelson is rarely regarded as a trendsetter, he nevertheless made major contribution with his professionalism and sheer volume of chart entries over long period.

Hit Singles:

	US	UK
I'm Walkin'/A Teenager's Romance, 1957	2	—
A Teenager's Romance/I'm Walkin', 1957	4	—
Be Bop Baby, 1957	3	—
Stood Up/Waitin' In School, 1958	2	—
Waitin' In School/Stood Up, 1958	18	—
My Bucket's Got A Hole In It/Believe What You Say, 1958	12	—
Believe What You Say/My Bucket's Got A Hole In It, 1958	4	—
Poor Little Fool, 1958	1	4
Lonesome Town/I Got A Feeling, 1958	7	—
I Got A Feeling/Lonesome Town, 1958	10	27
Someday, 1958	—	9
It's Late/Never Be Anyone Else But You, 1959	9	3
Never Be Anyone Else But You/It's Late, 1959	6	14
Sweeter Than You/Just A Little Too Much, 1959	9	19
Just A Little Too Much/Sweeter Than You, 1959	9	11
I Wanna Be Loved, 1959	20	—
Young Emotions, 1960	12	—
Travelin' Man/Hello Mary Lou, 1961	1	2
Hello Mary Lou/Travelin' Man, 1961	9	2
Everlovin'/A Wonder Like You, 1961	16	—
A Wonder Like You/Everlovin' 1961	11	—
Young World, 1962	5	19
Teenage Idol, 1962	5	39
It's Up To You, 1963	6	22
Fools Rush In, 1963	12	12
For You, 1964	6	14
Garden Party, 1972	6	41

Albums:
Ricky (Liberty/London), 1957
Decca Years (MCA/—), 1971
Intakes (Epic), 1977
The Rick Nelson Singles Album (Fame), 1978
Rockin' Rock (MCA), 1979
Playing To Win (Capitol/—), 1981

Worth Searching Out:
Garden Party (MCA), 1974

Sandy Nelson

US drummer.
Born Sander Nelson, Santa Monica, California, December 1, 1938.

Career: Nelson grew up in LA; went to high school with Nancy Sinatra, Phil Spector and Jan and Dean(▶). Made recording debut as member of local outfit Kip Tyler and the Flips. Group also included Bruce Johnson — later one of the Beach Boys(▶) — on piano and schoolmate Spector. Recorded for Ebb and Challenge labels.

Played on the Teddy Bears' million-selling

To Know Him Is To Love Him. Was session drummer on Gene Vincent's(▶) 1959 album **Crazy Times**.

Solo debut **Teenbeat** sold a million copies on Original Sound. He was then snapped up by major Imperial label. His compulsive, if repetitive, **Let There Be Drums** — recorded shortly after he lost his left foot in a car crash — was a massive hit.

Nelson went on to record plethora of albums for first Imperial, then its parent label Liberty. These usually provided instrumental covers of established hit tunes. Nelson's somewhat limited drumming style veered towards R&B but mostly verged on bland MOR.

Hit Singles:

	US	UK
Teenbeat, 1959	4	9
Let There Be Drums, 1961	7	3

Albums:
Worth Searching Out:
Teenbeat (Imperial/—), 1960
Let There Be Drums (Imperial/—), 1961

Willie Nelson

US vocalist, composer, guitarist.
Born Abbott, Texas, April 30, 1933.

Career: Learned guitar chords from grandparents, who raised him. On discharge from US Air Force in early '50s, married Cherokee Indian girl. Settled in Waco, Texas, working as salesman before becoming radio announcer. Graduated to bigger station in Fort Worth, hosting country shows. Began playing in local honky-tonks. His classic songs **Night Life** and **Family Bible** were written at this time. On moving to Nashville he got job as bass player in Ray Price's band; Price made **Night Life** his theme tune. Earning reputation for perceptive songwriting, Nelson penned **Hello Walls**, a big hit for Faron Young, and **Crazy**, which Patsy Cline charted.

Taking over core of Price's band, Nelson went on road in own right. His marriage broke up and he took up with wife of a DJ Association president. They eventually married, living in Fort Worth, Nashville and Los Angeles.

In early years Nelson also helped career of

Below: Rick Nelson, who proved he was more than just a pretty face.

Charly Pride(▶). He featured the black country singer on his shows in the deep South.

During '60s, Nelson's abrasive tough-life, hard-living style did not fit in with increasingly smooth RCA Nashville sound. He consequently determined to get out of RCA contract; switched to Atlantic who had just opened Nashville office and whose roots were in blues and R&B (Nelson's music has been dubbed 'white man's blues'). Atlantic's Jerry Wexler produced Nelson in New York. **Phases And Stages** album fully established intense, brooding style and chillingly lonesome songs.

Moving with third wife Connie to Austin, Texas, Nelson became leader of so-called 'Outlaw' country movement there. A switch to Columbia brought him crossover hits of which **Blue Eyes Cryin' In The Rain** made him major star.

Along with Waylon Jennings and handful of others, Nelson has done much to bridge gap between rock and country. However, when he tried to further broaden outlook with **Stardust** album, a collection of re-makes of MOR standards, many critics accused him of selling out. But a listen to a selection of his near 20 albums confirms that he has been uncompromisingly his own man. Major pop-chart success came in 1980 with **On The Road Again** and in 1982 with **Always On My Mind**.

Combines work in studio with movie roles — featured in Robert Redford's 'Electric Horseman', 'Honeysuckle Rose' and starred in 'Barbarosa', released 1983.

Hit Singles:

	US	UK
On The Road Again, 1980	20	—
Always On My Mind, 1982	5	49

Albums (selected):
Best Of* (United Artists/—), 1973
Classic Willie Nelson (—/Sunset), 1979
Sings Kristofferson (Columbia/CBS), 1979
Honeysuckle Rose (Columbia/CBS), 1980
Always On My Mind (Columbia/CBS), 1982
Greatest Hits (Columbia/CBS), 1982
20 Of The Best (RCA), 1982
*Originally titled **And Then I Wrote**

With Waylon Jennings:
Waylon And Willie (RCA), 1978

With Leon Russell:
One For The Road (Columbia/CBS), 1979

New Riders Of The Purple Sage

US group formed 1970.

Original line-up: David Nelson, vocals, guitar; John Dawson, vocals, guitar; Jerry Garcia, steel pedal guitar; Phil Lesh, bass; Mickey Hart, drums.

Career: As part of Grateful Dead's(▶) loose structure, Garcia sought some outlet for exploring country music considerd inappropriate to Dead's image. He joined with Nelson and Dawson and launched NRPS as opening act for Dead in 1970.

Following record-industry interest, Dead members (except Garcia) were replaced by Dave Torbert (bass) and ex-Jefferson Airplane(▶) drummer Spencer Dryden.

This line-up recorded countrified rock on first LP. Within year Garcia found he couldn't handle both bands and Buddy Cage took his place for next four albums; **Home, Home On the Road** was excellent live set.

In February 1974, Torbert left to form Kingfish and bass slot was taken over by ex-Byrds(▶) Skip Battin. He recorded next two LPs with band before leaving to push country rock even further with Flying Burrito Brothers (▶) (he was replaced by Steve Love.)

Band then moved to MCA and despite several above-average LPs has slowly disappeared.

Final line-up: Nelson; Dawson, vocals, guitar; Buddy Cage, steel guitar; Spencer Dryden, drums; Steve Love, bass.

Albums:
New Riders Of The Purple Sage (Columbia/CBS), 1971
Powerglide (Columbia/CBS), 1972
Gypsy Cowboy (Columbia/CBS), 1972
Adventures Of Panama Red (Columbia/CBS), 1973
Home, Home On The Road (Columbia/CBS), 1974*
Oh, What A Mighty Time (Columbia/CBS), 1975
Best Of NRPS (Columbia/CBS), 1976
Marin County Line (MCA), 1978
Feelin' All Right, (A&M/—), 1981
*Live

Randy Newman

US composer, pianist, vocalist.
Born Los Angeles, November 28, 1943.

Career: Born into musical family, took piano lessons from age seven. Graduated from University of California in music composition.

Started career as arranger and songwriter and quickly gained reputation among fellow musicians as perceptive and unusually intelligent writer. Early supporters of his work included Judy Collins(▶), who recorded **I Think It's Going To Rain Today** in 1966, and Britain's Alan Price(▶) who hit in 1967 with **Simon Smith And His Amazing Dancing Bear.**

Newman signed with Warner Bros in 1968 and released **Randy Newman,** which featured his striking compositions with large orchestra. It created interest but had little commercial appeal, which could also be said about **Twelve Songs,** his next album (originally a collection of demos recorded before **Randy Newman**). This album contained **Mama Told Me Not To Come,** later a hit for Three Dog Night(▶).

After **Live**, concert versions of songs from first two albums, **Sail Away** and **Good Old Boys**, consolidated Newman's reputation as writer of pointed, oblique songs with sharp edge of satire. His subject matter—nuclear bombs, racism, pollution—although stuff of protest, was dealt with in wry, ambiguous manner that set Newman apart from run-of-the-mill protest singers. Rather than preaching, he has always preferred subtlety, creating miniature tableaux that make their own telling point.

In 1977 his album **Little Criminals** yielded hit single in **Short People**, a satire on bigotry which nevertheless was mistaken for bigotry itself by many people, including variety of organisations for midgets and dwarves. Despite controversy, **Little Criminals** won Newman much wider audience.

Never a prolific artist, Newman made further impact with **Born Again** in 1979, then released nothing until **Trouble In Paradise** in early 1983. Regarded by most critics as brilliant return to form of **Little Criminals,** album puts Newman's sardonic voice and spare piano accompaniment into context of LA session-rock ethos.

Although recorded work has become steadily more elaborate, Newman invariably undertakes live work accompanied only by his own piano. Complex, self-effacing man who is one of few truly original talents in rock, Randy Newman will probably eventually be regarded as one of most important artists of '70s and '80s.

Hit Singles:

	US	UK
Short People, 1978	2	—

Albums:
Randy Newman (Reprise), 1968
Twelve Songs (Reprise), 1969
Live (Reprise), 1971
Sail Away (Reprise), 1972
Good Old Boys (Warner Bros), 1974
Little Criminals (Warner Bros), 1977
Born Again (Warner Bros), 1979
Trouble In Paradise (Warner Bros), 1983

Olivia Newton-John

Australian vocalist.
Born Cambridge, England, September 26, 1948.

Career: British-born, Australian-raised, and now an American show-business institution, Olivia Newton-John has straddled the musical fields of pop, middle-of-the-road and country. Starred in movies 'Grease' and 'Xanadu' (for which she recorded title song, along with ELO, which hit No. 1 on UK charts).

Grandfather was Nobel prize winner, father was principal of Ormond College in Melbourne, where she grew up. Winning trip to England as first prize in talent contest at 16, she appeared in cabaret and on TV as one half of girl duo (with Pat Carrol) which broke up when partner's visa expired. She was also part of short-lived Tomorrow group, formed for abortive television series of same name.

Debut single, Dylan's **If Not For You**, made international noise and follow-up **Banks Of The Ohio** earned Grammy award. After touring Europe with Cliff Richard(▶), she became regular on his TV show. Third hit, **Let Me Be There**, won Grammy for Best Country Vocalist and America quickly became her strongest market.

Movie 'Grease' yielded her three huge hits: **You're The One That I Want** (a duet with co-star John Travolta(▶)), **Summer Nights** and **Hopelessly Devoted To You**.

From much criticised 'Xanadu', **Magic** was also international hit, while her '80s album **Physical** contained three hits and was accompanied by massive-selling video. Has also recorded successful duets with Bee Gees(▶), Andy Gibb and Cliff Richard.

Hit Singles:

	US	UK
If Not For You, 1971	25	7
Banks Of The Ohio, 1971	—	6
What Is Life, 1972	—	16
Take Me Home Country Roads, 1973	—	15
Let Me Be There, 1974	6	—
Long Live Love, 1974	—	11
If You Love Me (Let Me Know), 1974	5	—
I Honestly Love You, 1974	1	22
Please Mr Please, 1975	3	—
Something Better To Do, 1975	13	—
Sam, 1977	20	6
Hopelessly Devoted To You, 1978	3	2
A Little More Love, 1978	3	4
Physical, 1981	1	7
Landslide, 1982	52	18
Make A Move On Me, 1982	5	43
Heart Attack, 1982	3	46
With John Travolta:		
You're The One That I Want, 1978	1	1
Summer Nights, 1978	5	1
With ELO:		
Xanadu, 1980	8	1
With Andy Gibb:		
I Can't Help It, 1980	12	—
With Cliff Richard:		
Suddenly, 1980	20	15

Albums:
Let Me Be There (MCA/—), 1973
If You Love Me Let Me Know (MCA/Pye), 1974
Long Live Love (MCA/EMI), 1974
First Impressions (MCA/EMI), 1974
Have You Never Been Mellow (EMI), 1975
Clearly Love (MCA/EMI), 1975
Come On Over (MCA/EMI), 1976

Left: Olivia Newton-John, whose looks only added to her vocal talent.

Don't Stop Believin' (MCA/EMI), 1976
Making A Good Thing Better (MCA/EMI),
    1977
Greatest Hits (EMI), 1977
Totally Hot (MCA/EMI), 1978
Grease Soundtrack (RSO), 1978
Xanadu Soundtrack (MCA), 1980
Physical (EMI), 1981
Greatest Hits (EMI), 1982

Harry Nilsson

US vocalist, composer.
Born New York, June 15, 1941.

Career: Moved to California during teens, started writing songs. After some early success — he wrote **Cuddly Toy** for Monkees(▶) — he was signed by RCA in 1968.

Early albums showed Nilsson to be distinctive singer/writer of idiosyncratic promise, but first hit **Everybody's Talkin'** was theme tune of film 'Midnight Cowboy' (1969), written by Fred Neil. **Nilsson Schmilsson** became platinum album in US, yielding hit single (No. 1 in both US and UK) in Badfinger-composed song **Without You. Son Of Schmilsson** LP did nearly as well.

Next quirky turn in Nilsson's career came with release of **A Little Touch Of Schmilsson In The Night**, an album of cover versions of standard songs like **Makin' Whoopee**. Seemingly aimed somewhere between satire and tribute, album sold well to MOR audiences.

A Little Touch Of Schmilsson In The Night. Courtesy of RCA Records.

Since mid-'70s, however, artist seems to have been casting around for direction. In between bouts of well-publicised partying with friends like Ringo Starr(▶) he has continued to record with varying degrees of success. 'The Point', soundtrack of full-length animated film for TV, was adapted and presented successfully at London's Mermaid Theatre in 1976.

Latterly Nilsson has had success as songwriter while keeping generally low profile. Lack of discipline seems likely to remain obstacle to consistent achievement.

Hit Singles:

	US	UK
Everybody's Talkin', 1969	6	23
Without You, 1972	1	1
Coconut, 1972	8	42

Albums:
Pandemonium Shadow Show (RCA), 1967
Aerial Ballet (RCA), 1968
Harry (RCA), 1969
Nilsson Sings Newman (RCA), 1970
Nilsson Schmilsson (RCA), 1971
Son Of Schmilsson (RCA), 1972
A Little Touch Of Schmilsson In The Night
    (RCA), 1973
Du It On Mon Dei (RCA), 1975
Son Of Dracula (RCA), 1974
The Sandman (RCA), 1975

That's The Way It Is (RCA), 1976
Knillssonn (RCA), 1977
Early Times (Mercury/DSM), 1977
Greatest Hits (RCA), 1978
Nilsson's Greatest Music (RCA), 1981

Nitty Gritty Dirt Band

US group formed 1966.

Original line-up: Jeffrey Hanna, washboard, harmonica, vocals, guitar; Bruce Kunkel, guitar, kazoo, washboard, bass; Jimmy Fadden, drums, harp, vocals; Ralph Barr, guitar, clarinet, banjo; Les Thompson, guitar, mandolin; John McEuen, banjo, mandolin, guitar, accordion.

Career: Kunkel and Hanna started as high-school folk duo. Fellow students joined loosely formed Illegitimate Jug Band (name based on absence of jug in band). On leaving school, group settled down in Long Beach, California, with above line-up and new name, the Nitty Gritty Dirt Band. McEuen's older brother Bill took over management.

The Nitty Gritty Dirt Band. Courtesy Liberty Records.

Humorous, zany and good-time approach to music attracted Liberty Records. First single, **Buy For Me The Rain**, became instant US hit but really missed band's flair for jumping from bluegrass to folk to music-hall material. Band returned to club work and except for appearance in film 'Paint Your Wagon' seemed curious one-hit wonder.

Same line-up released second LP, **Ricochet**. Without catchy pop tune, album was ignored and remains one of rock's forgotten gems. By time of third album **Rare Junk**, Kunkel had left to be replaced by Darrow, who subsequently quit with Barr. Jim Ibbotson joined to replace Barr and provide band with steady bass player.

Band returned to US national attention with cover of Jerry Jeff Walker's(▶) **Mr Bojangles**, followed by Kenny Loggins(▶) tune **House at Pooh Corner**. This helped album **Uncle Charlie And His Dog Teddy** into charts.

Relocation to Colorado is reflected in title of next LP, **All The Good Times**. The true eclectic taste of band reached peak on **Will The Circle Be Unbroken**? This ambitious triple record set of American bluegrass and country music was recorded in Nashville with original artists of material selected for project. Rolling Stones raved about significance of album, which was too far from rock mainstream for general audience.

Thompson left before release of **Stars And Stripes Forever** and band continued as foursome until 1976. Hanna then left. Remaining members shortened name to Dirt Band and recruited John Cable and Jackie Clark.

Dirt, Silver and Gold commemorated tenth year of band in 1976. In 1977, tour of USSR (first American band to do so) provided

Above: The Motor City Madman, mayhem merchant Ted Nugent.

inspiration for McEuen track, **White Russia**, on **Dirt Band** LP. Albums since have continued to maintain high standards of craftsmanship. Linda Ronstadt(▶) appeared on **American Dream**, and **Make A Little Magic** LP provided Top 30 single of same name.

Dirt Band is now American institution with far-flung credentials and steady following. By following Doc Watson and Roy Acuff instead of Little Richard or Elvis, Dirt Band has limited its audience; but that does not negate skill and quality of band's music.

Current line-up: McEuen; Fadden; Jim Ibbotson, vocals, bass; John Cable, guitar, vocals; Jackie Clarke, bass.

Hit Singles:

	US	UK
Mr Bojangles, 1970	9	—
An American Dream, 1979	13	—

Albums:
Uncle Charlie And His Dog Teddy (Liberty),
    1970
All The Good Times (United Artists), 1972
Will The Circle Be Unbroken (United Artists),
    1973
Stars And Stripes Forever (United Artists),
    1974
Dream (United Artists), 1975
Dirt, Silver And Gold (United Artists), 1976*
The Dirt Band (United Artists), 1978
Wild Nights (Liberty), 1978
American Dream (United Artists), 1979
Make A Little Magic (United Artists), 1980
Jealousy (United Artists), 1981
*Triple compilation

Worth Searching Out:
The Nitty Gritty Dirt Band (Liberty/—), 1967
Ricochet (Liberty/—), 1967
Dead & Alive (—/Liberty), 1969

Ted Nugent

US guitarist, bandleader, vocalist, composer.
Born Detroit, December 13, 1949.

Career: Self-styled 'wild man of rock', Nugent's antics (including hunting with bow and arrow and wearing a loin cloth) over his decade and a half of recording have almost justified epithet. He acquired first guitar at eight; joined first major band, Amboy Dukes, in 1965. Dukes played quasi-psychedelic music

appropriate to times, but with extra Detroit metal quotient. Group scored US Top 20 hit in summer 1968 with **Journey To The Centre Of The Mind**, later included on notable **Nuggets** double LP. Early LPs became collectors' items when greater '60s consciousness returned in late '70s.

Group continued through '60s, eventually adopting name of Ted Nugent and the Amboy Dukes — Nugent in typical manner had altered nature of band from democracy to dictatorship, with himself as dictator. Band's most famous member (other than Nugent) was probably Rusty Day, later in Cactus, although perhaps 10 people were members at one time or another. Despite label changes, group had little success and even two-year period without record deal. After signing with Epic in 1975, fortunes improved; Amboy Dukes tag dropped. First LP for new label was Nugent's first to make US Top 30, using quite long-lived band (by Nugent standards): Derek St Holmes, rhythm guitar, vocals; Rob Grange, bass; Cliff Davies, drums.

Scream Dream, Ted Nugent. Courtesy Epic Records.

1976 LP **Free For All** featured Meat Loaf(▶) (then less than household name) as guest vocalist and again reached Top 30. By 1978 LP **Weekend Warriors** band beginning to change again, although only Cliff Davies remained as drummer and sometime producer through 1981 live LP **Intensities In Ten Cities**.

During 1982, Nugent changed labels after seven successful years with Epic, and formed new band of previous members Dave Kiswiney (bass) and Derek St Holmes (lead vocals), plus noted drummer Carmine Appice (ex-Vanilla Fudge(▶) etc.). With his lengthy experience and nearly 20 LPs behind him, Nugent is difficult to criticise, especially as his guitar playing is exemplary, if ear-splitting. However, to move into mega-platinum zone occupied by very few hard rock acts, a greater degree of light and shade is required. Even so, fan following faithful and substantial, if often close to deafness (like Nugent himself). Guitar: Gibson Les Paul.

Hit Single: US UK
With Amboy Dukes:
Journey To The Centre Of The
Mind, 1969 16 —

Albums:
With Amboy Dukes:
Marriage On The Rocks — Rock Bottom
(Polydor), 1970

Ted Nugent and the Amboy Dukes:
Call Of The Wild, 1973*
Tooth, Fang & Claw, 1974*
Ted Nugent (Epic), 1975
Free For All (Epic), 1976
Cat Scratch Fever (Epic), 1977
Double Live Gonzo (Epic), 1978
Weekend Warriors (Epic), 1978
State Of Shock (Epic), 1979
Scream Dream (Epic), 1980
Intensities In Ten Cities (Epic), 1981
Great Gonzos The Best Of (Epic), 1981
Nugent (Atlantic), 1982
*Released as double album set (Discreet), 1977

Worth Searching Out:
The Amboy Dukes:
The Amboy Dukes (Mainstream/London), 1967
Journey To The Centre Of The Mind (Mainstream/London), 1968
Migration (Mainstream/London), 1969

Ted Nugent and the Amboy Dukes:
Survival Of The Fittest Live (Polydor), 1971

Gary Numan

UK vocalist, instrumentalist.
Born Gary Anthony James Webb, London, March 8, 1958.

Career: Joined first band the Lasers, a punk outfit, in keeping with times in 1976. By 1977, had assumed control, renaming band Tubeway Army, with trio format: Numan front man (singer, writer, guitar, keyboards) with Paul Gardiner (bass) and Numan's uncle Jess Lidyard (drums). First single was **That's Too**

Bad, recorded later that year. Signed with small Beggar's Banquet label in 1978.
Gigged around London, with drummer Bob Simmonds replacing Lidyard, then Barry Benn replacing Simmonds; Sean Burke (guitar) added by mid-1978. Second single **Bombers** released, but Numan decided to disband group. Album's worth of demos (recorded before dissolution) impressed record company so much that these were released as debut LP in late 1978.
Early in 1979, Numan, Gardiner and Lidyard cut second and final Tubeway Army LP, **Replicas**, which included No. 1 single **Are Friends Electric?** — as a result, LP topped UK chart. After this, Numan decided to record under own name, and next LP **The Pleasure Principle** also topped chart, as did extracted single **Cars**. Numan's heavily synthesised sound and unworldly material, this time augmented by Chris Payne (keyboards, viola), captured public's imagination. During autumn 1979 first tour as star with stage set of fluorescent tubes was huge success.
In 1980 toured Europe, North America, Japan and Australasia. Hit with three more Top 10 singles in UK, as well as releasing one of earliest rock video cassettes. Cracked US Top 10 with **Cars** single (although American success remains comparatively limited). UK success tailed off, and during 1981, while still scoring hits, Numan was obviously less fashionable. By this time, drummer Cedric Sharpley (ex-Druid) had joined, replacing Lidyard. Halfway through year, Numan had decided to stop live work but two live LPs (issued separately and as boxed set) were released to coincide, but Numan was seemingly more interested in gaining private pilot's licence (he subsequently flew around the world). Released new LP **Dance** and single **She's Got Claws**, with help from numerous guest musicians, including Mick Karn (Japan(▶)), Roger Taylor of Queen(▶) and Canadian violinist (and Numan discovery) Nash the Slash. Wrote and produced hit single **Stormtrooper In Drag** for ex-colleague Paul Gardiner, as well as singing on hit single **Love Needs No Disguise** by Dramatis, group composed of his ex-band (Russell Bell, guitar; Dennis Haines, keyboards; Chris Payne, keyboards, viola; Cedric Sharpley, drums).
Numan spent much of 1982 as tax exile in

Below: Gary Numan, perhaps the first super-star of the synthesiser.

US, but released three more UK Top 20 singles, plus new LP **I Assassin**, which made UK Top 10. On return from US, decided to resume live work; began work on LP for 1983. It is tempting for many critics to suggest that Numan experienced his five minutes of fame at start of the '80s, but his rather well-timed absence from Britain may easily result in his returning to the top before the mid-'80s.

Hit Singles: US UK
With Tubeway Army:
Are Friends Electric?, 1979 — 1

Solo:
Cars, 1979 9 1
Complex, 1979 — 6
We Are Glass, 1980 — 5
I Die; You Die, 1980 — 6
This Wreckage, 1980 — 20
She's Got Claws, 1981 — 6
Music For Chameleons, 1982 — 19
We Take Mystery, 1982 — 9
White Boys And Heroes, 1982 — 20

Albums:
With Tubeway Army:
Tubeway Army (—/Beggar's Banquet), 1979
Replicas (—/Beggar's Banquet), 1979

Solo:
The Pleasure Principle (—/Beggar's Banquet), 1979
Telekon (—/Beggar's Banquet), 1980
Dance (Atco/Beggar's Banquet), 1981
I Assassin (Atco/Beggar's Banquet), 1982

Hazel O'Connor

UK vocalist, composer, actress.
Born Coventry, May 16, 1955.

Career: Studied art after leaving school (as well as posing as nude model). Travelled around Europe and North Africa in early '70s; worked in Japan as dancer and English teacher. Began singing around time of punk explosion; signed with Albion Records in 1978. Early singles unsuccessful, but landed starring role in punk rock feature film 'Breaking Glass', achieving much acclaim, plus first hits **Eighth Day** (UK Top 10) and **Give Me An Inch**. Also won 'Best New Actress' award from trade paper 'Variety', while **Breaking Glass** soundtrack LP (written completely by O'Connor) went gold.
In 1980, recorded first solo LP, **Sons And Lovers**, with group Megahype: Ed Case, drums; Andy Qunta (now Icehouse(▶)), drums; Wesley Magoohan (now the Beat(▶)) saxophone; Neil O'Connor (brother), guitar; plus various bass players. LP failed to chart, but spawned hit single **D-Days** (another Top 10) 1981 saw three more hit singles and LP **Cover Plus**, which briefly charted. At this time, Steve Kinch became permanent bass player with Megahype.
Very little action during 1982, with no new records, due to changing management and record company, etc; group disbanded. O'Connor appeared in late 1982 charity gig in Manchester, using backing tapes, and at CND concert in spring 1983, but musical appearances limited by theatrical work and TV series 'Jangles'. In mid-1983 recorded with Ed Case and Neil O'Connor, plus various friends, with view to acquiring new record deal. Without some substantial impetus (eg another major film role à la 'Breaking Glass'), it is difficult to see Hazel returning to major stardom, despite songwriting ability.

Hit Singles: US UK
Eighth Day, 1980 — 5
D-Days, 1981 — 10
Will You, 1981 — 8

Albums:
Breaking Glass (A&M), 1980
Sons And Lovers (A&M), 1980
Cover Plus (—/A&M), 1981

The O'Jays

US vocal group formed 1962.
Original line-up: Eddie Levert; Walter Williams; William Powell; Bobby Massey; Bill Isles.

Career: Originally doo-wop outfit formed at High School in Canton, Ohio. Quintet first recorded together as the Mascots in 1958; around 1962 they changed name to the O'Jays after Cleveland radio DJ Eddie O'Jay.
During early '60s they recorded for variety of labels with only sporadic success, and Isles left group in 1966. In late '60s group fared little better, but signed with independent Gamble-Huff Productions in 1968. Minor hits on Gamble-Huff's Neptune label included **One Night Affair** and **Looky Looky**, but label folded leaving O'Jays in limbo.

My Favorite Person, The O'Jays. Courtesy Philly Intl. Records.

In 1971 Bobby Massey left to concentrate on record production, and a year later remaining trio signed with Gamble and Huff's new operation, Philadelphia International Records. Things then started to look up for group. First album, **O'Jays In Philadelphia,** created some interest, but second LP **Backstabbers**, finally pulled it all together for them. Distinctive vocalising and excellent writing and production by Gamble and Huff provided slew of hits from album.
1974 album **Ship Ahoy** featured extended titletrack and lyrics concerned with ecological/political matters. Albums since then have further reflected humanitarian concerns, sometimes ad nauseam. In 1975 illness forced William Powell into retirement, to be replaced by former member of Little Anthony and the Imperials, Sammy Strain.
Excellent albums like **The Year 2000** and continuing ability to come up with hit singles seem likely to ensure further success of group. Practically a black music institution, the O'Jays at their best are equal to any outfit of their type.

Current line-up: Levert; Williams; Sammy Strain.

Hit Singles: US UK
Backstabbers, 1972 3 14
Love Train, 1973 1 9
Put Your Hands Together, 1974 10 —
For The Love Of Money, 1974 9 —
I Love Music, 1976 5 13
Livin' For The Weekend, 1976 20 —
Used Ta Be My Girl, 1978 4 12

Albums:
Greatest Hits (Liberty/—), 1970
Backstabbers (Philly Intl.), 1973

Ship Ahoy (Philly Intl.), 1974
Peace (—/Phoenix), 1975
Family Reunion (Philly Intl.), 1976
Message In The Music (Philly Intl.), 1976
Travellin' At The Speed Of Thought (Philly Intl.), 1976
Collector's Items: Greatest Hits (Philly Intl.) 1978
So Full Of Love (Philly Intl.), 1978
Identify Yourself (Philly Intl.), 1979
The Year 2000 (Philly Intl.), 1980
My Favorite Person (Philly Intl.), 1982

The Oak Ridge Boys

US vocal group formed 1957.

Career: In 1964, baritone Bill Golden joined original Oak Ridge Boys, a white gospel outfit formed by Smitty Gatlin. Personnel changes in '60s and early '70s resulted in current line-up of Golden, lead vocalist Duane Allen, tenor Joe Bonsall and bass Richard Sterban (former member of Presley backing group Stamp Quartet).

Group became leading purveyors of gospel and in mid-'70s began to move into country cross-over area. Result was string of country hit singles and considerable album success. At same time, group built up excellent reputation as live act, helped by superb Oak Ridge Band. On record they use top Nashville musicians such as Kenny Buttrey and Weldon Myrick.

Although none of the singers (except possibly bass Sterban) has outstanding solo voices, their rich and immaculate harmony work is musically arresting. Despite recent increasing pop success, boys still have large country following. Professionalism and ear for good song seem likely to ensure longevity of already well-established act.

Current line-up: Bill Golden; Duane Allen; Joe Bonsall; Richard Sterban.

Hit Singles:

	US	UK
Elvira, 1981	5	—
Bobbie Sue, 1982	12	—

Albums (selected):
Best Of (Columbia/—), 1970
Y'All Come Back Saloon (MCA), 1978
Room Service (MCA), 1978
Have Arrived (MCA), 1979
Together (MCA), 1980
Fancy Free (MCA), 1981
All Our Favourite Songs (Columbia/—), 1982
Bobbie Sue (MCA), 1982
Christmas (MCA), 1982

Phil Ochs

US vocalist, guitarist, composer.
Born El Paso, Texas, December 19, 1940; died April 8, 1976.

Career: Having studied journalism at Ohio State University, Ochs graduated to singing the news. He performed with pop group the Sundowners in Ohio clubs, but success of first song **The Cuban Invasion** in 1962 encouraged him to continue writing protest songs based on current events. In 1962-3 was considered Dylan's(▶) major rival on US folk scene. Helped by Bob Gibson (who also championed Joan Baez(▶)), Ochs moved to New York. After publishing in 'Broadside', singing in Greenwich Village folk clubs and performing at Newport Folk Festival, he recorded **All The News That's Fit To Sing** (1964). Album, which made charts, included

Talking Vietnam and **Talking Cuban Crisis**, plus songs about death of submarine crew and murders of civil rights worker Medger Evers and New York youth worker Lou Marsh.

Moralising was sometimes heavy-handed, but wit, satire and theatricality in lyrics (and in live performance style) lifted Ochs above ordinary protest singers and into charts, despite being blacklisted by most US radio and TV stations. On second LP, he set to music Alfred Noyes' poem 'The Highwayman', and began adding lyrical songs to repertoire. **There But For Fortune** became hit for Joan Baez in 1965. Recognising need to sing for, not just about, the people, Ochs defended Dylan's(▶) use of amplification. Later albums became more poetic, personal and disillusioned, had jazz and rock backings and were less successful. Articles, poems and songs by Ochs, plus an interview with him, were published in 'The War Is Over' (1968).

Desperate search for musical and personal identity culminated with **Phil Ochs Greatest Hits** in 1970, an ironically titled album of new songs featuring jacket photo of Ochs wearing glittering gold suit and clutching electric guitar à la Presley(▶) Eclectic to say the least, album had country cuts, pop and rock tracks, satirical songs and orchestrated ballads. 'God help the troubadour who tries to be a star', he sang in **Chords Of Fame**. At Carnegie Hall concert that year (recorded, but album never released), Ochs said 'What America needs is

Chords Of Fame, Phil Ochs. Courtesy A&M Records.

for Elvis Presley to become Che Guevara'. On April 8, 1976, Phil Ochs committed suicide. A commemorative double album was issued later that year.

Albums:
All The News That's Fit To Sing (Elektra/—), 1964
I Ain't Marching Anymore (Elektra/—), 1965
In Concert (Elektra/—), 1966
Pleasure Of The Harbour (A&M), 1967
Tape From California (A&M), 1968
Greatest Hits (A&M), 1970
Chords Of Fame (A&M), 1974
Greatest Hits (A&M), 1981
Songs For Broadside #10 (Folkways/—), 1976

Mike Oldfield

UK composer, multi-instrumentalist.
Born Reading, Berkshire, May 15, 1953.

Career: Started at age 14 in folk duo with sister Sally. Released acoustic **Sallyangie** in 1968 on Transatlantic. After forming short-lived Barefeet, joined Kevin Ayers and the Whole World as bassist/guitarist in 1970-71.

Above: The Oak Ridge Boys, wearing jackets no doubt designed by Nudie.

Composed 50-minute demo, which was rejected by most major companies. Work was eventually chosen to launch Richard Branson's new label, Virgin. Oldfield overdubbed all the instruments in the studio, creating collage of melodies and instrumental lines that formed basis of **Tubular Bells**, released in May 1973. Album was critically acclaimed and sold in extraordinary quantities, much to amazement of the rock business. US success was assured when **Tubular Bells** was chosen as theme for film 'The Exorcist'.

The less instantly appealing **Hergest Ridge** covered similar ground. Oldfield received critical backlash but survivied intact to produce best-selling **Ommadawn**, a more ambitious work incorporating African drums and Celtic pipes.

Friendship with avant-garde composer David Bedford, from Kevin Ayers days, led to work on **The Orchestrated Tubular Bells** with Royal Philharmonic Orchestra. In addition, Virgin released four-album set **Boxed**,

Below: A smouldering stare from Mike Oldfield.

which included all previous work, plus **Collaborations**. Meanwhile, Oldfield spent three years preparing **Incantations**, his most epic project to date.

Moving to London in '78, began experimenting with dance music, producing single **Guilty** with a New York rhythm section. First-ever tour followed, backed by 50 musicians, including string players and choir. Music was accompanied by set of films by Ian Eames; live double LP **Exposed** was culled from shows.

1980's **Platinum** was lighter work than its predecessors and included punk-rock parody **Punkadiddle**, juxtaposed alongside an Irish gig. To promote **Platinum**, Oldfield Music was formed; British debut (July '81) was followed by extensive European tour. New work, **QE2**, quickly followed and immediately went gold. World sales of **Tubular Bells** hit 10 million in 1981 and Oldfield was awarded The Freedom Of The City Of London in recognition of sales to exports and charity works. Further distinction came when he was entered in 'Who's Who', the only rock musician, bar McCartney(▶), to achieve recognition there. May 1982 saw formation of the Mike Oldfield Group (Maggie Reilly, vocals; Morris Pert, percussion/keyboards; Rick Fern, bass; Tim Cross, keyboards; and Pierre Moelen, drums). Eighth album **Five Miles Out** ended decade of extraordinary sales. In spite of criticism from mainstream rock press, Oldfield's popularity has never seriously waned, and seems likely to continue for many years, despite fluctuating 'live' audience.

Hit Singles:	US	UK
In Dulce Jubilo/On Horseback, 1975	—	4
Portsmouth, 1976	—	3
Blue Peter, 1979	—	19
Moonlight Shadow, 1983*	—	4

*with Maggie Reilly

Albums:
Tubular Bells (Virgin), 1973
Hergest Ridge (Virgin), 1974
Ommadawn (Virgin), 1975
The Orchestrated Tubular Bells (Virgin), 1975
Boxed (Virgin), 1975
Incantations (Virgin), 1978
Exposed (Virgin), 1979
Platinum (Virgin), 1980
QE2 (Virgin), 1980
Five Miles Out (Virgin), 1982
Crises (Virgin), 1983

Worth Searching Out:
Sallyangie (—/Transatlantic), 1968

Yoko Ono
Japanese vocalist.
Born Tokyo, February 18, 1933.

Career: Brought up in wealthy Japanese family, at 14 Yoko Ono moved to New York where in early '60s she became major figure on avant-garde art scene as poet, film-maker and conceptual artist.

But for her relationship with John Lennon(▶), her contribution to rock music would be regarded as minimal. However, there is no doubt that she provided a guiding force for him during their somewhat tempestuous time together.

Yoko Ono was married with a small child, Kyoko, when she met Lennon at one of her art exhibition 'happenings' in New York in 1968. After each divorced, they were married in Gibraltar on March 20, 1969, Lennon later changing his middle name from Winston to Ono.

Inseparable from Lennon, Ono appeared in 'Let It Be' movie and became constant source

of irritation to the Beatles(▶) final days of group.

Adopting image of being the ultimate couple, united in everything — dress, hairstyle, etc. — and never being photographed alone, they espoused cause of world peace and undertook series of bizarre stunts, appearing nude on album sleeve, and spending week in bed together at Amsterdam hotel.

When Lennon formed loose-knit Plastic Ono Band in 1969, Ono was constant member of its ever changing line-up, though her contribution was limited to coming out on stage in a plastic bag, from the depths of which she would emit series of highly unmusical grunts and squeals. Lennon's **Sometime In New York City** album featured one side recorded live by Plastic Ono Band at UNICEF Peace For Christmas concert held at London's Lyceum Ballroom, while ever-loving Lennon reckoned her composition **Don't Worry Kyoko (Mummy's Only Looking For A Hand In The Snow)** to be best rock 'n' roll song of all time!

In 1970, she published book of poems under title 'Grapefruit', and her movies 'Apotheosis' and 'Fly' were chosen for avant-garde section of 1972 Cannes Film Festival.

All the 'true-love' overkill took its toll; John and Yoko broke up for a year in 1974, although they were eventually reconciled and she presented him with a son. Their domestic bliss was ended when Lennon was assassinated in 1980 outside their New York apartment block.

Yoko Ono's spiritual influence on Lennon's work after they met is obvious. It was she who introduced him to both free-form jazz and the experimental use of electronics.

Since Lennon's death, she has played no real role in rock scene though she continues to command newspaper headlines.

Albums:
Season Of Glass (Geffen), 1981
It's Alright (Polydor), 1982

Roy Orbison
US vocalist, composer, guitarist.
Born Vernon, Texas, April 23, 1936.

Career: Formed first group, the Wink Westerners, at 13. Appeared on local radio talent shows, then formed the Teen Kings while at North Texas State University. First recordings made (after encouragement from college friend Pat Boone) at Norman Petty's Clovis, New Mexico, studio in 1955, including first version of **Ooby Dooby** released on Jewel. During 1956 recorded for Sun in Memphis; re-recording of **Ooby Dooby** reached lower part of US charts. Although regarded as classic rockabilly, Orbison's voice is better suited to ballads and much of later Sun material was weak by comparison.

Encouraged by some success as songwriter, mostly stemming from Everly Brothers'(▶) version of **Claudette**, Orbison moved to Nashville and signed with RCA. Two singles failed to make impression and in 1959 signed with Monument Records, beginning long partnership with producer Fred Foster. Although first two releases were not hits, Orbison and Foster found right formula with **Only The Lonely** in summer 1960; many hits followed in similar style.

Orbison's records are characterised by romantic themes and vocal crescendos, making best use of distinctive voice. Dramatic stage performer despite lack of movement and tendency towards shyness, emphasised by dark glasses. Personal life marked by tragedy of wife Claudette's death in motorcycle accident (1966) and death of two sons

in house fire (1968).

Popularity in US not maintained at quite the same level as in UK, but Orbison remains great performer, still touring to capacity audiences. Most recent album for Elektra failed to match earlier material, although duet single with Emmylou Harris(▶), **That Loving You Feeling**, was moderate success in 1980.

Hit Singles:	US	UK
Only The Lonely, 1960	2	1
Blue Angel, 1960	9	11
Running Scared, 1961	1	9
Crying, 1961	2	25
Dream Baby, 1962	4	2
In Dreams, 1963	7	6
Falling, 1963	22	9
Blue Bayou/Mean Woman Blues, 1963	29	3
Pretty Paper, 1963	15	6
Mean Woman Blues/Blue Bayou, 1963	5	3
Borne On The Wind, 1964	—	15
It's Over, 1964	9	1
Oh Pretty Woman, 1964	1	1
Goodnight, 1965	21	14
Crawlin' Back, 1965	46	19
Lana, 1966	—	15
Too Soon To Know, 1966	—	3
There Won't Be Many Coming Home, 1966	—	18

Albums:
Greatest Hits (Monument), 1972
All-Time Greatest Hits (Monument), 1973
The Big O (Charly), 1975
At The Rockhouse (Charly), 1980
Golden Days (Monument), 1981

Below: Roy Orbison, always capable of thrilling live audiences despite apparent shyness.

OMD (Orchestral Manoeuvres In The Dark)
UK group formed 1978.

Original line-up: Paul Humphreys and Andy McCluskey, various electronic instruments, vocals.

Career: Humphreys and McCluskey, both from Merseyside, formed first band, VCL XI, in 1976, when pair were 16. Interest stimulated by early German synthesiser bands like Kraftwerk(▶). Group never got beyond rehearsals, but duo joined Hitlers Underpantz, described as 'an assortment of musicians into doing things differently', although this band was no more successful than VCL XI. By end of 1977, duo became nucleus of the Id, an eight-piece band which soon folded.

In 1978, Humphreys and McCluskey adopted name of Orchestral Manoeuvres In The Dark (later abbreviated to OMD), using backing tapes played on tape recorder known as 'Winston'. Played debut gig in this formation at end of 1978 at 'Eric's' in Liverpool, then approached trendy independent label Factory Records of Manchester, who released single of **Electricity** as limited edition in June 1979. Signed by Virgin records subsidiary Dindisc, supported Gary Numan(▶) on UK tour. With proceeds built own recording studio, where they cut first LP, **Orchestral Manoeuvres In The Dark** (1980). After 'retiring' 'Winston', expanded line-up by adding drummer Malcolm Holmes (ex-the Id) and David Hughes (ex-Dalek I) on bass and keyboards.

1980 saw two minor hit singles followed by first Top 10 single **Enola Gay** (titled after

name of plane which dropped first atom bomb) from second LP **Organisation**. Hughes left during year, replaced by multi-instrumentalist (keyboards, saxophone) Martin Cooper. 1981 was big year for band — two Top 5 singles plus Top 3 LP, **Architecture And Morality**. Impetus continued into early 1982 with another Top 5 single. Rest of year spent recording fourth LP **Dazzle Ships**, which was less well received than earlier work; it seemed needlessly self-indulgent, although it contained another hit single, **Genetic Engineering**. OMD's main early strength was in catchy quality of their songs — later fame and consequent lack of urgency have produced loss of direct approach, and current records are cluttered with unnecessary effects (eg radio signals). However, lack of appreciation may hopefully force reversion to original style.

Current line-up: Humphreys; McCluskey; Martin Cooper, keyboards; Malcolm Holmes, drums.

Hit Singles:	US	UK
Enola Gay, 1980	—	8
Souvenirs, 1981	—	3
Joan Of Arc, 1981	—	5
Maid Of Orleans, 1982	—	4
Genetic Engineering, 1983	—	20

Albums:
Orchestral Manoeuvres In The Dark (—/Virgin), 1980
Organisation (—/Virgin), 1980
Architecture And Morality (Virgin-Epic/Virgin), 1981
Dazzle Ships (Virgin-Epic/Virgin), 1983

Orleans

US group fromed 1972.

Original line-up: Larry Hoppen, guitar; Wells Kelly, drums, keyboards; John Hall, guitar.

Career: Hoppen and Wells started in Ithica, New York, band called Boffalongo. In January 1972 they joined with Hall and formed Orleans. In November Lance Hoppen came in as bass player.

Became concert favourites in north-east. ABC release **Orleans** in 1973 won them further popularity.

In 1975 Asylum released **Let There Be Music** which produced major hit **Dance With Me** — as slick and smooth as any record from LA. 1976 saw addition of second drummer, Jerry Marotta, and **Still The One** single became million-seller.

Marotta and Hall left in 1977. Bob Leinback, who had been in Boffalongo with

Above: Orchestral Manoeuvres In The Dark, who shortened name to OMD.

Hoppen and Wells, joined on keyboards while R. A. Martin was recruited to play horns. This line-up released **Forever**. Orleans' music sounded innocuous to rock fans but struck a chord as band maintained strong AOR status throughout '70s.

John Hall left in 1977 and formed John Hall Band, which has been quite successful in early '80s in US.

Current line-up: Kelly; Larry Hoppen; Lance Hoppen, bass; Bob Leinback, keyboards; R. A. Martin, horns.

Hit Singles:	US	UK
Dance With Me, 1975	6	—
Still The One, 1976	5	—
Love Takes Time, 1979	11	—

Albums:
Orleans (ABC), 1973
Let There Be Music (Asylum), 1975
Before The Dance (ABC), 1977
Forever (Infinity), 1979
One Of A Kind (Radio/—), 1982

Ozzy Osbourne

UK vocalist.
Born John Osbourne, Birmingham, December 3, 1948.

Career: Ozzy Osbourne first won acclaim as Black Sabbath(▶) vocalist. Following departure in 1978 (under unpleasant terms) Sabbath fans have been delighted with both sides trying to outdo each other professionally.

Formed permanent band called Blizzard of Ozz; signed to Jet on strength of past history. Strong debut album released in 1980 featured Lee Kerslake (ex-Uriah Heep(▶)) on drums, Bob Daisley on bass and Randy Rhoads on guitar; **Blizzard Of Ozz** showed Osbourne had no intention of avoiding confrontation with old mates. **Ozz** featured same hard rock approach of Sabbath and provided impetus for that band to re-form and work again.

Diary Of A Madman indicated Ozzy and Rhoads had special talent for creating exciting, riveting heavy metal. But just as it seemed as if Ozzy would leave Sabbath in the dust, his luck turned sour. Publicity stunt of biting the head of a dead bat thrown on stage backfired when Ozzy had to undergo painful rabies inoculations. Worse, Randy Rhoads was killed in freak airplane accident and Blizzard of Ozz crumbled around Osbourne. Kerslake and Daisley went to Uriah Heep.

Refusing to give in, Ozzy recruited Brad

Gillis, guitar; Rudi Sarzo, bass; and Tommy Aldridge, drums. This line-up recorded blistering double live set **Talk of the Devil**, which included versions of early Sabbath material. These tracks in particular seemed to blow out Sabbath's recent live versions of same songs.

No publicist could have dreamed up a better idea. As Ozzy and Sabbath duel it out, fans are treated to a dazzling array of new, stronger recordings from both camps. Waiting for next development in this musical struggle is almost as exciting as waiting for Star Wars saga to unfold.

Albums:
Blizzard Of Ozz (Jet), 1980
Diary Of A Madman (Jet), 1981
Talk Of The Devil (Jet), 1982

The Osmonds

US vocal group formed 1960.

Original line-up: Alan Osmond; Wayne Osmond; Merrill Osmond; Jay Osmond.

Career: Encouraged by parents, brothers were taught to sing and play several instruments. They first started performing at various Mormon Church functions. Professional career started with residency at Disneyland. Walt Disney TV show led to regular spot on Andy Williams show where they were mainly featured doing barber shop quartet type numbers, which lasted from 1962 to 1966. That year group became regulars on Jerry Lewis Show, and younger brother Donny (then nine) joined group. Further TV work and worldwide touring followed.

In 1970 brothers signed with MGM, and following year scored US No. 1 with **One Bad Apple**. Record initiated string of hits (mainly cover versions) that lasted into mid-'70s, and elevation of group into 'teenybopper sensation' worldwide.

Success of group also spawned solo careers for Donny, younger brother Jimmy and sister Marie, as well as launching Donny and Marie as duo.

At best group were pale imitation of Jackson Five, although professionalism and polish could not be denied. Religious background ensured clean-living image, and in many quarters Osmonds became byword for safe, slick, showbiz approach to rock and pop.

Towards end of '70s appeal faded, and members pursued different career directions with varied success, Donny and Marie being the most successful with own TV show in late '70s. Jimmy has acted in films and TV, most recently seen on 'Fame' series.

Final line-up: Alan; Wayne; Merrill; Jay; Donny Osmond; Jimmy Osmond.

Below: The seven hitmakers of the Osmond Family, Donny fifth from left.

Hit Singles:	US	UK
One Bad Apple, 1971	1	43
Double Lovin', 1971	14	—
Yo-Yo, 1971	3	—
Down By The Lazy River, 1972	4	40
Hold Her Tight, 1972	14	—
Crazy Horses, 1972	14	2
Going Home, 1973	36	4
Let Me In, 1973	36	2
I Can't Stop, 1974	—	12
Love Me For A Reason, 1974	10	1
The Proud One, 1975	22	5
Donny Osmond Solo:		
Sweet And Innocent, 1971	7	—
Go Away Little Girl, 1971	1	—
Hey Girl, 1971	9	—
Puppy Love, 1972	3	1
Too Young, 1972	13	5
Why, 1972	13	3
Twelfth Of Never, 1973	8	1
Young Love, 1973	23	1
When I Fall In Love, 1973	14	4
Are You Lonesome Tonight, 1974	14	—
Where Did All The Good Times Go, 1974	—	18
Marie Osmond:		
Paper Roses, 1973	5	2
Donny And Marie Osmond:		
I'm Leaving It All Up To You, 1974	4	2
Morning Side Of The Mountain, 1974	8	5
Make The World Go Away, 1975	44	18
Deep Purple, 1976	14	25
Little Jimmy Osmond Solo:		
Long-Haired Lover From Liverpool, 1972	38	1
Tweedle Dee, 1973	59	4
I'm Gonna Knock On Your Door, 1974	—	11

Albums:
Our Best To You (MGM), 1974
Christmas Album (Polydor), 1976
Greatest Hits (Polydor), 1978

Donny Osmond Solo:
Donald Clark Osmond (Polydor), 1977

Marie Osmond Solo:
This Is The Way That I Feel (Polydor), 1977

Donny And Marie Osmond:
Growin' Coconuts (MGM), 1974
Deep Purple (Polydor), 1976
Winning Combination (Polydor), 1978

Johnny Otis

US vocalist, composer, multi-instrumentalist.
Born Johnny Veliotes, Vellejo, California, December 28, 1921.

Career: It may be paradoxical that a white man, son of Greek immigrant parents, should be known as 'The Godfather of Rhythm and Blues', but facts dictate that Johnny Otis is

eminently worthy of the accolade. Inspired by big band jazz of Count Basie and Ellington, Otis learned to play drums then moved on to piano and vibes. Played in bands with Harlan Leonard and Count Matthews. By mid-1940s had own band; scored hit with **Harlem Nocturne** on Excelsior in 1946. After spell touring, settled down in Los Angeles to open Barrelhouse Club in 1948, partnered by late Bardu Ali. Venue featured local R&B acts and Johnny proved to have ear for talent, discovering the Robins and Little Esther (Phillips).

By 1950 Otis and protegés were scoring numerous hits on Savoy. Early '50s saw him form touring Revue of R&B talent; he also found time to produce hits for Johnny Ace and Little Richard(▶) on Duke/Peacock Records in Houston, Texas. Travels took him to Detroit, where he spotted emergent singers Jackie Wilson(▶) ,Willie John and Hank Ballard.

Revue began recording for Capitol as rock 'n' roll years arrived. **Willie And The Hand Jive** was Top 10 smash for Otis in 1958. **Ma (He's Making Eyes At Me)** became popular for Marie Adams with the Revue. Further hits followed on Capitol for couple of years before Johnny moved to King; results were uninspiring and unsuccessful, so took break from performing.

Next Otis records were not until 1969; fine blues-based **Cold Shot** LP on Kent yielded R&B hit **Country Girl**. Featured his son Shuggie on guitar along with newer talents Delmar Evans and Gene Connors. Otis Band also connected with **Snatch And The Poontangs**, a risqué LP on Kent!

Success prompted Johnny to organise Revue to play 1970 Monterey Jazz Festival; featured veteran R&B giants Joe Turner, Little Esther and Roy Brown, among others. Show was committed to disc by Epic; label also signed Otis to contract. **The Watts Breakaway** appeared on Okeh.

In 1974 Otis launched own blues spectrum label, re-recording R&B greats like Charles Brown, Joe Turner, Pee Wee Clayton and Joe Liggins with his own combo, though not always with memorable results. After lull in activity, returned to disc with fresh Johnny Otis Show on Alligator in 1982.

Hit Singles:	US	UK
Ma He's Making Eyes At Me, 1957	—	2
Bye Bye Baby, 1958	—	20
Willie And The Hand Jive, 1958	9	—

Albums:
Original Show (Savoy), 1972
Original Show Volume 2 (Savoy/—), 1974
Johnny Otis (—/Bulldog), 1975
Rock 'n' Roll Hit Parade (—/Flyright), 1979

The Outlaws

US group formed mid-'70s.

Original line-up: Hughie Thomasson, guitar, vocals; Billy Jones, guitar, vocals; Henry Paul, guitar; Monto Yoho, drums; Frank O'Keefe, bass.

Career: Band began as bar group in Tampa, Florida. Allman Brothers(▶) and new Lynyrd Skynyrd(▶) had opened up market for southern rock. From the start Outlaws pushed image of stetsons and dual lead guitars. Harder edge meant band was acceptable to mainstream rock audience. Country influence and western clothes also made band accessible to mellower followers of Eagles(▶) and Southern California rock.

Excellent material such as **High Tides And Green Grass** and opening for acts such as the Who(▶) and Rolling Stones(▶) seemed to indicate bright future for Outlaws. Instead,

Above: Country rockers the Outlaws, popular despite lack of hit singles.

band began cranking out albums indistinguishable from each other. 1979 saw major overhaul as Yoho and O'Keefe left. David Dix became new drummer while Rick Cua joined on bass. Band expanded to three lead guitarists by adding Freddie Salem. These changes, however, placed Outlaws firmly in category of faceless US corporate rock.

Faithful following seems to keep Outlaws going but time seems past for band to have any major influence. Highest chart position achieved was No. 31 in 1981 with **(Ghost) Riders In The Sky.**

Current line-up: Thomasson; Freddie Salem, guitar, vocals; David Dix, drums; Rick Cua, bass.

Albums:
The Outlaws (Arista), 1975
Lady In Waiting (Arista), 1976
Hurry Sundown (Arista), 1977
Bring It Back Alive (Arista), 1977
Playin' To Win (Arista), 1978
In The Eye Of The Storm (Arista), 1979
Ghost Riders In The Sky (Arista), 1980
Wanted (Arista), 1981
Los Hombres Malo (Arista), 1982
Greatest Hits (Arista), 1982

Pablo Cruise

US group formed 1973.

Original line-up: Cory Lerios, keyboards, vocals; David Jenkins, guitar, vocals; Steve Price, drums, vocals; Bud Cockrell, bass, vocals.

Career: Cockrell (ex-It's A Beautiful Day) and Lerios (ex-Stoneground) formed Pablo Cruise with definite ideas about multi-textured, lush sound first explored in Beautiful Day. Band earned derisive moniker of 'Pablum Cruise' in hard rock set but struck chord with growing audience for Southern California 'mellow-rock'.

Band has placed some singles in US Top 40 (**Love Will Find A Way, Cool Love**) and does well on US AOR radio. Albums continue to sell quiet, easy-listening sound. Founding member Cockrell left during **Reflector** LP (replaced by John Pierce) but band continued with effortless approach to music.

Current line-up: Lerios; Jenkins; Price; John Pierce, bass, vocals; Angelo Rossi, guitars, vocals.

Albums:
Pablo Cruise (A&M), 1975
Lifeline (A&M), 1976
A Place In The Sun (A&M), 1977
Worlds Away (A&M), 1978
Parts Of The Game (A&M), 1979
Reflector (A&M), 1981

Robert Palmer

UK vocalist, composer, guitarist.
Born Batley, Yorkshire, January 19, 1949.

Career: Developed taste for American R&B as teenager; first band (at 15) was Mandrakes. After year working as graphic designer Palmer decided to go for musical career. In 1968 he took vocalist job with Alan Brown Set; next year he moved on to group DaDa, which provided his first visit to US. DaDa eventually transformed into Vinegar Joe for whom he played rhythm guitar and shared vocals with Elkie Brooks. By 1974 Palmer and Brooks were off on solo careers.

Palmer approached Chris Blackwell (Island Records) with some of his demos and Blackwell immediately packed him off to New Orleans and New York to record first LP. **Sneakin' Sally Thru The Alley** was released in September 1974 and won Palmer enough US audience support to convince him to move to America. (In 1976 he transferred to Nassau.)

Pressure Drop was released little over a year later and was lead-in to Palmer's first US nationwide tour. True US success came in 1978-79 when singles **Every Kinda People** (from **Double Fun**) and **Bad Case Of Lovin' You** (from **Secrets**) won approval of national audience.

Palmer expanded his activities in 1980 by doing some production work. This apparently reduced his own output because only two albums have appeared since.

Palmer has so closely copied his US influences that many fans assume he is Philadelphia blue-eyed soul; his albums are ultimately frustrating, however, because for every soulful classic there is another track which seems half-finished. His sound and LP covers project slick, almost dilettante, life style. Like any proper playboy, Palmer doesn't want to push himself too hard and every LP has air of casual under-achievement.

Hit Singles:	US	UK
Every Kinda People, 1978	16	53
Bad Case Of Lovin' You (Doctor, Doctor), 1979	14	—
Some Guys Have All The Luck, 1982	—	16

Albums:
Sneakin' Sally Thru The Alley (Island), 1974
Pressure Drop (Island), 1975
Some People Can Do What They Like (Island), 1976
Double Trouble (Island), 1978
Secrets (Island), 1979
Clues (Island), 1980
Maybe It's Alive (Island), 1982
Pride (Island), 1983

Graham Parker

UK vocalist, composer, guitarist.
Born London, 1950.

Career: Began playing in groups as early as 13 (the Deepcut Three). Formed mod-combo The Way Out in 1965. Played Camberley (Surrey) youth clubs until leaving school. Then quit music for a couple of years and worked in Animal Research Institute. Moved to Guernsey; began taking acid and playing acoustic guitar in imitation of the Incredible String Band. Returned home, then travelled to Morocco and Gibraltar, where he formed folk/R&B unit specialising in 'space rock'.

Returned to England in 1971. Signed publishing deal with Stuart Johnson and eventually met Dave Robinson, now head of Stiff Records (then operating Hope & Anchor Studio), who arranged some demos backed by assorted pub rockers; Brinsley Schwarz (guitar/keyboards/saxophone), Bob Andrews (keyboards), Martin Belmont (guitar), Andrew Bodner (bass) and Stephen Goulding (drums). As the Rumour, they subsequently became Parker's backing band.

Radio plug for **Between You And Me** caught attention of Phonogram A&R man Nigel Grainge, who signed them. With Nick Lowe(▶) as producer, **Howlin' Wind** (released in April 1976) was greeted with rapturous applause by music press. Reviews compared Parker style with Morrison, Springsteen and Dylan, and suggested he was potentially the most impressive British R&B vocalist to emerge in years.

Second album **Heat Treatment** (1977) was highly regarded as one of year's finest. Heavily R&B influenced, it indicated that Parker was no hype but a solid, durable vocalist. While punk rock reached its peak, Parker continued to rely on old-style blue-eyed R&B, but played with a passion and energy seldom seen in the repertoire of his more illustrious predecessors. His next two LPs, **Stick To Me** and **The Parkerilla**, both climbed into the Top 20 of UK album charts, though they lacked quality of previous works, and sold mainly on strength of acclaimed live performances.

Always a major live attraction, Parker's subsequent recordings failed to produce the excitement and high standard of his early work. After signing to RCA, **Another Grey Area** (1982) consolidated his position as one of Britain's foremost R&B vocalists, but failed to indicate any real possibility of major commercial breakthrough in '80s.

Graham Parker's Heat Treatment. Courtesy Vertigo Records.

Albums:
Howlin' Wind (Mercury/Vertigo), 1976
Heat Treatment (Mercury/Vertigo), 1976
Stick To Me (Mercury/Vertigo), 1977
The Parkerilla (Mercury/Vertigo), 1978
Squeezing Out Sparks (Arista/Vertigo), 1979
The Up Escalator (Arista/Stiff), 1980
Another Grey Area (RCA), 1982

Alan Parsons Project

UK group formed 1975.

Original/current line-up: Alan Parsons, guitars, keyboards, vocals, producer, engineer; Eric Woolfson, keyboards.

Career: Parsons was assistant engineer at EMI studios in 1968 when he worked on Beatles' **Abbey Road(▶)**. His involvement impressed Paul McCartney(▶) who used him to engineer several Wings LPs. Parsons also engineered various albums for the Hollies(▶) as well as Pink Floyds'(▶) **Dark Side Of The Moon.** Turning from engineering to production, cut Cockney Rebel, Pilot, and Al Stewart(▶).

Woolfson also worked at Abbey Road Studios where he met Parsons and together they began plans to create own music. Woolfson's previous experience had been as writer; became Project's idea man.

Woolfson's first idea seemed to borrow from Rick Wakeman(▶) who had begun electronic symphonic album concept in 1972 with **Six Wives Of Henry VIII.** Woolfson turned his attention to writing mood pieces to describe stories of Edgar Allen Poe. **Tales Of Mystery And Imagination** appeared in 1975 with highly innovative packaging scheme which almost caused music within to be overlooked.

Science fiction was motif of **I Robot** LP, while **Pyramid** was based on then popular pyramid power cult. **Eve** looked at relations with women, and bears close hearing as well as close look at surprising cover. **The Turn Of A Friendly Card** dealt with gaming and the role of fate in modern society. **Eye In The Sky** continued the concern with modern high-tech society by dealing with 1984 surveillance concepts.

Despite impeccable production and multi-talented session men, Project LPs tend to

Above: Alan Parsons (right) engineer of the Beatles' Abbey Road album.

grate after repeated listenings. In spite of this drawback, any new Project LP is worth at least an initial listen to see where Parsons and Woolfson's remarkable imaginations have travelled.

Hit Single:

	US	UK
Eye In The Sky, 1982	3	—

Albums:
Tales Of Mystery And Imagination (20th Century/Arista), 1975
I Robot (Arista), 1977
Pyramid (Arista), 1978
Eve (Arista), 1979

The Turn Of A Friendly Card (Arista), 1980
Eye In The Sky (Arista), 1982

Dolly Parton

US vocalist, guitarist, composer.
Born Locust Ridge, Tennessee, January 19, 1946.

Career: Born into large, poor rural family, showed early interest in music-making. Appeared on Grand Ole Opry at age 12; moved to Nashville after leaving high school at 18.

Contract with Monument Records led to little success, but break came when Parton formed partnership with country superstar Porter Wagoner in 1967. She became integral part of Wagoner's live show, and also recorded and made TV appearances with him. Under Wagoner's aegis Parton developed vivid 'blonde bombshell' persona that was to become her stock-in-trade.

In 1973 Parton left Wagoner show, although he continued to produce her solo records. In 1976 she split from Wagoner altogether, having signed contract with Los Angeles-based management company. In meantime, solo career began to take off, helped by endorsement of other female artists like Linda Ronstadt(▶), Emmylou Harris(▶) and Maria Muldaur(▶). (All three recorded Parton compositions on albums.)

Seeking to broaden appeal, Parton moved into rock territory with **New Harvest — First Gathering** in 1977. Featuring numbers like **My Girl** and **Higher And Higher**, album alienated country stalwarts but gained artist many new fans. Audience-widening process bore fruit when Parton scored platinum album with **Here You Come Again** in 1978. Elaborate West Coast production was far removed from country roots.

By beginning of '80s Parton had achieved dream of all-round stardom, with major role in

successful movie '9 to 5' (self-penned title song from film was US No. 1), string of awards, and ability to draw capacity crowds at virtually any type of venue. A chat-show favourite, Parton showed that lively and witty intelligence lurked beneath spectacular Mae-West-meets-Barbie-Doll appearance.

Movie 'Best Little Whorehouse In Texas' (co-starring Burt Reynolds) provided further vehicle for Parton's acting talent, and it seems likely that movies and music will vie for her attention in future (although throat trouble diagnosed in spring '83 was causing concern). Country aficionados and many critics rate early RCA recordings as her most appealing work. Both 'Best Of' compilations are of highest quality and show Parton's clear, distinctive voice to excellent effect.

Above: The diverse Dolly Parton, country/pop singer, TV/film actress.

Hit Singles:

	US	UK
Jolene, 1976	60	7
Here You Come Again, 1978	3	—
Two Doors Down, 1978	19	—
9 to 5, 1980	1	46

Albums (selected):
Best Of (with Porter Wagoner) (RCA), 1969
Best Of (RCA), 1970
My Tennessee Mountain Home (RCA), 1973
Jolene (RCA), 1974
Best Of Volume 2 (RCA), 1975
Love Is Like A Butterfly (RCA), 1975
Bargain Store (RCA), 1975
New Harvest—First Gathering (RCA), 1977
Here You Come Again (RCA), 1978
Both Sides Of (—/Lotus), 1979
The Dolly Parton Collection (Monument), 1980
9 to 5 And Odd Jobs (RA), 1981
The Very Best Of (RCA), 1981
Greatest Hits (RCA), 1982
Heartbreak Express (RCA), 1982

Les Paul

US guitarist, vocalist.
Born Lester Polfuss, Waukesha, Wisconsin, June 9, 1923.

Career: Best remembered as creator of Gibson Les Paul model guitar, beloved of many musicians, which he developed in 1941 while in hospital recovering from car crash.

After apprenticeship playing hillbilly, then jazz, Paul formed first Les Paul Trio in late '30s before working as guitarist for Fred Waring, then Bing Crosby.

Featuring a solid body and sustaining pick-ups, the Les Paul guitar appeared on the market in 1952. By this time Paul had made a series of unsuccessful singles for Decca and Columbia but then found major stardom in partnership with Mary Ford (born Colleen Summer, Pasadena, California, July 7, 1928). They married in 1948 and three years later sold a million copies of **Mockin' Bird Hill** (also a million-seller the same year for Patti Page) on Capitol.

The 'new sound', with Mary's voice matched to Paul's 'talking guitar' achieved by double track earned them two further million-sellers that year. **How High The Moon** and **The World Is Waiting For The Sunrise** and another in 1954 with **Vaya Con Dios** which topped Cashbox US charts for 11 weeks. Paul and Ford divorced in 1963, and Ford died in 1977.

Hit Singles

	US	UK
With Mary Ford:		
Vaya Con Dios, 1953	—	7
Hummingbird, 1955	7	—

Albums:
Multi-Trackin' /), N/A
Trio (Glendale/—), N/A
New Sound Of, Volume 2 (Capitol/—), N/A
The World Is Waiting For The Sunrise (Capitol/EMI), 1979

With Mary Ford:
The Very Best Of Les Paul And Mary Ford (Capitol), 1974

With Chet Atkins:
Chester And Lester (RCA), 1977
Guitar Monsters (RCA), 1978

Tom Paxton

US composer, guitarist, vocalist.
Born Chicago, Illinois, October 31, 1937.

Career: After University of Oklahoma and military service, Paxton moved to New York; became one of mainstays of Greenwich Village coffee-house folk music scene. Many of his early songs, including **The Last Thing On My Mind** and **Rambling Boy**, quickly became folk club standards.

Like many of his folk contemporaries — Tom Rush(▶), Phil Ochs(▶), Judy Collins(▶) — he first signed to Elektra Records, cutting seven fine albums in his seven years with them. He earned reputation as much for sensitive love songs (**My Lady's A Wild Flying Dove**) as for biting social commentary and protest (**Daily News**), satire (**Talking Vietnam Pot Luck Blues**) and even children's songs (**We're All Going To The Zoo**).

Paxton made triumphant appearance at 1971 Isle Of Wight Festival; since then has commanded faithful following among folk buffs and respect among other artists. His songs have been widely covered, though he has never strayed from folk roots and so never matched commercial success of Dylan(▶), Rush and other peers.

After spell with Reprise, Paxton signed to British label MAM (released via Vanguard in US) in 1975 and switched base to London where he began working in small-combo setting.

Whatever the theme of his songs, they are all marked by high-quality musicianship and tremendously perceptive lyrics.

Albums:
Ramblin' Boy (Elektra), 1964
Outward Bound (Elektra), 1966
Morning Again (Elektra), 1968
Things I Notice Now (Elektra), 1969
The Compleat Tom Paxton (Elektra), 1971
New Songs From The Briar Patch (Vanguard/MAM), 1977
Heroes (Vanguard), 1978
Up And Up (Mountain/Evolution), 1980

Below: Pendergrass, once lead singer of Harold Melvin and the Blue Notes.

Teddy Pendergrass

US vocalist, drummer.
Born Theodore Pendergrass, Philadelphia, 1950.

Career: Raised in gospel environment, Pendergrass began musical career as drummer with Philadelphia-based soul group the Cadillacs. In 1969, band were recruited en-bloc as back-up for local vocal team Harold Melvin and the Blue Notes.

During tour of French West Indies, Blue Notes split up. When Melvin put together new line-up he chose Pendergrass as lead singer, group being signed to Kenny Gamble and Leon Huff's Blue Note label. Pendergrass's passionately soulful wail gave group a distinctive sound; established them in front-rank of then hot 'Philadelphia Sound' with string of hits of which smouldering soul ballads like **If You Don't Know My By Now** and **I Miss You** stand out.

Label credit 'Harold Melvin and the Blue Notes featuring Teddy Pendergrass' was insufficient to satisfy Pendergrass' lust for limelight and in 1976 he signed solo to Philadelphia International after legal battle with erstwhile group.

Issuing one album a year from 1977 to 1980, Pendergrass carefully crafted emergent image as black America's No. 1 sex symbol. Aimed his charisma directly at the ladies; even gave 'ladies only' shows!

An affair with wife of Marvin Gaye(▶), who happened to be touring UK at time for same promoter, caused scheduled 1980 visit to Britain to be cancelled. In April 1981 Pendergrass crossed Atlantic and, despite lack of any great chart success in Britain, proceeded to turn British women on. Returned again early in 1982.

On March 26, 1982, shortly after his return to US, Pendergrass was involved in car crash while driving his Rolls Royce, reportedly on way home from watching basketball game. He suffered severe internal and spinal injuries and it was feared he had been crippled for life, but in ensuing months he made remarkable recovery and is now back on recording scene.

Hit Singles:	US	UK
As Harold Melvin And The Blue Notes Featuring Teddy Pendergrass:		
If You Don't Know Me By Now, 1972	3	9
The Love I Lost, 1973	7	21
Bad Luck, 1975	15	—
Wake Up Everybody, 1976	12	23
Don't Leave Me This Way, 1977	—	5

Albums (selected):
As Harold Melvin And The Blue Notes Featuring Teddy Pendergrass:
Greatest Hits (Philadelphia International), 1976

Solo:
Teddy Pendergrass (Philadelphia International), 1977
Life Is A Song Worth Singing (Philadelphia International), 1978
Teddy (Philadelphia International), 1979
Live — Coast To Coast (Philadelphia International), 1980
T.P. (Philadelphia International), 1980
It's Time For Love (Philadelphia International), 1981
Ready For Teddy (Philadelphia International), 1981
This One's For You (Philadelphia International), 1982

Above: Carl Perkins, composer of rock'n'roll gem Blue Suede Shoes.

Pentangle

UK group formed 1967.
Original/Final line-up: Bert Jansch, guitar, vocals; John Renbourn, guitar, sitar, vocals; Jacqui McShee, vocals; Danny Thompson, bass; Terry Cox, drums.

Career: Pentangle's formation resulted from collaboration between Jansch and Renbourn (**Bert And John**) in 1966. Both were established solo guitarists with short but auspicious histories on London folk scene. Jansch, who had moved down from Edinburgh several years earlier, was innovative force, heavily influencing career of Donovan(▶), amongst others. Renbourn, a rocker turned folkie, had approached solo vocalist McShee and sung on her second album, **Another Monday**. Thompson and Cox had extensive experience in various jazz/blues units, including Alexis Korner's Blues Inc.

in Tottenham Court Road quintet worked up repertoire of folk, blues and jazz instrumentals. In spite of these early experiments, group remained folk-based (though electric guitar was introduced on fourth album **Cruel Sister**). Always a crowd-puller on British folk circuit, they also received warm reception in US following tours in 1969 and early '70s. Third album **Basket Of Light** achieved greatest commercial success, and two Top 50 singles, **Once I Had A Sweetheart** and **Light Flight,** showed them capable of achieving mass audience. Activities extended to writing television/film scores including 'Tam Lin;, 'The Lion At World's End' and 'Take Three Girls'.

In spite of promising start, later work proved decidedly lightweight. Significantly, both Renbourn and Jansch had continued recording solo albums during stay in Pentangle, often outshining group's own work. Their industrious manager Jo Lustig continued to organise successful tours but, following release of **Solomon's Seal**, group fragmented. Not surprisingly, individual members returned to solo activities for which they had previously been famed.

Albums:
Pentangling (—/Transatlantic), 1973

Worth Searching Out:
The Pentangle (Reprise/Transatlantic), 1968
Sweet Child (Reprise/Transatlantic), 1968
Basket Of Light (Reprise/Transatlantic), 1969
Cruel Sister (Reprise/Transatlantic), 1970
Reflection (Reprise/Transatlantic), 1971
Solomon's Seal (Reprise), 1972
Pentangle History Book (—/Transatlantic), 1972

Carl Perkins

US vocalist, guitarist, composer.
Born Lake City, Tennessee, April 9, 1932.

Career: Began performing country and blues material in Tennessee in late 1940s. By early '50s had evolved own style, apparent in first recordings for Flip and Sun labels in Memphis in 1955. At first encouraged to record country material by Sun's Sam Phillips, but turned to rockabilly and achieved distinction of first national rockabilly hit with own composition **Blue Suede Shoes** in 1956. Major setback to career came when hospitalised following serious injury in car crash on way to first major television appearance; unable to consolidate chart success.

Despite quality material and distinctive vocal and guitar style, Perkins was overshadowed by Elvis Presley(▶) (who covered **Blue Suede Shoes** with some success) and was neglected at Sun in favour of Jerry Lee Lewis(▶). Moved to US Columbia with fellow Sun artist Johnny Cash(▶) in 1958 in joint deal, only to find himself overshadowed again, this time by Cash ,and despite minor hit with **Pointed Toe Shoes**, star status eluded him.

Death of elder brother Jay in 1958 was further setback, and Perkins turned increasingly to drink. Signed to US Decca in 1963, toured Europe and recorded with Beatles(▶), who regarded him as hero. Cut good material for various labels during '60s and became integral part of Johnny Cash Road Show, touring extensively. Encouraged by Cash, turned towards Christianity and away from pills and booze. Split with Cash in 1976 in order to return to touring and recording independently.

Highly regarded as guitarist, Perkins still impresses with live performances and occasionally records, most recently for his own Suede label. In business where current competition plays major part, Perkins can be regarded as somewhat unlucky not to make greater chart impact.

Guitars: Gibson Switchmaster, later Fender Telecaster.

Hit Singles:	US	UK
Blue Suede Shoes, 1956	2	10

Albums:
The Rocking Guitar Man (Charly), 1975
The Original Carl Perkins (Charly), 1976
Sun Sound Special (Charly), 1978
The Carl Perkins Dance Album (Charly), 1981
The Sun Years (3 LP box set) (Sun), 1982
Survivors (with Johnny Cash and Jerry Lee Lewis) (CBS), 1982

Peter, Paul And Mary

US group formed 1961.

Peter Yarrow, vocalist, guitarist; born New York City, May 31, 1938.
Paul (real name Noel) Stookey, vocalist, guitarist; born Baltimore, Maryland, November 30, 1937.
Mary Travers, vocalist; born Louisville, Kentucky, November 7, 1937.

Career: 'Antiseptic', complained those who thought trio's pretty harmonies and wholesome image diluted and softened impact of protest songs. 'Bringing message to mainstream', said others, noting that material was umcompromising and that group spoke out on civil rights and anti-war issues to wide audience, appearing on platform with Martin Luther King when civil rights leader made 1963 'I Have A Dream' speech.

Although P, P & M were manufactured in 1961 by Bob Dylan's(▶) manager Albert Grossman to emulate success of Kingston Trio, each had strong folk roots. Yarrow was exposed to folk scene at NY's High School of Music and Art, then studied and taught folklore while getting BA degree in psychology. Stookey led rock 'n' roll band while at school, compered and sang at student events at Michigan State, then came to NY for job in industry. Performing weekends as singer and comedian in Greenwich village clubs, met and was influenced by Tom Paxton(▶), Dave Van Ronk and others, becoming full-time performer in 1960. Travers grew up in progressive NY family, and at 14 belonged to Songswappers, a group which recorded three albums with Pete Seeger(▶).

With Milt Okun as musical director, trio's strong stage personality combined with intelligent material and arrangements to make them style-setters during 1960s. Programme mixed Yarrow/Stookey originals with traditional songs and compositions by others. First album **Peter, Paul and Mary** (1962) gave double-sided hit single of Seeger's **If I Had A Hammer** and **Lemon Tree**.

There were two 1963 albums, **Moving** and **In The Wind**, from which Dylan's **Blowin' In The Wind** went to No. 2 in US and No. 13 in UK, won Grammy and brought Dylan to public notice. Trio sang Dylan's song with him at memorable 1963 Newport Festival concert. Yarrow, member of Newport Folk foundation's initial board of directors, was compere when electric Dylan was booed off stage at 1965 Festival. 'He's gone to get his acoustic guitar,' he shouted, placating angry audience when Dylan stomped off.

Other major hits included **Puff The Magic Dragon** and John Denver's(▶) 1969 **Leaving On A Jet Plane**. Of ten albums, eight went gold; five of these were platinum. Then, after 1970 peace rally in Washington, DC, trio split up.

Each made solo albums and each managed Top 100 single, but no spectacular success. Yarrow co-produced Mary MacGregor's 1976 album **Torn Between Two Lovers**, from which his titletrack composition became major 1977 chart topper. Stookey produced folk albums, then formed Neworld Media, running a recording studio and doing film editing. Travers hosted US radio chat show in 1975 and wrote her autobiography.

In 1978 trio reunited for anti-nuclear rally in California, then gradually began performing together more frequently. During 1983 they have scheduled 50 concerts, including European tour, thus far receiving high praise from critics and full-capacity audiences, who find that old songs haven't gone stale. Some suggest that as revived peace movement brought them together again, Peter, Paul and Mary are heralding new era of social change, in need of balladeers.

Hit Singles:	US	UK
If I Had A Hammer, 1962	10	—
Puff The Magic Dragon, 1963	2	—
Blowin' In The Wind, 1963	2	13
Don't Think Twice, It's Allright, 1963	9	—
I Dig Rock And Roll Music, 1967	9	—
Leavin' On A Jet Plane, 1969	1	2

Albums:
Peter Paul & Mary (Warner Bros), 1962
In Concert (Warner Bros), 1965
Album 1700 (Warner Bros), 1967
Peter Paul & Mommy (Warner Bros), 1970
Ten Years Together (Warner Bros), 1974
Reunion (Warner Bros), 1978

Tom Petty & The Heartbreakers

US group formed 1976.

Original line-up: Tom Petty, vocals, Fender Stratocaster, Rickenbacker 12-string guitars; Stan Lynch, drums, vocals; Mike Campbell, guitar; Benmont Tench, keyboards, vocals; Ron Blair, bass.

Career: Petty grew up in Gainsville, Florida, and played for local group Epics in high school. He quit when band began posing instead of playing. After finishing high school he held variety of low-paid jobs while playing bass in Gainsville's premier band Mudcrutch, where he came across Campbell and Tench.

Mudcrutch elected to seek fortune in Los Angeles and moved there in April 1974. One single flopped and band folded. Trio kept in touch and in early 1976 were working on some of Tench's demos with Lynch and Blair (also from Gainsville) when they decided to try again. Group interested Shelter Records and released first LP, which received critical praise for Byrds(▶)-like feel with '70s technology. (Single from album, **American Girl**, ironically, was covered by Jim McGuinn.)

Exciting live shows and plenty of radio play ensured quick success for band, who responded by recording even stronger LP, **You're Gonna Get It!** Just as it seemed **That** single gave them first Top 10 hit), Shelter Records collapsed. Band became deeply involved in legal problems (Petty himself filing bankruptcy) and lost momentum. **Damn The Torpedoes** reflected band's tenacity and resilience in both title and sound. Doing much to pick up band again, album also brought approval of fellow musicians. Stevie Nicks, taking break from Fleetwood Mac(▶) used band on **Bella Donna** solo LP; Petty produced excellent, but obscure, Del Shannon(▶) LP; and Tench worked with Dylan(▶).

This outside activity may explain failure of **Hard Promises** to match earlier work. **Long After Dark** regained old balance, but also reflected Blair's waning interest in rock business. His place was taken by Howard Epstein.

Despite UK/European tours with good audience response, band has not been really successful in UK. Whether Tom Petty and the Heartbreakers are willing to take time to break UK is questionable. They are new megastars of '80s in US and can play anywhere they want. But Petty is known for liking hard work and stiff challenges, as reflected by high quality of his music, so he just may take on UK yet.

Current line-up: Petty; Campbell; Tench; Lynch; Howard Epstein, bass.

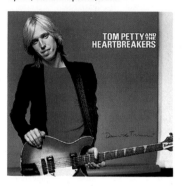

Damn The Torpedoes, Tom Petty. Courtesy Backstreet Records.

Hit Singles:	US	UK
Don't Do Me Like That, 1979	10	—
Refugee, 1980	15	—
The Waiting, 1981	19	—
You Got Lucky, 1983	20	—

With Stevie Nicks:
Stop Draggin' My Heart Around, 1981	3	—

Below: Guitarist/vocalist Tom Petty produced Del Shannon's 1982 album.

Albums:
Tom Petty & The Heartbreakers (Shelter/Island), 1976
You're Gonna Get It! (Shelter/Island), 1978
Damn The Torpedoes (Backstreet), 1979
Hard Promises (Backstreet), 1981
Long After Dark (Backstreet), 1982

Wilson Pickett

US vocalist, composer.
Born Prattville, Alabama, March 18, 1941.

Career: First made impression as lead singer for Detroit-based vocal group the Falcons; Falcons releases demonstrated full-blooded vocal style that was to become Pickett's stock-in-trade. After group split Pickett recorded **If You Need Me** and **It's Too Late** for Lloyd Price's Double L label; both were R&B hits.

Pickett signed with Atlantic in 1964 and after a couple of unsuccessful releases, company recorded him at Stax Studios in Memphis with Steve Cropper and Stax session mafia. Result was first major hit, the classic **In The Midnight Hour** (co-written by Cropper), which went to No. 21 in the US, 12 in the UK. **Hour**'s irresistible dance beat coupled with Pickett's cocky, macho vocalising established him as soul star on a par with '60s heroes like Otis Redding(▶).

The next four years saw slew of exciting soul hits, firmly based on solid dance beat (Pickett was underrated as an interpreter of soul ballads). He also toured extensively, with large soul revue show, and was particularly popular in UK.

Towards end of '60s Pickett's popularity waned as new flower-power ethos began to take effect (although strangely one of his biggest hits were cover of the Beatles(▶) mock gospel ballad **Hey Jude**. He signed with RCA in 1972, and has continued to record with varied success. Although there has been no diminution in the power of his voice, since the early '70s Pickett seems to have been searching for a direction that could open up a place for him in the era of Earth Wind and Fire(▶) and the Commodores(▶), but success has been only sporadic.

Pickett has continued to work live, but his aggressive personality has made him a less than bankable proposition; two recent trips to UK have been cancelled at last minute amid rumours of fisticuffs and/or ludicrous monetary demands.

One of the great soul performers of '60s, Wilson Pickett summed up for many what soul was all about. Sly, sexy, macho and aggressive, he had all the vocal equipment required to wring the last ounce out of a song. His hit singles collections demonstrate perfectly the raw exhilaration of '60s soul, and are essentials for any rounded record collection.

Hit Singles:	US	UK
In The Midnight Hour, 1965	21	12
634-5789, 1966	13	36
Land Of 1000 Dances, 1966	6	22
Funky Broadway, 1967	8	43
She's Lookin' Good, 1968	15	—
Hey Jude, 1969	23	16
Engine Number 9, 1970	14	—
Don't Let The Green Grass Fool You, 1971	17	—
Don't Knock My Love — Part 1, 1971	13	—

Albums:
If You Need Me (—/Joy), 1974
I Want You (United Artists), 1979
The Right Track (EMI), 1981
The Best Of (Atlantic), 1982

Pink Floyd

UK group formed 1966.

Original line-up: Syd Barrett, vocals, guitar; Roger Waters, bass; Richard Wright, keyboards; Nick Mason, drums.

Career: Barrett and Waters attended Cambridge High School for boys, along with future member Dave Gilmour. Barrett moved to art college in London, playing in Geoff Mott and the Mottos and the Hollering Blues, before forming short-lived duo with Gilmour. Waters, meanwhile, was studying architecture in London and had formed Sigma 6 with Mason and Wright.

Group evolved into T. Set, Meggadeath and the Screaming Abdabs, finally bringing in jazz guitarist Bob Close and Barrett. Latter dubbed group the Pink Floyd Sound, a name said to have been inspired by Georgia bluesmen Pink Anderson and Floyd Council. As they moved towards psychedelic music, Close was ousted.

Group spent late 1966 playing at variety of early underground haunts, including the Marquee, the London Free School's Sound/Light Workshop in All Saint's Church Hall, Notting Hill and, most notably, the Roundhouse. By end of year they were regular headliners at UFO, London's foremost hippie club. With new managers Peter Jenner and Andrew King, secured contract with EMI, recording first single in January 1967. **Arnold Layne**, written by Barrett, was amusing tale of transvestite who steals underwear. Novel sound and theme ensured Top 20 placing in UK charts, establishing Floyd as most successful group to emerge from Britain's underground scene.

During May 1967, ambitious **Games For May** was staged at London's Queen Elizabeth Hall, complete with quadrophonic sound system. **Games For May**, retitled **See Emily Play**, was released as single and reached UK No. 6 in July.

In August, first LP **Piper At The Gates Of Dawn** demonstrated Barrett's dominant role in group. Songs were full of childlike images, subtly echoing work of Lewis Carroll, combining the innocent and the menacing. Barrett's lead guitar work was impressive, neatly complementing Wright's unusual keyboards style. Prior to first US tour, Barrett's behaviour became increasingly erratic, possibly a side-effect of over-use of hallucinogens. In succeeding months, condition worsened; at some performances he would not play at all, remaining motionless on stage. By February 1968, Gilmour was brought in as replacement, Barrett finally leaving in April.

Without Barrett's lyrics, group had little chance of succeeding as singles act. Instead they concentrated on live work, appearing regularly at Middle Earth, and headlining free concert in London's Hyde Park in July. Second album, **A Saucerful Of Secrets**, demonstrated ability to survive. Used Waters instrumental/electronics/choral work to great effect, particularly during climactic **Set The Controls For The Heart Of The Sun**.

Subsequent concerts revealed increasing professionalism/imagination in use of lighting/sound. At Royal Festival Hall their presentation 'More Furious Madness From The Massed Gadgets Of Auximenes' featured the innovatory Azimuth Co-ordinator, a PA system that ingeniously projected the sound around auditorium. Increasing interest in soundtrack music led to scores for **More** (1969), **The Committee** (1969), **Zabriskie Point** (1970), **The Body** (1970) and **Obscured By Clouds** (1972).

Released double album **Ummagumma**, featuring two live sides (recorded at Mothers Club, Birmingham, and Manchester College

of Commerce, in June 1969) backed by studio contributions from every member. Work was self-indulgent in parts and erratic in quality. A period of relative quiet ended with release of **Atom Heart Mother** (1970) which topped UK LP charts. In spite of commercial success, it was least impressive offering to date. Successful concerts followed, including free concert in Hyde Park that attracted 100,000 people.

Early in 1971, Floyd appeared at Crystal Palace Garden Party amid fireworks and rain. Premiered **Return To The Son Of Nothing**, an extended hard rock/melodic improvisation that finally emerged as **Echoes**, the key track on their 1971 LP **Meddle**. Extra-curricular work was undertaken frequently during early '70s. A film of group at Pompeii (directed by Adrian Maben) was premiered at Edinburgh Festival, while they worked industriously on next album.

The Dark Side Of The Moon LP, the culmination of various ideas over the years, centred on death and emotional breakdown caused by fear, loneliness and spiritual impoverishment. Work also underlined dark pessimism evident in Waters' songwriting, perhaps consciously rejecting the escapist romanticism that had characterised and destroyed Barrett. Bleakness of theme was offset by stunning production, unparalleled for its period. An aesthetically rewarding venture, album also became their biggest seller. Remained in UK lists for over two years; has yet to drop from US charts, making it the longest running LP in recording history.

Following album's release, group played London's Earls Court before 18,000 people, then retired for six months. Re-emerged briefly for Robert Wyatt benefit. For most of 1974 group members embarked on various projects, but they returned to the States for another tour in 1975, before playing badly received set at Knebworth.

Wish You Were Here finally appeared in September 1975 after two and a half years. Work was rather anticlimactic and press reaction proved unfavourable. Sales wise, it was another triumph. During 1976 group toured Europe and States, and completed work on **Animals**, released January 1977. Further solo projects followed amid rumours of

Above: Pink Floyd, 1966, (from left) Nick Mason, Richard Wright, Roger Waters, and Syd Barrett.

impending dissolution. The release of **The Wall** in 1979 provided another phenomenal seller, including a Christmas single chart-

topper, **Another Brick In The Wall**. Spin-off film 'The Wall', starring Bob Geldof of Boomtown Rats(▶), receaeived mixed review, but fared no worse than others in the genre.

Latest work, **The Final Cut**, emphasises Waters' dominance of group with more bleak visions of present-day society. From early underground following group has gone on to receive worldwide acclaim, but its future largely depends on continued motivation and interest of members, particularly Waters. Mason has recently quit and current rumours indicate that Floyd is no more.

Final/Current line-up: Waters; Wright; David Gilmour, guitar.

Hit Singles:

	US	UK
Arnold Layne, 1967	—	20
See Emily Play, 1967	—	6
Money, 1973	13	—
Another Brick In The Wall, 1979	—	1

Albums:
The Piper At The Gates Of Dawn (Columbia), 1967
A Saucerful Of Secrets (Columbia), 1968
More (Columbia), 1969
Ummagumma (Harvest), 1969

Piper At The Gates Of Dawn, Pink Floyd. Courtesy EMI/Columbia Records.

Atom Heart Mother (Harvest), 1970
Relics (Regal Starline), 1971
Meddle (Harvest), 1971
Obscured By Clouds (Harvest), 1972
The Dark Side Of The Moon (Harvest), 1973
A Nice Pair (Harvest), 1973
Wish You Were Here (Harvest), 1975
Animals (Harvest), 1977
The Wall (Harvest), 1979
The Final Cut (EMI), 1983
Works (Capitol), 1983*
*compilation

With Various Artists:
Zabriskie Point (Soundtrack) (MGM), 1970
Worth Searching Out:
Syd Barrett Solo:
The Madcap Laughs And Barrett (Harvest), 1974
David Gilmour Solo:
David Gilmour (Columbia/CBS), 1978
Nick Mason Solo:
Fictitious Sports (Columbia/CBS), 1981

Gene Pitney

US vocalist, composer.
Born Rockville, Connecticut, February 17, 1941.

Career: Began as songwriter; first record **I Wanna Love My Life Away** was made as song demo and only released after several music publishers had rejected song. Track featured Pitney playing all instruments and multi-track vocals; it reached No.39 in US charts, becoming first of many chart appearances throughout '60s.

Wrote several hits for other artists, including Roy Orbison(▶), Ricky Nelson(▶) and the Crystals. Most of own recordings were self-penned and later published by own company.

Pitney's distinctive tenor vocals made records immediately identifiable, and regular tours consolidated position in UK as major US solo artist of '60s, second only to Orbison(▶). The Beatles liked Pitney and they toured the UK with him. He never did as well in the US, where audiences considered him a bit square.

In late '60s Pitney turned to country music, dueting with George Jones(▶) for one US chart appearance, while retaining following in UK, which is still considerable.

Hit Singles:

	US	UK
Town Without Pity, 1962	13	—
(The Man Who Shot) Liberty Valance, 1962	4	—
Only Love Can Break A Heart, 1962	2	—
Half Heaven-Half Heartache, 1963	12	—
Mecca, 1963	12	—
24 Hours From Tulsa, 1963	17	5
That Girl Belongs To Yesterday, 1964	49	7
It Hurts To Be In Love, 1964	7	36
I'm Gonna Be Strong, 1964	9	2
I Must Be Seeing Things, 1965	31	6
Last Chance To Turn Around, 1965	13	—
Looking Through The Eyes Of Love, 1965	28	3
Princess In Rags, 1965	—	9
Backstage, 1966	—	4
Nobody Needs Your Love, 1966	—	2
Just One Smile, 1966	—	8
Something's Gotten Hold Of My Heart, 1967	—	5
Somewhere In The Country, 1968	—	19
She's A Heartbreaker, 1968	16	—

Albums:
(Not including repetitious budget compilations)
The Best Of (Piccadilly/—), 1981
Greatest Hits Of All Time (—/Phoenix), 1982
20 Golden Pieces Of (—/Bulldog), 1983

The Plasmatics

US group formed 1979.

Original/Current line-up: Wendy O. Williams, vocals, sax, percussion; Ritchie Stotts, guitar; Wes Beech, guitar; Jean Beauvoir, bass; Stu Deutsch, drums.

Career: A theatrical punk band, the Plasmatics owe their fame more to spectacular antics than to music. The focal point of group is Wendy O. Williams who enlivens their stage act by blowing up used cars, and cutting television sets in half with chainsaw. Became folk heroine of sorts when arrested by Milwaukee police for indecent exposure and lewdness during performance (acquiring black eye in ensuing struggle). Williams sued and eventually won case, claiming, 'In a free country everyone ought to be able to express their art.'

Signed to Stiff America in 1982; **2nd Album** indicated that band had jelled. A truly excellent video from LP (featuring a car smashing through a wall of televisions) immediately became a favourite on MTV.

Albums:
New Hope For The Wretched(Stiff America/Stiff), 1980
2nd album (Stiff America/Stiff), 1982

The Platters

US vocal group formed 1953.
Original line-up: Tony Williams; Alex Hodge; David Lynch; Herb Reed.

Career: Perhaps the best-known of many vocal harmony groups who trod fabled 'rags-to-riches' path during rock 'n' roll years of '50s, Platters climbed from obscurity of regional R&B charts to worldwide stardom. Original quartet met entrepreneur Buck Ram in Los Angeles in 1953; signed to Federal Records, but met little success. Ram made some inspired personnel changes, replacing Hodge with Paul Robi and recruiting Zola Taylor as contrasting female voice.

Continued to record for Federal, picking up local sales. Ram placed them with Mercury as virtual 'make-weights' in deal involving the Penguins, who had just scored pop hit with **Earth Angel**. Platters' first four records on Mercury all reached national Top 5 between fall 1955 and late 1956. **Only You, The Magic Touch, The Great Pretender** and **My Prayer** were fine, lyrical ballads; latter two topped charts, led by Tony Williams' clear, soaring tenor.

Hits continued to flow during next five years; chart-toppers **Twilight Time** and **Smoke Gets In Your Eyes** became 'pop' standards in Platters' distinctive ballad styling/lush orchestrations.

In 1961 Tony Williams quit to pursue solo career; auditions yielded Sonny Turner as replacement. Despite maintaining similar mode of performance, hits did not come as readily. Group made good living on cabaret circuit, though, and continued steady output of LPs until leaving Mercury in 1965.

Change of musical direction followed more personnel changes; Sandra Dawn replaced Zola, Nate Nelson took over from Paul Robi. Group pacted with Musicor in 1966, taking more soulful inclination and switching uptempo; scored with lilting beaters like **I Love You 1000 Times** and **With This Ring**. Albums contained reworkings of their Mercury hits.

Subsequent years brought further personnel changes, record label switches, and profusion of lawsuits. 'Buck Ram Platters' are now touring minions of their ageing manager, who slaps injunctions on any original member who dares to quote Platters' name in show billings.

Final line-up: Lynch; Reed; Sonny Turner; Nate Nelson.

Hit Singles:

	US	UK
Only You, 1955	5	—
The Great Pretender, 1956	1	—
The Great Pretender/Only You, 1956	—	5
(You've Got) The Magic Touch, 1956	4	—
My Prayer, 1956	1	4
You'll Never Know/It Isn't Right, 1956	11	23
It Isn't Right/You'll Never Know, 1956	13	23
On My Word Of Honor/One In A Million, 1957	20	—
One In A Million/On My Word Of Honor, 1957	20	—
Only You, 1957	—	18
I'm Sorry/He's Mine, 1957	11	18
He's Mine/I'm Sorry, 1957	16	—
Twilight Time, 1958	1	3
Smoke Gets In Your Eyes, 1959	1	1
Harbour Lights, 1960	8	11

Albums (selected):
Best Of Volume 1 (—/Philips), 1973
Best Of Volume 2 (—/Philips), 1973
Encore (Mercury/—), 1976
More Encore Of Greatest Hits (Mercury), 1976
19 Hits (King/—), 1977

Poco

US group formed 1968.
Original line-up: Richie Furay, guitar, vocals; Jim Messina, guitar, vocals; Randy Meisner, bass, vocals; Rusty Young, pedal steel guitar; George Grantham, drums, vocals.

Career: When Buffalo Springfield(▶) broke up in 1967—Furay and Messina actually finishing off final LP by themselves—(changed named from Pogo to Poco after copyright problems over American cartoon figure of same name). They contacted Young whom they had used on Buffalo Springfield LP, and Young introduced Colorado friends Meisner and Grantham.

Audition for Apple missed, but band signed to Epic and released strong **Pickin' Up The Pieces** album. Meisner left (later to join Eagles(▶)) and Messina filled in on bass until Tim Schmit (also a 'future' Eagle) joined. Band continued to play for small, but loyal following.

Messina departed in 1970 to form Loggins and Messina(▶). Paul Cotton joined and began making major contributions with lead guitar, strong vocals and good songwriting abilities. This line-up recorded band's signature tune. **A Good Feelin' To Know.**

Above: Poco, part of the Californian country rock family.

Furay left in 1973, after six years of frustration with band which every critic liked, but which couldn't sell records. He tried Souther-Hillman-Furay supergroup for short time and then went solo.

Young and Cotton assumed leadership and with Schmit/Grantham rhythm section released two meandering LPs, **Seven** and **Cantamos**. In 1975 band changed labels and finally scored US chart success. Further personnel changes have left Young/Cotton focal point of band with steady following, ensuring band can make living out of countrified rock.

Current line-up: Young; Paul Cotton, guitar; Kim Bullard, keyboards; Charlie Harrison, bass; Steve Chapman, drums.

Hit Singles:

	US	UK
Crazy Love, 1979	17	—
Heat Of The Night, 1979	20	—

Albums:
Pickin' Up The Pieces (Epic), 1969
Poco (Epic/CBS), 1970
Deliverin' (Epic), 1970
From The Inside (Epic), 1971
A Good Feelin' To Know (Epic), 1972
Crazy Eyes (Epic), 1973
Cantamos (Epic), 1974
Head Over Heels (ABC), 1975
The Very Best Of Poco (Epic), 1975
Live (Epic), 1976
Rose Of Cimarron (ABC), 1976
Indian Summer (ABC), 1977
Legend (ABC), 1978
The Songs Of Paul Cotton (Epic), 1979
The Songs Of Richie Furay (Epic/CBS), 1979
Under The Gun (MCA), 1980
Blue And Grey (MCA), 1981
Cowboys And Englishmen (MCA), 1982
Ghost Town (Atlantic), 1982

Above: The Pointer Sisters, now successful as a trio.

Pointer Sisters

US vocal group formed 1973.
Original line-up: Bonnie Pointer; Anita Pointer; Ruth Pointer; June Pointer.

Career: Four genuine sisters, daughters of church ministers; born Oakland, California. Started singing in church, and formed Pointer Sisters after leaving school.

Through acquaintance with producer David Rubinson, they became involved with session work on West Coast, singing behind such artists as Boz Scaggs, Grace Slick and Esther Phillips. Eventually they decided to pursue career in own right and Rubinson negotiated deal with ABC/Blue Thumb in 1973.

Initially the sisters concentrated on jazzy nostalgia material and featured close-harmony scat singing; '40s image was followed through in clothes and presentation. They achieved considerable success in this mode, and showed versatility by scoring country hit with Grammy award-winning **Fairy Tale.** Also featured in movie **Car Wash.**

Eventually musical frustration set in, and the sisters left ABC/Blue Thumb in 1977. They disbanded for short period, Bonnie branching out to pursue moderately successful solo career. Remaining three regrouped in 1978 and signed deal with producer Richard Perry's Planet label.

First album **Energy** and hit single **Fire** both achieved gold status and showed total change of direction, drawing on rock writers like Bruce Springsteen(▶) and Steely Dan's(▶) Becker and Fagen. Career since has concentrated on mainstream rock orientation, with considerable success.

One of very few black female vocal groups to follow rock direction, Pointer Sisters look set for career longevity through talent and individuality. Group commands wide following among AOR audiences.

Current line-up: Anita Pointer; Ruth Pointer; June Pointer.

Hit Singles:

	US	UK
Yes We Can Can, 1973	11	—
Fairy Tale, 1974	13	—
How Long (Betcha' Got A Chick On The Side), 1975	20	—
Fire, 1979	2	34
Heaven Must Have Sent You, 1979	11	—
He's So Shy, 1980	3	5
Slow Hand, 1981	2	10
Should I Do It, 1982	13	50
American Music, 1982	16	—

Albums:
Live At The Opera House (ABC), 1974
Best Of . . . (Blue Thumb/ABC), 1976
Energy (Planet), 1978
Priority (Planet), 1979
Special Things (Planet), 1980
Black And White (Planet), 1981
Retrospect (MCA/—), 1981
So Excited (Planet), 1982
Greatest Hits (Planet), 1982

Retrospect, The Pointer Sisters. Courtesy MCA Records.

The Polecats

UK group formed 1980.
Original/Current line-up: Tim Worman, vocals, guitar; Boz (Martin Boorer), guitar; Phil Bloomberg, bass; Neil Rooney, drums.

Career: Worman and Boz had played together since 1976 at youth clubs; recruited Bloomberg in 1977 and Rooney in 1980, by which time they were known as promising young rockabilly group in London area. After initial single on independent Nervous label, signed with Phonogram in 1981 following growing reputation on European gig circuit. Recorded with producer Dave Edmunds(▶), then of Rockpile, whom Polecats had supported on tour.

Began major recording career with reasonable success: three Top 40 UK hit singles (**John, I'm Only Dancing, Rockabilly Guy** and **Jeepster**) plus minor hit album in 1981. However, disappeared from view subsequently, although rumours of imminent comeback heard in early 1983.

The Polecats were one of the more successful examples of the rebirth of British interest in rockabilly (as in Johnny Burnette(▶), etc) in early '80s, but also included among their hits cover versions of songs associated with David Bowie(▶) and Marc Bolan(▶). Since rockabilly revival appears to have evaporated, they may have to try a different approach to return to charts — as they are still in early twenties, this may well be possible.

Album:
Polecats (—/Mercury), 1981

The Police

UK group formed 1977.

Original line-up: Sting (Gordon Sumner), vocals, Ibanez bass; Henri Padovani, guitar; Stewart Copeland, drums.

Career: Band was formed by drummer Copeland, previously with moderately successful UK outfit Curved Air. Idea was to combine post-punk principles of simplicity and spontaneity with coherence and melodic sense. Copeland recruited Sting from Newcastle jazz and rock scene, and pair pulled in Padovani on guitar.

Band's first single was **Fall Out**, released in January 1977 on Illegal Records, an independent label formed by Copeland with brother Miles. (Miles Copeland had also served as manager throughout band's career.) Padovani's tenure was short-lived; he left in August 1977 to form Flying Padovani Brothers; replacement was Andy Summers, veteran of Zoot Money's Big Roll Band, the Animals(▶), Soft Machine(▶), Kevin Ayres and Kevin Coyne.

It was not until release of **Roxanne** on A&M in 1979 that band started to attract attention. Combining reggae-styled verse with rocking harmony chorus, single eventually went silver. It was first of string of major hit singles, each distinctive yet recognisable Police. By end of 1980 band was firmly established in UK and was making major inroads into US and international market.

Albums were as successful as singles. **Outlandos D'Amour** went double platinum in UK and gold in US, **Regatta De Blanc** made triple platinum in UK and gold in US, and third album, **Zenyatta Mondatta**, had massive sales figures all over the world — it achieved triple platinum status in UK, platinum status in US and went either gold or platinum in virtually every other territory.

Meanwhile, band had gained reputation as exciting live act and toured throughout world to wild acclaim during 1980-81. **Six Pack**, a package of the first five Police singles plus new release **The Bed's Too Big Without You** on A&M, went to No. 17 in the UK singles charts, a rather unique accomplishment.

1982 saw **Ghost In The Machine** LP riding high in charts, and hit singles from album soaring; **Every Little Thing She Does Is Magic** gave them their fourth UK No. 1, and **Invisible Sun** reached No. 2 in the UK despite BBC banning of accompanying video which depicted troubled streets of Belfast. Band kept relatively low profile as members went about various solo projects. Sting, natural front man of band, had already had major acting parts in the Who(▶) film 'Quadrophenia' and BBC-TV film 'Artemis '81', and received further acclaim for his lead role in Dennis Potter-written movie 'Brimstone And Treacle'. As if that were not enough, he scored hit with **Spread A Little Happiness**, the '30s song featured in film. Andy Summers recorded moderately successful instrumental LP, **I Advance Masked,** with Robert Fripp in 1982.

Below: Probably the most popular group in the world in the 1980s, The Police — Sting (bass), Stewart Copeland (drums) and Andy Summers (guitar).

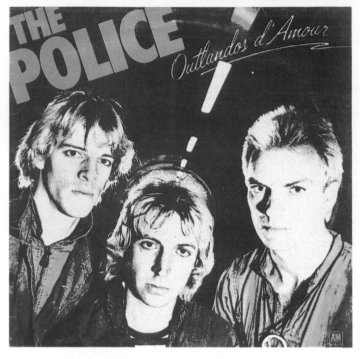

Outlandos d'Amour, the first Police album, which featured their first big hit, 'Roxanne'. Courtesy A&M Records.

Return to group work came in spring 1983. **Synchronicity** LP and single **Every Breath You Take** flew to No. 1 both sides of the Atlantic. **Synchronicity** was third Police LP in a row to enter UK album charts at No. 1.

Now one of world's biggest rock acts, the Police are in position to pick and choose what they do. Their intelligent approach to rock music and ability to keep coming up with fresh and appealing material seems likely to carry them well into '80s.

Current line-up: Sting; Copeland; Andy Summers, Fender Stratocaster, Gibson 335 guitars, vocals.

The second album by the Police with a second enigmatic title. Courtesy A&M Records.

Hit Singles:

	US	UK
Roxanne, 1979	32	12
Can't Stand Losing You, 1979	—	2
Message In A Bottle, 1979	—	1
Walking On The Moon, 1979	—	1
So Lonely, 1980	—	6
Six Pack, 1980	—	17
Don't Stand So Close To Me, 1980	10	1
De Do Do Do, De Da Da Da, 1980	10	5
Invisible Sun, 1981	—	2
Every Thing She Does Is Magic, 1981	3	1
Spirits In The Material World, 1982	11	12
Every Breath You Take, 1983	1	1
Wrapped Around Your Finger, 1983	—	7

Sting solo:

	US	UK
Spread A Little Happiness, 1982	—	16

Albums:

Outlandos D'Amour (A&M), 1978
Regatta De Blanc (A&M), 1979
Zenyatta Mondatta (A&M), 1980
Ghost In The Machine (A&M), 1981
Synchronicity (A&M), 1983

Sting Solo:

Brimstone And Treacle (soundtrack) (A&M), 1982

Andy Summers with Robert Fripp:

I Advance Masked (A&M), 1982

Bottom: Onstage in 1981 in the UK. Below: The Police in 1983 (left) Sting, (right) Andy Summers and (front) Stewart Copeland.

Right: During their 1980 World Tour and (below) taking Western rock music to India where it had rarely been heard before their 1980 concert.

A No. 1 album in both the US and UK. Courtesy A&M Records.

Elvis Presley

US vocalist, guitarist, composer, actor: Born Tupelo, Misssissippi, January 8 1935; died Memphis, Tennessee, August 16, 1977.

Career: Early influences included gospel concerts, church singing, R&B radio shows in hometown, and country singers of '40s. In first public appearance at age 10, came second singing **Old Shep** in State Fair talent contest. Following family move to Memphis and some experience singing with gospel groups, visited Sun Studios to cut acetate as gift to mother.

Sun's Sam Phillips recognised potential and eventually in 1954 teamed Presley with Scotty Moore (guitar) and Bill Black(▶) (bass). Resulting first single, **That's All Right,** became big enough hit locally for trio to begin touring Southern US and eventually appear on 'Louisiana Hayride' radio show.

Further Sun singles consolidated popularity and reports of excitement generated at live appearances prompted Colonel Tom Parker to become manager and RCA-Victor Records to purchase contract from Sun for $35,000. In retrospect, sum paid seems minimal, but was astronomical in 1955.

With better distribution and promotion than Sun could provide, coupled with controversial television appearances, Presley rapidly became most important artist in rock 'n' roll field and major threat to 'establishment' singers. First major hit, **Heartbreak Hotel,** in summer 1956 was rapidly followed by succession of No. 1s in similar style, mostly introduced on major TV shows.

Fan fervour resulted in unprecedented merchandising of Presley products and hysterical scenes at concerts and public appearances. Although management policy was criticised later, Colonel Parker successfully promoted hysteria while building solid career for Presley, typified by first movie contract guaranteeing advances of $450,000 for first three films.

Career interrupted for two years by draft into US Army in 1958. However, Presley's popularity was scarcely affected by lack of public appearances thanks to stockpile of recordings and continuing publicity resulting from Colonel Parker's activities on his behalf. By 1960, when Presley returned from service in Germany, rock 'n' roll had ceased to rule the charts. Subsequent releases followed the pattern set by **It's Now Or Never,** an almost-MOR ballad.

First movies had shown some acting promise coupled with fairly natural musical content, but as demand for anything featuring Presley increased, less importance was placed on scripts. Aim was to maintain flow of glossy films with box-office appeal. Thus best films 'Love Me Tender', 'Jailhouse Rock' and 'Loving You' quickly degenerated to opportunist pap of 'Girls Girls Girls' and "Paradise Hawaiian Style".

Presley was undoubtedly capable of succeeding with better acting parts, as in 'Flaming Star', but more money could be made linking soundtrack album with teen-appeal films. Resulting 'assembly line' material bored Presley and accelerated decline as movie actor. At same time recorded material became less adventurous, with movie soundtrack providing singles releases to exclusion of stronger unrelated material; by late '60s singles had ceased to be automatic hits.

Following marriage in 1967 to Priscilla Beaulieu, daughter of Army officer, hoped-for return to former greatness confirmed by first TV appearance since 1960, 'NBC Special'. Both material and physical appearance raised hopes of fans who had watched their idol decline. Unfortunately, early promise of single **If I Can Dream** and live appearances in Las Vagas with distinguished band, including guitarist James Burton(▶), failed to sustain momentum. During '70s records and stage shows again declined, although faithful fans maintained following.

In mid-'70s Presley increasingly withdrew to safety of Graceland estate in Memphis with family and bodyguards. He became dependent on drugs to control basic functions, and gained weight. Record releases were irregular and stage appearances a parody of former self. Many were convinced that drugs were major factor in death from 'natural causes' at age 42. Presley's personal doctor is believed to be somewhat suspect.

His Hand In Mine, Elvis Presley. Courtesy RCA Records. Presley holds the record for the most weeks at No. 1 in the UK.

As news of death spread, there were hysterical scenes outside home in Memphis and at funeral. RCA was unable to cope with demand for Presley product as sales broke all previous records. Cult following since death has continued unabated. Books, articles, films and TV documentaries on Presley's life abound; many attempt to investigate cause of demise.

Despite criticism of later career, it is undeniable that Presley's influence on others has been and remains enormous. He was first rock 'n' roll artist to successfully blend black and white musical influences and retain appeal to broad audience. Presley holds nearly every rock record in UK, including Most Hits, Most Weeks In Charts and Most Top 10 Hits.

With his good looks, vocal talent and sex appeal, Presley was a 'natural' pop idol, and it is a measure of his greatness that he remains the most important and adulated performer of the rock 'n' roll era.

Hit Singles:	US	UK
Heartbreak Hotel/I Was The One, 1956	1	2
Blue Suede Shoes (EP in US), 1956	20	9
I Was The One/Heartbreak Hotel, 1956	19	—
I Want You, I Need You, I Love You, 1956	1	14
Don't Be Cruel/Hound Dog, 1956	1	2
Hound Dog/Don't Be Cruel, 1956	1	2
Love Me/When My Blue Moon Turns To Gold (EP), 1956	2	—
When My Blue Moon Turns To Gold/Love Me, 1956	19	—
Love Me Tender/Any Way That You Want Me, 1956	1	11
Any Way That You Want Me/Love Me Tender, 1956	20	—
Blue Moon, 1956	—	9
Too Much, 1957	1	6
All Shook Up, 1957	1	1
(Let Me Be Your) Teddy Bear/Loving You, 1957	1	3
Loving You/(Let Me Be Your) Teddy Bear, 1957	20	—
Paralysed, 1957	—	8
Party, 1957	—	2
Got A Lot O' Livin' To Do, 1957	—	17
Trying To Get To You, 1957	—	16
Lawdy Miss Clawdy, 1957	—	15
Santa Bring My Baby Back To Me, 1957	—	7
Jailhouse Rock/Treat Me Nice, 1957	1	1
Treat Me Nice/Jailhouse Rock, 1957	18	—
Don't/I Beg Of You, 1958	1	2
I Beg Of You/Don't, 1958	8	—

It Won't Seem Like Christmas Without You, just part of Elvis Presley's vast discography. Courtesy RCA Victor.

Below: Elvis Presley, the King of rock'n'roll, who will remain a true legend. Photo from the late '50s.

Wear My Ring/Doncha Think It's Time, 1958	2	3
Doncha' Think It's Time/Wear My Ring, 1958	15	—
Hard Headed Woman, 1958	1	2
King Creole, 1958	—	2
One Night/I Got Stung, 1958	4	1
I Got Stung/One Night, 1958	8	—
A Fool Such As I/I Need Your Love Tonight, 1959	2	1
I Need Your Love Tonight/A Fool Such As I, 1959	4	—
A Big Hunk O'Love/My Wish Came True, 1959	1	4
My Wish Came True/A Big Hunk O'Love, 1959	12	—
Stuck On You/Fame And Fortune, 1960	1	3
Fame And Fortune/Stuck On You, 1960	17	—
It's Now Or Never, 1960	1	1
A Mess Of Blues, 1960	—	2
Are You Lonesome Tonight/I Gotta Know, 1960	1	1
I Gotta Know/Are You Lonesome Tonight, 1960	20	—
Surrender, 1961	1	1
Wooden Heart, 1961	—	1
Flaming Star (EP), 1961	14	—
I Feel So Bad/Wild In The Country, 1961	5	—
Wild In The Country/I Feel So Bad, 1961	—	4
(Marie's The Name) His Latest Flame/Little Sister, 1961	4	1
Little Sister/(Marie's The Name) His Latest Flame, 1961	5	—
Can't Help Falling In Love/Rock A Hula Baby, 1962	2	—
Rock A Hula Baby/Can't Help Falling In Love, 1962	—	1
Good Luck Charm, 1962	1	1
Follow That Dream (EP), 1962	15	34

She's Not You, 1962	5	1
Return To Sender, 1961	2	1
One Broken Heart For Sale, 1963	11	12
(You're The) Devil In Disguise, 1963	3	1
Bossa Nova Baby, 1963	8	13
Kiss Me Quick, 1963	—	14
Viva Las Vagas, 1964	29	17
Kissin' Cousins, 1964	12	10
Such A Night, 1964	16	13
Ask Me/Ain't That Loving You Baby, 1964	12	—
Ain't That Loving You Baby/Ask Me, 1964	16	15
Blue Christmas, 1964	—	11
Do The Clam, 1965	21	19
Crying In The Chapel, 1965	3	1
Easy Question, 1965	11	—
Tell Me Why, 1965	33	15
I'm Yours, 1965	11	—
Puppet On A String, 1965	14	—
Love Letters, 1966	19	6
All That I Am, 1966	41	18
If Every Day Was Like Christmas, 1966	—	13
Guitar Man, 1968	43	19
US Male, 1968	28	15
If I Can Dream, 1969	12	11
In The Ghetto, 1969	3	2
Clean Up Your Own Back Yard, 1969	35	2

Suspicious Minds, 1969	1	2
Don't Cry Daddy, 1970	6	8
Kentucky Rain, 1970	16	21
I've Lost You, 1970	32	9
The Wonder Of You, 1970	9	1
You Don't Have To Say You Love Me, 1970	11	9
There Goes My Everything, 1971	—	6
Rags To Riches, 1971	—	9
I Just Can't Help Believin', 1971	—	6
Until It's Time For You To Go, 1972	40	5
American Trilogy, 1972	—	8
Burning Love, 1972	2	7
Separate Ways/Always On My Mind, 1973	20	—
Always On My Mind/Separate Ways, 1973	—	9
Steamroller Blues/Fool, 1973	17	—
Fool/Steamroller Blues, 1973	—	15
If You Talk In Your Sleep, 1974	17	40
Promised Land, 1974	14	9
My Boy, 1975	20	5
Girl Of My Best Friend, 1976	—	9
Suspicion, 1976	—	9
Moody Blue, 1977	—	6
Way Down, 1977	18	1
My Way, 1977	—	9
It Won't Seem Like Christmas Without You, 1979	—	13
It's Only Love, 1980	—	3
(In order of US release)		

Albums:
(Not including budget releases)
Rock 'n' Roll (RCA), 1956
Elvis Presley (RCA), 1956
Elvis (RCA), 1956
Loving You (RCA), 1957
King Creole (RCA), 1958
For LP Fans Only (RCA), 1959
A Date With Elvis (RCA), 1959
Elvis Is Back (RCA), 1960
His Hand In Mine (RCA), 1960
Something For Everybody (RCA), 1961
Blue Hawaii (RCA), 1961
Pot Luck (RCA), 1962
It Happend At The World's Fair (RCA), 1963
Roustabout (RCA), 1964
Harem Holiday (RCA), 1965
Paradise, Hawaiian Style (RCA), 1966
How Great Thou Art (RCA), 1967
Clambake (RCA), 1967
Double Trouble (RCA), 1967
Speedway (RCA), 1968
Elvis — NBC Special (RCA), 1968
That's The Way It Is (RCA), 1970
I'm 10,000 Years Old, Elvis Country (RCA), 1971
Elvis Sings The Wonderful World Of Christmas (RCA), 1971
Elvis Live At Madison Square Garden (RCA), 1972
Aloha From Hawaii Via Satellite (RCA), 1973
Hits Of The '70s (RCA), 1974
Pictures Of Elvis (RCA), 1975
The Elvis Presley Sun Collection (RCA), 1975
Elvis In Demand (RCA), 1977
Elvis, Scotty and Bill — The First Year (Very Wonderful Golden Editions), 1979
Elvis Aaron Presley (RCA), 1980
Guitar Man (RCA), 1980
Elvis Presley Sings Leiber and Stoller (RCA), 1980
The Million Dollar Quartet (Sun), 1981
This Is Elvis (RCA), 1981

Right: The early Elvis Presley, whose brilliance was never surpassed by any other solo singer.

Below right: Elvis in decline — on stage during the 1970s.

Below: One of the few '60s artists who rivalled the Beatles in popularity.

Billy Preston

US organist, vocalist, composer.
Born Houston, Texas, September 9, 1946.

Career: By age 10 Preston, who had moved with family to Los Angeles, had already put in time as backing musician with gospel great Mahalia Jackson and taken a cameo role in movie 'St Louis Blues'.

After stints with backing bands of Little Richard(▶) and Sam Cooke(▶), which brought him to Britain at just 16 — he first met the Beatles(▶) on a Richard package tour in 1962 — Preston started recording his own organ instrumentals for Derby and Vee-Jay (including the classic **Billy's Bag**). A better contract with Capitol followed, plus regular appearances on US television's 'Shindig' show and tours with Ray Charles(▶), who pushed him into limelight and made Preston star in own right (one of his Vee-Jay sets appearing under *double-entendre* title **The Most Exciting Organ Ever!**).

Following UK trip with Charles for superb TV special, Preston signed to Beatles' Apple label and scored with vocal **That's The Way (God Planned It)**. He played on Beatles'(▶) **Get Back** and **Let It Be** hits and then featured as part of John Lennon's(▶) Plastic Ono Band, notably at the 1969 'Peace For Christmas' UNICEF charity concert at London's Lyceum Theatre (recorded as one side of Lennon's **Sometime In New York City** album), playing alongside John Lennon(▶), Yoko Ono(▶), George Harrison(▶), Eric Clapton(▶), Klaus Voorman, Keith Moon(▶), Alan White, Delaney and Bonnie(▶), and Bobby Keys.

When Apple went rotten, Preston switched to A&M, succeeding with **I Wrote A Simple Song, Outta Space, Will It Go Round In Circles** and other singles in early '70s. He also played on Sly and the Family Stone(▶) hits and guested on Rolling Stones'(▶) massive American tour in 1975.

Managed by Diana Ross's then husband Bob Silverstein, Preston switched to Motown in 1979. Since then he has logged steady run of hit records, including international chart-topper **With You I'm Born Again** with Syreeta, and guested on numerous sessions.

Hit Singles:

	US	UK
That's The Way (God Planned It), 1969	—	11
Outta-Space, 1972	2	44
Will It Go Round In Circles, 1973	1	—
Space Race, 1973	4	—
Nothing From Nothing, 1974	1	—

With Syreeta:

With You I'm Born Again, 1979	4	2

Albums:
Gospel In My Soul (MCA/Joy), 1964
Most Exciting Organ Ever! (Vee-Jay/Joy), 1967
The Apple Of Their Eye (—/President), 1969
Live European Tour (A&M), 1974
Whole New Thing (A&M), 1977
Behold (Myrrh), 1970
Late At Night (Motown), 1979
Soul'd Out (GNP/—), 1979
The Way I Am (Motown), 1981
Pressin' On (Motown), 1982
Best Of (A&M/—), 1982

With Syreeta:
Fast Break (Motown), 1979
Billy Preston And Syreeta (Motown), 1981

Right: The multi-talented Chrissie Hynde, soldiering on after the tragic deaths of Honeyman-Scott and Farndon.

Pretenders

UK group formed 1978.

Original line-up: Chrissie Hynde, vocals; James Honeyman-Scott, vocals, keyboards, guitar; Pete Farndon, bass; Martin Chambers, drums.

Career: In 1974, American-born Chrissie Hynde quit job on London-based rock paper 'New Musical Express' to sing with French band, which flopped; returned to US to join R&B group Jack Rabbit. Giving France another try, she joined rock 'n' roll band the Frenchies before returning to London again. Then worked as back-up singer on Stiff Records' national tour.

Impressed with her work, bosses of Real label introduced her to group of musicians from Hereford and groomed them as the Pretenders. Just cracking UK Top 30 with debut single, a re-make of Kinks' **Stop Your Sobbing**, band toured UK, released second single **Kid** (1979). With third record, catchy **Brass In Pocket** (highlighting Hynde's sensual vocals), topped chart.

Well-balanced debut album **Pretenders** went straight to No. 1. Appearance on all-star Kampuchean refugee charity concert heightened reputation; three of their songs appeared on resultant double album.

Tours of Europe and America (received accolade as 'Best New Artists' in 'Rolling

The Pretenders' classic first album. Courtesy WEA Records.

Stone' magazine) and release of another single, **Message Of Love**, and **Extended Play** (a five-track EP) preceded **Pretenders II** album (1981). Recorded in Paris and London and produced by Chris Thomas, nine of 12 songs were penned by Chrissie Hynde. She co-wrote two more with James Honeyman-Scott, but his death (drug-related) in mid-1982 put future of band in question. Soldiered on and late 1982 single **Back On The Chain Gang**, featuring Billy Bremner (guitar) and Tony Butler (bass), became Top 5 hit in US, with heavy airplay on MTV. Then suddenly, in April 1983, Farndon died. Two new members, Rob McIntosh (ex-Night) and Malcolm Foster (ex-Foster Brothers), were recruited in time for

Below: Originals (from left), Farndon, Chambers, Hynde and Honeyman-Scott.

Pretenders performance at Us Festival in May 1983.

Current line-up: Hynde; Chambers; Rob McIntosh, guitar; Malcolm Foster, bass.

Hit Singles:

	US	UK
Brass In Pocket, 1979	14	1
Talk Of The Town, 1980	—	8
Message Of Love, 1981	—	11
I Go To sleep, 1981	—	7
Back On The Chain Gang, 1982	5	17

Albums:
Pretenders (Sire/Real), 1980
Pretenders II (Sire/Real), 1981

Alan Price

UK keyboard player, vocalist, composer.
Born Fairfield, Durham, April 19, 1942.

Career: After leaving Animals(▶) in 1965, formed Alan Price Set, a more sophisticated ensemble which featured horns. Scored series of hits in late '60s with variety of material ranging from Screamin' Jay Hawkins' (▶) **I Put A Spell On You** to Randy Newman's(▶) **Simon Smith And His Amazing Dancing Bear**.

Following break-up of band, Price became involved in short-lived project with Georgie Fame called Fame And Price Together, which resulted in major hit single **Rosetta**. One album was also released.

In 1973 Price was asked by director Lindsay Anderson to score movie 'O Lucky Man', and result met with much acclaim. The following year he embarked on semi-concept album, **Between Yesterday And Today**, which delineated life of young man from North-East who makes good in London. A single from album, **Jarrow Song**, became major hit in 1975; album itself was also successful. **Jarrow Song**, probably one of the most unusual pop hits ever, is a complicated, elaborately produced saga about a hunger march that took place in 1926. At time of release, TV documentary about Price's life was broadcast.

Price left Warner Bros for Polydor and later Jet, and his record success since has been only sporadic. However, in late '70s his career developed to include writing music for theatre and television, and acting, and he has remained in demand as personality and as artist. 1983 reformation of Animals has added intriguing new chapter to Price's extensive and varied career.

Hit Singles:

	US	UK
I Put A Spell On You, 1966	—	9
Hi Lili Hi Lo, 1966	—	11
Simon Smith And His Amazing Dancing Bear, 1967	—	4
The House That Jack Built, 1967	—	4
Don't Stop The Carnival, 1968	—	13
Jarrow Song, 1974	—	6

Fame and Price Together:

Rosetta, 1971	—	11

Albums:
The World Of Alan Price (—/Decca), 1970
England My England (—/Jet), 1978
Alan Price (Jet), 1978
Focus On (—/Decca), 1979
Rising Sun (—/Jet), 1980
A Rock And Roll Night At The Royal Court (—/Key), 1981

Worth Searching Out:
O Lucky Man (Soundtrack) (Warner Bros), 1973
Between Yesterday And Today (Warner Bros), 1974

Charly Pride

US vocalist.
Born Sledge, Mississippi, March 18, 1938.

Career: As black performer in country music, Pride is rare, but not unique, and certainly not the first, as is widely chronicled — harmonica player Deford Bailey was featured at 'Grand Ole Opry' from 1925-41.

First interest was baseball; pitched for minor league team Memphis Red Sox in mid-'50s. After spell in military, returned to US seeking pro baseball career, while working at metal plant in adopted homestate of Montana.

Turned to music after trials with major league teams California Angels (ironically now owned by Gene Autry) and New York Mets proved negative. Signed to RCA by Chet Atkins(▶), who had heard impressive demos; tapes were cut at insistence of country star Red Sovine, who urged Pride to try Nashville when singer appeared as support on a show in Pride's hometown Helena, Montana.

With limited publicity, little was known of Pride's background. However, he scored his first hit within year of signing with RCA, **Just Between You And Me**; personal appearances were inevitable. Billed originally as 'Country' Charly Pride, he was launched at the Opry in 1967 having scored further C&W hits; he was, surprisingly, well received.

The recipient of countless CMA, Grammy awards and nominations, Pride is an integral part of mainstream country market. His distinctive baritone voice, delivered without tremelo (unusual for a black performer), has earned him a reputation which belies his roots.

Albums (selected):
The Sensational (RCA), 1969
Best Of Volume 1 (RCA), 1970
Best Of Volume 2 (RCA), 1972
I'm Just Me (RCA), 1972
Sings Everybody's Choice (RCA), 1972
Best Of Volume 3 (RCA), 1976

John Prine

US composer, vocalist, guitarist.
Born Maywood, Illinois, October 10, 1946.

Career: More respected by other artists than by record-buying public, Prine's twangy voice and engaging personality are at odds with subtle metaphor and quirky imagery of his writing. After stint with US Army followed by job with US Post Office, he began singing in Chicago folk clubs in 1969, where original, witty material about lost love, war and drugs attracted cult following. Along with Steve Goodman, Prine was discovered By Kris Kristofferson(▶), who helped him get record contract, and Paul Anka, who provided business advice.

**Diamonds In The Rough, John Prine.
Courtesy Atlantic Records.**

Numerous other performers, including Al Kooper(▶) and Bonnie Raitt(▶), have recorded Prine's songs. Everly Brothers(▶) covered **Paradise**, about evils of strip mining, a cause Prine became associatetd with, playing benefits for Kentucky miners. Another song on same topic, **Muhlenberg County**, was included by Tom T. Hall (an adept songwriter himself) in recent concerts. After first few albums, heavier rock backing was added but failed to achieve commercial success. Change from Atlantic to Asylum label in 1977 did little to increase popular appeal.

Albums:
John Prine (Atlantic), 1972
Diamonds In The Rough (Atlantic), 1972
Sweet Revenge (Atlantic), 1973
Common Sense (Atlantic), 1975
Prime Prine (Atlantic), 1976
Bruised Orange (Asylum), 1978
Pink Cadillac (Asylum), 1979
Storm Windows (Asylum/—), 1980

Procol Harum

UK group formed 1967.
Original line-up: Gary Brooker, vocals, piano; Ray Royer, guitar; Matthew Fisher, organ; David Knights bass; Bobby Harrison, drums.

Career: Brooker was singer with Southend R&B group the Paramounts, who worked club circuit between 1962-66 and had minor hit with re-working of Coasters'(▶) **Poison Ivy**. On break-up of group Brooker started col-

Above: Procol Harum in late 1967 with (left to right) a very young Robin Trower, Gary Brooker, Barry Wilson, Dave Knights, and Matthew Fisher.

laboration with lyricist Keith Reid and recruited above line-up to record songs under name Procol Harum.

Under aegis of producer-entrepreneur Denny Cordell, band released **A Whiter Shade Of Pale** in summer 1967. This highly individualistic cut featuring surrealistic lyrics against cantata-like organ part struck chord with newly psychedelia-orientated record buyers; **Pale** became enormous hit both sides of Atlantic.

Almost immediately line-up was re-shuffled; Royer and Harrison quit to form short-lived Freedom, and were replaced by ex-Paramount Robin Trower(▶) on guitar and B. J. Wilson on drums. This line-up hit with **Homburg** and cut first three Procol albums.

In UK band was regarded as something of one-hit wonder, but US audiences took Procol to heart and American tours were successful. Meanwhile, Matthew Fisher quit band to pursue solo career, followed by David Knights. Bassist Chris Copping, another ex-Paramount, replaced latter and **Home** and **Broken Barricades** were made with band as quartet. Heavier rock direction was in evidence at this time.

Trower left in 1971, finding band too restricting for guitar heroics, and eventually formed highly successful Robin Trower(▶) Band. Copping switched to organ and in came bassist Alan Cartwright and guitarist Dave Ball. In November 1971 band went to Canada to gig with Edmonton Symphony Orchestra. Resulting live album was huge success, especially in US. Extremely successful US tour followed.

In 1973 Mick Grabham replaced Dave Ball, and line-up remained stable until 1976 when Cartwright left. Copping returned to bass and Pete Solley joined on organ.

Final albums suffered from lack of direction and provided only few gems compared to earlier output. Procol Harum eventually disbanded in 1977; Gary Brooker surfaced with solo album **Lead Me To The Water** in 1982.

Procol Harum always cut individualistic path through rock undergrowth, artistic stability being provided by Brooker's music and Reid's lyrics. Characteristic sound of organ and piano topped by Brooker's soul-influenced vocals are best in evidence on early albums. Output is rarely less than interesting and band has considerable influence on development of self-consciously artistic strains of rock.

Final line-up: Brooker; Mick Grabham, guitar; Chris Copping, bass; Pete Solley, organ; B. J. Wilson, drums.

Hit Singles:	US	UK
A Whiter Shade Of Pale, 1967	5	1
Homburg, 1967	34	6
A Whiter Shade Of Pale, 1972	—	13
Conquistador, 1972	16	22
Pandora's Box, 1975	—	16

Albums:
Procol Harum (A&M/Regal Zonophone), 1967†‡
A Salty Dog (A&M/Regal Zonophone), 1969†
Shine On Brightly (A&M/Regal Zonophone), 1969*
Home (A&M/Regal Zonophone), 1970*
Broken Baricades (A&M/Chrysalis), 1971
Live In Concert (A&M/Crysalis), 1972
Grand Hotel (Chrysalis), 1973
Exotic Birds And Fruit (Chrysalis), 1974
Ninth (Chrysalis), 1975
Platinum Collection (—/Cube), 1981
Procol Harum (Greatest Hits) (—/Impact), 1982
†Available as double set (—/Cube), 1975
‡Now known as **A Whiter Shade Of Pale**
*Available as double set (—/Cube), 1975

Bernard Purdie

US drummer.
Born Elkton, Maryland, June 11, 1939.

Career: Bernard 'Pretty' Purdie learnt drums as child; played local gigs in teens. After graduating, moved to New York in 1961 for one week engagement with Mickey and Sylvia. Decided to stay and gained experience while paying rent with laundry job.

In next few years won reputation as first-class session drummer, particularly in soul style. By mid-'60s Purdie had become name in his own right, not least because of Muhammad Ali-style penchant for self-promotion (nickname 'Pretty' was self-awarded).

Purdie has played with many of biggest names in rock and soul, including James Brown(▶), Aretha Franklin(▶), Joe Cocker(▶), Nina Simone(▶), Larry Coryell(▶), Donny Hathaway(▶), Kate and Anna McGarrigle(▶), Steely Dan(▶) and Cat Stevens(▶). Although he has recorded sporadically as leader since 1967, Purdie's claim to fame is really as crème-de-la-crème session man.

Albums:
Worth Searching Out:
Shaft (Prestige), 1976

Pure Prairie League

US group formed 1971.
Original line-up: Craig Fuller, guitar, vocals; George Powell, guitar, vocals; John Call, pedal steel guitar; Jim Lanham, bass; Jim Caughlin, drums.

Career: Fuller and Powell wanted to explore country-rock field opened up by Byrds(▶) and Flying Burrito Brothers(▶). After above line-up settled down, band recorded strong first album. However, there was absolutely no public response and Lanham, Coughlan and Call quit.

Fuller and Powell used session musicians to record equally good follow-up LP, **Bustin' Out**; it also bombed and band began two-year stint working small venues.

In 1974, RCA released **Amie** as single from LP. It became sizeable US hit and band became 'overnight' success while on college circuit. Call returned, but Fuller left in 1975. Adding Michael Conner (keyboards), Larry Goshorm (guitar) and Michael Reilly (bass), band released some rather pedestrian albums. Call left again after **Dance** LP. By this time covers often held as much interest as records within.

1980 label change coincided with more personnel changes but also produced **Firin' Up** album, band's best effort for some time. Following example of Byrds and Flying Burrito Brothers, Pure Prairie League have pushed country and western rock to extreme which is no longer rock and no longer C&W but a unique hybrid.

Current line-up: Michael Reilly, bass; Jeff Wilson, guitar, vocals; Vince Gill, guitar, vocals; Billy Hinds, drums; Michael Connor, keyboards.

Hit Singles:

	US	UK
Let Me Love You Tonight, 1980	10	—

Albums:
Pure Prairie League (RCA), 1972
Bustin' Out (RCA), 1972
Two Lane Highway (RCA), 1975
If The Shoe Fits (RCA), 1976
Dance (RCA), 1976
Live Takin' The Stage (RCA), 1977
Just Fly (RCA), 1978
Firin' Up (RCA), 1980
Pure Prairie Collection (—/RCA), 1981
Something In The Night (Casablanca), 1981

Quarterflash

US group formed 1980.
Original/Current line-up: Rindy Ross, vocals, saxophone; Mark Ross, guitar; Jack Charles, vocals, guitar; Rich Gooch, bass; Rick DiGiallonardo, keyboards; Brian Willis, drums.

Career: Group formed by Mark and Rindy Ross, who had played music together since schooldays in Portland, Oregon, plus members of Pilot, another Portland band. Originally called Seafood Mama, group attracted attention for its obvious musical talent and particularly Rindy Ross' singing/saxophone playing.

Signed by newly formed Geffen Records in early 1981; recorded eponymous debut LP, which reached US Top 10, as did single **Harden My Heart**. Success much more limited in Britain, but group had scored another three progressively smaller US hit singles by late 1982. Quarterflash are shaping up to be classic example of American group playing early '70s rock while the world moves on to something different.

Hit Singles:

	US	UK
Harden My Heart, 1981	3	49
Find Another Fool, 1982	16	—

Album:
Quarterflash (Geffen), 1981

Left: Quarterflash with their focal point, Rindy Ross (holding saxophone).

Suzi Quatro

US vocalist, bass player, guitarist, actress.
Born Detroit, June 3, 1950.

Career: Made debut at eight playing bongos in father Art Quatro's jazz band. Left school at 14 to appear on TV as go-go dancer Suzi Soul. Formed all-girl group Suzi and the Pleasure Seekers at 15 with sisters Patti, Nancy and Arlene. They played all over US and even visited Vietnam for tour of US bases.

Changing name to Cradle, they performed at Detroit dance hall and were seen by British producer Mickie Most (in town to record Jeff Beck Group at Motown studios). Suzi's aggressive stage presence—despite her diminutive size—struck Most as star quality. He expressed interest in bringing her to Britain to sign for his Rak label.

Suzi toured UK working as support act. Most encouraged her songwriting, but, after 1972 debut single **Rolling Stone** flopped, decided to call on services of then amazingly successful British songwriters Nicky Chinn and Mike Chapman.

Encased in black leather jump suit, blatantly sensual legs astride her bass guitar, she thumped away aggressively. Her small figure fronted band of tough guys; this image as trend-setting raunchy female rock star provided perfect showcase for Chinn and Chapman's propulsively direct rockers like chart-toppers **Can The Can**, **48 Crash** and **Devil Gate Drive**.

Put together at time of her 1972 tour as support for Slade, Quatro's band comprised Len Tuckey, guitar; Dave Neal, drums; and keyboard player Alastair McKenzie (soon replaced by Mike Deacon from Vinegar Joe).

Efforts to break in America—had a hit single there with **All Shook Up** and toured widely—caused her to lose grip on UK charts. She has, however, remained major personality of rock scene thanks to wide TV exposure via chart shows, variety shows, panel games and appearances as actress, inititally through 'Happy Days' comedy series as character based on self, Leather Tuscadero, friend of The Fonz Has subsequently done serious plays.

Married her guitarist Len Tuckey in mid-'70s; they now have a baby girl. In 1982 she switched labels to Polydor.

Guitar: Fender Precision bass.

Hit Singles:

	US	UK
Can The Can, 1973	56	1
48 Crash, 1973	—	3
Daytona Demon, 1973	—	14

Above: Suzi Quatro (foreground) on stage with bass and all male backing band.

Devil Gate Drive, 1974	—	1
Too Big, 1974	—	14
The Wild One, 1974	—	7
If You Can't Give Me Love, 1978	—	4
She's In Love With You, 1979	—	11

Albums
Suzi Quatro (Bell/Rak), 1973
Aggro-phobia (—/Rak), 1977
If You Knew Suzie (—/Rak), 1978
Greatest Hits (—/Rak), 1980
Main Attraction (—/Polydor), 1982

Queen

UK group formed 1972.
Original/Current line-up: Brian May, self-made 'May Axe' guitar; Roger Meadows Taylor, drums; Freddie Mercury, vocals; John Deacon, bass.

Career: Evolved from college group Smile, featuring Brian May, Tim Staffell and Roger Meadows Taylor. Smile lasted long enough for series of gigs and one single, **Earth/Step On Me**, released only in US on Mercury. When group folded, Staffell persuaded flatmate Freddie Mercury to join May and Taylor in new venture. Several months later Deacon was added.

Group underwent strenuous rehearsals, playing occasionally at Imperial College, while Mercury masterminded flamboyant satin and silk image. Lucrative contract with EMI was quickly followed by debut single **Keep Yourself Mine**, which flopped. A month prior to its release, Mercury had recorded cover of Beach Boys'(▶) **I Can Hear Music** under pseudonym Larry Lurex, another rare cut.

First album **Queen** revealed group negotiating clever balance between early '70s glam rock and late '60s Zeppelin style heavy metal. With EMI publicity campaign in full swing, group eventually hit charts in early 1974 with **Seven Seas Of Rhye**. By end of 1974 two further LPs were issued, **Queen II** and **Sheer Heart Attack**. Latter attracted critical commendation from certain section of rock press, who praised group for aggressive rock and ingenious arrangements, courtesy of producer Roy Thomas Baker. Success of fifth single **Killer Queen** placed Queen in enviable position of achieving following from both Top 20 fans *and* heavy-metal enthusiasts.

Most of 1975 spent preparing **A Night At The Opera**, one of the most extravagant and expensive albums of era. Pilot single **Bohemian Rhapsody** was ultimate kitsch epic, an elaborate production brilliantly highlighting group's harmonies/guitar work and Mercury's falsetto vocal. Single became

Christmas chart-topper for nine weeks, the longest stay at top since Paul Anka's **Diana** in 1957. From that point on, Queen were established as one of UK's most popular and enduring groups.

Success of **Bohemian Rhapsody** encouraged group to pursue more elaborate and grandiloquent works in complete contrast to their heavy-metal-tinged first three albums. Determined not to be dismissed as '70s glam rock refugees, group have changed image/style frequently in recent years, particularly on singles **Another One Bites The Dust** (penned by Deacon) and rockabilly **Crazy Little Thing Called Love**. Queen have been frequently castigated for pretentiousness and absurd posturings, but their cleverness deserves respect and in Brian May they have one of rock's more stylish guitarists.

Group's single success in recent years has

been enhanced by imaginative use of video, for which their act seems particularly suited. Much-publicised 'Queen's Greatest Flix' has proved consistent No. 1 in video charts over last few years. Group also involved themselves in celluloid rock, writing soundtrack for film 'Flash Gordon' with lyrical/musical contributions from all four members.

International appeal of Queen has increased since late '70s, following gruelling tours of South America and the Far East, often visiting cities not normally associated with rock concerts. Their 75-ton gear and 30-strong road crew continue to provide one of rock's most expensive and spectacular live shows. Perhaps their greatest feat in terms of crossover appeal occurred in 1981 with inspired and bizarre team-up with David Bowie(▶), which produced impressive **Under Pressure**, their first No. 1 since **Bohemian Rhapsody**.

The First Queen album. Courtesy Elektra Records.

Jazz, Queen. Courtesy Elektra/Asylum. Records.

Hit Singles:

	US	UK
Seven Seas Of Rhye, 1974	—	10
Killer Queen, 1974	12	2
Now I'm Here, 1975	—	11
Bohemian Rhapsody, 1975	9	1
You're My Best Friend, 1976	16	7
Somebody To Love, 1976	13	2
Queen's First EP, 1977	—	17
We Are The Champions, 1977	18	2
Bicycle Race/Fat Bottomed Girls, 1978	—	11
Don't Stop Me Now, 1979	—	9
Crazy Little Thing Called Love, 1979	—	2
Save Me, 1980	—	11
Play The Game, 1980	—	14
Another One Bites The Dust, 1980	1	7
Flash, 1980	—	10
Las Palabras de Amor, 1982	—	17
Body Language, 1982	11	—

With David Bowie:

Under Pressure, 1981	29	1

Albums:

Queen (Elektra/EMI), 1973
Queen II (Elektra/EMI), 1974
Sheer Heart Attack (Elektra/EMI), 1974
A Night At The Opera (Elektra/EMI), 1975
A Day At The Races (Elektra/EMI), 1976
News Of The World (Elektra/EMI), 1977
Jazz (Elektra/EMI), 1978
Live Killers (Elektra/EMI), 1979
The Game (Elektra/EMI), 1980
Flash Gordon (Soundtrack) (Elektra/EMI), 1980
Greatest Hits (Elektra/EMI), 1981
Hot Space (Elektra/EMI), 1982

Quicksilver Messenger Service

US group formed 1965.

Original line-up: David Freiberg, bass; John Cipollina, guitar; Jim Murray, vocals; Casey Sonoban, drums; Alexander 'Skip' Spence, guitar, vocals.

Career: Individual members were either folksingers or refugees from prototype San Franciscan groups. Dino Valente was poised to join original line-up but was arrested and jailed on drug charges. By mid-1965, Sonoban and Spence had left, replaced by Gary Duncan (guitar/vocal) and Greg Elmore (drums). Establishing sizeable reputation following free concert appearances, group were wooed by record company A&R men. Resisted signing contract until Capitol coughed up large advance. Initially heard singing two songs on soundtrack of movie 'Revolution'. By October 1967 Murray had quit (later to re-emerge in Copperhead) and group continued as quartet.

Debut **Quicksilver Messenger Service** (May 1968) was seminal San Franciscan rock album, ably demonstrating complementary guitar work of Cipollina and Duncan. Follow-up **Happy Trails** (March 1969) was even better and is generally acknowledged as quintessential San Franciscan acid-rock album. The 25-minute re-working of Bo Diddley's(▶) R&B chestnut **Who Do You Love** remains finest recorded moment.

By January 1968, newly released Valente enticed Duncan away to join the Outlaws(▶), a group that never emerged. Meanwhile, British session-pianist Nicky Hopkins was drafted for less impressive **Shady Grove**. (Band had shortened name to simply 'Quicksilver' by this time.) Following New Year's Eve gig, Valente and Duncan returned, completed Stateside tour and recorded **Just For Love** as six-piece. With Valente assuming dominant role, Hopkins quit (replaced by Mark Naftalin) and group entered period of disillusionment. Cipollina then quit, along with manager Ron Polte, and next album **What About Me** was completed by session musicians.

While recording sixth album, Freiberg was convicted on marijuana charge and imprisoned for two months in July 1971. Following release, reverted to session work before joining Jefferson Starship(▶); replacement was Mark Ryan. During interim Naftalin also left; Chuck Steaks brought in on organ. Succeeding albums **Quicksilver** and **Comin' Thru** displayed little sign of artistic renaissance. A long period of inactivity only brought further line-up changes, involving John Nicolas (bass), Harold Acevas (drums), Bob Hogan (keyboards), Bob Fluria (bass) and Skip Olsen (bass).

Like many San Franciscan groups, Quicksilver's original energy and spark were dissipated amid succession of line-up changes as members sought vainly to recapture old spirit. By mid-'70s even the most die-hard enthusiasts were left with feeling that Quicksilver should have split after 1969 peak.

Attempting to rekindle past glories, a re-formed Quicksilver with Duncan, Cipollina, Freiberg, Elmore and Valente cut **Solid Silver**, a bitter disappointment. Failure of this grand design prompted final dissolution, though occasionally news filters through of Quicksilver re-formations. Valente and Duncan

Left: Queen (from left) Brian May, Freddie Mercury, John Deacon and Roger Taylor.

apparently teamed up with Rick Wetzel and Chris Myers in preparation for September 1977 Breman Festival, but failed to appear.

Final line-up: Freiberg; Cipollina; Gary Duncan, guitar; Greg Elmore, drums; Dino Valente, vocals.

Albums:
Quicksilver Messenger Service (Capitol), 1968
Happy Trails (Capitol), 1969
Shady Grove (Capitol), 1969
Just For Love (Capitol), 1970
What About Me (Capitol), 1971
Quicksilver (Capitol), 1971
Anthology (Capitol), 1973
Solid Silver (Capitol), 1975

REO Speedwagon

US group formed 1971.

Original line-up: Gary Richrath, Gibson Les Paul guitar, vocals; Neil Doughty, keyboards; Alan Gratzer, drums; Gregg Philbin, bass; Barry Luttnell, vocals.

Career: Formed in Champaign, Illinois, REO Speedwagon began years of local, then national, touring. Owing as much to Ted Nugent(▶) and Bob Seger(▶) as any English influence, REO played highly competent rock with no frills.

Stripped-down sound underwent various changes: Luttrell left after first album and Kevin Cronin brought more laid-back almost country feel when he took over vocals. (He was replaced by Michael Murphy in 1974-75 before returning to resume lead vocals.)

You Get What You Play For was live recording and attempted to translate energy of live REO onto vinyl. Widespread success continued to elude band until self-produced **Nine Lives** LP. With new bass player Bruce Hall, REO consolidated its growing popularity through another live album **A Decade Of Rock And Roll 1970-1980**.

Nothing suggested REO would ever produce massive hit, but **Hi Infidelity** roared to top of US charts and became REO's ticket to headlining large concerts. Unexpected success took REO by surprise and band spent over two years following up with next release. It could hardly match its predecessor and **Good Trouble** attracted criticism that REO was Frampton-like one-LP wonder.

Like Foghat, Journey(▶) and Styx(▶), REO suffers from faceless, 'corporate' band image. No individual stands out to grasp fans' attention although Richrath is a fine guitarist. When long years of hard work earned 'overnight success', band was in quandary on how to follow up. Playing hard rock on stage, but owing chart success to ballad-like singles, REO's problem is pleasing two audiences.

Current line-up: Richrath; Doughty; Gratzer; Kevin Cronin, vocals; Bruce Hall, bass.

The debut album. Courtesy Epic Records.

Hit Singles:	US	UK
Keep On Lovin' You, 1981	1	7
Take It On The Run, 1981	5	19
Keep The Fire Burnin', 1982	7	—

Albums:
REO Speedwagon (Epic), 1971
R.E.O. T.W.O. (Epic), 1972
Ridin' The Storm Out (Epic), 1973
Lost In A Dream (Epic), 1974
This Time We Mean It (Epic), 1975
REO (Epic), 1976
You Get What You Play For (Epic), 1977*
You Can Tune A Piano But You Can't Tuna Fish (Epic), 1978
Nine Lives (Epic), 1979
A Decade Of Rock 'n' Roll 1970-1980 (Epic), 1980*
Hi Infidelity (Epic), 1980
Good Trouble (Epic), 1982
*Live

Gerry Rafferty

UK vocalist, composer, guitarist.
Born Paisley, Scotland, April 16, 1947.

Career: Original member of Scottish folk trio Humblebums (with Billy Connolly and Tam Harvey), cutting two albums for ethnic UK label Transatlantic.

Debut solo album **Can I Have My Money Back**, released 1971, featured Joe Egan and Rab Noakes (guitars), and Roger Brown (bass), founding members of Stealers Wheel (with bassist Ian Campbell). Unit quickly disbanded. Rafferty and Egan then recruited Paul Pilnick, guitar, Tony Williams, bass, and Rod Coombes, drums, to supply additional instrumentation for 1973 **Stealers Wheel** album.

LP included **Stuck In The Middle**, a US/UK Top 10 single, and excellent example of legendary producers Leiber/Stoller's(▶) ear for a hit. Still under aegis of Leiber/Stoller, band recorded **Ferguslie Park** (1974) and then **Right Or Wrong** (1975), a Mentor Williams production which marked end of Rafferty/Egan partnership.

Shackled by legal problems resulting from **Stealers Wheel**, Rafferty did not re-surface until 1977, when **City To City** album was released. His melodic, easy-going approach is best demonstrated by **Baker Street**, the million-selling single culled from LP, featuring explosive tenor sax solo by Raphael Ravenscroft.

Sporadic album releases and reluctance to tour have made introverted Rafferty an enigmatic character, but a talent worth persevering with. Joe Egan's solo career has been less satisfactory, despite two acceptable albums for Ariola.

Hit Singles:	US	UK
Baker Street, 1978	2	3
Right Down The Line, 1978	12	—
Days Gone Down, 1979	17	—
Night Owl, 1979	—	5

With Stealers Wheel:
	US	UK
Stuck In The Middle, 1973	6	8

Albums:
Can I Have My Money Back (Blue Thumb/Transatlantic), 1971
Gerry Rafferty Revisited (—/Transatlantic), 1974
Gerry Rafferty (Visa/Logo), 1978
City To City (Liberty/United Artists), 1978
Night Owl (Liberty/United Artists), 1979
Snakes & Ladders (Liberty/United Artists), 1980
Sleepwalking (Liberty), 1982

Rainbow

UK group formed 1975.

Original line-up: Ritchie Blackmore, Fender Stratocaster guitar; Ronnie James Dio, vocals; Mickey Lee Soule, keyboards; Craig Gruber, bass; Gary Driscoll, drums.

Career: Virtuoso guitarist Blackmore was founder-member of Deep Purple(▶), but left amid much speculation in 1975. Joined forces with New York band Elf to form first version of Rainbow. Eponymous album released 1975.

Rainbow's first LP. Courtesy Polydor Records.

Summer of 1976 saw first of succession of personnel changes. Blackmore sacked entire band except Dio, and brought in Jimmy Bain on bass, Tony Carey on keyboards and Cozy Powell on drums. Line-up released **Rainbow Rising**, including tracks with Munich Philharmonic Orchestra. For **Long Live Rock 'n' Roll** LP, group added bassist Bob Daisley and keyboards man was David Stone.

Long Live Rock'n'Roll, Rainbow. Courtesy Polydor Records.

Above: One of the numerous line-ups of Rainbow, led by the unpredictable but charismatic Ritchie Blackmore (second from left) still searching for his perfect band.

The next album heralded reunion with former Purple bassist Roger Glover, while Don Airey replacing Stone and former half of Marbles hit-making duo Graham Bonnet taking over on vocals. This line-up was the most successful so far, scoring two major hit singles. These showed Rainbow to be masters of pop-metal sub-genre, able to combine heavy rock power with commercial melody lines. By now (1980) band had also become top-line live attraction, headlining summer's hugely successful Castle Donnington Festival.

However, further personnel changes were in store. Powell and Bonnet left to pursue solo careers and were replaced by Bob Rondinelli on drums and Joe Lynn Turner on vocals. Run of success continued with album **Difficult To Cure** and hit singles **I Surrender** and **Can't Happen Here**.

Record success continued throughout 1982, although band has yet to make major US impact (album **Straight Between The Eyes** made No. 30 in US album charts). At time of writing Bob Rondinelli had parted company with band.

Reputedly a hard taskmaster, Ritchie Blackmore seems to be searching for perfect line-up to execute his particular vision of the art of heavy metal. Nevertheless, all line-ups have followed roughly same musical direction, and Rainbow has carved out excellent reputation among aficionados of genre. To non-metallic ears, band is at its best executing vigorous and melodic pop-rock.

Current line-up: Blackmore; Joe Lynn Turner, vocals; Roger Glover, bass; Don Airey, keyboards.

Hit Singles:	US	UK
Since You've Been Gone, 1979	57	6
All Night Long, 1980	—	5
I Surrender, 1981	—	3
Can't Happen Here, 1981	—	20

Albums:
Ritchie Blackmore's Rainbow (Polydor), 1975
Rainbow Rising (Polydor), 1976
On Stage (Polydor), 1977
Long Live Rock 'n' Roll (Polydor), 1978
Down To Earth (Polydor), 1979
Difficult To Cure (Polydor), 1981
Jealous Lover (Polydor/—), 1981
The Best Of (Polydor), 1981
Straight Between The Eyes (Polydor), 1982

Bonnie Raitt

US guitarist, vocalist, composer.
Born Los Angeles, California, November 8, 1949.

Career: Grew up in musical family in LA, moved to Cambridge, Boston, area in 1967. Raitt selected Dick Waterman as manager because of his association with various blues artists ,her childhood heroes.

1971 debut LP set pattern of using wide variety of material and musicians for each recording. Subsequent LPs showed maturity, understanding and warmth in Raitt's reading of good contemporary material. Notable examples are: Jackson Browne's(▶) **Under The Falling Sky** and Eric Kaz's **Love Has No Pride** from second LP; Allen Toussaints'(▶) **What Is Success** on **Streetlights** LP; and Hayes-Porter's (▶) **Your Good Thing** from **Glow** album.

Raitt's performances and regular touring finally earned US success with **Sweet Forgiveness** album (1977). **The Glow** was carefully prepared as follow-up and included more original material than previous LPs. It failed to push Raitt towards bigger audience, which may be just as well since some artists have special flair for creating excitement in smaller, more intimate atmosphere. Raitt is a master who is true descendant of her blues heroes.

Albums:
Bonnie Raitt (Warner Bros), 1971
Give It Up (Warner Bros), 1972
Takin' My Time (Warner Bros), 1973
Streetlights (Warner Bros), 1974
Home Plate (Warner Bros), 1975
Sweet Forgiveness (Warner Bros), 1977
The Glow (Warner Bros), 1979
Green Light (Warner Bros), 1982

Ramones

US group formed 1974.

Original line-up: Joey Ramone (Jeffrey Hyman), drums; Dee Dee Ramone (Douglas Coldin), bass; Johnny Ramone (John Cummings), guitar.

Career: Began as a trio, first appearing at New York's Performance Studio in March 1974. Four months later, manager Tommy Ramone (Tommy Erdelyi) became drummer, with Joey switching to lead vocals (original and later members all changed from real names to 'Ramone'). Residency at CBGBs (new wave club in NY's Bowery) in summer allowed group to develop stage act, but on first attempt to spread wings—opening Johnny Winter(▶) concert—they were booed from stage. Danny Fields took over management in late 1975, having already worked with MC5(▶), the Stooges and Lou Reed(▶).

Record deal with Sire led to recording of debut **Ramones**, released in April 1976. Album served as catalyst by encouraging other companies to sign many of New York's up-and-coming young acts. Prototype new wave rockers, group received rapturous welcome in UK in summer of '76, heavily influencing emerging punk movement with their distinctive dress (leather jackets and torn jeans) and high-speed minimalist rock (17 song sets played in half an hour!).

Next two albums, **Leave Home** and **Rocket To Russia**, established familiar pattern of high-powered rock based on late '50s/early '60s themes. Singles were uniformly impressive, but neither **Sheena Is A Punk Rocker** nor **Swallow My Pride** cracked Top 20. Having championed pinheads, cretins and glue sniffing during 1977, group were swiftly becoming redundant following first flowering of punk. In May 1978, Tommy departed to become producer, playing memorable farewell gig at CBGBs. New drummer Marc Bell (Marty Ramone) debuted on 1978's **Road To Ruin** and LP proved most commercially successful to date, though met mixed response from critics, disturbed by mid-tempo material. Following in England was underlined by release of double **It's Alive** from Rainbow gigs of 1979.

Very much the spirit of CBGBs, Ramones have modified original formula to a minimal degree over the years, though union with producer Phil Spector resulted in less raucous material in **End Of The Century**. Group only finally broke into UK charts late in 1980 with uncharacteristic but memorable violin-steeped cover of Ronettes' 1964 hit, **Baby I Love You**, a complete contrast to earlier head-banging material. 1980 also saw release of first feature film 'Rock'n' Roll High School', the title of a track from **End Of The Century**.

Often dismissed as unintelligent and ephemeral, Ramones have survived '70s intact. 1981 album, **Pleasant Dreams**, a return to basics with 12 self-penned songs, showed group's astuteness in employing professional hitmaker Graham Gouldman (Mindbenders, 10 cc) as producer. Latest album, **Subterranean Jungle**, received strong support from critics, several of whom compared it favourably with the best of group's early work. Since recording the album, drummer Bell has been replaced by ex-Velveteen Richard Beau (now Ricky Ramone).

Current line-up: Joey; Dee Dee; Johnny; Ricky Ramone, drums.

Hit Single:

	US	UK
Baby I Love You, 1980	—	8

Albums:
Leave Home (Sire), 1977
Rocket To Russia (Sire), 1977

Below: The Ramones in a still from the 1980 'Rock'n'Roll High School' feature film in which they starred.

Road To Ruin (Sire), 1978
It's Alive (—/Sire), 1979
End Of The Century (Sire), 1980
Pleasant Dreams (Sire), 1981
Subterranean Jungle (Sire), 1983

Worth Searching Out:
Ramones (Sire), 1976

Johnnie Ray

US vocalist, pianist, actor.
Born John Alvin Ray, Dallas, Oregon, January 10, 1927.

Career: First professional appearance at age 15 with Jane Powell on Portland, Oregon, radio talent show. Moved south to California in 1949 and for next two years worked night clubs and bars in Hollywood. Moved to Detroit in 1951; discovered by DJ Robin Seymour who obtained record deal with Columbia Records. Following success of double-sided hit **Cry/The Little White Cloud That Cried**, many presumed singer was black as single was released on Columbia's R&B subsidiary Okeh.

Ray's vocal histrionics earned him nickname 'The Prince of Wails', and he rapidly became one of the most popular artists of early '50s. Inspired a fanatical, sometimes hysterical, fan following; near-riots resulted when he toured Britain just prior to the rock 'n' roll explosion.

First film with Ethel Merman, 'There's No Business Like Show Business', led to further film roles and major US theatre productions. Record sales waned in US but hits continued into rock 'n' roll era in UK, with **Yes Tonight Josephine** almost making permanent transition.

Since age 15 has worn hearing aid and has devoted much time to raising funds in aid of deaf children. In recent years has toured while continuing charity work and occasionally recording.

Hit Singles:

	US	UK
Cry/The Little White Cloud That Cried, 1951	*	*
Please Mr Sun/Here I Am Brokenhearted, 1952	*	*
What's The Use, 1952	*	*
Walking My Baby Back Home, 1952	*	*
Faith Can Move Mountains, 1952	*	*
Somebody Stole My Gal, 1953	*	*
Such A Night, 1954	*	*
If You Believe, 1955	—	*
Paths Of Paradise, 1955	—	20

Above: Johnnie Ray who has worn a hearing aid since 15, hands out presents at one of the schools for deaf children to which he gives financial aid.

Hey There, 1955	—	5
Song Of The Dreamer, 1955	—	10
Who's Sorry Now, 1956	—	17
Ain't Misbehavin', 1956	—	17
Just Walkin' In The Rain, 1956	2	1
You Don't Owe Me A Thing/ Look Homeward Angel, 1957	10	12
Look Homeward Angel/You Don't Owe Me A Thing, 1957	36	7
Yes Tonight Josephine, 1957	12	1
Build Your Love (On A Strong Foundation), 1957	58	18

Albums:
Best Of (—/Hallmark), 1968
Greatest Hits (Columbia/Embassy), 1977
An American Legend (—/Embassy), 1979
20 Golden Greats (—/MSD), 1979
Yesterday, Today And Tomorrow (RCA), 1981

Redbone

US group formed 1968.

Original/Final line-up: Lolly Vegas, lead guitar, vocals; Tony Bellamy, rhythm guitar, vocals; Pat Vegas, bass; Peter DePoe, drums.

Career: Formed on a Cheyenne reservation in Washington State, Redbone — the name was derived from rehbone, the cajun epithet for half-breed — exploited their Red Indian heritage while purveying potent mixture of soul and swamp rock.

Early years were split between working as migrant farm labourers and backing black artists, including John Lee Hooker and folk/gospel star Odetta. The Vegas brothers penned **Niki Hokey**, a hit for P. J. Proby and Bobbie Gentry, and wrote group's own world-wide smash **Witch Queen Of New Orleans** (1971). After initial string of worthwhile albums, moving gradually from highly rhythmic swamp rock to smooth soul, and 1975 million-seller **Come And Get Your Love**, their career rapidly declined.

Hit Singles:

	US	UK
Witch Queen Of New Orleans, 1971	21	2
Come And Get Your Love, 1974	5	—

Albums:
Worth Searching Out:
Potlatch (Columbia/CBS), 1970
Witch Queen Of New Orleans (Epic), 1971

Leon Redbone

Canadian guitarist, vocalist.
Real name/birthdate not available.

Career: Redbone first appeared in Toronto night-clubs in 1970. His act included ragtime, jazz and blues standards, all done as one-man band with funny wheezes, grunts and Groucho Marx poses. First Bob Dylan(▶), then other performers, began mentioning him as an original talent because of his bizarre interpretations. The intrigue grew when Redbone refused to provide any personal information, not even confirming Redbone as his real name.

The man from nowhere, of indeterminate age, continued to play music his way, either as publicity stunt or for personal reasons. He did consent (although reluctantly, he claimed) to sign Warner Bros record contract. TV appearances and tours followed, Redbone wisely keeping to folk circuit and small venues. His albums sold, not particularly well, but enough to keep him in business.

Following third album **Champagne Charles**, Redbone began appearing with two or more side musicians, but style remained the same and it seems Redbone is content to maintain low profile.

Albums:
On The Track (Warner Bros), 1975
Double Time (Warner Bros), 1976
Champagne Charles (Warner Bros), 1977
From Branch To Branch (Emerald City), 1981

Otis Redding

US vocalist, composer.
Born Macon, Georgia, September 9, 1941; died December 10, 1967.

Career: All-time soul great, Redding started musical career in time-honoured fashion, singing in local church choir and at gigs around his home town of Macon. Through school-friend Phil Walden (later to head up Capricorn Records), Redding was introduced to local band Johnny Jenkins and the Pinetoppers, and in 1959 joined them on the road as general assistant and occasional vocalist.

Redding recorded various sides over the next few years for several small labels, but did not taste success until 1962 when he cut **These Arms Of Mine** and **Hey Hey Baby** at the end of a Jenkins recording session at Stax Studios. Stax boss Jim Stewart was impressed by Redding's style and composing talent, releasing **These Arms Of Mine** in November 1962.

The single made impression on US charts, and paved way for succession of successful singles over next few years. Master of the soul ballad, Redding was particularly affecting on slow numbers like **Pain In My Heart, That's How Strong My Love Is**, the classic **I've Been Loving You Too Long** and the much-loved **My Girl**, but was capable of whipping up a storm of excitement on uptempo material. Classic Redding stompers include **Respect, I Can't Turn You Loose**, Sam Cooke's(▶) **Shake, Hard To Handle** and **Love Man**.

Many soul albums feature one or two hits and a lot of mediocre padding, but Redding's albums were of consistently high standard. The definitive Redding album is **Otis Blue**, a superbly balanced set of ballads and uptempo material which includes a magisterial version of B. B. King's **Rock Me Baby**.

Otis Redding also excelled as live performer, and toured regularly between 1964

Left: **The utterly enigmatic Leon Redbone, whose age has been variously put between 25 and 60, but whose music veers towards the latter extreme.**

and 1967. He headed the 1965 Stax-Volt tour of Europe and made other trips to UK with own band, and during this period was probably appreciated more in Britain than in his native country. Never giving less than 100% of himself, Otis Redding was the performer for whom the term 'soul' might have been invented. Dancing, dropping to his knees, running on the spot, urging on members of his band, he radiated energy and emotional commitment.

In 1967 Redding's career looked set to achieve new levels of success. His appearance at Monterey Pop Festival, recorded on 1970 Reprise LP **Monterey International Pop Festival: Otis Redding/The Jimi Hendrix Experience**, on bill which featured heavy rock acts like Jimi Hendrix(▶) and the Who(▶), was hailed by critics and fans alike, European tour later the same year won him more friends, so much so that he was voted top international male singer by Melody Maker readers. But just as everything seemed to be coming together for the soul star, Redding was killed when his plane crashed into Lake Monona in Wisconsin in 1967. Several members of his band, the Bar-Kays, also perished.

As often happens, Redding's tragic death seemed to improve his marketability. Posthumous single **Dock Of The Bay** reached top of American charts and became a million-seller, and made No. 3 in Britain. It was easily his biggest hit.

One of the most important and best-loved of the '60s soul heroes, Redding had an inimitable vocal style and ability to get to the heart of a song, particularly ballads. Scorned during the psychedelic and 'heavy rock' eras, he is now revered as one of the major influences of black music.

Hit Singles:	US	UK
My Girl, 1965	—	11
Tramp (with Carla Thomas), 1967	—	18
Dock Of The Bay, 1968	1	3
Hard To Handle, 1968	51	15

Albums:
Otis Blue (Atco/Atlantic), 1966

Otis Redding Live In Europe (Volt/Atlantic), 1966
The Immortal Otis Redding (Atco/Atlantic), 1968
Love Man (Atco/Atlantic), 1969
History Of Otis Redding (Atco/Atlantic), 1969
History Of Otis Redding (Volt/Atlantic), 1970
Best Of (Atco/Atlantic), 1972
Pure Otis (Atco/Atlantic), 1979
Recorded Live (Atlantic), 1982

Worth Searching Out:
Pain In My Heart (Atco/Atlantic), 1965
Dictionary Of Soul (Volt/Atlantic), 1966
Sings Soul Ballads (Atco/Atlantic), 1970

Jimmy Reed

US vocalist, guitarist, harmonica player, composer.
Born Mathis James Reed Leland, Mississippi, September 6, 1925; died August 29, 1976.

Career: Though often criticised for narrow spectrum of his creativity and at times monotonous nature of his style, Jimmy Reed was highly influential urban blues musician whose work influenced the Rolling Stones(▶), the Who(▶) and other rock bands.

Reed grew up in blues-rich Mississippi Delta country and learned guitar from friend

A Jimmy Reed reissue. Courtesy Charly Records.

Eddie Taylor. He also became adept harmonica player.

Reed moved to Chicago in 1943 but returned to South after discharge from Naval service. Three years later, on breakdown of marriage, he moved North again, to Gary, Indiana. Working local nightspots, he eventually broke into Chicago Southside blues club circuit where he played with John Brim, Eddie Taylor and Albert King (then a drummer).

DJ Vivian Carter and record-shop owner Jimmy Bracken signed Reed to their Vee-Jay label in 1953 and scored in late 1954 with **You Don't Have To Go**, first of string of 14 R&B chart entries of which 12 were pop hits.

Reed's lazy, hypnotic four-to-the-bar rhythms (later adopted most effectively by Slim Harpo) made him big concert draw as well as recording star, numbers like **Big Boss Man, Shame Shame Shame** (which made UK charts in 1964 and was shamelessly cribbed by the Rolling Stones as **Little By Little**), and **Baby What You Want Me To Do** (covered superbly by Little Richard(▶)) entered the repertoire of countless groups and solo artists, black and white alike.

Coping with epilepsy and his somewhat erratic personality, Reed became an alcoholic, often failing to show for dates, while his performances ranged from brilliant to dire. He died in 1976.

Albums:
At Soul City (Vee-Jay/Joy), 1960s
Big Boss Man (Bluesway/DJM), 1973
Best Of (GNP/Joy), 1974
Jimmy Reed Is Back (-/Joy), 1976

Lou Reed

US vocalist, guitarist, composer.
Born Long Island, New York, March 2, 1943.

Career: Born into rich middle-class family. Spent much of adolescence 'rebelling' in various punk/garage groups (Pasha and the Prophets, the Eldorados, the Shades and the Jades). Later attended Syracuse University; dropped out; dabbled in journalism, acting and music. Record companies refused songs because of their bizarre nature, so for time he wrote conventional love songs, but eventually organised new group with another disenchanted performer, John Cale/(▶). Velvet Underground(▶) achieved some measure of fame and notoriety, mainly in New York, but albums were too controversial for mass consumption; group eventually folded in 1970, after which their influence was increasingly felt.

Reed drifted for a year, even taking up employment at father's accountancy firm in Long Island, before signing RCA contract in late 1971. Moved to Britain to work on solo debut with aid of New York writer Richard Robinson. **Lou Reed** was effective in parts, but spoiled by uninspired production.

Luck changed when David Bowie(▶) took interest in Reed's career. With Bowie in producer's chair, sessions were completed for **Transformer**; Reed was invited to appear at Royal Festival Hall alongside the androgynous one. Album received great publicity, sold well, and spawned memorable and controversial hit **Walk On The Wild Side**. The appearance of Reed in eye liner, singing deliberately risqué songs, yet minus the true menace of his Velvet Underground work, led to accusations of commercial sell-out. Reed was clearly parodying himself, and has continued to do so

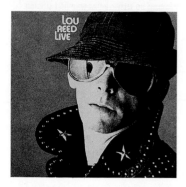

Live and Loud, 1975. Courtesy RCA Records.

**Lou or Liza Minelli?
Courtesy RCA Records.**

frequently over the years. **Berlin** was attempt to recapture power of Velvets' work, but in spite of some critical approbation, failed commercially. Nevertheless it remains Reed's most harrowing album in its analysis of sado/masochism and suicide.

Following **Berlin** sessions, Reed assembled touring group comprising Dick Wagner (guitar), Steve Hunter (guitar), Prakash John (bass) and Whitey Glan (drums). One of their better performances, at NY's Academy Of Music, released as **Rock 'n' Roll Animal**. Having partially restored credibility, Reed faltered with next work, **Sally Can't Dance**, his least inspired to this point. Another average effort followed before horrendous **Metal Machine Music**, a double album of 'electronic music', consisting almost entirely of tape hum. Rock's premier candidate for 'the worst album ever made', **Metal Machine Music** was ultimate example of artistic suicide.

Coney Island Baby was reasonable, yet hardly sufficient to repair damage done to career. Since then, Reed has had mixed fortunes, and Arista albums, including **Street Hassle** (co-produced by Richard Robinson), **The Bells** and **Growing Up In Public**, received merely lukewarm response from critics and public. In October 1981, recorded a new work with producer Sean Fuller at RCA's

New York studios; **The Blue Mask**, released in 1982, proved surprise return to form. Latest work, **Legendary Hearts**, though less impressive than its predecessor, indicates that Reed is not a completely spent force.

Hit Singles:	US	UK
Walk On The Wild Side, 1973	16	10

Albums:
Lou Reed (RCA), 1972
Transformer (RCA), 1972
Berlin (RCA), 1973
Rock 'n' Roll Animal (RCA), 1974
Sally Can't Dance (RCA), 1974
Lou Reed Live (RCA), 1975
Coney Island Baby (RCA), 1976
Rock And Roll Heart (Arista), 1976
Walk On The Wild Side — The Best Of Lou Reed (RCA), 1977
Street Hassle (Arista), 1978
Live — Take No Prisoners (Arista), 1978
The Bells (Arista), 1979
Growing Up In Public (Arista), 1980
Rock 'n' Roll Diary 1967-1980 (Arista), 1980
The Blue Mask (RCA), 1982
Legendary Hearts (RCA), 1983

Below: One of the original members of the Velvet Underground, Lou Reed, in the 1970s.

Jim Reeves
US vocalist.
Born Galloway, Texas, August 20, 1923; died July 31, 1964.

Career: Reeves' early life of rural poverty was relieved by interest in music, fuelled by Jimmie Rodgers records. He took up guitar at five, landed first radio broadcast at nine and by 15 was regular performer on local radio in Shreveport, Louisiana.

At University of Texas Reeves was outstanding baseball player and athlete, but passed up career as professional pitcher because of injury. Eventually he joined radio station in Henderson, Texas, as DJ/announcer, performing in local clubs in spare time.

In 1947 he met and married schoolteacher Mary White; pair moved to Shreveport where Reeves joined radio station KWKH, home of famous 'Louisiana Hayride'. Reeves announced show and was given occasional singing spot. Filling in one night for indisposed Hank Williams, he was heard by Abbott Records head Favor Robinson; immediate signing followed. Second release, **Mexican Joe**, was smash pop hit, the first of many country-pop crossover successes.

Reeves changed from Abbott to RCA in 1955, and became 'Grand Ole Opry' regular. Continued to broaden appeal throughout '50s with US and European touring; massive smash **He'll Have To Go** confirmed him as international star in 1959.

Further chart action followed until singer's death in plane crash in 1964. As ever, demise accelerated record sales, major international successes continuing through '60s into early '70s, particularly in Britain. Highest charting single was **Distant Drums**, No. 1 in the UK in 1966. He was voted into Country Music Hall of Fame in 1967.

Very much representative of easy-listening side of country music, Reeves' output is generally unacceptable to rock-orientated ears; even by country standards, many of his recordings are banal, saccharine ditties unredeemed by his obvious emotional commitment. Arrangements and production generally show Nashville at its most bland and uninventive. However, Reeves' pleasant baritone voice and 'Gentleman Jim' persona held strong appeal for millions, and he was one of first country-orientated artists to break pop and international markets. Much of his carefully chosen material has since become standard MOR fare; **He'll Have To Go** was featured on Ry Cooder's album **Chicken Skin Music**.

Hit Singles:	US	UK
Four Walls, 1957	11	—
He'll Have To Go, 1960	2	12
You're The Only Good Thing, 1961	—	17
Welcome To My World, 1963	—	6
I Love You Because, 1964	—	5
I Won't Forget You, 1964	—	3
There's A Heartache Following Me, 1964	—	6
It Hurts So Much, 1965	—	8
Not Until The Next Time, 1965	—	13
Is It Really Over, 1965	—	17
Distant Drums, 1966	45	1
I Won't Come In While He's There, 1967	—	12
When Two Worlds Collide, 1969	—	17
But You Love Me Daddy, 1969	—	15

Albums (selected):
Best Of (RCA), 1974
A Legendary Performer (RCA), 1976
Hits Of (RCA), 1977
Unforgettable (RCA), 1979
Greatest Hits (with Patsy Cline) (RCA), 1982

Renaissance
UK group formed 1969.
Original line-up: Keith Relf, vocals, harmonica; Jim McCarty, drums; Jane Relf, vocals; John Hawken, keyboards; Louis Cennamo, bass.

Career: Originally formed as minor league supergroup with ex-Yardbirds Keith Relf and Jim McCarty teaming up with Hawken (ex-Nashville Teens), and Relf's sister Jane as lead vocalist. Folk-based songs combined with classical, jazz and rock elements provided blueprint for **Renaissance** (1969). Results proved less than satisfactory and group dissolved. Keith Relf went on to form Armaggedon, then left after debut LP. Died in 1976 (accidental self-electrocution).

Early 1972, group re-formed with completely new line-up comprising Annie Haslam (vocals), Michael Dunford (guitar, vocals), John Camp (bass, vocals), John Tant (keyboards) and Terence Sullivan (percussion). **Prologue**, released same year, was ignored in UK but met favourable response Stateside. Not surprisingly, group emigrated to States, attracting a growing cult following during successive years. Original ideas of Relfs were still discernible in new line-up's attempts to synthesise classical, folk and rock. Musical pot-pourri was further complicated by inclusion of lyrics by poet Betty Thatcher.

Generally regarded as too contrived, even for rock mainstream, their relative success Stateside proved sufficient for group to survive '70s. A Top 10 single, **Northern Lights**, brought them belated but brief British recognition in 1978.

Current line-up: Mike Dunford, guitar, vocals; John Camp, vocals, guitar; John Tant, keyboards; Terence Sullivan, drums; Maggie Reilly, vocals.

Hit Single:	US	UK
Northern Lights, 1978	—	10

Albums:
Renaissance (Island), 1969
Prologue (Sovereign), 1972
Ashes Are Burning (Sovereign), 1973
Turn Of The Cards (BTM), 1975
Scheherazade & Other Stories (BTM), 1975
Renaissance Live At Carnegie Hall (BTM), 1975
Novella (WB), 1977
Illusion (—/Island), 1977*
A Song For All Seasons (WB), 1978
Azure D'Or (WB), 1979
Time Live (A&M), 1983
*First released 1970, making it second LP by original Renaissance line-up.

Charlie Rich
US vocalist, pianist, composer.
Born Colt, Arkansas, December 14, 1934.

Career: Rockabilly singer turned country music star, Rich's first music was jazz and blues. While with USAF in Oklahoma in early '50s, his group the Velvetones (with wife Margaret on vocals) worked on local TV. After discharge, he moved back to work on father's cotton farm in West Memphis, Arkansas.

Bill Justis (who scored with instrumental **Raunchy** in 1958) introduced Rich to Sam Philips at Sun Records' studio in Memphis. Philips thought Rich's style too sophisticated and loaned him pile of Jerry Lee Lewis(▶) records so he could learn rockabilly idiom. After sessions backing Warren Smith, Ray Smith, Billy Lee Riley and others, Rich came up with own 1959 rockabilly smash **Lonely Weekends**.

On demise of Sun, Justis took Rich to RCA's Groove subsidiary for which he was working and new association yielded 1963 hit **Big Boss Man**. Nashville-based Shelby Singleton signed Rich in 1965 to Mercury's Smash subsidiary and encouraged artist to broaden style utilising rock 'n' roll, country, R&B and soul influences. Result was classic **Mohair Sam** and superlative LP, including re-makes of earlier hits.

Moving into straight country vein Rich recorded sentimental ballads for Hi without success. Making concerted push into country music, Epic then signed Rich and teamed him with their ace Nashville producer Billy Sherrill. Initial releases gained only modest sales, but critical acclaim. In 1972, **I Take It On Home** with **Peace On You** on flip was country and pop smash and earned Grammy nomination.

Behind Closed Doors and chart-topping **The Most Beautiful Girl** singles along with album transformed Rich into country superstar; also crossed over into international pop charts.

A succession of similar sophisticated Nashville albums followed. In 1979 Rich switched to Elektra, scoring with **I'll Wake You Up When I Get Home** album. Since then, pop success has eluded Rich (nicknamed 'the Silver Fox') though he continues to be popular in country idiom.

Hit Singles:

	US	UK
Behind Closed Doors, 1973	15	16
The Most Beautiful Girl, 1973	1	2
There Won't Be Any More, 1974	18	—
A Very Special Love Song, 1974	11	—
Every Time You Touch Me (I Get High), 1975	19	—

Albums (selected):

Early Years (Sun/—), 1960s
Memphis Sound (Sun/—), 1960s
Sun's Best (Sun/—), 1960s
20 Golden Hits (Sun/—), 1960s
Lonely Weekends (Sun/Charly), 1975
Original Charlie Rich (Sun/Charly), 1978
Behind Closed Doors (Epic), 1973
Greatest Hits (Epic), 1976
A Trio Plus (with Jerry Lee Lewis and Carl Perkins) (Sun/Charly), 1980

Worth Searching Out:
Many Sides Of Charlie Rich Featuring Mohair Sam (Smash—), 1965
Silver Fox (Epic), 1977

Cliff Richard

UK vocalist, guitarist, composer.
Born Harry Rodger Webb, Lucknow, India, October 14, 1940.

Career: Spent childhood in colonial India where English father worked for catering company; returned to UK in 1948. Following early racial problems due to sunburnt skin, soon became integrated into post-war British life, discovering rock 'n' roll via Bill Haley(▶) and especially Elvis Presley(▶); played in local skiffle groups. Formed the Drifters in 1958, which included Terry Smart (drums), Norman Mitham (guitar) and Richard himself (guitar, vocals). Mitham then replaced by Ian Samwell. After impressing agent with neo-Presley style, signed to EMI's Columbia label in August 1958. First single **Move It**, written by Samwell, recorded with session musicians, is now regarded as first British rock 'n' roll record.

Booked to appear on national tour, recruited new band — Smart, Samwell (bass), plus guitarists Hank B. Marvin (real name

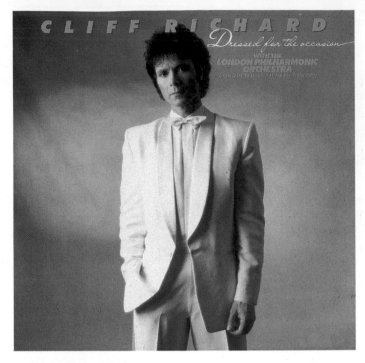

Dressed for the Occasion, 1983 LP by Cliff. Courtesy EMI Records

Brian Marvin) and Bruce Welch, both from Newcastle. After tour, Smart and Samwell were replaced by Jet Harris (bass) and Tony Meehan (drums) — entire band (including Cliff) was spawned by early London rock 'n' roll coffee bar, the '2Is'. Cliff and the Drifters became original British rock superstars, with ten Top 10 singles; by end of 1960, Drifters (changing name to Shadows to avoid confusion with black US vocal group) were chart-topping act in own right.

Cliff and Shadows appeared in several very popular films during '60s, including 'Expresso Bongo', 'The Young Ones', 'Summer Holiday', 'Wonderful Life' and 'Finder's Keepers'. By mid-1962 Harris and Meehan had left group for short-lived solo success, replaced by Brian Bennett (drums) and first Brian Locking, later John Rostill (bass). Hits continued in UK: 43 for Cliff, including eight No. 1's, plus 24 for Shadows, including five No. 1's, by 1968. Still very little US success. By end of '60s, Shadows had disbanded, but Cliff's success continued; his early rock 'n' roll was toned down to become 'family entertainment' and withstood Merseybeat/R&B crazes of early and mid-'60s. However, conversion to Christianity in '66 blunted his pop sensibility.

Continued (sometimes with re-formed Shadows, including Marvin, Welch and Bennett) as prime cabaret attraction with own TV series ,but seemed generally out of touch with youth during progressive rock years, although twice representing UK in Eurovision Song Contest. Rostill died in November 1973 from accidental electrocution. John Farrar, member of an Australian group based on Shadows, joined Marvin, Welch and Farrar group in 1970 and cut two albums. Farrar joined Shadows in 1972.

Cliff appeared close to retirement by mid-'70s; returned with strong material and arrangements **Miss You Nights** and **Devil**

Woman in 1976; latter was first US Top 10 hit. 1977 compilation LP **40 Golden Greats** was a huge seller which topped UK charts. Rest of '70s continued with 20th Anniversary celebrations by Cliff and Shadows, with end of decade providing Cliff's tenth No. 1 single, **We Don't Talk Anymore** (first chart topper since 1968), and growing US following.

In 1980 Richard was awarded OBE by Queen Elizabeth II. Charted with duet **Suddenly** from film 'Xanadu', with Olivia Newton-John(▶), whom he had helped to fame via his early '70s TV series. In 1983, Cliff celebrated 25 years as a rock star, having scored over 80 British hit singles, including ten No. 1's, plus numerous big-selling LPs. His appeal as clean, well-spoken boy next door seems undiminished by passage of time, and his fans range in age from eight to 80. It would appear that Cliff has no intention of retiring in near future — after dry chart period during '70s, he is now once again able to rely on every release becoming a hit, every concert a sell-out, although major US success continues to elude him.

Hit Singles:

	US	UK
Move It, 1958*	—	2
High Class Baby, 1958*	—	7
Livin' Lovin' Doll, 1959*	—	20
Mean Streak/Never Mind, 1959*	—	10
Living Doll, 1959*	30	1
Travellin' Light, 1959†	—	1
Dynamite, 1959†	—	16
Expresso Bongo (EP), 1960†	—	14
A Voice In The Wilderness, 1960†	—	2
Fall In Love With You, 1960†	—	2
Please Don't Tease, 1960†	—	1
Nine Times Out Of Ten, 1960†	—	3
I Love You, 1960†	—	1
Theme For A Dream, 1961†	—	3
Gee Whiz It's You, 1961†	—	4
A Girl Like You, 1961†	—	3
When The girl In Your Arms Is The Girl In Your Heart, 1961	—	3
The Young Ones, 1962†	—	1

Below: The Dorian Gray of rock'n'roll. Cliff and the Shadows in the early '60s (left to right) Jet Harris, Cliff Richard, Brian Bennett, Bruce Welch. It was obviously Hank Marvin's turn to make the tea...

	US	UK
I'm Looking Out The Window/ Do You Wanna Dance, 1962	—	2
It'll Be Me, 1962†	—	2
The Next Time/Bachelor Boy, 1962†	—	1
Summer Holiday, 1963†	—	1
Lucky Lips, 1963†	—	4
It's All In The Game, 1963	25	2
Don't Talk To Him, 1963†	—	2
I'm The Lonely One, 1964†	—	8
Constantly, 1964	—	4
On The Beach, 1964†	—	7
The Twelfth Of Never, 1964	—	8
I Could Easily Fall, 1964†	—	9
The Minute You're Gone, 1965	—	1
On My Word, 1965	—	12
Wind Me Up (Let Me Go), 1965	—	2
Blue Turns To Grey, 1966†	—	15
Visions, 1966	—	7
Time Drags By, 1966†	—	10
In The Country, 1966†	—	6
It's All Over, 1967	—	9
The Day I Met Marie, 1967	—	10
All My Love, 1967	—	6
Congratulations, 1968	—	1
Good Times (Better Times), 1969	—	12
Big Ship, 1969	—	8
Throw Down A Line, 1969**	—	7
With The Eyes Of A Child, 1969	—	20
Goodbye Sam, Hello Samantha, 1970	—	6
Sunny Honey Girl, 1971	—	19
Sing A Song Of Freedom, 1971	—	13
Living In Harmony, 1972	—	12
Power To All Our Friends, 1973	—	14
(You Keep Me) Hangin' On, 1974	—	13
Miss You Nights, 1976	—	15
Devil Woman, 1976	6	9
I Can't Ask For Anything More Than You Babe, 1976	—	17
My Kinda Life, 1977	—	15
We Don't Talk Anymore, 1979	7	1
Carrie, 1980	34	4
Dreamin', 1980	7	8
A Little In Love, 1981	11	15
Wired For Sound, 1981	—	4
Daddy's Home, 1981	23	2
The Only Way Out, 1982	—	10
Little Town, 1982	—	11
True Love Ways, 1983	—	8

With Olivia Newton-John
Suddenly, 1980	20	15

With Phil Everly:
She Means Nothing To Me, 1983	—	9

*with Shadows (As Drifters)
†with Shadows
**with Hank Marvin

Albums (selected):
The Young Ones (—/Columbia), 1961
Summer Holiday (Epic/Columbia), 1963
I'm Nearly Famous (Rocket/EMI), 1976
40 Golden Greats (—/EMI), 1977
Rock 'n' Roll Juvenile (—/EMI), 1979
Wired For Sound (EMI America/EMI), 1981
Dressed For The Occasion (—/EMI), 1983

Lionel Richie

US vocalist, composer, producer.
Born June 20, 1949.

Career: Former economics major, then lead singer of the Commodores(▶), Richie cited media pressure as reason for his departure for solo career.

Initial projects included production/writing brief for Kenny Rogers(▶) on **Shine On** set, which included **Lady** smash single, and duet with Diana Ross(▶) on movie score **Endless Love**.

First solo success was **Truly**, a typical piece of Richie balladeering, featuring his fractured, but precise, vocals.

Hit Singles:
	US	UK
Endless Love (with Diana Ross), 1981	1	7
Truly, 1982	1	6
You Are, 1983	4	44

Albums:
Lionel Richie (Motown), 1982

Jonathan Richman

US vocalist, composer.
Born Boston, May 16, 1951.

Career: First put together the Modern Lovers during late '60s, heavily influenced by '50s rock, girl groups and, most noticeably, Velvet Underground(▶). Lou Reed(▶)-style monotone vocals and aggressive three-chord garage-based rock ensured cult following. Modern Lovers also featured at various times future Cars drummer David Robinson, Talking Head(▶) Jerry Harrison (keyboards), bass player Ernie Brooks (later a member of the Necessaries) and guitarist John Felice, later founder of Boston's Real Kids.

Group recorded demos with Kim Fowley in 1972 (recently released on Bomp Records). Following year signed lucrative record deal with Warners, with ex-Velvet John Cale(▶) slated as producer. Disillusioned both with songs and record company, Richman lost interest and was dropped from label.

Richman returned to Boston and later joined Matthew Kaufman's Beserkley label. **Jonathan Richman And The Modern Lovers** was released in March 1976. Kaufman had meanwhile bought the Cale tapes, which were issued just prior to this under the confusing title **The Modern Lovers**. His backing musicians came and went — Robinson had been replaced by D. Sharpe; Greg 'Curly' Kerenen appeared on two LPs before replacement by Asa Brebner; while Leroy Radcliffe played on all four LPs, including live album recorded in Europe in 1977.

By 1977 Richman had achieved sizeable reputation in US and UK, strongly influencing current trends with his Velvet-inspired numbers and deliberate minimalism. **Roadrunner**, particularly, affected emerging punk movement in Britain. **Rock 'n' Roll With The Modern Lovers** subsequently paved way for Richman's celebrated unamplified performances.

In 1978, Richman dismissed entire group and took to road as solo, armed with electric guitar and mini-amp. Left Beserkley, finally forming new Modern Lovers which included Kerenen from old days. Now married and living in North Carolina, Richman is currently recording for Sire, produced by Peter Bernstein of Linda Rondstadt/Chic fame.

Although celebrated by most new wave critics, Richman has suffered somewhat from being accorded cult/novelty status during 1976/77 when he reached popularity peak in Europe. Repertoire ranges from classic Reed-influenced **Pablo Picasso** and **Roadrunner** to songs of childlike wonder celebrating ice-cream men, dinosaurs, martians and leprechauns. Musically, Richman has explored reggae and Chinese love songs in his ever-quirky style. A genuine original, it remains to be seen whether his lovable eccentricity can produce anything to rival his mid-70s work, as he has continued to release albums into the '80s.

Hit Singles:
	US	UK
Roadrunner, 1977	—	11
Egyptian Reggae, 1977	—	5

Albums:
The Modern Lovers (Beserkley), 1976
Back In Your Life (Beserkley), 1979
The Johnathan Richman Songbook (Beserkley), 1980
The Original Modern Lovers (Bomp), 1982

Worth Searching Out:
Jonathan Richman And The Modern Lovers (Beserkley), 1976
Rock 'n' Roll With The Modern Lovers (Beserkley), 1977
Modern Lovers Live (Beserkley), 1977

The Righteous Brothers

US vocal duo formed 1962.
Bill Medley born Los Angeles, September 19, 1940.
Bobby Hatfield, born Wisconsin, August 10, 1940.

Career: Bill Medley and Bobby Hatfield came together as blue-eyed soul duo in 1962. They undertook club gigs around Southern California, and had small hit in 1963 with Medley-penned **Little Latin Lupe Lu** on Moonglow. Originally called 'The Paramounts', changed name because early black fans called their music 'righteous'.

Although increasingly popular on home ground, they didn't gain national prominence until noticed by TV producer Jack Good who gave them regular spot on pop show 'Shindig'. At this point Phil Spector stepped in. Already hot, with big hits by Crystals and Ronettes under his belt, Spector took the Brothers into the studio and worked with them for three solid weeks on one song. The result of this concentrated effort was **You've Lost That Loving Feeling**.

Feeling was released on Spector's own Philles label, and by January 1965 had reached No. 1 spot on both sides of Atlantic. The combination of Bill Medley's Ray Charles-influenced baritone, Bobby Hatfield's impassioned high tenor and Spector's inspired production provided pop masterpiece and perennial favourite. A slew of successful, if not quite so brilliant, singles followed.

The Brothers eventually parted company in 1968 after farewell concert in Los Angeles. Bill Medley pursued solo career, making series of undistinguished and not particularly successful albums. Bobby Hatfield recorded solo and also attempted to keep the Brothers act together with new partner, Billy Walker, but with little success.

In 1974, however, Medley and Hatfield got together again and scored US Top 10 hit with **Rock 'n' Roll Heaven**, a novelty death disc, following it with **Give It To The People**. A couple of albums also ensued before they split again.

Without a doubt their best testimony is early work, particularly **You've Lost That Loving Feeling**. Rare among blue-eyed soul artists in that their delivery was 100% convincing, the Righteous Brothers offered unique, instantly recognisable sound with their perfect harmonies and helped to assimilate 'soul' approach into mainstream of pop music.

Hit Singles:
	US	UK
You've Lost That Loving Feeling, 1965	1	1
Just Once In My Life, 1965	9	—
Unchained Melody, 1965	4	14
Ebb Tide, 1965	5	48
(You Are My) Soul And Inspiration, 1966	1	15
He, 1966	18	—
You've Lost That Loving Feeling, 1969	—	10
Rock 'n' Roll Heaven, 1974	3	—
Give It To The People, 1974	20	—

Albums:
Greatest Hits Volume 1 (Verve), 1967
Volume 1 (Verve), 1967
Two By Two (Polydor) 1973

Worth Searching Out:
Soul And Inspiration (Verve), 1966

Marty Robbins

US vocalist, composer, guitarist.
Born Glendale, Arizona, September 26, 1925; died December 8, 1982.

Career: A genuine country & western performer, with emphasis on western. Robbins came from musical family, including harmonica virtuoso father. Had aspirations to emulate 'singing cowboys' of the '30s/'40s. Started singing in bars and clubs in legendary cowboy town of Phoenix, Arizona, following term in Navy.

Quickly earned local reputation, appearing on own TV show in area. Signed to Columbia after guest on his show Little Jimmy Dickens recommended him to company. First single **Love Me Or Leave Me Alone** released in 1952. After regular period in country charts, made Billboard 100 in 1956 with **Singing The Blues** (covered by Guy Mitchell in States and Tommy Steele in UK). Impressive run of cross-over hit singles continued until 1962 and included definitive cowboy ballad **El Paso**.

Appeared in several western 'B' movies and maintained hold on country charts throughout

One of Marty Robbins' last albums. Courtesy Columbia Records.

'60s and '70s. Re-entered US Top 60 in 1970 with powerful **My Woman, My Woman, My Wife**, a love opus which pulled at heart strings of middle America.

Robbins' dominant tenor voice and casual guitar playing made him a concert favourite. He was an Opry regular for nearly 30 years. Sadly, this prominent country performer died in 1982 after long battle with heart disease. His influence will endure as long as the saddled stars he worshipped.

Hit Singles:
	US	UK
Singing The Blues, 1956	17	—
A White Sport Coat (And A Pink Carnation), 1957	2	—
The Story Of My Life, 1957	15	—
El Paso, 1960	1	19
Don't Worry, 1961	3	—
Devil Woman, 1962	16	5
Ruby Ann, 1962	18	24

Albums (selected):
Gunfighter Ballads And Trail Songs (Columbia/CBS), 1962
El Paso (Columbia/Hallmark), 1962
Greatest Hits (Columbia/CBS), 1966
The Legend (Columbia/CBS), 1981
Come Back To Me (Columbia/CBS), 1981

Smokey Robinson

US vocalist, composer, executive.
Born William Robinson, Detroit, February 19, 1940.

Career: Formed Miracles (then called the Matadors) as high-school vocal group in 1955 with Bobbie and Emerson Rogers and Warren 'Pete' Moore; when Claudette Rogers replaced brother, became the Miracles. Met up with Berry Gordy in 1957 while latter was still working as independent producer. Collaboration led to release of **Got A Job**, through End Records, and **Bad Girl**, through Chess. Moderate success encouraged Gordy to set up Tammie — later Tamla — Records, with Robinson and Miracles as first signing. Group consisted of Robinson (lead vocals), Claudette and Bobbie Rogers (first and second tenors), Ronnie White (baritone), Warren More (bass) and Marvin Tarplin (guitar).

1960 saw first major success for Miracles and Tamla. **Shop Around**, written by Gordy and Robinson, reached No. 2 in US charts. Group was on its way, and next few years saw clutch of hit singles that included classics like **You've Really Got A Hold On Me** (covered by Beatles(▶)) and **Mickey's Monkey** (actually written by Holland/Dozier/Holland(▶)).

At the same time Robinson started writing for and producing other artists. Mary Wells scored with **Two Lovers** and **What's So Easy For Two**, and had her finest hour with **My Guy** in 1964. That same year

Robinson began two-year collaboration with Temptations(▶), which resulted in memorable classics such as **Get Ready, The Way You Do The Things You Do, It's Growing, Since I Lost My Baby** and evocative **My Girl** (covered by Otis Redding(▶) and many others). Incredibly, Robinson found time to work with other Motown artists like Marvin Gaye(▶) **(I'll Be Doggone, Ain't That Peculiar)** and the Marvelettes.

During second half of '60s Miracles continued to release hit after hit, including **Tracks Of My Tears**, considered one of all-time great singles. Robinson was by now regarded as important creative force, attracting particular attention for his lyrics. Although most of his songs (apart from straight dance tunes) were about hackneyed subject of love, unrequited or otherwise, fresh, vivid imagery, and felicitous turn of phrase ensured memorable impact. At same time, Robinson had established himself as one of pop's great voices, his plaintive high tenor providing some of its most moving moments. Group became known as Smokey Robinson and the Miracles.

However, Motown's impetus was being provided more and more by writing/production team of Holland/Dozier/Holland and their artists Supremes(▶) and Four Tops(▶), and by end of decade Robinson was thinking of leaving Miracles. In 1971, after series of farewell concerts, he did split from group, and started to concentrate on position as Vice-President of Motown Records with special responsibility for new talent.

Initially, Robinson continued to produce

Miracles, but they were soon handed over to other Motown 'house' producers and eventually left label for Columbia. Robinson himself worked on series of solo albums, which continued to make impression on black American market while being largely ignored by general pop audience. Often more experimental than his previous output, Robinson's '70s album repay listening and contain gems that are worth searching out.

However, in 1981 Robinson made return to pop spotlight with **Cruisin'** a US Top 10 hit This was only foretaste of 1981 success of **Being With You**, a romantic Robinson composition originally intended for Kim Carnes(▶). No. 1 both sides of the Atlantic, it brought Robinson to attention of new generation of record buyers and provided momentum for new career in '80s.

Writer of over 60 hit songs, possessor of one of pop's great voices, consistently successful for more than a quarter of a century, Smokey Robinson is a key figure of modern music. As revered by critics as he is accepted by record-buying public, Robinson has sufficient talent to continue making impression for further 25 years.

Hit Singles:	US	UK
Smokey Robinson and the Miracles:		
Shop Around, 1961	2	—
You Really Got A Hold On Me, 1963	8	—
Mickey's Monkey, 1963	8	—
Ooo Baby Baby, 1965	16	—
Tracks Of My Tears, 1965	16	—
My Girl Has Gone, 1965	14	—
Going To A Go-Go, 1966	11	44
(Come 'Round Here) I'm The One You Need, 1966	17	37
The Love I Saw In You Was Just A Mirage, 1967	20	—
I Second That Emotion, 1967	4	27
If You Can Want, 1968	11	50
Baby Baby Don't Cry, 1969	8	—
Tracks Of My Tears, 1969	—	9
Tears Of A Clown, 1970	1	1
(Come 'Round Here) I'm The One You Need, 1971	—	13
I Don't Blame You At All, 1971	18	11
Miracles		
Do It Baby, 1974	13	—
Love Machine, 1976	1	3
Solo:		
Being With You, 1981	1	1

Albums:
Smokey Robinson and the Miracles:
Anthology (Motown), 1974
Greatest Hits (Tamla/Motown), 1977

Smokey Robinson:
Smokey (Tamla/Motown), 1973
Smokin' (Tamla/—), 1978
Being With You (Motown), 1981
Yes It's You Lady (Motown), 1982

Below: The sublime, yet electrifying, Smokey Robinson (right) onstage with the Miracles in 1965. Smokey has few equals as a songwriter of sensitive and soulful lyrics.

Tom Robinson

UK vocalist, bass player, composer.
Born 1948.

Career: Gay activist and radical; formed Tom Robinson Band in mid-'70s as vehicle for political polemic. Having gained considerable cult following among disaffected youth in general as well as gays, Robinson was signed by EMI in 1977.

Strangely, first hit, **2-4-6-8- Motorway**, was not political piece but hard-rocking song about life on the road. Nevertheless further hits (**Don't Take No For An Answer, Up Against The Wall**) indicated tone of artist's politics. Best-known song outside hits was gay anthem **Glad To Be Gay**.

After two albums for EMI, Robinson folded band and formed Sector 27, claiming that he wished to merge into background and make group statement. New outfit failed to achieve major impact.

1982 release **Cabaret 79** is live recording dating from 1979, and contains all Robinson's best known work. Robinson himself compiled 1982 Fame (UK) release, and wrote comprehensive sleeve note — all material previously unavailable on album.

Latterly Robinson has been working small-time gigs again, despite 1983 return to limelight with **War Babies.** He is the type of outspoken character that helps to make rock more than simply entertaining.

Hit Singles:

	US	UK
Tom Robinson Band:		
2-4-6-8 Motorway, 1977	—	5
Don't Take No For An Answer, 1978	—	18
War Babies, 1983	—	6

Albums:
Power In The Darkness (Capitol/EMI), 1978
Tom Robinson Band 2 (Harvest/EMI), 1979
Sector 27 (International Recordings/Fontana), 1980
North By North West (International Recordings/—), 1981
Cabaret 79 (—/Panic), 1982
Tom Robinson Band (—/Fame), 1982

Jimmie Rodgers

US vocalist, guitarist, composer.
Born Meridian, Mississippi, September 8, 1897; died New York City, May 26, 1933.

Career: Won first prize in hometown talent contest in early teens; left home soon after to join travelling medicine show. First job was on railroad tracklaying gang with father; experience on railroads was source of much material recorded later.

By 1923 had joined Billy Terrell's touring tent show performing vaudeville standards professionally. Alternated appearances on stage and radio over next four years with railroad work, until first recording for RCA-Victor in August 1927. First single produced by Ralph Peer in Bristol, Tennessee, warehouse on portable equipment. Result was **Sleep Baby Sleep** and **The Soldier's Sweetheart**. Good sales resulted in further recordings, including Rodgers' first of many 'Blue Yodels', **T For Texas**, which rapidly became huge success in winter of 1928.

Soon established as 'America's Blue Yodeler', Rodgers continued to record similar material, inserting yodels into his own and other writers' songs. Simple style caught imagination of public, resulting in unrivalled sales for the period. Over next five years recorded 118 masters, mostly with simple guitar backing but some showing imaginative use of session musicians.

Above: Tom Robinson, who hit it big in 1977-78, then vanished until 1983.

Despite increasing discomfort resulting from poorly treated tuberculosis, toured extensively throughout career. Became first rural singer to bring country music to masses. Although primary appeal was to 'country folks', Rodgers was able to 'cross-over' to popular markets far away from his own origins, with record sales outside the US equalling the home market.

Death in 1933 from TB was inevitable, but accelerated by lifestyle and lack of effective treatment. After his death Rodgers achieved legendary status, with many country singers acknowledging influence. Songs continue to be recorded by contemporary artists, so that **Any Old Time, Mule Skinner Blues, In The Jailhouse Now** and others have become country and pop standards.

Widely regarded as father of country music, Rodgers was deservedly first performer to be honoured by election to Country Music Hall of Fame in 1961.

Hit Singles:
(Sales charts were not being compiled when Rodgers' singles were first issued.)

Albums:
This Is (RCA/—), early '60s
Best Of The Legendary (RCA/—), 1965
My Rough And Rowdy Ways (RCA/—), early '70s

Jimmie Rodgers

US vocalist, guitarist, composer.
Born Camus, Washington, September 18, 1933.

Career: Family background (father Hank Snow, named son after legendary Jimmie Rodgers) almost dictated career in music. During stint in US Air Force formed the Rhythm Kings; performed at US bases in Japan and Korea before returning to US.

Appearance on Arthur Godfrey talent show in 1957 prompted signing to Roulette Records. First release **Honeycomb** was US No. 1 followed by string of hits and own television show featuring simple folk style. Later appeared in country charts on Dot Records following last pop hit in UK with **English Country Garden** in 1962.

Suffered major setback in 1967 when injuries received in car accident forced retirement, but by 1969 had recovered sufficiently to host own TV show and begin recording again. Latterly has used religious material to support his role as evangelist.

Hit Singles:

	US	UK
Honeycomb, 1957	1	30
Kisses Sweeter Than Wine, 1957	3	7
Oh Oh I'm Falling In Love Again, 1958	3	—
Secretly/Make Me A Miracle, 1958	3	—
Are You Really Mine, 1958	10	—
Woman From Liberia, 1958	—	18
Bimbombey, 1958	11	—
English Country Garden, 1962	—	5

Albums:
Yours Truly (Roulette/-), 1960s
Both Sides Now (—/Mayfair), 1974

Kenny Rogers

US vocalist.
Born Houston, Texas, August 21, 1939.

Career: Early interest in music nurtured by singing with family in church choir; formed school group which recorded for small local label.

After leaving school, spent period with jazz group Bobby Doyle Trio before joining New Christy Minstrels in 1966. After year and a half, split to form Kenny Rogers and the First Edition with fellow Minstrels Terry Williams, Mike Settle and Thelma Camacho.

Signed by Reprise, group scored heavily internationally with 1969 release **Ruby, Don't Take Your Love To Town**. Written by country stalwart Mel Tillis, song reflected current unease with American involvement in Vietnam, and provided excellent showcase for Rogers' distinctively gruff vocals.

Several further hits followed, and group enjoyed considerable success in late '60s and early '70s. Following break-up in 1973, Rogers kept low profile until 1975 when he signed with United Artists via producer Larry Butler.

Under Butler's aegis, Rogers followed country/pop direction and had immediate success with singles releases. Massive hit **Lucille** in 1977 established him as international star.

Since that time Rogers has been premier country crossover artist, regularly hitting both pop and country charts. In 1978 he started recording partnership with female country star Dottie West, which provided another source of hit records, and has become in-demand TV and live performer.

Flexible, sincere vocals, obviously influenced by black artists, make Rogers one of country/pop's best vocalists. Casual, relaxed personality and careful choice of material ensure wide appeal among MOR audiences. At time of writing, artist was enjoying massive pop success in partnership with Scottish pop singer Sheena Easton(▶) with cover of Bob Seger's(▶) **We've Got Tonight**.

Hit Singles:

	US	UK
With the First Edition:		
Just Dropped In (To See What Condition My Condition Was In), 1968	5	—
But You Know I Love You, 1969	19	—
Ruby Don't Take Your Love To Town, 1969	6	2
Something's Burning, 1970	11	8
Tell It All Brother, 1970	17	—
Solo:		
Lucille, 1977	5	1
The Gambler, 1979	16	—
She Believes In Me, 1979	5	42
You Decorated My Life, 1979	7	—
Coward Of The County, 1979	3	1
Don't Fall In Love With A Dreamer (with Kim Carnes), 1980	4	—
Love The World Away, 1980	14	—
Lady, 1980	1	12
What Are We Doin' In Love (with Dottie West), 1981	14	—
I Don't Need You, 1981	3	—
Share Your Love With Me, 1981	14	—
Through The Years, 1982	13	—
Love Will Turn You Around, 1982	13	—
With Kim Carnes:		
Don't Fall In Love With A Dreamer, 1980	4	—
With Sheena Easton:		
We've Got tonight, 1983	6	—

Albums:
With First Edition:
Greatest Hits (Reprise/—), 1971
Solo:
Daytime Friends (Liberty/United Artists), 1977
Love Or Something Like It (Liberty/United Artists), 1978
The Gambler (Liberty/United Artists), 1979
The Singles Album (Liberty/United Artists), 1979
Greatest Hits (Liberty/—), 1979
Gideon (Liberty/United Artists), 1980
Kenny (Liberty/United Artists), 1980
Love Lifted Me (Liberty/United Artists), 1980
Share Your Love (Liberty), 1981
Ruby Don't Take Your Love To Town (—/MFP), 1981
Love Will Turn You Around (Liberty), 1982
With Dottie West:
Every Time Two Fools Collide (Liberty/United Artists), 1978
Classics (Liberty/United Artists), 1979
Lady (also with Kim Carnes) (Liberty/United Artists), 1981

181

Rolling Stones

UK group formed 1963.

Original line-up: Mick Jagger, vocals; Keith Richard, guitar, vocals; Brian Jones, guitar, vocals; Bill Wyman, bass; Ian Stewart, piano; Charlie Watts, drums.

Career: Jagger and Richard first met at primary school in Kent, then went their separate ways. In 1960, when Richard was attending Dartford Art School and Jagger the London School of Economics, they discovered mutual interest in blues and R&B. Pair moved in and out of ever-changing group line-ups that made up London's infant blues scene.

Line-up that was to become first version of Rolling Stones came together around Alexis Korner's Blues Incorporated, pioneer British blues outfit that had regular gig at Ealing Blues Club. Occasional sitter-in with outfit was Cheltenham-born guitarist Brian Jones. By early 1962 Jagger was regular singer with band, and was also rehearsing with Jones, Richard, and other like-minded musicians such as pianist Ian Stewart.

In June 1962 Blues Incorporated were booked for radio broadcast; budget only allowed for six players, so Jagger stepped down and instead deputised for Blues Incorporated at gig at London's Marquee Club; band was billed as Brian Jones and Mick Jagger and the Rollin' Stones. Line-up as above did not coalesce until following year when Charlie Watts made move

from Blues Incorporated, and Bill Wyman joined on bass after audition.

Turning-point was residency at Crawdaddy Club in Richmond. Reputation quickly spread by word of mouth, and band came to attention of former PR man Andrew Loog Oldham; he became band's manager and negotiated record contract with Decca. (First move was to oust pianist Stewart on the grounds that he looked too 'normal'—although he was to remain 'sixth Stone' throughout band's career, playing on records and at gigs.)

First release, version of Chuck Berry's(▶) **Come On,** came out in June 1963, and although not a major hit brought band to notice of public and, particularly, of media. Oldham pushed Stones as 'bad boys' compared to 'lovable moptop' Beatles(▶), and band swiftly became cult figures among youth. First album **The Rolling Stones**, largely covers of R&B material, reached top of UK charts and saw first US tour and first UK chart-topper, their version of Bobby Womack's **It's All Over Now**.

From this time onwards band quickly gathered momentum. From 1965 all singles were Jagger/Richard compositions, and band developed distinctive pop/rock style that still kept strong blues undertones. **The Last Time** made US Top 10, and paved way for first No. 1 on both sides of the Atlantic, the classic **(I Can't Get No) Satisfaction** (yet to be released in full stereo version).

By end of '60s Stones had become international attraction, second only to Beatles(▶) in importance. They were surrounded by almost permanent aura of publicity and notoriety: **Let's Spend The Night Together** was censored by the Ed Sullivan TV show; Jagger, Richard and

Below: Mick Jagger onstage at Leeds in 1982, proving that he can still excite a crowd 20 years later.

Right: An impressive stage setting at Wembley Stadium, 1982, for the return to London of the Stones.

Above: Mick Jagger (left) and Ron Wood onstage, 1976.

Inset above: Goat's Head Soup. Courtesy Rolling Stones Records.

Jones were all busted for drugs; Jagger's relationship with Marianne Faithfull provided gossip-column titillation; and virtually every 'pillar of decency' from Bournemouth to Wagga Wagga denounced band as corrupters of youth, tramplers on moral values, etc. End of decade also saw tragedy of Brian Jones' death, following his exit from group. Mick Taylor, formerly with John Mayall Band(▶), replaced him.

Musically, apart from 1967 flirtation with psychedelia manifested by **Their Satanic Majesties Request** album and **We Love You** single, band had gone from strength to strength. **Beggars Banquet** and **Let It Bleed** were both classic rock albums, regarded by many critics as together making up Stones' finest hour.

In '70s Stones became something of a rock 'n' roll institution, living life of jet-setting tax exiles and establishing new records for massively attended live performances. In 1974 Mick Taylor quit, to be replaced by Ron Wood, a member of Faces(▶). There was some toning down of former 'rebel' image, as members eased into mature years, their former 'two-fingers-to-the-world' stance being taken over by '70s punk outfits like Sex Pistols(▶). Record-wise, band continued to put out worthwhile albums (after 1971 on their own Rolling Stones label) that generally contained a couple of classics each, and maintained standard of singles with releases like **Brown Sugar** and **It's Only Rock And Roll.**

Although it might be assumed that band would be happy to coast into '80s, or even think about throwing in towel, 1981 saw US tour that broke all box-office records, while album **Tattoo You** made No. 1 in US charts, No. 2 in UK. **Still Life**, live album of '81 tour, was almost equally successful in following year.

Although Mick Jagger has never been technically a great singer — his on-stage antics have sometimes veered towards self-parody — and ensemble instrumental work can sometimes be somewhat sloppy, Stones can fairly lay claim to title of greatest rock 'n' roll band in the world. Now one of the longest-lived outfits, they have backlog of work which includes some of most exciting rock 'n' roll ever recorded, and look set to continue for at least foreseeable future. Presently recording 1983 LP.

Current line-up: Jagger; Richard; Wyman; Watts; Ron Wood, guitar, vocals.

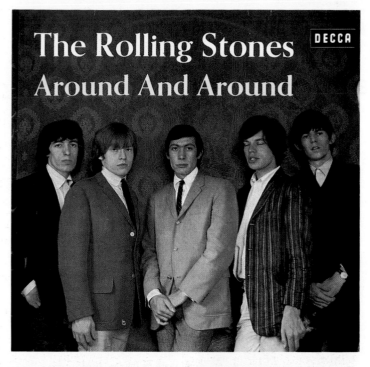

The Rolling Stones
Around And Around

DECCA

**Above: An early album sleeve reproduced courtesy of Decca Records.
Below: The controversial sleeve for 1978's Some Girls, which resulted in several law suits. Courtesy of Rolling Stones Records.**

Inset above: The classic Aftermath. Courtesy Decca Records.

Left: 'Thank Your Lucky Star' TV show, 1965. (From left) Brian Jones, Mick Jagger, Bill Wyman, Charlie Watts and Keith Richard.

Inset left: Still Life LP (1982). Courtesy Rolling Stones Records.

Hit Singles:

	US	UK
I Wanna Be Your Man, 1963	—	12
Not Fade Away, 1964	48	3
It's All Over Now, 1964	26	1
Little Red Rooster, 1964	—	1
Time Is On My Side, 1964	6	—
Heart Of Stone, 1965	19	—
The Last Time, 1965	9	1
(I Can't Get No) Satisfaction, 1965	1	1
Get Off My Cloud, 1965	1	1
As Tears Go By, 1966	6	—
19th Nervous Breakdown, 1966	2	2
Paint It Black, 1966	1	1
Mother's Little Helper, 1966	8	—
Have You Seen Your Mother Baby (Standing In The Shadows), 1966	9	5
Ruby Tuesday/Let's Spend The Night Together, 1967	1	3
Let's Spend The Night Together/ Ruby Tuesday, 1967	55	3
We Love You/Dandelion, 1967	14	8
Jumping Jack Flash, 1968	3	1
Honky Tonk Women, 1969	1	1
Brown Sugar/Bitch/Let It Rock, 1971	1	2
Tumbling Dice, 1972	7	5
Angie, 1973	1	5
Doo Doo Doo Doo Doo (Heartbreakers), 1974	16	—
It's Only Rock And Roll, 1974	16	10
Ain't Too Proud To Beg, 1974	17	—
Fool To Cry, 1976	10	6
Miss You/Far Away Eyes, 1978	1	3
Beast Of Burden, 1978	8	—
Emotional Rescue, 1980	3	9
Start Me Up, 1981	2	7
Waiting On A Friend, 1982	13	50

Albums:
The Rolling Stones (London/Decca), 1964
12x5 (London/—), 1965
The Rolling Stones Now (London/—), 1965
Out Of Our Heads (London/Decca), 1965
Decembers Children (London/—), 1965
Aftermath (London/Decca), 1966

Big Hits (High Tide And Green Grass) (London/Decca), 1966
Got Live If You Want It (London/—), 1967
Between The Buttons (London/Decca), 1967
Flowers (London/Decca), 1967
Their Satanic Majesties Request (London/ Decca), 1967
Beggars Banquet (London/Decca), 1968
Let It Bleed (London/Decca), 1969
Through The Past Darkly (Big Hits Volume 2) (London/Decca), 1969
Get Yer Ya Yas Out (London/Decca), 1970
Sticky Fingers (Rolling Stones), 1971
Stone Age (—/Decca), 1971
Gimme Shelter (—/Decca), 1971
Milestones (—/Decca), 1971
Exile On Main Street (Rolling Stones) Records), 1972
Rock 'n' Rollin' Stones (—/Decca), 1972
Hot Rocks: 1964-71 (London/—), 1972
More Hot Rocks (Big Hits And Fazed Cookies) (London/—), 1972

Goats Head Soup (Rolling Stones), 1973
No Stone Unturned (—/Decca), 1973
It's Only Rock'n'Roll (Rolling Stones), 1974
Rolled Gold (—/Decca), 1975
Metamorphosis (London/Decca), 1975
Made In The Shade (Rolling Stones), 1975
Black And Blue (Rolling Stones), 1976
Love You Live (Rolling Stones), 1977
Some Girls (Rolling Stones), 1978
Emotional Rescue (Rolling Stones), 1980
Sucking In The Seventies (Rolling Stones), 1981
Tattoo You (Rolling Stones), 1981
Still Life (Rolling Stones), 1982

Bill Wyman Solo:
Bill Wyman (A&M), 1982

Worth Searching Out:
Monkey Grip (Rolling Stones), 1974
Stone Alone (Rolling Stones), 1976

Ron Wood Solo:
(See Faces entry.)

Linda Ronstadt

US vocalist.
Born Tucson, Arizona, July 15, 1946.

Career: Daughter of guitar player; had musical upbringing. After attending Arizona State University, headed for California in 1964 to try luck in music business. She teamed up with old friend Bob Kimmel and LA musician Ken Edwards to form folk-rock group Stone Poneys. Band made three albums for Capitol between 1966 and 1968, scoring hit single with Mike Nesmith's **Different Drum**.

Encouraged by Capitol, Ronstadt decided to go solo in 1969. First two albums created considerable interest, and second, **Silk Purse**, provided first solo hit single **Long, Long Time**.

Prisoner In Disguise. Courtesy Asylum Records.

In 1971 she recruited Don Henley, Glenn Frey and Randy Meisner to form new backing band. All played on **Linda Ronstadt**, but split within six months to form Eagles(▶).

Career really began to take off when Ronstadt joined country-rock orientated West Coast label Asylum in 1973. Debut album **Don't Cry Now**, co-produced by Peter Asher, made US album charts. (Asher became manager and has produced all albums since.) 1974 album **Heart Like A Wheel** (contractually obligated to Capitol) eventually went platinum, spawning three gold singles inlcuding No. 1's **You're No Good** and **When Will I Be Loved.** At end of year Ronstadt

Get Closer. Courtesy Asylum Records.

had become America's top-selling female artist.

Further albums confirmed superstar status and Ronstadt also became huge concert attraction. In meantime, private life provoked much rumour and comment, and she became staple of gossip columns. Relationship with California Governor Jerry Brown elicited most column inches.

Although sometimes criticised for lack of rawness and passion, Ronstadt has made much fine music over last 10-year period. Undoubtedly greatly aided by relationship with Asher, Ronstadt has matured into excellent singer, and rarely chooses sub-standard material. Recently she has broadened scope of talents with appearance in hit version of Gilbert and Sullivan's 'Pirates Of Penzance' on Broadway; she also appears in film version. Now seems likely to become rock-orientated all-round entertainer.

Hit Singles:

	US	UK
Linda And The Stone Poneys:		
Different Drum, 1968	13	—
Solo:		
You're No Good, 1975	1	—
When Will I Be Loved, 1975	2	—
Heat Wave, 1975	5	—
That'll Be The Day, 1976	11	—
Blue Bayou, 1977	3	35
It's So Easy, 1977	5	—
Back In The USA, 1978	16	—
Ooh Baby Baby, 1979	17	—
How Do I Make You, 1980	10	—
Hurt So Bad, 1980	8	—

Albums:
Hand Sown, Home Grown (Capitol), 1969
Silk Purse (Capitol), 1970
Linda Ronstadt (Capitol), 1972
Don't Cry Now (Asylum), 1974
Heart Like A Wheel (Capitol), 1974
Different Drum (Capitol), 1975
Stone Poneys Featuring Linda Ronstadt (Capitol), 1975
Prisoner In Disguise (Asylum), 1975
Hasten Down The Wind (Asylum), 1976
Greatest Hits (Asylum), 1976
Simple Dream (Asylum), 1977
Retrospective (Capitol), 1977
Living In The USA (Asylum), 1978
Greatest Hits Volume 2 (Asylum), 1980
Mad Love (Asylum), 1980
Beginnings (Capitol/—),
Get Closer (Asylum), 1982

Above: Motown superstars (from left) Diana Ross, Marvin Gaye, Stevie Wonder.

Diana Ross

US vocalist, actress.
Born Detroit, March 26, 1944.

Career: Following endless speculation, Ross left record-breaking vocal group Supremes(▶) in December 1969. First solo single, **Reach Out And Touch**, was released in June 1970 and started string of hits which has continued to present.

Right from beginning, however, Ross and Motown label boss Berry Gordy collaborated to project Ross as more than merely successful pop singer. Pair envisaged all-round superstardom à la Streisand(▶). To this end Ross was presented as centrepiece of series of elaborately staged concerts and TV specials, at same time making debut in 'Lady Sings The Blues', a Motown-produced film about Billie Holiday.

While movie was not universally critically well received, it was commercially successful and Ross won general acclaim for her portrayal of the tragic jazz singer. Second foray into film acting was in the less successful 'Mahogany' (1975), although film did give Ross opportunity to wear variety of high-fashion costumes.

In meantime, hits continued apace — generally highly arranged ballads which allowed Ross to emote to good effect. In 1976, however, she surprised everyone with **Love Hangover**, a genuinely exciting upbeat disco stomper that reminded fans that Ross was not just a showbiz personality.

For third film, Ross played part of Dorothy in re-make of 'Wizard Of Oz' called 'The Wiz'. Again, movie was less than ecstatically received by critics but Ross herself garnered generally good reviews.

By 1980 relations with Motown were becoming strained, and Ross split from the company, signing with RCA for US and with Capitol for rest of world. However, this was not before artist had reasserted her dancefloor-filling credentials with Chic(▶)-produced album **Diana**, which yielded three hit singles.

Since changing companies Ross has gone from strength to strength, producing herself and continuing to chart heavily. (Although ironically her biggest hit of the '80s so far has been her duet from film soundtrack with Lionel Richie(▶) **Endless Love**, her swansong for Motown.) Like all survivors, Ross has adapted well, handling pop, soul, disco and rock masterfully. Now a major superstar who can fill world's largest venues many times over, Ross looks set to endure throughout '80s and beyond.

Hit Singles:

	US	UK
Reach Out And Touch (Somebody's Hand), 1970	20	33
Ain't No Mountain High Enough, 1970	1	6
Remember Me, 1970	16	7
I'm Still Waiting, 1971	—	1
Surrender, 1971	38	10
Doobedood'ndoobe Doobedood'ndoobe, 1972	—	12
Touch Me In The Morning, 1973	1	9
All Of My Life, 1974	—	9
Last Time I Saw Him, 1974	14	35
Do You Know Where You're Going To (Theme from 'Mahogany'), 1976	1	5
Love Hangover, 1976	1	10
The Boss, 1979	19	40
Upside Down, 1980	1	2
My Old Piano, 1980	—	5
I'm Coming Out, 1980	5	13
It's My Turn, 1981	9	16
Why Do Fools Fall In Love?, 1981	7	4
Mirror Mirror, 1982	8	36
Work That Body, 1982	44	7
Muscles, 1982	10	15
With Marvin Gaye:		
Youre A Special Part Of Me, 1973	12	—
You Are Everything, 1974	—	5
My Mistake (Was To Love You), 1974	19	—
With Lionel Richie:		
Endless Love, 1982	1	7

Albums:
Diana Ross (Motown), 1970
Everything Is Everything (Motown), 1971
I'm Still Waiting (Motown), 1971
Lady Sings The Blues (Motown), 1972
Touch Me In The Morning (Motown), 1973
Original Soundtrack Of Mahogany (Motown), 1975
Diana Ross (Motown), 1976
Greatest Hits (Motown), 1976
Greatest Hits Volume 2 (Motown), 1976
Baby It's Me (Motown), 1977
The Wiz (MCA), 1978
Ross (Motown), 1978
20 Golden Greats (Motown), 1979
The Boss (Motown), 1979
Diana (Motown), 1981
To Love Again (Motown), 1981
All The Great Hits (Motown), 1981
Why Do Fools Fall In Love? (RCA/Capitol), 1981
Silk Electric (RCA/Capitol), 1982

With Marvin Gaye:
Diana and Marvin (Motown), 1974

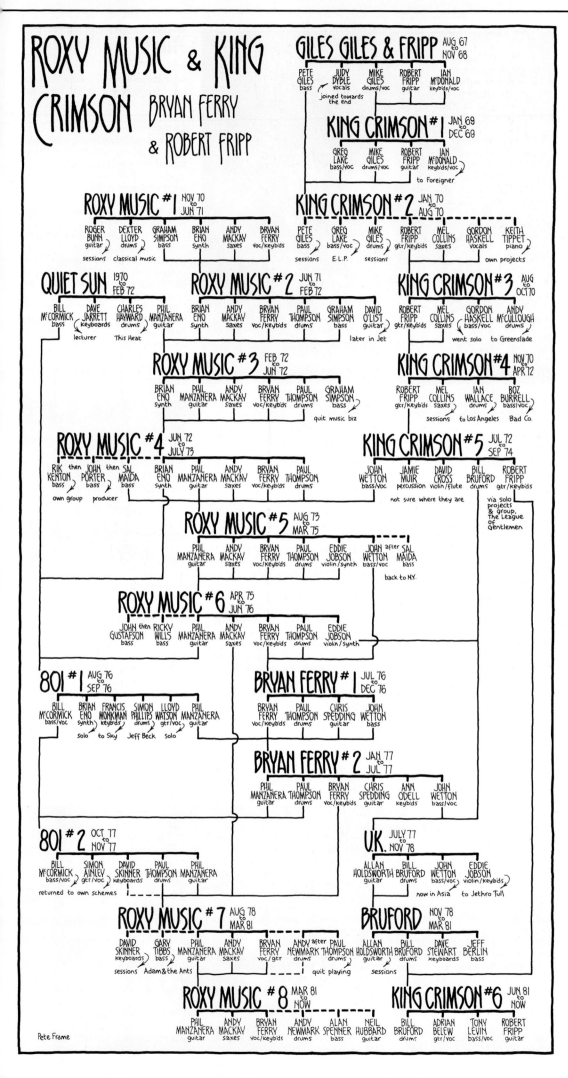

Pete Frame

Roxy Music

UK group formed 1970.

Original line-up: Bryan Ferry, vocals, keyboards; Graham Simpson, bass; Andy Mackay, bass; Brian Eno, synthesiser; Dexter Lloyd, drums; Roger Bunn, guitar.

Career: While working as teacher, Bryan Ferry(▶) spent free-time learning, playing and composing music. By 1970 he had decided to pursue full-time music career and sought out college friend Simpson to form band. MacKay was located in January 1971 through trade advert and he subsequently introduced Brian Eno(▶).

Original line-up lasted only few months. Paul Thompson (drums) answered 'Melody Maker' ad, following Lloyd's departure. Phil Manzanera wanted to join as second guitarist. He settled for sound-mixer when Ferry sought out ex-Nice guitarist, David O'List. Manzanera got his chance when Bunn, then O'List, left band.

Roxy Music tried to interest record companies with fully textured sound rather than relying on then standard lead guitar and over-emphasised bass. Island finally took chance and was rather surprised when debut LP was both critical and commercial success. Band's image and sound projected cool, calculating approach to rock as yet unseen.

Next bold move for early '70s was to release single which was not intended to be included on any LP. **Virginia Plain** made UK No. 4 and won band broad audience. This release also featured first of many new bass players, Rik Kenton. Within a few months, his place was taken by John Porter who lasted only first two months of 1973 while band recorded **For Your Pleasure.** During 1973 Europe/UK tours, Sal Maida filled in on bass.

Roxy Music took vacation for second half of 1973 due to Eno's departure for solo career and Ferry's growing interest in developing parallel solo venture. Eddie Jobson (ex Curved Air) assumed Eno's spot on keyboards and Roxy Music returned to stage work in autumn 1973. This time Ferry pushed 'cool' image to extreme by cutting long.hair and wearing tuxedo on stage.

Roxy's live efforts helped boost **Stranded** LP to UK No. 10. John Gustafson played bass on this album (and next two) but did so as session player and didn't tour with Roxy. John Wetton took on this role from autumn 1974 until April 1975 when he suddenly left for Uriah Heep(▶), and Gustafson at last went on the road. In late 1975 he was replaced by Rick Wills (later Small Faces(▶)).

Although **Country Life** and **Siren** were big success in UK and garnered critical praise in US, Ferry wanted to try solo tour. Roxy Music's break-up was never formally announced but band no longer existed after June 1976. Various solo projects failed to produce new careers for Roxy members but public interest in band remained high, as seen by UK chart success of live LP **Viva,** and then **Greatest Hits.**

In late 1978 Ferry gathered nucleus of MacKay, Manzanera and Thompson for Roxy Music re-union. Using ex-Vibrator Gary Tibbs (bass) and ex-Ace Paul Carrack (keyboards), band recorded **Manifesto.**

After extensive touring, Roxy Music entered new stage of career with **Flesh And Blood.** Although not radically different from past, this album marked new level of sophisticated lyrics with melodic background. Somehow Roxy achieved sound which fitted into '80s without destroying roots from '60s; they reworked classic old John Lennon(▶) song, **Jealous Guy,** and produced moving tribute for Lennon in early 1981.

By now Roxy Music had lost Thompson and remaining core used various session players to produce their finest effort, **Avalon. More Than This** and **Take A Chance With Me** are two classic cuts from LP which surpass bounds of rock and encourage hope that Roxy Music will remain strong influence on today's newer bands.

Current line-up: Ferry; Manzanera; Mackay.

Hit Singles:	US	UK
Virginia Plain, 1972	—	4
Pyjamarama, 1973	—	10
Street Life, 1973	—	9
All I Want Is You, 1974	—	12
Love Is The Drug, 1975	30	2
Virginia Plain, 1977	—	11
Dance Away, 1979	—	2
Angel Eyes, 1979	—	4
Over You, 1980	—	5
Oh Yeah (On The Radio), 1980	—	5
The Same Old Scene, 1980	—	12
Jealous Guy, 1981	—	1
More Than This, 1982	—	6
Avalon, 1982	27	13

Albums:
Roxy Music (Reprise/Island), 1972
For Your Pleasure (Warner Bros/Island), 1973
Stranded (Atco/Island), 1973
Country Life (Atco/Island), 1974

Greatest Hits. Courtesy Polydor.

Siren (Atco/Island), 1975
Viva Roxy Music (Live) (Atco/Island), 1976
Greatest Hits (Polydor), 1977
Manifesto (Polydor), 1979
Flesh And Blood (Polydor), 1980
The First Seven Albums (Polydor), 1981*
Avalon (Polydor), 1982
The High Road (Polydor), 1983†

*Boxed set
†Live mini-LP

Andy Mackay Solo:
In Search Of Eddie Riff (—/Island), 1974
Resolving Contradictions (—/Bronze), 1978

Phil Manzanera Solo:
Diamond Head (Atco/Island), 1975
Quiet Sun: Mainstream (Antilles/Island), 1975
801: Live (Polydor/Island), 1976
Listen Now (Polydor), 1977
K Scope (Polydor), 1978

Bryan Ferry Solo:
(See separate entry)

Todd Rundgren

US vocalist, composer, producer, guitarist. Born Upper Darby, Pennsylvania, June 22, 1948.

Career: Greatly influenced by 'British Invasion' spearheaded by Beatles and Rolling Stones; acquired first electric guitar at 17. First band was Woody's Truck Stop (for less than a year); by 1968 had left to form the

A Wizard, A True Star, Todd Rundgren. Courtesy Bearsville Records.

Nazz, legendary Philadelphia band who made three LPs between 1968 and 1970, now regarded as prime collectors' items (reissued in 1983 by Rhino Records, Los Angeles). However, Todd left group by mid-1969 to perfect ability as producer/engineer.

Produced only minor acts early on, but engineered for such as the Band(▶), Paul Butterfield(▶) Blues Band and Jesse Winchester, as well as embarking on personal solo career.

Had great success with 1972 LP **Something/Anything?**, plus production of debut LP by Sparks(▶) (then known as Halfnelson) and Badfinger.

1973 productions included New York Dolls, Grand Funk Railroad(▶) and Fanny. In 1974 formed Utopia (current/longest-lived line-up: Rundgren, guitar, vocals; Roger Powell, keyboards, vocals; Kasim Sulton, bass, vocals; Willie Wilcox, drums, vocals). Since 1974, group and Todd's solo LPs effectively interleaved. Musically and vocally, Rundgren has experimented with several styles; equally proficient backed solely by own guitar or piano. His lyrics are also varied, sometimes poignant, often witty, but always perceptive. During '70s, probably best known as producer, while own performing/recording career has largely retreated into cult status. Among notable productions during this period are those for Hall & Oates(▶), Tom Robinson(▶), Tubes(▶) , Patti Smith(▶), Shaun Cassidy and mega-selling **Bat Out Of Hell** by Meat Loaf(▶).

During early '80s, somewhat less active as producer; also cut down on live performances, probably due to major involvement in making videos — personally owns studio. (His award-winning **Time Heals** video must be seen.) Never an enormous record seller, as list below demonstrates, Todd retains very faithful following (which he no doubt prefers) always ensuring respectable sales. He perhaps deserves more than most the description (used as early LP title) 'A Wizard, A True Star'.

Hit Singles:	US	UK
We Gotta Get You A Woman, 1971	20	—
I Saw The Light, 1972	16	36
Hello It's Me, 1973	5	—

Albums:
With The Nazz:
Worth Searching Out:
Nazz (Screen Gems-Columbia/—), 1968
Nazz Nazz (Screen Gems-Columbia/—), 1969
Nazz III (Screen Gems-Columbia/—), 1970

Solo and with Utopia:
Something/Anything (Bearsville), 1972
A Wizard, A True Star (Bearsville/Island), 1973
Todd (Bearsville), 1973
Todd Rundgren's Utopia (Bearsville), 1974
Initiation (Bearsville), 1975
Another Life (Bearsville), 1975
Faithful (Bearsville), 1976
Ra (Bearsville), 1977
Oops! Wrong Planet (Bearsville), 1977
Hermit Of Mink Hollow (Bearsville/Island), 1978
Back To The Bars (Bearsville), 1978
Adventures In Utopia (Bearsville), 1980
Deface The Music (Bearsville), 1980
Healing (Bearsville), 1981
Swing To The Right (Bearsville), 1982
Utopia (Bearsville), 1982
The Ever Popular Tortured Artist Effect (Bearsville), 1983

Worth Searching Out:
Runt (Bearsville), 1970
The Ballad Of Todd Rundgren (Bearsville), 1971

Rush

Canadian group formed 1973.

Original line-up: Alex Lifeson, guitar; Geddy Lee, bass, keyboards, vocals; John Rutsey, drums.

Career: Band began playing bars in Toronto, using hard rock/heavy metal sound to project gothic images of sci-fi future. Privately produced first LP was rejected by major labels but received extensive airplay in Seattle. This led to some American bookings in Pacific Northwest and group caught attention of Mercury Records who had promoted fellow Canadians Bachman-Turner Overdrive(▶) to stardom.

Mercury released first album and set up national tour when Rutsey decided to leave. Neil Peart joined and expanded band's potential by adding lyric-writing abilities and vocal talents to what had been a rather limited range of sound.

Next two LPs spread band's reputation for hard rock; more importantly began expounding Rush's vision of the individual winning out against high-tech in some distant society. This approach culminated in extended work covering entire first side of **2112**, which tells the tale of a young man who discovers an

Hemispheres, Rush. Courtesy Mercury Records.

electric guitar and suddenly finds himself an outlaw for inventing music to go with it.

At this point, band stepped back and released live set **All The World's A Stage**. Subsequent LPs have continued to dabble in sci-fi motifs or space age trappings (excellent **Countdown** on **Signals** LP is good example). Group managed to avoid taking itself too seriously and have won over ever-growing audience with extensive touring. **Exit: Stage Left** indicates Rush's unwillingness to stray too far from studio sound when performing

Below: Rush frontmen Alex Lifeson (left) and Geddy Lee.

live which tends to make a Rush concert somewhat predictable.

In defense of band it must be said that few other groups can reproduce their studio sound on stage as faithfully as Rush can. Their fans seem to appreciate this and have pushed unit into megastar status which only shows signs of improving.

Current line-up: Lifeson; Lee; Neil Peart, percussion, vocals.

Hit Singles:

	US	UK
Spirit Of Radio, 1980	—	13

Albums:
Rush (Mercury), 1974
Fly By Night (Mercury), 1975
Caress Of Steel (Mercury), 1975
2112 (Mercury), 1976
All The World's A Stage (Double live), (Mercury), 1976
A Farewell To Kings (Mercury), 1977
Archives (Mercury), 1978*
Hemispheres (Mercury), 1978
Permanent Waves (Mercury), 1980
Rush Through Time (Mercury), 1980†
Moving Pictures (Mercury), 1981
Exit: State Left (Live) (Mercury), 1981
Signals (Mercury), 1982
*Re-issue of first three LPs
†Picture disc of previous material

Tom Rush

US composer, vocalist, guitarist.
Born Portsmouth, New Hampshire, February 8, 1941.

Career: Tom Rush emerged from same vibrant New York/Boston coffee-house folk scene which in early '60s saw Bob Dylan(▶), Tom Paxton, Phil Ochs(▶), Joan Baez(▶), Tim Hardin(▶) and Richie Havens(▶) emerge to stardom.

While studying at Harvard, Rush was discovered by Elektra Records' boss Jac

Blues, Songs And Ballads, Tom Rush. Courtesy Prestige Records.

Holzman and embarked on series of albums which fulfilled promise shown on earlier obscure recordings for Prestige label.

Unlike his contemporaries on the folk scene who restricted themselves to traditional material — including old rural blues songs — and originals, Rush wasn't ashamed to exploit material of more contemporary (and popular) black and white performers like Bo Diddley(▶) and Buddy Holly(▶). Nor was he afraid to use electric instrumentation where warranted (a diversion which later landed Bob Dylan in big trouble with folk purists while turning him into a major rock star).

Of all white folk singers, Rush seemed the one who most understood what the blues was really all about and his interpretations of songs like **Galveston Flood** provided spine-

chilling intensity of feeling. More restrained yet equally moving was his beautiful, sadly romantic song cycle, **The Circle Game**, which shook off folk roots and was one of first true concept albums. Included was the original of his best known song, **No Regrets**, a rendition which no other artist has yet matched.

Four well-received Elektra albums brought him deal with the more powerful Columbia company in 1970 and his work for them showed interest spreading across whole panoply of American popular music, including country and western. (Rush was the first major artist to record Jackson Browne's material.)

Six years with Columbia yielded just four albums and he was dropped from label's roster in 1975.

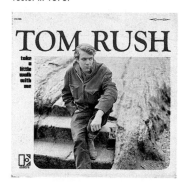

Take A Little Walk With Me, Tom Rush. Courtesy Elektra Records.

Albums:
Blues Songs And Ballads (Prestige/—), 1965
Tom Rush (Elektra), 1965
Take A Little Walk With Me (Elektra), 1966
I Got A Mind To Ramble (Prestige/ Transatlantic), 1968
Tom Rush (Fantasy/—), 1968
The Circle Game (Elektra), 1968
Classic Rush (Elektra), 1969
Tom Rush (Columbia/CBS), 1970
Ladies Love Outlaws (Columbia/CBS), 1976
Best Of (Columbia/CBS), 1976

Leon Russell

US composer, vocalist, pianist, guitarist.
Born Lawton, Oklahoma, April 2, 1941.

Career: Studied classical piano from early age; at 14 took up trumpet and formed own band. Other early experience included playing with Ronnie Hawkins(▶) and Jerry Lee Lewis(▶).

In 1958 Russell moved to Los Angeles and became session musician, working with artists like Glen Campbell(▶), Byrds(▶), Herb Alpert(▶), Crystals(▶) and Righteous Brothers(▶). In late '60s became friendly with blue-eyed soul duo Delaney and Bonnie(▶), and in 1969, along with numerous other West Coast session luminaries, joined Delaney and Bonnie's Friends for touring and recording.

Most of Friends eventually became part of Joe Cocker's(▶) touring band, Mad Dogs And Englishmen, which Russell led. Exposure made him cult figure, and solo career started to take off in 1970 with **Leon Russell** (released on his own Shelter label, formed with English producer/entrepreneur Denny Cordell).

Next few years saw enormous popularity for artist. Although technically limited singer, Russell made up for this with excellent production, superstar session line-ups and good, largely self-penned material. Already renowned for Joe Cocker hit **Delta Lady** — originally written for Rita Coolidge(▶), Russell

came up with several much-covered classics, notably **A Song For You, Superstar** and **This Masquerade.** Recording career peaked with gold album **Carney** (1972) and triple album **Live** (1973).

Despite striking stage personality — wispy grey hair and beard, stove-pipe hat — and evident talent, Russell's career quietened down in late '70s. Following an earlier country album in 1973—tribute to Hank Williams' **Hank Wilson's Back — Volume I** in recent years artist has turned to country roots with albums like **One For The Road** with Willie Nelson(▶) and **New Grass Revival Live.** Somewhat enigmatic figure, Russell has made much good music and earned honourable place in rock pantheon.

Hit Singles:

	US	UK
Tight Rope, 1972	11	—
Lady Blue, 1975	14	—

Albums:
Leon Russell (MCA), 1970
Leon Russell And The Shelter People (MCA), 1971
Carney (MCA), 1972
Will O' The Wisp (MCA), 1975
Best Of Leon Russell (MCA), 1976
Leon Russell And New Grass Revival Live (Paradise), 1981

With Marc Benno:
Asylum Choir (MCA), 1968

With Willie Nelson:
Willie And Leon (Columbia/CBS), 1979

Sad Cafe

UK group formed 1976.

Original line-up: Paul Young, percussion, vocals; Ian Wilson, guitar, vocals; Mike Hehir, guitar; Lenni, saxophone; Vic Emerson, keyboards; John Stimpson, bass; David Irving, drums.

Career: Formed out of two Manchester groups, Mandala and Gyro. Group took name from Carson McCullough book 'The Ballad Of Sad Café'. Signed to powerful local Kennedy Street Agency who got them RCA recording deal.

Debut album **Fanx Ta Ra** was well received. From follow-up **Misplaced Ideals** single **Run Home Girl** charted internationally winning group reputation in US. This took them there in 1979 for string of 54 club, college and theatre dates on bills with major acts like Rush(▶), Toto(▶) and Santana(▶).

Facades, Sad Cafe's 1979 album. Courtesy RCA Records.

10 cc's Eric Stewart produced third album **Facades** at Strawberry Studios; this work contained three hit singles, **Every Day Hurts**, **Strange Little Girl** and **My Oh My**. Album went gold as group ended triumphant 24-date UK tour with three sell-out shows at Apollo Theatre in home town. **A History Of**

Sad Cafe live album reflected their potency as live act; group featured in TV 'Rock Stage' series conceived to showcase bands of exceptional stage charisma.

In August 1980 band had switched from RCA to Polydor, at which time John Stimpson moved across to management of band, being replaced by Des Tong. In early 1981 band joined Swan Song roster for US and Canadian releases.

Current line-up: Young; Wilson; Hehir; Lenni; Emerson; Irving; Des Tong, bass.

Hit Singles:

	US	UK
Every Day Hurts, 1979	—	3
My Oh My, 1980	—	14

Albums:
Fanx Ta Ra (RCA), 1977
Misplaced Ideals (RCA), 1978
Facades (RCA), 1979
Sad Cafe (RCA), 1980
Live In Concert (RCA), 1981

Doug Sahm

US vocalist, guitarist, composer.
Born San Antonio, Texas, November 6, 1941.

Career: Inaugurated first band the Knights in 1955. Moved to San Francisco in early '60s and formed Sir Douglas Quintet, which had worldwide hit in 1965 with **She's About A Mover**, a simple but catchy piece of garage-band rock/R&B.

After some further success with **Mendocino**, band broke up in early '70s. Sahm signed with Atlantic for couple of albums of variable quality, then moved to Warner Bros for 1974 album **Groover's Paradise.** This LP with its Tex-Mex influences heralded Sahm's move back to his Texas roots.

Basing himself in Austin, Sahm has become pillar of local musical community, sporadically releasing albums which combine variety of musical forms, notably country, blues, R&B, cajun and Tex-Mex. Although too eclectic to have wide appeal, Sahm's music is rarely less than interesting, and most of his albums are worth looking out for in cut-out bins.

Hit Singles:

	US	UK
As Sir Douglas Quintet:		
She's About A Mover, 1965	13	15

Albums:
Hell Of A Spell (Takoma/Chrysalis), 1980
Sir Douglas Way Back (—/Charly), 1980

Worth Searching Out:
Groover's Paradise (Warner Bros), 1974

Sam And Dave

US vocal duo formed 1958.
Sam Moore born Miami, Florida, 1935.
David Prater, born Ocilla, Georgia, 1937.

Career: Sam Moore sang gospel with the Melonaires, then started doing solo club gigs around home town. Playing the King of Hearts Club in 1958, was joined onstage by Dave Prater and the partnership was born.

Duo signed to Roulette in 1960, without significant success. After switching to Atlantic in 1965, Jerry Wexler arranged for them to record at Stax studios in Memphis with famous Stax house-band, David Porter and Issac Hayes(▶) producing and writing.

Resultant singles, some issued on Atlantic, some on Stax, were among the most vibrant, exciting pop-soul records of '60s. The combination of Sam and Dave's intense, gospel-inflected harmonies and the tight Stax rhythm section on both uptempo numbers and soul ballads was irresistible. As a live act, Sam and Dave became legendary for their emotion-filled delivery and superslick dancing. Began to make their mark in 1966 with **Hold On (I'm Coming),** which went to No. 21 in US.

After Stax was sold to Gulf and Western in 1968, Sam and Dave continued to record for Atlantic, but later sides recorded in Miami were unsuccessful. By end of '60s the pair apparently were on bad terms, and broke up in 1970. Throughout '70s they came together and split, came together and split again, recording sporadically, but never recapturing great days of previous decade.

As '60s top soul duo, Sam and Dave occupy well-deserved niche in pop history. Never quite as heavyweight as Otis Redding(▶) or Aretha Franklin(▶), they nevertheless produced several classic records that can still set any dance floor alight.

Hit Singles:

	US	UK
Soul Man, 1967	2	24
I Thank You, 1968	9	34
Soul Sister Brown Sugar, 1969	41	15

Albums:
Best Of Sam And Dave (Atlantic), 1969

Worth Searching Out:
Double Dynamite (Stax/Atlantic), 1966
Soul Men (Stax/Atlantic), 1967

Santana

US guitarist, bandleader, composer.
Born Carlos Santana, Autlan, Jalisco, Mexico, July 20, 1947.

Career: Emerged as major local rock musician during San Francisco's Haight-Ashbury flower-power era; guested on seminal **The Live Adventures Of Mike Bloomfield And Al Kooper** album, then put together own band. Brought Latin flavour to rock through use of conga player Mike Carrabello and award-winning Central American percussionist José 'Chepito' Areas alongside Gregg Rolie, keyboards, vocals, David Brown, bass, and Mike Shrieve, drums.

Santana (the first album). Courtesy CBS Records.

Reputation was already made before 1969 debut album **Santana** which sold a million copies (most after Woodstock) in US alone. Band's appearance in 'Woodstock' concert and film, performing **Soul Sacrifice**, was one of the great moments of rock.

Oye Como Va, penned by Latin-music great Tito Puente, helped second album **Abraxas** (1970) to equally big sales. **Santana 3** (1972) brought Santana's guitarist protegé Neil Schon and Coke Escovedo into band. Live album jamming with Buddy Miles was less satisfying. Its realease co-incided with disbanding of original Santana group in wake of Santana's espousal of teach-

Above: Carlos Santana, one of the finest guitarists to emerge from San Francisco in the '60s.

ings of guru Sri Chinmoy at instigation of friend Mahavishnu John McLaughlin(▶), Santana adopted name Devadip.

Latin/jazz/rock fusion **Caravanserai** album used Rolie and Schon, along with studio musicians; they were not included in new band in 1973. This placed Santana originals Areas and Shrieve alongside Tom Coster, keyboard, James Mingo Lewis and Armando Peraza, percussion, and Doug Rauch, bass. Besides own band's work, Santana recorded **Love, Devotion, Surrender** album in partnership with McLaughlin, and **Illuminations** with Alice Coltrane.

Various line-up changes saw Santana band return from heady experimentation to simpler roots, which put albums back among bestsellers.

In 1977, Santana ditched existing band, except Coster; Schon and Rolie formed Journey(▶). Santana came under management of former Fillmore and Woodstock promoter Bill Graham, which led in 1977 to CBS Records' first 'Crystal Globe' Award for sale of five million units in Europe. 1982 brought Santana's output to 14 albums in 15 years, his guitar work remaining distinctive for its pure tone, and providing fluid solos to enhance his always melodic material. Carlos Santana is the Latin voice of rock.
Guitar: Gibson 335.

Hit Singles:

	US	UK
Evil Ways, 1970	9	—
Black Magic Woman, 1970	4	—
Oye Como Va, 1971	13	—
Everybody's Everything, 1971	12	—
She's Not There, 1977	27	11
Winning, 1981	17	—
Hold On, 1982	15	—

Albums:
Santana (Columbia/CBS), 1969
Abraxas (Columbia/CBS), 1970
Santana III (Columbia/CBS), 1971
Caravanserai (Columbia/CBS), 1972
Welcome (Columbia/CBS), 1973
Greatest Hits (Columbia/CBS), 1974
Bortboletta (Columbia/CBS), 1976
Amigos (Columbia/CBS), 1976
Moonflower (Columbia/CBS), 1977
Inner Secrets (Columbia/CBS), 1978
Marathon (Columbia/CBS), 1979
Swing Of Delight (Columbia/CBS), 1980
Zebop! (Columbia/CBS), 1981
Shango (Columbia/CBS), 1982
Havana Moon (Columbia/CBS), 1983

Savoy Brown

UK group formed 1966.

Original line-up: Kim Simmonds, guitar; Martin Stone, guitar; Bryce Portius, vocals; Bob Hall, keyboards; Ray Chappell, bass; Leo Mannings, drums.

Career: Contemporaries of Fleetwood Mac(▶), Chicken Shack, John Dummer Band and Jellybone in British blues revival of mid-'60s; moved to heavy rock. Following in US never matched in UK.

During turbulent decade of existence, Savoy Brown had constantly changing line-up. Guitarist Kim Simmonds (whose brother Harry managed group) was only founder member to survive until demise.

First album **Shake Down** was not released in US but follow-up set **Getting To The Point** began to establish following there. For this LP Chris Youlden replaced Portius as vocalist; he was destined to write much of future material with Simmonds. Brassy **Train To Nowhere** from 1969 **Blue Matter** album became band's theme. With **A Step Further** and **Raw Sienna** band tapped kind of audiences built by Hendrix(▶) and his contemporaries.

Lonesome Dave, vocals, piano, replaced Youlden in 1970; line-up then cmprised Tony Stevens, bass; Roger Earl, drums, and Simmonds. Latter found himself alone when other three left to form popular US-based Foghat.

Simmonds put together new band in 1971 from remnants of defunct Chicken Shack: Dave Walker, vocals; Paul Raymond, keyboards; Andy Sylvester, bass; Dave Bidwell, drums. American reputation continued to flourish.

In 1973, Andy Pyle replaced Sylvester but Simmonds broke band up at year's end. In spring 1974, Savoy Brown was raised from dead. Simmonds joined with former Chicken Shack leader Stan Webb, guitar, and Miller Anderson, guitar (ex-Keef Hartley Band). They brought in James Leverton, bass, and Eric Dillon, drums. This latest conglomerate was short-lived; Anderson rejoined Keef Hartley and Webb and Dillon left to start Broken Glass.

Final line-up: Simmonds; Stan Webb, guitar; Miller Anderson, guitar; James Leverton, bass; Eric Dillon, drums.

Albums:
Shake Down (—/Decca), 1967
Getting To The Point (Parrot/Decca), 1968
Blue Matter (Parrot/Decca), 1968
Raw Sienna (Parrot/Decca), 1970
Looking In (Parrot/Decca), 1970
Street Corner Talking (Parrot/Decca), 1970
Hellbound Train (Parrot/Decca), 1972
Jack The Toad (Parrot/Decca), 1973

Boogie Brothers (London/Decca), 1974
Best Of (London/Decca), 1978
Blues Roots (—/Decca), 1978
Greatest Hits Live In Concert (Townhouse/—), 1981
Rock & Roll Warriors (Townhouse/—), 1981

Saxon

UK group formed 1977.

Original line-up: Peter 'Biff' Byford, vocals; Paul Quinn, guitar; Graham Oliver, guitar; Steve Dawson, bass; Pete Gill, drums.

Career: Yorkshire lads who, refusing to cash in on punk or new wave syndrome, played power chord riffs with a vengeance few others could attain. Carrere signed band in 1979 and released **Saxon** LP same year. Despite typical heavy-metal posing (i.e., standardised logo, long hair, lots of leather), Saxon actually played decent, but loud, songs with tight arrangements and above-average lyrics.

Wheels Of Steel was released in May 1980 and became long-running hit. Next album saw Gill replaced by Nigel Glockler. It was no surprise when fourth LP, **Denim And Leather,** became international hit and proved band to be excellent example of hard rock at its best.

Extensive touring interfered with recording schedule, so band released commendable live set, **The Eagle Has Landed.** But this was only filler, as good as it was. With **Power And The Glory** (1983) band has picked up again and provided another superb studio set.

Saxon have brash, rugged sound and the skill to remain interesting. So far they have mixed volume with right amount of humour and variety to earn deserved success. A few live shows should win over US audiences as well.

Current line-up: Byford; Quinn; Oliver; Dawson; Nigel Glockler, drums.

Hit Singles:

	US	UK
Wheels Of Fire, 1980	—	20
747 (Strangers In The Night), 1980	—	13
And The Bands Played On, 1981	—	12
Never Surrender, 1981	—	18

Albums:
Saxon (—/Carrere), 1979
Wheels Of Steel (—/Carrere), 1980
Strong Arm Of The Law (Carrere), 1980
Denim And Leather (Carrere), 1981
The Eagle Has Landed (—/Carrere), 1982
Power And The Glory (—/Carrere), 1983

Below: Saxon in concert and full flight at full volume.

Leo Sayer

UK vocalist, composer.
Born Gerard Sayer, Shoreham, Sussex, May 21, 1948.

Career: After period as busker, was discovered in 1972 by musician/agent Dave Courtney and singer/actor Adam Faith(▶) Courtney and Sayer formed songwriting partnership, with Faith managing Sayer. First break came when Faith produced Roger Daltrey's(▶) first solo album **Daltrey** in 1973, Sayer's composition from LP **Giving It All Away** became UK Top 5 single.

First album **Silver Bird** made UK charts, helped by success of single **The Show Must Go On.** Sayer's strong material and idiosyncratic singing style often employing falsetto quickly established him as successful new contender in pop-rock field, with string of hit singles. His chirpy personality (he originally wore clown make-up) also ensured TV exposure as guest on various shows.

In 1975 Sayer ended his association with Courtney (although he worked with him again later), and in 1976 joined forces with ace producer Richard Perry for album **Endless Flight.** Project was great success, resulting in huge disco-orientated hit single **You Make Me Feel Like Dancing,** which broke Sayer in US market. Collaboration with Perry continued successfully into late '70s, with Sayer spending much of his time in US.

Latterly Sayer has had his own show on UK TV, which has showcased his likeable unassuming personality and distinctive musical talents. Although not a major artist, Sayer provides pleasant music in lightweight vein and has talent to sustain career into foreseeable future either as performer or songwriter.

Hit Singles:

	US	UK
The Show Must Go On, 1973	—	2
One Man Band, 1974	—	6
Long Tall Glasses, 1974	9	4
Moonlighting, 1975	—	2
You Make Me Feel Like Dancing, 1973	1	2
When I Need You, 1977	1	1
How Much Love, 1977	17	10
I Can't Stop Loving You, 1978	—	6
More Than I Can Say, 1980	2	2
Have You Ever Been In Love, 1982	—	10

Albums:
Silverbird (Warner Bros/Chrysalis), 1973
Just A Boy (Warner Bros/Chrysalis), 1974
Another Year (Warner Bros/Chrysalis), 1975
Endless Flight (Warner Bros/Chrysalis), 1976
Thunder In My Heart (Warner Bros/Chrysalis), 1977
Leo Sayer (Warner Bros/Chrysalis), 1978
The Very Best Of (Chrysalis), 1979
Here (Chrysalis), 1979
The Show Must Go On (—/Pickwick), 1979
Living In A Fantasy (Chrysalis), 1980
When I Need You (—/Hallmark), 1982
World Radio (Warner Bros/Chrysalis), 1982

Boz Scaggs

US vocalist, guitarist, composer.
Born William Royce Scaggs, Ohio, June 8, 1944.

Career: William 'Boz' Scaggs was brought up in Texas, and met Steve Miller(▶) at high school in Dallas. Joined Miller's band the Marksmen in 1959.

Scaggs and Miller moved on to University of Wisconsin; formed band (the Ardells) to play local gigs. Scaggs quit college in 1963 to return to Texas and put together short-lived outfit called the Wigs, playing R&B. From 1964 to 1966 Scaggs was in Europe, scraping living as solo act (as folk singer). First album, **Boz**, recorded in Stockholm.

In 1967 Scaggs returned to America to join Steve Miller in San Francisco, collaborating on two highly acclaimed albums, **Children Of The Future** and **Sailor**. Left in late 1968, citing musical differences.

After one Atlantic album, Scaggs signed with CBS and started to move towards R&B stylings that would eventually make his name. During early '70s Scaggs continued to build following with albums like **My Time** and **Slow Dancer**; but it was not until 1976 release of **Silk Degrees** that he hit big time.

Featuring musicians now famous as members of Toto(▶), **Degrees** was soul-influenced without being slavishly imitative, and full of memorable songs. Album contained several hit singles, including much-covered semi-standard **We're All Alone**, and went on to sell over five million copies.

Two Down Then Left followed similar musical pattern and scored comparable

Above: The sophisticated Boz Scaggs pictured on stage.

success. Scaggs consolidated position by touring extensively (material performed even better live) throughout US and rest of world. 1980 album **Middle Man** featured guest guitarist Carlos Santana, and was followed by compilation **Hits!**

At time of writing, Scaggs was keeping relatively low profile. He is thoughtful artist with real facility for combining intelligent commercial songs with R&B feel. Well-crafted and played on only best musicians, Scaggs' music appeals to extremely wide audience, ensuring longevity.

Hit Singles:

	US	UK
Lowdown, 1976	3	28
What Can I Say, 1977	42	10
Lido Shuffle, 1977	11	13
Breakdown Dead ahead, 1980	15	—
Jojo, 1980	17	—
Look What You've Done To Me, 1980	14	—
Miss Sun, 1980	14	—

Albums:
Boz Scaggs (Atlantic), 1969
Moments (Columbia/CBS), 1971
Boz Scaggs And Band (Columbia/CBS), 1971
My Time (Columbia/CBS), 1972
Slow Dancer (Columbia/CBS), 1974
Silk Degrees (Columbia/CBS), 1976
Two Down Then Left (Columbia/CBS), 1977
Middle Man (Columbia/CBS), 1980
Hits! (Columbia/CBS), 1980

Silk Degrees, Boz Scaggs. Courtesy CBS Records.

Michael Schenker Group

European group formed 1980.

Original line-up: Michael Schenker, guitar; Gary Barden, vocals; Simon Phillips, drums; Mo Foster, bass; Don Airey, keyboards.

Career: Schenker (born Saustedt, West Germany, January 10, 1955) joined brother's band, Scorpions(▶), who opened for UFO(▶) on one of their early German tours. UFO was impressed enough to ask Schenker to join them. From 1974 until 1979, helped develop UFO into excellent hard rock band, culminating in brilliant live LP, **Strangers In The Night**.

By time of its release in early 1979, Schenker had left group. Briefly touring with Scorpions again, he then guested on their **Love Drive** LP before finally deciding on solo career.

Following jamming sessions with Aerosmith (▶) in September 1979, Schenker was free to work on solo LP. Rehearsals began with Gary Barden and Denny Carmassi (ex-Montrose(▶)) on drums, as well as Billy Sheehan on bass. Schenker then went into hospital because of personal problems and project fell apart. Within a year, had formed line-up above; hired Roger Glover as producer, and released first solo LP. (Phillips' previous notable work included sessions for Jack Bruce(▶), Nazareth(▶), Roger Glover, Art Garfunkel(▶), Jeff Beck(▶), Roxy Music(▶), and Pete Townshend(▶).

Although strong, line-up was never meant to be permanent and Schenker recruited touring unit of Barden; Chris Glen, bass; famous session drummer Cozy Powell (Jeff Beck(▶) and Rainbow(▶) among many others); and his own replacement in UFO, Paul Raymond.

In 1981, this line-up struggled to produce second studio LP. **MSG** was expensive flop and, as expected, line-up again changed. However, old line-up was featured on double-

live LP, **One Night At Budokan**.

Raymond left for full-time duties with UFO and Graham Bonnet stepped in for vocalist Barden. Bonnet helped band present a very strong Reading Festival performance, then recorded **Assault Attack**. For some reason, Bonnet's vocals failed to live up to either his earlier solo work or live efforts with Schenker. Barden returned on vocals and Ted McKenna replaced Cozy Powell. This line-up should be steady enough for Michael Schenker to finally reach his potential as rock musician. Anyone capable of creating the exciting sounds of UFO's '70s LPs surely can't be a spent force just yet.

Current line-up: Schenker; Barden; Chris Glen, bass; Ted McKenna, drums.

Albums:
The Michael Schenker Group (Chrysalis), 1980
MSG (Chrysalis), 1981
One Night At Bukodan (Chrysalis), 1981
Dancer (Chrysalis), 1982
Assault Attack (Chrysalis), 1983

Scorpions

German group formed 1970.

Original line-up: Michael Schenker, Gibson Flying 'V' guitar; Rudolph Schenker, guitar; Klaus Meine, vocals; Luthar Heimber, bass; Wolfgang Dziony, drums.

Career: Rudolph Schenker had own band Copernicus in 1965; his brother Michael(▶) joined Cry. In 1970 they formed Scorpions. Line-up above recorded **Lonesome Crow** in 1972 and earned strong sales in Germany. Michael left to join UFO(▶) and Scorpions fell apart. Rudolph Schenker and Meine found Francis Bucholz (bass) and this trio became mainstay of re-formed gorup (to present day).

For most of 1974 Scorpions opened for bands on European tours. Late 1975 saw their first appearances in London; band was already extremely successful in home country and had strong following in Japan. Their 1978 Japanese tour provided live material for **Tokyo Tapes**.

A switch to EMI in 1979 provided better distribution system for band's recordings, and **Lovedrive** introduced Teutonic heavy metal to American audiences on Ted Nugent(▶) tour. **Animal Magnetism** received surprisingly good reviews and band has worked steadily since. **Blackout** LP even made US Top 10.

Like Krokus(▶), the Scorpions' hard work has yet to gain extensive following in UK/US. Except for Abba(▶) and a handful of Australian bands, rock world remains predominantly British/American domain.

Current line-up: Rudolph Schenker; Meine; Francis Bucholz, bass; Mathias Jabs, guitar; Herman Rarebell, drums.

Albums:
Fly To The Rainbow (RCA), 1976
In Trance (RCA), 1976
Virgin Killer (RCA), 1976
Taken By Force (RCA), 1978
Tokyo Tapes (RCA), 1978
Best Of (RCA), 1979
Lonesome Crow (—/RCA), 1979
Lovedrive (Mercury/Harvest), 1979
Animal Magnetism (Mercury/Harvest), 1979
Blackout (Mercury/Harvest), 1982

Left: Guitar star Michael Schenker, who worked with both the Scorpions and UFO before embarking on his own successful career.

Seals And Crofts

US vocal/instrumental duo.
Jim Seals guitar, fiddle, alto sax;
born Sidney, Texas, 1940; Dash Crofts,
mandolin, drums, keyboard, guitar; born
Cisco, Texas, 1940.

Career: Both precocious musicians; Seals won Texas state fiddle championship at nine; played in many country groups, learning tenor sax along the way. Duo moved to California in 1958 and joined the Champs, whose **Tequila** was currently an international smash, selling estimated six million copies worldwide.

By 1965, duo had formed seven-piece Dawnbreakers, which included Louis Shelton (guitar) and Joey Edwards (bass). Group gradually fragmented following entire ensemble's conversion to the Bah'ai faith. Late '60 were spent in prayer/meditation while deciding whether to continue as musicians.

Early in 1970 duo performed new material, Crofts having mastered mandolin during interim. Albums on the TA label, **Seals And Crofts** and **Down Home,** attracted Warner Bros, who signed them in 1971.Since then, they have produced string of gold albums and two US Top 10 singles, **Summer Breeze** (1972) and **Diamond Girl** (1973). Former also supplied Isley Brothers(▶) with sizeable hit.

Their enormous appeal in US has perplexed many rock writers, who tend to dismiss duo for their saccharine sincerity and sanctimonious tone. Totally ignored in Britain, their sales steadily increased in US until late '70s. Songs/albums of social concern, such as **Unborn Child,** a comment on the evils of abortion, have partly filled the gap left by demise of Simon and Garfunkel.

Hit Singles:

	US	UK
Summer Breeze, 1972	6	—
Hummingbird, 1973	20	—
Diamond Girl, 1973	6	—
I'll Play For You, 1975	18	—
Get Closer, 1976	6	—

Albums:
Summer Breeze (Warner Bros), 1972
Diamond Girl (Warner Bros), 1973
Greatest Hits (Warner Bros), 1975
Sudan Village (Warner Bros), 1976
One For One (Warner Bros), 1977
Takin' It Easy (Warner Bros), 1978
The Longest Road (Warner Bros/—), 1980

The Searchers

UK group formed 1962.
Original line-up: Mike Pender, vocals, guitar; John McNally, vocals, guitar; Tony Jackson, vocals, bass; Chris Curtis, drums.

Career: On Merseyside in early '60s the Searchers were second only to Beatles in terms of local popularity; they specialised in high, keening harmonies and immaculate stage presentation.

National attention came after signing to Pye in 1963; group's cover of Drifters' **Sweets For My Sweet** soared to No. 1 spot and made group integral part of Merseybeat boom.

Group did not write own material and generally relied on covering suitable American hits like Jackie De Shannon's **Needles And Pins** (co-written by Sonny Bono of Sonny and Cher(▶)), Orlons' **Don't Throw Your Love Away** and **When You Walk In The Room,** also a hit for De Shannon. Group had considerable American success on Kapp label, making Top 40 on five occasions in 1964.

By 1965 group seemed unable to find right material and hits dried up. Jackson left to form Tony Jackson and the Vibrations (one minor hit), and was replaced by Frank Allen, formerly with Cliff Bennett's Rebel Rousers. At this time band started to move into lucrative club and cabaret circuit, where they continue to make substantial living to this day. Chris Curtis left in 1969 and was replaced by American drummer Billy Adamson.

In their time the Searchers were one of the best-loved British 'beat groups', appealing to wide audience with their soaring harmonies and jangling guitar sound. In musical approach if not image they anticipated later folk-rock harmony outfits like Byrds(▶) and Mamas and Papas(▶). In early 1983 group celebrated 21 years in the music business with a series of special concerts, and look set to continue for another 21 years.

Current line-up: Pender; McNally; Frank Allen, bass; Bob Jackson, keyboards; Billy Adamson, drums.

Hit Singles:

	US	UK
Sweets For My Sweet, 1963	—	1
Sugar And Spice, 1963	44	2
Needles And Pins, 1964	13	1
Don't Throw Your Love Away, 1964	16	1
Some Day We're Gonna Love Again, 1964	34	11
When You Walk In The Room, 1964	35	3
Love Potion No. 9, 1964	3	—
What Have They Done To The Rain, 1964	29	13
Goodbye My Love, 1965	52	4
He's Got No Love, 1965	—	12
Take Me For What I'm Worth, 1966	—	20

Albums:
Meet The Searchers (Kapp/Pye), 1963
Sugar And Spice (—/Pye), 1963
When You Walk In The Room (—/Pye), 1964
It's The Searchers (—/Pye), 1964
Sounds Like The Searchers (—/Pye), 1964
Take Me For What I'm Worth (—/Pye), 1965
The Searchers (Sire), 1980
Needles And Pins (—/Hallmark), 1971
The Searchers File (—/Pye), 1977
100 Minutes (—/Pye), 1982
Loves Melodies (Sire/—), N/A

Golden Hour Of The Searchers. Courtesy Golden Hour/Pye Records.

Neil Sedaka

US vocalist, composer, pianist.
Born Brooklyn, New York, March 13, 1939.

Career: Piano prodigy at eight, this son of a taxi driver studied at prestigious Juilliard School and had promising future as classical pianist. At 13 began writing songs with neighbour Howard Greenfield, who remained lyric-writing partner for over 20 years (until

replaced by Phil Cody after 1973). Sedaka and Greenfield were one of several teams working at Brill Building in New York, turning out high-quality music which bridged gap between Tin Pan Alley and rock'n'roll for teen market's top performers. Then, in 1958, Connie Frances(▶) had hit with their **Stupid Cupid.**

Sedaka began recording own songs and between 1959 and 1963 hits like **The Diary, Calendar Girl, Oh Carol** (dedicated to friend and fellow Brill Building writer Carole King(▶)), **Stairway To Heaven, Breaking Up Is Hard To Do** and **Happy Birthday Sweet Sixteen** sold over 20 million copies. Never succumbing to pitfalls of stardom, Sedaka lived and worked in father's unpretentious Brooklyn apartment, writing over 500 songs before Beatles-influenced music caused his popularity as performer to fade. Composing talent was still in demand, however, and he wrote for Tom Jones, the Fifth Dimension and Andy Williams.

Oh Carol, Neil Sedaka. Courtesy RCA Records.

Always popular in Britain (his second record, **I Go Ape,** made No. 5 in UK), Sedaka was persuaded in 1971 to do come-back concert at Albert Hall in London; show successfully combined new songs with oldies. While in Britain he recorded two albums with group called Hot Legs (who became 10cc(▶), then returned to Los Angeles to record third album—all for Britain. When Elton John(▶) realised Sedaka had no US record company, he signed him to own label, Rocket Records. Gold-rated **Sedaka's Back** and **The Hungry Years,** combining songs from three British LPs, was well received in US and Sedaka had his first US No. 1 hit single in ten years with **Laughter In The Rain** (1975) followed by hit **Bad Blood,** which featured Elton John on backing vocals. **Breaking Up Is Hard To Do** returned to charts in 1976 after 14 years.

Sedaka's songs for Captain and Tenille, **Love Will Keep Us Together** and **You Never Done It Like That,** further enhanced revived reputation. First NBC-TV special in 1976 received both critical and popular acclaim. Since then, Sedaka has continued to write, record, appear on television and play to full houses in Las Vegas, Lake Tahoe and around the world. A star at 20 and a has-been at 25, Sedaka has accepted ups and downs with equanimity. His new songs remain fresh and original, and his music is enjoyed by widest possible audience.

Hit Singles:

	US	UK
The Diary, 1959	14	—
I Go Ape, 1959	42	9
Oh! Carol, 1959	9	3
Stairway To Heaven, 1960	9	8
You Mean Everything To Me, 1960	17	45
Calendar Girl, 1961	4	8
Little Devil, 1961	11	9
Happy Birthday, Sweet Sixteen, 1961	6	3
Breaking Up Is Hard To Do, 1962	1	7
Next Door To An Angel, 1962	5	29
Alice In Wonderland, 1963	17	—
Oh Carol/Breaking Up Is Hard To Do/Little Devil, 1972	—	19
That's When The Music Takes Me, 1973	27	18
Laughter In The Rain, 1974	1	15
Bad Blood, 1975	1	—
Breaking Up Is Hard To Do, 1976	8	—
Love In The Shadows, 1976	16	—

Albums:
Oh Carol (—/Camden), 1970
Stupid Cupid (—/Camden), 1972
Tra-La Days Are Over (Polydor), 1974
Live At The Royal Festival Hall, With The Royal Philharmonic Ochestra (Polydor), 1974
Laughter In The Rain (Polydor), 1974
Let's Go Steady Again (—/Pickwick), 1975
Laughter And Tears (Polydor), 1976
Neil Sedaka Collection (—/Pickwick), 1976
And Songs—A Solo Concert (Polydor), 1977
Sedaka '50s and '60s (RCA), 1977
A Song (Elektra/Polydor), 1977
All You Need Is The Music (Polydor), 1978
Many Sides Of (RCA), 1979
Neil Sedaka's Greatest Hits (RCA), 1980
In The Pocket (Elektra/Polydor), 1980
Now (Elektra/Polydor), 1981
Singer, Songwriter, Melody Maker (Accord/—), 1982
20 Golden Pieces Of (—/Bulldog), 1982

Laughter And Tears, Neil Sedaka. Courtesy Polydor Records.

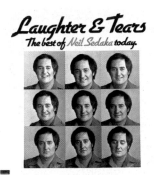

Pete Seeger

US composer, vocalist, guitarist, banjoist.
Born New York City, May 3, 1919.

Career: Born into musical family (sister Peggy is known in UK for musical partnership with Ewan McColl, while youngest brother Mike was fiddler for New Lost City Ramblers), Seeger learned banjo as child, then studied traditional ballads at Library of Congress in teens. Travelled with Woody Guthrie(▶) and Almanac Singers from 1940, often giving free performances at union meetings and strikers' demonstrations. After serving in US Army during World War II, in 1948 he co-founded Weavers, committed yet commercially popular folk group which, despite blacklisting, continued performing and recording sporadically until 1964.

When People's Songs, union of progressive songwriters, was formed in late '40s, Seeger became president. During '50s, he was guiding light of 'Sing Out!' publication and helped found 'Broadside' magazine, where most singer-songwriters of '60s first gained notice. With his help, Newport Folk Festival was reorganised in 1961 to use profits for encouraging folk music. Seeger privately published 'How To Play The Five-String Banjo', refusing to copyright book because 'the banjo belongs to everyone'. Popular target for US witch hunters, Seeger's humanity was so unusual it seemed threatening Particularly 'suspicious' was custom of learning song from every country where he gave concerts. When ABC-TV's 'Hootenanny' blacklisted him in 1962, many young folk performers boycotted programme. Seeger was later given own show on Public Broadcasting.

Probably as close to sainthood as anyone the music world has produced, Seeger has spent over 40 years directing music towards social change for peace, equality and decency. Using song to inform, rally and entertain, he has performed on stages throughout the world, hosted own television show, sung from rickety platforms and grassy fields, alongside protest marches (like 1970 March On Washington when he led singing of Lennon's(▶) **Give Peace A Chance**), and from deck of sloop Clearwater, which sailed along Hudson River publicising danger of pollution.

Not exclusively an up-front activist, Seeger has worked quietly behind scenes, too. For example, he arranged for steel drummer from Trinidad to teach at New York settlement houses and reform schools, then helped resulting bands to get bookings. Writer of such songs as **If I Had A Hammer, Turn, Turn, Turn** and **Where Have All The Flowers Gone**, which became hits for others, Seeger still continues to encourage new writers by performing their songs.

Seeger's performing and recording career, spanning five decades, would be enough to entitle him to inclusion in any book about popular music. As important, however, are his tireless efforts to keep musical path open for new talent like Dylan(▶), Baez(▶) and hundreds of others who have repeatedly expressed gratitude and friendship, and who continue to perform with him. Married with three children, Seeger lives along the Hudson River in Beacon, New York.

Albums (selected):
American Ballads (Folkways/—), 1957
At Village Gate Volume I (Folkways/—), 1960
At Village Gate Volume II (Folkways/—), 1962
Broadsides (Folkways/—), 1963
Little Boxes (Folkways/—), 1964
Struggle And Protest (Folkways/—), 1964
Greatest Hits (Columbia/Embassy), 1967

Bob Seger

US vocalist, composer, guitarist.
Born Detroit, Michigan, 1947.

Career: Seger grew up in Detroit and played in local band, Last Heard. 1966 saw release of solo material. Several tracks received good critical notice or became regional hits (**Heavy Music** (1966), **2+2=?** (1967) and **Ramblin' Gamblin' Man** (1968)). After four LPs and many, many mid-Western gigs, Seger quit music in 1969 and went to college.

Stranger In Town, Bob Seger. Courtesy Capitol Records.

By 1971 he was on the road again, with same results; critical praise, regional hits—and always just out of the running.

Third phase of career began when he formed permanent backing group, the Silver Bullet Band. This aggregation produced **Beautiful Loser,** but again national success just eluded Seger. He decided to try Frampton's(▶) approach of using live LP to sell sound rather than collection of old hits.

Live Bullet proved to be key and Seger was sudden overnight success some 12 years after first attempts. He quickly followed up with **Night Moves** and both albums stayed in US charts for some time, (**Night Moves** went platinum).

Anxious to give fans same musical diet, Seger finally found time in heavy touring schedule to record **Stranger In Town,** which went triple platinum.

Against The Wind went to No. 1 in US LP charts, but seemed to suffer from platinum overdosage. Seger sensed this and offered another live set, **Nine Tonight,** a collection of old hits, giving him time to rejuvenate his creative forces. In 1983, he released his personal masterpiece, **The Distance.**

Hit Singles:		US	UK
Ramblin' Gamblin' Man, 1969		17	—
Night Moves, 1977		4	—
Still The Same, 1978		4	—
Hollywood Nights, 1978		12	42
We've Got Tonite, 1979		13	41
Fire Lake, 1980		6	—
Against The Wind, 1980		5	—
You'll Accomp'ny Me, 1980		14	—
Tryin' To Live My Life Without You, 1981		5	—
Shame On The Moon, 1983		2	—

Albums:
Ramblin' Gamblin' Man (Capitol), 1969
Noah (Capitol/—), 1969
Mongrel (Capitol), 1970
Smokin' O.P.'s (Reprise), 1972
Seven (Reprise), 1974
Beautiful Loser (Capitol), 1975
Live Bullet (Capitol), 1976
Night Moves (Capitol), 1976
Stranger In The Town (Capitol), 1980
Against The Wind (Capitol), 1980
Nine Tonight (Capitol), 1982
The Distance (Captiol), 1983

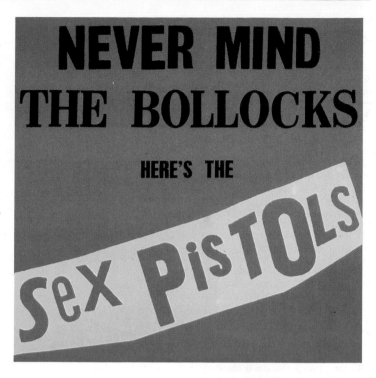

The Sex Pistols

UK group formed 1975.
Original line-up: Steve Jones, guitar, vocals; Glen Matlock, bass; Paul Cook, drums; Johnny Rotten, vocals.

Career: Jones, Cook and Matlock used to hang around Malcolm McLaren's clothes store; there they met John Lydon whom McLaren suggested as band's vocalist. McLaren became manager and began developing strong image by encouraging tough, ragged street dress (which rebelled against decadent glam look of '70s acts). He renamed Lydon 'Rotten' and coined moniker Sex Pistols.

Early gigs were hardly professional but full of explosive energy. McLaren capitalised on group's inexperience and used it to promote image of angry young men only refused to copy established rock stars (megabands in particular).

Never Mind The Bollocks, Sex Pistols. Courtesy Virgin Records.

1976 gigs not only enhanced band's reputation for being 'anti' everything but began involving audience in violence on regular basis. November 1976 turned Sex Pistols loose on centre of rock world. A few days after signing EMI contract, and readying **Anarchy In The UK** single, Pistols were provoked into swearing on live Thames TV programme. Uproar made them front page items of all newspapers, not just music weeklies. Kids loved it and the 'punk' revolution was on.

EMI dropped band in January 1977, losing £40,000 advance. A&M stepped in to sign band, but gave up £75,000 advance a few days later. By time Virgin offered £50,000

Below: The very lovely Sex Pistols (from left) Sid Vicious, Paul Cook, Johnny Rotten, Steve Jones.

advance in May 1977, band had collected over £150,000 for one single.

In interim, Rotten replaced Matlock with friend Sid Vicious. Pistols were banned practically everywhere which meant there was no way to follow up notoriety with a little rock'n'roll. Subsequent recordings ensured Pistol's place in chart histories, but on concluding first American tour, Rotten announced group's break up. Other three carried on temporary, even using infamous Great Train Robber Ronald Biggs for vocal or two. All this was pointless; it became macabre when Vicious was arrested for murder of girlfriend. He died in ugly overdose incident while awaiting trial.

Several post-Pistols solo projects (Rich Kids, Professionals, Public Image Ltd.) have all failed to win either wide critical acclaim or the popular support afforded Pistols. Ironically, Pistols influenced entire rock industry but accomplished little musically. Band's assault on established rock heroes forced these stars to question their secure status and make more of an effort to remain fresh.

The Sex Pistols raw style inspired many young musicians/singers, previously inhibited by lack of money or finesse, to form back-to-the-basics bands. The Pistols were not only a shot in the arm to the music industry, but (with McLaren's foresight, which he continues to demonstrate) helped bring back the fashion/music connection that had been so exciting in the '60s. Most importantly, the Sex Pistols encouraged audiences and performers to question the music scene, and brought them back together.

Final line-up: Jones, guitar, vocals; Cook, drums; Sid Vicious, bass, vocals.

Hit Singles:

	US	UK
God Save The Queen, 1977	—	2
Pretty Vacant, 1977	—	6
Holidays In The Sun, 1977	—	8
No One Is Innocent/My Way, 1978	—	7
Something Else/Friggin' In The Riggin', 1979	—	3
Silly Thing/Who Killed Bambi, 1979	—	6
C'mon Everybody, 1979	—	3

Albums:
Never Mind The Bollocks, Here's The Sex Pistols (Warner Bros/Virgin), 1977*
The Great Rock'n'Roll Swindle (—/Virgin), 1978
Some Product (—/Virgin), 1979
Carry On Sex Pistols (—/Virgin), 1979
Flogging A Dead Horse (—/Virgin), 1979
*Only LP released while band was working unit.

Sha Na Na

US group formed 1969.

Original line-up: Don York, vocals; Frederick Greene, vocals; Rich Joffe, vocals; Chris Donald, guitar; Screamin' Scott Symon, piano; John 'Bowzer' Bauman, piano; Lennie Baker, saxophone; Elliot Cahn, vocals, guitar; Henry Gross, vocals, guitar; Bruce Clarke, bass; Jocko Marcellino, drums.

Career: Lovingly sending up great '50s era of rock'n'roll, Sha Na Na (originally Eddie and the Evergreens) had highly visual stage act which made them sensation of 1969 Woodstock Festival. However, self-proclaimed 'Dirty Dozen' were unable to capture effectively on albums or singles the fun of stage show.

Baker was only true rocker, having been member of '50s hit-makers Danny and the Juniors (of **At The Hop** renown). Rest

affected gold-lamé costumes, slicked down hairstyles, crepe-soled shoes, and dance styles of golden era, while re-working Presley(▶), Vincent(▶) and Cochran(▶) material. Hilariously parodied not just music of rock 'n' roll but teen-lifestyle of '50s; show was like set for 'West Side Story'. Sha Na Na were classy musicians and brilliant actors, coming across as hoodlums, incarnate.

Original **Bounce In Your Buggy** was near UK hit but records generally lacked dynamism of British rivals Showaddywaddy(▶) (who also based style on '50s nostalgia but re-worked oldies in own inimitable way).

In 1970, Chris Donald was replaced by Vinnie Taylor. (Henry Gross left for solo career. This has yielded various albums, including **Henry Gross** and **Plug Me Into Something**, and **Release** which included US hit **Shannon** in 1976.) Further changes came in 1973 when Elliot Cahn and Ritch Joffe left; Chico Ryan replaced Bruce Clarke. Band started to affect pseudonyms; Cahn had been Gino, Scott Powell became Captain Outrageous, then Tony Santini, Elliott Randall (who also had some success on Polydor) replaced Vinnie Taylor when latter died of heroin overdose in 1974; adopted name Enrico Ronzoni. Further problems came with nervous breakdown of Scott Symon, and John Bauman's operation for collapsed lungs.

Sha Na Na's own product amounted to seven albums plus a compilation but has now dried up in an age when records have become much harder to sell. Group will pass into rock history as one of the great live bands. Repeats of their 1977 music/comedy TV series are still popular in the US — though mostly with 6-12 age group. True lovers of rock 'n' roll will prefer, however, to have the originals rather than Sha Na Na's covers in their record collection.

Final line-up: York; Greene; Syman; Bauman; Baker; Marcellino; Chico Ryan, bass; Elliott Randall, guitar.

Hit Singles:

	US	UK
Henry Gross Solo:		
Shannon, 1976	6	—

Albums:
Here To Stay (Buddah/Kama Sutra), 1969
Best Of (Buddah/—), 1976
Rock 'n' Roll Revival (—/Golden Hour), 1977
Remember Then (Accord/—), 1978

Henry Gross Solo:
Plug Me Into Something (A&M), 1970

The Shadows

UK group formed 1959.

Original line-up: Hank Marvin, Fender Stratocaster guitar; Bruce Welch, Fender Telecaster guitar; Jet Harris, bass; Tony Meehan, drums.

Career: In 1958 Marvin and Welch were members of Cliff Richard's(▶) backing group the Drifters. By following year personnel had stabilised as above, and group had changed name to Shadows to avoid confusion with American Drifters(▶).

Although band continued to back Richard, they started to record independently from 1959. During a 1960 British tour, Jerry Lordan, artist on same bill, gave them instrumental piece he had written called **Apache**. Their version of song reached No. 1 in July 1960, and set pattern for instrumental hits that would last until psychedelia era of 1967. Formula was simple yet effective; Marvin's lead guitar would carry melody, while others provided clipped, efficient backing.

Almost completely arranged, Shadows music could be clinical; yet it provided example for thousands of young instrumentalists, especially, of course, guitar players. Image-wise, Shadows relied on matching mohair suits and laid-back nonchalance; wildness of ensuing beat and R&B era was in many cases reaction to their uniformed neatness.

During this period several personnel changes took place. Tony Meehan left in 1961 to be replaced by Brian Bennett. Jet Harris quit in 1962 and almost immediately joined up with Meehan again — duo produced three Top 10 singles in 1963 before Harris retired from scene due to ill health. For short while Harris was replaced in Shadows by Brian 'Licquorice' Locking; he in turn was followed by John Rostill.

In 1968, after hits had dried up, outfit ceased to exist as regular working aggregation. During '70s members got involved in other musical activities; among many other projects, Bruce Welch wrote for and produced Cliff Richard(▶), John Farrar produced Olivia Newton-John(▶), and Brian Bennett became

Left: The surviving Shadows (left to right) Bruce Welch, Brian Bennett and Hank B. Marvin, in the 1980s.

in-demand session musician. However, band continued to record and work together sporadically, with various bass players.

In 1977 **Twenty Golden Greats** compilation album topped UK charts, and following year group returned to singles chart in big way with version of show tune **Don't Cry For Me Argentina**. Since that time group has made sporadic chart appearances, and tours continue to be guaranteed sell-outs.

Although their music has not been that influential — few rock guitarists actually play *like* Hank Marvin — Shadows encouraged generation of young men to take up instruments and make music for themselves. Many current axe heroes point to Hank Marvin as their first role model. Now elder statesmen of rock and pop, Shadows will undoubtedly clock up more hits before drawing final curtain.

Current line-up: Marvin; Welch; Brian Bennett, drums.

Hit Singles:

	US	UK
Apache, 1960	—	1
Man Of Mystery/The Stranger, 1960	—	5
F.B.I., 1961	—	6
Frightened City, 1961	—	3
Kon-Tiki, 1961	—	1
The Savage, 1961	—	10
Wonderful Land, 1962	—	1
Guitar Tango, 1962	—	4
Dance On!, 1962	—	1
Foot Tapper, 1963	—	1
Atlantis, 1963	—	2
Shindig, 1963	—	6
Geronimo, 1963	—	11
Theme For Young Lovers, 1964	—	12
The Rise And Fall Of Flingel Bunt, 1964	—	5
Genie With The Light Brown Lamp, 1964	—	17
The Next Time I See Mary Anne, 1965	—	17
Stingray, 1965	—	19
Don't Make My Baby Blue, 1965	—	10
War Lord, 1965	—	18
Let Me Be The One, 1975	—	12
Don't Cry For Me Argentina, 1978	—	5
Theme From The Deer Hunter (Cavatina), 1979	—	9
Riders In The Sky, 1980	—	12

Albums:
The Shadows (—/Columbia), 1962
Greatest Hits (—/Columbia), 1963
Dance With The Shadows (—/Columbia), 1964
The Sound Of The Shadows (—/Columbia), 1965
More Hits (—/Columbia), 1965
Shadow Music (—/Columbia), 1966
Jigsaw (—/Columbia), 1967
Established 1958 (—/Columbia), 1968
Something Else (—/Columbia), 1969
Shades Of Rock (—/Columbia), 1970
Rockin' With Curly Leads (—/EMI), 1973
Specs Appeal (—/EMI), 1975
The Shadows (—/Ember), 1975
Live At Paris Olympia (—/EMI), 1975
Rarities (—/NUT), 1976
Tasty (—/EMI), 1977
20 Golden Greats (—/EMI), 1977
At The Movies (—/MFP), 1978
String Of Hits (—/EMI), 1979
Change Of Address (—/Polydor), 1980
Another String Of Hot Hits (—/EMI), 1980
Rock On With (—/MFP), 1980
Hits Right Up Your Street (—/Rollover), 1981
Live (—/MFP), 1981
Life In The Jungle (—/Polydor), 1982

Shalamar

US group formed 1978.

Original/current line-up: Jody Watley, vocals; Jeffrey Daniels, vocals, guitar; Howard Hewett, vocals, bass.

Career: Encouraged by British music entrepreneur Simon Soussan, black American entrepreneur Dick Griffey put together Los Angeles session singers and musicians to record medley of Motown oldies. Titled **Uptown Festival**, disc was aimed directly at Britain's 'Northern Soul' cult market. Griffey chose name Shalamar for non-existent group.

Griffey moved on from booking acts for TV show 'Soul Train' to running own Solar (Sound Of Los Angeles Records) label. He decided to create group to capitalise on record's success; announced on 'Soul Train' that show was to form new group. Chicago-born model Jody Watley and LA native Jeffrey Daniels had made name via superb dancing on programme; they were picked for Shalamar along with bassist Howard Hewett.

Take That To The Bank, from group's second Solar album, was chart breakthrough. Earned gold disc for **The Second Time Around** from third album. By fourth LP **Shot Of Love**, trio had developed as songwriters and musicians. Their marvellously choreographed stage act conplemented their vocal talents.

Friends album moved them into ranks of true supergroups of black music, spawning several hit singles. Shalamar have shown remarkable development for what had been a manufactured group. They are particularly popular in UK, though rumours of imminent split abound.

Hit Singles:

	US	UK
Take That To The Bank, 1978	—	20
Second Time Around, 1979	8	45
I Owe You One, 1980	—	13
I Can Make You Feel Good, 1982	—	7
A Night To Remember, 1982	44	5
There It Is, 1982	—	5
Friends, 1982	—	12

Albums:
Uptown Festival (Soul Train), 1977
Disco Gardens (Solar), 1978
Big Fun (Solar), 1979
Three For Love (Solar), 1981
Friends (Solar), 1982
Greatest Hits (Solar), 1982

Del Shannon

US vocalist, composer.
Born Charles Westover, Grand Rapids, Michigan, December 30, 1939.

Career: Shannon took up singing and guitar in early teens. First real experience was gained in US Army, where he performed on Armed Forces Network's 'Get Up and Go' programme. After discharge returned to his home state, and began singing professionally in local clubs.

Discovered by Detroit agents Harry Balk and Irving Micahnik, Shannon was soon signed to Big Top Records. His first and biggest hit, **Runaway**, was recorded almost immediately. Shannon and keyboard player Max Crook had worked out song in clubs with an electric organ called the Musitron. Single made No. 1 in US in early 1961, remaining on chart for 17 weeks; hit in UK during June of that year, staying on charts for 22 weeks. Shannon had further Top 20 singles, including **Hats Off To Larry, Little Town Flirt** and **Keep Searchin'**.

Chart success declined after 1965, although English duo Peter and Gordon scored with his **I Go To Pieces**. Shannon's sharp, early '60s sound was considered dated by 1967; he tried varying sound by recording album with producer Andrew Loog Oldham; though interesting, it was a commercial failure. Shannon produced other artists with considerable success; Brian Hyland's Shannon-produced **Gypsy Woman** was No. 1 in UK, Top 5 in US. Continued to tour, particularly in England; a fine live album was released in 1972.

In '70s Shannon released singles produced by Jeff Lynn (of ELO(▶)) and Dave Edmunds(▶)), again with little commercial success. In 1982 signed with Elektra records who released album produced by long-time admirer Tom Petty(▶), **Drop Down and Get Me**, which met with critical approval.

Hit Singles:

	US	UK
Runaway, 1961	1	1
Hats Off To Larry, 1961	5	6
So Long Baby, 1961	28	10
Hey Little girl, 1962	38	2
Swiss Maid, 1962	—	2
Little Town Flirt, 1963	12	4
Two Kinds Of Teardrops, 1963	50	5
Keep Searchin' (We'll Follow The Sun), 1965	9	3

Albums:
The Del Shannon Hit Parade (—/London), 1980
Live In England (—/Fame), 1982
Drop Down And Get Me (Elektra/Demon), 1982

Shooting Star

US group formed 1977.

Original/current line-up: Van McClain, vocals, guitar; Charles Waltz, vocals, violin, keyboards; Bill Guffey, keyboards; Steve Thomas, drums; Ron Verlin, bass; Gary West, vocals, keyboards, guitar, percussion.

Career: Hard rock band very popular with American teenagers, especially in the Midwest. Formed in Kansas City; quickly became local favourites. Signed to Virgin/Atlantic; first album, self titled, was released in 1978. Received ample airplay, but sales were limited. Band toured US to receptive audiences.

Due to record company shake-ups and re-shuffling, band switched to Virgin/Epic; recorded successful **Hang On For Your Life** LP stayed in US chart for 35 weeks. Shooting Star toured to support product; Virgin/Epic re-released first album, which had quickly gone out of print. Third album **Three Wishes**, released in 1982, was accompanied by videos played heavily on MTV.

Albums:
Shooting Star (Virgin-Atlantic/Virgin), 1978
Hang On For Your Life (Virgin-Epic/Virgin), 1980
Three Wishes (Virgin-Epic/Virgin), 1982

Showaddywaddy

UK group formed 1973.

Original/Current line-up: Dave Bartram, vocals; Buddy Gask, vocals; Russ Field, guitar; Trevor Oakes, guitar; Al James, bass; Rod Deas, bass; Romeo Challenger, drums; Malcolm Allured, drums.

Career: Formed by merger of two Leicester bands, the Choice and the Hammers. From beginning pursued policy of reviving rock 'n' roll and '50s pop.

The Greatest Hits, Del Shannon. Courtesy Line Records.

After winning talent contest, band signed with Bell (later Arista) Records, and began phenomenal run of hit singles with **Hey Rock And Roll** in May 1974. Strangely, first four hits were self-penned, but further releases were all cover versions.

Band also quickly became in-demand live act, attracting 'family' type audience. As yet band has made no impression in US, but it has considerable following in Europe and Eastern bloc countries.

Although competent and versatile (doubling of instruments makes for varied stage show), Showaddywaddy lack conviction of other revivalist bands like Darts(▶) and Sha Na Na(▶). Nevertheless, cheerful, colourful image and knack for picking right material should ensure continued success. (Recent singles do not show in our Top 20 based chart, but band is still regularly hitting UK Top 40.)

Hit Singles:

	US	UK
Hey Rock And roll, 1974	—	2
Rock 'n' Roll Lady, 1974	—	15
Hey Mr Christmas, 1974	—	13
Sweet Music, 1975	—	14
Three Steps To Heaven, 1975	—	2
Heartbeat, 1975	—	7
Under The Moon Of Love, 1976	—	1
When, 1977	—	3
You Got What It Takes, 1977	—	2
Dancin' Party, 1977	—	4
I Wonder Why, 1978	—	2
A Little Bit Of Soap, 1978	—	5
Pretty Little Angel Eyes, 1978	—	5
Remember Then, 1979	—	17
Sweet Little Rock 'n' Roller, 1979	—	15

Albums:
Step Two (—/Bell), 1975
Trocadero (—/Bell), 1976
Greatest Hits (—/Arista), 1976
Showaddywaddy (—/MFP), 1977
Red Star (—/Arista), 1977
Greatest Hits '76-78 (—/Arista), 1978
Crepes And Drapes (—/Arista), 1979

Bright Lights (—/Arista), 1980
Good Times (—/Arista), 1981
Living Legends (—/RCA), 1983

Simon & Garfunkel

US duo formed 1957.

Career: During late '50s, a bouncy little guy named Paul Simon(▶) was hustling for fraternity party gigs around Forest Hills High School in New York. Unfashionable and uncool, his vocal harmony duo Tom and Jerry had few takers. (When he and partner Art Garfunkel(▶) became famous in 1965 as Simon and Garfunkel, lots of people were kicking themselves.) As Paul and Jerry they actually reached No. 54 in charts with late 1957 **Hey Schoolgirl** but, despite appearance on 'American Bandstand', follow-ups failed to take off. They went separate ways, Paul Simon to Queens College and Art Garfunkel to New York's Columbia University.

While at college, Simon and fellow-student Carole King(▶) made demo tapes for publishers, which taught him techniques like overdubbing. Single **The Lone Teen Ranger** (recorded in 1962 as Jerry Landis) got to 97 in US charts. Dropping out of law school in 1964, Simon left for England to perform on folk circuit. Another single **He Was My Brother** (recorded as Paul Kane) was heard in New York by Columbia Records, who agreed to produce Simon and Garfunkel album. Simon returned to US where **Wednesday Morning 3 AM** was recorded under real names. Garfunkel had recorded for Octavia, then Warwick as Arty Garr. Mixing traditional and modern folk songs plus original numbers by Simon, album was less than successful. Simon therefore returned to UK, where he recorded solo album **The Paul Simon Songbook**, containing own material, including **I Am A Rock** and, like **3 AM**, using only guitar accompaniment.

Producer Tom Wilson, who had helped electrify Dylan, saw possibilities in one track on **3 AM**. Adding electric guitar, bass and drums, Wilson released **Sounds Of Silence** as single, which shot to US No. 1. Hearing of success while in Europe, Simon again returned to US. In 1966 he and Garfunkel recorded **Sounds Of Silence** album, including material from **Songbook**, but with rock backing. **Homeward Bound**, written while waiting for train in Lancashire, became duo's first UK hit single, reaching No. 9 (No. 5 in US).

Below: Showaddywaddy, rock 'n' roll revivalists supreme for the cabaret circuits of Britain.

Simon's literate, poetic yet aggressive lyrics, filled with introspection, isolation and ironic protest, combined perfectly with Garfunkel's delicate vocal arrangements to create a sound that appealed to increasingly sophisticated young listeners. Tour of US and UK was followed by **Bookends,** then **The Graduate** soundtrack album which won Grammy for Best Original Motion Picture Score. Also received Grammy for **Mrs Robinson** (Best Record), supposedly written almost by accident while working on film score: new song had gap which, by chance, had same number of beats as name of character in Mike Nichols' film, so Simon jokingly used her name to fill gap. When Nichols heard there was song called Mrs Robinson, he demanded to hear it, and it went straight into film.

By now Simon and Garfunkel were so popular that **3 AM** was finally released in UK. In 1970 **Bridge Over Troubled Water** became extraordinarily successful, title track reaching No. 1 in US and UK, and album selling over 9 million copies. Despite success, duo felt constrained by partnership, so split up after final concert in Garfunkel's home town of Forest Hills. Although Garfunkel occasionally did guest numbers with Simon, it was 11 years before they reunited for 1981 free concert in New York's Central Park. Nearly half a million people, including the Mayor, gathered there to be reminded of, as New York Times said, 'distinct musical identities that complement each other in a very special way'. Double-record, video and six-week European tour followed, giving much-needed boost to stagnating solo careers.

Hit Singles:

	US	UK
The Sounds Of Silence, 1966	1	—
Homeward Bound, 1966	5	9
I Am A Rock, 1966	3	17
A Hazy Shade Of Winter, 1966	13	—
At The Zoo, 1967	16	—
Scarborough Fair (Canticle), 1968	11	—
Mrs Robinson, 1968	1	4
Mrs Robinson (EP), 1969	—	9
The Boxer, 1969	7	6
Bridge Over Troubled Water, 1970	1	1
Cecilia, 1970	4	—
El Condor Pasa, 1970	18	—
My Little Town, 1975	9	—

Albums:

Wednesday Morning 3 AM (Columbia/CBS), 1966
The Sounds Of Silence (Columbia/CBS), 1966
Parsley, Sage, Rosemary And Thyme (Columbia/CBS), 1966
Bookends (Columbia/CBS), 1968
The Graduate (Soundtrack) (Columbia/CBS), 1968
Bridge Over Troubled Water (Columbia/CBS), 1970
Greatest Hits (Columbia/CBS), 1972
Collected Works (Columbia/—), 1981
Collection (—/CBS), 1981
Concert In Central Park (Warner Bros), 1982

Greatest Hits, Simon And Garfunkel '60s classics. Courtesy CBS Records.

Carly Simon

US vocalist.
Born New York, June 25, 1945.

Career: Carly emerged on New York folk scene in mid-'60s with sister Lucy as the Simon Sisters. Enjoyed minor hit on Kapp in 1964 with **Winkin', Blinkin' And Nod** while still studying at exclusive Sarah Lawrence College.

When Lucy got married, Carly went to France; did not return to singing until she met Bob Dylan's manager Albert Grossman. He brought in Dylan's producer Bob Johnson, and his regular backing musicians, including the Band(▶), Al Kooper(▶) and Mike Bloomfield(▶). He persuaded Dylan(▶) himself to write one song for 1966 New York session aimed at establishing Carly as 'The female Dylan'.

The pair fell out, however, and tracks were never released. Carly was re-discovered by Elektra Records' boss Jac Holtzman at party in late 1969.

'Esquire' magazine film critic and screenplay writer Jacob Brackman had been writing material with her for some time. This provided

Below: Art Garfunkel (left) and his partner Paul Simon, who remain one of the most popular duos in the history of rock music.

Hit Singles:

	US	UK
That's The Way I've Always Heard It Should Be, 1971	10	—
Anticipation, 1972	13	—
You're So Vain, 1972	1	3
The Right Thing To Do, 1973	17	17
Haven't Got Time For The Pain, 1974	14	—
Nobody Does It Better, 1977	2	7
You Belong To Me, 1978	6	—
Jesse, 1980	11	—
Why, 1982	—	10

With James Taylor:

Mockingbird, 1974	5	34

Albums:

Carly Simon (Elektra), 1971
Anticipation (Elektra), 1971
No Secrets (Elektra), 1972
Hot Cakes (Elektra), 1974
Playing Possum (Elektra), 1975
Best Of (Elektra), 1976
Another Passage (Elektra), 1976
Boys In The Trees (Elektra), 1978
Spy (Elektra), 1979
Come Upstairs (Warner Bros), 1980
Torch (Warner Bros), 1981
You're So Vain (—/Hallmark), 1981

Above: The sensuous Carly Simon in a rare onstage performance.

content for debut album which included smash single **That's The Way I've Always Heard It Should Be**, a pensive song about difference between childhood dreams and adult realities. Theme was fully exploited in subsequent albums, notably on follow-up set **Anticipation**.

1972s **No Secrets** album made Simon international star thanks to classic single **You're So Vain** (featuring Mick Jagger on backing vocals). Reportedly, its anonymous non-hero was film star Warren Beatty though Carly refused to confirm this.

Married to singer/songwriter James Taylor(▶) in 1973, the couple duetted on 1974 hit single **Mockingbird**, a mirror copy of Inez and Charlie Fox's original. Following that year's **Hotcakes** album, had 18-month hiatus before appearance of **Playing Possum**, Simon's third LP with ace producer Richard Perry. After **Another Passenger** album (produced by Ted Templeman in 1976) returned to Richard Perry in following year for Oscar and Grammy nomination song **Nobody Does It Better**, theme for James Bond film 'The Spy Who Loved Me'.

Carly finished long contract with Elektra with **Boys In The Tree**, produced by Arif Mardin. Switched to parent Warner Bros label for most recent albums; unfortunately these have shown steadily declining quality, maybe due in part to break-up with Taylor.

Paul Simon

US composer, vocalist, guitarist
Born Newark, New Jersey, October 13, 1941.

Career: Musical career began as schoolboy with, in 1964, startlingly successful partnership of Simon and Garfunkel(▶). Far from remaining with Garfunkel throughout early years, Simon recorded on his own as Paul Kane, Jerry Landis and True Taylor, toured European folk circuit and made solo album of own material in London before duo's hit single **Sounds Of Silence** became US No. 1 in 1966. Pair then continued to record and toured together until splitting up amicably in 1970, at height of success.

Freed from constraints of partnership, Simon became more musically complex, incorporating variety of influences, including South American group Los Incas, jazz violin of Stephane Grapelli and Jamaican reggae. 1972 album **Paul Simon** not only provided US/UK hit single **Mother And Child Reunion,** but reached No. 1 in UK. Dixie Hummingbirds gospel group and top quality session musicians were added to second LP **There Goes Rhymin' Simon.** Lyrically more relaxed, simpler and funkier, album gave Simon hit singles on both sides of Atlantic. Concert album **Live Rhymin** from 1973 tour featured Jesse Dixon gospel group and South American band Urubamba performing new versions of his old songs.

In 1975, **Still Crazy After All These Years** blended musical changes with starkly precise personal songs. Containing US No. 1 single **50 Ways To Leave Your Lover,** album won two Grammys (Best Album And Best Male Pop Vocal Performance), bringing Simon's Grammy award total to 12. Disappointed that critical attention still focused on lyrics rather than musical ideas. Simon toured again with top-rated session musicians.

Having made acting debut in Woody Allen's 'Annie Hall,'' Simon produced, were starred in and scored 1980 film 'One Trick Pony', which faded from sight shortly after release. Album from film, first original release in five years, fared only a little better. When Central Park concert attracted over 500,000 to Simon and Garfunkel reunion, it seemed perfect time to revitalise career by renewing partnership.

One Trick Pony, Paul Simon. Courtesy Warner Bros Records. Simon scored and starred in film.

Hit Singles:

	US	UK
Mother And Child Reunion, 1972	4	5
Me And Julio Down By The Schoolyard, 1972	22	15
Take Me To The Mardi Gras, 1973	—	7
Kodachrome, 1973	2	—
Love Me Like A Rock, 1973	2	39
50 Ways To Leave Your Lover, 1976	1	23
Slip Slidin' Away, 1977	5	36
(What A) Wonderful World (with Art Garfunkel and James Taylor), 1978	17	—
Late In The Evening, 1980	6	58

Albums:
Paul Simon (Columbia/CBS), 1972*
There Goes Rhymin' Simon (Columbia/CBS), 1973*
Live Rhymin' (Columbia/CBS), 1974*
Still Crazy After All These Years (Columbia/ CBS),1975*
Greatest Hits, etc (Columbia/CBS), 1977
One Trick Pony (soundtrack) (Warner Bros), 1980
*Available as 5 LP set **Collected Works** (Columbia/—), 1981, with **Paul Simon Songbook** LP.

Paul Simon's first album without Arty, which featured his first two solo hits. Courtesy CBS Records.

Nina Simone

US vocalist, pianist.
Born Eunice Wayman, Tryon, North Carolina, February 21, 1933.

Career: By age of seven Nina Simone had taught herself piano and organ. She sang in church choir, but received formal music training at high school in Asheville, Carolina, and at famed Juilliard School of Music.

When her family moved to Philadelphia, Simone began working East Coast clubs. She gained contract with Bethlehem Records, which led to million-selling version of **I Loves You Porgy** in 1959. On moving to Colpix in 1960 numerous albums and couple of minor hits followed. A period with Philips between 1965 and 1967 resulted in hits **Don't Let Me Be Misunderstood** and Screamin' Jay Hawkins' **I Put A Spell On You.** Latter established Simone internationally.

In 1967 Simone switched labels again, to RCA, and entered her most productive and commercially successful period with further hit singles, and number of albums which combined high-quality material with classy, often jazz-influenced arrangements. Despite stringently maintained musical standards, albums were generally easy to listen to and found ready market as high-class adult MOR. Simone's distinctive jazz and gospel-tinged voice and more than competent piano playing provided consistently attractive focal points.

In '70s, she began to devote more time to political work, and from mid-'70s to present day she has worked and recorded only sporadically. Superb 1978 album **Baltimore**

Baltimore, Nina Simone. Courtesy CTI/Polydor Records. Simone became more political in the '70s.

showed that her talent remained undimmed, although recent reports of serious financial and personal problems give cause for concern.

A genuinely talented and committed artist, Nina Simone deserves greater recognition than she has as yet received. Nevertheless, it seems likely that her personality will always come between her and wide international acclaim.

Hit Singles:

	US	UK
I Loves You Porgy, 1959	18	—
Ain't Got No/I Got Life, 1968	—	2
To Love Somebody, 1969	—	5

Albums:
Here Comes the Sun (RCA), 1969
Best Of Nina Simone (Philips/—), 1970
Best Of Nina Simone (RCA/—), 1972
Gifted And Black (—/Contempo), 1974
I Loves You Porgy (Bethlehem/CBS), 1977
Baltimore (CTI), 1978
Pure Gold (—/RCA), 1979
Cry Before I Go (—/Manhattan), 1980
My Baby Just Cares For Me (—/Charly), 1982
Artistry Of Nine Simone (—/RCA), 1982
Nina Simone (—/Dakota), 1982

Frank Sinatra

US vocalist, actor.
Born Francis Albert Sinatra, Hoboken, New Jersey, December 12, 1915.

Career: Sang in Glee Club while at high school; after graduating, formed vocal quartet called Hoboken Four. Outfit made Major Bowes' 'Amateur Hour' on radio; Sinatra gained attention with solo rendition of **Night And Day**.

Following vaudeville tour for Bowes, Sinatra undertook life of freelance vocalist, working around New York area. Period as MC at Rustic Cabin Roadhouse was followed by stint as vocalist for Harry James Band.

Time with Tommy Dorsey Band led to recording, first with Pied Pipers, later as

Above: The incredible Frank Sinatra, who has survived changes of musical fashion for over forty years.

soloist. At this point, in latter '30s. Sinatra began rapid rise to stardom, becoming first singer to evoke hysteria among young females on wide scale. 'The Voice', as he became known, specialised in moody renditions of good standard songs. Not a jazz singer, although influenced by great performers like Billie Holiday, Sinatra became biggest act of '40s, recording first for RCA, then Columbia.

In 1953, switched labels to Capitol, and initiated change of image from romantic to sophisticate; result was some of Sinatra's most famous albums (**Come Fly With Me, Songs For Swingin' Lovers**). In 1961 he founded own record company, Reprise, and during '60s continued to make good records despite tendency to pick dubious contemporary material. Continued successful film career; Earned Academy Award for 'From Here To Eternity'. By late '60s singer was also well-known for charity work, not to mention volatile private life.

In early '70s, having conquered virtually every height available to popular entertainer, Sinatra announced intention to retire. However, it quickly became apparent that this meant no more than cutting down on workload, and artist has made appearances and records sporadically ever since.

Although operating in totally different field musically, Sinatra is on par with two other solo colossi of post-war music, Presley and Dylan, in terms of influence. Genuinely a legend in his own lifetime, Sinatra at his peak was superb technician who could also plumb emotional depths. 'The Voice' does not have the flexibility it used to have, but 'threats' of retirement can now surely be dismissed.

Hit Singles:

	US	UK
(Love Is) The Tender Trap, 1956	7	2
Hey! Jealous Lover, 1956	3	—
Can I Steal A Little Love, 1957	15	—
All The Way, 1957	2	3
Witchcraft, 1958	6	12
French Foreign Legion, 1959	—	18
High Hopes, 1959	30	6
River, Stay 'Way From My Door, 1960	—	18
Nice 'n' Easy, 1960	60	15
Ol' MacDonald, 1960	25	11
Granada, 1961	—	13
Strangers In The Night, 1966	1	1
That's Life, 1966	4	46
My Way, 1969	27	5
Love's Been Good To Me, 1969	—	8
I Will Drink The Wine, 1971	—	16

With Sammy Davis Jr:

Me And My Shadow, 1962	—	20

With Nancy Sinatra:

Somethin' Stupid, 1967	1	1

Albums:
Songs For Swingin' Lovers (Capitol), 1956
Come Dance With Me (Capitol), 1959
Come Fly With Me (Capitol), 1962
Moonlight (Reprise), 1966
Greatest Hits (Reprise), 1968
My Way (Reprise), 1969
Greatest Hits, Volume 2 (Reprise) 1970

Siouxsie And The Banshees

US group formed 1976.

Original line-up: Siouxsie Sioux, vocals; Steve Severin, bass; Sid Vicious, drums; Marco Pirroni, guitar.

Career: Siouxsie had closely followed Sex Pistols(▶) attack on polished, professional sound of established rock bands; without rehearsal formed above line-up for one gig. Within two months Vicious and Perroni were gone, Vicious to infamy with latter-day Sex Pistols and Perroni to play in the Motels, then with Adam and the Ants(▶). Kenny Morris took over drums and Peter Fenton assumed guitar. This line-up won wide critical and public support as one of London's premier punk bands.

Refusal to sign standard recording contract meant band was ignored by major firms. Plans to sign with Kit Lambert's Track label (Who(▶)) fell through when Track folded. By July 1977 Fenton was replaced by John McKay.

Polydor finally signed Siouxsie and promptly found itself in confrontation with band. ('I wouldn't piss on our record company if their building was on fire', was widely quoted as indication of band's regard for their label.)

Following release of two LPs, McKay and Morris quit in autumn 1979 just as band started extensive tour. Ex-Slits member 'Budgie' was quickly taken on as permanent

Above: Siouxsie Sioux, an original punk-ette who outlived punk and now works with Budgie as the Creatures.

drummer, Cure guitarist Robert Smith was 'loaned' to meet tour dates. John McGeoch (ex-Magazine) then joined as permanent guitarist. **Kaleidoscope** LP also featured great guitar work from Steve Jones (ex-Pistols, Professionals), yet studio work did not seem to quite fit band's no-compromise approach; never matched live enthusiasm of Siouxsie on stage. Despite strong LP **Ju Ju**, spirit of band is best experienced on **Once Upon A Time/The Singles**.

Siouxsie and Budgie began side band, the Creatures and McGeoch left in late 1982. Despite these distractions, Siouxsie maintains that her primary commitment is to keeping Banshees alive. Considering her continuous refusal to knuckle under (despite re-signing with Polydor), she might pull the whole thing off, though doctors have ordered her to temporarily stop singing to preserve voice. Released Creatures single **Right Now** in summer 1983.

Current line-up: Siouxsie; Severin; Budgie, drums.

Hit Singles:

	US	UK
Hong Kong Garden, 1978	—	7
Happy House, 1980	—	17

Albums:
The Scream (—/Polydor), 1978
Join Hands (—/Polydor), 1979
Kaleidoscope (Gem/Polydor), 1980
Ju Ju (Gem/Polydor), 1981
Once Upon A Time/The Singles (Gem/Polydor), 1981

Siouxsie & Budgie as the Creatures:
Wild Thing EP (—/Polydor), 1981
Feast (—/Polydor), 1983

Sky

UK group formed 1978.

Original line-up: John Williams, guitar; Francis Monkman, keyboards; Kevin Peek, guitar; Tristan Fry, percussion; Herbie Flowers, bass.

Career: John Williams is regarded by many as world's finest classical guitarist, while Herbie Flowers is one of the most respected session men in British rock/pop. Their coming together in Sky was result of mutual desire to broaden creative horizons. Fellow group members are from equally diverse backgrounds. Williams' Australian compatriot Kevin Peek has played on records by Cliff Richard(▶), Peter Skellern and Shirley Bassey. Tristan Fry was classically trained and played with London Philharmonic Orchestra as well as recording with Duke Ellington, Frank Sinatra(▶) and Elton John(▶). Steve Gray is another seasoned sessioneer, having worked with Paul McCartney(▶), Roger Daltrey(▶), Neil Diamond(▶) and John Denver(▶). Flowers is no stranger to charts — he had been member of another successful amalgam of session musicians, Blue Mink, in '60s.

Idea of Sky was to show that sheer musicianship could win out over pop dross without show-business hype. Consequently, Sky is a band without a leader. Their music has evolved quite naturally from the diverse talents of members.

Self-produced debut album was cut at EMI's famed Abbey Road Studios in late 1978. Tapes were taken to Midem music industry fair by manager Peter Lyster-Todd in January 1979. Ariola Records signed group and album hit Top 10 within weeks of release in April; eventually achieved double-gold standard. In May, band embarked on ambitious UK tour, closing with acclaimed London date at Royal Albert Hall. Followed

through with 'Sky At Night' tour in autumn. This culminated in five nights at London's Dominion Theatre to rapturous reception.

Fifo, an imaginative conceptual piece by Monkman, was included in **Sky 2** (1980), an 80-minute double album. Chart single **Toccata** followed. Sky toured overseas, including visit to Williams' and Peek's Australian homeland. They put in further major British tour before release of third LP **Sky 3** in February 1981. A live album in 1983 showed they could reproduce studio sound on stage.

Sky's music is kaleidoscopic in range, reflecting group's membership and proves that a gimmick-free marriage between rock, jazz and classical elements can not only produce good music but also big-selling records.

Note: UK Sky not to be confused with early '70s US band of same name.

Current line-up: Williams; Peek; Fry; Flowers; Steve Gray, keyboards.

Hit Singles:

	US	UK
Toccata, 1980	—	5

Albums:
Sky (Arista/Ariola), 1979
Sky 2 (—/Ariola), 1980
Sky 3 (Arista/Ariola), 1981
Sky Box Set (first three albums) (—/Ariola), 1981
Forthcoming (Arista/Ariola), 1982
Sky Five Live (—/Arista), 1983

Slade

UK group formed 1968.

Original/Current line-up: Noddy Holder vocals, guitar; Dave Hill, John Birch, guitar; Jimmy Lea, bass, piano; Don Powell, drums.

Career: Group started out playing routine material in Midlands clubs as 'N Betweens. Changed name to Ambrose Slade; discovered in 1969 at Rasputin's Club in London's Bond Street by Chas Chandler, during era of original skinhead cult. Chandler, who had been member of Animals(▶) and had already turned Jimi Hendrix(▶) into a superstar, decided on cash-in image. Short-cropped hair, 'bovver boots', rolled-up jeans etc. were adopted. Audiences saw it as pure marketing ploy and gambit failed.

Chandler persevered, hanging on to Polydor contract while shortening band's name to Slade. Re-make of Bobby Marchan's **Get Down And Get With It,** also a US R&B hit for Little Richard, got them into chart. Image now was of aggressive glitter, heavy stomping and loud guitar. Adopting gimmick of misspelt song titles, band were projected as teen working-class heroes. **Look Wot You Dun, Take Me Bak 'Ome, Mama Weer All Crazee Now, Cum On Feel The Noize** and others made them Britain's top pop band of

Old, New, Borrowed And Blue, Slade. Courtesy Polydor Records.

Above: Slade on stage (left to right) Jimmy Lea, Noddy Holder, Dave Hill and Don Powell. Their succession of hits in the early '70s tells its own story.

1972-74. Between October 1971 and October 1974 released 12 singles, all of which made UK Top 5, six of them reaching No 1. 1973 Christmas hit **Merry Xmas Everybody** also made No. 1 and charted again in December 1980, 1981, and 1982.

Songwriting partnership of Lea and Holder now mentioned in same breath as Lennon/McCartney, while band were touted as new Beatles(▶) However, despite success, songs elicited few cover versions and Slade never showed Beatles' diversity of musical talent.

Attempts to broaden base of appeal served only to dampen fires of Slade fever. Spent tail-end of 1974 working on 'Flame' movie project in which they starred as mythical band. Despite some flair for acting and good script, movie made little impact though yielded hit semi-ballad **Far Far Away**. Time spent trying to crack Stateside market served only to further weaken grasp on UK. 1975 was bad year, but Slade bounced back in 1976 with stomping **Let's Call It Quits**. Title was somewhat prophetic as emergence of new wave pushed them into background. Slade didn't listen to own message and revived career on back of heavy metal boom with big 1981 hit **Lock Up Your Daughters**.

Having always managed to find faithful stage audience somewhere in world, Slade are soldiering on into '80s.

Hit Singles:

	US	UK
Get Down And Get With It, 1971	—	16
Coz I Luv You, 1971	—	1
Look Wot You Dun, 1972	—	4
Take Me Bak 'Ome, 1972	—	1
Mama Weer All Crazee Now, 1972	—	1
Good Buy T' Jane, 1972	—	2
Cum On Feel The Noize, 1973	—	1
Skweeze Me Pleeze Me, 1973	—	1
My Friend Stan, 1973	—	2
Merry Xmas Everybody, 1973	—	1
Everyday, 1974	—	3
Bangin' Man, 1974	—	3
Far Far Away, 1974	—	2
How Does It Feel, 1975	—	15
Thanks For The Memory (Wham Bam Thankyou Mam), 1975	—	7
In For A Penny, 1975	—	11
Let's Call It Quits, 1976	—	11
We'll Bring The House Down, 1981	—	10

Albums:
Slade Alive (Polydor), 1972
Slade Alive Volume 2 (—/Barn), 1978
Return To Base (—/Barn), 1979
We'll Bring The House Down (—/Cheapskate), 1981
Lock Up Your Daughters (—/RCA), 1981
Slade On Stage (—/RCA), 1982

Sly And The Family Stone

US group formed 1966.

Original line-up: Sly Stone, vocals, keyboards, guitar; Freddie Stone, guitar; Cynthia Robinson, trumpet; Jerry Martini, saxophone; Rosie Stone, piano, vocals; Larry Graham, bass; Greg Errico, drums.

Career: The history of Sly and the Family Stone is virtually the history of founder and guiding light Sly Stone. Born Sylvester Stewart in 1944 in Dallas, Texas, he played in various bands with brother Freddie after family had moved to California. As lead singer for group called the Viscanes, he made his recording debut with **Yellow Moon,** which became small local hit.

In late teens and early twenties Sly gained experience in many areas of the music business, writing and producing successfully for artists like Bobby Freeman, the Mojo Men and the Beau Brummels, and working as DJ on San Francisco radio. In 1966 he put together own band, the Stoners, which was forerunner of Family Stone.

Formation of Family Stone coincided with upsurge of psychedelia centred in San Francisco. An inter-racial, male and female band, Family Stone pioneered acid-soul-rock, combining punch brass riffs and stinging rock guitar with wild vocal harmonies and an irresistible dance beat. Finding their audience among newly liberated white kids rather than in black dance halls, band was in tune with times.

Success came in early 1968. Signed to Epic, band released LP **A Whole New Thing,** and single **Dance To The Music. Dance** was an exhilarating rock/soul amalgam that brought breath of fresh air to charts both sides of Atlantic.

Follow-up single **M'Lady** did better in UK than US, where it only just made Top 100, but third single, **Everyday People**, topped American charts. **Strand,** the album from which it was taken, went gold, and titletrack was also hit.

Sly and the Family Stone become in-demand concert act, and were a high point of 1969 Woodstock Festival. Sly's **I Want To Take You Higher** became Festival's anthem, but the Festival turned out to be zenith of band's career. More record success was still to come, but personality clashes and drug problems led to band (in particular Sly, who often failed to show up at scheduled concerts) becoming increasingly unreliable. Sly's darker side was reflected in pessimistic vision of 1971 album **There's A Riot Going On**.

Following years saw band undergo various personnel changes (with Larry Graham carving successful solo career). Subsequent albums were less than convincing. Collection of Sly's old hits, **Back On The Right Track**, was issued in 1979, and in 1982 he surfaced in partnership with George Clinton. Seminal cultural figure of his time, Sly Stone showed that rock could be funky as well as heavy, and that there was still a place for dance music in '60s and early '70s.

Final line-up: Sly Stone; Freddie Stone; Cynthia Robinson; Rusty Allen, bass; Bill Lordan, drums; Rosie Stone; Jerry Martini; Pat Rizzo, saxophone; Sid Page, violin.

Hit Singles:

	US	UK
Dance To The Music, 1968	8	7
Everyday People, 1969	1	36
Hot Fun In The Summertime, 1969	2	-
Thank You Falettinme Be Mice Elf Agin, 1970	1	—
Family Affair, 1971	1	15
Runnin' Away, 1972	23	17
If You Want Me To Stay, 1973	12	—

Albums:
Dance To The Music (Epic/Direction), 1968
Life (Epic), 1968
A Whole New Thing (Epic), 1970
High Energy (Epic), 1975
Back On The Right Track (Warner Bros), 1979
Recorded 64/67 (Sculpture), 1979
Greatest Hits (Epic), 1981

Worth Searching Out:
Stand (Epic), 1969
There's A Riot Going On (Epic), 1971

Small Faces

UK group formed 1965.

Original line-up: Steve Marriott, vocals, guitar; Jimmy Winston, organ; Ronnie 'Plonk' Lane, bass; Kenny Jones, drums.

Career: The Who(▶) were group that adopted mod image as sales ploy; the Small Faces were mods who became a group.

Formed in London's East End, Small Faces (so called because of members diminutive size, 'faces' being flash mods) were built round lead singer, former child actor Marriott. Wearing razor-sharp clothes group initially set out to re-create the American R&B soul music espoused by fellow mods. Borrowing riff from Solomon Burke's **Everybody Needs Somebody To Love** they came up with potent **Watcha Gonna Do About It?** to crash chart in September 1965. Ian MacLagan replaced Winston for follow-up **I've Got Mine**, which flopped but was quickly followed by successes, **Sha La La La Lee**, **Hey Girl**, the chart-topping **All Or Nothing** and **My Mind's Eye**. All were co-written by Marriott and Lane (one of the strongest songwriting duos of the '60s), moving increasingly into straight pop vein.

Switching to Immediate label, set up by Rolling Stones(▶) manager Andrew Loog-Oldham, and Tony Calder, Small Faces came up with more interesting material with clever and evocative **Itchycoo Park** (1967), their only US Top 20 record, and the perceptive **Lazy Sunday** (1968). Then came superlative **Ogden's Nut Gone Flake** album (1968), its classic circular fold-out sleeve a replica of the familiar UK tobacco brand.

Marriott left in early 1969 to join Peter Frampton(▶) in formation of Humble Pie(▶). Lane, Jones and MacLagan soldiered on. Went through very rough patch but turned down offers to work as backing band for solo artists, linking up with Jeff Beck Group emigrés Rod Stewart(▶) and Ron Wood later the next year as the Faces(▶).

Small Faces re-formed in 1976 with following line-up: Marriott; Jones; MacLagan; audience in UK since the late '70s mod revival.

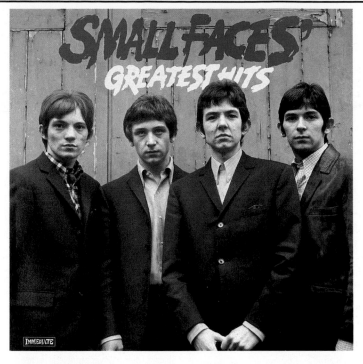

Rick Wills (Roxy Music(▶)) bass. Cut two mediocre LPs **Playmates** and **78 In The Shade**. Still the penultimate mod band, Small Faces have gained a whole new

Final line-up: Marriott; Jones; Ian MacLagan, organ; Rick Wills, bass.

Hit Singles:

	US	UK
Watcha Gonna Do About It?, 1965	—	14
Sha La La La Lee, 1966	—	3
Hey Girl, 1966	—	10
All Or Nothing, 1966	—	1
My Mind's Eye, 1966	—	4
Here Comes The Nice, 1967	—	12
Itchycoo Park, 1967	16	3
Tin Soldier, 1967	—	9
Lazy Sunday, 1968	—	2
Universal, 1968	—	16
Itchycoo Park, 1975	—	9

Albums:
Small Faces (—/Decca), 1966
Ogden's Nut Gone Flake (Immediate), 1967
Rock Roots: The Small Faces (—/Decca) 1976*
Greatest Hits (—/Immediate), 1977
Playmates (Atlantic), 1977
78 In The Shade (Atlantic), 1978
Big Hits (—/Virgin), 1980
For Your Delight (—/Virgin), 1981
By Appointment (Accord/—), 1981
Sha La La La Lee (—/Decca), 1981
*Features all Decca A&B sides.

With Amen Corner:
Amen Corner And Small Faces (—/New World), 1975

Worth Searching Out:
There Are But Four Small Faces (Immediate), 1967
Autumn Stone (—/Immediate), 1969

Greatest Hits, a Small Faces reissue. Courtesy Immediate Records.

Jimmy Smith

US organist, vocalist.
Born Norristown, Pennsylvania, December 8, 1925.

Career: Despite experimental work of Fats Waller, Wild Bill Davis and others, the Hammond electric organ was regarded as mere novelty instrument before arrival of Jimmy Smith. Despite fierce disapproval of purist critics, Smith established the instrument as mainstay of modern-jazz scene, besides influencing countless R&B players. He can be credited as man who first achieved jazz/R&B/soul crossover and helped make funk part of black music language.

Taught piano by father, Smith played in various minor jazz and R&B groups around home state between 1941 and 1951 when he moved to Philadelphia to attend music school.

Inspired by Wild Bill Davis, Smith switched to organ and played in various bands, including one led by emergent soul singer Don Gardner.

New York-based Blue Note was then THE jazz label and in 1954 they signed Smith and his first trio (Thornel Schwartz, guitar; Donald Bailey, drums). He started issuing flood of albums featuring fluid line-up, Bailey appearing on most but Schwartz being replaced by Quentin Warren and then a variety of guest guitarists, including Kenny Burrell, Eddie McFadden and Wes Montgomery. Smith prominently featured guests such as sax players Stanley Turrentine, Lou Donaldson and Jackie McLean, on other instruments.

From a small combo base, Smith experimented increasingly with bigger line-ups and on switching to Verve in 1962 was recorded under aegis of ace jazz producer Creed Taylor with full-blown Oliver Nelson Orchestra. Their highly inventive—and exciting—collaboration on Elmer Bernstein's **Walk On The Wild Side** made pop as well as jazz and R&B charts. Smith's work became commercially orientated; he even laid down gruff-voiced vocals on several Muddy Waters' (▶) blues standards.

Smith's emergence as major figure led to

Left: The Small Faces' 1966 debut album. Courtesy Immediate Records.

host of other organists breaking through to prominence, including Brother Jack McDuff, Jimmy McGriff, John Patton, Richard 'Groove' Holmes and Lonnie Smith, all of whom owed stylistic debt to the innovator.

Smith's artistry lay in his spectacular exploitation of the Hammond keyboard, not only in terms of the wild scat-style phrases but also in the underlying solid bass riffs. Thanks to Smith's influence, at one point in late '60s it seemed that virtually every commerically successful jazz album featured the Hammond organ in line-up.

Midnight Special, Jimmy Smith. Courtesy Blue Note Records.

This overkill led to sudden fall from favour, hastened by emergence of the synthesiser in its varied guises. But in early '80s, the Hammond organ has seen something of a revival and this has brought Smith back from semi-retirement. Recent somewhat sparsely released albums lack sheer excitement of period when it seemed every other week brought a new Jimmy Smith album (more than 80 in all).

Albums (selected):
Midnight Special (Blue Note), 1961
Organ Grinder Swing (Verve), 1965
Greatest Hits (Blue Note), 1968
Cat Strikes Again (Inner City/—), 1981

Patti Smith

US vocalist, poet, lyricist.
Born Chicago, December 30, 1946.

Career: Raised in New Jersey; moved to New York in 1967. Evolved own form of rock 'n' roll poetry through influences of Dylan, Hendrix, Stones and Jim Morrison, allied to writings of William Burroughs and Art Rimbaud.

Co-writer of play 'Cowboy Mouth' with Sam Shepard in 1971; also appeared in BBC-TV special that year. Through boyfriend Allen Lanier of Blue Oyster Cult(▶) she was encouraged to venture into songwriting and singing. Co-penned Cult's famed **Career Of Evil** on 1974 album **Secret Treaties** and two cuts on their 1976 set **Agents Of Fortune**, on which she was also guest vocalist.

Smith began to attract cult following through poetry readings at St Mark's Church, New York, and own publications in Creem Magazine. Two volumes of her writings, 'Seventh Heaven' and 'Witt', were published.

With encouragement from long-time mentor Lenny Kaye, moved increasingly into songwriting and began playing New York club dates, backed by Kaye on guitar and Richard Sohl on piano. Adding Ivan Kral, guitar, bass, and Jay Daugherty, drums, she became darling of New York's emergent new wave/punk scene.

Anarchical debut album **Horses**, produced by John Cale(▶) was potent if disturbing statement.

Self-indulgence soon became downfall, however, and subsequent less rewarding albums coupled with unfortunate public manner saw her star soon fade. Smith's fourth, and to date last, album **Waves** (1979) found little success. Single **Because The Night** (written by Bruce Springsteen(▶)) probably her best known work, was re-released in 1983. Married Fred 'Sonic' Smith from MC5 in late '70s.

Hit Singles:

	US	UK
Because The Night, 1978	13	5

Albums:
Horses (Arista), 1975
Radio Ethiopa (Arista), 1976
Easter (Arista), 1978
Waves (Arista), 1979

Phoebe Snow

US vocalist, composer.
Born Manhattan, New York, July 17, 1952.

Career: Began to take interest in music, especially jazz, blues and folk, in late '60s. Played Greenwich Village folk clubs in early '70s, coming to attention of newly formed Shelter Records. First album **Phoebe Snow**, released in 1974, was almost immediate success. Single **Poetry Man** became US Top 5 entry; album eventually went gold.

Individualistic new talent had arrived on scene; critics and public were impressed by Snow's limpid, flexible voice and strong compositions. Paul Simon(▶) featured her on record and in live performance; Snow moved to his record company Columbia for next album, **Second Childhood**. This also went gold, despite more muted critical acclaim.

Further albums showed certain lack of direction and were only moderately successful, but 1979 saw minor UK hit with Paul McCartney(▶) album track **Every Night**. Snow's distinctive treatment of song regained attention of public, but again she failed to capitalise commercially. A move to Mirage in 1981 has so far resulted in only minor success, but Snow remains respected vocalist who could make major resurgence at any time.

Hit Singles:

	US	UK
Poetry Man, 1975	5	—

Albums:
Phoebe Snow (MCA), 1974
Second Childhood (Columbia/CBS), 1976
It Looks Like Snow (Columbia/CBS), 1976
Against The Grain (Columbia/CBS), 1978
Never Letting Go (Columbia/CBS), 1978
Best Of (Columbia/CBS), 1981
Rock Away (Mirage), 1981

Soft Cell

UK group formed 1980

Original/Current line-up: Marc Almond, vocals; Dave Ball, synthesisers, keyboards, drum machine.

Career: Marc Almond and Dave Ball met in Leeds where Almond was doing night-club cabaret. Ball provided background support and duo began using video tapes and stage props—dropped after audience started paying more attention to gimmicks than to music. Using old Gloria Jones song, **Tainted Love,** Soft Cell tried for popular success and failed; six months later track was re-issued and became UK No.1. Massive press interest followed. Refusing to buckle under as one-hit wonder, band produced carefully crafted debut LP **Cabaret.**

Almond also showed eclectic taste by working with Mari Wilson, Genesis P. Orridge and the The's Matt Johnson. Still works in separate musical venture, Marc and the Mambas. Soft Cell continued series of hits in UK before **Tainted Love** connected in America. 1982 single **Where The Heart Is** reached No. 21 in the UK. **Numbers** made it to No. 25 in 1983.

Approach may seem light, even superficial at first, but beneath the surface, Soft Cell manage to marry emotion and technology, fun with thought. Each release is a bit of a send-up and yet... somehow deserves to be taken seriously. Without trying, Soft Cell may be one of UK's more important bands of '80s.

Hit Singles:

	US	UK
Tainted Love, 1981	8	1
Bed Sitter, 1981	—	4
Say Hello, Wave Goodbye, 1982	—	3
Torch, 1982	—	2
What, 1982	—	3

Albums:
Non-stop Erotic Cabaret (Sire/Some Bizzare), 1982
Non-stop Ecstatic Dancing (Sire/Some Bizzare), 1982
The Art Of Falling Apart (Sire/Some Bizzare), 1983

Soft Machine

UK group formed 1966.

Original line-up: Robert Wyatt, drums, vocals; Kevin Ayers, bass, vocals; Mike Ratledge, keyboards; Daevid Allen, guitar; Larry Nolan, guitar.

Career: Evolved from jazz-orientated Wilde Flowers, which had included Wyatt, Ayers, Richard Sinclair, Brian and Hugh Hopper, Graham Flight, Pye Hastings and Richard Coughlan. Wyatt had enrolled at Canterbury College of Art before bumming around Europe where he met Daevid Allen, an Australian beatnik heavily influenced by Terry Riley's 'tape-loop' experimentation. Meanwhile, Ratledge had abandoned his studies at Oxford and returned to Canterbury. Original line-up above settled on name Soft Machine, taken from a William Burroughs novel.

After only a few gigs Nolan quit, later returning to native California. Meanwhile, group appeared regularly with Pink Floyd(▶) at London's UFO club (later known as the Roundhouse) **Love Makes Sweet Music**, produced by former Animal(▶) Chas Chandler, was a shot at commercial market. Flip side **Feelin' Reelin' Squeelin'** was produced by notorious Kim Fowley and featured Jimi Hendrix(▶) on rhythm guitar. Commercial failure of single was followed by visit to France; their improvisation was put to good use in Alan Zion's production of passion play 'Desire Attrappé Par La Queue'. Allen failed to gain re-entry into England, so returned to Paris and later founded Gong).

Soft Machine augmented by Andy Summers, later to achieve superstardom in the Police(▶), toured US as Jimi Hendrix support, but broke up after recording debut **The Soft Machine** with Tom Wilson in New York. Individual members scattered: Ratledge returned to England; Ayers moved to Ibiza; and Wyatt divided time between New York and Los Angeles. Probe Records released album in December 1968 and successful results prompted re-formation.

With Ayers unavailable, Wyatt recruited Hugh Hopper and along with Ratledge cut **Soft Machine Volume II** in early 1969. Album highlighted Wyatt's songs and Ratledge's experimental work. Series of gigs

saw line-up gradually increased to seven-piece with introduction of Elton Dean (saxophone), Nick Evans (trombone), Marc Charig (trumpet) and Lynn Dobson (flute, saxophone, sitar). Group became increasingly jazz-orientated and were chosen to represent rock at London Proms in 1970. Financial considerations precluded use of additional members on record, so they departed. 1971's **Fourth** revealed fewer Wyatt vocals and following recording he left to form Matching Mole.

Group suffered series of personnel upheavals during 1972. Phil Howard took over on drums, only to be replaced by Nucleus' John Marshall during sessions for **Fifth**. Elton Dean was replaced by Nucleus' Karl Jenkins, and after **Sixth** Hopper embarked on solo career. New bassist Roy Babbington appeared for heavily jazz-influenced **Seven**, following which Allen Holdsworth (violin/guitar) was added to inject energy into Harvest debut, **Bundles**. The thirteenth Soft Machine line-up saw departure of remaining original member Mike Ratledge, and further instability followed with changes involving John Ethridge (guitar), Alan Wakeman (brother of Rick on sax), Steve Cooke (bass) and Rick Sanders (violin). Group's free-form improvisation (and fre-form fluid line-up) ensured continued respect, particularly in Europe. Generally accepted that finest work can be heard on innovative early albums.

Final line-up (1979): Ratledge; Elton Dean, alto sax, electric piano; Hugh Hopper, bass; Phil Howard, drums; John Marshall, drums; Roy Babbington, double bass.

Albums:
The Soft Machine (Probe), 1968
Third (Columbia/CBS), 1970
Fourth (Columbia/CBS), 1971
Fifth (Columbia/Embassy), 1972
Sixth (Columbia/CBS), 1973
Seventh (Columbia/CBS), 1973
Bundles (—/Harvest), 1975
Softs (—/Harvest), 1976
Triple Echo (—/Harvest), 1977

Sonny And Cher

US vocal duo formed 1963.
Sonny, born Salvatore Bono, Detroit, Michigan, February 12, 1935;
Cher, born Cherilyn Sakasian La Pierre, El Centro, California, May 20, 1946.

Career: Sonny wrote his first song in 1951, and by early '60s was making inroads into music business as writer, and as house producer for Specialty Records. In 1963, he co-wrote **Needles And Pins,** later to become huge international hit for the Searchers(▶), and started work as assistant to Phil Spector. Cher moved from her home town to

Hollywood to be an actress and took up session singing to pay for acting lessons. She met Sonny at a Ronettes' recording session, and the duo's professional and personal partnership started. They married in 1963.

Recording as Caesar and Cleo for Reprise and as Sonny and Cher for Vault, the pair eventually landed contract with Atco in 1965, which was to prove the turning point. In summer 1965 **I Got You Babe** was released and raced to No. 1 spot both sides of the Atlantic. Written, arranged and produced by Sonny, it contained every ingredient needed for success in '65, a strong melody, lyrics that were vaguely anti-authoritarian yet romantic, and a catchy, easily recognisable oboe riff.

Visually, Sonny and Cher came on as the acceptable face of hippiedom—colourful but not totally outrageous, groovy but not threatening. The combination proved irresistible, and their career took off. However, despite their long hair and 'flower-child' appearance, Sonny and Cher, weren't particularly interested in substance of '60s 'alternative' ethos, and veered increasingly towards 'all round entertainer' position.

Following career lull in late '60s, they began to move into supper-club work, and started own TV show in 1972. Meanwhile, a couple more hit singles kept their names before the pop public.

Sonny and Cher each recorded supposedly solo singles, though even where credited only to one, both were actually featured. Ultimately, however, it became increasingly obvious that Cher was likely to become lasting star, and the duo's personal and professional partnership foundered in 1974. Cher has since become major star of TV, cabaret and gossip columns; she also received many positive reviews of her role in the 1982 film 'Come Back To The Five And Dime, Jimmy Dean, Jimmy Dean'.

While in no way an 'important' act, Sonny and Cher made their mark on the '60s music scene and left behind some well-crafted, memorable records.

Hit Singles:

	US	UK
I Got You Babe, 1965	1	1
Baby Don't Go, 1965	8	11
Just You, 1965	20	—
But You're Mine, 1965	15	17
What Now My Love, 1966	14	13
Little Man, 1966	21	4
The Beat Goes On, 1967	6	29
All I Ever Need Is You, 1971	7	8
A Cowboy's Work Is Never Done, 1972	8	—

Sonny:

	US	UK
Laugh At Me, 1965	10	9

Cher:

	US	UK
Bang Bang, 1966	2	3
You Better Sit Down Kids, 1967	9	—

Below: Sonny and Cher, who ended their personal and professional relationships.

Gypsys, Tramps, and Thieves,
1971   1   4
The Way Of Love, 1972   7   —
Half-Breed, 1973   1   —

Albums:
The Very Best Of Sonny And Cher
(—/Hallmark), 1981

Joe South

US vocalist, guitarist, composer, producer.
Born Atlanta, Georgia, February 28, 1940.

Career: Joe South's emergence as a recording artist in 1958 with blatant cash-in novelty
record **The Purple People Eater Meets
The Witch Doctor** was to prove nadir of a
career which saw him not only score in own
right, notably with **The Games People Play**
and **Rose Garden** (both 1968), but play
major role in rock scene as session guitarist,
songwriter and producer.

Starting as DJ on local Atlanta radio station
South got into session scene with local acts,
black and white. He penned the Tams' 1962
hit **Untie Me** as well as hits for Billy Joe
Royal (**Hush, Down In The Boondocks,
Deep Purple**), Johnny Rivers (**These Are
Not My People**) and Dorsey Burnette (**The
Greatest Love**). He produced prolifically for
Billy Joe Royal, the Tams, the Classics Four
and Tommy Roe, and played guitar on
Dylan(▶)'s classic **Blonde On Blonde**
album as well as on hits for Aretha Franklin(▶),
Simon and Garfunkel(▶), Tommy Roe and
others.

With own backing band the Believers,
South landed contract with Capitol which led
to classic blue-eyed soul album **Introspection**
which included Top-10 hits **Games People
Play** and **Rose Garden**.

Follow-up album **Don't It Make You
Want To Go Home** brought more of South's
incisively perceptive songwriting, notably on
Walk A Mile In My Shoes and **These Are
Not My People**, but he failed to maintain
this momentum depsite a switch to Island in
1975 and has slid into obscurity.

Hit Singles: US   UK
Games People Play, 1969   12   6
Walk A Mile In My Shoes, 1970   12   —

Albums:
Greatest Hits (Capitol), 1974

Southside Johnny & The Asbury Jukes

US group formed 1975.

Original line-up: Johnny Lyon, vocals;
'Miami' Steve Van Zandt, guitar, vocals; Kevin
Kavanaugh, keyboards, vocals; Billy Rush,
guitar; Alan Berger, bass; Kenny Pentifallo,
drums, vocals; Carlo Novi, tenor sax; Ricky
Gazda, trumpet; Deacon Earl Gardner,
trumpet; Bob Malach, tenor sax; Louie
Parente, trombone; Bill Zacagni, baritone
saxophone.

Career: 'Southside' Johnny Lyon (born December 4, 1948) was besotted by blues and
R&B from an early age. Lyon joined Sonny
Kenn Blues Band at 16, then various other
groups until early '70s, when he, Bruce
Springsteen(▶) and Miami Steve Van Zandt
were all in Sundance Blues Band and then in
Dr. Zoom and the Sonic Boom (where Lyon
acquired 'Southside' epithet). March 1972
saw Lyon plus others from Ashbury Park, New

Jersey, moving to Richmond, Virginia, to join
Studio B—band failed to conquer world.

In 1973, back in New Jersey, formed
acoustic blues duo, Southside Johnny and the
Kid (Van Zandt), then Bank Street Blues Band,
which also included Kevin Kavanaugh. Van
Zandt left in 1974 to play with Dovells, where
he met Alan Berger, while Lyon joined
Blackberry Booze Band, which included
Kenny Pentifallo. BBB became resident band
at now legendary Asbury Park night spot
Stone Poney in December 1974. Van Zandt
returned to co-lead in early 1975, and name
changed to Asbury Jukes in mid-1975,
although soon afterwards Van Zandt joined
Springsteen's E Street Band; during time off
from Springsteen, Van Zandt produced demos
with Asbury Jukes.

First LP soon followed, featuring guest
spots from Ronnie Spector and Lee Dorsey.
Group's impressive R&B sound indicated
major success to follow, but live shows
seemingly made more impact than records,
despite inclusion of unreleased Springsteen
material. Second LP featured guest tracks
from Drifters(▶), Coasters(▶) and five Satins,
but still no hits; ditto third album. In 1979,
moved to Mercury label (from Epic) and
discontinued use of Van Zandt as producer.
At this point, band line-up included Lyon,
Kavanaugh, Rush, Berger, Gazda, plus Steve
Becker, drums; Ed Manion, baritone sax;
Richie 'La Bamba' Rosenberg, trombone; Joel
Gramolini, guitar; Bob Muckin, trumpet; Stan
Harrison, tenor sax. Material, now written by
Lyon, Rush and Berger, noticeably inferior,
although first LP for new label produced minor
hit single.

For 1980 LP, Rush and Lyon took over
production, to no great improvement — band
still hot, but material sadly lame. After
impressive double live LP (using some of
earlier material), group appear to have
vanished, possibly returning to New Jersey
circuit—Lyon himself perhaps unable to
accept that his undoubted talent as R&B
singer/front man did not extend to songwriting
or production. Nevertheless, destined for semi-
legendary status on basis of early recordings.

Current line-up: Lyon; Rush; Kavanaugh;
Richie Rosenberg, trombone; Steven Becker,
drums; Joel Gramolini, guitar; Rick Gazda,
trumpet; Ed Manion, saxophones; Steve
Buslowe, bass.

Albums:
I Don't Want To Go Home (Epic), 1976
This Time It's For Real (Epic), 1977
Hearts Of Stone (Epic), 1978
The Jukes (Mercury), 1979
Havin' A Party With Southside Johnny (Epic/
CBS), 1979*
Love Is A Sacrifice (Mercury), 1980
Reach Up And Touch The Sky (Mercury),
1981
*compilation

**I Don't Want To Go Home, Southside
Johnny. Courtesy Epic Records.**

Spandau Ballet

US group formed 1979.

Original/Current line-up: Tony Hadley,
vocals; Gary Kemp, guitar; Martin Kemp,
bass; Steve Norman, saxophone; John Keeble,
drums.

Career: Formed by young Londoners to provide soundtrack for 'futurist'/'new romantic'
activities in ultra fashion-conscious London
night-clubs. Early on managed by Steve
Strange, before latter formed Visage. Band
refused to publicise early gigs other than by
word of mouth, creating elitist image which
led to exposure on TV documentary about
London scene. Played gig on HMS Belfast
moored on River Thames.

Signed with Chrysalis Records in mid-1980,
given own label identity, Reformation Records
— such a distinction for unknown band that
success was assured. First single and album
both made Top 5. Third single showed that
band could provide more than 'futurist' sound.
One side, **Glow**, using jazz funk, provided
new direction for next single, **Chant No. 1**,
which reached Top 3, using black London
horn section Beggar and Co. Bubble seemed
to be bursting in early 1982, but second LP
was released in normal form and as boxed set
of 12in singles. Worked live in Europe and
America, while **Instinction** and **Lifeline**
were both remixed from LP to become Top 10
singles.

Success continued in 1983 with release of
third LP **True**; title track topped singles chart
in first half of year. Despite having been
dismissed as shallow hype in early days,
Spandau Ballet have persevered; they now
rank with Duran Duran(▶) as major attraction in
Britain. Rest of world likely to follow before
long, due to exotic videos and improved
quality of material, largely written by Gary
Kemp.

Hit Singles: US   UK
To Cut A Long Story Short, 1980   —   5
The Freeze, 1981   —   17
Muscle Bound/Glow, 1981   —   10
Chant No. 1 (I Don't Need This
Presure On), 1981   —   3
Instinction, 1982   —   10
Lifeline, 1982   —   7
Communication, 1983   —   12
True, 1983   —   1

Albums:
Journeys To Glory (Chrysalis), 1981
Diamond (—/Chrysalis), 1982
True (—/Chrysalis), 1983

**Above: Spandau Ballet, dismissed as a
hype at the start, but who later came
through with numerous hits.**

Sparks

US/UK group formed 1974.

Original line-up: Russell Mael, vocals; Ron
Mael, keyboards; Trevor White, guitar; Ian
Hampton, bass; Dinky Diamond, drums.

Career: Former child models, the Mael
brothers (Ron, born Los Angeles, 1948, and
Russell, born Santa Monica, 1953) recorded
first as Halfnelson, a trio formed in 1968 with
guitarist Earl Mankey. Demo tape sent to
Todd Rundgren(▶) led to contract with Albert
Grossman's Bearsville label. On album produced in Hollywood by Rundgren the Maels
were augmented by bass player Jim Mankey
(younger brother of Earl) and drummer Harley
Feinstein. Album sold poorly on release in
January 1971 and again failed to take off
when group changed management and re-
released album under new name Sparks,
through single **Wonder Girl** did chart.

Following three-month UK tour, group
released second Bearsville album, **A Tweeter
In Woofer's Clothing**, again to little success.
Shifted base to London and concluded new
deal with Island Records. Work-permit
problems prevented rest of band joining them.
Mael brothers consequently advertised in
music press and put together British band for
widely hailed Muff Winwood-produced
Kimono My House, from which **This Town
Ain't Big Enough For Both Of Us** scored
big.

Witty lyrics, bizarre arrangements and a
novel, high-pitched vocal approach, plus an
eye-catching stage image (Ron Mael, sporting
a Charlie Chaplin moustache and slicked-down

**Below: The Mael Brothers, Russell and
Ron, joint leaders of Sparks.**

hair, sitting impassively at the keyboards, long-haired Russell Mael cavorting around) struck receptive chord. Audience, however, consisted mainly of teenyboppers. Frustrated at being unable to reach out to adult rock audiences, the brothers returned to California to form American version of Sparks. They had no success and once more returned to Europe. Linked up with Donna Summer(▶)'s German-based Italian producer Giorgio Moroder for big-selling albums **Number One In Heaven** (1979) and **Terminal Jive** (1980), and hit singles **The Number One Song** and **Beat The Clock**.

Finding strong audience in France, they have subsequently concentrated on that market, their 1980 **When I'm With You** single having sold 750,000 copies in that country alone.

Current line-up: Russell Mael; Ron Mael.

Hit Singles:	US	UK
This Town Ain't Big Enough For Both Of Us, 1974	—	2
Amateur Hour, 1974	—	7
Never Turn Your Back On Mother Earth, 1974	—	13
Something For The Girl With Everything, 1975	—	17
The Number One Song In Heaven, 1979	—	14
Beat The Clock, 1979	—	10

Albums:
Best Of (—/Island), 1979
No. 1 In Heaven (—/Virgin), 1979
In Outer Space (Atlantic), 1983

Worth Searching Out:
Kimono My House (—/Island), 1974

The Specials

UK group formed 1977.

Original line-up: Terry Hall, vocals; Lynval Golding, guitar, vocals; Jerry Dammers, keyboards; Roddy Radiation, guitar; Horace 'Gentleman' Parker, bass; Neville Staples, percussion, vocals; John Bradbury, drums.

Career: Exploited Jamaican ska style, which pre-dated reggae; the Specials struck a chord with British youth—black and white—and especially, the unemployed. Dubbed their up-dated and racially integrated dance music style 'Two-Tone'. Band, formed in Coventry mid-'77, seemed set to lead nationwide ska revival with **Message To You Rudy** hit. Instead they evolved own lyrically strong 'lounge music' style, featuring veteran Jamaican trombone player Rico Rodriguez as regular guest.

Too Much Too Young, Rat Race, Do Nothing and other hits showed way for UB40(▶), Madness(▶), Bad Manners(▶), and other like-conveived groups. As keyboard player Jerry Dammers increasingly dom-

Specials (debut album). Courtesy 2 Tone/Chrysalis Records.

Above: The Specials on stage, with Terry Hall (left) and Jerry Dammers (extreme right).

inated proceedings as songwriter and producer, discontent flared. In summer 1981 singers Neville Staples and Terry Hall and guitarist Lynval Golding were already preparing to split and form Fun Boy Three(▶). They laid down tracks for debut album while the Specials' superb **Ghost Town** — which summed up riot-torn summer — was soaring to UK No. 1.

Remnants of the Specials, now totally Dammers-dominated, revived earlier name the Specials aka. Backed girl singer Rhoda on controversially acidic **The Boiler**, but have found it hard to maintain status. Roddy Radiation went on to form Roddy Radiation and the Tearjerkers.

Current line-up: Dammers; Bradbury; Stan Campbell, vocals; Rhoda Dakar, vocals; Gary McManus, bass; John Shipley, guitar.

Hit Singles:	US	UK
Gangsters, 1979	—	6
A Message To You Ruby/Nite Club, 1979	—	10
Too Much Too Young (EP), 1980	—	1
Rat Race/Rude Boys Outa Jail, 1980	—	5
Stereotype/International Jet Set, 1980	—	6
Do Nothing/Maggies Farm, 1981	—	4
Ghost Town, 1981	—	1

Albums:
Specials (Chrysalis), 1979
More Specials (Chrysalis/Two Tone), 1980

Spirit

US group formed 1967.

Original line-up: Randy California, guitar, vocals; Ed Cassidy, drums; Mark Andes, bass; Jay Ferguson, vocals; John Locke, piano.

Career: Nucleus of Spirit formed in 1965 when Ferguson, Cassidy, California and Andes played together in electric folk group, the Red Roosters. Secured gigs at various Hollywood clubs before Andes and Ferguson quit to form Western Union and, later, Yellow Balloon. California moved to New York and

gained useful experience jamming with Jimi Hendrix(▶). Meanwhile, Cassidy (California's step-father), a jazz veteran (previously sideman for Cannonball Adderly, Gerry Mulligan, Thelonius Monk, Zoot Sims, the New Jazz Trio and the Rising Sons), returned to jazz roots with various short-lived groups.

Cassidy teamed up with John Locke, formerly of 11-piece avant-garde New World Jazz Company, and in April 1967 reunited former colleagues as Spirits Rebellious, later abbreviated to Spirit. An extraordinary amalgam of jazz/rock made them one of most innovative and challenging groups of '60s.

They were signed by Lou Adler to new Ode label; Adler produced first album, **Spirit,** a dense, intriguing work for the period, highlighting Ferguson's writing talent.

Next two albums, **The Family That Plays Together Stays Together** and **Clear,** were almost equally adventurous, with California gradually emerging as dynamic guitar player/songwriter. **The Twelve Dreams Of Dr Sardonicus** (February 1971) hit unforeseen heights and is rightly regarded as one of finest albums ever released.

California's exotic, sometimes bizarre, arrangements alienated Ferguson whose influence on Spirit's musical direction was waning, and the group divided prior to release of **Sardonicus**. Andes and Ferguson formed the briefly successful Jo Jo Gunne. Meanwhile, California had sustained a fractured skull in a riding accident, which put him out of action for over a year.

Cassidy soldiered on, recruiting Texas duo Al and Christian Staehely, with whom he recorded disappointing **Feedback**. Disillusioned, he quit, as did John Locke in February 1973. Contractual complexities allowed Staehely Brothers to continue using Spirit's name for a brief period, but no albums were recorded.

Having almost formed a new group with Noel Redding, California put together Kaptain Kopter And The Fabulous Twirlybirds, reuniting with Cassidy during the sessions. Resulting album was Hendrix-inspired heavy-metal blow-out with unusual covers of such Beatle songs as **Day Tripper** and **Rain,** and Paul Simon's **Mother And Child Reunion.**

Streamlined to a trio, with addition of bassist Larry 'Fuzzy' Knight, Kaptain Kopter toured UK in March/April 1973, illegally using the name Spirit. During visit, a depressed California jumped off Chelsea Bridge, but survived. He recorded **A Jour-**

ney Through Potatoland, a bizarre concept album that remained unreleased for eight years.

Spirit re-formed in 1975, to cut double LP **Spirit Of '76,** an astonishing comeback with some of California's finest work to date. New bassist Barry Keene remained for staunch **Son Of Spirit;** he was later replaced by Larry Knight. Follow-up album **Farther Along** proved partially successful 'reunion' with John Locke, Mark Andes, and additional guitarist Matthew Andes. Ferguson's solo commitments precluded involvement, but complete original line-up did play much-publicised gig at Santa Monica Civic Auditorium on August 28, 1976. It was during this show that California became involved in fracas with Neil Young(▶).

Original line-up failed to record album, though Spirit trio continued. Excellent **Future Games** followed, but after further tours and a couple of live albums, Spirit again split. California is currently pursuing a solo career, in the old tradition of Kaptain Kopter, but Spirit will no doubt resurface again in the future.

Final line-up: California; Cassidy; Larry Knight, bass.

Albums:
Spirit (Epic), 1968
The Twelve Dreams Of Dr Sardonicus (Epic), 1971
Feedback (Epic), 1971
Best Of (Epic), 1973
Spirit Of '76 (Mercury), 1975
Farther Along (Mercury), 1976
Future Games (Mercury), 1977
Spirit Live (Potato/Illegal), 1977
Potatoland (Rhino/Beggar's Banquet), 1978

Worth Searching Out:
The Family That Plays Together Stays Together (Epic), 1968

Split Enz

New Zealand group formed 1974.

Original line-up: Timothy Finn, vocals, piano; Philip Judd, vocals, guitars; Eddie Rayner, keyboards; Wally Wilkinson, guitar; Jonathan Chunn, bass; Noel Crombie, drums.

Career: Split Enz had reputation for exciting stage act throughout native New Zealand by end of 1975. Above unit moved to Australia in early 1975. Made-up faces and costumes set band apart from anything happening in the Antipodes.

Mental Notes was recorded in mid-1975; LP attracted attention of Roxy Music's(▶) Phil Manzanera. He produced **Second Thoughts** in England which mainly featured alternative version of songs on first LP.

Band came to UK in May 1977 and stayed until end of 1978. During this time, Phil Judd quit and was replaced by Tim's brother Neil Finn. Chunn and Wilkinson also left. Group added two British musicians, Nigel Griggs, bass, and Malcolm Green, drums. **Dizrythmai** was released and the extended UK stay was mainly spent on tour as support act.

Despite favourable reviews in British music weeklies, band's off-putting appearance fit neither new punk image nor older format. Result was fall from critical and popular grace as end of 1978 drew near. Phil Judd rejoined, then quit; band was dropped by Chrysalis. Singing with Mushroom Records, band recorded **Frenzy** and then returned to Australia. **I See Red** became Australian Top 10 single and band spent most of 1979 touring Australia. After beginning new studio LP in September 1979, **Beginning Of The Enz**

Right: Kiwi eccentrics Split Enz, who broke through with True Colours.

was released with early mixes and unreleased material.

True Colours, issued in late 1979, finally broke band in US. Gimmicky cover colour scheme was unnecessary but LP produced UK Top 10 **I Got You**. Most importantly, US tour had to add extra dates to meet growing demand for band's music. A&M then stepped in and offered Enz worldwide contract. **Waiata** and **Time And Tide** followed, but seemed to miss spark of **True Colours**. Question now is whether Splitz Enz can maintain momentum and conquer world like they did the South Pacific.

Current line-up: Tim Finn; Rayner; Neil Finn, guitar, vocals; Nigel Griggs, bass; Crombie.

Hit Singles:

	US	UK
I Got You, 1980	53	12

Albums:
Second Thoughts (Chrysalis), 1977
Dizrythmai (Chrysalis), 1977
Frenzy (CA&M/—), 1978
Beginning Of The End (Chrysalis), 1979
True Colours (Mushroom, then A&N), 1980
Waiata (A&M), 1981
Time And Tide (A&M), 1982

Worth Searching Out:
Mental Notes (Chrysalis), 1976

Dusty Springfield

UK vocalist.
Born Mary O'Brien, London, April 16, 1939.

Career: First made impression as part of pop-folk trio the Springfields which had handful of hits in early '60s. Group broke up in September 1963, and Springfield embarked on solo career. Forsaking folksiness for more soulful style (then being popularised by Motown), she was responsible for series of hit singles which combined commercial catchiness with distinctive vocalising. More than any other British female singer of the time she made an impression on the US market; five singles made US Top 20.

Well thought of by critics and fellow professionals, Springfield was better equipped vocally than most of her contemporaries, and could make creditable job of more demanding soul material. This ability was best displayed on 1969 LP **Dusty In Memphis**, produced by Jerry Wexler, featuring Memphis session mafia. Although in retrospect not as brilliant as made out to be at the time, it remains one of the best blue-eyed soul efforts of this era.

Son Of A Preacher Man in late 1968 was Springfield's last major chart success; she then began to fade from sight amid rumours of personal problems. During '70s she lived somewhat reclusively in America, occasionally recording and acting as back-up for other singers. A flurry of activity in 1978/79 resulted in couple of LPs and promotional appearances. Latterly, Springfield has again been keeping her head down, surfacing only to prove that her voice is still in excellent shape.

Very much one of Britain's 'swinging '60s' figureheads, at peak of fame Springfield was as well known to public for 'panda' eye make-up and elaborate coiffure as for vocal prowess. Nevertheless, she is a talented vocalist with a distinctive style who, given right material and will to succeed, could still make a mark on music scene of '80s.

Hit Singles:

	US	UK
I Only Want To Be With You, 1963	12	4
Stay Awhile, 1964	38	13
I Just Don't Know What To Do With Myself, 1964	—	3
Wishin' And Hopin', 1964	6	—
Losing You, 1964	—	9
In The Middle Of Nowhere, 1965	—	8
Some Of Your Lovin', 1965	—	8
Little By Little, 1966	—	17
You Don't Have To Say You Love Me, 1966	4	1
Going Back, 1966	—	10
All I See Is You, 1966	20	9
I'll Try Anything, 1967	40	13
I Close My Eyes And Count To Ten, 1968	—	4
Son Of A Preacher Man, 1968	10	9

Albums:
Golden Hits (Philips), 1966
This Is Dusty Springfield Volume 2—The Magic Garden (—/Philips), 1973
You Don't Have To Say You Love Me (—/Contour), 1976
It Begins Again (Liberty/Mercury), 1978
Greatest Hits (Mercury/Phonogram), 1979
Living Without Your Love (Liberty/Mecury), 1979
Memphis Plus (Mercury), 1980
The Very Best Of Dusty Springfield (—/K-Tel), 1981
Whiteheat (Casablanca/—), 1982

Worth Searching out:
Dusty In Memphis (Atlantic/Philips), 1969

Bruce Springsteen

US composer, vocalist, guitarist.
Born Freehold, New Jersey, September 23, 1949.

Career: Springsteen grew up watching Beatles(▶) revolutionising rock 'n' roll and decided he wanted to be a rock star. Started gigging in New York clubs, formed various bands, went to California, returned to East Coast, and missed completely.

In 1972 he hired Mick Appel to manage him. Appel took him to John Hammond of Columbia Records who supposedly was as impressed with Springsteen as he had been years ago with Bob Dylan(▶) Result was recording of folkish **Greetings From Asbury Park, New Jersey.** Bruce still missed.

Second LP, **The Wild, The Innocent And The E-Street Shuffle,** carried the seeds for

developing back-up group, the E Street Band. It also marked Springsteen as original talent rather than another Dylan soundalike.

Live shows began to take on marathon proportions of epic tales, true-life ballads, whispered intimacies and buckets of sweat. If it seemed as pre-arranged as a James Brown(▶) stage faint, it was still exciting, warm and sincere.

American critic Jon Landau had become acquainted with Springsteen and liked his shows. In May 1974 he wrote review citing Springsteen as 'rock and roll future'. The phrase caught and, aided by Columbia, pushed Springsteen into glare of mass media publicity.

Landau and Springsteen became friends and when sessions for next LP bogged down, Springsteen asked Landau to help out production. **Born To Run** finally justified media hype and deservedly became instant success. It also continued maturation process begun

Darkness On The Edge Of Town, Bruce Springsteen. Courtesy CBS Records. Bruce 'The Boss' must be seen live.

on second album, while holding on to b[...] and immediacy of garage bands.

The LP ensured sell-out tours for 1975, during which Springsteen honed down live act to professional perfection. It was obviously time to start on follow-up album. Instead, Springsteen's career came to halt when he and Appel became involved in contract dispute. This delayed new releases until 1978, when **Darkness On The Edge Of Town** appeared. It naturally reflected loss of innocence, but expressed hope for some ultimate workable future.

Springsteen's vision of everyman's future

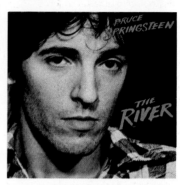

The River, Bruce Springsteen. Courtesy CBS Records.

continued on excellent album **The River**. His willingness to continue to take chances was proved by 1982 release **Nebraska**.

Having finished demo tapes for E Street Band, Springsteen decided studio recordings were losing raw edge he intended. Against advice, he decided demos would be released. After LP went to No. 1 in US charts, his decision was vindicated, but it could have proved disastrous. Revived Gary 'US Bonds'(▶) career (as co-producer with Miami Steve van Zandt) with two raw-edged albums in early '80s.

Springsteen is one of America's greatest current talents. He has reached goal of being rock star by remaining street-wise, questioning, East Coast kid. As long as he avoids becoming too slick or too sentimental, he will be, at very least, 'rock and roll present'.

Hit Singles:

	US	UK
Hungry Heart, 1980	5	—
Fade Away, 1981	20	—

Park, New Jersey
973
nt and The E-Street
CBS), 1973
ia/CBS), 1975
Darkness   ge Of Town (Columbia/
CBS), 1978
The River (Columbia/CBS), 1980
Nebraska (Columbia/CBS), 1982

Squeeze

UK group formed 1974.

Original line-up: Jools Holland, keyboards; Harry Kakoulli, bass; Gilson Lavis, drums; Chris Difford, guitar, vocals; Glenn Tilbrook, guitar, vocals.

Career: Until their demise in autumn 1982, Squeeze (band known as UK Squeeze in US until American band of same name split up) had successfully re-written teenage anthem songbook expounding love in the back seat.

The enterprising South East London quintet first recorded for independent Deptford Fun City label with EP **Packet Of Three** in 1974, carving out a solid local reputation.

First album **Squeeze** released on A&M in 1978 contained hit single **Take Me I'm Yours**, first in series of cockney, adolescent anecdotes from pens of Difford and Tilbrook.

Personnel changes (John Bentley replacing Kalkoulli, Paul Carrack (ex-Ace) coming in for Holland) established line-up which scored with singles **Up The Junction, Another Nail In My Heart** and **Pulling Mussels.**

Fourth album **East Side Story** earned group breakthrough in States, and included new keyboard player Don Snow (ex-Sinceros) following departure of Carrack to Carlene Carter's band. Carrack then toured with Nick Lowe(▶) and pursued solo career.

Ironically, soon after American success, band went into swift demise. Difford and Tilbrook went on to do London play 'Labelled With Love' based on Squeeze songs. Jools Holland formed Millionaires and had spell as co-host on UK music show 'The Tube.'

Final line-up: Lavis; Difford; Tilbrook; John Bentley, bass; Don Snow, keyboards.

Hit Singles:	US	UK
Take Me I'm Yours, 1978	—	19
Cool For Cats, 1979	—	2
Up The Junction, 1979	—	2
Another Nail In My Heart, 1980	—	17
Labelled With Love, 1981	—	4

Albums:
Squeeze (A&M), 1978
Cool For cats (A&M), 1979
Argy Bargy (A&M), 1980
East Side Story (A&M), 1981
Singles (A&M), 1982

East Side Story, Squeeze. Courtesy A&M Records.

The Staple Singers

US vocal group formed 1954.

Original line-up: Roebuck 'Pop' Staples, guitar, vocals; Pervis Staples; Cleotha Staples; Mavis Staples.

Career: Blues guitarist in teens, Pop Staples turned to gospel, joining Golden Trumpets touring group in 1931. He then moved from Missouri to Chicago where his children were born. Family group first recorded for United in 1954, then had six-year stint with Vee-Jay during which reputation was made, second release **Uncloudy Day** being major gospel smash. Yvonne joined group in 1961 when Pervis was serving in Army (he left group a decade later). Joining Riverside in 1961, they cut in excess of 400 tracks in just two years before being signed to major Epic label.

In 1967 they entered pop Hot 100 with ultra-soulful **Why Am I Treated So Bad**, produced by erstwhile rock 'n' roller Larry Williams, who was also responsible for their classic version of Stephen Stills'(▶) **For What It's Worth**.

In 1968, group were signed to Stax Records who proceeded to turn them into major pop act, though their material was still mainly inspirational in nature. **Respect Yourself** and other hits made them one of label's top groups and their appearance in massive 'Soul To Soul' concert in Ghana cemented reputation.

Since demise of Stax in mid-'70s, the Staples have been unable to repeat earlier triumphs through recordings for Warner Bros or 20th Century. Mavis Staples' solo career, which saw several superb albums on Stax's Volt subsidiary, has also gone into doldrums.

Current line-up: As above with Yvonne Staples replacing Pervis Staples.

Hit Singles:	US	UK
Respect Yourself, 1971	12	—
I'll Take You There, 1972	1	30
If You're Ready (Come Go With Me), 1973	9	34
Let's Do It Again, 1975	1	—

Albums (selected):
Hold On To Your Dream (20th Century), 1981
This Time Around (Stax), 1981
At Their Best (—/Stax), 1982

Worth Searching Out:
Be Altitude — Respect Yourself (Stax), 1971

Ringo Starr

UK drummer, vocalist, composer, actor.
Born Richard Starkey, Liverpool, July 7, 1940.

Career: The only member of the Beatles(▶) to have played in other bands (notably Rory Storme and the Hurricanes) before Beatles; Ringo only joined most famous group of all immediately before first Parlophone recording session (which produced **Love Me Do**). Throughout Beatles era, was never taken seriously as writer, although occasional songs were set aside for him to sing, like **Honey Don't** on **Beatles For Sale** LP and especially singalong **Yellow Submarine**. Shortly before Beatles split, he released extremely poor LP of standards **Sentimental Journal**, supposedly recorded because his mother liked such songs as **Night And Day** and **Bye Bye Blackbird**.

Ringo continued to work with both John Lennon(▶) and George Harrison(▶) after split, appearing on most of their early solo records. In 1970 released second solo effort, country

& western flavoured **Beaucoups Of Blues**, produced by Nashville star Pete Drake. It was major improvement over debut, if still somewhat obscure. During this period, made several appearances in films, including Frank Zappa's(▶) '200 Motels', 'Blind Man' and 'Born To Boogie' starring Marc Bolan(▶), but best of all, 'That'll Be The Day', which launched David Essex(▶) as major movie star. Next LP, excellent **Ringo**, produced by Richard Perry, was incredibly successful, spawning two US chart-topping singles, plus participation from other three ex-Beatles (although not altogether). Follow-up LP, **Goodnight Vienna**, used same recipe, but with fewer hits.

1976's **Ringo's Rotogravure** LP was far less interesting; subsequent LPs show little sign of return to mid-'70s form. Own label Ognir proved unsuccessful. Seemingly, Ringo has now outlived the advantages of being a Beatle, and while his drumming remains object lesson in unostentatious brilliance, as a vocalist he is now regarded as merely adequate. He looks unlikely to return to chart contention unless he teams up with Richard Perry (or someone like him). Movie career has continued with appalling 'Cave Man', co-starring Barbara Bach, whom Ringo married in 1982.

Hit Singles:	US	UK
It Don't come Easy, 1971	4	4
Back Off Boogaloo, 1972	9	2
Photograph, 1973	1	8
You're Sixteen, 1974	1	4
Oh My My, 1974	5	—
Only You, 1974	6	28
No No Song, 1975	3	—

Albums:
Sentimental Journey (Apple), 1970
Beaucoup Of Blues (Apple), 1970
Ringo (Apple), 1973
Goodnight Vienna (Apple), 1974
Blast From Your Past (Apple), 1975*
Ringo's Rotogravure (Atco/Polydor), 1976
Ringo The 4th (Atco/Polydor), 1977
Bad Boy (Portrait/Polydor), 1978
Stop And Smell The Roses (Boardwalk/RCA), 1981

*Compilation

Status Quo

UK group formed 1967.

Original line-up: Rick Parfitt, guitar, vocals; Francis Rossi, guitar, vocals; Alan Lancaster, bass, vocals; John Coghlan, drums; Roy Lynes, organ, vocals.

Career: Rossi (originally known as Mike) met Lancaster at school in spring 1962. As young 12-year-olds, they formed first band, Scorpions. Within four months, band's guitarist quit. Rossi and Lancaster recruited another schoolmate to carry on. This second band

Above: Ringo Starr at his drums on Dutch television in 1976.

came across Coghlan in September 1962 when his own group was practising next door.

Going through several personnel changes in the merge, the Spectres, as they called themselves, began playing holiday camps. In April 1965 Roy Lynes took over organ spot. The line-up of Rossi, Lancaster, Coghlan and Lynes actually recorded three flop singles for Pye. Parfitt was added in May 1967 after career in various South London outfits.

Group changed name to Traffic, then to Traffic Jam because of Winwood's group. Another single flopped and to earn living band had to assume backing duties for US artists.

In August 1967, group took new name of Status Quo. They recorded Rossi number, **Pictures Of Matchstick Men**, and quietly resumed duties as back-up band. Early 1968 found Status Quo sudden pop stars as single became international hit, but subsequent work failed to maintain success.

Lynes left in 1970 when Quo was at nadir of career. A year later band moved to Vertigo Records with no noticeable change in fortunes. Instead, they began building up following by playing relentless (some say, repetitious) boogie. Despite critical write-off, Status Quo's audience put band back in UK Top 10 with **Paper Plane. Piledriver** LP charted shortly after and everything band did seemed to go gold. Single **Down, Down** went to No. 1 in UK and album **On The Level** charted in late '74. Andy Bown played keyboards on and off from 1974-79. Since 1974 every new LP on Vertigo has made UK Top 5.

The long tours and hard work seemed to have no effect on rock's longest established line-up. So it was surprising that 1982 began with announcement of Coghlan's retirement. Pete Kirchner (ex-Original Mirrors) stepped in and Quo promptly released two further chart albums. **From The Makers Of. . .** included live performances before big fan, HRH Prince Charles. At this rate, Quo will still be making big hits long after Charles becomes King.

Current line-up: Parfitt; Rossi; Lancaster; Pete Kirchner, drums.

Hit Singles:	US	UK
Pictures Of Matchstick Men, 1968	12	7
Ice In The Sun, 1968	—	8
Down The Dustpipe, 1970	—	12
Paper Plane, 1973	—	8
Mean Girl, 1973	—	20
Caroline, 1973	—	5
Break The Rules, 1974	—	8
Down, Down, 1974	—	1
Roll Over Lay Down, 1975	—	9
Rain, 1976	—	7
Mystery Song, 1976	—	11
Wild Side Of Life, 1976	—	9
Rockin' All Over The World, 1977	—	3

Again And Again, 1978	—	13
Whatever You Want, 1979	—	4
Living On An Island, 1979	—	16
What You're Proposing, 1980	—	2
Lies/Don't Drive My Car, 1981	—	11
Something 'Bout You Baby I Like, 1981	—	7
Rock'n'Roll, 1981	—	8
Dear John, 1982	—	10
Caroline (live), 1982	—	13

Albums:
(not including various repetitious compilations)
Ma Kelly's Greasy Spoon (—/Pye), 1970
Dog Of Two Heads (—/Pye), 1971
Piledriver (A&M/Vertigo), 1973
Hello (A&M/Vertigo), 1973
Quo (A&M/Vertigo), 1974
On The Level (Capitol/Vertigo), 1975
Blue For You (—/Vertigo), 1976
Status Quo Live (Capitol/Vertigo), 1977
Rockin' All Over The World (Capitol/Vertigo, 1977
Status Quo File (—/Pye), 1977
If You Can't Stand The Heat (—/Vertigo), 1978
Whatever You Want (—/Vertigo), 1979
Twelve Gold Bars (—/Vertigo), 1980
Just Supposin' (—/Vertigo), 1980
Never Too Late (—/Vertigo), 1981
1+9+8+2=XX Years (—/Vertigo), 1982
'From The Makers Of. . .' (—/Vertigo), 1982

Steeleye Span

UK group formed 1969.

Original line-up: Maddy Prior, vocals; Tim Hart, vocals, guitar, dulcimer; Ashley 'Tyger' Hutchings, bass; Gay Woods, vocals, concertina; Terry Woods, vocals, mandolin.

Career: Having just left Fairport Convention(▶) Ashley 'Tyger' Hutchings teamed up in 1969 with duos Tim Hart and Maddy Prior (who had already cut three folk albums) and Gay and Terry Woods (from ill-fated Sweeney's Men electric folk band) to form Steeleye Span. Band's aim was to pioneer electronic concept of folk music.

Debut album **Hark! The Village Wait**, produced by Sandy Roberton, revealed that the Woods were at odds with other three and they quit to return to Ireland; replaced by leading folk revival figure Martin Carthy (guitar, keyboards, vocals) and Peter Knight (keyboards, vocals, fiddle, mandolin). Band became full-time touring and recording outfit. They appeared in Keith Dewhurst's play 'Coruna' to widen audience beyond folk confines.

More interested in purist acoustic music, Hutchings left band. Carthy also split in December 1971 following differences over whether group should look for another electric bass player or multi-instrumentalist. Rock-orientated musicians Rick Kemp, bass, and Bob Johnson, electric guitar, came in.

Right: Walter Becker (left) and Donald Fagen of Steely Dan.

With Roberton replaced as manager by Joe Lustig, a new deal with Chrysalis was forged; careful exploitation made group major act by ealy '70s. Addition of hard-rocking drummer Nigel Pegrum in 1974 for appropriately titled **Now We Are Six** set (produced by Jethro Tull's Ian Anderson) added momentum.

Showing gift for theatrics, group included a mummers' play in stage presentations, and Peter Sellers appeared as guest musician on **New York Girls**, playing ukelele. Five-part harmonies behind Prior's piping lead vocals gave group distinctive if predictable vocal sound.

Switched management to Tony Secunda in 1975; moved onto fresh ground when Wombles' producer Mike Batt was brought in for **All Around My Hat**, a UK smash and their American breakthrough. They also experimented with reggae backings and heavier rock flavour to move yet further from folk roots.

After commercial failure of artistically creditable **Rocket Cottage** album (1976), band took six-month rest. Johnson and Knight worked on their **King Of Elfland's Daughter** concept album project (with Alexis Korner, Frankie Miller and Mary Hopkin guesting).

Span re-formed (Prior and Kemp now married), Carthy rejoining and accordionist John Kirkpatrick being added. Kemp and Johnson left. Group continued to record, with Knight concentrating on keyboards rather than fiddle, and style became yet more rock orientated.

Final line-up: Prior; Kemp; Peter Knight, keyboards, vocals, fiddle, mandolin; Bob Johnson, guitar; Martin Carthy, vocals, guitar; John Kirkpatrick, accordion.

Hit Singles:	US	UK
Gaudete, 1973	—	14
All Around My Hat, 1975	—	5

Albums:
Hark The Village Wait (Chrysalis/Mooncrest), 1970
Please To See The King (Chrysalis/Mooncrest), 1971
Ten Man Mop (Chrysalis), 1971
Below The Salt (Chrysalis), 1972
Parcel Of Rogues (Chrysalis), 1973
Now We Are Six (Chrysalis), 1974
Commoners Crown (Chrysalis), 1975
All Around My Hat (Chrysalis), 1975
Rocket Cottage (Chrysalis), 1976
Storm Force 10 (Chrysalis), 1977
Live At Last (Chrysalis), 1978
Steeleye Story (Chrysalis/—), 1977
Original Masters (Chrysalis), 1977*
Sails Of Silver (—/Chrysalis), 1980
Steeleye Span (—/Pickwick), 1980
*Double compilation

Below: Status Quo (from left) Andy Bown (keyboards), Rossi, Parfitt, Kircher, Lancaster.

Steely Dan

US group formed 1972.

Original line-up: Donald Fagen, keyboards, vocals; Walter Becker, bass, vocals; Denny Dias, guitar; Jeff 'Skunk' Baxter, guitar, pedal steel guitar; Jim Hodder, drums; David Palmer, vocals.

Career: Formed around dual writing/performing talents of Fagen and Becker, both former students at Bard College, New York. First band included Denny Dias; joined Jay And Americans back-up band when group split. First recorded work was soundtrack for off-beat Zalman King movie 'You Gotta Walk It Like You Talk It (Or You'll Loose That Beat)'. Took name Steely Dan from a William Burroughs novel.

Moved to West Coast at insistence of producer Gary Katz; signed as writers to ABC/Dunhill Records. Katz/Fagen/Becker assembled group comprising Dias, fellow New Yorker Palmer, and Bostonians Baxter and Hodder.

Debut album **Can't Buy A Thrill** (1972) set pattern for jazz-structured melodies and succinct, Runyonesque lyrics. Singles from LP **Do It Again** and **Reelin' In The Years** made US Top 20.

Palmer quit (forming Wha Koo in 1977) before second album **Countdown To Ecstacy**, leaving vocals exclusively to Fagen. Quintet completed **Pretzel Logic** (with notable session musicians such as Michael Omartian, Jeff Porcaro (now in Toto(▶)), Chuck Rainey, Dean Parks, Vic Feldman and Crusaders'(▶), Wilton Felder). Album included classic **Rikki Don't Lose That Number**, a US Top 10 single.

With Fagen and Becker deriving more pleasure from recording than touring, Baxter and Hodder departed; Baxter subsequently joined Doobie Brothers(▶). For **Katy Lied**, group added Michael McDonald (also later to join Doobies), vocals, and Jeff Porcaro, drums. McDonald had previously toured both US and UK with band.

By now almost permanent studio unit, group cut **The Royal Scam** with addition of session players but without departed Dias. Chart success maintained with track **Haitian Divorce**.

Aja (1977) saw Fagen/Becker firmly in control; musicians included drummer Bernard Purdie(▶) guitarists Larry Carlton(▶) and Lee Ritenour, and guest appearance by Dias, veteran Feldman on percussion and keyboards, and surprisingly Chuck Rainey on bass, depriving Becker of his role for all but one track. McDonald supplied back-up vocals.

Steely Dan's final album to date, **Gaucho**

(1980), returned duo to singles chart with track **Babylon Sisters.** Becker again limited on bass contribution, with Rainey and Anthony Jackson (a Simon & Garfunkel(▶) favourite) stepping in.

Band's tenuous story further confused by Donald Fagen solo set **Nightfly** (1982); songs were exclusively Fagen's (except Leiber/Stoller's **Ruby Baby**) but sound was definitive Steely Dan.

Nightfly explored fantasies of teen America; sound complemented by Porcaro, Brecker Bros (trumpet and sax), Carlton, Hugh McCracker, guitar, and bassists Rainey Jackson, Marcus Miller, Abe Laboriel and Will Lee. Becker could take heart from the talent it took to replace him.

Fagen maintains band could re-form, despite solo success.

Current/Final line-up: Fagen; Becker; plus session players.

Hit Singles:	US	UK
Do It Again, 1973	6	39
Reelin' In The Years, 1973	11	—
Rikki Don't Lose That Number, 1974 (1979)	4	58
Haitian Divorce, 1976	3	17
FM (No Static At All), 1978	7	49
Babylon Sisters, 1980	2	—

Albums:
You Gotta Walk It (Visa/—), 1969
Can't Buy A Thrill (MCA), 1972
Countdown To Ecstasy (MCA), 1973
Pretzel Logic (MCA), 1974
Katy Lied (MCA), 1975
The Royal Scam (MCA), 1976
Aja (MCA), 1977
Greatest Hits (MCA), 1979
Gaucho (MCA), 1980

Donald Fagen Solo:
The Nightfly (Warner Bros), 1982

Steely Dan's Gaucho, featuring single Babylon Sisters. Courtesy MCA Records.

Above: John Kay, lead singer of US hard rock band Steppenwolf.

Steppenwolf

US group formed 1967.

Original line-up: John Kay, guitar, vocals; Jerry Edmonton, drums; Goldy McJohn, organ; Michael Monarch, guitar; Rushton Moreve, bass.

Career: East German-born John Kay and his family fled to Canada when he was 14. There he discovered Western music and formed blues group Sparrow. Realising limited chances in Toronto, Kay took band to New York, the California.

Sparrow began adapting style to blues-based gritty rock made popular by English bands. By mid-1967 they had become Steppenwolf and the first of many bass player changes occurred as John Russell Morgan replace Moreve.

When band recorded debut LP in late '67, they had several years of road experience and original material stored up. **Born To Be Wild** single was released as crisis in Czechoslovakia led to Russian invasion. Rough vocals, outrageous lyrics and grinding music epitomised political atmosphere of tanks in the street and worldwide call to break free.

The first Steppenwolf album. Courtesy RCA Records.

Magic Carpet Ride, released barely three months later, enhanced image of bold, creative force at large.

Albums by Steppenwolf were patchy and uneven until 1969 release, **Monster.** This represented band at its most political as well as its most cohesive musically. Instead of pushing ahead, frenzied past few years caught up and group began more extensive personnel changes. Monarch's guitar spot was taken by Larry Byrom, then Kent Henry. Bass player duties were handed over to Nick St. Nicholas, then to George Biondo. This caused break-up of tight-knit sound forged by early band, and in February 1972 came announcement of Steppenwolf's demise.

When Kay's solo career failed to take hold, he reorganised band in 1974 with McJohn, Edmonton, Biondo and guitarist Bobby Cochran. After **Slow Flux** LP Wayne Cook replaced McJohn. **Hour Of The World** album proved band could sometimes recapture old sound, but Kay failed to come up with material that matched magic days of 1967-1969. Despite further efforts, band never regained old form.

Steppenwolf's place in rock history depends as much on political climate of '60s as on music. As memories fade, band's music seems less potent, less a call to arms. Nevertheless, underlying sound still has powerful hold as seen by many successful greatest hits and compilation releases.

Final Line Up: Kay; Edmonton; Bobby Cochran, guitar; George Biondo, bass; Wayne Cook, keyboards.

Hit Singles:

	US	UK
Born To Be Wild, 1968	2	30
Magic Carpet Ride, 1968	3	—
Rock Me, 1969	10	—

Albums:
Steppenwolf (Dunhill/Stateside), 1968
Steppenwolf The Second (Dunhill/Stateside), 1968
Live Steppenwolf (Dunhill/Probe), 1970
Steppenwolf 7 (Dunhill/Probe), 1970
Steppenwolf Gold (MCA), 1971
16 Greatest Hits (ABC), 1973

Cat Stevens

UK vocalist, composer, guitarist.
Born Steven Georgiou, London, July 21, 1947.

Career: Son of a Greek restaurateur father and Swedish mother, Stevens enjoyed two distinct musical careers, first as straightforward folk-influenced pop artist then, following time off scene seriously ill, as folk-rock album star experimenting heavily with ethnic Greek instruments which give his style unique dimension.

He became involved in folk scene while studying at Hammersmith College and met former Springfields' folk group member Mike Hurst, then working as independent record producer. Instead of emigrating to America as intended, Hurst invested his savings in recording Stevens' own composition, **I Love My Dog,** which he then licensed to Tony Hall for Decca's newly formed Deram (progressive music subsidiary) as label's debut release. The record charted and follow-up **Matthew And Son** did even better, reaching No. 2 in early 1967.

Stevens toured with both Jimi Hendrix(▶) and Englebert Humperdinck and his perceptive

songs were snapped up by other recording stars (notably P.P. Arnold with **The First Cut Is The Deepest** and the Tremeloes with **Here Comes My Baby).** In early 1968 he scored third Deram hit with **I'm Gonna Get Me A Gun.**

After contracting TB, Stevens spent year recuperating, using the time to develop new ideas and songs in almost classical manner. Taking time to get everything just right, Stevens eventually signed to Island and released the landmark **Mona Bone Jakon** in 1970. From that set, **Lady d'Arbanville** (written about a former girlfriend) emerged as hit single, but Stevens had truly matured into album artist and subsequent sets made him a superstar both sides of Atlantic.

Massive earnings from records and concerts led to tax exile in Brazil during which time he became heavily involved with UNESCO and various charities.

By mid-'70s, Stevens had become very much the recluse, developing a passionate interest in mysticism. He converted to Moslem faith and married girl he had seen at a London mosque but never spoken to.

The Old School Yard (1977) was his last hit single; subsequently he retired completely from music scene, devoting himself to religious studies and adopting the name Yusef Islam.

Hit Singles:

	US	UK
Matthew And Son, 1967	—	2
I'm Gonna Get Me A Gun, 1967	—	6
A Bad Night, 1967	—	20
Lady D'Arbanville, 1970	—	8
Wild World, 1971	11	—
Peace Train, 1971	7	—
Morning Has Broken, 1972	6	9
Can't Keep It In, 1972	—	13
Sitting, 1972	16	—
Oh Very Young, 1974	10	—
Another Saturday Night, 1974	6	19

Albums:
Matthew And Son (—/Deram), 1967
New Masters (—/Deram), 1968
World Of (—/Decca), 1970
Mona Bone Jakon (A&M/Island), 1970
Tea For The Tillerman (A&M/Island), 1971
Teaser & The Firecat (A&M/Island), 1971
Catch Bull At Four (A&M/Island), 1972
Foreigner (A&M/Island), 1973
Buddha & The Chocolate Box (A&M/Island), 1974
View From The Top (—/Deram), 1974
Numbers (A&M/Island), 1975
Greatest Hits (A&M/Island), 1975
Izitso (A&M/Island), 1977
Back To Earth (A&M/Island), 1978
Cat's Cradle (London/—) '70s
The First Cut Is The Deepest (—/Decca), 1981

Below: Cat Stevens, a chart star of two decades, but now retired.

Shakin' Stevens

UK vocalist, composer.
Born Michael Barratt, Ely, Wales, March 4, 1948.

Career: Formed first band, the Sunsets, in 1969; toured pubs/clubs establishing reputation as premier rock 'n' roll revivalist. Signed to Parlophone records in 1970; first album **A Legend** produced by Dave Edmunds(▶).

Over next six years recorded for variety of major and minor labels mostly in same 'revival' style with some success, notably in Europe. Similarity to Presley(▶) resulted in starring role in London Musical 'Elvis', followed by regular spot on revived 'Oh Boy!' TV show.

Signed to Track Records during Elvis show for first album without Sunsets; moved to Epic following 'Oh Boy' appearances. First singles

This Ole House, Shakin' Stevens. Courtesy Epic Records.

on Epic unsuccessful but fourth single became Top 30 hit in February 1980. **Marie, Marie** fared better. Finally consolidated popularity in 1981 with **This Ole House.**

Although initially regarded as rockabilly artist, Stevens has since softened image somewhat, at same time retaining obvious affection for '50s music, carefully produced by Stuart Coleman.

Hit Singles:

	US	UK
Marie, Marie, 1980	—	19
This Ole House, 1981	—	1
You Drive Me Crazy, 1981	—	2
Green Door, 1981	—	1
It's Raining, 1981	—	10
Oh Julie, 1982	—	1
Shirley, 1982	—	6
Give Me Your Heart Tonight, 1982	—	11
I'll Be Satisfied, 1982	—	10
Blue Christmas (EP), 1982	—	2

Albums:
Shakin' Stevens (—/Polydor), 1978
Shakin' Stevens & The Sunsets — A Legend (—/Nut), 1979
Shakin' Stevens & The Sunsets — Tiger (Everest), 1980

Shaky, Shakin' Stevens. Courtesy Epic Records.

Marie Marie (—/Epic), 1980
Take One (—/Epic), 1980
Shakin' Stevens & The Sunsets at
   The Rockhouse (—/Magnum), 1981
Shakin' Stevens & The Sunsets (—/Mint),
   1981
Manhattan Melodrama (—/Mint), 1981
Shakin' Stevens (—/Hallmark), 1981
Rock On With A Legend (—/MFP), 1981
Shatterin', Volume II (—/Contour), 1981
Shaky (—/Epic), 1981
This Ole House (Epic), 1981
You Drive Me Crazy (Epic/—), 1981
Get Shakin' (Epic/—), 1982
Hot Dog (—/Epic), 1982
Give Me Your Heart Tonight (—/Epic), 1982

Al Stewart

UK vocalist, composer, guitarist.
Born Glasgow, Scotland,

Career: Public school drop out, originally
studied guitar with Robert Fripp and played
lead in Bournemouth group Tony Blackburn &
the Sabres. Moved to London, establishing
small following after solo folk club appearances at Bunjies and Les Cousins in mid-'60s.
Signed to CBS, recorded Dylan-influenced
Bedsitter Images, a slight work, sweetened
by orchestral backing. Grand attempt to
launch Stewart at Festival Hall with elaborate
rock group/orchestral accompaniment proved
premature.

Love Chronicles continued artist's near
obsession with unrequited love as major
theme. 18-minute titletrack gained some
notoriety for 'artistic' use of swear word
'fucking' and established Stewart as troubadour of London's bedsitter land. 1970's
Zero She Files followed familiar self-
analytical style of predecessors as Stewart
gradually won favour on college circuit.
Transitional **Orange** hinted at possible development, not fully realised until 1974's
Past, Present And Future, his most ambitious work to date. Concept album, inspired
by Erika Cheetham's book **The Centuries Of
Nostradamus**, featured series of songs
based on important historical events of 20th
century. Two of longer cuts, **Roads To
Moscow** and **Nostradamus**, highlighted
Stewart's talent as writer/guitarist/arranger.

Past, Present And Future was first work
to be released in US, prompting an ambitious
March '74 tour, for which backing group was
assembled from recently defunct Home.
Mid-'70s albums **Modern Times** and RCA
debut **Year Of The Cat** revealed Stewart
attempting to shed old folkie image in favour
of more contemporary sound.

His preoccupation with time as theme
continued in **Time Passages**, which included
songs focusing on French Revolution, 16th
century England and contemporary America.
Incorporation of jazz/reggae elements alongside familiar acoustic work proved sufficiently
successful to secure breakthrough into US
mainstream where all Stewart's RCA albums
have sold well — **The Year Of The Cat**
climbing to Top 5.

In spite of recent American successes,
Stewart is often dismissed in his home country
for lack of aggression and conservatism. His
early self-indulgence has alienated most
British critics but at his rare best he deserves
greater respect.

Hit Singles:		US	UK
Year Of The Cat, 1977		8	31
Time Passages, 1978		7	—

Albums:
Love Chronicles (—/RCA), 1969
Orange (CBS), 1972
Past, Present And Future (Arista/CBS), 1974
Modern Times (Arista/CBS), 1975
Year Of The Cat (Arista/RCA), 1976
The Early Years (Arista/RCA), 1978
Time Passages (Arista/RCA), 1978
24 Carrots (Arista/RCA), 1980
Live; Indian Summer (Arista/RCA), 1981

John Stewart

US vocalist, composer, guitarist, producer.
Born San Diego, California, September 5,
1939.

Career: Early professional career included
membership in Cumberland Trio and Kingston
Trio. As writer produced hits for the
Monkees(▶) and the Lovin' Spoonful(▶) in
'60s. Became solo artist in early '70s, cutting
three albums for Capitol. Switched to RCA in
1973. Recorded **Cannons In The Rain** and
a live album in 1974; met only moderate success. Stewart toured frequently in
1975-76. Cut **Fire In The Wind** (1977) for
RSO/Polydor.

In 1979, he met up most fruitfully with
Fleetwood Mac(▶); recorded two duets with
Stevie Nicks, **Gold**, which made Top 20 (and
many critics 10-best lists), and **Midnight
Wind**. **Bombs Away Dream Baby** (1979)
was followed by **Dream Babies Go To
Hollywood** (1980).

Stewart's efforts with Stevie Nicks have
seen most productive period. Though glossy,
well-played, and well-produced, with all-star
back-up singers like Nicolette Larsen, and
musicians like Lindsay Buckingham, Stewart's
albums lack both force and focus without the
presence of a stronger musical personality.

Hit Single:	US	UK
Gold, 1979	5	43

Albums:
California Bloodlines (Capitol), 1971
Willard (Capitol), 1972
Cannons In The Rain (RCA), 1973
Fire In The Wind (RSO), 1977
Bombs Away Dream Baby (RSO), 1979
Dream Babies Go To Hollywood (RSO), 1980

Rod Stewart

UK vocalist, guitarist.
Born London, January 10, 1945.

Career: London born, but eternally proud of
Scottish ancestry (his brothers were born
North of the border). Attended same school as
Ray and Dave Davies of the Kinks.

After spells as fence-erector and grave-
digger, signed apprentice forms with Brentford
Football Club but was soon disillusioned by
poor pay and having to clean boots of senior
players. However, he is still a soccer fanatic.

While travelling around Europe, met folk
singer Wizz Jones in Spain who taught him to
play harmonica. Repatriated as destitute
Stewart learned guitar and joined Birmingham
outfit Jimmy Powell and the Dimensions; sang
and played harmonica.

In 1964 Stewart recorded obscure but
superb version of R&B clasic **Good Morning
Little Schoolgirl** for Decca. Joined Long
John Baldry's band the Hoochie Coochie Men
as second vocalist. Fronted Soul Agents for
while before joining Brian Auger, Julie Driscoll
and Reginald Dwight (better known as Elton
John(▶)), in Steampacket in mid-'65. Also
had spell in Steampacket's next form, Bluesology. Backed by Auger's organ playing,
Stewart cut version of his hero Sam Cooke's(▶)
Shake for Columbia in 1966. Quit to sing
alongside Beryl Marsden in Shotgun Express
with Peter Green(▶) (guitar), Peter Bardens

(keyboards); Dave Ambrose (bass) and Mick
Fleetwood (drums). Despite classy line-up,
band failed. While continuing as-yet-unsuc-
cessful solo recording career, Stewart joined
Jeff Beck Group(▶).

After disastrous London concerts, band
found feet in America. Stewart featured on
lauded albums **Truth** (1968) and **Beck-Ola**
(1969). This led to solo contract with Mercury
in 1969.

Stewart quit Beck's band when latter
wanted to fire Ronnie Wood with whom
Stewart had struck up friendship and strong
working relationship. Soon after, Stewart and
Wood were added to line-up of the Faces(▶).

While Faces, with Stewart singing lead,
turned out patchy albums, Stewart's solo
efforts for Mercury were outstanding. After
initial break in US via **An Old Raincoat
Won't Let You Down** (titled the **Rod
Stewart Album** in US) and **Gasoline Alley**
LP in 1970, he quickly built similar reputation
in homeland. Hit big with **Maggie May** from
dynamic 1971 album **Every Picture Tells A
Story**. In September 1971, Stewart achieved
distinction of topping both album and single
charts on both sides of the Atlantic in same
week.

Fronting Faces for live appearances, Stewart
built band into massive concert attraction.
Generated frenetic atmosphere and built
legion of fanatical followers who followed him
in adopting the tartan symbol — and espousing football. Group regularly kicked footballs
into audience and Stewart always took time
out to attend major games.

In 1972, **Never A Dull Moment** LP and
You Wear It Well single struck gold. An
astute minor label dug out an old track
Stewart had recorded, for session fee alone,
with studio group Python Lee Jackon back in
1968. They could not use Stewart's name but
his reputation was enough and **In A Broken
Dream** made No. 3 in UK charts.

Recording material first made famous by
his heroes in rock 'n' roll, soul and R&B
(ranging from Jerry Lee Lewis to Chuck Berry

to Sam Cooke), Stewart always added his own
inimitable touch. Cover versions and new
material alike showed enormous creativity
and fully exploited merits of his gravelly
vocals.

Court wrangles between Mercury and
Warner Bros (to whom Faces were signed) led
to delays in release of next album. Time was
filled in by **Sing It Again, Rod**, a compilation
set of old tracks which also included Stewart's
version of **Pinball Wizard** from Lou Reizner's
Rainbow Theatre stage presentation of Pete
Townshend's rock musical 'Tommy' in which
Stewart had appeared. Ever the ligger,
Stewart indulged in notorious boozing sessions with Elton John and other cohorts.

Issued late in 1974, Stewart's **Smiler**
album was disappointing. In December 1975
he announced he was leaving Faces to give
solo career more impetus. Debut Warner
Bros' album Tom Dowd-produced **Atlantic
Crossing**, recorded largely in Muscle Shoals,
Alabama (he had moved home base to
Hollywood), was good start. 1976 follow-up,
A Night On The Town, appeared on
manager Billy Gaff's Riva label (through
Warner Bros) and was hugely successful,
yielding three US chart-topping singles:
**Tonight's The Night, The Killing Of
Georgie** and **The First Cut Is The Deepest**.
The first equalled achievement of the Beatles'
Hey Jude in topping US charts for eight
weeks.

Sailing brought another UK No. 1 in
1979, but on personal front Stewart had
problems. He broke up long-standing but tempestuous relationship with Swedish actress
Britt Eckland amid much acrimony and
married Alana Hamilton.

Stewart seemed happier and more con-
fident as undisputed leader of own band
rather than as member of a group. Strutting in
front of classy but disciplined musicians like

**Below: Rod Stewart, a chart topping
artist from 1973 onwards, and one of
the biggest stars still active.**

Phillip Chenn (bass), Carmine Appice (drums) and Jim Cregan (guitar), he oozed extrovert showmanship and throughout subsequent line-up changes he has managed to maintain equilibrium. With his tight leopard-skin pants, spiky blond hair and emaciated yet sensual looks, he can rest assured that fans from the '70s to the '80s given a resounding yes to his recorded question **Do You Think I'm Sexy?**

Hit Singles:

	US	UK
Reason To Believe/Maggie May, 1971	—	19
Maggie May/Reason To Believe, 1971	1	1
You Wear It Well, 1972	13	1
Angel/What Made Milwaukee Famous, 1972	40	4
Oh No Not My Baby, 1973	59	6
Farewell/Bring It On Home To Me/ You Send Me, 1974	—	7
Sailing, 1975	58	1
This Ole Heart Of Mine, 1975	—	4
Tonight's The Night, 1976	1	5
The Killing of Georgie, 1976	30	2
Get Back, 1976	—	11
I Don't Want To Talk About It/ The First Cut Is The Deepest, 1977	21	1
You're In My Heart, 1977	4	3
Hotlegs/I Was Only Joking, 1978	28	5
Ole Ola (Muhler Brasileira), 1978	—	4
Do Ya Think I'm Sexy?, 1978	1	1
Ain't Love A Bitch, 1979	22	11
Passion, 1980	5	9
Tonight I'm Yours (Don't Hurt Me), 1981	—	8
Young Turks, 1981	5	11
Baby Jane, 1983	15	1

Best Of Rod Stewart, '70s hits from the highly adaptable 'Rod The Mod'. Courtesy Mercury Records.

Albums:
An Old Raincoat Won't Ever Let You Down (Vertigo), 1970*
Gasoline Alley (Mercury/Vertigo), 1970
Every Picture Tells A Story (Mercury), 1971
Never A Dull Moment (Mercury), 1972
Sing It Again, Rod (Mercury), 1973
Smiler (Mercury), 1974
Atlantic Crossing (Warner Bros/Riva), 1975
A Night On The Town (Warner Bros/Riva), 1976
Foot Loose & Fancy Free (Warner Bros/Riva), 1977
Best Of (Mercury), 1977†
Best of, Volume II (Mercury), 1977†
Blondes Have More Fun (Warner Bros/Riva), 1978
Greatest Hits (Warner Bros), 1979
Foolish Behaviour (Warner Bros/Riva), 1980
Tonight I'm Yours (Warner Bros/Riva), 1981
Rod The Mod (Accord), 1981
Maggie May (—/Contour), 1981
Absolutely Live (Warner Bros/Riva), 1982
Body Wishes (WEA), 1983
*Titled **Rod Stewart Album** aka **Thin** (Mercury) in US.
†Double compilations

Stiff Little Fingers
UK group formed 1977.
Original line-up: Jake Burns, guitar, vocals; Henry Cluney, guitar, vocals; Ali McMordie, bass; Brian Faloan, drums.

Career: Jake Burns had assembled SLF in Belfast, Northern Ireland, by November 1977, when they were seen by Daily Express reporter Gordon Ogilvie. He was impressed by their self-confidence and relative competence, considering level of experience, and encouraged Burns to write songs which took life in Ireland as their subject. **Suspect Device/Wasted Life** was pressed on private label.

Ogilive sent copy to BBC Radio One DJ John Peel who also was taken with SLF. Peel began playing the obscure single on his Rock Show and sales increased to point that independent label Rough Trade took over distribution.

Local fanzine, 'Alternative Ulster', asked SLF to write them free flexi-disc. Band did, but deal fell through, and Rough Trade was happy to release **Alternative Ulster/78 R.P.M.** as second single. Cut attracted enough attention for Tom Robinson(▶) to invite band on his autumn 1978 UK tour and for Rough Trade to ask for an LP's worth of material. **Inflammable Material** appeared in late 1978. Faloan decided to shift from Ireland to England was not for him and quit. Jim Reilly joined and appeared on last Rough Trade single, **Gotta Gettaway/ Bloody Sunday.**

Chrysalis Records offered better opportunity and SLF switched distribution again. **Nobody's Heroes** incorporated brash sound from first LP with new material indicating SLF was no longer bound by self-limiting subject matter. One single from LP, **At The Edge**, made UK Top 20. Live shows continued to be special events of energy and power. **Hanx** LP attempted to capture this and marks fitting conclusion to SLF's earlier period.

Go For It album signalled SLF's arrival as major talent. Singles continued to expand subject matter from 'the troubles' to more personal relationships as well as sound from abrasive to lyrical. Excellent example is **Listen** from **R.E.P. One Pound Ten Pence Or Less** EP which featured new drummer, Dolphin Taylor. Despite 'Top of the Pops' TV exposure, EP failed to score as deserved. **Now Then. . .** LP provided even stronger material than before. SLF looked set to gain

major success following strong reviews, but breakthrough never came.

Burns seemed more interested in other activities. (His appearance on BBC TV's 'Mike Read's Pop Quiz' show revealed photographic memory, active curiosity covering wide range of subjects and intelligence to pursue them.) In early 1983, announcement that Burns was leaving effectively ended group.

All The Best is superb collection of all SLF singles and essential to anyone following rock since 1976.

SLF were powerful, underrated outfit who matured from coarse, brash sound to high-energy melody. Not punk, not pop, they were hopeful group who could re-build bridges between many musical factions of '80s.

Final line-up: Burns; Cluney; McMordie; Dolphin Taylor, drums.

Hit Singles:

	US	UK
At The Edge, 1980	—	15

Albums:
Inflammable Material (—/Rough Trade), 1978
Nobody's Heroes (Chrysalis), 1980
Hanx (—/Chrysalis), 1980
Go For It (—/Chrysalis), 1981
Now Then. . . (—/Chrysalis), 1982
All The Best (—/Chrysalis), 1983

Stephen Stills
US guitarist, vocalist, songwriter. Born Dallas, Texas, January 3, 1945.

Career: Moved about Southern US as child, attending variety of schools, eventually entering University of Florida. After playing part-time in local folk circles, Stills quit college and moved to New York for its reputed folk scene. Perceiving changing musical climate, he left for Los Angeles. After several projects (one of which was to fail audition for Monkees(▶)), he helped found Buffalo Springfield(▶). Stills wrote band's major hit, **For What It's Worth.**

Following Buffalo's demise, Stills recorded **Supersession** with Al Kooper(▶) and Mike Bloomfield(▶), toured with girlfriend Judy Collins(▶), played on one of her albums and did sessions for Joni Mitchell(▶).

End of 1968 brought announcement of Crosby, Stills and Nash(▶) supergroup (CSN). Still's ode to Judy Collins became their first hit, **Suite: Judy Blue Eyes.** When CSN reunited Stills with old Buffalo Springfield mate Neil Young(▶), band became top heavy

with egos, and Stills began working on first solo LP, recorded while he was living in London. Stills employed number of major musicians, including Jimi Hendrix(▶), who died before album's release; LP was dedicated to him. Second solo album used CSN&Y sidemen whom Stills organised into loose confederation he called Manassas. After two releases, part of band left with Chris Hillman who was to form Souther-Hillman-Furay Band.

Stills reorganised back-up band but broke off activity for 1974 CSN&Y reunion tour. Since then Stills has released several LPs, most notable being joint venture with Neil Young as Stills-Young Band. He has also rejoined CSN, whenever that happens along, but of late his influence is diminishing as '60s recede.

Hit Singles:

	US	UK
Love The One You're With, 1971	14	37

Albums:
Stephen Stills (Atlantic), 1970
Stephen Stills II (Atlantic), 1971
Stills (Columbia/CBS), 1975
Stlls Live (Atlantic), 1976
Illegal Stills (Columbia/CBS), 1976
The Best Of Stephen Stills (Atlantic), 1976
Long May You Run (with Stills-Young Band) (Reprise), 1976
Thoroughfare Gap (Columbia/CBS), 1978

Manassas:
Manassas (Atlantic), 1975
Down The Road (Atlantic), 1973

Worth Searching Out:
Supersession (with Al Kooper and Mike Bloomfield) (Columbia/CBS), 1968

The Stranglers
UK group formed 1975.
Original/Current line-up: Hugh Cornwell, vocals, Fender Telecaster guitar; Jean-Jacques Burnel, vocals, bass; Dave Greenfield, keyboards; Jet Black, drums.

Career: Following formation in village near Guildford, Surrey, supported Patti Smith(▶) on 1975 UK tour. During 1976 played more than 200 gigs, mainly around London, and built up reputation as powerful live act. Benefited from interest in 'new wave' despite having little in common with punk outfits.

Two years hard work paid off with release of first album **Rattus Norvegicus**, which leapt to No. 4 in UK charts. Simultaneously, single **Peaches/Go Buddy Go** reached No. 8 in singles charts.

Winning streak continued throughout 1977 and 1978, but from 1979 to beginning of 1981 band seemed to slip from limelight somewhat. Had no major singles success during this time, but continued touring regularly. Low point came when, following series of legal wrangles, band was imprisoned in Nice, France.

Although successful within their field, band seemed destined to remain something of unknown quantity to average record buyer. Some were already beginning to dismiss Stranglers as 'punk revivalists' when band bounced back in 1981 with two major albums, **The Meninblack** and **La Folie**. More surprising was single from **La Folie, Golden Brown**. In contrast to tough black leather visual image and usual output it was gentle, floating summery waltz that appealed to many who had never before bought Stranglers records. Single was huge hit all over world;

Left: The Stranglers (from left) Dave Greenfield, Jet Black, Jean-Jacques Burnel, Hugh Cornwell.

few months later band followed with almost as succesful **Strange Little Girl** single.

Always unpredictable, Stranglers have potential to become one of '80s biggest acts; however, US has as yet largely resisted their charms. Tendency toward naive political philosophising and often churlish attitude towards media do not help band's cause, but basics of talent and originality are much in evidence.

Hit Singles:	US	UK
Peaches/Go Buddy Go, 1977	—	8
Something Better Change/ Straighten Out, 1977	—	9
No More Heroes, 1977	—	8
Five Minutes, 1978	—	11
Nice 'n' Sleazy, 1978	—	18
Duchess, 1979	—	14
Golden Brown, 1982	—	2
Strange Little Girl, 1982	—	7

Albums:
Rattus Norvegicus (A&M/United Artists), 1977
No More Heroes (A&M/United Artists), 1977
Black And White (A&M/United Artists), 1978
Live (X Cert) (A&M/United Artists), 1979
The Raven (A&M/United Artists), 1979
The Meninblack (EMI), 1981
La Folie (EMI), 1981
The Collection 1977-1982 (—/Liberty), 1982
Feline (Epic), 1983

Feline, The Stranglers. Courtesy Epic Records.

Strawbs

UK group formed 1967.

Original line-up: Dave Cousins, vocals, guitar, banjo, dulcimer; Tony Hooper, guitar, vocals; Arthur Philips, mandolin.

Career: Originally called Strawberry Hill Boys (after the London suburb where they rehearsed), Strawbs were brainchild of folkie Dave Cousins. Playing mixture of folk and bluegrass, band gigged around folk clubs in late '60s and underwent series of personnel changes. Mandolin player Philips left, while Ron Chesterman joined on bass. Rated folk singer and writer Sandy Denny also joined for a while, but had left to join folk-rockers Fairport Convention(▶) by time Strawbs signed with A&M in 1969.

Strawbs, the band's first A&M album, was released in 1969 to considerable acclaim in folk circles, but **Dragonfly** (1970) failed to consolidate its impact. In move away from folk orientation, Cousins virtually re-formed the band. Hooper stayed, but John Ford replaced Chesterman on bass and Richard Hudson joined on drums. Most significantly, ex-Royal College of Music graduate Rick Wakeman(▶) who had contributed to **Dragonfly**, joined on keyboards.

Just A Collection Of Antiques And Curios (1970) and **From The Witchwood**

(1971) saw critical attention being focused on Wakeman, and he quite to join Yes(▶). His replacement was Blue Weaver, formerly of Amen Corner.

Although tensions had begun to build up within band over course of 1971, Strawbs enjoyed their greatest success the next year in 1972. **Grave New World**, a powerful mixture of folk, classical and rock influences, became their biggest-selling album, and band started to present themselves more as rock band on stage, using lights, back projection and other effects. Tony Hooper, dismayed by band's move away from folk roots, left to be replaced by another former folkie, Dave Lambert. Late 1972 saw chart success with single **Lay Down**, and in January 1973 band made No.2 in UK charts with **Part Of The Union**, a satirical semi-novelty song, though Strawbs remained obscure in US.

However, the next few years were bedevilled by lack of direction and multiple personnel changes. Band's appeal waned. **Deadlines**, released on Arista in 1978, was Strawbs' swansong. Dave Cousins returned to more folk-orientated style for 1979 solo release **Old School Songs**, but little has been heard of him since.

Although they never looked like a long-term proposition, Strawbs were one of the '70s more interesting folk-rock aggregations, largely due to the original talent of Cousins.

Final line-up: Cousins, Rod Coombes, drums; Dave Lambert, guitar, vocals; Chas Cronk, bass.

Hit Singles:	US	UK
Lay Down, 1972	—	12
Part Of The Union, 1973	—	2

Albums:
Dragonfly (A&M), 1970
Just A Collection Of Antiques And Curios (A&M), 1970
From The Witchwood (A&M), 1971
Grave New World (A&M), 1972
Bursting At The Seams (A&M), 1973
Hero And Heroine (A&M), 1974
By Choice (A&M), 1974
Ghosts (A&M), 1975
Nomadness (A&M), 1976
Burning For You (Oyster), 1977
Deadlines (Arista), 1978
Best Of (A&M), 1978

Above: The Stray Cats with Brian Setzer (centre).

Stray Cats

US group formed 1980.

Original/Current line-up: Brian Setzer, guitar, vocals; Lee Rocker, bass; Slim Jim Phantom, drums.

Career: Teenage New Yorker Setzer, ex-Bloodless Pharaohs, recruited fellow New Yorker Rocker on upright bass and Phantom on minimal drum kit to play rockabilly. With manager Tony Bidgood came to London in summer 1980. Although penniless, initial UK gigs caused great excitement, and group were signed by Arista before end of 1980. Experienced acclaimed rock 'n' roller Dave Edmunds(▶) produced first LP, **Stray Cats**, which not only went gold all over Europe, but also spawned three UK Top 10 hits, **Runaway Boys**, **Rock This Town** and **Stray Cat Strut**.

After highly successful 1981, released second LP **Gonna Ball**, produced by band and Hein Hovan, but both LP and extracted singles vanished almost without trace. At this point, group had no releases in US, but in mid-1982, they were signed for US by EMI-America. Remained on Arista in UK. In US, compilation LP **Built For Speed**, with most of first LP plus some of second, took off in summer 1982, and reached No. 2 in US LP chart, while **Rock This Town** made Top 10 in singles chart. Meanwhile, group returned to Dave Edmunds to produce third LP, completed before end of 1982. Release delayed because of success of **Built For Speed**. Having established highly commercial sound with first album, group apparently decided to forego supervision for follow-up; reports indicate that third LP will be in same mould as debut, and group's standing in US should make it great success.

Hit Singles:	US	UK
Runaway Boys, 1980	—	9
Rock This Town, 1981	9	9
Stray Cat Strut, 1981	3	11

Albums:
Stray Cats (—/Arista), 1981
Gonna Ball (—/Arista), 1982
Built For Speed (EMI/—), 1982
Rant 'n' Rave (EMI/Arista), 1983

Barbra Streisand

US vocalist, actress.
Born Barbara Joan Streisand, Brooklyn, New York, April 24, 1942.

Career: Worked as switchboard operator and theatre usherette before winning talent competition in Greenwich Village night club. Played cabaret circuit before joining an off-Broadway revue. Made Broadway debut in 1962 in 'I Can Get It For You Wholesale' playing Yetta Tessye Marmel Stein opposite Elliot Gould whom she later married (and later divorced). Barbra stole show with her singing and clowning, winning New York critics' award and becoming star overnight.

In 1964 she played/sang role of Fanny Bryce in Broadway musical 'Funny Girl'. Same year signed multi-million dollar recording contract with Columbia. Soon had first hit record with **People**.

Film debut was 1968 film version of 'Funny Girl'; tied with Katherine Hepburn for an Academy Award as Best Actress.

In 1977 Streisand won an Oscar for her music for song **Evergreen** (co-written with Paul Williams) featured in re-make of movie 'A Star Is Born' in which she starred as a rock singer, opposite Kris Kristofferson(▶).

Other notable movie appearances have included 'Hello Dolly' (with Louis Armstrong), 'The Owl And The Pussycat' (with George Segal), 'What's Up Doc' and 'The Main Event' (with Ryan O'Neill), 'The Way We Were' (starring Robert Redford and for which she sang the US chart-topping title song) and 'Funny Lady'.

Her first venture out of world of MOR and showbiz music was in 1970 when she entered Top 10 with her version of Laura Nyro's **Stoney End**. In late '70s she had hit single with **No More Tears/Enough Is Enough**, a duet with Donna Summer(▶), Barry Gibb produced her in rock/pop vein on **Guilty** LP, which gave her three hit singles.

In 1976 she entered classical music world with album of Leider and classical art songs which outraged critics but sold a million.

Now active in production, she has devoted past year or so to film version of 'Yentl'.

Hit Singles:	US	UK
People, 1964	5	—
Second Hand Rose, 1966	32	14
Stoney End, 1971	6	27
The Way We Were, 1974	1	31
Love Theme From A Star Is Born (Evergreen), 1977	1	3
My Heart Belongs To Me, 1977	1	—
The Main Event/Fight, 1979	3	—
Woman In Love, 1980	1	1
Comin' In And Out Of Your Life, 1981	11	—
With Neil Diamond:		
You Don't Bring Me Flowers, 1978	1	5
With Donna Summer:		
No More Tears (Enough Is Enough), 1979	1	3
With Barry Gibb		
Guilty, 1980	3	34
What Kind Of Fool, 1981	10	—

Albums (selected):
My Name Is Barbra (Columbia/Embassy), 1964
Simply Streisand (Columbia/CBS), 1967
Greatest Hits (Columbia/CBS), 1969
Stoney End (Columbia/CBS), 1971
The Way We Were (Columbia/CBS), 1974
Greatest Hits Vol. II (Columbia/CBS), 1979
Guilty (Columbia/CBS), 1980*
Memories (Columbia/CBS), 1981
*With Barry Gibb

Styx

US group formed 1970.

Original line-up: Chuck Panozzo, bass; John Panozzo, drums; Denis de Young, keyboards; John Curulewski, guitar; James Young, guitar.

Career: The Panozzos played in garage bands with neighbour de Young as far back as 1963. By 1968 above line-up had established local Chicago reputation as Tradewinds.

In 1970 they signed with small Wooden Nickel label. By 1974 they had recorded four LPs, none of which was successful. In mid-'70s, **Lady** was picked up by US radio from second LP. Styx back catalogue made belated sales. Curulewski left after fifth album **Equinox,** and Tommy Shaw took over lead vocals.

Styx seemed to represent typical US faceless rock; becoming purveyors of the worst traits of '70s music. **Crystal Ball,** and then 1977's **The Grand Illusion,** were huge sellers. Subsequent LPs became ever more grandiose, ever more popular, and ever more the same.

Styx are presently as contrived and as smooth as ever, and still as successful. Who buys these records?

Current line-up: C. Panozzo; J. Panozzo; de Young; Young; Tommy Shaw, vocals.

Hit Singles:	US	UK
Lady, 1975	6	—
Come Sail Away, 1978	8	—
Renegade, 1979	16	—
Babe, 1979	1	6
The Best Of Times, 1981	3	42
Too Much Time On My Hands, 1981	9	—
Mr. Roboto, 1983	7	—

Albums:
Styx I (RCA), 1972
Lady Styx II (RCA), 1973
The Serpent Is Rising (RCA/—), 1973
Man Of Miracles (RCA/—), 1974
Equinox (A&M), 1975
Crystal Ball (A&M), 1976
The Grand Illusion (A&M), 1977
Pieces Of Eight (A&M), 1978
Cornerstone (A&M), 1979
Best Of Styx (RCA), 1979
Paradise Theater (A&M), 1980
Kilroy Was Here (A&M), 1983

Donna Summer

US vocalist, composer.
Born Boston, Massachusetts, September, 1950.

Career: Dropped out of high school to pursue ambition to become singer. Joined rock group and played small-time gigs around Boston.

Above: Styx, monsters in America, but still almost unknown in Britain.

Eventually moved to New York, auditioning for part in Broadway production of 'Hair'. Instead was offered part in German version of show and moved to Germany. Roles in several European productions followed, and Summer settled in Mannheim.

In 1975 started recording with Oasis Records producers Giorgio Moroder and Pete Belotte. Result was disco-sex epic **Love To Love You Baby,** a repetitive electronic-orientated single that united quasi-orgasmic moans and groans with metronomic disco beat. Picked up by Casablanca in US, single became enormous worldwide hit, despite protests from various moralist groups.

Greatly helped by astute business and musical sense of Moroder and Belotte, Summer quickly became acknowledged Queen of '70s disco, releasing series of singles and albums that combined memorable melodies, robotic rhythms and sensual lyrics.

Love To Love You Baby, Donna Summer. Courtesy Oasis/Casablanca Records.

Perhaps surprisingly, in late '70s Summer began to show she was not simply disco puppet. Records revealed more maturity, and 1979 duet with Barbra Streisand(▶), **No More Tears (Enough Is Enough),** matched her with vocal talents of Streisand.

In 1980 Summer signed with Geffen and entered new phase: recorded more of her own material, and became devout Christian, dropping overtly sexual image. Her **State Of Independence** was widely reckoned to be one of best singles of 1982, and at time of writing future looks bright. Avowed intention of becoming all-round enterainer seems more than likely to bear fruit. 1983 single **She Works Hard For The Money** made US Top 10.

Hit Singles:	US	UK
Love To Love You Baby, 1975	2	4
I Feel Love, 1977	6	1
Down Deep Inside (Theme from The Deep), 1977	—	5
I Remember Yesterday, 1977	—	14
Love's Unkind, 1977	—	3
I Love You, 1977	37	10
Rumour Has It, 1978	53	19
Last Dance, 1978	3	51
MacArthur Park, 1978	1	5
Heaven Knows, 1979	4	34
Hot Stuff, 1979	1	11
Bad Girls, 1979	1	14
Dim All The Lights, 1979	2	29
On The Radio, 1980	5	32
The Wanderer, 1980	3	48
Love Is In Control (Finger On The Trigger), 1982	10	18
State Of Independence, 1982	41	14
I Feel Love, 1982	—	22
She Works Hard For The Money, 1983	10	25

With Barbra Streisand:

No More Tears (Enough Is Enough), 1979	1	3

Albums:
Love To Love You Baby (Oasis/Casablanca), 1975
A Trilogy Of Love (Casablanca), 1977
Four Seasons Of Love (Casablanca), 1977
I Remember Yesterday (Casablanca/Embassy), 1979
The Deep (Casablanca), 1977
Once Upon A Time (Casablanca), 1977
Shutout (with Paul Jabara) (Casablanca), 1977
Live And More (Casablanca), 1978
Bad Girls (Casablanca), 1979
On The Radio (Casablanca), 1979
The Wanderer (Geffen), 1980
Walk Away (Casablanca), 1980
Greatest Hits Volume 1 (Casablanca), 1980
Greatest Hits Volume 2 (Casablanca), 1980
Donna Summer (Geffen), 1982

Supertramp

UK group formed 1969.

Original line-up: Roger Hodgson, vocals, bass, keyboards; Richard Davies, vocals, keyboards; Dave Winthrop, reeds; Richard Palmer, guitar; Bob Miller, drums.

Career: Hodgson and Davies formed band with aid of wealthy benefactor and convinced A&M to take chance on recording them. A&M wasn't particularly impressed with first effort and didn't release it in US. Miller left and was replaced by Kevin Currie. Frank Farrell joined on bass to allow Hodgson's move to guitar on second album. Band broke up after LP failed to dent charts and Scandinavian tour met with indifferent audiences.

Hodgson and Davies regrouped with Doug-las Thompson on bass and John Anthony Helliwell on reeds (both ex-members of Alan Brown set). Bob Benberg (ex-Bees Make Honey) took over drums. Using production talents of Ken Scott, band recorded million-selling **Crime Of The Century**.

After two more albums, band moved to US—hence title of next LP, **Breakfast In America**. Group began enjoying singles success and settled in as major concert draw. However, despite megastar success, individuals in group shun publicity. Supertramp has retreated into irregular LP/tour schedule.

Spring 1983 brought announcement that band would tour homeland UK in summer 1983, before splitting permanently.

Current/Final line-up: Davies; Douglas Thompson, bass; John Helliwell; Bob Benberg, drums.

Hit Singles:	US	UK
Dreamer, 1975	—	13
Give A Little Bit, 1977	15	29
The Logical Song, 1979	6	7
Goodbye Stranger, 1979	15	—
Take The Long Way Home, 1979	10	—
Breakfast In America, 1979	—	9
Dreamer, 1980	—	15
It's Raining Again, 1983	11	26

Albums:
Supertramp (A&M), 1970
Indelibly Stamped (A&M), 1971
Crime Of The Century (A&M), 1974
Crisis? What Crisis? (A&M), 1975
Even In The Quietest Moments (A&M), 1977
Breakfast In America (A&M), 1979
Paris (A&M), 1980
...Famous Last Words (A&M), 1982

...Famous Last Words, Supertramp. Courtesy A&M Records.

Below: Supertramp model the bearded millionaire look.

The Supremes

US vocal group formed 1959.

Original line-up: Diana Ross; Mary Wilson; Florence Ballard; Barbara Martin.

Career: Originally known as Primettes, formed by Mary Wilson, Florence Ballard, Diane (Diana) Ross(▶) and Betty Anderson in Detroit. Anderson quickly replaced by Barbara Martin. Group did local gigs with male group the Primes (later the Temptations(▶)) and recorded for Lupine without great success.

In 1960 they came to attention of emerging local entrepreneur Berry Gordy, who signed them to Tamla Motown. Over the next few years group acted as back-up singers and recorded handful of moderately successful singles. Barbara Martin dropped out in 1962 and group carried on as trio.

Turning-point came when Gordy assigned writing/production team Holland/Dozier/Holland(▶) to group in 1963; **Where Did Our Love Go** became US No. 1 and massive worldwide hit in 1964. Next three years saw trio become most successful female vocal group in pop history, with slew of international chart-toppers.

From 1966 group was billed as Diana Ross and the Supremes, Gordy already singling out Ross as potential solo superstar. Florence Ballard left to pursue unsuccessful solo career (ending in untimely death of heart attack in 1976). Replacement was Cindy Birdsong, formerly of Patti LaBelle and the Bluebelles. Hits continued, although not on such a massive scale, until Diana Ross left group in 1969 to achieve superstardom. Between 1964 and 1969 group had notched up 12 No. 1 hits.

Although Ross' departure (she was replaced by Jean Terrell) was expected to deal mortal blow to group's success, more major hits were forthcoming, starting with **Up The Ladder To The Roof** in 1970. Couplings with Temptations and Four Tops(▶) also helped keep Supremes at forefront during this period.

After 1972 group began to look slightly old-fashioned against new, more militant stance of black music; it also suffered from personnel changes. Mary Wilson continued to tour and record with various line-ups until 1977 when group broke up. Wilson pursued as yet not particularly successful solo career.

Supremes' '60s output with Holland/Dozier/Holland ranks among finest pop music ever. They were also influential in making black music a major international force, combining glamour, real talent and touch of soul hitherto missing from female vocal line-ups.

Final line-up: Mary Wilson; Cindy Birdsong; Jean Terrell.

Hit Singles:	US	UK
Where Did Our Love Go, 1964	1	3
Baby Love, 1964	1	1
Come See About Me, 1964	1	27
Stop! In The Name Of Love, 1965	1	7
Back In My Arms Again, 1965	1	40
Nothing But Heartaches, 1965	11	—
I Hear A Symphony, 1965	1	39
My World Is Empty Without You, 1966	5	—
Love Is Like An Itching In My Heart, 1966	9	—
You Can't Hurry Love, 1966	1	3
You Keep Me Hangin' On, 1966	1	8
Love Is Here And Now You're Gone, 1967	1	17
The Happening, 1967	1	6
Reflections, 1967	2	5
In And Out Of Love, 1967	9	13
Love Child, 1968	1	15
I'm Livin' In Shame, 1969	10	14
Some Day We'll Be Together, 1969	1	13
Up The Ladder To The Roof, 1970	10	6
Stoned Love, 1970	7	3
Nathan Jones, 1971	16	5
Floy Joy, 1972	16	9
Automatically Sunshine, 1972	37	10
Baby Love, 1974	—	12

With The Four Tops

River Deep Mountain High, 1971	14	4

With The Temptations:

I'm Gonna Make You Love Me, 1969	11	3
I Second That Emotion, 1969	—	18

Albums:
Live At The Talk Of The Town (Motown), 1968
Greatest Hits (Motown), 1968
Love Child (Motown), 1969
Greatest Hits Volume 2 (Motown), 1970
Baby Love (—/MFP), 1973
Anthology (Motown), 1974
At Their Best (Motown), 1978
Stoned Love (—/MFP), 1979
Greatest Hits (featuring Mary Wilson) (Motown), 1981
Motown Superstars Series Volume 1 (Motown/—), 1982

With The Temptations:
TCB (Motown), 1969

With The Four Tops:
The Magnificent Seven (Motown), 1971

Talking Heads

US group formed 1976.

Original/Current line-up: David Byrne, vocals, guitar; Chris Frantz, drums; Tina Weymouth, vocals, bass, synthesiser; Jerry Harrison, vocals, guitar, keyboards.

Career: Byrne, Frantz and Weymouth met at Rhode Island School of Design in early '70s. Trio began working, living, and then playing music together. In 1976 they decided to expand line-up and asked ex-Modern Lovers Harrison to join. Harrison had grave doubts about any further involvement with music business and had applied for graduate school, but later agreed to join provided he could finish semester.

Band cashed in on Sire Records' search for 'new wave' groups and recorded **Talking Heads: 77**. Upon release it was clear Heads didn't fit into neat category. (Interestingly, Sire's other new wave groups, such as Dead Boys, also failed.)

Next album, **More Songs About Buildings And Food**, may have overloaded on ideas Byrne picked up while studying design (cover was modern mosaic of band made up of polaroid prints), but it also contained music which moved mind and soul. Single **Take Me To The River** earned heavy radio play and opened up audience. Band had become intellectual favourites. **Fear Of Music** LP was instant critical success and won notice in UK.

Band members became involved in variety of private projects. Byrne worked on albums with Brian Eno(▶), Harrison released solo LP. Weymouth/Frantz enjoyed considerable outside success with Tom Tom Club(▶).

This activity alone could have caused a delay before next release, but **Remain In Light** was soon out, and went beyond sparse sound of previous LPs. **Light** explored African rhythms, added side group of music-

ians, and generally destroyed any possible preconceptions about band. Supporting tour included expanded line-up so that audiences could hear new efforts. Band emphasised change by including live material going back to early days as well as new material for LP, **The Name Of This Band Is Talking Heads.**

One of few new bands content to let their music be predominant feature, Talking Heads should continue to produce innovative music.

Hit Singles:	US	UK
Once In A Lifetime, 1981	—	14

Albums:
Talking Heads: 77 (Sire), 1977
More Songs About Buildings And Food (Sire), 1978
Fear Of Music (Sire), 1979
Remain In Light (Sire), 1980
The Name Of This Band Is Talking Heads (Sire), 1982
Speaking With Tongues (Sire), 1983

James Taylor

US vocalist, composer, guitarist.
Born Boston, Massachusetts, March 12, 1948.

Career: Taylor's mother passed her interest in music on to her children—thus Taylor's decision to try musical career following high school. In 1967 he recorded some tapes with friend Danny Kortchmar in New York as the Flying Machine. He moved to Notting Hill area of London and passed demos of his work to new Beatles company, Apple Ltd. **James Taylor** was released and ignored, though it included his excellent **Carolina In My Mind**.

Mud Slide Slim, James Taylor. Courtesy Warner Bros Records.

With Apple falling into disarray, Taylor returned to US. After bouts of depression, and another round of mental institutions (his first had been while still in high school), with support of producer Peter Asher (Linda Ronstadt(▶)), he finally signed with Warner Bros. Taylor's painful expression, deep introspection and laid-back delivery began selling

Above: Talking Heads in concert, with group leader David Byrne (foreground) partly obscuring Jerry Harrison.

well. **You've Got A Friend** single reached No.1 in US and his popularity peaked in 1972. In 1973 he married Carly Simon(▶) (they divorced in late '70s). He branched out and encouraged siblings Livingston and Kate Taylor in their musical careers.

By 1976 Eagles(▶) and Linda Ronstandt pre-empted Taylor's easy-listening style and he began experimenting with more rock-orientated material. Despite mid-'70s success, Taylor hasn't weathered well. Along with Melanie(▶) and Donovan(▶), Taylor's personal baring of his soul now seems sentimental, even mawkish.

Hit Singles:	US	UK
Fire And Rain, 1970	3	42
You've Got A Friend, 1971	1	4
Don't Let Me Be Lonely Tonight, 1973	14	—
Mockingbird (with Carly Simon), 1974	5	34
How Sweet It Is, 1975	5	—
Handy Man, 1977	4	—
Your Smiling Face, 1977	20	—
(What A) Wonderful World, 1978	17	—

Albums:
James Taylor (Apple), 1968
Sweet Baby James* (Warner Bros), 1970
James Taylor & The Original Flying Machine (Springboard/DJM), 1971
Mud Slide Slim* (Warner Bros), 1971
One Man Dog (Warner Bros), 1972
Walking Man (Warner Bros), 1974
Rainy Day Man (Trip/DJM), 1975
Gorilla (Warner Bros), 1975
In The Pocket (Warner Bros), 1976
The Best Of James Taylor (Warner Bros), 1976
J.T. (Columbia/CBS), 1977
Greatest Hits (Warner Bros), 1977
Flag (Columbia/CBS), 1979
Dad Loves His Work (Columbia/CBS), 1981

*Released as double album, UK only, 1975

Below: James Taylor, an anachronism in 1983, but a major star of the '70s.

The Teardrop Explodes

UK group formed 1978.

Original line-up: Julian Cope, bass, vocals; Paul Simpson, guitar; Mike Finkler, guitar; Gary Dwyer, drums.

Career: Welsh-born Cope, at college in Liverpool, formed the Crucial Three in 1977 with Ian McCulloch and Pete Wylie. By end of 1978, McCulloch had left to form Echo & the Bunnymen(▶), and Wylie to form Wah!Heat (later simply Wah!). Cope then formed Teardrop Explodes (name taken from a DC comic) with Simpson, guitarist Pete Johnson, who soon left to be replaced by Finkler, and Dwyer.

After first gig in November 1978, recorded **debut single Sleeping Gas** for Zoo, a just-formed local independent label. March 1979 saw Simpson replaced by Dave Balfe, co-director of Zoo. Second single **Bouncing Babies** released in mid-1979, by which time group was gaining recognition as leading light of 'new Merseybeat' phenomenon (although music more inclined to '60s US West Coast style).

Third single **Treason**, released early 1980, met huge critical success, but soon after Finkler left, replaced by Alan Gill (ex-Dalek I). Group played New York to great acclaim, signed with major label (Mercury) for first LP **Kilimanjaro**, released October 1980. After single tour, Balfe and Gill quit.

Cope and Dwyer recruited new band — Troy Tate, guitar; Jeff Hammer, keyboards; Alfie Agius (ex-Interview), bass; Cope took over as vocalist/guitarist. **Reward**, single made before line-up change, was first Top 10 hit in early 1981, followed by four smaller hits, plus second LP **Wilder**, released end of year. Cope had become neo-teen idol, but decided to split band during latter half of 1982. Faithful Dwyer apparently remains with him, but future plans for Cope are uncertain.

Final line-up: Cope; Dwyer; session musicians.

Hit Singles:	US	UK
Reward, 1981	—	6
Treason, 1981	—	18

Albums:
Kilimanjaro (Mercury), 1980
Wilder (Mercury), 1981

The Temptations

US vocal group formed 1961.

Original line-up: Otis Williams; Melvin Franklin; Eldridge Bryant; Eddie Kendricks; Paul Williams.

Career: Formed in Detroit in 1961 from amalgam of elements from Otis Williams and the Distants (Otis Williams, Franklin, Bryant) and the Primes (Kendricks, Paul Williams). Temptations were recording for Tamla Motown a year later but it was not until David Ruffin replaced Bryant in 1963 (his brother Jimmy Ruffin had been offered job but declined) that breakthrough came. The contrast between lead vocals of Kendricks — high, sweet and soft — and Ruffin — gritty and emotion-laden — provided formula for success; thanks were also due to young songwriter/producer Smokey Robinson(▶).

The Robinson-penned, Kendricks-led **The Way You Do The Things You Do** gave them 1963 hit. Two years later, with Ruffin singing lead, **My Girl** brought them to forefront

among black vocal groups, overtaking Curtis Mayfield's Impressions(▶) in mass popularity.

In 1966 group started working with writer/producer Norman Whitfield who exploited more biting version of Motown sound with ballsy **Ain't Too Proud To Beg, I Know (I'm Losing You)** and others, counter-balanced by some smooth ballad efforts.

After Ruffin split for solo career, Dennis Edwards was brought in from the Contours and Whitfield took opportunity to push Temptations in new musical direction. So-called 'psychedelic soul' style evolved, with dramatic use of recording effects and rock-influenced arrangements which made **Cloud Nine, Runaway Child, Running Wild, Can't Get Next To You, Psychedelic Shack** and **Ball Of Confusion** such totally distinctive hits.

A return to soft balladry saw **Just My Imagination** earn Temptations first platinum single award, and marked last appearance of solo-bound Kendricks; now seriously ill, Paul Williams also left (he died soon after). Their replacements were Damon Harris (the Vandals) and Richard Street (the Monitors).

Further Whitfield-produced progressive soul hits came with **Superstar, Take A Look Around, Papa Was A Rolling Stone** and the monumental **Masterpiece** album.

Following departure of Harris (replaced by Glenn Leonard in 1975) and Edwards (in 1979), group seemed to lose much of its fire. Whitfield having moved on to mastermind Undisputed Truth, then Rose Royce, plus his own label, Temptations' subsequent work lacked sense of direction.

After unsuccessful stint with Atlantic, Temptations returned to home base in 1980, recording **Power** album for Motown with Dennis Edwards back as lead singer. But, despite recent efforts, group have failed to regain earlier stature; live shows retain slick presentation and dazzling choreography.

Current line-up: Franklin; Dennis Edwards; Glen Edwards; Richard Street.

Hit Singles:	US	UK
The Way You Do The Things You Do, 1964	11	—
My Girl, 1965	1	43
It's Growing, 1965	18	45
Since I Lost My Baby, 1965	17	—
My Baby, 1965	13	—
Ain't Too Proud To Beg, 1966	13	21
Beauty Is Only Skin Deep, 1966	3	18
(I Know) I'm Losing You, 1966	8	19
All I Need, 1967	8	—
You're My Everything, 1967	6	26
(Loneliness Made Me Realise) It's You That I Need, 1967	14	—
I Wish It Would Rain, 1968	4	45
I Could Never Love Another (After Loving You), 1968	13	47
Cloud Nine, 1968	6	15
Run Away Child, Running Wild, 1969	6	—
Get Ready, 1969*	29	10
Don't Let The Joneses Get You Down, 1969	20	—
I Can't Get Next To You, 1969	1	13
Psychedelic Shack, 1970	7	33
Ball Of Confusion (That's The World Is Today), 1970	3	7
Just My Imagination (Running Away With Me), 1971	1	8
Superstar (Remember How You Got Where You Are), 1971	18	32
Take A Look Around, 1972	30	13
Papa Was A Rollin' Stone, 1972	1	14
Masterpiece, 1973	7	—
*In 1966, US		

With Diana Ross and Supremes:

	US	UK
I'm Gonna Make You Love Me, 1969	2	3
I Second That Emotion, 1969	—	18

Albums:
Greatest Hits (Gordy/Motown), 1967
Cloud Nine (Gordy/Motown), 1969
Psychedelic Shack (Gordy/Motown), 1970
Puzzle People (Gordy/Motown), 1970
Greatest Hits Volume II (Gordy/Motown), 1972
All Directions (Gordy/Motown), 1972
Masterpiece (Gordy/Motown), 1973
Anthology (Motown), 1977
Temptations (—/Motown), 1977
Sing Smokey (—/Motown), 1979
Power (Gordy/Motown), 1980
20 Golden Greats (—/Motown), 1980
Reunion (Gordy/—), 1981
All The Million Sellers (Gordy/Motown), 1982
Get Ready (—/Pickwick), 1982
Give Love At Christmas (—/Motown), 1982
Surface Thrills (Motown), 1983

With The Supremes:
TCB (Tamla Motown), 1969

10 cc

UK group formed 1972.

Original line-up: Eric Stewart, guitar, vocals; Graham Gouldman, bass, vocals; Lol Creme, guitar, vocals; Kevin Godley, drums, vocals.

Career: In June 1970, Stewart, Creme and Godley had worldwide hit as Hotlegs with **Neanderthal Man**. Godley and Creme had first met at art school; Stewart had been in the Mindbenders (who had 1966 UK Top 5 hit with **Groovy Kind Of Love**). Graham Gouldman, another Mindbenders, joined Hotlegs for 1970 UK tour supporting Moody Blues(▶);

Sheet Music, 10cc. Courtesy Mercury Records.

wrote Yardbirds(▶) hit **For Your Love**. Stewart had set up Strawberry Studios in Stockport, Cheshire, and in 1971 Neil Sedaka(▶) recorded his comeback album **Solitaire** there with Stewart, Gouldman, Godley and Creme. Returned following year to cut **The Tra La Days Are Over** (Gouldman had met Sedaka while working as songwriter for Kasenatz-Katz organisation in New York's Brill Building).

Godley and Creme came up with **Donna**, a clever parody (as much of their work is) of US '50s hits, and took song to Jonathan King who released it on his new UK label, King, changing band's name to 10 cc. Record made No. 2. First chart-topper **Rubber Bullets** scored in 1973.

Following debut album **10 cc**, band played first live gigs at Douglas, Isle Of Man, in August 1973, adding Paul Burgess on drums; toured US twice in 1974.

Switching to Phonogram early in 1975 for third album, **The Original Soundtrack**, group continued run of hits; peaked creatively with classic single **I'm Not In Love.**

After guesting with Rolling Stones(▶) at Knebworth in August 1976, band was depleted in October when Godley and Creme

10cc (debut LP with Rubber Bullets). Courtesy UK Records.

decided to leave for subsequently successful career as duo.

With Stewart and Gouldman now firmly in control of creative aspect, Stuart Tosh, Rick Fenn and Tony O'Malley joined 10 cc in April 1977, debuting on May UK tour. Duncan Mackay was added 10 months later.

Group's planned Japan/Australia tour was cancelled after motorcycle accident to Gouldman in Japan. He was soon back in action writing and recording score for that year's 'Animalympics' movie and title song for movie 'Sunburn'. Stewart produced Sad Cafe's(▶) second album as well as songs for French movie 'Girls'; recorded own solo album in 1981. Further outside production work came for Gouldman with the Ramones and Gilbert O'Sullivan in 1981.

Despite loss of Godley and Creme's highly imaginative writing talents (they now make videos for several big acts), Stewart and Gouldman proved capable of maintaining 10 cc's reputation as entertaining, satirical pop/rock band.

Current line-up: Stewart; Gouldman; Stuart Tosh, drums; Rick Fenn, guitar; Tony O'Malley, keyboards; Duncan Mackay, keyboards.

Hit Singles:	US	UK
Donna, 1972	—	2
Rubber Bullets, 1973	—	1
The Dean And I, 1973	—	10
Wall Street Shuffle, 1974	—	10
Life Is A Minestrone, 1975	—	7
I'm Not In Love, 1975	1	1
Art For Art's Sake, 1975	—	5
I'm Mandy Fly Me, 1976	60	6
Things We Do For Love, 1976	5	6
Good Morning Judge, 1977	—	5
Dreadlock Holiday, 1978	44	1

Albums:
10 cc (UK), 1973
Sheet Music (UK), 1974
Original Soundtrack (Mercury), 1975
How Dare You (Mercury), 1976
Deceptive Bends (Mercury), 1977
Live And Let Live (Mercury), 1977
Bloody Tourists (Mercury), 1978
Greatest Hits (Mercury), 1979
Things We Do For Love (Mercury), 1979
Look Hear (Warner Bros/Mercury), 1980
Greatest Hits, 71-78 (Polydor/—), 1981
Ten Out Of Ten (Warner Bros/Mercury), 1981
In Concert (—/Contour), 1982

Ten Years After

UK group formed 1967.

Original/Final line-up: Alvin Lee, Gibson ES 335 guitar, vocals; Chick Churchill, keyboards; Leo Lyons, bass; Rick Lee, drums.

Career: One of major bands to emerge from mid-'60s blues revival movement in UK.

Formed by Lee and Lyons who met in Nottingham and worked together in Hamburg for a time. On returning to Britain; met music scholar Ric Lee while working in West End production and formed the Jaybirds. Adding Chick Churchill, changed name and came to critics' attention via appearances at London's Marquee Club. Group signed to Decca's Deram subsidiary who put out first album without waiting to score any hit singles (an unusual move in those days).

Famed American promoter Bill Graham heard album and booked group for his Fillmore Auditorium venues in US. Subsequent albums and appearance at massive Woodstock rock festival (and in the 'Woodstock' movie in which their 11-minute opus **Goin' Home** scored heavily) established world reputation for fast and furious blend of blues and heavy rock.

Introduced electronic effects for **A Space In Time** and moved into more pensive direction; album was US smash. But, by 1973, Lee was disillusioned with group's direction and exhaustive tour schedules (a record 28 US tours before they broke up), describing band as 'a travelling jukebox'.

Members took time off for solo projects and Lee retired to 15th-century country home to build studio and record gospel singer Mylon Lefevre. Churchill's solo album **You And Me** appeared in 1973. **Ten Years After** set that year was live album compiled from concerts in Amsterdam, Rotterdam, Frankfurt and Paris.

A month before band's scheduled spring 1974 UK tour, Lee appeared at London's Rainbow with own hastily assembled nine-piece band. Show was released on disc as **Alvin Lee And Co In Flight**.

Ten Years After's own Rainbow appearance a month later was sell-out. It proved to be their

Above: Alvin Lee, leader of Ten Years After in 1967, and of Ten Years Later in 1977, although the latter band did not equal the former's fame.

last British stage appearance as Lee set off to tour world as Alvin Lee And Co.

In May 1975, Alvin Lee declared Ten Years After defunct and Ric Lee formed own band. However, just one month later Ten Years After were back on road for US tour to fulfill contractual obligations before final split. Lee formed Ten Years Later in 1977 with Tom Compton drums, and Mick Hawksworth, bass; released two LPs, **Rocket Fuel** 1978) and **Ride On** (1979). Since then, Alvin Lee has recorded further solo efforts; Chick Churchill has become professional manager at Chrysalis Music; and Leo Lyons has worked as producer, notably with UFO.

At time of writing, Lee has agreed to re-unite original line-up for one night show at London's Marquee in summer 1983.

Hit Singles:

	US	UK
Love Like A Man, 1970	—	10

Albums:

Ten Years After:
Ten Years After (Deram), 1967
Undead (Deram), 1968
Stonehenge (Deram), 1969
Ssssssh (Chrysalis), 1969
Cricklewood Green (Chrysalis), 1970
Watt (Chrysalis), 1970
Alvin Lee & Co (Deram), 1972
A Space In Time (Columbia/Crysalis), 1972
Rock 'n' Roll To The World (Columbia/Chrysalis), 1972
Recorded Live (Columbia/Chrysalis), 1973
Positive Vibrations (Columbia/Chrysalis), 1974
Goin' Home (Deram/Chrysalis), 1975
Classic Performances (Columbia/Chrysalis), 1977
Hear Me Calling (—/Decca), 1981
Goin' Home, Their Greatest Hits (London/—), 1975

Ten Years Later:
Rocket Fuel (Polydor), 1978
Ride On (Polydor), 1979

Alvin Lee Solo:
Free Fall (—/Avatar), 1980
RX5 (Atlantic/—), 1981

With Mylon Lefevre:
Road To Freedom (Columbia/CBS), 1973

Thin Lizzy

UK group formed 1970

Original line-up: Phil Lynott, Fender Precision, Ibanez basses, lead vocals; Eric Bell, lead guitar; Brian Downey, drums.

Career: Hard-rocking group equally at home with blues ballads, Thin Lizzy is accessible and eclectic on record, skillfully showmanlike in concert.

First hit was **Whiskey In The Jar.** Hard-driving 1972 version of traditional folk song reached No. 6, staying in charts for eight weeks, but next three singles flopped. By then

Vagabonds Of The Western World, Thin Lizzy. Courtesy London Records.

Above: Phil Lynott (left) and Scott Gorham of Thin Lizzy.

Eric Bell, disturbed by Irish troubles, left group after Belfast concert, to be briefly replaced by Gary Moore, until Scott Gorham and Brian Robertson were added as guitarists.

In summer 1974 band signed with Vertigo label and made Reading Festival debut. More albums followed and UK, European and US tours, but three more singles failed to make charts. Then, five years and five LPs after first release, **Jailbreak** album provided **The Boys Are Back In Town** single, which entered Top 10 in UK and US charts. Title single also made charts and album reached Top 10 on both sides of Atlantic. 'Melody Maker's' readers' poll voted band 'brightest hope'. However, summer 1976 US tour was cancelled when Lynott contracted hepatitis

Thin Lizzy (debut album). Courtesy London Records.

and winter US tour was postponed when Robertson injured hand in brawl.

Next two singles made 1977 charts. Band headlined Reading Festival, topped bill on US tour, and **Bad Reputation,** their eighth album, reached No. 4, Video of Rainbow Theatre concert in March 1978 was shown on television in many countries but not in Britain. Albums and singles continued to reach charts; pick-up band called the Greedy Bastards formed and Robertson left the group going on to Motorhead(▶), to be replaced by Gary Moore. Moore's single, **Parisienne Walkways** co-written by Lynott, reached No. 8 in 1979. Thin Lizzy's **Black Rose**, released same month, topped album charts.

Tours still beset by troubles; three European dates were cancelled when Lynott got food poisoning and Moore was sacked for missing two US dates. Ex-Pink Floyd(▶) guitarist Snowy White joined group in 1980. The same year Lynott's solo album **Solo In Soho** reached No. 28 Band toured Japan and Australia, and further albums and singles made UK Top 30. In 1981 **The Adventures Of Thin Lizzy**, compilation of 10 years of hits, was successful (helped by £250,000 television advertising campaign). **The Philip Lynott Album,** Lynott's second solo endea-

vour, was released in August 1982. Recent additions Darren Warton (keyboards, synthesiser) and John Sykes (guitar) had short membership; band announced split in early 1983.

Final line-up: Lynott; Downey; Darren Wharton, keyboards; John Sykes, guitar.

Hit Singles:

	US	UK
Whiskey In The Jar, 1973	—	6
The Boys Are Back In Town, 1976	12	8
Don't Believe A Word, 1977	—	12
Dancin' In The Moonlight (It's Caught Me In The Spotlight), 1977	—	14
Rosalie—Cowgirl's Song, 1978	—	20
Waiting For An Alibi, 1979	—	9
Do Anything You Want To, 1979	—	14
Killer On The Loose, 1980	—	10
Killers Live (EP), 1981	—	19
Gary Moore Solo:		
Parisienne Walkways, 1979	—	8
Phil Lynott Solo:		
Yellow Pearl, 1981	—	14

Albums:
Thin Lizzy (London/Decca), 1971
Shades Of A Blue Orphanage (—/Decca), 1972
Vagabonds Of The Western World (London/Decca), 1973
Night Life (Mercury/Vertigo), 1974
Fighting (Mercury/Vertigo), 1975
Jailbreak (Mercury/Vertigo), 1976
Johnny The Fox (Mercury/Vertigo), 1976
Remembering (—/Decca), 1976
Bad Reputation (Mercury/Vertigo), 1977
Live And Dangerous (Warner Bros/Vertigo), 1978
Rocker (1971-1974) (London/—), 1978
Black Rose (Warner Bros/Vertigo), 1979
Chinatown (Warner Bros/Vertigo), 1980
Renegade (Warner Bros/Vertigo), 1981
Adventures Of (—/Vertigo), 1981
Thunder And Lightning (Warner Bros/Vertigo), 1983

Phil Lynott Solo:
Solo In Soho (Warner Bros/Vertigo), 1980
The Philip Lynott Album (Warner Bros/Vertigo), 1982
Making Love From Memory (MCA/—), 1982

Third World

Jamaican group formed 1973.

Original/Current line-up: Michael 'Ibo' Cooper, keyboards; Stephen 'Cat' Coore, guitar; Bunny 'Rugs' Clarke, vocals; Orvin 'Carrot' Jarrett, percussion; Willie Stewart, drums; Richard Daley, bass.

Career: Splinter group from Inner Circle(▶), Third World left Jamaica for UK in 1975 hoping to further aim of creating new musical fusion and were signed to Island, joining labelmates Bob Marley(▶) and the Wailers on British tour. They gained sufficient reputation from debut album to tour US as support for Stevie Wonder(▶), introducing dreadlocks and reggae beat to whole new audience.

Success of **96 Degrees In The Shade** album took group back to homeland for triumphant West Indian tour (1977), climaxed by critically acclaimed 'Explanitations' shows at Little Theatre, Kingston, Jamaica, where, aided by choreography of Jamaican National Dance Theatre's Thomas Pinnock, they explored full theatrical potential of their most spiritually important songs.

Third Island album, **Journey To Addis**, spawned sensational **Now That We've Found Love** single, extended version of

Above: Delaware slide boy—blues influence reflected in the playing style of George Thorogood.

which was one of disco scene's major records of 1978 thanks to totally compulsive rhythm track with brilliant percussive work.

Switching to CBS/Columbia in 1981 they issued generally weaker material, though **Dancing On The Floor** (produced by Stevie Wonder) was another disco smash. Their set at the Reggae Sunsplash festival in Montego Bay, Jamaica, where Stevie Wonder joined them on-stage, has led to more work with him.

Third World can claim to be the act which created reggae/soul/disco fusion (Wonder's **Boogie On Reggae Woman** helping point the way) in commercially viable form.

Hit Singles:	US	UK
Now That We've Found Love, 1978	47	10
Cool Meditation, 1979	—	17
Dancing On The Floor (Hooked On Love), 1981	—	10

Albums:
Aiye-Keta (—/Help), 1973
Third World (Island), 1976
96 Degrees In The Shade (Island), 1977
Journey To Addis (Island), 1978
Story's Been Told (Island), 1979
Prisoner In The Street (Island), 1980
Arise In Harmony (Island/—), 1980
Rock The World (Columbia/CBS), 1981
You Got The Power (Columbia/CBS), 1982

.38 Special

US group formed 1979.

Original line-up: Donnie van Zant, guitar, vocals; Don Barnes, guitar, vocals; Jeff Carlisi, guitar; Steve Brookins, drums; Ken Lyon, bass.

Career: Founded by van Zant, younger brother of late Ronnie, vocalist with Lynyrd Skynyrd(▶). Band follows same route as illustrious predecessors — triple lead guitar breaks, macho bar-room 'proud to be Southern' lyrics — albeit somewhat mellower.

First self-titled album was released in 1977; featured guest spot from Dan Hartman on vocals. For third album **Rockin' Into The Night**, Lyon was replaced by Larry Lundstrom. Title track made 43 in US singles chart. Band consolidated position in US pop lists with two further entries in 1981. **Hold On Loosely** made No. 27, **Fantasy Girl**, 52.

.38 Special broke through to first division in '82 when album **Special Forces** made US Top 10. LP cuts **Caught Up In You** and **You Keep Runnin' Away** earned singles placings.

Ironically more successful than their splinter, the Rossington-Collins Band, .38 Special are filling void left by Skynyrd.

Current line-up: van Zant; Barnes; Carlisi; Brookins; Larry Lundstrom, bass, vocals.

Hit Singles:	US	UK
Caught Up In You, 1982	10	—

Albums:
.38 Special (A&M), 1977
Special Delivery (A&M), 1978
Rockin' Into The Night (A&M), 1979
Wild Eyed Southern Boys (A&M), 1981
Special Forces (A&M), 1982

Richard And Linda Thompson

UK duo formed 1971.

Richard Thompson, guitar, vocals: born April 3, 1949; Linda Thompson, vocals: born ??

Career: Richard Thompson left Fairport Convention(▶) in January 1971, having established himself as major songwriter in group. Retreated to folk club and studio work, which included appearances on Nick Drake's **Bryter Layter**, Sandy Denny's solo albums, and various works by Mike Heron, John Martyn(▶), John Cale(▶) and Ian Matthews(▶). Also appeared as part of folkie superstar group, the Bunch, contributing to **Rock On**, an album of rock 'n' roll numbers. A contrasting LP of traditional dance music, **Morris On**, led directly to formation of the Albion Country Band, with whom he toured in late 1972.

Earlier that year, Richard had promoted first solo album, the celebrated **Henry The Human Fly**, with appearances on folk circuit, accompanied by Simon Nicol and Linda Peters — now Thompson's wife. Backed Sandy Denny on national tour, then put together Sour Grapes with Linda, Nicol, Willie Murray (drums) and Steve Borrell (bass). Group folded after support tour with Traffic(▶) in spring 1974.

Joint album with Linda, **I Want To See The Bright Lights Again**, critically acclaimed as classic of British folk/rock genre. Contained some of Thompson's most famous songs, including the rarely performed **End Of The Rainbow**, generally regarded as his bleakest composition. Music hall-inspired **Hokey Pokey** followed, as eccentric and idiosyncratic as any of his works.

In 1973, duo converted to Sufi faith, celebrating new austere lifestyle on stark, sombre **Pour Down Like Silver**. Toured UK twice with Dave Pegg (bass), Dave Mattacks (drums) and John Kirkpatrick (accordian), before three-year hibernation, broken only by 1976 anthology double, **Guitar, Vocal**, which included rare, unreleased material. Work fully revealed Thompson's importance as one of most original and interesting guitarists working in British pop music.

First Light proved welcome comeback

album and satiric **Sunnyvista** showed Thompson had lost none of his former wit, but in spite of critical respect and commendation, he remains a cult figure on fringes of 'rock' world. His songs have been covered by such artists as Julie Covington, Arlo Guthrie(▶) Any Trouble and the Pointer Sisters(▶), however he still shows no inclination to extend appeal to mass audience.

Following widely praised US tour, 'Rolling Stone' magazine nominated duo's 1982 LP **Shoot Out The Lights** as year's finest album. The subsequent break-up of their marriage suggests that this may have been their last recording together.

Albums:
Richard and Linda Thompson:
I Want To See The Bright Lights Again (—/Island), 1974
First Light (Chrysalis), 1978
Sunnyvista (—/Chrysalis), 1979
Shoot Out The Lights (Hannibal), 1982

Richard Thompson solo:
Strict Tempo (—/Elixir), 1981
Hand Of Kindness (Hannibal), 1983

Worth Searching Out:
Henry The Human Fly (—/Island), 1972
Guitar, Vocal (—/Island), 1976

George Thorogood And The Destroyers

US group formed 1974.

Original line-up: George Thorogood, guitar, harmonica; Jeff Simon, drums; Bill Blough, bass.

Career: Thorogood began by playing bars and small clubs in Wilmington, Delaware, then up and down East Coast. Music was rockin' R&B with early Stones(▶) influence. John Forward saw band at Joe's Place (Cambridge, Mass.) in summer 1975 and was struck by 'feel' they had for old standards, achieved by deliberate choice of small amps and by avoiding state of art electronics.

Two years of deals and negotiations by Forward led to contract with small ethnic blue grass label, Rounder Records. Self-titled album startled Rounder by selling strongly in every city where band had recently played. Second album also overloaded Rounder's independent distribution system as sales picked up nationally by word of mouth.

Move It On Over, George Thorogood & The Destroyers. Courtesy Sonet Records.

Recognising his limits, Thorogood refused to take his 'traditional rock'n'roll' to larger venues; band had to use phoney names so crowds could get into their usual gigs. (MCA released set of early demo tapes made in 1974 (with bassist Michael Lenn) when considering whether to sign band; group has

subsequently rejected any connection with effort.)

Third Rounder LP sold well enough for label to turn band over to Capitol Records and go back to folk/bluegrass artists. With **Bad To The Bone**, band had an album likely to be found in most US record shops. Real forte has always been live performances. Nothing on record can capture fire of Thorogood playing slide guitar in small crowded atmosphere. As opening act for Rolling Stones' 1981 US tour, George Thorogood may have won wider exposure, but with same sense of compromise the Glimmer Twins may have felt when leaving behind Crawdaddy Club.

Current line-up: Thorogood; Blough; Simon; Hank Carter, saxophone.

Albums:
George Thorogood And The Destroyers (Rounder/—), 1978
Move It On Over (Rounder/Sonet), 1978
Better Than The Rest (MCA), 1979
More George Thorogood And The Destroyers (Rounder/Sonet), 1980
Bad To The Bone (EMI America/—), 1982

Three Dog Night

US group formed 1968.

Original line-up: Danny Hutton, vocals; Cory Wells, vocals; Chuck Negron, vocals; Joe Schermie, bass; Floyd Sneed, drums; Jim Greenspoon, keyboards; Mike Allsop, guitar.

Career: Original members were all LA-based musicians passing through small local groups and doing session work. Hutton instigated idea of group based on three lead vocalists and recruited Wells and Negron. According to Eskimo lore, the colder the night, the more dogs are brought in to sleep with, coldest being 'three dog night'. Despite name, however, band was far from cold and almost immediately began picking up US gold records.

Although albums sold extremely well, group remained primarily a singles factory. **Joy To The World** was *the* No. 1 US single of 1971. By 1972 when hits stopped, band became disjointed. Jack Ryland replaced Schermie, and second keyboards player, Skip Konte, joined. Then band disappeared.

Nova-like career came at time when singles were disdained by 'serious' rock crowd, so it was easy to dismiss band as having little or no impact. Yet Three Dog Night must be fondly remembered for turning non-original material into joyful celebration all their own. Possibility of re-formation was being discussed when this volume went to press.

Final line-up: Hutton; Wells; Negron; Sneed; Greenspoon; Jack Ryland, guitar; Kip Konte, keyboards.

Hit Singles:	US	UK
One, 1969	5	—
Easy To Be Hard, 1969	4	—
Eli's Coming, 1969	10	—
Celebrate, 1970	15	—
Mama Told Me (Not To Come), 1970	1	3
Out In The Country, 1970	15	—
One Man Band, 1970	19	—
Joy To The World, 1971	1	24
Liar, 1971	7	—
An Old Fashioned Love Song, 1971	4	—
Never Been To Spain, 1971	5	—
The Family Of Man, 1972	12	—
Black And White, 1972	1	—
Pieces Of April, 1972	19	—
Shambala, 1973	3	—
Let Me Serenade, 1973	17	—

Albums:
Joy To The World—Greatest Hits
(MCA/Anchor), 1974
Best Of (MCA/—), 1975

Worth Searching Out:
It Ain't Easy (Dunhill/Stateside), 1970
Harmony (Dunhill/Probe), 1971

Tom Tom Club

US group formed 1981.

Original/Current line-up: Tina Weymouth,
bass, keyboards, vocals; Chris Frantz, drums;
session players.

Career: Weymouth and Frantz are active
members of Talking Heads(▶). Part of that
band's success rests on creative tension
between Weymouth and David Byrne and as
early as 1977 Weymouth hinted she might
enjoy a break from that situation.

Talking Heads LP **Remain In Light** indicated band was opening up Afro rhythms for
exploration. Weymouth and Frantz asked
some session players from LP to their home in
Bahamas. This led to formation of Tom Tom
Club, who had mammoth hit in US and UK with
Wordy Rappinghood.

So far Tom Tom Club (named after rehearsal
hall where they recorded) remains in back
seat to Weymouth/Frantz's commitment to
Talking Heads. Future of band depends on
duo's proclivity for solo work or their desire to
continue working with David Byrne. May have
found formula for rock survival by working in
both.

Hit Singles:	US	UK
Wordy Rappinghood, 1981	2	7

Albums:
The Tom Tom Club (Sire/Island), 1981

Toots And The Maytals

Jamaican vocal group formed 1962.

Original/Final line-up: Frederick 'Toots'
Hibbert; Raleigh Gordon; Nathaniel 'Jerry'
Mathias.

Career: Group put together by Toots Hibbert;
first named Vikings. Started recording career
with Clement 'Sir Coxsone' Dodd in Kingston.
Scored immediate success, but after several
records joined forces with legendary Prince
Buster(▶). Buster-produced records include
ska classics such as **Pain In My Belly** and
Dog War.

Further move to Byron Lee's organisation in
1966 resulted in string of Jamaican hits and
victory in Jamaican Song Festival. Changed
name to Maytals. First phase of career
brought to close when Toots fell foul of drug
laws and spent two years in prison.

Following Toots' release Maytals recorded
for yet another top producer, Leslie Kong,
staying with him throughout 'rock-steady'
period and into the beginning of reggae.
Classics from this period include **54-46
That's My Number, Pressure Drop,
Sweet And Dandy** and **Monkey Man**.

When Kong died (after long-term heart
trouble) in 1971, group turned again to Byron
Lee and recorded album **Kingston**, greatly
acclaimed record that brought group to
international notice. Next album, **In The
Dark**, consolidated success. By mid-'70s
Toots and Maytals had considerable following
in UK and US, and were playing to full and
enthusiastic audiences.

Since that time group has continued to
gratify its following with excellent records and

**Above: Toots Hibbert and the Maytals,
second only to Bob Marley as local
musical heroes in Jamaica.**

exciting live performances, without garnering
the huge international acceptance of Bob
Marley and Wailers. Toots has reggae's
greatest voice, rivalling Otis Redding's in
gritty soulfulness, but his down-to-earth
persona does not seem to inspire the
semi-mystical devotion that accrued to Marley.

In 1983 Toots Hibbert embarked on solo
career.

Albums:
Funky Kingston (Mango/Island), 1973
In The Dark (—/Island), 1974
Reggae Got Soul (Mango/Island), 1976
Best Of (—/Trojan), 1979
Toots Live (Mango/Island), 1980

Peter Tosh

Jamaican vocalist, composer, guitarist.
Born Peter McIntosh, Kingston, Jamaica,
October 19, 1944.

Career: A fervent preacher of Rastafarian
ethic, Peter Tosh has established himself as
leading figure of Jamaica's alternative culture,
first as member of influential Wailers, alongside late Bob Marley(▶) and Bunny (Wailer)
Livingstone, then as solo artist allied—in
somewhat unlikely fashion—to Mick Jagger
and Keith Richard via Rolling Stones(▶)
Records.

An adept musician by early teens, playing
steel guitar, acoustic guitar and keyboards,
Tosh met fellow Wailers in Kingston ghetto
suburb Trenchtown, sharing socially aware
songwriting, taking themes from politics,
religion, poverty and social repression. Among
his songs for Wailers were **Get Up, Stand
Up, One Foundation** and **400 Years**.

When trio split up (1974) Tosh's work took
on increasingly revolutionary nature which
led to beating by Jamaican police in 1975.
From this experience came his banned **Mark
Of The Beast** and an ever more radical
stance as in **Legalise It** (also banned, but big
JA hit nonetheless) which called for legal-
isation of marijuana. 1977 album **Equal
Rights** summed up Tosh's crusade against
racism and oppression with outspoken demand
for recognition by blacks of Africa as the true
homeland.

Switching from Virgin to Rolling Stones
Records in 1978 brought Tosh support of
Jagger and Richard. He teamed with revered
reggae sidemen Sly Dunbar(▶) (bass) and
Robbie Shakespeare(▶) (drums) to guest on
Stones' American tour. His classic **Bush
Doctor** album of 1978 included the superb
(You Gotta Walk) Don't Look Back single
which, in limited-release dub version, featured

Jagger and Richard on back-up vocals to
Smokey Robinson(▶) composition.

Two more Rolling Stones Records LPs and
1981 appearances at London's Rainbow
Theatre furthered Tosh's international appeal
while love-song duet with Gwen Guthrie on
Nothing But Love showed a softening in his
lyrical approach.

Albums:
Legalise It (Columbia/Virgin), 1976
Equal Rights (Columbia/Virgin), 1978
Bush Doctor (Rolling Stones), 1978
Mystic Man (Rolling Stones), 1979
Wanted Dread And Alive (EMI/Rolling
Stones), 1981

Toto

US group formed 1978.

Original line-up: Bobby Kimball, vocals;
Steve Lukather, guitar; David Paich, key-
boards; Steve Porcaro, keyboards; David
Hungate, bass; Jeff Porcaro, drums.

Career: All original line-up bar Kimball were
notable Los Angeles session musicians —
credits for various members include Steely
Dan, Boz Scaggs, Aretha Franklin, Leo Sayer,
Earth, Wind & Fire, Jackson Browne, Barbra
Streisand and many more. Group named
either after Dorothy's dog in 'Wizard Of Oz'
film, or Kimball's real surname (supposedly
'Toteaux'). Successful first LP featured in
US LP chart for most of 1979 and spawned
three US hit singles, but second and third LPs
were rather less notable; due, according to
Lukather, to fame arriving too quickly for
group to adapt to it.

However, 1982 LP gave group highest
placing in album chart in US, plus three US
and two UK hit singles. Resulted in domination
of 1983 Grammy Award Ceremony, winning

**Above: "Legalise it and I will advertise
it" said Peter Tosh, but they didn't
...unfortunately.**

seven categories; group also returned to UK
charts. This coincided with another Porcaro
brother, Mike, replacing Hungate on bass.
Group appear to have overcome bad patch, at
least as regards US. UK fame seems to
depend on audience reaction to each record,
since track record regarded as negligible
outside US (group are, however, reportedly
superstars in Japan). Music sometimes
epitome of US AOR syndrome.

Current line-up: Kimball; Lukather; Paich;
Steve Porcaro; Jeff Porcaro; Mike Porcaro,
bass.

Hit Singles:	US	UK
Hold The Line, 1978	5	14
Rosanna, 1982	2	12
Africa, 1982	1	3

Albums:
Toto (Columbia/CBS), 1978
Hydra (Columbia/CBS), 1979
Turn Back (Columbia/CBS), 1981
Toto IV (Columbia/CBS), 1982

**Toto (debut album). Courtesy CBS
Records.**

Pete Townshend

UK guitarist, composer, vocalist, multi-
instrumentalist.
Born London, May 19, 1945.

Career: Townshend grew up in Ealing, West
London, son of singer Betty Dennis and sax
player Cliff Townshend, who played with the
Squadronaires. Spent summers at holiday
camps where father played in bands. His
grandmother bought him his first guitar when
he was 12.

Townshend wrote his first song, **It Was
You,** at 16 (actually recorded by the very
early Who, in 1963, before Keith Moon
joined, but never released). In 1965 he began
20-year career writing for the Who(▶).

Townshend's first departure from the band
came in 1972 when he released **Who Came
First,** an album of songs either about his

Above: A young Pete Townshend (circa 1964) and a Rickenbacker he no doubt smashed to pieces later.

Indian master Meher Baba, or included because Baba liked them. (Various Baba-orientated LPs done with other Baba-lovers were previously recorded, but these were never intended as official Townshend releases.) **Who Came First** gave the public a very different taste of Townshend. Playing guitar without vengeance known as trademark in Who, Townshend created an atmosphere of relaxation with excellent acoustic sound accompanied by a clear and sincere, if not technically magnificent, voice. Up until this point, Townshend's voice was not often heard at length, as Roger Daltrey(▶) handled Who vocals.

Next official solo release, **Rough Mix**, didn't come until 1977, when Townshend teamed up with ex-Small Faces(▶), Faces(▶) singer/composer/bass player Ronnie Lane. Though LP had a 'Baba flavour', the references were quite subtle, and the sound was more upbeat. Only mildly successful initially,it has remained a steady seller, and has been re-released several times.

In 1980 Townshend truly made his mark as solo artist with **Empty Glass**. The single **Let My Love Open The Door**, made it into the US Top 10, (matching most successful Who single in US, **I Can See For Miles**) and several other tracks received massive US airplay. Townshend's voice, under producer Chris Thomas, had improved dramatically. Lyrical content was more intellectual and more personally revealing than Daltrey would have agreed to had the material been offered the Who. Many expected great things from Townshend's future solo work; there was no doubt about who was the main creative force behind the Who.

Unfortunately, the much-anticipated **All The Best Cowboys Have Chinese Eyes** LP in 1982 didn't quite measure up to **Empty Glass**. A bit too heady and abstract for some, it confused the general public with its experimental song structure, and sometimes bizarre lyrics. The stream-of-consciousness effect was balanced by a couple of energetic, almost Who-style tracks, but overall the LP lacked cohesiveness. When around the time of its release, Townshend gave several confessional interviews attesting to personal confusion and unhappiness, and even alcohol and drug addiction during much of its recording, this was understandable.

Early 1983 brought new LP of old material, a double LP collection of Townshend's personal demos, some done for the Who, some just for himself, entitled **Scoop.** In February '83, Townshend received the Lifetime Achievement Award from the British Record Industry.

Townshend has done some solo live shows, usually for charity (Rock Against Racism and Amnesty International gigs in '79), and performs and records with a wide variety of artists. He also owns two recording studios in London.

Guitars: 1964-66: Rickenbacker 6 and 12 strings, 1967-68: Fender Stratocaster, Telecaster, 1969-71: Gibson SG, 1972: Gibson Les Paul Deluxe, 1979: Schecters.

Hit Singles:

	US	UK
Let My Love Open The Door, 1980	9	—

Scoop, Pete Townshend's demos. Courtesy Atco Records.

Albums:
Who Came First (Decca/Track), 1972
Rough Mix (MCA/Polydor), 1977
Empty Glass (Atco/WEA), 1980
All The Best Cowboys Have Chinese Eyes (Atco/WEA), 1982
Pete Townshend Scoop (Atco/Atco), 1983

Toyah

UK vocalist, composer.
Born Toyah Ann Wilcox, Kings Heath, Birmingham, May 18, 1958.

Career: Left school in 1976 to take up place at Birmingham Old Rep Drama School; two months later was offered co-starring role in BBC-TV play 'Glitter'. Appearance in this led to place with National Theatre, and Toyah never returned to drama school.

Career as actress burgeoned, and in 1978 Toyah developed musical side of talent by forming eponymous band. Started gigging between acting jobs, one of which was a part in the Who(▶)'s 1979 film 'Quadrophenia'.

In 1979 she signed to Safari Records and released single **Victims Of The Riddle** and 33rpm six-track single **Sheep Farming In Barnet**. Both attracted critical attention and generated sales in alternative outlets.

1980 saw album **The Blue Meaning** make UK Top 40, and later in year **Toyah Toyah Toyah,** a collection of live tracks, confirmed success.

Breakthrough to wider public came in 1981 with release of four-track EP **Four From Toyah,** featuring **It's A Mystery.** It was a major hit, a were next three single releases (**Four More From Toyah** also being an EP). **Anthem** made No. 2 in album charts.

In 1982 Toyah consolidated record success while continuing to be greatly in demand as an actress. Voted top female vocalist in several UK polls, though she has yet to make any impact in US.

Without doubt extremely talented (and a particularly convincing actress), Toyah appeals to wide audience with her very personal brand of sophisto-punk. Her vivid appearance (in particular her amazing hairstyles and brilliant make-up which she does herself) and energetic stage act guarantee strong following for live work, and her versatility indicates continued success. At time of writing she had just taken over starring role in West End hit play 'Trafford Tanzi'.

Hit Singles:

	US	UK
Four From Toyah (EP), 1981	—	4
I Want To Be Free, 1981	—	8
Thunder In The Mountains, 1981	—	4
Four More From Toyah (EP), 1981	—	14

Albums:
The Blue Meaning (—/Safari), 1980
Toyah Toyah Toyah (—/Safari), 1980
Anthem (—/Safari), 1981
The Changeling (—/Safari), 1982
Warrior Rock (Toyah On Tour) (—/Safari), 1982

Traffic

UK group formed 1967

Original line-up: Steve Winwood, guitar, keyboards, vocals; Dave Mason, guitar; Jim Capaldi, drums; Chris Wood, saxophone, flute.

Career: Traffic emerged following Winwood's(▶) departure for Spencer Davis Group(▶) in which Winwood played dominant role. Mason(▶) and Capaldi previously played in Birmingham group Deep Feeling. Wood had played sax in ska-influenced Locomotive. In spring 1967, retired to a Berkshire cottage in Aston Tirrold, coining cliché 'getting it together in the country'.

Six months later, debut **Paper Sun**, a powerful and evocative summer single, climbed to No. 5 in UK charts. Follow-up **Hole In My Shoe**, with its dream-like imagery and schoolgirl's voice, was even more commercial and reached No. 2.

First album **Mr Fantasy** revealed individual talents of all members, indicating this was no one-man band. Another Top 10 single, film theme **Here We Go Round The Mulberry Bush**, revealed Mason's ability to pen commercial tunes, in contrast to others' heavy jazz leanings. This apparently caused incompatibility, culminating in Mason's departure in December 1967. Within six months he returned, contributing four songs to **Traffic**, but left again in October 1968 and group folded. Live/studio **Last Exit** was erratic and unsatisfactory finale.

After short stay in ill-fated Blind Faith(▶), Winwood worked on projected solo album **Mad Shadows**, which ended up as Traffic reunion, minus Mason. Re-formed trio released **John Barleycorn Must Die** in April 1970, a superb fusion of jazz, rock, R&B and folk. Unit was bolstered by induction of Rick Grech (ex-Family(▶), Blind Faith), and later Jim Gordon (session drummer) and Reebop Kwaku-Baah (congas). Mason again returned temporarily and this short-lived aggregation played six gigs, captured for posterity on **Welcome To The Canteen**, a surprisingly impressive live album.

During December 1971 US tour, **The Low Spark Of High Heeled Boys** met critical acclaim. However, Grech and Gordon quit and Winwood fell ill with peritonitis amid rumours of Traffic's imminent dissolution. During lull in group activity, Capaldi cut solo **Oh How We Danced** at Muscle Shoals. Formed partnership with rhythm section David Hood and Roger Hawkins, who joined Traffic for Jamaican-recorded **Shoot Out At The Fantasy Factory**. Muscle Shoals sessioneer Barry Beckett was added on keyboards for 1973 world tour, which included some of their finest live performances as evidenced on German-recorded **On The Road**.

When Shoalsmen returned to States in autumn 1973, Rosko Gee from Gonzales was brought in as bassist. As quartet (Winwood/Wood/Capaldi/Gee) cut final album **When The Eagle Flies**, which revealed

Below: Traffic (from left) Steve Winwood, Chris Wood, Jim Capaldi, Dave Mason — the original quartet.

Winwood concentrating heavily on keyboards/synthesiser. Period of indecision ended in December 1974 with Capaldi and Winwood pursuing solo careers.

Traffic were responsible for some of the finest music to emerge from Britain in the late '60s/early '70s. While many contemporaries fell into self-parody or became victims of self-indulgent '70s art rock, Traffic continued to produce music of increasing complexity, originality and quality.

Chris Wood died in July 1983 of liver failure.

Final line-up: Winwood; Capaldi; Wood; Rosko Gee, bass.

Hit Singles:

	US	UK
Paper Sun, 1967	—	5
Hole In My Shoe, 1967	—	2
Here We Go Round The Mulberry Bush, 1967	—	8

Jim Capaldi Solo:

Love Hurts,	—	4

(see also Mason and Winwood entries)

Albums:
Mr Fantasy (Island(, 1967
Traffic (Island), 1968
Last Exit (Island), 1969
Best Of Traffic (Island), 1969
John Barleycorn Must Die (Island), 1970
Welcome To The Canteen (Island), 1971
Low Spark Of High Heeled Boys (Island), 1971
Shoot Out At The Fantasy Factory (Island), 1973
On The Road (Island), 1973*
Where The Eagle Flies (Island), 1974
*Issued in single *and* double LP form.

Jim Capaldi Solo:
Oh How We Danced (—/Island), 1972
Short Cut Draw Blood (Antilles/Island), 1975
The Contender (—/Polydor), 1978
Electric Nights (Polydor), 1979
Sweet Smell Of Success (—/Carrere), 1980

John Travolta

US vocalist, actor.
Born Englewood, New Jersey, February 18, 1954.

Career: Of Italian/Irish parentage; dropped out of high school at 16 to pursue acting career. After gaining experience in summer stock, commercials and off-Broadway shows, made way to Hollywood where he played bit parts in various movies.

Part in touring version of 'Grease' led to role in Broadway version. First important break was leading role in TV show 'Welcome Back Kotter' in 1975. Next two years also saw parts in movies 'Devil's Rain', 'Boy in the Plastic Bubble' and 'Carrie'. During this period signed recording contract with Midsong, gaining three Top 40 entries.

Major turning-point came with main role in massively successful 1977 movie 'Saturday Night Fever'. Although Travolta did not sing in film, it established him as teen idol, and paved way for impact in 'Grease' in 1978. Travolta and co-star Olivia Newton-John(▶) scored hugely with songs from movie; Travolta's solo efforts also charted internationally.

Follow-up movies 'Moment By Moment' and 'Urban Cowboy' were comparatively disastrous; at time of writing Travolta is hoping to regain status with sequel to 'Saturday Night Fever', 'Stayin' Alive'.

Although primarily an actor, Travolta possesses pleasant if unspectacular singing voice. Hits with Newton-John were classics of lightweight pop-rock genre.

Hit Singles:

	US	UK
Let Her In, 1976	10	—
Sandy, 1978	—	2
Greased Lightnin', 1978	47	11

With Olivia Newton-John:

You're The One That I Want, 1978	1	1
Summer Nights, 1978	5	1

Albums:
Grease Soundtrack (RSO), 1978

Triumph

Canadian group formed 1975.
Original/current line-up: Rik Emmett, vocals, guitar; Mike Levine, bass, keyboards; Gil Moore, drums, vocals.

Career: Formed in Streetsville, Ontario, Triumph was inspired by fellow Canadians Rush(▶) to play thunderous music in small clubs and venues throughout province. Two LPs provided modicum of interest in Canada, but little elsewhere. Major problem was impact of punk/new wave music in 1976.

Extensive touring in US honed down band's sound and finally sparked audience support. **Progression Of Power** album suggested Triumph might yet produce unique image worthy of heavy-metal success. This was further indicated on excellent **Allied Force** and **Never Surrender** LPs.

In UK, Triumph remains relatively unknown. Early material was released collectively in 1979 but failure to tour in UK provides little opportunity for impact.

Hard work and exciting stage act have improved Triumph to point that band deserves a listen. Further improvement might yet win support needed to move group out of 'just another band' category.

Albums:
Triumph (RCA/Attic), 1976
Just A Game (RCA), 1979
Rock'n'Roll Machine* (RCA/Attic), 1979
Progression Of Power (RCA), 1980
Allied Forces (RCA), 1980
Never Surrender (RCA), 1982

*Debut LP **Triumph** with one track less

The Troggs

UK group formed 1966.
Original line-up: Reg Presley, vocals; Chris Britton, guitar; Pete Staples, bass; Ronnie Bond, drums.

Career: Formed in Andover, Hants, the Troggs were discovered by record producer Larry Page who signed them to management deal and secured recording contract with Fontana.

After debut on BBC Radio's 'Saturday Club' and TV's 'Thank Your Lucky Star', they recorded American writer Chips Taylor's **Wild Thing**. Featuring Reg Presley's moody vocal and ocarina playing, the record lived up to title, being one of wildest records ever cut in UK. Its originality was rewarded with a million sales and American chart-topping status (where it was, most unusually, available on two different record labels—Fontana and Atco).

Presley himself penned the follow-up **With A Girl Like You**, a UK chart-topper which also went gold, and again available on both Fontana and Atco in US.

The classic **I Can't Control Myself** and **Any Way That You Want Me** gave them four UK Top-10 hits in very first year. Another million-seller came in 1967 with **Love Is All**

Around (also a Presley composition).

Peter Staples was replaced by Tony Murray in 1969 and group's recording career went into decline despite mini-hit with novel version of Beach Boys(▶) **Good Vibrations.**

However, stunning stage act created fanatically loyal following in Germany, France, Holland, Britain and, particularly, in America, which sustained them through the '70s despite lack of activity.

With no further line-up changes, group today continues to earn good money on cabaret/club circuits, despite lack of recording success.

Current line-up: Presley; Britton; Bond; Tony Murray, bass.

Hit Singles:

	US	UK
Wild Thing, 1966	1	2
With A Girl Like You, 1966	29	1
I Can't Control Myself, 1966	43	2
Any Way That You Want Me, 1968	—	8
Give It To Me, 1967	—	12
Night Of The Long Grass, 1967	—	17
Love Is All Around, 1967	7	5

Albums:
The Troggs Tapes (Private Stock/Penny Farthing), 1975
Live At Max's Kansas City (Max's Kansas City), 1979

Worth Searching Out:
Wild Thing (Atco/Fontana), 1966
Best Of (—/Page One), 1967

Wild Thing, Troggs. Courtesy Fontana Records.

Robin Trower

UK guitarist, composer.
Born London, March 9, 1945.

Career: Trower began in a Southend band, Paramounts. Co-member Gary Brooker went on to form Procol Harum(▶). After recording **Whiter Shade Of Pale**, Brooker asked Trower to join Harum and he stayed from 1967-71. He left because of dissatisfaction with limited guitar sound.

Trower had become a great admirer of Jimi Hendrix(▶), as evidenced by his **Song For A Dreamer**, which he contributed to his final Harum LP, **Broken Barricades**. Instead of going for guitar hero role, Trower tried to form group to be called Jude. This effort failed, but introduced him to ex-Stone The Crow bassist/vocalist Jim Dewar. In mid-1972, he and Dewar formed Robin Trower Band with drummer Reg Isadore. First LP, **Twice Removed From Yesterday**, produced some spacy riffs which some found exhilarating, but others considered a Hendrix rip-off.

Band was ignored in UK, but did well in the US. Unfortunately, each subsequent release pushed Trower further into axe hero role. Ex-Sly Stone drummer Bill London replaced Reg Isadore on third LP, **For Earth Below**.

Twice Removed From Yesterday, Robin Trower. Courtesy Chrysalis Records.

This line-up recorded next five LPs, by which time recycled Hendrix lines were no longer interesting.

Trower then teamed up with London and Jack Bruce(▶) to form BLT. LP of same name made US Top 40 in 1981. Isadore joined band for **Truce** LP.

Trower's guitar work can be interesting, if highly derivative. Among peers (Pat Travers, Mahogany Rush), he clearly ranks as one of the best. US following will keep him employed for some time to come.

Guitar: Fender Stratocaster.

Albums:
Twice Removed From Yesterday (Chrysalis), 1973
Bridge Of Sighs (Chrysalis), 1974
For Earth Below (Chrysalis), 1975
Robin Trower Live (Chrysalis), 1975
Long Misty Days (Chrysalis), 1976
In City Dreams (Chrysalis), 1977
Caravan To Midnight (Chrysalis), 1978
Victim Of Fury (Chrysalis), 1980
Time Is Short (Chrysalis), 1983

Bruce, London, Trower:
BLT (Chrysalis), 1981

Bruce/Trower:
Truce (Chrysalis), 1982

The Tubes

US group formed 1972.

Original/current line-up: Fee Waybill, vocals; Bill Spooner, guitar; Vince Welnick, keyboards; Rich Anderson, bass; Michael Cotten, synthesiser; Roger Steen, guitar; Prairie Prince, percussion.

Career: Formed by Bill Spooner with art school friends, group immediately gained devoted following in San Francisco's Bay Area. Combined often heavy rock with outrageous satire and became known for bizarre creations such as Quay Lude (drugged-out superstar) and Dr Strangekiss (a crippled Nazi, sounding not unlike Tom Jones). Sexist parody also played important role in act, with semi-clad girls and a leather-and-chains production called 'Mondo Bondage' Notoriety was increased following cameo appearance in porno movie 'The Resurrection Of Eve'.

Signed record deal with A&M in 1975, releasing **The Tubes** same year. With Al Kooper as producer, set included Rocky Horror style classics, notably **White Punks On Dope**, later a Top 30 UK hit. As following increased, Tubes invested in innumerable props to bolster stage act, including glitter rainstorm, fog machines and elaborate electronics. Often individual sets would be required for single numbers, and theatrical presentations proved gruelling.

By third album **Now**, Tubes had recruited

Minge Lewis to produce more mainstream work. Late '70s also saw them tempering theatrical outrage by limiting appearances of dancing girls, possibly to avoid accusations of blatant sexism. Braved a purely musical, non-theatrical, club tour in 1980, which was only partially successful. Very much part of '70s glam rock mentality, even though appearance was late in decade, Tubes proved amusing spectacle, but their charm seems decidedly ephemeral.

Fourth album **Remote Control**, produced by Todd Rundgren(▶), failed to break any new ground and caused renewed friction with record company. Finally recorded unreleased album for A&M, for which Waybill refused to contribute vocals. Reputedly left their record company following finance dispute.

Signed deal with Capitol, which led to 1981-82 tour, taking in Sweden, Norway, Germany, France, Holland, Portugal, Italy and Britain. **The Completion Backward Principle** (a phrase borrowed from the methodology of salesmanship) saw group assigned to producer David Foster (Boz Scaggs, Hall & Oates) in attempt to record hit album. Although work showed flashes of old humour, it was obvious compromise, as even the group admit. Ironically, Tubes now seem part of the very system they once parodied so effectively, confirmed by 1983 US AOR hit **She's A Beauty**.

Hit Singles:
She's A Beauty, 1983   10   —

Albums:
The Tubes (A&M), 1975
Young And Rich (A&M), 1976
Now (A&M), 1977
What Do You Want From Live (A&M), 1978
Remote Control (A&M), 1979
The Completion Backward Principle (Capitol), 1981
Outside Inside (Capitol), 1983

Ike And Tina Turner

US duo formed 1959.
Ike Turner, guitarist, keyboard player, producer: born Clarksdale, Mississippi, November 5, 1931.
Tina Turner, vocals: born Annie Mae Bullock, Brownsville, Tennessee, November 26, 1938.

Career: One of the most exciting R&B acts for over two decades, Ike and Tina Turner had volatile relationship which ended in both personal and professional divorce. Since then Tina has continued with relatively unsuccessful solo career while Ike has concentrated on production work at his Bolic Sound Studios.

Above: The outrageous Tubes toned down their act to find success.

A gifted guitarist/pianist, Ike Turner is equally famed as talent scout for Modern Records, recruiting B. B. King(▶), Howlin' Wolf(▶) and Bobby Bland. But most important of all was his discovery of Tina in 1959. The magic combination yielded debut hit **A Fool In Love** on Sue in 1960.

The Ikettes (P. P. Arnold, Merry Clayton and Bonnie Bramlett were sometime members) was formed as backing vocal group with Turner's Kings Of Rhythm band.

Churning out numerous singles and more than 30 albums for Sonja, Innis, Kent, Loma, Warner, Modern, Tangerine and Cenco, the duo sailed successfully through '60s, winning even wider audience when touring UK with Rolling Stones(▶) in '66. They cut classic **River Deep Mountain High** for Phil Spector's Philles label (Ike was actually barred from studio so that Spector could inject his own unbridled 'Wall Of Sound' into what has been cited as greatest pop record of all time).

Stints with Pompeii, Blue Thumb (who steered them towards both blues and heavy rock) and Minit led Ike and Tina to a rich spell with Liberty/United Artists. Pop chart action came with **Sexy Ida, Sweet Rhode Island Red** and **Nutbush City Limits** which brought adulation from rock audiences and appearance for Tina as Acid Queen in screen version of the Who's(▶) rock opera 'Tommy'.

As well as for his classics with Tina, Ike Turner demands respect as man behind Jackie Brenston's 1951 Chess hit **Rocket 88**, often cited as history's first rock 'n' roll record.

Hit Singles:

		US	UK
It's Gonna Work Out Fine	1961	14	—
River Deep Mountain High	1966	—	3
A Love Like Yours	1966	—	16
Proud Mary	1971	4	—
Nutbush City Limits	1973	22	4

Albums:
River Deep Mountain High (A&M), 1966
Airwaves (Liberty/—), '70s
Her Man, His Woman (—/Capitol), 1970
The Ike And Tina Turner Revue (—/New World), 1975
Souled From The Vaults (—/DJM), 1975
Soul Sellers (—/United Artists), 1979
Hot 'N' Sassy (Accord/—), 1982

Left: Ike and Tina Turner in happier days before their divorce.

The Turtles

US group formed 1965.
Original line-up: Howard Kaylan, vocals; Mark Volman, vocals; Al Nichol, guitar; Chuck Portz, bass; Jim Tucker, guitar; Don Murray, drums.

Career: While still at Westchester High School (LA) in 1962, Kaplan (change to Kaylan came later), Nichol and Portz formed surf band, the Nightriders. Murray, who attended nearby school, joined on drums. In February 1963 band added Volman, and changed name to Crossfires.

With various rhythm guitarists, this line-up recorded some obscure singles, and played at local high-school dances. Jim Tucker eventually took rhythm guitar spot. (Band occasionally billed itself as folk group, Crosswind Singers.) The new, but very small, White Whale label offered a contract on condition that name be changed yet again. Band's manager suggested 'Tyrtles' to cash in on UK-sounding name; band agreed on 'Turtles'.

The Byrds(▶) had just hit with Dylan cover,

Happy Together, The Turtles. Courtesy White Whale Records.

Mr Tambourine Man, so Turtles' first release, **It Ain't Me, Babe**, sounded like perfect progression in folk-rock fusion. **Let Me Be** and **You Baby**, both written by 'protest' songwriter P. F. Sloan, followed debut into charts. First LP was released in 1965 and, as was typical of time, carried lots of covers and some filler. The surprise is that the jangling sound on **Wanderin' Kind** and **Love Minus Zero** sounds as fresh and novel today as it did then.

Next single was self-penned **Grim Reaper Of Love**; being different in texture and sound from expected Turtles mould, it barely made charts. White Whale regrettably put pressure on Kaylan/Volman to stop releasing original material. Next release, **Outside Chance,** missed completely, but included new drummer John Barbata (later of Jefferson Starship(▶)). Then Portz left; Jim Pons (ex-Leaves) took his place.

By early 1967, band had been a year without a hit, a bad sign in the golden age of singles. However, **Happy Together** went to US No. 1, and put band back in spotlight. Turtles' next release, **She'd Rather Be With Me**, made No. 3 in US.

By 1968, band wanted to assume self-production. After two misses, they came up with US No. 6 **Elenore**, but the public seemed to miss ironic mockery of song, so band overloaded potshots on next LP. **The Turtles Present The Battle Of The Bands** was unequalled in its loving snipes at rock styles until Nick Lowe's(▶) **Jesus Of Cool/Pure Pop For Now People** LP.

The Turtles lost Tucker while touring UK, (he wasn't replaced). As sessions were to begin for new LP, Barbata also quit and John Seiter (ex-Spanky And Our Gang) came in. Line-up of

Kaylan, Volman, Nichol, Pons and Seiter lasted rest of band's lifetime. New LP was to be straight-ahead rock, and admirer Ray Davies (Kinks(▶)) agreed to produce it. Despite strong material and Davies credentials, album failed to hit at a time when LPs were beginning to determine success and status.

Band continued to tour with greatest hits package, making 'unhip' decision to play White House at Tricia Nixon's request. Failure to produce hit records caused growing problems with White Whale, which led to legal hassles; band quietly disappeared sometime in 1970.

Kaylan and Volman have most interesting Turtles history. Unable to record under their own name because of lawsuits, the duo took names of two Turtles roadies and joined Frank Zappa(▶) as Phlorescent Leech and Eddie. Their appearance in '200 Motels' was promising and promoted comic image. As Flo & Eddie, they released several LPs, backed Marc Bolan(▶), promoted a radio show, and in general maintained zany side of Turtles into '70s and '80s.

Considering their brilliant sound and good sense of humour, it is puzzling that the Turtles haven't exerted greater influence. They remain a highly underrated cult band; though recordings during their heyday have become somewhat collectable.

Final line-up: Kaylan; Volman; Nichol; Jim Pons, bass; John Seiter, drums.

Hit Singles:	US	UK
It Ain't Me Babe, 1965	8	—
You Baby, 1966	20	—
Happy Together, 1967	1	12
She'd Rather Be With Me, 1967	3	4
You Know What I Mean, 1967	12	—
She's My Girl, 1967	14	—
Elenore, 1968	6	7
You Showed Me, 1969	6	—

Albums:
As The Crossfires:
Out Of Control (Rhino/—), 1981

As The Turtles:
Happy Together Again (—/Philips), 1975
It Ain't Me Babe (Rhino/—), 1982
Great Hits Of The Turtles (Rhino/—), 1982

Worth Searching Out:
You Baby (White Whale/—), 1966
Happy Together (White Whale/London), 1967
Golden Hits (White Whale/—), 1967
Battle Of The Bands (White Whale/London), 1968
More Golden Hits (White Whale/—), 1969
Turtle Soup (White Whale/—), 1969
Wooden Head (White Whale/—), 1970
Happy Together Again (Sire/—), 1975

Conway Twitty

US vocalist, guitarist, composer.
Born Harold Lloyd Jenkins, Friars Point, Mississippi, September 1, 1935.

Career: Former rock 'n' roll singer, turned country performer, Twitty scored in late '50s with teen anthems **I Need Your Lovin'** and **It's Only Make Believe** (which he co-wrote).

Transition to country started in mid-'60s. First C&W chart record was **Guess My Eyes Were Bigger Than My Heart** (1966), and since then he has maintained continuous stream of hit singles and albums.

Twitty was coupled with Loretta Lynn(▶) for series of duets in early '70s, and pair earned Country Music Association Vocal Duo Of The Year awards in '72, '73, '74 and '75.

A baseball protegé (he turned down chance of going pro), Twitty is welcome change

Above: Conway Twitty, rock'n'roller turned country music superstar.

from the schmaltz-laden stereotypes rife in Nashville. His powerful baritone is still a major draw at concerts.

Hit Singles:	US	UK
It's Only Make Believe, 1958	1	1
Mona Lisa, 1959	29	5
Danny Boy, 1959	10	—
Lonely Blue Boy, 1960	6	—

Albums (selected):
Looking Back (—/Polydor), 1975
Georgia Keeps Pulling On My Ring (MCA), 1978
It's Only Make Believe (—/Pickwick), 1981
Southern Comfort (Elektra/—), 1982
Greatest Hits (MGM/—), 1982
No. 1 Classics Volume 1 (Elektra), 1982
Early Favourites (Accord/—), 1982
Number Ones (MCA/—), 1982
Shake It Up Baby (—/Bulldog), 1982

With Loretta Lynn (selected):
Feelins (MCA), 1975
United Talent (MCA), 1976
Very Best Of (MCA/—), 1976

U2

UK group formed 1979.
Original/Current line-up: Bono 'Vox' Hewson, vocals; Dave 'The Edge' Evans guitar, keyboards; Adam Clayton, bass; Larry Mullen, drums.

Career: Inspired by London's new, young bands in 1976, Bono and the 'The Edge' decided to form own group in Dublin. Fellow mates Clayton and Mullen joined, and name U2 was taken, with implication that every fan could join as well.

Bono described band as beginning with three chords, but with special enthusiasm. Pub gigs led to local record contract with CBS. Two singles, released in Ireland only, gained cult status in UK. Island Records became interested and took over band, releasing **11 O'clock Tick Tock** in May 1980.

UK critics began falling over themselves to cite U2 as next big thing. When **Boy** LP was released, U2 were hailed as *the* hope of rock's future. Band ignored press and pushed on, establishing close rapport with audiences. **I Will Follow** was issued as strong single.

Touring in US brought band into contact with producer Sandy Pearlman (Blue Oyster Cult/Dictators/Clash) and for time he was considered for second LP. Some New York sessions were produced but ultimately band returned to Steve Lilywhite.

1981 single **Gloria** received heavy airplay

and made UK Top 40. When **October** LP was released, expected revisionism set in and critics carped that U2 was really just another '60s band because of basic guitar, bass, drum sound. Band continued to ignore press and found audiences growing everywhere.

U2 went on road in December 1982 and started playing new LP before its February 1983 release. **War** entered UK charts at No. 1 and featured U2's best effort so far. **Sunday Bloody Sunday** and **New Year's Day** singles had band confronting its Irish background, as do many U2 compositions. Like the Clash(▶) and the Jam(▶), U2 are politically/socially aware and though sometimes regarded as a bit preachy, generally manage to make their music entertaining as well as informative.

Liking U2 requires taking risk. Band assumes music matters, and is brutally honest in living up to that assumption. So far band has delivered, being rewarded with young, committed, level-headed audience. Have recenty toured US to appease new fans there.

Albums:
Boy (Island), 1980
October (Island), 1981
War (Island), 1983

UB40

UK group formed 1977.
Original line-up: Ali Campbell, vocals, guitar; Robin Campbell, guitar, vocals; Brian Travers, saxophone; Earl Falconer, bass; Jimmy Lynn, keyboards; Jim Brown, drums; Norman Hassan, percussion; 'Yomi' Babayemi, percussion.

Career: Band came together in West Midlands; as most members were unemployed, took name UB40 from unemployment benefit form.

Inter-racial outfit, UB40 pioneered specifically British brand of melodic reggae, combining smooth vocals and liquid saxophone fill-ins with relaxed reggae beat. At first amateurish band quickly tightened up sound and by 1979 were undertaking gigs. That same year Lynn left, replaced by Michael Virtue, Babayemi returned to his native Nigeria; Astro joined as resident toaster/vocalist. That year group also signed to local Graduate label; second single, **King/Food For Thought**, took them into Top 5.

From then on, success came quickly. Touring with Pretenders(▶) led to series of tours as headliners, and debut album **Signing Off** reached UK Top 20.

At end of 1980 band decided to quit Graduate and form own Dep label. Product released under new arrangement made more

chart impact and UB40 has become one of most successful of new British bands in '80s. Genuinely original, in tune with harsh realities of times, UB40 deserve to go from strength to strength. Only problem might be slight tendency to 'sameness' in material.

Current line-up: Ali Campbell; Robin Campbell; Travers; Falconer; Brown; Hassan; Astro, toaster, vocals; Michael Virtue, keyboards.

Hit Singles:	US	UK
King/Food For Thought, 1980	—	4
My Way Of Thinking/I Think It's Going To Rain, 1980	—	6
The Earth Dies Screaming/ Dream A Lie, 1980	—	10
Don't Slow Down/Don't Let It Pass You By, 1981	—	16
One In Ten, 1981	—	7

Albums:
Signing Off (—/Graduate), 1980
Present Arms (—/Dep International), 1981
Present Arms In Dub (—/Dep International), 1981
The Singles Album (—/Graduate), 1982
UB44 (—/Dep International), 1982

UFO

UK group formed 1970.
Original line-up: Phil Mogg, vocals; Pete Way, bass; Andy Parker, drums; Mick Bolton, guitar.

Career: When UFO formed, their style of music was called hard rock. **UFO 1** and **Flying** were totally ignored in UK/US but became popular in Germany and Japan. Bolton left and remaining trio became core of UFO through various personnel changes. Michael Schenker(▶) met UFO while with Scorpions, who opened a German tour. He took guitar spot on **Phenomenon** which became underground cult LP in US.

Force It and **No Heavy Petting** LPs showed off Schenker's growing heavy-metal guitar abilities; the latter album also saw band expand range by adding Danny Peyronel on keyboards. **Lights Out** album provided stage favourites **Love To Love** and title song. Paul Raymond was now on keyboards and band developed highly competent stage show. In UK they had become major draw without compromising to punk or new wave.

Growing reputation was boosted by **Obsession**, but live **Stranger In The Night** finally broke band in US. For exciting heavy metal, this LP is excellent introduction.

Below: Ireland's finest export of the '80s, U2, with Bono (right).

arked departure of Schenker
Michael Schenker Group.
ho had guested on LP, took
time.
his period begins demise of
band. **No Place To Run** saw Raymond
replaced by Neil Carter. LP was too slickly
produced by George Martin and missed edge
given by Schenker. **The Wild, The Willing
And The Innocent** album met fair reviews
but did nothing new or exciting. Worse,
Mogg's stage performances were becoming
erratic because of personal problems and
pressures. Way managed to contend with
deteriorating situation for one more LP, but
mid-1982 brought announcement he was
leaving to form Fastway with ex-Motorhead(▶)
guitarist, Fast Eddie Clarke.

**Strangers In The Night, UFO. Courtesy
Chrysalis Records.**

Band recorded **Making Contact** in 1983
with Carter doubling on keyboards and bass.
UFO set off on European tour with Billy
Sheehan as guest bassist. Then at February
1983 Athens show Mogg collapsed, and
audience nearly rioted. Cutting short tour,
group quickly returned to UK so that Mogg
could rest up. A month later plans were
announced for several UK 'thank you' gigs in
summer 1983, following which UFO would
disband. Despite disappointment to loyal
fans, it's probably best thing for UFO at this
point.

Current line-up: Mogg; Parker; Paul
Chapman, guitar; Neil Carter, bass, keyboards.

Albums:
UFO 1 (—/Beacon), 1971
Flying (—/Beacon), 1972
Phenomenon (Chrysalis), 1973
Force It (Chrysalis), 1975
No Heavy Petting (Chrysalis), 1976
Lights Out (Chrysalis), 1977
Obsession (Chrysalis), 1978
Strangers In The Night (double, live),
  (Chrysalis), 1979
No Place To Run (Chrysalis), 1979
The Wild, The Willing And The Innocent
  (Chrysalis), 1981
Mechanix (Chrysalis), 1982
Making Contact (Chrysalis), 1983

Ultravox

UK group formed 1975.

Original line-up: John Foxx (real name
Dennis Leigh), vocals; Billy Currie, violin,
keyboards, synthesiser; Chris Cross (aka
Chris St John), bass; Stevie Shears, guitar;
Warren Cann, drums.

Career: Foxx, from Chorley, Lancs, met Cross
when latter moved from London to join
Preston band Stoned Rose. After recruiting
other three (Cann born in Canada, others
British), formed band named Tiger Lily, with
intention of playing like early Roxy Music(▶).

Signed with small Gull label, released version
of Fats Waller's **Ain't Misbehavin'**, title
music to X-rated film of same name. No
success, but single reissued in '80s on even
smaller Scottish label, Dead Good Records.
Band also known in early days by such
names as the Zips, the Innocents, London
Soundtrack and Fire Of London, but by 1976
had settled on name of Ultravox! (exclamation
mark later dropped).
Signed with Island in 1976, releasing three
LPs and numerous singles, all unsuccessful,
despite growing cult following. In 1978,
Shears left, replaced until 1979 by Robin
Simon. That same year, Foxx departed to
embark on partially successful solo career,
which continues today. Currie, Cross and
Cann decided to stay together, even though
group dropped by Island at this time. Recruited
James 'Midge' Ure as singer/guitarist — Ure
had played with Currie in Visage, part time
band for both, led by Steve Strange. Ure's
previous career had included Slik, a Scottish
pop band who topped UK charts in 1976 with
Forever And Ever, Rich Kids, formed by
ex-Sex Pistol(▶) bassist Glen Matlock (Ure
was also invited at one point to join Sex
Pistols, but declined), and temporary work
with Thin Lizzy(▶).
When Ure joined Ultravox, group adopted
fresh direction with synthesisers, which had
started when Foxx was singer, and signed with
Chrysalis. Ever since, they have enjoyed
substantial success in UK, and to a lesser
extent in other countries, with unbroken run of
hit singles, plus several successful LPs.
While they have also worked on outside
projects (Currie with Visage until early 1983,

**Above: Ultravox (from left) Cross, Currie,
Ure, Cann.**

Ure also with Visage, as well as solo records
and 1983 collaboration with Mick Karn of
Japan, Cross making videos with Ure, and
Cann writing film music), suspicion exists that
group may have become too set in their ways,
and liberal plundering of albums for single
releases (which rely heavily on excellent
videos) could result in fall from 1983 position
as superstars.

Current line-up: Midge Ure, vocals, guitar,
synthesiser; Currie; Cross; Cann.

Hit Singles:	US	UK
Vienna, 1981	—	2
All Stood Still, 1981	—	8
The Thin Wall, 1981	—	14
The Voice, 1981	—	16
Reap The Wild Wind, 1982	—	12
Hymn, 1982	—	11
Visions In Blue, 1983	—	15

Midge Ure Solo:

	US	UK
No Regrets, 1982	—	9

Albums:
Ultravox! (Island), 1977
System Of Romance (Antilles/Island), 1978
Vienna (Chrysalis), 1980
Three Into One (Antilles/Island), 1980*
Rage In Eden (Chrysalis), 1981
Quartet (Chrysalis), 1982
*compilation

Worth Searching Out:
Ha! Ha! Ha! (Island), 1977

Undertones

UK group formed 1975.

Original/Final line-up: Feargal Sharkey,
vocals; John O'Neill, guitar; Damian 'Dee'
O'Neil, guitar; Mike Bradley, bass; Billy
Doherty, drums.

Career: Formed in Derry, Northern Ireland,
band went unnoticed until mid-1978 when UK
press discovered Irish music scene. **Teenage
Kicks** EP was put out on independent label;
John Peel played a role in getting band
exposure by including EP on his radio show.
Undertones' first LP captured brash, young
sound. With a cover deliberately derivative of
Who's(▶) **My Generation** LP, Undertones
struck pose of an '80s band aware of rock's
past. Critics praised band's freshness, and UK
concerts won large audiences.
Focus of band was Sharkey's quavering
vocals, which always seemed ready to break
down but just managed to last to end of each
song. This kept concerts interesting, but band
stalled on record. **Hypnotised** was termed
average by critics but **Positive Touch** was
condemned as repetitive.
Undertones retreated to Northern Ireland in
1982 and took time to rework sound. **The Sin
Of Pride** may refer to band's early cockiness,
but it also revealed group's maturity and
awareness of its own limitations. This LP
astounded critics for its assimilation of
diverse styles and its handling of complex
subjects; it may prove to be one of '80s best
albums.
With their honesty and conviction, they could
probably have become major influence, but
group split up in 1983.

Hit Singles:	US	UK
Jimmy, Jimmy, 1979	—	16
My Perfect Cousin, 1980	—	9
Wednesday Week, 1980	—	11
It's Going To Happen, 1981	—	18

Albums:
The Undertones (—/Sire), 1979
Hypnotised (Sire), 1980
Positive Touch (Harvest/EMI), 1981
The Sin Of Pride (—/Ardeck), 1983

Uriah Heep

UK group formed 1969

Original line-up: Mick Box, guitar; David
Byron, vocals; Ken Hensley, keyboards; Alex
Napier, drums; Paul Newton, bass, vocals.

Career: Box and Byron asked Ken Hensley to
leave Toe Fat and formed Uriah Heep. Napier
and Newton had been with Box and Byron in
their old band Spice; Newton had known
Hensley in earlier band, Gods, and introduced
him to Heep. While recording first LP, Napier
left, to be replaced by Nigel Olsson, who quit
after recording sessions for Elton John(▶).
Heep auditioned Keith Baker as new drummer.
Following second LP, Baker left. Ian Clarke
joined for one year and one album. Hensley
finally convinced Toe Fat mate, Lee Kerslake,
to take drums. Band also replaced Newton
with Mark Clarke who quit after few months.
Throughout this flux, band was object of
critical attack rivalled only by that directed
towards Grand Funk Railroad(▶). Gary Thain
joined on bass and band took off as international stars. Based on vague sorcery,
Demons And Wizards and **The Magician's
Birthday** LPs were full of mystic connota-

**Left: Uriah Heep must be termed sur-
vivors, despite continual line up changes
in the band.**

tions. The same line-up also recorded highly underrated **Uriah Heep Live** LP which predates heavy metal without the boring repetition that sometimes plagues genre.

Thain developed drug problems which led to his firing in early 1975. (He died in December 1975.) John Wetton (later of Asia(▶)) joined for 18 months. **Return To Fantasy** and **High And Mighty** were recorded during this period.

Even though LPs were as strong as ever Heep lost audience and internal dissent began tearing band apart. Wetton and Byron left in August 1976. Box, Hensley and Kerslake signed up John Lawton for vocals and Trevor Bolder (ex-David Bowie(▶)) on bass. This line-up recorded **Firefly**, **Innocent Victim** and **Fallen Angel** as band continued downward slide. Reshuffle again occurred before recording of excellent **Abominog**, which appeared after most fans assumed band was gone for good.

Uriah Heep stand in class all their own for determination, stubbornness — and eternal hope of a big hit.

Current line-up: Box; Lee Kerslake, drums; Peter Goalby, vocals; Bob Daisley, bass; John Sinclair, keyboards.

Albums:
Very 'Eavy, Very 'Umble (—/Vertigo), 1970
Uriah Heep (Mercury/—), 1970
Salisbury (Mercury/Vertigo), 1971
Look At Yourself (Mercury/Bronze), 1971
Demons And Wizards (Mercury/Bronze), 1972
The Magician's Birthday (Mercury/Bronze), 1972
Uriah Heep Live (Mercury/Bronze), 1973
Sweet Freedom (Warner Bros/Bronze), 1973
Wonderworld (Warner Bros/Bronze), 1974
Return To Fantasy (Warner Bros/Bronze), 1975
The Best Of (Mercury/Bronze), 1975
High And Mighty (Warner Bros/Bronze), 1976
Firefly (Warner Bros/Bronze), 1977
Innocent Victim (Warner Bros/Bronze), 1977
Fallen Angel (Chrysalis/Bronze), 1978
Conquest (—/Bronze), 1980
Abominog (Mercury/Bronze), 1982
Dreamer (—/Bronze), 1982
Head First (Mercury/Bronze), 1983

Ritchie Valens

US vocalist, guitarist, composer.
Born Los Angeles, California, May 13, 1941; died February 3, 1959.

Career: Took up guitar age nine; became popular entertainer while in high school, appearing at school functions and local dances with own group, the Silhouettes. Spotted by Bob Keene of Del-Fi Records and signed to contract. First single **Come On Let's Go** was moderate success in US with cover version by Tommy Steele reaching UK Top 10.

Mexican background apparent in many recordings, with adaptation of traditional Mexican song **La Bamba** becoming best-known example; released with **Donna**, which became Valens' biggest hit. Made film debut in late 1958 singing **Ooh My Head** in rock 'n' roll teen drama movie 'Go Johnny Go'.

Embarked on first major tour through Mid-West US in January 1959. Halfway through tour, co-star Buddy Holly(▶) chartered plane to fly to next engagement; Valens won seat on aircraft by flipping coin with guitarist Tommy Allsup. Valens died with Holly and Big Bopper when plane crashed into snow-covered cornfield.

Death at age 17 cut short promising career

and left few recordings to evaluate importance but his influence is evident, in particular on Chris Montez who took Valens' style into charts in early '60s.

Hit Singles:

	US	UK
Donna/La Bamba, 1958	2	—

Albums:
His Greatest Hits (—/President), 1970
Rock Lil' Darlin' (—/Joy), 1971

Van Halen

US group formed 1974.

Original/Current line-up: David Lee Roth, vocals; Edward Van Halen, Gibson Flying V guitar; Mike Anthony, bass; Alex Van Halen, drums.

Career: Netherlands-born Van Halen brothers originally trained as concert pianists; family relocated in Pasadena, California. Formed group (originally known as Mammoth) with Roth and Anthony (both born in US Mid-West), and became popular local attraction through combination of loud and energetic heavy metal and Roth's very tight trousers. Due to inability to attract record deal, began promoting own gigs; used every possible attention-grabbing trick — like parachuting into stadium gig in successful attempt to upstage headlining band.

By 1977, group were attracting audiences of 3,000. Warners Bros' A&R man Ted Templeman saw them playing in Hollywood club and signed them immediately.

Below: Jon Anderson (left) and Vangelis Papathanassiou joined forces in 1980.

First single was cover of Kinks(▶) **All Day And All Of The Night.**

Subsequently, five LPs were released, all produced by Templeman, with major US chart success—first Top 20, rest Top 10—and somewhat smaller success in singles chart. Van Halen are archetypal latterday heavy metal exponents (though they prefer skintight silk to black leather); Roth and Eddie Van Halen had spell as major US teeny bopper heartthrobs. Group seem likely to remain major US draw, even if success in UK considerably less. Eddie Van Halen regarded domestically as hottest US guitar player; recently guested on Michael Jackson's(▶) No. 1 single **Beat It.**

Hit Singles:

	US	UK
Dance The Night Away, 1979	15	—
Pretty Woman, 1982	12	—

Albums:
Van Halen (Warner Bros), 1978
Van Halen II (Warner Bros), 1979
Women And Children First (Warner Bros), 1980
Fair Warning (Warner Bros), 1981
Diver Down (Warner Bros), 1982

Vangelis

Greek composer, keyboard player.
Born Vangelis Papathanassiou.

Career: During '60s came to prominence in native land as leader of Aphrodite's Child, who scored notable Euro hit with **Rain And Tears** single (1968) and **666** double LP (1972). Another member of group Demis Roussos later became famous for easy-listening hits in mid-'70s.

Left: Van Halen, with extrovert singer David Lee Roth in scarf.

After group split, Vangelis relocated to Paris to establish reputation as serious composer. Worked on score for film 'L'Apocalypse Des Animaux' with director Frederick Rossiff for notable LP. Moved to London in 1974. Initially regarded as flatulent upstart, Vangelis ignored major commercial failure and continued to work on electronic/synthesiser music through several poor-selling albums.

By 1980, had teamed up with ex-Yes(▶) vocalist Jon Anderson — Vangelis tipped to join Yes some years before — for series of album projects which have enjoyed much more success. Crowning achievement is his music composition for multiple Oscar-winning 'Chariots Of Fire' movie, which also won Vangelis Oscar for best score.

Hit Singles:

	US	UK
Chariots Of Fire (Main Theme), 1981	—	12
Chariots Of Fire — Titles, 1982	1	41

With Jon Anderson:

	US	UK
I'll Find My Way Home, 1981	51	6

Albums:
Heaven And Hell (RCA), 1975
Albedo 0.39 (RCA), 1976
Spiral (RCA), 1977
Beauborg (RCA), 1978
Hypothesis (Affinity), 1978
Best Of (RCA), 1978
China (Polydor), 1979
See You Later (Polydor), 1980
Short Stories (Polydor), 1979
Chariots Of Fire (Polydor), 1981
Friends Of Mr. Cairo (Polydor), 1981
Private Collection (Polydor), 1983

Vanilla Fudge

US group formed 1967.

Original/Final line-up: Carmine Appice, drums; Tim Bogart, bass; Vinnie Martell, guitar; Mark Stein, organ.

Career: East Coast contemporaries of Rascals. Vanilla Fudge's brief fling at fame was to take someone else's (preferably fast-tempoed) song, slow it down, slow it down again; and *then* play it with tortured guitar and fugue-like organ. Five albums, progressively more pretentious and tedious, and one hit single make the band only marginally interesting, mostly for the subsequent careers of members Bogart and Appice (Cactus, Jeff Beck(▶)), Boxer, and Rod Stewart(▶)).

Hit Singles:

	US	UK
You Keep Me Hangin' On, 1967	6	18

Albums:
Vanilla Fudge (Atco/Atlantic), 1967

Bobby Vee

US vocalist.
Born Robert Velline, Fargo, North Dakota, April 30, 1943.

Career: Formed first band the Shadows in 1959. Made first appearance in hometown as direct result of Buddy Holly's(▶) death in plane crash on February 3. Holly and rest of 'Winter Dance Party' had been due to appear in Fargo that evening; Vee's group brought in as replacement. First record on local label, **Suzy Baby**, became local hit and was released nationally on Liberty, who signed

Vee to long-term deal. In attempt to take over where Buddy Holly had left off, producer Snuff Garrett had Vee cover Adam Faith's(▶) UK hit **What Do You Want**, which in turn had been inspired by Holly's last recordings with pizzicato strings. Release failed but next single, **Devil Or Angel**, made Top 10, followed by Hollyish **Rubber Ball**, which became first of many UK hits.

During next three years, Vee became established as purveyor of Brill Building pop songs, with best material from Gerry Goffin and Carole King(▶), who wrote biggest hit **Take Good Care Of My Baby**. Although records and image were 'manufactured' to appeal to same market as Frankie Avalon(▶) and Fabian(▶), Vee's records had more lasting appeal due to careful production. Collaboration with Crickets in 1962 resulted in excellent **Bobby Vee Meets Crickets** album and sell-out tour of UK, with guests spots in 'Just For Fun' teen-movie. Appeal faded in mid-'60s despite attempts to score with contemporary material and 'fluke' comeback in 1967 with **Come Back When You Grow Up**.

Attempted further comeback in '70s under real name, but despite interesting album failed to make impression. Became Bobby Vee again in order to capitalise on old hits in nostalgia market.

Although following in his idol's musical footsteps led Bobby Vee to be much less innovative than Holly himself, it proved the right formula in the pre-Beatle era; good looks, grooming and a supply of Tin Pan Alley hit machine songs were of more value than creativity.

Hit Singles:	US	UK
Devil Or Angel, 1960	6	—
Rubber Ball, 1960	6	4
How Many Tears, 1961	—	10
Take Good Care Of My Baby, 1961	1	3
Run To Him, 1961	2	6
Please Don't Ask About Barbara, 1962	15	29
Sharing You, 1962	15	10
Punish Her, 1962	20	—
A Forever Kind Of Love, 1962	—	13
The Night Has A Thousand Eyes, 1962	3	3
Charms, 1963	13	—
Come Back When You Grow Up, 1967	3	—

Albums:
Golden Greats (Liberty/—), 1968
Singles Album (—/Fame), 1982

The Velvet Underground

US group formed 1966.

Original line-up: Nico, vocals; Lou Reed, guitar, vocals; John Cale, guitar, bass; Maureen Tucker, drums, percussion.

Career: Ill-assorted group of talented subversives came together in New York's fertile and bustling 'alternative' music scene in 1966 — Cale(▶), a Welsh child prodigy, Reed(▶), a classically trained trumpet player, and Tucker, one of few female drummers in rock.

Outlook was direct and dramatic opposite of the 'flower power' scene that was burgeoning at that time. Group mercilessly spotlighted drugs, death and the bizarre. Struggled in NYC's underground clubs until discovery by media idol/artist Andy Warhol. He added Nico, one of his protegées, promoted them, and designed cover of first album, **The Velvet Underground And Nico** (1967).

Group's image, outlook and sound were shocking and incomprehensible at times. Literate, half-spoken vocals and dark slashing sound did not suit audience looking for peace and love, and connection with Warhol led some to view them as publicity stunt. Their pervading influence is now obvious in punk, new wave and Euro-pop, however.

Nico left after first album. Group recorded two more albums on Verve/Polydor, **White Light/White Heat** 1968 and **The Velvet Underground** (1969), but they were too controversial to meet with commercial success. In 1970 Cale and Reed left, both to pursue varied and lengthy solo careers. Morrison was joined by Bill and Doug Yule briefly, but the Velvets' natural life had come to an end by 1972.

Final line-up: Morrison; Bill Yule, drums; Doug Yule, guitar, bass, keyboards.

Albums:
White Light/White Heat (Verve), 1968
The Velvet Underground (MGM), 1969
Loaded (Cotillion/Atlantic), 1970
Live (with Lou Reed) (Mercury), 1969
Velvet Underground Live (Cotillion/Atlantic), 1970

Worth Searching Out:
The Velvet Underground And Nico (Verve), 1967

The Ventures

US group formed 1960.

Original line-up: Don Wilson, guitar; Bob Bogle, guitar; Nokie Edwards, guitar; Howie Johnson, drums.

Career: Unable to secure recording deal from Fleetwoods Manager Bob Reisdoff with demo tapes (then calling themselves ('Versatones'), Don Wilson's mother Jonie formed own Blue Horizon label and mailed copies of their infectious, guitar-laden instrumental **Walk Don't Run** to DJs. DJ Pat O'Day of KJR Seattle played re-recorded song as outro to newcasts. Bob Reisdoff called KJR to ask identify of band and ended up signing them to Dolton Records, who took it to No. 2 in US charts and million-seller status.

Walk Don't Run, The Ventures. Courtesy Liberty Records.

Perfidia, re-make of 1939 Latin composition by Alberto Dominguez, gave them second gold disc and led to steady outpouring of albums through the '60s, exploiting their distinctive style which relied on very clean sound and heavy use of tremolo arm effect also used by British counterparts the Shadows.

In 1962 group toured Japan for first time and found their major market. Specialising in instrumental cover versions of current hits they churned out no fewer than 50 albums between 1960 and 1973, many of which went gold (their total sales in Japan have exceeded 40 million copies).

Victim of a car crash, Howie Johnson was replaced on drums in 1963 by Mel Taylor while same year saw Bob Bogle, lead guitarist on early hits, swap roles with bassist Nokie Edwards whose clean-picking style smacked of Chet Atkins(▶).

The Ventures capitalised on surf-music craze and in 1964 earned another gold disc for **Walk—Don't Run '64,** re-make of their earlier million-seller. **In Space** album introduced the Mosrite guitar they had been developing for a decade, and earned them a cool million dollars that year.

Such luminaries as Leon Russell(▶), Glen Campbell(▶), David Gates, B. Bumble and Red Rhodes were all used on Ventures' sessions, on organ or second guitar. Ex-John Mayall(▶) and Canned Heat(▶) players Harvey Mandell and Larry Taylor along with ex-Fortune Dave Carr were featured on **Rock 'N' Roll Forever** album.

Jerry McGhee — respected session man for Elvis Presley(▶), the Everly Brothers(▶), Rick Nelson(▶), Delaney and Bonnie(▶) and others — replaced Nokie Edwards in 1967, at which time a pronounced R&B flavour entered their work. After spell in retirement, Edwards returned to fold in 1972. Altogether, group has recorded 13 albums solely for Japanese market; they were first foreigners elected to the Conservatory of Music of Japan, while back home in the US they were presented with special award in 1972 for selling a million albums there annually every year since 1960.

Despite enormous commercial success, the Ventures were an enigma. What had, with **Walk Don't Run,** been a totally innovative and excitingly different sound has long since become a stilted cliché, and their teenage pioneering, middle-aged MOR tedium.

Final line-up: Jerry McGhee, guitar; Edwards; Mel Taylor, drums; Bogle, bass guitar.

Hit Singles:	US	UK
Walk Don't Run, 1960	2	8
Perfidia, 1960	15	4
Walk — Don't Run '64, 1964	8	—
Hawaii Five-O, 1969	4	—

Albums
Walk—Dont' Run (Liberty/—), 1960
Play Telstar, The Lonely Bull, And Others (Liberty/—), 1963
Golden Greats (Liberty), 1974
Very Best Of (Liberty/Sunset), 1976
Super Double Disc Of The Ventures (—/A&M), 1979
Play The Country Classics (Liberty/—), 1982

Tom Verlaine

US vocalist, guitarist, multi-instrumentalist, composer.
Born Thomas Miller, Mount Morris, New Jersey, December 13, 1949.

Career: Grew up in Wilmington, Delaware; learned piano, sax and guitar before mid-teens. Moved to New York in 1968, working as banana packer/despatcher. Formed Neon Boys (1972) with long-time friend Richard Hell, bass, and Billy Ficca, drums. Hell had previously published Verlaine's poetry in magazine he ran. Adding Richard Lloyd on guitar, band changed name to Television.

Cut debut single **Little Johnny Jewel** on local Ork Records in 1975; Fred Smith (later of Blondie(▶)) had replaced Hell. (Verlaine had previously played guitar on obscure Patti Smith track **Hey Joe,** 1974.) Signed to Elektra 1976; first album **Marquee Moon** released year later. LP saw much critical success, with Verlaine's futuristic playing a focal point; album often cited by young

Above: Tom Verlaine, Television's leader and now a solo artist.

musicians as most influential to new wave.

After second album **Adventure** (which made UK Top 10), band split. Lloyd cut solo **Alchemy** for Elektra (1979), Smith moved to sessions (played on Verlaine's LPs), Hell formed Richard Hell and the Voidoids, 1977.

Verlaine's first solo album **Tom Verlaine** saw further journalistic praise, but limited appeal outside of East Coast. Two-year hiatus followed before release of **Dreamtime**, on Warner Bros. Current album **Words From The Front** attracted interest in UK with might of Virgin Records behind release (Verlaine still signed to Warner Bros in US).

An extravagant guitarist who has considerable following among fellow-musicians, Verlaine may need to polish edges before universal acceptance.

Albums:
With Television:
Marquee Moon (Elektra), 1977
Adventure (Elektra), 1978

Solo:
Tom Verlaine (Elektra), 1979
Dreamtime (Warner Bros), 1981
Words From The Front (Warner Bros/Virgin), 1982

Tom Verlaine. Courtesy Elektra Records.

Gene Vincent

US vocalist, composer.
Born Vincent Eugene Craddock, Norfolk, Virginia, February 11, 1935; died Hollywood, California, October 12, 1971.

Career: Took up music seriously following disablement due to leg injuries received in motorcycle accident at Norfolk Naval Base while merchant seaman. By 1956 secured regular spot on country music station WCMS with DJ 'Sheriff' Tex Davis acting as manager. Recorded demo of **Be-Bop-A-Lula** at WCMS studio and won contract with Capitol Records, who regarded Vincent as 'answer' to Elvis Presley. **Lula** rapidly became hit but despite making charts again in 1957 Vincent's popularity declined in US.

During short-lived road career with Blue Caps, Vincent was regarded as wildest rock 'n' roll act on and off stage, leaving wrecked hotels and dressing rooms in wake. Poor management and money problems with group forced him to cease touring in US. Continued to record for Capitol, occasionally producing classic tracks. Generally recording career lacked direction, with producer Ken Nelson veering towards MOR standards in attempt to broaden appeal.

During 1960 found new popularity in Britain with appearances on Jack Good's 'Boy Meets Girl' TV show. Despite setback of further injuries received in April 1960 car crash that killed Eddie Cochran(▶), continued to tour UK regularly and became hero of teddy-boy movement; scored several minor UK hits on Capitol before final decline to smaller labels and smaller club dates.

By 1969 Vincent was shadow of former self, beset by personal problems and alcoholism. Returned to California in 1971, where attempts to once again revive career failed. He died later that year from heart failure undoubtedly related to drink problems.

Cult following established during lifetime shows no sign of diminishing and echoes of Vincent's stye are still found in many rockabilly revival groups, notably in recent chart successes of the Stray Cats(▶).

Hit Singles:	US	UK
Be-Bop-A-Lula, 1956	7	16
Bluejean Bop, 1956	—	16
Lotta Lovin', 1957	13	—
My Heart, 1960	—	16
Pistol Packin' Mama, 1960	—	15

Albums:
Gene Vincent's Greatest (Fame), 1977
The Gene Vincent Singles Album (Capitol), 1981
Gene Vincent and Eddie Cochran — Together Again (Capitol), 1980
Gene Vincent and Eddie Cochran — Rock 'n' Roll Heroes (Rockstar), 1981
The Bop They Couldn't Stop (Magnum Force), 1981
Dressed in Black (Magnum Force), 1982
Ain't That Too Much (Everest), 1982
Birdoggin' (Bulldog), 1982

Gene Vincent and the Shouts:
Shakin' Up A Storm (EMI), 1983

Loudon Wainwright III

US composer, guitarist, vocalist.
Born Chapel Hill, North Carolina, September 5, 1947.

Career: Wainwright began appearing in East Coast clubs and bars in the late '60s. He clearly emphasised the folk side of rock by relying on acoustic guitar and funny between-songs patter. In 1971 Atlantic brought out **Album I** which continued folk trend with macabre subject matter. **Album II** emphasised outrage for sake of outrage à la Lenny Bruce.

Switching to Columbia, Wainwright found sense of balance between humour and making a point. **Album III** captured Wainwright at his best; **Red Guitar** tipped hat to Pete Townshend's(▶) stage antics, and **Dead Skunk** got into US Top 20. Wainwright also had realised limits of self-accompaniment and on this LP began using session musicians for recording and as back-up group on stage. He married Kate McGarrigle(▶) in 1973 and she

appeared on **Unrequited** LP. (They had separated by 1978.)

Following albums always had something to say but appealed only to limited audience. At this point it appears that Wainwright will remain minor figure. Perhaps the barbs behind the humour are too sharp for mass audience.

Hit Singles:	US	UK
Dead Skunk, 1973	16	—

Albums:
Album I (Atlantic), 1971
Album II (Atlantic), 1972
Album III (Columbia/CBS), 1973
Attempted Moustache (Columbia/CBS), 1974
Unrequited (Columbia/CBS), 1975
T-Shirt (Arista), 1976
Final Exam (Arista), 1978
Live One (—/Radar), 1979
Fame And Wealth (—/Demon), 1983

Tom Waits

US composer, vocalist, pianist.
Born Pomona, California, December 7, 1949.

Career: Waits entertained small audiences on West Coast in early '70s. His rough voice and sparse back-up (usually piano, stand-up bass, drums and sax) evoked atmosphere of '50s Beatniks rather than '60s rock. Waits' tales of survival on other sides of tracks drew attention of Elektra, who signed him in 1973.

Waits' compositions started to get recorded by other artists and he opened for variety of acts from Charlie Rich to Frank Zappa. He has continued working throughout US and Europe but, despite rave critical approval, he remains cult figure on outskirts of rock. Waits' songs about lowlife are perceptive and poignant observations rather than critical judgements and his music seems best suited to dark,

Heartattack And Vine, Tom Waits. Courtesy Asylum Records.

Left: The charismatic Gene Vincent, in Capitol Studios during the '50s.

smoke-filled basement clubs and Bohemian cafes. This perhaps limits his potential for mass appeal, though he recently contributed to score for Francis Ford Coppola film; 'One From The Heart'.

Albums:
Closing Time (Elektra), 1973
The Heart Of A Saturday Night (Elektra/Asylum), 1974
Nighthawks At The Diner (Asylum), 1975
Small Change (Asylum), 1976
Foreign Affairs (Elektra), 1977
Blue Valentine (Asylum), 1978
Heartattack And Vine (Asylum), 1980

Rick Wakeman

UK keyboard player, composer.
Born London, May 18, 1949.

Career: Born into musical family; father was professional pianist. Studied piano from age four. On leaving school attended Royal College of Music when he started to make mark as session musician. Eventually gave up studies in favour of recording world. Provided keyboards expertise for many top artists, including David Bowie(▶), T. Rex(▶) and Cat Stevens(▶) during late '60s/early '70s.

In 1970 Wakeman was asked to join emergent Strawbs(▶), and stayed with band for 16 months. But after Yes(▶) lost keyboards man Tony Kaye, they persuaded Wakeman to quit Strawbs(▶) and join them, which he did in summer 1971.

While with Yes, Wakeman became keyboard star, adding prodigious technique and classical influence to Yes' sometimes flatulent music. But, having already released one solo album, **Six Wives Of Henry VIII**, Wakeman split to pursue solo career in 1974.

Next album, **Journey To The Centre Of The Earth**, was huge success on both sides of Atlantic, and Wakoman built spectacular stage show around it. With following album, **The Myths And Legends Of King Arthur**, he went step further and produced musical spectacular on ice at London's Empire Pool, complete with 45-piece orchestra and 48-piece choir.

Below: Keyboard maestro Rick Wakeman, an electro-pop pioneer.

Continuing to make solo records, Wakeman nevertheless rejoined Yes in 1976, staying with group until end of 1979. During this period suffered from number of health, personal and financial problems.

Quitting long-time label A&M in 1979, Wakeman did not record for two years until he came up with elaborate visionary work **1984** for Charisma. This became Top 30 UK album, and put Wakeman back on path of success. Following earlier excursions into film music **Lisztomania** (1975) and **White Rock** (1976), he scored horror movie 'The Burning' in 1982, following it with music for World Cup movie **G'Olé** in spring 1983.

Wakeman has also recently hosted Channel 4 rock/chat show 'Gastank', and appears to be in good shape to make success of '80s. Although his music can be rather baroque for some tastes, Wakeman is influential instrumentalist who helped to bring keyboards to forefront of rock.

Albums:
Six Wives Of Henry VIII (A&M), 1973
Journey To The Centre Of The Earth (A&M), 1974
Myths And Legends Of King Arthur (A&M), 1975
Lisztomania (A&M), 1975
No Earthly Connection (A&M), 1976
White Rock (Soundtrack) (A&M), 1976
Criminal Record (A&M), 1977
Best Known Works (A&M), 1978
Rhapsodies (A&M), 1979
1984 (Charisma), 1981
The Burning (Charisma), 1982
G'Olé (Charisma), 1983

The Walker Brothers

US group formed 1964.

Original/final line-up: Gary Walker, born Gary Leeds, Glendale, California, September 3, 1944, drums; John Walker, born John Maus, New York City, November 12, 1943, guitar; Scott Walker, born Scott Engel, Hamilton, Ohio, January 9, 1944, bass.

Career: Only indirectly related, Walker Brothers met in Hollywood when Gary returned from UK tour with P. J. Proby and formed trio with intention of reversing British domination of beat group scene.

Letting hair grow for eight months they appeared on nationwide TV show 'Hollywood A Go-Go' and developed strong act helped by prior experience; Gary had played drums for Elvis Presley(▶) for short stint; Scott had been discovered by Eddie Fisher who featured him on several TV shows, and worked with both Phil Spector and Sonny Bono; and John had featured in TV series 'Hallo Mom' with Betty Hutton at age 12.

Gary persuaded partners that they would find ready market in UK so they shifted base to London and signed with Philips, swiftly scoring million-seller with big-beat ballad **Make It Easy On Yourself** (a Bacharach/David composition), after initial hit **Love Her**. Although they were largely ignored in US, Walker Brothers had huge UK pop (particularly female) following.

After several more top 30 records, Scott split for solo career which gave him three UK Top 20 records between 1968-1969. His somewhat histrionic big voice style soon lost mass appeal, however, and personal and business wrangles hastened chart decline.

Group re-formed briefly in 1976 scoring UK Top 10 hit with Tom Rush(▶) song **No Regrets**.

Hit Singles:	US	UK
Love Her, 1965	—	20
Make It Easy On Yourself, 1965	16	1
My Ship Is Coming In, 1965	—	3
The Sun Ain't Gonna Shine Anymore, 1966	13	1
(Baby) You Don't Have To Tell Me, 1966	—	13
Another Tear Falls, 1966	—	12
No Regrets, 1976	—	7

Albums:
Spotlight On (—/Philips), 1975

Jerry Jeff Walker

US composer, guitarist, vocalist.
Born Onetona, New York, March 16, 1942.

Career: Legend has it that Walker left home as soon as possible to seek fame and fortune as folk singer. Several years of work followed until Beatles(▶) and Dylan(▶) killed off coffeehouse scene. Various folk groups began transmuting into the Byrds(▶), Lovin' Spoonful(▶), Mamas And Papas(▶), Buffalo Springfield(▶). In this atmosphere Walker formed Circus Maximus in 1966. he made one good if unoriginal, folk-rock album, then left as rest of band wanted to follow on to next 'in' thing: jazz rock.

Returning to his first love, Walker made country-folk LP for Circus Maximus label, then split to ATCO when Vanguard showed no

Above: The highly individual Jerry Jeff Walker, pictured in the '70s.

interest in releasing his style of music. It was while recording three ATCO LPs that Walker wrote **Mr Bojangles**, since covered countless times and US Top 10 hit for Nitty Gritty Dirt Band(▶).

On moving to Austin, Texas, Walker began exploring local talent and developing cowboy music in Willie Nelson(▶)/Waylon Jennings(▶) mould. His low-key approach hardly meshes with rock's high-powered business cycle of record, tour, record. His reluctance to sacrifice private life for life on road has kept following extremely limited. MCA (his label since 1972) seems content with this approach and Walker continues to play game his own way, i.e. to make music for fun and not to worry about size of audience.

Albums:
Mr Bojangles (Bainbridge/—), 1968
Driftin' My Way Of Life (Vanguard), 1969
Jerry Jeff Walker (MCA), 1972
Viva Terlingua (MCA/—), 1973
Walker's Collectables (MCA), 1974
Ridin' High (MCA), 1975
It's A Good Night For Singing (MCA/—), 1976
A Man Must Carry On (MCA), 1977
Contrary To Ordinary (MCA), 1978
Jerry Jeff (Elektra), 1978
Too Old To Change (Elektra), 1979

Best Of (MCA/—), 1980
Reunion (MCA), 1981
Cowjazz (MCA/—), 1982

Junior Walker

US saxophonist, composer, vocalist.
Born Autrey de Walt, Blythesville, Arkansas, 1942.

Career: Started playing saxophone while still at school and put together first band in 1961. Soon signed to Harvey Fuqua's label, shortly to be incorporated in nascent Motown company.

Back Street Boogie, Jr. Walker. Courtesy Warner Bros Records.

Shotgun, released in 1965 on Motown's Soul label, was Walker's first major hit. A raucous, raw soul belter featuring chicken-scratching tenor and shouted, basic vocals, it set pattern for output for next several years. Walker's records contrasted vividly with output of Motown's more sophisticated artists like the Supremes(▶) and the Four Tops(▶).

In late '60s Walker smoothed off rough edges of his style and evolved more relaxed formula to take him into '70s. Since mid-'70s he and band have continued to record for Motown, then Warner Bros with varying success, but no major hits. He continues to tour regularly both in US and Europe,

although venues are likely to be small clubs.

Along with King Curtis, Junior Walker represents a continuation of tradition initiated by big band and R&B tenor players of '40s and '50s, 'honkers and screamers' like Sil Austin, Red Prysock and Hal 'Cornbread' Singer. Junior Walker is progenitor of some of most exciting dance records of '60s.

Hit Singles:	US	UK
Shotgun, 1965	4	—
(I'm A) Roadrunner, 1966	20	—
How Sweet It Is, 1966	18	22
What Does It Take (To Win Your Love), 1969	4	13
These Eyes, 1969	16	—
Walk In The Night, 1972	46	16
Take Me Girl I'm Ready, 1973	—	16

Albums:
Shotgun (Soul/—), 1965
Greatest Hits (Soul/Tamla), 1966
Anthology (Motown/Tamla), 1974
Whopper Bopper Show Stopper (Soul/Tamla), 1976
Smooth Soul (Soul/Tamla), 1978
Back Street Boogie (Warner Bros), 1980

Worth Searching Out:
Road Runner (Soul/Tamla), 1966
Peace And Understanding (Soul/Tamla), 1973

Joe Walsh

US guitarist, vocalist, composer.
Born Wichita, Kansas, November 20, 1947.

Career: First gained attention as star of the James Gang(▶), a Cleveland-based band who toured with the Who(▶) gathering critical raves. Walsh was propelling force of group, providing songs and fierce hard-rock guitar. Quit in 1971 and with drummer Joe Vitale and bassist Kenny Passarelli recorded solo LP, **Barnstorm**. After idea of developing Barnstorm into a working band fell apart, he

Below: Jr. Walker with the sax that filled thousands of dance floors.

So What, Joe Walsh. Courtesy ABC Records.

recorded two albums. One, **The Smoker You Drink, The Player You Get,** went gold in 1973; from it came Top 30 single **Rocky Mountain Way**.

Signed with MCA in 1974. Released fairly interesting live LP, **You Can't Argue With A Sick Mind** (1976). Joined the Eagles(▶) same year, becoming part of that group's best line-up, Walsh's guitar adding bite to band's progressive LA harmonies. Continued with his solo projects; contributed theme song for movie 'The Warriors' in 1978, and played on sessions for Randy Newman(▶), Emerson, Lake and Palmer(▶), and Warren Zevon(▶), among others. Had hit single with **Life's Been Good to Me** from **But Seriously Folks** LP.

In 1982 the Eagles announced their break-up (though rumours of a reunion concert are already buzzing). Walsh worked with John Entwistle(▶) on his **Too Late The Hero** album the same year. In spring 1983 he began major US tour opening for Stevie Nicks.

Hit Single:

	US	UK
Life's Been Good To Me, 1978	12	14

Albums:
Barnstorm:
Barnstorm (Dunhill/Probe), 1972
(See also James Gang, Eagles)

Solo:
The Smoker You Drink, The Player You Get (Dunhill/Probe), 1973
So What (Dunhill/Probe), 1974

You Can't Argue With A Sick Mind (ABC-MCA/Anchor), 1976
But Serously Folks . . . (Asylum), 1978
Best Of (ABC-MCA/—), 1978

War

US group formed 1970.
Original line-up: Eric Burdon, vocals; Harold Brown, drums, percussion, vocals; Howard Scott, guitar, percussion, vocals; B. B. Dickerson, bass, percussion, vocals; Lonnie Jordan, keyboards, synthesiser, vocals; Charles Miller, saxophone, vocals; Lee Oskar, harmonica, vocals.

Career: Formed in San Pedro, California, high school. Original members worked as the Creators, the Romeos, Senor Soul and Night Shift, playing black clubs and recording for minor labels. Then member Peter Rosen (bass) introduced group to producer Jerry Goldstein who was looking for new band to work with Eric Burdon(▶), who had just broken up the New Animals.

Burdon brought in Danish-born white harmonica player Lee Oskar and War was born. Existing horn section of Night Shift was dropped, with exception of Charles Miller. Rosen died of drug overdose; B. B. Dickerson was brought back from Hawaii to rejoin old friends.

Debut single, **Spill The Wine**, topped US chart and two albums with Burdon (**Eric Burdon Declares War** and **Black Man's Burdon**) charted. Burdon brought band to Europe in 1970, where they jammed with Jimi Hendrix(▶) at Ronnie Scott's Jazz Club in London. Suffering from exhaustion, Burdon dropped out of return tour in 1971 and War completed the dates alone.

Under guidance of Goldstein and partner Steve Gold, War then evolved unique and hypnotic blend of jazz, funk, Afro-Latin, soul and R&B to earn accolade 'The Music Band'. Debut albums without Burdon, **All Day Music** and **The World Is A Ghetto** led way for subsequent tally of more than 10 platinum and gold awards.

After much success with United Artists, band had year-long lay-off in 1974 due to arguments with management which were, happily, resolved to mutual satisfaction. Compulsive 1975 hit **Low Rider** saw them on new label, Island, in UK, and in 1976 the song became their first British hit.

Moving to MCA, band scored with **Galaxy** (1977) and **The Music Band** (1979), by which time Dickerson had been replaced by Luther Rabb. Girl singer Tweed Smith, horn player Pat Rizzo and extra drummer Ron Hammaon were added; band switched to RCA in 1981.

Alongside their activities within War, Lee Oskar, Lonnie Jordan and Luther Rabb have all had successful solo recordings.

Current line-up: Brown; Scott; Jordan; Miller; Oskar; Luther Rabb, bass; Tweed Smith, vocals; Pat Rizzo, saxophone; Ron Hammaon, drums.

Hit Singles:

	US	UK
Spill The Wine, 1970	3	—
Slippin' Into Darkness, 1972	16	—
The World Is A Ghetto, 1973	7	—
Gypsy Man, 1973	8	—
The Cisco Kid, 1973	2	—
Me And Baby Brother, 1974	15	21
Why Can't We Be Friends, 1975	6	—
Low Rider, 1975	7	12
Summer, 1976	7	—
Galaxy, 1978	39	14

Albums:
All Day Music (Lax/MCA), 1972
The World Is A Ghetto (Lax/MCA), 1973
Live (MCA), 1974
Why Can't We Be Friends (Lax/MCA), 1975
Galaxy (MCA), 1978
The Music Band (MCA), 1979
The Music Band 2 (MCA), 1979
Best Of The Music Band (MCA/—), 1981
Outlaw (RCA), 1982

Below: War, originally formed as a backing band for Eric Burdon, soon proved that they could make it on their own.

Dionne Warwick

US vocalist.
Born East Orange, New Jersey, December 12, 1941.

Career: Studied music from age six. Sang with family gospel group Drinkard Singers. After further music training at Hart College of Music in Connecticut, Warwick (she has gone back and forth between Warwick and Warwicke spellings) moved to New York and became in-demand back-up singer. Often worked with sister Dee Dee, and aunt Cissy Houston.

Songwriters/producers Burt Bacharach and Hal David were impressed by her work on Drifters'(▶) session and arranged contract with Sceptre Records. Warwick's first solo release, written by them, was **Don't Make Me Over**; it became US hit and started huge run of success for Bacharach-David-Warwick partnership. Team created some of clas- siest romantic pop music ever recorded; Bacharach's distinctive and often subtle melodies, David's above-average lyrics and Warwick's ethereal but soulful voice com- bined to produce clutch of classics.

Nevertheless, by late '60s formula was wearing thin and Warwick attempted to revive flagging career by switching to Warner Bros and experimenting with various producers. Arrived back in limelight through pairing with Spinners on **Then Came You**, a 1974 No. 1.

Second major phase of career started with signing to Arista. Barry Manilow(▶)-produced 1979 LP **Dionne** was million-seller, and further Arista albums have also scored heavily. Latterly Warwick has enjoyed greater than ever success with Barry Gibb-produced and written album **Heartbreaker**, which spawned international hit singles.

**Heartbreaker, Dionne Warwick.
Courtesy Arista Records.**

A talented artist with truly distinctive vocal approach, Warwick has managed to avoid worst excesses of MOR while at same time steering clear of disco route. Her perfectionist approach ensures that she will be able to pursue successful career for years to come.

Hit Singles:	US	UK
Anyone Who Had A Heart, 1964	8	42
Walk On By, 1964	6	9
You'll Never Get To Heaven, 1964	34	20
Reach Out For Me, 1964	20	23
Message To Michael, 1966	8	—
Alfie, 1967	15	—
I Say A Little Prayer/Valley of The Dolls, 1967	4	—
Valley Of The Dolls/I Say A Little Prayer, 1968	2	28
Do You Know The Way To San Jose, 1968	10	8
Promises Promises, 1968	19	—
This Girl's In Love With You, 1969	7	—
You've Lost That Lovin' Feeling, 1969	16	—
I'll Never Fall In Love Again, 1970	6	—
I'll Never Love This Way Again, 1979	5	—
Deja Vu, 1979	15	—
Heartbreaker, 1982	10	
All The Love In The world, 1983	—	12

With Detroit Spinners:

Then Came You, 1974	1	9

Albums:

Greatest Hits Volume 1 (—/Hallmark), 1973
Greatest Hits Volume 2 (—/Hallmark), 1973
Greatest Hits Volume 3 (—/Hallmark), 1974
Greatest Hits Volume 4 (—/Hallmark), 1975
Collection (—/Pickwick), 1976
Dionne (Arista), 1979
No Night So Long (Arista), 1980
Golden Collection (—/K-Tel), 1981
Hot Live & Otherwise (Arista), 1981
Friends In Love (Arista), 1982
Heartbreaker (Arista), 1982
Golden Hits Volume 1 (—/Phoenix), 1982
Golden Hits Volume 2 (—/Phoenix), 1982
20 Golden Pieces Of Dionne Warwick (—/Bulldog), 1982

With Isaac Hayes:
A Man And A Woman (MCA), 1977

Muddy Waters

US vocalist, guitarist, composer.
Born McKinley Morganfield, Rolling Fork, Mississippi, April 4, 1915; died April 30, 1983.

Career: Raised on a plantation in Clarksdale, Mississippi, where he was discovered and recorded by folklorist Alan Lomax for the Library of Congress in 1941, Walters joined the great wartime black exodus to the Northern industrial cities, settling in Chicago

**Muddy Mississippi Waters Live.
Courtesy Blue Sky Records.**

in 1943 and quickly establishing himself in its vibrantly exciting blues circuit.

Leonard and Phil Chess signed Waters to their Aristocrat label (soon re-named Chess) in 1945. He became company's musical father figure, helping to nurture many careers, including those of his sidemen Otis Spann (his half-brother), Little Walter, Jimmie Rodgers(▶), and emergent R&B/rockers Bo Diddley(▶) and Chuck Berry(▶).

Waters, a true giant of the blues, was indisputably the major figure of Chicago blues scene through the '50s (when he logged 12 American R&B chart hits) and into '60s. Some of his best-known songs, **Rollin' Stone, Got My Mojo Working**, and **Mannish Boy**, became fodder for countless British and American R&B/rock bands, most notably the Rolling Stones(▶) (named after Waters' hit) and Johnny Winter(▶). In recent years he recorded for Winter's Blue Sky label, and still showed enormous musical powers despite ailing health, which culminated in death from heart failure in 1983.

Albums (selected):
Can't Get No Grinding (Chess), 1973
Back In The Early Days (—/Syndicate), 1977
Hard Again (Blue Sky), 1977
I'm Ready (Blue Sky), 1977
Live (Blue Sky), 1977
Chess Masters (Chess), 1981
King Bee (Blue Sky), 1981

Worth Searching Out:
Electric Mud (Cadet), 1968

Weather Report

US group formed 1970.

Original line-up: Josef Zawinul, keyboards, synthesiser; Wayne Shorter, saxophones; Miroslav Vitous, bass; Alphonse Mouzon, drums; Airto Moreira, percussion.

Career: Most durable of all jazz/rock ag- gregations that sprung to life in late '60s/ early '70s. Formed by Austrian (born Vienna) Zawinul and Shorter (born Newark, NJ).

Hold impressive jazz credentials: Zawinul worked with Cannonball Adderley, Miles Davis (recorded **Bitches Brew**); composed standards **Mercy Mercy Mercy** and **In A Silent Way**; earned Grammy in 1967 for best instrumental performance. Shorter (ex- Art Blakey, Miles Davis) was prominent tenor player before switching affection to alto sax. Czech-born Vitous had recorded/ performed with Art Farmer, Freddie Hubbard, Brookmeyer-Terry Quintet, Miles Davis, Stan Getz and Herbie Mann. Brazilian Airto worked with Lee Morgan and Miles Davis. South Carolinan Mouzon recorded/performed with

Above: Muddy Waters on stage in the '70s with his trusty Fender Telecaster.

Roy Ayers and did sessions for Roberta Flack(▶) and Gene McDaniels.

Moreiro quit shortly after release of debut **Weather Report** (1970). LP earned plaudits from jazz and rock critics alike; set recording pattern of tight percussive music with em- phasis on interplay between Zawinul and Shorter. Tracks were totally melodic, opening new avenues for those usually reluctant to listen to normal complexity of jazz

Unit has subsequently undergone various personnel changes: Vitous left in 1974 after release of **Mysterious Traveller**. Replace- ment Jaco Pastorius remained until 1979 and **Mr Gone** set. Bass duties were taken over by Abe Laboriel. Mouzon moved to McCoy Tyner group in '72, and then Larry Coryell's 11th House. Is now prominent session player and sometime leader of own band. Drum seat was permanently filled by Pete Erskine (ex-Stan Kenton and Maynard Ferguson) in 1978. Percussionists who have graced group's work include Alex Acuna, Ishmael Wilburn, Tony Willians, Steve Gadd and Eric Garratt, group drummer from 1972-76.

Weather Reoprt have earned various poll honours throughout world; are regular re- cipients of 'Downbeat' magazine's Best Group plaudit. Debut album also won Downbeat award. Entered 1983 with new line-up for **Procession** set.

Unit's popularity has extended worldwide,

Below: Joe Zawinul, founder member of jazz/rockers Weather Report.

particularly Japan; they are infrequent but welcome visitors to Europe. Weather Report's authority in jazz/rock market has outlasted all contemporaries.

Current line-up: Zawinul; Shorter.

Albums:
Weather Report (Columbia/CBS), 1970
I Sing The Body Electric (Columbia/CBS), 1972
Sweetnighter (Columbia/CBS), 1973
Mysterious Traveller (Columbia/CBS), 1974
Tail Spinnin' (Columbia/CBS), 1975
Black Market (Columbia/CBS), 1976
Heavy Weather (Columbia/CBS), 1977
Mr Gone (Columbia/CBS), 1978
8.30 (Columbia/CBS), 1979
Night Passage (Columbia/CBS), 1980
Weather Report (Columbia/CBS), 1981
Procession (Columbia/CBS), 1983

Wham

UK duo formed 1982.
George Michael, vocals; born George Michael Panos, London, June 26, 1963.
Andrew Ridgeley, guitar; born Jan. 1963.

Career: Michael and Ridgeley as teenage North Londoners had been in various no-hope groups before joining forces in summer 1982 and recording as duo, co-writing material. First single **Wham! Rap (Enjoy What You Do)** was well received by pop press and in clubs, but not played on daytime radio due to so-called contentious lyrics concerning problems faced by jobless youth.

Second single **Young Guns (Go For It)** covered lyrical ground, but achieved radio play to become Top 3 hit at end of 1982. Follow-up **Bad Boys**, released March 1983, made No. 2 in UK; first LP **Fantastic** followed.

Wham's musical style combines popular elements of generally black musical styles (funk, rap), apparently appropriate for '80s teenage generation in Britain—highly danceable, with hopeful lyrical message.

Hit Singles:	US	UK
Young Guns (Go For It), 1982	—	3
Bad Boys, 1983	—	2

Album:
Fantastic (—/Innervision), 1983

Tony Joe White

US vocalist, composer, guitarist.
Born Oak Grove, Louisiana, July 23, 1943.

Career: Along with Creedence Clearwater Revival(▶), J. J. Cale(▶), Link Wray and the Kershaw Brothers, Tony Joe White was prime exponent of so-called swamp-rock style, a hauntingly powerful blend of R&B, funk and country influences.

Formed first band, Tony Joe and the Mojos, while in his teens. Then formed new outfit called Tony and the Twilights and headed for Texas where he remained as solo artist and songwriter when band broke up.

In 1968 White moved to Nashville, and with help from then unknown Billy Swan, started laying tracks for debut album which was picked up by Monument Records. Recording in Nashville and Memphis, using best of local sessioneers, White came up with three masterful albums for label, featuring his imaginative songwriting, rich-voiced (if mumbled) vocals and a strange guitar technique, dubbed by him as 'whomper stomping', which made much use of the wah-wah pedal.

The funky **Polk Salad Annie** (later covered by Elvis Presley(▶)), catapulted him into the charts and was followed by such masterpieces as **Soul Francisco**, the message ballad **Willie And Laura Mae Jones** and his original **Rainy Night In Georgia** (covered successfully by Brook Benton).

Switching to Warner Bros in 1972, White's music became less soul and more country, losing cutting edge, though the lilting **I've Got A Thing About You Baby** had plenty of appeal.

After three Warner albums, White signed to 20th Century in 1976 but his debut album for them, **Eyes** (1977), was somewhat mundane and he quickly slipped from the recording scene.

Hit Singles:	US	UK
Polk Salad Annie, 1969	8	—

Albums:
The Best Of Tony Joe White (Warner Bros), 1975
Tony Joe White (20th Century/—), 1978

Barry White

US vocalist, pianist, composer, arranger, producer.
Born Galveston, Texas, 1944.

Career: Raised in Los Angeles, sang in local group during teens. In 1961 joined Rampart Records as house arranger and keyboard player. Played on Bob and Earl classic **Harlem Shuffle**. In 1966 moved to Mustang/Bronco Records, where he produced Felice Taylor's big hit **I Feel Love Coming On** and sides for Viola Wills.

When label folded in 1969 White recruited Linda and Glodean James (Glodean later became his wife) and Diana Taylor to form Love Unlimited. Under White's aegis, group scored No. 1 hit with **Walking In The Rain (With The One I Love)** on Uni. Outcome was major deal for White and group with 20th Century records in 1973.

White immediately became major hitmaker himself, evolving formula that consisted of catchy song with strong hook and sexy/romantic lyrics, backed by slow, semi-disco beat and banked strings. White's deep rich voice, strongly influenced by Isaac Hayes(▶), was major selling point. Despite gargantuan build, singer built up strong female following and inspired hysteria at concert appearances.

Success began to diminish in late '70s, but in meantime singer had earned 60 gold and 15 platinum records from worldwide sales. Still active on all fronts, and actually more talented than most of his output would suggest, White could return to chart form at any time. He is classic example of artist almost having to become self-parody to maintain commercial success.

Hit Singles:	US	UK
I'm Gonna Love You Just A Little Bit More Baby, 1973	3	23
Never, Never Gonna Give Ya Up, 1974	7	14
Can't Get Enough Of Your Love Babe, 1974	1	8
You're The First, The Last, My Everything, 1974	2	1
What Am I Gonna Do With You, 1975	8	5
I'll Do For You Anything You Want Me To, 1975	40	20

Below: Former boutique salesman David Coverdale (front) proudly unveils the 1983 version of his band Whitesnake.

	US	UK
Let The Music Play, 1975	32	9
You See The Trouble With Me, 1976	—	2
Baby We Better Try And Get It Together, 1976	—	15
Don't Make Me Wait Too Long, 1976	—	17
Just The Way You Are, 1978	—	12

Albums:
Rhapsody In White (with Love Unlimited Orchestra) (Philly Intl/Pye), 1973
Can't Get Enough (20th Century), 1974
Sings For Someone You Love (20th Century), 1977
Barry White The Man (20th Century), 1978
Greatest Hits (20th Century), 1979
I Love To Sing The Songs I Sing (20th Century), 1979
The Message Is Love (Unlimited Gold), 1979
Sheet Music (Unlimited Gold), 1980
The Best Of Our Love (Unlimited Gold), 1981
Change (Unlimited Gold), 1982

With Glodean James:
Barry And Glodean (Unlimited Gold), 1981

Whitesnake

UK group formed 1978.

Original line-up: David Coverdale, vocals; Micky Moody, guitar; Bernie Marsden, guitar; Jon Lord, keyboards; Neil Murray, bass; David Dowle, drums.

Career: Coverdale joined 1973 Deep Purple(▶) line-up and stayed with band until its demise in 1976. 1977 saw release of solo LP, **Whitesnake**. It disappeared but Coverdale had more success with next solo project, **Northwinds**. Once legal problems were sorted out (allowing him to play live again), Coverdale formed stable line-up. Band released **Trouble** while undertaking extensive UK tour. Sound was basic R&B-influenced rock, pioneered decade before by Deep Purple and others.

Snakebite and **Love Hunter** continued in same style with danger of Whitesnake becoming cliché. Dowle was replaced by Purple-mate Ian Paice to roughen up edges of band's backbeat.

Fool For Your Loving single proved band could reach mass appeal. **Ready An' Willing** sold well enough to encourage recording of double live set, **Live In The Heart Of The City** (title reflected place of origin: Hammersmith Odeon, London). **Come An' Get It** was next release and revealed basic problem: music was loud and energetic, but it sounded as if everyone could play it in their sleep. **Saints An' Sinners** tried to find solution by changing band's line-up.

Until Whitesnake sounds as if it is taking chances, it will remain UK equivalent of US faceless rock (Styx(▶), REO Speedwagon(▶) and the like).

Current line-up: Coverdale; Moody; Lord; Colin Hodgkinson, bass; Mel Galley, guitar.

Hit Singles:	US	UK
Fool For Your Loving, 1980	53	13
Don't Break My Heart Again, 1981	—	17

Albums:
Trouble (United Artists), 1978
Love Hunter (United Artists), 1979
Ready An' Willing (Mirage/United Artists), 1980
Live In The Heart Of The City (Mirage/United Artists), 1980
Come An' Get It (Atlantic/Liberty), 1981
Saints An' Sinners (—/Liberty), 1982

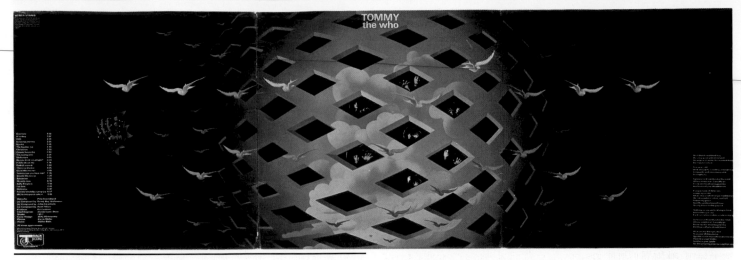

The Who

UK group formed 1964.

Original line-up: Pete Townshend, guitar, keyboards, vocals; Roger Daltrey, vocals; John Entwistle, bass, horns, vocals; Keith Moon, drums.

Career: While at Acton County Grammar School, Townshend(▶) and Entwistle(▶) joined Daltrey's(▶) band the Detours in 1962. Townshend's mother got boys audition with Commercial Entertainments Ltd's Bob Druce; they were soon doing gigs on his club circuit, playing mostly R&B and Top 10 covers. Originally a five-piece, Detours went through several singers and guitarists until Daltrey switched from guitar to vocals; they then stayed a four-piece with Townshend on lead, Entwistle on bass, and Dougie Sandom on drums. Became Who when they saw another band named Detours on TV. Were introduced to Helmut Gorden, an enterprising door-knob manufacturer; he became manager, took all earnings and put band on weekly wage.

More influential, however, was Pete Meaden, a fast-talking, pill-popping freelance publicist enamoured with the world of 'mods' — Meaden decided Who were perfect for mod audience; convinced band to change name to High Numbers (a 'number' being a mod). He introduced them to the fashions of Carnaby Street. Wrote and produced a mod single for them, **I'm The Face/Zoot Suit**, on Fontana in July 1964; it flopped, despite widespread publicity, probably because Meaden had simply written new lyrics to Slim Harpo's **Got Love If You Want It**.

Band didn't really arrive at the perfect formula until one night at the Royal Oldfield Hotel. A cocky young kid in the audience announced he could play drums better than their drummer (a substitute — Sandem had left band), and proved it by demolishing the drumkit in the interval; Keith Moon(▶) was in.

Meaden had ideas, but no money, so when Kit Lambert stopped by the Railway Hotel in Harrow to see High Numbers, he persuaded them to let him, and his partner Chris Stamp, take over management. Meaden was dropped, and band became Who again. It was at the Railway that Townshend smashed his first guitar: he accidentally broke the neck of his 12-string Rickenbacker on very low ceiling; mishap getting no reaction from audience, Townshend proceeded to smash it to smithereens. This got such a reaction that Lambert encouraged Townshend (and Moon, who followed suit and kicked over his drumkit) to continue instrument-destroying as a publicity stunt. Became the traditional ending to a Who performance.

Lambert bought Townshend two Vortexian tape recorders; he came up with first demo, **I**

Can't Explain, which later sold itself to Kinks(▶) producer Shel Talmy. Talmy became Who producer; got band recording contract with US Decca, then UK Decca. While in residency Tuesday nights at Marquee Club in Soho in early '65, still playing mostly R&B covers, Who recorded **I Can't Explain** at Pye Studios. Helped by first 'Top of the Pops' appearance, single went to No. 8 in UK. From then on Townshend continued to write 90% of Who material (Entwistle contributed remainder).

Four months later, second single, **Anyway, Anyhow, Anywhere**, which featured feedback (then so revolutionary that their record company sent it back, convinced strange noises were a mistake), went to No. 10 in the UK and became signature tune for TV's music show 'Ready, Steady, Go'. Third single that year not only surpassed others in sales, reaching No. 2 in UK, but also in notoriety. **My Generation** was soon adopted as anthem for the young with its controversial angry, stuttered lyric, 'Hope I die before I get old'.

With three hit singles and first LP, **My Generation (The Who Sing My Generation** in US), doing well, bookings were up. Earnings trebled, yet Who remained in debt because of continued instrument smashing. On top of financial worries, there were personality clashes, internal power struggles, constant threats to split up (which continued for 20 years), and management/producer problems. With conflict on all sides, Who ended up in legal battle with Shel Talmy over **Substitute**, their next single. Despite being released on two different labels it reached No. 5 in Britain, and Talmy bowed out for a percentage. Lambert produced single that followed, **I'm A Boy**, which climbed to No. 2 in UK. Later that year, band had first US hit, **Happy Jack**, followed by success with seemingly innocent song about masturbation, **Pictures Of Lily**, and slightly psychedelic Top 10 hit both sides of the Atlantic, **I Can See For Miles**. The Who had moved away from mod, and after brief pop art phase (Union Jack jackets, target T-shirts, slightly longer hair) dabbled briefly in semi-hippie look until late '60s.

First live dates in America were with Murray the K show in New York. Later that year toured extensively in US as support for Herman's Hermits(▶), a tour that made them rather unpopular with hotel managers. It was their appearance at Monterey Pop Festival, aided by first national US TV appearance on the Smothers Brothers Show, that sold them to America. Both shows made use of smoke bombs and self-destrucion.

Until **Tommy**, the Who were basically a singles band. Neither **A Quick One** nor **The Who Sell Out** LPs did particularly well. Though **Sell Out** had brilliant basis for an album — a radio station format with adverts and jingles between tracks — the cover, with Daltrey sitting in bath of baked beans, drew more attention.

Top: The triptych cover of Tommy. The Who. Courtesy Polydor Records. Left: The Who, circa 1965-what youthful innocence!

Above: A feature of early Who shows was an instrument destroying finale, apparently conceived by the group in order to avoid encores.

In 1969 Who released their long-awaited double LP **Tommy**; A 'rock opera' concept album chronicling the adventures of a deaf, dumb and blind boy, with spiritual overtones, it was dedicated to Townshend's Indian master Meher Baba. From now on Who music was more obsessed with problems of adolescent males, as lyrics grew more politically, socially and spiritually thought-provoking. Daltrey became more of a front man; band spent two years performing **Tommy** live in its entirety, taking it eventually to several European opera houses. Received 14-minute standing ovation at NY's Metropolitan Opera House. One of the most familiar Who images of era was Daltrey in long blonde curls and leather fringe twirling his mike, and Townshend in white boiler suit doing scissor leaps, performing **Tommy**, was part of the Woodstock festival; Woodstock absolutely confirmed Who's future success in US.

In 1970 released **Live at Leeds**; many critics regard it as fine example of live Who concert. The Who have long been considered one of the top live acts in rock 'n' roll. Few can match their intensity and versatility and few moments in rock are more universally moving than the **See Me, Feel Me** finale.

After very trying work on another ambitious concept LP, **Lifehouse**, failed, remains were salvaged to make **Who's Next**, first LP produced by Glyn Johns, and first to feature synthesisers, used frequently thereafter.

The next major project, **Quadrophenia**, returned to sound of band's early days, and again used mod culture as vehicle to address adolescence. **Quadrophenia** was vastly underrated (criticised mostly for over-orchestration), only fully appreciated in 1979 when repackaged as movie soundtrack for Who film of same name, which coincided with the UK rebirth of the mod movement.

By 1975, all four Who members had made at least one solo album. Entwistle put together **Odds & Sods**, an LP of old Who rarities to appease fans, but no new Who material was being recorded.

It seemed that nothing could match the success of **Tommy**; in 1975 it was Ken Russell's 'Tommy' film, with Daltrey in leading role, and soundtrack LP, which brought band whole new following, rather than new album, **Who By Numbers**. Poorly received, melancholy **Numbers** addressed problems of ageing; single **Squeeze Box** made US Top 20 and UK Top 10.

Back on the road in 1975-76, the Who were selling out soccer stadiums; May '76 concert at Charlton Athletic Ground earned them a place in the Guinness Book of World Records for loudest concert.

After problems with Lambert and Stamp, Bill Curbishley stepped in as manager. There was a long lull in recording until 1978 when **Who Are You** was completed. The LP and single of the

The original Quadrophenia album, The Who. Courtesy Polydor Records.

The Kids Are Alright, soundtrack compilation. Courtesy Polydor Records.

same name were Who's biggest sellers since original **Tommy**.

Untimely death of drummer Keith Moon on September 7, 1978 forced Who to consider folding, but by early '79 pressed on with ex-Small Faces(▶), Faces(▶) drummer Kenney Jones. Jones made live debut with new Who at London's Rainbow; soon press was hailing 1979 'Year of the Who'. Extensive touring and two successful Who films 'The Kids Are Alright', a film biography of the band, and 'Quadrophenia' with accompanying Who soundtracks put Who back in business. However, year ended in tragedy when 11 Who fans were crushed to death at Cincinnati concert on December 3, 1979. Devastated, Who again considered disbanding, but continued US tour well into 1980.

Face Dances in 1981, the first new material in three years, was produced by Bill Szymcyzk. Some thought it innovative, but most considered it wrong for the Who. Single **You Better, You Bet** made US Top 20, but at this point the Who were being largely ignored in UK. Worry over responsibility of the band and the efforts of balancing stardom with family life drove Townshend to drink and drugs. Some felt the Who were finished. But Townshend pulled himself together, going completely straight in early '82. Much relieved, the other members were anxious to contribute to next LP (returning to producer Glyn Johns) **It's Hard**, which erased bad press of **Face Dances**; in conjunction with tours in US, LP proved band was still strong.

Since punk/new wave movements of late '70s, the Who's popularity has wained considerably in the UK, but they continue to be one of the top three acts in America. Their 1982 US 'Farewell Tour' was the biggest draw of the year, grossing 40 million dollars. Although the Who refuse to do any more extensive touring, they plan miscellaneous live dates and another two albums.

Authorized biography by Richard Barnes, 'The Who: Maximum R&B' is essential reading for any more extensive touring, they plan miscellaneous live dates, a live LP and possibly one more studio album.

Current line-up: Townshend; Daltrey; Entwistle; Kenney Jones, drums.

Hit Singles:	US	UK
I Can't Explain, 1965	—	8
Anyway, Anyhow, Anywhere, 1965	—	10
My Generation, 1965	—	2
Substitute, 1966	—	5
I'm A Boy,1966	—	2
Happy Jack, 1966	24	3
Pictures Of Lily, 1967	51	4
I Can See For Miles, 1967	9	10
Pinball Wizard, 1969	19	4
The Seeker, 1970	44	19
See Me Feel Me/Overture From Tommy, 1970	12	—
Won't Get Fooled Again, 1971	15	9
Let's See Action, 1971	—	16
Join Together, 1972	17	9
5.15, 1973	45	20
Squeeze Box, 1975 US, 1976 UK	16	10
Substitute (re-issue), 1976	—	7
Who Are You, 1978	14	18
You Better, You Bet, 1981	18	—

Left: Meaty, Beaty, Big & Bouncy (back cover), The Who. Courtesy Polydor.

Below left: Bearded Pete Townshend onstage in 1971.

Below: US Tour 1980, with Pete Townshend (right) and Kenney Jones.

Albums:
Tommy (Decca/Track), 1969
Live At Leeds (Decca/Track), 1970
Who's Next (Decca/Track), 1971
Meaty, Beaty, Big & Bouncy (Decca/Track), 1971†
Quadrophenia (MCA/Track), 1973
Odds & Sods (MCA/Track), 1974
A Quick One/Sell Out (MCA/Track), 1974*
Magic Bus/My Generation, 1974*
Tommy (soundtrack) (Polydor/Polydor), 1975
The Who By Numbers (MCA/Polydor), 1975
The Story Of The Who (—/Polydor), 1976†
Who Are You (MCA/Polydor), 1978
The Kids Are Alright (soundtrack) (MCA/Polydor), 1979
Quadrophenia (soundtrack) (Polydor/Polydor), 1979
My Generation (re-issue) (—/Virgin), 1979
Live At Leeds/Who Are You (—/Polydor), 1980*
Face Dances (Warner Bros/Polydor), 1981
Hooligans (MCA/—), 1981†
It's Hard (Warner Bros/Polydor), 1982
Who's Greatest Hits (MCA/—), 1983†
Rarities (—/Polydor), 1983
*Double Re-issues
†Compilations

Kim Wilde

UK vocalist.
Born Kim Smith, London, November 18, 1960.

Career: Daughter of seminal UK rock 'n' roller Marty Wilde, Kim embarked on training for non-musical career at Hertfordshire Art College. After singing on demos made by brother Ricky, attracted attention of notable producer/record company owner Mickie Most. He supervised mixing of **Kids In America**, produced by Ricky and written by Marty and Ricky. Single released on Most's RAK label in early 1981 reached No. 2; hit with three further singles in UK Top 20 during 1981 — **Chequered Love, Water On Glass** and **Cambodia** — all created by same family team.

First LP reached Top 3 in UK in 1981; less successful in US when released where in 1982, although **Kids In America** was sizeable US hit 18 months after UK release. 1982 was far less successful—two smaller hit singles and **Select** LP minor chart item—but Kim embarked on first tour which was generally well received. A very attractive blonde (sometimes compared to French sex symbol Brigitte Bardot), it is conceivable that Kim's future may be in films, although her currently flagging singing career could perhaps be revived by use of outside material/production. A superior pop singer, her enormous potential is at present not totally fulfilled.

Hit Singles:

	US	UK
Kids In America, 1981	25	2
Chequered Love, 1981	—	4
Water On Glass, 1981	—	11
Cambodia, 1981	—	12
View From A Bridge, 1982	—	16

Albums:
Kim Wilde (EMI/RAK), 1981
Select (—/RAK), 1982

Don Williams

US composer, vocalist, guitarist.
Born Floydada, Texas, May 27, 1939.

Career: Williams, the most laid-back singer in country music, worked as debt collector, truck driver, oilman and at other jobs before making it full-time in music.

In 1964 he formed Pozo Seco Singers in Corpus Christi, Texas, with Lofton Cline and Susan Taylor. First single, **Time**, went to US Top 10 in country charts and trio became major folk/country act before disbanding in 1971.

Williams moved to Nashville and first solo record **Don't You Believe** appeared in 1973 on JMI who gave him three hit singles from first album.

Signed to ABC-Dot in 1974, Williams has been astutely guided in his career by agent Jim Halsey. When MCA bought out ABC they proceeded to turn Williams into major international act via succession of critically acclaimed self-produced albums.

He co-starred with Burt Reynolds in 'W.W. And The Dixie Dancekings', during which he was presented with the cowboy hat which has since become his trade mark along with his denim suits. He also appeared in 'Smokey And The Bandit II'.

Williams songs have been recorded by Eric Clapton(▶), Kenny Rogers(▶) and Jeanne Pruitt, Pete Townshend(▶), Johnny Cash(▶) and Sonny James. Though his material is firmly rooted in country music, his deep rich voice and relaxing songs with astute lyrics have spread his appeal far beyond that market.

Hit Singles:

	US	UK
I Recall A Gypsy Woman	—	13

Below: The Texan with the deep voice who only removes his hat when he goes to bed, Don Williams, a prodigious album seller in the '70s.

Albums (selected):
Volume I (Dot/MCA), 1977
Volume II (MCA), 1977
Volume III (MCA), 1977
Greatest Hits (—/ABC), 1977
Country Boy (Dot/ABC), 1977
I Believe In You (MCA), 1980
Especially For You (MCA), 1981
Listen To The Radio (MCA), 1982

Hank Williams

US vocalist, composer, guitarist.
Born Hiram King Williams, Georgiana, Alabama, September 17, 1923; died January 1, 1953.

Career: The first country superstar; learned guitar at seven from blues performer Rufe Payne aka Tee-Tot. Formed band the Drifting Cowboys in teens; earned residency at local radio station in Montgomery. Signed with local label Sterling Records in 1946 before moving to MGM.

Secured regular billing at Grand Ole Opry after single **Lovesick Blues** made national impact (later sacked due to drink problem). Established as major performer after run of best-selling cuts, including **My Bucket's Got A Hole In It**, **Mind Your Own Business**, **Kaw-Liga**, **Wedding Bells**, oft-covered **Cold Cold Heart, Hey Good Lookin', Jambalaya** and classics **Your Cheating Heart** and **Take These Chains From My Heart**. Williams' emotive tenor was definitive country 'sound', particularly effective on ballad sides. All tracks were produced by C&W entrepreneur Fred Rose of famed Acuff-Rose publishing house.

A long-time alcoholic, Williams disguised his condition from all but closest friends and maintained frenetic touring schedule. Died, aged 29, in back seat of car on way to show in Ohio. After hasty autopsy, cause of death listed as heart attack. Evidence indicated Williams choked on own vomit caused by combination of drink/drugs.

Immortality secured by enshrinement at Country Music Hall Of Fame in 1961. His son Hank Williams Jr has enjoyed moderate success, more recently with country-rock band.

Stage show 'The Show He Never Gave' based on Williams' hectic life enjoyed success in US and London's West End in 1981. Former cab driver Carl Chase played Williams with some skill in UK production. Williams' biography by Chet Flippo is absorbing reading.

Albums (selected):
24 Greatest Hits (MGM), 1970

Jackie Wilson

US vocalist.
Born Detroit, Michigan, June 9, 1934.

Career: Possessor of one of the finest tenor voices in popular music idiom Wilson's hit record career has spanned three decades. During brief spell as boxer in late 1940s, won amateur Golden Gloves welterweight title.

Singing began in church. Performed with Ever Ready Gospel Singers before taking secular path in 1951 for session with Dizzy Gillespie's Dee Gee label. Later that year sang in talent show at Paradise Theatre, Detroit; heard by Billy Ward, whose group the Dominoes were then hot with **Sixty Minute Man**. Ward, impressed, took phone number then called months later when Clyde McPhatter quit Dominoes. Wilson replaced him to sing lead/second tenor; sang with group for four years on King/Federal Records, his soaring tenor tones distinctive in melismatic delivery of ballads like **Rags To Riches**.

When Dominoes moved to Decca in 1956,

Below: Hank Williams, who died before the rock'n'roll era began, but whose many classic songs are still covered by today's stars.

Wilson stayed with them for while then left for solo career. Sang in local clubs until spotted by Al Green, manager of Johnny Ray and LaVerne Baker. Signed with Brunswick Records under supervision of house band-leader Dick Jacobs; has remained Brunswick artist. Wilson was mainstay of roster for more than a decade with lengthy succession of hits, adapting style to keep up with times. Hits included **Reet Petite** (1957), **Lonely Teardrops** and classy ballad **To Be Loved** (1958).

Maintained stylistic variations and fought with orchestration over the years until 1963, when he injected R&B feeling with **Baby Workout**.

In 1966 Wilson began recording in Chicago (instead of New York); with move came transfusion of new ideas from producers Carl Davis and Sonny Sanders. More main-stream soul output of danceable songs like **Whispers, Higher and Higher** and **I Get The Sweetest Feeling** resulted. Wilson was transformed into soul star.

Formula lost commercial impact by early '70s and Wilson began searching for new ideas and material. Brief liaison with Eugene Records and Chi-Lites was unsuccessful.

On September 29, 1975, Jackie suffered heart-attack while singing at Latin Casino in Camden, New Jersey; lapsed into coma, suffered severe brain damage, and has since been confined to Cherry Hill Medical Centre in NJ.

Hit Singles:

	US	UK
Reet Petite, 1957	—	6
Lonely Teardrops, 1959		7
That's Why (I Love You So), 1959	13	—
I'll Be Satisfied, 1959	20	—
Night/Doggin' Around, 1960	4	—
Doggin' Around/Night, 1960	15	—
(You Were Made For) All My Love/ A Woman, A Lover, A Friend, 1960	12	—
A Woman, A Lover, A Friend/ (You Were Made For) All My Love, 1960	15	—
Alone At Last, 1960	8	50
My Empty Arms, 1961	9	—
Please Tell Me Why, 1961	20	—
I'm Comin' On Back To you, 1961	19	—
Baby Workout, 1963	5	—
Whispers (Gettin' Louder), 1966	11	—
(Your Love Keeps Lifting Me) Higher And Higher, 1967	6	—
I Get The Sweetest Feeling, 1972	35*	9
(Your Love Keeps Lifting Me) Higher And Higher, 1969	—	11

*Charted in US in 1968

Albums (selected):
My Golden Favourites (Brunswick/Coral), 1962
My Golden Favourites Volume 2 (Brunswick/ Coral), 1962
Greatest Hits (Brunswick), 1968

Worth Searching Out:
Baby Workout (Brunswick/—), 1964
Higher And Higher (Brunswick/MCA), 1967

Edgar Winter

US keyboards and saxophone player, composer, vocalist.
Born Beaumont, Texas, December 28, 1946.

Career: Brother of Johnny Winter(▶) who shared interest in R&B but preferred jazz This led to Edgar's interest in piano. Played with brother in local band Black Plague before pursuing education, while Johnny moved on to rock. Edgar dropped out of college to play jazz professionally, rejoined Johnny when

Columbia offered major contract.

Following excellent contributions to brother's first two Columbia LPs, Edgar produced jazz-fusion solo LP **Entrance**. It failed to win public notice and Edgar returned to rock format, organising own band.

Edgar Winter's White Trash began with Jerry La Croix (vocals, sax, harp), Jon Smith (vocals, sax), Mike McLellan (vocals, trumpet), Bobby Ramirez (drums), George Sheck (bass) and Floyd Radford (guitar). **White Trash** appeared in spring 1971 and received adequate response to merit further development. Although **Roadwork** was excellent live double LP, it also showed up problems of managing seven-man outfit. Unwieldy size and Winter's continuing insistence on dropping R&B background led to band's break-up in mid-1972.

Winter immediately formed Edgar Winter Group with Dan Hartman (bass, vocals), Chuck Ruff (drums) and Ronnie Montrose(▶) (guitar). Within one week new band was recording **They Only Come Out At Night** LP, released in November 1972. Preview LP cut **Hanging Around** was released as single. Radio stations began playing B-side **Frankenstein** so an edited version was rushed out as A-side single and became 'monster' hit in both US and UK.

Jerry Weems replaced Montrose on guitar then decided to quit. Winter asked his producer Rick Derringer(▶) to fill in. This combination became instant hit on large concert circuit in US and produced excellent **Shock Treatment** LP.

1975 saw Winter's energies diluted over wide range of projects. All-solo **Jasmine Nightdreams** continued in vein of **Entrance**, while **The Edgar Winter Group With Rick Derringer** returned to basic rock format, without experimental efforts of **Shock Treatment**. Both Derringer and Hartman began full-time solo careers in 1976, leaving Winter without anyone to challenge and direct his many talents.

Following average live LP with brother Johnny in 1976, Edgar temporarily disappeared. In 1979 he re-formed the Edgar Winter Group and has since released several LPs. Though technically good, Edgar Winter has so far failed to find right mixture to create dynamic, aggressive sound of band's first two albums.

Edgar has also recorded with Meatloaf(▶) and Montrose.

Hit Singles:

	US	UK
Frankenstein, 1972	1	18
Free Ride, 1973	14	—

Albums:
Edgar Winter:
Entrance (Epic), 1970

Edgar Winter's White Trash:
Road Work (Epic), 1972
Recycled (Epic), 1977*

Edgar Winter Group:
They Only Come Out At Night (Epic), 1972
Standing On Rock (Blue Sky), 1981

With Johnny Winter:
See Johnny Winter entry

Worth Searching Out:
Edgar Winter's White Trash:
White Trash (Epic), 1971

Edgar Winter Group:
Shock Treatment (Epic), 1974
The Edgar Winter Group With Rick Derringer (Blue Sky), 1975
The Edgar Winter Album (Blue Sky), 1979
*compilation

Johnny Winter

US guitarist, vocalist, composer.
Born Leland, Mississippi, January 23, 1944.

Career: Fluid guitarist who lived for traditional blues and R&B; spent teens playing with younger brother Edgar(▶) in local Texan bands. Later began working as session player and recorded several LPs for regional release in South. **Austin, Texas, About Blues, Early Times, Before The Storm, First Winter, The Johnny Winter Story** and **The Progressive Blues Experiment** all contain material from this period.

Johnny Winter And, Johnny Winter. Courtesy CBS Records. The Winter Brothers had their heyday in the '70s.

One of these albums was mentioned in 'Rolling Stone' article covering local scene in Texas; New York Scene club owner Steve Paul then located Winter and signed him to management contract. He proclaimed Winter next rock 'superstar' and the hype was on.

Columbia offered one of largest recording contract's ever given new talent and promptly packed Winter off on national tour. When Winter's atmospheric blues did not transpose to large concert halls, he overhauled his back-up band. Steve Paul took the Scene's house band and reorganised the McCoys (**Hang On Sloopy**) to back Winter; key figure in line-up was Rick Derringer(▶).

Columbia was faced with competition from Winter's old material, which had been bought up and re-issued by various cash-in outfits. As a result, Winter's new material failed to mark up expected sales. More importantly, music tastes began to change in US as younger kids failed to support blues revival. Despite several excellent LPs (**Johnny Winter And, Johnny Winter And Live**), strain on Winter exceeded his ability to cope and rock's 'next superstar' retired with drug habit.

Still Alive And Well didn't appear until 1973 but showed Winter was still talented and capable of recording strong effort. However, its critical success failed to produce significant sales and next two Johnny Winter LPs began to sound as if he was desperately trying to produce a commercial success.

In 1977, Winter began extended collaboration with Muddy Waters(▶). If this signalled end of Winter's hopes for superstardom, it also marked his return to true strength as blues guitarist: simple, clean and traditional music which revitalised interest in Muddy Waters' career.

Like so many other 'next big thing' hypes, Winter never came close to matching the stupendous expectations placed on him. Only now can his early Columbia masterpieces be appreciated.

Albums:
Johnny Winter (Columbia/CBS), 1969
Second Winter (Columbia/CBS), 1969
Johnny Winter And (Columbia/CBS), 1970

Johnny Winter And . . . Live (Columbia/CBS), 1971
Still Alive And Well (Columbia/CBS), 1973
Saints And Sinners (Columbia/CBS), 1974
Captured Live (Blue Sky), 1976
Nothin' But The Blues (Blue Sky), 1977
White, Hot, And Blue (Blue Sky), 1978
Ready For Winter (Accord/—), 1981
Raised On Rock (Blue Sky), 1981

With Edgar Winter:
Together Live (Blue Sky), 1976

Worth Searching Out:
The Johnny Winter Story (double) (Blue Sky), 1980

Stevie Winwood

UK vocalist, composer, multi-instrumentalist.
Born Birmingham, England, May 12, 1948.

Career: Generally acclaimed as one of Britain's greatest white R&B vocalists. Career began in 1961, playing with trombonist Rico and later the Muff Woody Jazz Band (featuring his brother Muff Winwood). At 15, Steve and Muff joined Spencer Davis Rhythm 'n' Blues Quartet.

Professional career began following year, by which time Winwood had assimilated many musical influences, including folk, jazz, pop, blues and soul. Newly named Spencer Davis Group(▶) achieved some lowly chart placings before breaking big in 1965/66 with string of hits and two No. 1s, **Keep On Running** and **Somebody Help Me**. In spite of title, it was Winwood who gained critical attention and approval for powerhouse vocals and impressive guitar and piano work; it came as no surprise when he announced his decision to form new unit in 1967.

Traffic(▶) provided Winwood with greater freedom to develop his musical ideas. Two highly acclaimed albums, **Mr Fantasy** and **Traffic**, were boosted by three hit singles: **Paper Sun, Hole In My Shoe** and **Here We Go Round The Mulberry Bush**. By early 1969, Winwood was tempted by a more ambitious plan and formed world's first supergroup — Blind Faith(▶), with Cream's Eric Clapton and Ginger Baker, and Family's Rick Grech. Group were hyped to ludicrous proportions and individual egos suffocated natural talents. After recording one album, and touring America (following much-publicised appearance in Hyde Park), Faith folded.

Winwood began '70s guesting with Ginger Baker's(▶) Air Force, but soon began work on solo album **Mad Shadows**, which finally emerged as Traffic re-formation. Over next four years, Traffic recorded four more studio albums, all critically acclaimed.

Winwood's solo career was preceded by two years of silence, punctuated by appearances on albums by Viv Stanshall, Jim Capaldi, Sandy Denny, Toots and the Maytals (▶) and George Harrison(▶). Such eclectic

Arc Of A Diver, Steve Winwood. Courtesy Island Records.

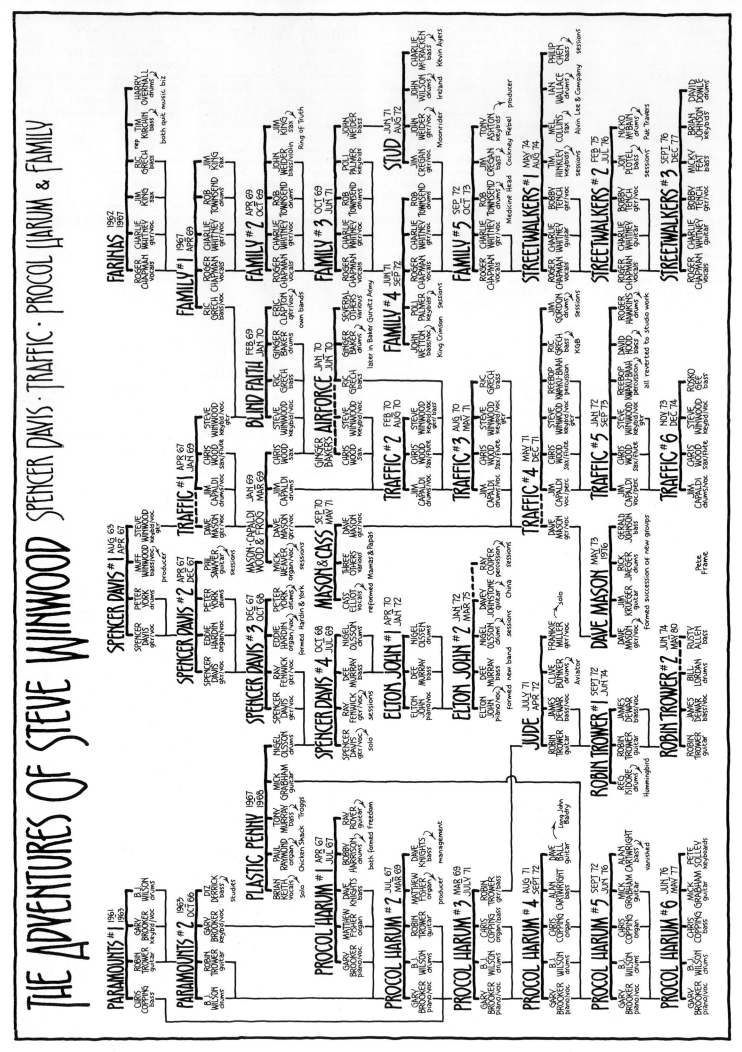

Above: Steve Winwood, man of many bands and solo star of the '80s.

musical activities proved sufficient inspiration for first solo, finally released in 1977. Ever restless, Winwood continued with related projects, including concert with Georgie Fame(▶) and appearances on Stomu Yamashta's **Go Live From Paris** and Marianne Faithful's **Broken English**.

Second solo **Arc Of A Diver**, a Top 5 US hit, revealed imaginative use of electronic keyboard instruments and synthesiser, continuing experiments begun on first effort. Lyrical contributions by Will Jennings, George Fleming and Viv Stanshall seemed erratic in quality, but hit single **While You See A Chance** made US Top 10. Latest work, **Talking Back To The Night**, consolidated rather than improved solo reputation. Accompanied by group of hot session men, Winwood undertook his first tour as solo artist during summer 1983. In spite of illustrious history, the once precocious teenage talent has yet to produce the work of genius of which many believe him still capable. Nevertheless, high quality of artist shows little sign of atrophying as middle age beckons.

Hit Singles:

	US	UK
With Traffic:		
(See separate entry)		
Solo:		
While You See A Chance, 1980	9	—

Albums:
With Traffic:
(See separate entry)

With Blind Faith:
Blind Faith (Polydor), 1969

Solo:
Steve Winwood (Island), 1977
Arc Of A Diver (Island), 1980
Talking Back To The Night (Island), 1982

Wishbone Ash

UK group formed 1969.
Original line-up: Steve Upton, drums; Martin Turner, bass; Glen Turner, guitar.

Career: Locally successful Torquay (Devon)-based trio moved to London following replacement of Glen Turner by Andy Powell. Recruiting Ted Turner (unrelated to Glen and Martin), established twin lead-guitar line-up in imitation of Page and Beck in Yardbirds(▶).

After nine months solid gigging, released debut **Wishbone Ash** in 1970. Highly praised for its solid and occasionally imaginative guitar arrangements, album was surprise

Right: Wishbone Ash on stage with (foreground) Andy Powell.

hit. Group capitalised on reputation with extensive touring on club and college circuit, establishing sizeable student following in early '70s. Fairly anonymous bunch, their mainstream British rock ensured comfortably long career, almost threatening an important work with 1972 **Argus**, which reached No. 3 in UK album charts. **Wishbone 4** was anticlimactic return to basics, indicating acceptance of role as middling college group. Temporarily lost direction following departure of Ted Turner, who was replaced by Laurie Wisefield (formerly of Home). Group travelled to Miami for 1974 **There's The Rub**, produced by Bill Szymczyk.

In 1975, manager Miles Copeland arranged the 'Star Trucking' European tour, designed to give group greater exposure. When bill-topper Lou Reed pulled out, tour ended in series of disastrous financial losses, with group's management on verge of bankruptcy. Disillusioned, Wishbone Ash took up residency in States where they concentrated on establishing strong cult following. Subsequent infrequent appearances in Europe proved reasonably successful.

Following US deal with Atlantic, recorded **Locked In** (1976) with producer Tom Dowd. Outdated album work has not seriously affected drawing power on corporate US rock circuit where they have achieved modicum of success, promoting myriad albums. After long career with MCA, group were allowed to compile their own **Best Of Wishbone Ash** LP, released in 1982.

Current line-up: Upton; Laurie Wisefield, guitar; Trevor Bolder, bass; Andy Powell, guitar; Claire Hamill, vocals.

Albums:
Wishbone Ash (MCA), 1970
Pilgrimage (MCA), 1971
Argus (MCA), 1972
Wishbone 4 (MCA), 1973
Live Dates (MCA), 1974
There's The Rub (MCA), 1974
New England (MCA), 1976
Locked In (MCA), 1976
Front Page News (MCA), 1977
Classic Ash (MCA), 1977
No Smoke Without Fire (MCA), 1978
Just Testing (MCA), 1979
Number The Brave (MCA), 1981
Twin Barrels Burning (AVM), 1982
Best Of (MCA), 1982

Bill Withers

US vocalist, composer, guitarist.
Born Slab Fork, West Virginia, July 4, 1938.

Career: Born into rural family, Withers showed no particular aptitude for music as child. Served in US navy for nine years, only started singing and playing guitar afterwards, in 1964.

While working in aircraft factory he began composing songs, and was eventually signed by independent Sussex label in 1971. First album, **Just As I Am**, was produced by Booker T. Jones and featured clutch of sensitive and original songs. Single from album, **Ain't No Sunshine**, eventually went gold and has since become a standard, recorded by everyone from Michael Jackson(▶) to Roland Kirk.

Second album, **Still Bill**, confirmed emergence of major new talent and notched up even greater success. By now Withers was also performing live with superb rhythm section (guitarist Benorce Blackman, bass player Melvin Dunlap and drummer James Gadson), winning over audiences with combination of appealingly unstylised voice, distinctive material and modest, almost diffident manner. Style coalesced best elements of black music and singer/songwriter tradition.

After a superb live double album and one more studio album, Withers split from Sussex to join Columbia roster. Since that time his

Left: Bill Withers can afford to smile after charting for ten years.

career has progressed in fits and starts. His albums have generally been little more than pleasant, and sales have not been spectacular. However, in 1978 he scored major international hit with **Lovely Day**.

Most recent success has been as guest artist on two superb singles, **Soul Shadows** by Crusaders(▶) and **Just The Two Of Us** by Grover Washington. Both showed his vocal prowess to be undiminished, and had they been released under his own name would have undoubtedly put him right back at top. Bill Withers continues to be held in high regard, both as songwriter and vocalist, and is likely to be in demand for some time to come.

Greatest Hits, Bill Withers. Courtesy Columbia Records.

Hit Singles:

	US	UK
Ain't No Sunshine, 1971	3	—
Lean On Me, 1972	1	18
Use Me, 1972	2	—
Lovely Day, 1978	30	7
Just The Two Of Us (with Grover Washington Jr.), 1981	2	34

Albums:
Best Of (Sussex), 1975
Menagerie (Columbia/CBS), 1978
'Bout Love (Columbia/CBS), 1978
Greatest Hits (Columbia/CBS), 1980

Worth Searching Out:
Just As I Am (Sussex), 1971
Still Bill (Sussex), 1972
Live At Carnegie Hall (Sussex), 1973

Stevie Wonder

US vocalist, composer, multi-instrumentalist.
Born Steveland Morris, Saginaw, Michigan, May 3, 1950.

Career: One of the most important and consistent of contemporary artists, Stevie Wonder showed early interest in music. Although blind since birth, by age eight was proficient on piano, harmonica, drums and bongoes.

Family moved to Detroit when Wonder was child; at age 10 he was introduced to nascent Tamla Motown label by family friend Ronald White, one of the Miracles. Period of grooming followed, during which time several moderately successful singles were released. Wonder gained experience of live work on Motown's touring 'revues', quickly winning reputation as exciting vocal/instrumental act.

First major success came in 1963 with **Fingertips**, recorded live and featuring Stevie's urgent vocalising and harmonica playing against jumping brass background. Record made No. 1, as did album from which it was taken, **Twelve Year Old Genius**. Nevertheless, next few singles were not particularly successful: right format for youthful prodigy had not yet been found.

Wonder solved problem himself with **Uptight**, released in 1966. Self-penned, and featuring vocals without harmonica, it made No. 3 in US and became massive international hit. It heralded string of international successes, most self-written, others taken from wide range of sources, including Bob Dylan(▶) (**Blowin' In The Wind**) and cabaret repertoire (**For Once In My Life**).

By end of '60s Wonder was becoming somewhat restless within confines of Motown 'family', although reluctant to make break completely. He was already producing other artists, and felt capable of taking full control of his career. Crucial point was release of album **Signed, Sealed And Delivered** in 1970. Entirely produced by Wonder, it won award for best soul album of 1970 and gave him confidence to pursue own path.

In 1970 Wonder met and married Syreeta Wright (marriage later broke up). Syreeta contributed to **Where I'm Coming From** album, which heralded new phase of Wonder music in experimental direction.

Following year saw Wonder attain majority, at which time all previous earnings became available to him. Artist then set up Taurus Productions; although gaining independence from Motown, company remained as distributor of all Wonder products.

New freedom prompted important musical leap forward with **Music Of My Mind**, a one-man tour-de-force featuring variety of electronic keyboards. Album alienated some old fans, but brought Wonder to attention of new rock audience, and eventually went gold. It also paved way for album which established commercial viability of new Wonder music, **Talking Book**. Full of songs which have since become standards—**You Are The Sunshine Of My Life, You've Got It Bad, Girl, Superstition, I Believe (When I Fall In Love It Will Be Forever)**—**Talking Book** was first in series of award-winning platinum albums that became synonymous with name Stevie Wonder in '70s.

'70s also saw Wonder sign record-breaking financial agreement with Motown—a guaranteed $13 million between 1975 and 1982. He became one of most often-awarded artists, with 14 Grammies between 1974 and 1977 alone. He gained reputation for keen socio-political awareness (particularly of black issues) and became symbol of spirit of liberation. Double album **Songs In The Key Of Life,** was regarded by many as one of *the* albums of the decade.

Entering '80s as strongly as ever with **Hotter Than July**, Wonder continued to exert huge influence. In 1982 he was given Award of Merit by American Music Awards, a citation which only does scant justice to enormous contribution he has made to popular music. Revered by his peers as much as by public, Wonder is sure to continue to push back boundaries throughout '80s and beyond.

Latest album, **Stevie Wonder's Original Musiquarium 1**, contains 12 classics from previous albums, plus four new songs.

Below: Steveland Morris, aka Stevie Wonder, circa 1966.

Hit Singles:	US	UK
Fingertips Part 2, 1963	1	—
Uptight (Everything's Alright), 1966	3	14
Nothing's Tood Good For My Baby, 1966	20	—
Blowin' In The Wind, 1966	9	36
A Place In The Sun, 1966	9	20
I Was Made To Love Her, 1967	2	5
I'm Wondering, 1967	12	22
Shoo-Be-Doo-Be-Doo-Da-Day, 1968	9	46
For Once In My Life, 1968	2	3
I Don't Know Why, 1969	39	14
My Cherie Amour, 1969	4	4
Yester-Me, Yester-You, Yesterday, 1969	7	2
Never Had A Dream Come True, 1970	26	6
Signed, Sealed, Delivered, I'm Yours, 1970	3	15
Heaven Help Us All, 1970	9	29
We Can Work It Out, 1971	13	27
If You Really Love Me, 1971	8	20
Superstition, 1973	1	11
You Are The Sunshine Of My Life, 1973	1	7
Higher Ground, 1973	4	29
Living For The City, 1974	8	15
He's Misstra Know It All, 1974	—	10
Don't You Worry 'Bout A Thing, 1974	16	—
You Haven't Done Nothing, 1974	1	30
Boogie On Reggae Woman, 1975	3	12
I Wish, 1976	1	5
Sir Duke, 1977	1	2
Send One Your Love, 1979	4	52
Masterblaster (Jammin'), 1980	5	2
I Ain't Gonna Stand For It, 1980	11	10
Lately, 1981	—	3
Happy Birthday, 1981	—	2
That Girl, 1982	4	39
Do I Do, 1982	13	10

With Paul McCartney:

	US	UK
Ebony And Ivory, 1982	1	1

Albums:
Tribute To Uncle Ray (Motown), 1963
Jazz Soul Of Little Stevie (Motown), 1963
Twelve Year Old Genius Recorded Live (Motown), 1963
With A Song In My Heart (Motown), 1964
Uptight (Motown), 1966
Down To Earth (Motown), 1966
I Was Made To Love Her (Motown), 1967
Some Day At Christmas (Motown), 1967
For Once In My Life (Motown), 1969
My Cherie Amour (Motown), 1969
Live At The Talk Of The Town (Motown), 1970
Stevie Wonder Live (Motown), 1970
Where I'm Coming From (Motown), 1971
Greatest Hits (Motown), 1972
Greatest Hits Volume 2 (Motown), 1972
Music Of My Mind (Motown), 1972
Talking Book (Motown), 1972
Innervisions (Motown), 1973
Fulfillingness First Finale (Motown), 1974
Songs In The Key Of Life (Motown), 1976
Anthology (Motown), 1977
The Secret Life Of Plants (Motown), 1979
Light My Fire (—/MFP), 1979
Hotter Than July (Motown), 1980
Stevie Wonder's Original Musiquarium 1 (Motown), 1982

Below: Little Stevie Wonder had his first No. 1, Fingertips, at age 13.

Lower Right Hand Page: Stevie going strong in the '70s.

Inset Far Opposite: For Once In My Life. Courtesy Tamla-Motown Records.

Inset Opposite: Original Musiquarium 1. Courtesy Motown Records.

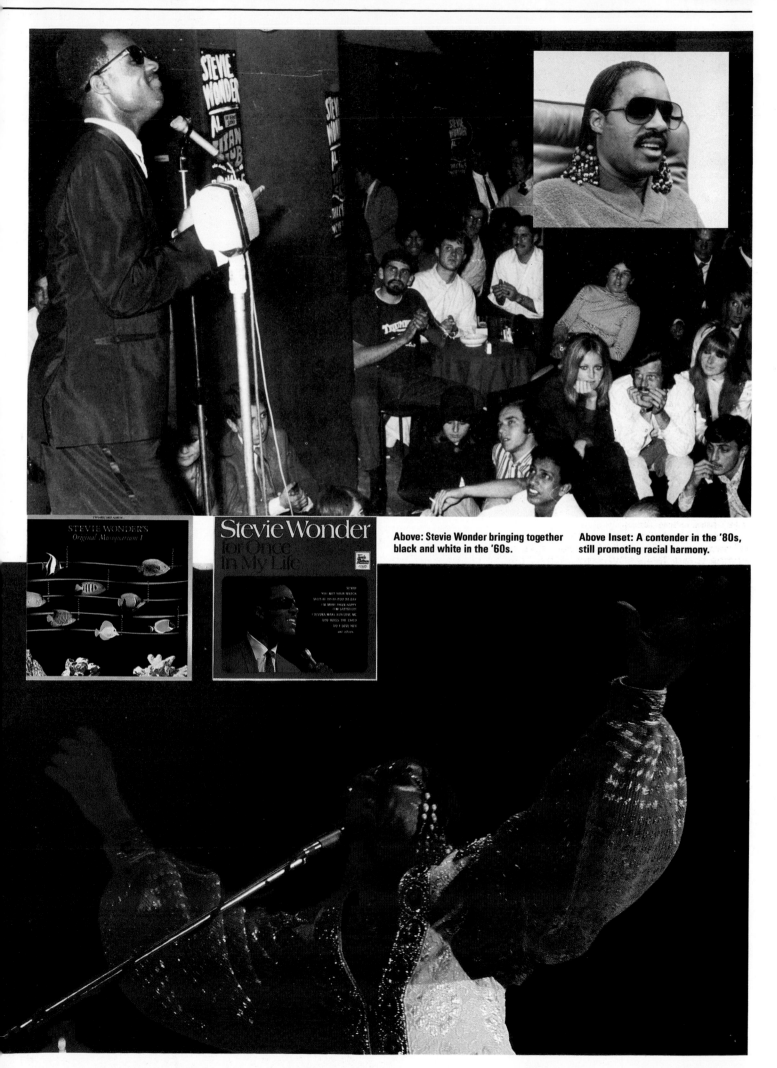

Above: Stevie Wonder bringing together black and white in the '60s.

Above Inset: A contender in the '80s, still promoting racial harmony.

Roy Wood

UK vocalist, composer, multi-instrumentalist. Born Ulysses Adrian Wood, Birmingham, November 8, 1946.

Career: Learned guitar in early teens and joined/formed numerous groups, including the Falcons, the Lawmen, Gerry Levene and the Avengers, and Mike Sheridan and the Nightriders (who recorded Wood's composition **Make Them Understand**). Following expulsion from Moseley College of Art, Wood became more involved in group work, finally forming the Move(▶) in 1964. Impressive line-up of Bev Bevan (drums), Carl Wayne (vocals), Chris 'Ace' Kefford (bass) and Trevor Burton (guitar) was enlisted from cream of small-time Birmingham groups. Signed to opportunist manager Tony Secunda, they established themselves via residency at London's Marquee Club. Burgeoning interest led to recording contract with Deram. First single, **Night Of Fear,** reached No. 2 in early 1967, and was followed by eight other hits, all composed by Wood, one of the cleverest and most appealing songwriters of the era. Psychedelia, flower power, early rock 'n' roll and classical pastiche were some of the themes explored on successive single releases.

As years passed, Wood's influence over group increased. From **Fire Brigade** onwards he assumed lead vocals as well as songwriting credits.

Following two essentially pop albums, **The Move** and **Shazam,** Wood was anxious to undertake more ambitious work. Acknowledged as a singles group in Britain, Move were gradually accepted as serious musicians in the States (despite limited popularity). Musical direction became increasingly diverse and uncertain towards end of decade; during final stage of career they flirted with heavy metal (**Brontosaurus, When Alice Comes Down To The Farm**) and rock revivalism (**Californian Man**). Wood's desire for music of greater complexity resulted in creation of Electric Light Orchestra(▶), whose aim was to continue the exploratory work begun by the Beatles(▶) on such songs as **Strawberry Fields Forever** and **I Am The Walrus.**

After recording one hit album and single (**10538 Overture**), the ever-restless Wood left ELO in the hands of Jeff Lynne in order to pursue another new project. Soon a new group, Wizzard, emerged, comprising Rick Price (guitar), Bill Hunt (piano/harpsichord/French horn), Hugh McDowell (electric cello), Nick Pentelow (sax), Mike Burney (sax), Keith Smart (drums) and Charlie Grima (drums). Wood took lead role with new image, including multi-coloured hair and warpaint. First single, **Ball Park Incident,** was an intriguing production, echoing Phil Spector's wall-of-sound '60s work.

Subsequent singles were even more impressive and included two celebrated No. 1's, **See My Baby Jive** and **Angel Fingers.** These and the haunting Spector-like festive hit, **I Wish It Could Be Christmas Everyday,** confirmed Wood's ability to write/produce hits that were the equal of his finest '60s work. Nevertheless, inability to produce albums of equivalent interest remained a failing from the early days. A brave attempt at rock revivalism, **Eddy And The Falcons,** proved commercially unsuccessful, causing Wood to lose interest.

In mid-70s he revived the pseudo-heavy metal experimentation of **Brontosaurus** in a revamped Wizzo, but his work was ill-timed. A simultaneous shot at solo fame produced the impressive hit **Forever,** an affectionate tribute to Neil Sedaka(▶) and the Beach

Boys(▶). Solo albums **Boulders** (1970) and **Mustard** (1975) were again erratic, though they demonstrated his total control as producer, engineer and designer (he even painted the cover!).

Late '70s and '80s proved barren for Wood, while his protegée Lynne has reaped a fortune with ELO. Wood's great strength and weakness has always been his peripatetic nature, but his past record remains exemplary—composer of all Move's hits, the mastermind behind the original ELO, and the creator of some of early '70s finest UK singles via Wizzard. A multi-talented producer, arranger, singer, songwriter and manipulator of pop genres, it would be a mistake to write him off despite his inconspicuous profile on the current scene.

Hit Singles:	US	UK
(See also Move and ELO)		
With Move:		
(See separate entry)		
With ELO:		
10538 Overture, 1972	—	9
With Wizzard:		
Ball Park Incident, 1972	—	6
See My Baby Jive, 1973	—	1
Angel Fingers, 1973	—	1
I Wish It Could Be Christmas Everyday, 1973	—	4
Rock'n'Roll Winter (Looney's Tune), 1974	—	6
Are You Ready To Rock, 1974	—	8
Solo:		
Dear Elaine, 1973	—	18
Forever, 1973	—	8
Going Down The Road, 1974	—	13
Oh What A Shame, 1975	—	13

Albums:
With Move:
(See separate entry)

With ELO:
The Electric Light Orchestra (Harvest), 1971

Solo:
Boulders (Harvest), 1973
Mustard (Jet), 1975
The Roy Wood Story (Harvard), 1976
On The Road Again (Automatic), 1979

With Wizzard:
Wizzard Brew (Harvest), 1973
Eddy And The Falcons (Warner Bros), 1974
See My Baby Jive (Harvest), 1974

Roy Wood Wizzo Band:
Super Active Wizzo (Warner Bros), 1977

Tammy Wynette

US vocalist, composer, guitarist, pianist. Born Virginia Wynette Pugh, Itawamba County, Mississippi, May 5, 1942.

Career: In custom-designed luxury bus, Tammy Wynette travels 100,000 miles a year to sing, with a sob in her voice, songs of love and loss which seem to reflect her highly publicised private life. Market research revealed that her fans are mostly married women between 22 and 45. It is for this audience that she writes country songs of shattered romance, with outstanding success.

Raised on rundown farm by grandparents while widowed mother worked in town, Wynette had extensive music lessons on piano and guitar that were father's legacy. Dreaming of fame, she organised trio which sang on local radio. Teenage marriage resulted in three children and poverty, so she learned hairdressing (and still keeps beautician's licence up-to-date, just in case). After splitting up with husband, she worked as Birmingham beautician and sang on local television while trying to procure recording contract.

Moving to Nashville with three children and no money, Wynette struggled as club singer and song-plugger for nearly a year before Epic Records' Billy Sherrill agreed to record **Apartment Number 9**, 1966 single which immediately made charts. **Your Good Girl's Gonna Go Bad** went to top of country charts, soon followed by 15 more hit singles and 11 albums.

Wynette's career is filled with firsts, bests and mosts: **Stand By Your Man** is one of the biggest selling country music singles ever, making a US Top 20 in 1969 and UK No.1 in 1975. She has topped US country chart 35 times, sold over 30 million records and won two Grammys. Chosen three times as Female Vocalist of the Year by Country Music Association (1968-70), she was also first female country singer to achieve platinum album. **Greatest Hits** album earned over one million dollars and, overall, her records have grossed more than a hundred million dollars.

For over 12 years producer Sherrill continued to select and, in some instances, write or co-write songs like **I Don't Wanna Play House, Take Me To Your World,** the phenomenally successful **Stand By Your Man** and **D.I.V.O.R.C.E.** (parodied in 1975 by Billy Connolly's UK No. 1 single of same title). In 1968 Wynette married country star

George Jones(▶) and Sherrill produced well-received duet albums. When stormy, headline-grabbing marriage ended, as was responsible for apparently autobiographical hits like Wynette's composition **'Til I Can Make It On My Own,** which also reached No. 1 for Kenny Rogers(▶) and Dottie West.

Since divorce from hard-drinking Jones in 1975, Wynette has developed as live performer, belting out her heartbreak on Las Vegas stages, television and city-by-city US 1982 tour. As songwriter, too, her success increases, and her material has been recorded by her ex-husband Jones, Julie Andrews and Debbie Boone.

In 1978 she married George Richey, who co-wrote several of her past hits. Former music director for television series 'Hee Haw', Richey has taken over as Wynette's producer. Two 1982 albums have resulted: **Soft Touch** and **Good Love And Heartbreak.** Autobiography 'Stand By Your Man' was published in 1979 and, made into CBS-TV movie, which aired in US in 1981.

Hit Singles:	US	UK
Stand By Your Man, 1969	19	—
Stand By Your Man, 1975	—	1
D.I.V.O.R.C.E., 1975	—	12

The Best Of Tammy Wynette. Courtesy Epic Records.

Albums (selected):
Greatest Hits Volume I (Epic/—), '70s
Greatest Hits Volume II (Epic/—), '70s
Greatest Hits Volume III (Epic/—), '70s
Greatest Hits Volume IV (Epic/—), '70s
The Best Of (Epic), 1981
Soft Touch (Epic), 1982
The Classic Collection (Epic), 1982

XTC

UK group formed 1977.

Original/Current line-up: Andy Partridge, guitar, vocals; Colin Moulding, bass, vocals; Barry Andrews, keyboards; Terry Chambers, drums.

Career: Partridge organised XTC as punk band in Swindon, near London. **This Is Pop?** single attracted some attention and revealed XTC to be power-pop group in punk clothing. This became more apparent by time solid third album, **Drums And Wires,** appeared in 1979.

Next LP yielded minor hit, **Sergeant Rock,** which earned some US airplay and write-off as lightweight by UK press. In 1982 **Senses Working Overtime** put band back in UK charts, and double LP **English Settlement** (cut to single LP for US market) received critical approval. End of 1982 produced singles compilation (UK only) **Waxworks.** In promotional move, this album was issued for

Left: A mug shot of XTC, with prime mover Andy Partridge (with glasses) looking less than amused.

limited time with second LP, **Beeswax**, comprising B-side.

Hit Singles:

	US	UK
Making Plans For Nigel, 1979	—	17
Sergeant Rock, 1981	—	16
Senses Working Overtime, 1982	—	10

Drums And Wires, XTC. Courtesy Virgin Records.

Albums:
White Music (Virgin-Epic/Virgin), 1978
Go 2 (Virgin-Epic/Virgin), 1978
Drums And Wires (Virgin-Epic/Virgin), 1979
Black Sea (Virgin), 1980
English Settlement (—/Virgin), 1982
English Settlement (Single) (Virgin-Epic/—), 1982
Waxworks: Some Singles 1977-1982 (—/Virgin), 1982
Beeswax: Some B-sides 1977-1982 (—/Virgin), 1982

The Yardbirds

UK group formed 1963.

Original line-up: Keith Relf, vocals, harmonica; Anthony 'Top' Topham, guitar; Chris Dreja, guitar; Paul Samwell-Smith, bass; Jim McCarty, drums.

Career: First version of Yardbirds grew out of Kingston Art School band, the Metropolitan Blues Quartet. Eric Clapton(▶) replaced Topham in late 1963, before band took over residency vacated by Rolling Stones(▶) at Crawdaddy Club in Richmond. Band generated strong cult following on London and Home Counties club circuit, and toured Europe with blues legend Sonny Boy Williamson.

Signed by Columbia, they released **Five Live Yardbirds** in 1964 (only in UK), essential listening for anyone wanting to know what British R&B was all about. Album increased their following, as did **Sonny Boy Williamson And The Yardbirds,** released same year. 1965 saw shift in direction when band recorded **For Your Love,** written by Graham Gouldman then of Mindbenders, later of 10 cc(▶). An unusual yet thoroughly commercial rock/pop song, far removed from band's R&B orientation, it catapulted the Yardbirds into charts on both sides of Atlantic, making No. 3 in UK and No. 6 in US.

Success was consolidated by release of two more Graham Gouldman singles, **Heart Full Of Soul** and **Evil Hearted You**. Clapton, however, quit after **For Your Love**, unable to reconcile himself to move away from band's roots, and joined John Mayall's(▶) Bluesbreakers. Jimmy Page was asked to replace Clapton, but declined and recommended Jeff Beck(▶), another ex-art college musician, who accepted.

1966 saw further stresses and personnel changes. Now a hot live act, band was continually touring, which didn't suit Paul Samwell-Smith. He pulled out to concentrate on production. Chris Dreja moved to bass, and

Jimmy Page, then an in-demand session musician, agreed to second offer, joining Beck on guitar. Relatively minor hit **Happenings Ten Years Time Ago** was only single with this line-up.

By end of year Beck had also left. Following fairly disastrous album produced by Mickey Most, and a couple of unsuccessful American singles, Relf, McCarty, Page and Dreja called it a day in July 1968.

Relf and McCarty formed folk duo Together, then founded Renaissance(▶), but their post-Yardbirds career was not particularly auspicious, Relf died in accident at home in 1976. Dreja became a photographer, while Page formed New Yardbirds which metamorphosised into supergroup Led Zeppelin(▶) (managed by former Yardbirds road manager Peter Grant).

Yardbirds' influence was greater than their actual success and paved the way for guitar-dominated psychedelic/heavy rock bands of late '60s and '70s. Now, virtually all recordings have become collectors' items, and Yardbirds are regarded as one of all-time legendary rock bands.

Final line-up: Relf; McCarty; Jimmy Page, guitar; Dreja.

Hit Singles:

	US	UK
For Your Love, 1965	6	3
Heart Full Of Soul, 1965	9	2
Evil Hearted You/Still I'm Sad, 1965	—	3
I'm A Man, 1965	17	—
Shapes Of Things, 1966	11	3
Over Under Sideways Down, 1966	13	10

Albums:
Yardbirds With Sonny boy Williamson (Mercury/Fontana), 1964
Five Live Yardbirds (—/Charly), 1964
The Yardbirds (—/CBS), 1966
Great Hits (Epic/—), 1967
Remember (—/Starline), 1971
Eric Clapton And The Yardbirds (Springboard/—), 1972
Yardbirds Favourites (Epic), 1972
Yardbirds Featuring Eric Clapton (—/Charly), 1975
Yardbirds Featuring Jeff Beck (—/Charly), 1975
Shapes Of Things (Springboard/Charly), 1977
Single Hits (—/Charly), 1982
Afternoon Tea (Rhino/—), 1982
For Your Love (Accord/—), 1982

Five Live Yardbirds. Courtesy EMI Records.

Worth Searching Out:
Having A Rave-up With The Yardbirds (Epic/—), 1971
Live Yardbirds Featuring Jimmy Page (Epic), 1971*
*Withdrawn

Yazoo

UK duo formed 1982.

Original line-up: Alison (Alf) Moyet, vocals; Vince Clarke, keyboards, synthesisers, computerised drums.

Career: Clarke, originally main man of Depeche Mode(▶), left group after writing first three hits and much of first album, theoretically to embark on solo career. Alf (nickname contributed by French father) had sung around Southend area R&B scene in such bands as the Vicars and the Screaming Abdabs. Not having achieved ambition of working on London circuit, advertised in music press for 'rootsy blues band'. Vince, antithesis of this description, answered advert, and duo decided to make single to see whether anything would happen.

Only You reached No. 2 in UK charts; follow-up **Don't Go** also made Top 3, while debut LP entered album chart at No. 2. By this time, Alf (regarded as simply a vocalist) had also begun to write songs. Duo embarked on successful UK tour in September '82, then performed in New York, where they had to be renamed Yaz, as ethnic US record label had already registered name of Yazoo. B-side of **Only You, Situation**, became first (minor) US hit single (MTV led to further US success); album also registered in chart. Third UK single

reached Top 20. With recording in progress for second LP and fourth UK single released, announcement was made that duo would split to work on solo projects, although reunions are by no means out of the question.

Alf seems likely to achieve solo success as her talent (a Janis Joplinesque voice and image) is unique in 1983. Predicting future success for Vince more problematic in view of vast number of synthesiser acts in UK charts.

Hit Singles:

	US	UK
Only You, 1982	—	2
Don't Go, 1982	—	3
The Other Side Of Love, 1982	—	13
Nobody's Diary, 1983	—	7

Albums:
Upstairs At Eric's (Sire/Mute), 1982

Upstairs At Eric's, Yazoo. Courtesy Mute Records.

Yes

UK group formed 1968.

Original line-up: Jon Anderson, vocals; Chris Squire, bass; Peter Banks, guitar; Tony Kaye, organ; Bill Bruford, drums.

Career: After 12 years in nowhere bands Anderson chanced upon Squire in Soho night-club; line-up of Yes was completed by members of their previous bands. Debut LP **Yes** took Beatles(▶)/Byrds(▶) originals and expanded them into almost unrecognisable baroque extravaganzas; sound deliberately emulated classical influence of ELP's(▶) Keith Emerson.

Follow-up **Time And A Word** LP added superfluous strings and did not sound innovative as intended. In 1971 Banks left; he was replaced by Steve Howe (ex-Syndicate, In Crowd, Budast, Tomorrow). This line-up produced **The Yes Album**, which showed that original intention to fuse rock/classical music remained band's driving force. Significantly, Banks added synthesiser and Yes recorded completely original music for the LP.

Kaye was replaced by Rick Wakeman(▶) (ex-Strawbs) whose classical training coincided with band's direction. **Fragile** LP took on symphonic sound closely associated with Yes. In 1972 Alan White (ex-Plastic Ono Band) took over drums for what many consider best Yes line-up.

Growing integration of technological advances and classical idioms exploded on **Close To The Edge** (recorded before Bruford had left drum slot to play with King Crimson(▶)). New line-up proved that complex, orchestral compositions translated well on stage with live set, **Yessongs**. This triple set also betrayed problem with Yes music: the line between innovative exploration and overblown pretension.

Left: The highly contrasting due which made up Yazoo—Alf (right) and Vince Clarke.

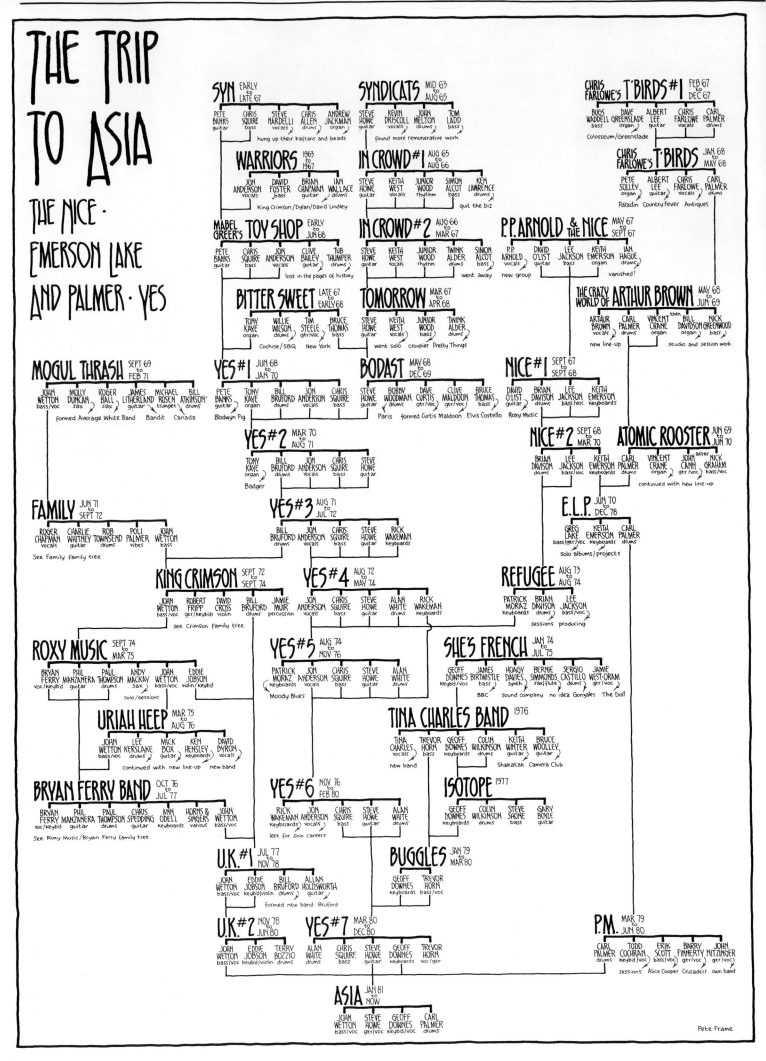

Next double LP **Topographic Oceans** sunk under its own weight and convinced Wakeman to jump ship. (He had released successful solo album **Six Wives Of Henry VIII** in 1973.) Patrick Moraz (keyboards) joined August 1974. His classical training allowed him to assume Wakeman's mantle with little difficulty, as evidenced on **Relayer** LP and in live shows. Wakeman rejoined in 1976 when Moraz quit Yes as fans were flooded with plethora of various solo efforts and spin-offs.

1977's **Going For The One** dredged up same old Yes conventions and music seemed slightly foolish in light of new wave. Wakeman left after **Tormato** and then — a shock to Yes fans — so did Anderson; Anderson went on to solo work and Vangelis(▶). Buggles duo Trevor Horne (guitars) and Geoff Downes (keyboards) joined in 1980 for US/UK tours and recording of **Drama** LP. Then not with a bang, but with a short press announcement, Yes folded altogether. Howe and Downes reappeared in Asia(▶) with Carl Palmer and John Wetton in 1981.

At their best, Yes was an exciting, thrilling band whose techno-rock explorations gave rock a bit of 'high art' gloss and foreshadowed synth bands of '80s.

Final line-up: Squire; Trevor Horne, guitar, vocals; Steve Howe, Gibson Howe Model guitar (based on Switchmaster); Geoff Downes, keyboards; Alan White, drums.

Hit Singles:

	US	UK
Roundabout, 1972	13	—
Wonderous Stories, 1977	—	7

Albums:
Yes (Atlantic), 1969

Below: Yes on stage shortly before they succumbed to the inevitable and split up in the early 1980s.

Time And A Word (Atlantic), 1970
The Yes Album (Atlantic), 1971
Fragile (Atlantic), 1971
Close To The Edge (Atlantic), 1972
Yessongs (Atlantic), 1973
Tales From Topographic Oceans (Atlantic), 1973
Relayer (Atlantic), 1974
Yesterdays (Atlantic), 1975
Going For The One (Atlantic), 1977
Tormato (Atlantic), 1978
Drama (Atlantic), 1980
Yesshows (Atlantic), 1980
Classic Yes (Atlantic), 1981

Neil Young

Canadian vocalist, composer, guitarist.
Born Toronto, Ontario, November 12, 1945.

Career: Son of well-known Toronto sports writer, who gave Neil ukelele for Xmas, 1958. Graduated to banjo, then guitar soon after. Early influence was Hank Marvin of Shadows(▶). After short-lived group the Jades, joined first real band the Squires in 1963. By late 1964 began to arrange and write for them. During this period, met Stephen Stills(▶) and Richie Furay, whom he would later join in Buffalo Springfield(▶). Became coffee-bar folk singer in New York, then met Bruce Palmer, a member of Mynah Birds (led by Rick Matthews, who later found fame as Rick James(▶) in '80s). Mynah Birds, with Young a member, cut several still unreleased tracks for Motown, but arrest of James as deserter from US Navy effectively killed group.

Young moved to Los Angeles with Palmer in early 1966; reunited with Stills and Furay in freeway traffic jam. Quartet decided to form group the Herd, with drummer Dewey Martin (ex-Dillards). Changed group name to Buffalo Springfield after steamroller of same name; began gigging in spring 1966. After meeting

Byrds(▶), became embroiled in LA folk/rock and country/rock scenes.

With several line-up changes in rhythm section (Palmer departed and later returned, Young left and rejoined, Jim Messina joined early 1968), Buffalo Springfield lasted until May 1968, leaving three excellent LPs and five hit singles, only one of which, **For What It's Worth**, made US Top 10.

After working as folkie, Young acquired record deal with Reprise. First solo LP released start of 1969. Then formed band Crazy Horse(▶), who provided backing for second classic LP, **Everybody Knows This Is Nowhere**. After recording third LP, Young was invited to join Crosby, Stills & Nash, and briefly group became Crosby, Stills, Nash & Young(▶) for **Deja Vu** LP, double live album and performance at Woodstock Festival. Personality clashes led Young back to solo career; **After The Goldrush** and **Harvest** were commercially and artistically successful. But Young turned back on success with 1973 release of **Journey Through The Past**, soundtrack to film produced by Young. Subsequent three LPs permeated by melancholy songs and performances, as Young refused to follow easy commercial path.

Late 1975 LP **Zuma** saw return to form of earlier LPs, with attacking guitar solos and instantly recognisable vocals from Young. Briefly worked with Stephen Stills, but union short-lived. Next LP, **American Stars 'n' Bars**, included assistance from Linda Ronstadt(▶) and Emmylou Harris(▶), joining stellar list of guests on previous Young records such as Crosby, Stills, Nash, Jack Nitzsche, Rick Danko and Levon Helm (the Band(▶)), Nils Lofgren(▶) and others. Three-LP set **Decade**, a self-compiled retrospective, released in late 1977, almost whole year before **Comes A Time**, which encountered many delays due to track changes, remixes, cover art alteration, etc. New era arrived with **Rust Never Sleeps** and **Live Rust**, once

Above: Neil Young, dwarfed by his stage equipment, from his strange film, Rust Never Sleeps.

again with backing from Crazy Horse, to whom Young has returned several times in his career. Concept included major tour, made into film 'Rust Never Sleeps'.

Young then worked at length on film project 'Human Highway'. Directed and acted in movie, along with Dean Stockwell, Russ Tamblyn and Devo(▶). During this period (1980-81) also released two more albums. In 1982, began using synthesisers and electronic instruments; eventually invited many of past friends from backing bands to assist him in making **Trans**, including Nils Lofgren, guitar; Ben Keith, pedal steel, keyboards; Bruce Palmer, bass; Joe Lala, percussion; and Ralph Molina, drums. Group toured in

support of **Trans**. While new electronic direction admirable in some ways, peculiar sounds tended to alienate long-standing Young fans, who preferred his earlier work. However, following is extremely faithful, and new direciton regarded by many as experiment from which their hero will emerge and return to intense electric rock of most influential periods (1969-1973 and 1975-1979).

Hit Singles:

	US	UK
With Buffalo Springfield:		
(See separate entry)		
Crosby, Stills, Nash & Young		
Woodstock, 1970	11	—
Teach Your Children, 1970	16	—
Ohio, 1970	14	—
Solo:		
Heart Of Gold, 1972	1	10

Albums:
With Buffalo Springfield:
(See separate entry)

Crosby, Stills, Nash & Young:
Deja Vu (Atlantic), 1970
Four Way Street (Atlantic), 1971
So Far (Atlantic), 1974*
*Compilation

Solo:
Neil Young (Reprise), 1968
Everybody Knows This Is Nowhere (Reprise), 1969
After The Goldrush (Reprise), 1970
Harvest (Reprise), 1971
Journey Through The Past (Reprise), 1972
Time Fades Away (Reprise), 1973
On The Beach (Reprise), 1974
Tonight's The Night (Reprise), 1975
Zuma (Reprise), 1975
Long May You Run (Stills/Young Band), 1976
American Stars 'n' Bars (Reprise), 1977
Decade (Reprise), 1977*
Comes A Time (Reprise), 1978
Rust Never Sleeps (Reprise), 1979
Live Rust (Reprise), 1979
Hawks And Doves (Warner Bros), 1980
Re-ac-tor (Warner Bros), 1981
Trans (Warner Bros), 1982
*Compilation

ZZ Top

US group formed 1970.

Original/Current line-up: Billy Gibbons, Gibson Les Paul guitar, vocals; Dusty Hill, Fender Telecaster bass, vocals; Frank Beard, drums.

Career: Gibbons was exciting guitarist in local Houston, Texas, band of late '60s, Moving Sidewalks. When that project fell apart, he and manager Bill Ham planned new group. Beard joined and, after failure to find right combination through auditions, recommended Hill. Drawing on traditional country blues and delta music, ZZ Top added hard white rock to come up with own version of high-energy music. Band quickly established reputation as powerful opening act, challenging headliners to match their performances.

First Album received only local interest but **Rio Grande Mud** reflected growing audience by eventually going gold. **Tres Hombres** in 1973 put band into big time and provided US hit single **La Grange**. Forever touring as boogie band, ZZ Top now headlined massive concerts and **Fandango!** quickly followed **Tres Hombres** to platinum. From studio side of LP **Tush,** with its raunchy euphemisms, merited heavy airplay. Following **Téjas** LP and massive World Wide Texas Tour (1976-77), ZZ Top decided to take a vacation which turned into three-year hiatus.

Changes in music could have precluded any significant return. Instead, 1979's **Dequello** was instant success. ZZ Top seem immune to fashion, like all great cowboys, and, free to do what they want.

Hit Singles:

	US	UK
Tush, 1974	20	—

Albums:
First Album (Warner Bros), 1971
Rio Grande Mud (Warner Bros), 1972
Tres Hombres (Warner Bros), 1973
Fandango! (Warner Bros), 1974
Téjas (Warner Bros), 1976
Best Of (Warner Bros), 1977
Dequello (Warner Bros), 1979
El Loco (Warner Bros), 1981
Eliminator (Warner Bros/—), 1983

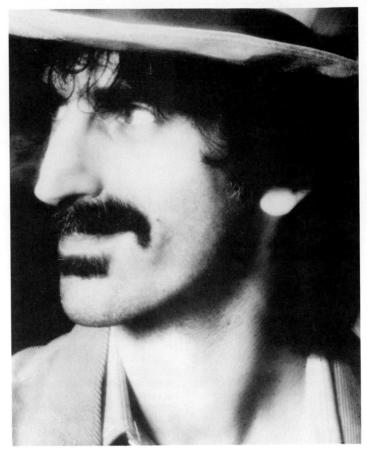

Frank Zappa

US composer, guitarist, vocalist.
Born Francis Vincent Zappa Jr., Baltimore, Maryland, December 21, 1940.

Career: Raised on East Coast until age 10, then moved to West Coast with family, which may explain schizoid musical career. Early interests ranged from Edgar Varese to R&B to '50s Do-Wop. Practical experience included high-school band Blackouts, recording Don Von Vliet (also ex-Blackout and re-named Captain Beefheart(▶) by Zappa), and producing naughty sex tape for local vice squad

Above: The enigmatic Frank Zappa, surely the most consistently adventurous figure in rock music today.

(which earned light jail sentence and draft exemption).

Zappa joined group Soul Giants which, according to legend, played first gig on Mothers' Day. MGM couldn't cope with name 'the Mothers' so added 'of Invention'. Original line-up of Ray Collins, Jimmy Carl 'Token Indian' Black, Roy Estrada and Dave Coranda immediately went for record number of personnel changes. Coranda left in horror at Zappa's master plan for world domination.

Tom Wilson (Dylan(▶), Velvet Underground(▶), producer) recorded debut **Freak Out** in early 1966. Double bonanza of over-the-top social commentry, **Freak Out** demanded a little thinking to get behind satire to strange music underlying it. Zappa became touted as rock's sharpest sociologist. The highly intelligent interviews he gave revealed distaste for any trends or fashions. With further personnel changes, Zappa recorded **Absolutely Free** which questioned lack of freedom in modern society. If rock fans felt smug, claiming to be outside that society, they missed point of **We're Only In It For The Money** which lampooned Beatles(▶) **Sgt. Pepper** and rock's under-30 audience in one blow.

Claiming all his work was one extended piece, Zappa overloaded his modern classical influences into free-form solo **Lumpy Gravy** LP. Zappa's band seemed to disappear although he continued to use many of the same musicians. In late 1967 he started work on two simultaneous recording projects. **Cruising With Ruben And The Jets** appeared first and provided return to satire of early albums. In fact, Zappa reproduced '50s feel so faithfully from cover and liner notes to sound itself, it's questionable whether he

Left: Texan hard rockers Z.Z. Top on stage (left to right) Dusty Hill, Frank Beard, Billy Gibbons.

intended a put-down or tribute; Sha-Na-Na(▶) or Rocky and the Replays never did better. **Uncle Meat**, soundtrack for never made movie, indicated Zappa's fascination for all forms of media.

Burnt Weeny Sandwich proved to be Mothers' last album. **Weasels Ripped My Flesh** (1970) was released under Mothers name but was compilation of old and live material. Zappa formally announced Mothers' demise in October 1969 press release, and promptly buried himself in running two new labels (Bizarre and Straight) while producing groups on outer fringe of rock respectability (early Alice Cooper(▶), GTO's, Beefheart, Wild Man Fischer). Old Mothers Lowell George and Roy Estrada went on to form Little Feat(▶). Jimmy Carl Black and Bunk Gardner formed Geronimo Black, while Art Tripp joined Captain Beefheart.

Zappa kept Ian Underwood (guitar, keyboards) for second solo album **Hot Rats.** When released, it was hard to tell difference between Zappa alone and Zappa with Mothers. This was apparent when next LP, **Chunga's Revenge,** featured many musicians who eventually made up the Mothers used in **200 Motels** movie and soundtrack. These last two projects made particular use of vocalists Howard Kaylan and Mark Volman (ex-Turtles(▶)).

Zappa jammed with John Lennon(▶) and appeared on **Sometime In New York** LP (1972). Then he took Mothers (who, of course had undergone several more personnel changes) on tour and released two live albums: **The Mothers: Fillmore East-June 1971** and **Just Another Band From LA.** End of '71 saw poor European tour (band's equipment lost in Montreux fire) and serious injury to Zappa when pushed from stage at Rainbow Theatre, London. Zappa continued to release (some say grind out) material, either solo **(Waka Jawaka)** or with Mothers **(Grand Wazoo)**. Although assured of certain level of sales, Zappa seemed to want wider approval of his ideas. His writing moved closer to simple rock. Lyrics began to lose bite and became more scatological. If shock tactics didn't get him into Top 10, he'd titillate his way there.

New record deal with Warners emphasised

The classic cover of Weasels Ripped My Flesh, Mothers Of Invention. Courtesy Bizarre/Reprise Records.

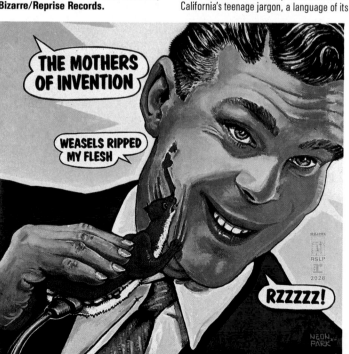

efforts to make hit record. **Overnite Sensation** missed mark but **Apostrophe** finally rose high in US charts. In gratitude Zappa hired marching band to play past Warners' office. Next two LPs, **Roxy And Elsewhere** and **One Size Fits All**, took step back to live recordings as if Zappa was content to resume his role outside mainstream rock. **Bongo Fury** was also primarily live but featured reunion with old friend Captain Beefheart. Beefheart's appearance signalled end of dispute between the two stretching back to Zappa's production of the Captain in late '60s. One year passed before **Zoot Allures** appeared. Then as if possessed, Zappa began releasing albums every few months. **Sheik Yerbouti** (1979), **Joe's Garage Act 1** (1979) and **You Are What You Is** (1981) are all excellent. **Ship Arriving Too Late To Save A Drowning Witch** (1982) contains **Valley Girl** single by Zappa and Moon Unit (his daughter). It was counterculture's answer to Frank/Nancy Sinatra(▶) duet of '60s, comprised of Southern California's teenage jargon, a language of its

own. Problem with Zappa's recent outpouring is the difficulty even Zappa fans have in assimilating it all. But be assured, it is just another step in master plan for world domination.
Guitars: D'mini-Les Paul, the Strate.

Albums:
Uncle Meat (Bizarre/Reprise), 1969
Hot Rats (Bizarre/Reprise), 1969
Burnt Weeny Sandwich (Bizarre/Reprise), 1969
Weasels Ripped My Flesh (Bizarre/Reprise), 1970
Chunga's Revenge (Bizarre/Reprise), 1970
The Mothers: Fillmore East, June 1971 (Bizarre/Reprise), 1971
200 Motels (United Artists), 1971
Just Another Band From LA (Bizarre/Reprise), 1972
Waka/Jawaka — Hot Rats (Bizarre/Reprise), 1972
Grand Wazoo (Bizarre/Reprise), 1972
Overnite Sensation (DiscReet), 1973
Apostrophe (DiscReet), 1974
Roxy And Elsewhere (DiscReet), 1974
One Size Fits All (DiscReet), 1975
Bongo Fury (DiscReet), 1975
Zoot Allures (DiscReet), 1976
Zappa In New York (DiscReet), 1978
Studio Tan (DiscReet), 1978
Sheik Yerbouti (DiscReet), 1979
Sleep Dirt (DiscReet), 1979
Orchestral Favourites (DiscReet), 1979
Joe's Garage Act I (Zappa/CBS), 1979
Joe's Garage Acts II & III (Zappa/CBS), 1979
Tinsel Town Rebellion (Barking Pumpkins/CBS), 1980
You Are What You Is (Zappa/CBS), 1981
Shut Up And Play Yer Guitar (Barking Pumpkin/CBS), 1981
Ship Arrived To Late To Save A Drowning Witch (Barking Pumpkin/CBS), 1982
The Man From Utopia (Barking Pumpkin/CBS), 1983
Rare Meat —Early Productions of Frank Zappa (Del Fi/—), 1983

Worth Searching Out:
Freak Out (MGM/Verve), 1966
Absolutely Free (MGM/Verve), 1967

Cruising With Ruben & The Jets, Mothers Of Invention. Courtesy Verve Records.

We're Only In It For The Money (MGM/Verve), 1968
Lumpy Gravy (MGM/Verve), 1968
Cruising With Ruben And The Jets (MGM/Verve), 1968
Mothermania — The Best Of The Mothers (MGM/Verve), 1968

The Zombies
UK group formed 1963.

Original/Final line-up: Colin Blunstone, vocals; Rod Argent, keyboards; Paul Atkinson, guitar; Chris White, bass; Hugh Grundy, drums.

Career: Formed by five grammar school boys in St Albans (first bass player Paul Arnold was almost immediately replaced by White), the Zombies started off with a bang when they won 'beat group' competition organised by London evening newspaper.

Band was subsequently signed to Decca, and first single, **She's Not There**, was immediate success, making UK Top 20 and actually topping singles charts in US. Composed by Argent(▶), it featured unusual syncopated melody line and highlighted Blunstone's breathy, ethereal vocals.

Follow-up single, **Tell Her No**, provided second US Top 10 hit — although oddly it was far less successful in Britain. By 1967, band had been virtually forgotten in their homeland, though still appreciated in US. However, momentum had been lost, and in 1967 the various members went their separate ways.

Before splitting band recorded excellent and innovative album, **Odyssey And Oracle**, which ironically spawned huge hit single **Time Of The Season. Time** became million-seller in US and Japan, over a year after band had ceased to exist.

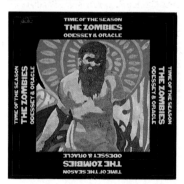

Odyssey And Oracle, The Zombies. Courtesy Date Records.

Colin Blunstone dropped out of music until the early '70s, when he returned to take up a solo career. Argent formed band of same name which had moderate success, and continued with variegated solo career.

Although relatively short-lived, the Zombies made their mark on music of '60s and helped to establish British acts as world-wide contenders. They added intelligence and subtlety to 'beat group' format, and produced some music which still sounds fresh and interesting today.

Hit Singles:	US	UK
She's Not There, 1964	2	12
Tell Her No, 1965	6	42
Time Of The Season, 1969	3	—

Albums:
Time Of The Zombies (Epic), 1973
She's Not There (—/Decca), 1982

Worth Searching Out:
Odyssey And Oracle (Columbia/CBS), 1968

Appendix

Sheer lack of space prevents us including a full entry on the following acts, but we would like to recognise their contributions to rock music.

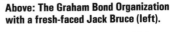

Above: The Graham Bond Organization with a fresh-faced Jack Bruce (left).

A

ACE – Short-lived British soul-influenced group. Topped US charts in 1975 with moody **How Long** from **Five-A-Side** album.
MOSE ALLISON – Highly individual white blues jazz singer/pianist. Much recorded and a major influence on British stars such as Georgie Fame.
CARLOS ALOMAR – US guitarist, leader of David Bowie's stage band, with whom he's been for eight years. Has also worked with John Lennon, Bette Midler, Chuck Berry and R&B greats Wilson Pickett and James Brown. Married to former Chic vocalist Robin Clark.
ALTERED IMAGES – UK synth band behind cutesy, squeaky, goo-goo vocals of Clare Grogan (who had part in film 'Gregory's Girl'). Had promising start with 1981 hits **Happy Birthday** and **I Could Be Happy,** but sound now wearing thin.
AMEN CORNER – Cardiff-based mod band which topped UK charts with **Half As Nice** (1969) and enjoyed four other Top 20 records. Name changed to Fairweather (after lead singer Andy Fairweather-Low) in 1970 when they had Top 5 hit with **Natural Sinner.**
THE AMERICAN BREED – Scored in 1967 with **Bend Me Shape Me.** Originally called Gary and the Nite Lights, they hailed from Chicago.
AMON DUUL II – First German rock band to make it big in US. Influenced by Pink Floyd, their '70s music was strongly avant-garde in form.
LAURIE ANDERSON – One woman show from America, best known for socially perceptive lyrics and electric sound. Most recent success was single **O Superman,** which reached No.2 in the UK in 1981.
PAUL ANKA – Canadian teen idol who topped US/UK charts in 1957 with **Diana.** Subsequently scored 35 further Top 60 entries in America before settling down on nightclub circuit. Wrote English lyrics to **My Way,** which assured already wealthy artist (art collection, property) of royalties in old age.
ANNETTE – Annette Funicello was regular face in '60s spate of 'beach party' movies. Launched with Top 10 US single **Tall Paul** on Walt Disney's Vista label; followed through with string of crass but commercially successful singles.
ARRIVAL – Liverpool pop band. Scored in 1970 with **Friends** and **I Will Survive,** but folded three years later, three of members becoming nucleus of Kokomo.
ASSOCIATION – Slick pop group who featured their five-part harmonies on series of major hits throughout late '60s. Topped US charts twice with **Windy** (1967) and **Cherish** (1966). Rumours of band's reunion have been rife since 1975, but still no show.
ATLANTA RHYTHM SECTION – Distinguished band of session musicians (featuring guitarist Barry Bailey) who scored five US Top 20 hits in late '70s. Re-make of **Spooky,** originally recorded by Classics IV, (whose line-up included current ARS guitarist J.R. Cobb and group's manager Buddy Buie), was group's last major success.
AUDIENCE – US tour supporting the Faces won them strong following but dissension within band led to break-up before full potential was realised.
BRIAN AUGER – From jazz pianist to R&B organist, he featured John McLaughlin in his first group. Then formed Brian Auger Trinity which by mid-1965 had become Steampacket with Long John Baldry, Rod Stewart and Julie Driscoll fronting on vocals. After band split, Auger and Driscoll had 1968 hit with **This Wheel's On Fire.**
HOYT AXTON – Best known as songwriter with hits for Steppenwolf, Three Dog Night, Ringo Starr, Tiny Tim and Joan Baez. Cut series of fine country rock albums in own right. His mother wrote Elvis Presley's hit **Heartbreak Hotel,** and was partner in formation of Stax label.

B

B-52's – One of the earliest US new wave bands who sprung to fame with wacky **Rock Lobster** (1979). Continued in similar vein with songs like **Party Gone Out Of Bounds.** Hilarious lyrics, but sound gets repetitive after first LP.
BURT BACHARACH – Enormously successful New York-based songwriter, notably in partnership with Hal David. On Staff at Scepter/Wand Records they wrote hits for Chuck Jackson, Tommy Hunt, Maxine Brown and, most notably, Dionne Warwick – including classics **Anyone Who Had A Heart, Walk On By** and **You'll Never Get To Heaven.** Partnership dissolved after 'Promises Promises' musical. From 1963 on, Bacharach recorded own albums for MCA and A&M and starred in countless TV specials. Last major success was with B.J. Thomas's chart-topping **Raindrops Keep Falling On My Head** for 'Butch Cassidy And The Sundance Kid' flick in 1969.
THE BACHELORS – Irish balladeer group (brothers Declan and Con Clusky plus Sean Stokes). Their old-hat 'Tin Pan Alley' format competed successfully with Merseybeat explosion; had 10 Top 20 hits between 1963-1967.
BADFINGER – Beatles' protegés; scored in 1970 with McCartney's **Come And Get It.** Founder and songwriter Peter Ham committed suicide in 1975.
LONG JOHN BALDRY – Seminal figure on British R&B scene. Served with Cyril Davies R&B All Stars, taking over band and re-naming it the Hoochie Coochie Men on Davies' death in January 1964. Gave Rod Stewart his first break (as second singer) and then joined Steampacket, also with Stewart. From Bluesology (which also included Elton John), moved into pop with 1967 UK chart-topper **Let The Heartaches Begin.** Football anthem **Mexico** marked by big, full voice.
KENNY BALL – Five UK Top 10s in 12 months with commercial slant on traditional jazz, starting with **Samantha** (1961), ending with **Suki Yaki** (1963).
BANANARAMA – UK all-girl trio paired with Fun Boy Three for 1982 hit **Really Saying Something.** Also hit with **Shy Boy** on own. A bit weak vocally, lacking energy overall. Probably best-suited to back-up work.
BARCLAY JAMES HARVEST – Manchester-based British cult band with critically acclaimed albums for EMI's Harvest label and Polydor.
H.B. BARNUM – Major US black arranger, composer. Had hits with Robins, Lou Rawls, Irma Thomas, the Osmonds and many Motown acts. Recorded own piano/vocal albums for RCA in '60s.
BOBBY BARE – First hit, **The All-American Boy,** a parody on Elvis Presley, made US No. 2 in 1958 but label credit went to his friend Bill Parsons. Subsequently became major pop/country artist with classic **Detroit City** and **500 Miles Away From Home,** plus brilliant reading of Kris Kristofferson's **Me And Bobby McGhee.**
JOHN BARRY – John Barry Seven instrumental group backed countless British pop package shows between 1957-1962 before wider fame was won with TV and movie film tunes, most notably work on the 'James Bond' series.
LEN BARRY – Had big hit as member of Dovells with **Bristol Stomp** (1961), then became successful blue-eyed soul singer on own with Philadelphia classics **1-2-3** and **Cry Like A Baby.**
SHIRLEY BASSEY – Welsh-born daughter of West Indian seaman. Made UK charts with cover of Harry Belafonte's **Banana Boat Song.** After two-year chart hiatus, London Palladium appearances helped establish her as major recording, concert and cabaret star with torch-ballad successes **As Long As He Needs Me, You'll Never Know, What Now My Love** and **I (Who Have Nothing).**
MIKE BATT – Producer of psychedelic band Hapshash and the Coloured Coat, moved into lushly-orchestrated own-name albums of rock covers. Had 1975 solo hit with **Summertime City,** then captured weeny-bopper market with his music for 'The Wombles' TV series.
THE BEAU BRUMMELS – Launched as 'America's answer to the British invasion', their soft-rock approach paved way for the Byrds, Turtles and others with 1965 hits **Laugh Laugh** and **Just A Little.**
HARRY BELAFONTE – Harlem-born but strongly influenced by West Indies where he spent five years of his childhood. 1956 classic album **Calypso** went gold and included memorable single **Banana Boat Song.** Also a successful actor.
FREDDIE BELL AND THE BELLBOYS – Pioneer rock 'n' rollers. Appeared with Bill Haley in 1955 'Rock Around The Clock' movie and were first US rockers to visit UK, touring with Tommy Steele in 1956. Scored on British charts with **Giddy Up A Ding Dong.**
MAGGIE BELL – Blues and soul-laced Scottish singer. Fronted admirable Stone the Crows which featured Les Harvey on lead guitar. After band split, following Harvey's death from electrocution on-stage at Swansea, she released superb if uncommercial solo albums.
BELLESTARS – Seven-piece all-girl group evolved from Bodysnatchers who make funky, brassy dance music. Early hit singles were covers **Iko Iko** and **The Clapping Song.** Strong single **Sign Of The Times** (1983) indicates some originality.
CLIFF BENNETT – UK blue-eyed soulster, his brassy Rebel group scored with covers of the Drifters' **One Way Love** and Beatles' **Got To Get You Into My Life.** Later formed heavier Toe Thumb with little success.
BROOK BENTON – Gospel-rooted black rock 'n' roll balladeer. With Belford Hendricks and producer Clyde Otis he co-wrote his first three big hits **It's Just A Matter Of Time, Endlessly** and **Thank You Pretty Baby** in 1959. Consistently in charts (including million-selling duets **Baby (You've Got What It Takes)** and **Rockin' Good Way** with Dinah Washington) until 1963. Bounced back in 1970 with classic rendition of Tony Joe White's **Rainy Night In Georgia.**
BIG BOPPER – One-hit wonder J.P. Richardson, alias the Big Bopper, was top Texan radio DJ. Scored worldwide with rock 'n' roll novelty **Chantilly Lace** (1958). Had minor success with follow-up **The Big Bopper's Wedding,** but died February 3, 1959, in air crash (with Buddy Holly and Ritchie Valens). Also a successful songwriter, he penned Johnny Preston's **Running Bear** hit.

Below: Bananarama are best known for their work with the Fun Boy Three.

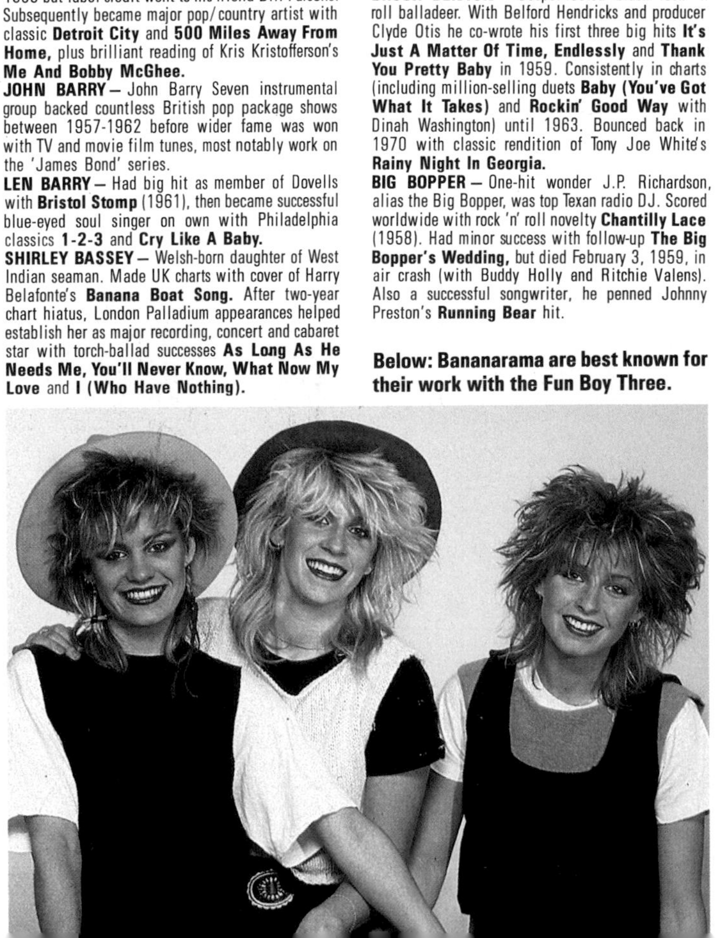

BIG BROTHER AND THE HOLDING COMPANY – The San Francisco-based group which spring-boarded Janis Joplin to superstardom.
BIG STAR – 1972 resurrection of the Box Tops. Switch to soft-rock format lacked appeal of earlier band's superior blue-eyed soul, and despite critical acclaim for **No. 1 Record** album band failed to crack big-time.
THE BIG THREE – Highly respected Liverpool group of early '60s that failed to follow Beatles and others to international success, despite Brian Epstein's management.
ACKER BILK – Replaced Monty Sunshine as clarinettist in legendary Ken Colyer trad jazz band before forming own combo in 1958. Commercial slant plus strong image – bowler hats and striped waistcoats – helped him to eight UK Top 20 hits, including chart-topping TV theme **Stranger On The Shore,** which also made No. 1 in America.
ELVIN BISHOP – Emerged from Paul Butterfield Blues Band to form own highly respected funky rock band highlighting his delicious guitar style and solid vocals.
CILLA BLACK – Friend and close associate of the Beatles, launched to stardom by Brian Epstein with covers of US soul hits, then veered towards MOR via cabaret and regular TV shows.
BLACK OAK ARKANSAS – Raunchy Southern boogie band. Earned gold in 1974 for **High On The Hog** album.
BLANCMANGE – UK duo Neil Arthur and Stephen Luscombe make lighthearted pop in style of biggest hit **Living On The Ceiling.** Check out 1982 single **God's Kitchen/I've Seen The World.**
DAVID BLUE – Singer/songwriter, friend of Bob Dylan and stalwart of Greenwich Village folk-rock scene. Classy albums on Warner Bros, Elektra and Asylum.
BLUES PROJECT – New York white blues band formed by Danny Kalb and featuring Al Kooper and Steve Katz (who went on to create Blood Sweat and Tears). Influence far exceeded their record sales.
COLIN BLUNSTONE – Classy British singer/songwriter remembered as lead singer of the Zombies and for 1971 solo hit **Say You Don't Mind.**
GRAHAM BOND – Early days as modern jazz alto-sax player led him into British R&B boom of early '60s. Switching to organ he replaced the deceased Cyril Davies in Blues Incorporated before forming own group, which included Ginger Baker, Jack Bruce and John McLaughlin. After demise of Graham Bond Organization he was involved in several bands, including Ginger Baker's Airforce before falling to death under London Underground train in 1974.
BONEY M – West Indian vocal/instrumental group with several semi-religious UK pop hits, including **Daddy Cool, Sunny, Ma Baker, Belfast, Rivers Of Babylon/Brown Girl In The Ring** (No. 1), **Rasputin, Mary's Boy Child** (also No. 1) and **Hooray! Hooray! It's A Holi Holiday** in the late '70s.
BONZO DOG (DOO DAH) BAND – British rock band with penchant for humorous material, led by Viv Stanshall, Neil Innes and Roger Ruskin Spear. Had outrageously funny stage act and UK Top 5 single with **The Urban Spaceman** in 1968.
PAT BOONE – Next to Elvis, the most successful US solo singer of the rock 'n' roll era (though his music was somewhat right of MOR and relied on clean-cut 'all-American Boy' image). Raised in Nashville and married to daughter of country star Red Foley; came to prominence with bland cover versions of black rock 'n' roll hits by Fats Domino **(Ain't That A Shame)** and Little Richard **(Tutti Frutti, Long Tall Sally).** Then switched to 'moon in June' romantic ballads with **Love Letters In The Sand, April Love** and others. Had 24 Top 20 hits of which novelty item **Speedy Gonzales** was

best credential for his inclusion in a rock book. Daughter Debbie had major hit in 1977 with **You Light Up My Life.**

THE BOX TOPS — Super Memphis-based blue-eyed soul band. Topped charts in 1967 with **The Letter.** As much a vehicle for songwriting/arranging/producing talents of Dan Penn, Spooner Oldham and Chips Moman as for Alex Chilton's distinctively husky lead vocals.

BRECKER BROS — Mike (tenor sax, flute, soprano sax) and Randy (trumpet) Brecker are stalwarts of US session scene. Worked with Stevie Wonder, Janis Joplin, James Taylor, Johnny and Edgar Winter, John Lennon, Carly Simon, David Allen, Patti Austin and countless others. Recorded own selection of jazz-funk albums for Arista.

BRINZLEY SCHWARZ — Launched with biggest PR hype of all-time (a complete jet-load of UK journalists being flown out to see them perform at New York's Fillmore East). Backlash worked against them. Despite some fine mixtures of blues-rock and soft-rock harmonies they could not fight way into major league and broke up in 1975.

DAVID BROMBERG — American guitarist, also dobro player (though inferior vocalist) who has worked with Bob Dylan, Willie Nelson, Gordon Lightfoot, Rick Derringer, and Sha Na Na among others. Large selection of solo LPs recorded for Columbia and Fantasy (from 1971-1977) feature many live recordings.

ELKIE BROOKS — Superior smokey-voiced songstress. Emerged from Da Da and Vinegar Joe to become major solo concert attraction and notch massive-selling albums, notably **Pearl.**

ARTHUR BROWN — Zany UK rock personality who scored with powerful **Fire** (1968). The Crazy World Of Arthur Brown was staggering in-concert spectacle but was never properly captured on disc.

FELICE AND BOUDLEAUX BRYANT — Nashville-based composers who wrote **Bye Bye Love, Wake Up Little Suzie, Bird Dog** and other hits for Everly Brothers, **Raining In My Heart** for Buddy Holly and **Let's Think About Living** for Bob Luman. Recorded own albums in '60s.

ROY BUCHANAN — Served on rock 'n' roll session scene (with Dale Hawkins, Bob Luman, Freddie Cannon, etc.) before re-emerging in '70s as highly acclaimed guitar star on Polydor.

BUCK'S FIZZ — 1981 Eurovision winners with **Making Your Mind Up.** Highly produced pop in Abba mould has done well in the UK since, with such hits as **The Land Of Make Believe** and **My Camera Never Lies** (both No. 1s).

JIMMY BUFFET — purveyor of laid-back California-style tunes such as **Margaritaville** (1977).

DORSEY BURNETTE — Bass player in brother Johnny's famed rock 'n' roll trio. Had own hits with big ballads **Tall Oak Tree** and **Big Rock Candy Mountain.** Also wrote hits for Jerry Lee Lewis and Ricky Nelson.

JERRY BYRNE — White New Orleans rock 'n' roller. Cut 1958 pounding classic **Lights Out** with black producer Harold Battiste.

C

FREDDIE CANNON — Boston native brought to fame via Philadelphia-based Swan Records and 'American Bandstand' TV show. 18 hits in a row — notably hard-rocking **Tallahassie Lassie** and **Way Down Yonder In New Orleans. Palisades Park** made him major star of tail-end of rock 'n' roll's golden '50s.

If I Could Do It All Over Again, I'd Do It All Over You, Caravan. Courtesy Decca Records.

CARAVAN — Long-established Canterbury-based outfit formed around guitarist Pye Hastings and keyboard-player Dave Sinclair (who quit in 1971, and again in 1975 after short reunion with group). Popular concert act during '70s, who never made impact on charts despite excellent albums, particularly **If I Could Do It All Over Again I'd Do It All Over You.**

CARLENE CARTER — Talented country rock singer, daughter of country star June Carter. Now married to Nick Lowe. Paul Carrack played keyboards in her excellent backing band.

DAVID CASSIDY — Star of popular 'The Partridge Family' US TV series. Became massive hero of teeny-bopper audiences in early '70s before being ousted by Donny Osmond and Michael Jackson. Continues to act.

CATE BROS — Ernie (keyboards) and Earl (guitar) Cate received acclaim in late '70s as powerful live act. Record sales proved sporadic, despite excellent Steve Cropper-produced albums.

Below: British vocalist Elkie Brooks charted mostly in the late '70s.

THE CHAMPS — Highly rated US instrumental combo who topped charts with debut hit **Tequila** (1958). Their raunchy singles are now prized collectors' items. Latter-day members Jimmy Seals and Dash Crofts went on to further success as Seals and Crofts duo.

BRUCE CHANNEL — R&B-flavoured rocker. **Hey Baby** made US No. 1 in 1962. Went on to tour UK with Beatles in same year. Fluid harmonica playing set Channel apart from dozens of contemporaries.

CHAS AND DAVE — Modern-day Flanagan and Allan, Chas Hodges (ex-Heads Hands & Feat) (piano, vocals) and Dave Peacock (bass, vocals), both former session musicians, have achieved record and concert success with clever cockney patois lyrics, which they call 'Rockney', coupled with solid rock base.

CHEECH AND CHONG — Popular hippy comic duo discovered by Lou Adler (who produced their recent movie). Tommy Chong was once member of Canadian soul outfit Bobby Taylor and the Vancouvers and co-wrote their classic Motown cut **Does Your Mama Know About Me.** Pair (Cheech Marin is Mexican/American, Chong Chinese/American) are now cult film stars through appearances in series of US Government drug abuse movies.

CHIEFTANS — Traditional Irish folk outfit led by Paddy Maloney (uillean pipes, tin whistle) who have been major concert attraction for 15 years. Album releases have been sporadic in recent past after long tenure with Island and then Columbia. Contributed to Stanley Kubrick's 'Barry Lyndon' movie soundtrack in 1975.

CHILLIWACK — Your basic US band with better than average harmonies; most recently enjoying US success with '80s hits like **My Girl (Gone, Gone, Gone)** and **Whatcha Gonna Do (With My Heart).**

CHINA CRISIS — Unusually dreamy, soft sound sets them apart from other UK '80s groups. Gary Daly and Eddie Lundon provide peaceful respite with relaxing singles like **Christian** and **Tragedy And Mystery.**

THE CHIPMUNKS — Studio creation (sounding like a 33 rpm record on 45 speed) of David Seville. The perky **Chipmunk Song** sold three and a half million copies proving that either poor taste was alive and well in 1958, or that a lot of children talked parents into buying it.

JIMMY CLANTON — White New Orleans kid who scored initially with black-sounding R&B ballad **Just A Dream;** then promoted as all-American boy-next-door with million-selling **Venus In Blue Jeans** (1962).

CLASSICS IV — Backing band on hits for Billy Joe Royal and the Tams, they scored in 1967 with ballady **Spooky.** Guitarist James Cobb and group's arranger/producer Buddy Buie went on to join the Atlanta Rhythm Section.

PERRY COMO — King of the crooners — with '50s hits like **Tina Marie, Magic Moments** and **Catch A Falling Star.** His top-rated TV show provided admirable showcase for many emergent R&B and rock acts as well as influencing teen fashion trends.

THE COWSILLS — Pop-harmony family group earned gold discs for **The Rain, The Park And Other Things** (1967) and **Hair** (1969).

FLOYD CRAMER — Top session pianist at RCA's Nashville Studios. Backed hits by Elvis Presley, Chet Atkins, Jim Reeves and others, and enjoyed million-seller in own right with atmospheric **Last Date** (1960).

THE CREATION — UK mod/pop group in Who mould; Shel Talmy produced their minor hits in 1966. Now mostly of interest to '60s collectors.

THE CRICKETS — With guitarist/singer Sonny Curtis and drummer Jerry Allison (the constant core of a changing line-up), the Crickets started out as Buddy Holly's backing group, splitting from him shortly before his death. In 1962 they toured and recorded with Bobby Vee, enjoying two UK hits. After break-up in 1975, Curtis and Allison played on Eric Clapton's 1970 solo albums, following which Crickets were re-formed.

THE CRITTERS — Covered John Sebastian's **Younger Girl** from debut Lovin' Spoonful album to score memorable if minor 1966 hit.

ARTHUR 'BIG BOY' CRUDUP — Mississippi bluesman whose originals, **That's All Right** and **My Baby Left Me,** provided early hit material for Elvis Presley.

CURLY LEADS & SWITCHES — Legendary R&B outfit who produced classic **Plug Me In** album in early '60s. Curly (real name Maximillian De Frost) was grandson of French Ambassador to US who joined with local black musicians after moving to Louisiana. Now noted chef in French quarter of New Orleans, but still playing part-time.

JOHNNY CYMBAL — Tribute to those mainstays of the '50s black R&B group sound, **Hey Mr Bass Man,** made Top 20 in 1963.

D

DALE AND GRADE — Their 1963 cover of Don and Dewey's R&B hit **I'm Leaving It Up To You** took the Lousiana duo to top of US charts.

DANNY AND THE JUNIORS — Group of Italian Americans from Philadelphia whose **At The Hop** (1957) remains one of the all-time great rock 'n' roll waxings.

JAMES DARREN — Philadelphia contemporary of Frankie Avalon, Steve Alaimo and Fabian. His corny but catchy **Goodbye Cruel World** made him a star in 1961.

DARTS — London-based doo-wop revivalists who charted a dozen times in UK between 1977 and 1980, including a trio of No. 2s **Come Back My Love, Boy From New York City** and **It's Raining** in 1978.

DAVE DEE, DOZY, BEAKY, MICK AND TICH — British mid-'60s pop band with 10 UK Top 20 entries to credit, including 1968 chart-topper **The Legend Of Xanadu.**

BILLIE DAVIS — Teamed with Mike Sarne for novelty item **Will I What?,** then charted as solo in 1963 with **Tell Him** before linking up with ex-Shadows' bass player Jet Harris for long and traumatic relationship. In 1967 cut classic soulful version of **Angel Of The Morning.**

JOEY DEE AND THE STARLIGHTERS — Resident band at the Peppermint Lounge in New York, their **Peppermint Twist** rode the dance craze wave in 1961. Felix Cavaliere, Eddie Brigati and Gene Cornish were in group in 1963 before moving on to form the Young Rascals.

KIKI DEE — Powerful English vocalist who has never attained deserved recognition. Biggest chart record **Don't Go Breaking My Heart** (1976) cut with Elton John, but **Amoreuse** remains her classic track. Once signed to Motown.

JACKIE DE SHANNON — Enormously talented — and underrated — Californian singer/songwriter prolifically recorded by Liberty. **Needles And Pins** was major hit for British group the Searchers.

WILLIE DIXON — Long-time producer and composer at Chess Studios where he nurtured major talent. A workmanlike double bass player, has released many quality blues albums. Best known composing credits include **I'm A Man, Hootchie Kootchie Man,** and **Wang Dang Doodle.**

THOMAS DOLBY — UK vocalist electro-pop wizzard with mad-scientist looks to match. First UK hit was **Windpower.** Actually broke in the US first with **She Blinded Me With Science** (1982) accompanied by fantastic video featuring Magnus Pyke.

DOLLAR — UK male/female duo with several hits from 1978-1982, most notably **Love's Got A Hold On Me, Mirror Mirror** and **Give Me Back My Heart.** Have recently split.

RAL DONNER — Chicago-born, New York-based Elvis Presley soundalike. 1963's **I Got Burned** was best effort among string of chart entries.

THE DOVELLS — Philadelphian blue-eyed soul group with penchant for dance craze discs which earned them eight hits in four years. Lead singer Len Barry went on to solo fame.

JULIE DRISCOLL — Started as secretary of the Yardbirds' fan club and climbed to stardom as a singer. Fronted Steampacket with Rod Stewart and Long John Baldry, then in partnership with Brian Auger had 1968 hit with cover of Dylan's **This Wheel's On Fire.** Married to jazz/classical composer Keith Tippett.

LES DUDEK — Talented US guitarist/producer who has been involved with various projects throughout '70s and '80s. Has cut several solo albums, as well as recording with Allman Bros, Steve Miller. Had own Dudek, Finnegan, Krueger Band before joining Cher for **Black Rose** LP and group of same name.

JOHNNY DUNCAN — Tennessee-born country singer/guitarist. Married British girl and settled in UK on discharge from army. Replaced Lonnie Donegan as resident skiffle singer in Chris Barber's band, then formed own Blue Grass Boys making UK No. 2 with **Last Train To San Fernando** (1957).

JAMES DUNLAP — US drummer, former member of Watts 103rd Street Rhythm Band. Joined Bill Withers group in early '70s. Now leading session player and Michael Jackson's regular studio drummer.

E

THE EASYBEATS — Formed in Australia where they had four chart-toppers in quick succession. Went to Britain in 1966 and cut worldwide hit **Friday On My Mind.** After lesser hits, group broke up in 1969.

RANDY EDELMAN — US singer/songwriter, and excellent piano player, particularly popular in UK. Charted in UK during 1976 with re-make of **Concrete And Clay** and **Uptown Uptempo Woman.**

ELECTRIC FLAG — Rock/soul supergroup bringing together guitar wizard Mike Bloomfield, Nick 'The Greek' Gravenites and black drummer Buddy Miles, plus brass. Hard-hitting sound wowed audience at 1967 Monterey Pop Festival but albums disappointed.

RAMBLING JACK ELLIOTT — Itinerant American folk singer/songwriter. Companion to Woody Guthrie while in teens and major influence over Bob Dylan.

JOE ELY — Powerful country rock singer whose MCA albums have shown snatches of lyrical genius.

THE EQUALS — UK pop-soul band (two blacks, two whites). Topped chart with **Baby Come Back** (1968); had further hits with **Viva Bobby Joe** and **Black Skin Blue Eyed Boys.** Eddy Grant went on to solo stardom in '80s.

F

MARIANNE FAITHFULL — Ex-convent schoolgirl most remembered for notorious liaison with Mick Jagger. The Jagger-Richard song **As Tears Go By** was her best and biggest record.
CHRIS FARLOWE — UK male vocalist with hits in the mid-'60s, namely No. 1 single **Out Of Time.**
CHARLIE FEATHERS — Influential Mississippi rockabilly singer/guitarist. Never a hitmaker but a cult figure during '70s.
THE FIXX — UK group now getting exposure in the US with melancholy hit **Stand Or Fall** (1982).
FLAMIN' GROOVIES — San Franciscan favourites of Continental audiences having built cult following for their purist approach to rock 'n' roll in '50s/Beatles' mould.
FLASH AND THE PAN — Australian group formed from remnants of Easybeats. Unusual sound is readily identifiable by nasal vocals that sound as if singer is locked in a box. Recently re-entered US/UK chart scene with **Waiting For A Train** (1983).
FLASH CADILLAC AND THE CONTINENTAL KIDS — Rock 'n' roll revivalists from Colorado.
FOCUS — First Dutch band to become rock superstars thanks to distinctive blend of rock, modern jazz and the classics. **Sylvia** and **Hocus Pocus** both scored in 1973. Thijs van Leet (keyboards, flute) and Jan Akkerman (guitar) had some solo success.
FOGHAT — US/UK aggregation formed by ex-patriot Brits — Tony Stevens, Dave Peverett and Roger Earl (all ex-Savoy Brown) in 1972. Group enjoyed album/concert success in US during '70s while being totally ignored in Britain.
WAYNE FONTANA — Leader of the Mindbenders. Hit UK No. 2 with cover of Major Lance's **Um Um Um Um Um Um'** then went to No. 1 in US, No. 2 in UK, with **Game Of Love** (1965). Had solo charters after group broke up in 1966.
FRANKIE FORD — Black New Orleans stalwart Huey 'Piano' Smith cut **Sea Cruise** for Ace Records. Label wiped off his vocals and substituted those of their great white hope Frankie Ford for 1959 Top 20 classic. Same format was adopted for follow-up **Alimony.**
THE FORTUNES — Birmingham, England, group that cut Coca Cola's familiar theme **It's The Real Thing,** as well as the pirate radio theme **Caroline.** Scored big US/UK hits with **You've Got Your Troubles, Here It Comes Again** and **This Golden Ring,** thanks to their classy harmonies.
THE FOUR PREPS — Barber-shop harmonies won them late '50s hits and made them major influence on nascent Beach Boys.
FOURMOST — Early '60s UK pop/Mersey group, produced by Brian Epstein, who scored with hits **Hello Little Girl** and **A Little Loving.**
KIM FOWLEY — Important figure of Los Angeles 'garage rock' scene. Wrote and produced for Jayhawks, B. Bumble and the Stingers, Hollywood Argyles, Rivingtons, and Paul Revere and the Raiders. Worked in England throughout 1965, producing Rockin' Berries, P.J. Proby, Cat Stevens, Soft Machine and others. Worked Stateside on first Mothers Of Invention album. Cut run of solo albums besides writing hit songs for Byrds, Emerson, Lake and Palmer, Helen Reddy and many more.
STAN FREBERG — Recorded classic send-ups of Presley's **Heartbreak Hotel,** the Platters' **The Great Pretender** and Harry Belafonte's **Banana Boat Song** in '50s.
JOHN FRED AND THE PLAYBOY BAND — White Louisiana band had brief moment of glory with international 1967 hit **Judy In Disguise (With Glasses)** in 1967.
FREDDIE AND THE DREAMERS — Lightweight British pop act of '60s. Freddy Garrity's on-stage leapings inspired Chubby Checker record **Do The Freddie,** which group then recorded as their seventh and final hit. Still active on cabaret circuit.
BOBBY FULLER FOUR — Recorded 1966 hits **I Fought The Law** and **Love's Made A Fool Of You,** but Fuller was shot dead within months.
JERRY FULLER — Managed minor hits of his own but wrote biggies for Ricky Nelson (including **It's A Young World)** and Gary Puckett and the Union Gap **(Young Girl).**

G

STEVE GADD — Premier New York session drummer. Worked with Joe Cocker, Stanley Clarke, Paul Simon, Ringo Starr (sic), Dr John, Lee Ritenour, Steely Dan, Kate and Anna McGarrigle. Was featured in Simon & Garfunkel Central Park concert in 1981. Member of Stuff.
MICKEY GILLEY — Cousin of Jerry Lee Lewis and regular entrant in lower reaches of country charts; enjoys cult status thanks to '50s rockabilly cuts.
JIMMY GILMER AND THE FIREBALLS — Studio musicians at Norman Petty's new Mexico base; they provided him with over-dubs for unreleased Buddy Holly demo tapes before scoring four US hits between 1959 and '61 and three more in 1968-69. **Sugar Shack** (1963) made US No. 1.
GERRY GOFFIN — Major '60s songwriter with then wife Carole King. Made several unsuccessful solo albums.

Above: Marianne Faithful in the '60s. Maintaining a lower profile in the '80s.

GOLDEN EARRING — Dutch band who've been around for a while, mostly in the background except for big transatlantic hit **Radar Love** (1973 and 1977). Have had recent US success via MTV with **Twilight Zone** (1982).
GONG — Adventurous French/Australian/English band that included Bill Bruford (ex-Yes) and guitarists Steve Hillage and Allan Holdsworth among its members. Officially split in 1977, but re-formed temporarily until 1979.
CHARLIE GRACIE — Pretender to Presley's throne while the king was on military service. Biggest hit came with **Butterfly** (1957).
GRANDMASTER FLASH AND THE FURIOUS FIVE — US vocalist and back-up men. Scored with rapping single **The Message** in the UK in 1982.
RICK GRECH — French-born bass guitarist; emerged from Family to join short-lived Blind Faith with Eric Clapton. Progressed to Ginger Baker's Airforce, Traffic and the Crickets before working with Eric Clapton again in 1973.
ELLIE GREENWICH — Major writer from New York's famed Brill Building school, in partnership with Jeff Barry. Came up with hits for such Phil Spector acts as the Crystals, the Ronettes and Bob B. Soxx and the Blue Jeans, and for acts on legendary Red Bird and Bang labels. Since divorce from Barry, she has cut albums in singer/songwriter mould.
THE GROUNDHOGS — Earthy British R&B band (taking name from John Lee Hooker song) led by wizard guitarist Tony McPhee. Admirable albums for United Artists.
JAMES GUERCIO — Chicago catalyst. Produced **Kind Of A Drag** hit for Buckingham in 1966. Joined Mothers Of Invention on guitar in 1968. Produced second and biggest-selling Blood Sweat and Tears album. Masterminded Chicago Transit Authority (Chicago). Set up Caribou studios in Colorado (where Elton John and others recorded). Produced, directed and scored 'Elektra Glide In Blue' movie. Became Beach Boys' manager in 1975 and appeared on stage with them.
ADRIAN GURVITZ — Flash guitarist and former member of Gun, Three Man Army, Baker-Gurvitz Army and Moody Blues' drummer Graeme Edge's Band. Made UK Top 10 in 1982 with trite single, **Classic.**

H

H.P. LOVECRAFT — Chicago acid-rock outfit formed in 1966. Hauntingly mystic albums.
TOM T. HALL — Influential country performer/songwriter with string of superb albums. Wrote Jeannie C. Riley hit **Harper Valley PTA.**
JOHNNY HALLYDAY — France's answer to Elvis Presley — with a lot of Gene Vincent influence thrown in. Cut countless major American and British hit songs in French and managed to stay at top during two decades, but found little recognition beyond Continent, where he enjoyed superstar status.
ALBERT HAMMOND — London-born, Gibralter-raised US West Coast stalwart. Hit big in 1972 with **It Never Rains In Southern California.**
JOHN HAMMOND JR — Son of Columbia/CBS's venerated A&R man. Among best — and most esoteric — of white blues singers to emerge in '60s. String of superior albums, including **Triumverate,** cut in 1973 with Mike Bloomfield and Dr John.
HARPERS BIZARRE — Purveyors of lightweight but classy five-part pop harmonies. Scored with Paul Simon's **59th Street Bridge Song (Feelin' Groovy)** and re-makes of Cole Porter's **Anything Goes** and Glenn Miller's **Chatanooga Choo Choo.** Producer Ted Templeman was outfit's drummer.
JET HARRIS AND TONY MEEHAN — Erstwhile members of the Shadows. Guitarist Harris and drummer Meehan had three monster instrumental singles: **Diamonds, Scarlet O'Hara** and **Applejack** in 1963.
DALE HAWKINS — Superior Louisiana rockabilly singer who injected heavy R&B flavour into his 1957 masterpiece **Susie Q.**
LEE HAZLEWOOD — Arizona radio DJ turned songwriter, producer, recording star. Owner of Philadelphia's renowned Jamie label in '60s. Produced Nancy Sinatra's hit **These Boots Are Made For Walking** then recorded smash Jackson duet with her.
HEAD EAST — Obscure US outfit despite some enterprising material and a fine series of albums for A&M since **Flat As A Pancake** (1975).
ROY HEAD — White Texan R&B singer remembered for **Treat Her Right** biggie.
HEAVEN 17 — Stylish UK band formed from remains of original Human League (Martyn Ware, Ian Craig Marsh), now based around lead singer Glenn Gregory. Appealing disco-electronic sound and futuristic/socio-ecological lyrics have provided hits **(We Don't Need This) Fascist Groove Thing** and **Temptation.** Debut LP **Penthouse And Pavement** (1891) deserves a listen.
BOBBY HEBB — As youngster once played spoons with Bo Diddley! Reputed to be first black artist to appear on Nashville's Grand Ol' Opry show. Had UK No. 2 with soul ballad **Sunny.**
DICK HECKSTALL-SMITH — Graduated from jazz and rock 'n' roll into R&B as sax player with Blues Incorporated before progressing through Graham Bond Organization, John Mayall's Bluesbreakers and Colosseum to solo albums and session work.
THE HERD — Built by songwriters Ken Howard and Alan Blakeley around teen-appeal good looks of Peter Frampton (billed as 'The Face Of 1968'). After run of hits, Frampton left to form Humble Pie with Steve Marriott, then found subsequent solo success while the Herd fell apart.
HOOKFOOT — Superior British rock band formed from session men working behind Elton John and others at DJM Records.
NICKY HOPKINS — Britain's most respected rock session pianist. Responsible for dazzling electric piano solo on Cyril Davies' classic **Country Line Special.** Became major name through work on Rolling Stones' sessions and was member of Jeff Beck Group through 1968. Moved to California and joined Quicksilver Messenger Service for two albums, returning to UK for further work with Stones and solo album. Also featured on various Who LPs, most notably **Who's Next.**
JOHNNY HORTON — Country-pop singer best remembered for epic **Battle Of New Orleans.** Died in November 1960 car crash.
ENGLEBERT HUMPERDINCK — Transformed from unsuccessful pop singer Jerry Dorsey into every mum's favourite by astute management of Gordon Mills (who also guided Tom Jones and Gilbert O'Sullivan). Covered Esther Phillips' version of country classic **Release Me** for 1967 monster, which paved way to career as major TV artist and Las Vegas draw.
BRIAN HYLAND — Scored at 15 with crass **Itsy Bitsy Teeny Weeny Yellow Polka Dot Bikini.** Friend and protegé of Del Shannon, he redeemed himself with **Sealed With A Kiss** (1962) and superb Shannon-produced version of Curtis Mayfield-penned **Gypsy Woman** (1970).

I

FRANK IFIELD — British-born (Coventry), raised in Australia. Returned to UK in 1959 to establish himself with falsetto flavour ballads and outbreaks of yodelling. Hit No. 1 with **I Remember You, I'm Confessin' Lovesick** and **Wayward Wind.**
INCREDIBLE STRING BAND — Glasgow-based jug band. Flowered into fully fledged folk rock outfit with well-made hippy-orientated albums.
INNER CIRCLE — Jamaican reggae outfit destined for superstardom until death of founder Jacob Miller. Recorded **Everything Is Great** UK chart hit in 1979.
IT'S A BEAUTIFUL DAY — Superior San Francisco post-psychedelia rock band hinged around violin sound of classically trained leader David La Flamme.

Below: Dutch band Golden Earring finally made it in the US via MTV.

Above: Johnny Kidd, here with the Pirates, penned Shakin' All Over.

J

TERRY JACKS — Rod McKuen translated **Seasons In The Sun** from the Jaques Brel French original for the Beach Boys. They recorded but never released it. Instead a version by Canadian Terry Jacks crashed the charts. Previously he had sold more than four million records in partnership with his wife Susan Pesklevits as the Poppy Family.

TOMMY JAMES AND THE SHONDELLS — Their cover of Raindrops' **Hanky Panky** on local Michigan label Snap remained obscure for two years; it was then picked up for national distribution by Roulette and rocketed to No. 1. Subsequent hits included **Money Money, Crimson And Clover** and **Crystal Blue Persuasion.**

JAY AND THE AMERICANS — Had 18 US chart entries between 1962 and 1977. Clean-cut all-American image was fostered by ace producer Wes Farrell.

PAUL JONES — After role as lead singer with Manfred Mann, enjoyed British solo hits and went on to rewarding career as actor. Founder member of Blues Band.

TOM JONES — Started out as Presley-style rock 'n' roller. After years in obscurity, discovered by Gordon Mills who took him to London, changed his name (from Thomas J. Woodward) and took him to No. 1 with Mills-penned **It's Not Unusual** (1965). Seven weeks at No. 1 the following year, **Green Green Grass Of Home** paved way to Las Vegas, TV spectaculars and superstardom. Though his performances were often over-the-top, at his best Jones could be extremely soulful and commanded wide respect from black American R&B artists.

JUICY LUCY — Blues-based UK band fronted by vocals of former Zoot Money Big Roll Band bass player Paul Williams. Scored with 1970 version of Bo Diddley's **Who Do You Love?**

BILL JUSTIS — Birmingham, Alabama-born Memphis rock 'n' roll session stalwart. Booting alto-sax playing earned him 1957 million-seller with **Raunchy.**

K

KC AND SUNSHINE BAND — Good-time US disco outfit led by Harry Casey who were dance favourites throughout '70s. Casey secured songwriting reputation with Grammy for Betty Wright's **Where Is The Love?** in 1975. Resurfaced in 1983 with UK No. 1 **Give It Up.**

KAJAGOOGOO — '80s version of the Bay City Rollers. Weak, contrived pop from the makers of Duran Duran, nevertheless popular in the UK (particularly with the pre-teen set). Now breaking in US as well with hits **Too Shy** and **Ooh To Be Ah.** Future doubtful as lead singer Limahl was sacked in summer 1983.

THE KALIN TWINS — A five-week stint at No. 1 in UK with **When** (1958) led to a British tour, but despite success of follow-up **Forget Me Not,** they quickly sank into obscurity.

EDEN KANE — Richard Sarstedt took his stage name from title of Orson Wells' movie 'Citizen Kane'. Run of UK hits from 1961 to '62 included No. 1 **Well I Ask You.** Re-emerged in '70s with brothers Clive and Peter as the Sarstedt brothers.

JERRY KELLER — Scored with delightful **Here Comes Summer** in 1959. Also wrote 1965 hit

Almost There for Andy Williams.

JOHNNY KIDD AND THE PIRATES — Image-laden British rockers. Kidd (Frederick Heath) co-penned their 1960 debut hit **Shakin' All Over,** arguably the most authentic rock 'n' roll original ever cut in Britain. Influenced early '60s bands. Johnny Kidd died in 1966, but Pirates continued.

THE KINGSMEN — Place in rock history assured by superlative 1964 re-make of Richard Berry's R&B number **Louie Louie.**

THE KINGSTON TRIO — Folksy pop harmony group. Made No. 1 in 1958 with Civil War movie theme **Tom Dooley.**

KNACK — Short-lived LA pop band that never lived up to critics' expectations after 1979 hit **My Sharona.**

BUDDY KNOX — Texan country singer turned rock 'n' roller. Cut his 1957 **Party Doll** and **Hula Love** hits at Norman Petty's studio in Clovis, New Mexico.

ALEXIS KORNER — Father figure of British R&B explosion of '60s. Later sang lead with successful studio band CCS. Now has own excellent R&B/Blues programme on BBC Radio One.

BILLY J. KRAMER AND THE DAKOTAS — Members of Brian Epstein's Merseybeat stable. Six British Top 20 records in two years, included Lennon/McCartney songs **Do You Want To Know A Secret, Bad To Me, I'll Keep You Satisfied** and **From A Widow.**

L

RONNIE LANE — Originally half of Small Faces songwriting duo with Steve Marriott. Went on to Faces, then quit to work with own back-up band Slim Chance. Scored in 1974 with **How Come** and **The Poacher.** In 1977 recorded mellow **Rough Mix** LP with Pete Townshend. Despite handicap of multiple sclerosis continues to write and occasionally perform.

RONNIE LAWS — Former member of Earth Wind & Fire who is regular in US R&B and pop charts with his classy alto playing and vocalising.

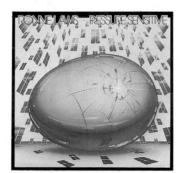

**Pressure Sensitive, Ronnie Laws.
Courtesy Blue Note Records.**

ALBERT LEE — Highly respected London guitarist who emerged from Chris Farlowe's Thunderbirds and was later member of Poet and the One Man Band and Head Hands and Feet before stint with the Crickets, and permanent role with Emmylou Harris band.

GARY LEWIS AND THE PLAYBOYS — Son of Hollywood comedian Jerry Lewis, Gary and his group had seven breezy US pop hits in just two years in mid-'60s.

JOHN LEYTON — UK TV actor who scored in 1961 with Joe Meek-produced No. 1 **Johnny Remember Me.** Went back to acting for roles in major movies including 'The Great Escape' 'Von Ryan's Express', and 'Krakatoa: East of Java'.

LOBO — Aka Kent Lavoie, had million-seller in 1971 with **Me And You And A Dog Named Boo.**

JACKIE LOMAX — Emerged from Liverpool group the Undertakers to record for Apple under aegis of George Harrison.

TRINI LOPEZ — A folksy sing-along style with a Latin flavour was the format which took Trini Lopez to success with **If I Had A Hammer, La Bamba** and **Lemon Tree** in early to mid-'60s.

FRANKIE LYMON AND THE TEENAGERS — Young lead singer Frankie Lymon sadly ended up an unknown after period as child star with '50s group. Big hits **Why Do Fools Fall In Love** (1956), **I'm Not A Juvenile Delinquent,** and **Baby Baby** (both 1957) are now classics.

M

MAISONETTES — London group who scored with clever Motown soundalike **Heartache Avenue** in 1982.

HARVEY MANDEL — White Detroit blues rock guitarist who has recorded prolifically under own name and as member of Canned Heat and John Mayall's Bluesbreakers. Also did session work with Love, the Ventures, Charlie Musselwhite and others.

AL MARTINO — American balladeer. Had '70s UK hit with **Spanish Eyes,** which he originally recorded in 1955.

CHARLIE McCOY — Superb country-rock harmonica player who has appeared on many of Bob Dylan's records, as well as being member of Nashville sessioneers' group Area Code 615.

THE McCOYS — Covered the Vibrations' **My Girl Sloopy** as **Hang On Sloopy** for 1965 gold disc. Later became back-up band for Johnny Winter. Guitarist Rick Derringer went on to work with Edgar Winter and cut solo album **All American Boy.**

SCOTT McKENZIE — The man who sang the 1967 hippy flower-power love and peace anthem **San Francisco (Be Sure To Wear Some Flowers In Your Hair).**

RALPH McTELL — Long-established UK folk purveyor whose loyalty to that music has prevented consistent national attention. Made UK charts in 1974 with **Streets Of London.**

THE MEMBERS — UK white reggae band formed around lead singer Nick Tesco. Enjoyed some US success with lighthearted single and popular MTV video **Working Girl,** until Tesco left in 1983.

MENTAL AS ANYTHING — Up and coming Australian version of Madness, currently getting exposure in US via amusing MTV videos like **Let's Cook.**

THE MERSEYBEATS — Liverpool band. Scored with cover of Jackie De Shannon-penned Dionne Warwick hit **Wishin' And Hopin'** and **I Think Of You** in 1964. After brief break-up, re-emerged as Merseys duo to score with **Sorrow.**

LEE MICHAELS — Multi-instrumentalist (mainly guitar, keyboards) who enjoyed long tenure with A&M label. Scored US Top 10 in 1971 with **Do You Know What I Mean.** His band once featured Doobie drummer Keith Knudsen.

JOHN MILES — UK guitarist/vocalist from Jarrow who scored with ambitious **Music** in 1975, and disco-oriented **Slowdown** a year later. Has subsequently remained in second division of rock performers despite undoubted talent.

ROGER MILLER — Novelty country-pop hits out of Nashville with **Dang Me** (1969), King Of The Road (1965) and **England Swings** (1965).

THE MINDBENDERS — Originally led by Wayne Fontana, they split from him and found success in 1965 with **Groovy Kind Of Love.** Guitarist Eric Stewart later became member of 10cc.

GUY MITCHELL — Tin Pan Alley-styled pop singer who dabbled in rock 'n' roll, notably with **Singing The Blues** (1956), covered in UK by Tommy Steele.

MODERN ROMANCE — Up-tempo '80s combo with brassy-heavy, latin-tinged party music approach, evident on UK hits **Everybody Salsa, Ay Ay Ay Ay Moosey,** and **Best Years Of Our Lives.** Also quite popular in foreign regions, such as South America.

ZOOT MONEY — With his powerful Big Roll Band, was a mainstay of British R&B/soul club scene and cut some fine records of which only **Big Time Operator** made chart impact. From his band, Paul Williams went on to front Juicy Lucy while Andy Somers (Summers) ended up in the Police. Money now makes regular appearances as actor in British TV commercials and shorts.

MONSOON — Unique blend of traditional East Indian music and pop, with inspired vocals from young Indian beauty Sheila Chandra. 1982 singles **Ever So Lonely** and **Shakti** definitely worth a listen.

CHRIS MONTEZ — Mexicano Californian. Punchy **Let's Dance** was 1962 million-seller as follow-up **Some Kind Of Fun.**

SCOTTY MOORE — Elvis Presley's first manager and his backing guitarist on Sun hits and early tours.

MOTHER EARTH — Rock/blues/country showcase for superbly soulful voice of Tracy Nelson. Recorded admirable late '60s albums on Mercury.

MOTORS — UK band formed from remnants of Ducks De-Luxe. Charted in UK during 1978 with **Airport** and **Forget About You.** Strong material supplied by bassist Andy McMaster and guitarist Nick Garvey.

MUD — Basic British beat group used as vehicle for the songs of Nicky Chinn and Mike Chapman, before going into self-production and achieving run of Top 20 singles. Mud's two No. 1 singles in the UK were **Tiger Feet** (1974) and **Oh Boy** (1975).

MUNGO JERRY — Up-dated jug band with skiffle flavour made Mungo Jerry rave success of 1970 open-air concerts; led to million-selling smash **In The Summertime.** Further hits established big following on Continent, which band's leader Ray Dorset has exploited skilfully through to '80s.

ANNE MURRAY — Nova Scotia-born easy-listening country singer with enormous following. From first big hit **Snowbird** in 1970, material has crossed over into pop charts.

**Below: Ronnie Lane left the Faces
and formed Slim Chance, then went solo.**

N

FRED NEIL — Influential component of Greenwich Village folk scene. From his debut Elektra album **Bleeker And MacDougal, Candy Man** was later covered by roy Orbison and **The Other Side Of Life** by the Lovin' Spoonful. Most successful song was **Everybody's Talkin',** recorded by Harry Nilsson for soundtrack of 'Midnight Cowboy'.
MICHAEL NESMITH — Left the super-successful Monkees pop outfit to find solo recognition for his polished brand of country rock and his First National Band. Best known solo hits are **Joanne** and **Rio.** Now successful with film/video production.
THE NEW YORK DOLLS — Flashy glam-rock band with strong transvestite overtones and ear-splitting sound, which won lots of publicity but limited record sales. They broke up in 1975. David Johansen went on to US solo success in '80s.
THE NEWBEATS — Perky falsetto sound made **Bread And Butter, Everything's Alright** and **Run Baby Run** (1964-65) into hits for this Nashville-based trio.
MICKEY NEWBURY — Superior country writer who adapted **American Trilogy** single covered successfully by Elvis Presley. His own material has been recorded by Andy Williams, Kenny Rogers, Jerry Lee Lewis and Ray Charles among others. His finest work can be found on Elektra LPs.
THE NICE — Formed as backing band for P.P. Arnold they made showy rock albums. Caused controversy by burning the Stars and Stripes during their stage renditions of **America.** Keyboard virtuoso Keith Emerson went on to found Emerson Lake And Palmer.
NIGHT RANGER — Yet another band caught in '70s time warp. **Don't Tell Me You Love Me** video showcases them as one of the most unbearable bunch of poseurs on MTV. However, someone in America's buying this stuff.
LAURA NYRO — New York singer who cut masterpiece **Eli And The Thirteenth Coming,** since when she has recorded only sporadically. Wrote pop classics **Stoned Soul Picnic, Wedding Bell Blues, And When I Die, Stoney End** and **Eli's Coming.**

O

TONY ORLANDO — Worked for Don Kirshner cutting demos before being launched as artist in own right in 1961 with **Halfway To Paradise.** Following solo hits in '60s he was re-launched as lead singer of Dawn in '70s for further triumphs. Biggest US/UK Dawn hits were **Knock Three Times** and **Tie A Yellow Ribbon Round The Old Oak Tree.** Also had US weekly TV variety show.
OSIBISSA — Introduced African rock music to British audiences and commanded large following from 1970 to 1976 when **Sunshine Day** gave them their first chart single.
GILBERT O'SULLIVAN — Managed to get break with Gordon Mills management outfit by squatting in MAM office reception. Given short-trousers and cloth cap working-class image he scored with thoughtful and melodious songs, hitting pinnacle with transatlantic hit **Alone Again (Naturally)** (1972). Enjoyed total of 12 UK Top 20 records between 1970-1974, including No. 1's **Clair** and **Get Down.**
OZARK MOUNTAIN DAREDEVILS — Country-rock exponents who enjoyed major success in mid-'70s. Charted, however, with pure pop **Jackie Blue** in 1975.

P

PAUL AND PAULA — Twee **Hey Paula** hit summit of American charts in 1962, but cloying unisex teenager image saw them quickly fade from prominence.
PAVLOV'S DOG — Adventurous US band from New York featuring dual keyboards and falsetto vocalising of David Surkamp. Band split after two eccentric albums recorded in mid-'70s.
PEARLS BEFORE SWINE — US cult band led by Tom Rapp which enjoyed underground success in late '60s/early '70s. After couple of solo albums, Rapp moved to Europe and quit recording scene.
PETER AND GORDON — Peter Asher's actress sister Jane was Paul McCartney's girlfriend, which explains how duo got to record fresh Lennon/McCartney material, bringing them hits with **World Without Love** and **Nobody I Know.** Peter Asher went on to manage James Taylor and Linda Ronstadt.
BOBBY 'BORIS' PICKETT — Pickett's imitation of Boris Karloff's spooky voice took **Monster Mash** to the top in 1961.
JOHNNY PRESTON — Recorded solo in 1959, scoring internationally with **Running Bear,** on which vocal chant effects were contributed by the Big Bopper.
THE PRETTY THINGS — Anarchic UK R&B/rock band who tried to be even more outrageous than the Rolling Stones. Made some interesting but usually excessively noisy singles, plus competent **S.F. Sorrow** and **Parachute** albums.
P.J. PROBY — US vocalist probably more famous for his then outrageous hairstyles and splitting trousers than his hits **Hold Me, Together, Somewhere** (all 1964) and **Maria** (1965).
PSYCHEDELIC FURS — UK new wave band now enjoying US success courtesy of MTV with most successful single to date **Love My Way** (1982).
GARY PUCKETT AND THE UNION GAP — Civil War-inspired stage uniforms and breezy Jerry Fuller-produced pop songs gave this San Diego group their moments of glory, notably with 1968 chart-topper **Young Girl.**

Q

QUESTION MARK AND THE MYSTERIANS — Basic garage-rock sounds of **96 Tears** (1966) gave this Flint, Michigan-based Tex-Mex group their lone smash hit.
QUINTESSENCE — Eastern-flavoured jazz-rock outfit formed via 'Melody Maker' adverts in 1969. Series of Island albums were aimed at underground hippy audiences.

R

EDDIE RABBIT — Country artist who has made regular inroads into US pop charts. Best known for **Every Which Way But Loose** movie theme, which enjoyed Top 50 status in both US/UK in 1979.
RARE EARTH — Bringing heavy rock flavour to essentially soul material, this band launched Motown's Rare Earth label (named after them). Under ace black producer Norman Whitfield, cut classic long versions of such Motown classics as **Get Ready, (I Know) I'm Losing You** and **Ma** in early '70s.
THE RASCALS — Pioneer blue-eyed soul band on Atlantic, formed in 1966 as the Young Rascals. Topped charts year later with **Good Lovin'; Groovin'** was 1967 classic. Sheer musicianship made them delightful live attraction. Organist Felix Cavaliere, singer Eddie Brigati and guitarist Gene Cornish had all previously been with Joey Dee and the Starlighters.
CHRIS REA — Powerful Newcastle vocalist and songwriter who has been on fringes of major success for some time. His self-titled **Magnet LP** made UK Top 60 in 1982.
PAUL REVERE AND THE RAIDERS — US band who thanks to their colourful American Revolutionary War garb (including long hair in ponytails) and strong musicianship made immediate impact when they appeared in 18th-century costumes on Dick Clark's 'Where The Action Is' TV show. Recorded string of pop classics in long career, including American No. 1 **Indian Reservation** in 1971. Band saw many personnel changes, but lead singer Mark Lindsay remained constant factor. Lindsay enjoyed some solo success, including own US TV show in early '70s.
JEANNIE C. RILEY — Tom T. Hall's superb lyric of liberated womanhood made **Harper Valley PTA** 1968 the ideal vehicle to take Jeannie soaring up the charts.
LEE RITENOUR — Ace session guitarist who has made impact with own jazz-rock LPs. Has recorded with George Duke, Seals & Crofts, B.B. King, Art Garfunkel, Alessi Bros, George Benson (with whom he shares Ibanez endorsement), Stephen Bishop and Bobby Bland.
JOHNNY RIVERS — Personable vocalist/guitarist who became US teen idol in mid-'60s with clever re-makes of R&B hits, including **Memphis, Baby I Need Your Lovin', Maybellene** and **Rockin' Pneumonia-Boogie Woogie Flu.**
TOMMY ROE — Buddy Holly soundalike from Atlanta, Georgia, who scored a couple of US No. 1s with his own composition in the '60s, **Sheila** (1962) and **Dizzy** (1969). Now works on US club circuit with own trio.
TIM ROSE — A member of Big Three folk group with Mama Cass, Rose composed classic **Morning Dew** for his debut/solo album. Also included brilliant **Hey Joe,** which Jimi Hendrix covered successfully. Rose later settled in Britain, setting up band there.
RUFUS — Successfully overcame loss of Chaka Khan with **Numbers** set in 1977; band rejoined Chaka for 1981 set **Camouflage.**
BOBBY RYDELL — The original Robert Lewis Ridarelli had sensational period in US charts from 1959-64, scoring 22 Top 60 hits, including teen classics **Wild One, Volare** and **The Cha-Cha-Cha.** Still active on supper-club circuit.
MITCH RYDER AND THE DETROIT WHEELS — White soul-tinted US '60s group that specialised in up-dated Little Richard-flavoured material, scoring with **Sock It To Me Baby!, Jenny Take A Ride, Devil With A Blue Dress On** and its flip **Good Golly Miss Molly.** Ryder (real name Billy LaVere) retired to car-production line after short-lived venture Detroit, where he aggravated already damaged throat.

Above: '60s group Paul Revere and the Raiders, more pop than revolutionary.

Left: P. J. Proby, pony-tailed heart-throb of the mid-'60s.

S

SAGA — Another formula, heavy-metal band kept in business by the fans of faceless rock in the tradition of Triumph, Rush and the like.
SCREAMING LORD SUTCH — An anachronism throughout his long career and master of the publicity stunt. His **Jack The Ripper** parody kept him in work for two decades, although he enjoyed US success with Atlantic album **Lord Sutch And Heavy Friends,** which included his ex-band members Jimmy Page, Nicky Hopkins and Ritchie Blackmore. Now prospective UK parliamentary candidate and founder of Monster Raving Loony Party.
SELECTER — British two-tone reggae band from the Midlands who enjoyed couple of minor hits in UK before disbanding. Vocalist Pauline Black is a promising talent who should re-surface.
SHAM 69 — Creation of vocalist Jimmy Pursey whose lyrical content decried social conditions of British working class. Biggest hits were **If The Kids Are United** and **Hurry Up Harry** in 1978. Pursey has subsequently pursued solo career with negligible success.
HELEN SHAPIRO — Husky-voiced singer who charted with melodic teen material in early '60s. Topped UK charts with **You Don't Know** and **Walkin' Back To Happiness** in 1961. Still active on cabaret/supper-club circuit.
PETE SHELLEY — Formerly lead singer with the Buzzcocks with several hits from 1978-80 such as **Ever Fallen In Love (With Someone That You Shouldn't Have)** and **Promises.** Most notable solo single **Homosapien.**
BOBBY SHERMAN — Launched via 'Shindig' TV series, Sherman was archetypal American teen idol and his records were predictably unadventurous though they gave him a 1969-1970 chart run.
SIMPLE MINDS — Somewhat avant-garde band formed in 1979 with lead singer Jim Kerr. Unique, rather undefinable sound, best exemplified by hits **Promised You a Miracle** and **Glittering Prize.**
PETER SKELLERN — UK singer/songwriter/pianist from Lancaster with a penchant for wistful '30s-flavoured material. Won UK/US success with debut single **You're A Lady.** Has cut run of highly entertaining albums, often using softly muted brass band to add Northern England feel.
J.D. SOUTHER — Guitarist founder of ill-fated Souther (John David), Hillman (Chris), Furay (Richie) band which did not live up to enormous potential during two-album 18-month tenure. Has enjoyed modicum of solo success while recording with Linda Ronstadt (for whom he wrote superb **Heart Like A Wheel**), Warren Zevon, Joe Walsh and Christopher Cross.
CHRIS SPEDDING — Anonymous guitar hero of countless recording sessions, had taste of solo glory with **Motorbiking** hit on Mickie Most's Rak label in 1975.
SPINNERS — Superb US black vocal group known as the Detroit Spinners in the UK; formed in the '50s

and still working in the '80s. Enjoyed most chart success between 1961 and 1978 with US/UK hits like **It's A Shame, Could It Be I'm Falling In Love, Ghetto Child, Rubberband Man** and US No.1 **Then Came You.** Best work featured lead vocalist Phillipe Wynne.
SPOOKY TOOTH – Major band on late '60s progressive rock scene in Britain; had only moderate success with albums. Dogged by frequent personnel changes, including loss of American-born founder Gary Wright. Three-year hiatus from 1970-1973 didn't help.
RICK SPRINGFIELD – US singer/guitarist who's never quite made the big time, but who's hung in there for over a decade with such hits as **Speak To The Sky** (1972), and more recently **Jessie's Girl** (a No. 1 in 1981), **I've Done Everything For You** (1981), **Don't Talk To Strangers** (No.2 in 1982) and **Affair Of The Heart** (1983). Plays Dr. Noah Drake on US soap 'General Hospital'.
BILLY SQUIER – Annoying poseur who relies mostly on good looks for appeal. Nevertheless has come up with some good hooks on recent US hits like **Everybody Wants You** (1982).
ALVIN STARDUST – A '60s star as Shane Fenton, he burst into charts with new name and black leather image. Chart-topping **Jealous Mind** and further hits were also written by Shelley.
STEVE STRANGE – Poseur extraordinaire who landed recording contract. Charted (as Visage, with Midge Ure of Ultravox) in UK with **Fade To Gray** (1980), **Mind Of A Toy** (1981), **Damned Don't Cry** (1982) and **Night Train** (1982).His main talent lies in attracting similarly precious individuals to various London nightspots.
STUFF – Aggregation of superstar sessioneers, including Steve Gadd (drums) Cornell Dupree (guitar), Eric Gale (guitar), Richard Tee (keyboards), Gordon Edwards (bass) and Chris Parker (drums). Their Warner Bros albums have, naturally enough, contained magical moments.
STYLISTICS – Excellent US black vocal group who've managed several US/UK pop singles from 1972-76, including **I'm Stone In Love With You, Break Up To Make Up, Rock 'N' Roll Baby, You Make Me Feel Brand New, Let's Put It All Together, Sing Baby Sing, Can't Give You Anything (But My Love)**, and more.
SURVIVOR – Two-hit wonders in '70s style. Achieved US/UK No.1 with soundtrack tune **Eye Of The Tiger** (1982) from 'Rocky III'. Reached Top 20 with follow-up **American Heartbeat.**
SUTHERLAND BROS AND QUIVER – Iain and Gavin Sutherland amalgamated their own unit with pub-rock band Quiver in 1972, remaining on fringe of national success for seven years. Brothers are best known for composition **Sailing**, an international hit for Rod Stewart, and their own soulful **Arms Of Mary**, a UK Top 10 entry in 1976.
BILLY SWAN – Bill Black Combo and Clyde McPhatter both scored with Swan's composition **Lover Please.** After stint as roadie for country stars, became Monument Records' staff producer, working on Tony Joe White's **Polk Salad Annie** hit. As an artist he adopted soft-rocking style to achieve No. 1 with **I Can Help** (1974).
SWEET – Unpretentious pop band who secured regular UK chart placings from 1971 to 1978. Brainchild of Nickey Chinn, Michael Chapman songwriting/production partnership, who wrote **Blockbuster** No. 1 for group in 1973.
SWINGING BLUE JEANS – Liverpool band led by vocalist/ guitarist Ray Ennis who had string of UK hits, **Hippy Hippy Shake, You're No Good,** etc. (and couple of minor US chart entries) in mid-'60s.

T

TANGERINE DREAM – German synthesiser outfit popular in Europe since formation in 1967. Current members Edgar Froese, Christoph Frank and Johannes Schmoelling have also been active on solo projects. Recorded soundtrack for James Caan movie 'Thief' ('Violent Streets' in UK) in 1981.
TEARS FOR FEARS – Curt Smith and Roland Orzabel make synth music with just the right amount of gloom. UK singles **Mad World** and **Change** (1982) seem to indicate promising future. Currently emerging in US.
TOMMY TEDASCO – The 'man of 1000 jingles' (as well as countless TV and music scores) is probably most often-hired guitarist on West Coast, having started out in '60s with Jan & Dean. Has also worked for Beach Boys, Fats Domino, Stephen Bishop, Judy Henske, Maria Muldaur, Michael Nesmith, Dory Previn and Elvis Presley. Contributes regular 'Studio Log' column for US magazine 'Guitar Player' and is author of guitar instruction volume. Has cut a couple of solo albums in jazz vein.
NINO TEMPO AND APRIL STEVENS – Tempo played sax on Bobby Darin records before signing to Atco as duo with his sister and notching No. 1 with Deep Purple. In late '70s, Tempo came back to prominence as an instrumentalist, riding disco boom with his Fifth Avenue Sax band.
TENPOLE TUDOR – Tartan punk from Eddie Tenpole and his look-alike band. Specialise in raucous, sing-along pub-style tunes, anachronistic clothes and Scottish nationalism. 1981 hits **Swords Of A Thousand Men** and **Wunderbar** are typical of sound. Good fun.
B.J. THOMAS – One of pop's anomalies, a soulful singer who has contented himself with lifeless MOR material. His anthem is whimpish **Raindrops Keep Fallin' On My Head**, but also enjoyed seven other US Top 20 entries from 1969-75.
THOMPSON TWINS – UK trio consisting of two males (one black) and one female – no twins – no matter how you look at it. Tom Bailey, Alannah Currie and Joe Leeway make funky pop with innovative percussion as on hits **In The Name Of Love, Lies, Love On Your Side** and **We Are Detective** (1983). Have recently broken into US market.
THUNDERCLAP NEWMAN – Andy Newman met The Who's Pete Townshend at art college. Formed Thunderclap Newman with Jimmy McCullough and Speedy Keene. Townshend produced through the Who's Track label; group scored in 1969 with **Something In The Air** but success was not sustained. McCullough went on to play with Stone the Crows, then Wings.
JOHNNY TILLOTSON – Melodic **Poetry In Motion** (1958) made star of this former country singer. Eight-year run found him consistently on the American charts, his other biggie being **It Keeps Right On A-Hurtin'.**
TINY TIM – Long-time Greenwich Village weirdo. Appeared in 1968 'You Are What You Eat' movie and 'Laugh-In' TV series before bizarre re-make of **Tiptoe Through The Tulips** single and **God Bless Tiny Tim** album shot him to international prominence.
KEITH TIPPETT – Respected jazz and neo-classical composer. Has played keyboards on King Crimson and Soft Machine albums. Married to Julie Driscoll, of **This Wheel's On Fire** fame.
THE TOKENS – Originally purely a studio outfit, with such luminaries as Neil Diamond, Neil Sedaka and Carole King playing on records. Eventually working band of Hank Medress, Jay Seigel, Phil Matgo and Mitch Margo was formed. Folksy style gave them American No. 1 with **The Lion Sleeps Tonight.**
THE TORNADOS – Put together as London-based session band by producer Joe Meek; became the Tornados when they started to work as Billy Fury's backing outfit. 1962 brought enormous organ-dominated space-flavoured instrumental hit **Telstar.** Guitarist Heinz left for solo career with material based on his fascination with Eddie Cochran, scoring with single **Just Like Eddie** (1963).
TOWER OF POWER – San Francisco-based R&B rock outfit at forefront of brass-laced bands of early '70s. Original vocalist Lenny Williams has enjoyed chart status with enterprising soul material.
THE TREMELOES – As backing group to Brian Poole they had UK No. 1 with cover of Contours' US soul hit **Do You Love Me?** Poole quit in 1965 for solo stardom but soon sank – returning to job as a butcher – while his erstwhile support went on to run of seven Top 10 hits from 1967-1970, including chart-topping cover of Four Seasons' oldie **Silence Is Golden.**
BONNIE TYLER – Gifted Welsh vocalist who returned to charts with a bang with Jim Steinman-penned **Total Eclipse Of The Heart** in 1983. First hit **Lost In France** made No. 9 in UK during 1976, while **It's A Heartache** (1977) made both UK/US Top 10.

U

THE UNITED STATES OF AMERICA – Lone eponymous album (1968) for Columbia was superbly innovative slice of progressive rock, parodying everything from **Sargeant Pepper** to Jefferson Airplane.
PHIL UPCHURCH – Noted US session guitarist (Cat Stevens, Howlin' Wolf, George Benson, Quincy Jones, etc) who charted in 1962 with million-selling dance opus **You Can't Sit Down.** Has released sporadic solo albums.

V

VANDENBERG – **Burning Heart** single/video typifies the deluge of hard rock/hippy clones in the US.
BOBBY VINTON – Major US pop artist in early '60s with decidedly MOR ballad material like **Roses Are Red, Blue Velvet, Blue On Blue** and **I Love How You Love Me.** Makes maximum use of Polish heritage in well-worked, but corny, cabaret show.

W

WALL OF VOODOO – Mexican/American LA band with unique blend of cultures evident in off-the-wall music. Video of hit single **Mexican Radio** (1982) not to be missed.
CLIFFORD T. WARD – Singer/songwriter from English Midlands who went Top 10 with melodious debut single **Gaye** in 1973; scored again in 1975 with **Jigsaw Girl.**
JIMMY WEBB – Wrote songs for Johnny Rivers and Fifth Dimension, who recorded for Rivers' Soul City label, to establish self as major LA-based writer. Fifth Dimension's **Up Up And Away,** Glen Campbell's **By The Time I Get To Phoenix** and Richard Harris's **MacArthur Park** were among his formidable triumphs. In 1970 Webb started touring and signed own contract with Reprise the following year leading to albums for variety of labels.
BERT WEEDON – Veteran British session guitarist who charted with cover of Virtues' **Guitar Boogie Shuffle** in 1959 to make him one of longest-toothed rock 'n' rollers. Has wielded considerable influence over younger musicians thanks to his highly proficient technique.
IAN WHITCOMB – Active on UK R&B scene, Whitcomb went to US West Coast on holiday, recording version of **Sporting Life** to notch minor hit. Jerry Dennon flew to Dublin, where Whitcomb was studying, to record **You Turn Me On.** A US Top 10 hit in 1965, it failed to register in the artist's home territory.

Below: '80s synth band, the Thompson Twins, (from left) Joe Leeway, Tom Bailey, and Alannah Currie.

MARTY WILDE – Member of the Larry Parnes school of British rock 'n' rollers. Resident on TV's 'Oh Boy!' and 'Boy Meets Girl' shows, he had string of British hits at tail-end of '60s, starting with **Endless Sleep** in 1957. Tried to launch son Ricky as British teeny-bopper idol, without success; did better with daughter Kim Wilde who ranks as major artist of '80s in own right.
PAUL WILLIAMS – Diminutive US writer who, wrote hits for Carpenters and Barbra Streisand among others. Is currently carving out successful career as singer/writer/ actor in movies and on television. In demand as soundtrack composer as well.

Above: One of the finest voices of the '80s, so far in a '60s style, Mari Wilson.

MARI WILSON AND THE WILSATIONS – Mari Wilson is the Queen of the beehive hairdo – in keeping with distinctly '60s image: female vocalist with back-up singers set up. Biggest hit so far **Just What I Always Wanted** (1982) displays promising vocal talent. Definitely worth seeing live.
PETE WINGFIELD – Keyboard player with British R&B band Jellybread, diverted into sessions for Freddie King, Van Morrison, Colin Blunstone and others before own 1975 transatlantic hit **Eighteen With A Bullet.** Later a member of the Olympic Runners soul band. Toured with Van Morrison in '70s.
LINK WRAY – Legendary swamp-rock guitarist of Shawnee Indian extraction. Big hit with **Rumble** instrumental in 1958 followed by long spell in obscurity before re-emergence with hypnotic if at times strangely metered albums.
GARY WRIGHT – Former member of Spooky Tooth (keyboards, vocals) who stormed US charts in 1976 with **Dream Weaver** album and single. Currently records in own home studio.
ROBERT WYATT – Soft Machine drummer turned British progressive rock guru. Scored in 1974 with surprise Cockney version of **I'm A Believer.** Re-emerged in 1983 with Elvis Costello-penned Falklands War comment **Shipbuilding.**

Y

PAUL YOUNG – Founder and lead singer of the now defunct Q-Tips. Most promising new blue-eyed soul singer in the UK with No.1 cover in 1983 of Marvin Gaye's **Wherever I Lay My Hat.**
THE YOUNGBLOODS – Formed by talented New York singers Jesse Colin Young and Jerry Corbitt, who shared lead vocal role. Expanded group became resident at Cafe A Go Go in 1966 with strong jug-band/folk-rock flavour. After cutting Dino Valenti's **Get Together** in 1957 (Top 10 in 1959 on re-release) they moved to West Coast, cutting much acclaimed **Elephant Mountain** and other fine albums before folding in 1973, leaving Young to continue as respected solo artist.
TIMI YURO – Diminutive white girl singer with amazingly soulful voice, reminiscent of black star Esther Phillips. At her finest on R&B ballads, she benefited from lush yet totally sympathetic Nashville string arrangements. Scored with **Hurt** (1961) and superb albums, before moving into MOR and disappearing from scene due to marital problems.

Z

ZAGER AND EVANS – Fashionably futuristic lyrics of **In The Year 2525** made this duo from Omaha, Nebraska, 1969's most successful one-hit wonders.
WARREN ZEVON – US singer/songwriter best known for 1978 single **Werewolves Of London.** Somewhat of a cult figure.

Lee Abrams

US consultant.

As a highly paid consultant to scores of radio stations across the US, Abrams is generally considered to have removed the last traces of 'freedom' from free-form FM rock radio in the States.

He invented the 'Superstars' formula, based on demographic research and surveys, promoting the notion that constant rotation of recognisable album cuts, mostly from the late '60s and early '70s, and regulated dollops of big-name 'product', was the way for FM radio to hang onto its audience. This became the norm; a form that was once genuinely experimental, and genuinely music-orientated, whatever its excesses, became locked into limited playlists and rigid repetiton.

At first this seemed successful; but in the late '70s, record sales and ratio ratings began to decline almost mysteriously. Radio had ceased to be a sales and promotion tool for any new music, and suddenly everyone was hurting. The logjam was broken, after a few years of confusion, by the recent surprising achievements of one or two 'New Music' stations on both the East and West Coasts; radio programmers found that a little daring would not, after all, lose them their listeners. When last heard from, Abrams was trying to come up with a way to formularise this development too.

Lou Adler

US producer, executive.

Prime mover in development of West Coast rock. Managed Jan and Dean in the early part of their career, before teaming with Herb Alpert. As 'Barbara Campbell' duo co-wrote **Only Sixteen** with Sam Cooke.

Formed Dunhill Productions in 1964, recording the Mamas and Papas, P.F. Sloan, Richard Harris and Barry McGuire. Most of the hit material was supplied by Sloan and Steve Barri.

Compounded success in late '60s with new label Ode, as Dunhill had been sold to ABC Records. Company's initial hit was Scott McKenzie's flower power anthem **San Francisco (Be Sure To Wear Some Flowers In Your Hair)**. Signed Carole King, whose album **Tapestry** launched singer/songwriter album vogue.

Later produced Cheech and Chong (whom he directed in their recent movie, Ode released soundtrack of **Tommy** stage show, produced by Lou Reizner.

Adler now spreads his talent across several fields, including movies, stage shows, theatre and night clubs.

Peter Asher

UK producer.

One half of pop duo Peter & Gordon in '60s; scored series of hits in UK/US charts, including **A World Without Love**, **Lady Godiva**, **Nobody I Know** and **I Go To Pieces.**

Made head of A&R at Apple, partly due to relationship between Paul McCartney and Asher's actress sister Jane. However, took decision to sign James Taylor, justifying appointment.

Unhappy at undisciplined business system at Apple, moved to Los Angeles with Taylor, who became first act to come under Asher's production wing. Asher immediately earned platinum awards for Taylor's first two albums for Warner Bros, before accepting production role with Linda Ronstadt, who also became major album artist. Subsequently managed both acts.

Roy Thomas Baker

UK producer.

Learned engineering at Decca studios in early '60s, where he worked with Rolling Stones, T. Rex, Dr John, Frank Zappa and Eric Clapton.

As producer, Baker was responsible for Queen (**Queen, Queen II, Sheer Heart Attack, A Night At The Opera** and **Jazz**), Nazareth, Welsh band Man, Lindisfarne, Be-Bop De Luxe, Pilot, Ian Hunter, Dusty Springfield and, more recently, the Cars, Journey, Ron Wood (**Gimme Some Neck**), Foreigner (**Head Games**) and Alice Cooper (**Flush The Fashion**).

Retired in 1980, in order to re-charge batteries, although now back in action with Cars, his current long-term project.

Frank Barselona

US agent.

Owner of Premier Talent Agency, New York-based operation prominent in promotion of major rock acts, such as ELP, Ten Years After, Herman's Hermits and the Who. With assistant Barbara Skydell has excellent relationship with managers, notably Peter Grant; Led Zeppelin and Bad Company both toured for Premier.

An insomniac, Barselona is live-wire when all around are dozing, both metaphorically and physically.

Bert Berns

US publisher, executive, composer, producer.

Influential part of New York R&B scene in late '50s/early '60s. Wrote classic **Twist And Shout** with Phil Medley, and subsequently supplied material for Don Covay, Marv Johnson, Garnett Mimms and Solomon Burke. Also co-wrote **My Girl Sloopy** and **Under The Boardwalk** with other co-habitants of Brill Building in New York, where Berns had his office.

Formed own soul/R&B labels Shout and Bang, which released material by Roy C. Erma Franklin and Freddy Scott. Berns died in 1967 after suffering a heart attack.

Chris Blackwell

Jamaican executive, producer.

White Jamaican, heir to baked bean empire. Formed Island Records in '60s to promote reggae (or blue beat/ska as it was called then before it was popularized). Also gave British R&B movement a boost.

Leased single **My Boy Lollipop** by Millie to Fontana Records to provide funds for ailing company. Record helped popularise West Indian music, and opened market for other acts, including Desmond Dekker.

Signed Bob Marley in 1973, and launched the struggling artist into reggae superstardom. Blackwell was fascinated with Rastafarian religion, and the musical message of its disciples; he felt Marley could 'speak' to the masses.

Divergence into rock proved equally successful, with Island now a premier international company. Blackwell recently instigated one plus one pre-recorded tape (one side blank) which infuriated rivals, but was logical step in face of home pirating.

As producer, Blackwell has worked with Free, Traffic and, more recently, the B-52s.

Richard Branson

UK executive.

Former public schoolboy who launched Virgin empire in early '70s. Operation now encompasses record company, book and music publishing, and record stores.

Had set-backs, albeit temporary, with TV Records, whose product was available via massive television-based advertising, and 'Event', short-lived weekly, started during temporary absence of London's 'what, where, when' publication 'Time Out'.

Branson now lives in Berkshire in mansion which houses impressive recording studio.

Mel Bush

UK promoter.

Bournemouth-based promoter, who, with Harvey Goldsmith, could claim to be premier rock impresario in UK. Started promoting at local ballroom in nearby Boscombe in late '60s.

His impressive list of tours includes Roxy Music, Slade and David Essex.

Chess Brothers

US executives, producers.

Polish immigrants Leonard and Phil Chess founded Chess Records in 1950. Company became forerunner of urban blues movement out of Chicago, the operation's base.

Chess recorded all major blues talent throughout the '50s, including Muddy Waters, Howlin' Wolf, Elmore James, Sonny Boy Williamson, Buddy Guy, Little Walter, Otis Spann, John Lee Hooker and bass player Willie Dixon, who became the in-house producer, writer and arranger.

The Chess/Checker combine also moved in to rock'n'roll field, establishing two of its finest exponents in Chuck Berry and Bo Diddley. Also active in soul market (on subsidiary Cadet) with the Dells, Radiants, Etta James, Koko Taylor and Fontella Bass.

Chess was sold to the GRT tape company shortly after the death of Leonard Chess in 1969; Phil Chess continued to run the radio station they owned in Chicago.

Chinn and Chapman

UK producers, composers.

Phenomenally successful pop production/ writing team of '70s, Nicky Chinn and Mike Chapman were responsible for chart action of Sweet, Mud, Suzi Quatro and Smokie between 1971-79.

Sweet had 16 Top 50 chart singles in UK, Mud had 15, and Smokie had 12, earning Chinn and Chapman nickname of 'hit factory'.

Despite teen influence of material and artists, adapted satisfactorily to rock acts Exile, Blondie and vocalists Tanya Tucker and Pat Benatar from 1978.

Collectively known as Chinnichap, formed Dreamland Company, which was unable to equal success of duo's independent work.

Dick Clark

US DJ.

Once described as the single most influential person in the popular music industry. From start as radio announcer, Clark got into TV and became host of local Philadelphia Show 'Bandstand' in 1956. The musical format and the presentation—the show was recorded with a participatory audience of jiving teen-agers—caught mood of the times. In 1957 show won nationwide slot via ABC and proved instrumental in furthering the rock'n'roll ex-

Below: Dick Clark, host of 'American Bandstand', informing and entertaining teenagers of the '50s, '60s, '70s and '80s.

plosion which the likes of Alan Freed had set in motion a few years earlier.

Despite national audience, show tended to push local artists (Fabian, Frankie Avalon, etc), and helped make Philadelphia major pop music centre. Clark pursued wide range of activities, including a syndicated newspaper column, the weekly 'Dick Clark Show' and Hollywood-based 'Where The Action's At' on TV, the 'World Of Talent' and work as a MC on pop and rock tours, as well as a series of pop movies.

Following the Congressional probe into the music industry's payola scandal of early '60s, Clark was ordered to divest himself of some of his peripheral business interests.

'American Bandstand' continues to this day as a major promotional outlet for musical talent.

Miles Copeland
US manager.

Brother of Stewart of the Police and Ian, who runs the US booking agency, FBI, Miles Copeland was born in London in 1944. He spent his childhood travelling around the world, as his father worked for the CIA.

While at univeristy in Beruit, he was asked to provide a light show for visiting band Ruperts People. When he later moved to London, they asked him to become their manager. Miles went on to work with the Climax Blues Band, Renaissance, and Wishbone Ash, and run British Talent Management.

In 1974 Miles became manager of Curved Air and suggested brother Stewart as drummer. When Stewart became interested in punk, Miles saw it as marketable and set up Faulty Products to handle new acts. Founded IRS record label.

Since then Miles has been the guiding light of the most successful band of the '80s, the Police.

Most recently, he formed his own music publishing company, Illegal Songs.

Above: Miles Copeland, who manages the most successful band of the '80s.

Bob Crewe
US producer.

After stints as male model, interior decorator and singer, Crewe teamed up with Texan songwriter Frank Slay Jr in 1953. Crewe made demos of Slay's compositions and had unsuccessful records released by BBS Jubilee and Spotlight. In 1956, Crewe and Slay set up as independent producers in Philadelphia, notably with the Rays for Chess. They also established own XYZ label. Their 1957 song **Silhouettes** made the Rays a major act. First released on XYZ, it was leased to the more

powerful Cameo label and sold a million copies.

Freddie Cannon's hits for Swan Records, including **Tallahassie Lassie** and **Way Down Yonder In New Orleans**, were further Crewe/Slay collaborations. In 1959 partnership split, Crewe making unsuccessful attempt to become movie actor before scoring own debut hit for Warwick with **The Wiffenpoof Song** (1961).

Crewe masterminded creation of the Four Seasons, produced their debut **Bermuda** for Gone then switched them to Vee-Jay for the million-selling **Sherry**. For next six years, Crewe produced all the Four Seasons' hits and co-wrote most of the material with group member Bob Gaudio. Forming own New Voice label, Crewe had mid-'60s hits with Norma Tanega (**Walking My Cat Named Dog**) and Mitch Ryder and the Detroit Wheels (**Jenny Take A Ride**). In 1967 had instrumental Top 20 hit in own right with **Music To Watch Girls By**.

Launched in 1969, his Crewe label had minor success with Ben E. King and Oliver. In mid-'70s he made strong comeback with independent productions for Disco Tex and the Sex-O-Lettes and the Four Seasons' lead singer Frankie Valli.

Mike Curb
US executive.

It won't surprise Mike Curb's many antagonists to know that he began his career as an advertising jingle writer, and made his fortune—his first fortune, it should be noted—as the founder of Sidewalk Productions, an outfit that produced soundtracks for sleazy drive-in movies such as 'Mondo Hollywood'.

He sold this extraordinarily successful company in 1968 for millions, and became president of MGM Records. From that position he caused a wave of controversy and outrage by announcing that the prestigious label would 'release from their contracts' any 'drug-orientated' rock acts—unless, it turned out, they were particularly popular. This was the most spectacular of Curb's public moves—apart from the entertainment he organised for Richard M. Nixon's Inaugural Ball.

After several years at the top in the record business, promoting such artists as Debby Boone, Shaun Cassidy(▶) and the Osmond Family, he left it for the world of right-wing politics, much to music-lovers' relief and Governor Jerry Brown's dismay; Curb became Lieutenant Governor of California in 1979, and a constant thorn-in-the-side to the liberal Brown. It is possible that music-lovers relaxed too soon, however; Mike Curb Records is still an active company, though it doesn't seem to have produced anything of note yet.

Bill Curbishley
UK manager.

Originally managing director at Track Records in the early '70s, Curbishley was involved with the Who while working under Kit Lambert and Chris Stamp. Became Roger Daltrey's personal manager when he undertook solo career. From 1973 onwards gradually took over Lambert and Stamp's duties and after their departure became official manager of the band in 1976. Seven years later still performs one of the most unenviable duties in rock: trying to manage the Who.

Above: Formerly with Columbia, Clive Davis started Arista in the mid-'70s.

Clive Davis
US executive.

Established reputation with Columbia Records during '60s and '70s with phenomenal AOR, MOR roster, including Simon & Garfunkel, Barbra Streisand, Santana, Byrds, Chicago (recently ceremoniously dumped by label), Leornard Cohen, Earth, Wind And Fire, Johnny Winter and Weather Report.

Left Columbia in 1974 after allegations of unjustifiable expense payments relating to son's Bar Mitzvah. Promptly formed Arista Records, who were soon challenging his previous employees in the lucrative album market.

Davis signed Barry Manilow, Kinks, Dionne Warwick, Grateful Dead, Aretha Franklin, Stray Cats, Alan Parsons, Three Degrees, Sky, Air Supply (for whom he co-penned a couple of songs), giving Arista a large slice of the major international LP markets.

Tom Dowd
US engineer, producer.

New York native who shared success of Atlantic Records from late '40s, as freelance engineer. Artists he worked with include the

Coasters, the Drifters, LaVern Baker, Modern Jazz Quartet, Wilson Pickett (cut **In The Midnight Hour**), Ray Charles, Bobby Darin, Solomon Burke, the Clovers, Chuck Willis, Otis Redding (**Otis Blue** album), Aretha Franklin and King Curtis.

Moved into rock field with more emphasis as producer during mid-'60s. Engineered the Young Rascals, Cream (**Disraeli Gears, Wheels Of Fire**), Jerry Jeff Walker. Produced Cher, Allman Bros (including superb **Live At The Fillmore East**), Delaney & Bonnie, Lulu, Derek and the Dominoes (**Layla**), Dr John, Tony Joe White, Eric Clapton, Rod Stewart, Lynyrd Skynyrd, Kenny Loggins, Pablo Cruise and Abba. In many cases, co-produced with Jerry Wexler and Arif Mardin, and, of course, with acts themselves.

Brian Epstein
UK manager.

Liverpudlian born in 1934. Father owned successful chain of record shops in area, one of which Epstein managed. After receiving requests for **My Bonnie**, an early Beatles single cut in Germany, decided to track down unknown outfit.

Was surprised to find group were local, and signed them to management contract after seeing gig at the Cavern Club. Group signed

Below: Brian Epstein (far right), best known as the Beatles' manager, died in 1967.

to Parlophone after rejection by Decca. Success of Beatles prompted activity with other Liverpool acts, including Cilla Black, Gerry & the Pacemakers and Billy J. Kramer and the Dakotas. Epstein was certainly responsible for establishing the 'Liverpool Sound' internationally.

Founded the NEMS agency, and subsequently bought London West End theatre the Savile, where he promoted a series of rock concerts in mid-'60s.

Died in London in 1967 after taking accidental overdose of drugs. With Colonel Tom Parker, rates as most successful manager in pop history.

Ahmet Ertegun
US executive, producer, writer.

Founded Atlantic Records with Herb Abramson in late '40s. Son of Turkish Ambassador to US, was brought up in Washington where he was involved in promotion of jazz concerts.

Enthusiasm for R&B and jazz took Atlantic to forefront of indie labels in '50s; adopted policy of royalty payments, earning longevity of contract with artists.

As writer, had biggest success with **Stand By Me**, now an R&B standard, but first a hit for Ben E. King in 1960. Also involved in production during '50s.

A shrewd negotiator, Ertegun signed Swan Song and Rolling Stone labels for distribution in US. After Kinney takeover in 1972, remained head of board, moving into other fields, including ownership of New York Cosmos soccer team.

Above: Nesuhi Ertegun of Atlantic. His brother Ahmet founded the label.

Nesuhi Ertegun
US executive, producer.

Brother of Ahmet, and active member of Atlantic since early '50s, Nesuhi inaugurated company's strong jazz catalogue (signing Modern Jazz Quartet). With Ahmet and Jerry Wexler, bought out original Atlantic partner Herb Abramson in late '50s.

Enthusiastic international operator, Nesuhi is now President of New York Cosmos soccer team.

Leonard Feather
US author, composer, pianist.

Regarded as doyen of jazz critics. Feather has contributed to dozens of periodicals including 'Down Beat', 'Esquire', 'Gallery' and 'Los Angeles Times', which column is syndicated to over 300 papers worldwide. His books include 'Inside Jazz', 'The Book Of Jazz From Then Till Now', 'Laughter From The Hip', 'From Satchmo To Miles', 'The Pleasures Of Jazz', and the definitive jazz work 'The Encyclopedia Of Jazz'.

His compositions have been recorded by Louis Armstrong, Duke Ellington, Ella Fitzgerald, Sarah Vaughan, Yusef Lateef and Roland Kirk. Also recorded with Armstrong as pianist.

Feather is prominent speaker on jazz at US colleges/universities, and has acted as MC at the Newport Jazz Festival. His TV programme 'The Jazz Show' received an Emmy nomination.

Alan Freed
US DJ.

Nearly twenty years after his death in disgrace, Freed's name is one of the best remembered and respected of early rock'n'roll. Starting his career as a radio announcer, he became a DJ on station WJW in Cleveland, Ohio, in 1951, playing the black R&B music he loved. This proved unexpectedly popular with white teenagers.

No documentation exists, of course, but it is here that Freed coined the term 'rock'n'roll' as a description of music. Here, also, he began producing rock concerts, starting with a bang in 1952 with rock's first riot.

Freed moved to New York City and WINS in 1954; the station soon became the most popular in the city. His programmes during that time are still remembered; listeners could hear him beating time and even singing along with the music. Sometimes he would play a record he particularly loved three of four times in a row, and he was famous for never ever playing white 'cover' versions of black hits.

He became even more familiar to audiences through his appearances in many early rock movies, introducing his favourite groups (portraying himself generally), and in one memorable moment playing drums with Chuck Berry's combo for **Little Queenie**.

Freed was brought down by the 'payola' scandal of 1959-60. A wave of anti-rock feeling—certainly not unrelated to the large share of the market the music establishment, unions and corporations alike, felt it was losing to 'white trash' and blacks, and fuelled by an unfortunate series of riots at rock shows (by now almost a tradition)—swept the US. Undeniably, DJs, Freed included, *did* take money from record promoters to play their products on the air. But Freed, being the most popular and, paradoxically, the most honest offender, was a scapegoat of the 'payola' investigation; many well-known names got off scott free. He was indicted in 1960 for taking bribes and, his career effectively over, he pleaded guilty to a lesser charge in 1963. He disappeared from the music scene, and died in 1965, at the age of 42.

Gamble And Huff
US producers, composers.

In 1964 Kenny Gamble composed **The 81** for Philadelphia group Candy and the Kisses. Leon Huff, who had been working as session musician in New York for Leiber and Stoller, played piano on the record. Thus one of most important partnerships in black music began, the duo forming core of the Romeos group, then producing, notably for Cameo-Parkway and Jamie-Guyden, and setting up own Excel label (1966). After local hit with the Intruders, label name changed to Gamble and their productions turned Intruders into national soul act. In 1968, duo made new deal with Chess for national distribution and label name became Neptune, but deal foundered on death of Leonard Chess and sale of Chess company to GRT. Undaunted, Gamble and Huff secured new, and even bigger, deal with Columbia and set up Philadelphia International Records.

PIR became to '70s pop-soul music what Motown had been in the '60s. A string of international hits came from Billy Paul, Harold Melvin and the Blue Notes, the O'Jays, the Three Degrees and others. Gamble and Huff were also much in demand producing for other labels. They scored notably for Atlantic with Archie Bell and the Drells (who later switched to PIR), for Mercury with Jerry Butler, Spring with Joe Simon, Columbia with Johnny Mathis, imbuing all their records with distinctive 'Philly Sound'. Classy session-musician aggregation MFSB, plus the local symphony orchestra, were widely employed on PIR recordings, almost all of these were cut at Philadelphia's Sigma Sound studios.

Success continued into '80s with Teddy Prendergrass, the Jones Girls and others, but financial problems caused demise of label in 1982.

Kenny Gamble is married to '60s soul star Dee Dee Sharpe.

Tommy 'Snuff' Garrett
US producer.

Texan who produced **Dreamin'** for Johnny Burnette in 1960, before launching Bobby Vee to stardom. At 22, was made head of A&R at Liberty Records, where he hired then unknown Phil Spector.

Further success came with Jerry Lewis' son Gary Lewis (and the Playboys) for whom Garrett produced 10 major US chart hits in mid-'60s (with arrangements by a young Leon Russell).

Formed own Viva label after leaving Liberty, before retiring. Returned to production in '70s with Sonny & Cher.

As performer, Garrett cut several MOR albums, including **50 Guitars Of Tommy Garrett**.

David Geffen
US executive, producer.

Founded Asylum Records in 1971. Impressive roster included key West Coast talent Jo Jo Gunne, Jackson Browne, David Blue and Judee Sill. Remained president of company after Warner Bros takeover in 1973. Further signings included Eagles, Linda Ronstadt and Joni Mitchell (whom he managed, along with Crosby, Stills, Nash & Young).

Pacted Bob Dylan for two albums (**Planet Waves** and **Before The Flood**) after persuading him to tour after eight-year absence from road. Geffen was replaced by Joe Smith in 1975, and after flirtation with films, started own Geffen label in 1980. Like its predecessor, Geffen immediately attracted major talent, including Donna Summer, Elton John, Neil Diamond, Peter Gabriel, Quarterflash and Asia.

Charlie Gillett
UK journalist, broadcaster.

Lancashire-born Gillett first came to prominence as author of 'Sound Of The City' (1970), an accurate and thorough journey through development of rock music and its roots; book was written as part of MA thesis, completed at New York's Columbia University.

His other titles include the history of Atlantic Records, 'Making Tracks' and 'Rock Files' ('Rock Almanac' in US), a four-volume set of chart/historical detail.

Briefly acted as manager of London pub band Kilburn and the High Roads. He has been an avid enthusiast of UK rock club scene. Formed own record company Oval in 1973.

More recently, Gillett has been most-informed DJ on Greater London radio stations, Radio London (BBC subsidiary) and Capital Radio.

Harvey Goldsmith
UK promoter.

In the late '60s sold posters in Kensington market; has since moved up considerably in the business world.

Generally considered one of the leading promoters in Britain; has also handled US, Australian and European tours/shows. Responsible for some of the biggest, most successful rock festivals, including the 1976 'Who Put The Boot In' shows (and the heavily criticised Charlton set-up). Goldsmith often promotes charity gigs in tours he handles. Organised the benefit concerts for the People of Kampuchea in 1979, which featured the Who, Queen, the Pretenders, Paul McCartney and Wings, Elvis Costello, Ian Dury, Rockpile and others. Promoted Bob Dylan's Blackbushe (UK) show in 1978. Has most recently promoted the tours of the Who (1981), the Rolling Stones (1982) and David Bowie, Wham and Robert Plant (1983).

Above: promoter Harvey Goldsmith.

Jack Good
UK television producer, actor.

Former graduate of Oxford University, Good launched classic rock programme '6.5 Special' in 1957. Moving from BBC, Good joined infant commercial television where he devised 'Oh Boy', 'Boy Meets Girl' and 'Wham' rock shows.

Moving to US, Good produced 'Around The Beatles', 'Shindig' and one-off specials for Monkees and Andy Williams.

Played Othello in stage musical 'Catch My Hair' (which also featured Lance Le Gault and P.J. Proby) in 1970, before attempt to transfer show to film.

More recently worked on revival rock show 'Oh Boy' with Lulu and Alvin Stardust.

Above: Berry Gordy, the man who formed the major R&B and soul label, Motown.

Berry Gordy
US executive.

Former employee of Ford Motor Co. As an independent writer/producer, scored several R&B hits throughout the '50s, including Jackie Wilson's **Reet Petite** and **Lonely Teardrops** and Marv Johnson's **You Got What It Takes**.

Formed Motown label in 1960, an abbreviation of Motor Town, Detroit, the company base. Motown subsequently became major R&B and soul outfit throughout '60s and '70s, launching such acts as Stevie Wonder, Marvin Gaye, Smokey Robinson, Supremes, Diana Ross, Temptations, Four Tops, Martha and the Vandellas, Rick James and Commodores.

Delved into film with 'The Lady Sings The Blues', starring Diana Ross; follow-up 'Mahogany' flopped badly. Company moved to California in early '70s, since when several top names quit the label, including Ross and Marvin Gaye.

Motown's phenomenal and continued success earned Gordy accolade as premier black executive in music business.

Bill Graham
US promoter.

Career: Graham is the ultimate rock impresario, with an idiosyncratic style compounded of toughness, honesty and devotion to music. His first and greatest fame, of course, was gained as owner and manager of the Fillmores East and West; the first Fillmore, a disused San Francisco skating rink, opened in 1965, and the Fillmore East, an old theatre in Greenwich Village, New York City, soon afterwards.

Another venue, the Winterland Ballroom, also in San Francisco, opened in 1968. Graham also managed archetypal West Coast groups such as the Jefferson Airplane, Hot Tuna and Quicksilver Messenger Service in the '60s.

The strain of living a dual-coast existence (he took a personal interest in his theatres and visted them regularly) eventually became too much, even for Graham, and he closed both halls in 1971, with acerbic comments on the state of rock.

Winterland remained in service and highly regarded, but Graham turned his attention to concert promotion, presenting some of the biggest and best-known tours and festivals in rock throughout '70s. In 1980 he bought the Old Waldorf, the most popular rock club in San Francisco, a departure from ballrooms and arenas.

In 1982 he demonstrated that his power and influence were practically undiminished when he managed, with great success and no little controversy, the first giant UNUSON Music and Electronics Festival in California. There he provided rock-watchers with a little nostalgia, fighting with the backers, the bands and the press from the first announcement of his involvement (though the complex event went off like clockwork).

Peter Grant
UK manager.

Former wrestler/tour manager (Little Richard, Gene Vincent, etc) with stature to match. Assumed management of Led Zeppelin in 1969, signing group to Atlantic after being turned down by Polydor (UK).

Formerly partner of Mickie Most, then Mark London. With London, managed Stone the Crows and, later, group's vocalist Maggie Bell.

Founded Swan Song Records with Zeppelin in 1974, opening offices in New York and London's New Kings Road. Label signed Dave Edmunds and Pretty Things. Also released product by another Grant band, Bad Company.

Owner of huge sixteenth-century mansion in Sussex (complete with drawbridge), Grant now spends time in low-key operation of individual Zeppelin members.

Jay Graydon
US guitarist, arranger, producer.

Multi-talented Graydon has worked with Joe Cocker, Jennifer Warnes, Lee Ritenour and Flora Purim.

Produced magnificent Manhattan Transfer album **Extensions**, which included **Birdland** and **Twilight Zones** singles. Currently working with Al Jarreau.

John Hammond
US producer, executive.

When Columbia's head of A&R signed then relatively unknown Bob Dylan to lucrative recording contract in 1962, deal was known within company as 'Hammond's folly'. Hammond's ear for worthy new talent was, however, proved right again.

Bessie Smith, Count Basie, Billie Holiday, Lester Young, Charlie Christian (all pre-war) and Aretha Franklin, Pete Seeger, Dylan and Bruce Springsteen in the rock era were all developed as recording stars by New Yorker John Hammond.

Educated at Yale, Hammond then studied music at New York's renowned Julliard Academy. A white with a deep love of black music—particularly jazz and blues—he gave black artists a break in his own theatre by promoting integrated tours and recording sessions at time when racial segregation was rife in US. His legendary 'Spirituals To Swing' concerts at Carnegie Hall, New York, in 1938 and 1939 introduced such artists as jazzmen Benny Goodman, Charlie Christian and Lester Young, and blues artists Big Bill Broonzy and Sonny Terry, to a wider audience.

Hammond hoped to present obscure but legendary bluesman Robert Johnson at the 1938 concert. After sending people scouring the South for the elusive Johnson, his efforts were thwarted by Johnson's murder at hands of a jealous woman. Subsequently, Hammond compiled the classic Columbia album **Robert Johnson, King Of The Delta Blues Singers**. This showcased the bluesman's sparse but ultra-influential recorded work.

Besides work as producer (of Dylan's debut album among many others), Hammond has been respected music journalist, contributing to 'Melody Maker' and 'The Gramaphone' in the UK and 'Down Beat' in the US. Has also written widely on race relations. He has been a vice president of the National Association For The Advancement Of Coloured People. His autobiography 'John Hammond On Record' was published in 1982. Hammond's son, John Hammond Jr, is among the best—and more esoteric—of the white blues singers to emerge during the '60s.

Jac Holzman
US executive, producer.

Founder of Elektra Records in 1950. Initially a folk-orientated label, acts included Tom Paxton, Judy Collins and, a decade earlier, Jean Ritchie and Theodore Bikel.

Moved into rock mainstream with Paul Butterfield Blues Band and West Coast outfits Love and the Doors. Later signings included Bread and Carly Simon.

Elektra came under Kinney group umbrella in 1970, and Holzman subsequently moved from the label to become senior vice-president of the parent company; involving himself in development of quadrophonic sound systems.

Hugo And Luigi
US producers, composers, executives.

Influential duo who carved out impressive career in R&B and soul markets from mid-'50s. Hugo (Peretti) and Luigi (Creatore) originally recorded as artists, scoring with **Young Abe Lincoln** in 1955.

Pair (both New York Italians) then bought Roulette Records, where they wrote (under pseudonym Mark Markwell) and produced many chart entries, including million-selling **Falling In Love Again** for Jimmie Rodgers.

Moving to RCA, couple worked with both Sam Cooke and Isley Bros before joining Avco Embassy in 1973 as vice-presidents (later owned company) and beginning fruitful association with Stylistics, for whom they wrote and produced.

Jimmy Iovine
US producer, engineer.

Exciting new production talent who cut teeth engineering for Bruce Springsteen and John Lennon. Impressive roster since late '70s has included Patti Smith, Tom Petty, Golden Earring, Motors, Dire Straits, Graham Parker and Meat Loaf.

Glyn Johns
UK producer, engineer.

Major British rock producer/engineer of '60s, having linked with Steve Miller (**Children Of The Future, Sailor, Brave New World, Your Saving Grace**), Traffic, Led Zeppelin, Family and Joe Cocker.

Worked with Rolling Stones for **Get Yer Ya-Yas Out, Sticky Fingers, Black And Blue** and **Exile On Main Street**, the Beatles (engineered **Let It Be**), the Who (**Who's Next, Who By Numbers** and **Who Are You**), Faces, Boz Scaggs, the Eagles (**Eagles, Desperado, On The Border**), Gallagher & Lyle, Eric Clapton, Ozark Mountain Daredevils, Wings (**Red Rose Speedway**), Fairport Convention and Joan Armatrading.

Entered '80s with somewhat less frenetic schedule, producing Live Wire, former Fairport Tim Renwick, Nine Below Zero, and continuing work with the Who.

Above: John of all trades, Jonathan King. You either love him or you hate him.

Jonathan King
UK executive, producer, broadcaster.

Master of self-parody with successful initial career as producer/writer/performer. First hit was **Everyone's Gone To The Moon** (1965), which made US/UK Top 20. Subsequent chart records have included **It's Good News Week** (1965), Hedgehoppers Anonymous (in fact a group of RAF servicemen), **Sugar Sugar** (1971), Sakkarin, **Una**

Paloma Blanca (1975). King himself recorded variously as Bubblerock, 53rd and 3rd, Shag, 100 Ton & A Feather, Weathermen, Sound 9418, Father Abraphart and the Smurps.

Formed own UK label in 1972, signing 10cc and Kursaal Flyers. An astute observer of pure 'pop' market, was instrumental in setting Bay City Rollers off on their long-term residency in charts.

The dubious quality of his output belies his 'good time' message. Has recently earned a more honourable living as broadcaster. His series 'Entertainment USA' for BBC received excellent reviews. Divides time between New York and London.

Don Kirshner
US publisher, TV producer, manager.

Manager of Bobby Darin and Connie Francis in mid-'50s. With partner Al Nevins, set up the Brill Building complex in New York, where writers would compete in battle for potential hit songs. Composers involved included Gerry Goffin, Carole King, Neil Sedaka, Howard Greenfield, Barry Mann and Cynthia Weill. All were dominant in charts during early '60s; the music was published by Kirshner's company Aldon Music.

Created the Monkees for American TV consumption in 1966, a US alternative to the Beatles. Needless to say, the Monkees music was published by Kirshner and, for the most part, written by contract writers Tommy Boyce and Bobby Hart. Subsequently created cartoon series the Archies, which spawned teenybopper hits, including **Sugar Sugar** in 1969.

With advent of AOR market, Kirshner inaugurated syndicated TV show 'Don Kirshner's Rock Concert', which featured prominent performers throughout the '70s. Is now involved in cable TV operation, as well as own Kirshner label, for whom Kansas records.

Below: Kit Lambert, manager and producer of the Who in the '60s and '70s, with Pete Townshend (right) and Pete's younger brother Simon in 1972.

Kit Lambert
UK manager, producer.

Best known as manager/producer of the Who. Son of composer/arranger Constant Lambert. Attended Lansing Public School. Spent some time as an officer in the British Army. Went on a rather harrowing journey up the Amazon, during which his best friend was killed.

Interest in film led to job as assistant director. Met Chris Stamp, another assistant director at Shepperton Studios. Duo discovered the Who at the Railway Hotel in Harrow in summer 1964 while looking for a band to star in their film about the current music/fashion scene. Convinced band to let them take over management from Pete Meaden/Helmut Gorden. Duo ousted producer Shel Talmy by 1966. Lambert's first Who production was **I'm A Boy** single. Founded Track Records in 1967; launched label with Jimi Hendrix's **Hey Joe**. Lambert also worked with the Merseybeats, Arthur Brown and Thunderclap Newman among others.

In early '70s went to New York to produce Labelle. Between 1973 and 1976 Lambert and Stamp became somewhat less efficient in their duties for the Who (who by then had reached megaband status), and after legal wrangles with group, were replaced by Bill Curbishley. Lambert went on to produce some early punk bands, while Stamp returned to film. Lambert died on April 7, 1981, of a brain haemorrhage after falling down the stairs at his mother's flat.

Far more instrumental in the image/concepts behind the Who than many realise, Kit Lambert was not only responsible for the guitar-smashing publicity stunts, but was a major contributor to 'Tommy'. He in fact presented Townshend with a script early on; with the laurels of his composer father hanging over him, Lambert pushed for the rock-opera concept, and he and Townshend worked very closely on the project. When one examines the post-1975 work of the Who, Lambert's absence is sadly evident. Along with Brian Epstein, Lambert was one of the major management figures of the '60s.

Leiber & Stoller
US composers, producers.

Baltimore-raised Jerry Leiber and Mike Stoller were prime movers in R&B development in '50s and '60s. As writers/producers, duo cut countless hits with the Coasters, the Drifters, Ben E. King, Ruth Brown, LaVern Baker, Joe Turner, the Robins and many others. Wrote **Hound Dog** and **Jailhouse Rock**, both successfully worked by Elvis Presley.

Formed Red Bird label in 1963 with George Goldner, and had chart action with the Dixie Cups and Shangri-Las.

During '70s, worked with British acts, including Stealers Wheel, Procol Harum and Elkie Brooks. Have threatened move to musicals for some time — 'Only In America' played at the Roundhouse Theatre, London, for a short run in 1980.

Mark London
Canadian producer, writer, publisher.

Came to London in mid-'60s as singer. Began

Above: Martha Quinn, an MTV 'VJ', chats with Elton John.

career in New York's Catskill mountains as comic/MC. First break in UK was as co-star with Jean Shrimpton and Paul Jones (ex-Manfred Mann) in rock movie 'Privilege'. Subsequently featured in various TV sitcoms/dramas.

Wrote titletrack of movie 'To Sir With Love' with lyricist Don Black, which Lulu took to top of US charts for five-week stay. Subsequently married singer's manager Marian Massey; took active part in career as producer, returning Lulu to American charts with **I Could Never Miss You** in 1981. Album **Lulu** earned Grammy nomination for track **Who's Fooling Who**.

As publisher, London is now teamed with prominent keyboard player/composer Mike Moran, and duo have long-term commitments to film and TV work. Currently writing music for comic Kenny Everett's film debut; penned **Snot Rap**, UK Top 10 for that artist in 1983.

MTV
US cable television station.

A service of Warner Amex Satellite Entertainment Company in New York, MTV (Music Television) is a 24-hour-a-day video music channel (with stereo radio hook-ups available), funded by advertising. Launched on August 1, 1981. MTV now boasts 13.5 million viewers in the US, mostly between the ages of 12 and 34.

With five 'VJs' (JJ Jackson, Martha Quinn, Nina Blackwood, Mark Goodman and Alan Hunter) MTV offers videos (mostly of current singles with some archive footage), music industry news (record releases, tour dates, gossip), interviews with pop/rock artists, music documentaries/biographies, live concerts and various contests, with prizes like stereo/video equipment and trips to meet the stars. Also features a monthly talent contest for unknown acts called 'The Basement Tapes'; viewers vote for the best new band/artist and the winner receives an EMI-America recording contract.

MTV has been instrumental in breaking

new and foreign (particularly British) acts in the US. In an age when gruelling tours as a means of exposure are becoming a less than profitable venture, MTV videos have served as an effective means of introducing performers to the vast US market. The opportunity to project their visual image/sound to a national audience has resulted in improved radio airplay, record distribution and sales for many hitherto unsuccessful artists, due to demand from MTV viewers.

Mandolin Brothers
US instrument specialists.

Neither brothers, nor named Mandolin, former competitors Stan Jay and Harold Kuffner opened their store on Staten Island, New York, in 1971, initially as an instrument 'spare part' operation.

Subsequent development saw pair becoming leading purveyors of antique and collectors' instruments. The shop's huge stock includes vintage mandolins and banjos (predominantly Gibson) and guitars, of which Gibson and Martin are the premier attraction. Mandolin Bros have also been responsible for the re-issue of classic Martin models, including the Herringbone D-28 and 1939 D-45.

Although originally stockists of electric instruments, the company inaugurated a policy change in summer 1982, whereby only classic electric guitars would be available.

Mandolin Bros store is now owned solely by Jay, Kuffner having left at the end of 1981.

Barry Mann
US composer.

One of the most successful pop writers of all time. Like many New Yorkers, a product of the Brill Building set-up. With wife Cynthia Weill, composed many Top 50 hits, including **Bless You** (Tony Orlando), **I Love How You Love Me** (the Paris Sisters), **Uptown** (the Crystals), **Blame It On The Bossa Nova** (Eydie Gorme), **On Broadway** (the Drifters), **You've Lost That Loving Feeling** (with Phil Spector), **We Gotta Get Out Of This Place** (Animals) and **I Just Can't Help Believing** (B.J. Thomas).

Ventured briefly into performing when he cut **Who Put The Bomp** in 1961; had unsuccessful venture as singer/songwriter in mid-'70s.

Arif Mardin

Turkish arranger, producer, engineer.

Former staff man at Atlantic, Mardin was responsible for arrangements/production of many soul classics by artists including Aretha Franklin, Wilson Pickett and King Curtis. Also turned to freelancing in early '70s, and subsequently worked with Bee Gees, Rolling Stones, James Gang, Jackie DeShannon, Tony Joe White, Willie Nelson, Average White Band, Stephen Stills and Chaka Khan. His own **Glass Onion** instrumental LP is worth searching out in record stores.

George Martin

UK producer.

Started as producer at EMI, whom he joined in 1950, on classic British comedy acts Flanders and Swann, and Goons Peter Sellers and Spike Milligan. Formerly a student at Guildhall School of Music, where he studied oboe.

Instrumental in signing the Beatles to Parlophone—the group had been turned down by two other EMI labels—and insisting drummer Pete Best be replaced. Produced arguably the greatest pop music of all time with the band from 1962-70, including definitive rock collection **Sgt. Pepper**.

Also responsible for Beatles' manager Brian Epstein's other acts, including Gerry and the Pacemakers, Billy J. Kramer and the Dakotas, and Cilla Black.

Produced **Sentimental Journey** for Ringo Starr after Beatles' split, moving into burgeoning rock scene in early '70s with Sea Train, Stackridge and John McLaughlin.

Was involved in disastrous **Sgt. Pepper** movie soundtrack (which at least was better than the film, but hardly a satisfactory testament to the music's originators).

Cut UK-domiciled trio America from 1974-79, as well as Jeff Beck (**Blow By Blow, Wired**), Neil Sedaka, Gary Brooker and, more recently, UFO and Cheap Trick. Renewed acquaintance with Paul McCartney for 1982 **Tug Of War** album.

Partner in AIR studio set-ups in London and Montserrat.

Below: Manager, producer, seeker of talent, promoter of fads, Malcolm McLaren.

Malcolm McLaren

UK manager, producer.

Notorious as manager of Sex Pistols, who secured advances from EMI and A&M before being unceremoniously dumped. McLaren banked £175,000 for his protegés with barely a single in sight. The story was later chronicled in the movie 'The Great Rock 'N' Roll Swindle'.

Formerly owner of 'Sex' fashion store in London's Kings Road (instrumental in choice of Adam Ant image), McLaren has subsequently found success with Bow Wow Wow (attracting further notoriety for promotion of group's teenage vocalist Annabella Lwin).

Now a performer in his own right, McLaren debuted with rap disco single **Buffalo Gals** in 1983. The man who described the Sex Pistols as 'Britain's answer to Elvis Presley' is, it seems, capable of anything.

Joe Meek

UK producer.

After RAF service as radio technician, Gloucester-born Meek entered music business as engineer at London's IBC studios.

Worked on records by Shirley Bassey, Petula Clark, Anne Shelton, Denis Lotis, Frankie Vaughan and others. Becoming engineer at Dennis Preston's Lansdowne Studios in 1956, Meek worked on trad-jazz records by Chris Barber and Humphrey Lyttleton and Lonnie Donegan's early skiffle hits. In 1958 he wrote Tommy Steele hit **Put A Ring On Her Finger**.

Meeke opened own studio above a flat in North London's Holloway Road, using second-hand equipment. At same time, started Triumph, one of few independent British labels, in 1960. Michael Cox covered US hit **Angela Jones** to make UK Top 10, but other Triumph recordings failed. Meek reverted to lease-tape deals with major companies. In 1960 he scored with John Leyton's **Johnny Remember Me** and **Wild Wind**, Mike Berry's **Tribute To Buddy Holly** and minor hits for the Outlaws, who were his regular studio band.

A group of Meek session-men cut **Telstar** in 1962. With label credit to the Tornados it topped charts in both Britain and US, as well as being one of most technically advanced recordings of its era.

Further Tornados records had moderate success and group's Heinz became solo star. In 1963, Meek scored with Mike Berry's **You Think It's Time** and the Honeycombs gave him another hit in 1964 with **Have I The Right**.

1966 found his magic touch waning and none of Meek's records became hits. Increasing business/personal problems led to his suicide on February 3, 1967.

Terry Melcher

US producer.

The son of film-star Doris Day, Melcher recorded unsuccessfully as singer for Columbia in 1962 using name Terry Day. Based in Hollywood (but born in New York) and switching to production, he worked with Wayne Newton, Pat Boone and surf/drag-strip group the Rip Chords in early '60s. He also made further records as duo with future Beach Boy Bruce Johnston under tag Bruce and Terry.

It was his production work with Paul Revere and the Raiders and then with the Byrds which established his reputation. Among his successes during the eight years from 1963 onwards were all the Byrds albums, eight albums for Paul Revere and the Raiders, two albums for the Rip Chords, and one for his mother.

Returning to singing, Melcher used all-star session team, including Ry Cooder, Roger McGuinn and Chris Hillman, for his 1973 introspective Reprise album **Terry Melcher**, but it sold poorly. Melcher then concentrated on his own Equinox label and outside production work for such diverse artists as David Cassidy and Barry Mann.

Daniel Miller

US producer.

Founder of Mute Records, and producer of label's premier acts Yazoo and Depeche Mode. Former DJ (in Switzerland) and TV commercial editor.

Built own home studio around TEAC four-track machine, and began recording synthesiser music. Miller pressed 500 copies of first single **TVOD/Warm Leatherette** (as the Normal), before handling Rough Trade distribution rights. Cut has now sold in excess of 30,000 units. Miller also records as the Silicon Teens.

Mike Moran

UK keyboards player, arranger, producer.

Graduate of the Royal College Of Music. Has performed/recorded with George Harrison, Paul McCartney, Leo Sayer, Cliff Richard and Lulu. Composed 'Time Bandits' movie score, as well as various themes for British TV series including 'The Consultant' and 'Harry's Game'. Currently working on UK comic Kenny Everett's horror film 'Blood Bath At The House Of Death'; wrote Everett's 1983 UK Top 10 single **Snot Rap** (with Mark London).

As performer, Moran scored success with Lynsey De Paul on 1977 British Eurovision song contest entry **Rock Bottom**. Resides in Hertfordshire, where he records at own self-built studio.

Bruce Morrow

US DJ.

Any American who was a teenager in the New York area in the '60s would instantly recognise the voice of 'Cousin Brucie'; he practically personified rock'n'roll AM radio at that time. His rapid delivery, word-play and vocabulary of odd shrieks and noises have never been—and probably *couldn't* be—closely imitated.

Morrow began his New York career at WINS, moving to WABC, then the largest and most powerful (in terms of wattage and influence) Top 40 AM station in the area, in 1961. He stayed there for 13 successful years.

With the waning of AM in the '70s, Morrow frankly professed himself 'bored' with the new 'Superstar' formats and playlists; like all great DJs, he truly has a passion for rock music. He left New York radio in 1977, and, having invested wisely, soon realised his dream of buying his own station. He currently owns four radio stations and one television station; he has a daily show on New Jersey's WRAN-AM (one of his), and a regular 'oldies' programme on WCBS-FM in New York City, both of which receive amazing response from his old fans.

Jerry Moss

US executive, producer.

Former promoter/independent producer who, with trumpeter Herb Alpert, founded A (Alpert) & M (Moss) Records. Initially called Carnival, the label scored with its third single, Alpert's **The Lonely Bull**.

After capturing a major slice of the MOR market throughout the '60s and '70s, most notably with the Carpenters, A&M made impressive inroads into rock with the development of Supertramp and, more recently, Police, Joan Armatrading and Squeeze. The company's AOR roster continued with Styx and Elkie Brooks.

A skilled negotiator, Moss is acknowledged as one of record business's 'major' operators.

Mickie Most

UK producer.

Englishman who emigrated to South Africa in late '50s after period as Most Bros with Alex Murray. Scored many hits in that country with covers of US/UK hits as vocalist.

Returned to UK in 1962 where he began incredibly successful career as producer, starting with the Animals and including Lulu, Herman's Hermits, Donovan, Jeff Beck, and more recently, Mud, Suzi Quatro and Hot Chocolate.

Formed own RAK label in 1969; opened studio in 1977. Often seen on TV as knowledgeable 'inside man' on panel shows. Was regular on 'New Faces' talent show, where his honest comments/predictions proved correct with 99% of artists.

Russell Mulcahy

Australian video director.

Most prominent of current crop of pop video directors. Has filmed Paul McCartney, Bonnie Tyler, Fun Boy Three, Ultravox, Fleetwood Mac, Billy Joel, Spandau Ballet, and, particularly, Duran Duran, whose **Rio** and **Hungry Like The Wolf** were major video chart entries in 1982.

Mulcahy is also active in commercials field, and is planning to direct first feature movie 'Razorback' in 1983.

Murray The K

US DJ, promoter.

Murray Kaufman was one of the best-loved and most influential DJs in American rock. His fast patter, special slang, straw hat and excellent taste in rock'n'roll made his programme on New York's City's WINS one of the most popular in the country in the early '60s. He hosted a series of legendary rock shows at the Brooklyn Fox and the Brooklyn Paramount theatres, the last of the great package shows with truly all-star line-ups. But he gained greatest fame when the Beatles hit—Murray was ready for them. Infiltrating himself (somehow) into their entourage, he broadcast an endless flow of short interviews and 'Beatle news' that had New York teenagers glued to their radios, promoting himself forever after as 'the fifth Beatle'.

After the first hysteria of Beatlemania, Murray was more popular than ever. In 1965 he made an important move to WOR-FM in New York. Here he pioneered free-form 'album-orientated' rock radio. The constraints of sales-promoting AM's narrow Top-40 playlists disappeared, at least temporarily. Murray played whatever he liked, sometimes whole album sides at a time, uninterrupted. It couldn't last, of course, and didn't, but for a few years in the late '60s, FM radio enjoyed a real golden age, and Murray Kaufman was an important part of it.

By the '70s, advertising pressure and ratings wars had caught up with FM, and most stations reacted by instituting playlists, the 'album Top-40' format, the 'Superstars' format, and other limits on the form. Murray the K left radio and took to producing concerts, some television specials and nostalgia shows. He died in 1982, aged 60, after a long and debilitating struggle with cancer.

Colonel Tom Parker

US manager.

Oft-criticised individual whose resolute pursuit of immortality for himself and client Elvis Presley has been partially achieved.

Parker replaced Bob Neal as Presley's manager in November 1955, signing 'the King' to RCA after paying Sam Phillips compensation of $35,000 for rights to all recorded Sun Material.

Despite period during mid-'60s when Presley was in danger of being digested by appalling 'B' movies, his position as most popular performer in pop history was never seriously challenged. Parker's reluctance to let Presley tour UK (against the artist's wishes)

Above: Colonel Tom Parker (left), Elvis' controversial manager from 1955.

was considered a naive judgement, however; Parker thought a tour would crack the Presley image in a major record territory.

After Presley's death, Parker was the target of much mud-slinging, including an attack on his birthright; it was claimed he was Dutch, and did not have a US passport, a sure-fire reason for his unwillingness to leave the country.

Richard Perry

US producer, percussionist.

Most prominent of young AOR producers to develop in the '70s. Started as an independent in New York, and supplied finished cuts to Leiber/Stoller's Red Bird label among others.

Broke through after move to West Coast, producing Captain Beefheart classic **Safe As Milk**. In late '60s, worked with acts as varied as Tiny Tim, Fats Domino, Ella Fitzgerald and folk singer Theodore Bikel.

Established reputation internationally with Carly Simon LPs **No Secrets** and **Hot Cakes**, as well as work with Barbra Streisand (including **Stoney End**), Nilsson classics **Nilsson Schmilsson** and **Son Of Schmilsson**, and trio of albums for Fanny, first major all-girl rock group.

Perry's magic touch then continued throughout '70s with Ringo Starr (**Ringo** and **Goodnight Vienna**), Art Garfunkel, Manhattan Transfer, Leo Sayer, Diana Ross and, into the '80s, with the Pointer Sisters.

Formed own label Planet in 1978 with offices on Sunset Boulevard, Los Angeles.

Norman Petty

US producer, engineer, manager.

Best known as producer/co-writer on early Buddy Holly and Crickets (whom he also managed) material, including **That'll Be The Day, Peggy Sue, Everyday, Oh Boy, Maybe Baby** and **It's So Easy**. Also recorded Roy Orbison, Buddy Knox and Jimmy Bowen at his studio in Clovis, New Mexico.

After Holly's death, Petty re-mastered and re-mixed several of artists' sessions, releasing material throughout '60s. Other Petty-produced artists included Stringalongs and Jimmy Gilmer and Fireballs.

Sam Phillips

US producer, engineer.

As responsible as any individual for rock'n'roll explosion in mid-'50s. His Sun studios and label featured work by Elvis Presley, whose contract he later sold to RCA records, Jerry Lee Lewis, Carl Perkins, Charlie Rich and Roy Orbison.

Phillips was prime mover in rockabilly sound popularised by Presley, guitarist Scotty Moore and bass player Bill Black. Innovative use of echo marked Phillips as unique production talent.

Classic Sun singles include **Blue Suede Shoes** Carl Perkins, **Whole Lotta Shakin' Going On** and **Great Balls Of Fire**, Jerry Lee Lewis, **Lonely Weekends**, Charlie Rich and **Good Rockin' Tonight**, Elvis Presley.

Pomus And Shuman

US composers.

Although respected as suppliers of some of Presley's most memorable material—**A Mess Of Blues, Surrender, She's Not You**—duo initially had success with **A Teenager In Love** (Dion and the Belmonts) in 1959.

Both New Yorkers, Doc Pomus (confined to a wheelchair since teens) and Mort Shuman

joined forces in the late '50s. Pomus had previously recorded as blues artist; Shuman had tasted success as writer with Charlie Gracie.

While signed to Leiber and Stoller's Aberdach set-up, pair wrote **Save The Last Dance For Me, This Magic Moment** and **I Count The Tears** for the Drifters, as well as countless R&B hits for performers such as Gary 'US' Bonds, Ben E. King and Gene McDaniels.

Kal Rudman

US journalist, analyst.

Bespectacled author of 'Friday Morning Quarterback' and 'FMGB Album Report', trade tip sheets which have major influence on radio planning in US.

Rudman exploits his unique judgement of potential hit records in the journals (started in the '70s), virtually eliminating chances of any singles given his personal 'thumbs down'.

A regular on the Merv Griffin chat show, Rudman has become a personality in his own right with his outspoken views on music business.

Martin Rushent

UK producer, engineer.

Persuaded to cut moody UK band the Stranglers, after much debate, which launched successful production career in mid-'70s. Formerly engineer at several studios.

Moved into '80s with Human League and Altered Images. Owns studio, record company and publishing firm Genetic.

Shelby Singleton

US producer, executive.

Country pop producer who turned Mercury's Smash subsidiary into a leading label of the '60s. After becoming VP of Mercury, Singleton signed Jerry Lee Lewis and Charlie Rich to the label.

At the end of the '60s, Singleton had formed his own Plantation, Silver Fox (named after Charlie Rich) and SSS labels, scoring with performers such as Jeannie C. Riley, Jo Jo Benson and Johnny Adams. He also purchased Sun Records, revitalising the label's classic '50s product of artists such as Johnny Cash and Jerry Lee Lewis.

Below: Phil Spector, the 'mad genius' behind the 'wall of sound'.

Phil Spector

US producer, composer, pianist, guitarist.

Born in the Bronx, New York, began career as member of Teddy Bears, who hit with **To Know Him Is To Love Him** in 1959. After spell with Leiber/Stoller (co-wrote Ben E. King hit **Spanish Harlem** with Leiber), moved into solo production. After several minor hits, including singles with Gene Pitney and Connie Francis, started regular visit to charts with the Crystals on his own label Philles.

Spector's 'Wall Of Sound' was formulated during late '50s, but first used to maximum effect on singles by Ronettes (he later married Ronnie from that group), Bob B. Soxx and the Blue Jeans and, later, the Righteous Bros (**You've Lost That Lovin' Feeling** which he co-wrote) and Ike & Tina Turner (**River Deep Mountain High**).

Revived (in part) this production technique with the Ramones for 1980 LP **End Of The Century**. During '70s, worked with the Beatles (**Let It Be**), George Harrison (**All Things Must Pass, Concert For Bangla Desh**), John Lennon (**Plastic Ono Band,** the classic **Imagine, Some Time In New York City, Rock'n'Roll, Roots**), Dion and Leonard Cohen.

Robert Stigwood

Australian manager.

First worked in UK for Brian Epstein's NEMS organisation, suffering a bankruptcy before establishing managerial credentials with Bee Gees, Cream and Eric Clapton.

Formed own RSO label as natural progression through management. The Bee Gees and Clapton remain company's mainstays.

Stigwood has also achieved success with theatrical ventures 'Hair', 'Jesus Christ Superstar' and London production of 'John Paul George Ringo and . . . Bert'.

Continued his magical touch with movies 'Grease', 'Saturday Night Fever' and 'Tommy', although struck sand with 'Sgt. Pepper's Lonely Hearts Club Band', (which he had produced on stage in New York), 'Times Square' and the abysmal 'Moment by Moment', which starred Stigwood favourite John Travolta.

Another initially-fated venture was launch of TV-AM breakfast television in UK—programme failed to register on audience measuring scale during formative months.

Bill Szymczyk

US producer.

Former electronics student who started as engineer on spate of folk albums (Phil Ochs, Eric Anderson) in mid-'60s. Joined ABC Records in 1967, linking successfully with B.B. King two years later on some of the blues maestro's classic albums, including **Live And Well** (which included majestic **The Thrill Is Gone**), **Completely Well, Indianola Mississippi Seeds** and **Live At Cook County Jail**.

Also responsible for James Gang's LPs from 1969-72, later producing Joe Walsh solo sets between 1972-80. Szymczyk also produced other major West Coast acts Jo Jo Gunne and Rick Derringer, before linking with the Eagles for the **On The Border** album.

Enjoyed worldwide chart status with Eagles until band's demise, linking once again with Joe Walsh. Produced group's **One Of These Nights, Hotel California, The Long Run** and **Live**.

Other Szymczyk credits from the '70s include Michael Stanley, Dan Fogelberg, Wishbone Ash, Elvin Bishop, former Spirit Jay Ferguson and the Outlaws. Cut **Face Dances** with the Who in 1981, making Szymczyk as near a household name as it can ever be.

Own studio complex, Pandora Productions, based in Miami Florida.

Creed Taylor

US executive, producer.

Former head of A&R at ABC Paramount Records, where he founded Impulse jazz label. Moved to Verve in 1962, producing one of the largest-selling jazz albums of all time, with Astrud Gilberto and Stan Getz.

After short spell at A&M, formed own CTI (Creed Taylor Industries), Kudu and Salvation labels.

Company became forerunner of jazz-funk and jazz-rock movement, recording outstanding talent, including Grover Washington Jr, Hubert Laws, Freddie Hubbard, Stanley Turrentine, Deodato, George Benson, Esther Phillips and Bob James.

Above: Robert Stigwood (far left), who brings you RSO records and films.

Ted Templeman

US producer, drummer.

Former member of Harpers Bizarre, featured on group's hit **The 59th Street Bridge Song (Feelin' Groovy)**. Now staff producer for Warner Bros, has guided careers of Doobie Bros and Van Halen.

With Doobie Bros, cut all classic hits—**Black Water, Long Train Runnin', Listen To The Music, Minute By Minute, What A Fool Believes**, etc—as well as solo LPs by Tom Johnston and Michael McDonald. Began association with Van Halen in 1978.

Other credits include Captain Beefheart, Montrose and Nicolette Larson. Competent instrumentalist (notably drums, but also trumpet).

Chris Thomas

UK producer.

Former student at the Royal Academy Of Music (violin). Started career as engineer in AIR studios complex, cutting teeth with George Martin on the Beatles **White** album.

Debuted as producer with British R&B outfit Climax Blues Band, before encompassing

Procol Harum (from 1970), Roxy Music (**For Your Pleasure, Stranded, Country Life, Siren, Viva**), Badfinger, John Cale and Frankie Miller. Also mixed Pink Floyd's classic 1973 collection **Dark Side Of The Moon**.

Earned notoriety in 1977 with production of Sex Pistols' **Never Mind The Bollocks**, before returning to rock mainstream with Wings (**Back To The Egg**), the ill-fated Pretenders (first two albums), Pete Townshend (**Empty Glass, Chinese Eyes**) and Elton John (**The Fox, Jump Up**).

Allen Toussaint

US arranger, producer, pianist, composer.

An unassuming linchpin of the 'New Orleans Sound', Toussaint came to prominence as an arranger and producer in the early '60s. With no formal musical training, he started on trumpet and trombone as a teenager—which may in part account for the sympathetic clarity of his horn sounds—before taking up his real instrument, the piano.

He became a well-known session musician and songwriter, directing recording in the small, homey, and extremely productive studio of Cosimo Matassa in New Orleans' French Quarter.

Hits by Irma Thomas, Ernie K-Doe, Lee Dorsey and Aaron Neville sprang from these

sessions, having in common a neatly controlled exuberance and a rhythmic complexity very characteristic of the city's ever-likely ethnic mix. Toussaint went on to produce Dr John, Joe Cocker, Frankie Miller, the Neville Bros, his own renowned house band, the Meters, and LaBelle, for whom he arranged one of his—and their—biggest hits, **Lady Marmalade**.

In 1973, he and partner Marshall Sehorn opened their own Sea-Saint Studio in New Orleans. Sea-Saint is as modern, gadget-filled, and electronically up-to-date as any studio in the country, but Toussaint's sound still reaches for a distinctive balance of spareness, intricacy and a good beat.

Tony Visconti

US producer, arranger, guitarist.

UK resident (born Brooklyn, New York) who made mark with leading British acts T. Rex, Strawbs and particularly David Bowie in the late '60s/early '70s.

Cut **Space Oddity, The Man Who Sold The World, David Live, Young Americans, Low, Heroes, Lodger** and **Scary Monsters**

Above: Allen Toussaint has produced Dr. John, Joe Cocker, and Thin Lizzy.

with Bowie, taking artist successfully into '80s.

Worked with acts as diverse as Tom Paxton and Osibisa during early '70s, and confirmed reputation as producer with LPs for Ralph McTell, Gentle Giant, Sparks, Thin Lizzy, Iggy Pop, Steve Gibbons Band and Hazel O'Conner (**Breaking Glass** soundtrack and **Cover Plus**). Also arranged and conducted Wings' **Band On The Run** (1973). Joined new wave movement in '80s with Boomtown Rats (**Mondo Bongo**) and Stranglers (**La Folie**). Married to former McCartney prodigy Mary Hopkin.

Jerry Wexler

US producer, executive.

Joined Atlantic Records in early '50s after period as journalist for US trade paper 'Billboard'. Undertook production duties with Ahmet Ertegun and engineer Tom Dowd from 1953. First act was the Drifters, with Clyde McPhatter, followed by Ray Charles; worked with numerous R&B outfits throughout '50s.

Most impressive work was with Aretha Franklin, including definitive soul album **Lady Soul** (1967). The Wexler/Franklin liaison earned the producer several industry awards.

Other Wexler credits include Willie Nelson, Kim Carnes, Dire Straits and Bob Dylan.

Norman Whitfield

US composer, arranger, producer.

New York-born Whitfield was kingpin in development of Motown. Wrote **Pride And Joy** for Marvin Gaye, and oft-covered **I Heard It Through The Grapevine**.

Prime mover with Barrett Strong in development of Temptations through 'psychedelic' era. Masterminded success of his protegés Undisputed Truth before leaving Motown and starting own Whitfield label.

Continued success througout '70s, notably with Rose Royce.

A&M Records

UK: 136 New Kings Road
London SW6
US: 1412 North La Brea Avenue
Hollywood, CA 90028

Founded in 1962 by trumpeter Herb Alpert and indie producer Jerry Moss. Ultra successful MOR/AOR operation, with Alpert and the Carpenters providing solid catalogue. The company operates out of the old Charlie Chaplin film studio in Hollywood.

Major Artists: Police, Herb Alpert, Joan Armatrading, Styx, Supertramp, Squeeze, Joe Jackson.

Ace Records

UK: 3-5 Kentish Town Road
London NW1

Owned by Ted Carroll, specialises in re-issues, mostly in '50s rock'n'roll vein.

Ariola Records

UK: 3 Cavendish Square
London W1

Associated Label: Go Feet, I Spy, Hansa, Bell.
Major Artists: Sky

Arista Records

US: 6 West 57th Street
New York, NY 10019
1888 Century Park East
Los Angeles, CA 90067
UK: 3 Cavendish Square
London W1

Formed by Clive Davis after his hasty exit from Columbia for alleged irregularities in expenses payments. Arista's roster parallels his former employer's catalogue of artists, namely dependable rock acts and classy MOR performers.

Associated Labels: Ariola US, Buddah, Jive, GRP, Savoy.
Major Artists: Air Supply, Barry Manilow, Alan Parsons Project, Aretha Franklin, Kinks, Flock of Seagulls, Haircut 100, Dionne Warwick.

Atlantic Records

US: 75 Rockefeller Plaza
New York, NY 10019
9229 Sunset Boulevard
Los Angeles, CA 90069

Pioneering R&B label started by brothers

Ahmet and Nesuhi Ertegun, and Herb Abramson. After first major signing Ray Charles, company kept in the forefront of soul music with distribution/recording pact signed with Stax in '60s. Moved into rock with major acts like Iron Butterfly, Yes and Led Zeppelin. Run under the WEA umbrella in UK, part of the Kinney group.

Associated Labels: Atco, Cotillion, Modern, Rolling Stones, Swan Song, Duke.
Major Artists: Roberta Flack, Foreigner, Crosby, Stills & Nash, Abba, Phil Collins, Buffalo Springfield.
Atco: Pete Townshend, Genesis.
Swansong: Led Zeppelin, Bad Company.

BBC Records

UK: Portland Place
London W1

Primarily an outlet for material recorded for television and radio shows. Will happily advertise their own product on the box, while steadfastly refusing to accept other commercials.

Beggar's Banquet

UK: 8 Hogarth Road
London SW5

A label for the '80s.
Major Artists: Bauhaus, Gary Numan.

Bizarre Records

UK: 20 Broadwick Street
London W1
US: 3300 Warner Boulevard
Burbank, CA 91510

Frank Zappa's answer to the conglomerate.

Associated Labels: Straight.
Major Artists: Alice Cooper, Captain Beefheart, GTO's.

Bronze Records

UK: 100 Chalk Farm Road
London NW1

Formed in '60s by husband and wife team Lillian and Gerry Bron.
Major Artists: Uriah Heep, Manfred Mann, Motorhead.

Buddah Records

US: 1790 Broadway
New York, NY 10019

Major pop operation in '60s and '70s which also boasted solid soul roster, including Curtis Mayfield and Gladys Knight.

Associated Labels: Kama Sutra.
Major Artists: Melanie, Curtis Mayfield, Lovin' Spoonful.

CBS Records

US: 51 West 52nd Street
New York, NY 10019.
1801 Century Park West
Los Angeles, CA 90067
UK: 17 Soho Square
London W1

Major operation with particular emphasis on MOR and AOR artists. Columbia Broadcasting Systems began business in 1965. With artists like Simon & Garfunkel and Barbra Streisand on the label, could happily cease operation and live on the catalogue material.

Associated Labels: Philadelphia Intl., Scoti Bros, Geffen, Epic, Monument, T.C., Columbia.
Major Artists: Julio Iglesias, Barbra Streissand, Johnny Mathis, Simon and Garfunkel, Santana, Willie Nelson, Al Di Meola, the Clash, Bob Dylan, Journey, Adam Ant, Frank Zappa.
Epic: Michael Jackson, Adam Ant, Abba, Shakin' Stevens, REO Speedwagon, Culture Club.

Capitol Records

US: 1750 North Vine Street
Hollywood, CA 90028
1370 Sixth Avenue
New York, NY 10019

Distributed by EMI in UK. Long established, with solid artist roster.

Associated Labels: Blue Note, Harvest, Spector, Seraphim, Sunbird.
Major Artists: Beatles, Little River Band, Motels, Steve Miller.

Carrere Records

UK: 20 Queen Street
London W1

Major Artists: Saxon.

Below: Dionne Warwick with several Arista executives.

Charisma Records Ltd.

Charisma Records

UK: 90 Wardour Street
London W1

Started by entrepreneur/horse-racing fanatic/
journalist Tony Stratton-Smith in late '60s.
Had early success with Monty Python albums.

Major Artists: Genesis, Peter Gabriel,
Malcolm McLaren.

Charly Records

UK: 156 Ilderton Road
London SE15

Innovative young company who concentrate
on re-issue of classic rock and R&B material,
particularly Jerry Lee Lewis, Buddy Holly,
Carl Perkins, John Lee Hooker.

Chiswick Records

UK: 3 Kentish Town Road
London NW1

Will listen to all and sundry. Have released all
and sundry. Forerunner of punk movement.

Chrysalis Records

UK: 12 Stratford Place
London W1
645 Madison Avenue
New York , NY 10022

Founded by Chris Ellis and Chris Wright. Built
catalogue on impressive '60s/early '70s
success of Jethro Tull.

Associated Labels: 2-Tone.
Major Artists: Jethro Tull, Blondie, Spandau
Ballet, Lynx ,Ultravox, Icehouse, Fun Boy
Three, Pat Benatar.
2-Tone: The Specials.

**Above: Terry Ellis (left) and Chris Wright
(right) of Chrysalis.**

Cream Records

US: 8025 Melrose Avenue
Los Angeles, CA 90046

Owners of top-flight R&B label Hi.

DJM Records

UK: 5 Theobalds Road
London WC1

Formed by ex-crooner Dick James (DJ), and
funded by fortune earned by his publishing
company which signed the Beatles (and
Northern Songs). Elton John maintained
company's prominence in '70s.

Major Artists: Elton John, Jasper Carrot.

Decca Records

UK: 50 New Bond Street
London W1

Part of vast conglomerate. Forced to trim
operation in late '70s and sold to Polygram in
1981. Now rely on impressive MOR catalogue (Semprini, etc). Success with Stones
made up in part for decision to pass on the
Beatles.

Associated Labels: Ace Of Clubs, Ace Of
Diamonds, Argo, Deram, London, Vocalion.
Major Artists: Rolling Stones, The Who.

EMI Records

UK: 20 Manchester Square
London W1
US: 6920 Sunset Boulevard
Los Angeles, CA 90028
1370 Sixth Avenue
New York, NY 10019

Beatles, Cliff Richard, Pink Floyd, Rolling
Stones—what more could you ask for. Made
several dodgy corporate moves (in development of stereo system, albums, etc) but have
made more than a few 'correct' decisions. In

the States, EMI is part of Capitol operation in
conjunction with Liberty Records. Elvis
Costello's dad Henry Mortimer has been with
the label 60 years, Cliff 25.

Associated Labels: Harvest, Parlophone,
Capitol, Liberty, HMV, Music For Pleasure,
Rolling Stones Records.
Major Artists: Beatles, Cliff Richard, Pink
Floyd, Scorpions, Kim Carnes, J. Geils.

Elektra/Asylum/
Nonesuch Records

US: 962 North La Cienaga Avenue
Los Angeles, CA 90069
665 Fifth Avenue
New York, NY 10022

Elektra (founded by Jac Holzman) and Asylum
(David Geffen) represent the best in quality
rock. Holzman started with acts like the
Doors, Geffen with the Eagles, Joni Mitchell.

Associated Labels: Musician, Curb, Solar,
Full Moon.
Major Artists: Queen, Cars, Jackson
Browne, Bread, Linda Ronstadt.

Fantasy Records

US: 10 and Parker Street
Berkeley, CA 94710

Now allied to sister jazz labels Prestige and
Milestone. Also handling Stax catalogue.

Major Artist: Creedence Clearwater Revival.

Geffen Records

US: 9126 Sunset Boulevard
Los Angeles, CA 90069

David Geffen's second major label (after
Asylum). Quality performers, excellent product.

Major Artists: Elton John, Peter Gabriel,
John Lennon, Donna Summer, Joni Mitchell,
Sammy Hagar.

Ice Records

UK: 85 Richmond Avenue
London N1

Owned by reggae star Eddy Grant; run by
brother Rudy.
Major Artist: Eddy Grant.

International
Record Syndicate

US: 1416 North La Brea Avenue
Los Angeles, CA 90028

Forerunner of the UK punk/new wave movement. American equivalent of Stiff, founded
by Police manager Miles Copeland.

Major Artists: Wall of Voodoo, Cramps.

ISLAND

Island Records

UK: 22 St. Peters Square
London W6
US: 444 Madison Avenue
New York, NY 10022
7720 Sunset Boulevard
Los Angeles, CA 90046

Formed by baked bean heir Chris Blackwell
in '60s. Blue Beat/Ska (forerunner to reggae)
pioneers. Had considerable influence in
development of British R&B in mid-'60s with
distribution of Guy Stevens Sue label. Bob
Marley, Free and Bad Co. maintained label
through '70s.

Associated Labels: Mango, Antilles, Shelter,
Grove Muzic, Black & Gold.
Major Artists: Cat Stevens, Bad Co., Steve
Winwood, Bob Marley.

K-Tel Records

UK: 620 Western Avenue
London W3
US: 11311 K-Tel Drive
Minnetonka, MN 55343

King of the TV advertised album companies,
spending upwards of half a million pounds per
LP on promotion.

Lightning Records

UK: 841 Harrow Road
London NW10

Revivalist company. Hot on rock 'n' roll.

Associated Labels: Old Gold, Revival.

255

MCA RECORDS

MCA Records

US: 70 Universal City Plaza
Universal City, CA 91608
10 East 53rd Street
New York, NY 10022
UK: 1 Great Pulteney Street
London W1

Independent of film company apart from odd soundtrack album. Solid country repertoire, plus, of course, Buddy Holly.

Associated Labels: ABC, Blue Thumb, Magnet, Coral, Dot, Dunhill, Impulse, Paramount.
Major Artists: Buddy Holly, the Who, Merle Haggard, Crusaders, Diamond Head, Musical Youth, Olivia Newton-John.

Magnet Records

UK: 22 York Street
London W1

Had major success in mid-'70s with lightweight pop material.

Major Artists: Bad Manners, Alvin Stardust, Darts.

Motown Records

US: 6255 Sunset Boulevard
Los Angeles, CA 90028
UK: 16 Curzon Street
London W1

The doyen of soul labels. Founded by Berry Gordy in 1959, who introduced the then 'Little' Stevie Wonder to the label. Wonder is still Motown's premier performer. Another Tamla star Smokey Robinson is on the board. Moved to the West Coast from Detroit (the Motor City) in 1967.

Associated Labels: Gordy, Tamla, Prodigal, Rare Earth, Soul.
Major Artists: Stevie Wonder, Supremes, Commodores, Lionel Richie, Jose Feliciano, Four Tops, Temptations, Miracles, Smokey Robinson, Marvin Gaye.

Music For Pleasure

UK: 1 Uxbridge Road,
Hayes, Middlesex.

Budget label with vast catalogue, mostly reissues through EMI such as the Beach Boys and Cliff Richard.

Mute

UK: 49-53 Kensington Gardens Square,
London W2

Adventurous young British company who seem to have finger on pulse of current UK musical trends. First single **TVOD/Warm Leatherette** by the Normal, now considered a classic.

Mute founder Daniel Miller (who records as the Normal and Silicon Teens) also produces company's premier acts Depeche Mode and Yazoo (Yaz in US).

Major Artists: Depeche Mode, Fad Gadget, Yazoo, Duet Emmo, Deutsch Amerikanische Freundschaft, Silicon Teens.

PRT

UK: 19 Upper Brook Street
London W1

Formerly Pye, now major record/tape/video manufacturers/distributors under PRT (Precision Records & Tapes) banner. Good catalogue on varied labels.

Associated Labels: Golden Hour, Precision, Piccadilly, Buddah, Chess, Cadet, All Platinum, Hi/Cream, R&B, Roulette, Sugarhill, Vanguard, Vogue.

Phonogram

UK: 50 New Bond Street
London W1A 2BR
US: 810 7th Avenue
New York, NY 10019

Prime label used to be Philips (Dusty Springfield, Status Quo, etc). Quality material now issued on Mercury, Casablanca, Vertigo and De-Lite via distribution deals. Dutch operation Philips were prime movers in video, laservision (whoops!) and general electrical goods.

Associated Labels: Mercury, Casablanca, De-Lite, Charisma, Philips, Vertigo, Fontana.
Major Artists: Dire Straits, David Essex, Four Tops, Steve Miller, Kool & the Gang.

Below: Motown artists group shot.

Pickwick

UK: Hyde Industrial Estate
The Hyde
London NW9

As their address suggests, more a factory than a record company. Specialist budget labels abound.

Associated Labels: Hallmark, Contour, Marble Arch, Camden.

Polydor

UK: 13 George Street
London W1

Company's variable sales figures put on upward trend by astute management in early '70s. Strong artist roster includes catalogue acts like James Last, and major rock performers like the Who, Rainbow, Jon & Vangelis and Bee Gees (Polydor distributes Robert Stigwood's RSO label). Major classical pioneers with Deutsche Grammaphone.

Associated Labels: RSO, CTI, Spring, MGM, Verve, Capricorn.
Major Artists: Bee Gees, the Who, Rainbow, Jon & Vangelis, Roxy Music, the Jam, James Last.

Above: Russ Regan, West Coast VP and GM of Polygram Record Operations.

PolyGram Records

Polygram

US: 810 Seventh Avenue
New York, NY 10019.
1930 Century Park West
Los Angeles, CA 90067

Holding company that owns Polydor. Prominent distribution deals have kept operation in charts continually.

Associated Labels: Mercury, Polydor, Casablanca, MGM, Verve, Riva, Spring RSO, De-Lite, Chocolate City.

President

UK: 21 Panton Street
London SW1

Seem to pick up all sorts of various specialist labels, including top-flight R&B and gospel.
Associated Labels: Bulldog, Energy, Enterprise, Jayboy, Joy, Manhattan, New World.

Rak

UK: 42 Charlotte Street
London NW8

Mickie Most's successful independent label, still turning out the hits. Acts have included (either on label or under Most's production) Lulu, Herman's Hermits, Suzi Quatro, Smokie and Hot Chocolate.

Major Artists: Hot Chocolate, Suzi Quatro.

RCA Records

US: 1133 Sixth Avenue
New York, NY 10036
6363 Sunset Boulevard
Hollywood, CA 90028
UK: 1 Bedford Avenue
London WC1

Impressive country roster plus Presley makes company major catalogue operation. Notable pop performers in current market include Hall & Oates, Bucks Fizz, Eurythmics and Jo Boxers. Distribute Motown label in UK.

Associated Labels: Ensign, Grunt, 20th Century, Chi-Sound, Salsoul, Millenium.
Major Artists: Elvis Presley, Jim Reeves, Hall & Oates, Alabama, David Bowie, Jefferson Starship, Bucks Fizz.

Riva

UK: 2 New Kings Road
London SW8

Founded by Rod Stewart and his then manager Billy Gaff in mid-'70s. Label busted wide open with US success of John Cougar in 1982.
Major Artists: Rod Stewart, John Cougar.

Rocket

UK: 104 Lancaster Gate
London W2

Owned by Elton John. Sporadic success against diminishing record sales.

Rounder Records

US: 186 Willow Avenue
Somerville, MA 02144

Responsible for rejuvenating bluegrass in US. Recorded David Grisman, Ricky Scaggs and Tony Rice. Strong folk and blues output.
Major Artist: George Thorogood.

Slash

US: 7381 Beverly Boulevard
Los Angeles, CA 90036

Prominent new independent which concentrates on new wave.
Major Artists: Blasters, 'X', Gun Club.

Sonet

UK: 121 Ledbury Road
London W11

The company that claims a hit every two years. Started by two jazz enthusiasts in Sweden in 1956. Catalogue includes specialist labels Specialty (R&B) and Rounder (bluegrass).

Associated Labels: Specialty, Takoma, Rounder, Alligator, Red Stripe.

Below: Dave Robinson, who took over from Jake Riviera at Stiff.

Stiff Records

UK: 115-123 Bayham Street
London NW1

Innovative, progressive outfit founded by Jake Riviera now run by Dave Robinson. Promoted acts with successful package tours.

Major Artists: Elvis Costello, Ian Dury, Madness, Lene Lovich, Wreckless Eric, Ian Gomm, Rachel Sweet, Graham Parker, the Damned.

Sugarhill Records

US: 96 West Street
Englewood, NJ 07631

Influential soul/disco outfit and leaders in rap movement.
Major Artist: Sugarhill Gang.

Takoma

US: 9255 Sunset Boulevard
Los Angeles, CA 90069

Country, rockabilly, rock'n'roll, bluegrass—generally ethnic, owned by John Fahey.

Major Artists: John Fahey, Leo Kottke, Sir Douglas Quintet.

Trojan Records

UK: 104 High Street
London NW10

Long-established reggae label. Ska/Bluebeat innovators in '60s.

Major Artists: Bob Marley (early).

Virgin Records

UK: 2 Vernon Yard
Portobello Road
London W11

Founded by latter-day Louis B. Meyer, Richard Branson. Young, enthusiastic staff have put company in forefront of UK market. Not afraid to take risks—reputedly lost a few million in abortive TV-advertised record deal. Ultra successful publishing company work hand in hand with record personnel.

Associated Labels: Secret, Ripe, Radial-choice, Focus, Dep, Gypsy.

Major Artists: Culture Club, Phil Collins, Gillan, Mike Oldfield.

Records Limited

WEA Records

UK: 20 Broadwick Street
London W1

Umbrella outfit in UK for Warner Bros, Elektra and Atlantic.

Associated Labels: Asylum, Discreet, Radar, Westbound, Sire, Beggar's Banquet, F-Beat, Riva, Swan-Song.

Above: Managing Director of WEA Music in the UK, Mike Heap.

Warner Bros Records

US: 3300 Warner Boulevard
Burbank, CA 91510
3 East 54th Street
New York, NY 10022

Despite Groucho Marx's famous letter to the company (where he doubts that they were real brothers) Harry, Sam and Jack were indeed kin. The three Warner brothers founded their operation in 1925 to develop sound movies ('Don Juan', 'The Jazz Singer'). A short-lived venture with Brunswick Records in 1930 curtailed the company's record operation until the late '50s. Now a giant in the industry, with acts and clout to match.

Associated Labels: Reprise, Sire, Bearsville, Dark Horse, ECM, Slash, Geffen, Curb.
Major Artists: The Who, Fleetwood Mac, Frank Sinatra, Doobie Bros, Randy Crawford, Ry Cooder, Christopher Cross, George Benson, Emmylou Harris, Rod Stewart, Soft Cell, George Harrison, Devo, Randy Newman, Foghat.

Alembic

45 Foley Street
Santa Rosa, CA 95401
USA
Founded US 1969.

Husband and wife team Ron and Susan Wickersham started the Alembic guitar company at instigation of the Grateful Dead, for whom the couple worked as sound specialists. Initially offering a customising serviced, the Wickershams soon began building their own instruments, with emphasis on active electronic circuitry.

Alembic specialise in bass guitars, which are made at the company's plant in Santa Rosa, California. Bass virtuoso Stanley Clarke leads the pack of Alembic enthusiasts.

Main guitars: Long Scale Point, Long Scale Omega, Series II.

Above: Collector John Entwistle (the Who) with Alembic 'Explorer' bass.

Ampeg

Box 310
Elkhart IN 46515
USA
Founded US 1950.

Primarily an amplification company, Ampeg launched their first instrument in 1962, an upright cello-styled electric bass, and began importing Burns guitars to the US.

An association with Dan Armstrong produced the unique 'See-Through' plastic-bodied guitars and basses, which gained notoriety in late '60s (and an avid fan in Stones' Keith Richard).

Ampeg and Armstrong split in 1971, and the company reverted to more traditional guitar styling, albeit with a scroll peghead.

Main guitar: Dan Armstrong Clear Body, Dan Armstrong Fretless Bass.

Aria

41 1-chome Kandacho
Chikusaku
Nagoya
Japan
Founded Japan 1956.

Japanese concert guitarist Shiro Aria launched his company as a specialist classical guitar operation before following the Japanese tradition of copying, and then perfecting, electric instruments.

SB 1000 bass has been a mainstay of Jack

Bruce's armoury for some time, while the Les Paul-styled PE-R80 has found particular favour in the US.

Main guitars: Rev Sound Series, Super Twin Series, Tri Sound Series, Pro Electric Series, Cardinal Series, Urchin Series, TX Series, Rock Series, Super Bass Series, Rock Bass Series, Western Acoustic Series.

Dan Armstrong

Founded US 1972.

Long-time active repairman/designer (and articulate salesman for his products), Armstrong popularised the sliding pick-up (first used on his 'See-Through' Ampeg instruments).

Armstrong's other liaisons have been with Danelectro, and Fender, for whom he modified the Stratocaster circuitry. He is also an avid special effects instigator.

B.C. Rich

4770 Valley Blvd, No. 117
Los Angeles, CA 90032
USA
Founded US 1969.

Bernardo Chavez Rico started out in his father's workshop in late '40s, opening his own electric guitar operation in 1969 in Los Angeles.

Most of the construction is done by hand, limiting production to approximately 2,000 guitars per year, although the B.C. Rico line is manufactured in Japan.

Superior workmanship has attracted the likes of Neil Geraldo (Pat Benatar) and Craig Chaquitco (Jefferson Starship) to the B.C. Rich fold.

Main guitar: The Bich, Eagle, Mockingbird, Wave, Warlock, Seagull.

Burns

Actualisers Ltd.
Padnal Road
Littleport, Ely
Cambridge
England
Founded UK late 1950s.

Burns guitars were Fender's closest rivals in the UK during '60s, and were even played (for a time) by erstwhile Fender devotees, the Shadows. It was a Burns' 12 string that provided the classic intros to the Searcher's

Needles And Pins and **When You Walk In The Room**.

British designer James Burns sold his company to Baldwin (US) in 1965, whereupon the famous Bison range established an international reputation.

Main guitars: Bison, Sonic, Scorpion.

D'Angelico

Founded US 1932.

New Yorker John D'Angelico began building guitars in 1914 as apprentice to his luthier uncle before embarking on his own, and establishing a reputation as a supreme craftsman.

His hand-made guitars were usually built to order, and were played by many prominent jazz guitarists of the day, despite stiff competition from Gibson.

D'Angelico died in 1964, leaving a legacy of immaculate workmanship.

Main guitars: Style 'A', Style 'B', Excel, New Yorker.

D'Aquisto

14 Willow Park Center
Farmingdale, NY 11735
USA
Founded US 1960s.

A former apprentice to fellow New Yorker John D'Angelico, James D'Aquisto followed his tutor's tradition of fine acoustic guitars, which he now supplements with the very occasional electric solidbody, and a range of strings.

D'Aquisto's reputation has instigated a four-year waiting list for his instruments, which grace many a hit recording. Studio guitarist Sal DiTroia (who worked with Paul Simon and Don McLean among others) is a leading D'Aquisto exponent.

Main guitar: New Yorker Special.

Daion

5-358 Motomachi
Naniwa-Ku, Osaka 556
Japan
Founded Japan 1978.

Because of the way in which they have been marketed, most Japanese guitars are not produced or designed by personalities. One major exception is the range produced by Hirotsugu Teradaira of Daion. His company has made the policy of issuing a specific 'Year Series' of instruments—the '81 Series was designed in 1981 by Teradaira, the '82 in 1982, and so on, having commenced in 1978 with a solid cedar topped acoustic guitars set.

Daion have also produced their own range of solid bodied electric models, although they are best known for their acoustics and semi-acoustics.

Main guitars: Year series 1978 on, Mugen, Power X Series.

Danelectro

Founded US 1948.

If you didn't play a Futurama, then you probably bought a Danelectro as your first

guitar. The famous Danelectro Silvertone was sold by Sears, Roebuck through their mail-order catalogue, and endeared two generations in '50s and '60s.

Nathan Daniel started Danelectro after a period building amps for other manufacturers (notably Epiphone). His first guitar was introduced in 1965, and production was maintained until 1968, when MCA, who had taken the company over a year previously, shut down the operation.

The Danelectro name was maintained for a time by Dan Armstrong, who acquired manufacturing equipment and part-completed guitars from the factory.

Top session player Tommy Tedasco uses a '60s Danelectro 6-string Buss.

Main guitars: Silvertone, Pro 1, Convertible, Short Horn Bass, Slimline, Coral Firefly, Coral Long Horn.

Dean

6417 North Ravenswood Avenue
Chicago, IL 60626
USA
Founded US 1970s.

Dean Zelinsky's space-age styling has not overshadowed a quality range of instruments favoured by John McFee (Doobie Bros).

Chicago-based Zelinsky was manufacturing in his late teens, after an apprenticeship customising, repairing and collecting guitars.

Main guitars: ML, Baby Series.

EKO

EKO SpA
1/3 via Ceccaroni
62019 Recanati
Italy
Founded Italy 1962.

EKO acoustics have maintained popularity as a cheap, reliable beginners' instrument, with the Acoustic Bass (fretless or standard) earning a particularly good reputation.

Main guitars: Ranger 6 Acoustic, CO2, BX7 Bass, Acoustic Bass.

Epiphone

Norlin Music Inc.
7373 North Cicero Avenue
Lincolnwood IL 60646
USA
Founded US 1928.

Now part of the Gibson conglomerate, Epiphone originated from the House of Stahapoulo, a banjo/mandolin/violin company based in New York.

Concentrating primarily on arch-top 'F'-hole acoustics, Epiphone nevertheless took advantage of the move to electric models in late '30s under the guidance of inventor Herb Sunshine. He was responsible for the company's individual polepiece pick-up.

Epiphone was acquired by Gibson in 1957, and began offering similar but cheaper models in direct competition to the parent company.

Although never enormously popular with rock musicians, certain models earned respect during '60s, notably the Casino, Riviera, and Sheraton.

The majority of Epiphone instruments (which still include banjos and mandolins) are now made in Japan, although the American Series of guitars, launched in 1982, re-introduced production to Kalamazoo.

Main guitars: Casino, Sheraton, Texas Acoustic, Howard Roberts, Wilshire, Coronet, Riviera, Broadway, Rivoli Bass.

Fender

1402 E. Chestnut,
Santa Ana, CA 92701
USA
Founded US, 1945.

Leo Fender, born in California in 1907, was aware that amplification would begin to make the traditional guitar designs redundant, and that the changing musical styles in the late '40s would require a purpose-built instrument. After a period of experimentation, Fender settled on a one piece ash body, with a laminated maple neck and fingerboard, and launched the Fender Broadcaster in 1948.

The unique cutaway in the guitar's design enabled guitarists to extend their range, adding nearly half an octave to the now completely accessible fingerboard. The sound was achieved by an individually wound pick-up, and a solid brass bridge, where each string could be individually balanced for harmonics, and also raised or lowered to suit the player.

The immediate success of this guitar set other American manufacturers into a quandary, and none so more than Gibson, who had turned down the idea of a solid-body when guitar virtuoso Les Paul had initiated the idea to the company before the Second World War.

Fender's master stroke came in 1950, when he introduced the Stratocaster, the Broadcaster's "big brother", which had the same ash/maple configuration, but a more stylish contoured body, with twin cutaway and three pick-ups. Available in a variety of flashy colours, the Stratocaster quickly became *the* guitar to play in the burgeoning rock 'n' roll market.

The Broadcaster (later superseded by the Telecaster) and Stratocaster were joined by two bass guitars, the Precision and Jazz basses, a logical progression as the double bass was becoming largely inaudible in the electronic climate, now dominated by Fender guitars and amplification.

Jimi Hendrix's affinity with the Stratocaster began when he was discharged from the US Army and began working as a back-up musician for various rock 'n' roll and R&B performers. This intense performer started a series of "Sound-alikes", and wailing Fender Stratocasters (or Strats as they are affectionately called) could be heard from Sausalito to Southend-on-Sea. None, however, had the same desire, emotion or ability. The sight of Hendrix in full swing picking the guitar strings with his teeth while still coaxing a fluid melody, may yet prove to be the Stratocaster's eventual epitaph.

The jangling rhythm guitar of Buddy Holly was a trade mark of all his classic rock 'n' roll records. The spiralling introduction on **That'll Be The Day**, and the loosely picked chords of **Words Of Love** have the classic Stratocaster sound, and he most certainly took the guitar as a lead instrument to a whole new audience.

The Shadow's Hank Marvin is one who has acknowledged a debt to Buddy Holly but Marvin saw further potential with the "three guitar group", and the Shadows began to dominate the charts in the early '60s with a series of pop instrumentals, ranging from the haunting **Wonderful Land** to their most identifiable recording **Apache**. The Shadows had a full complement of Fender guitars, for apart from Marvin's Stratocaster, rhythm guitarist Bruce Welch played a Telecaster, and bassist Jet Harris a Jazz bass.

Leo Fender sold his company to CBS in 1965, bringing to an end nearly 20 years of unbridled imagination and quality to the guitar industry. Fender is still active in the business, and now has his own G&L company, after a period as consultant for Music Man.

Main Guitars: Stratocaster, Telecaster, Musicmaster.

Basses: Jazz, Precision, Musicmaster.

G & L

2548 East Fender Avenue
Unit G
Fullerton, CA 92631
USA
Founded US 1980.

G & L marked Leo Fender's return to autonomous guitar production, in collaboratin with his long-time associate George Fullerton. They are based in Fullerton, California.

The F100-1 range has all the Fender hallmarks, complete with integral vibrato.

Main guitars: F100-1 Series, L1000 Series, L2000 Series, G200 Series, S500 Series, SC-3.

Above: Steve Howe, (Yes, Asia) and custom Gibson, based on the 400 CES.

Gibson

244 Parsons Street
Kalamazoo, MI
USA
Founded US, 1902.

Founded over 80 years ago in Kalamazoo, Michigan, by Orville Gibson, the Gibson Mandolin-Guitar Manufacturing Co. Ltd, as it was originally known, has preserved a tradition of excellence.

The blossoming guitar and mandolin market in the early 1900s meant instant success for the Gibson company, and the purchase of a three-storey building in the town established a link with Kalamazoo which is inherent to this day. In fact, Gibson are still based in the same building on Parsons Street.

Aggressive marketing by this pioneering business established Orville Gibson and his designers (most notably Lloyd Loar, instigator of the exquisite F-5 archtop mandolin) as trend setters. They recruited leading musicians with endorsement contracts, and formed their own groups like Gibsonites, who toured the States proclaiming the excellent of the instruments they were using. Gibson even introduced the Army and Navy Mandolin, having secured a contract with the American Armed Forces before the First World War.

The advent of dance bands and jazz took the guitar out of the parlour in the '20s, and the instrument enjoyed halcyon days. Gibson introduced the first known "signature" model guitar in 1925, the Nick Lucas Special, named after a popular radio performer of the time.

The Lucas Special was produced for over ten years, and Gibson achieved further commercial and aesthetic advances with their L-5 guitar an archtop acoustic with F-soundholes, which gave the instrument more attack than conventional roundhole models. It proved the ideal tool for jazz guitarists, who needed clarity and volume in a big-band environment.

The '30s saw Gibson experiment with electric guitars, although in their infancy these were little more than acoustics with an attached microphone, or pick-up. It wasn't until Les Paul encouraged the company to enter the electric market with his own solidbody model in 1952 that Gibson truly entered a new era of guitar manufacture. The parallel success of the Les Paul models and jazz acoustics, most notably the ES-150 (which had been electrified by Charlie Christian in the '30s), Super 400 and L-5 confirmed Gibson as the consummate guitar company during the '50s, although there was considerable opposition from Rickenbacker, Harmony, Kay, Epiphone, Guild, Gretsch and particularly Fender.

Although Gibson went through a period in the late '50s and early '60s when their instruments were considered "old-fashioned", the rock boom re-introduced the Les Paul to a new generation, and this guitar quickly secured a position, shared with the Fender Stratocaster, as the ultimate weapon for the rock'n'roll guitarist.

The single cutaway, and relatively small-bodied Les Paul, contained all the elements needed for the thunderous onslaught of the heavy metal era. Controlled sustain and feedback by the bucket load became trade-marks of the headbanging 200mph HM brigade. Guitarists like Led Zeppelin's Jimmy Page and the Allman Brothers' Band Dickie Betts set the pattern for a million upstart axemen who are today trading riff for riff with their peers.

Gibson were also fortunate in having one of music's finest ambassadors in B.B. King to endorse their instruments. King has for many years played a Gibson ES-355, a stereo model which he controls effortlessly, and there is no question that he and his sound were the single most important influence on guitarists in rock bands of the '60s and '70s.

The semi-solid thin-bodied 355 is also favoured by other standout musicians including Larry Carlton, Eric Gale and George Benson, and Chuck Berry has never taken a duck walk without this model in his hands.

Main Guitars: ES-355, SG Range, Firebrand Range, Les Paul Signature Range, HR Range.

Below: Jimi Hendrix gave Fenders a new voice.

Below: Guitar hero Eric Clapton frequently uses Fender Strats.

Below: John Deacon (left) of Queen onstage with a Fender Jazz bass.

Below: Yet another famous Fender customer, veteran Jeff Beck.

Gordon Smith

10 Dawson Road
Broad Heath
Altrincham, Cheshire
England
Founded UK 1970s.

Gordon Smith is an independent operation run by a collective of British luthiers based in Lancashire.

Instruments are hand built and carry a 25-year guarantee.

Main guitars: GS Series, Flying V, Explorer, Gypsy Series, Gemini.

Gretsch

908 West Chestnut
Chanute, KS 66720
USA
Founded US 1883.

Guitar manufacture did not play an important part in Gretsch's progress until the mid-'30s, the company concentrating on its successful drum and cymbal (having bought out Zildjian) operation.

A variety of arch- and flat-top acoustics paved the way for the Gretsch hollow-bodied electrics, made famous by the legendary Chet Atkins, who lent his name to model 6120. This guitar has been played by Eddie Cochran, Pete Townshend and Scotty Moore.

Atkins later endorsed the Country Gentleman, the Super Chet, Super Axe and Chet Atkins' Solid Body. All have become classics, with Atkins himself expressing a penchant for the Country Gentleman.

After a series of business transactions, most notably Gretsch's acquisition by Baldwin, and calamitous fires, the company ceased guitar making in 1981.

Main guitars: Chet Atkins Hollow Body, Corvette, Astro-Jet, Duo-Jet, Rancher, White Falcon, White Penguin, Country Club, Country Gentleman, Anniversary, Tennessean, Gretsch Electric Bass, Super Chet, Gretsch Monkees model (named after the Monkees pop group).

Guild

225 West Grand Street
Box 203
Elizabeth, NJ 07207
USA
Founded US 1952.

Guild soon outgrew its early New York premises, moving to New Jersey in 1956 and establish-

ing a range that was to include 50 models in early '60s.

Always one to recognise the power of endorsement, Dronge, himself a talented classical player, recruited rock 'n' roll instrumentalist Duane Eddy to expound the virtues of Guild. Two Eddy signature models, the DE-500 Deluxe and DE-400 Standard, became synonymous with the 'King of Twang'.

The success of the Duane Eddy/Guild partnership prompted the company into further liaisons, and Richie Havens, Charlie Byrd, George Benson and Eric Clapton joined the Guild fold.

Guild are probably more renowned for acoustic, rather than electric, guitars, although the S-100 solidbody (similar to the Gibson SG series) became a popular rock instrument in mid-'70s.

Main guitars: F-20 acoustic, F-50 acoustic, Artist, Duane Eddy DE-500 Deluxe, Starfire, S-100, X-500, S-60D.

Hagström

Hagström Musik
P.O. Box 1140
S-11181
Stockholm
Sweden
Founded Sweden 1920s.

Swedish farmhand Albin Hagström began making piano accordians in '20s as a hobby, moving to guitar production — on the instigation of his son Karl — in late '50s.

Apart from Hagström acoustics, their most famous brand name was the Futurama, a cheap, but solid line of instruments which was the predecessor of the Japanese 'copies'

Above: Pete Townshend (the Who) now uses a variety of Fender, Gibson, Gretsch, and Schecter models.

available today.

Despite a move into synthesiser electronics, Hagström found the pace too fast, and ceased production in mid-'70s.

Main guitars: Futurama I, Futurama II, Hagström 8 String Bass.

Hamer

835 West University Drive
Arlington Heights, IL 60004
USA
Founded US 1970s.

Hamer's first entry into guitar production was an excellent copy of the Gibson Explorer, a flashy instrument which found immediate

Above: 'Abominable Showman' Nick Lowe, shows off his Hamer 8-string bass.

approval from Cheap Trick's avid axe collector Rick Nielson.

The Hamer company, named after Paul Hamer (whose partner is Joel Dantzig), is based in Illinois, where they have maintained their affinity with Gibson, and developed a specialised custom order business.

Main guitars: Sunburst, Prototype, Special, Vector, Standard, Cruise Bass.

Harmony

International Music Corp.
P.O. Box 2344
Fort Worth, TX 76113
USA
Founded US 1892.

At one time, Harmony produced half of American guitar output, and was producing over one quarter million instruments (including mandolins, violins and banjos) per year during early '20s.

Willie Schultz, a German immigrant who had previously worked for the Knapp Drum Co., operated out of a loft in downtown Chicago, initially producing ukeleles.

Schultz' fast-growing operation was acquired by Sears, Roebuck in 1916 who quickly increased the company's range of guitars.

Throughout '20s and '30s, Harmony was as synonymous with guitars as Ford was with cars, and sales spiralled upward until '60s, when Japanese imports threatened the US home market. At this time, Harmony were manufacturing a wide range of solidbodys and semi-acoustics, albeit along Gibson-style lines.

The Japanese competition finally proved too much for Harmony, who shut down in 1975, just 10 years after producing 350,000 guitars in one 12-month stretch.

Main guitars: H61 Meteor, H22 Bass, Stratotone, H-62, Stella 12 String, Cremona, Roy Smeck Vita, Roy Smeck Grand Concert.

Harptone

Founded US 1893.

Long-established acoustic specialists, who also produced a limited range of electrics, notably their large-bodied George Harrison/Ringo Starr endorsed model.

Production switched from New Jersey to Virginia when the Harptone name was sold to Diamond S in 1975.

Main guitars: D-10 Acoustic, D-20 Acoustic, D-30 Acoustic, C-20 Jumbo, B-4 Acoustic Bass, T-20.

Höfner

Schoenbacherstrasse 56
D 8521 Bubenreuth
West Germany
Founded Germany 1957.

Paul McCartney's Höfner violin bass may go down in history as the most identifiable instrument ever played by a rock band.

McCartney's affinity for his guitar allowed Höfner a sizeable share of the UK market during '60s, but the line soon became unfashionable and now fills a role as a respectable beginner's instrument.

Main guitars: Verithin, Violin Bass, President, Galaxie, S9C.

Hohner

Hohner A.G.
P.O. Box
D 7218 Trossingen
West Germany
Founded Germany 1857.

Primarily a keyboard/harmonica company, Hohner produce a range of economy electric guitars and basses and acoustic models.

Hohner celebrated their 125th anniversary in 1982.

Main guitars: MS Series, MF-250, MB Basses.

Hondo

International Music Corp.
P.O. Box 2344
Fort Worth, TX 76113
USA
Founded Japan 1969.

Hondo (trade name of International Music Corporation) instruments are made in either Japan or South Korea, and as such have a variable quality control. They are, however, reasonably priced instruments which have some individual body styling. Hondo Chiquita 'travel' guitars have found favour as practice instruments, and the CH-4 doubles effectively as a guitar or bass with a change of strings and nut.

Main guitars: Chiquita, Professional Series, De Luxe Series, H830S Bass, Encore Series, H 781 Flame.

Ibanez

Fuji Gen-Gakki
793 Yoshikawa Hirata
Matsumoto-shi
Nagan Pref. 499-65
Japan
Founded Japan 1960s.

In mid-'60s, the rock 'n' roll boom created an insatiable demand for leading American brands of guitars, a trend quickly followed by Far East manufacturers. They produced copies of the favourite axes of the period — notably the Fender Stratocaster — and for a price that every aspiring rock guitarist could afford.

Although many of these companies quickly disappeared, Ibanez maintained production and developed their own models. These were

Above: Sting (Police) uses both an upright bass and an Ibanez.

endorsed by the likes of Lee Ritenour, George Benson and Joe Pass—a notable trio in anyone's books—and Ibanez moved into frontline of guitar innovators. Other Ibanez guitar users include Steve Hillage, Phil Lynott ,Pat Simmons, Jim Cregan, Steve Miller, Bob Weir and Sting.

To some extent, Ibanez have maintained their penchant for imitation, notably the Stratocaster-like Blazer series, and now enjoy the best of both worlds with a range that is as large and varied as any leading US company.

Main guitars: Artist Range, Musician Range, Jazz Series ,Artist Semi-Acoustic Rnage, Personality Series, Destroyer Range, Iceman Range, Blazer Range, Studio Range, Rock 'n' Roll Range, Artwood Acoustic Range, CR10, JP20, GB20.

Jay Dee

Unit 2, 153 Brighton Road
Moseley, Birmingham B12 8QN
England
Founded UK 1970s.

John Diggens ('Jay Dee' or J.D.) served his guitar making apprenticeship with luthier John Birch. Diggens eventually went solo and

his remarkable craftsmanship became acknowledged by an impressive list of players, including Tony Iommi and Geezer Butler (Black Sabbath), John Thomas (Budgie), Mark King (Level 42) and Angus Young (AC/DC). Jay Dee guitars are also noted for their elaborate decorations; mother of pearl rings of Saturn as fretboard inlays, flashing LED's, Union Jack colours, even a six foot flying 'V' for Budgie!

Main guitars: Roadie, Hooligan.

Kay

3057 North Rockwell Street
Chicago, IL 60618
USA
Founded US 1931.

Chicago-based company that sprung to prominence in mid-'30s with good value acoustic and electric guitars.

Founded by Henry Kay Kuhrmeyer (former President of the Stromberg-Voisinet guitar/mandolin company, which evolved into Kay on Kuhrmeyer's appointment), the company had to work hard to stay the pace with Gibson, Martin and Harmony.

Some innovative designs (including a contraption that would form a chord at the push of a button) enabled Kay to expand well into '60s.

Kay changed hands a couple of times before being shut down in 1968 as a result of a depression in the American guitar industry and an influx of Japanese imports.

The Kay trade name now appears on the very same imported guitars that caused its decline.

Main guitars: K310, K-155, Kay Kraft Range, Kay/Kessell Gold Kay Series, Pro, Artist, Jazz Special, Flying V.

Kramer

BKL International Corp.
1111 Green Grove Road
Neptune, NJ 07753.
USA
Founded US 1975.

Young American company whose guitars feature a detachable aluminium neck. Gary Kramer, Dennis Barardi and Peter LaPlaca started Kramer as a contender for the quality end of the guitar market, although they had struggled in the face of opposition from the likes of Gibson, B. C. Rich and Fender.

Despite lending his name to the company, Kramer left in 1976 to join Travis Bean as a designer/consultant/partner.

Main guitar: V Bass, Voyager, 650 Series, 420 Series.

Lowden

K. Irving Distributors
67-71 Dublin Road
Belfast BT2 7LU
Northern Ireland
Founded UK 1981.

George Lowden, a young Northern Irishman, had already built himself a reputation in his native country as a maker of traditional folk instruments when the opportunity came to him to design and develop a whole range of

acoustic guitars to be manufactured in Japan to his designs and under his guidance.

Lowden guitars have quickly established an enviable reputation, combining the qualities of a hand-made guitar in a production-built instrument. Lowdens sell, although at a fairly high price by mass market standards, for considerably less than similar handmade models.

Main guitars: L25, L34.

Manson

Windsor Place, Jarvis Brook
Crowborough, Sussex TN6 2HU
England
Founded UK 1970s.

Two brothers, Hugh and Andy Manson, working from a small workshop in Sussex, have established a tremendous following in the past few years. The Mansons divide their work between Hugh, who makes the acoustic instruments, and Andy, who specialises in electrics.

Early devotees of Manson guitars included John Paul Jones of Led Zeppelin, who went to them for a triple neck guitar. Since then they have even made four-necked models, in both acoustic and solid body formats. They have even made a fold-down guitar which fits into a suitcase!

Main guitars: Kestrel, Sandpiper Acoustic, Magpie Acoustic.

Martin

Box 329
Nazareth, PA 18064
USA
Founded US 1833.

The Grandaddy of all acoustic guitar manufacturers, the C. F. Martin Co. was started by German émigré Christian Friedrich Martin.

Martin opened a shop in New York on his arrival in the States, where he put his previous experience as a workshop foreman for a violin/guitar luthier in Vienna to good use.

Martin moved to Nazareth six years later, and this valley town in Eastern Pennsylvania has housed the company ever since. The business still remains in the Martin family.

The extraordinary success of Martin guitars goes way beyond a traditional 'rags to riches' story, and is reflected in the feeling that to own a Martin is like owning a Rolls Royce. Cost has nothing to do with it. After all, Martins retail at an average $850, and many an independent guitar maker charges more than four times that price (the most expensive Martins, the

D-45 and OM-45, retail for $2,200).

Until recently, the company offered a lifetime warranty (to the original owner) on all models, and this added an aura of confidence for any prospective purchaser.

The adage 'the older they get the better they get' can certainly be applied to a Martin; the noted acoustic instrument store Mandolin Bros, of Staten Island, New York, were charging upwards of $6,000 for a 1938 D-28 herringbone model (current list price $1,400) in their summer '82 catalogue.

Perhaps the answer lies in their continued use (and without endorsement) by the world's leading musicians. Almost without exception, leading members of the rock guitarist fraternity own Martins.

The current range of Martin acoustics, which include the famous Dreadnought and 'M' series, is supplemented by four solidbody electrics introduced in 1979.

Appreciating the problems caused by the influx of cheap Far Eastern imports, Martin now supplement their catalogue with the Sigma line, which are inspected at their Nazareth factory complex after manufacture in Japan.

Main guitars: D (Dreadnought) Series: 18, 19, 28, 35, HD-28, HD-35, DC-28 (cutaway), D-41 (Pearl inlay), D-45 (Pearl inlay); small-bodied Dreadnoughts: 7-28, 7-37K; D & OM Series: M-36, M-38, MC-28 (cutaway), OM-45; 12-strings: D-12-18, D-12-28; Koa Wood Dreadnoughts: D-25K, D-25K2, D-37K,

D-37K2; Re-issues: D-28 Herringbone, OM-28 (1930), D-45 (1939); Electrics: EM-18, E-18, EM-18 Bass, E-18 Bass.

Above: Much-respected Chet Atkins 'picks' a Martin acoustic.

Mosrite

Founded US 1959.

An extraordinary publicity campaign by the Ventures turned Semie Moseley's small custom-guitar business into a full-scale manufacturing operation in early '60s.

On the instigation of Ventures' lead guitarist Nokie Edwards (and with $75,000 of the group's money), Moseley designed a range of guitars that bore the legend 'The Ventures play only the Mosrite guitar'. Bearing in mind that the Ventures had begun a period of chart success unprecedented for a US instrumental group, one can see why the Mosrite instruments quickly scaled the sales charts.

A deal for amplification by the Ventures, which Moseley endorsed, was for the most part responsible for the downfall of Mosrite. Amplifiers were an alien world to Moseley, and the Mosrite Award model received considerable criticism. The investment was soon lost, and Moseley began looking around for assistance.

A short-lived tenure with Dobro had ceased, and Moseley approached country star Buck Owens, Buddy Ross of the Kustom company, Pacific Music (Guild's distributors) and the Japanese outfit Hiro before setting up a deal which ensured a further period of production.

Hiro now produce a limited range of Mosrite guitars, primarily for home consumption, where the Ventures — and the Mosrite guitar — have retained immense popularity.

Main guitars: Mosrite Ventures range, V-1, CO Mk 1 3000, Celebrity 111, Joe Maphis Model, Mk V Model 101, D-1000 Californian.

Music Man

1338 State College Parkway
Anaheim, CA 92803
USA
Founded US 1972.

Noted primarily for their association with Leo Fender, Music Man entered the mainstream of guitar manufacture with a range designed and built by Fender, featuring, not surprisingly, all the maestro's ideas and innovations.

The company is owned by former Fender employees Forrest White and Thomas Walker and is based in Southern California.

Main guitars: Stingray bass, Sabre II.

National

National (Dobro)
Original Musical Instrument Co.
18108 Redondo Circle
Huntington Beach, CA 92648
USA
Founded US 1972.

Known mainly for their resonator-bodied acoustic guitars, National, and close relatives Dobro, were also involved in a range of solid and semi-acoustic electrics in the '60s.

Czechoslovakian immigrant John Dopyera is generally recognised as the inventor of the resophonic guitar, and, with his brothers, he developed the uniquely styled and innovative instruments for more than 50 years.

Dobro guitars are now distributed by OMI (Original Musical Instrument Company) of Long Beach, California.

Below: George Harrison's collection includes several Dobros.

Main guitars: Dobro Model 66, Dobro 33H, Dobro 33D, Supro Folk Star, Regal-Dobro Artist, Dobro 27G, Dobro 37G, Dobro 45G, National Trojan, National Estrelita, National El Trovador, National Style I, National Style O. Electrics: Dobro Electric Hawaiian Guitar, National Aristocrat, National Sonora, National Dynamic, National Debonaire, National Town & Country, Supro Dual-Tone, National Stylist, National Glenwood 98, Supro Belmont, Supro Bermuda, National Bel-Aire, National 84, National 85, bass.

Ovation

Blue Hills Avenue
Bloomfield, CT 06002
USA
Founded US, 1963.

The round-backed, fibre-glass bodied Ovation guitars introduced by designer Charles Kaman in 1966, were the first major innovation in guitar construction since the research into sound braces at the end of the last century.

Kaman, an avid amateur guitarist, runs his own aerospace company. Part of his manufacturing business involved fusing fibreglass and Sitka spruce into strong, yet flexible helicopter rotor blades. Kaman took this process a step further, utilising the material lyrachord for the bowl-shaped backs which were married to Sitka spruce soundboards.

Traditionalists were both surprised and amused by the Ovation guitar, and even more astonished when the idea gained almost immediate acceptance from a variety of established performers, notably Glen Campbell.

Initial production for the guitars was carried out in New Hartford, New England, although the operation has now diversified into various parts of North-East America, including a research/engineering plant at Bloomfield, Connecticut, near Kaman's Corporate headquarters.

The Ovation range was extended to include acoustic/electric guitars based on the standard models, but including a built-in pickup mounted directly beneath the saddle.

Kaman has since introduced more traditional methods for Ovation solidbody electric guitars, whilst veering further into the space age with the Adamas series, a guitar with soundholes in the upper body, and a soundboard constructed from epoxy-graphite.

Amongst the fine guitarists who use Ovation/Adamas are jazz virtuoso Larry Coryell, country star Roy Clark and jazz-rock exponent Al Di Meola.

Main guitars: 6-string acoustic, acoustic/electrics: Balladeer, Custom Balladeer, Artist, Legend, Glen Campbell, Anniversary, Legend Ltd., Custom Legend, Elite, Folklore.

Above: Virtuoso John McLaughlin onstage with an Ovation acoustic.

12-string acoustic, acoustic/electric: Custom Balladeer 12, Legend 12, Custom Legend 12.
Nylon-string acoustic, acoustic/electric: Country Arist Artist, Concert Classic, Classic. Cutaway acoustic/electric: Country Artist, Classic, Balladeer, Legend, Legend Shallow Bowl, Custom Legend.
Solidbody electrics: Viper, Magnum bass, Adamas Range, Preacher Series.

Peavey

Peavey Electronics
711 A Street
Meridian, MS 39301
USA
Founded US 1966.

A graduate of Mississippi State University, Hartley Peavey began building amplifiers, a domestic operation that was at last challenging the influx of Far Eastern imports.

By the end of '70s, Peavey had launched a range of guitars which mirrored his amplifier operation—'build 'em cheap, but build 'em good'. The guitars were designed with the help of computers, bringing space-age technology to the rock musician.

Main guitar: T-Series.

Rickenbacker

3895 South Main
Santa Ana, CA 92707
USA
Founded US 1932.

Like many of the historical American guitar companies, Rickenbacker was started by a European émigré. Adolph Rickenbacker, a Swiss tool craftsman, inaugurated the Electro String Instrument Corporation initially to produce the Hawaiian lap steel guitar.

Credit for the invention of the electric guitar has often been laid at Rickenbacker's door, although with the frantic development of the instrument in early '30s, this has never been definitely confirmed.

With a steady business built around sales of pick-ups, steel guitars and amplifiers, Rickenbacker did not enter the pop and rock market until late '50s, when his distinctive double-cutaway solids and semi-acoustic models were issued.

Rickenbacker's unique styling attracted some notable performers, finding favour first with Ricky Nelson and, in mid-'60s, with Roger McGuinn of the Byrds, whose jangling 12-string Rickenbacker earned this American band an immediately identifiable sound.

John Lennon was another Rickenbacker advocate and Paul McCartney used a Rickenbacker bass after dispensing with his Höfner violin model; they were followed by Credence Clearwater's John Fogerty and Pete Townshend whose destructive antics were monitored by a generation of young guitar freaks.

Particularly well-known for their rhythm guitars, Rickenbacker have had occasional surges in popularity, especially when guitar heroes act as unpaid advocates of their axes. More recently, Paul Weller from the Jam, Tom Petty and Spandau Ballet's Gary Kemp have voiced their attachment to Rickenbacker.

Introduced in 1964, the 330 remains the archetypal Rickenbacker, a twin cutaway semi-acoustic with two pick-ups that has seen little modification in its near 20-year lifespan.

Main guitars: 330, Capri, Capri 12 String, 365, 375, 325 (¾ size), 366-12, 320, 360, 360-12, 366-12, 370, 4080, 4001, 4001 bass, 4000 bass, 4005/6 6 string bass, 4002 bass, 4080/12 bass/12 string doubleneck, Combo 1000, 450, Combo 850, BD Lap Steel.

Schecter

Schecter Guitar Research
6164 Sepulveda Blvd.
Van Nuys, CA 91411
USA
Founded US 1977.

Repairman/toolmaker David Schecter was in demand with LA studio musicians as a 'guitar doctor' when he started his customised spare-parts business.

Schecter's 'bolt on' range for Fender and Gibson guitars now encompasses 900 items, none of which requires any modification for a perfect 'fit'.

Schecter guitars were developed as a public relations exercise to demonstrate the innumerable spare-parts catalogue. Based on well-known Fender bodies, Schecters quickly found favour with legendary axemen such as Jeff Beck and Mark Knopfler.

Main guitar: Schecter Custom Bodies

Shergold

9 Avenue Industrial Estate
Southend Arterial Road
Harold Wood, Romford
Essex RM3 0BY
England
Founded UK 1960s.

Long-established British manufacturers, Shergold remain the UK's main rival to the American/Japanese influx.

Started by Jack Golder and Norman Holder, the company received a boost when Genesis' Mike Rutherford appeared on stage with a Shergold double-neck (bass/guitar), although the company's most popular model is the Masquerader, which resembles a cross between a Burns Bison and a Fender Stratocaster.

Main guitars: Modulator Series, Masquerader Series, Custom Double Neck Series, Marathon Series, Activator Series.

Steinberger

475 Oakland Avenue
Staten Island City, NY 11105
USA
Founded US 1978.

The introduction of industrial engineer Ned Steinberger's bass guitar caused a revolution in the instrument world. The bass had no headstock, the strings were tuned from machine heads on the guitar's tiny body and the instrument itself had no wood in it at all—the whole body/neck assembly being moulded from carbon graphite fibre and glass fibre reinforced expoxy resin. These materials endow the Steinberger with an unmatched sustain and harmonic purity, not to mention a physical strength many times greater than is possible with any type of wood. The 24 fret Steinberger measures a mere 38″ in overall length and weighs eight pounds (slightly less than a Fender Precision) although Steinberger claim that their bass has twice the density of wood.

So successful was the Steinberger that a host of imitators followed—many of which were laughable imitations and only one of which, the British-made Strata bass, (which features wooden side pieces mounted on the carbon graphite body and has some shared patented features from Steinberger used under licence) was commendable.

Users of Steinberger basses include John Entwistle, Gerald V. Casale (Devo), Tony Levin, Marcus Miller (Miles Davis), Sting, and Bill Wyman.

Steinberger have recently introduced a six string guitar version of their concept.

Main guitars: Steinberger bass (L2).

Takamine

Takamine Gakki Co. Ltd.
933 Sakashita-cho Ena
Gifu-Pref
Japan
Founded Japan 1968.

Takamine make no solid bodied instruments and do not have the typical industrial production set-up; their plant is in the Japanese countryside. Headed by founder, Mass Hirade, Takamine produces only high quality instruments, with apparent disregard for the mass market.

Takamine have an older workforce than most guitar making companies, only skilled craftsmen being employed by Hirade. The classical range takes his name.

The major breakthrough into the international marketplace came when Takamine became involved with Kaman (makers of Ovation guitars) on the development of transducer technology. As a result, Takamine have now become a major name throughout Europe and the US. Perhaps their most respected customer is classical/popular guitarist John Williams.

Main guitars: Hirade classics, EF3605 6-string electric acoustic.

Above: '60s fan Paul Weller (Jam, Style Council) plays Rickenbackers.

Tokai

36 Terawaki-cho
Hamamatsu
Shizuoka 430
Japan
Founded Japan 1980.

Superior copyists of US brands. Somewhat more expensive than most Eastern imitators.

Main guitar: Flying 'V'.

Travis Bean

11671 Sheldon Street
Sun Valley, CA 91352
USA
Founded US 1974.

Former professional motorcycle racer, Travis Bean started his business in mid-'70s with partners Marc McElwee and Gary Kramer (instigator of the aluminium-necked Kramer guitars).

Based in Sun Valley, California, Travis Bean's aluminium-necked guitars were manufactured until 1979, when Bean left the guitar world after disagreements with his business and financial advisers.

Main guitar: Artist 1000.

Vigier

Capelle M.I. Ltd.
333A London Road
Hadleigh, Essex
England
Founded France 1970s.

Patrice Vigier heads a team of six craftsmen, who, apart from turning extremely fine quality woods into handsome instruments, are experts in the electronics field. They have devised a system of active powered tone controls which function particularly well. Vigier have some unique constructional ideas too, such as a metal plate beneath the fingerboard to increase sustain and harmonic transference through to the pickups.

Vigier are soon to launch a long-awaited development in the guitar world—an active instrument with a programmable memory, which could possibly become the guitar or bass player's answer to the synthesiser and put Vigier at the forefront of a technological revolution.

Main guitars: Arpege guitar and bass.

Vox

32/34 Gordon House Road
London NW5 1NE
England
Founded UK 1958.

The Tom Jennings designed Vox AC 30 amp has passed into legend among rock guitarists, and is still favoured as studio and stage equipment — Rory Gallagher swears by them. The Vox guitar range was launched in mid-'60s to supplement the company's amplifier range, finding immediate favour with English 'beat groups' of the time.

The unique Tear Drop model had a certain curiosity value, and Vox also launched the organ guitar, a short-lived project which satisfied neither guitarists nor keyboard players.

Vox ceased manufacture in 1969, reappearing some 10 years later with production transferred to Japan.

Main guitars: Phantom Series, Tear Drop Series, Standard Series, Custom Series.

Wal

Electric Wood
Sandown Works
Chairborough Road
High Wycombe,
Bucks HP12 3HH
England
Founded UK 1977.

John Perry and Ian Waller founded their company Electric Wood in order to produce a range of high-quality, British-made bass guitars.

Favoured by such musicians as Percy Jones (Brand X), John Illsley (Dire Straits) and Mike Kahn, the Wal bass has proved a strong rival to the prominent American manufacturer Alembic.

Main guitars: Custom, Pro 1E, Pro 1.

Washburn

Fretted Instruments Inc.
1415 Waukegan Road
Northbrook, IL 60062
USA
Founded US 1876.

A major manufacturer of acoustic guitars and mandolins (under the aegis of the Lyon and

Healey brand name), the Washburn name was acquired by a Japanese company in early '70s, who instigated a range of solid-body electric, and acoustic/electric guitars. Washburn mandolins are now endorsed by famed jazz/bluegrass exponent Jethro Burns, while the Moody Blues' John Lodge plays the Festival acoustic/electric.

All instruments are vetted at the Fretted Industries factory in Northbrook, Illinois.

Main guitars: Wing Series, Stage Series, Festival Acoustic/Electric range.

Westone

11 Namiayangi
Matsumoto
Japan
Founded Japan 1980.

Value-for-money outfit currently earning a solid reputation in the UK. The Westone Paduak (named after the wood used for the

Below: The men of Men At Work, Colin Hay (left), and Ron Strykert (right), work with Yamahas.

body) has active electronic circuitry for a price that other manufacturers only dream about.

Main guitars: Paduak, Concorde Series, Rainbow Series, Thunder Series.

Yamaha

Nippon Gakki Co. Ltd.
10-1 Nakazawa-cho
Hamamatsu
Shizuoka 430
Japan
Founded Japan 1887.

Yamaha did not mass produce guitars until the '60s, and then, ironically (but typical of the Far East) moved actively in the 'facsimile' market.

Their product is now considered preeminent among Japanese competitors, having secured a reputation for innovative electronics, and solid styling. Yamaha's acoustic guitar range has satisfied many leading players; the solidbody electric SBG2000 series has attracted top rock axemen, notably Carlos Santana.

Main guitars: SBG Series, SHB Series, SSC Series, SC Series, SA Series, BB bass Series, L-20 Acoustic Series, Classic and Folk Series Acoustics.

Gretsch

908 West Chestnut
Chanute, KS 66720
USA

Founded by German immigrant, Fred Gretsch, the company's history began with the manufacture of banjos and other stringed instruments though they were probably the *first* drum makers in the US.

Gretsch have always had the reputation of producing high-quality kits, much favoured by jazz players and session percussionists who enjoy the traditional 'wooden' sound which the kits produce. A suprisingly large number of well-known drummers who actually endorse other kits, and use them on stage, keep Gretsch kits for their fabled recorded sound.

Probably the major Gretsch endorsees down the years have been American star Chico Hamilton and Charlie Watts of the Rolling Stones.

The Baldwin company (owners of the Gretsch name for some time) have done little with the product—their UK branch having been for some reason particularly reluctant to promote it. Recently, however, the Gretsch company has been sold to Charlie Roy (owner of the American amp makers Kustom) and it seems as if some life could soon be injected into this illustrious name.

Ludwig

Ludwig International Ltd.
1728 Damen Avenue
Chicago, IL 60647
Founded US 1930s.

William F. Ludwig Sr travelled with his parents from Germany to the New World in 1887. He was trained as a musician (at his father's insistence).

William later teamed up with his father in the Wood Brothers Circus, playing one-night stands, 14 shows a week, travelling by wagon across the country from venue to venue.

Eventually, Ludwig found himself faced with a musical form which his primitive equipment couldn't handle. This was back in the Follies of 1907, when he encountered 'syncopation'. His old-fashioned wooden bass drum pedal wouldn't allow him to keep up with the beat.

Ludwig cast around for a pedal fast enough to handle this new rhythmical pattern—and failed. In the end he made his own. With the help of his brother-in-law, he established a small production base for his newly-designed pedal in a barn on the Northwest side of Chicago.

By 1909, William F. Ludwig had risen to the ranks of the Pittsburgh Symphony Orchestra as a timpanist. Again, Ludwig decided that he should make his own timpani pedal. Three years later the first set was developed and sold to the St Paul Symphony Orchestra. The first proper factory owned by the Ludwig Company was eventually established on North Lincoln Street, Chicago (the city the company has been established in and associated with ever since).

Ragtime and jazz started to capture American hearts and minds, and Ludwig even made banjos for a few years while this instrument was all the rage (some of these all-steel models are still being used today).

The Great Depression forced Ludwig into a merger with brass makers C.G. Conn in 1930, but, frustrated with being little more than a

Above: Keith Moon of the Who destroyed several Premier kits.

salesman, he parted company with Conn and once more struck out on his own.

The first product of the new Ludwig company was the 'Speed King' foot pedal—probably *still* the most famous and highly regarded foot pedal today. Individual drums and full kits followed, and Ludwig was eventually able to buy his own company name back from Conn in 1955.

Progress was steady, Ludwig growing slowly in stature through the years, until a little-known English drummer from Liverpool was seen using Ludwig with an equally unheard of band—the Beatles. It was 1963 and Ludwig was shot to the top of the tree on the crest of the British invasion of America.

For the next few years Ludwig was *the* drum manufacturer whose products it was essential to be seen with.

But times changed. The Japanese were advancing and by the 1970s the emergence of Pearl, Tama and other oriental percussion firms had begun to take a heavy toll of Ludwig's market. Today, Ludwig's prices seem exorbitant in comparison with those of the Japanese. The firm is now owned by the gigantic Vincent Bach Company and sales are relatively small compared with the oriental brand leaders.

Paiste

Paiste Ltd.
6207 Nottwil
Switzerland
Founded Switzerland 19??.

Precise details about Paiste's origins are difficult to obtain, but it seems this Swiss-based manufacturer came into existence during the early part of this century via the emigration of a Russian gong-maker to Switzerland. Orchestral cymbals were a natural product for Paiste to move into and the company achieved

a notable role in this field (which they have maintained to this day).

Jazz drummers picked up the Paiste line later on; rock drummers followed. Among notable endorsees are Stewart Copeland (Police), Cozy Powell, Carmine Appice and Carl Palmer.

Although Paiste have been around for a long while, they are trying hard to cater to the demands of modern percussionists. Much of a cymbal's sound depends on the precise nature of the metallurgical mix which goes into the cymbal. Both Zildjian and Paiste have their own formulae and hence a very different sound. Many drummers (unless naturally favouring one product over the other) tend to mix their cymbals makes to obtain the sounds they desire.

In recent years Paiste have worked very hard to establish themselves among the rock fraternity. A recent development is the 'Rude' range of cymbals, specifically designed for heavy metal drummers. They also have a virtual monopoly on the massive gongs rock drummers love to begin and end their sets with.

Pearl

Pearl Musical Instrument Co.
16-64-chome
Narihira, Sumida-ku
Tokyo 130
Japan
Founded Japan 1970s.

Alongside Tama, Pearl drums have a similarly phenomenal range of endorsees among top-name musicians. Japanese-based, the Pearl Corporation offers a range of products throughout the world, but it is their drums which seem to have caught the public's imagination. As with other Japanese makers, Pearl have based their reputation on the reliability and sturdiness of their hardware, as well as on a very active policy of co-operation with leading percussionists. They are noted

for providing a first-rate back-up service for Pearl users and this, plus the quality and reliability of their equipment, has led to a string of endorsements by such names as Phil Collins, Narada Michael Walden and Chester Thompson.

Premier

Blaby Road
South Wigston
Leicester LE8 2DF
England
Founded UK 1920s.

Premier was started by Albert Della Porta in the early 1920s. Trained as an engineer, but having weak eyesight which ill-equipped him for the job, Della Porta took up music, eking-out his meagre earnings by helping at the Boyle Drum Co. Della Porta eventually persuaded Boyle's foreman, George J. Smith, to come with him and develop his ideas in a new company which he had decided to start—the Premier Drum Co. Ltd. Their first premises were a basement in Berwick Street, Soho.

Premier came up with the idea of replacing the old rope-tension military drums with properly tensioned ones and, after much initial ridicule from north of the border, they were widely adopted by the major Scottish Pipe bands of the era. This began a history of Premier's associations with this type of drum. Some 30 years later the Royal Marines also adopted them as suppliers.

During WWII, Premier turned their attention away from manually played percussion to the high-explosive kind, making radar and gunsights for 16- and 25-pounder guns. The factory (by now situated in Park Royal) later succumbed to an air raid and the company was relocated in Leicester. One benefit Premier gained from the war was learning to work to exacting tolerances.

A major boost to the company's prestige came via Mitch Mitchell (playing with Jimi Hendrix) and Keith Moon—both leading Premier users and both fine drummers who influenced a whole generation of percussionists in the '60s.

Premier continue to develop new products at a rate which shows them to be still a very vital force. Several leading players actively endorse Premier, including Ted McKenna (from the Michael Schenker Group), Pete York, Kenney Jones of the Who, Carl Palmer (a tremendous enthusiast about Premier and currently playing in Asia), and many others in fields as varied as jazz and new wave (the latter including players like Hugo Burnham from the Gang of Four).

Rogers

1000 East 2nd Street
Dayton, OH 45402
USA
Founded US late 1800s.

Formed over 100 years ago by Joseph Rogers in Cleveland, Ohio, the Rogers kits prospered during the big band era and had some notable users among 'name' drummers. Down the years they have been responsible for numerous innovations in percussion, notably in the introduction of what is the basis of virtually all Japanese drum pedals. Some time during the 1960s, Rogers moved to

California where they continued to innovate without, perhaps, ever achieving the kudos gained by such makers as Gretsch and Ludwig. One of Rogers' major inventions was the application of ball and socket devices to tom tom holders (dubbed the Swivomatic system); this won them many fans as it was a considerable improvement over previous types. The Dynasonic snare, using a principle which enabled the snares to be kept under tension while away from the head, was another Rogers development.

Eventually, like Fender, Harold Rhodes and others, the Rogers company was absorbed into the giant CBS conglomerate, and today many of their lesser kits are virtually 'badge engineered'—being produced in Japan and shipped to the Rogers plant in California. Compared with other Japanese kits like Tama and Pearl, they haven't found very much favour in the UK. The top-flight Rogers kits are still, however, made in the US and include such lines as the XP-8 Power Shells. These are manufactured from eight layers of maple and the stands feature the Rogers Memriloc system which 'remembers' the exact position in which the respective accessories (toms, cymbals, etc) are set, so that they can be re-set at a later date quickly and simply.

Continuing to innovate (especially in the field of hardware), Rogers kits have had some well-known users, including Buddy Rich, Dave Clarke, Bill Lordan (with Robin Trower) and Rod Morgenstein.

Rototoms

Remo Inc.
12804 Raymer Street
North Hollywood, CA 91605
USA
Founded US 1968.

More of an accessory than a drum kit, the profound effect of the Rototom makes it worth covering in an overview of percussion equipment. Developed by US drum head/skin specialists, Remo, it is a tunable tom tom-type unit with a tuning mechanism actuated by rotating the drum. First introduced in the US in 1968, they rapidly gained a following among jazz, rock and classical players.

Sizes available from Rototoms currently cover models from 6-18"—each drum having a tunable range of over 1 octave. The practical spread of a set is said to be around 3½ octaves. Endorsees include Billy Cobham, Bev Bevan and Bill Bruford.

Sabian

Meductic, New Brunswick,
Canada

Operating from a plant in Canada, Sabian cymbals are a direct offshoot of Zildjian, headed by former boss Bob Zildjian.

Still a very new name, Sabian have only a small range of products, comprising cast bronze cymbals available in both hand and machine finished types.

Current users include some prestigious names among modern drummers: Phil Collins, Kenney Jones, Ted McKenna (formerly with Michael Schenker) and Topper Headon (the Clash).

Simmons

Musicaid
176 Hatfield Road
St. Albans, Herts.
England

Simmons are undoubtedly the world leaders in electronic drums and percussion equipment. Located in St Albans, UK, the Simmons electronic drum kit caused a sensation when it first appeared, and numerous refinements have taken place on the original concept since its introduction. The Simmons V was probably the world's first fully electronic drum kit, using polycarbonate surfaces for natural 'feel and response'. The kits were also available in a wide range of colours, which assisted their appeal.

The electronics which come with Simmons kits are equipped with memory functions and a great variety of sounds, suiting them to both stage and studio applications.

Following their move into fully electronic drum kits (some of which come in amazing custom shapes), Simmons have developed the SDS6, a sequencer unit for their drums. For obvious reasons, their success has mainly lain with the 'new wave' synthesiser groups, but in bringing drums into the electronic world they have made what remains the most significant contribution to date.

Slingerland

6633 North Milwaukee Avenue
Niles, IL 60648
USA
Founded US 1918.

Based in Niles, Illinois, Slingerland have been operating for around 65 years. They first came to major prominence when they started teaming-up with noted drummers, using the players' skills in the design stage before putting their new products on the market. One of the first 'names' they worked with was the legendary Gene Krupa. This policy of close co-operation was continued with another great drummer, Louis Bellson, who was the first player, legend has it, to use a double bass drum set-up, a style which was to re-emerge briefly during the 1960s and '70s but which has slipped once again since then.

Probably Slingerland's biggest success

came with their Radio King kit, a set of drums with solid maple shells. Later on, Slingerland claimed that they pioneered the 5-ply construction with their TDR drum.

Slingerland can claim to have been involved in quite a few significant innovations down the years, and they have also had their fair share of well-known users. They remain a high-class drum-maker, rather than a mass-producer, keeping a fairly low profile compared with other American manufacturers like Ludwig and Rogers. Among noted rock drummers who have used Slingerland at some stage in their career is Bev Bevan of ELO.

Sonor Drums

Zum Heilbach 5
D-5920 Bad Berleberg-Aue
West Germany
Founded West Germany.

West German manufacturers Sonor produce the Rolls-Royce of drum kits, with a price to match. Refusal to sacrifice quality to lower price has restricted sales. However, they are reputed to make the strongest drums. Supporters include Steve Smith (Journey), Bernard Purdie, and Phil Rudd (AC/DC).

Tama

Hoshino Gakki Co. Ltd.
3-22 Shumokucho
Higashi-ku
Nagoya,
Japan
Founded Japan 1961

One of the many Japanese manufacturers to establish themselves as leading drum and percussion makers during the 1970s, Tama are part of the gigantic Hoshino set-up, also responsible for Ibanez guitars. Making their name initially from their very early 'Star' kits, Tama developed extremely strong hardware and well-made drums shells which soon endeared them to leading players such as Simon Phillips, Bill Bruford, Brian Downey, Lenny White, Mick Fleetwood and Neil Peart.

Probably the first major 'name' drummer to begin playing Tama (certainly in UK) was current Police drummer, Stewart Copeland,

who began using and endorsing Tama while resident with Curved Air.

In operation since 1961 the major turning-point, in many people's eyes, was when drummer supreme, Billy Cobham, changed over to Tama and began actively endorsing the range.

Yamaha

Nippon Gakki Co. Ltd.
10-1 Nakazawa-cho
Hamamatsu
Shizuoka 430
Japan
Founded 1887.

Despite being one of the oldest musical-instrument manufacturing companies in the world (and now, possibly, the biggest) Yamaha have never quite risen to the challenge of establishing themselves alongside other Japanese drum manufacturers like Tama and Pearl. For all that, however, the giant corporation continues to offer an enormous range of products, which has a small, but influential, list of devotees.

The consensus regarding Yamaha drums is that they are of the first quality, so it remains something of a puzzle why the company has managed to capture so much of the guitar and keyboard market and yet remains, in proportion to its size, relatively unsuccessful in the drum world.

Nevertheless, major endorsees of Yamaha drums include some particularly noteworthy players: Cozy Powell, Peter Erskine (Weather Report), Al Davis (reputedly Miles Davis' favourite) and session drummer extraordinaire Steve Gadd.

Zildjian

39 Fayetts Street,
North Quincy, MA 02171
USA
Founded Turkey 1623.

The original company was founded in 1623 in Constantinople, Turkey, by a Mr Avedis who, so the story goes, discovered a secret process of alloy manufacture which enabled him to produce cymbals of a quality previously unheard of in the Turkish Empire. It is important to realise that prior to this period in musical history, cymbals were not regarded as an integral part of instrumentation, and it wasn't until the 1680s that German composers began to introduce this 'novel' sound into their music.

The modern-day history of Avedis-Zildjian begins in the 20th century; an American descendant of Mr Avedis re-discovered the formulae used by his ancestor and began to introduce his cymbals to the early jazz drummers who, prior to that point, had been using just one cymbal type of extremely limited quality and range.

The newly formed Avedis-Zildjian company established itself in Quincy, Massachusetts and began a series of cymbal innovations which continues to this day. The Hi-hat, Crash, Ride and almost any cymbal type you care to think of, came from the Zildjian factory. The brand rapidly established itself with the jazz drummers of the era—players like Gene Krupa, Joe Jones and Chick Webb. Current players include Simon Phillips, Steve Gadd, Pete Erskine and just about anyone who is anyone in drumming.

Below: Stewart Copeland (Police) has used Tama drums since Curved Air.

Alpha-Syntauri

Syntauri Corp.
3506 Waverley Street
Palo Alto, CA 94305
USA
Founded US 1980.

Established in 1980, in Palo Alto, California, the Syntauri Corporation designed what was probably the world's first microcomputer keyboard synthesiser system. Designed by inventor Charles Kellner, the Alpha-Syntauri uses an Apple computer with specially developed 'software' to control it.

A highly sophisticated computerised concept, the Alpha-Syntauri is, surprisingly, quite straightforward to operate. Four or five-octave keyboards are offered, alongside growing amounts of computer software, which enables the Syntauri to be used in computerised multi-track recording applications, as well as for more conventional stage use. Various models are available. A leading advocate of the Syntauri approach is American keyboard star Herbie Hancock. The Syntauri also sells at a remarkably low price.

Casio

2-6-1 Nishishin Juku
Shinjuku-ku
Tokyo 160
Japan
Founded Japan 1979.

Casio's background lies in massive volume consumer electronics, mainly calculators. Almost unbelievably (considering the impact they have made on the market since then) Casio only made the decision to enter the keyboard market in 1979. The first Casiotone keyboards appeared a year later.

The initial models produced by the company (the CT-201 and the M-10 Mini) caught the rest of the keyboard world totally by surprise. Priced at a mere £79 (in the UK), the M-10 was a remarkable little unit which rapidly gained phenomenal popularity with keyboard players of all kinds—and many non-keyboard players too.

A virtual avalanche of new products appeared, the CT-301 in 1980 being followed by eight products the following year and countless more in 1983. Every few months Casio seem to be launching yet another series of keyboards. The product range is best understood by breaking it down into three distinct types: the VLs (fitted with calculator type keys), the Mini keyboards, and the standard size units.

Casio's use of silicon chip technology is startling. From the tiniest models to their standard stage-size keyboards, the features offered by Casio seem to grow so fast that it is hard to grasp. By 1982 they had already launched the CT-701, which was capable of reading coded music with a light-pen (probably the first keyboard of its type to be capable of such 'bar code' reading). They rapidly progressed from there to develop other novel ideas, like the enormously successful PT-30 keyboard (costing well under £100) which can be programmed to play. The programmes (as opposed to the notes themselves) were 'dumpable' onto standard cassette recorders for eventual replay, or, alternatively, internal storage in a digital memory.

Casio are extremely popular with musicians, from beginners through to professional players, who either take the portable models on tour with them, or use them in home studios, while the full-size versions are used on stage and in the studio. They may not offer the voice quality of instruments from manufacturers like Moog, Yamaha, Rhodes/Chroma and others, but their cost is extremely low and they are packed with innovative design features.

Crumar

Crumar SpA
P.O. Box 98
1-60022 Castelfidardo
Italy
Founded Italy 1970s.

The Crumar range of products embraces electronic pianos (like the hugely successful Roadrunner), organs (like the Performer) and polyphonic synthesisers (the Trilogy, the Status and the Composer). While they have never actually led the market, Crumar have always been present in it, offering excellent value for money for the semi-pro player.

The Emulator

E-mu Systems
417 Broadway
Santa Cruz, CA 95060
USA
Founded US 1981.

February 1981 saw the birth of what was to become one of the most advanced synthesisers ever produced—the Emulator. Originally picked up and used by Stevie Wonder, the Emulator has rapidly become the vanguard keyboard of the latest breed of synthesisers and has gained followers and users among such artists as Jethro Tull, Captain and Tenille, Orchestral Manoevres in the Dark and Ultravox.

The Emulator has an enormous 'library' of sounds on floppy discs, and can be used for sampling techniques of required sounds. Its extensive sequencer capabilities can be interfaced with almost any other synthesiser.

The Emulator is at the very forefront of computerised synthesisers and is, at present, the 'State Of The Art' machine, beloved of the new wave of synthesiser bands.

Elka-Orla

via Squartabue
62019 Recananti
Italy
Founded Italy 1960.

Most of Elka's considerable commercial achievement has been due to their electronic organs, which have proved to be very acceptably priced for the home organ and club-type organ market.

Based in Castelfidardo, Elka-Orla are actually three Italian companies (Elka, Orla and S.E.M.), joined together for the purposes of marketing their respective products in this, and other markets. They have always had some presence in the professional keyboards market with their Elka organs (back in the 1960s models like the Capri and Panther were occasionally seen with pop groups of that era).

The range of Elka keyboards, which provides a good and inexpensive bridge between the home organ market and the beginner's rock

Above: A young Stevie Wonder and an early Hohner organ.

keyboard field, has grown over the years. Models like the portable Micropiano and Elkatwin have gained some following among younger players, offering good sounds at fair prices, rather than outstanding technical features.

However, Elka shocked the keyboard market in 1982 when they announced the Elka Synthex. From a background almost solely in relatively low-tech organs, electronic pianos and string machines, Elka suddenly delivered a very capable synthesiser, which received good reviews from a surprised music press.

Other areas in which Elka have contributed to the rock keyboard market in recent years are electronic pianos and string machines. The Elka Micropiano 16, the Elkatwin 61 and the twin manual X109 portable organ, all have a strong following. Elka remain viable and rather underrated manufacturers who, particularly judging by the quality of some of their recent professional products, like the X-50 and the Synthex, are a good deal further advanced technically than many probably realise.

Fairlight CMI

15 Boundary Street
Rushcutters Bay
New South Wales 2011
Australia
Founded Australia 1981.

Along with the E-Mu, the Australian designed and manufactured Fairlight computer/synthesiser is currently about the most highly regarded keyboard system around. With synths as complex and capable as the Fairlight it is hard to say where the keyboard begins and the computer ends; the Fairlight is every bit a full-blown computerised keyboard system of the most advanced kind.

Following the announcement of the Fairlight in 1981, the team behind it (Peter Vogel, Kim Ryrie and Tony Furse) who spent several years on research, achieved instant recognition throughout the world. Early on it was picked-up by Stevie Wonder and since that point the company has never looked back.

Utilising disc drives (as do computers in the micro computer world) the Fairlight is capable of digitally producing some astonishing sounds, and (again in common with the best computers) it has a tremendous library of available 'software' to back it.

The Fairlight, viewed at its most simple level, is basically a digital re-processor of digitally stored sounds. From a floppy disc, the machine can recall sounds and reproduce them; a light pen can be used on the Fairlight's monitor screen. Real sounds can also be recorded into it by various means; a brass or woodwind instrument, for example, could be miked-up and the sound recorded (via an analogue to digital conversion process) into the Fairlight itself, for reproduction at a later date. Unlike early attempts at the same idea (for example the Mellotron/Novatron) the Fairlight will reproduce these sounds *exactly* as they are recorded with no significant alteration. More interestingly, the sound recorded for later reproduction could be as unconventional as a thunderstorm or birdsong, which could later be used in a concert or on a record.

If this were all the Fairlight were capable of, however, it would be little more than a fairly reasonable digital recorder. In fact, the system has far more complex and far-reaching abilities, such as generation of artificial sounds and composing aids. For example, someone with theoretical knowledge of music but no ability to play an instrument could both compose and play via the light pen system.

Because of its enormous cost the Fairlight will never be an instrument for anyone other than the wealthy professional musician. And, because of its ability to virtually do away with musical skills (all you really need is patience, a small amount of flair for computer systems and imagination), it has many detractors among musicians.

(Fender) Rhodes

Fender Rhodes
1300 East Valencia
Fullerton, CA 92631
USA
Founded US 1940s.

The Rhodes story goes back to 1942, when Harold Rhodes (then a piano teacher) had the idea of developing a truly portable piano, small enough to be played in bed by wounded servicemen. Using discarded aeroplane parts he made a series of three-octave instruments and went round hospitals demonstrating his new invention.

After several false starts, Rhodes eventually developed a revolutionary tone bar generator which he patented—the Rhodes piano was properly born.

Touch sensitive (like a 'real' piano) the Rhodes didn't really begin to take off until the '60s, and then mainly among jazz players. The instrument had a sound of its own and was picked up by a list of musicians which today includes Chick Corea, Herbie Hancock and Joe Zawinul.

The basic operating principle of the Rhodes (subsequently known as the 'Fender Rhodes' following Harold Rhodes' absorption into the mighty CBS Empire) is the use of a tone bar, developed from the basic idea of a tuning fork. These generators are struck by hammers (much as strings are hit on a conventional piano) and each tone bar can be individually adjusted for the optimum sound and touch sensitivity—something offered by no ordinary electronic piano.

From the original Rhodes electric piano, much development work has been undertaken and there are now many different versions of the basic theme, including 73 and 88-note 'stage' models, 'suitcase' pianos and others.

Recently, the Rhodes name has been applied to a truly revolutionary instrument—the Rhodes Chroma. This keyboard was, in fact, developed by the ailing ARP Company—synthesiser pioneers who were eventually absorbed into the CBS conglomerate. The Chroma is a keyboard with, as yet, still unexplored potential. In essence it is a 16 channel, programmable polyphonic synthesiser with a 'dynamic' keyboard; in other words, unlike most synthesisers it has a truly touch-sensitive operational feel to it.

As well as offering a truly astonishing range of capabilities for programming in its own right, the Chroma will also work with an Apple Computer, with the keyboard's sounds and uses being programmed from the Apple itself. These include multi-track recording via the computer interface, expanded data storage and much more.

Right: Rick Wakeman has used several keyboards in combination, including the Hammond here.

Hammond

4200 West Diversey
Chicago, IL 60639
USA
Founded US 1934.

Invented by engineer Laurens Hammond, the basic operating principle of this organ was a development of Hammond's earlier experiments with clocks and timing systems generally—the tone-wheel generator.

The sound produced by this revolutionary system (granted a US patent in 1934) was unique in that it enabled the player to blend both harmonics and fundamentals of notes. Originally sold for use at home, the Hammond was picked up and used widely by entertainers of all kinds, and then began to find its way onto rock stages.

One of the major factors behind the 'Hammond Sound' was the use of the Leslie tone cabinet, which produced a swirling, almost 'phased' sound when used in conjunction with the Hammond. It worked by employing a rotating chamber inside a vented wooden enclosure, the sound being directed from the speaker through the vents in the chamber as it moved. Musicians other than keyboard players have also used this speaker system from time to time, notably guitarist Jimi Hendrix who frequently put it to good use.

The leading rock-orientated exponent of the Hammond was Keith Emerson, whose physical abuse of the keyboard involved hurling knives into it and literally throwing the organ around on stage! The Hammond not only produced a rich sound, full of harmonics, which few (if any) other organs could emulate, but also produced feedback (like an electric guitar).

Despite its tremendous popularity with rock keyboard players, the enormous cost of producing what was, after all, a largely electro-mechanical system, led to Hammond abandoning the original tone-wheel generator principle in favour of purely electronic tone production systems. For the home organ

market this was fine—the new models were cheaper to manufacture, buy and service—but the rock players soon found that the new Hammonds had lost that characteristic 'Hammond Sound'.

Meanwhile Robert Moog was busy leading the way to the future with the still relatively novel synthesiser—the day of the Hammond had largely passed. Still, even today, some notable rock keyboard players manage to keep their Hammond tone-wheel models working and make extensive use of them—a leading example being ex-Deep Purple player Jon Lord (currently working with Whitesnake).

Hohner

Hohner A.G.
P.O. Box
D-7218 Trossingen
West Germany
Founded Germany 1857.

Although not associated with the 'high-tech' movement of keyboards, the two major Hohner products widely used in rock, the Pianet and the Clavinet, have a long and honourable pedigree. Simplicity of tone production has led to relatively low cost and ease of use. Devotees of the two Hohner models are legion, but perhaps the best example of the Clavinet's sound is on Stevie Wonder's **Superstition**.

Korg

Keio Electronic Laboratory
15-12 Shimotakaido 1-chome
Suginamu-ku
Tokyo 168
Japan
Founded Japan 1965.

The Korg name began to emerge some 15 years ago, when the company produced the first of its many drum machine/rhythm units.

The company then became a kind of electronics laboratory.

Perhaps the most notable 'first' from Korg was their original instrument tuner/meter, a field in which they have taken the lead and held it ever since.

The first Korg electronic keyboard product to make significant waves in the West was the Mini-Korg synthesiser. Since then they have gone from strength to strength, securing prestigious endorsees as Rick Wakeman and Keith Emerson, plus bands like UFO and Duran Duran.

The current Poly-6 and Poly-61 are extremely popular polyphonic synthesisers, and the programmable drum machine commands very respectable sales.

Korg also have a good reputation among piano devotees with their EPS-1 touch-sensitive keyboards.

Mellotron/ Novatron

Streetly Electronics
388 Aldridge Road
Streetly
Sutton Coldfield
West Midlands B74 2DT
England
Founded UK 1960s.

In the early 1960s (before the synthesiser was even a glint in Robert Moog's eye) a new keyboard, using taped recordings or real instruments and voices, was being developed in the English Midlands.

A twin manual keyboard instrument, the Mellotron worked by having every key trigger a tape recording. Because there was a finite length to the tapes used, the notes would not play indefinitely and there were many early problems created by tape-stretch (which could alter the fundamental tuning of the instrument).

Nevertheless, the three-section form of the

sounds the Mellotron produced (melody, rhythms and accompaniment) endowed it with a remarkable sound which was seized upon by numerous '60s bands.

The Beatles used it to enormous advantage on **Strawberry Fields**, the Moody Blues on most of their tracks (notably **Knights In White Satin**). Musicians of the calibre of Patrick Moraz employ the equipment.

Due to various legal problems, the original manufacturers of the Mellotron are no longer allowed to call the instrument by that name and it is now being produced in England as the Novatron, although it remains, essentially, much the same instrument.

Moog broke the next barrier against synthesisers when they developed the truly polyphonic Polymoog (a synthesiser which could play more than one note at a time—thus making it more akin to a conventional keyboard instrument), which they launched with somewhat limited success due to cost and rumoured reliability problems.

Moog also produced one of a tiny number of pedal-operated synthesisers—the Taurus system, which has been employed by numerous players whose hands were otherwise occupied with guitars and basses. Notable users are Geddy Lee and Alex Lifeson of the Canadian band Rush.

Moog

Moog Music Inc.
2500 Walden Avenue
Buffalo NY 14225
USA
Founded US 1964.

Despite some earlier work undertaken in the US, the first proper synthesiser was developed by Dr Robert Moog (properly pronounced it should rhyme with 'rogue'), who announced his invention back in 1964. Early versions of Moog's device circulated among esoteric circles, but the first truly commericial use of the original 'Moog synthesiser' was on **Switched On Bach**, released in 1968.

Probably the first truly universal application of Moog's ideas in a reliable and usable form came with the introduction of the legendary Mini-Moog which entered production in 1971. This instrument has probably appeared on more stages and on more records than any other synthesiser.

Although only a monophonic synthesiser (i.e. it could only handle one note at one time), the Mini-Moog had a touch of real genius about it in the form of a note 'bending' device, giving keyboard players, to some extent, the facility long-envied of guitarists, who had always been able to bend their notes away from natural pitch by literally bending their strings as they played them.

Moog's operation was eventually absorbed by the giant Norlin corporation (which also owned Gibson, the guitar makers) and the Mini-Moog was phased out of production in 1981. Despite this, many players still use Mini-Moogs.

Above: Manfred Mann, seen here in the '70s, with a combination of synthesisers by early manufacturers Moog and ARP.

Moog have recently begun to hit back against Japanese competition with some interesting developments such as the Memory Moog, a completely polyphonic synthesiser with a considerable memory. Unlike most of the current 'new wave' synthesiser manufacturers, Moog appear to have decided that digital synthesis is not for them, and they have lost considerable ground to other makers like Fairlight, Yamaha and EMU. For all that, however, Moog are heavily promoting their popular 'Source' model, which has programmes available for it developed by, and featuring the playing of, such notable instrumentalists as Jan Hammer and Gary Wright.

Oberheim

2250 South Barrington Ave.
Los Angeles, CA 90064
USA
Founded US 1980.

Oberheim started by electronics engineer Tom Oberheim in California. Various products preceded the first significant 'hit' for Oberheim—the OB-1, one of the first programmable machines on the market. Following that success, came the OB-1A and then a move towards polyphonics like the OBX, OBSX and the OB-8, an eight-voice type. Oberheim keyboards are well liked and very widely used by

rock players—particularly for their characteristic rather brassy sounds.

A recent development from the company has been the introduction of the DX digital drum machine. This has all the usual features of this type of machine but it scores in its ability to directly interface into the rest of the Oberheim system notably the DSX polyphonic synth and the OB-8.

Roland

7-13 Shinkitajima 3-chome
Suminoe-ku
Osaka 559
Japan
Founded Japan 1972.

Currently, Roland policy with regard to employment in Japan is that a 15% minimum of staff should be actively working in research and development, and this has undoubtedly paid handsome dividends. The product range they offer is probably the widest from any Japanese maker, covering synthesisers and computer peripherals, instrument amps, effects units, mixers and PA equipment—even down to 'own brand' Roland batteries to power the effects.

The first Roland synthesisers (the semi preset SH1000 and SH2000) were reasonably successful and had begun to develop a reputation among semi-professional musicians. The sum total of the Roland product range at that point was, perhaps, six or seven lines—by 1983 that had grown to a figure in excess of 300, with an average of one new product being released every month.

Spreading out across almost the whole field of instrumentation, Roland synthesisers and electronic systems began to catch on swiftly both in the UK and US. By the late '70s the range already included what was to become the only commercially successful guitar synthesiser, a 'micro-composer', synthesisers like the SH 1000, electronic pianos (the EP 30), string machines and electronic organs.

Perhaps the real breakthrough for Roland

came in the early 1980s when the rate of introduction of new products began to approach that of current levels. It wasn't so much that they offered a massive range of synthesisers and electronic pianos—more that their accepted technological prowess across the board aided their relatively small keyboard range by contributing to the whole company image. This image was re-inforced by such complex and technically advanced products as the huge System 700.

New products, like the Juno Series of polyphonic synthesisers, the Jupiter range, and individual models like the monophonic SH-09 and, lately, the very successful SH-101, a portable relatively low-cost monophonic model which can be worn on a strap like a guitar, have put Roland's keyboards firmly in the forefront of the market—particularly with the modern 'synth' bands.

Lately the company has been at the head of the movement to introduce the 'Midi' system—a common interface standard which should enable synthesiser players to link together many different manufacturers' electronic key-

Sequential Circuits

3051 North First Street
San Jose, CA 95134
USA
Founded US 1977.

In 1977 a newly formed company, Sequential Circuits, unleashed what was to instigate a total revolution in the keyboard market—a keyboard system that could remember note sequences. Their synthesiser, the Prophet, rapidly established itself in world markets.

Since the launch of the Prophet synthesiser, the basic model 5 has been repeatedly updated to enable it to compete with other manufacturers' products. Curiously, despite

Below: '80s equipment from Roland, the Juno and Jupiter lines.

the overwhelming success of this keyboard, the company launched the 5 alongside a two-manual version, the Prophet 10 (which had to be withdrawn due to various technical problems—not least of which was a tendency for the tuning to drift).

Today the SC range still only comprises the come and Sequential Circuits managed to successfully re-launch the Prophet 10. In fact, one of the major features of the Prophet range now is its ability to check the tuning of the oscillators via a self-checking and adjusting programme.

Today the SC range still only comprises the latest up-dated versions of the Prophet, plus an excellent polyphonic sequencer, which has opened up the machine's market potential even further.

Synclavier

New England Digital Corp.
P.O. Box 305
Norwich, VT 05055.
USA
Founded 1980.

Manufactured by New England Digital. The Synclavier offers computerised operation and has already earned itself a considerable following among leading musicians. Bands such as the Human League and individual players like Gerry Rafferty and Tony Banks (Genesis) are numbered among Synclavier users to date.

A complete programming language ('MAX') is offered on the Synclavier, which also comes with a 16-track digital memory recorder (one of the ultra-modern types which enables the player to multi-track, record or compose in a digital form with the keyboard operating on its own). As with many of the ultra-advanced keyboards, the cost of the Synclavier is phenomenal, which restricts its use.

Synergy

Music Tech.
105 5th Avenue
Garden City Park, NY 11040
USA
Founded US.

Built by Digital Keyboards of New York Synergy is quite a different keyboard from the usually static Fairlight and Alpha Syntauri synths, being a perfect instrument for stage work.

The storage system for the Synergy's polyphonic operation utilises cartridges containing magnetic recording media rather than floppy discs. 32 digital oscillators are employed. The Synergy has 24 voices preprogrammed into it (any four of which can be used simultaneously) and the unit comes with a 74-key keyboard all for a low cost.

The basic sounds of the Synergy are developed in the US on a large music computer and these are supplied to the Synergy user already recorded on cartridges. If the user wishes to have his own sounds on the machine he can have these processed for him by the manufacturer and supplied ready for use.

Basic built-in abilities of the Synergy include a 'Rhodes' sound, a Crumar 'T20' organ sound, flutes, chimes, and so on. This makes the Synergy ideal for use on stage

Above: Duran Duran members Nick Rhodes (keyboards) and Andy Taylor (guitar) are comfortable with Yamaha equipment.

where it can be employed to replace a whole host of other products.

Wurlitzer

403 East Gurler Road
De Kalb, IL 60115
USA
Founded 1800s.

The term 'the mighty Wurlitzer' dates back to the era of the cinema/theatre organ, and the company has a place in any run-down of rock-orientated keyboards on account of its widely used EP 200 model electronic piano.

The Wurlitzer uses hammers to strike very unsophisticated electronic reeds, which gives it the characteristic 'Wurlitzer' sound. Developed and introduced in the early '60s, the Wurlitzer has retained a small but vitally important following, and is still being used today, and in fact has made somewhat of a comeback with musicians in the '80s. Supertramps' **Dreamer** is perhaps the most notable recorded example of the Wurltizer piano sound.

Yamaha

Nippon Gakki Co. Ltd.
10-1 Nakazawa-cho
Hamamatsu
Shizuoka 430
Japan
Founded Japan 1887.

Until relatively recently, Yamaha's prominence lay firmly in the field of acoustic pianos, to such an extent that they are inextricably involved in the UK with veteran piano manufacturers Kemble.

Their first venture into modern keyboard technology began way back at the turn of the century, when they made a reed organ. This was a natural progression from the pianos which Yamaha had been manufacturing since 1897.

The first major product to hit the rock market was the CP30, launched in the UK as recently as 1978. This instrument established Yamaha, in one move, as a major force. Before that the company had been heavily involved with electronic organs, but the CP30 was the first product to make a significant impact among Western rock players. But it was really Yamaha's electric grand piano that consolidated their reputation. This was a grand piano which could be split, taking the harp off the action, and was fitted with transducers on each string.

Before 1978 Yamaha had already produced

synthesisers, but it was the launch of the CS80 which firmly established them in that field. Perhaps the first really expressive polyphonic synthesiser, the CS80 put to rest some of the criticisms that synths were basically rather sterile sounding. Although now long out of production, the CS80 appealed to players of all kinds—even today a CS80 in good condition will fetch reasonable money.

Even while the Yamaha Company was developing these products, they had begun to invest considerable amounts of money and research in digital FM synthesis, following the publication of the first technical paper on the subject in 1973. Seeing the need for synthesisers which didn't make too many electronics and programming demands on keyboard players, Yamaha began to research and develop the principle.

Previous Yamahas (the GS and CE ranges) offer many ease of use advantages, but nothing to date has combined the low cost and sound quality of the DX series of FM Digital types with the main feature—they are now fully programmable. Their operation requires a little understanding of computer technology as an algorithmic system is used. Rather than floppy discs or some other storage mechanism, the DX Series employs plug-in ROM (Read Only Memory) cartridges which come with preprogrammed sounds. An optional extra is a device which allows one to store sounds inside and EPROM (Erasable Programmable ROM).

Index

The performers in this book appear in alphabetical order. Therefore, this index serves mainly as a comprehensive cross-referencing system, listing page number only when performers appear in an entry other than their own. Several performers and personalities who do not have their own entries but who are referred to in the book are also listed.